THE SCOUTING REPORT: 1991

Produced by STATS, Inc.
(Sports Team Analysis and Tracking Systems, Inc.)

John Dewan, Editor
Don Zminda, Associate Editor

Statistics by STATS, Inc.

HarperPerennial
A Division of HarperCollins*Publishers*

The player photographs which appear in THE SCOUTING REPORT: 1991 were furnished individually by the 26 teams that comprise Major League Baseball. Their cooperation is gratefully acknowledged: Baltimore Orioles, Boston Red Sox, California Angels, Chicago White Sox, Cleveland Indians, Detroit Tigers, Kansas City Royals, Milwaukee Brewers, Minnesota Twins, New York Yankees, Oakland A's, Seattle Mariners, Texas Rangers, Toronto Blue Jays, Atlanta Braves, Chicago Cubs, Cincinnati Reds, Houston Astros, Los Angeles Dodgers, Montreal Expos, New York Mets, Philadelphia Phillies, Pittsburgh Pirates, St. Louis Cardinals, San Diego Padres and San Francisco Giants. Our appreciation is also extended to the Columbus Clippers, Colorado Springs Sky Sox, Louisville Redbirds, Pawtucket Red Sox and Phoenix Firebirds for their assistance in obtaining additional photographs. New York Mets' photographs by Marc Levine. Los Angeles Dodgers' photographs by Jon SooHoo.

FIRST EDITION

Designed by STATS, Inc.

ISSN 0743-1309

ISBN 0-06-273002-9

91 92 93 94 95 RRD 10 9 8 7 6 5 4 3 2 1

Table of Contents

Acknowledgments

Looking back to the spring of 1990, we didn't know what the baseball season would bring, or even if the lockout would end in time to have a 1990 season. It seems like a long time ago, much longer than the few months that have passed. In that short time a new chapter was written in baseball. We saw the Cincinnati Reds' surprising victory over the A's. Cecil Fielder's mighty bat hit 51 home runs. Bob Welch racked up 27 victories. Bobby Thigpen saved 57 games. After a shaky start, it was a great season. We're glad you are taking this journey with us as we look back at the players of the 1990 season and we look foward with anticipation to what the 1991 season will bring. Let me tell you about the folks who make this journey possible.

Don Zminda is the associate editor for this book and Director of Publications at STATS, Inc. He coordinated the scouts (no small task) and was the first and primary editor of the reports, giving each essay, written by so many diverse analysts, a high level of consistency. Don's baseball knowledge and writing skills are more than indispensable to this book.

Dr. Richard Cramer is the founder and Chairman of the Board of STATS, Inc. He is also our chief technical wizard, always tinkering with the baseball information and finding new and interesting ways to present it. Dick is responsible for the graphics as well as the statistical rankings you find in the book.

Bob Mecca is the statistical editor. Bob drew upon his extensive baseball background and computer expertise to verify and enhance the statistical references. Bob has also played a key role in generating creative statistical information for many of STATS' clients.

Ross Schaufelberger is this year's copy editor. He batted 1.000 in that role. While putting the final touches on the essays, he continually went beyond the call of duty, insuring that this year's edition of the book is better than ever. His input was a valued addition to this book. Ross was also responsible for working with the Major League Teams in obtaining player photos.

Others at STATS who worked directly on the book include Arthur Ashley, Assistant Vice President, who found the time between all of his other responsibilities to lend his help on this book wherever it was needed. Matt Greenberger assisted in the copy editing and player photos. Suzette Neily typed many of the reports into computer readable form for editing.

Thanks to the STATS Staff that kept the office going while we got the book done. Sue Dewan, Vice President (and my wonderful wife), worked with our computer systems daily as they digested the baseball games each night. David Pinto, Senior Analyst, brought STATS' information into your living rooms nightly with his creative and detailed support of ESPN broadcasts. Marge Morra and Nadine Sanchez, along with Michael Canter and Jon Passman, stayed on top of the daily operations of the office.

Thanks to Bill James for his insightful formulas for projecting player performance which helped us formulate the stars, bums and sleepers of 1991, our new section this year.

And once again, thanks to our editor at HarperCollins, Dan Bial. It's always a pleasure to work with him.

— John Dewan

The Scouting Staff

Producing a book of this magnitude requires writers who are experts on the strengths and weaknesses of major league players. Our staff is composed of both newspaper beat writers and our own STATS' reporters, who cover games for us from the press box. Not all of them are as famous as Peter Gammons, who graciously volunteered to write the Red Sox reports for us, but they all have the same dedication to making this a good book. The writers are the unsung heroes of The Scouting Report, and we are deeply grateful to them.

The scouting reports in this book were written by the following people, in conjunction with our board of editors:

Baltimore Orioles	Kent Baker *Baltimore Morning Sun*
Boston Red Sox	Peter Gammons *Boston Globe*
California Angels	Dave King *STATS, Inc.*
Chicago White Sox	Bob Mecca *STATS, Inc.*
Cleveland Indians	Paul Hoynes *Cleveland Plain Dealer*
Detroit Tigers	Bob Duff *Windsor Star*
Kansas City Royals	Marc Bowman *STATS, Inc.*
Milwaukee Brewers	Tom Flaherty *Milwaukee Journal*
Minnesota Twins	Howard Sinker and Dennis Brackin *Minneapolis Star-Tribune*
New York Yankees	John Benson *Diamond Analytics*
Oakland Athletics	Chuck Hildebrand *Peninsula Times-Tribune*
Seattle Mariners	Bob Finnigan *Seattle Times*
Texas Rangers	Allen Sheffield *STATS, Inc.*
Toronto Blue Jays	Howard Sinker *Minneapolis Star-Tribune*
Atlanta Braves	Corey Seeman *STATS, Inc.*
Chicago Cubs	Dave Srinivasan *STATS, Inc.*
Cincinnati Reds	Sam Carchidi *Philadelphia Inquirer*
Houston Astros	Joe Heiling *Beaumont Enterprise & Journal*
Los Angeles Dodgers	Mark Langill *Pasadena Star-News*
Montreal Expos	Jack Romanelli *Montreal Gazette*
New York Mets	John Benson *Diamond Analytics*
Philadelphia Phillies	Pete DeCoursey *Reading Eagle-Times*
Pittsburgh Pirates	John Perrotto *Beaver County Times*
St. Louis Cardinals	Rollie Loewen *STATS, Inc.*
San Diego Padres	Barry Bloom *San Diego Tribune*
San Francisco Giants	Chuck Hildebrand *Peninsula Times-Tribune*

On a personal level, I'd like to thank Ross Schaufelberger, who worked tirelessly on the minute details that help make a project of this scope become a reality. Thanks, Ross.

Finally, I'd like to thank Dick Cramer and John and Sue Dewan, the driving forces behind STATS. This is our second edition of The Scouting Report; we think it's even better than the first one, and our goal is to continue to improve every year. It's easier to achieve that goal when you work with people like Dick, John and Sue, who never stop trying to make a good operation even better. Thanks again to all of you.

— Don Zminda

Introduction

To all of you previous readers of ***The Scouting Report***, welcome back! To you new readers, we're glad to have you along. Once again, we have scouting reports on over 700 major league baseball players included in this book. They are the most complete and detailed reports the general public has ever had the opportunity to see.

We've got some new stuff this year. Our biggest additions are the pitcher charts for the key hurlers on each team. You've heard radio and TV announcers make statements such as "This guy's main problem is that he doesn't throw strikes" and "He's not getting that first pitch in there for a strike." We've decided to answer that question directly. Rather than speculating that a guy seems to be throwing strikes, we measured it directly. (See below for a more thorough discussion of the pitcher strike charts.)

We've also added a new section this year, Stars, Bums and Sleepers. Here we look at all the players in the book and give you a flavor for what we expect them to do in 1991 compared to 1990. We also show you who the sleepers are -- the guys who might come out of nowhere to have good seasons in '91. This section is especially good for all you fantasy/rotisserie players out there.

The Players

For each major league team, there are 25 to 30 players scouted here. Most of the players are covered in depth, with a full page of scouting information. They are listed alphabetically with the team they last played for in 1990. The lesser players, four to seven per team, follow the primary players on each team.

The Scouting Report Page

The Scouting Report page for primary players has two parts. The left side of the page provides an in-depth report by one of our expert scout/analysts who cover the teams on a daily basis. These reports are drawn from their day-to-day observation of the players.

The right-hand side of the page is chock full of information from the STATS computer. Starting at the top of the column it lists:

Position: The first position shown is the player's most common position in 1990. If a position player played at any other positions in 10 or more games, those positions are shown also. For pitchers, SP stands for starting pitcher and RP stands for relief pitcher. A second pitching position is shown if a starting pitcher relieved at least four times or a relief pitcher started at least twice.

Bats and Throws: L=left-handed, R=right-handed, B=both (switch-hitter).

Opening Day Age: This is the player's age on April 8, 1991.

Born: Birth date and place.

ML Seasons: This number indicates the number of different major league seasons in which this player has actually appeared. For example, if a player was called up to play in September in each of the last three seasons, the number shown would be three (3). Note that this is different from the term Major League Service, which only counts the actual number of days a player appears on a major league roster.

Overall Statistics: These are traditional statistics for the player's 1990 season, and his career through 1990.

Pitcher Strike Charts

The pitcher strike charts answer the question "How Often Does He Throw Strikes?" The charts are constructed based on the most extreme pitchers at throwing strikes in baseball. Dennis Eckersley throws 75% of his pitches for strikes overall, and 82% for strikes when he's behind on the count (which, of course, is very rare). At the other extreme, Scott Bankhead threw only 42% of his pitches for strikes when he was ahead on the count in 1990. Therefore we've constructed the chart to represent the 40-80% range of throwing strikes.

Here are some gound rules: When you read your USA Today box score or hear an announcer state that a certain pitcher has thrown 97 pitches, 62 of them for strikes, the strike count includes swinging strikes, taken strikes, foul balls **and** balls hit in play. Even though not all balls hit into play are strikes, the theory is that most of them are, and the ones that aren't would be difficult to judge. Our charts reflect this. The charts are then broken into four categories. **All Pitches** is straight forward, as is **First Pitch.** We define **Ahead** as being any time there are more strikes than balls in the count (0-1, 0-2, 1-2). **Behind** includes all counts with more balls than strikes (1-0, 2-0, 3-0, 2-1, 3-1, 3-2).

League averages are also shown in each chart. If the pitcher is listed with an American League team, the AL average is shown. The NL average is shown for players whose scouting report is with a National League team. Here are the league averages for 1990:

Strike Percentage by League — 1990

	American	National
All Pitches	61.7%	62.7%
First Pitch	56.2%	57.1%
Ahead in the Count	56.7%	58.8%
Behind in the Count	68.1%	68.6%

You'll notice the National League throws a slightly higher percentage of strikes in all cases.

Hitting Diagrams

The hitting diagrams shown in these reports are the most advanced of their kind in baseball. For every game and every ball hit into play last year (both hits and outs), STATS' trained reporters entered data into the STATS computer. They kept track of the kind of batted ball -- ground ball, fly ball, pop-up, line drive or bunt, as well as the distance of each ball. Direction is kept by dividing the field into 26 "wedges" angling out from home plate. Distance is measured in 10-foot increments from home plate

Below are Gregg Jefferies' hitting diagrams. One chart shows where Jefferies hit the ball against left-handed pitchers; the other shows him against righties.

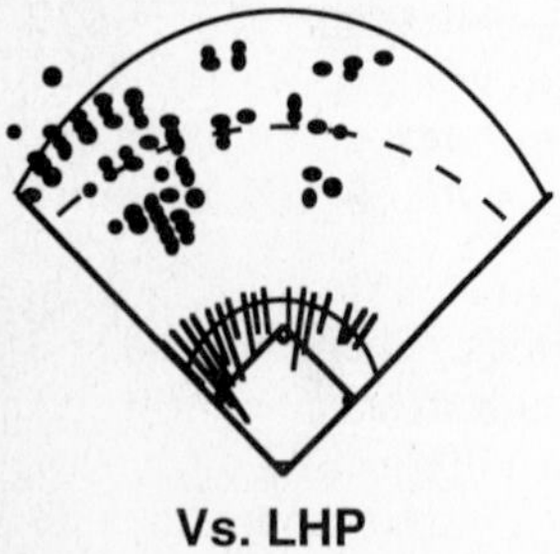
Vs. LHP

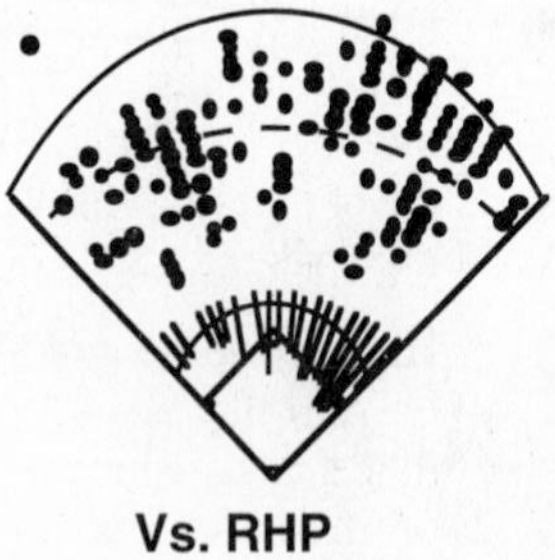
Vs. RHP

In the diagrams, ground balls and short line drives are shown by the various length lines in the infield: the longer the line, the more ground balls and liners hit in that direction. Jefferies is a switch-hitter, and from either side of the plate, the majority of his batted balls to the infield are pulled; there are very few balls down the opposite lines. When Jefferies is batting right-handed, the third baseman and shortstop should remain in their positions, but the second baseman should move toward the second base bag and the first baseman should move well off the line. To defense Jefferies in the infield when he's batting left-handed, the second and first basemen should stay put, the shortstop should move toward the center of the diamond, and the third baseman should move off the line to cover the hole.

In the outfield, batted balls are shown by dots. The dotted line in the outfield is 300 feet away from home plate, indicating how deep an outfield normally plays. As you can see, Jefferies is strictly a pull hitter against a LHP (batting right-handed). The outfield should play at normal depth, but shift well to the left. If Jefferies should dump a hit down the right field line, it'd be news. Batting left-handed, Jefferies has excellent power to right field -- the right fielder should play straight-away and deep -- but can hit the ball the opposite way as well. The left fielder should play at medium depth but slightly off the line.

Technical Information on the Diagrams

A lot of experimentation went into producing these charts. When we first started, we tried to show every single batted ball that was hit into play by each player. We found that the charts became very cluttered for everyday players. We began experimenting with trying to show only the most meaningful information. When all was said and done, here's what we ended up with:

a. Pop-ups and bunts are excluded. We excluded pop-ups because 95% of these are caught regardless of how fielders are positioned. We excluded bunts because defensing a bunt is a whole different strategy that is primarily used on a select number of players and situations.

b. Groundballs under 50 feet are excluded. These are swinging bunts and are somewhat rare. We exclude them because they don't provide a true indication of the direction of a batted ball reaching an infielder or going through the infield.

c. For everyday players, we excluded what we call isolated points in the outfield. If a player hit only one ball in a given area of the field with no other batted balls in the vicinity all season, we exclude it from the chart. We felt that one ball does not give a true indication of a tendency. This rule did not apply to balls hit farther than 380 feet; all batted balls over 380 feet are shown.

d. Similarly, for players who play infrequently, we expanded the data sample to create a larger pattern of dots in the outfield when he tended to hit in a given area more frequently.

e. For ground balls over 50 feet, we excluded only the rare isolated ground ball. For most players, almost all of their ground balls are shown.

Other notes of interest:

The field itself is drawn to precise scale, with the outfield fence reaching 400 feet in centerfield and 330 feet down the lines. Keep in mind that parks are configured differently so that a dot that is shown inside of the diagram might actually have been a home run. Similarly, a dot outside the fence in the diagram might actually have been in play.

Liners under 170 feet are part of the infield. We give responsibility for short line drives to the infielders.

No distinction is made between hits and outs.

1990 Situational Stats

There are eight situational breakdowns for every primary player. **Home** and **Road** show performance between playing in his home park versus on the road. **Day** and **Night** show performance in day games versus night games. For hitters, **LHP** and **RHP** show the player's performance versus left-handed pitchers and right-handed pitchers respectively. For pitchers, **LHB** and **RHB** show how the opposition batters hit against that pitcher based on the side of the plate from which they hit. **Sc Pos** stands for Scoring Position. It shows batting performance when hitting with runners in scoring position. For pitchers, Sc Pos shows the opposition's batting statistics when there are men in scoring position against that pitcher.

The definition we use for **Clutch** here can be simply restated as the late innings of a close game. For those of you interested in the exact definition, clutch is when it is the seventh inning or later and the batting team is up by one run, tied, or has the tying run on base, at bat, or on deck. You'll notice a similarity to the save definition. This is intentional; it allows our definition of Clutch to be consistent with a very well-known statistic, the save.

1990 Rankings

This section shows how the player ranked against the league, against his teammates, and by position in significant categories. Thanks to the power of the STATS computer, we not only include traditional categories, but also the less traditional categories as shown in the Major League Leaders section of this book. The Defintions and Qualifications section below provides some details on these lesser known categories. Due to space considerations, when a player ranked high in numerous categories, we omitted some of the less interesting rankings.

Major League Leaders

The chapter immediately following this introduction is a complete listing of Major League Leaders. The top three players in each category are shown for each league separately. You'll notice a STATS flavor to these leaders. Not only do we show the leaders for the common categories like batting average, home runs and ERA, but you'll also find less traditional categories like steals of third, percentage of extra bases taken as a runner and pitches thrown.

Definitions and Qualifications

The following are definitions and qualifications for the Major League Leaders and Rankings.

Definitions:

Times on Base -- Hits plus walks plus hit by pitch.

Groundball/Flyball Ratio -- The ratio of all ground balls hit to fly balls and pop-ups hit. Bunts and line drives are excluded completely.

Percentage of extra bases taken as a runner -- This figure measures how often a player takes an extra base on a single or double, advances on a groundout, or advances on a fly out.

Runs scored per time reached base -- This is calculated by dividing Runs Scored by Times on Base.

Clutch -- This category shows a player's batting average in the late innings of close games: the seventh inning or later with the batting team ahead by one, tied, or has the tying run on base, at bat, or on deck.

Bases Loaded -- This category shows a player's batting average in bases loaded situations.

GDP per GDP situation -- A GDP situation exists any

time there is a man on first with less than two outs. This statistic measures how often a player grounds into a double play in that situation.

Percentage of Pitches Taken -- This tells you how often a player lets a pitch go by without swinging.

Percentage of Swings Put into Play -- This tells you how often a player hits the ball into fair territory when he swings.

Run Support per Nine Innings -- This figure indicates how many runs are scored for a pitcher by his team while he was pitching translated into a per nine inning figure.

Baserunners per Nine Innings -- These are the hits, walks and hit batsmen allowed per nine innings.

Strikeout/Walk Ratio -- This is simply a pitcher's strikeouts divided by his walks allowed.

Stolen Base Percentage Allowed -- This figure indicates how successful opposing baseunners are when attempting a stolen base. It's stolen bases divided by stolen base attempts.

Save Percentage -- This is saves divided by save opportunities. Save opportunities include saves plus blown saves.

Blown Saves -- A blown save is given any time a pitcher comes into a game where a save situation is in place and he loses the lead.

Holds -- A hold is given to a pitcher when he comes into the game in a save situation, but is removed before the end of the game while maintaining his team's lead. The pitcher must retire at least one batter to get a hold.

Percentage of Inherited Runners Scored -- When a pitcher comes into a game with men already on base, these runners are called inherited runners. This statistic measures the percentage of these inherited runners that the relief pitcher allows to score.

First Batter Efficiency -- This statistic tells you the batting average allowed by a relief pitcher to the first batter he faces.

Qualifications:

In order to be ranked, a player had to qualify with a minimum number of opportunities. The qualifications are as follows:

Batters

Batting average, slugging percentage, on-base average, home run frequency, ground ball/fly ball ratio, runs scored per time reached base, pitches seen per plate appearance, percentage of pitches taken, lowest percentage of swings that missed and percentage of swings put into play -- 502 plate appearances

Percentage of extra bases taken as a runner -- 40 opportunities to advance

Stolen base percentage -- 20 stolen base attempts

Runners in scoring position -- 100 plate appearances with runners in scoring position

Clutch -- 50 plate appearances in the clutch

Bases loaded -- 10 plate appearances with the bases loaded

GDP per GDP situation -- 50 plate appearances with a man on first and less than two outs

Vs LHP -- 125 plate appearances against left-handed pitchers

Vs RHP -- 377 plate appearances against right-handed pitchers

BA at home -- 252 plate appearances at home

BA on the road -- 252 plate appearances on the road

BA on 3-1 count -- 20 plate appearances putting the ball into play or walking on a 3-1 count

BA with 2 strikes -- 150 plate appearances with 2 strikes

BA on 0-2 count -- 10 plate appearances putting the ball into play or striking out on a 0-2 count

BA on 3-2 count -- 20 plate appearances with a 3-2 count

Pitchers

Earned run average, run support per nine innings, baserunners per nine innings, batting average allowed, on-base average allowed, slugging percentage allowed, home runs per nine innings, strikeouts per nine innings, strikeout/walk ratio, stolen base percentage allowed, GDPs per nine innings and groundball/flyball ratio off -- 162 innings pitched

GDPs induced per GDP situation -- pitchers facing 30 batters in GDP situations

Save Percentage -- 20 save opportunities

Percentage of inherited runners scoring -- 30 inherited runners

First batter efficiency -- 40 games in relief

BA allowed, runners in scoring position -- pitchers facing 100 batters with men in scoring position

ERA at home -- 81 innings pitched at home

ERA on the road -- 81 innings pitched on the road

Vs LHB -- 125 left-handed batters faced

Vs RHB -- 377 right-handed batters faced

Fielders

Percentage caught stealing by catchers -- catchers with 75 stolen base attempts against them

Major League Leaders

1990 American League Leaders

Batters

Batting Average
George Brett	**.329**
Rickey Henderson	.325
Rafael Palmeiro	.319

Home Runs
Cecil Fielder	**51**
Mark McGwire	39
Jose Canseco	37

Runs Batted In
Cecil Fielder	**132**
Kelly Gruber	118
Mark McGwire	108

Games Played
Roberto Kelly	**162**
Tony Fernandez	161
Cal Ripken	161

At Bats
Harold Reynolds	**642**
Roberto Kelly	641
Tony Fernandez	635

Runs Scored
Rickey Henderson	**119**
Cecil Fielder	104
Harold Reynolds	100

Hits
Rafael Palmeiro	**191**
Wade Boggs	187
Roberto Kelly	183

Singles
Rafael Palmeiro	**136**
Julio Franco	133
Wade Boggs	132
Roberto Kelly	132

Doubles
Jody Reed	**45**
George Brett	**45**
Wade Boggs	44
Ivan Calderon	44

Triples
Tony Fernandez	**17**
Sammy Sosa	10
Lance Johnson	9
Nelson Liriano	9
Luis Polonia	9

Stolen Bases
Rickey Henderson	**65**
Steve Sax	43
Roberto Kelly	42

Caught Stealing
Lance Johnson	**22**
Roberto Kelly	17
Ozzie Guillen	17

Walks
Mark McGwire	**110**
Mickey Tettleton	106
Tony Phillips	99

Intentional Walks
Wade Boggs	**19**
Cal Ripken	18
George Brett	14

Hit by Pitch
Phil Bradley	**11**
Pete Incaviglia	9
Kelly Gruber	8

Strikeouts
Cecil Fielder	**182**
Mickey Tettleton	160
Jose Canseco	158

Ground into Double Play
Ivan Calderon	**26**
Rafael Palmeiro	24
Tony Pena	23

Sacrifice Bunts
Mike Gallego	**17**
Billy Ripken	**17**
Ozzie Guillen	15

Sacrifice Flies
Dave Parker	**14**
Kelly Gruber	13
George Bell	11
Jerry Browne	11

Batter Plate Appearances
Harold Reynolds	**737**
Tony Fernandez	721
Wade Boggs	713

Times on Base
Wade Boggs	**275**
Fred McGriff	263
Rickey Henderson	260

Total Bases
Cecil Fielder	**339**
Kelly Gruber	303
Fred McGriff	295

Slugging Percentage
Cecil Fielder	**.592**
Rickey Henderson	.577
Jose Canseco	.543

On-Base Average
Rickey Henderson	**.439**
Fred McGriff	.400
Edgar Martinez	.397

HR Frequency - AB/HR
Cecil Fielder	**11.2**
Jose Canseco	13.0
Mark McGwire	13.4

Groundball/Flyball Ratio
Steve Sax	**2.8**
Tony Pena	2.5
Kirby Puckett	2.4

Extra Bases Taken as Runner
Mike Devereaux	**63.9%**
Mike Felder	61.5
Bo Jackson	60.5

Runs/Time Reached Base
Rickey Henderson	**45.8%**
Sammy Sosa	44.2
Jerry Browne	43.6

SB Success %
Henry Cotto	**87.5%**
Rickey Henderson	86.7
Paul Molitor	85.7
Jim Gantner	85.7

Steals of Third
Rickey Henderson	**17**
Steve Sax	11
Alex Cole	9

BA Scoring Position
Alan Trammell	**.379**
George Brett	.360
Lance Johnson	.345

BA Late & Close
Rickey Henderson	**.426**
Walt Weiss	.405
Gary Sheffield	.397

BA Bases Loaded
Luis Rivera	**.600**
Terry Steinbach	.579
Johnny Ray	.556

GDP/GDP Situation
Rob Deer	**0.0%**
Kevin Maas	3.9
Jack Howell	4.8

BA vs LH Pitchers
Sandy Alomar Jr	**.376**
Cecil Fielder	.371
Shane Mack	.370

BA vs RH Pitchers

Luis Polonia	**.341**
George Brett	.336
Rickey Henderson	.330

BA at Home

Wade Boggs	**.359**
Kirby Puckett	.344
Tom Brunansky	.340

BA on the Road

Rafael Palmeiro	**.350**
Rickey Henderson	.342
George Brett	.340

BA on 3-1 Count

Sam Horn	**1.000**
Charlie O'Brien	.800
Cory Snyder	.750
Felix Jose	.750

BA With 2 Strikes

Rickey Henderson	**.310**
Felix Fermin	.277
Edgar Martinez	.270

BA on 0-2 Count

Chili Davis	**.409**
Luis Polonia	.353
Sandy Alomar Jr	.351

BA on 3-2 Count

Rance Mulliniks	**.417**
Felix Fermin	.412
Bill Spiers	.412

Pitches Seen

Wade Boggs	**3,067**
Tony Phillips	2,784
Cecil Fielder	2,749

Pitches Seen per PA

Mickey Tettleton	**4.4**
Wade Boggs	4.3
Rickey Henderson	4.3

% Pitches Taken

Rickey Henderson	**66.3%**
Mickey Tettleton	65.4
Alvin Davis	64.7

% of Swings that Missed

Jody Reed	**7.0%**
Wade Boggs	7.3
Edgar Martinez	8.3

% Swings Put Into Play

Lance Johnson	**59.3%**
B.J. Surhoff	57.5
Jody Reed	57.4

Bunts in Play

Steve Finley	**34**
Mitch Webster	32
Billy Ripken	31

Pitchers

Earned Run Average

Roger Clemens	**1.93**
Chuck Finley	2.40
Dave Stewart	2.56

Wins

Bob Welch	**27**
Dave Stewart	22
Roger Clemens	21

Losses

Tim Leary	**19**
Jack Morris	18
Matt Young	18
Allan Anderson	18

Win-Loss Percentage

Bob Welch	**.818**
Roger Clemens	.778
Dave Stieb	.750

Games Pitched

Bobby Thigpen	**77**
Duane Ward	73
Jeff Montgomery	73

Games Started

Jack Morris	**36**
Dave Stewart	**36**
Bob Welch	35
Melido Perez	35

Complete Games

Jack Morris	**11**
Dave Stewart	**11**
Ron Robinson	7
Chuck Finley	7
Bobby Witt	7
Matt Young	7
Roger Clemens	7

Shutouts

Dave Stewart	**4**
Roger Clemens	**4**
Jack Morris	3
Melido Perez	3
Kevin Appier	3

Saves

Bobby Thigpen	**57**
Dennis Eckersley	48
Doug Jones	43

Games Finished

Bobby Thigpen	**73**
Doug Jones	64
Dennis Eckersley	61

Innings Pitched

Dave Stewart	**267.0**
Jack Morris	249.2
Bob Welch	238.0

Hits Allowed

Jim Abbott	**246**
Greg Swindell	245
Jack Morris	231

Batters Faced

Dave Stewart	**1,088**
Jack Morris	1,073
Bob Welch	979

Runs Allowed

Jack Morris	**144**
Mark Langston	120
Jim Abbott	116

Earned Runs Allowed

Jack Morris	**125**
Mark Langston	109
Jim Abbott	106

Home Runs Allowed

Dave Johnson	**30**
Greg Swindell	27
Scott Sanderson	27

Walks Allowed

Randy Johnson	**120**
Charlie Hough	119
Bobby Witt	110

Hit Batters

Charlie Hough	**11**
Mike Boddicker	10
Dave Stieb	10

Strikeouts

Nolan Ryan	**232**
Bobby Witt	221
Erik Hanson	211

Wild Pitches

Tim Leary	**23**
Jack Morris	16
Matt Young	16
Jeff M. Robinson	16

Balks

Jaime Navarro	**5**
Melido Perez	4
5 Pitchers with	3

Run Support per 9 IP

Bob Welch	**5.9**
Todd Stottlemyre	5.8
Pete Harnisch	5.8

Baserunners per 9 IP

Nolan Ryan	**9.6**
Roger Clemens	10.0
David Wells	10.1

Batting Average Allowed

Nolan Ryan	**.188**
Randy Johnson	.216
Roger Clemens	.228

Slugging Pct Allowed

Roger Clemens	**.306**
Dave Stieb	.320
Nolan Ryan	.322

On-Base Average Allowed

Nolan Ryan	**.268**
Roger Clemens	.278
David Wells	.283

Home Runs per 9 IP

Roger Clemens	**.276**
Kirk McCaskill	.465
Greg Hibbard	.469

Strikeouts per 9 IP

Nolan Ryan	**10.2**
Bobby Witt	9.0
Roger Clemens	8.2

Strikeout/Walk Ratio

Roger Clemens	**3.9**
Nolan Ryan	3.1
Erik Hanson	3.1

Stolen Bases Allowed

Jack Morris	**45**
Bobby Witt	36
Charlie Hough	33

Caught Stealing Off

Chuck Finley	**18**
Greg Cadaret	17
Frank Tanana	15

SB Pct Allowed

Greg Swindell	**20.0%**
Dave Johnson	20.0
Frank Tanana	37.5

GDPs Induced

Matt Young	**27**
Jim Abbott	**27**
Greg Hibbard	25
Bob Welch	25

GDPs Induced per 9 IP

Kevin Brown	**1.2**
Jim Abbott	1.1
Matt Young	1.1

GDPs Induced/GDP Situation

Luis Aquino	**24.4%**
Craig McMurtry	21.9
Brian DuBois	21.8

Grd/Fly Ratio Off

Kevin Brown	**3.4**
Matt Young	2.2
Jim Abbott	2.0

Save Opportunities

Bobby Thigpen	**65**
Doug Jones	51
Dennis Eckersley	50

Save Percentage

Dennis Eckersley	**96.0%**
Dave Righetti	92.3
Mike Schooler	88.2

Blown Saves

Dan Plesac	**10**
Jeff Montgomery	**10**
Mike Jackson	9

Holds

Barry Jones	**30**
Rick Honeycutt	27
Chuck Crim	19

% Inherited Runners Scored

Joe Klink	**12.9%**
Kevin Hickey	17.1
Bobby Thigpen	17.7

First Batter Efficiency

Terry Leach	**.125**
Bobby Thigpen	.127
Duane Ward	.129

BA Allowed Scoring Position

Nolan Ryan	**.157**
Steve Farr	.157
Roger Clemens	.172

Pitches Thrown

Dave Stewart	**3,977**
Bobby Witt	3,780
Jack Morris	3,753

Pitches Thrown per Batter

Kevin Brown	**3.4**
Dave Johnson	3.4
Allan Anderson	3.5

Pickoff Throws

Charlie Hough	**368**
Roger Clemens	269
Kevin Brown	209
Jack McDowell	209

ERA at Home

Roger Clemens	**1.53**
Chuck Finley	1.63
Dave Stewart	1.74

ERA on the Road

Dana Kiecker	**2.14**
Roger Clemens	2.31
Dave Stieb	2.73

BA Off by LH Batters

Ben McDonald	**.181**
Doug Jones	.200
Gregg Olson	.200

BA Off by RH Batters

Nolan Ryan	**.158**
Dave Stieb	.205
Roger Clemens	.213

Fielders

Errors by Pitcher

Matt Young	**9**
Bobby Witt	5
Chuck Finley	5
Randy Johnson	5

Errors by Catcher

Sandy Alomar Jr	**14**
Mike Heath	13
Brian Harper	11

Errors by First Base

Carlos Quintana	**17**
Cecil Fielder	14
Kevin Maas	9
Randy Milligan	9

Errors by Second Base

Julio Franco	**19**
Harold Reynolds	**19**
Nelson Liriano	11

Errors by Third Base

Edgar Martinez	**27**
Robin Ventura	25
Gary Sheffield	25

Errors by Shortstop

Kurt Stillwell	**24**
Luis Rivera	18
Ozzie Guillen	17
Alvaro Espinoza	17
Jeff Huson	17
Dick Schofield	17

Errors by Left Field

Pete Incaviglia	**7**
Mike Greenwell	**7**
Ivan Calderon	**7**
Greg Vaughn	**7**

Errors by Center Field

Lance Johnson	**10**
Devon White	9
Ken Griffey Jr	7

Errors by Right Field

Sammy Sosa	**13**
Ruben Sierra	10
Junior Felix	9

% CS off Catchers

Lance Parrish	**47.0%**
Bob Geren	43.3
Pat Borders	42.6

1990 National League Leaders

Batters

Batting Average

Willie McGee	**.335**
Eddie Murray	.330
Dave Magadan	.328

Home Runs

Ryne Sandberg	**40**
Darryl Strawberry	37
Kevin Mitchell	35

Runs Batted In

Matt D. Williams	**122**
Bobby Bonilla	120
Joe Carter	115

Games Played

Joe Carter	**162**
Tim Wallach	161
Brett Butler	160
Bobby Bonilla	160

At Bats

Joe Carter	**634**
Tim Wallach	626
Bobby Bonilla	625

Runs Scored

Ryne Sandberg	**116**
Bobby Bonilla	112
Brett Butler	108

Hits

Brett Butler	**192**
Lenny Dykstra	**192**
Ryne Sandberg	188

Singles

Brett Butler	**160**
Barry Larkin	147
Lenny Dykstra	145

Doubles

Gregg Jefferies	**40**
Bobby Bonilla	39
Chris Sabo	38

Triples

Mariano Duncan	**11**
Tony Gwynn	10
Vince Coleman	9
Brett Butler	9
Lonnie Smith	9

Stolen Bases

Vince Coleman	**77**
Eric Yelding	64
Barry Bonds	52

Caught Stealing

Eric Yelding	**25**
Delino DeShields	22
Juan Samuel	20

Walks

Jack Clark	**104**
Barry Bonds	93
Brett Butler	90

Intentional Walks

Eddie Murray	**21**
Andre Dawson	**21**
Tony Gwynn	20

Hit by Pitch

Glenn Davis	**8**
Joe Carter	7
Lenny Dykstra	7
Matt D. Williams	7
Barry Larkin	7

Strikeouts

Andres Galarraga	**169**
Matt D. Williams	138
Jim Presley	130
Dale Murphy	130

Ground into Double Play

Dale Murphy	**22**
Jose Lind	20
Eddie Murray	19

Sacrifice Bunts

Jay Bell	**39**
Dwight Gooden	14
Jack Armstrong	13
Ed Whitson	13

Sacrifice Flies

Bobby Bonilla	**15**
Will Clark	13
Pedro Guerrero	11
Hubie Brooks	11

Batter Plate Appearances

Brett Butler	**732**
Joe Carter	697
Jay Bell	696

Times on Base

Brett Butler	**288**
Lenny Dykstra	**288**
Eddie Murray	267

Total Bases

Ryne Sandberg	**344**
Bobby Bonilla	324
Ron Gant	310

Slugging Percentage

Barry Bonds	**.564**
Ryne Sandberg	.559
Kevin Mitchell	.544

On-Base Average

Lenny Dykstra	**.418**
Dave Magadan	.417
Eddie Murray	.414

HR Frequency - AB/HR

Darryl Strawberry	**14.6**
Kevin Mitchell	15.0
Ryne Sandberg	15.4

Groundball/Flyball Ratio

Willie McGee	**3.3**
Brett Butler	2.2
Delino DeShields	2.1

Extra Bases Taken as Runner

Daryl Boston	**66.7%**
Stan Javier	64.6
Eric Yelding	64.4

Runs/Time Reached Base

Bobby Bonilla	**50.7%**
Ryne Sandberg	48.5
Ron Gant	47.6

SB Success %

Kirk Gibson	**92.9%**
Marquis Grissom	91.7
Eric Davis	87.5

Steals of third

Vince Coleman	**18**
Otis Nixon	13
Barry Bonds	12

BA Scoring Position

Lenny Dykstra	**.427**
Dave Magadan	.382
Barry Bonds	.377

BA Late & Close

Benito Santiago	**.433**
Randy Ready	.407
Dave Magadan	.391

BA Bases Loaded

Kevin McReynolds	**.800**
Ozzie Smith	.571
Tony Gwynn	.556

GDP/GDP Situation

Dave Justice	**2.7%**
Lonnie Smith	2.7
Todd Benzinger	3.9

BA vs LH Pitchers

Mariano Duncan	**.410**
Jack Clark	.377
Dave Justice	.366

BA vs RH Pitchers

Lenny Dykstra	**.344**
Eddie Murray	.338
Ryne Sandberg	.334

BA at Home

Ryne Sandberg	**.357**
Willie McGee	.348
Eddie Murray	.343

BA on the Road

Dave Magadan	**.372**
Bip Roberts	.338
Barry Larkin	.326

BA on 3-1 Count

Hubie Brooks	**.750**
Jim Presley	.667
Franklin Stubbs	.636

BA With 2 Strikes

Dave Magadan	**.309**
Tony Gwynn	.282
Lenny Harris	.275

BA on 0-2 Count

Tony Gwynn	**.435**
Lonnie Smith	.381
Rafael Ramirez	.314

BA on 3-2 Count

Hal Morris	**.526**
Domingo Ramos	.461
Dwight Smith	.444

Pitches Seen

Brett Butler	**2,902**
Jay Bell	2,671
Lenny Dykstra	2,551

Pitches Seen per PA

Kal Daniels	**4.1**
Dave Magadan	4.1
Delino DeShields	4.0

% Pitches Taken

Dave Magadan	**65.9%**
Todd Zeile	63.3
Barry Bonds	62.9

% of Swings that Missed

Lenny Dykstra	**5.9%**
Tony Gwynn	6.5
Ozzie Smith	7.1

% Swings Put Into Play

Tony Gwynn	**61.6%**
Ozzie Smith	59.3
Mike Scioscia	57.5

Bunts in Play

Brett Butler	**55**
Jay Bell	51
Craig Biggio	31

Pitchers

Earned Run Average

Danny Darwin	**2.21**
Zane Smith	2.55
Ed Whitson	2.60

Wins

Doug Drabek	**22**
Ramon Martinez	20
Frank Viola	20

Losses

Jose DeLeon	**19**
Joe Magrane	17
Greg Maddux	15
Mike Morgan	15
Dennis Rasmussen	15

Win-Loss Percentage

Doug Drabek	**.786**
Ramon Martinez	.769
John Tudor	.750

Games Pitched

Juan Agosto	**82**
Paul Assenmacher	74
Greg W. Harris	73

Games Started

Frank Viola	**35**
Tom Browning	**35**
Greg Maddux	**35**

Complete Games

Ramon Martinez	**12**
Bruce Hurst	9
Doug Drabek	9

Shutouts

Bruce Hurst	**4**
Mike Morgan	**4**
6 Pitchers with	3

Saves

John Franco	**33**
Randy Myers	31
Lee Smith	27

Games Finished

Roger McDowell	**60**
Randy Myers	59
Steve Bedrosian	53

Innings Pitched

Frank Viola	**249.0**
Greg Maddux	237.1
Ramon Martinez	234.2

Hits Allowed

Greg Maddux	**242**
Tom Browning	235
Tom Glavine	232

Batters Faced

Frank Viola	**1,016**
Greg Maddux	1,011
Dwight Gooden	983

Runs Allowed

Greg Maddux	**116**
Fernando Valenzuela	112
Tom Glavine	111

Earned Runs Allowed

Fernando Valenzuela	**104**
Tom Glavine	102
John Smoltz	99
Dwight Gooden	99

Home Runs Allowed

Dennis Rasmussen	**28**
Mike Scott	27
Tom Browning	24

Walks Allowed

John Smoltz	**90**
Jose DeLeon	86
Pat Combs	86

Hit Batters

Mark Gardner	**9**
Joe Magrane	8
Jim Deshaies	8

Strikeouts

David Cone	**233**
Ramon Martinez	223
Dwight Gooden	223

Wild Pitches

John Smoltz	**14**
Fernando Valenzuela	13
Joe Magrane	11
Frank Viola	11
Mike Bielecki	11

Balks

Dave Smith	**5**
Andy Benes	**5**
Jack Armstrong	**5**
Bob Kipper	**5**
Jose Rijo	**5**

Run Support per 9 IP

Dwight Gooden	**6.8**
Doug Drabek	5.9
Dennis Rasmussen	5.7

Baserunners per 9 IP

Danny Darwin	**9.5**
Doug Drabek	9.7
Dennis Martinez	9.8

Batting Average Allowed

Sid Fernandez	**.200**
Jose Rijo	.212
Ramon Martinez	.221

Slugging Pct Allowed

Jose Rijo	**.313**
Danny Darwin	.331
Doug Drabek	.331

On-Base Average Allowed

Danny Darwin	**.266**
Doug Drabek	.274
Dennis Martinez	.274

Home Runs per 9 IP

Dwight Gooden	**.387**
Greg Maddux	.418
Joe Magrane	.443

Strikeouts per 9 IP

David Cone	**9.9**
Sid Fernandez	9.1
Dwight Gooden	8.6

Strikeout/Walk Ratio

David Cone	**3.6**
Danny Darwin	3.5
Ramon Martinez	3.3

Stolen Bases Allowed

Dwight Gooden	**60**
Mike Scott	53
Kevin Gross	31
John Smoltz	31

Caught Stealing Off

Dennis Rasmussen	**16**
Dwight Gooden	**16**
Joe Magrane	**16**

SB Pct Allowed

Terry Mulholland	**50.0%**
Pat Combs	52.4
Tom Browning	54.5

GDPs induced

Zane Smith	**34**
Greg Maddux	27
Tom Glavine	23

GDPs Induced per 9 IP

Zane Smith	**1.4**
Scott Garrelts	1.1
Greg Maddux	1.0

GDPs Induced/GDP Situation

Zane Smith	**24.3%**
Atlee Hammaker	23.7
Ricky Horton	18.4

Grd/Fly Ratio Off

Mike Morgan	**2.7**
Greg Maddux	2.6
Zane Smith	2.1

Save Opportunities

John Franco	**39**
Randy Myers	37
Lee Smith	32

Save Percentage

John Franco	**84.6%**
Lee Smith	84.4
Randy Myers	83.8

Blown Saves

Paul Assenmacher	**10**
Jay Howell	8
Craig Lefferts	7
Greg W. Harris	7

Holds

Rob Dibble	**17**
Juan Agosto	16
Scott Ruskin	15

% Inherited Runners Scored

Randy Myers	**9.4%**
Juan Agosto	17.0
Stan Belinda	22.0

First Batter Efficiency

Darrel Akerfelds	**.133**
Stan Belinda	.146
Don Carman	.149

BA Allowed Scoring Position

Oil Can Boyd	**.169**
David Cone	.183
Danny Darwin	.200

Pitches Thrown

Ramon Martinez	**3,802**
Dwight Gooden	3,690
Frank Viola	3,684

Pitches Thrown per Batter

Ed Whitson	**3.2**
Tom Browning	3.2
Bill Gullickson	3.3

Pickoff Throws

Jim Deshaies	**341**
John Burkett	280
Tom Glavine	272

ERA at Home

Mark Portugal	**1.78**
Zane Smith	2.05
Jose Rijo	2.24

ERA on the Road

Danny Darwin	**2.02**
Dennis Martinez	2.27
Doug Drabek	2.51

BA Off by LH Batters

Zane Smith	**.164**
Joe Boever	.182
Rob Dibble	.185

BA Off by RH Batters

Sid Fernandez	**.195**
John Smoltz	.198
Trevor Wilson	.218

Fielders

Errors by Pitcher

Roger McDowell	**5**
Dwight Gooden	4
Jeff Parrett	4

Errors by Catcher

Mackey Sasser	**14**
Benito Santiago	12
Joe Girardi	11

Errors by First Base

Pedro Guerrero	**13**
Mark Grace	12
Will Clark	12

Errors by Second Base

Roberto Alomar	**17**
Mariano Duncan	15
Jeff Treadway	15

Errors by Third Base

Jim Presley	**25**
Ken Caminiti	21
Tim Wallach	21

Errors by Shortstop

Alfredo Griffin	**26**
Garry Templeton	**26**
Rafael Ramirez	25
Dickie Thon	25

Errors by Left Field

Lonnie Smith	**12**
Kevin Mitchell	9
Barry Bonds	6
Tim Raines	6

Errors by Center Field

Willie McGee	**16**
Andy Van Slyke	8
Eric Yelding	7

Errors by Right Field

Bobby Bonilla	**12**
Hubie Brooks	10
Dale Murphy	5
Andre Dawson	5
Glenn Wilson	5
Tony Gwynn	5
Milt Thompson	5

% CS off Catchers

Joe Oliver	**40.2%**
Joe Girardi	37.0
Darren Daulton	35.0

Stars, Bums and Sleepers — Who's Who in 1991

This is the section of the book where we're going to have a little fun. Here at STATS, we think we know a little about baseball and especially about individual players. After all, this is the most comprehensive scouting report of all major league baseball players that there is. So we decided to give you our player evaluations and prognostications in a summarized form. If you play fantasy or rotisserie baseball, you might find this section especially useful.

How To Use This Section

Every position is broken into four groups: Expect A Better Year in '91, Look for Consistency, Production Will Drop and 1991 Sleepers. Here's the key point to remember when looking at the first three of these categories. **A player is put into one of these three groups based on his 1990 performance.** For example, Ryne Sandberg is shown in the category Production Will Drop. That means that you probably shouldn't expect Ryno to hit 40 homers again, especially in conjunction with a .300+ batting average and 25 stolen bases. However, we still believe that Ryne Sandberg could easily have the best year among all second basemen in baseball. If he hits 25 dingers with 85 RBIs while batting .280 and tossing in 20 stolen bases, that would be a significant drop in production -- for him. It would probably still be the best offensive numbers among all second basemen in baseball.

For 1991 Sleepers, we've done something a little bit different. The numbers we show in this section are each player's combined minor and major league performance for 1990. The idea here is to show what this player is **capable** of doing. We've tried to factor in playing time into the equation, but you'll get a better idea as the season starts as to who's playing and who's not.

Finally, within each grouping (for example, catchers listed under Expect A Better Year) we've ranked the players based on our own expectations of performance from best performance to worst. Taking this example, we rank Craig Biggio ahead of Todd Zeile and Benito Santiago. But we leave it up to you to determine how an improved season by Craig Biggio will compare to our expected production drop from Lance Parrish.

How We Developed This Section

We broke down all 719 players in this book into their most common position played in 1990. We then looked at every player in two basic ways: statistical analysis and subjective rating.

For our statistical model, we looked at historical patterns of performance to help us project performance for each player. Here are some of the factors that we plugged into our computer:

Career trends -- A player should not be judged simply based on his most recent year of performance. While it is possible that a player who had a good year in relation to the rest of his career has suddenly become a better ballplayer, it's much more likely that it was simply a good year. Meaning, of course, that it's likely he'll come down to a more normal performance the following year. While it is possible for a .280 career hitter like Lenny Dykstra to hit .325 again, it's much more likely he'll come back down to the .270-.290 range that he's established for his career. The same is true about a bad season for most players. If their playing time does not get severely cut, a player with a bad season will usually rebound.

Player Age -- The best age for a player in baseball is 26 or 27. Based on historical studies, this is the age when players have their best years. So, the rule of thumb is that if a player is less than 26, you can expect some improvement over the level of play he's established so far in his career. If a player is over 27, you can expect some decrease in his playing performance from **the level of play he has established in recent years and over his career.**

Minor League Performance -- In his book ***The Bill James Abstract***, Bill has found that minor league performance, when properly adjusted, is just as reliable in predicting major league performance as is prior major league performance. Therefore, we've looked at minor league performance here to help us project 1991, especially for the players we called sleepers.

We then added our own subjective considerations:

Playing Time -- When considering how good a player will be in a given year, you first have to determine how often he'll get a chance to play. This we've done by evaluating players compared to their teammates.

Pitchers' Inconsistency -- For every five hitters you can name as being reasonably consistent from year to year, there is probably only one pitcher who can compare in consistency. All things considered, Jose DeLeon was one of the top pitchers in the National League in 1989. He probably compares to other NL pitchers in 1989 as Will Clark compared to other 1989 hitters. Will Clark dropped off in 1990, but Jose DeLeon felt so low about his 7-19 season that he could crawl under a snake standing up. The key point is this: predicting pitcher performance is a very inexact science. We used a lot of subjective considerations when we came up with our pitcher evaluations.

Catcher

Expect A Better Year in '91

	1990 Statistics			
	Avg.	HR	RBI	SB
Craig Biggio	.276	4	42	25
Todd Zeile	.244	15	57	2
Benito Santiago	.270	11	53	5
Terry Steinbach	.251	9	57	0
Matt Nokes	.248	11	40	2
Dave Valle	.214	7	33	1
Tom Pagnozzi	.277	2	23	1
Bob Geren	.213	8	31	0
Ron Karkovice	.246	6	20	2
Greg Myers	.236	5	22	0
Scott Bradley	.223	1	28	0

Look for Consistency

	1990 Statistics			
	Avg.	HR	RBI	SB
Tony Pena	.263	7	56	8
Mickey Tettleton	.223	15	51	2
Sandy Alomar Jr	.290	9	66	4
B.J. Surhoff	.276	6	59	18
Pat Borders	.286	15	49	0
Joe Oliver	.231	8	52	1
Mike Fitzgerald	.243	9	41	8
Joe Girardi	.270	1	38	8
Greg Olson	.262	7	36	1
Mike LaValliere	.258	3	31	0
Geno Petralli	.255	0	21	0

Production Will Drop

	1990 Statistics			
	Avg.	HR	RBI	SB
Lance Parrish	.268	24	70	2
Carlton Fisk	.285	18	65	7
Darren Daulton	.268	12	57	7
Mike Scioscia	.264	12	66	4
Brian Harper	.294	6	54	3
Mike Macfarlane	.255	6	58	1
Don Slaught	.300	4	29	0
Gary Carter	.254	9	27	1
Mike Heath	.270	7	38	7
Mackey Sasser	.307	6	41	0
Terry Kennedy	.277	2	26	1

1991 Sleepers

	1990 Statistics (includes minor leagues)			
	Avg.	HR	RBI	SB
Steve Decker	.293	18	88	3
Darrin Fletcher	.282	13	66	1
Damon Berryhill	.234	7	23	0
Todd Hundley	.254	1	37	5
Hector Villanueva	.268	15	52	1

First Base

Expect A Better Year in '91

	1990 Statistics			
	Avg.	HR	RBI	SB
Will Clark	.295	19	95	8
Don Mattingly	.256	5	42	1
Glenn Davis	.251	22	64	8
Carlos Quintana	.287	7	67	1
Wally Joyner	.268	8	41	2
Mike Marshall	.258	10	39	0
Pete O'Brien	.224	5	27	0
Dion James	.274	1	22	5
Todd Benzinger	.253	5	46	3
Gary Redus	.247	6	23	11
Carmelo Martinez	.240	10	35	2

Look for Consistency

	1990 Statistics			
	Avg.	HR	RBI	SB
Fred McGriff	.300	35	88	5
Mark McGwire	.235	39	108	2
Dave Justice	.282	28	78	11
Mark Grace	.309	9	82	15
Kent Hrbek	.287	22	79	5
Jack Clark	.266	25	62	4
Randy Milligan	.265	20	60	6
Andres Galarraga	.256	20	87	10
Pedro Guerrero	.281	13	80	1

Production Will Drop

	1990 Statistics			
	Avg.	HR	RBI	SB
Cecil Fielder	.277	51	132	0
Eddie Murray	.330	26	95	8
Rafael Palmeiro	.319	14	89	3
George Brett	.329	14	87	9
Dave Magadan	.328	6	72	2
Franklin Stubbs	.261	23	71	19
Sid Bream	.270	15	67	8
Greg Brock	.248	7	50	4

1991 Sleepers

	1990 Statistics (includes minor leagues)			
	Avg.	HR	RBI	SB
Frank Thomas	.325	25	102	7
Francisco Cabrera	.253	14	45	3
Kevin Maas	.266	34	79	3
Jeff Conine	.318	15	97	21
Hal Morris	.340	8	46	13
Tino Martinez	.307	17	98	8
Ricky Jordan	.250	7	55	2
Jeff Manto	.283	20	96	10
Lee Stevens	.259	23	98	2

Second Base

Expect A Better Year in '91

	1990 Statistics			
	Avg.	HR	RBI	SB
Delino DeShields	.289	4	45	42
Roberto Alomar	.287	6	60	24
Steve Sax	.260	4	42	43
Paul Molitor	.285	12	45	18
Juan Samuel	.242	13	52	38
Johnny Ray	.277	5	43	2
Jose Oquendo	.252	1	37	1
Manny Lee	.243	6	41	3
Nelson Liriano	.234	1	28	8
Jim Gantner	.263	0	25	18

Look for Consistency

	1990 Statistics			
	Avg.	HR	RBI	SB
Julio Franco	.296	11	69	31
Jody Reed	.289	5	51	4
Gregg Jefferies	.283	15	68	11
Lou Whitaker	.237	18	60	8
Jerry Browne	.267	6	50	12
Robby Thompson	.245	15	56	14
Harold Reynolds	.252	5	55	31
Billy Doran	.300	7	37	23
Jose Lind	.261	1	48	8
Jeff Treadway	.283	11	59	3
Willie Randolph	.260	2	30	7
Mike Gallego	.206	3	34	5
Casey Candaele	.286	3	22	7

Production Will Drop

	1990 Statistics			
	Avg.	HR	RBI	SB
Ryne Sandberg	.306	40	100	25
Scott Fletcher	.242	4	56	1
Tommy Herr	.261	5	60	7
Mariano Duncan	.306	10	55	13
Billy Ripken	.291	3	38	5
Al Newman	.242	0	30	13
Bill Pecota	.242	5	20	8

1991 Sleepers

	1990 Statistics (includes minor leagues)			
	Avg.	HR	RBI	SB
Mickey Morandini	.258	2	34	19
Terry Shumpert	.262	2	20	21
Geronimo Pena	.248	6	37	25

Third Base

Expect A Better Year in '91

	1990 Statistics			
	Avg.	HR	RBI	SB
Wade Boggs	.302	6	63	0
Kevin Seitzer	.275	6	38	7
Carney Lansford	.268	3	50	16
Robin Ventura	.249	5	54	1
Jeff King	.245	14	53	3
Craig Worthington	.226	8	44	1
Mike Pagliarulo	.254	7	38	1
Jack Howell	.228	8	33	3

Look for Consistency

	1990 Statistics			
	Avg.	HR	RBI	SB
Howard Johnson	.244	23	90	34
Gary Sheffield	.294	10	67	25
Tony Phillips	.251	8	55	19
Edgar Martinez	.302	11	49	1
Gary Gaetti	.229	16	85	6
Charlie Hayes	.258	10	57	4
Jim Presley	.242	19	72	1
Ken Caminiti	.242	4	51	9
Terry Pendleton	.230	6	58	7
Carlos Baerga	.260	7	47	0

Production Will Drop

	1990 Statistics			
	Avg.	HR	RBI	SB
Matt D. Williams	.277	33	122	7
Kelly Gruber	.274	31	118	14
Chris Sabo	.270	25	71	25
Brook Jacoby	.293	14	75	1
Tim Wallach	.296	21	98	6
Lenny Harris	.304	2	29	15
Mike Sharperson	.297	3	36	15
Wally Backman	.292	2	28	6
Luis Salazar	.254	12	47	3

1991 Sleepers

	1990 Statistics (includes minor leagues)			
	Avg.	HR	RBI	SB
Travis Fryman	.274	19	80	7
Leo Gomez	.273	26	98	2
Jim Leyritz	.270	13	57	6
Steve Buechele	.210	8	31	1

Shortstop

Expect A Better Year in '91

	1990 Statistics			
	Avg.	HR	RBI	SB
Cal Ripken	.250	21	84	3
Jeff Blauser	.269	8	39	3
Kurt Stillwell	.249	3	51	0
Greg Gagne	.235	7	38	8
Dick Schofield	.255	1	18	3
Bill Spiers	.242	2	36	11
Alvaro Espinoza	.224	2	20	1
Kevin Elster	.207	9	45	2
Andres Thomas	.219	5	30	2

Look for Consistency

	1990 Statistics			
	Avg.	HR	RBI	SB
Barry Larkin	.301	7	67	30
Tony Fernandez	.276	4	66	26
Jay Bell	.254	7	52	10
Shawon Dunston	.262	17	66	25
Ozzie Guillen	.279	1	58	13
Dickie Thon	.255	8	48	12
Ozzie Smith	.254	1	50	32
Spike Owen	.234	5	35	8
Walt Weiss	.265	2	35	9
Felix Fermin	.256	1	40	3
Rafael Ramirez	.261	2	37	10
Luis Rivera	.225	7	45	4
Jeff Huson	.240	0	28	12
Jose Uribe	.248	1	24	5

Production Will Drop

	1990 Statistics			
	Avg.	HR	RBI	SB
Alan Trammell	.304	14	89	12
Garry Templeton	.248	9	59	1

1991 Sleepers

	1990 Statistics (includes minor leagues)			
	Avg.	HR	RBI	SB
Tim Naehring	.269	17	59	0
Jose Offerman	.307	1	63	61
Omar Vizquel	.244	2	29	9

Left Field

Expect A Better Year in '91

	1990 Statistics			
	Avg.	HR	RBI	SB
Mike Greenwell	.297	14	73	8
Tim Raines	.287	9	62	49
George Bell	.265	21	86	3
Pete Incaviglia	.233	24	85	3
Greg Vaughn	.220	17	61	7
Dwight Smith	.262	6	27	11
Phil Bradley	.256	4	31	17
Daryl Hamilton	.295	1	18	10
Brady Anderson	.231	3	24	15

Look for Consistency

	1990 Statistics			
	Avg.	HR	RBI	SB
Kevin Mitchell	.290	35	93	4
Kal Daniels	.296	27	94	4
Ivan Calderon	.273	14	74	32
Kevin McReynolds	.269	24	82	9
Vince Coleman	.292	6	39	77
Luis Polonia	.335	2	35	21
John Kruk	.291	7	67	10
Billy Hatcher	.276	5	25	30
Willie Wilson	.290	2	42	24
Larry Sheets	.261	10	52	1
Mike Felder	.274	3	27	20

Production Will Drop

	1990 Statistics			
	Avg.	HR	RBI	SB
Barry Bonds	.301	33	114	52
Rickey Henderson	.325	28	61	65
Bip Roberts	.309	9	44	46
Candy Maldonado	.273	22	95	3
Lonnie Smith	.305	9	42	10
Dan Gladden	.275	5	40	25
Jim Eisenreich	.280	5	51	12
Jeff Leonard	.251	10	75	4
Gary Ward	.256	9	46	2

1991 Sleepers

	1990 Statistics (includes minor leagues)			
	Avg.	HR	RBI	SB
Bernard Gilkey	.295	4	49	51
Hensley Meulens	.279	29	106	7
Wes Chamberlain	.253	8	56	18
Oscar Azocar	.276	10	71	15
Javier Ortiz	.328	6	49	3

Center Field

Expect A Better Year in '91

	1990 Statistics			
	Avg.	HR	RBI	SB
Ellis Burks	.296	21	89	9
Kirby Puckett	.298	12	80	5
Roberto Kelly	.285	15	61	42
Eric Davis	.260	24	86	21
Jerome Walton	.263	2	21	14
Kirk Gibson	.260	8	38	26
Oddibe McDowell	.243	7	25	13
Devon White	.217	11	44	21
Mike Devereaux	.240	12	49	13
Mark Carreon	.250	10	26	1

Look for Consistency

	1990 Statistics			
	Avg.	HR	RBI	SB
Ken Griffey Jr	.300	22	80	16
Robin Yount	.247	17	77	15
Joe Carter	.232	24	115	22
Bo Jackson	.272	28	78	15
Lloyd Moseby	.248	14	51	17
Lance Johnson	.285	1	51	36
Dave Henderson	.271	20	63	3
Dave Martinez	.279	11	39	13
Eric Yelding	.254	1	28	64

Production Will Drop

	1990 Statistics			
	Avg.	HR	RBI	SB
Lenny Dykstra	.325	9	60	33
Ron Gant	.303	32	84	33
Brett Butler	.309	3	44	51
Andy Van Slyke	.284	17	77	14
Willie McGee	.324	3	77	31
Mitch Webster	.252	12	55	22
Daryl Boston	.272	12	45	19
Mookie Wilson	.265	3	51	23
Gary Pettis	.239	3	31	38
Stan Javier	.298	3	27	15
Otis Nixon	.251	1	20	50
Doug Dascenzo	.253	1	26	15

1991 Sleepers

	1990 Statistics (includes minor leagues)			
	Avg.	HR	RBI	SB
Ray Lankford	.265	13	84	37
Juan Gonzalez	.263	33	113	2
Brian McRae	.273	12	87	25
Alex Cole	.305	0	44	78
Milt Cuyler	.258	2	50	53
Gerald Young	.261	1	28	20

Right Field

Expect A Better Year in '91

	1990 Statistics			
	Avg.	HR	RBI	SB
Jose Canseco	.274	37	101	19
Ruben Sierra	.280	16	96	9
Danny Tartabull	.268	15	60	1
Paul O'Neill	.270	16	78	13
Tom Brunansky	.255	16	73	5
Larry Walker	.241	19	51	21
Rob Deer	.209	27	69	2
Felix Jose	.265	11	52	12
Glenn Braggs	.280	9	41	8
Greg Briley	.246	5	29	16
Glenallen Hill	.231	12	32	8
Rex Hudler	.282	7	22	18
Kevin Romine	.272	2	14	4

Look for Consistency

	1990 Statistics			
	Avg.	HR	RBI	SB
Darryl Strawberry	.277	37	108	15
Tony Gwynn	.309	4	72	17
Jesse Barfield	.246	25	78	4
Von Hayes	.261	17	73	16
Dale Murphy	.245	24	83	9
Sammy Sosa	.233	15	70	32
Junior Felix	.263	15	65	13
Joe Orsulak	.269	11	57	6
Steve Finley	.256	3	37	22
Cory Snyder	.233	14	55	1
Chet Lemon	.258	5	32	3
Milt Thompson	.218	6	30	25

Production Will Drop

	1990 Statistics			
	Avg.	HR	RBI	SB
Bobby Bonilla	.280	32	120	4
Andre Dawson	.310	27	100	16
Dave Winfield	.267	21	78	0
Hubie Brooks	.266	20	91	2
Shane Mack	.326	8	44	13
Glenn Wilson	.245	10	55	0
Gene Larkin	.269	5	42	5
Dante Bichette	.255	15	53	5
Henry Cotto	.259	4	33	21

1991 Sleepers

	1990 Statistics (includes minor leagues)			
	Avg.	HR	RBI	SB
Eric Anthony	.228	17	58	13
Pedro Munoz	.311	12	82	27
Marquis Grissom	.252	5	32	23
Mark Whiten	.287	16	55	16
Jay Buhner	.264	9	38	2
Kevin Bass	.260	7	40	4
Randy Bush	.242	6	19	0

Designated Hitter

Expect A Better Year in '91

	1990 Statistics			
	Avg.	HR	RBI	SB
Alvin Davis	.283	17	68	0
Harold Baines	.284	16	65	0
John Olerud	.265	14	48	0
Chili Davis	.265	12	58	1

Look for Consistency

	1990 Statistics			
	Avg.	HR	RBI	SB
Dwight Evans	.249	13	63	3
Mel Hall	.258	12	46	0
Sam Horn	.248	14	45	0
Steve Balboni	.192	17	34	0

Production Will Drop

	1990 Statistics			
	Avg.	HR	RBI	SB
Chris James	.299	12	70	4
Dave Parker	.289	21	92	4
Brian Downing	.273	14	51	0
Dan Pasqua	.274	13	58	1
Gerald Perry	.254	8	57	17

1991 Sleepers

	1990 Statistics (includes minor leagues)			
	Avg.	HR	RBI	SB
Paul Sorrento	.278	24	85	4
Matt Stark	.307	14	112	3

Starting Pitchers

Expect A Better Year in '91

	1990 Statistics				
	W	L	ERA	Sv	BR/9
Sid Fernandez	9	14	3.46	0	10.14
Bret Saberhagen	5	9	3.27	0	11.67
Tim Belcher	9	9	4.00	0	10.94
Kelly Downs	3	2	3.43	0	11.14
Mike Scott	9	13	3.81	0	11.42
Jim Deshaies	7	12	3.78	0	11.95
Danny Jackson	6	6	3.61	0	12.35
Tim Leary	9	19	4.11	0	12.42
Greg Swindell	12	9	4.40	0	12.28
Bryn Smith	9	8	4.27	0	12.35
Orel Hershiser	1	1	4.26	0	11.01
Don Robinson	10	7	4.57	0	12.27
John Smiley	9	10	4.64	0	11.99
Mark Langston	10	17	4.40	0	13.08
Mike Moore	13	15	4.65	0	13.14
Chris Nabholz	6	2	2.83	0	9.90
Chris Bosio	4	9	4.00	0	11.67
Allan Anderson	7	18	4.53	0	12.31
Mike LaCoss	6	4	3.94	0	13.21
Jose DeLeon	7	19	4.43	0	12.76
Ron Darling	7	9	4.50	0	13.14
Rick Reuschel	3	6	3.93	1	13.86
Storm Davis	7	10	4.74	0	13.18
Bob Milacki	5	8	4.46	0	13.57
Mark Gubicza	4	7	4.50	0	13.69
Shawn Boskie	5	6	3.69	0	12.07
Bert Blyleven	8	7	5.24	0	13.10
Andy Hawkins	5	12	5.37	0	13.70
Rick Sutcliffe	0	2	5.91	0	15.61
Paul Abbott	0	5	5.97	0	17.13

Look for Consistency

	1990 Statistics				
	W	L	ERA	Sv	BR/9
Doug Drabek	22	6	2.76	0	9.69
Dave Stewart	22	11	2.56	0	10.58
Frank Viola	20	12	2.67	0	10.42
Ed Whitson	14	9	2.60	0	10.35
Dave Stieb	18	6	2.93	0	10.91
Jose Rijo	14	8	2.70	0	10.55
Dennis Martinez	10	11	2.95	0	9.80
Nolan Ryan	13	9	3.44	0	9.62
David Cone	14	10	3.23	0	10.33
Dwight Gooden	19	7	3.83	0	11.84
Erik Hanson	18	9	3.24	0	10.49
Bruce Hurst	11	9	3.14	0	10.14
Greg Hibbard	14	9	3.16	0	11.22
Mike Boddicker	17	8	3.36	0	12.00
Bud Black	13	11	3.57	0	10.76
Greg Maddux	15	15	3.46	0	12.04
Tom Candiotti	15	11	3.65	0	11.94
Tom Browning	15	9	3.80	0	11.54
Ben McDonald	8	5	2.43	0	9.33
Kirk McCaskill	12	11	3.25	0	12.13
John Burkett	14	7	3.79	1	11.74
John Smoltz	14	11	3.85	0	11.55
Jack McDowell	14	9	3.82	0	11.99
Andy Benes	10	11	3.60	0	11.56
Eric King	12	4	3.28	0	10.79
Kevin Brown	12	10	3.60	0	11.90
Charlie Leibrandt	9	11	3.16	0	11.25
Mark Portugal	11	10	3.62	0	11.81
Kevin Tapani	12	8	4.07	0	11.01
Ted Higuera	11	10	3.76	0	11.65
Joe Magrane	10	17	3.59	0	12.00
Mike Morgan	11	15	3.75	0	11.99
Jimmy Key	13	7	4.25	0	11.17
Dave Johnson	13	9	4.10	0	12.10
Jack Morris	15	18	4.51	0	12.04
Bob Walk	7	5	3.75	1	12.22
Brian Holman	11	11	4.03	0	12.34
Dana Kiecker	8	9	3.97	0	12.32
Greg Harris	13	9	4.00	0	13.13
Mark Guthrie	7	9	3.79	0	12.07
Tom Gordon	12	11	3.73	0	13.55
Mark Knudson	10	9	4.12	0	12.30
Charlie Hough	12	12	4.07	0	13.17
Mike Witt	5	9	4.00	1	12.15
Melido Perez	13	14	4.61	0	12.11
Bill Gullickson	10	14	3.82	0	13.22
Scott Garrelts	12	11	4.15	0	13.01
Pat Combs	10	10	4.07	0	13.21
Chuck Cary	6	12	4.19	0	12.12
Tom Glavine	10	12	4.28	0	13.06

Fernando Valenzuela	13	13	4.59	0	13.24
Dennis Rasmussen	11	15	4.51	0	13.52
Jaime Navarro	8	7	4.46	1	13.32
Dave LaPoint	7	10	4.11	0	13.59
Kevin Gross	9	12	4.57	0	13.22
Jim Abbott	10	14	4.51	0	13.73
Pete Smith	5	6	4.79	0	11.81
Curt Young	9	6	4.85	0	12.96
Ken Howell	8	7	4.64	0	13.33
Jeff M. Robinson	10	9	5.96	0	14.59
John Cerutti	9	9	4.76	0	13.82
Frank Tanana	9	8	5.31	1	13.53
Mike Bielecki	8	11	4.93	1	14.09
Roy Smith	5	10	4.81	0	13.97
Walt Terrell	8	11	5.24	0	14.41
Derek Lilliquist	5	11	5.31	0	13.35
Ken Hill	5	6	5.49	0	12.93
Tommy Greene	3	3	5.08	0	13.50
Bruce Ruffin	6	13	5.38	0	14.56
Al Nipper	2	3	6.75	0	21.00

Production Will Drop

	1990 Statistics				
	W	L	ERA	Sv	BR/9
Roger Clemens	21	6	1.93	0	10.01
Bob Welch	27	6	2.95	0	11.19
Ramon Martinez	20	6	2.92	0	10.06
Chuck Finley	18	9	2.40	0	11.17
Zane Smith	12	9	2.55	0	10.41
David Wells	11	6	3.14	3	10.10
Oil Can Boyd	10	6	2.93	0	10.34
Kevin Appier	12	8	2.76	0	11.59
Bob Tewksbury	10	9	3.47	1	10.47
Mike Harkey	12	6	3.26	0	11.35
Terry Mulholland	9	10	3.34	0	10.76
Bobby Witt	17	10	3.36	0	12.61
Neal Heaton	12	9	3.45	0	11.28
Jack Armstrong	12	9	3.42	0	11.71
Ron Robinson	14	7	3.26	0	12.57
Scott Sanderson	17	11	3.88	0	12.00
Randy Johnson	14	11	3.65	0	12.25
Tom Bolton	10	5	3.38	0	12.11

Mark Gardner	7	9	3.42	0	11.73
Matt Young	8	18	3.51	0	12.42
Trevor Wilson	8	7	4.00	0	11.18
Dave Eiland	2	1	3.56	0	10.68
Jose DeJesus	7	8	3.74	0	11.91
Todd Stottlemyre	13	17	4.34	0	12.90
Pete Harnisch	11	11	4.34	0	13.17
Russ Swan	2	4	3.65	0	12.77
Bill Krueger	6	8	3.98	0	13.53
Dan Petry	10	9	4.45	0	13.59
Adam Peterson	2	5	4.55	0	12.49
John Mitchell	6	6	4.64	0	14.48
David West	7	9	5.10	0	13.78
John Farrell	4	5	4.28	0	13.13
Steve Searcy	2	7	4.66	0	15.17
Mike Walker	2	6	4.88	0	15.46

1991 Sleepers

	1990 Statistics (includes minor leagues)				
	W	L	ERA	Sv	BR/9
Pascual Perez	1	2	2.12	0	7.94
Randy Tomlin	13	10	2.42	0	9.72
Rich Delucia	13	11	2.31	0	9.80
Jim Neidlinger	13	8	3.90	0	11.48
Brian Barnes	14	8	2.79	0	10.67
Scott Erickson	16	7	2.94	0	11.27
Alex Fernandez	10	6	3.08	0	11.60
Scott Chiamparino	14	11	3.16	0	12.86
Omar Olivares	11	12	2.85	0	11.17
Larry Casian	11	10	4.32	0	13.22
Jose Mesa	9	9	3.38	0	12.22
Paul Marak	10	10	2.74	0	11.70
Bill Wegman	3	2	4.17	0	12.31
Anthony Telford	17	7	2.47	0	10.69
Joe Grahe	13	9	4.36	0	13.61
Steve Avery	8	16	4.67	0	13.70
Steve Adkins	16	9	3.31	0	13.61
Julio Valera	11	11	3.32	0	11.42
Chris Hammond	15	3	2.47	0	11.84
Scott Bankhead	0	3	9.45	0	16.65

Relief Pitchers

Expect A Better Year in '91

	1990 Statistics				
	W	L	ERA	Sv	BR/9
Tom Henke	2	4	2.17	32	9.40
Mike Schooler	1	4	2.25	30	10.29
Jay Howell	5	5	2.18	16	11.59
Tim Burke	3	3	2.52	20	11.28
Dave Righetti	1	1	3.57	36	12.91
Mark Williamson	8	2	2.21	1	9.81
Lee Guetterman	11	7	3.39	2	10.26
Duane Ward	2	8	3.45	11	10.15
Chuck Crim	3	5	3.47	11	11.87
Alejandro Pena	3	3	3.20	5	11.13
Terry Leach	2	5	3.20	2	11.68
Todd Burns	3	3	2.97	3	12.58
Ken Dayley	4	4	3.56	2	11.41
Ted Power	1	3	3.66	7	11.67
Jeff Robinson	3	6	3.45	0	11.88
Bobby Ojeda	7	6	3.66	0	12.58
Mitch Williams	1	8	3.93	16	15.06
Atlee Hammaker	4	9	4.36	0	11.63

Jesse Orosco	5	4	3.90	2	13.36
Mike Jackson	5	7	4.54	3	12.80
Gary Wayne	1	1	4.19	1	12.10
Dennis Lamp	3	5	4.68	0	12.52
Scott Terry	2	6	4.75	2	13.25
John Wetteland	2	4	4.81	0	13.60
Joe Hesketh	1	6	4.53	5	14.33
Calvin Schiraldi	3	8	4.41	1	14.37
Jeff Parrett	5	10	4.64	2	14.58
Wes Gardner	3	7	4.89	0	13.27
Jamie Moyer	2	6	4.66	0	13.90
Jeff Ballard	2	11	4.93	0	13.30
Mark Grant	2	3	4.73	3	14.39
Tim Birtsas	1	3	3.86	0	16.48
Eric Show	6	8	5.76	1	14.90
Mark Davis	2	7	5.11	6	16.65
Doug Bair	0	0	4.81	0	15.16
Martin Clary	1	10	5.67	0	14.87
Rick Luecken	1	4	5.83	1	18.17
Rob Murphy	0	6	6.32	7	18.63

Look for Consistency

	1990 Statistics				
	W	L	ERA	Sv	BR/9
Doug Jones	5	5	2.56	43	9.60
Randy Myers	4	6	2.08	31	10.38
Gregg Olson	6	5	2.42	37	11.02
Dave Smith	6	6	2.39	23	9.70
John Franco	5	3	2.53	33	11.57
Rob Dibble	8	3	1.74	11	8.91
Danny Darwin	11	4	2.21	2	9.46
Jeff Montgomery	6	5	2.39	24	11.45
Jeff Reardon	5	3	3.16	21	10.34
Mike Henneman	8	6	3.05	22	12.02
Bryan Harvey	4	4	3.22	25	11.19
Steve Farr	13	7	1.98	1	10.77
Rick Honeycutt	2	2	2.70	7	9.81
Barry Jones	11	4	2.31	1	11.68
Roger McDowell	6	8	3.86	22	13.45
Bill Sampen	12	7	2.99	2	12.85
Joe Klink	0	0	2.04	1	11.80
Donn Pall	3	5	3.32	2	10.78
Dan Plesac	3	7	4.43	24	13.17
Steve Bedrosian	9	9	4.20	17	13.39
Stan Belinda	3	4	3.55	8	12.03
Joe Boever	3	6	3.36	14	13.04
Lance McCullers	2	0	3.02	0	10.28
Eric Plunk	6	3	2.72	0	12.76
Luis Aquino	4	1	3.16	0	11.85
Reggie Harris	1	0	3.48	0	10.45
John Candelaria	7	6	3.95	5	12.31
Steve Olin	4	4	3.41	1	12.48
Scott Ruskin	3	2	2.75	2	13.74
Juan Berenguer	8	5	3.41	0	13.01
Rick Mahler	7	6	4.28	4	11.76
Clay Parker	3	3	3.58	0	11.96
Tim Layana	5	3	3.49	2	13.16
Ken Patterson	2	1	3.39	2	12.75
Dale Mohorcic	1	2	3.23	2	13.25
Joe Price	3	4	3.58	0	11.85
Juan Agosto	9	8	4.29	4	13.35
Les Lancaster	9	5	4.62	6	13.38
Jim Acker	4	4	3.83	1	13.35
Gary Mielke	0	3	3.73	0	12.95
Greg Cadaret	5	4	4.15	3	13.72
Dan Schatzeder	1	3	2.20	0	11.50
Tom Niedenfuer	0	6	3.46	2	12.60
Steve Wilson	4	9	4.79	1	11.98
Bill Long	6	2	4.55	5	14.09
Frank Wills	6	4	4.73	0	12.73
Frank DiPino	5	2	4.56	3	13.78
Xavier Hernandez	2	1	4.62	0	12.71
Paul Mirabella	4	2	3.97	0	14.49
Sergio Valdez	6	6	4.85	0	12.87
Randy O'Neal	1	0	3.83	0	14.55
Scott Radinsky	6	1	4.82	4	14.62
Jim Clancy	2	8	6.51	1	16.11
Scott Scudder	5	5	4.90	0	13.44
Jeff Pico	4	4	4.79	2	15.46
Gene Harris	1	2	4.74	0	14.68
Craig McMurtry	0	3	4.32	0	15.98
Brent Knackert	1	1	6.51	0	17.60

Production Will Drop

	1990 Statistics				
	W	L	ERA	Sv	BR/9
Dennis Eckersley	4	2	0.61	48	5.52
Bobby Thigpen	4	6	1.83	57	9.44
Lee Smith	5	5	2.06	31	10.84
Rick Aguilera	5	3	2.76	32	10.74
Craig Lefferts	7	5	2.52	23	10.41
Jeff Brantley	5	3	1.56	19	11.73
Norm Charlton	12	9	2.74	2	11.95
Gene Nelson	3	3	1.57	5	9.04
Larry Andersen	5	2	1.79	7	10.16
Bill Landrum	7	3	2.13	13	11.30
Greg W. Harris	8	8	2.30	9	11.12
Steve Frey	8	2	2.10	9	11.96
Jerry Don Gleaton	1	3	2.94	13	9.80
Paul Assenmacher	7	2	2.80	10	11.10
Bill Swift	6	4	2.39	6	11.46
Kenny Rogers	10	6	3.13	15	12.53
Bob Patterson	8	5	2.95	5	10.65
Tim Crews	4	5	2.77	5	10.31
Edwin Nunez	3	1	2.24	6	11.65
Mike Hartley	6	3	2.95	1	10.21
Keith Comstock	7	4	2.89	2	10.61
Bob Kipper	5	2	3.02	3	10.48
Dave Schmidt	3	3	4.31	13	13.31
Brad Arnsberg	6	1	2.15	5	13.07
Curt Schilling	1	2	2.54	3	11.15
Willie Fraser	5	4	3.08	2	11.01
Francisco Oliveras	2	2	2.77	2	11.39
Mark Eichhorn	2	5	3.08	13	13.50
Julio Machado	4	1	2.47	3	12.93
Wally Whitehurst	1	0	3.29	2	9.87
Steve Ontiveros	0	0	2.70	0	10.80
Kent Mercker	4	7	3.17	7	12.85
Wayne Edwards	5	3	3.22	2	11.84
Mark Thurmond	2	3	3.34	4	11.28
Darrel Akerfelds	5	2	3.77	3	11.81
Paul Gibson	5	4	3.05	3	13.32
Dennis Cook	9	4	3.92	1	12.29
Don Carman	6	2	4.15	1	11.53
Steve Crawford	5	4	4.16	1	11.81
Jeff Gray	2	4	4.44	9	12.26
Randy Veres	0	3	3.67	1	11.88
Mike Jeffcoat	5	6	4.47	5	12.36
John Barfield	4	3	4.67	1	11.37
Tony Castillo	5	1	4.23	1	13.38
Mike Fetters	1	1	4.12	1	13.17
Drew Hall	4	7	5.09	3	12.50
Tim Drummond	3	5	4.35	1	13.95
Dwayne Henry	2	2	5.63	0	15.50
Jose Nunez	4	7	6.53	0	14.09

1991 Sleepers

	1990 Statistics (includes minor leagues)				
	W	L	ERA	Sv	BR/9
Rich Garces	4	3	1.85	38	10.31
Jeff Russell	1	6	4.62	10	14.21
Jim Gott	3	5	2.88	3	13.32
Mike Perez	8	7	4.22	32	12.67
Rich Rodriguez	4	5	3.21	9	11.98
Andy McGaffigan	6	4	3.86	1	13.19
Tom Edens	5	6	4.73	6	12.89
Mike Stanton	0	4	10.66	2	22.03

American League Players

BRADY ANDERSON

Position: LF/CF
Bats: L **Throws:** L
Ht: 6' 1" **Wt:** 186

Opening Day Age: 27
Born: 1/18/64 in Silver Spring, MD
ML Seasons: 3

HITTING:

The Orioles are still waiting for the big explosion from Brady Anderson, whom they obtained from Boston three years ago in the Mike Boddicker deal. Injuries (shoulder, sprained ankle) restricted Anderson to fewer than 90 games in 1990 and impeded the running style which he needs in order to thrive.

Anderson hasn't yet shown much at the plate in the majors. He will take a walk occasionally, but his on-base average is not high enough to be a leadoff man. Sometimes he believes he is a cleanup hitter, going for home runs when he should settle for singles and doubles. He is still learning how to use the entire field, using his speed as much as possible.

Anderson went through a stretch last year in which he hit .500 for a few weeks. At that point his season average was well over .300 and he looked to be on his way at last. But then he slumped badly again. Until he accepts his limitations, Anderson will probably never hit consistently. He keeps himself in excellent shape and is solidly built, but so far he hasn't hit over any long period of time.

BASERUNNING:

Anderson has solid baserunning instincts, reads pitchers well and steals with a high success rate. During one stretch last season, he swiped 12 bases in a row. He has the potential to get 40 with more playing time. Anderson must stay healthy because speed is a huge part of his game.

FIELDING:

Anderson's time in the field last year was impaired by early-season shoulder problems which restricted his throwing. He is a daring player who isn't afraid to run into walls or dive for the ball at any time, but he occasionally does so unwisely. His speed allows him to get a good jump on balls and catch drives that other players could never reach. A natural center fielder, he can play either of the corners as well. Anderson has a quick release, but his arm is not much better than average, making him more suitable for left or center.

OVERALL:

The Orioles were experimenting with Anderson and Steve Finley in September to determine if either or both could play regularly. It was likely that one would be used in a trade to obtain some much needed power. Since they are virtual clones, one of the two would figure to be expendable. Anderson may well be the odd man out, since the Orioles are growing weary of waiting for his bat to arrive.

Overall Statistics

	G	AB	R	H	D	T	HR	RBI	SB	BB	SO	AVG
1990	89	234	24	54	5	2	3	24	15	31	46	.231
Career	277	825	99	178	30	8	8	61	41	97	166	.216

Where He Hits the Ball

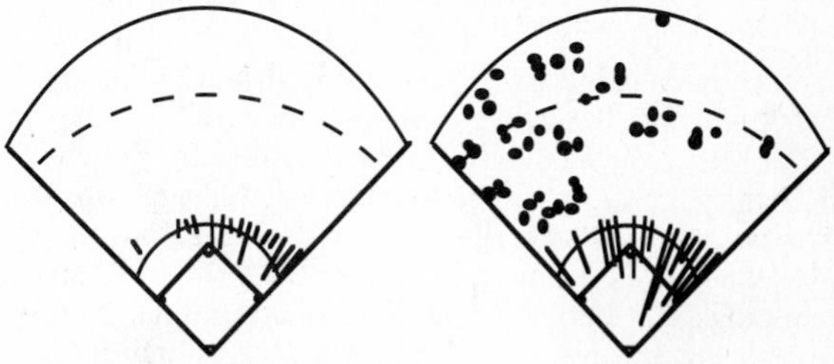

1990 Situational Stats

	AB	H	HR	RBI	AVG		AB	H	HR	RBI	AVG
Home	126	22	1	10	.175	LHP	46	7	0	4	.152
Road	108	32	2	14	.296	RHP	188	47	3	20	.250
Day	70	20	1	9	.286	Sc Pos	61	17	1	20	.279
Night	164	34	2	15	.207	Clutch	31	8	0	6	.258

1990 Rankings (American League)

- Did not rank near the top or bottom in any category

JEFF BALLARD

Position: RP/SP
Bats: L **Throws:** L
Ht: 6' 2" **Wt:** 198

Opening Day Age: 27
Born: 8/13/63 in Billings, MT
ML Seasons: 4

Overall Statistics

	W	L	ERA	G	GS	Sv	IP	H	R	BB	SO	HR
1990	2	11	4.93	44	17	0	133.1	152	79	42	50	22
Career	30	39	4.42	118	91	0	571.2	659	317	176	180	68

How Often He Throws Strikes

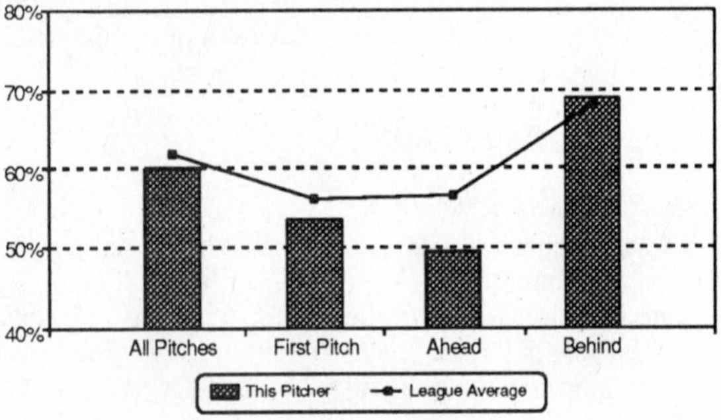

1990 Situational Stats

	W	L	ERA	Sv	IP		AB	H	HR	RBI	AVG
Home	1	5	4.52	0	67.2	LHB	136	40	4	15	.294
Road	1	6	5.35	0	65.2	RHB	390	112	18	52	.287
Day	1	2	6.19	0	32.0	Sc Pos	121	33	6	44	.273
Night	1	9	4.53	0	101.1	Clutch	53	16	1	6	.302

1990 Rankings (American League)

➠ Led the Orioles in losses (11) and hit batsmen (3)

PITCHING:

Jeff Ballard went from the penthouse to the outhouse last season. A finesse pitcher who must depend on control, Ballard yields few walks but needs to throw more quality strikes in order to re-establish himself as one of the staff aces. Ballard won more games than any other American League lefthander in 1989 (18), but had only two victories in 1990, one as a starter.

Conspiring against Ballard were two off-season elbow operations, the shortened spring training, and his role as the team's player representative. He gave up nine home runs in his first six starts and by May 28 was in the bullpen working in long relief and spotting against left-handed hitters. A month later he had a 1-9 record. Ballard lost some zip off the sinker that had served him well in his big season and he tended to spot the ball instead of throwing it. In addition, the run support provided by Ballard's teammates dropped dramatically while he was a starter.

The combination was disastrous. Left-handed batters actually hit higher against him than righthanders (.294 to .287), an indication that the movement on his four pitches -- sinker, slider, curve and change-up -- wasn't as lively. He wound up allowing 22 homers, second on the team, averaging one nearly every six innings. But Ballard's walk and strikeout totals were both low again, evidence that his control may have been too good.

Ballard's problems last year must have the Orioles wondering whether his 1989 success was a fluke. He was 18-8 in '89, but for the rest of his career his record is a horrendous 12-31. And winning 18 games while striking out only 62 batters -- as Ballard did in 1989 -- is a highly unusual combination. The last pitcher to win so many games with so few strikeouts was Dick Newsome of the 1941 Red Sox.

FIELDING AND HOLDING RUNNERS:

Ballard is a gifted athlete who uses his intelligence and instincts well in the field. As a lefthander, he has a natural advantage in holding runners and he can spring off the mound quickly in either direction. He is usually aware of the game situation, and few runners take liberties with him on the mound.

OVERALL:

Ballard hopes a winter of rest, rehabilitation and throwing will help him regain his spot in a starting rotation that was devoid of lefthanders after he left. But he must regain his total health, consistency, and the ability to change speeds and pitch selection that he had in 1989. With his stuff, he is not really suited to relief work, and he'll need to pitch a lot better to win as a starter.

HITTING:

The Orioles are somewhat exasperated by Mike Devereaux, a player they see as having great potential with the bat. Devereaux got off to an extremely slow start last year, then had a hamstring injury and never shifted into gear until a late-season spate of home runs.

Devereaux fashions himself a power hitter, and that often leads him into bad habits. So far, the majority of his homers have come directly down the left field line, a cozy 309-foot shot at Baltimore's Memorial Stadium. That tempts Devereaux into trying to pull everything. As a result, he often bails out and becomes susceptible to breaking pitches outside.

Devereaux's minor league record led the Orioles to expect a lot more. As a Dodger farm hand he batted over .300 four times, and he hit 26 home runs at San Antonio in 1987. After months of effort, the Orioles finally landed Devereaux in exchange for Mike Morgan before the start of the '89 season. They've given him considerable playing time, but if anything, he's regressed, batting .266 and then .240.

As a hitter Devereaux still walks too little, strikes out too often and finds it difficult to air his problems. The Orioles, who gave him a long look in the leadoff spot in 1989, would prefer he be more of an all-fields hitter and let the home runs come naturally. But thus far he hasn't been able to change his style.

BASERUNNING:

Devereaux has excellent speed, but was held back last year by the hamstring problem. He stole only 13 bases after swiping 22 in 1989. Devereaux is still learning how to get a good lead, but he accelerates rapidly when he takes off. No one on the team is better at going from home to first or first to third.

FIELDING:

The best on the team at getting a jump on fly balls, Devereaux has settled in center field despite some stiff competition. With his speed, he can make difficult plays look easy. His arm is adequate, though sometimes erratic. Overall he's outstanding, and if he played every day, Devereaux would be among the top glovemen at his position.

OVERALL:

Intelligent, polite and popular among his teammates, Devereaux is highly regarded in the Oriole organization. But he still hasn't proven he is an everyday player, partially because of injuries, partially because he is prone to batting slumps. If he ever puts everything together and begins to curb his tendency to try to pull the ball, look out.

MIKE DEVEREAUX

Position: CF
Bats: R **Throws:** R
Ht: 6' 0" **Wt:** 195

Opening Day Age: 28
Born: 4/10/63 in Casper, WY
ML Seasons: 4

Overall Statistics

	G	AB	R	H	D	T	HR	RBI	SB	BB	SO	AVG
1990	108	367	48	88	18	1	12	49	13	28	48	.240
Career	279	855	114	209	36	4	20	101	38	69	128	.244

Where He Hits the Ball

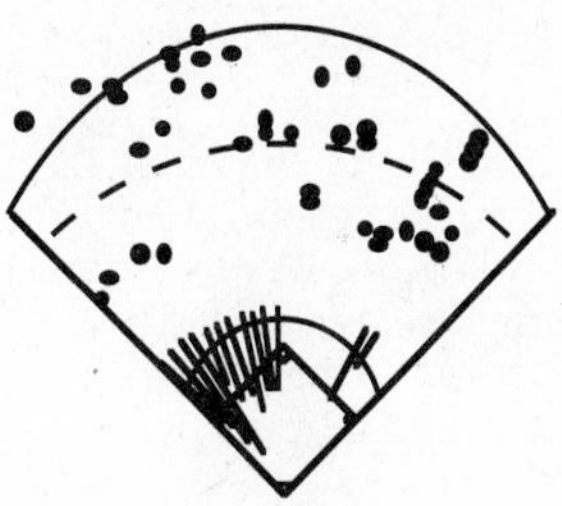

Vs. LHP

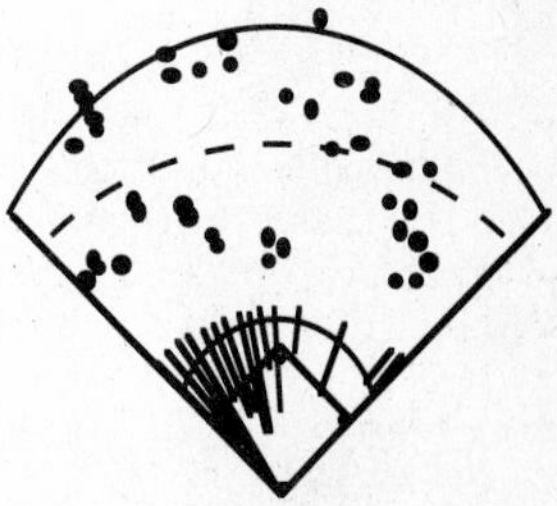

Vs. RHP

1990 Situational Stats

	AB	H	HR	RBI	AVG		AB	H	HR	RBI	AVG
Home	150	35	6	21	.233	LHP	160	37	7	22	.231
Road	217	53	6	28	.244	RHP	207	51	5	27	.246
Day	109	32	4	20	.294	Sc Pos	92	22	3	37	.239
Night	258	56	8	29	.217	Clutch	64	19	1	6	.297

1990 Rankings (American League)

- 1st in percentage of extra bases taken as a runner (63.9%)
- 4th worst in stolen base percentage (52.0%)
- Led the Orioles in caught stealing (12) and percentage of extra bases taken as a runner

HITTING:

The Baltimore organization likes what it saw of Steve Finley in a late-season test to see if he could be a regular. Finley could settle into the leadoff spot this season if continues to improve as a hitter. It would also help if he could learn to bunt effectively and uncork his speed, a major part of his game.

Finley batted nearly .300 down the stretch after moving back to the deepest part of the batter's box. The change allowed him to wait a little more before committing himself, especially on breaking balls. In addition, Finley bunted more often -- with poor results, but at least he was trying. Finley also took more pitches, though he has a long way to go in that area. If he learns to be more selective, he could eventually be a .300 hitter over the course of a season. Because of his speed, he could also become an effective leadoff hitter, which the Orioles would love. Since he drew only 32 walks last year, he's still got a long way to go.

Eventually, the Orioles believe Finley can hit 10-12 home runs, even though he's produced mostly singles in his two major league seasons. However, hitting home runs is not a high priority with Finley; his future is as a line drive hitter with power to the gaps.

BASERUNNING:

With Finley, as with Brady Anderson and Mike Devereaux, the Orioles can play run-and-hit instead of hit-and-run, a maneuver left over from the days of Earl Weaver. He has superior speed, reads pitchers well and is on his own most of the time. He led the team in steals and can fly on the base paths.

FIELDING:

Finley has the versatility and skill to play any of the three outfield positions. With a better than average arm, his most frequent spot is right field. He is fundamentally sound and his speed serves him well, giving him the ability to catch up to a lot of fly balls. He rarely misses a cutoff man or throws to the wrong base. He has a reckless style, often ignoring his health to make a diving catch.

OVERALL:

A gifted player, Finley could be on the trading block in the Orioles' quest for a power hitter. But they will not part with him easily, because they see signs of the breakthrough everyone has predicted for him. Finley has been a prospect long enough; perhaps his time for stardom has arrived.

STEVE FINLEY

Position: RF/LF/CF
Bats: L **Throws:** L
Ht: 6' 2" **Wt:** 175

Opening Day Age: 25
Born: 5/12/65 in Union City, TN
ML Seasons: 2

Overall Statistics

	G	AB	R	H	D	T	HR	RBI	SB	BB	SO	AVG
1990	142	464	46	119	16	4	3	37	22	32	53	.256
Career	223	681	81	173	21	6	5	62	39	47	83	.254

Where He Hits the Ball

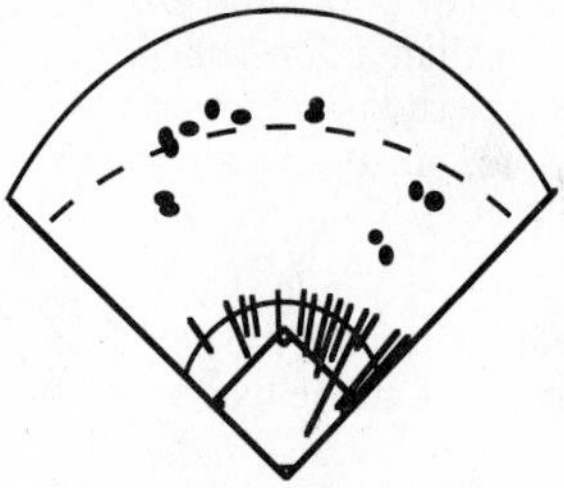

Vs. LHP

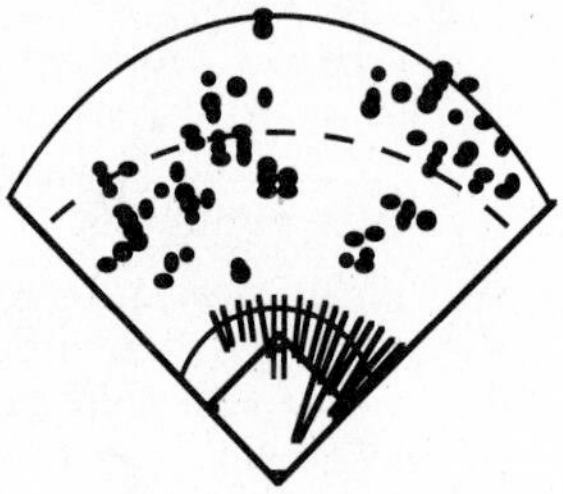

Vs. RHP

1990 Situational Stats

	AB	H	HR	RBI	AVG		AB	H	HR	RBI	AVG
Home	247	57	1	14	.231	LHP	114	22	1	9	.193
Road	217	62	2	23	.286	RHP	350	97	2	28	.277
Day	124	29	0	7	.234	Sc Pos	102	26	0	34	.255
Night	340	90	3	30	.265	Clutch	69	14	1	4	.203

1990 Rankings (American League)

- 1st in bunts in play (34)
- 2nd worst batting average on an 0-2 count (.028)
- 5th worst batting average with the bases loaded (.091)
- Led the Orioles in triples (4), stolen bases (22) and bunts in play
- Led AL right fielders in sacrifice bunts (10) and bunts in play

PETE HARNISCH

Position: SP
Bats: R **Throws:** R
Ht: 6' 0" **Wt:** 207

Opening Day Age: 24
Born: 9/23/66 in Commack, NY
ML Seasons: 3

PITCHING:

A bulldog who always wants the ball, Pete Harnisch was the only Oriole to stay in the rotation all year until manager Frank Robinson shut him down in late September when his arm wore down. Harnisch's impressive minor league numbers finally began to show in the big leagues when he began to harness both himself and his excellent stuff. The jitters he took to the mound began to disappear and he gained more confidence with each start.

A big 207-pounder, Harnisch has been considered an outstanding prospect since he led Fordham to a berth in the NCAA playoffs. He only pitched three years in the minors, but he averaged nearly a strikeout an inning at every stop. On his way up Harnisch was never a big winner, but at every stop he learned a little more about how to pitch.

Harnisch is a power pitcher; he can throw in the low 90's with great movement and he has more of an idea of what to do with his slider, curveball and change-up. Now, when his fastball is taking an off day, Harnisch can survive with his other pitches. He still has a tendency to permit a lot of baserunners because of a high walk total and often has to pitch out of the jams he creates. But he had several tough-luck losses last year or he might have had a winning record.

Harnisch is extremely tough on right-handed hitters (.222). He could be a number three starter on almost any team right now and his future is bright. The important thing is his sense of belonging. Harnisch no longer has to wonder whether he has major-league talent.

FIELDING AND HOLDING RUNNERS:

Harnisch is improving, but he has some distance to go. His follow-through from the pitching motion leaves him in an awkward position for defense, especially on balls hit up the middle, and he is prone to an occasional mental breakdown. He still has trouble holding runners consistently although his timing to first has improved. Runners are eager to capitalize on his tardy release to the plate.

OVERALL:

The talent Harnisch demonstrated on his way up is manifesting itself. He proved extremely durable last season and his eagerness to pitch rewarded the faith and patience the Orioles have shown in him. If he can curb his wildness and continue to progress as a fielder, he will be a solid pitcher. Maturity is setting in.

Overall Statistics

	W	L	ERA	G	GS	Sv	IP	H	R	BB	SO	HR
1990	11	11	4.34	31	31	0	188.2	189	96	86	122	17
Career	16	22	4.49	51	50	0	305.0	299	159	159	202	28

How Often He Throws Strikes

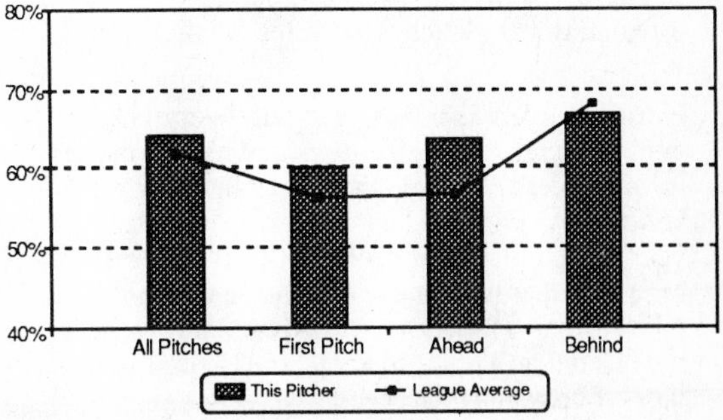

1990 Situational Stats

	W	L	ERA	Sv	IP		AB	H	HR	RBI	AVG
Home	7	6	4.63	0	89.1	LHB	435	125	10	50	.287
Road	4	5	4.08	0	99.1	RHB	288	64	7	30	.222
Day	3	0	3.77	0	31.0	Sc Pos	164	42	5	59	.256
Night	8	11	4.45	0	157.2	Clutch	48	12	2	5	.250

1990 Rankings (American League)

- 3rd in run support per 9 innings (5.77)
- 4th in most pitches thrown per batter (3.94)
- 5th in worst strikeout/walk ratio (1.42) and most baserunners allowed per 9 IP (13.2)
- 9th in walks allowed (86)
- Led the Orioles in losses (11), games started (31), complete games (3), innings (188.2), batters faced (821), walks allowed, strikeouts (122), pitches thrown (3,237), runners caught stealing (10) and run support per 9 innings

SAM HORN

Position: DH
Bats: L **Throws:** L
Ht: 6' 5" **Wt:** 240

Opening Day Age: 27
Born: 11/2/63 in Dallas, TX
ML Seasons: 4

HITTING:

At age 27, Sam Horn is a big free-swinger with awesome power and still-unfulfilled potential. As a Red Sox farm hand, Horn seemed to have it all together in 1987 when he belted 30 homers in only 94 games at Pawtucket; when called up to the big club late that year, he continued to blast 14 more in a 46-game shot. But when Horn slumped badly the next two years, hitting an anemic .148 in limited duty in both '88 and '89, the Bosox finally gave up on him.

The Orioles, desperate for some power, offered Horn another opportunity last spring. As with Boston, he started out in blazing fashion, with two homers and six RBI on opening day. But again he went into a funk and had to be sent back to the minors. Horn returned in midseason and finished with respectable numbers, playing almost exclusively against right-handed pitching. His average was low, but he was a constant longball threat, which is what the Orioles were looking for.

Horn's problem is he wants to pull everything. Pitchers continually work him away, and he gets messed up trying to jerk those pitches to right when he could simply be driving the ball wherever it's pitched. Last year Reggie Jackson seemed to convince Horn, at long last, that he could go the other way and still hit the ball out. Horn took the advice and made some strides, but he'll have to keep doing it on a consistent basis if he wants to succeed.

BASERUNNING:

Horn is a one-base-at-a-time kind of runner, a lumbering type who should not take chances. He is not a threat to steal and is easily doubled up on ground balls. With any play behind him, caution is the word on the base paths.

FIELDING:

As a defensive player, Horn has little value. He has tried to improve at first base, but he has limited agility and trouble with low throws. The Orioles did use him a little at first after Randy Milligan was injured, but Horn's future is as a DH.

OVERALL:

Horn has hit 30 homers in 519 lifetime at-bats scattered over four seasons -- figures very similar to what Cecil Fielder had accomplished going into the 1990 season. Horn's weakness against lefties will probably prevent him from becoming another Fielder, but there is little doubt that his power can help the Orioles. If he dedicates himself more and works on using the entire field, he can be an effective cleanup hitter.

Overall Statistics

	G	AB	R	H	D	T	HR	RBI	SB	BB	SO	AVG
1990	79	246	30	61	13	0	14	45	0	32	62	.248
Career	182	519	66	122	22	0	30	91	0	68	153	.235

Where He Hits the Ball

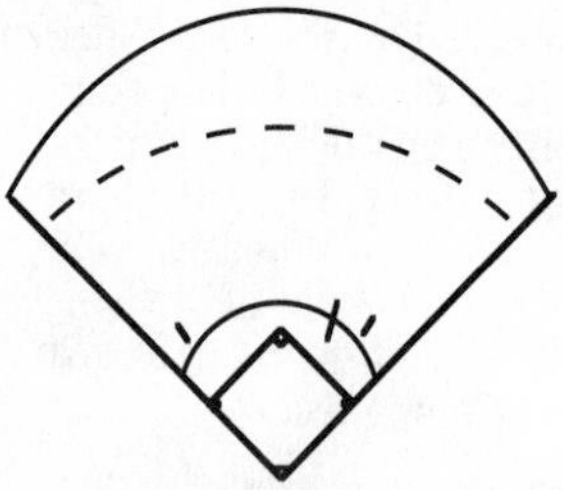

Vs. LHP

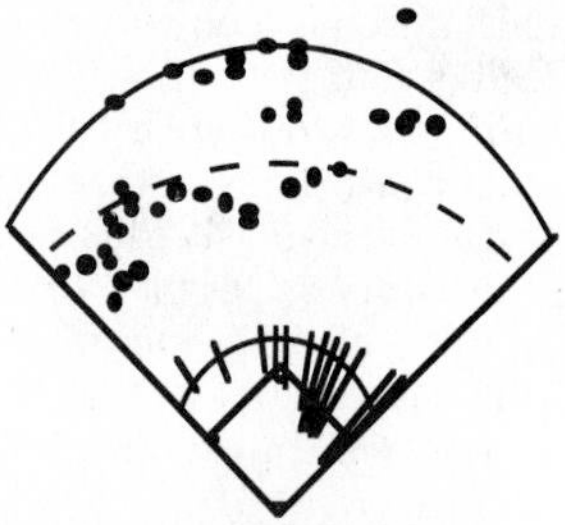

Vs. RHP

1990 Situational Stats

	AB	H	HR	RBI	AVG		AB	H	HR	RBI	AVG
Home	120	30	8	21	.250	LHP	17	1	0	0	.059
Road	126	31	6	24	.246	RHP	229	60	14	45	.262
Day	76	19	4	13	.250	Sc Pos	68	18	5	34	.265
Night	170	42	10	32	.247	Clutch	41	12	2	9	.293

1990 Rankings (American League)

- ➟ 1st in batting average on a 3-1 count (1.000)
- ➟ Led the Orioles in batting average on a 3-1 count

DAVE JOHNSON

Position: SP
Bats: R **Throws:** R
Ht: 5'11" **Wt:** 180

Opening Day Age: 31
Born: 10/24/59 in Baltimore, MD
ML Seasons: 3

PITCHING:

Here is the shining example of the little train that could. Dave Johnson spent eight years in the minor leagues and kept pursuing the dream. Finally, it seems to have paid off. At 31, he is a relic on a team overflowing with young pitchers. But the man is a self-believer who has become a hometown favorite with his gritty underdog image and dedication to the community. Last year, on a staff that struggled all year long, Johnson was the steady veteran, leading the club with 13 wins.

Johnson has to pitch to spots because his stuff is average. He throws a fastball, curve, slider and change and isn't overly impressive with any of them. But he has a wealth of experience that allows him to locate pitches effectively. Another factor is that he throws from unconventional positions (sidearm, three quarters) that keep hitters guessing. Further, he has a knack for making the big pitch in crucial situations. He sometimes appears to be pitching in a backward pattern, but knows exactly what he's doing.

Johnson was restricted to 29 starts last year by some back problems, but he was one was one of only two Orioles to reach double figures in wins (Pete Harnisch was the other). Underscoring his bulldog reputation, Johnson was 8-0 after Oriole losses. The one Achilles heel in Johnson's makeup is his tendency to allow too many hits and homers. He led the league by allowing 30 home runs. He compensates for this tendency with pinpoint control. Most of all, he realizes his limitations, doesn't overdo anything, and is honest about his physical condition.

FIELDING AND HOLDING RUNNERS:

Johnson is the toughest pitcher in baseball to steal on, and his unusual set-up position is the key. He stands facing the plate at an angle, giving him an excellent view of baserunners. Most runners simply look at Johnson's motion and stay glued to first base. In two years, no one had stolen a base against him until late last season. Johnson is very quick to first base and keeps runners off balance by taking away their first step. With the glove, he is aware of what needs to be done and uses his ability well.

OVERALL:

His tenure in the minors has given Johnson a sense of insecurity because he knows he has to prove himself every spring, especially in an organization accenting youth. But his tenacity, heart and know-how have earned him a lot of backers. When the season starts, Johnson figures to be starting along with it.

Overall Statistics

	W	L	ERA	G	GS	Sv	IP	H	R	BB	SO	HR
1990	13	9	4.10	30	29	0	180.0	196	83	43	68	30
Career	17	16	4.28	49	43	0	275.2	299	134	73	98	42

How Often He Throws Strikes

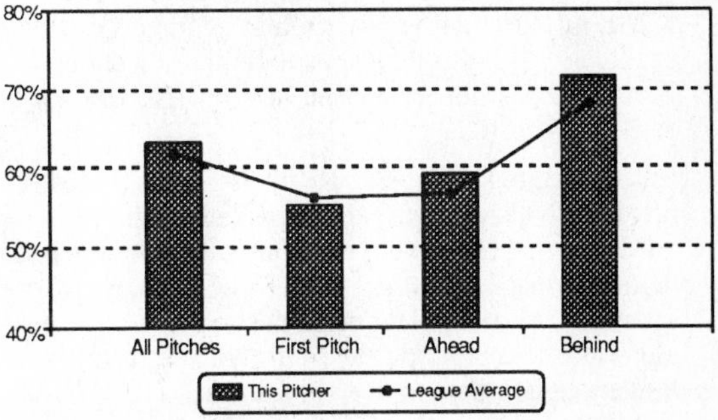

1990 Situational Stats

	W	L	ERA	Sv	IP		AB	H	HR	RBI	AVG
Home	5	6	3.72	0	87.0	LHB	347	103	15	37	.297
Road	8	3	4.45	0	93.0	RHB	353	93	15	36	.263
Day	5	1	3.47	0	70.0	Sc Pos	131	31	3	39	.237
Night	8	8	4.50	0	110.0	Clutch	35	11	4	4	.314

1990 Rankings (American League)

- 1st in home runs allowed (30), highest slugging percentage allowed (.476), lowest groundball/flyball ratio (.79) and most home runs allowed per 9 IP (1.50)
- 2nd in lowest stolen base percentage allowed (20.0%) and least pitches thrown per batter (3.42)
- 3rd in least strikeouts per 9 IP (3.4)
- Led the Orioles in wins (13), complete games (3), hits allowed (196), home runs allowed, hit batsmen (3), GDPs induced (18), lowest stolen base percentage allowed and least pitches thrown per batter

RON KITTLE

Position: DH/1B
Bats: R **Throws:** R
Ht: 6' 4" **Wt:** 220

Opening Day Age: 33
Born: 1/5/58 in Gary, IN
ML Seasons: 9

HITTING:

Acquired for Phil Bradley in a mid-season deal last year, Ron Kittle was a big disappointment to the Orioles. Leading the White Sox in home runs at the time of the trade, Kittle reported with a groin injury that hindered him at the plate. He seldom played during the last month of the season, and didn't produce much when he was put into the lineup. Kittle hit only two home runs for the Orioles and had the club wondering about his motivation. Kittle is a Chicago-area boy who was unhappy to leave the contending White Sox. He blasted the Sox brass after the deal and never seemed at home in Baltimore.

At his best, Kittle is a hitter with prodigious power. Working with White Sox hitting coach Walt Hriniak in 1989, Kittle hit for the best average of his career (.302), while retaining most of his longball ability. Maybe it was the injury, but once he left Hriniak, Kittle hit for neither power nor average. Kittle is capable of going to the opposite field often enough to keep defenses honest, but he has to drive in runs to earn his keep.

Like most big sluggers, Kittle is often fooled by breaking balls and will chase pitches in the dirt. He needs playing time to get into a groove, but there is no evidence that he will get it with the Orioles, whose accent is on speed. His best shot appears to be in a platoon role against lefties, but that might not give him enough at-bats to keep him sharp.

BASERUNNING:

Kittle is slow on the bases and lumbers along one base at a time. Injuries in recent seasons have robbed him of what little speed he once had, and he hasn't stolen a base since 1986. Last year he didn't even make an attempt. Third-base coaches have to be careful about trying to score Kittle from second on a single.

FIELDING:

Once an adequate outfielder, Kittle has only one position besides designated hitter now: first base. He is not extremely agile, but he does an acceptable job in the field. With his mounting injury problems and lack of mobility, he won't be seen on defense too often.

OVERALL:

The Orioles are a team which needs a slugger, and Kittle could still be the guy. His track record is proven, but his inconsistency may be his downfall. Kittle is still young enough to be a valuable player, but he won't help much unless his bat is working.

Overall Statistics

	G	AB	R	H	D	T	HR	RBI	SB	BB	SO	AVG
1990	105	338	33	78	16	0	18	46	0	26	91	.231
Career	826	2661	349	639	100	3	174	453	16	231	735	.240

Where He Hits the Ball

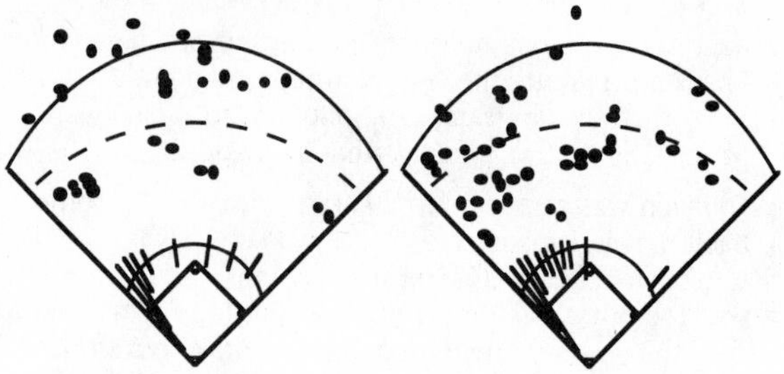

Vs. LHP   Vs. RHP

1990 Situational Stats

	AB	H	HR	RBI	AVG		AB	H	HR	RBI	AVG
Home	185	42	8	20	.227	LHP	151	34	13	25	.225
Road	153	36	10	26	.235	RHP	187	44	5	21	.235
Day	106	25	4	11	.236	Sc Pos	82	17	1	23	.207
Night	232	53	14	35	.228	Clutch	51	10	2	6	.196

1990 Rankings (American League)

- Did not rank near the top or bottom in any category

CY YOUNG STUFF

BEN McDONALD

Position: SP/RP
Bats: R **Throws:** R
Ht: 6' 7" **Wt:** 212

Opening Day Age: 23
Born: 11/24/67 in Baton Rouge, LA
ML Seasons: 2

PITCHING:

Ben McDonald is a young man on his way to stardom -- perhaps superstardom. The Orioles were cautious last year with the nation's number one draft choice of 1989, and with good reason. As a college and Olympic star at LSU, McDonald had been given a heavy workload, even for someone with his strength and stamina. Wanting to take no chances, the Orioles babied him a bit. Last year McDonald strained a lateral oblique muscle in his side during spring training, then had some blister problems on his pitching hand while at Class AAA Rochester. The cure for the blister problem was his call-up to the big leagues, where the seams on a baseball are not as pronounced as in the minor leagues. McDonald didn't arrive in the big leagues until mid-season and didn't start until after the All-Star break.

Once he got going, McDonald showed why he is a cornerstone of the staff's future. He won his first five starts, a club record, and went on to an 8-5 record, allowing only 88 hits in 118.2 innings and a team-low .205 opposing bating average. McDonald throws a fastball in the mid 90's -- but his sharp breaking curve is the key to his success. If the curve is getting over, he is extremely tough to hit. This season McDonald figures to go more often to the change-up, which thus far he has used sparingly. That will make his fastball even more devastating.

McDonald sometimes displays his emotions on the mound, particularly after getting out of a key inning. That is a reflection of his youthful enthusiasm. He is still learning and has a tendency at times to want to overpower every hitter. But he is only getting better. Someday, this former college basketball player will be a 20-game winner.

FIELDING AND HOLDING RUNNERS:

Despite being 6-7, McDonald is an agile athlete who knows the value of defense. But he has a tendency to fall off the mound at the end of his delivery and must recover with his quickness; that's not always easy, and sometimes he winds up out of position. McDonald has a high leg kick, which can give him trouble at holding runners. He is also slow to home plate, but he is improving. Adopting the slide step and a more open stance toward first have helped.

OVERALL:

The sky is the limit for McDonald, who undoubtedly will take his place in the rotation this season, and possibly the head of the rotation before too long. Barring injury and with a more varied pitch selection, he could cross the threshold in a big way. American League hitters already respect his overpowering stuff. He needs only refinement and experience.

Overall Statistics

	W	L	ERA	G	GS	Sv	IP	H	R	BB	SO	HR
1990	8	5	2.43	21	15	0	118.2	88	36	35	65	9
Career	9	5	2.79	27	15	0	126.0	96	43	39	68	11

How Often He Throws Strikes

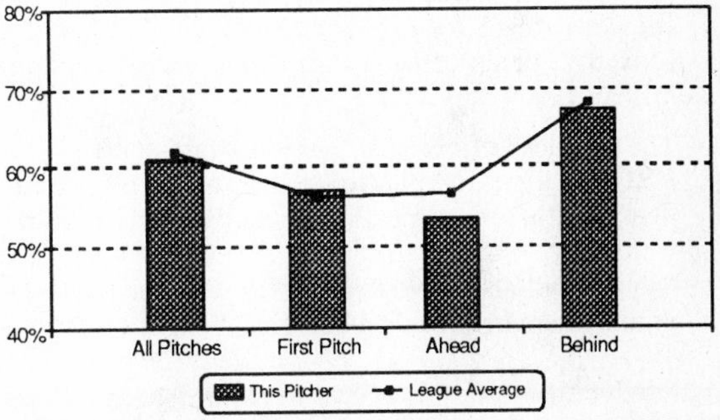

1990 Situational Stats

	W	L	ERA	Sv	IP		AB	H	HR	RBI	AVG
Home	4	3	2.41	0	74.2	LHB	216	39	2	8	.181
Road	4	2	2.45	0	44.0	RHB	213	49	7	23	.230
Day	1	1	4.63	0	11.2	Sc Pos	78	10	1	19	.128
Night	7	4	2.19	0	107.0	Clutch	75	13	3	7	.173

1990 Rankings (American League)

- 1st in lowest batting average vs. left-handed batters (.181)
- 6th in shutouts (2)
- Led the Orioles in complete games (3), shutouts, wild pitches (5) and lowest batting average vs. left-handed batters

HITTING:

Although not acquired for his offense, Bob Melvin does have some run-producing ability. The Orioles' number two catcher has been slowly improving as a hitter the last few years, raising his average each season (.199, .234, .241, .243). Over the last two seasons, he has totaled 69 RBI in 579 at-bats. That's not Carlton Fisk territory, but it's plenty good for a guy who makes his living with his glove.

Melvin has some definite weaknesses as a hitter and is still working to overcome them. He is a good high-ball hitter who can drive the ball to all fields. Thus, pitchers tend to work him low in the strike zone, trying to make him chase offerings he can't handle. An impatient type who seldom walks, Melvin often takes the bait. But he has the desire to be a better hitter, and his efforts are paying off. Last year he increased his home run total from one to five and showed a knack for getting key hits with two out. He proved to be an offensive asset, particularly against lefthanders.

The Orioles believe that Melvin could increase his RBI total to nearly 50, even in his backup role. To do that he'll have to improve his terrible strikeout-to-walk ratio, which was almost five to one last year. Melvin will also have to hit better at Memorial Stadium, where he batted an anemic .174 last year.

BASERUNNING:

Melvin is a typical catcher, a runner who needs the momentum of the hit-and-run or bunt to get a jump on the next base. He's large and certainly won't steal many bases. He's been caught 11 times out of his last 12 attempts (since 1987)! But, because of his conservatism, he doesn't make silly mistakes.

FIELDING:

No one questions Melvin's ability with the glove. Pitchers love to throw to him, he calls an excellent game and he blocks balls in the dirt very well. He also has the perfect temperament to deal with the young Oriole pitching staff -- he encourages without being bossy. And Melvin has a strong throwing arm, important on a team with youngsters still dealing with how to hold runners. Melvin is always in the game from behind the plate.

OVERALL:

Melvin accepts his platoon role with equanimity and realizes his limitations. He is a valuable man to have as the pitchers mature. If he could only hit a tad better, he'd be the quintessential number two catcher.

BOB MELVIN

Position: C
Bats: R **Throws:** R
Ht: 6' 4" **Wt:** 205

Opening Day Age: 29
Born: 10/28/61 in Palo Alto, CA
ML Seasons: 6

Overall Statistics

	G	AB	R	H	D	T	HR	RBI	SB	BB	SO	AVG
1990	93	301	30	73	14	1	5	37	0	11	53	.243
Career	484	1448	140	331	63	6	30	156	4	74	286	.229

Where He Hits the Ball

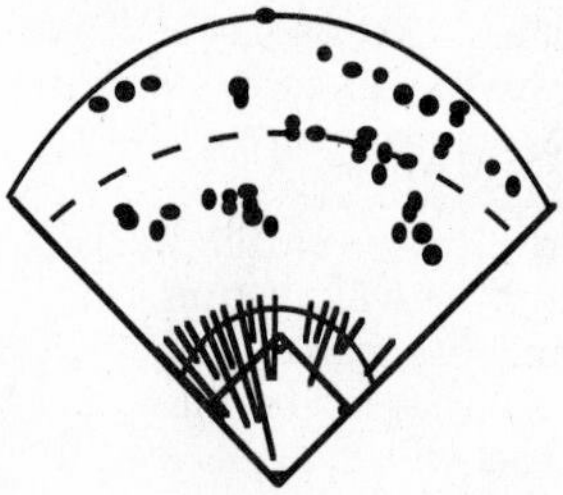

Vs. LHP

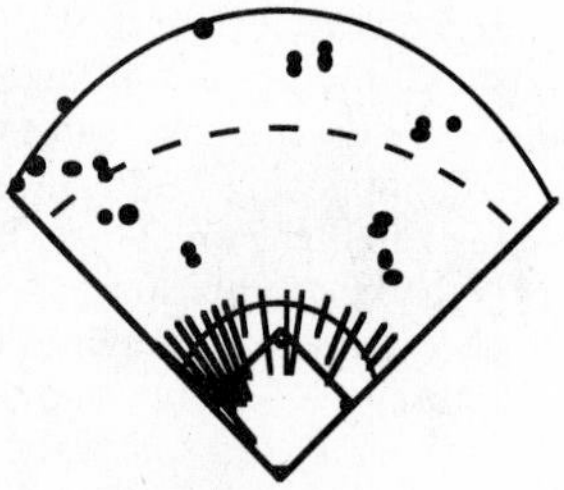

Vs. RHP

1990 Situational Stats

	AB	H	HR	RBI	AVG		AB	H	HR	RBI	AVG
Home	121	21	3	13	.174	LHP	152	42	3	16	.276
Road	180	52	2	24	.289	RHP	149	31	2	21	.208
Day	90	31	1	12	.344	Sc Pos	98	27	2	32	.276
Night	211	42	4	25	.199	Clutch	54	10	1	6	.185

1990 Rankings (American League)

- 4th in lowest percentage of extra bases taken as a runner (26.8%)

PITCHING:

Bob Milacki took a step backward in 1990. He was plagued by injuries and an atypical lack of control. As a rookie in 1989, Milacki had been the staff workhorse. The big righthander had won 14 games, hurled 243 innings, and tied for the league lead with 36 starts. He was the first rookie in 71 years to lead the league in games started. The heavy workload didn't seem to bother him at all, as Milacki was outstanding late in the year. Down the stretch, when the Orioles were battling unsuccessfully for a division title, Milacki was the staff leader, going 5-0 with a 2.33 ERA in his last seven '89 starts.

Maybe that heavy workload didn't bother Milacki in '89, but it was a different story in 1990. All season long he was hampered by assorted ailments, the most serious of which was an inflamed rotator cuff late in the year. A tenacious type, Milacki tried to pitch through the problem, but probably hurt himself by doing so. He ended up working only 135.1 innings and won only five games all year.

Milacki has a lot of weapons. He has a 90 mile-per-hour fastball, a big sweeping curve, a slider and a change. At 6-4 and 225, he looks like he could break bats -- and batters -- in half. But last year Milacki got into a habit of trying to fool too many hitters with the change-up and perhaps underestimated his other pitches. He nibbled too often and walked more batters than he struck out, while frequently pitching from behind in the count. Strangely, Milacki gave up twice as many homers to right-handed batters as he did to lefties in virtually the same number of at bats. What he needs is a full spring training to recapture the rhythm that stamped him as the best pure pitcher on the staff.

FIELDING AND HOLDING BASERUNNERS:

For his size, Milacki is very agile and handles the glove well. Regarding his move to first base, however, his concentration sometimes lapses and he undergoes stretches when runners get the jump on him. Part of the problem last year was that he was behind in the count so much.

OVERALL:

In '89 Milacki won 14 games without much offensive support and was a pillar of strength, even on three days' rest. But that's part of the problem. He wants the ball so badly, and the Orioles are so eager to give it to him, that there's a real danger of him being overworked. Milacki's 1990 experience indicates that he needs to be handled a little more tenderly. His strong right arm is too talented to waste.

BOB MILACKI

Position: SP
Bats: R **Throws:** R
Ht: 6' 4" **Wt:** 220

Opening Day Age: 26
Born: 7/28/64 in Trenton, NJ
ML Seasons: 3

Overall Statistics

	W	L	ERA	G	GS	Sv	IP	H	R	BB	SO	HR
1990	5	8	4.46	27	24	0	135.1	143	73	61	60	18
Career	21	20	3.79	67	63	0	403.1	385	180	158	191	40

How Often He Throws Strikes

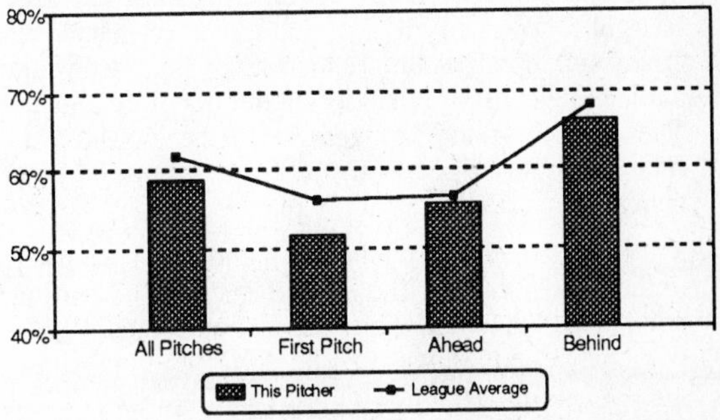

1990 Situational Stats

	W	L	ERA	Sv	IP		AB	H	HR	RBI	AVG
Home	1	3	5.29	0	49.1	LHB	261	72	6	26	.276
Road	4	5	3.98	0	86.0	RHB	262	71	12	41	.271
Day	2	3	4.72	0	47.2	Sc Pos	115	32	2	41	.278
Night	3	5	4.31	0	87.2	Clutch	31	12	2	3	.387

1990 Rankings (American League)

- 10th in most stolen bases allowed (19)
- Led the Orioles in most stolen bases allowed

RANDY MILLIGAN

Position: 1B
Bats: R **Throws:** R
Ht: 6' 2" **Wt:** 225

Opening Day Age: 29
Born: 11/27/61 in San Diego, CA
ML Seasons: 4

HITTING:

There's no telling what Randy Milligan might have accomplished had he not dislocated his shoulder in a home-plate collision with Oakland catcher Ron Hassey on August 7. That injury knocked Milligan out of the lineup until the final few games of the season, when he came back just to re-assure himself that he was sound again. Milligan was leading the Orioles in virtually every offensive category except batting average up until the injury. Despite missing nearly two months, he still finished with 20 homers, one short of Cal Ripken's team-high 21. Although the injury kept him from having a monster season, it was a successful year for the big slugger. Milligan labored eight long years in the minors before getting his first real chance with the Cinderella Orioles of 1989.

Milligan is a selective hitter who was leading the majors in walks when he went on the disabled list. He has good power to all fields and is a tough man in clutch situations because of his batting eye. Two years ago, Milligan hit righthanders better than lefthanders. That turned around last year, when he led the club with a .330 average against lefties and reached base nearly every other time at the plate.

Milligan hits outside pitches well and can drive them to the opposite field. The big difference in his hitting between 1989, when he hit only 12 homers, and 1990, when he belted 20, was that he didn't let himself get jammed as much with inside stuff. Milligan proved he could pull with considerable power, eliminating the only real weakness in his hitting.

BASERUNNING:

For a big man, Milligan has surprising speed, especially when he gets underway. He's not much of a base-stealer, but can take advantage if he's given too much freedom. He catches opponents napping occasionally and is usually quick around the paths.

FIELDING:

No Gold Glover, Milligan is at worst adequate and at best above average. Milligan won't embarrass a team with his glove very often, but he's prone to occasional mental lapses and dropped balls. He hustles on defense and tries hard to improve, but he is not a polished first baseman.

OVERALL:

Milligan is one of those guys who always seems to be in a good mood. A positive influence, he brings harmony to the clubhouse. If he hits like he did last year and stays healthy, he has the potential to be a 30-homer, 90-RBI man. He may have to share some time with David Segui, but first base is his until proven otherwise.

Overall Statistics

	G	AB	R	H	D	T	HR	RBI	SB	BB	SO	AVG
1990	109	362	64	96	20	1	20	60	6	88	68	.265
Career	276	810	130	212	48	6	35	113	16	183	168	.262

Where He Hits the Ball

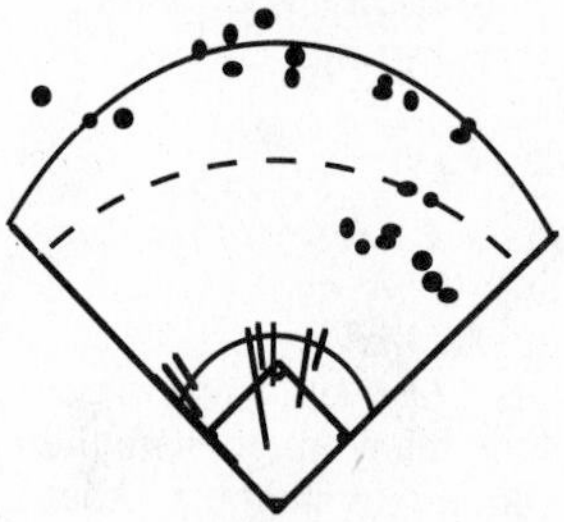

Vs. LHP

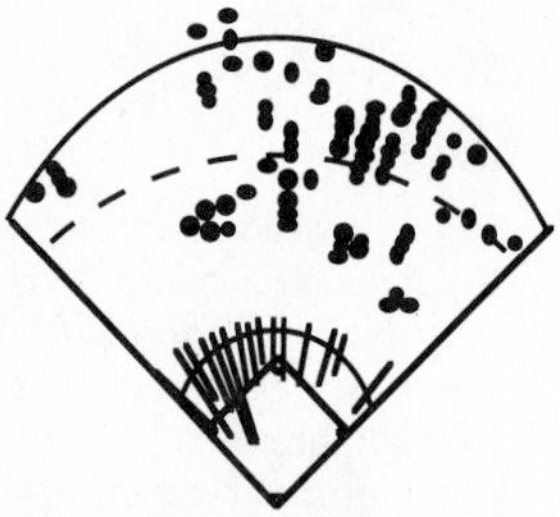

Vs. RHP

1990 Situational Stats

	AB	H	HR	RBI	AVG		AB	H	HR	RBI	AVG
Home	166	44	11	31	.265	LHP	100	33	8	22	.330
Road	196	52	9	29	.265	RHP	262	63	12	38	.240
Day	98	30	5	20	.306	Sc Pos	95	24	3	39	.253
Night	264	66	15	40	.250	Clutch	60	15	4	11	.250

1990 Rankings (American League)

- 2nd in on-base average vs. left-handed pitchers (.473) and slugging percentage vs. left-handed pitchers (.680)
- 7th in walks (88)
- 10th highest batting average vs. left-handed pitchers (.330)
- Led the Orioles in batting average vs. left-handed pitchers, on-base average vs. left-handed pitchersand slugging percentage vs. left-handed pitchers

JOHN MITCHELL

Position: SP/RP
Bats: R **Throws:** R
Ht: 6' 2" **Wt:** 195

Opening Day Age: 25
Born: 8/11/65 in Dickson, TN
ML Seasons: 5

PITCHING:

John Mitchell broke into the Oriole rotation in the middle of last season and had up-and-down results. Mitchell started off well, winning three games in July as the Orioles briefly moved into contention. In August he won three more, but had a 5.35 ERA in seven starts and was hammered for 53 hits in only 37 innings. Mitchell soon lost his job in the rotation and finished the year as a little-used reliever.

A pitcher who always threw a lot of innings in the Mets' minor-league system, Mitchell relies basically on a sinking fastball and a curveball, with an occasional slider and change-up mixed in. Mitchell's stuff is not overpowering, and he has to get movement and location to be successful. Last year he simply wasn't sharp enough, walking more batters than he struck out.

As a minor leaguer, Mitchell was a consistent winner. In six seasons from '84 thru '89, he won in double figures five times, always had good ERAs, and led his league in innings pitched twice. At age 25, he's had eight seasons of professional experience and figures to be about as ready as he'll ever be. But despite his minor league success, Mitchell has yet to prove he can win at the major league level. After 240 major league innings, his lifetime record is 9-14 with a 4.35 ERA, and he's allowed well over one hit per inning.

In 1990 Mitchell struggled with his control, was hit hard (.300 opposing average), and never settled into a long-term groove. Lefthanders battered him at a .317 clip, primarily because he often fell behind and had to go at them. He has an opportunity with an up-and-coming team, but must make the necessary adjustments to finding the plate.

FIELDING AND HOLDING RUNNERS:

Mitchell could stand some improvement at keeping runners close, but he isn't all that bad. His move to first is decent. Coming off the mound, Mitchell falls far to the left, and that makes it difficult for him to field balls hit to his right. But, on balance, he is better than average defensively.

OVERALL:

Mitchell will have to scramble to earn a spot on the big-league roster with a team loaded with young pitching. He doesn't have superior stuff, but he has a resilient arm that lends itself to starting or long relief. Though he struggled as a starter last year, he was reasonably effective out of the pen, with a 3.60 ERA. If he regains his control, he has a chance.

Overall Statistics

	W	L	ERA	G	GS	Sv	IP	H	R	BB	SO	HR
1990	6	6	4.64	24	17	0	114.1	133	63	48	43	7
Career	9	14	4.35	51	37	0	240.0	272	138	93	107	14

How Often He Throws Strikes

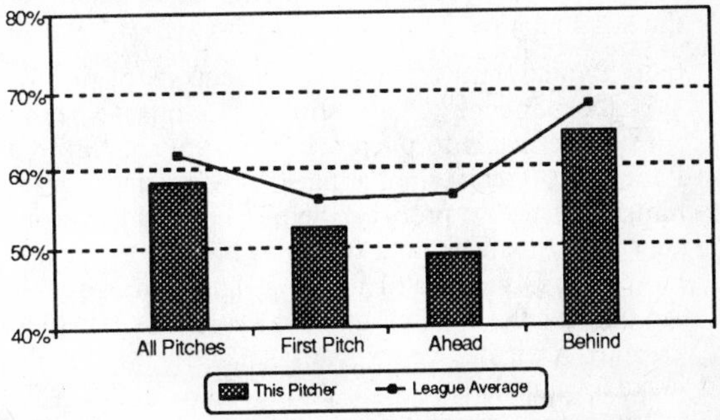

1990 Situational Stats

	W	L	ERA	Sv	IP		AB	H	HR	RBI	AVG
Home	2	2	4.47	0	50.1	LHB	202	64	4	23	.317
Road	4	4	4.78	0	64.0	RHB	242	69	3	33	.285
Day	2	1	4.74	0	24.2	Sc Pos	120	34	2	48	.283
Night	4	5	4.62	0	89.2	Clutch	25	11	0	3	.440

1990 Rankings (American League)

- Led the Orioles in hit batsmen (3)

STOPPER

GREGG OLSON

Position: RP
Bats: R **Throws:** R
Ht: 6' 4" **Wt:** 211

Opening Day Age: 24
Born: 10/11/66 in Omaha, NE
ML Seasons: 3

PITCHING:

Last year Gregg Olson had quite an act to follow -- his own -- and he acquitted himself well. Despite a short stretch after the All-Star break in which he was hit and hit hard, Olson broke Don Aase's club save record by racking up 37. All in all Olson was not quite as effective as in his rookie season, when he was all but unhittable. Still, Olson remained one of the league's top closers except for the one fallow period when his elbow had stiffened and he was pitching in pain. He's expected to be fully recovered after a winter of rest.

In 1990 Olson proved human at times, allowing his first two home runs at home after 41 innings without one. He had a propensity for digging himself holes, then digging out of them. His was the type of pitching which occasionally stopped heartbeats. But Olson retained that 95 MPH fastball and a set of curves, including the big one, Uncle Charlie, that he uses for the kill.

Only 24 and with less than three seasons of professional experience, Olson still has things to learn. Mostly, he needs to pitch a little more and throw a little less, thereby eliminating some wear and tear on himself. It would probably help if he could learn to spot his fastball without trying to blow it by everybody. But Olson is still learning, has a tremendous attitude for the bullpen and always wants the ball. Coupled with his overwhelming talent, that would make a valuable asset to any team. The Orioles want to try to remove some pressure from him by finding another short man.

FIELDING AND HOLDING RUNNERS:

This is an area where Olson has room for improvement. He is poor at holding runners on first and is not as effective to the hitter when he concentrates too much on runners. It is a Catch 22 situation. Some minor changes could help him, but the last thing the Orioles want to do is tinker too much and cut down his ability to get out batters. With the glove, Olson tends to rush on ground balls and needs to decrease his body motion.

OVERALL:

Pure, raw ability to blow away the opposition will keep Olson as a closer for some time. He can refine his fastball to the point where location and not velocity will do the job. He also has a way to go defensively. But Olson is certainly on the fast track with nothing but success to look forward to in his future.

Overall Statistics

	W	L	ERA	G	GS	Sv	IP	H	R	BB	SO	HR
1990	6	5	2.42	64	0	37	74.1	57	20	31	74	3
Career	12	8	2.11	138	0	64	170.1	124	41	87	173	5

How Often He Throws Strikes

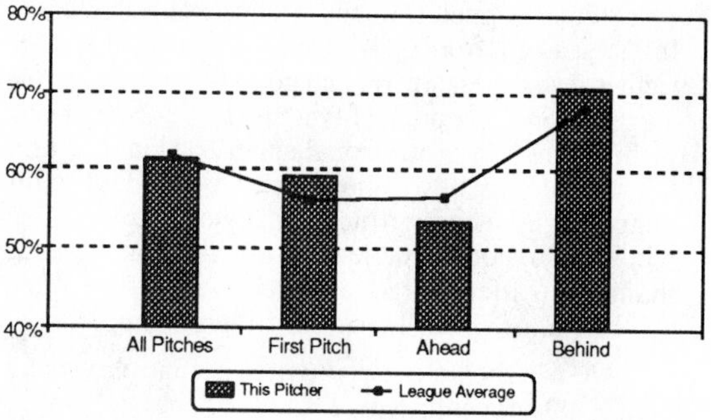

1990 Situational Stats

	W	L	ERA	Sv	IP		AB	H	HR	RBI	AVG
Home	5	0	2.93	13	30.2	LHB	145	29	1	13	.200
Road	1	5	2.06	24	43.2	RHB	123	28	2	14	.228
Day	1	1	1.75	17	25.2	Sc Pos	82	17	1	24	.207
Night	5	4	2.77	20	48.2	Clutch	201	43	3	24	.214

1990 Rankings (American League)

- 3rd lowest batting average vs. left-handed batters (.200)
- 4th in saves (37), save opportunities (42) and save percentage (88.1%)
- 5th in games finished (58)
- Led the Orioles in games (64), saves, games finished, hit batsmen (3), wild pitches (5), save opportunities and save percentage

JOE ORSULAK

Position: RF/LF
Bats: L **Throws:** L
Ht: 6' 1" **Wt:** 186

Opening Day Age: 28
Born: 5/31/62 in Glen Ridge, NJ
ML Seasons: 7

HITTING:

Joe Orsulak was the Orioles' top hitter for two straight seasons, 1988 and 1989. He appeared headed for a third such crown before a late-season swoon that was probably the result of a back injury. When healthy, the man can flat out hit. Orsulak was among the league's top ten in late May with a .339 average. That's a lofty level for him, but Orsulak has proven himself to be a solid .280-.290 type.

A bona fide contact hitter, Orsulak takes advantage of the entire field and seems to hit a line drive (even if foul) in every at-bat. He flashed a little more power in 1990 with 11 home runs and he is versatile enough to play in any spot in the batting order.

Whether jerking a double down the line or spraying a line drive to left, Orsulak never gets cheated at the plate and is tough to strike out. He can reach effectively for the outside pitch and will surprise with an occasional bunt. Probably the key to his game is concentration. He follows each pitch intently, and does his best to get the maximum out of every appearance. His strength is hitting fastballs on the inside half of the plate. Though he battles every pitch, he is less successful against outside fastballs, and low curves tend to give him problems.

BASERUNNING:

Orsulak had two 24-stolen base seasons with the Pirates, but he's been less successful with Baltimore. He wasn't even successful in half his attempts in 1990. A little better than average to first, Orsulak has sensibly run less often as his speed has diminished. Orsulak is an intelligent player, and he runs the bases well.

FIELDING:

Once a liability, Orsulak has worked hard to improve this phase of his game, perhaps picking up the beat from his speedy counterparts. He can play left or right field in keeping with the Orioles' philosophy of multi-position players. Orsulak has a tendency to make a lot of sliding catches because he sometimes gets a late break. But he is not afraid of walls and accepts the challenge when runners test his arm.

OVERALL:

Orsulak is a man who shuns the spotlight and does his job with the least amount of fanfare. He always seems to come out of spring training as a reserve, yet winds up with as many at-bats as the other outfielders because he can deliver at the plate. As long as Orsulak can hit, he'll have a job. Even if his fielding skills and baserunning diminish, he'll make a solid designated and pinch hitter.

Overall Statistics

	G	AB	R	H	D	T	HR	RBI	SB	BB	SO	AVG
1990	124	413	49	111	14	3	11	57	6	46	48	.269
Career	670	2058	282	569	91	25	28	183	71	165	187	.276

Where He Hits the Ball

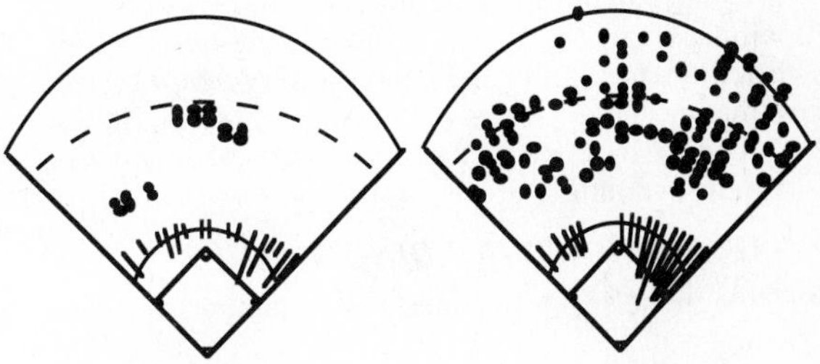

Vs. LHP   Vs. RHP

1990 Situational Stats

	AB	H	HR	RBI	AVG		AB	H	HR	RBI	AVG
Home	202	55	9	34	.272	LHP	72	18	0	7	.250
Road	211	56	2	23	.265	RHP	341	93	11	50	.273
Day	108	26	3	14	.241	Sc Pos	110	33	4	47	.300
Night	305	85	8	43	.279	Clutch	61	13	1	3	.213

1990 Rankings (American League)

- 7th highest batting average on a 3-1 count (.571)

PITCHING:

An 11-year veteran at age 34, Joe Price remains a valuable commodity because of his versatility. Though he was used mostly as a middle man in 1990, Price can start, work middle and long relief, or face lefthanders in situational duty. There's a place on anyone's team for a lefthander who can do all that, and Price made himself right at home in his first year with the O's.

Not overpowering, Price primarily relies on a sweeping breaking ball. His other pitches are nothing spectacular: an average fastball and a slider that he needs to position well. Price can strike out people when he's right, but he's susceptible to the home run when he hangs his breaking ball.

Price is a veteran with a solid knowledge of the game. His value extends to the clubhouse where he is a good influence on the young Oriole pitchers. He is always willing to give them tips without being overbearing. Price still has ability and figures to survive for several more seasons, provided his health cooperates. He was forced out by some back stiffness last year and missed almost a month.

FIELDING AND HOLDING RUNNERS:

Though he's a lefthander, Price has a surprising amount of difficulty holding baserunners. His 1989 stint with the Red Sox was noted, as much as anything, for one harrowing sequence in which Devon White of the Angels stole second, third and home off Price in the same inning. There were no such incidents in 1990, but opponents were not afraid to gamble against Price. His repertoire accents the breaking ball, giving them more time to steal; Price knows this and is working on varying his move to give them more to think about. He is an average fielder who doesn't get that many opportunities because of the short length of his appearances and his knack for throwing a lot of fly balls.

OVERALL:

Though he had some well-documented difficulties with Red Sox manager Joe Morgan, Price has been a solid citizen with Baltimore and is regarded as a student of baseball. He can substitute in a number of roles, making him very valuable when healthy. While improvement in his control would aid his cause, a strong point for Price was his effectiveness last year against both righties and lefties. Opposing pinch hitters from both sides of the plate were less dangerous to him overall.

JOE PRICE

Position: RP
Bats: R **Throws:** L
Ht: 6' 4" **Wt:** 215

Opening Day Age: 34
Born: 11/29/56 in Inglewood, CA
ML Seasons: 11

Overall Statistics

	W	L	ERA	G	GS	Sv	IP	H	R	BB	SO	HR
1990	3	4	3.58	50	0	0	65.1	62	29	24	54	8
Career	45	49	3.65	372	84	13	906.0	839	408	337	657	95

How Often He Throws Strikes

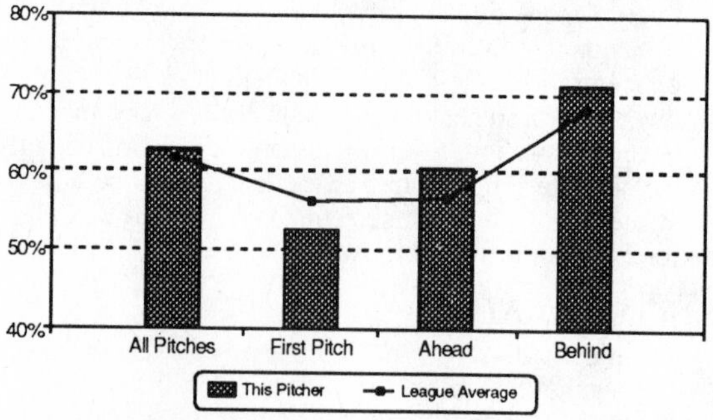

1990 Situational Stats

	W	L	ERA	Sv	IP		AB	H	HR	RBI	AVG
Home	2	1	2.06	0	39.1	LHB	90	24	1	6	.267
Road	1	3	5.88	0	26.0	RHB	155	38	7	22	.245
Day	0	2	7.08	0	20.1	Sc Pos	70	15	3	22	.214
Night	3	2	2.00	0	45.0	Clutch	54	17	2	8	.315

1990 Rankings (American League)

- 4th lowest percentage of inherited runners scoring (18.0%)

HITTING:

When discipline at the plate became his byword last season, Bill Ripken flourished. He led the Orioles in batting average, climbing 52 points over his previous career average, by adhering to his lessons and becoming a successful spray hitter. Despite a foot injury that kept him out of the lineup for two weeks, Ripken tied for the American League lead in sacrifices and showed an eagerness to play hit-and-run baseball. More than ever before, Ripken went to right field with outside pitches. By stopping his inclination to pull the ball, he became a much more effective batter.

Ripken's improvement was surprising to some, but perhaps it shouldn't have been. Though he's had three and a half years of major league experience, Ripken is still only 26. He obviously comes from a family with both intelligence and athletic skill. He's a student of the game: even in the minor leagues, where he broke in at age 17, Ripken's career was one of steady progress.

Always a good low fastball hitter, Ripken has never been strong against either breaking pitches or high fastballs. Though he still didn't draw many walks, Ripken stopped chasing the pitches he couldn't handle and thus became a much improved hitter. A good bunter, he adapted himself well to both the No. 2 and No. 9 spots in the batting order.

BASERUNNING:

Ripken does not have blinding speed for a middle infielder, but he is well schooled in basic baseball fundamentals and gets the job done. He can score from first on a double and beat out a few ground balls. While he doesn't try to steal a lot, when he does he usually makes it.

FIELDING:

There was never any question about Ripken's glove. He has outstanding range, dives for the ball adroitly and is a master at taking the slowly-hit grounder and whipping a throw across his body for an out. Alongside his brother Cal, the Ripken double-play combination is as good as any because they know each other so well. They committed only 11 errors between them last year.

OVERALL:

If he continues to improve with the bat, Bill Ripken could well become an All-Star player. He took a giant step in that direction with his play last season, but must guard against falling into old batting habits. The club prankster, he is regarded as a comic by some, not-so-funny by older baseball people. But Ripken is a fixture, so his detractors might as well get used to him.

BILLY RIPKEN

Position: 2B
Bats: R **Throws:** R
Ht: 6' 1" **Wt:** 183

Opening Day Age: 26
Born: 12/16/64 in Havre de Grace, MD
ML Seasons: 4

Overall Statistics

	G	AB	R	H	D	T	HR	RBI	SB	BB	SO	AVG
1990	129	406	48	118	28	1	3	38	5	28	43	.291
Career	452	1470	158	372	66	4	9	118	18	104	182	.253

Where He Hits the Ball

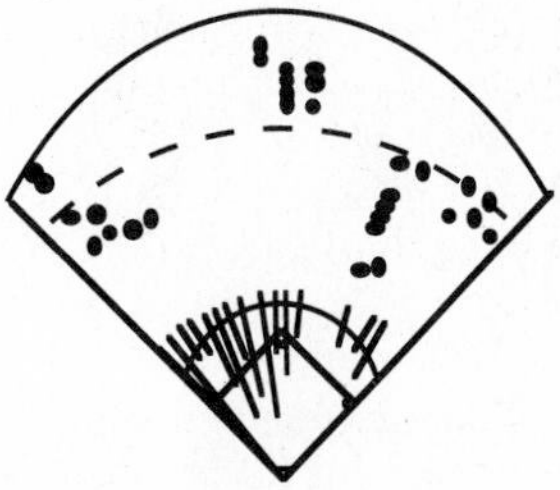

Vs. LHP

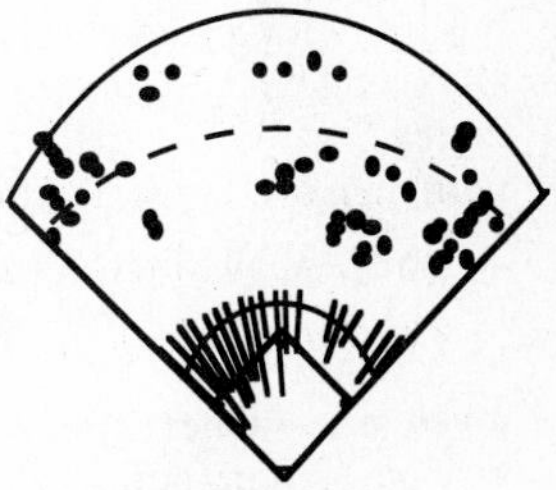

Vs. RHP

1990 Situational Stats

	AB	H	HR	RBI	AVG		AB	H	HR	RBI	AVG
Home	198	55	2	20	.278	LHP	140	44	2	11	.314
Road	208	63	1	18	.303	RHP	266	74	1	27	.278
Day	102	34	1	10	.333	Sc Pos	100	31	0	32	.310
Night	304	84	2	28	.276	Clutch	58	21	0	5	.362

1990 Rankings (American League)

- 1st in sacrifice bunts (17)
- 3rd in bunts in play (31)
- 6th highest batting average in the clutch (.362)
- Led the Orioles in doubles (28), sacrifice bunts, batting average with runners in scoring position (.310), batting average in the clutch and percentage of swings put into play (53.8%)
- Led AL second basemen in sacrifice bunts, hit by pitch (4), batting average in the clutch and bunts in play

HALL OF FAMER

CAL RIPKEN

Position: SS
Bats: R **Throws:** R
Ht: 6' 4" **Wt:** 225

Opening Day Age: 30
Born: 8/24/60 in Havre de Grace, MD
ML Seasons: 10

HITTING:

It's hard to believe that Cal Ripken, the former Rookie of the Year and MVP, is already 30. But it's not hard to believe that the steady Ripken is well on his way to becoming one of the most prolific offensive shortstops in history. Last year Ripken recorded his ninth straight 20-homer season, becoming only the third current major leaguer to accomplish that feat (Dale Murphy and Dwight Evans are the others.) He already has the career record for American League shortstops.

Ripken's average has leveled off in the .250-.260 range the last four seasons, a sharp drop from the .318 mark he reached in his MVP year of 1983. Many believe that Ripken would hit higher if he took an occasional day off. But there may be another reason for the decline. Ripken changes his stance frequently and sometimes gets impatient because he feels that he must drive in runs. In short, he takes on too heavy a burden, with results that are opposite from his intent. Opposing pitchers tended to pitch around him often, increasing his frustration. Ripken batted only .204 with men in scoring position last year.

A good fastball hitter, Ripken likes the ball inside and low. He has some problems with outside pitches and high, inside fastballs. But he tinkers with his style so much that pitchers have to work constantly to find ways to get him out.

BASERUNNING:

As a baserunner, Ripken's biggest asset is his deep knowledge of the game. He lacks the speed to be a base stealer, but runs the bases well. Ripken has the innate ability to realize when and how far to go, which slide to use, and to know where the batted ball is headed. He is far from the fastest man on the team, but he is the smartest baserunner.

FIELDING:

Cal Ripken is the steadiest, most consistent shortstop in baseball. It is difficult to envision a shortstop playing in every game for an entire season while making only three errors, but that's what Ripken accomplished in 1990. He had the highest fielding percentage ever by a shortstop. Being a big man, he gives up a little range, but Ripken positions and reacts very well and uses his rifle arm to compensate.

OVERALL:

Ripken is a model for the young Orioles. He goes about his job with dignity, but does not badger others into following. He simply considers it part of the job and expects the same of teammates. The season he had defensively was almost too good to be true. Now, if he can relax at the plate, he just might win another MVP award.

Overall Statistics

	G	AB	R	H	D	T	HR	RBI	SB	BB	SO	AVG
1990	161	600	78	150	28	4	21	84	3	82	66	.250
Career	1476	5655	871	1552	294	28	225	828	22	635	701	.274

Where He Hits the Ball

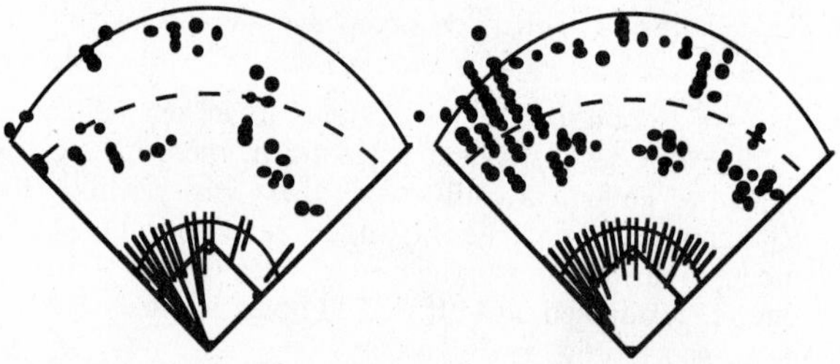

Vs. LHP Vs. RHP

1990 Situational Stats

	AB	H	HR	RBI	AVG		AB	H	HR	RBI	AVG
Home	300	64	8	42	.213	LHP	182	48	9	24	.264
Road	300	86	13	42	.287	RHP	418	102	12	60	.244
Day	162	47	9	21	.290	Sc Pos	167	34	2	59	.204
Night	438	103	12	63	.235	Clutch	98	27	4	13	.276

1990 Rankings (American League)

- 2nd in intentional walks (18) and games (161)
- 2nd worst batting average at home (.213)
- 5th in plate appearances (695)
- 7th in pitches seen (2,564)
- Led the Orioles in home runs (21), at-bats (600), runs (78), hits (150), singles (97), doubles (28), triples (4), total bases (249), RBI (84), sacrifice flies (7), intentional walks, time on base (237), pitches seen, plate appearances and games
- Led AL shortstops in fielding percentage (.996), home runs, sacrifice flies, walks, intentional walks and games

MICKEY TETTLETON

Position: C/DH
Bats: B **Throws:** R
Ht: 6' 2" **Wt:** 214

Opening Day Age: 30
Born: 9/16/60 in Oklahoma City, OK
ML Seasons: 7

HITTING:

Mickey Tettleton, the surprise of 1989, backslid into a disappointment in 1990. Many people expected Tettleton to repeat his 26-homer year of '89, but what he did was more in keeping with his history. While "Fruit Loops" cereal was credited with Tettleton's upsurge, "Special K" must have been what he ate during his downfall. Tettleton hit only 15 homers last year and went a stretch of nearly two months without one. He set an Orioles record for strikeouts with 160 and another dubious record for strikeouts by a switch-hitter. After June 23-24, Tettleton never went two consecutive starts without a whiff.

The Orioles' cleanup hitter at the beginning of last year, Tettleton took far too many hittable pitches and was frequently behind in the count. He drew 106 walks, obviously helping his team in the process, but became, at the same time, too much of a defensive hitter. Tettleton's batting average and RBIs diminished and he seemed, all too often, to be waiting for the perfect pitch. The Orioles know that Tettleton will never be a high-average hitter. But as one of their key hitters, they'd like more power production from him.

As with many switch-hitters, Tettleton likes the ball low as a lefty swinger, high as a righty. He has a long swing, one which produces power. It also produces strikeouts, since once it's started, it's hard to stop. The Orioles will live with the strikeouts; what they'd like is more of the power.

BASERUNNING:

Tettleton is decent on the base paths and better than average when he gets a headstart from first to third. He has average speed for a catcher and seldom is daring. He won't steal more than a couple of times a year, but he won't hurt a team when he's on base, either. For his size, he's not a bad overall baserunner.

FIELDING:

Pitchers don't mind throwing to Tettleton because he is soft-spoken and easy to work with. Last year he was bothered at times by a knee operation which sometimes made catching excruciating for him. He throws fairly well. Bob Melvin is considered the superior defensive catcher, but Tettleton has improved.

OVERALL:

A free agent at year's end, there was some question as to whether the Orioles would offer Tettleton what he wanted to stay. He likes Baltimore and would prefer to remain an Oriole. If he does, he will have to be more aggressive at the plate and swing at more strikes. His home run range is probably 15-20, but simple contact would be enough to satisfy the O's in most situations.

Overall Statistics

	G	AB	R	H	D	T	HR	RBI	SB	BB	SO	AVG
1990	135	444	68	99	21	2	15	51	2	106	160	.223
Career	621	1847	249	436	79	6	74	234	15	315	543	.236

Where He Hits the Ball

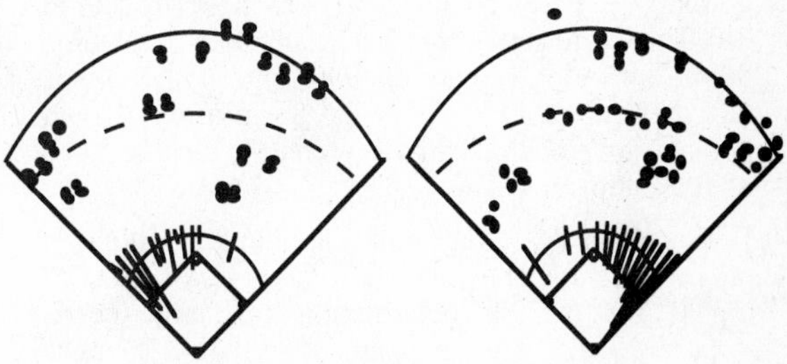

Vs. LHP Vs. RHP

1990 Situational Stats

	AB	H	HR	RBI	AVG		AB	H	HR	RBI	AVG
Home	215	51	8	27	.237	LHP	128	30	5	18	.234
Road	229	48	7	24	.210	RHP	316	69	10	33	.218
Day	135	31	4	12	.230	Sc Pos	110	17	3	34	.155
Night	309	68	11	39	.220	Clutch	78	14	6	13	.179

1990 Rankings (American League)

- 1st in lowest batting average with runners in scoring position (.155), lowest batting average vs. right-handed pitchers (.218), lowest cleanup slugging percentage (.333) and most pitches seen per plate appearance (4.44)
- 2nd in walks (106), strikeouts (160), lowest batting average on the road (.210) and highest percentage of pitches taken (65.4%)
- 3rd lowest batting average (.223)
- Led the Orioles in walks, strikeouts, on-base average vs. right-handed pitchers (.385) and highest percentage of pitches taken
- Led AL catchers in runs scored (68), walks, times on base (210), strikeouts, pitches seen (2,482) and plate appearances (559)

MARK WILLIAMSON

Position: RP
Bats: R **Throws:** R
Ht: 6' 0" **Wt:** 171

Opening Day Age: 31
Born: 7/21/59 in Corpus Christi, TX
ML Seasons: 4

PITCHING:

Mark Williamson has a firmly established role as the Orioles' premier set-up man . . . between injuries, that is. Last year Williamson was slowed by a strained hip coming out of spring training. Later, he sustained a fractured hand that ended his season prematurely. In between, Williamson was just as effective as ever. He had a 1.65 earned run average and 8-2 record at the end of July. Those numbers regressed slightly, but he still had another outstanding year. Over the last two seasons Williamson is 18-7 with a 2.62 ERA and ten saves, setting the table superbly for closer Gregg Olson.

In 1990 Williamson allowed opponents to hit only .215 against him; that was a sharp improvement over 1989, when the opposition hit .261. His strikeout-to-walk ratio (60-28) improved as well. Most importantly, his ERA shrank from 2.93 in '89 to 2.21 in '90. The one negative was that he allowed more home runs (four in 1989, eight in 1990), but that total was still better than his '87 and '88 figures. Given Williamson's overall improvement, the Orioles have no reason to complain.

Williamson's basic stuff (fastball, palmball, slider) is only a little above average. His fastball will seldom top 90 miles per hour, but his ability to change speeds -- particularly with the palmball -- makes it more effective. Looking for even more variety, he has started using a curve. More than anything, his ability to keep hitters off balance is the key to his success.

Williamson has the skill, experience and arm to fit into any slot on the staff, but is so vital in the set-up mode that the Orioles no longer consider moving him. He's the bridge between the young starters and Gregg Olson. He has the determination to fight through injuries and the temperament to handle any role.

FIELDING AND HOLDING RUNNERS:

Williamson can be counted on to field his position well and is always aware of the game situation. He is not afraid to throw as often as necessary to hold runners, rarely goes to the wrong base and takes defense seriously. One thing he could improve is mixing up his timing to home plate, because baserunners can occasionally gauge his delivery.

OVERALL:

Whenever Williamson is hurt, the Orioles have trouble filling his spot. He has shown the effects of the grind in the late stages of the last two seasons. But that's more a testimony to his willingness to pitch every day if necessary than to his brittleness. Replacements don't come easily for this type of pitcher who, though often unrecognized, is as valuable as anyone.

Overall Statistics

	W	L	ERA	G	GS	Sv	IP	H	R	BB	SO	HR
1990	8	2	2.21	49	0	1	85.1	65	25	28	60	8
Career	31	24	3.64	212	12	15	435.1	417	189	139	257	38

How Often He Throws Strikes

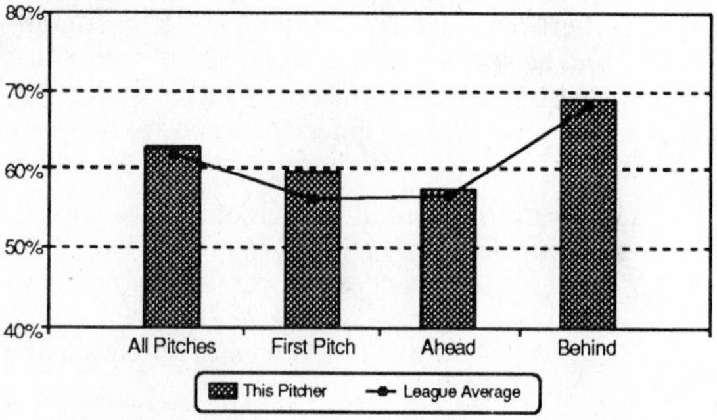

1990 Situational Stats

	W	L	ERA	Sv	IP		AB	H	HR	RBI	AVG
Home	5	0	1.35	0	46.2	LHB	139	31	6	19	.223
Road	3	2	3.26	1	38.2	RHB	163	34	2	18	.209
Day	3	2	2.86	1	22.0	Sc Pos	82	15	3	30	.183
Night	5	0	1.99	0	63.1	Clutch	146	31	4	21	.212

1990 Rankings (American League)

- 8th in first batter efficiency (.175)
- Led the Orioles in holds (8) and first batter efficiency

CRAIG WORTHINGTON

Position: 3B
Bats: R **Throws:** R
Ht: 6' 0" **Wt:** 190

Opening Day Age: 25
Born: 4/17/65 in Los Angeles, CA
ML Seasons: 3

Overall Statistics

	G	AB	R	H	D	T	HR	RBI	SB	BB	SO	AVG
1990	133	425	46	96	17	0	8	44	1	63	96	.226
Career	304	1003	108	234	42	0	25	118	3	133	234	.233

Where He Hits the Ball

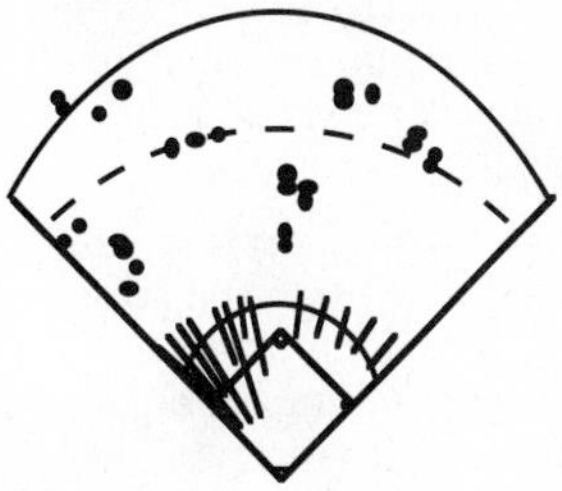

Vs. LHP

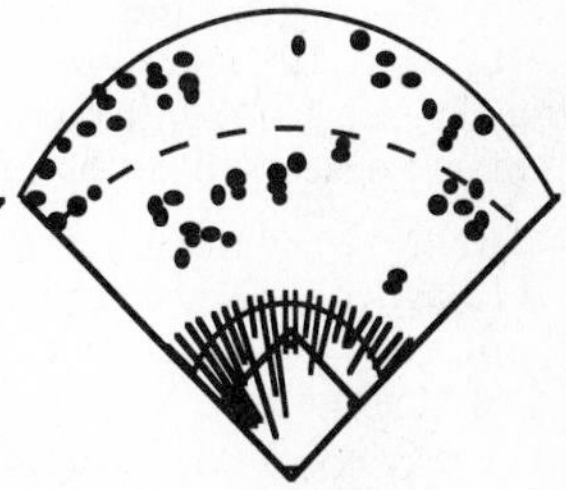

Vs. RHP

1990 Situational Stats

	AB	H	HR	RBI	AVG		AB	H	HR	RBI	AVG
Home	209	49	3	20	.234	LHP	126	32	2	12	.254
Road	216	47	5	24	.218	RHP	299	64	6	32	.214
Day	121	31	5	17	.256	Sc Pos	112	22	0	35	.196
Night	304	65	3	27	.214	Clutch	82	21	4	8	.256

1990 Rankings (American League)

- 4th worst batting average with runners in scoring position (.196) and 4th worst batting average on the road (.218)
- Led the Orioles in GDPs (13)

HITTING:

One of the more promising rookies of 1989, Craig Worthington lost ground last year. Like many second-year players, Worthington's problem was that he didn't adjust to the changes pitchers made in their approach to him. As a rookie, he proved he could handle fastballs, especially ones on the inside part of the plate. But breaking balls were another story, and Worthington got a steady diet of them last year. He's a good enough hitter to adjust, but last year he simply couldn't get untracked.

It didn't help that Worthington got a late start in an already-late spring training and couldn't seem to recover. He did reasonably well for awhile, but then he went into a long slump. Worthington had an up-and-down second half, but he didn't hit a homer after July 28. It's true that he had some injury problems, but they were no excuse for a horrific offensive season.

Perhaps it was the sophomore jinx, perhaps it was simply a matter of Worthington taking too much for granted. He batted only .196 with men in scoring position, a situation in which he thrived the previous year. Worthington hit poorly at home, away, on grass and on turf -- a real equal-opportunity out. Worthington has a compact swing and good bat speed, but had trouble figuring out what pitchers were trying to do. After awhile, the Orioles began to question his dedication.

BASERUNNING:

Simply slow, Worthington is not a force on the base paths. Manager Frank Robinson, who likes the running game, will send him on the run-and-hit play, but he'll almost never attempt a straight steal. Caution is the word to use with Worthington on the base paths.

FIELDING:

Along with his bat, Worthington's fielding suffered a trifle last season. He seemed concerned about his lack of success at the plate and occasionally took it with him on defense. Nevertheless, he still is a solid glove man who has decent range and a usually accurate arm. His sidearm throws are sometimes errant, but overall, fielding is not a problem for Worthington.

OVERALL:

Since he doesn't get leg hits, the Orioles want Worthington to apply himself to becoming a tougher out. In 1989, he easily matched what had been forecast for him -- that he'd have a moderate average, but be a strong RBI man. Now, after a lackluster sophomore campaign, he needs to motivate himself. Leo Gomez, a minor-league power hitter, finished the year at third. His presence in camp may spur a Worthington resurgence.

DAVE GALLAGHER

Position: CF/LF
Bats: R **Throws:** R
Ht: 6' 0" **Wt:** 180

Opening Day Age: 30
Born: 9/20/60 in Trenton, NJ
ML Seasons: 4

Overall Statistics

	G	AB	R	H	D	T	HR	RBI	SB	BB	SO	AVG
1990	67	126	12	32	4	1	0	7	1	7	12	.254
Career	344	1110	147	301	42	7	6	85	13	84	136	.271

HITTING, FIELDING, BASERUNNING:

Claimed on waivers from the White Sox in August, Dave Gallagher wound up in a fill-in role in the Oriole outfield. Gallagher barely played down the stretch and appears too similar to younger men to make much of an impact on this team.

Strictly a singles hitter who has to spray the ball, Gallagher has leadoff potential if he can hit as he did in 1988, when he batted .303. He's not a patient hitter and doesn't draw many walks, so hitting for a good average is essential to his success. He is an intelligent player who can handle the bat and bunt, and he always hustles. He is aggressive running the bases, but is not an overwhelming threat to steal.

In the outfield, Gallagher is very sure-handed. He won three minor league fielding titles and has committed only six errors in four major league season. He sometimes has fundamental lapses and lacks blazing speed, so he is no longer suited to center field. But he catches what he gets to and has a decent arm.

OVERALL:

Neither powerful nor very fast, Gallagher needs to hit around .300 to merit a regular position. But his hitting has slipped the last two years, regulating him to a life of pinch running and late-inning defensive work. He is probably best suited as a fourth or fifth outfielder at this stage of his career and probably won't get much playing time except against the occasional lefthander.

LEO GOMEZ

Position: 3B
Bats: R **Throws:** R
Ht: 6' 0" **Wt:** 180

Opening Day Age: 24
Born: 3/2/67 in Canovanas, Puerto Rico
ML Seasons: 1

Overall Statistics

	G	AB	R	H	D	T	HR	RBI	SB	BB	SO	AVG
1990	12	39	3	9	0	0	0	1	0	8	7	.231
Career	12	39	3	9	0	0	0	1	0	8	7	.231

HITTING, FIELDING, BASERUNNING:

The long shadow of Brooks Robinson has been a curse to all his successors at third base for the Orioles. Even Doug DeCinces' steady play didn't satisfy Orioles followers. The latest to be tried and found wanting has been the highly-touted Craig Worthington. Now the Birds may be ready to switch third basemen again, this time to Leo Gomez.

Only 24, Gomez has hit well at every level of the Baltimore system since being signed as an undrafted free agent in 1985. His averages have declined as he's moved up the minor league ladder, but he still batted .277 at AAA Rochester last year. What has impressed the Orioles, however, is that Gomez' home run production has been increasing. He belted 26 homers at Rochester in 1990 and displayed good power to all fields. Very dedicated, he has lost weight while increasing his strength through an exercise program. Unlike most young sluggers, he's a very disciplined hitter who drew 89 walks last year.

Gomez' defense was once a question mark, but he has worked hard to improve that part of his game. He has a strong arm and now looks more than adequate at the position. He's not a fast runner, however, and won't steal many bases.

OVERALL:

Gomez will go into spring training with an excellent chance to replace Worthington at third. Capable of hitting 20 or more homers at the big league level, he's been compared to Ron Cey. Gomez just hopes that Oriole fans can avoid comparing him to Brooks Robinson.

RENE GONZALES

Position: 2B
Bats: R **Throws:** R
Ht: 6' 2" **Wt:** 191

Opening Day Age: 29
Born: 9/3/61 in Austin, TX
ML Seasons: 6

Overall Statistics

	G	AB	R	H	D	T	HR	RBI	SB	BB	SO	AVG
1990	67	103	13	22	3	1	1	12	1	12	14	.214
Career	307	622	62	135	16	2	5	47	9	44	99	.217

HITTING, FIELDING, BASERUNNING:

Rene Gonzales wears uniform number 88 because the man he rarely replaces at shortstop, Cal Ripken, Jr., has his favorite number, 8. Ripken has Gonzales' favorite position as well, so he has to be content with being Mr. Utility. Gonzales handles that job well.

As a hitter, about all you can say about Gonzales is that you know what to expect from him. He's batted .215, .217 and .214 the last three seasons, while getting increasingly less playing time. Gonzales could probably improve at the plate if he stopped trying to pull the ball so often. The result is a few home runs -- very few -- but many more instances of poor contact.

Since he possesses fine speed, Gonzales is often used as a pinch runner. He's not much of a base stealing threat, but he runs the bases intelligently. Gonzales' main strength, however, is with the leather. In the field, he is quick and agile, a player who came up as a shortstop but can also handle second and third with skill. He has a strong, accurate arm and can turn the double play.

OVERALL:

Gonzales has value in his versatility and has accepted his back-up assignment despite his yearning to start somewhere. There is no drop-off on defense when he is inserted, but he doesn't hit enough to justify further duty. Barring some sudden, unexpected improvement with the bat, he'll probably never be more than a utility man.

TIM HULETT

Position: 3B/2B
Bats: R **Throws:** R
Ht: 6' 0" **Wt:** 185

Opening Day Age: 31
Born: 1/12/60 in Springfield, IL
ML Seasons: 7

Overall Statistics

	G	AB	R	H	D	T	HR	RBI	SB	BB	SO	AVG
1990	53	153	16	39	7	1	3	16	1	15	41	.255
Career	459	1417	154	345	57	10	35	143	13	87	275	.243

HITTING, FIELDING, BASERUNNING:

Tim Hulett missed nearly half of 1990 after suffering a broken bone in spring training. After coming back, he played predictably, showing occasional pop in his bat and hitting .297 with men in scoring position. Hulett's strong suits are his perseverance at the plate, and his ability to hit even when his playing time is limited. He has fine power for an infielder, and belted 17 homers for the White Sox in 1986. He likes to look for a fastball and pull it with power. Hulett was once a wild swinger, but he has developed a little patience over the years.

When he reaches base Hulett is no base stealing threat, but he doesn't embarrass the team with silly mistakes when he gets aboard. In the field, he can play second or third with average ability, limited range and adequate results. Another of the White Sox connection to general manager Roland Hemond, Hulett's track record is sound, but not extraordinary.

OVERALL:

It does not appear Hulett will ever be a starter with the Orioles. He's a decent hitter, but not outstanding enough to force his way into the lineup, especially since the regular Oriole infielders are all better with the glove. But for the Orioles, Hulett is an excellent bench player because he can hit even when used infrequently. Those skills are especially attractive to a team that was next-to-last in the league in batting average.

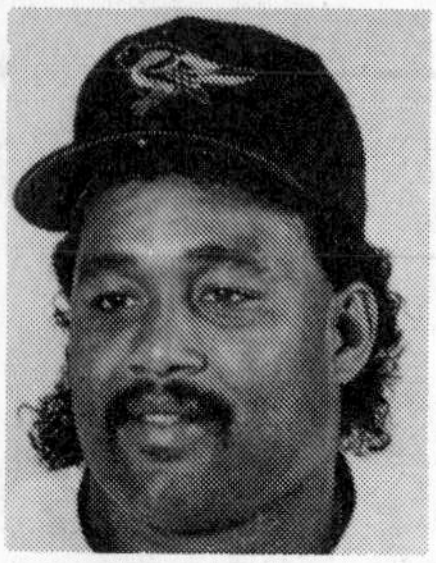

JOSE MESA

Position: SP
Bats: R **Throws:** R
Ht: 6' 3" **Wt:** 210

Opening Day Age: 24
Born: 5/22/66 in Azua, Dominican Republic
ML Seasons: 2

Overall Statistics

	W	L	ERA	G	GS	Sv	IP	H	R	BB	SO	HR
1990	3	2	3.86	7	7	0	46.2	37	20	27	24	2
Career	4	5	4.73	13	12	0	78.0	75	43	42	41	9

PITCHING, FIELDING & HOLDING RUNNERS:

Jose Mesa has completely recovered from two serious elbow operations that threatened to end his career. Acquired in the Mike Flanagan trade in 1987, Mesa recorded his first major league victory that September, but then was out of the majors for almost three years. After years of struggle, Mesa finally made it back for seven starts last season, recording his second major league victory and two more for good measure. Mesa's performance, and especially his live arm, impressed the Oriole staff. He has four good pitches: two different fastballs, a breaking curve and a change-up. He is also experimenting with a slider. So far, the elbow has withstood the tests and Mesa seems qualified to pitch in almost any role. He showed he could handle the big game, pitching well in two starts against a Toronto team fighting for a division title. That was no fluke, as Mesa's win in '87 -- an impressive, eight and two-thirds inning start -- came in the last week against a Detroit club battling for a crown. He was adequate holding baserunners last year, but hasn't been tested enough to determine the quality of his fielding.

OVERALL:

Don't count Mesa out as the Orioles' surprise of 1991. He's always had ability, and he showed it at the end of a season he started at Class AA Hagerstown just hoping his elbow was all right. If things break right, Mesa could be in the Orioles' starting rotation.

CURT SCHILLING

Position: RP
Bats: R **Throws:** R
Ht: 6' 4" **Wt:** 215

Opening Day Age: 24
Born: 11/14/66 in Anchorage, AK
ML Seasons: 3

Overall Statistics

	W	L	ERA	G	GS	Sv	IP	H	R	BB	SO	HR
1990	1	2	2.54	35	0	3	46.0	38	13	19	32	1
Career	1	6	4.54	44	5	3	69.1	70	38	32	42	6

PITCHING, FIELDING & HOLDING RUNNERS:

Curt Schilling longs to be a starter on a team loaded with candidates. He may get his chance this spring. Schilling has the equipment -- a fastball in the 90's, a slider and a split-finger pitch. He is on the brink of becoming an effective power pitcher if he can steadily mature. But Schilling may be needed too much in the bullpen to be given that starting shot. The Orioles are tinkering with the idea of making Schilling Gregg Olson's sidekick in the closing role, which would take some of the pressure off Olson's tender elbow. The O's are withholding a decision until they see more of Schilling, who has been effective at the minor-league level.

Schilling was used in Mark Williamson's spot -- as a set-up man -- after being brought up in the middle of last year. He started well and had a strong stretch in which he didn't allow a run. Schilling cooled off a little after that, but he finished with one the lowest earned run averages on the team and allowed only one homer. He is a decent fielder with good athletic ability and is working to copy Dave Johnson's move to hold runners. But he hasn't perfected it yet.

OVERALL:

Schilling has a bundle of talent and needs only to harness it and be patient. If he gets too anxious to be a starter, he may not flourish as he did in Williamson's role. Schilling appears to have the makeup for closing duty, so he may wind up there on a part-time basis.

DAVID SEGUI

Position: 1B
Bats: B **Throws:** L
Ht: 6' 1" **Wt:** 170

Opening Day Age: 24
Born: 7/19/66 in Kansas City, KS
ML Seasons: 1

Overall Statistics

	G	AB	R	H	D	T	HR	RBI	SB	BB	SO	AVG
1990	40	123	14	30	7	0	2	15	0	11	15	.244
Career	40	123	14	30	7	0	2	15	0	11	15	.244

HITTING, FIELDING, BASERUNNING:

Though David Segui has had less than three full seasons of professional experience, the Orioles are very high on his future prospects. Segui had two stints with Baltimore last year. At first he looked over-matched, but he began stinging the ball in his second trip to the majors. A line-drive hitter from both sides of the plate, Segui only belted two homers in his 40 game trial last year. Still, the Orioles like his power potential, and feel he may eventually be a 15-homer man in the majors.

The son of former major league pitcher Diego Segui, David has a lot of poise for a young player. He's been a solid hitter at every minor-league plateau, and that's partly because of his makeup: he is intense, intelligent and highly coachable. In his brief trial last year, Segui looked like he'd be a good clutch hitter. He's not particularly fast, but he uses his knowledge to his advantage on the bases and is rarely caught in a baserunning mistake. It is doubtful he will ever steal more than a few bases. Defensively, he is already major league caliber with quick reactions and an ability to go either way for the diving stop.

OVERALL:

One of the youngsters on whom the Orioles are banking heavily, Segui's problem right now is that he plays the same position as Randy Milligan. But if Segui continues to progress as a hitter, he will stay around, particularly since he bats from both sides of the plate.

ANTHONY TELFORD

Position: SP
Bats: R **Throws:** R
Ht: 6' 0" **Wt:** 175

Opening Day Age: 25
Born: 3/6/66 in San Jose, CA
ML Seasons: 1

Overall Statistics

	W	L	ERA	G	GS	Sv	IP	H	R	BB	SO	HR
1990	3	3	4.95	8	8	0	36.1	43	22	19	20	4
Career	3	3	4.95	8	8	0	36.1	43	22	19	20	4

PITCHING, FIELDING & HOLDING RUNNERS:

Anthony Telford began last year in Class A, but by August he was starting for the Orioles. Telford came back from shoulder surgery that shelved him for 15 months. Otherwise, he might have already been firmly established with the O's. The injury cost him speed on his fastball, but it had a side benefit: Telford learned how to pitch.

Telford still throws in the high 80's and has a curve and change-up which he is not afraid to throw on any count. Occasionally, he will use his slider as something to show the hitter. Despite the injury, Telford has a high confidence level that borders on cockiness. He is strong-willed, knows what he wants to do and how to do it. But he is no longer the young phenom drafted in 1987; he has to have more than one pitch working to be successful.

Telford is a good athlete who can field, but had some mental lapses last year in coverage. He is average at holding runners and his assortment of breaking stuff, which gets to the plate slowly, doesn't help him keep runners close.

OVERALL:

Telford was once considered one of the organization's brightest pitching prospects. He is still rated highly, but is looked at differently because he is more of a Mike Boddicker-type of pitcher than the imposing sort he once was. But Telford believes in himself and he has a way of making others believe in him as well.

PITCHING:

When the Red Sox acquired 37-year-old Larry Andersen from Houston on August 31 for one of their top prospects, third baseman Jeff Bagwell, they thought they were buying the pennant for the league's most incendiary bullpen. At the time, they didn't know if Jeff Reardon could come back off the disabled list and their closers were Jeff Gray and Darryl Irvine. Andersen hadn't been a closer -- he has only 34 career saves -- but his ERAs of 2.94, 1.54 and 1.79 and his 244 strikeouts in 266 innings over the last three seasons indicated that he is still very tough.

In his first appearance with Boston, Andersen struck out six Athletics in three innings. But, as time wore on, while he pitched well for Boston -- a 1.23 ERA in 22 innings, with 25 strikeouts and a save -- he got worn out. He allowed 50% of inherited runners to score and first batters with runners in scoring position were 4-for-7 against him.

On the right staff, Andersen is one of the premier set-up men in the game. He is predominantly a slider pitcher, actually a two slider pitcher, one that breaks big, and one that is tighter. His sliders are so unhittable that he will throw them nine out of every ten pitches, and batters still don't hit him.

However, at Andersen's age, there is a limit to his endurance, and the book on him is that once he gets warmed up, a manager either has to pitch him or sit him down. Joe Morgan goes by his own book, and when Andersen arrived and showed that great slider, Morgan warmed him up at least once in 19 consecutive games. By the end of the season, he was exhausted, his arm "like hamburger."

HOLDING RUNNERS AND FIELDING:

Because of his high leg kick, Andersen can be run on, although he will hold the ball and vary his moves to first to confuse runners. He is a good fielder, with quick reactions on balls hit back through the box.

OVERALL:

Though he is 37, Andersen has pitched better than ever the last two seasons, while averaging 63 appearances a year. After the '90 season he was granted a "new look" free agency. If anyone comes up with a salary comparable to what he was making in Boston, Andersen will be elsewhere. He'd like to pitch another year.

LARRY ANDERSEN

Position: RP
Bats: R **Throws:** R
Ht: 6' 3" **Wt:** 205

Opening Day Age: 37
Born: 5/6/53 in Portland, OR
ML Seasons: 13

Overall Statistics

	W	L	ERA	G	GS	Sv	IP	H	R	BB	SO	HR
1990	5	2	1.79	65	0	7	95.2	79	22	27	93	2
Career	32	30	3.15	534	1	34	819.2	780	333	254	589	50

How Often He Throws Strikes

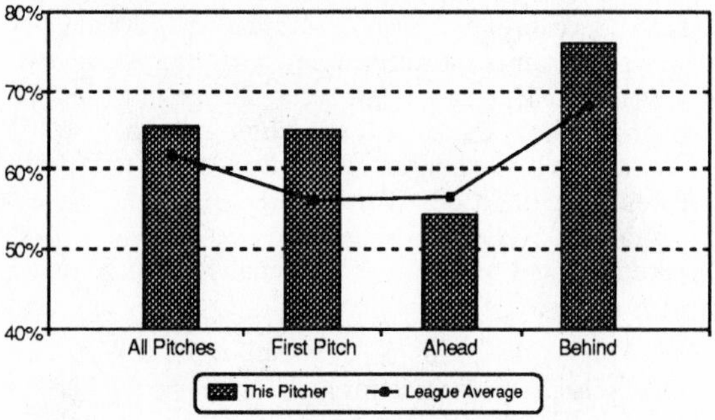

1990 Situational Stats

	W	L	ERA	Sv	IP		AB	H	HR	RBI	AVG
Home	4	0	0.68	3	53.1	LHB	168	47	2	23	.280
Road	1	2	3.19	4	42.1	RHB	180	32	0	15	.178
Day	3	1	4.09	2	22.0	Sc Pos	108	25	0	34	.231
Night	2	1	1.10	5	73.2	Clutch	189	47	1	25	.249

1990 Rankings (American League)

- 5th (in the National League) in first batter efficiency (.167)

MARTY BARRETT

Position: 2B
Bats: R **Throws:** R
Ht: 5'10" **Wt:** 175

Opening Day Age: 32
Born: 6/23/58 in Arcadia, CA
ML Seasons: 9

Overall Statistics

	G	AB	R	H	D	T	HR	RBI	SB	BB	SO	AVG
1990	62	159	15	36	4	0	0	13	4	15	13	.226
Career	929	3362	417	935	162	9	17	311	57	304	206	.278

Where He Hits the Ball

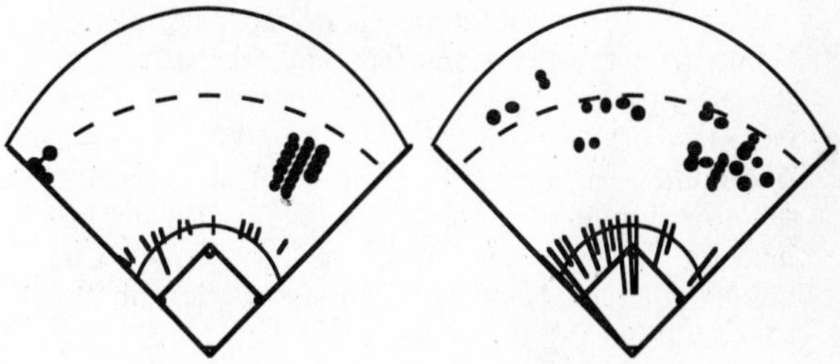

Vs. LHP **Vs. RHP**

1990 Situational Stats

	AB	H	HR	RBI	AVG		AB	H	HR	RBI	AVG
Home	68	17	0	5	.250	LHP	37	9	0	3	.243
Road	91	19	0	8	.209	RHP	122	27	0	10	.221
Day	55	12	0	4	.218	Sc Pos	41	12	0	13	.293
Night	104	24	0	9	.231	Clutch	26	9	0	3	.346

1990 Rankings (American League)

→ 9th in sacrifice bunts (11)

HITTING:

Marty Barrett's saga in Boston in 1990 became a sad story, though not from a financial point of view: Barrett was in the first of a two year, $2.7 million guaranteed contract. In May, he lost his starting position. He tried to get the club to release him by speaking out, then when the season ended, ripped the manager and the club, saying "no one on the team has any respect for Joe (Morgan)."

Barrett is a highly intelligent, limited-skills player whose skills may or may not have evaporated. But he's got to play to be useful, as he cannot jump out of bed and move, and he can only play one position. Barrett's average has gone from .293 to .283 to .256 to .226 the last four years. He still can do things with the bat when he plays -- bunt, hit-and-run, play situations. Barrett was often used as a specialist in bunting situations last year, and laid down 11 sacrifices despite playing only 62 games.

Even in limited duty, Barrett continued to be an excellent contact hitter last year, striking out only 13 times in 159 at-bats. But even that was a high ratio for him. In 1989, Barrett struck out only 12 times in more than twice as many at-bats, 336. Clearly his timing was off, not surprising given the limited usage. Pitchers tend to work him high and inside, but not too many hurlers can overpower him.

BASERUNNING:

Barrett never could run, but he could always steal a few bases. He doesn't run much any more, but he'll go if a pitcher ignores him, and was a perfect four-for-four last year. Like most of the Red Sox, he is a fairly conservative runner, but he will take as many bases as hit feet will allow.

FIELDING:

This is Barrett's main problem now. Always lacking range, he had to play close to second base and his arm was below average for the position. But now, between a knee operation, age, and lack of playing time, his range is even more reduced. If he could play 125 games it might come back, because he's a rhythm infielder, and rhythm infielders have to play to be effective.

OVERALL:

It could well be that at the age of 32, Barrett's career is almost over. If the Red Sox cannot give him away, they will release him in spring training. But Barrett is smart enough to know that if he sits for another year, he will be done. When he gets released, he will pop up somewhere on a club that needs an experienced, winning hand.

MIKE BODDICKER

Position: SP
Bats: R **Throws:** R
Ht: 5'11" **Wt:** 186

Opening Day Age: 33
Born: 8/23/57 in Cedar Rapids, IA
ML Seasons: 11

<u>PITCHING:</u>

One of the best trades Boston GM Lou Gorman ever made came on July 29, 1988, when he traded Curt Schilling and Brady Anderson for Mike Boddicker. In two-and-a-half years, the Red Sox have had a 39-22 pitcher who has pitched big game after big game. Last year Boddicker was 17-8 -- the second-best record on the club after Roger Clemens -- and was the winner in the crucial last-night game against Chicago which gave the Red Sox the AL East title.

Last year was Boddicker's best since he won 20 for the '84 Orioles. But in seven full seasons (after spending many extra years in the minors because of Baltimore's great pitching), he's averaged 226 innings and 14 wins. This past season he won 10 in a row from April 30 to July 2, then was 6-0 in his final nine starts of the season. He learned Fenway, throwing strikes and letting opponents hit fly balls to center (where the new configuration of the park has accounted for fewer homers than any AL park except Royals Stadium and Comiskey Park the last two years). Boddicker had a 2.97 ERA and allowed only five homers at home. He was third in the league in seven-inning quality starts (minimum seven innings, three or fewer earned runs), and the weak Boston bullpen allowed 12 of the 23 runners he left on base to score.

People think of Boddicker as a breaking-ball pitcher, with a great curve and his "fosh," an offspeed, dead fish screwball change. But he still works off a very decent fastball, and throws everything -- including pitches he invents in his windup -- from every position at every conceivable speed. His curveballs break every plane, sometimes landing like ducks on a lake. His fosh change isn't as good, but lights a lot of speeds on the radar gun. Boddicker has shown a tendency to run out of gas after three times through the order, usually in the seventh or eighth.

<u>HOLDING RUNNERS AND FIELDING:</u>

One of the best fielders in the game, Boddicker was an all-Big Ten third baseman at Iowa. Because he is such a good athlete, he is tough to run on, with a quick move and a slide-step to the plate.

<u>OVERALL:</u>

Boddicker went into the free agent market as one of the best. He isn't Roger Clemens. He is, however, as good a number-two starter as you'd want. He eats up innings, loves big games and brings that wonderful old Baltimore pitching knowledge to a team's younger pitchers.

Overall Statistics

	W	L	ERA	G	GS	Sv	IP	H	R	BB	SO	HR
1990	17	8	3.36	34	34	0	228.0	225	92	69	143	16
Career	118	95	3.66	273	262	0	1802.1	1725	818	610	1180	164

How Often He Throws Strikes

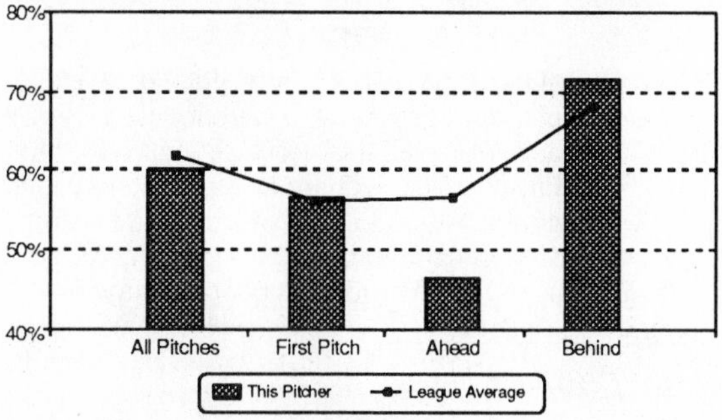

1990 Situational Stats

	W	L	ERA	Sv	IP		AB	H	HR	RBI	AVG
Home	11	5	2.97	0	136.1	LHB	464	121	7	44	.261
Road	6	3	3.93	0	91.2	RHB	409	104	9	33	.254
Day	6	1	2.47	0	51.0	Sc Pos	198	51	4	60	.258
Night	11	7	3.61	0	177.0	Clutch	81	15	0	3	.185

1990 Rankings (American League)

- 2nd in hit batsmen (10)
- 4th in run support per 9 innings (5.41)
- 5th in games started (34) and hits allowed (225)
- 7th in innings (228.0), wins (17), batters faced (956) and winning percentage (.680)
- Led the Red Sox in games started, hits allowed, batters faced, home runs allowed (16), hit batsmen, wild pitches (10), pitches thrown (3,552), GDPs induced (21) and run support per 9 innings

WADE BOGGS

Position: 3B
Bats: L **Throws:** R
Ht: 6' 2" **Wt:** 197

Opening Day Age: 32
Born: 6/15/58 in Omaha, NE
ML Seasons: 9

HITTING:

Before the second game of the American League Championship series, Wade Boggs said, "I've got to make dramatic changes over the offseason. I've completely wasted two full years of my life." For the first time since he played part-time as a rookie in 1982, Boggs didn't have 200 hits. For the first time in five seasons, he didn't walk 100 times. In the years 1988-89-90, his average fell from .366 to .333 to .302, his hits from 214 to 205 to 187, his walks from 125 to 107 to 97, his on-base average from .476 to .430 to .386.

While still a tough out, after ankle, foot and back injuries Boggs was fed a steady stream of fastballs on his fists. In the past, he'd inside-out those balls off The Wall. Last year Boggs took a lot of fastballs down and over the middle, and his power came from breaking balls down in the strike zone, another change. For one reason or another, he swung through more balls than ever, and his 68 whiffs doubled his '88 total.

Part of it may have been Boggs' quest for 200 hits. Before the All-Star break, he walked once every 6.6 plate appearances; after the break, he walked once every 11 appearances, as he began chasing bad pitches. "Mechanically, I was completely screwed up. Johnny Bench asked me why my hands were where they were; I didn't even know. I didn't know where my hands, knees, head. . . anything. . .were. If it takes millions of dollars or videotape equipment, I'll get back to where I was."

BASERUNNING:

Boggs still gets down to first base in about 4.1 seconds, because he's in full stride at the completion of his swing. But, like so many Red Sox players, he is tentative on the bases and runs to not get thrown out. Boggs did not attempt a stolen base in 1990.

FIELDING:

Even though he made 20 errors, anyone who watches Boggs play third base day-in and day-out would argue that he deserves a Gold Glove. He has worked hard at his position, and it has paid off. Boggs goes to the line exceptionally well, makes the bunt/topper play, and has a strong, accurate arm that he uses to start the 5-4-3 double play without peer.

OVERALL:

There has always been a lot of debate about Boggs' real worth because he hasn't been a production hitter and because he's always hit 75-100 points higher at Fenway. When he was hitting .366, the arguments were hot and heavy. When he hit .302 with 63 RBI, they became less interesting. Boggs says "the electronic era is coming to Wade Boggs." He'll be 33 in June. He hopes it works.

Overall Statistics

	G	AB	R	H	D	T	HR	RBI	SB	BB	SO	AVG
1990	155	619	89	187	44	5	6	63	0	87	68	.302
Career	1338	5153	912	1784	358	41	70	586	14	841	407	.346

Where He Hits the Ball

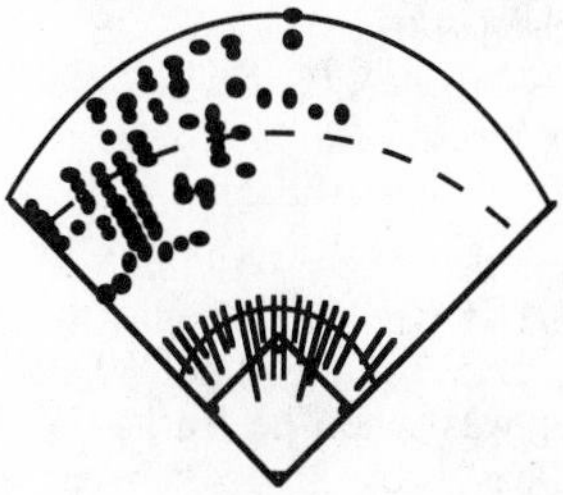

Vs. LHP

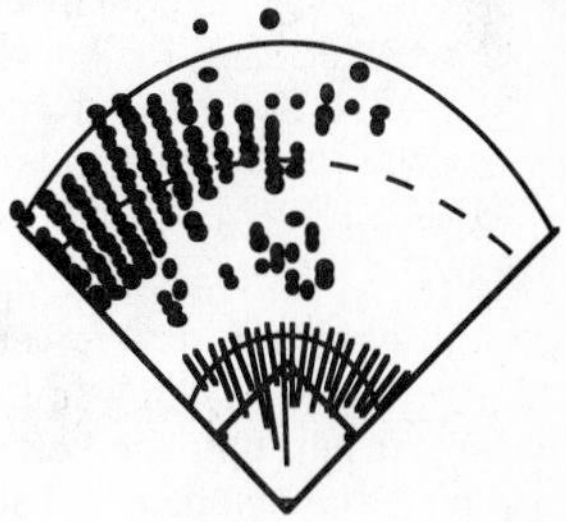

Vs. RHP

1990 Situational Stats

	AB	H	HR	RBI	AVG		AB	H	HR	RBI	AVG
Home	309	111	3	32	.359	LHP	230	63	1	30	.274
Road	310	76	3	31	.245	RHP	389	124	5	33	.319
Day	204	67	3	22	.328	Sc Pos	139	47	1	55	.338
Night	415	120	3	41	.289	Clutch	103	30	0	7	.291

1990 Rankings (American League)

- 1st in intentional walks (19), times on base (275), pitches seen (3,067) and batting average at home (.359)
- 2nd in hits (187), leadoff on-base average (.402), pitches seen per plate appearance (4.30) and lowest percentage of swings that missed (7.3%)
- Led the Red Sox in batting average (.302), at-bats (619), runs (89), hits, singles (132), walks (87), intentional walks, times on base, pitches seen, plate appearances (713), on-base average (.386), pitches seen per plate appearance, batting average with runners in scoring position (.338), batting average at home and batting average with 2 strikes (.256)

PITCHING:

Before the 1990 season, Tom Bolton, Greg Harris and Dana Kiecker had won a total of 10 games as starters. They won 28 starts between them last year. All three had labored long and hard to reach this point, but especially Bolton, who pitched for ten seasons in the minors. Bolton may have been the victim of circumstances, as everything went wrong for him in his minor league career. He suffered a shattered jaw, had a bad shoulder, underwent a serious kidney reconstruction. . . not only that, but every time the Red Sox brought him up, it was as a reliever, and it is apparent that Bolton is a starter, not a guy who gets that one left-handed batter out.

Sure, Tom Bolton was a shock. This is a guy who in his ten minor league seasons had won 53 and lost 42, never winning more than nine games through 1988. Yawn. But in '89, finally healthy, he was 12-5, 2.89 at Pawtucket. The problem was, no one really cared. But when the Sox had no one else, he did the job. He allowed three earned runs or less in 14 of his 16 starts. He had a 1.99 ERA as a starter in Fenway.

Like so many major league left-handed starters, Bolton is not a hard thrower. But when he's right, he never throws a ball near the center of the plate. What helped him turn the corner was when he learned a change-up that he could at least show hitters, as well as enough confidence to begin throwing inside. His fastball is in the 84 MPH area with sinking motion. He has a good curveball that he runs in on righthanders, but he sometimes has trouble throwing it for strikes against lefties.

HOLDING RUNNERS AND FIELDING:

Bolton can be slow to the plate and easier to run on than some of the righthanders on this staff. He is an average fielder. committing only one error last year.

OVERALL:

The 1991 season is a big one for Bolton, because we will find out if his '90 run was a fluke. Make-up is important, and Tom Bolton is a tough guy who's been through many a tough time. If he can win in double figures again, the Red Sox will probably be more than happy.

TOM BOLTON

Position: SP/RP
Bats: L **Throws:** L
Ht: 6' 3" **Wt:** 175

Opening Day Age: 28
Born: 5/6/62 in Nashville, TN
ML Seasons: 4

Overall Statistics

	W	L	ERA	G	GS	Sv	IP	H	R	BB	SO	HR
1990	10	5	3.38	21	16	0	119.2	111	46	47	65	6
Career	12	12	4.21	82	20	1	229.0	250	114	98	144	13

How Often He Throws Strikes

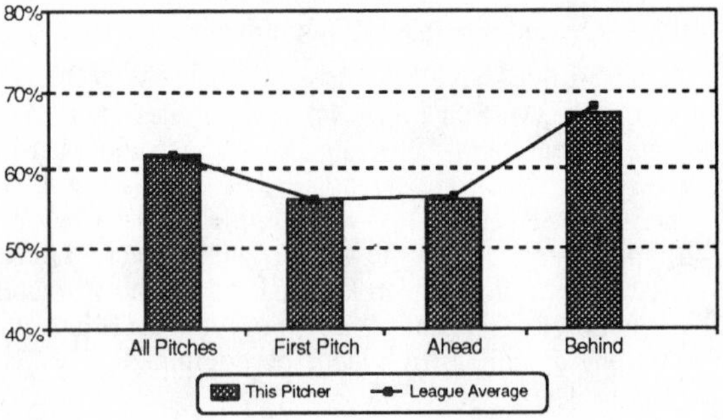

1990 Situational Stats

	W	L	ERA	Sv	IP		AB	H	HR	RBI	AVG
Home	6	1	1.99	0	54.1	LHB	99	24	1	9	.242
Road	4	4	4.55	0	65.1	RHB	344	87	5	36	.253
Day	3	2	2.84	0	31.2	Sc Pos	101	32	2	40	.317
Night	7	3	3.58	0	88.0	Clutch	51	16	2	7	.314

1990 Rankings (American League)

- 11th in winning percentage (.667)
- Led the Red Sox in GDPs induced per GDP situation (.154)

TOM BRUNANSKY

Position: RF
Bats: R **Throws:** R
Ht: 6' 4" **Wt:** 216

Opening Day Age: 30
Born: 8/20/60 in Covina, CA
ML Seasons: 10

Overall Statistics

	G	AB	R	H	D	T	HR	RBI	SB	BB	SO	AVG
1990	148	518	66	132	27	5	16	73	5	66	115	.255
Career	1376	4943	659	1227	232	25	224	712	63	606	903	.248

Where He Hits the Ball

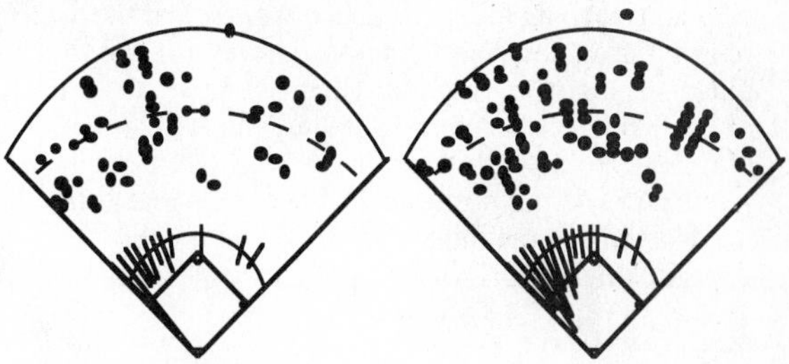

Vs. LHP   Vs. RHP

1990 Situational Stats

	AB	H	HR	RBI	AVG		AB	H	HR	RBI	AVG
Home	252	84	13	52	.333	LHP	179	51	6	29	.285
Road	266	48	3	21	.180	RHP	339	81	10	44	.239
Day	150	42	9	33	.280	Sc Pos	150	32	7	59	.213
Night	368	90	7	40	.245	Clutch	86	20	0	4	.233

1990 Rankings (American League)

- 1st lowest batting average on the road (.190)
- 3rd highest batting average at home (.340) and lowest groundball/flyball ratio (.73)
- 8th in sacrifice flies (8)
- Led the Red Sox in sacrifice flies, strikeouts (105), least GDPs per GDP situation (9.6%) and slugging percentage vs. left-handed pitchers (.527)
- Led AL right fielders in sacrifice flies, batting average on an 0-2 count (.214), batting average at home and highest percentage of pitches taken (58.1%)

HITTING:

When the Red Sox acquired Tom Brunansky for Lee Smith last May 4, he was hailed as a savior, the slugging cleanup hitter they needed. In Brunansky's second game in Fenway, he had two homers and seven RBI, and by June 16 was hitting .328. Members of the media daily asked Bruno how he liked Boston, because he was a free agent that the club claimed it wanted to keep for years. By November, Brunansky was saying he was "insulted" by the club's offer, and GM Lou Gorman privately was saying he wouldn't mind getting a draft choice if someone were to sign the 30-year-old right fielder.

On June 16, Brunansky hurt his shoulder diving for a fly ball; he eventually had to alter his hitting style, suffered through an 0-for-34 streak and until the last weekend of the season had only 10 home runs. Then he hit five in a crucial three game series against Toronto. Sure, Brunansky's skills have diminished slightly, but he was too classy to say his shoulder was to blame for his slump. Sure, his hitting zone is essentially a small area down and over the plate, and the Blue Jays found that zone pitch after pitch after pitch in that final weekend. Sure, he is .206 lifetime with the bases loaded, which tells you how easily he can be pitched. But he is a money man who knows how to play. He's a dead guess hitter and Whitey Herzog says he has "the best instincts and baseball intelligence of anyone I've ever managed."

BASERUNNING:

Brunansky's instincts carry over to baserunning, where he has only average speed but is an excellent baserunner who can take extra bases, read outfielders and even steal if pitchers allow him.

FIELDING:

Brunansky is a good, solid outfielder who plays hitters, pitchers and counts. Notice that in left and center in Fenway there are small brown circles where Mike Greenwell and Ellis Burks play almost everyone because they're never moved. Brunansky learned elsewhere, so there's no brown circle in right. The catch he made to clinch the division was a classic example of a tough, understated play by an outfielder with anticipation and guile.

OVERALL:

Brunansky is a complimentary player, a sixth hitter, fine outfielder and winner. He brings to teams an unselfish, professional attitude that makes him a more valuable player than his stats -- and slightly declining skills - - indicate.

FUTURE MVP?

ELLIS BURKS

Position: CF
Bats: R **Throws:** R
Ht: 6' 2" **Wt:** 188

Opening Day Age: 26
Born: 9/11/64 in Vicksburg, MS
ML Seasons: 4

HITTING:

He is the enigma. On the one hand, Ellis Burks is clearly Boston's best player, a loping, graceful center fielder who led them in homers, RBI, slugging and key RBI. On the other, there is always the feeling that Ellis Burks should be even better, that his shy, laconic personality is holding back a tremendous talent.

"No matter what I do, in Boston they'll always say, 'he should have done more,'" says Burks. He is right, too. In 1990, after being slowed down by a bad ankle and two different shoulder injuries his first two seasons, Burks emerged as a powerful and productive hitter who ended up in the fourth spot in the order. His big adjustment came when he learned to go the other way with the ball down and away.

Burks' great bat speed makes him a dangerous inside-half, fastball pull hitter, but he can also put the ball in play and try to let his speed do the work. Near the end of last season, he too often pressed, swung at bad first pitches and got himself out. He drove in an abysmal 11 of 33 runners from third with less than two out, but did lead the club with a .341 average with two out and runners in scoring position. The feeling is that Burks needs a big veteran thumper behind him to take some pressure off.

BASERUNNING:

Burks' stolen bases have gone from 27 to 25 to 21 to 9. Unfortunately, he doesn't have a great first step, and has lost all confidence. The problem is that he's become afraid to be thrown out, and a base stealer cannot steal while thinking that way.

FIELDING:

Part of Burks' enigma has come from an odd reticence in center field. When he first came up, he looked as if he would quickly become the league's premier defensive center fielder. He used to play shallow and challenge hitters, but injuries, particularly to his shoulder, have made him less reckless on balls in front of him in center; thus, he tends to play deeper. Burks' shoulder left him a below-average thrower for more than a year, but near the end of last season he started to improve.

OVERALL:

No Red Sox everyday player has more trade value, respect or talent than Ellis Burks. He is a very good player. Can he be a great player who hits 35 homers, knocks in 120 runs and steals 35 bases? Probably, but perhaps not in Boston, where this quiet Texan is befuddled by the maniacal nature of the city's folk.

Overall Statistics

	G	AB	R	H	D	T	HR	RBI	SB	BB	SO	AVG
1990	152	588	89	174	33	8	21	89	9	48	82	.296
Career	526	2085	349	606	119	21	71	301	82	187	321	.291

Where He Hits the Ball

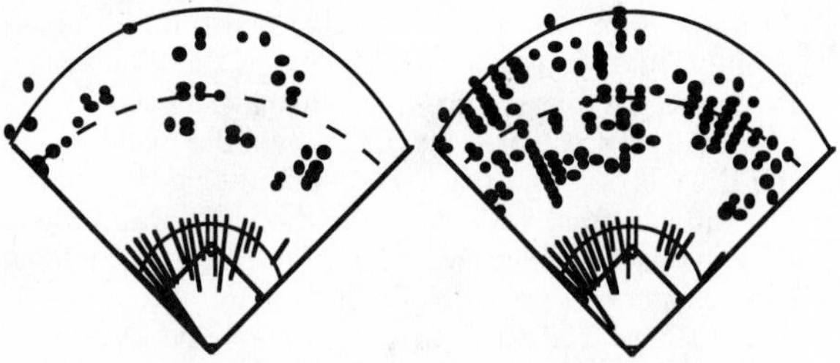

1990 Situational Stats

	AB	H	HR	RBI	AVG		AB	H	HR	RBI	AVG
Home	297	91	10	48	.306	LHP	188	56	5	24	.298
Road	291	83	11	41	.285	RHP	400	118	16	65	.295
Day	184	54	5	29	.293	Sc Pos	170	52	7	72	.306
Night	404	120	16	60	.297	Clutch	93	26	1	9	.280

1990 Rankings (American League)

- 2nd lowest stolen base percentage (45.0%)
- 5th in total bases (286)
- 6th in triples (8) and slugging percentage vs. right-handed pitchers (.502)
- Led the Red Sox in home runs (21), runs (89), triples, totals bases, RBIs (89), stolen bases (9), caught stealing (11), slugging percentage (.486), HR frequency (28 ABs per HR), runs scored per time reached base (39.9%) and slugging percentage vs. right-handed pitchers
- Led AL center fielders in RBIs, GDPs (18), slugging percentage, batting average with 2 strikes (.249) and fielding percentage (.994)

PITCHING:

At the time Roger Clemens felt his shoulder going in his last August start in Cleveland, he was 20-6 with a 1.95 ERA. He was the leader in the Cy Young Award race. But on September 4, he went out to face Dave Stewart and Oakland hurting more than he let his manager, Joe Morgan, or pitching coach, Bill Fischer, know. Clemens started only twice more, plus two starts -- one a six inning shutout, one that he'd like to forget -- against his nemesis Stewart, against whom he's 0-8 since Stew signed with the Athletics.

If you were to look at videotapes of Clemens in 1984 and 1990 you'd see the difference between a free-wheeling kid with full range of movement and a beast of a competitor who muscles the ball to the plate. But, when healthy, the man is simply brilliant. Clemens isn't the hardest thrower in the league, but he is a 90-92 MPH fireballer with incredible control. He is always around the plate, in, out, up, down. He likes the strikeouts he gets with his cross-seam fastball up in the strike zone, but his sinking, running fastball is just as effective. He has a nasty forkball that he threw more often with Tony Pena, as well as a slider and curveball. What's also amazing about a pitcher around the plate as consistently as Clemens is that he didn't allow a home run in his last 12 games.

A few statistical reminders on just what kind of season Clemens had in 1990: the Sox were 22-9 in his starts, he led all major league pitchers in six-inning quality starts, his teammates gave him their lowest run support, (he won four games in which his teammates scored one or two runs), his ERA in the 10 games he started and didn't win was 2.86, and his Fenway ERA was 1.53.

HOLDING RUNNERS AND FIELDING:

Clemens is an average fielder, and despite his big delivery, he has become adept at keeping runners at bay between a slide-step, countless throws to first base and a variation in his move to the plate. Understand that this man works at every part of his game, every day.

OVERALL:

Clemens is a franchise pitcher with the constant worrisome reminder that he has suffered some sort of injury in five different seasons. He also takes care of himself as fanatically as anyone alive, so it could also be that the best is yet to come.

ROGER CLEMENS

Position: SP
Bats: R **Throws:** R
Ht: 6' 4" **Wt:** 220

Opening Day Age: 28
Born: 8/4/62 in Dayton, OH
ML Seasons: 7

Overall Statistics

	W	L	ERA	G	GS	Sv	IP	H	R	BB	SO	HR
1990	21	6	1.93	31	31	0	228.1	193	59	54	209	7
Career	116	51	2.89	206	205	0	1513.0	1281	535	425	1424	102

How Often He Throws Strikes

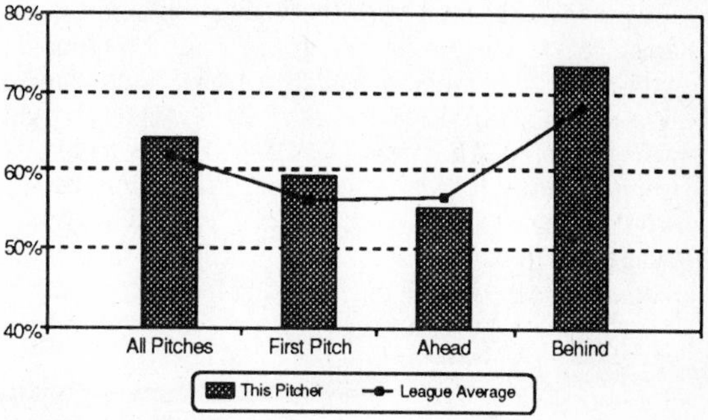

1990 Situational Stats

	W	L	ERA	Sv	IP		AB	H	HR	RBI	AVG
Home	11	2	1.53	0	111.2	LHB	443	107	7	28	.242
Road	10	4	2.31	0	116.2	RHB	404	86	0	18	.213
Day	9	1	1.09	0	91.0	Sc Pos	186	32	1	36	.172
Night	12	5	2.49	0	137.1	Clutch	120	19	1	3	.158

1990 Rankings (American League)

- 1st in ERA (1.93), shutouts (4), strikeout/walk ratio (3.87), lowest slugging percentage allowed (.306), least HRs per 9 innings (.28) and ERA at home (1.53)
- 2nd in pickoff throws (269), winning percentage (.778), lowest on-base average allowed (.278), least baserunners per 9 innings (10.0) and ERA on the road (2.31)
- Led the Red Sox in ERA, wins (21), complete games (7), shutouts, innings (228.1), strikeouts (209), pickoff throws, runners caught stealing (14), winnings percentage, striekout/walk ratio, lowest batting average allowed, strikeouts per 9 innings and lowest batting average allowed with runners in scoring position (.172)

DWIGHT EVANS

Position: DH
Bats: R **Throws:** R
Ht: 6' 3" **Wt:** 208

Opening Day Age: 39
Born: 11/3/51 in Santa Monica, CA
ML Seasons: 19

HITTING:

There were flashes of the old Dwight Evans during the 1990 season: eighth and tenth inning homers off Dave Johnson and Gregg Olson to beat Baltimore on June 23, a fourteenth inning homer off Mike Schooler to beat the Mariners in Seattle, an Aug. 24 homer that beat David Wells 1-0. But, for the most part, it was a long, hard season fighting back injuries. The struggle ended bitterly when the Red Sox released him after the World Series because Manager Joe Morgan didn't want him back despite more than 18 stellar seasons.

Because his back restricted his ability to go out and drive the pitch away from him, Evans changed to his old style -- look for mistakes on the inner half of the plate and try to jerk them. Near the end of the season he tried to fight through the back pain and drive tough pitches through the middle.

Evans was disabled with the back problems in August. When he had his old friend Carl Yastrzemski work with him, General Manager Lou Gorman called Yaz and told him not to come to Fenway when Dwight was activated. That prompted Yaz to call a local talk show and say it would be "a long, long time before you see me around the Red Sox." Evans' winter plan was to try to have a minor back procedure, then come back. He may be able to.

BASERUNNING:

Evans cannot move the way he once did, but he is still an average runner. He never was a base stealer, but while he used to get confused when he was younger -- he was picked off third twice in the same game -- he matured into a fine baserunner who could read plays in front of him very well.

FIELDING:

With all due respect to Dave Winfield, Dwight Evans was the finest defensive right fielder of his time, winning eight Gold Gloves in what may be -- because of the area, angles, sun, etc. -- the toughest right field in the business. As a DH, Evans did not go to the field last year, but he can probably play there again if his back is okay. The arm isn't there any more, but people still respect it anyway.

OVERALL:

Is Evans done? In his physical condition at the age of 39, all that would be needed to finish him is the back. Evans has 379 homers and one less total base than Jim Rice. If he were to have one or two more productive seasons and went over the 400 homer mark, he would be a borderline Hall of Famer.

Overall Statistics

	G	AB	R	H	D	T	HR	RBI	SB	BB	SO	AVG
1990	123	445	66	111	18	3	13	63	3	67	73	.249
Career	2505	8726	1435	2373	474	72	379	1346	76	1337	1643	.272

Where He Hits the Ball

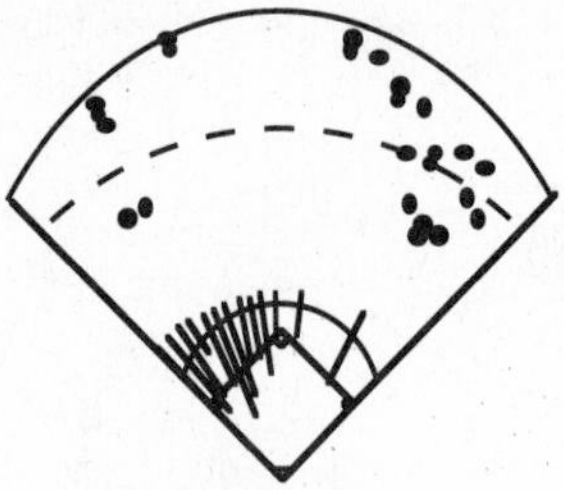

Vs. LHP

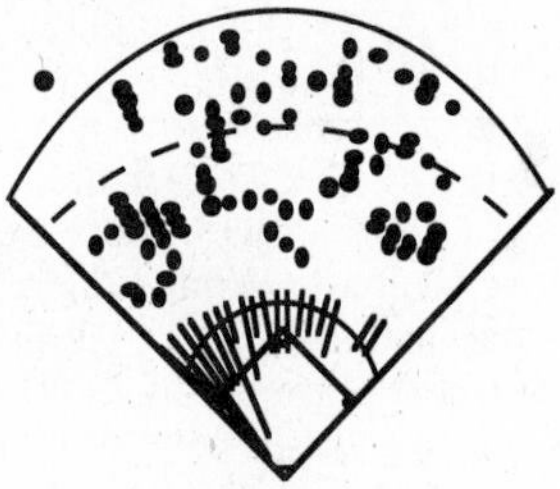

Vs. RHP

1990 Situational Stats

	AB	H	HR	RBI	AVG		AB	H	HR	RBI	AVG
Home	218	55	7	31	.252	LHP	147	39	3	16	.265
Road	227	56	6	32	.247	RHP	298	72	10	47	.242
Day	141	43	10	36	.305	Sc Pos	123	33	5	51	.268
Night	304	68	3	27	.224	Clutch	85	25	8	24	.294

1990 Rankings (American League)

- 9th in highest percentage of pitches taken (61.3%)
- Led the Red Sox in hit by pitch (4)
- Led designated hitters in GDPs (18) and runs scored per time reached base (36.3%)

PITCHING:

At the end of spring training last year, Jeff Gray was told by the Phillies that he hadn't made the club. Not only that, they asked him to go onto their AA Reading roster for a couple of days for bookkeeping purposes. Gray asked for his release, signed on with Pawtucket and on June 5 arrived in Boston to become a significant contributor to the division winners.

Gray had nine saves, but seven came in seven chances from Aug. 19 through Sept. 10 as he filled in for Jeff Reardon. His 4.44 ERA is a little deceiving, for Gray went through a period in July where he was hammered because he was afraid to tell management that he had a pulled rib cage muscle. He was the best on the staff preventing inherited runners from scoring (77.8%), held opposing hitters to a .131 average entering in the middle of innings and held first batters overall to a .231 mark.

Looking at Gray, he hardly resembles the Rob Dibble/Dick Radatz monster reliever, and it's probably the comparison to some of those hard-throwers that got him nowhere in the Reds organization before moving to the Phillies and on to the Red Sox. A former Florida State teammate of Jody Reed, Gray isn't a hard thrower, but he is deceiving. He works everything off his forkball, and because he has a slow, deliberate delivery, the ball seems to explode out of his hand after the hitter has been lulled to sleep. His forkball isn't a sharp breaking darter, but it has a late break, and usually it looks like a fastball until the last second. Gray usually works backwards -- he tries to get ahead of hitters with his forkball, then come back and get them out with his fastball or slider.

HOLDING RUNNERS AND FIELDING:

Though he's one of the slowest workers around, Gray has good defensive reactions and fielded his position well last year, committing no errors. He pays attention to runners, but his slow delivery makes him easy to steal on.

OVERALL:

Some scouts feel that Gray is the type of pitcher who's effective life is one-half a season, while he tricks people with his unusual delivery and sequence. Then, after that, when the batters get used to him, he could have trouble. Maybe so, but the Red Sox saw enough to know he warrants another chance. Sometimes makeup is more important that arm strength, and Gray believes he is a premium big-league closer.

JEFF GRAY

Position: RP
Bats: R **Throws:** R
Ht: 6' 1" **Wt:** 175

Opening Day Age: 28
Born: 4/10/63 in Richmond, VA
ML Seasons: 2

Overall Statistics

	W	L	ERA	G	GS	Sv	IP	H	R	BB	SO	HR
1990	2	4	4.44	41	0	9	50.2	53	27	15	50	3
Career	2	4	4.35	46	0	9	60.0	65	31	19	55	3

How Often He Throws Strikes

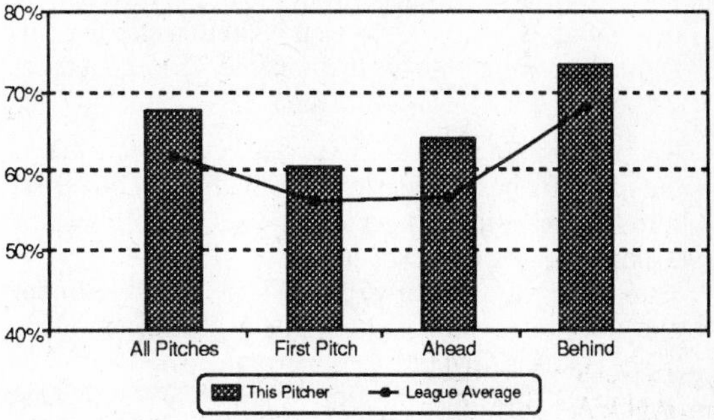

1990 Situational Stats

	W	L	ERA	Sv	IP		AB	H	HR	RBI	AVG
Home	2	2	4.01	6	24.2	LHB	98	27	2	11	.276
Road	0	2	4.85	3	26.0	RHB	100	26	1	13	.260
Day	1	0	1.56	3	17.1	Sc Pos	60	17	0	18	.283
Night	1	4	5.94	6	33.1	Clutch	107	27	2	11	.252

1990 Rankings (American League)

- Did not rank near the top or bottom in any category

HITTING:

For more than a year, every time a Red Sox deal has been rumored, it's involved Mike Greenwell. It's true that Greenwell hasn't fulfilled the great expectations he projected in '88 when he was runner-up for MVP and batted .325 with 119 RBI. His average has gone from .328 to .325 to .308 to .297, his RBI from 119 to 95 to 78. He's hit only 20 homers since June 24, 1989. But there were physical adjustments and maturing adjustments that had to be made. After a tough first half in which he had only two homers at the All-Star break, Greenwell hit .344 over the last 72 games and finished with respectable numbers.

Early last season when his left foot was killing him, Greenwell became a front foot, arms hitter who lost his power and his ability to pull the fastball. While he'd always been a dead fastball hitter who liked to pull the gas on the inner half of the plate, then use the rest of the field, he was being pounded inside. He said he needed surgery on his left ankle and foot, but at the end of the season it was postponed.

Regardless, by September he was close to normal at the plate. He has learned to get the ball away and drive it to the opposite field, which he does so well because his bat's so quick he can stay back exceptionally well. How many hitters can be in the middle of the lineup and over three years have a 208-115 walk-strikeout ratio? The day GM Lou Gorman arrived at the general managers' meetings the first week of November, he said, "there is a lot of interest in Greenwell, and I'm talking."

BASERUNNING:

When Greenwell is healthy, he is an average runner who is unusually aggressive for the plodding Bosox. If he were on a running team, he could triple his average of seven steals a season. The only problem sometimes is that he tends to run the bases like a Boston driver.

FIELDING:

Greenwell also tends to play left field like a Boston driver. He is a very erratic left fielder, albeit sometimes aggressive, and when he gets out of the confines of Fenway, it really shows. His arm is stronger than his judgement.

OVERALL:

There are a lot of holes in Mike Greenwell's game, but the fact remains he is a rarity -- a productive left-handed hitter for the middle of anyone's order with a lifetime average of .313 who has averaged 96 RBI a year for the last three years. That's why so many teams want him.

MIKE GREENWELL

Position: LF
Bats: L **Throws:** R
Ht: 6' 0" **Wt:** 195

Opening Day Age: 27
Born: 7/18/63 in Louisville, KY
ML Seasons: 6

Overall Statistics

	G	AB	R	H	D	T	HR	RBI	SB	BB	SO	AVG
1990	159	610	71	181	30	6	14	73	8	65	43	.297
Career	635	2256	326	707	139	20	73	388	43	251	176	.313

Where He Hits the Ball

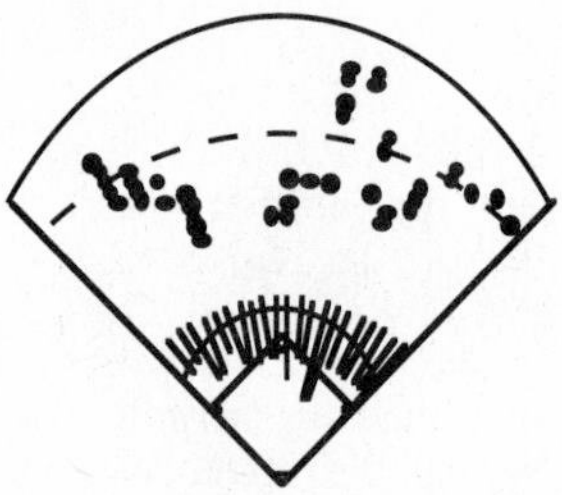

Vs. LHP

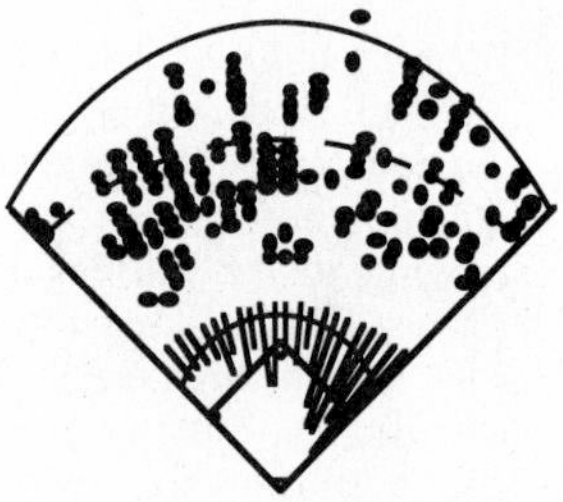

Vs. RHP

1990 Situational Stats

	AB	H	HR	RBI	AVG		AB	H	HR	RBI	AVG
Home	306	95	6	41	.310	LHP	202	52	3	22	.257
Road	304	86	8	32	.283	RHP	408	129	11	51	.316
Day	179	61	3	21	.341	Sc Pos	162	37	1	52	.228
Night	431	120	11	52	.278	Clutch	99	23	3	13	.232

1990 Rankings (American League)

- 4th in hits (181)
- 5th in singles (131)
- 6th in intentional walks (12), games (159), least pitches seen per plate appearance (3.22), batting average vs. right-handed pitchers (..316) and lowest percentage of swings that missed (9.5%)
- 7th in at-bats (610)
- Led the Red Sox in hit by pitch (4), games and batting average on a 3-2 count (.318)
- Led AL left fielders in at-bats, hits, singles, intentional walks, plate appearances (682), games, batting average at home (.310), errors (7) and highest percentage of swings put into play (54.2%)

GREG HARRIS

Position: SP
Bats: B **Throws:** R
Ht: 5'11" **Wt:** 165
Opening Day Age: 35
Born: 11/2/55 in Lynwood, CA
ML Seasons: 10

PITCHING:

Some have wondered how the Red Sox finished first for the third time in five years in 1990. The answer, pure and simple, was starting pitching, and Greg Harris was a key to the pitching success. Boston starters had the best ERA in baseball, 3.32; Montreal was next at 3.47, Toronto was next in the AL East at 3.93 and no other divisional rival was under 4.00. They were a close third to Seattle and Oakland in quality starts in the American League. Think about that. Yes, they were 44-53 in games Roger Clemens and Mike Boddicker didn't start, but three guys named Harris, Dana Kiecker and Tom Bolton kept them in the race.

Harris, who has been released four times, was thrust into the rotation in a moment of desperation. Though he'd worked some in the Texas rotation in 1987, Harris hadn't been primarily a starter since his rookie year of 1981, when he was breaking in with the Mets. Surprising almost everyone, Harris won 12 games as a starter; he'd previously won a total of eight in starting roles in his career, and he's 35 years old. He pitched the final of three straight shutouts over the Blue Jays in Toronto the last week of August. And the bullpen allowed 15 of his 34 runners left on base to score.

Harris is sort of a hybrid between Boddicker and Kiecker. He has a terrific big curveball, spots his fastball, cuts some, and now has a change like Boddicker. Curveball pitchers often are tougher for hitters from the opposite side, and while Harris is ambidextrous and would like to pitch left-handed, lefties batted .239 against him, righties .291. His arm tired after the 150-inning mark, and everything slowed down at the same time. Hitters started laying off his cutter. He was winless after Sept. 10.

HOLDING RUNNERS AND FIELDING:

Always a good athlete, Harris fields his position very well, and being ambidextrous helps give him a quick glove hand. He also has a good move to first.

OVERALL:

There is the feeling that after signing a two-year, $2.8 million contract, Harris will be different; hitters will lay off his cut fastball. But, the facts of life -- a 4.07 ERA as a starter, his quality starts (12 in 30, 40%, the club's worst percentage), his 4.45 ERA in Fenway -- are bad signs. GM Lou Gorman was criticized for what many felt was a panic signing of Harris. "He's as good a second or third starter as there is," said Gorman. We shall see. But Harris is better than a releasee, and may return to long relief.

Overall Statistics

	W	L	ERA	G	GS	Sv	IP	H	R	BB	SO	HR
1990	13	9	4.00	34	30	0	184.1	186	90	77	117	13
Career	48	54	3.61	417	75	38	975.1	886	450	421	743	88

How Often He Throws Strikes

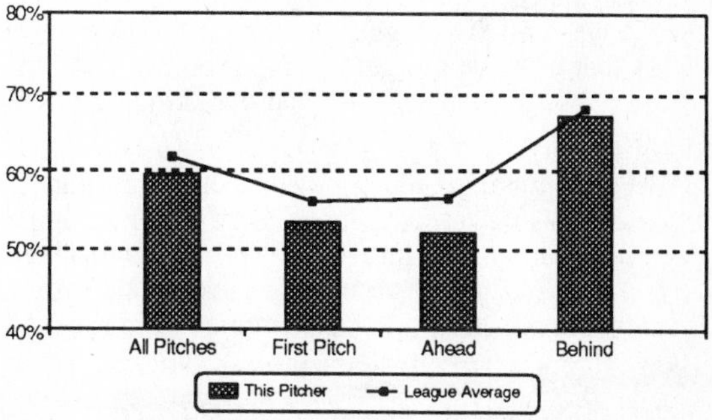

1990 Situational Stats

	W	L	ERA	Sv	IP		AB	H	HR	RBI	AVG
Home	8	5	4.45	0	89.0	LHB	352	84	5	29	.239
Road	5	4	3.59	0	95.1	RHB	351	102	8	42	.291
Day	7	0	2.41	0	52.1	Sc Pos	164	41	1	54	.250
Night	6	9	4.64	0	132.0	Clutch	50	12	0	2	.240

1990 Rankings (American League)

- 5th in highest groundball/flyball ratio (1.74)
- 6th in pickoff throws (201)
- 7th in highest on-base average allowed (.338) and most baserunners allowed per 9 innings (13.1)
- 8th in lowest strikeout/walk ratio (1.52)
- 9th in highest batting average allowed (.265)
- Led the Red Sox in losses (9), walks allowed (77), stolen bases allowed (15), groundball/flyball ratio, least pitches thrown per batter (3.69), GDPs induced per 9 innings (.83) and lowest batting average vs. left-handed batters (.239)

PITCHING:

Dana Kiecker was one of the best stories in baseball last year. Kiecker was put on the Red Sox roster because they had several open spots and he had been a minor league free agent. He had never pitched for a team with a winning record, and he hadn't had a winning record of his own since his rookie-ball season way back in 1983, when he signed out of St. Cloud (Minn.) State. As the 1990 season wore on, he became increasingly valuable, worked his way into the rotation and actually started the second game of the American League Championship series.

The 30-year-old Kiecker is a three-quarter, sinker/sweeping slurve thrower. He's much tougher on right-handed batters (.183) than lefties (.318), and is smart enough to pitch around lefties he knows can hurt him. The stat that got a lot of attention during the season was that his Fenway ERA was 6.50, his road ERA was 2.14. The biggest reason for this difference was that he tended to get too hyper before his home starts, though he eventually had two strong Fenway starts down the stretch.

Kiecker's running, sinking fastball is better than he sometimes realizes. He became a master of dropping down on all kinds of hitters. White Sox' hitters claim right-handed hitters can usually pick up his grip -- fastball or breaking ball --as he brings his right hand over his leg in his delivery, so he may improve on that.

HOLDING RUNNERS AND FIELDING:

Kiecker does not have a good move to first and is easy to run on -- a particular problem for a pitcher who allows a lot of baserunners. Kiecker responds well to balls up the middle, but sometimes can get careless. He committed two errors last year.

OVERALL:

Some feel that Kiecker was a shot-in-the-dark fluke, but he also may be the classic late bloomer. A lot of pitchers move up quickly, but Kiecker needed two years in A ball, two in AA and two in AAA, and he learned his lessons well. He's tough to hit out of the park (only seven homers in 152 IP). His ERA as a starter was 3.68 -- and that might have been better had his relievers not allowed 14 of the 27 runners he left on base to score. Give Mike Boddicker a lot of credit -- he was invaluable helping both Kiecker and Greg Harris.

DANA KIECKER

Position: SP/RP
Bats: R **Throws:** R
Ht: 6' 3" **Wt:** 180

Opening Day Age: 30
Born: 2/25/61 in Sleepy Eye, MN
ML Seasons: 1

Overall Statistics

	W	L	ERA	G	GS	Sv	IP	H	R	BB	SO	HR
1990	8	9	3.97	32	25	0	152.0	145	74	54	93	7
Career	8	9	3.97	32	25	0	152.0	145	74	54	93	7

How Often He Throws Strikes

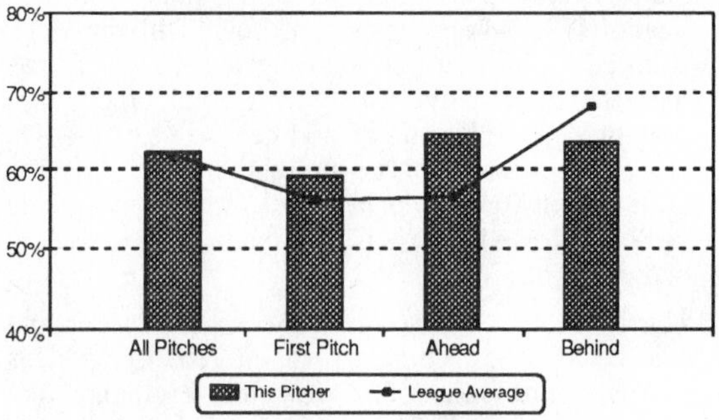

1990 Situational Stats

	W	L	ERA	Sv	IP		AB	H	HR	RBI	AVG
Home	3	5	6.50	0	63.2	LHB	299	95	4	34	.318
Road	5	4	2.14	0	88.1	RHB	273	50	3	26	.183
Day	1	3	4.78	0	49.0	Sc Pos	144	41	2	52	.285
Night	7	6	3.58	0	103.0	Clutch	31	9	0	3	.290

1990 Rankings (American League)

- → 1st in ERA on the road (2.14)
- → 4th in hit batsmen (9)
- → 7th in highest batting average vs. left-handed batters (.318)
- → Led the Red Sox in losses (9), stolen bases allowed (15) and ERA on the road

PITCHING:

In the third-to-last game of the 1990 season, with the Red Sox a game in front of the Toronto Blue Jays, Dennis Lamp warmed up on seven separate occasions before manager Joe Morgan brought him in to start the 11th inning against the White Sox. Inevitably, Lamp gave up the winning run, and afterwards all the animosity that had built up during the season between Morgan and his relievers exploded. "No one can work this way," Lamp said. "It is a joke. This guy has no idea how to manage a bullpen."

It got worse during the playoffs, when Larry Andersen, Jeff Gray and Jeff Reardon joined in the Morgan-bashing; after the third game of the playoffs, when the media arrived in the Boston clubhouse, there were five Boston relievers sitting in front of their lockers with ice packs on their shoulders -- and none of them even got into the game.

The Red Sox bullpen was atrocious in 1990. It blew 51 leads. First batters hit .297 against the Boston bullpen, first batters with runners in scoring position an astonishing .353 and the bullpen ERA of 4.62 was the worst in the American League. Lamp was a big part of those problems, too. After going 4-2, 2.32 in 112.1 innings in 1989, he struggled in '90, finishing with a 4.68 ERA, a .350 average by first batters and a simmering feud with the manager.

Lamp is your basic sinker-slider pitcher with good control. He has long carried the reputation of being the classic middle man who pitches much better two runs down than he does one run ahead.

HOLDING RUNNERS AND FIELDING:

The fact that he doesn't hold runners on well and is a poor fielder, slow off the mound (and sometimes covering first base), makes Lamp vulnerable to running, bunting games. Last year runners stole 12 bases off him in 16 attempts.

OVERALL:

At the age of 38, one inclination is to toss Lamp to the wind, especially when the Red Sox have a host of middle relief types. But Lamp has drifted back and forth with good and bad years over a career that dates back to the Cubs in 1977. So while he wasn't throwing anywhere near as hard as he did in 1989, there is reason to believe that with his two-year contract up at the end of 1990, Lamp could come back close to what he was in '89. He has one of those arms.

DENNIS LAMP

Position: RP
Bats: R **Throws:** R
Ht: 6' 3" **Wt:** 215

Opening Day Age: 38
Born: 9/23/52 in Los Angeles, CA
ML Seasons: 14

Overall Statistics

	W	L	ERA	G	GS	Sv	IP	H	R	BB	SO	HR
1990	3	5	4.68	47	1	0	105.2	114	61	30	49	10
Career	89	92	3.87	567	163	35	1711.0	1842	845	509	785	111

How Often He Throws Strikes

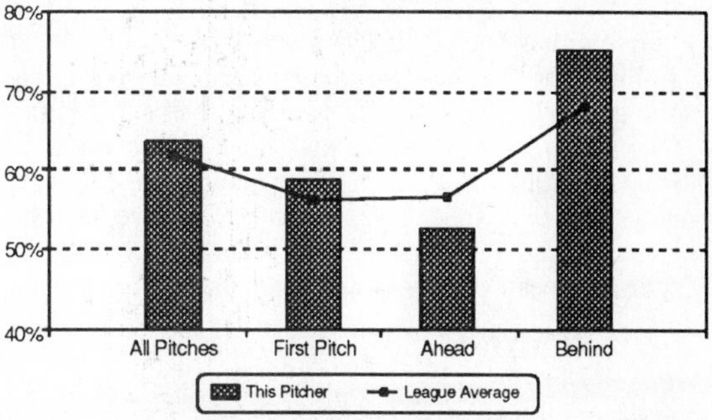

1990 Situational Stats

	W	L	ERA	Sv	IP		AB	H	HR	RBI	AVG
Home	2	2	4.40	0	57.1	LHB	194	58	3	26	.299
Road	1	3	5.03	0	48.1	RHB	214	56	7	47	.262
Day	1	2	5.40	0	36.2	Sc Pos	138	46	2	59	.333
Night	2	3	4.30	0	69.0	Clutch	83	23	4	11	.277

1990 Rankings (American League)

- 1st in highest percentage of inherited runners scored (43.3%)
- 2nd in highest batting average allowed with runners in scoring position (.333)
- 4th in worst first batter efficiency (.350)

MIKE MARSHALL

Position: 1B/DH
Bats: R **Throws:** R
Ht: 6' 5" **Wt:** 220

Opening Day Age: 31
Born: 1/12/60 in Libertyville, IL
ML Seasons: 10

Overall Statistics

	G	AB	R	H	D	T	HR	RBI	SB	BB	SO	AVG
1990	83	275	34	71	14	2	10	39	0	11	66	.258
Career	1011	3524	429	953	169	8	147	523	26	247	790	.270

Where He Hits the Ball

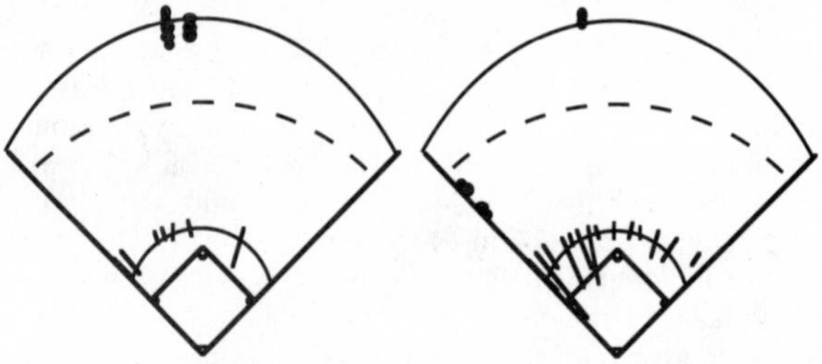

Vs. LHP Vs. RHP

1990 Situational Stats

	AB	H	HR	RBI	AVG		AB	H	HR	RBI	AVG
Home	146	37	7	22	.253	LHP	96	21	4	9	.219
Road	129	34	3	17	.264	RHP	179	50	6	30	.279
Day	92	24	1	12	.261	Sc Pos	78	16	1	25	.205
Night	183	47	9	27	.257	Clutch	43	10	1	10	.233

1990 Rankings (American League)

- Did not rank near the top or bottom in any category

HITTING:

Near the end of last season, Mike Marshall went in to see Manager Joe Morgan to ask about his future with the club. "He told me he doesn't see me in his plans as an everyday player," said Marshall. "At least he's honest." Marshall then sought to go to Japan.

It has been a strange road for the 31-year-old outfielder-first baseman since he played so well in the 1988 World Series. He was restricted much of the 1989 season by a back injury, and hit only 11 homers and knocked in 42 runs. He was then traded to the Mets and lost his job to Dave Magadan. Then on July 28, he was sent to Boston for three minor leaguers -- two of whom, Greg Hansell and Ender Peroza -- are top prospects. On the 1990 season, Marshall had only 10 homers and 39 RBI, which means his 1989-90 totals of 21 homers and 81 RBI are within a HR and an RBI of his '88 totals.

Marshall has been disabled seven times in his career and has chronic back problems, but is he done? He always was a low, out-over-the-plate fastball and mistake breaking ball hitter, and his .286 average in Boston indicated he may still be able to hit. But now it's a matter of finding someone who'll give him the chance. The fact that he's a high strikeout, free-swinger doesn't help him when he plays sporadically.

BASERUNNER:

At 6-5 and 220 pounds, Marshall was not exactly the Maury Wills kind of Dodger. He was zero for two stealing in 1990, and is a career 44 percent base stealer. He has decent instincts on the bases, but has a basic problem -- lack of speed.

FIELDING:

One problem Marshall has is that he really doesn't have a position. He is too slow to play right field, especially in Fenway Park. His back restricts him at first base; in fact, Tommy Lasorda had to move him off first and put him in right field because of his back, which weakened the Dodgers and angered Lasorda at one point.

OVERALL:

There are people in baseball who think Marshall is at the end of the line. One National League GM who was offered Marshall during the season said, "I wouldn't take him for nothing, which is what I was offered him for." But Marshall does have a history of being a pretty good clutch hitter; he has hit 147 home runs and he is only 31. Done? Maybe not. But he needs a chance to prove himself.

PITCHING:

How bad was Rob Murphy's 1990 season? One August night in Kansas City, when Joe Morgan came to relieve him, Murphy fired his glove into the outfield. In September, when Murphy was warming up and Morgan went to the mound to discuss relieving Dennis Lamp, the entire bleacher crowd at Fenway looked like a USC student section, waving their arms and chanting, "No, no, no. . . ."

Murphy has appeared in more games the last four years (305) than any major league reliever, and since he's worked for reliever-abusers Pete Rose and Morgan, many fear his arm is shot. His fastball was down five MPH from 1989. How bad was he? He was 0-6, 6.32. First batters hit .371 against him, and first batters with runners in scoring position hit .391. Righthanders hit him at a .404 rate, and slugged him at .677. In September, he tried different release points, offspeed pitches and most anything he could, but he was a shell of his old reliable self. He allowed 118 baserunners in 57 innings. The league hit .348 against him. The last time he came into a game when it mattered, Mark McGwire greeted him with a grand slam off the Budweiser sign in the Oakland Coliseum.

Murphy is an excitable, hyper sort who may create some of his own problems. He feels that he is the type who should be used often, for one, two or three left-handed batters, but Morgan doesn't believe in that sort of specialization. Murphy is a fastball/slider pitcher who used to throw 88-90 MPH, but after all these years of abuse, his erratic work habits, and what his coaches feel is an increasing attachment to his racehorse business, there are those who feel he may never get it back.

HOLDING RUNNERS AND FIELDING:

Slow to react, Murphy is not quick off the mound on balls hit back through the middle. He controls the running game well, however, with a good move to first and a quick delivery to the plate.

OVERALL:

If Rob Murphy is going to return to the status of a first rate lefthanded reliever, he may have to get out of Fenway, get away from Morgan, and find a manager who will use him to get lefties out and see what happens. Don't count him out.

ROB MURPHY

Position: RP
Bats: L **Throws:** L
Ht: 6' 2" **Wt:** 205

Opening Day Age: 30
Born: 5/26/60 in Miami, FL
ML Seasons: 6

Overall Statistics

	W	L	ERA	G	GS	Sv	IP	H	R	BB	SO	HR
1990	0	6	6.32	68	0	7	57.0	85	46	32	54	10
Career	19	24	3.17	341	0	23	400.2	370	158	166	371	28

How Often He Throws Strikes

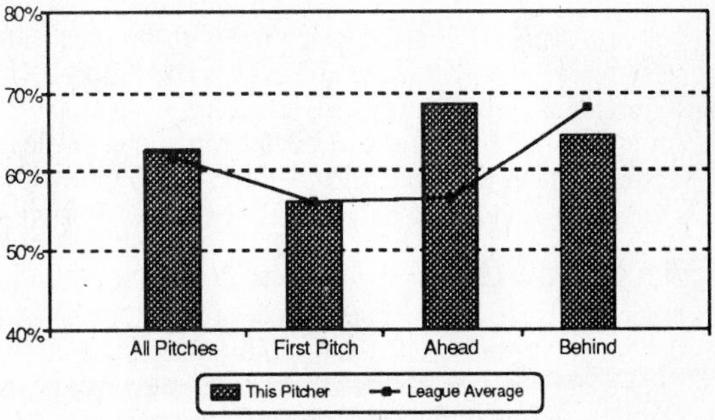

1990 Situational Stats

	W	L	ERA	Sv	IP		AB	H	HR	RBI	AVG
Home	0	2	5.10	2	30.0	LHB	83	20	0	6	.241
Road	0	4	7.67	5	27.0	RHB	161	65	10	43	.404
Day	0	2	4.32	3	16.2	Sc Pos	89	30	2	39	.337
Night	0	4	7.14	4	40.1	Clutch	122	39	5	27	.320

1990 Rankings (American League)

- 3rd worst first batter efficiency (.371)
- 5th in holds (16)
- 6th in games pitched (68)
- Led the Red Sox in games pitched, holds and lowest percentage of inherited runners scored (30.6%)

TIM NAEHRING

Position: SS
Bats: R **Throws:** R
Ht: 6' 2" **Wt:** 190

Opening Day Age: 24
Born: 2/1/67 in Cincinnati, OH
ML Seasons: 1

HITTING:

The Red Sox are very excited about this 23-year-old shortstop out of the University of Miami, Ohio. Tim Naehring is big (6-2, 190), weight- lifting strong and just looks like a ballplayer. The late scout Tony Lucadello likened Naehring to fellow alumnus Mike Schmidt when he was in college. That's a bit of an exaggeration, but Naehring is an intriguing shortstop because he has enough power to have hit 15 homers in less than half a season at Pawtucket and two more in 85 at-bats last year in Boston.

Boston's eighth round pick in the 1988 draft, Naehring has moved up in the Red Sox minor league system very quickly. He skipped AA ball, moving from Class A Lynchberg to AAA Pawtucket in midseason 1989. Despite his inexperience he shows a lot of polish as a hitter. Naehring is patient for a young hitter and won't swing at a lot of offerings.

Naehring missed considerable time with injuries last year, however, and there are questions about his back. After he got to Boston last summer, he had back problems. A California doctor determined that one leg is shorter than the other and that he will be fine with a lift in his shoe, but a bad back is always worrisome.

BASERUNNING:

Naehring has only average speed, at best, but he's a decent baserunner with the size to break up the double play. He's not a base stealer, however, never having swiped more than four in a professional season.

FIELDING:

The question in everyone's mind is whether or not Naehring is a shortstop or a third baseman. Some think he is too big and his range too limited to play short and feel he is a third baseman. Others feel that he will offer only Steve Buechele-kind of power, and, anyway, the Red Sox already have Wade Boggs. The Red Sox would love to use Naehring at short, where his size and power potential would be the best the Sox have had at the position since Rico Petrocelli. He has the arm for the position.

OVERALL:

If Naehring is healthy this year, watch him. He has a good swing, sure hands, a strong arm and outstanding instincts. With the soft grass in Fenway Park, Naehring could play shortstop, and if he hits .260 with 12-15 homers, he will add a big dimension to the Red Sox. He's got a reputation for wearing down, but Luis Rivera is an ideal twice-a-week player.

Overall Statistics

	G	AB	R	H	D	T	HR	RBI	SB	BB	SO	AVG
1990	24	85	10	23	6	0	2	12	0	8	15	.271
Career	24	85	10	23	6	0	2	12	0	8	15	.271

Where He Hits the Ball

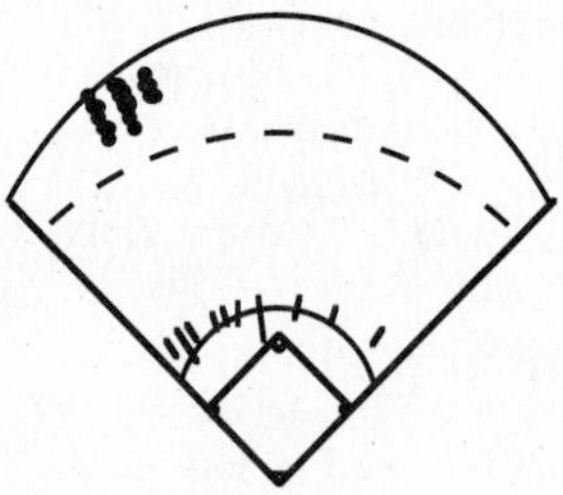

Vs. LHP

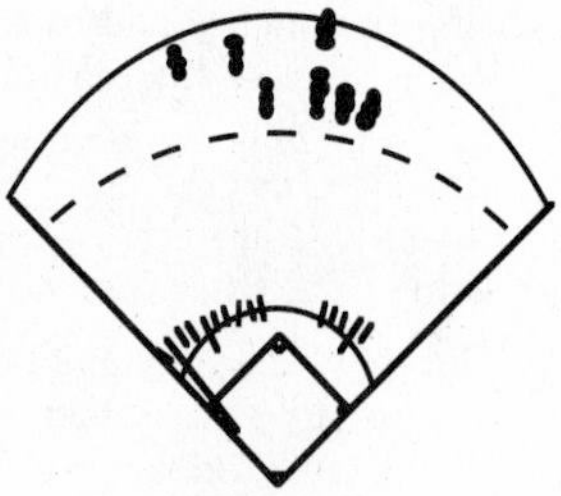

Vs. RHP

1990 Situational Stats

	AB	H	HR	RBI	AVG		AB	H	HR	RBI	AVG
Home	20	6	2	6	.300	LHP	29	12	1	7	.414
Road	65	17	0	6	.262	RHP	56	11	1	5	.196
Day	21	4	0	3	.190	Sc Pos	18	6	0	8	.333
Night	64	19	2	9	.297	Clutch	12	3	0	0	.250

1990 Rankings (American League)

- Did not rank near the top or bottom in any category

TONY PENA

Position: C
Bats: R **Throws:** R
Ht: 6' 0" **Wt:** 184

Opening Day Age: 33
Born: 6/4/57 in Monte Cristi, Dominican Republic
ML Seasons: 11

Overall Statistics

	G	AB	R	H	D	T	HR	RBI	SB	BB	SO	AVG
1990	143	491	62	129	19	1	7	56	8	43	71	.263
Career	1350	4676	500	1275	212	23	89	528	67	321	590	.273

Where He Hits the Ball

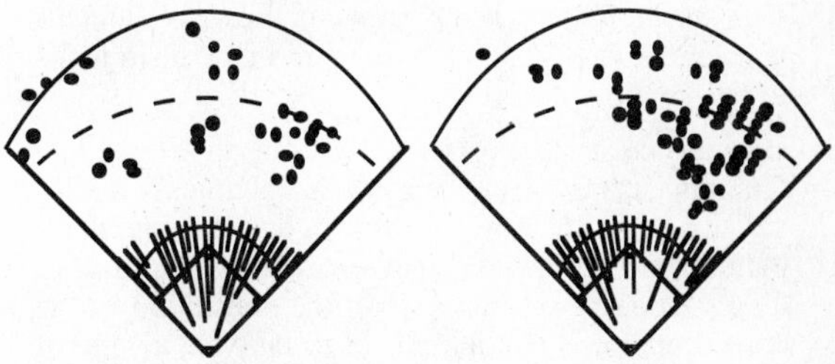

Vs. LHP   Vs. RHP

1990 Situational Stats

	AB	H	HR	RBI	AVG		AB	H	HR	RBI	AVG
Home	247	68	3	30	.275	LHP	155	45	5	22	.290
Road	244	61	4	26	.250	RHP	336	84	2	34	.250
Day	128	30	1	10	.234	Sc Pos	127	38	2	50	.299
Night	363	99	6	46	.273	Clutch	99	29	0	10	.293

1990 Rankings (American League)

- 2nd in groundball/flyball ratio (2.50)
- 3rd in GDPs (23)
- 7th in most GDPs per GDP situation (18.9%)
- Led the Red Sox in GDPs and groundball/flyball ratio
- Led AL catchers in at-bats (491), singles (102), GDPs, games played and groundball/flyball ratio

HITTING:

Many considered Tony Pena Boston's most valuable player last year, for his defensive contributions as well as his off-field enthusiasm. Pena did not have a great year at bat, but there was a reason: he tore up his thumb in a home plate collision in May and was never the same. No one can ever question how hard he plays, and while he is a wild swinger and can be pitched to, he battled his way to hit .301 in the final month and finish at .263.

Pena likes the ball away, but fights off pitches and fists a lot of important hits to the opposite field. There are times when he's hit 0-2 pitches over his head or off his toe. He definitely is **not** a pull hitter, as he hit The Wall only once all season and pulled three homers -- all on offspeed pitches up in the strike zone -- into the net. His power comes against lefties, as he hit five of his seven homers against them.

For a free swinger, Pena was pretty good getting runners in from third with less than two outs, succeeding in 19 of 33 situations. He hit near .300 with runners in scoring position and in clutch situations, a tribute to the way he plays.

BASERUNNING:

No one will ever accuse Pena of being a Ray Schalk or John Wathan as a running receiver, although he did steal 12 bases back in 1985. He stole eight last year, mainly by surprise and seizing situations; his speed has been worn down by all the innings he's been behind the plate.

FIELDING:

It was behind the plate that Pena earned MVP consideration. Between Clemens' forkball and the rest of the staff's breaking balls (Boddicker, Harris, Kiecker, Reardon), he saved countless wild pitches and encouraged nothing but the hardest breakers. A lot of hanging breaking balls are the result of pitchers' fears of catchers not catching them with runners on base, and the Red Sox pitchers were never afraid of bouncing balls in the dirt. He may not throw the way he once did, but he still throws well. He battles and he always hustles. He's also very good at going out to the mound and getting on his pitchers.

OVERALL:

Pena's body is banged up like something out of the Red Badge of Courage. While he's a wild, unpredictable swinger, he gets big hits and has turned the personality of the team around. Some players didn't always appreciate his enthusiasm. Tough.

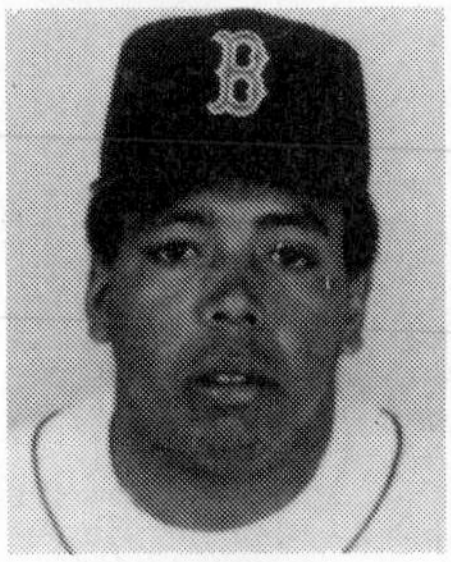

CARLOS QUINTANA

Position: 1B
Bats: R **Throws:** R
Ht: 6' 2" **Wt:** 195

Opening Day Age: 25
Born: 8/26/65 in Miranda, Venezuela
ML Seasons: 3

HITTING:

Conjure up the image of the prototypical second hitter and you think of Nellie Fox, Dick Groat, Ted Sizemore . . . and then there's Carlos Quintana. Quintana is 6-2, close to 215 pounds (not the "official weight" of 195 as reported in the Boston media guide), runs like he's in the Senior League, and yet he became something of a cult hero in his first full season in Boston. Joe Morgan put him into the second spot on July 29, mainly because there wasn't anyone else to hit between Jody Reed and Wade Boggs. In one way, Quintana fit the mold -- he's an opposite-field hitter with little power. The homer he hit in his second day in the second spot was his seventh of the season, and also his last. Quintana hit only three balls off and three balls over The Green Monster the entire season.

Quintana got a lot of big hits by driving tough pitches to the opposite field in the first four months of last season, and he was hitting .318 on August 9. But from then on he was a pretty easy out. Fastballs are his problem, and anything from the middle half in tends to tie him up.

Hitting coach Richie Hebner intends to try to help Quintana learn to drop the bat head out quicker to take advantage of his strength and pull some balls. He batted only .245 with eight extra base hits and 11 GDPs the last two months, so if he doesn't adjust he could become a platoon player to take advantage of his apparent ability to hit lefties (.352).

BASERUNNING:

We'd like to see the catchers in the Western Carolina League in 1986, because Quintana stole 26 bases. He's stolen 16 in the other five years combined, last year stealing once in three attempts. He has decent instincts, but is the classic Boston baserunner -- one base, stop, next base, stop.

FIELDING:

Quintana had been an outfielder throughout his minor league career, but when the Red Sox lost Nick Esasky to free agency, they asked Quintana to make the transition to first base. Considering he'd played the position only a handful of times in the minors and in winter ball, he did pretty well, showing surprising athletic ability and aggressiveness.

OVERALL:

This could be a pivotal season for Quintana, because unless he begins to show more power, he might end up a platoon player. However, if he can learn to pull the fastball and drive it, his good bat control and eye could make him an interesting hitter for years to come. After all, how many 6-2, 215 guys could handle the second spot in the order as a rookie?

Overall Statistics

	G	AB	R	H	D	T	HR	RBI	SB	BB	SO	AVG
1990	149	512	56	147	28	0	7	67	1	52	74	.287
Career	188	595	63	165	33	0	7	75	1	61	89	.277

Where He Hits the Ball

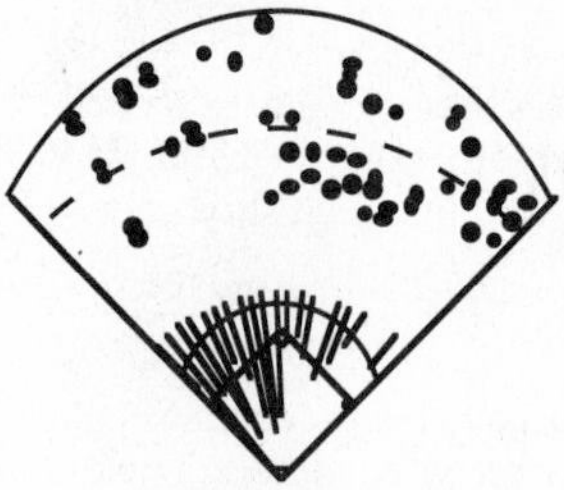

Vs. LHP

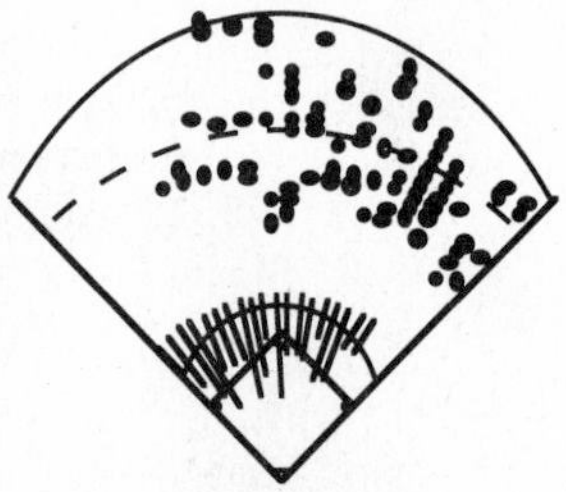

Vs. RHP

1990 Situational Stats

	AB	H	HR	RBI	AVG		AB	H	HR	RBI	AVG
Home	251	75	3	31	.299	LHP	182	64	3	27	.352
Road	261	72	4	36	.276	RHP	330	83	4	40	.252
Day	150	45	3	29	.300	Sc Pos	129	40	1	52	.310
Night	362	102	4	38	.282	Clutch	82	25	1	9	.305

1990 Rankings (American League)

- 5th in least runs scored per time reached base (27.9%), highest batting average vs. left-handed pitchers (.352) and lowest batting average on a 3-1 count (.067)
- 7th in groundball/flyball ratio (2.04)
- 8th in GDPs (19)
- Led the Red Sox in batting average in the clutch (.305), batting average vs. left-handed pitchers and on-base average vs. left- handed pitchers (.407)
- Led AL first basemen in sacrifice bunts (4), grounder/flyball ratio and errors (17)

PITCHING:

The end of Jeff Reardon's 1990 season was right out of a John R. Tunis novel. During the previous winter Reardon had signed a three year, $6.8 million contract with the Red Sox because he wanted to return home and pitch for the team he idolized while growing up in the small Western Massachusetts town of Dalton. When the season began, the Sox still hadn't traded Lee Smith, so Smith was still the closer. Then after Smith was dealt for Tom Brunansky, Reardon was plagued by a succession of injuries until his long-troublesome back gave out in late July. On August 4, Reardon underwent back surgery. His season was pronounced over.

But Reardon insisted on trying to come back, and by mid-September returned to save the bullpen. Had he not returned, Boston never would have won the division, as Reardon won or saved their last five victories and was standing on the mound when they recorded the final out against the White Sox on the final night of the season. Heart is something Reardon has never lacked, one reason he was the top reliever of the eighties and, along with Bruce Sutter, one of two relievers ever to record 20 or more saves in nine straight seasons.

This is not the old, overpowering Jeff Reardon; but then, he wasn't overpowering when he was on the mound when the Twins won the division, pennant and World Series in 1987. He's still a high fastball, curveball, change-up pitcher. His fastball is often in the 85-87 MPH range and is dangerous, but he has excellent location. The curveball is now his best pitch, a hard sideways breaker that eats lefties (they batted .143 against him). The change-up has made his fastball a lot better.

HOLDING RUNNERS AND FIELDING:

Reardon is not a good fielder, with a motion that leaves him out of position on comebackers. He is not good at holding runners, either. Last year, runners were successful eight times in nine attempts with Reardon on the mound.

OVERALL:

After Reardon came back, he wasn't thrilled with the way he was used, warming up as early as the sixth inning and entering in the seventh on an occasion. In Minnesota he was managed by Tom Kelly the way Dennis Eckersley is handled by Tony La Russa. Over a full season, at the age of 35, with 287 saves behind him, the wear and tear may begin to take its toll.

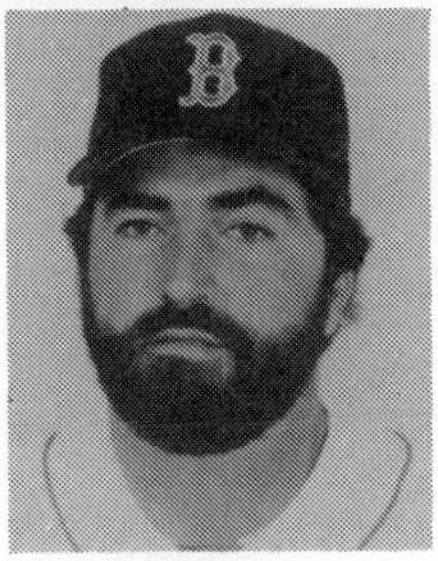

JEFF REARDON

Position: RP
Bats: R **Throws:** R
Ht: 6' 0" **Wt:** 200

Opening Day Age: 35
Born: 10/1/55 in Dalton, MA
ML Seasons: 12

Overall Statistics

	W	L	ERA	G	GS	Sv	IP	H	R	BB	SO	HR
1990	5	3	3.16	47	0	21	51.1	39	19	19	33	5
Career	62	65	3.03	694	0	287	943.2	796	340	320	755	87

How Often He Throws Strikes

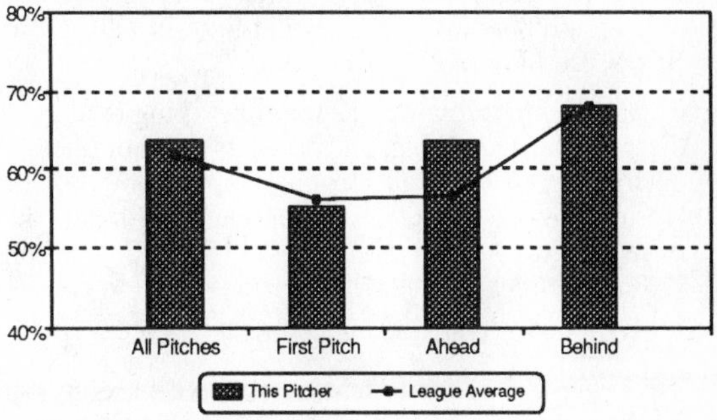

1990 Situational Stats

	W	L	ERA	Sv	IP		AB	H	HR	RBI	AVG
Home	5	1	2.03	12	26.2	LHB	91	13	1	6	.143
Road	0	2	4.38	9	24.2	RHB	98	26	4	19	.265
Day	0	1	3.38	2	10.2	Sc Pos	59	18	2	22	.305
Night	5	2	3.10	19	40.2	Clutch	139	30	4	22	.216

1990 Rankings (American League)

- 4th lowest save percentage (75.0%)
- 7th in blown saves (7)
- Led the Red Sox in saves (21), games finished (37), save opportunites (28), save percentage, blown saves and first batter efficiency (.209)

JODY REED

Position: 2B/SS
Bats: R **Throws:** R
Ht: 5' 9" **Wt:** 160

Opening Day Age: 28
Born: 7/26/62 in Tampa, FL
ML Seasons: 4

HITTING:

When he finally stopped being moved between second base and shortstop last year, Jody Reed established himself as one of -- if not **the** -- best second basemen in the American League. Throw him a fastball, any fastball on the inner half of the plate, and he'll pull it hard into the corner or off The Wall. Reed's 45 doubles -- which tied him with George Brett for the major league lead -- prove it; in fact, he hit more balls off The Wall (nine) than anyone but Wade Boggs.

However, Fenway doesn't make Reed, because he batted only seven points lower (.293-.286) on the road and still managed 19 road doubles. He didn't get many fastballs on the inside half of the plate the last two months, but made adjustments and rapped balls all over the park. He finally wore down in the last couple of weeks, and on the final day of the season his average dropped to .289, the first time it was below .290 since June 15.

Pitchers try to throw Reed a lot of breaking balls, but his strike zone isn't big, and he waits them out. He is a very tough out, and a good situation player who was Boston's most efficient regular getting runners in from third with less than two out (16 of 30, five for six in the clutch).

BASERUNNING:

Reed is a highly intelligent, instinctive baserunner, but he is not a base stealer. In the past three seasons, he has stolen nine times and been caught 12. Unlike most of the Red Sox, Reed is an aggressive baserunner and will go from first to third whenever he can.

FIELDING:

The transition from short has been natural for Reed, and he's made himself an extraordinary second baseman with superb agility. In 118 games at second, he made just six errors in his first full season playing there. This is one second baseman who isn't afraid to hang in on double plays, and is adept at getting the ball to the shortstop in a position where he can make a strong throw.

OVERALL:

Often overlooked, Reed is Boston's heart and soul, the personification of a mediocre team that came back to win their second divisional title in three years. If you think back, the one change Joe Morgan made after taking over for John McNamara after the All-Star Break in 1988 was to install Reed at short in place of Spike Owen. It was then that the Red Sox took off and won that division as well.

Overall Statistics

	G	AB	R	H	D	T	HR	RBI	SB	BB	SO	AVG
1990	155	598	70	173	45	0	5	51	4	75	65	.289
Career	419	1490	210	432	111	4	9	127	10	197	130	.290

Where He Hits the Ball

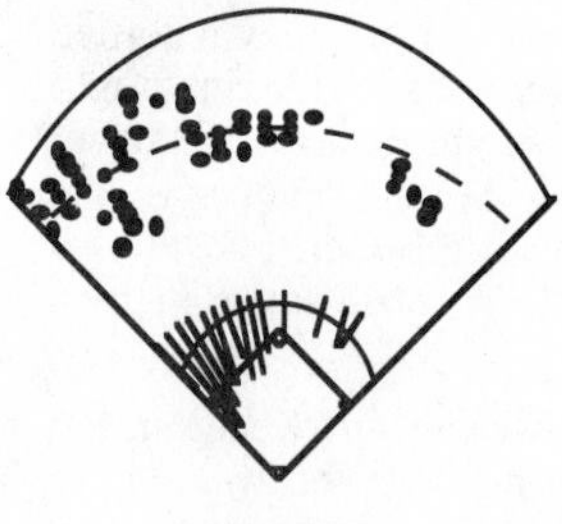

Vs. LHP

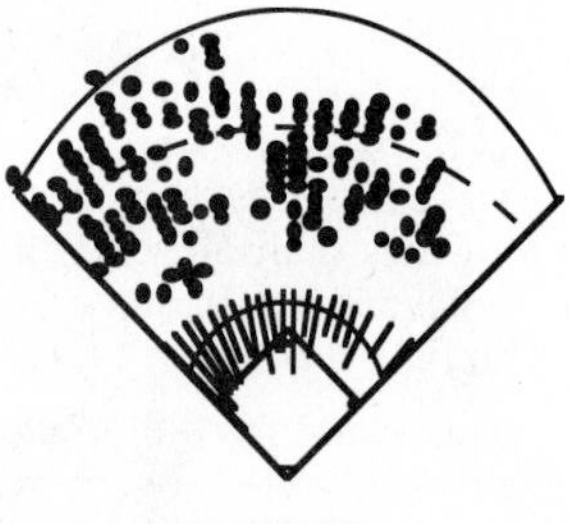

Vs. RHP

1990 Situational Stats

	AB	H	HR	RBI	AVG		AB	H	HR	RBI	AVG
Home	311	91	3	31	.293	LHP	184	55	0	14	.299
Road	287	82	2	20	.286	RHP	414	118	5	37	.285
Day	180	59	1	23	.328	Sc Pos	119	33	0	44	.277
Night	418	114	4	28	.273	Clutch	91	27	1	13	.297

1990 Rankings (American League)

- 1st in doubles (45) and lowest percentage of swings that missed (7.0%)
- 3rd in highest percentage of swings put into play (57.4%)
- 4th in least runs scored per time reached base (27.8%)
- Led the Red Sox in doubles, hit by pitch (4), batting average on a 3-1 count (.438), batting average on the road (.286), highest percentage of pitches taken,(64.5%)
- Led AL second basemen in hits (173), doubles, hit by pitch, GDPs (19), batting average on the road and batting average with 2 strikes (.256)

LUIS RIVERA

Position: SS
Bats: R **Throws:** R
Ht: 5' 9" **Wt:** 165

Opening Day Age: 27
Born: 1/3/64 in Cidra, Puerto Rico
ML Seasons: 5

Overall Statistics

	G	AB	R	H	D	T	HR	RBI	SB	BB	SO	AVG
1990	118	346	38	78	20	0	7	45	4	25	58	.225
Career	407	1238	128	283	67	5	16	118	10	87	228	.229

Where He Hits the Ball

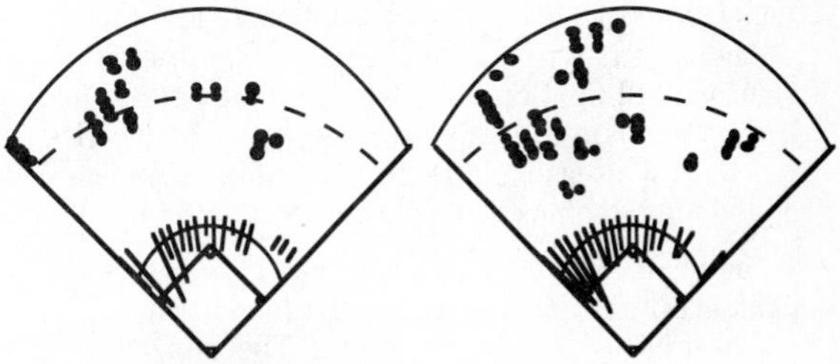

Vs. LHP Vs. RHP

1990 Situational Stats

	AB	H	HR	RBI	AVG		AB	H	HR	RBI	AVG
Home	177	41	4	32	.232	LHP	116	20	2	15	.172
Road	169	37	3	13	.219	RHP	230	58	5	30	.252
Day	100	22	3	12	.220	Sc Pos	105	26	3	40	.248
Night	246	56	4	33	.228	Clutch	55	13	1	6	.236

1990 Rankings (American League)

- 1st in batting average with the bases loaded (.600), lowest batting average vs. left-handed pitchers (.172) and lowest on-base percentage vs. left-handed pitchers (.226)
- 5th in lowest slugging percentage vs. left-handed pitchers (.267)
- 7th in sacrifice bunts (12)
- Led the Red Sox in sacrifice bunts, batting average with the bases loaded, batting average on an 0-2 count (.238), bunts in play (17) and percentage of extra bases taken as a runner (51.6%)
- Led AL shortstops in batting average with the bases loaded

HITTING:

The Red Sox started last season with Jody Reed at short and Marty Barrett at second, but when it became increasingly evident that Barrett's range -- which Boston Globe columnist Mike Barnicle compared to that of Margaret Thatcher -- had badly dwindled, they moved Reed to second and gave Luis Rivera the regular shortstop job. Rivera hit .333 in the 21 games in May and stayed over .300 until June 9, but he eventually found his level and finished at .225.

To Rivera's credit, there were some surprising pluses: he got 13 of 23 runners in from third with less than two out and six of his seven homers came from the seventh inning on. But the feeling is that if he plays every day, those numbers could drift down. Rivera's basically a high fastball hitter who likes the ball on the inner half of the plate. Since he's a little guy, he sometimes gets those pitches, and bails and wails with surprising power. But if he sees a lot of breaking balls and fastballs away, he can go into dreadful slumps.

Rivera is also a decent bunter, and Joe Morgan used him on the squeeze once; with more situations, Morgan might do it more often, for Morgan loves the squeeze. Hit and run? No. Rivera swings and misses too often. Anyone with a career .281 on-base percentage isn't patient, or a very good hitter.

BASERUNNING:

Despite decent quickness in the field, Rivera is not fast on the base paths, is seldom a threat to steal, and has very average instincts on the bases.

FIELDING:

Rivera will make some of the best plays you'll ever see -- ranging far into the hole and throwing on the run, scooping balls in center field and throwing back across his body . . . But the last five weeks of the season, anyone rooting for the Red Sox gasped every time the ball was hit to him. Rivera's play down the stretch recalled an Expos' official's contention that he has "scared eyes under pressure."

OVERALL:

When the Red Sox and Expos were discussing a Spike Owen-John Dopson trade, Red Sox GM Lou Gorman said he needed a shortstop to back up Reed. Montreal GM Dave Dombrowski offered Rivera. Neither Gorman nor Morgan had ever heard of him. "He's our (---) regular shortstop," said Buck Rodgers, so the Sox took him. And Rivera's turned out to be a decent throw-in. Not great, but okay. He's one of those guys who's good enough to play, but when you play him, you're always looking for someone better.

WES GARDNER

Position: RP/SP
Bats: R **Throws:** R
Ht: 6' 4" **Wt:** 203

Opening Day Age: 29
Born: 4/29/61 in Benton, AR
ML Seasons: 7

Overall Statistics

	W	L	ERA	G	GS	Sv	IP	H	R	BB	SO	HR
1990	3	7	4.89	34	9	0	77.1	77	43	35	58	6
Career	18	29	4.84	172	44	13	440.1	444	257	204	346	51

PITCHING, FIELDING & HOLDING RUNNERS:

Wes Gardner is the classic tease. People always say, "Wow, he has a great arm." Every once in a while, Gardner will light up your eyes. But the bottom line is that this is a guy who's going to be 30 the first month of the season, is 18-29, 4.84 lifetime and cannot be left in games when they mean anything.

To be blunt, Gardner can't close games. He can only pitch in relief when three runs down, and he can't start because he always breaks down. The hope is that someone can get hold of him and carefully use him the way the Athletics use Gene Nelson, when they're behind in games. The raw ability is there -- an 89- 92 MPH fastball, plus a hard, nasty slider. Gardner was supposed to be a premier closer coming out of the Mets system, but players and coaches say that was Mets buildup that was used to talk the Boston GM into accepting Calvin Schiraldi and Gardner for a winner, Bobby Ojeda. That's one trade the Red Sox wish they could take back. He's a bad fielder, easy to run on and he breaks down with injuries.

OVERALL:

As much as the Sox have needed a closer, they've had enough of Gardner's act. He was 0-for-2 in save situations last year and hasn't had a save for three years. "But he has a great arm . . ."

JOE HESKETH

Position: RP
Bats: L **Throws:** L
Ht: 6' 2" **Wt:** 170

Opening Day Age: 32
Born: 2/15/59 in Lackawanna, NY
ML Seasons: 7

Overall Statistics

	W	L	ERA	G	GS	Sv	IP	H	R	BB	SO	HR
1990	1	6	4.53	45	2	5	59.2	69	35	25	50	7
Career	29	25	3.51	217	47	19	492.1	464	221	192	401	38

PITCHING, FIELDING & HOLDING RUNNERS:

Ah, to be free and left-handed! Joe Hesketh was released by Montreal last year and a half-dozen teams claimed him, so he ended up in Atlanta by virtue of the Braves' standing. Then, although he'd recorded five saves, the Braves released Hesketh after 31 appearances. Once more, he wasn't out of work long, as the Red Sox quickly signed him.

Despite the five saves, Hesketh believes that his best role is as a starter, and his two decent starts for Boston in the stretch opened some eyes. He hurt his shoulder with the Expos years back, and feels the strains of getting up and down in the pen weaken him considerably. He's also not the classic left-handed middle man, either, because he doesn't get left-handed batters out -- they hit .407 off him in a Boston uniform. He also allowed eight of the 12 runners he inherited to score. However, he is left-handed.

Hesketh fields his position well, but for a lefty does not do a great job of controlling the running game.

OVERALL:

It's been six years since Hesketh was 10-5 for the Expos in 25 starts, allowing just 125 hits in 155.1 innings. At 32, this could be his last chance to hook on, and somewhere down the line that chance will best come if a Boston starter is hurt.

JOHN MARZANO

Position: C
Bats: R **Throws:** R
Ht: 5'11" **Wt:** 197

Opening Day Age: 28
Born: 2/14/63 in Philadelphia, PA
ML Seasons: 4

Overall Statistics

	G	AB	R	H	D	T	HR	RBI	SB	BB	SO	AVG
1990	32	83	8	20	4	0	0	6	0	5	10	.241
Career	101	298	36	73	19	0	6	34	0	13	56	.245

HITTING, FIELDING, BASERUNNING:

When the Red Sox finally and mercifully traded Rich Gedman to Houston last June 7, John Marzano came up and got a chance as Tony Pena's backup. It's been a rocky road to the big leagues for Boston's number-one pick in 1984, when he was a member of the U.S. Olympic team that won the silver medal in Los Angeles.

Marzano came up with some fanfare in 1987, but was sent back in '88 when John McNamara suggested he needed work. Marzano pouted instead of worked and hit .198, .205 and .211 in 1988-89 at Pawtucket, New Britain and Pawtucket again. Nonetheless, Marzano could be a decent backup. He can catch, his arm is average by American League standards (he threw out eight of 27) and he batted .241. He has little running speed and has never stolen a base in the majors.

Curiously, when Marzano was in college, he showed signs of 20 home run power, and it wasn't just the aluminum bat; he used to work in the offseason at Veterans Stadium with then-Philly batting coach Deron Johnson. But he's never shown that power professionally, and has but 9 homers the last three years, combined.

OVERALL:

If Tony Pena gets hurt, it will be interesting to see how Marzano responds, or whether the Red Sox will soon be shopping for a proven receiver. Last year the Sox pitchers had a 3.65 ERA with Pena, 4.07 with Marzano.

PHIL PLANTIER

Position: DH
Bats: L **Throws:** R
Ht: 6' 0" **Wt:** 175

Opening Day Age: 22
Born: 1/27/69 in Manchester, NH
ML Seasons: 1

Overall Statistics

	G	AB	R	H	D	T	HR	RBI	SB	BB	SO	AVG
1990	14	15	1	2	1	0	0	3	0	4	6	.133
Career	14	15	1	2	1	0	0	3	0	4	6	.133

HITTING, FIELDING, BASERUNNING:

The Red Sox have three rookies they hope will be contributing by the end of the 1991 season: shortstop Tim Naehring, first baseman Maurice (Mo) Vaughn and Phil Plantier. Plantier is a strong, slugging left fielder -- or could be with a lot of hard work -- who jumped all the way from the A Carolina league to the AAA International League last year. Plantier led all minor league hitters with 33 homers. However, the jump had its affect on him, as he batted only .253 at Pawtucket and struck out once every three at-bats.

Plantier has a classic, quick, fly ball swing with extraordinary power to left-center, and when he gets to know the strike zone, should be a big threat in Boston. But International League pitchers constantly got him out with pitches down and out of the strike zone mixed in with breaking balls, and major league pitchers did the same; in 15 at-bats with the Red Sox, Plantier struck out six times. Naturally, he has only average speed. He is a converted third baseman who needs a lot of work in the outfield.

OVERALL:

Only 22, Plantier has less than four seasons of professional experience, and he's still pretty raw. But he has shown a penchant to work hard, and for a kid built like Carl Yastrzemski, he looks like he may have big-time Fenway Park power.

KEVIN ROMINE

Position: RF/CF
Bats: R **Throws:** R
Ht: 5'11" **Wt:** 185

Opening Day Age: 29
Born: 5/23/61 in Exeter, NH
ML Seasons: 6

Overall Statistics

	G	AB	R	H	D	T	HR	RBI	SB	BB	SO	AVG
1990	70	136	21	37	7	0	2	14	4	12	27	.272
Career	287	575	82	149	28	1	4	48	10	46	114	.259

HITTING, FIELDING, BASERUNNING:

Kevin Romine is one of the more under-appreciated players in the game, but by the time he finally gets a chance to play everyday against left-handed pitching, he may have slowed down and be but a shell of the player he once was. There was a time when Romine could **really** run -- he was the top high school running back in Southern California -- but he tore a hamstring muscle in A ball with the Boston organization and lost a couple of steps. He still has above-average speed and outstanding baserunning instincts.

Romine is an above-average to excellent right fielder with an average arm, although his quickness getting rid of the ball helps him hold baserunners on the base paths. He can play center and left. He hits lefthanders; does a .329 lifetime average against left-handed pitching intrigue you? He's had a penchant for big hits: three of his four career homers are ninth inning game-winners, and he was six-of-nine getting runners in from third with less than two out.

OVERALL:

Romine's not going to hit much against righthanders, but there is a place on a National League team for this guy. He might earn a platoon job in Fenway's tough right field if they had power elsewhere. Unfortunately, the former Arizona State star will turn 30 on May 23. It may soon be too late; the Red Sox feel he's too valuable to trade, but lacks enough power to play.

JIM ABBOTT

Position: SP
Bats: L **Throws:** L
Ht: 6' 3" **Wt:** 200

Opening Day Age: 23
Born: 9/19/67 in Flint, MI
ML Seasons: 2

PITCHING:

In 1990, Jim Abbott continued to prove that he is a legitimate major league pitcher, with possible 17 or 18-win seasons ahead of him. However, 1990 also brought some concerns about Abbott. He backslid last year from his strong rookie season, and hitters belted him around at a .295 clip.

Abbott won 10 games last season, a downturn from the 12 he won in his freshman campaign. Velocity was no problem, as he continued to have success with his 90 MPH fastball. But Abbott's breaking pitches were not consistently sharp and his lack of a true change-up often allowed opposing batters to sit on the fastball. Abbott continued to get lots of ground ball outs and numerous double plays as well, but that was partly because he allowed so many baserunners.

As with most pitchers, location is probably more important to Abbott than speed. When he is on his game, he is uncanny at hitting the corners with his breaking pitches. Abbott can also pitch inside, a trait not shared by many of his colleagues from the aluminum bat world of college. Abbott will sometimes groove his first pitch in an effort to get ahead of a batter -- five of his 16 home runs allowed were on the first pitch. Fatigue has also become somewhat of a concern. Although Abbott completed four games, the third best total on the team, opponents lit him up at a .333 clip once he'd thrown 90 pitches.

HOLDING RUNNERS AND FIELDING:

Though some baseball people refuse to believe it, Abbott is an above average fielder for his position. Abbott's handicap (he does not care for his condition to be called that) rarely, if ever, comes into play during a baseball game. Holding runners, however, is another story. For the second year in a row, Abbott was among the league's worst in stolen base percentage allowed (78.9%). This on a team whose catcher was the most successful in the A.L. at throwing out runners. It is certainly an area in which Abbott needs to work very hard.

OVERALL:

Abbott has so much poise that it's hard to remember he's only 23, with only two years of professional experience under his belt. He probably needs another pitch, improved technique at holding runners, and some better offensive support before he moves into the top ranks of American League pitchers. His third season will be a crucial one. Abbott needs some polish, and much more consistency, if he's going to become the dominating hurler that so many people envisioned.

Overall Statistics

	W	L	ERA	G	GS	Sv	IP	H	R	BB	SO	HR
1990	10	14	4.51	33	33	0	211.2	246	116	72	105	16
Career	22	26	4.24	62	62	0	393.0	436	211	146	220	29

How Often He Throws Strikes

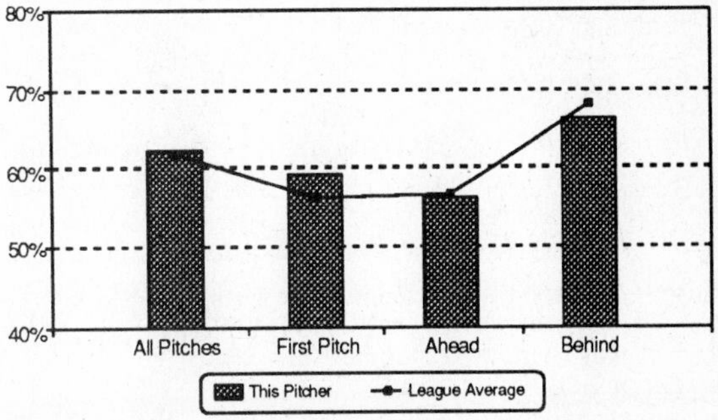

1990 Situational Stats

	W	L	ERA	Sv	IP		AB	H	HR	RBI	AVG
Home	4	7	4.75	0	110.0	LHB	110	35	3	20	.318
Road	6	7	4.25	0	101.2	RHB	723	211	13	76	.292
Day	1	4	3.00	0	39.0	Sc Pos	182	52	1	75	.286
Night	9	10	4.85	0	172.2	Clutch	74	19	2	9	.257

1990 Rankings (American League)

- 1st in most hits allowed (246), most GDPs induced (27), highest batting average allowed (.295), highest on-base average allowed (.353) and most baserunners allowed per 9 innings (13.7)
- 2nd in most GDPs induced per 9 innings (1.15)
- 3rd highest groundball/flyball ratio (1.95)
- 4th highest batting average allowed vs. right-handed batters (.292)
- Led the Angels in games started (33), hits allowed, balks (3), GDPs induced, groundball/flyball ratio, least pitches thrown per batter (3.52) and most GDPs induced per 9 innings

DANTE BICHETTE

Position: RF/LF/CF
Bats: R **Throws:** R
Ht: 6' 3" **Wt:** 215

Opening Day Age: 27
Born: 11/18/63 in West Palm Beach, FL
ML Seasons: 3

Overall Statistics

	G	AB	R	H	D	T	HR	RBI	SB	BB	SO	AVG
1990	109	349	40	89	15	1	15	53	5	16	79	.255
Career	178	533	54	130	24	1	18	76	8	22	110	.244

Where He Hits the Ball

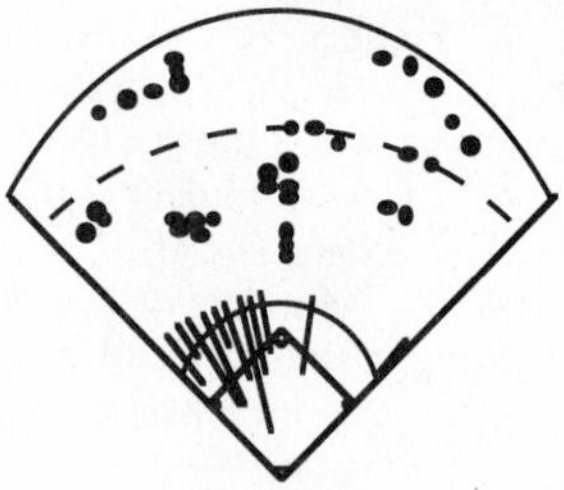

Vs. LHP

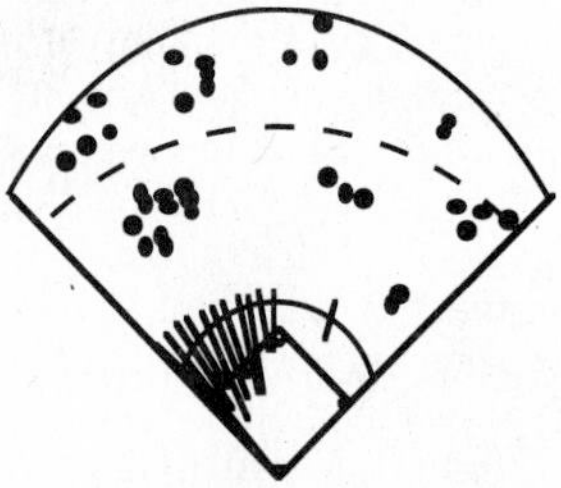

Vs. RHP

1990 Situational Stats

	AB	H	HR	RBI	AVG		AB	H	HR	RBI	AVG
Home	159	41	8	26	.258	LHP	146	40	5	21	.274
Road	190	48	7	27	.253	RHP	203	49	10	32	.241
Day	81	13	4	9	.160	Sc Pos	95	24	5	40	.253
Night	268	76	11	44	.284	Clutch	59	19	3	13	.322

1990 Rankings (American League)

→ Did not rank near the top or bottom in any category

HITTING:

Dante Bichette began last season in spectacular fashion, both at the plate and in the field. Playing every day, he batted with power and provided numerous big hits. When Dave Winfield was acquired from the Yankees, Bichette found his playing time greatly reduced. Not coincidentally, he slumped and didn't find his swing again until August. Bichette never really regained his spot in the lineup and ended up with only 349 at-bats.

Although no longer a youngster at 27, Bichette clearly still has much to learn at the plate. He almost always tries to pull the ball, and as a result strikes out frequently. He does not have good command of the strike zone (he walked just 16 times all last year) and will chase the high fastball or bad breaking ball with regularity. He had some problems against right-handers, but Bichette did hit 10 of his 15 homers off righties. He appears to have the ability to avoid the platoon role that Doug Rader seems to have in mind for him.

Bichette loves to look for the fastball on the first offering, but pitchers know that. Last year they stopped feeding him the heater, and Bichette did not hit a home run off the first pitch all season. He is an extremely competitive player who hates to sit on the bench. If the Angels don't play him early in 1991, look for Bichette to demand a trade.

BASERUNNING:

Bichette is not very fast, although he did steal five out of seven bases. At the beginning of last season, when Rader was desperately trying to manufacture some runs, he often had Bichette running. But Bichette's lack of speed put an end to the idea.

FIELDING:

Bichette has one of the strongest arms in all of baseball, and possibly the best. He led the Angels in assists and foiled many opposing clubs' plans to advance an extra base. He also has enough range to be considered a possible center fielder. But the Angels, stocked with outfielders, are considering moving Bichette to third base. Bichette has played third in the minors, but hardly with satisfying results. In his longest stint at third -- 54 games for Palm Springs and Midland in 1986 -- his fielding average was below .900.

OVERALL:

Bichette has talent, but his future with California is up for grabs. If he can make the conversion to third base, he would presumably platoon with Jack Howell. His tremendous play in the outfield and his promising bat makes one wonder why the Angels would want to move Bichette anywhere.

BERT BLYLEVEN

Position: SP
Bats: R **Throws:** R
Ht: 6' 3" **Wt:** 205

Opening Day Age: 40
Born: 4/6/51 in Zeist, Netherlands
ML Seasons: 21

Overall Statistics

	W	L	ERA	G	GS	Sv	IP	H	R	BB	SO	HR
1990	8	7	5.24	23	23	0	134.0	163	85	25	69	15
Career	279	238	3.28	667	661	0	4836.1	4482	1953	1293	3631	413

How Often He Throws Strikes

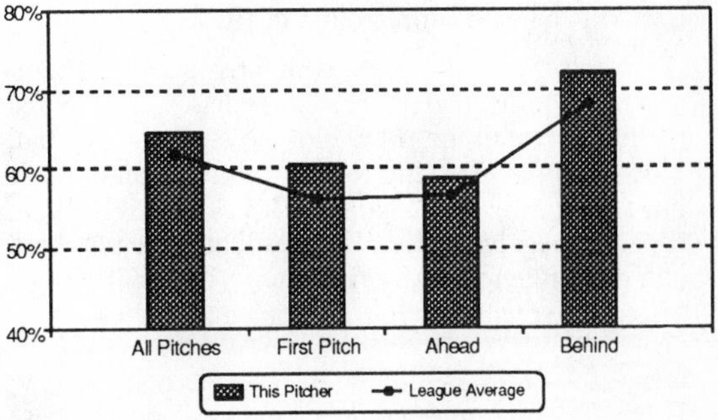

1990 Situational Stats

	W	L	ERA	Sv	IP		AB	H	HR	RBI	AVG
Home	4	2	3.82	0	70.2	LHB	270	84	8	35	.311
Road	4	5	6.82	0	63.1	RHB	268	79	7	38	.295
Day	0	3	11.05	0	22.0	Sc Pos	130	41	5	58	.315
Night	8	4	4.10	0	112.0	Clutch	12	3	0	2	.250

1990 Rankings (American League)

- 8th in hit batsmen (7)
- Led the Angels in hit batsmen

PITCHING:

Perhaps the largest single difference between the surprising Angels of 1989 and the frustrating Angels of 1990 was the performance of Bert Blyleven. In '89, it looked as though Blyleven's career would continue into his forties and that he would easily reach the magic 300-win mark. Now, just a year later, Blyleven's career is in jeopardy. He was having a very rough time of things when a shoulder injury ended his season last August.

The best explanation for Blyleven's lackluster year is that his curveball, once the most feared breaking ball in the league, lacked most of its old snap. It was apparent early in the 1990 campaign that Blyleven's curve was just not breaking like it did in 1989. Indeed, it was hanging, not breaking, resulting in more home run balls. The shoulder troubles might have been the root cause, but the Angels have to wonder.

When Blyleven was not throwing his curve, his fastball was getting hit hard. Lefthanders hammered him for a .311 average and righthanders were not far behind. Blyleven completed just two of his 23 starts, and often was not around for the sixth inning. He continued to battle as always, but was very fortunate to win eight of his 15 decisions.

Blyleven ranks fourth on the all-time strikeout list and needs just ten more K's to pass Tom Seaver and move into third. But his strikeout rate showed a sharp decline in 1989, and last year he could barely manage one punchout every two innings. While he retains the ability to notch the key strikeout, Blyleven has become more of a control pitcher, putting very few men on base via the walk. One suspects that if he could once again find his best curveball, more strikeouts would follow.

HOLDING RUNNERS AND FIELDING:

Neither of these areas are among Blyleven's strongest attributes. He can generally catch what is hit to him, but his reactions have dulled and he is a little slow covering first base. Blyleven has been helped by Lance Parrish's gun behind the plate, but is not adept at holding runners. A consummate professional, Blyleven almost never fails to back up a play at third or the plate.

OVERALL:

The Angels cannot afford to be too patient with Blyleven in 1991, given the level of competition in the A.L. West. If he can't regain command of his curveball, look for the Halos to put the pressure on Blyleven to retire. Blyleven might then be faced with having to either hang up his spikes, or leave his California home if he wants to continue pitching.

HITTING:

A sore lower back put a damper on Chili Davis' 1990 season. When he was healthy, Davis continued to put up productive numbers, but he wasn't in the lineup enough to help a team dependent on his power. For the first time in his career, Davis failed to play in at least 136 games. It was also his second poorest season in terms of RBIs (58). Prior to 1990, Davis had been one of the most consistent players in baseball, and could usually be counted on for 80-90 RBIs and 20 to 25 home runs.

When Davis did play last year, which was mainly in the first half, he was one of the Angels' best offensive players. He kept his average around the .270 mark until the All-Star break, was hitting with power and drawing a lot of walks. Uncharacteristic of a Chili Davis season was his batting average with runners in scoring position, which was below .220. The Angels need this figure to turn around in 1991.

A switch-hitter, Davis is a slightly stronger hitter against right-handed pitchers, as he has been for most of his career. From either side he's a good lowball hitter, and pitchers tend to work him upstairs. Davis has good power to the gaps and loves to pull the ball, especially against lefties. He is patient at the plate and is a good role model for the young Angel hitters -- a power hitter who is willing to let a bad pitch go by.

BASERUNNING:

Davis has become a complete liability on the base paths. The 31-year old hasn't stolen in double figures since 1987 and last year swiped only a single sack. Davis is a station-to-station man on the bases, but has pretty good judgement on when to advance. Davis grounded into 14 double plays in 412 at-bats, second on the team to Dave Winfield.

FIELDING:

Davis is entering the stage of his career where his days in left field are ending and his days of designated hitting are just beginning. He has a tough time with almost every aspect of outfield play, especially charging hard ground hits and balls hit into the corner. His arm is not adequate for a major league outfielder.

OVERALL:

Davis is one of many players on the Angels whose status is unclear. If healthy, he is clearly one of California's best hitters and should be in the lineup daily. However, his lack of defensive ability and the Angels' logjam of designated hitter candidates could make Davis expendable in the near future.

CHILI DAVIS

Position: DH/LF
Bats: B **Throws:** R
Ht: 6' 3" **Wt:** 210

Opening Day Age: 31
Born: 1/17/60 in Kingston, Jamaica
ML Seasons: 10

Overall Statistics

	G	AB	R	H	D	T	HR	RBI	SB	BB	SO	AVG
1990	113	412	58	109	17	1	12	58	1	61	89	.265
Career	1299	4720	652	1262	214	25	156	659	108	539	894	.267

Where He Hits the Ball

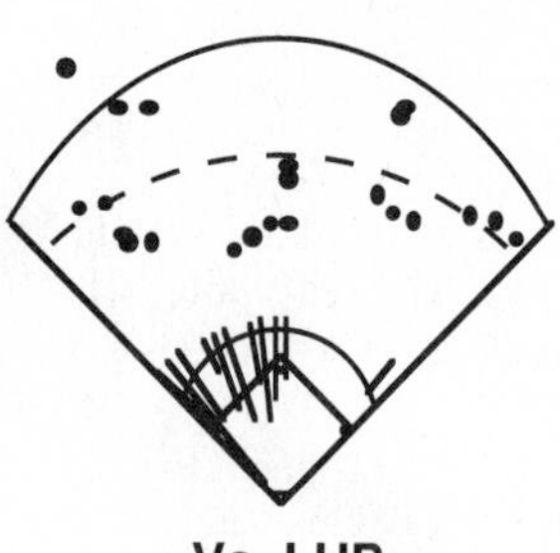
Vs. LHP

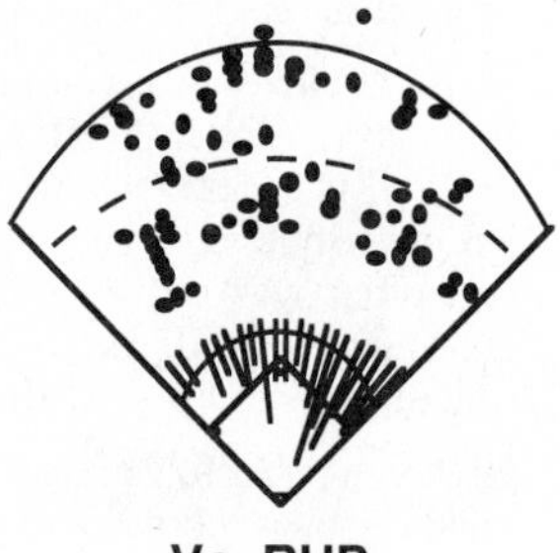
Vs. RHP

1990 Situational Stats

	AB	H	HR	RBI	AVG		AB	H	HR	RBI	AVG
Home	216	66	10	39	.306	LHP	126	32	4	20	.254
Road	196	43	2	19	.219	RHP	286	77	8	38	.269
Day	97	23	1	11	.237	Sc Pos	105	23	4	44	.219
Night	315	86	11	47	.273	Clutch	54	16	0	8	.296

1990 Rankings (American League)

- ➡ 1st in batting average on an 0-2 count (.409)
- ➡ 8th in batting average on a 3-1 count (.571)
- ➡ Led the Angels in walks (61), batting average on an 0-2 count and batting average on a 3-1 count
- ➡ Led designated hitters in batting average with the bases loaded (.429) and batting average with an 0-2 count

BRIAN DOWNING

Position: DH
Bats: R **Throws:** R
Ht: 5'10" **Wt:** 194

Opening Day Age: 40
Born: 10/9/50 in Los Angeles, CA
ML Seasons: 18

Overall Statistics

	G	AB	R	H	D	T	HR	RBI	SB	BB	SO	AVG
1990	96	330	47	90	18	2	14	51	0	50	45	.273
Career	2114	7126	1059	1897	325	26	248	985	48	1077	999	.266

Where He Hits the Ball

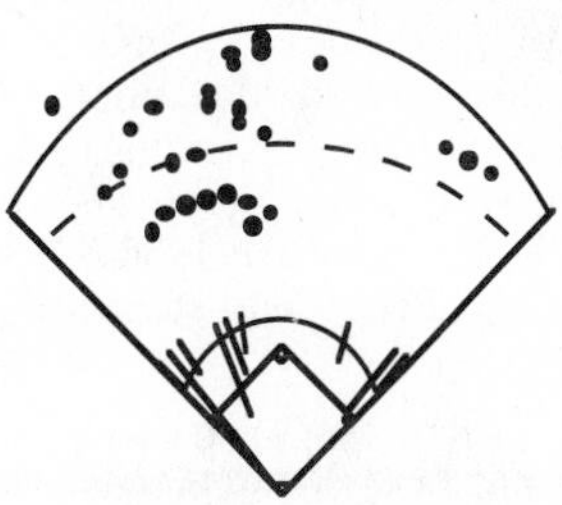

Vs. LHP

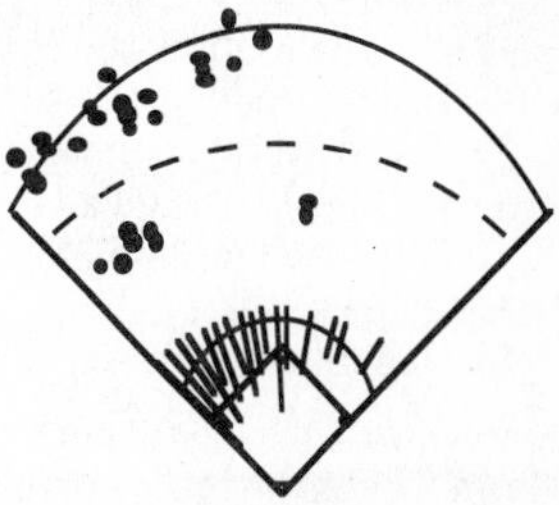

Vs. RHP

1990 Situational Stats

	AB	H	HR	RBI	AVG		AB	H	HR	RBI	AVG
Home	162	49	11	26	.302	LHP	119	41	5	16	.345
Road	168	41	3	25	.244	RHP	211	49	9	35	.232
Day	103	25	2	16	.243	Sc Pos	79	23	3	35	.291
Night	227	65	12	35	.286	Clutch	65	16	3	6	.246

1990 Rankings (American League)

- 3rd highest leadoff on-base average (.382) and on-base average vs. left-handed pitchers (.466)
- 6th highest batting average vs. left-handed pitchers (.345)
- 7th highest slugging percentage vs. left-handed pitchers (.555)
- Led the Angels in hit by pitch (6), batting average/on-base average/slugging percentage vs. left-handed pitchers and percentage of pitches taken (60.6%)

HITTING:

Although it does not bode well for the Angels' future, 40-year old Brian Downing might have been California's most productive offensive player in 1990. If he wasn't, he was certainly close. To many people's amazement, Downing's game refuses to sink to the point where the Angels could consider releasing him or forcing him into retirement. Still more remarkable, Downing could make an argument for everyday play as designated hitter, though a platoon role would be the best arrangement.

Downing was unforgiving against left-handed pitchers last year, hitting them for a .345 batting average and a .555 slugging percentage. As one might suspect of a 17-year veteran, Downing can hurt a pitcher with almost any pitch, although he feasts on fastballs up in the strike zone. Once considered a dead-pull hitter, it is now common for Downing to go the other way when necessary. Undoubtedly the Angels' most patient hitter, Downing was one of three Angels who walked more often than they struck out.

Downing has lost some of his power, though he might still be capable of a 20 home run season with more playing time. He has reached that mark six times, including a five year streak from 1984 thru 1988. Downing continues to be a tough man in the clutch.

BASERUNNING:

When Downing leads off (he had more at-bats in the number one position than anywhere else), it is not to take advantage of his speed. He no longer even attempts to steal. Nonetheless, Downing is an intelligent base runner who picks and chooses his advancements carefully. He is capable of stretching a double into a triple now and then.

FIELDING:

Downing did not play in the field in 1990. Always sure-handed, he could probably still play left field (and not much worse than the Angels who played there last year), but his lack of mobility makes him best suited for DH duty. Downing, one of the few players to publicly campaign for a DH role, has no complaint with that.

OVERALL:

Downing was almost traded to the Athletics late in the 1990 season, and he wants desperately to play for a champion once in his career. Downing has said he will play in 1991 and it is quite likely that he will continue to hurt left-handed pitchers. If California doesn't contend, Downing, one of the most popular Angels of all-time, may end up with another club, one which could help him realize his wish of playing in a World Series.

PITCHING:

The career of Mark Eichhorn, which hit rock bottom at Atlanta in '89, picked up a bit at Anaheim in 1990. Signed as a free agent by the Angels, Eichhorn was unexpectedly thrust into the position of part-time closer when Bryan Harvey was ineffective early in the year. Eichhorn responded by recording a career high 13 saves, doing his best work since his fantastic seasons of 1986 and '87 with Toronto. However, all 13 of Eichhorn's saves came in the first three months of the season. As the season wore on, he became increasingly inconsistent. That strengthened the old argument that Eichhorn can only be effective for short periods of time because hitters figure him out quickly.

Eichhorn's trademark is a sidearm delivery which, these days, serves up tantalizingly slow pitches. When hitters try to sit on his inappropriately named fastball, Eichhorn will throw a change-up which has many batters jumping out of their shoes. During his early days with Toronto, Eichhorn could throw pretty hard, and averaged more than a strikeout per inning as a rookie in 1986. But an extremely heavy workload -- 158 appearances and 284.2 relief innings in 1986-87 -- took its toll. Eichhorn lost velocity and stopped fooling hitters.

The fastball had still not returned by 1990, and Eichhorn is probably going to have to make do by changing speeds and fooling hitters with his tricky motion. It won't be easy. Despite some statistics that look good at first glance, Eichhorn put more men on base per inning last year than at any year of his major league career except 1988. Eichhorn had been historically tough on right-handers because of his delivery, but was hit very hard by righties in '90 (.288). Although Eichhorn's control is usually excellent (23 walks in 84.2 innings), he has displayed a penchant for hitting left-handed batters. Eichhorn was second on the team in hit batters with six, all against lefties.

HOLDING RUNNERS AND FIELDING:

When he first emerged as a legitimate major league pitcher in 1986, Eichhorn was among the league's worst pitchers at holding runners on base. But that has not been the case over the past two years. In 1990, Eichhorn allowed just four stolen bases while three were caught. As a fielder, Eichhorn has limited range, but is sure-handed and rarely commits an error.

OVERALL:

Doug Rader lost confidence in Eichhorn when he began struggling last July. With his current stuff, he simply isn't suited for duty as a closer. But although Eichhorn will probably never be a star again, his ability to change speeds might allow him to stay in the majors as a middle reliever.

MARK EICHHORN

Position: RP
Bats: R **Throws:** R
Ht: 6' 3" **Wt:** 200

Opening Day Age: 30
Born: 11/21/60 in San Jose, CA
ML Seasons: 6

Overall Statistics

	W	L	ERA	G	GS	Sv	IP	H	R	BB	SO	HR
1990	2	5	3.08	60	0	13	84.2	98	36	23	69	2
Career	31	28	3.17	307	7	28	542.1	502	211	180	424	37

How Often He Throws Strikes

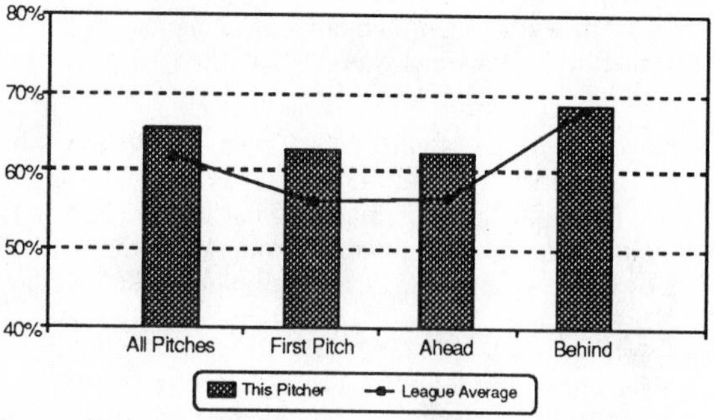

1990 Situational Stats

	W	L	ERA	Sv	IP		AB	H	HR	RBI	AVG
Home	2	4	2.82	3	38.1	LHB	155	45	1	19	.290
Road	0	1	3.30	10	46.1	RHB	184	53	1	31	.288
Day	0	0	4.13	3	24.0	Sc Pos	153	38	1	48	.248
Night	2	5	2.67	10	60.2	Clutch	160	42	1	22	.262

1990 Rankings (American League)

- Led the Angels in games pitched (60)

STAFF ACE

CHUCK FINLEY

Position: SP
Bats: L **Throws:** L
Ht: 6' 6" **Wt:** 215

Opening Day Age: 28
Born: 11/26/62 in Monroe, LA
ML Seasons: 5

PITCHING:

Chuck Finley was the outstanding left-handed starter in the American League last season, and maybe all of baseball. Not bad for a pitcher whom many considered the second best lefty on the team (to Mark Langston) at the start of the season. Just 28 years old, Finley should now be entering his prime pitching years -- a prospect which will keep A.L. batters awake at night.

A five year veteran, Finley has improved steadily since his rocky sophomore season of 1987, when he was 2-7 with a 4.67 ERA. The improvement has often been dramatic. Many baseball people felt that Finley's 1989 performance was about his peak. That year he set career highs in wins (16), ERA (2.57), complete games (9), innings pitched (199.2) and strikeouts (156). Except for the complete games, Finley surpassed each of those totals in 1990. The 6-6 Finley has improved his strikeout totals each year in the majors. He had 177 a year ago, and must now be considered a possible 200 strikeout pitcher.

Finley's fastball is deceptive. Although it reaches the low nineties, it is helped greatly by a change-up that is probably the best on the Angels staff. Along with a curve, Finley has developed a split-fingered fastball which has helped him get more strikeouts; the splitter also gets him into trouble occasionally, however. He is the perfect example of a four-pitch pitcher who does not dominate with any one pitch, but can get you out with all of them.

Finley allowed 17 home runs in 1990, a career high, but he has not allowed a home run to a left-handed batter since 1988. Lefties hit Finley for a .256 average last year after batting only .172 in '89. But this cannot be considered too troublesome, considering that he gave up just two extra base hits to southpaws in 1990 (both doubles).

HOLDING RUNNERS AND FIELDING:

Fielding is one of the weak spots in Finley's game. He is awkward coming off the mound and is very erratic with his throws, especially to second base. Holding runners on is another story, however. Finley has a very good move, rarely balks and was seventh in the A.L. in lowest stolen base percentage allowed at 45.5%.

OVERALL:

Chuck Finley has come a very long way in just five years, especially considering his lack of seasoning (just 28 games in Class A ball before being called up to the bigs). If the Angels contend for the A.L. West crown in the next several years, look for Finley to collect 20-25 wins and possibly a Cy Young Award as well.

Overall Statistics

	W	L	ERA	G	GS	Sv	IP	H	R	BB	SO	HR
1990	18	9	2.40	32	32	0	236.0	210	77	81	177	17
Career	48	41	3.22	152	95	0	767.0	714	307	311	544	54

How Often He Throws Strikes

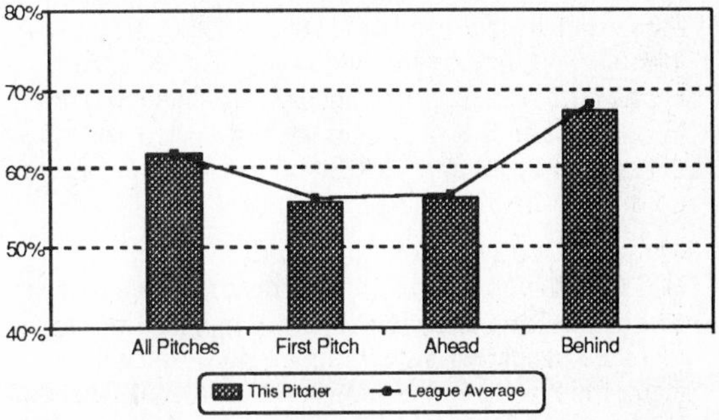

1990 Situational Stats

	W	L	ERA	Sv	IP		AB	H	HR	RBI	AVG
Home	11	4	1.63	0	132.1	LHB	121	31	0	6	.256
Road	7	5	3.39	0	103.2	RHB	743	179	17	57	.241
Day	8	5	3.05	0	100.1	Sc Pos	182	43	2	46	.236
Night	10	4	1.92	0	135.2	Clutch	144	41	0	8	.285

1990 Rankings (American League)

- 1st in runners caught stealing (18)
- 2nd in ERA (2.40) and most errors by a pitcher (5)
- 3rd in complete games (7)
- 4th in wins (18) and innings (236.0)
- Led the Angels in ERA, wins, complete games, shutouts (2), innings, batters faced (962), home runs allowed (17), wild pitches (9), runners caught stealing, winning percentage (.667), strikeout/walk ratio (2.2) and least baserunners allowed per 9 innings (11.2)

WILLIE FRASER

Position: RP
Bats: R **Throws:** R
Ht: 6' 1" **Wt:** 208

Opening Day Age: 26
Born: 5/26/64 in New York, NY
ML Seasons: 5

Overall Statistics

	W	L	ERA	G	GS	Sv	IP	H	R	BB	SO	HR
1990	5	4	3.08	45	0	2	76.0	69	29	24	32	4
Career	31	34	4.26	160	56	5	543.1	518	280	191	272	69

How Often He Throws Strikes

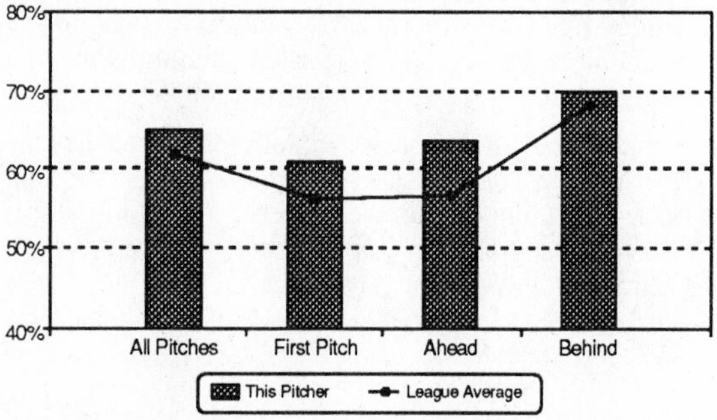

1990 Situational Stats

	W	L	ERA	Sv	IP		AB	H	HR	RBI	AVG
Home	4	1	2.62	1	44.2	LHB	121	25	1	12	.207
Road	1	3	3.73	1	31.1	RHB	165	44	3	23	.267
Day	1	1	3.00	1	15.0	Sc Pos	70	22	2	30	.314
Night	4	3	3.10	1	61.0	Clutch	121	35	1	16	.289

1990 Rankings (American League)

- 4th in lowest batting average vs. left-handed batters (.207)
- 5th in first batter efficiency (.154)
- Led the Angels in lowest batting average vs. left-handed batters, holds (5) and first batter efficiency

PITCHING:

Willie Fraser is still trying to undo the damage of his 1988 season, when he started 32 games, gave up 33 home runs in 194 innings and posted an astronomical 5.41 ERA. Though he was groomed as a starting pitcher, Fraser hasn't started a game since then. But he's slowly climbing back to respectability after two solid, if unspectacular, years in middle relief. Still only 26, Fraser has had some dramatic ups and downs in his short major league career.

Fraser's recent success can be attributed mainly to his development of a split-fingered fastball. Unlike some hurlers, Fraser doesn't get many strikeouts with the splitter. But he does get a lot of outs, and that's all the Angels care about. By successfully controlling the split-finger, Fraser is able to keep the ball down and consequently in the ballpark. Probably the most encouraging sign for Fraser is that he gave up just six home runs in 1989 and only four in 1990, after yielding those 33 dingers in 1988 (and 26 in 1987). Fraser has also improved greatly against left-handed batters, holding them to a .207 average last year. Fraser was very effective after the All-Star break in 1990, picking up three of his five wins in August.

Manager Doug Rader has used Fraser effectively as a middle reliever, and he appears destined to remain in that role as long as he is with the Angels. Although he matched his career high with two saves in '90, Fraser is not the type to finish games, nor is he really needed to close in Anaheim. A workhorse, Fraser is capable of working long stints out of the bullpen. He's remained injury-free also and has not been placed on the disabled list since his call-up in September of 1986.

HOLDING RUNNERS AND FIELDING:

Neither area is troublesome for Fraser. Although he once had problems preventing stolen bases, Fraser allowed only four men to steal in 1990. He is also a capable fielder, with a good follow-through which allows him to get to more ground balls than the average pitcher.

OVERALL:

After two straight solid seasons, Fraser's career is on the upswing again. Used cautiously by Rader, he's probably not going to get many more innings than he did last season, barring an injury to one or more of the Angels' five starters. But thanks to the split-finger, Fraser has improved his pitching to the point that he may be trade material for a team which needs a fourth or fifth starter.

PITCHING:

Nobody plays loud rock songs when he enters a game, and nobody's given him a nasty nickname. Perhaps that's why nobody knows that Bryan Harvey has emerged as one of the outstanding short relievers in baseball. Inconsistency continues to plague Harvey, but when this hard-throwing hurler has command of his pitches, there are very few people who can hit him.

American League hitters batted only .201 against Harvey last year, and just .183 the year before. His fastball is consistently over 90 MPH, and occasionally reaches 95. Harvey combines his heater with a split-fingered fastball which has incredible movement. It's a devastating combination, and when both pitches are working batters have trouble even making contact, much less hitting the ball hard. For the second straight year, Harvey struck out well over one batter per inning, while allowing well under one hit per frame.

Some American League observers are skeptical of Harvey because of his wildness. In '89 he actually allowed more walks than hits. Harvey's control improved in 1990, but there's still plenty of room for additional improvement. In one game against Detroit last year, Harvey walked the bases loaded in extra innings and then forced home the winning run with yet another free pass. Harvey's inconsistency can be overstated, as he was ninth in the league in save percentage (80.7%, 25 saves in 31 opportunities). But he goes into a few slumps over the course of a season. Last year, for instance, Harvey started slowly and was forced to share the closer's role with Mark Eichhorn until he finally straightened himself out.

Despite his intermittent control problems, Harvey seldom gets behind in the count. His problems frequently stem from getting ahead 0-1 or 1-2 and then losing concentration. Harvey is not prone to losing his head for long periods of time, however, and has a good presence on the mound.

HOLDING RUNNERS AND FIELDING:

Harvey's move is adequate. He does not pick many men off base, but because of his outstanding speed to the plate, not many run on him either. He comes off the mound surprisingly well and leaves himself in good position to field ground balls.

OVERALL:

Although he continues to be a well-kept secret, Harvey is now the all-time Angels leader in saves, and he's overdue for some acclaim. If the Angels ever mount a challenge to the Athletics, Harvey might just put up some very impressive numbers -- especially if he can avoid those maddening bouts of wildness.

BRYAN HARVEY

Position: RP
Bats: R **Throws:** R
Ht: 6' 2" **Wt:** 212

Opening Day Age: 27
Born: 6/2/63 in Chattanooga, TN
ML Seasons: 4

Overall Statistics

	W	L	ERA	G	GS	Sv	IP	H	R	BB	SO	HR
1990	4	4	3.22	54	0	25	64.1	45	24	35	82	4
Career	14	12	2.79	158	0	67	200.1	146	67	98	230	14

How Often He Throws Strikes

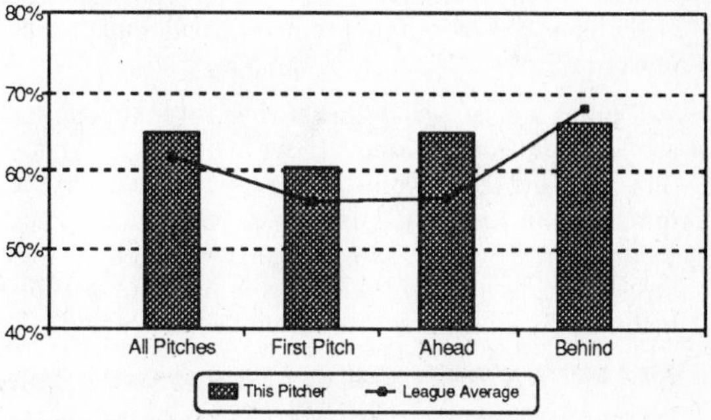

1990 Situational Stats

	W	L	ERA	Sv	IP		AB	H	HR	RBI	AVG
Home	3	1	4.00	10	36.0	LHB	106	22	1	14	.208
Road	1	3	2.22	15	28.1	RHB	118	23	3	11	.195
Day	1	1	2.37	9	19.0	Sc Pos	59	13	1	21	.220
Night	3	3	3.57	16	45.1	Clutch	135	27	3	21	.200

1990 Rankings (American League)

- 7th in lowest batter average vs. left-handed batters (.208)
- 9th in saves (25) and save percentage (80.7%)
- Led the Angels in saves, games finished (47), save opportunities (31), holds (6), save percentage and blown saves (7)

DONNIE HILL

Position: 2B/3B/SS
Bats: B **Throws:** R
Ht: 5'10" **Wt:** 160

Opening Day Age: 30
Born: 11/12/60 in Pomona, CA
ML Seasons: 7

HITTING:

The up-and-down career of Donnie Hill resumed in Anaheim in 1990. Signed as a free-agent before the season began, Hill played an integral role for California, filling in around the infield on an oft-injured squad. Hill took full advantage of Dick Schofield's spring injury, leading the Angels in hitting through much of April. His playing time increased until September, when the infield finally got healthy again. Hill had just 37 at-bats after September 1st, but by then his season was clearly a success.

Hill is a fastball hitter who depends greatly on being ahead in the count. Doug Rader used him primarily in the number two spot because of his ability to make contact. But because Hill suffers if he takes strikes to benefit a base stealer, Rader may find that Hill is more valuable in the number eight or nine slot. Rader used Hill predominantly against right-handed pitchers, and Hill responded by hitting them 41 points higher than lefties (.276 to .235).

Hill takes a surprisingly big swing for someone his size. But he rarely connects with much power, although he did take Dennis Eckersley deep in an extra-inning game in July. His home/road numbers are worth note; 23 of his 32 RBIs and 14 of his 23 extra base hits came away from Anaheim Stadium. In 1989, he hit .377 on the road for Oakland.

BASERUNNING:

Hill has never been a base-stealing threat. He never stole more than 15 bases in the minors, and has not reached double figures in the majors. He is fairly aggressive once he gets going, however, and has an impressive number of triples over his career.

FIELDING:

Hill was the starting shortstop on Arizona State's 1981 NCAA Championship team, but has been moved to second base for most of his professional career. He is capable of playing both positions adequately as a fill-in, but is probably not solid enough anywhere to earn a full-time position with most major league teams. The ambidextrous Hill has a quick glove hand and a decent arm, but his range is limited.

OVERALL:

Hill proved his value to the Angels last season, providing important substitute roles during some hard times. The Angels traded longtime prospect Mark McLemore in part because of Hill's 1990 performance. Hill is still only 29, and since he's versatile and swings a decent bat, his place in baseball looks pretty secure.

Overall Statistics

	G	AB	R	H	D	T	HR	RBI	SB	BB	SO	AVG
1990	102	352	36	93	18	2	3	32	1	29	27	.264
Career	653	2047	233	529	80	13	25	206	21	140	198	.258

Where He Hits the Ball

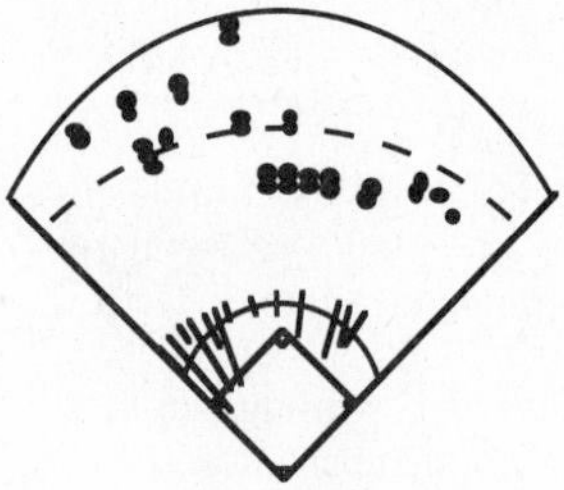

Vs. LHP

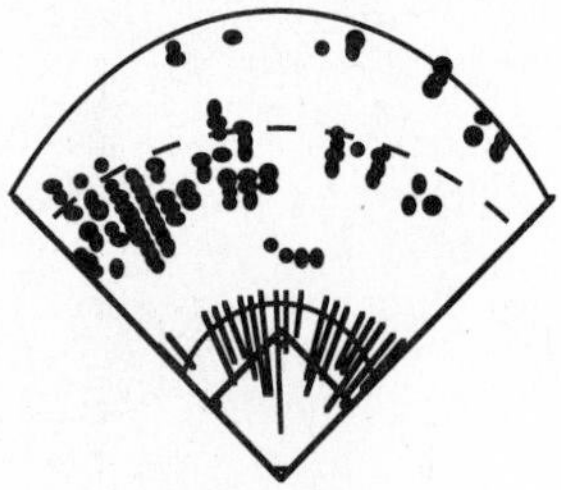

Vs. RHP

1990 Situational Stats

	AB	H	HR	RBI	AVG		AB	H	HR	RBI	AVG
Home	169	42	0	9	.249	LHP	98	23	1	12	.235
Road	183	51	3	23	.279	RHP	254	70	2	20	.276
Day	99	28	1	6	.283	Sc Pos	80	20	1	29	.250
Night	253	65	2	26	.257	Clutch	54	16	1	7	.296

1990 Rankings (American League)

- Did not rank near the top or bottom in any category

HITTING:

Jack Howell continued his downward slide in 1990, spending part of the season in AAA Edmonton and finishing the year with plenty of speculation surrounding his status at third base with the Angels. Any hope that Howell would hit lefthanders has vanished; he hit just .177 against them a year ago and .140 the year before that. The dilemma the Angels face is whether to continue using Howell against righthanders. Howell, previously a career .262 hitter with good power against righties, slumped to a .240 batting average with just eight home runs in 254 at-bats.

When you look at Howell's numbers over the past several seasons, you might picture a mammoth man who tries to pull the ball out of the park on each pitch, and missing with increasing frequency. This is not completely accurate. Howell is not a huge person, but he does have good power, especially to straightaway center. He has improved noticeably at going with an outside pitch to the opposite field. And despite the backslide in many aspects of his game in 1990, Howell dramatically improved his strikeout to walk ratio. After three straight season with at least 118 strikeouts, Howell fanned only 61 times. That's one strikeout every 5.2 at-bats in 1990, one every 3.8 in the previous three years.

BASERUNNING:

Howell has been successful on just five of 14 stolen base attempts over the past three years. He's not speedy, but if a pitcher falls asleep, Howell will occasionally take off. Howell gets out of the box pretty well and is one of the Angels' most aggressive players on the base paths.

FIELDING:

The Angels might be inclined to give Howell more time if they felt that he had continued his solid glove work despite his hitting slump. But Howell, previously an excellent fielder, slumped on defense as well as at bat in 1990. He continued to show tremendous reflexes, especially on balls down the line. However, Howell committed 18 errors in just 105 games, after making just 11 in 144 games in 1989. Maybe he just had a bad year, but California won't wait long to get the answer.

OVERALL:

Howell had the worst year of his career last season. Every aspect of his game, except his judgement of the strike zone, regressed. Howell is now 29, and after six seasons of largely-unfulfilled potential, the Angels are about out of patience. If California is serious about playing Dante Bichette at third, Howell may be among the first casualties in an Angel overhaul.

JACK HOWELL

Position: 3B
Bats: L **Throws:** R
Ht: 6' 0" **Wt:** 201

Opening Day Age: 29
Born: 8/18/61 in Tucson, AZ
ML Seasons: 6

Overall Statistics

	G	AB	R	H	D	T	HR	RBI	SB	BB	SO	AVG
1990	105	316	35	72	19	1	8	33	3	46	61	.228
Career	647	2027	259	485	106	14	76	251	12	236	495	.239

Where He Hits the Ball

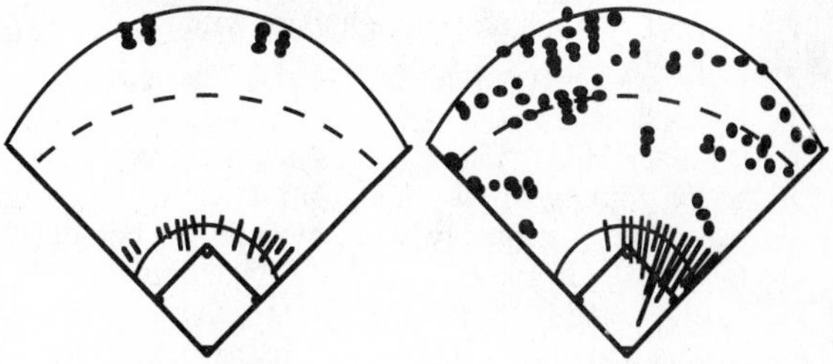

Vs. LHP

Vs. RHP

1990 Situational Stats

	AB	H	HR	RBI	AVG		AB	H	HR	RBI	AVG
Home	156	34	3	17	.218	LHP	62	11	0	5	.177
Road	160	38	5	16	.237	RHP	254	61	8	28	.240
Day	72	21	2	7	.292	Sc Pos	66	11	1	21	.167
Night	244	51	6	26	.209	Clutch	57	12	1	3	.211

1990 Rankings (American League)

- 3rd in least GDPs per GDP situation (4.8%)
- 4th lowest batting average with the bases loaded (.071)
- Led the Angels in intentional walks (5) and least GDPs per GDP situation
- Led AL third basemen in least GDPs per GDP situation

WALLY JOYNER

Position: 1B
Bats: L **Throws:** L
Ht: 6' 2" **Wt:** 198

Opening Day Age: 28
Born: 6/16/62 in Atlanta, GA
ML Seasons: 5

Overall Statistics

	G	AB	R	H	D	T	HR	RBI	SB	BB	SO	AVG
1990	83	310	35	83	15	0	8	41	2	41	34	.268
Career	703	2657	376	759	136	8	93	422	26	271	265	.286

Where He Hits the Ball

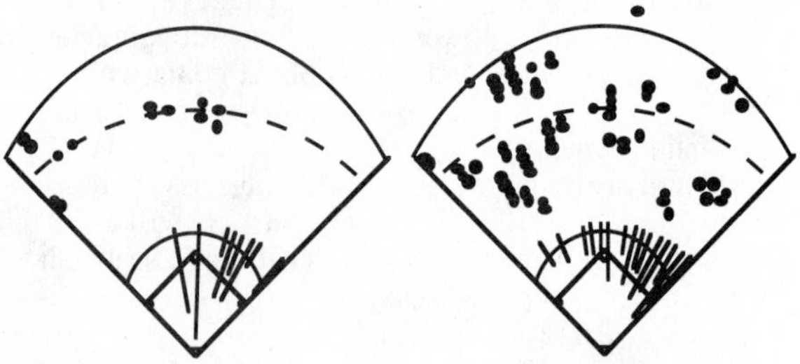

Vs. LHP   Vs. RHP

1990 Situational Stats

	AB	H	HR	RBI	AVG		AB	H	HR	RBI	AVG
Home	135	37	5	21	.274	LHP	106	24	2	17	.226
Road	175	46	3	20	.263	RHP	204	59	6	24	.289
Day	68	18	2	13	.265	Sc Pos	78	22	1	33	.282
Night	242	65	6	28	.269	Clutch	55	13	2	9	.236

1990 Rankings (American League)

- 9th in batting average on a 3-2 count (.360) and percentage of extra bases taken as a runner (57.1%)
- Led the Angels in batting average on a 3-2 count
- Led AL first basemen in percentage of extra bases taken as a runner

HITTING:

For the first time in his major league career, Wally Joyner failed to play in at least 149 games. His season-ending knee injury in July left the Angels reeling for an offensive replacement (they never found one) and kept Joyner from enjoying another All-Star season at first base.

Despite the injury, Joyner continued to show American League fans what to expect from him -- a good batting average with line drive power and a mastery of the strike zone. Joyner followed the pattern of his career by hitting lefthanders about 60 points lower than righthanders. Armed with one of the sweetest swings in the game, Joyner has good bat speed and will put the ball almost anywhere on the diamond. The one exception is against lefties -- Joyner will almost always go to left field against southpaws. Pitchers, especially lefties, tend to work him away, and Joyner is intelligent enough to go with the pitch.

Though he's never batted .300 -- his .268 mark last year was a career low -- Joyner is a very reliable clutch hitter. He is almost always near the team lead in batting with men in scoring position and with men on base. Joyner probably will never hit 34 homers again, as he did in 1987. But he has outstanding power to the alleys and is far more than just a singles hitter. Wally has tremendous bat control and is one of the Halos' top hit-and-run men.

BASERUNNING:

Joyner has never stolen more than eight bases in a season, but his career stolen base rate is just under 75%. He could conceivably steal 10 or more if he ran more often. Since he's recovering from knee surgery, that's unlikely. Joyner is one of the Angels' smarter baserunners and is deceptively fast for a first baseman.

FIELDING:

Joyner has been regarded as one of the A.L.'s best fielding first basemen, but his game is not quite on a level with a Mattingly or Hernandez. His arm is strong but not always accurate and he does not always set himself up for the throw to first base on plays wide of the bag. His range is outstanding, however, and he is certainly among the league's elite.

OVERALL:

For the first time in his career, Joyner's name came up in trade rumors around Anaheim Stadium. It is clear that California is high on Lee Stevens, which might make Joyner expendable. Don't count on it. A fan favorite, Joyner is just entering his prime hitting years and should continue to put up reliable numbers for many seasons in the future.

PITCHING:

Mark Langston was supposed to be the man who would finally lead Gene Autry to a World Series. When Langston combined for a no-hitter with Mike Witt in his first Angel start last year, expectations could not have been any higher. But as is so often the case with the Angels, the auspicious beginning was only a tease. All year long, Langston seemed to be alternately the victim of poor defense behind him or poor offense supporting him. In June he was involved in three straight 2-1 losses while striking out a total of 33 men, and that started him on a skid of nine straight losses. The Angels offense managed only 19 runs for him during the streak, nine of those in one game. Langston finished the year receiving the fifth worst run support in the A.L. (3.9 runs per game). However, he had no excuse for his 4.40 ERA.

As in the past, Langston's lack of control caught up with him. He walked 104 men in 223 innings and walked four or more in a game 13 times. Adding his walks to the hits he allowed, Langston put 319 men on base in 1990. His wildness was especially acute early in the year, and many speculated that the lockout may have had a strong affect on Langston's season (despite his well-publicized workouts on Late Night with David Letterman).

Early in the season, Langston was not consistent with either his fastball or slider. In fact, it was not until late in the year that he was dependable with both pitches. Langston was very shaky early in games (he failed to reach the fifth inning four times), but did manage to complete five of his 33 starts. He probably would have completed more with better control.

HOLDING RUNNERS AND FIELDING:

Langston won two Gold Gloves with Seattle, and is widely considered one of the outstanding fielding pitchers in baseball. His one weakness is questionable judgement on sacrifices -- he sometimes tries to nail the lead runner when he shouldn't. Langston has a decent move to first, but runners have some success stealing on him because of his high leg kick.

OVERALL:

Overlooked in his frustrating season is the fact that Langston won five of his last seven decisions. With the combination of the lockout, some harsh criticism from ex-manager Dick Williams and the pressure he put on himself in his new surroundings, Langston took most of the year to get untracked. It probably won't take long to determine whether 1990 was an aberration, or the symptom of a much larger problem.

MARK LANGSTON

Position: SP
Bats: R **Throws:** L
Ht: 6' 2" **Wt:** 183

Opening Day Age: 30
Born: 8/20/60 in San Diego, CA
ML Seasons: 7

Overall Statistics

	W	L	ERA	G	GS	Sv	IP	H	R	BB	SO	HR
1990	10	17	4.40	33	33	0	223.0	215	120	104	195	13
Career	96	93	3.88	233	230	0	1597.1	1421	773	772	1448	159

How Often He Throws Strikes

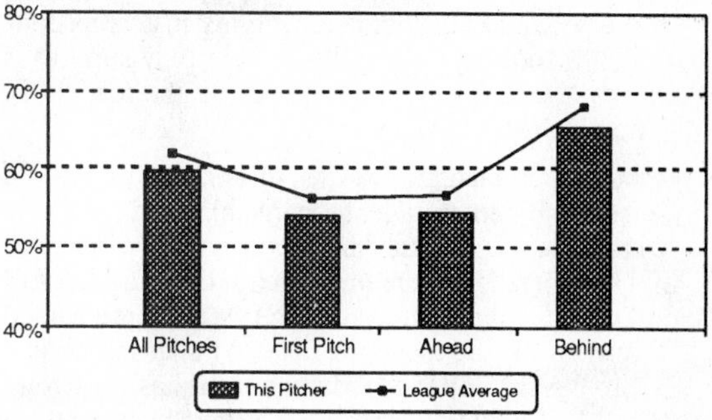

1990 Situational Stats

	W	L	ERA	Sv	IP		AB	H	HR	RBI	AVG
Home	3	11	4.55	0	118.2	LHB	138	34	1	15	.246
Road	7	6	4.23	0	104.1	RHB	691	181	12	89	.262
Day	2	5	6.55	0	45.1	Sc Pos	205	58	4	91	.283
Night	8	12	3.85	0	177.2	Clutch	67	20	4	14	.299

1990 Rankings (American League)

- 4th in pitches thrown (3,743), runners caught stealing (14) and highest on-base average allowed (.343)
- 5th in most losses (17), walks allowed (104), strikeouts (195), most pitches thrown per batter (3.94) and least run support per 9 innings (3.92)
- 6th in hits allowed (215) and least HRs allowed per 9 innings (.53)
- 7th in pickoff throws (183) and most strikeouts per 9 innings (7.87)
- Led the Angels in losses (17), games started (33), walks allowed, strikeouts, pitches thrown, pickoff throws, stolen bases allowed (22) and strikeouts per 9 innings

PITCHING:

When the Angels look back on the disappointment of 1990, one player who won't have many fingers pointed at him is Kirk McCaskill. The current version of McCaskill is a much different pitcher than he was in his first full season, 1986. In those days, McCaskill had a 90 mile-an-hour fastball which simply overpowered hitters (he struck out nine or more 10 times that season). Surgery to remove bone chips in 1987 and a radial nerve irritation in 1988 forced a change, however. Since then McCaskill has relied on an assortment of breaking pitches to get batters out.

McCaskill has four pitches: a fastball, curve, change and slider. While the fastball remains effective, it is his curve and slider that have become his best pitches. No longer able to overpower hitters, McCaskill is prone to trouble when he falls behind in the count. His strength these days is keeping the ball down. Last year he yielded only nine home runs, tying his career low. Not surprisingly, McCaskill's double play support is excellent, and he is regularly among the leaders in ground ball/fly ball ratio.

Anyone who watches McCaskill knows the tell-tale sign of imminent trouble: he starts missing high in the strike-zone. Often that happens around the seventh inning, when he's thrown 90 pitches or so. McCaskill completed only two games in 1990 and depended heavily on his bullpen. He lacks the stamina he had before his arm injuries, though he still has his strong days. McCaskill tied for the league lead in shutouts in 1989 with four, and posted another in 1990.

One thing to look for from McCaskill is a fast start on the season. Over the past two years, McCaskill is 6-1 in April with an ERA under 1.00 (0.88). Knowing that, one might think he is likely to experience problems late in the season, but McCaskill has also been effective the last two Septembers.

HOLDING RUNNERS AND FIELDING:

McCaskill was a fourth round draft pick of the NHL Winnipeg Jets, and often resembles a sprawling goalie while fielding his position. Outstanding defensively, he also helps himself greatly by keeping baserunners close to first. He probably holds runners as well as any other righthander in the American League.

OVERALL:

Over the past two seasons, McCaskill has quietly forged himself into the upper echelon of right-handed pitchers in the American League. However, he needed arthroscopic surgery in the off season. If he recovers, there is no reason that the 29-year old shouldn't continue to be the Angels' outstanding righty for several years to come.

KIRK McCASKILL

Position: SP
Bats: R **Throws:** R
Ht: 6' 1" **Wt:** 195

Opening Day Age: 30
Born: 4/9/61 in Kapuskasing, Ontario
ML Seasons: 6

Overall Statistics

	W	L	ERA	G	GS	Sv	IP	H	R	BB	SO	HR
1990	12	11	3.25	29	29	0	174.1	161	77	72	78	9
Career	68	55	3.80	162	159	0	1043.1	998	483	382	643	90

How Often He Throws Strikes

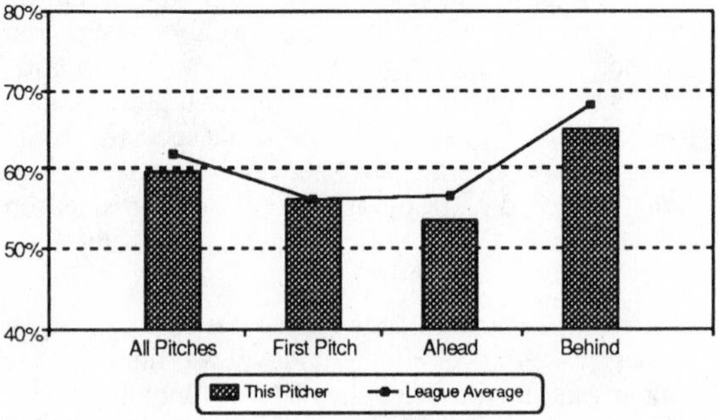

1990 Situational Stats

	W	L	ERA	Sv	IP		AB	H	HR	RBI	AVG
Home	7	3	2.77	0	81.1	LHB	334	84	6	35	.251
Road	5	8	3.68	0	93.0	RHB	326	77	3	32	.236
Day	3	1	1.65	0	27.1	Sc Pos	148	39	2	56	.264
Night	9	10	3.55	0	147.0	Clutch	40	11	0	4	.275

1990 Rankings (American League)

- 2nd in least HRs allowed per 9 innings (.47)
- 3rd lowest strikeout/walk ratio (1.08)
- 4th lowest stolen base percentage allowed (37.5%)
- 7th most GDPs per 9 innings (.98)
- Led the Angels in lowest slugging percentage allowed (.332), lowest stolen base percentage allowed, highest run support per 9 innings (4.54) and least HRs allowed per 9 innings

LANCE PARRISH

Position: C
Bats: R **Throws:** R
Ht: 6' 3" **Wt:** 220

Opening Day Age: 34
Born: 6/15/56 in Clairton, PA
ML Seasons: 14

HITTING:

After a decent first season on the West Coast in 1989, Lance Parrish solidified the Angels' catching position in 1990. He provided them with top-flight defense and a reliable bat in the middle of the lineup. It's now hard to believe that just two years ago many baseball experts were writing off Parrish's career.

Parrish's .268 average was a thirty point jump over 1989 and a 53 point increase from his disastrous 1988 season with Philadelphia. Parrish brings good power to the plate; his 24 home run total in '90 was his highest since 1985, when he hit 28 with Detroit in 79 more at-bats. As has been his history, Parrish cleaned up on left-handed pitchers in 1990, belting them around for a .304 average and a .488 slugging mark.

Almost all of Parrish's power is to left field. Because of that, opposing pitchers try to keep the ball away from him most of the time. He comes up to the plate swinging -- Parrish will jump all over the first pitch fastball. He has two distinct weaknesses, which both stem from a lack of patience at the plate: chasing high fastballs and breaking pitches away. But pitchers know that Parrish will punish a mistake left over the plate, especially up in the strike zone.

BASERUNNING:

Parrish is among the slowest men in the American League, as he would be the first to admit. He stole two bases in four attempts last year, but is very slow out of the batter's box and will almost never take the extra base.

FIELDING:

Parrish was the A.L. leader in throwing out opposing runners last year. He is extremely quick coming out of his crouch and his arm is both strong and very accurate. When Parrish first came to California in 1989, he was widely credited by his teammates for the improvement in the Angel pitching performance -- in large part because they claim he prefers the inside pitch more than former Angel backstop Bob Boone.

OVERALL:

Catcher is one of the few positions at which California can feel comfortable for 1991. Parrish suffered through a late-season slump in '90 which appeared to be caused by fatigue. He has had a history of back troubles, and to prevent those injuries from becoming troublesome, the Angels may need to rest him more this season. Otherwise, Parrish should be able to provide the Angels with several more years of All-Star catching while they try to acquire a worthy replacement.

Overall Statistics

	G	AB	R	H	D	T	HR	RBI	SB	BB	SO	AVG
1990	133	470	54	126	14	0	24	70	2	46	107	.268
Career	1656	6066	765	1557	265	26	285	947	25	516	1255	.257

Where He Hits the Ball

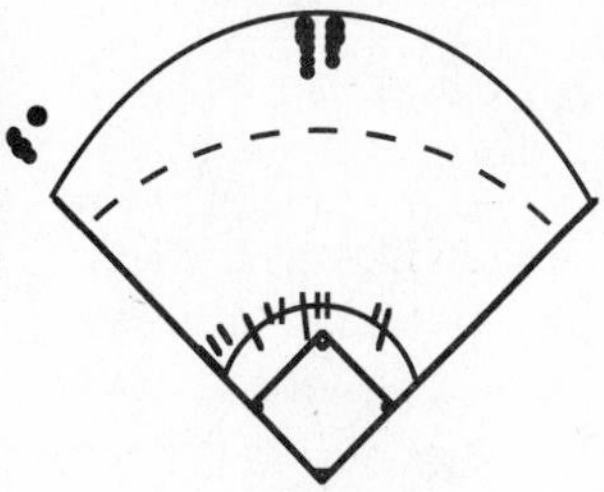

Vs. LHP

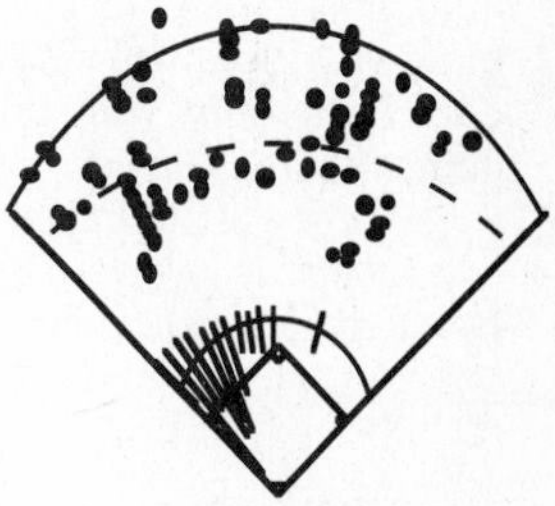

Vs. RHP

1990 Situational Stats

	AB	H	HR	RBI	AVG		AB	H	HR	RBI	AVG
Home	235	65	14	39	.277	LHP	125	38	7	17	.304
Road	235	61	10	31	.260	RHP	345	88	17	53	.255
Day	72	15	5	16	.208	Sc Pos	115	29	5	41	.252
Night	398	111	19	54	.279	Clutch	85	20	5	12	.235

1990 Rankings (American League)

- 1st in throwing out basestealers (47.0%)
- 9th in home run frequency (19.6 ABs per HR)
- 10th in home runs (24)
- Led the Angels in at-bats (470), home runs, total bases (212), slugging percentage (.451), and on-base percentage (.338), games (133) and home run frequency

LUIS POLONIA

Position: LF/CF/DH
Bats: L **Throws:** L
Ht: 5' 8" **Wt:** 155

Opening Day Age: 26
Born: 10/12/64 in Santiago City, Dominican Republic
ML Seasons: 4

HITTING:

When California traded for Luis Polonia early in the 1990 season, they were in great need of a run-scoring outfielder. And while he may not have been the answer to all of the Angels' problems, Polonia was certainly a valuable addition. He proved to be the most consistent performer of all the Halos' everyday players.

Polonia was once a switch-hitter, but he now bats exclusively from the left side of the plate. Although that has basically landed him a platoon role, Polonia did lead the A.L. in batting versus right-handed pitchers. Polonia's excellent speed and obvious hitting ability make him a natural for the leadoff spot. But with his lack of patience at the plate, Polonia needs to hit well over .300 to get on base enough to justify batting first. In 1990, he did just that.

Polonia is a slap hitter who rarely hits the gaps and picks up many hits in the infield. Pitchers work him outside, usually with breaking stuff, and Polonia dumps the ball to left field often. He's one of the league's best at putting the ball into play, and he loves to go the other way at any point in the count. When Doug Rader flashes the hit-and-run sign, it is quite possible that Polonia will be involved on one end or the other.

BASERUNNING:

Despite excellent speed, Polonia gets into plenty of trouble on the base paths. He's a very aggressive baserunner, and to an extent, that's good. But Polonia's value to the team would increase if he would pick and choose his advancements (especially on ground outs) a little more carefully. He was caught stealing 14 times in 35 attempts last year, and that's not going to help his club.

FIELDING:

Polonia's outfield work also needs lots of polish. His range is nowhere near where it should be for someone of his athletic ability, and his arm is very weak. Polonia is prone to overrunning ground balls in the outfield and misplaying singles into doubles. With his speed, it seems like a waste to move him to DH, but his outfield play is poor enough to make the Angels consider it.

OVERALL:

Only 26, Polonia is capable of being a long-time major leaguer. There's always room on a roster for someone who can hit, and Polonia's offensive skills are very solid. He quickly became a crowd favorite in Anaheim because of his aggressive style of baseball, and seems to have been well worth the trade of Claudell Washington and Rich Monteleone.

Overall Statistics

	G	AB	R	H	D	T	HR	RBI	SB	BB	SO	AVG
1990	120	403	52	135	7	9	2	35	21	25	43	.335
Career	454	1559	251	474	51	29	11	157	96	103	191	.304

Where He Hits the Ball

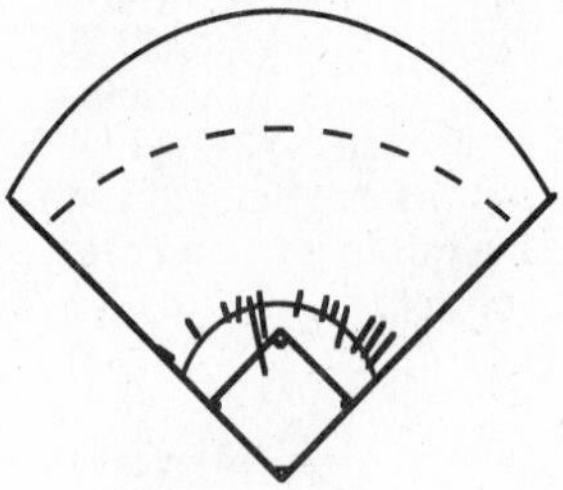

Vs. LHP

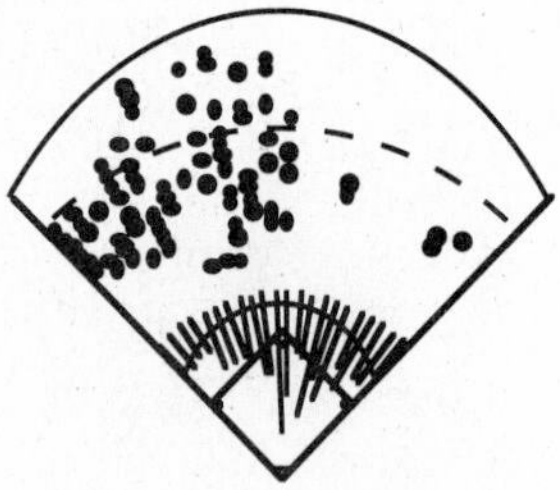

Vs. RHP

1990 Situational Stats

	AB	H	HR	RBI	AVG		AB	H	HR	RBI	AVG
Home	207	73	2	23	.353	LHP	51	15	0	3	.294
Road	196	62	0	12	.316	RHP	352	120	2	32	.341
Day	99	34	0	7	.343	Sc Pos	83	27	1	34	.325
Night	304	101	2	28	.332	Clutch	55	14	0	6	.255

1990 Rankings (American League)

- ➡ 1st in batting average vs. right-handed pitchers (.341)
- ➡ 2nd in batting average on an 0-2 count (.353)
- ➡ 3rd in triples (9)
- ➡ 8th in caught stealing (14)
- ➡ Led the Angels in hits (128), singles (110), triples, caught stealing and batting average with 2 strikes (.250)

JOHNNY RAY

Position: 2B
Bats: B **Throws:** R
Ht: 5'11" **Wt:** 189

Opening Day Age: 34
Born: 3/1/57 in Chouteau, OK
ML Seasons: 10

HITTING:

By the end of 1990, Johnny Ray was one of the most disgruntled players on the Angels. His season was marred by injury, several frustrating slumps and quite a bit of time on the bench. Ray continued to hit for a respectable average but saw several facets of his game decline.

Ray has always been among the best contact hitters in baseball. Last year, though, he struck out 44 times in 404 at-bats, a fine ratio for most players but by far the worst in Ray's career. Along with the increase in strikeouts came a decrease in walks, leading to his career low on-base average of .308. Meanwhile, another one of Ray's strengths -- line drive power to the gaps -- has declined noticeably. In 1988 Ray belted 42 doubles, but in '89 and '90 combined, he managed only 39.

The switch-hitting Ray has historically been a better hitter from the left side, but that turned around slightly last year. Ray's style of hitting changes when he switches sides of the plate. As a right-hander, he is little more than a slap hitter who just tries to make contact. From the left side, Ray stands in a little stronger and shows pretty good power. By any standard he is a spray hitter who rarely pulls the ball down the lines but often puts the ball into play. Ray has always been a fine breaking ball hitter, and pitchers generally try to jam him with fastballs.

BASERUNNING:

Once a respected base-stealer, Ray's running skills have deteriorated in a hurry. He stole a career low two bases in five attempts in 1990. Ray's lack of speed in the number two spot in the lineup hurts the Angels because he often requires an extra base hit to be driven in, rather than a single.

FIELDING:

Throughout his career, Ray has taken a beating for his lack of range. That's a fair criticism, although he is more valuable with California than he was with Pittsburgh because he sees much less artificial turf. In Ray's defense, he is a very smart fielder who positions himself well (sometimes unbelievably well) and doesn't make a lot of mistakes once he gets to the ball.

OVERALL:

Very little went right for Ray last season. By year's end, he was suggesting that a trade might be best for all parties involved. The Angels have also been rumored to be considering a change at second base. Despite some decline in his game, Ray should continue to produce for someone in 1991 and beyond.

Overall Statistics

	G	AB	R	H	D	T	HR	RBI	SB	BB	SO	AVG
1990	105	404	47	112	23	0	5	43	2	19	44	.277
Career	1353	5188	604	1502	294	36	53	594	80	353	329	.290

Where He Hits the Ball

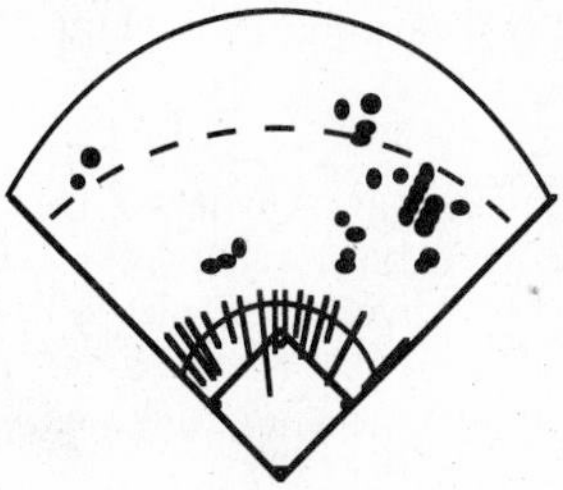

Vs. LHP

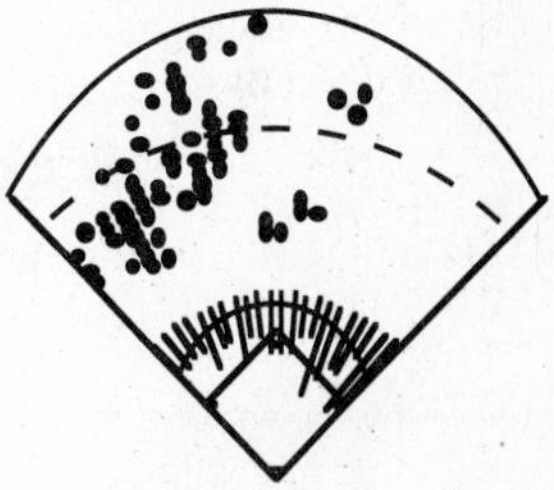

Vs. RHP

1990 Situational Stats

	AB	H	HR	RBI	AVG		AB	H	HR	RBI	AVG
Home	210	57	5	21	.271	LHP	120	36	0	15	.300
Road	194	55	0	22	.284	RHP	284	76	5	28	.268
Day	90	28	2	8	.311	Sc Pos	101	29	1	39	.287
Night	314	84	3	35	.268	Clutch	76	19	2	14	.250

1990 Rankings (American League)

- 3rd highest batting average with the bases loaded (.556)
- Led the Angels in doubles (23), batting average with the bases loaded, lowest percentage of swings that missed (10.7%) and highest percentage of swings put into play (48.9%)
- Led AL second basemen in batting average with the bases loaded

DICK SCHOFIELD

Position: SS
Bats: R **Throws:** R
Ht: 5'10" **Wt:** 175

Opening Day Age: 28
Born: 11/21/62 in Springfield, IL
ML Seasons: 8

HITTING:

After seven seasons as their regular shortstop, Dick Schofield continues to bewilder the Angels. For the second year in a row, Schofield played fewer than 100 games due to injury. After assorted ailments in 1989, a groin problem kept him out of the lineup in 1990 until June. When he returned, Schofield looked like a completely different ballplayer -- better in many ways, but puzzlingly worse in others.

Offensively, the rap on Schofield was that he was always trying to pull the ball. But last season, Schofield finally started going to the opposite field. As a result, he raised his average by 27 points over 1989, to a career-high .255. That wasn't the only breakthrough Schofield made in 1990. Schofield made a real effort to be more selective, taking more pitches than ever before. He consequently walked a career high 52 times despite his short season and recorded an on-base average of .363, a personal best by a whopping 42 points.

Unfortunately, Schofield's adjustments also had their downside: what Schofield picked up in patience, he lost in power. Schofield had never been a slugger, but this was ridiculous: only one homer, eight doubles, 18 RBIs and an anemic .297 slugging percentage, a career low. It was hard for the Angels to believe this was the same guy who belted 13 homers in 1986.

BASERUNNING:

From '86 thru '88, Schofield averaged 21 steals per year, with outstanding success rates. Weakened by injuries, he swiped only nine in 1989, and just three in 1990. He continues to be a very smart baserunner and is always a threat to take the extra base.

FIELDING:

As with teammate Jack Howell, Schofield's fielding took a downward turn in 1990. He was second to Howell with 17 errors in just 99 games. Could this be the same player who led the A.L. in fielding percentage in 1987 and '88? Though his range was still good overall, Schofield had some trouble going to his right, and his arm was erratic. The Angels hope that last year's performance was just an anomaly and that he will return to his normally steady self in 1991.

OVERALL:

Will the real Dick Schofield please stand up? From 1989 to 1990, he changed from a strong-fielding, pull-hitting, free-swinging shortstop to an opposite-field singles hitter who walks a lot but carries a shaky glove. The Angels can only hope that Schofield will regain his power and his defensive magic while retaining his new-found ability to get on base.

Overall Statistics

	G	AB	R	H	D	T	HR	RBI	SB	BB	SO	AVG
1990	99	310	41	79	8	1	1	18	3	52	61	.255
Career	926	2968	356	692	95	24	48	247	90	279	440	.233

Where He Hits the Ball

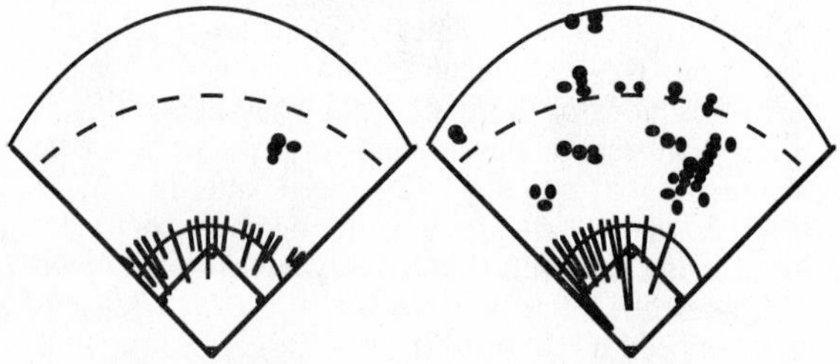

Vs. LHP Vs. RHP

1990 Situational Stats

	AB	H	HR	RBI	AVG		AB	H	HR	RBI	AVG
Home	158	43	1	12	.272	LHP	89	25	1	6	.281
Road	152	36	0	6	.237	RHP	221	54	0	12	.244
Day	77	16	0	6	.208	Sc Pos	54	16	0	17	.296
Night	233	63	1	12	.270	Clutch	50	11	0	2	.220

1990 Rankings (American League)

- 4th in sacrifice bunts (13)
- 6th in least GDPs per GDP situation as a hitter (5.4%)
- Led the Angels in sacrifice bunts and bunts in play (19)
- Led AL shortstops in least GDPs per GDP situation as a hitter (5.4%)

LEE STEVENS

Position: 1B
Bats: L **Throws:** L
Ht: 6' 4" **Wt:** 205

Opening Day Age: 23
Born: 7/10/67 in Kansas City, Mo
ML Seasons: 1

Overall Statistics

	G	AB	R	H	D	T	HR	RBI	SB	BB	SO	AVG
1990	67	248	28	53	10	0	7	32	1	22	75	.214
Career	67	248	28	53	10	0	7	32	1	22	75	.214

Where He Hits the Ball

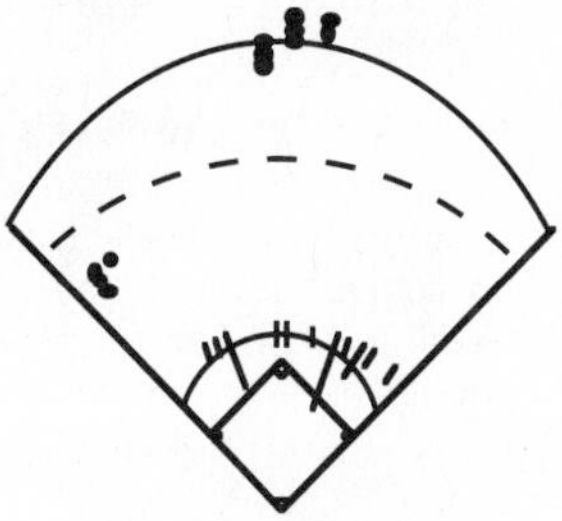
Vs. LHP

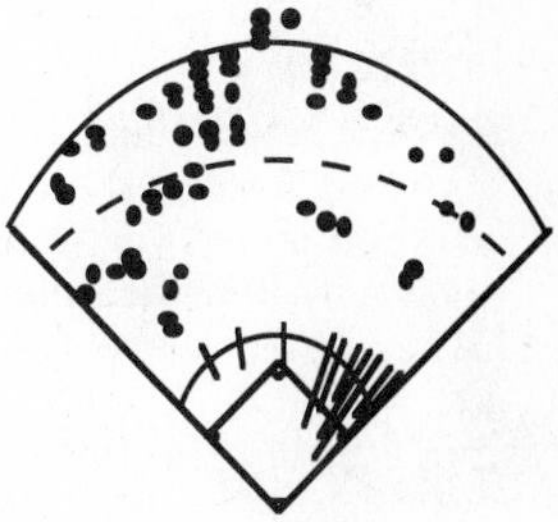
Vs. RHP

1990 Situational Stats

	AB	H	HR	RBI	AVG		AB	H	HR	RBI	AVG
Home	133	34	4	20	.256	LHP	54	11	1	9	.204
Road	115	19	3	12	.165	RHP	194	42	6	23	.216
Day	69	9	0	4	.130	Sc Pos	68	16	4	28	.235
Night	179	44	7	28	.246	Clutch	36	7	1	5	.194

1990 Rankings (American League)

➟ Did not rank near the top or bottom in any category

HITTING:

If nothing else, Lee Stevens certainly looks the part. The 6-4, 205 pound first baseman/outfielder has one of the sweetest natural swings in the game. But if Stevens is to take over first base at Anaheim Stadium and force the trade of All-Star Wally Joyner, he is going to have to produce a lot more than in 1990. Otherwise, GM Mike Port and the Angels will be vilified for a long time to come.

Stevens got his call-up from AAA in July, and for a time was the most welcome arrival from Edmonton in Southern California since Wayne Gretzky. When he made contact, Stevens was driving in runs and hitting for some power. The problem was that he was striking out in nearly a third of his at-bats. Stevens got off to a decent start, but pitchers began figuring him out and he struggled badly in late August and September. Stevens had a terrible time with left-handed pitchers in particular, and may be best suited for a platoon role during the early stages of his career.

Despite his smooth, beautiful swing, American League pitchers began throwing everything inside on him, and Stevens had difficulty adjusting. Leave the ball over the plate and Stevens will hit it, but the pitchers don't always oblige. He has very good power to the opposite field and might have 25 home run power when he fully develops.

BASERUNNING:

Stevens is a fairly gifted athlete (he was an all-state basketball player in Kansas during high school) and appears competent on the base paths. But he's not a base stealer, and thus far has been pretty cautious in his baserunning. He's still learning his trade, however.

FIELDING:

Stevens was drafted as an outfielder and remained one until his second year in pro ball, when he picked up first base on a part-time basis. Right now his range at first is very poor, and he committed a couple of errors on ground balls to his right last year. In '89 Stevens made just one error in the outfield for Edmonton. But the Angels have a crowded outfield; unfortunately, Stevens is no Wally Joyner at first.

OVERALL:

At 23, it is clear that Stevens has some productive seasons in front of him. He should develop good power to all fields and hit for an acceptable average. It is important to note, however, that Stevens is almost unplayable against lefthanders right now. Forcing him into an everyday situation at first base might be a tremendous mistake.

DEVON WHITE

Position: CF
Bats: B **Throws:** R
Ht: 6' 2" **Wt:** 178

Opening Day Age: 28
Born: 12/29/62 in Kingston, Jamaica
ML Seasons: 6

Overall Statistics

	G	AB	R	H	D	T	HR	RBI	SB	BB	SO	AVG
1990	125	443	57	96	17	3	11	44	21	44	116	.217
Career	612	2231	337	551	91	24	59	241	123	144	475	.247

Where He Hits the Ball

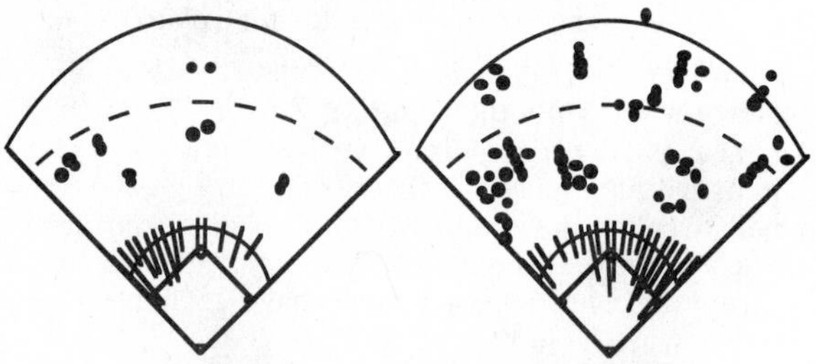

Vs. LHP　　Vs. RHP

1990 Situational Stats

	AB	H	HR	RBI	AVG		AB	H	HR	RBI	AVG
Home	219	47	5	20	.215	LHP	130	32	3	10	.246
Road	224	49	6	24	.219	RHP	313	64	8	34	.204
Day	87	20	2	8	.230	Sc Pos	112	22	3	34	.196
Night	356	76	9	36	.213	Clutch	87	17	3	8	.195

1990 Rankings (American League)

- 2nd lowest batting average (.217)
- 3rd lowest on-base average (.290)
- 5th in lowest batting average with runners in scoring position (.196), lowest lowest batting average on the road (.219) and highest percentage of extra bases taken as a runner (57.7%)
- Led the Angels in stolen bases (21), intentional walks (5), strikeouts (116), pitches seen (1,996), runs scored per time reached base (39.9%), bunts in play (19) and percnetage of extra bases taken as a runner

HITTING:

Devon White gives testament to the fact that no matter how many skills a player brings to a ballpark, baseball is still a game in which hitting is of the utmost importance. White possesses great speed, tremendous leaping ability and a fantastic arm -- but he's never shown he can hit major league pitching. And Angel executives must be wondering if he ever will.

By now most of baseball knows about the weak spots in White's game: he can't hit a breaking ball, and he doesn't have a good idea of the strike zone. The problems are intertwined, because if White could get ahead in the count a little more, he'd see a lot more fastballs. With his speed, White has been told to just make contact with the ball and that the rest would follow. But for White, that's easier said than done. Last year he struck out 116 times in 125 games and was even sent back to the minors to try to correct the flaws in his swing.

A switch hitter, White was almost completely useless from the left side last year, hitting around .200. While he's more successful batting right, he also loses much of his power. White's one improvement in 1990 was his number of walks (a career-high 44 in just 125 games). But that's not nearly enough.

BASERUNNING:

Without a doubt, White is one of the fastest men in the game. He is a very bright baserunner who will very rarely even draw a throw on advancements. His stolen base total was down in 1990, but one suspects that in a better season, White would revert back to his former numbers.

FIELDING:

White is a perennial Gold Glove candidate who electrifies crowds with his defensive ability. He gets a superb jump on fly balls and charges ground hits unlike most players in the league. Perhaps no player in the game is as adept as White at going over the wall to steal home runs. His arm is excellent and he rarely throws to the wrong base. He is simply a superior defensive player who is a pleasure to watch.

OVERALL:

Can the Angels, full of outfielders, continue to play White everyday? It seems like just yesterday that they faced a similar dilemma with another speedy Gold Glove center fielder who didn't reach base enough. California hopes that Devon White, unlike Gary Pettis before him, will turn things around and show some of the ability he displayed in 1987. If he can't, his fate with the Angels may be similar to that of Pettis.

DAVE WINFIELD

Position: RF
Bats: R **Throws:** R
Ht: 6' 6" **Wt:** 220
Opening Day Age: 39
Born: 10/3/51 in St. paul, MN
ML Seasons: 17

Overall Statistics

	G	AB	R	H	D	T	HR	RBI	SB	BB	SO	AVG
1990	132	475	70	127	21	2	21	78	0	52	81	.267
Career	2401	8896	1384	2548	433	76	378	1516	209	988	1305	.286

Where He Hits the Ball

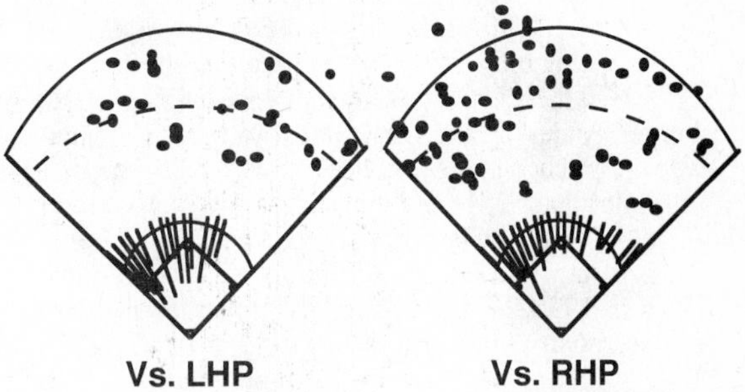

1990 Situational Stats

	AB	H	HR	RBI	AVG		AB	H	HR	RBI	AVG
Home	238	62	13	41	.261	LHP	156	45	5	32	.288
Road	237	65	8	37	.274	RHP	319	82	16	46	.257
Day	129	30	3	16	.233	Sc Pos	125	31	5	55	.248
Night	346	97	18	62	.280	Clutch	82	25	4	14	.305

1990 Rankings (American League)

- Led AL right fielders in GDPs (18) and fielding percentage (.988)

HITTING:

Last year was certainly an eventful one for Dave Winfield. He came back from a career-threatening injury, was traded early in the year and eventually found himself implicated in the George Steinbrenner-Howard Spira mess. In retrospect, that makes Winfield's impressive 1990 season look even better.

In April it appeared that Winfield's career might be over. He looked bad in the early going, swinging at a lot of questionable pitches and failing to hit the ball hard. Then, just when he seemed to be shaking off the rust he'd accumulated while missing the entire '89 season, Winfield was dealt to California. Once he reported to the Angels, Winfield's season started turning dramatically. He closed with a rush and finished the season with some very respectable numbers.

At this point in his career, Winfield tries to pull almost everything. For that reason, pitchers work him outside with breaking pitches and fastballs about 75 percent of the time. Though he performed well with the Angels, Winfield has noticeably less bat speed than his younger days, resulting in more strikeouts. Nonetheless, Winfield has retained many of his potent offensive skills. He still has tremendous power, and he continues to hit lefthanders well. Despite a somewhat dissatisfying performance with runners in scoring position (.248), Winfield continues to drive in runs and score them at a decent rate.

BASERUNNING:

For the first time in his career, Winfield failed to steal a base in a full season. In fact, he made only one attempt. While he could probably still steal a few bases, no manager would want to take the risk of re-injuring Winfield's back. Winfield can still build up some speed on the base paths, though, and is still an absolute terror breaking up a double play.

FIELDING:

Winfield has won seven Gold Gloves over his career, and it's not a knock on him to say that he won't win any more. His play in right field may not be up to the level of his younger days, but it's still acceptable. The Angels weren't complaining about the way Winfield played in 1990. He made just two errors in 132 games and displayed an adequate arm.

OVERALL:

Even at age 39, you get the feeling that Winfield might have at least one big season left in him. Any club would welcome a Hall of Fame candidate who's still a strong player, and the Angels felt that they needed Winfield's experience and leadership ability to make a run at the Athletics. They may just get a lot more than that in 1991 if Winfield stays healthy.

KENT ANDERSON

Position: SS/3B
Bats: R **Throws:** R
Ht: 6' 1" **Wt:** 180

Opening Day Age: 27
Born: 8/12/63 in Florence, SC
ML Seasons: 2

Overall Statistics

	G	AB	R	H	D	T	HR	RBI	SB	BB	SO	AVG
1990	49	143	16	44	6	1	1	5	0	13	19	.308
Career	135	366	43	95	12	2	1	22	1	30	61	.260

HITTING, FIELDING, BASERUNNING:

Kent Anderson enjoyed a very successful 1990, even though his utility role diminished due to injury. While batting only 143 times, Anderson hit a surprising .308, a career high for his professional career. No slugger, Anderson is a slap hitter who will take whatever the pitcher gives him and go with it. Since he's hit higher than .251 only one other time in his career -- and that was in Class A ball -- Anderson isn't being counted on to hit .300 again. Though he looked much better in 1990, he still can be overmatched by hard throwers, particularly when they work the ball inside. Anderson normally has decent bat control and is among the Angels' best bunters.

Anderson is primarily a shortstop, but can play any infield position which he is asked to play. He made nine errors in limited defensive time last year, and is very suspect in the field. His range and mobility are far below average. He is not a baserunning threat either, with a professional high of 10 stolen bases in AAA Edmonton and questionable speed.

OVERALL:

At age 27, 1991 could be Anderson's make or break season in the majors. What may determine his future is his ability to put the ball in play; his minor league figures suggest that he has occasional problems doing so. Nevertheless, it is safe to say that if he continues to hit the way he did in 1991, someone will find a place on their roster for him.

PETE COACHMAN

Position: 3B
Bats: R **Throws:** R
Ht: 5' 9" **Wt:** 175

Opening Day Age: 29
Born: 11/11/61 in Cottonwood, AL
ML Seasons: 1

Overall Statistics

	G	AB	R	H	D	T	HR	RBI	SB	BB	SO	AVG
1990	16	45	3	14	3	0	0	5	0	1	7	.311
Career	16	45	3	14	3	0	0	5	0	1	7	.311

HITTING, FIELDING, BASERUNNING:

Pete Coachman is a 29-year old career minor-leaguer who seized his first opportunity in the big leagues by hitting .311 in sixteen games. Coachman made a strong attempt to prove to the Angels that he belongs in their uniform. He was recalled on August 17th and delivered immediately -- his first four starts were multiple hit games. Although that performance obviously came as a pleasant surprise to the Halos, they shouldn't have been too surprised. Coachman has hit at every level at which he has played. In 1986 at AA Midland, Coachman batted .349 in 249 at bats and even popped five home runs. Generally speaking, however, he has very little home run power.

Coachman stole 69 bases at single-A in 1985. He remains a very fast baserunner, although his stolen base totals have decreased at each level of professional baseball. He was used by the Angels as a pinch runner late in the season. At third base Coachman looked to have decent reactions in both directions.

OVERALL:

To have a chance to play much in 1991, Coachman will have to put on a hitting display in the spring. Given his consistently solid minor league statistics and the Angels' uncertainty at third base, it remains a possibility.

MIKE FETTERS

Position: RP
Bats: R **Throws:** R
Ht: 6' 4" **Wt:** 200

Opening Day Age: 26
Born: 12/19/64 in Van Nuys, CA
ML Seasons: 2

Overall Statistics

	W	L	ERA	G	GS	Sv	IP	H	R	BB	SO	HR
1990	1	1	4.12	26	2	1	67.2	77	33	20	35	9
Career	1	1	4.31	27	2	1	71.0	82	37	21	39	10

PITCHING, FIELDING & HOLDING RUNNERS:

A heralded prospect who was a first round selection in 1986, Mike Fetters has already sampled a bit of the good life: he was born in southern California, moved to Hawaii (where he currently lives) and then trekked off to college at Pepperdine on Malibu Beach. Fetters finally reached the majors last year, appearing in 26 games. The results were mixed. Fetters had a decent ERA and showed much better control than he'd demonstrated in the minors, but he allowed a lot of hits and was very prone to the home run ball. Though Fetters led the PCL in strikeouts in 1989, he didn't show much ability to punch out major league hitters. Another negative sign was that lefthanders hit Fetters very hard (.328 average with seven home runs allowed in 128 at bats). Doug Rader liked using Fetters in long stints, but he might be more effective facing a couple of batters and giving way. Fetters has had a problem holding runners on base. He also threw a lot of wild pitches in the minors and continued to have that problem last season with California.

OVERALL:

Fetters was called up in May and remained on the roster for the rest of the season. His career is right on track after spending a year at each minor league level. His work last year was hardly sensational, but the Angels appear to think enough of him to give him a chance.

JOE GRAHE

Position: SP
Bats: R **Throws:** R
Ht: 6' 0" **Wt:** 195

Opening Day Age: 23
Born: 8/14/67 in West Palm Beach, FL
ML Seasons: 1

Overall Statistics

	W	L	ERA	G	GS	Sv	IP	H	R	BB	SO	HR
1990	3	4	4.98	8	8	0	43.1	51	30	23	25	3
Career	3	4	4.98	8	8	0	43.1	51	30	23	25	3

PITCHING, FIELDING & HOLDING RUNNERS:

At 23, Joe Grahe is on the fast track to major league success. Just one year removed from the University of Miami, Grahe made the sixth most starts on the Angels (eight) after being called up in August. Chosen in the second round of the 1989 draft, Grahe had a stellar final collegiate year, finishing third in the NCAA in strikeouts with 195 in 173 innings, while giving up just 124 hits.

With California, the hard-throwing righthander had some trouble getting the ball over the plate. He walked 23 men in 43 innings and managed to plunk three batters in the process. Grahe pitched impressively against the Athletics on two occasions, including an 8.1 inning, three-hit shutout performance which turned the heads of many Angels' fans. Grahe was very tough on right-handed hitters, but lefties pounded him. Not many baserunners tried to steal off of Grahe in his short time with the Angels.

OVERALL:

Though he spent his collegiate career in the top level at the University of Miami, Grahe has barely half a year of minor league experience. The Angels got a good look at the youngster during the latter stages of the season, and he'll undoubtedly get another look in spring training. If he doesn't make the team at that point, look for Grahe to stay around awhile the next time he gets the chance.

BILL SCHROEDER

Position: C
Bats: R **Throws:** R
Ht: 6' 2" **Wt:** 200

Opening Day Age: 32
Born: 9/7/58 in Baltimore, MD
ML Seasons: 8

Overall Statistics

	G	AB	R	H	D	T	HR	RBI	SB	BB	SO	AVG
1990	18	58	7	13	3	0	4	9	0	1	10	.224
Career	376	1262	153	303	49	1	61	152	6	58	343	.240

HITTING, FIELDING, BASERUNNING:

While the Angels continue to field All-Star starting catchers, they remain unable to successfully fill the backup slot. Bill Schroeder had the job for most of the last two years, but hardly played in 1990 (18 games) and was released immediately after the season. After being acquired from Milwaukee following the 1988 season, Schroeder hit with some power, but for a very low average. Probably what sealed his doom was his amazingly bad strikeout to walk ratio. In two seasons, Schroeder had 54 strikeouts in 196 at bats while walking just four times. Schroeder's best asset has always been his strength -- he has tremendous power to left-center and right-center fields -- but with the Angels it was longball or nothing.

Slow on the bases, Schroeder has not attempted a steal since 1987, and is strictly a base-to-base guy. His defense is more than acceptable at the major league level. Despite several operations on his throwing elbow, Schroeder has an above average arm and very good instincts behind the plate.

OVERALL:

Despite his release by the Angels, it is extremely likely that Schroeder will end up with somebody by the time spring training rolls around. Quality backup catchers are hard to come by, and Schroeder has hit fairly well in the past. He has hit lefthanders well over his career and could end up as part of a backup platoon.

MAX VENABLE

Position: CF/LF
Bats: L **Throws:** R
Ht: 5'10" **Wt:** 185

Opening Day Age: 33
Born: 6/6/57 in Phoenix, AZ
ML Seasons: 11

Overall Statistics

	G	AB	R	H	D	T	HR	RBI	SB	BB	SO	AVG
1990	93	189	26	49	9	3	4	21	5	24	31	.259
Career	645	1210	152	291	49	15	15	107	62	109	188	.240

HITTING, FIELDING, BASERUNNING:

For only the third time in his fifteen year professional career, Max Venable spent the entire season on a major league roster. While Venable performed capably for the Angels in 1990, he came nowhere close to his '89 season, when he batted .358 in 20 games. Nonetheless Venable's role increased in 1990, and he showed some signs of sticking around at the major league level. Used strictly as a platoon player for the last two seasons, Venable showed unexpected power last year. He popped four home runs, the second highest total of his career, and tied for second on the Angels with three triples. He also set a career high in walks with 24.

In the field, Venable's arm is questionable and he gets a poor jump on the ball. He covers some of his mistakes with above-average speed, but his fielding, overall, is below average. Venable's career stolen base rate is around 80%, although he has never stolen more than 15 bases in a major league season. He is capable of more than that, given the chance.

OVERALL:

One of several backup players on the Angels whose future may hinge on expansion, Venable's role on the team is in doubt because of an abundance of outfielders. Doug Rader seems to like Venable, though, and he will certainly contend for a spare outfield slot in 1991.

PHIL BRADLEY

Position: LF/CF
Bats: R **Throws:** R
Ht: 6' 0" **Wt:** 185

Opening Day Age: 32
Born: 3/11/59 in Bloomington, IN
ML Seasons: 8

HITTING:

Phil Bradley struggled in 1990 with a wrist injury that hampered his swing and finally landed him on the disabled list. He was acquired from the Orioles for Ron Kittle and Dave Gallagher in late July, a trade prompted by Bradley's rebuff at what he felt was an insulting contract offer from the Orioles. The White Sox were hoping that Bradley, a talented athlete, would be able to be a full-time fill-in player, plugging various offensive and defensive holes while giving the White Sox regulars much needed rest.

Throughout his career, Bradley has been an excellent breaking ball hitter, and has a knack for driving the inside fastball through the right side for base hits. However, his bad wrist slowed his bat speed and reduced his strength. The results were the lowest batting average (.256) and slugging percentage (.327) of his career. The White Sox, in need of a consistent leadoff hitter, liked the idea of having the patient Bradley (50 walks in 422 at-bats) at the top spot in the order. For the season, his on-base percentage in the number one spot in the order was a solid .353.

Bradley stands close to the plate and is one of those rare hitters for whom the hit by pitch is a legitimate offensive weapon. He was plunked 11 times last year. He's a very good bunter, and laid down 11 sacrifice hits during the year. When healthy, Bradley has good bat control, and his inside-out swing makes him an ideal hit-and-run man.

BASERUNNING:

Bradley hasn't lost much of his speed, and he can still run the bases well. He stole 17 bases in 24 attempts, a typical success rate for him. Bradley is an excellent baserunner, and can calculate the odds of making the extra base as soon as the ball is hit. He'll rarely, if ever, run his team out of an inning.

FIELDING:

Bradley has established himself as one of the finest defensive left fielders in the game, and has good instincts on defense in general. Bradley never looks like he's moving fast, but he can close an outfield gap or run under a long fly ball in a hurry. Bradley has a decent, accurate throwing arm which is best suited for left field.

OVERALL:

Bradley was a free agent at season's end, and it was quite possible the White Sox would not be willing to pay him what he wanted. He would be an ideal bench player for the White Sox, but Bradley might well prefer to play with a team that would give him more of a chance to play regularly.

Overall Statistics

	G	AB	R	H	D	T	HR	RBI	SB	BB	SO	AVG
1990	117	422	59	108	14	2	4	31	17	50	61	.256
Career	1022	3695	565	1058	179	43	78	376	155	432	718	.286

Where He Hits the Ball

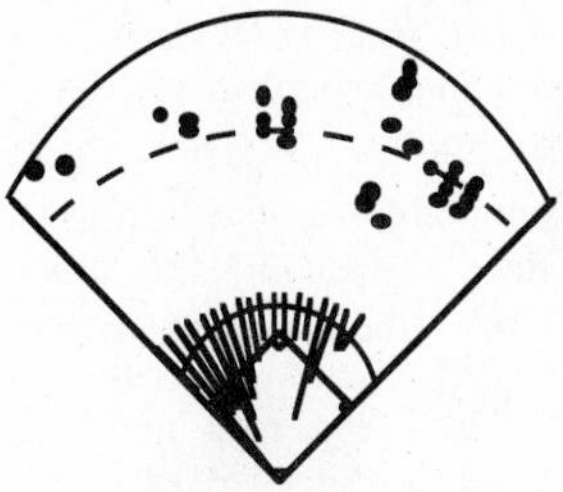

Vs. LHP

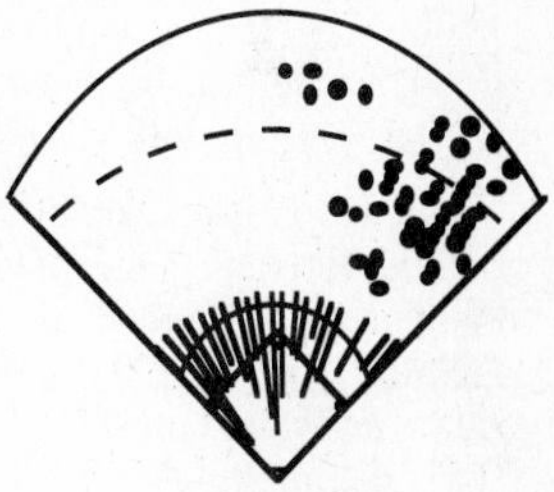

Vs. RHP

1990 Situational Stats

	AB	H	HR	RBI	AVG		AB	H	HR	RBI	AVG
Home	190	45	4	16	.237	LHP	161	38	2	9	.236
Road	232	63	0	15	.272	RHP	261	70	2	22	.268
Day	121	33	0	7	.273	Sc Pos	76	20	2	27	.263
Night	301	75	4	24	.249	Clutch	68	21	1	14	.309

1990 Rankings (American League)

- 1st in hit by pitch (11)
- 9th in sacrifice bunts (11) and batting average on an 0-2 count (.273)
- Led AL left fielders in hit by pitch, sacrifice bunts and batting average on a 3-1 count (.545)

HITTING:

Ivan Calderon lost both his arbitration case and fifteen pounds over the winter of 1989. His losses were the White Sox' gain: through hard work, aggressive play, and natural ability, Calderon posted career highs in stolen bases (32) and doubles (44), while becoming one of the American League's best left fielders.

In an organization indoctrinated into the Walt Hriniak Church of Hitting -- "Keep thine Head down, release top hand at the end of thy swing (Walt 1:1)" -- Calderon is a heretic. When he's going well, Calderon is able to use his strong arms and big swing to produce a lot of hard line drives distributed from left to right center field. His swing, though, can make him look awful when he doesn't make contact. Calderon's an excellent fastball hitter, and can drive the curve or offspeed pitch if the pitcher gets it a little too close to the plate. His weaknesses are the letter-high heater, which he'll chase, and offspeed pitches: his swing doesn't give him much of a chance when the pitcher crosses him up with a breaking pitch.

The old Comiskey Park cut down on Calderon's long ball output, but he accepted the parks dimensions, and banged out 44 doubles instead. No one knows yet how the new Comiskey will affect hitters, but Calderon is smart and adaptable, and figures to make the necessary adjustments.

BASERUNNING:

Lighter by fifteen pounds, Calderon's new-found aggressiveness was readily apparent on the bases. He stole more bases, 32, than he had in six previous major league seasons combined (29). Calderon is not slow -- he has above average speed -- but he has to be the slowest man ever to steal 32 bases. On the bases, Calderon is extremely aggressive, often challenging fielders, but he doesn't run into many outs.

FIELDING:

Out of place in right, Calderon became a very good left fielder despite making seven errors. The image of him belly-flopping in left-center field to make a game-saving catch was not only a favorite White Sox highlight, but indicative of Calderon's all-out style of play. His arm, more accurate than strong, is an excellent match for a left fielder.

OVERALL:

While his salary loss may prove only temporary, Calderon and the White Sox are hoping that the gains in his performance will be permanent. Aggressive at the plate, on the bases, and in the field, Calderon has been, arguably, the White Sox best player over the last two seasons. The Sox will need him to remain at this level of play if they have any hope of catching the A's.

IVAN CALDERON

Position: LF/DH
Bats: R **Throws:** R
Ht: 6' 1" **Wt:** 221

Opening Day Age: 29
Born: 3/19/62 in Fajardo, Puerto Rico
ML Seasons: 7

Overall Statistics

	G	AB	R	H	D	T	HR	RBI	SB	BB	SO	AVG
1990	158	607	85	166	44	2	14	74	32	51	79	.273
Career	660	2433	356	665	154	18	81	323	61	218	437	.273

Where He Hits the Ball

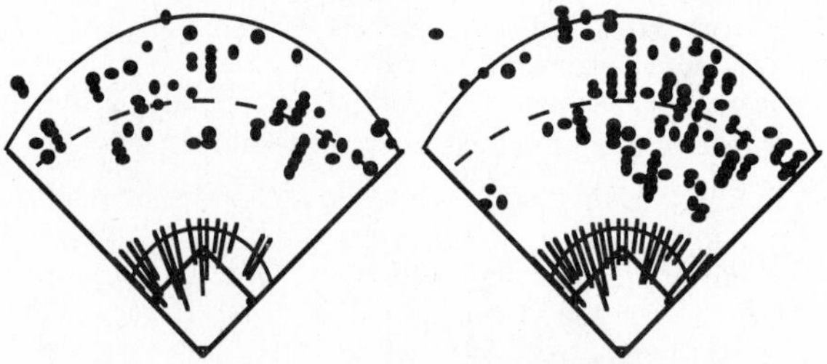

Vs. LHP Vs. RHP

1990 Situational Stats

	AB	H	HR	RBI	AVG		AB	H	HR	RBI	AVG
Home	284	87	6	40	.306	LHP	227	67	6	27	.295
Road	323	79	8	34	.245	RHP	380	99	8	47	.261
Day	154	41	2	15	.266	Sc Pos	131	43	8	60	.328
Night	453	125	12	59	.276	Clutch	88	19	1	6	.216

1990 Rankings (American League)

- 3rd in doubles (44)
- 4th in caught stealing (16)
- 5th in most GDPs per GDP situation (20.2%)
- 7th in stolen bases (32)
- Led the White Sox in at-bats (607), runs (85), hits (166), doubles, total bases (256), RBI (74), sacrifice flies (8), times on base (218), GDPs (26), pitches seen (2,201), plate appearances (667), stolen base success percentage (66.7%), slugging percentage vs. right-handed pitchers (.389) and batting average at home (.306)
- Led AL left fielders in doubles, caught stealing, GDPs, batting average with runners in scoring position (.328) and errors (7)

PITCHING:

Alex Fernandez has the chance to be the White Sox' ace pitcher for 1991 -- and years to come. Just 20 years old when called up last August, Fernandez impressed everyone with his maturity, poise, and repertoire. He gave the White Sox a chance to win in nearly every one of his starts, registering 10 quality starts in his 13 outings. In that sense, his final record, 5-5 with a 3.80 ERA, doesn't reflect how well he pitched. Fernandez got roughed up a bit in August, but compiled a 3.06 ERA in September and October.

Fernandez has great confidence in his 90 MPH fastball, which he tries to throw alternately high in the strike zone and on the inside part of the plate (he hit three batters in only 87.2 innings). Fernandez also surprises hitters with his curveball, which he'll throw at any time in the count. Unlike many rookie pitchers, Fernandez felt no compulsion to serve the opposition pastries when he found himself behind in the count.

Comparisons between Fernandez and Tom Seaver have become commonplace. He and Seaver are alike in build, and Fernandez' pitching motion, while not as dramatic as Seaver's, is similar in delivery and follow through. Like Seaver in most seasons, Fernandez was a workhorse in 1990, pitching 120 innings at college, 50 innings in the minors, and 90 more at Chicago. There's concern that he was overworked last year, but (also like Seaver) Fernandez derives a lot of power from his legs rather than his shoulder and arm, and that should save wear and tear on his arm. Fernandez got better as the game went on, as well. Opponents batted .305 through his first 75 pitches, but only .198 afterwards.

HOLDING BASERUNNERS AND FIELDING:

Fernandez did not acquit himself well in the field last year, despite a pitching motion which placed him in a good position to become the fifth infielder. He made two errors in his 17 chances. He played it safe when fielding the ball, taking the sure out when an alternate choice presented itself. Fernandez keeps a close watch on the baserunners, and has a very good move to first. Opponents stole only one base in five attempts against him.

OVERALL:

The White Sox are counting on the young Fernandez, hoping that he'll step in and fill the "ace pitcher" void. He has the poise and stamina to be a complete game pitcher, and it appears that hitting Fernandez early in the game might be the only way to beat him. Fernandez looks like the year-in, year-out big winner the White Sox have not had since the early 1970s.

ALEX FERNANDEZ

Position: SP
Bats: R **Throws:** R
Ht: 6' 0" **Wt:** 190

Opening Day Age: 21
Born: 1/1/70 in Miami Beach, FL
ML Seasons: 1

Overall Statistics

	W	L	ERA	G	GS	Sv	IP	H	R	BB	SO	HR
1990	5	5	3.80	13	13	0	87.2	89	40	34	61	6
Career	5	5	3.80	13	13	0	87.2	89	40	34	61	6

How Often He Throws Strikes

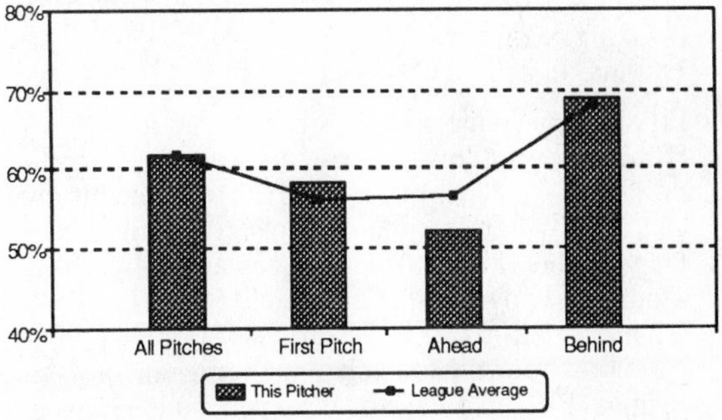

1990 Situational Stats

	W	L	ERA	Sv	IP		AB	H	HR	RBI	AVG
Home	2	1	3.67	0	27.0	LHB	176	48	3	12	.273
Road	3	4	3.86	0	60.2	RHB	160	41	3	21	.256
Day	1	2	1.50	0	24.0	Sc Pos	70	21	1	26	.300
Night	4	3	4.66	0	63.2	Clutch	27	3	0	1	.111

1990 Rankings (American League)

- Did not rank near the top or bottom in any category

HALL OF FAMER

CARLTON FISK

Position: C/DH
Bats: R **Throws:** R
Ht: 6' 2" **Wt:** 225

Opening Day Age: 43
Born: 12/26/47 in Bellows Falls, VT
ML Seasons: 21

Overall Statistics

	G	AB	R	H	D	T	HR	RBI	SB	BB	SO	AVG
1990	137	452	65	129	21	0	18	65	7	61	73	.285
Career	2278	8055	1220	2192	392	46	354	1231	124	792	1251	.272

Where He Hits the Ball

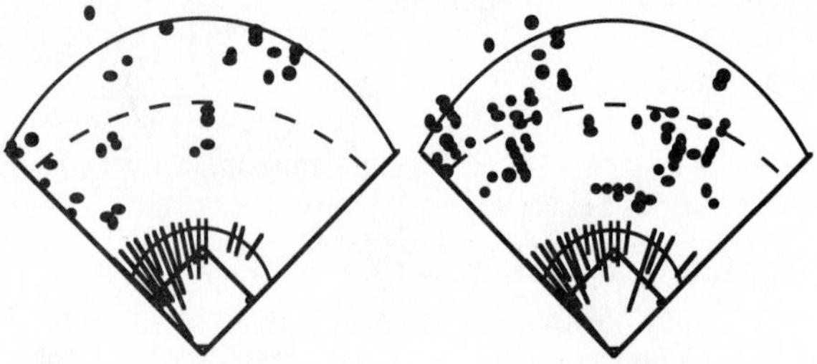

Vs. LHP Vs. RHP

1990 Situational Stats

	AB	H	HR	RBI	AVG		AB	H	HR	RBI	AVG
Home	219	63	5	37	.288	LHP	165	52	9	30	.315
Road	233	66	13	28	.283	RHP	287	77	9	35	.268
Day	79	21	2	3	.266	Sc Pos	131	29	3	47	.221
Night	373	108	16	62	.290	Clutch	70	16	3	12	.229

1990 Rankings (American League)

- 4th in hit by pitch (7)
- 8th in on-base average (.378)
- Led the White Sox in batting average (.285), home runs (18), walks (61), intentional walks (8), hit by pitch, slugging percentage (.451), on-base average (.378), HR frequency (25.1 ABs per HR), on-base average vs. left-handed pitchers (.397) and batting average on the road (.283)
- Led AL catchers in intentional walks, hit by pitch, slugging percentage and on-base average

HITTING:

Healthy all season for the first time since 1987, Carlton Fisk turned in the best all-around season of any catcher in the major leagues last year. While he was at it, he also set the new major league record for home runs by a catcher (332), surpassing Hall-of-Famer Johnny Bench's mark of 327.

Fisk batted .285, his highest full-season average since 1983. Though his slugging percentage was slightly below his career mark of .464, he drew 61 bases on balls, only the third time in his career he had drawn sixty or more. His on-base percentage of .378, 34 points above his lifetime mark, placed him eighth in the American League.

The way to get Fisk out is to outguess him with breaking balls, because he can still hit the fastball a long way. He stands back in the box, with his weight on his back foot. This allows him to stay back on the breaking ball and the change-up, which he often parlays into line drive hits to left and center.

Fisk has even adopted some of the techniques of Walt Hriniak -- head down, release one hand at the end of the swing -- and has managed to fit them into his own batting stroke, rather than completely giving one up for the other. Hriniak's techniques are criticized for sapping the power out of hitters, but Fisk's 18 dingers are proof that it ain't necessarily so. Comiskey Park has more to do with holding down home run rates than Hriniak. Fisk hit 13 of his 18 homers on the road.

BASERUNNING:

Though "catcher" pretty much sums up Fisk's running speed, it doesn't do justice to his baserunning instincts. Fisk was only 4-for-12 base stealing from 1986-1989, but he was 7-for-9 in 1990. He's careful picking his spots to steal. On the bases, Fisk knows his limitations, but he can tell when the defense isn't alert. Then, he'll steal or take the extra base.

FIELDING:

Fisk is very deliberate in calling a game, and that drives some people crazy, but it's definitely helped settle down the White Sox young pitchers. The knowledge he brings to a young staff is invaluable. Fisk still is a decent catcher at throwing out baserunners, nabbing 42 of 113 (37%).

OVERALL:

Fisk's newest moniker, "The Commander," fits him as well as his old one, "Pudge." A commanding presence both on the field and in the clubhouse, Fisk is more than just a veteran there to provide clubhouse leadership. He still has the tools which make him an excellent major league ballplayer, both at the plate and behind it.

SCOTT FLETCHER

Position: 2B
Bats: R **Throws:** R
Ht: 5'11" **Wt:** 173

Opening Day Age: 32
Born: 7/30/58 in Fort Walton Beach, FL
ML Seasons: 10

Overall Statistics

	G	AB	R	H	D	T	HR	RBI	SB	BB	SO	AVG
1990	151	509	54	123	18	3	4	56	1	45	63	.242
Career	1148	3777	490	998	165	27	21	358	57	395	406	.264

Where He Hits the Ball

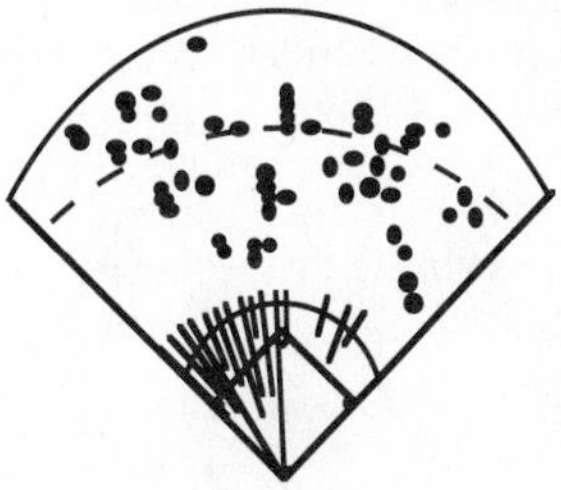

Vs. LHP

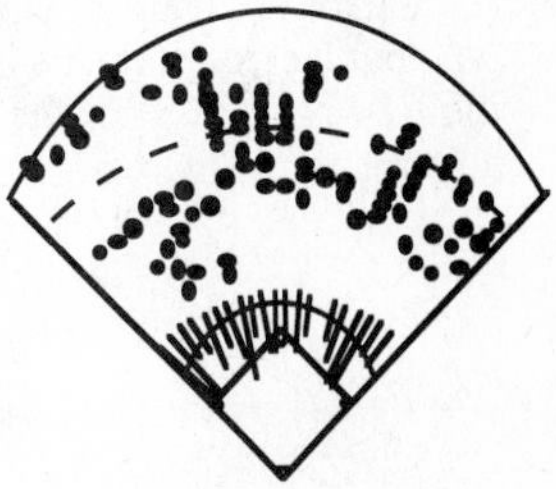

Vs. RHP

1990 Situational Stats

	AB	H	HR	RBI	AVG		AB	H	HR	RBI	AVG
Home	265	64	1	29	.242	LHP	173	49	1	13	.283
Road	244	59	3	27	.242	RHP	336	74	3	43	.220
Day	128	34	0	17	.266	Sc Pos	127	34	2	50	.268
Night	381	89	4	39	.234	Clutch	83	19	1	8	.229

1990 Rankings (American League)

- 1st in lowest slugging percentage (.312)
- 4th in bunts in play (29)
- 9th in worst batting average (.242), sacrifice bunts (11) and worst on-base average (.304)
- Led the White Sox in bunts in play

HITTING:

Scott Fletcher's seasonal batting averages form a very nice bell curve. Unfortunately, the apex of the Fletcher Curve was reached six years ago, and it's been on the downslope ever since. Since hitting .300 with the Rangers in 1986, Fletcher's batting averages have been .287, .276, .253, and, in 1990, .242.

Fletcher has been primarily a ground ball hitter, and he excelled in the number-two spot in the order for the White Sox in 1989. He can execute the bunt (11 sacrifice hits) and the hit-and-run, and take advantage of the moving baserunners to find holes in the infield. He hit the ball in the air quite a bit more last season, resulting in more home runs (four) than in the previous two seasons combined (one), but also a lot more easy fly outs.

Fletcher continued to be aggressive at the plate, but the results weren't as good. He was overwhelmed by the fastball, and chased a lot of them high in the strike zone. His bases on balls dropped all the way down to 45 last year, and he registered the second highest strikeout total of his career (63). White Sox infield offensive production was weak in 1990, and Fletcher needs to contribute more than 25 extra base hits to the cause.

BASERUNNING:

Fletcher has average speed, but is smart when he does get on base. The White Sox will occasionally hit-and-run with Fletcher on first and Ozzie Guillen up, taking advantage of the hole on the right side, but Fletcher is not a base stealer. In a career filled with bell curves, Fletcher's stolen bases reached a peak in 1987 with 13, and have been dropping ever since: eight to two and then hitting bottom last year with one.

FIELDING:

Fletcher was moved from shortstop to second base upon his return from the Rangers in 1989 and became paired with Ozzie Guillen. It has been a wonderful marriage. Fletcher's arm wasn't very good for a shortstop, but it's more than adequate at second. With excellent range, soft hands and the ability to hang in at second on the pivot, Fletcher also led all American League second basemen in double plays with 115.

OVERALL:

Despite his offensive drop, Fletcher will be the starting second baseman for the White Sox in 1990. His other offensive skills -- putting the ball in play, moving runners, executing the bunt and hit-and-run -- are valuable enough to keep him in the lineup. His defensive skills, which are considerable, combined with his hustling style and scrappy attitude, are a plus for the White Sox.

OZZIE GUILLEN

Position: SS
Bats: L **Throws:** R
Ht: 5'11" **Wt:** 153

Opening Day Age: 27
Born: 1/20/64 in Ocumare del Tuy, Venezuela
ML Seasons: 6

Overall Statistics

	G	AB	R	H	D	T	HR	RBI	SB	BB	SO	AVG
1990	160	516	61	144	21	4	1	58	13	26	37	.279
Career	929	3277	375	870	119	39	7	282	114	112	265	.265

Where He Hits the Ball

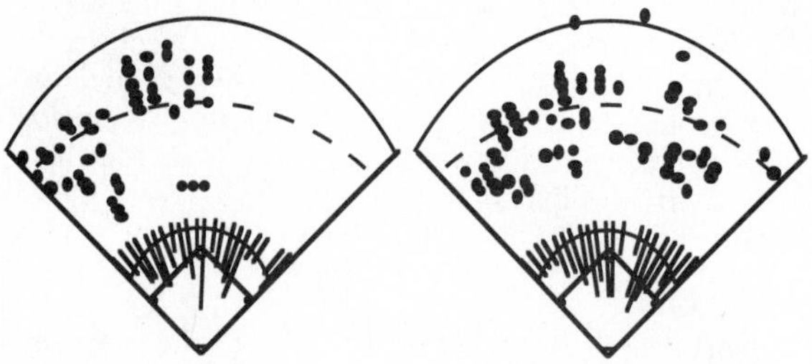

Vs. LHP Vs. RHP

1990 Situational Stats

	AB	H	HR	RBI	AVG		AB	H	HR	RBI	AVG
Home	247	69	1	25	.279	LHP	206	55	0	28	.267
Road	269	75	0	33	.279	RHP	310	89	1	30	.287
Day	131	37	0	20	.282	Sc Pos	133	44	0	56	.331
Night	385	107	1	38	.278	Clutch	90	27	0	14	.300

1990 Rankings (American League)

- 1st in lowest percentage of pitches taken (40.0%), lowest stolen base success percentage (43.3%) and fewest pitches seen per plate appearance (2.85)
- 2nd in caught stealing (17) and lowest HR frequency (516 ABs per HR)
- Led the White Sox in sacrifice bunts (15), intentional walks (8), games (160), batting average in the clutch (.300) and batting average with the bases loaded (.500)
- Led AL shortstops in sacrifice bunts, caught stealing, runs scored per time reached base (35.7%), bunts in play (27) and lowest percentage of swings that missed (10.2%)

HITTING:

Ozzie Guillen was hitting .351 on June 1, but the heights were a bit too much for him. Guillen returned to earth, batting .250 the rest of the way, and had to settle for the highest batting average of his career (.279), rather than of the American League.

Guillen hunches in the batter's box, and his bat, hands, and feet all have the tendency to fidget before the pitcher begins his delivery. When the ball arrives, Guillen will tighten up and look for a pitch he can drive to the left side of the diamond. Guillen is best when he's hitting the ball that way, or up the middle and on the ground. Outfielders should play him in and around to the left, where they'll catch more shallow fly balls and sinking line drives playing close. Guillen won't hit many over their heads.

While Guillen had his best year at the plate, he has more than his share of weaknesses. Lack of power is one, but lack of patience is another. Guillen swung at the first pitch 50% of the time, the highest figure of any regular American League player. Although he drew a career high 26 walks, eight of them were intentional. While Guillen was able to hit the fastball, breaking pitches gave him trouble, especially from lefthanders.

BASERUNNING:

After posting a career high 36 stolen bases in 1989, Guillen managed just barely one-third that amount in 1990 (13). Worse, he was caught 17 times for a dismal 43% success rate. Bad jumps and slow feet were the main culprits. Guillen is fine running the bases, rarely getting thrown out trying to stretch the point needlessly. However, Guillen will have to relearn how to steal bases or quit trying altogether if he's going to make effective use of his speed.

FIELDING:

In an age of great shortstop play, Ozzie Guillen may be the best. He will have lapses, as 17 errors attests, but if the ball is hit anywhere to the left of second base, there's always the chance that Guillen can get it. He turned 100 double plays, many unassisted, many spectacular.

OVERALL:

Guillen, with his infectious personality and irreverent sense of humor, was made co-captain with veteran Carlton Fisk last year, and a more curious pair can't be found in all of baseball. It shows how much respect Guillen, only 27, has acquired among White Sox players, management, and fans. Guillen will be the starting shortstop on the next White Sox team to win the AL West.

GREG HIBBARD

Position: SP
Bats: L **Throws:** L
Ht: 6' 0" **Wt:** 180

Opening Day Age: 26
Born: 9/13/64 in New Orleans, LA
ML Seasons: 2

PITCHING:

Greg Hibbard was the most consistent starting pitcher on the White Sox in 1990. While others may have been better for shorter bursts of time, Hibbard gave the club a chance to win more often. His final record, 14-9, could have been better had he received a few more runs (the White Sox scored three runs or less in 23 of Hibbard's 33 starts) or not been victimized by his bullpen, which lost three leads while Hibbard was on the bench.

A finesse hurler, Hibbard is a curveball and change-up pitcher who can pop a fastball by a hitter if the situation calls for it. Like former Orioles lefthander Scott McGregor, his soft deliveries belie an intense, competitive nature. Keeping hitters off-stride is Hibbard's game plan, and when it's working, he makes pitching look effortless.

While he's no fire-baller, Hibbard's motion allows him to get some smoke on his fastball when he needs it. His fastball isn't quite good enough to rely on for an entire game, though. His key pitches are the change-up, which gets the lefthanders out in front, and a back-door curve, which floats on the outer edges of the plate to righthanders. He has yet to allow a home run to a left-handed batter in his carrer, and held them to a .209 batting average and a meager .275 slugging percentage in 1990.

Hibbard gets into trouble when his offspeed stuff isn't working and his curve breaks back over the plate a little too much. Another side-effect is that Hibbard will start missing with the pitch, resulting in more walks than usual. He's usually a master of control, and early bases on balls are a sign that Hibbard isn't in top form for the evening.

HOLDING RUNNERS AND FIELDING:

Because his game features a lot of ground balls, it's a plus that Hibbard fields his position well. His quick reflexes help him on balls hit back through the box, and he's better than average on bunts as well. Hibbard's move to first could be a little better. But while he doesn't pick off many runners, he keeps runners close. Baserunners were 11 of 19 (58%) in 1990, almost identical to their 9 of 15 (60%) mark in '89.

OVERALL:

Hibbard was a little-publicized part of the 1987 deal which brought him, Melido Perez and two other hurlers from Kansas City. At 26, he's established himself not only as a solid member of the White Sox staff, but as one of the best left-handed starters in the American League. With better support, Hibbard could easily move up to the 15-18 victory level.

Overall Statistics

	W	L	ERA	G	GS	Sv	IP	H	R	BB	SO	HR
1990	14	9	3.16	33	33	0	211.0	202	80	55	92	11
Career	20	16	3.18	56	56	0	348.1	344	138	96	147	16

How Often He Throws Strikes

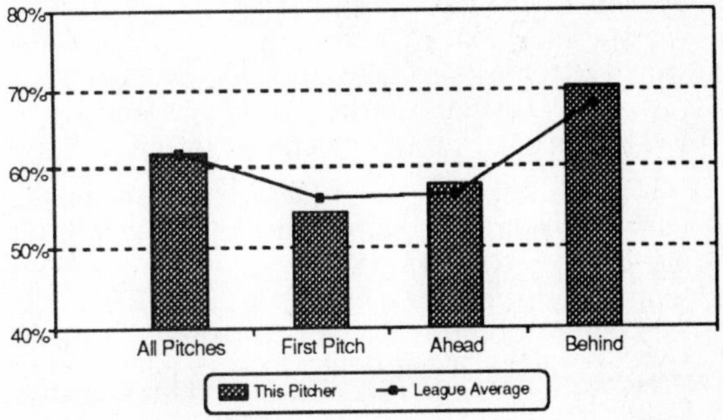

1990 Situational Stats

	W	L	ERA	Sv	IP		AB	H	HR	RBI	AVG
Home	8	5	2.98	0	120.2	LHB	91	19	0	7	.209
Road	6	4	3.39	0	90.1	RHB	701	183	11	59	.261
Day	2	2	2.74	0	46.0	Sc Pos	147	37	0	48	.252
Night	12	7	3.27	0	165.0	Clutch	88	21	1	3	.239

1990 Rankings (American League)

- 3rd in GDPs induced (25), lowest run support per 9 innings (3.75) and least HRs per 9 innings (.47)
- 4th in most GDPs induced per 9 innings (1.07)
- 5th in least strikeouts per 9 innings (3.9)
- Led the White Sox in ERA (3.16), wins (14), innings (211.0), hits allowed (202), batters faced (871), GDPs induced, lowest slugging percentage allowed (.355), lowest on-base average allowed (.305), groundball/flyball ratio (1.49), least baserunners allowed per 9 innings (11.2), least HRs allowed per 9 innings (.47), most GDPs induced per 9 innings

LANCE JOHNSON

Position: CF
Bats: L **Throws:** L
Ht: 5'11" **Wt:** 155

Opening Day Age: 27
Born: 7/7/63 in Lincoln Heights, OH
ML Seasons: 4

Overall Statistics

	G	AB	R	H	D	T	HR	RBI	SB	BB	SO	AVG
1990	151	541	76	154	18	9	1	51	36	33	45	.285
Career	267	904	119	244	32	13	1	80	64	60	86	.270

Where He Hits the Ball

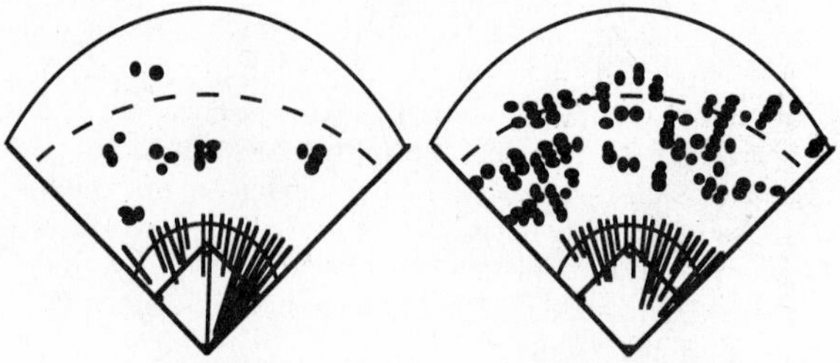

Vs. LHP Vs. RHP

HITTING:

Last year the White Sox finally gave speedy, free-swinging Lance Johnson a chance to play full time. Johnson was everything the White Sox could have hoped for -- except a leadoff man.

Early in the season, Johnson alternated with Sammy Sosa in the leadoff spot. However, he wasn't able to utilize his great speed because he couldn't get on base. Johnson batted only .234 in the number one spot, and his .274 on-base percentage while batting first was the third worst among major league leadoff hitters. He was both more comfortable and more effective in the second spot, where he spent 205 at-bats and batted a lofty .337.

It appeared that Johnson was wearing down as the season warmed up in the summer. Playing every day for the first time may have been a factor in slowing down Johnson's bat, and his batting average dropped every month from May through August, his worst month of the season (.235). But just when everyone thought he was finished, Johnson turned around and had a great September-October, batting .359.

Despite his lack of patience, Johnson was a tough out in the clutch, and he contributed a lot of key RBI for the White Sox. His .345 average with runners in scoring position enabled him to top the 50 RBI mark. Johnson also surprised everyone by batting 51 points higher against lefthanders than righthanders, a 180 degree turn from his 1989 season.

BASERUNNING:

Not shy about using his speed, Johnson stole 36 bases, and was usually able to take the extra base when the situation allowed. But he was caught stealing 22 times, and he was barely above 50% (12 for 22) with a lefthander pitching. This indicates that Johnson has a bit more to learn about the art of stealing bases.

FIELDING:

Johnson, who led American League center fielders in errors (10), lacks both the instincts and the arm to make him a great center fielder, but his quickness provides some compensation. Johnson made some breathtaking catches on balls hit in the alley and over his head, and his range fit well in the vast expanses of Comiskey Park. However, Johnson has a habit of making his first step in rather than towards the ball, and some possible outs wound up as extra-base hits.

OVERALL:

The White Sox, out of necessity, may give Johnson another chance to bat leadoff this year, but his demonstrated inability to get on base from that position is one big reason to avoid it. If he keeps hitting like he did in 1990, however, he'll be a positive contributor.

1990 Situational Stats

	AB	H	HR	RBI	AVG		AB	H	HR	RBI	AVG
Home	265	80	0	25	.302	LHP	156	50	0	19	.321
Road	276	74	1	26	.268	RHP	385	104	1	32	.270
Day	141	42	0	17	.298	Sc Pos	116	40	1	49	.345
Night	400	112	1	34	.280	Clutch	85	23	0	8	.271

1990 Rankings (American League)

- 1st in caught stealing (22), lowest HR frequency (541 ABs per HR) and highest percentage of swings put into play (59.3%)
- 2nd lowest leadoff on-base percentage (.274) and least pitches seen per plate appearance (3.01)
- 3rd in triples (9) and batting average with runners in scoring position (.345)
- Led the White Sox in singles (126), stolen bases (36), caught stealing, groundball/flyball ratio (2.26), batting average with runners in scoring position, lowest percentage of swings that missed (9.8%), highest percentage of swings put into play and percentage of extra bases taken as a runner (57.7%)

PITCHING:

A healthy Barry Jones was a key to both the White Sox success and Bobby Thigpen's record 57 saves last year. Jones and the eighth inning were an inseparable pair throughout the season (42 of Jones' 74 innings were in the eighth), and his effectiveness earned him a major league leading 30 holds.

Jones missed the middle four months of the 1989 season due to an elbow injury, but he pitched well in April and September of that year, just as he had pitched effectively for the White Sox in 1988. In fact, Jones has recorded ERAs well under 3.00 in four of his five major league seasons, so his success last year should not have been a surprise. Jones's record last year (11-3), which earned him the nickname "Vulture," was mainly due to his role as set-up man for Thigpen, and to the fact that the White Sox always seemed to put on their hitting shoes whenever Jones took the mound. The record was not undeserved, as he allowed only 19 of 56 inherited runners to score.

While Jones has a Goose Gossage-type build, he doesn't rely on hard stuff to get batters out. He isn't flashy, mixing a good curveball in with a sinking fastball and change-up. Jones is much more effective against right-handed batters, who chased his low offerings to the tune of a .184 batting average. His weakness is lefthanders, who can often get a bead on his pitches and drive them. When his nibbling pitches are missing, and he has to come in to the lefthanders, he can be hit. Another consequence of Jones's style is bases on balls: he allowed 26 unintentional walks in 74 innings pitched.

HOLDING BASERUNNERS AND FIELDING:

Jones is a big, lumbering man, and he is not quick off the mound. He generally fields everything within arm's length and lets his infielders do the rest. He's slow, but sure: he handled 24 chances flawlessly during the season. A righthander, Jones is at a natural disadvantage at holding baserunners, but his move is strong and with the help of Ron Karkovice, baserunners were only three out of five against him.

OVERALL:

While lack of a blazing fastball has kept Jones from becoming a star closer, he is nonetheless a fine set-up man. An injury-free Jones was a big part of the success of the White Sox pitching staff last year, and at 28, he is in his prime. Used wisely, against mainly righthanders, Jones will continue to be an effective and valuable part of any bullpen.

BARRY JONES

Position: RP
Bats: R **Throws:** R
Ht: 6' 4" **Wt:** 225

Opening Day Age: 28
Born: 2/15/63 in Centerville, IN
ML Seasons: 5

Overall Statistics

	W	L	ERA	G	GS	Sv	IP	H	R	BB	SO	HR
1990	11	4	2.31	65	0	1	74.0	62	20	33	45	2
Career	22	17	3.10	204	0	9	267.1	240	110	123	167	19

How Often He Throws Strikes

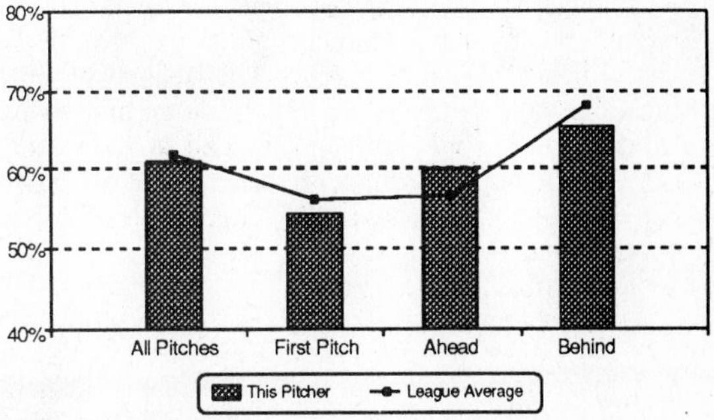

1990 Situational Stats

	W	L	ERA	Sv	IP		AB	H	HR	RBI	AVG
Home	8	1	2.18	0	45.1	LHB	112	34	2	19	.304
Road	3	3	2.51	1	28.2	RHB	152	28	0	14	.184
Day	2	0	1.59	1	22.2	Sc Pos	83	21	0	31	.253
Night	9	4	2.63	0	51.1	Clutch	227	54	0	30	.238

1990 Rankings (American League)

- 1st in holds (30)
- 5th in winning percentage (.733)
- 7th in blown saves (7)
- 10th in games pitched (65)

RON KARKOVICE

Position: C
Bats: R **Throws:** R
Ht: 6' 1" **Wt:** 215

Opening Day Age: 27
Born: 8/8/63 in Union, NJ
ML Seasons: 5

HITTING:

Playing the role of backup catcher is not an easy task, but Ron Karkovice acquitted himself well in 1990, turning in his second solid offensive season in a row for the White Sox. Despite playing only 68 games in spots mainly to spell Carlton Fisk, Karkovice was able to keep his batting stroke steady.

Though he slumped late in the season (.162 in September/October), Karkovice doubled his 1989 home run output from three to six in the same number of at-bats, and also made double figures in two-baggers for first time in his career (10). He hit all of his home runs on the road, and has only three of his 15 career dingers at Comiskey, which lends more credence to the theory that Comiskey Park, not Hriniak, is most responsible for low home run totals by Sox players.

Karkovice is a good fastball hitter, but won't chase a lot rising fastballs. He is developing something of a batting eye, drawing a career high 16 bases on balls last year, six more than in 1989. His weakness is the breaking ball, which he will chase down and away from the strike zone. Lefthanders, who stayed on the outer edge of the plate with breaking stuff, gave Karkovice a lot of trouble in 1990. Karkovice is also a very good bunter, registering seven sacrifice hits and six bunt singles last year.

BASERUNNING:

Karkovice has above average speed . . . for a catcher. He stole two bases in his only two attempts last year, making him 10 out of 12 for his career. Karkovice is surprisingly adept at getting around the bases. He scored 30 runs in only 183 at-bats, and will take the extra base more than occasionally.

FIELDING:

Since 1987, Karkovice has thrown out 67 of 131 baserunners, and he was 18 out of 36 in 1990. He is aggressive on defense, and his powerful arm enables him to turn more than a few bunts and slow choppers into outs. Also, let the record show that the White Sox ERA was 3.40 when Karkovice was catching and the team was 34-16 when he started. Karkovice has taken advantage of both the White Sox' intense game preparation regimen and Carlton Fisk's knowledge to improve himself as a handler of pitchers.

OVERALL:

There were never any questions about Karkovice's defense, and another solid year at the plate has gone a long way towards allaying the fears which arose following his 1987 and 1988 seasons when he hit .071 and .174, respectively. He's ready to be a regular, but there's only one problem: Carlton Fisk is planning to play forever.

Overall Statistics

	G	AB	R	H	D	T	HR	RBI	SB	BB	SO	AVG
1990	68	183	30	45	10	0	6	20	2	16	52	.246
Career	261	662	81	143	30	2	18	73	10	49	215	.216

Where He Hits the Ball

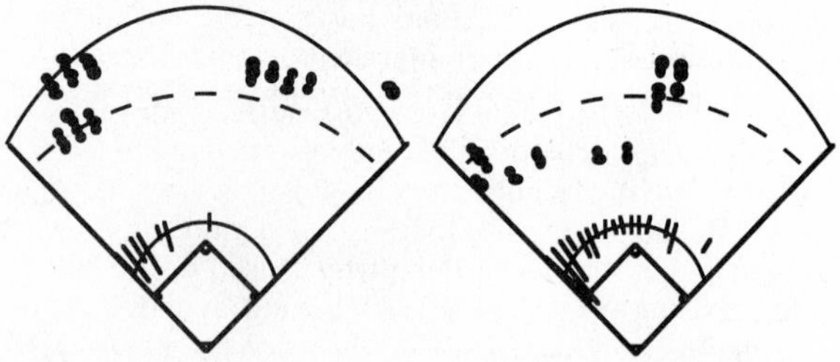

1990 Situational Stats

	AB	H	HR	RBI	AVG		AB	H	HR	RBI	AVG
Home	83	18	0	6	.217	LHP	64	14	2	9	.219
Road	100	27	6	14	.270	RHP	119	31	4	11	.261
Day	84	24	4	12	.286	Sc Pos	44	10	1	15	.227
Night	99	21	2	8	.212	Clutch	35	15	1	2	.429

1990 Rankings (American League)

- 1st in lowest batting average on a 3-2 count (.063)
- Led AL catchers in bunts in play (19)

PITCHING:

Eric King possesses one of the most valuable arms on the White Sox pitching staff, but also the most fragile one. King missed a portion of the 1989 season with a sore right shoulder, and in order to keep him healthy for the entire 1990 season, Manager Jeff Torborg devised a pitching rotation giving him as many days rest between starts as possible. King wound up pitching nine times on four days rest, seven times on five days rest, and nine times on six or more days rest. In addition, Torborg kept a close eye on King's pitch totals. He threw more than 100 pitches in only six of his 25 starts. Unfortunately, not even the extra rest was able to keep King off the disabled list. Following a fast 8-1 start, King began to lose something off his pitches. His ERA soared in July, and soon after King was back on the DL.

When King is going well, he'll use his two fastballs and a hard curve in tandem to keep hitters guessing. One fastball will run up and in on righthanders, while he'll try to throw the other down and away to lefthanders. One key to King's early effectiveness last year was his curveball, which he was getting over for strikes more often. While his hits and strikeouts per nine innings remained consistent, King walked 24 fewer batters than in 1989 in roughly the same number of innings. When his arm began to tire in late June, King lost both speed off his fastball and bite off his curve. The effects were not subtle. King was rocked in July (0-3, 6.97 ERA) and didn't return until September.

Opposition managers tried to stack their lineups with lefthanders against King, but this was not a good strategy. Facing nearly the same number of batters from each side of the plate, King held lefthanders to a .216 average, almost 40 points below that of righthanders.

HOLDING BASERUNNERS AND FIELDING:

King is a decent fielder, usually in good position at the end of his delivery. Despite being a righthander, he holds runners very well. He doesn't have a big motion, which gives his catchers at least a good chance at the baserunner.

OVERALL:

King has now had two good seasons in a row, but he's been injured in each one. Last year Jeff Torborg did everything he could to keep King healthy, and unless the White Sox go to an NFL schedule of one game per week, it's doubtful he can do much more. White Sox watchers should keep a close eye on King around the All-Star break for signs of weakening.

ERIC KING

Position: SP
Bats: R **Throws:** R
Ht: 6' 2" **Wt:** 180

Opening Day Age: 27
Born: 4/10/64 in Oxnard, CA
ML Seasons: 5

Overall Statistics

	W	L	ERA	G	GS	Sv	IP	H	R	BB	SO	HR
1990	12	4	3.28	25	25	0	151.0	135	59	40	70	10
Career	42	28	3.67	161	75	15	633.1	558	277	261	355	54

How Often He Throws Strikes

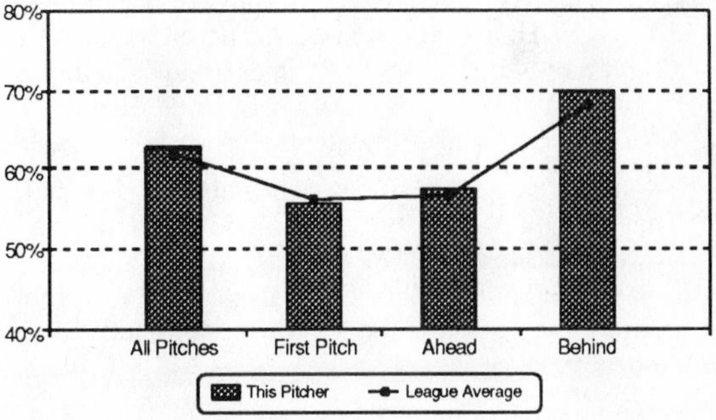

1990 Situational Stats

	W	L	ERA	Sv	IP		AB	H	HR	RBI	AVG
Home	5	3	3.93	0	75.2	LHB	268	58	5	27	.216
Road	7	1	2.63	0	75.1	RHB	302	77	5	27	.255
Day	3	1	4.99	0	39.2	Sc Pos	109	25	2	38	.229
Night	9	3	2.67	0	111.1	Clutch	26	5	1	5	.192

1990 Rankings (American League)

- 4th in winning percentage (.750)
- 6th in shutouts (2)
- Led the White Sox in winning percentage

HITTING:

After batting .300 in his rookie season of 1989, Carlos Martinez found himself limited to part-time duty last year. Martinez had personal problems in his native Venezuela, and lacked concentration in the early going. Never able to get in a groove, Martinez finished the disappointing campaign with a .224 average.

Martinez can hit the fastball, as he has shown in both his rookie year and during part of 1990. Following a dismal May, in which he hit .145, he began to rebound. Martinez batted .294 in June and .270 in July. But a .190 August pretty much relegated him to the bench for September, when he got only 12 at-bats.

Martinez is not a patient hitter, and the pressure to produce or be benched only compounded the problem. He drew an unintentional walk once every 34 at-bats, even worse than his poor 1989 ratio of 1 every 18 at-bats. He was down no balls and one strike after nearly half of his at-bats (130 times), and once behind in the count, Martinez was all but finished. He hit .115 with 2 strikes, well below the major league average.

Though he is 6'5", Martinez only weighs 175 pounds. That may explain why he hasn't hit for extra-base power. Martinez had 27 extra-base hits in 350 at-bats in 1989, and only 15 in 272 at-bats in 1990. A weight-training program to put on some extra pounds might be beneficial.

BASERUNNING:

Martinez is a big man but he has good speed. He's aggressive on the bases, and his big strides enabled him to leg out five triples. He once stole 24 bases in the minor leagues, and was five for six before the 1990 season. However, his abilities as a base stealer went south with his batting average; he was thrown out in all four of his attempts.

FIELDING:

Martinez was tried at a variety of positions his rookie year, but he played first base exclusively in 1990, with the exception of two innings in left field. He does not look comfortable at first base, however, and made eight errors there. On the whole, Martinez looks uncomfortable in his own body and it shows when he plays defense.

OVERALL:

The 1990 season was pretty much a lost one for Martinez, who bore up well under the pressure of personal problems and professional regression. His best positions are first base and left field, however, and he's not going to beat out Frank Thomas or Ivan Calderon. He may have to get used to being a part-time player again, unless the White Sox swing a deal.

CARLOS MARTINEZ

Position: 1B
Bats: R **Throws:** R
Ht: 6' 5" **Wt:** 175

Opening Day Age: 25
Born: 8/11/65 in La Guaira, Venezuela
ML Seasons: 3

Overall Statistics

	G	AB	R	H	D	T	HR	RBI	SB	BB	SO	AVG
1990	92	272	18	61	6	5	4	24	0	10	40	.224
Career	218	677	67	175	29	5	9	56	5	31	109	.258

Where He Hits the Ball

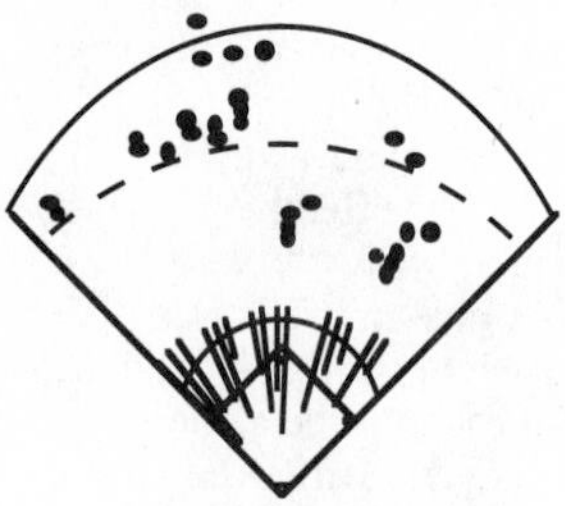

Vs. LHP

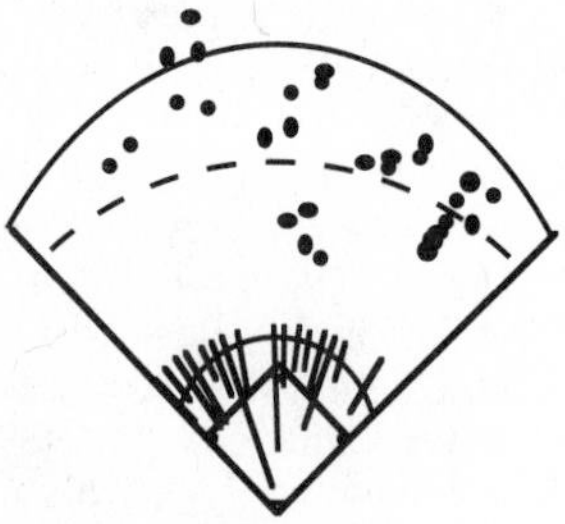

Vs. RHP

1990 Situational Stats

	AB	H	HR	RBI	AVG		AB	H	HR	RBI	AVG
Home	147	33	2	16	.224	LHP	140	31	2	7	.221
Road	125	28	2	8	.224	RHP	132	30	2	17	.227
Day	66	10	2	8	.152	Sc Pos	65	19	1	21	.292
Night	206	51	2	16	.248	Clutch	28	4	0	2	.143

1990 Rankings (American League)

- 3rd lowest on-base average vs. left-handed pitchers (.248)
- 4th lowest batting average with 2 strikes (.115)
- 6th lowest batting average on a 0-2 count (.038)
- Led AL first basemen in caught stealing (4)

PITCHING:

Jack McDowell, the White Sox' rock-and-roll righthander, returned to the big leagues in 1990 following a year-long stay in the minors. A former number-one pick out of Stanford, McDowell had been a member of the club's rotation in 1988, but was a big disappointment with a 5-10 record that was partially due to injuries and lack of support. The Sox let McDowell spend 1989 at AAA Vancouver, letting him work on his mechanics while his sore hip healed. They were also sending him a message to improve what they saw as an immature attitude.

McDowell came back last year, and he was everything the club had hoped for. Leading the young pitching staff with 14 wins, the tall, lanky McDowell impressed everyone with his aggressive, go-right-at-the-hitters attitude. In the heady days of August when the Sox still had dreams of dethroning Oakland, McDowell won six straight games (Aug. 5-Sept. 4).

Fearless to the point of being cocky, McDowell loves to pitch inside. When he plunked notorious plate-crowders Jose Canseco and Mark McGwire in a game at Oakland, he set the tone for a Sox sweep. His fastball rides up and in, and he balances it with a split fingered fastball and a hard breaking ball which dives down and in on lefthanders. With that repertoire, he was equally effective against lefthanders (.243) and righthanders (.245).

With McDowell, however, mechanics are everything. His long gangly motion sometimes gets out of sync, causing his right shoulder to fly open. When that happens, his pitches get up in the strike zone, and he either walks batters or gives up home runs. McDowell went through several stretches of ineffectiveness last year, resulting in a fairly high ERA (3.82).

HOLDING RUNNERS AND FIELDING:

McDowell's aggressive style carries over to his abilities as a fielder. He's quick off the mound, knows where he should be on every play, and always throws to the right base. A righthander with a deliberate motion, McDowell held runners close with a quick, purposeful move to first. He even worked the rarely successful fake-to-third-and-throw-to-first move, nabbing five baserunners during the year.

OVERALL:

When the Sox were sweeping Oakland last June, Dave Stewart was contemptuous of McDowell, saying "he should be in AAA." The next time the two hooked up, McDowell fired a three-hitter at Stewart, winning 11-1. That's the sort of in-your-face pitching the Sox love from McDowell. He could be their ace in 1991, if his mechanics continue to improve.

JACK McDOWELL

Position: SP
Bats: R **Throws:** R
Ht: 6' 5" **Wt:** 179

Opening Day Age: 25
Born: 1/16/66 in Van Nuys, CA
ML Seasons: 3

Overall Statistics

	W	L	ERA	G	GS	Sv	IP	H	R	BB	SO	HR
1990	14	9	3.82	33	33	0	205.0	189	93	77	165	20
Career	22	19	3.75	63	63	0	391.2	352	184	151	264	33

How Often He Throws Strikes

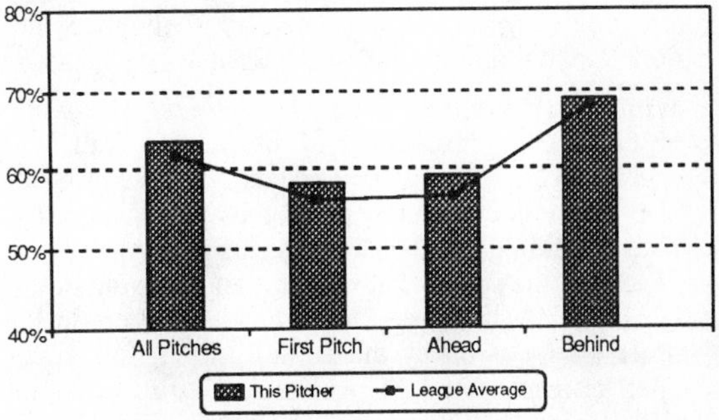

1990 Situational Stats

	W	L	ERA	Sv	IP		AB	H	HR	RBI	AVG
Home	9	4	3.30	0	128.1	LHB	408	99	11	37	.243
Road	5	5	4.70	0	76.2	RHB	368	90	9	46	.245
Day	5	2	3.90	0	64.2	Sc Pos	162	40	6	62	.247
Night	9	7	3.78	0	140.1	Clutch	58	13	0	3	.224

1990 Rankings (American League)

- 3rd in pickoff throws (209)
- 6th in stolen bases allowed (23)
- 7th in run support per 9 innings (5.22)
- 8th in games started (33), hit batsmen (7) and least GDPs per 9 innings (.53)
- Led the White Sox in wins (14), complete games (4), home runs allowed (20), hit batsmen (7), strikeouts (165), pitches thrown (3,362), pickoff throws, stolen bases allowed, caught stealing (11), strikeout/walk ratio (2.14) and run support per 9 innings

PITCHING:

Donn Pall grew up as a White Sox fan in Chicago's south suburbs and then attended the University of Illinois. He's a loyal, local boy, and like the folks on the no-nonsense South Side, a model of consistency. Since arriving late in 1988, Pall has turned in three nearly identical, good quality seasons. Last year, as usual, he excelled as a middle reliever in the record-setting White Sox bullpen.

Pall uses a fastball and curve to set up his split-finger pitch, which induces opponent batters to beat ground balls to the sure-handed White Sox infielders. Pall's ground ball-fly ball ratio was 2.5-to-1, one of the highest in the major leagues, and nearly twice the American League average (1.27-to-1). His main value lies in his ability to get the double play when the White Sox need it: he faced 70 batters in a double play situation (a man on first and less than two out -- no sacrifice hit), and got 13 of them to bounce into double plays, an outstanding 18.6%.

While Pall is effective when he first enters the game, he becomes less so the more he pitches. Pall held opposing hitters to a .210 average through his first 15 pitches, but once past that mark, they hit him at a .264 clip. Two things tend to happen: his pitches begin to stay up in the strike zone rather than dropping out of it, and he starts facing the lefthanded batters in the order. Pall was bit by the home run bug four times after he reached the 15 pitch mark. Lefthanders hit .278 against Pall, 81 points higher than righthanders.

The split-finger is sometimes hard to control, but Pall does a decent job; last year he walked only 16 batters unintentionally over 76 innings (fewer than two per nine innings). But working the inside part of the plate with his fastball, Pall will hit more than his share of batters.

FIELDING AND HOLDING BASERUNNERS:

Pall is a decent fielder, and will get a lot of chances because of the opposition's tendency to hit the ball on the ground. Last year he recorded 12 chances without an error, and started two double plays. But Pall needs some help from his catchers at keeping runners close: seven out of 10 runners were successful stealing against him.

OVERALL:

Pall's remarkable skill at getting the double play ball is a valuable asset to the White Sox, and he should remain an integral part of their middle relief corps. Pall can occasionally be effective in longer relief stints, but he's most effective when used for one inning or less, primarily against righthanded hitters.

DONN PALL

Position: RP
Bats: R **Throws:** R
Ht: 6' 1" **Wt:** 180

Opening Day Age: 29
Born: 1/11/62 in Chicago, IL
ML Seasons: 3

Overall Statistics

	W	L	ERA	G	GS	Sv	IP	H	R	BB	SO	HR
1990	3	5	3.32	56	0	2	76.0	63	33	24	39	7
Career	7	12	3.33	126	0	8	191.2	192	79	51	113	17

How Often He Throws Strikes

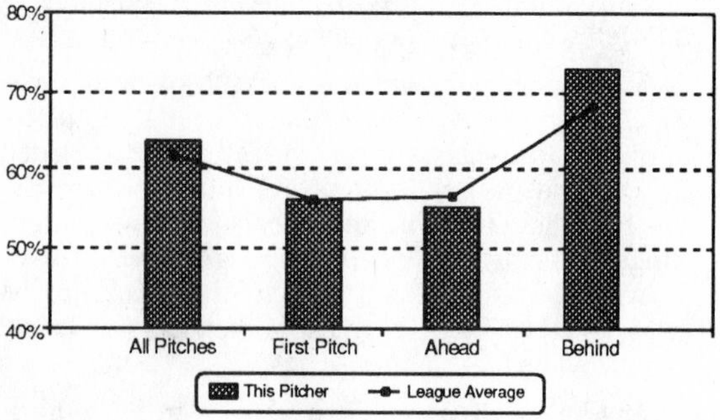

1990 Situational Stats

	W	L	ERA	Sv	IP		AB	H	HR	RBI	AVG
Home	0	3	4.50	1	44.0	LHB	115	32	1	17	.278
Road	3	2	1.69	1	32.0	RHB	157	31	6	19	.197
Day	1	3	4.81	0	24.1	Sc Pos	81	20	3	32	.247
Night	2	2	2.61	2	51.2	Clutch	101	25	4	12	.248

1990 Rankings (American League)

- 12th in GDPs induced per GDP situation (18.6%)
- Led the White Sox in GDPs induced per GDP situation

HITTING:

Injured during much of 1989, Dan Pasqua stayed healthy for the entire season last year, and was a potent left-handed bat in the middle of the White Sox order. He exhibited the same abilities he showed in 1986 when he had his best year with the Yankees. Playing mostly against righthanders in 1990, Pasqua posted career second-bests in batting average (.274), on-base percentage (.347), and slugging percentage (.495). A late-season 16-for-68 slump prevented him from finishing with better numbers.

Pasqua is an excellent fastball hitter with a good eye at the plate and tremendous power. Comiskey Park and limited playing time conspired to keep him from the 20-home run club. Despite hitting 86 points higher at home, Pasqua hit for more power on the road. Pasqua hit well for extra bases, getting 43 extra-base hits in 325 at-bats.

Though his strikeout total was high (66), Pasqua was a tough out most of the time. He made the most of his RBI opportunities, batting .283 with runners in scoring position and driving in a career high 58 runs. A patient hitter, Pasqua drew 37 walks and saw 3.9 pitches per plate appearance, one of the highest figures in the American League. Pasqua has never been able to get over the "platoon" label, mainly because of his inability to hit lefthanders. In 1990, he was given little opportunity to remove the label, squeezing in only 31 at-bats and a .194 average against southpaws.

BASERUNNING:

Pasqua has never been much of a threat on the bases, and it's a surprise when he actually takes off for second. He was one for two in 1990, and he's holding steady at 50% for his career. Pasqua is slow, and he was wise to play it safe on the bases.

FIELDING:

Left field is Pasqua's natural position, but he was rusty in 1990, playing only 136 innings. Pasqua's speed is a liability in the outfield, and he made three errors in only 43 chances in left field. Pasqua probably has the ability to play first base, where lack of foot speed wouldn't be as much of a problem, but the White Sox first base situation is filled at the moment.

OVERALL:

The White Sox need Pasqua's left-handed bat in the middle of the order, and he will likely be the full-time designated hitter against right-handed pitching. It's doubtful whether Pasqua will be given a full-time chance against lefthanders, however. Should the new Comiskey Park prove a little more kind to fly ball hitters like Pasqua, he could reach the 20-home run mark.

DAN PASQUA

Position: DH/LF/RF
Bats: L **Throws:** L
Ht: 6' 0" **Wt:** 205

Opening Day Age: 29
Born: 10/17/61 in Yonkers, NY
ML Seasons: 6

Overall Statistics

	G	AB	R	H	D	T	HR	RBI	SB	BB	SO	AVG
1990	112	325	43	89	27	3	13	58	1	37	66	.274
Career	589	1739	220	433	79	8	86	267	5	211	439	.249

Where He Hits the Ball

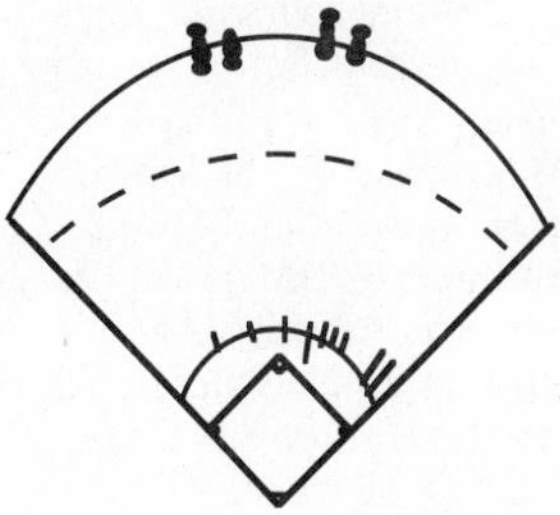

Vs. LHP

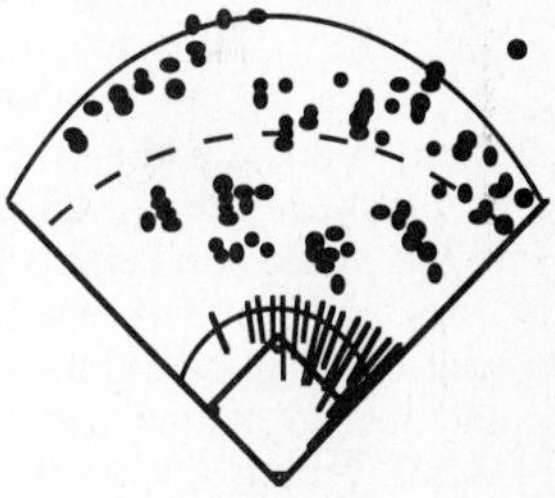

Vs. RHP

1990 Situational Stats

	AB	H	HR	RBI	AVG		AB	H	HR	RBI	AVG
Home	157	50	4	29	.318	LHP	31	6	0	4	.194
Road	168	39	9	29	.232	RHP	294	83	13	54	.282
Day	85	28	4	16	.329	Sc Pos	92	26	3	42	.283
Night	240	61	9	42	.254	Clutch	49	11	3	8	.224

1990 Rankings (American League)

- 5th lowest batting average with the bases loaded (.091)
- Led the White Sox in batting average on a 3-1 count (.429)

PITCHING:

If the 1990 White Sox were a science fiction television series, Melido Perez would be its obligatory "evil twin" episode. When he pitched well, Perez was downright brilliant (1.33 ERA in wins). Other times it seemed as if an imposter had knocked the real Melido Perez out, stuffed him in a locker for the evening, and took to the mound (9.57 ERA in losses).

Perez' early inning adventures became so well-documented (he didn't make it out of the third inning in 8 of his 35 starts) that it became a psychological barrier for him. Everyone wanted to see what Perez would do in the first inning; if he let a batter get on base, Sox fans would let out a collective "here-we-go-again" groan. While Perez would sometimes get himself together, people had a right to feel nervous.

You can usually tell which Perez has shown up in the early innings. He needs to get batters swinging at his fastball, thrown high in the strike zone, before he can effectively use the rest of his repertoire, which includes a curve and a split-finger fastball. In contrast to teammate Jack McDowell, who mainly works hitters in and out, Perez works them up and down. His letter high fastball is a perfect complement to his split-finger pitch, which starts out at knee-high level and then drops out of sight. In 1989, Perez was throwing the "splitter" too fast. In 1990, he took a little bit off and didn't throw it with the same hard motion as his regular fastball. The results were much more control over the pitch. Sometimes.

HOLDING RUNNERS AND FIELDING:

Most of the time, Perez' delivery allows him to finish in an upright position, fully facing the plate. Thus, he's usually in position to field come-backers and bunts. When he's over-throwing, though, his body will fly off to the left of the mound, putting him in poor position to field. Perez has a fast move toward first which makes runners know he's aware, and with the help of his catchers, he was able to hold opponent baserunners to a 52% success rate.

OVERALL:

At his best Perez is armed with a mitt-popping fastball, surprising curve, and a brutal split-finger pitch, arguably one the American League's best. At his worst he's a guy with several pitches and no control over any of them. But despite a wretched second half, Perez still managed 13 wins for the White Sox. It seems too early to give up on him.

MELIDO PEREZ

Position: SP
Bats: R **Throws:** R
Ht: 6' 4" **Wt:** 180

Opening Day Age: 25
Born: 2/15/66 in San Cristobal, Dominican Republic
ML Seasons: 4

Overall Statistics

	W	L	ERA	G	GS	Sv	IP	H	R	BB	SO	HR
1990	13	14	4.61	35	35	0	197.0	177	111	86	161	14
Career	37	39	4.52	101	101	0	587.2	568	334	253	445	65

How Often He Throws Strikes

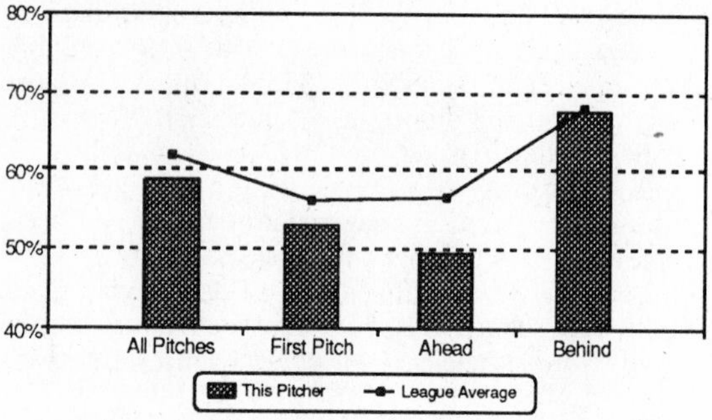

1990 Situational Stats

	W	L	ERA	Sv	IP		AB	H	HR	RBI	AVG
Home	5	6	5.11	0	81.0	LHB	380	95	6	47	.250
Road	8	8	4.27	0	116.0	RHB	355	82	8	36	.231
Day	2	3	5.58	0	50.0	Sc Pos	159	46	2	65	.289
Night	11	11	4.29	0	147.0	Clutch	40	9	1	3	.225

1990 Rankings (American League)

- 2nd in balks (4)
- 3rd in worst ERA (4.61), games started (35) and shutouts (3)
- 4th in worst ERA at home (5.11)
- 8th in losses (14) and strikeouts per 9 innings (7.36)
- Led the White Sox in loses, games started, shutouts, walks allowed (86), wild pitches (8), balks, caught stealing (11), lowest batting average allowed (.241), lowest stolen base percentage allowed (52.2%), strikeouts per 9 innings and lowest batting average allowed vs. right- handed batters (.231)

PITCHING:

Scott Radinsky is one of three young lefthanders the White Sox use out their bullpen. A rookie straight out of Class A, Radinsky got off to a sensational start last year. But then he faded, and by season's end clearly ranked behind both Ken Patterson and Wayne Edwards.

Radinsky showed the stuff that bullpen stoppers are made of in the early going. Relying mainly on a blazing fastball, he had 25 strikeouts in his first 29 innings pitched. His record stood at 5-1 with a 2.15 ERA, and he was a big reason the White Sox were in the pennant race. Everything looked rosy, but there were already cracks in Radinsky's armor. He had given up 16 walks over the same span and hitters had begun to hit his fastball. Radinsky gave up only eight hits over his first 19 innings, but yielded 10 in 10 innings in June.

Things took a turn for the worse in July. Radinsky's inconsistency with his breaking pitches forced him to be a one-pitch pitcher, and hitters caught up with him. They were able to sit on his fastball, and clocked Radinsky for a .459 batting average when the count was in their favor. In addition, the longer Radinsky stayed in the game, the more the hitters were able to figure him out. He held hitters to a .228 average through his first 15 pitches, but got lit up at .280 afterward.

Radinsky continued to falter, and was reduced to a mop-up man in September, when he managed only three innings in six appearances. Overall, Radinsky held lefthanders to a low .177 average, but righthanders batted .271 with a .402 on-base percentage.

FIELDING AND HOLDING RUNNERS:

While Radinsky didn't distinguish himself in the field, neither was he an embarrassment. He fielded 11 chances without an error. He's quick off the mound, and actually accomplished the rare feat of recording more putouts (seven) than assists (four). He has a good move to first, despite the fact that runners were two for two in stolen base attempts.

OVERALL:

Radinsky struck out the side with two runners on in one relief appearance against the Orioles, and afterward commented that he didn't think about the hitter or the pitches, but just threw as hard as he could. Radinsky is going to have to think a little more if wants to get major league hitters out. He already has a top-notch fastball, and if he can begin throwing his breaking pitch for strikes consistently, he could develop into a reliable closer.

SCOTT RADINSKY

Position: RP
Bats: L **Throws:** L
Ht: 6' 3" **Wt:** 190

Opening Day Age: 23
Born: 3/3/68 in Glendale, CA
ML Seasons: 1

Overall Statistics

	W	L	ERA	G	GS	Sv	IP	H	R	BB	SO	HR
1990	6	1	4.82	62	0	4	52.1	47	29	36	46	1
Career	6	1	4.82	62	0	4	52.1	47	29	36	46	1

How Often He Throws Strikes

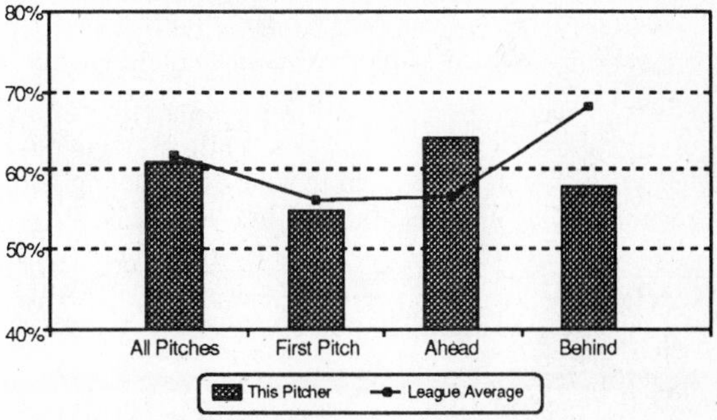

1990 Situational Stats

	W	L	ERA	Sv	IP		AB	H	HR	RBI	AVG
Home	2	1	4.50	3	26.0	LHB	62	11	0	8	.177
Road	4	0	5.13	1	26.1	RHB	133	36	1	19	.271
Day	3	1	7.47	1	15.2	Sc Pos	71	16	0	25	.225
Night	3	0	3.68	3	36.2	Clutch	74	12	0	5	.162

1990 Rankings (American League)

- 11th in lowest percentage of inherited runners scored (23.7%)

HITTING:

While no one was chanting "Sam-my! Sam-my!" enough to erase the memories of the traded Harold Baines, Sammy Sosa acquitted himself rather well in 1990. He managed the mythical "quadruple double," making double figures in doubles (26), triples (10), home runs (15), and stolen bases (32), all while finishing second on the White Sox in RBIs (70). Not bad for a 21-year-old in his first full major league season.

That Sosa accomplished this while hitting only .233 is, on the one hand, incredible, and on the other, disturbing. Sosa had an outstanding West Coast trip in mid-June, painting California red and giving White Sox fans a glimpse of the possibilities. His average was up to .271, and he was hitting with power. But it didn't stay that high. Sosa can hit a fastball a mile, but he looked positively weak-kneed on the breaking stuff. Righthanders began throwing Sosa more and more breaking pitches, and he never really adjusted, mustering only a .211 batting average against them.

Strike zone judgement is still Sosa's major problem. He struck out 150 times last year while drawing only 33 walks, figures which remind one of the young Juan Samuel. The White Sox used Sosa as a leadoff man against lefties for much of last season. But he'll never last in that role until he can learn to lay off bad pitches.

BASERUNNING:

Sosa has great speed. He stole 32 bases and was caught 16 times last year, not bad for a player with his limited major league experience. Like teammate Ivan Calderon, Sosa goes after every extra base he can. He has good instincts on the bases, and his speed can cover up for the times when his youthful enthusiasm gets the better of him.

FIELDING:

Sosa recorded 14 assists in right field last year, second only to Jesse Barfield, and comparisons to Barfield are appropriate: his arm is that good. His speed and aggressiveness are also assets, enabling him to cover a lot of ground. But Sosa committed 13 errors, 11 of the fielding variety, and that's way too many. His outfield problems are mostly due to inexperience, however, and you can bet on Sosa becoming one of the best right fielders in the game.

OVERALL:

Many of the 22-year-old Sosa's current shortcomings can be chalked up to inexperience. However, his poor strike zone judgement should be watched. Whether it will improve, or remain at the level established in his five year professional career, is a big question mark. It could mean the difference between a good and a great major league career.

SAMMY SOSA

Position: RF
Bats: R **Throws:** R
Ht: 6' 0" **Wt:** 165

Opening Day Age: 22
Born: 11/10/68 in San Pedro de Macoris, Dominican Republic
ML Seasons: 2

Overall Statistics

	G	AB	R	H	D	T	HR	RBI	SB	BB	SO	AVG
1990	153	532	72	124	26	10	15	70	32	33	150	.233
Career	211	715	99	171	34	10	19	83	39	44	197	.239

Where He Hits the Ball

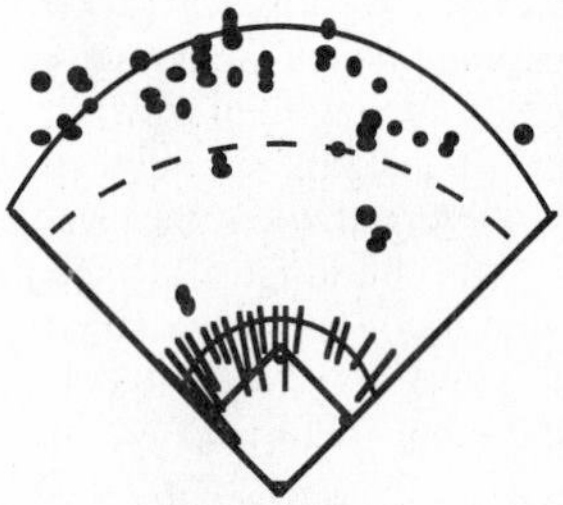

Vs. LHP

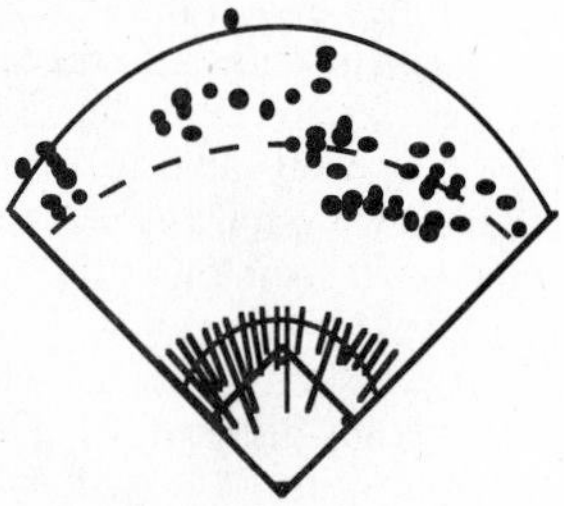

Vs. RHP

1990 Situational Stats

	AB	H	HR	RBI	AVG		AB	H	HR	RBI	AVG
Home	266	68	10	36	.256	LHP	233	61	12	37	.262
Road	266	56	5	34	.211	RHP	299	63	3	33	.211
Day	133	25	3	19	.188	Sc Pos	140	34	4	53	.243
Night	399	99	12	51	.248	Clutch	82	15	0	3	.183

1990 Rankings (American League)

- 2nd in triples (10), lowest on-base average (.282) and most runs scored per time reached base (44.2%)
- 3rd lowest batting average on the road (.211)
- 4th in caught stealing (16), strikeouts (150), and highest percentage of swings that missed (34.3%)
- Led the White Sox in triples, strikeouts, stolen base percentage (66.7%), runs scored per time reached base and steals of third (6)
- Led AL right fielders in triples, stolen bases (32), caught stealing, hit by pitch (6), runs scored per time reached base, errors (13) and steals of third

STOPPER

BOBBY THIGPEN

Position: RP
Bats: R **Throws:** R
Ht: 6' 3" **Wt:** 195

Opening Day Age: 27
Born: 7/17/63 in Tallahassee, FL
ML Seasons: 5

Overall Statistics

	W	L	ERA	G	GS	Sv	IP	H	R	BB	SO	HR
1990	4	6	1.83	77	0	57	88.2	60	20	32	70	5
Career	20	25	2.78	277	0	148	382.1	330	129	141	251	32

How Often He Throws Strikes

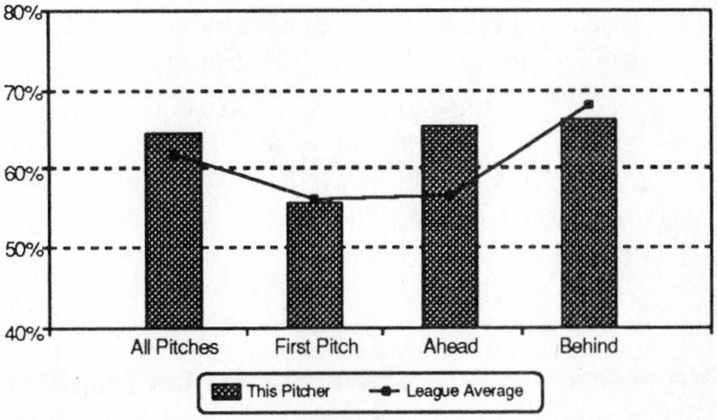

1990 Situational Stats

	W	L	ERA	Sv	IP		AB	H	HR	RBI	AVG
Home	3	3	1.94	27	46.1	LHB	158	34	3	12	.215
Road	1	3	1.70	30	42.1	RHB	149	26	2	13	.174
Day	1	2	3.05	14	20.2	Sc Pos	75	13	2	20	.173
Night	3	4	1.46	43	68.0	Clutch	253	47	5	25	.186

1990 Rankings (American League)

- 1st in games pitched (77), saves (57), games finished (73) and save opportunites (65)
- 2nd in first batter efficiency (.127)
- 3rd in lowest percentage of inherited runners scored (17.6%)
- 4th in blown saves (8)
- 5th in save percentage (87.7%)
- Led the White Sox in games pitched, saves, games finished, save opportunities, save percentage, blown saves, lowest batting average allowed vs. left-handed batters (.215), first batter efficiency and lowest percentage of inherited runners scored

PITCHING:

Not since Mike Marshall pitched in 106 games for the 1974 Los Angeles Dodgers has a relief pitcher been as valuable to a team as Bobby Thigpen was to the White Sox in 1990. Thigpen took advantage of natural talent and Jeff Torborg's handling to obliterate the old save record of 46, moving it all the way up to 57.

Torborg decided on a game plan early last season: use the rest of the bullpen to hold the line until the arrival of Thigpen in the ninth. Torborg never wavered, and Thigpen rarely faltered: he registered 57 saves in an incredible 65 opportunities (90%). Thigpen also finished 73 of the 77 games he appeared in.

Pitching with more leads than ever before, Thigpen was at his best. In the past, his concentration sometimes wavered when he found himself pitching in meaningless games, resulting in some pretty high ERAs for a guy with more than 30 saves. Many people questioned the workload put on Thigpen in 1990, but his 88.2 innings matched his yearly average prior to the season, and he registered the best ERA of his career (1.83).

Thigpen has four pitches: a 90-plus fastball, an excellent slider, a change and a curve. He uses them in that order. All his pitches tend to be flat if he doesn't work regularly. Thigpen challenges every hitter, using his moving fastball up in the strike zone, but his out pitch is the slider.

While he gave up fewer home runs last year (five) than in previous seasons, Thigpen is susceptible to the longball. Three of his defeats were due to the home run. A change-up left a little too far out over the plate resulted in a back-breaking three-run home run to the Angels' Lee Stevens in late August. Thigpen has also admitted to being a little too hyperactive when he first enters a game, occasionally exhibiting streaks of wildness.

HOLDING RUNNERS AND FIELDING:

Because it's late in the game and they're behind, runners will rarely be stealing when Thigpen is pitching. However, he is always conscious of baserunners and will keep them close with strong throws to first. He's an excellent fielder, one who rarely makes mistakes.

OVERALL:

When the White Sox were struggling a few years ago, a lot of people in Chicago called for the White Sox to trade Thigpen, figuring he was being wasted on a losing team. Now the White Sox are contenders, in good part because they built a pitching staff and a game plan around Thigpen. His strong right arm will again be the key to the Sox pitching staff in 1991.

FUTURE MVP?

FRANK THOMAS

Position: 1B
Bats: R **Throws:** R
Ht: 6' 5" **Wt:** 240

Opening Day Age: 22
Born: 5/27/68 in Columbus, GA
ML Seasons: 1

Overall Statistics

	G	AB	R	H	D	T	HR	RBI	SB	BB	SO	AVG
1990	60	191	39	63	11	3	7	31	0	44	54	.330
Career	60	191	39	63	11	3	7	31	0	44	54	.330

Where He Hits the Ball

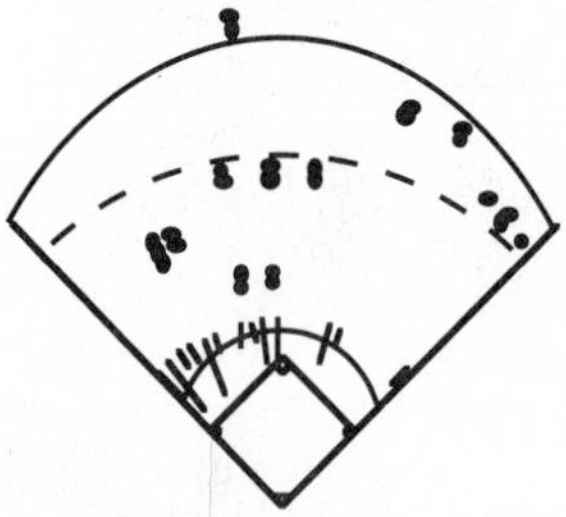

Vs. LHP

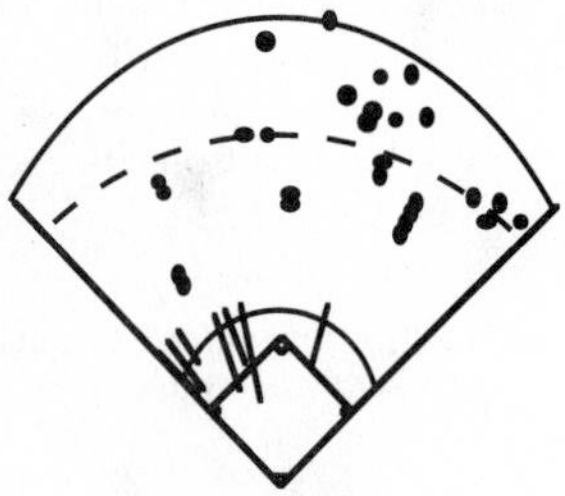

Vs. RHP

1990 Situational Stats

	AB	H	HR	RBI	AVG		AB	H	HR	RBI	AVG
Home	73	25	2	13	.342	LHP	71	29	5	12	.408
Road	118	38	5	18	.322	RHP	120	34	2	19	.283
Day	42	13	2	3	.310	Sc Pos	53	18	1	24	.340
Night	149	50	5	28	.336	Clutch	28	10	2	12	.357

1990 Rankings (American League)

➟ Did not rank near the top or bottom in any category

HITTING:

Frank Thomas could be the top first baseman in the American League this year. His awesome two-month performance last year made quite an impression, and left more than a few people wondering what took the White Sox so long to bring him up from the minors. He terrorized the Southern League and, moving up to major league pitching, Thomas showed no decline in performance, posting a .330 batting average and a .529 slugging percentage in 191 at-bats.

At 6-5 and about 240, Thomas is an intimidating presence at the plate. He never takes his eyes off the pitcher, even between pitches, and is a picture of concentration. His 44 walks were due to his own batting eye, the best per at-bat for any young player in a long time, and his patience keeps him ahead in the count much more often than not. Thomas was caught looking 26 times out of his 54 strikeouts, mainly because he thought the pitches were balls, not because he was fooled.

Thomas began hitting for power in September, winding up with seven home runs. The old Comiskey Park was responsible for taking a few dingers away. Thomas is not a pull hitter, and he has tremendous power to right-center field.

BASERUNNING:

Thomas has the speed and ability to steal 10 bases, depending upon how daring the White Sox want to be. He attempted only one stolen base for the White Sox, and was caught. In the minors, he was eight of 14. On the bases, Thomas is aggressive and intelligent. Out of the box at the crack of the bat, Thomas seems to have an immediate idea of which base he can make. He managed three triples for the White Sox.

FIELDING:

If there's a weakness in Thomas' game, it's his arm. It isn't very strong, and a few times runners went from first to third on ground outs to the infield. Otherwise, Thomas is a good fielder who should get better. Unlike many of the other recent White Sox tryouts at first base, Thomas looks comfortable at the position, and he has good range to his right.

OVERALL:

Thomas is the best hitter to come out of the White Sox farm system since Harold Baines, and he could generate more excitement on the South Side than any single player since Dick Allen. It could be scary for American League pitchers if Thomas gets any better than he is already. Only 22, he appears destined to be a fixture at first base for the White Sox, batting fourth, for many years to come.

ROBIN VENTURA

Position: 3B
Bats: L **Throws:** R
Ht: 6' 1" **Wt:** 185

Opening Day Age: 23
Born: 7/14/67 in Santa Maria, CA
ML Seasons: 2

Overall Statistics

	G	AB	R	H	D	T	HR	RBI	SB	BB	SO	AVG
1990	150	493	48	123	17	1	5	54	1	55	53	.249
Career	166	538	53	131	20	1	5	61	1	63	59	.243

Where He Hits the Ball

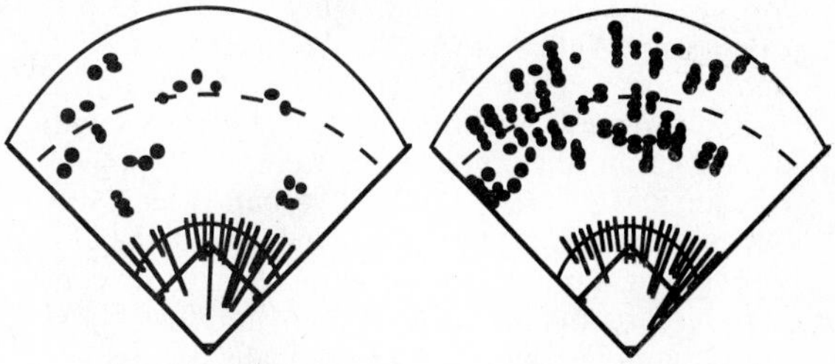

Vs. LHP   Vs. RHP

1990 Situational Stats

	AB	H	HR	RBI	AVG		AB	H	HR	RBI	AVG
Home	238	65	2	25	.273	LHP	154	34	0	12	.221
Road	255	58	3	29	.227	RHP	339	89	5	42	.263
Day	129	31	0	14	.240	Sc Pos	120	36	0	43	.300
Night	364	92	5	40	.253	Clutch	68	17	0	10	.250

1990 Rankings (American League)

- 2nd lowest slugging percentage (.319)
- 4th in sacrifice bunts (13) and lowest slugging percentage vs. left-handed pitchers (.247)
- 5th in highest percentage of swings put into play (55.2%)
- 8th lowest batting average on the road (.227)
- Led the White Sox in pitches seen per plate appearance (3.76), on-base average vs. right-handed pitchers (.329) and highest percentage of pitches taken (60.2%)
- Led AL third basemen in sacrifice bunts (13) and highest percentage of swings put into play

HITTING:

Robin Ventura's bat finally came around after a horrendous start last season, and the third baseman showed some of the form that made him an offensive powerhouse at the college level. Ventura put together a 58-game hitting streak while at Oklahoma State, but nothing could have prepared him for the 0-for-41 drought he suffered in May, which was quickly followed by another 1-for-19 lapse.

Ventura batted .249 for the season, but a flourish in September (.356) put him at .272 from June to the end of the season. Ventura had trouble getting his batting average above .175 in April and May; he wasn't hitting in "bad luck," he simply wasn't stroking the ball with any authority. Part of the problem was his lack of power. Ventura had only 23 extra base hits in close to 500 at-bats, not a particularly strong showing for someone with his credentials.

There are many positive signs that Ventura will improve. After finally climbing out of the black hole where his batting average disappeared, he was a good to very good hitter, stroking pitches into the outfield gaps. He also has a good eye and drew 55 walks. Ventura puts the ball in play and can handle the breaking pitch, striking out only 53 times. For a young player, Ventura was surprisingly tough with runners in scoring position (.300), finishing the season with 54 runs batted in.

BASERUNNING:

Ventura has only average speed, and at his present rate, shouldn't be asked to steal more than a dozen or so times. He was only one out of five in 1990. On the bases, Ventura isn't reckless. He'll take the extra base with two outs, or with fewer if the situation calls for it.

FIELDING:

Ventura was a plus in the White Sox infield. He showed excellent range toward and away from the line, and was very good on bunts and slow rollers hit in front of him. Ventura's fielding problems came early in the season (he made 14 of his 25 errors before the All-Star break) on throws across the diamond. He committed 14 throwing errors in all, and the ball had a tendency to sail.

OVERALL:

Ventura looks like he'll be holding down the White Sox third base job for a while. He's got good instincts on the bases and in the field, and, given his record after June 1st, he should improve at the plate. Ventura already is an intelligent and patient hitter, and if can increase his power output, he could become a top-flight third baseman.

WAYNE EDWARDS

Position: RP/SP
Bats: L **Throws:** L
Ht: 6' 5" **Wt:** 185

Opening Day Age: 27
Born: 3/7/64 in Burbank, CA
ML Seasons: 2

Overall Statistics

	W	L	ERA	G	GS	Sv	IP	H	R	BB	SO	HR
1990	5	3	3.22	42	5	2	95.0	81	39	41	63	6
Career	5	3	3.25	49	5	2	102.1	88	42	44	72	7

PITCHING, FIELDING & HOLDING RUNNERS:

Wayne Edwards was a tall, skinny, left-handed surprise for the White Sox in 1990. Edwards worked 95 innings and compiled a fine 3.22 ERA in various roles. He was able to get major league hitters out with his fastball, and that's good news. Complementing his fastball, Edwards has a fine curve ball, which was especially devastating to left-handed batters; they hit only .183 against him. While Edwards gave up considerably less than a hit an inning, he often found himself in trouble via the bases on balls. He walked 41 in 95 innings.

The White Sox used Edwards as a relief pitcher, but he responded well as a starter during the month of August, going 3-1 with a 2.54 ERA. One question is Edwards' stamina. He's thin for his height, and he averaged just under six innings per start.

Edwards didn't show a lot of skill as a fielder, but he should be categorized as average. Edwards has a good move to first, and being left-handed puts him at a natural advantage at holding runners. Opposing runners stole nine bases in 14 tries (64%) with Edwards on the hill.

OVERALL:

Too good to be a mop-up man or long reliever, Edwards was groomed as a starting pitcher in the minors, and showed he could be effective in that role at the major league level. The White Sox starting rotation is getting crowded, however, with more established pitchers already in place. Lefthanders are a commodity, and a lot of teams would be willing to give the 27-year-old Edwards a chance.

CRAIG GREBECK

Position: 3B/SS
Bats: R **Throws:** R
Ht: 5' 8" **Wt:** 160

Opening Day Age: 26
Born: 12/29/64 in Johnstown, PA
ML Seasons: 1

Overall Statistics

	G	AB	R	H	D	T	HR	RBI	SB	BB	SO	AVG
1990	59	119	7	20	3	1	1	9	0	8	24	.168
Career	59	119	7	20	3	1	1	9	0	8	24	.168

HITTING, FIELDING, BASERUNNING:

Craig Grebeck only stands about 5-6, and when he made the White Sox roster last spring, there were a few joking comparisons to Harry Chappas, the diminutive but notably unsuccessful Sox infielder of the late seventies. The jokes stopped in August when Grebeck took Nolan Ryan deep for his first major league homer. Ryan even paid Grebeck a compliment, one Grebeck could have done without, by drilling him with a fastball the next time the two hooked up.

As that home run showed, Grebeck can hit the fastball deep on occasion. Despite his size, he's belted 30 minor league homers, and he's been a consistent .280 minor league hitter; his .168 average with the Sox last year came in only 119 scattered at-bats. Grebeck is not a good base stealer (23 for 51 in the minors), but he runs the bases alertly.

Grebeck showed good range and good hands during a brief time platooning at third base with Robin Ventura. He displayed less ability at short, his primary position in the minors. He doesn't have the range or arm to play there regularly.

OVERALL:

The White Sox need backup infielders, and Grebeck is a sure bet to stick with the team in 1991. Since Ozzie Guillen and Robin Ventura are established on the left side, Grebeck's best shot at a regular job appears to be second base, where 32-year-old Scott Fletcher resides. It would be Grebeck's best position, and if he can wake up his bat to major league pitching, he should be around the major leagues for a little while.

STEVE LYONS

Position: 1B/2B
Bats: L **Throws:** R
Ht: 6' 3" **Wt:** 195

Opening Day Age: 30
Born: 6/3/60 in Tacoma, WA
ML Seasons: 6

Overall Statistics

	G	AB	R	H	D	T	HR	RBI	SB	BB	SO	AVG
1990	93	146	22	28	6	1	1	11	1	10	41	.192
Career	689	1872	240	480	89	14	15	175	30	140	316	.256

HITTING, FIELDING, BASERUNNING:

In a .192 season, Steve Lyons had only two highlights. He played all nine positions in an exhibition game against the Cubs, and he dropped his pants in front of the Tigers faithful in Detroit. The Detroit incident made a lot of folks laugh, but after it happened, the White Sox pretty much kept Lyons (and his trousers) nailed to the bench.

Lyons has some skills. He's hit as high as .280, he can run, and he's obviously versatile. He's been a regular at both second and third, but he's not good enough with the glove to handle those skill positions. He's much better defensively at first and the outfield, but at those spots, he doesn't hit with enough power. Lyons longs to be a regular again, as he was in 1988 and 1989. But he forgets that in those days, the White Sox were league doormats, and didn't have anybody better.

As for his baserunning, they don't call Lyons "Psycho" for nothing. He's only 30-for-54 (56%) as a base stealer in his career, and putting Lyons in to pinch run is like playing Russian Roulette with your scoring opportunity.

OVERALL:

By the end of last season, Lyons' main job consisted of being the catcher whenever someone threw out the first ball. He handled it superbly. It would be astonishing if Lyons were to play an important role on the 1991 White Sox, and not so astonishing if he wasn't with them team at the time you're reading this book.

KEN PATTERSON

Position: RP
Bats: L **Throws:** L
Ht: 6' 4" **Wt:** 210

Opening Day Age: 26
Born: 7/8/64 in Costa Mesa, CA
ML Seasons: 3

Overall Statistics

	W	L	ERA	G	GS	Sv	IP	H	R	BB	SO	HR
1990	2	1	3.39	43	0	2	66.1	58	27	34	40	6
Career	8	4	4.07	102	3	3	152.2	147	75	69	91	19

PITCHING, FIELDING & HOLDING RUNNERS:

Ken Patterson had two jobs out of the White Sox bullpen in 1990. One was the thankless role of long relief, but the other was as a situational pitcher, coming in to get one or two left-handed batters out. Patterson performed both admirably, and turned in the best performance of his brief three-year career. His ERA was 3.39, down over one run since 1989.

Patterson is a fly ball pitcher with a good fastball. He has gained confidence in his heater and last year it proved very effective against left-handed batters, who hit only .194 with no extra base hits against him. Righthanders fared much better; versus righties, Patterson was prone to leaving his pitches a little too far out over the plate, and they touched him for six home runs in only 66.1 innings of work. Another weakness Patterson developed was the base on balls. A decent strikeout pitcher, he walked almost as many batters (34) as he struck out (40).

Patterson is a good fielder. Like a lot of the other White Sox pitchers, he wisely lets his infielders make most of the plays. He is also good at holding baserunners, and his quick move to the plate helped hold opponents to five stolen bases out of eight tries.

OVERALL:

The White Sox now have three good lefthanders coming out of the bullpen: Patterson, Wayne Edwards, and Scott Radinsky. Patterson's value lies in his versatility. Even mediocre lefties seem to hang around forever, and Patterson is a lot better than that.

ADAM PETERSON

Position: SP/RP
Bats: R **Throws:** R
Ht: 6' 3" **Wt:** 190

Opening Day Age: 25
Born: 12/11/65 in Long Beach, CA
ML Seasons: 4

Overall Statistics

	W	L	ERA	G	GS	Sv	IP	H	R	BB	SO	HR
1990	2	5	4.55	20	11	0	85.0	90	46	26	29	12
Career	2	7	6.01	26	16	0	100.1	117	70	37	38	14

PITCHING, FIELDING & HOLDING RUNNERS:

Still only 25, Adam Peterson has pitched for the White Sox during each of the last four seasons. During the first three years, Peterson's earned run averages in brief action looked more like Dow Jones averages (13.50, 13.50, 15.19). He was better in 1990 (4.55), pitching well in spots as both a starter and long reliever. Peterson showed some stamina in his final five outings, going eight, five, eight, seven, and 6.2 innings. Aside from a four-inning, eight-run disaster, he pitched well out of the bullpen.

Peterson has a decent fastball and breaking pitch, but he has to mix them and outguess hitters to be effective. He's not a strikeout pitcher, but he has good control, meaning he's usually around the plate. That explains his high home run total (12). Peterson wasn't very effective against left-handed batters, who scalded him for a .354 average, but he was very tough on righthanders, who batted only .215.

Peterson's a decent fielder, and was effective in giving his catchers a chance to throw out would-be base stealers. Only two runners made it safely, while five were thrown out.

OVERALL:

It's hard to know where Peterson fits in with the White Sox, who have a whole group of young pitchers with equal or better raw talent. Peterson showed he could be effective in both a starting role -- he could be used if one of the regular starters becomes injured -- and in long relief. But he'll need to get lefthanders out more consistently if he wants to stay in the big leagues.

MATT STARK

Position: DH
Bats: R **Throws:** R
Ht: 6' 4" **Wt:** 220

Opening Day Age: 26
Born: 1/21/65 in Whittier, CA
ML Seasons: 2

Overall Statistics

	G	AB	R	H	D	T	HR	RBI	SB	BB	SO	AVG
1990	8	16	0	4	1	0	0	3	0	1	6	.250
Career	13	28	0	5	1	0	0	3	0	1	6	.179

HITTING, FIELDING, BASERUNNING:

Matt Stark made his return to the big leagues in 1990 following a three-year absence. Stark made his debut with Toronto in 1987, and must not have impressed a lot of Blue Jays people, because he lasted all of 12 at-bats, securing one lone single. Stark spent the next two years in the minors before his return last September. The White Sox were eager to see what he could do in the majors after a big season at AA Birmingham: .309 average, 14 home runs and 109 RBIs. Used as a pinch-hitter and designated hitter, Stark managed four hits in 16 trips to the plate.

Stark, 26, is 6-4 and 220 pounds. He's built like a catcher, his primary position, and the earth shakes whenever he runs; if he stayed with the White Sox, he would surely be one of the slowest players in the major leagues. Stark has hit into four double plays in only 28 major league at-bats. He was solid but not spectacular defensively in the minors, and the White have yet to give him any playing time at the position.

OVERALL:

There's always room in the majors for guys who can hit, and Stark appears to have the credentials. But he's right-handed, and the Sox have plenty of righty swingers, and he's a catcher; they already have Carlton Fisk and Ron Karkovice. Stark will probably go back to the minors this year as a good insurance policy in case of injury.

SANDY ALOMAR JR

Position: C
Bats: R **Throws:** R
Ht: 6' 5" **Wt:** 200

Opening Day Age: 24
Born: 6/18/66 in Salinas, Puerto Rico
ML Seasons: 3

Overall Statistics

	G	AB	R	H	D	T	HR	RBI	SB	BB	SO	AVG
1990	132	445	60	129	26	2	9	66	4	25	46	.290
Career	140	465	61	133	27	2	10	72	4	28	50	.286

Where He Hits the Ball

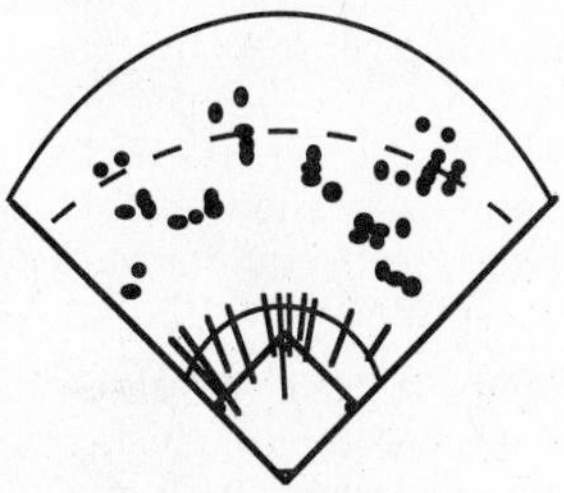

Vs. LHP

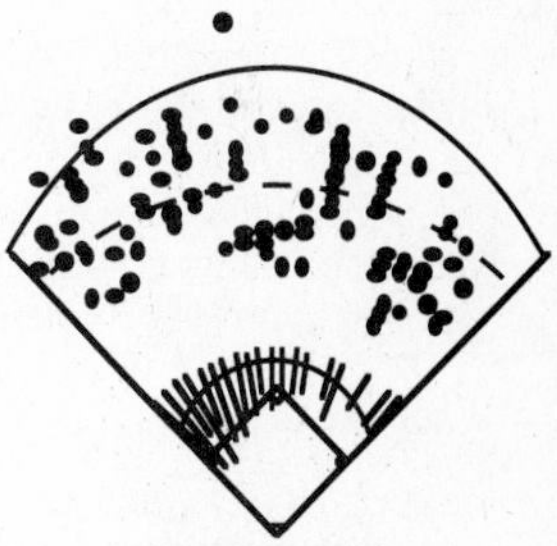

Vs. RHP

1990 Situational Stats

	AB	H	HR	RBI	AVG		AB	H	HR	RBI	AVG
Home	227	68	5	30	.300	LHP	117	44	2	18	.376
Road	218	61	4	36	.280	RHP	328	85	7	48	.259
Day	113	34	3	23	.301	Sc Pos	127	39	0	54	.307
Night	332	95	6	43	.286	Clutch	86	27	3	15	.314

1990 Rankings (American League)

- 1st in batting average vs. left-handed pitchers (.376)
- 3rd in batting average on an 0-2 count (.351)
- Led the Indians in batting average in the clutch (.314), batting average vs. left-handed pitchers, batting average on an 0-2 count and on-base average vs. left-handed pitchers (.403)
- Led AL catchers in batting average with runners in scoring position (.307), batting average in the clutch, batting average vs. left-handed pitchers, batting average on an 0-2 count, on-base average vs. left-handed pitchers, errors (14) and percentage of extra bases taken as a runner (50.0%)

HITTING:

Sandy Alomar Jr. came to spring training last year already pegged as the American League Rookie of the Year. He turned out to be the real deal, becoming the fourth Indian to win the award. Alomar drew good reviews as a defensive catcher in two straight seasons in Class AAA with San Diego, but no one knew for sure what he'd do offensively. Even the Indians said they'd be satisfied if he hit between .250 and .260. Alomar did much more.

The 6-foot-5 right-handed hitter batted .290 with nine homers and 66 runs batted in. In 1989, Andy Allanson and Joel Skinner, the Tribe's top two catchers, combined for four homers and 30 RBI. Not only was Alomar consistent -- his average was never lower than .275 after April 27 -- but he was also dangerous in the clutch. Alomar had success in tough situations because he concentrated on putting the ball in play, not over-swinging and trying to hit home runs. He also pasted lefties at a .376 clip, the highest such mark for all American League regulars.

Alomar played most of the second half with a badly bruised left thumb. He had to adjust his grip on the bat, splitting his hands so the top hand wouldn't irritate the thumb, but he still produced runs and hit for average. The only time he looked like a rookie was when he got overanxious and tried to hit homers. When Alomar does that, he tries to pull everything to left field and hits a lot of pop ups. But those stretches didn't last long.

BASERUNNING:

Alomar's not dangerous on the bases, but he did steal four bags -- most of them coming at crucial times. He can go from first to third on a single to right and will go into second base hard to break up a double play.

FIELDING:

The Cleveland pitching staff raved about Alomar's ability to block balls in the dirt. Knuckleballer Tom Candiotti said he was the best he's ever seen. Alomar's arm also lived up to its advance billing. He committed 14 errors, 11 on errant throws, but he threw out 35 percent (41 for 118) of the would-be base stealers to face him. His snap throw to second base from his knees will take your breath away. He's not afraid to block the plate on bang-bang plays.

OVERALL:

Alomar did everything well last year. He still needs work on calling a game, but he learns fast and works well with pitchers. After a loss to Milwaukee, he ripped up the clubhouse and challenged the rest of the ball club. It was a bold move for a rookie, but it's part of Alomar's makeup.

CARLOS BAERGA

Position: 3B/SS
Bats: B **Throws:** R
Ht: 5'11" **Wt:** 165

Opening Day Age: 22
Born: 11/4/68 in San Juan, Puerto Rico
ML Seasons: 1

Overall Statistics

	G	AB	R	H	D	T	HR	RBI	SB	BB	SO	AVG
1990	108	312	46	81	17	2	7	47	0	16	57	.260
Career	108	312	46	81	17	2	7	47	0	16	57	.260

Where He Hits the Ball

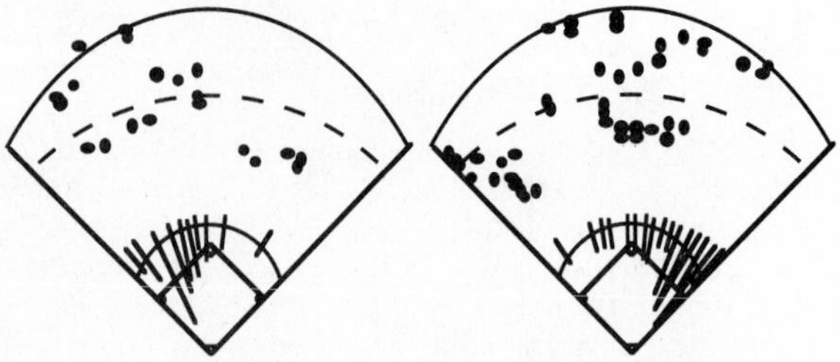

Vs. LHP   Vs. RHP

1990 Situational Stats

	AB	H	HR	RBI	AVG		AB	H	HR	RBI	AVG
Home	150	45	3	28	.300	LHP	103	25	2	16	.243
Road	162	36	4	19	.222	RHP	209	56	5	31	.268
Day	112	29	3	19	.259	Sc Pos	87	23	3	37	.264
Night	200	52	4	28	.260	Clutch	60	15	1	12	.250

1990 Rankings (American League)

- 7th in batting average with the bases loaded (.500)
- Led the Indians in batting average with the bases loaded
- Led AL third basemen in batting average with the bases loaded

HITTING:

Rookies like Carlos Baerga aren't supposed to be good pinch hitters. They're supposed to be too scared to come off the bench and be productive in the big leagues. Not Baerga. Displaying toughness under pressure, the switch-hitting rookie led Indians pinch hitters with a .355 (11-for-31) batting average. Only 22, Baerga can hit no matter how he's used. Last year 32 percent of his 81 hits went for extra bases.

Baerga started last season with the Indians, but, after getting off to a .208 start, was sent to Class AAA on July 25. The Indians wanted him to go down to get some regular playing time and work on hitting the breaking ball. The plan worked. Baerga returned on Aug. 11 and hit .319 the rest of the season to end up at .260 overall.

Baerga is a line drive hitter. A free swinger, he's still a sucker for high fastballs. But he has a compact stroke and can drive the ball in the gaps. As he gets older, he should develop more power. When Baerga pinch hits, he almost always swings at the first pitch. But after his return from the minors, he showed more patience at the plate when used in the starting lineup.

Although it may be too soon to tell, Baerga could be the number-three hitter the Indians spent all season looking for. He makes enough contact to advance runners, but also has the pop to drive some runs home.

BASERUNNING:

Baerga is built thick and low to the ground. He's 5-11, weighs close to 210 pounds (don't believe his "official weight of 165!) and looks like a penguin when he runs. He's not a base stealer, but he can run. He has just enough speed to beat out an infield single and more than enough to go from first to third. He goes hard into second base.

FIELDING:

Baerga played second, short and third last season. His best position is third and that's where he's expected to start this season. His arm is exceptional and his range is good. He loves to dive for balls. But he has a problem with wild throws. He made 17 errors in just 108 games last year. He could easily commit 30 as an everyday third baseman if he doesn't correct the problem.

OVERALL:

Baerga is one of several young Indians acquired through trades who offer hope for the future. He has the potential to be the kind of hitter who hits for average and drives in runs. Still young enough to overcome his defensive problems, he has a good, aggressive attitude. Putting on weight, however, could be a problem if he doesn't play every day.

TOM BROOKENS

Position: 3B/2B
Bats: R **Throws:** R
Ht: 5'10" **Wt:** 170

Opening Day Age: 37
Born: 8/10/53 in Chambersburg, PA
ML Seasons: 12

HITTING:

The Indians spent the last half of the 1980s looking for a utility infielder once Mike Fischlin had outlived his usefulness. Raise your hand if you remember these names: Luis Aguayo, Ron Washington, Junior Noboa, Tommy Hinzo, Fran Mullins, Domingo Ramos, Paul Zuvella and Houston Jimenez. They all came to Cleveland and flopped.

Tom Brookens didn't. Brookens, 37, signed a free agent contract with the Indians and the search ended. He did everything the Indians wanted -- played defense, helped the clubhouse run smoothly, ran the bases well, talked to the rookies (especially lockermate Sandy Alomar Jr.) and hit when it counted.

Brookens is a good offspeed hitter, and still has enough pop to drive the ball in the alleys. More importantly, he showed the ability to handle the toughest job in baseball -- sit for six or seven days and then come into a game and make something happen.

At 37, he's lost some of his bat speed. Brookens is sometimes overmatched by a high fastball, but he can spray the ball to all fields. Last year he always seemed to get an important hit when it was needed. Here's an example: On Aug. 22 against Milwaukee, Brookens hit his only home run of the season in the eighth inning. It broke a 2-2 tie and ended a four-game Cleveland losing streak. When asked why he started Brookens that day, manager John McNamara said, "Because I wanted to win."

BASERUNNING:

Brookens can still get down the first base line quickly, though his base stealing days are behind him. He goes from first to third well and can break up a double play.

FIELDING:

The versatile Brookens played first, second, short and third last year. Third is his best position; he can still pick the ball in the field and make a good strong throw. Short is probably his weakest spot, and that worries the Indians because they feel a utility infielder has to be able to play short. Brookens turns the double play pretty well, but he tends to wear down defensively when he has to play more than two or three days in a row.

OVERALL:

Brookens helped the Indians a lot last year. But being a free agent after the season, there was some question whether he would return. The Indians said they wanted him back, but hinted Brookens might have to take a salary cut. They also talked about using a younger player with more speed, one who could play shortstop. But Brookens figures to help someone in 1991.

Overall Statistics

	G	AB	R	H	D	T	HR	RBI	SB	BB	SO	AVG
1990	64	154	18	41	7	2	1	20	0	14	25	.266
Career	1336	3865	477	950	175	40	71	431	86	281	605	.246

Where He Hits the Ball

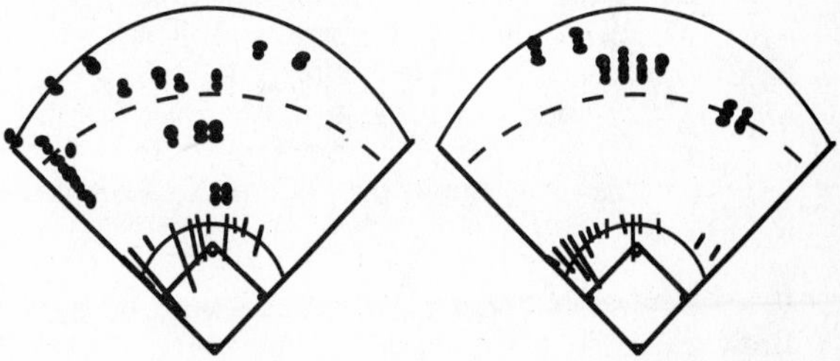

Vs. LHP Vs. RHP

1990 Situational Stats

	AB	H	HR	RBI	AVG		AB	H	HR	RBI	AVG
Home	71	16	0	10	.225	LHP	93	24	1	11	.258
Road	83	25	1	10	.301	RHP	61	17	0	9	.279
Day	43	12	1	4	.279	Sc Pos	43	13	0	19	.302
Night	111	29	0	16	.261	Clutch	26	8	1	5	.308

1990 Rankings (American League)

- 1st in worst batting average on a 3-1 count (.000)

HITTING:

Jerry Browne had an erratic but productive season in his second year with the Indians. Compared to 1989, Browne's batting average (.299-.267), games played (153-140), stolen bases (14-12) and on-base average (.370-.353) all dropped, but his runs (83-90), homers (5-6), runs batted in (45-50) and walks (68-72) all increased. On the whole, he had another good year.

The switch-hitting Browne was plagued by leg injuries last year. He was also benched several times in the first half because of a weak bat. However, he finished strongly -- hitting .281 with 40 runs and 32 RBI after the All-Star break. Browne's hitting took off after he was moved out of the leadoff role, where he was never comfortable. When the Indians brought up Alex Cole from Class AAA on July 25 to hit number-one, Browne dropped to the number-two hole and relaxed.

Browne became much more patient at the plate last season. Hitting behind Cole, he was called on to hit-and-run, sacrifice and take more pitches in order to give Cole a better chance to steal. It's a role he still needs to work on. Browne has more power from the left side of the plate. But he hits for a higher average right-handed.

BASERUNNING:

Browne has above-average speed, but below-average instincts when it comes to running the bases. No one gambled on the base paths more than Browne did last year. Unfortunately, no one lost more than Browne did either. Yes, he can steal a base, and he may one day be able to steal 20-25 bags a year. But his decision-making process has to improve or he'll continue to run his team out of potentially big innings.

FIELDING:

Browne has a good arm and great range at second base. His concentration on routine plays also improved last year. Yet, he still has a problem turning the double play. Some say it's his footwork. Others say he doesn't get the ball out of his glove fast enough to turn the pivot. No one has ever said it's because Browne is afraid of an oncoming baserunner. It's a problem Browne and infield coach Rich Dauer must address.

OVERALL:

With the release of Dion James, Browne is the only remaining player on the Tribe's big-league roster who was involved in the Julio Franco deal of 1988. The Indians shipped Franco -- perhaps the best pure hitter to wear an Indians' uniform in the last 20 years -- to Texas for Browne, Pete O'Brien and Oddibe McDowell. Were the Indians robbed? Maybe. But Browne, four years Franco's junior, remains a player on the rise.

JERRY BROWNE

Position: 2B
Bats: B **Throws:** R
Ht: 5'10" **Wt:** 170

Opening Day Age: 25
Born: 2/13/66 in St. Croix, Virgin Islands
ML Seasons: 5

Overall Statistics

	G	AB	R	H	D	T	HR	RBI	SB	BB	SO	AVG
1990	140	513	92	137	26	5	6	50	12	72	46	.267
Career	510	1803	270	498	84	17	13	153	60	227	196	.276

Where He Hits the Ball

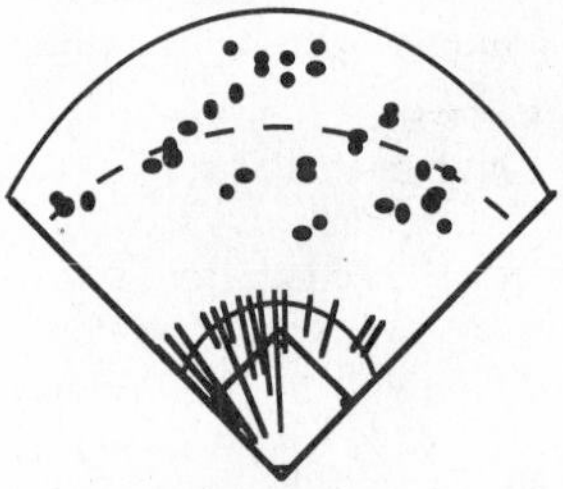

Vs. LHP

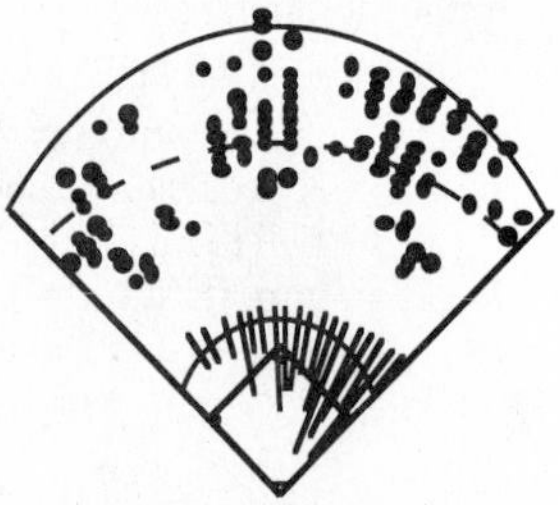

Vs. RHP

1990 Situational Stats

	AB	H	HR	RBI	AVG		AB	H	HR	RBI	AVG
Home	250	68	2	22	.272	LHP	139	39	0	14	.281
Road	263	69	4	28	.262	RHP	374	98	6	36	.262
Day	146	36	0	13	.247	Sc Pos	100	26	1	42	.260
Night	367	101	6	37	.275	Clutch	82	20	1	7	.244

1990 Rankings (American League)

- 3rd in sacrifice flies (11) and runs scored per time reached base (43.6%)
- 7th in runs scored (92) and sacrifice bunts (12)
- 8th in highest percentage of swings put into play (54.4%)
- Led the Indians in runs scored, sacrifice flies, walks (72), groundball/flyball ratio (1.42), runs scored per time reached base, highest percentage of pitches taken (59.7%), lowest percentage of swings that missed (11.2%) and highest percentage of swings put into play
- Led AL second basemen in sacrifice flies and runs scored per time reached base

TOM CANDIOTTI

Position: SP
Bats: R **Throws:** R
Ht: 6' 2" **Wt:** 200

Opening Day Age: 33
Born: 8/31/57 in Walnut Creek, CA
ML Seasons: 7

PITCHING:

Tom Candiotti has always been caught between the knuckleball and his other pitches. The knuckleball kept him in the big leagues, but Candiotti felt he was too young and talented to be considered strictly a knuckleball pitcher. So he kept throwing curveballs, sliders, fastballs and cut fastballs. He liked to keep a 50-50 mix between the knuckler and his other pitches in the first half of the season.

But at the All-Star break last season, Candiotti decided to concentrate on the knuckleball. He started throwing it almost 80 percent of the time and turned in his third consecutive winning season with the Indians. By the end of the year, Candiotti said he'd made the conversion to a full-time knuckleball pitcher. The change in style resulted in shoulder tightness in the latter part of the season and prevented Candiotti from equalling or surpassing his career high 16 victories of 1986.

Candiotti has spent time on the disabled list the last three seasons because of shoulder and elbow problems. Yet he is the first Indian to pitch 200 innings or more in five consecutive seasons since Sam McDowell in 1967-1971. The condition of his shoulder and elbow is a concern for the Indians. Candiotti went on the disabled list last May for an inflamed elbow. In years past, he's been on the DL for a strained rotator cuff and sore shoulder. The Indians have learned to watch him carefully. At the first sign of arm problems, they shut down "The Candy Man."

Candiotti throws three kind of knucklers -- hard, medium and slow. The slow knuckler travels between 50-60 MPH. He also throws a curveball at about the same speed, and the two pitches are hard to tell apart.

HOLDING RUNNERS AND FIELDING:

Candiotti works extra hard at holding runners because he knows how easy it is to get a jump on one of his slow-motion knucklers. He isn't afraid to throw to first base six or seven times to keep a runner close. An excellent fielder, he always covers the right base.

OVERALL:

Candiotti, who likes to pitch at Cleveland Stadium, went only 7-6 at home last season. Overall, he's 39-28 at the Stadium. The Candy Man prefers to face free-swinging power hitters. The knuckler eats them up and does terrible things to their swings. Patient hitters, guys who hit singles and line drives, are the ones that give him problems. Though he throws such an unpredictable pitch, Candiotti has good control. In his five seasons with the Indians, he's never had more walks than strikeouts.

Overall Statistics

	W	L	ERA	G	GS	Sv	IP	H	R	BB	SO	HR
1990	15	11	3.65	31	29	0	202.0	207	92	55	128	23
Career	71	65	3.69	179	171	0	1166.2	1147	544	388	711	103

How Often He Throws Strikes

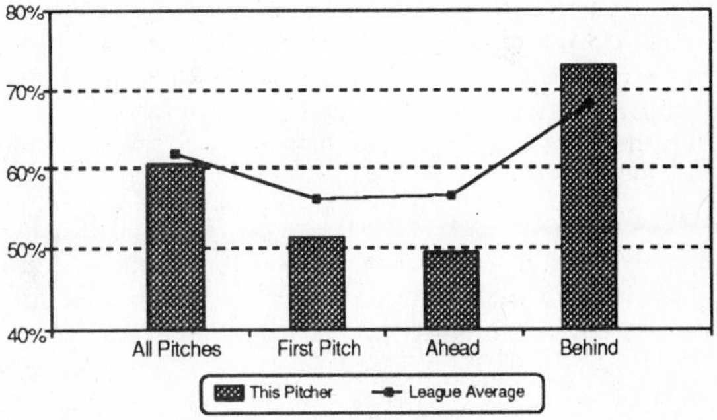

1990 Situational Stats

	W	L	ERA	Sv	IP		AB	H	HR	RBI	AVG
Home	7	6	4.10	0	112.0	LHB	403	103	9	38	.256
Road	8	5	3.10	0	90.0	RHB	385	104	14	48	.270
Day	6	1	3.55	0	50.2	Sc Pos	170	54	5	61	.318
Night	9	10	3.69	0	151.1	Clutch	58	18	1	7	.310

1990 Rankings (American League)

- 5th in highest run support per 9 innings (5.30) and highest batting average allowed with runners in scoring position (.318)
- 6th in most HRs allowed per 9 innings (1.03)
- 9th in most HRs allowed (23)
- 10th in wins (15)
- Led the Indians in wins, losses (11), hit batsmen (6), wild pitches (9), pitches thrown (3,296), stolen bases allowed (18), GDPs induced (17), winning percentage (.577), groundball/flyball ratio allowed (1.46), run support per 9 innings, GDPs induced per 9 innings (.76) and strikeouts per 9 innings (5.7)

ALEX COLE

Position: CF
Bats: L **Throws:** L
Ht: 6' 2" **Wt:** 183

Opening Day Age: 25
Born: 8/17/65 in Fayetteville, NC
ML Seasons: 1

HITTING:

No one changed the chemistry of the Indians more than Alex Cole in 1990. He did it with a quick bat and blazing feet. The Indians had been searching for a swift leadoff hitter/center fielder since the start of spring training last year. Their search ended when they obtained Cole from San Diego during the All-Star break in a minor league trade.

Cole, a left-handed hitter, isn't going to overpower anyone at the plate. But he's just not a slap-and-run hitter either. He hits line drives mostly to left field and up the middle. The Indians would like to see him pull the ball more because defenses started shifting against him, but Cole feels more comfortable going the opposite way.

Cole has a good eye at the plate and can take a pitcher deep in the count. He took several called third strikes while working the pitcher in such a fashion, but no one complained because the Indians wanted him to try to draw some walks. Cole had trouble bunting and the Indians arranged for him to take some lessons from former batting champion Rod Carew, a great bunter.

Though Cole finished the year at .300, the Indians aren't sure he can stay at that level. But they figure that if he can hit between .270 and .290, he can still kick-start the offense from the leadoff spot because of his speed.

BASERUNNING:

Cole makes his living with his feet. In his eighth appearance with the Indians, he set a club record by stealing five bases in one game. In his next game, he stole two more to tie an American League record for the most steals in consecutive games. Cole's 40 steals set a club record for rookies. And he did it in just 63 games. Cole didn't get a particularly good jump last year because he didn't know American League pitchers, but he's so fast that some catchers didn't even bother to make a throw.

FIELDING:

Cole isn't a great outfielder, but his speed allows him to outrun most of his mistakes. He has great range going into the alleys. His arm is below average, and he has some problems going back to the fence.

OVERALL:

Cole changed the Indians from a club with so-so speed to a running, take-the-extra-base ball club. In 63 games, he not only led the club in stolen bases, but finished fourth in the league. The Indians can't wait to see what he'll do in a full season. They went 31-35 after he was put in the starting lineup.

Overall Statistics

	G	AB	R	H	D	T	HR	RBI	SB	BB	SO	AVG
1990	63	227	43	68	5	4	0	13	40	28	38	.300
Career	63	227	43	68	5	4	0	13	40	28	38	.300

Where He Hits the Ball

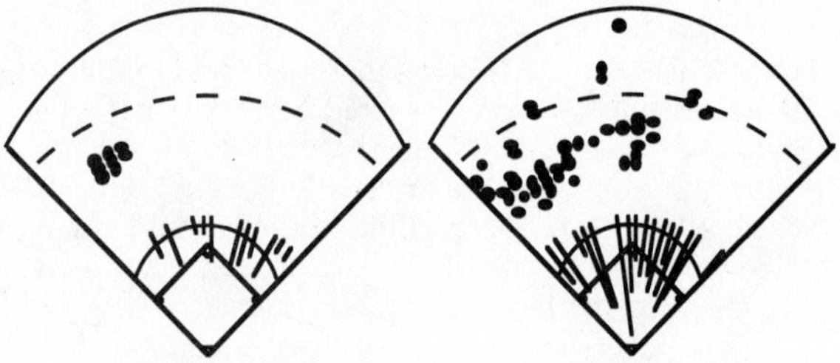

Vs. LHP　　Vs. RHP

1990 Situational Stats

	AB	H	HR	RBI	AVG		AB	H	HR	RBI	AVG
Home	121	37	0	9	.306	LHP	52	13	0	4	.250
Road	106	31	0	4	.292	RHP	175	55	0	9	.314
Day	32	12	0	2	.375	Sc Pos	50	16	0	11	.320
Night	195	56	0	11	.287	Clutch	22	6	0	0	.273

1990 Rankings (American League)

- 3rd in steals of third (9)
- 4th in stolen bases (40) and leadoff on-base average (.379)
- 7th in stolen base percentage (81.6%)
- Led the Indians in stolen bases, caught stealing (9), stolen base percentage and steals of third
- Led AL center fieldings in batting average on a 3-2 count (.321) and steals of third

JOHN FARRELL

Position: SP
Bats: R **Throws:** R
Ht: 6' 4" **Wt:** 210

Opening Day Age: 28
Born: 8/4/62 in Monmouth PK, NJ
ML Seasons: 4

PITCHING:

Hard times turned harder last season for John Farrell. After 15 starts, he went on the disabled list with tendinitis in his right elbow for the third straight season. On June 24, the day before he went on the disabled list, Farrell had thrown five solid innings against Milwaukee to win his first game since May 13.

At the time, the Indians were still optimistic. They figured Farrell could return right after the All-Star break and help pitch them into contention in the American League East. They figured wrong. When Farrell made his next start on Sept. 21, the Indians had long since faded in the AL East. Farrell threw five scoreless innings against Toronto and the club felt better about the 1991 season. In his next start, however, Farrell left after 4.1 innings with more elbow pain. This time the pain was in a different place. A few days after the season ended, Farrell had exploratory surgery on the elbow. A torn ligament was found. So was a bone chip. And the ulna nerve had to be re-routed. Farrell, who has the body of a linebacker, but Pee Wee Herman's right elbow, is expected to miss most of the 1991 season.

When healthy, Farrell can be a dominating pitcher. After changing the grip on his fastball in the second half of the 1989 season, he became one of the hardest throwers in the league. He has a good slider and a killer change up to go along with his fastball. His change-up is especially effective against right-handed hitters.

Farrell is very competitive, maybe too much so. When his elbow problems first began in 1988, he didn't tell anyone that something was wrong until late August. After spending nearly four years in the minors, Farrell wasn't going to blow his shot at the big leagues because his elbow hurt. In 1990 his elbow wasn't right either. But Farrell kept pitching. Give him an A for valor and a D for dumb.

HOLDING RUNNERS AND FIELDING:

Farrell is a good fielder, with a decent move to first base. He doesn't always concentrate as well as he should when it comes to holding runners. He gets off the mound quickly and always covers first base.

OVERALL:

Farrell's injury has put his career in jeopardy and the Indians' starting rotation in limbo. At the start of the 1990 season, the Tribe had one of the best rotations in the league with Greg Swindell, Tom Candiotti, Bud Black and Farrell. But with Farrell hurt and Black gone, they find themselves in a pitching crisis.

Overall Statistics

	W	L	ERA	G	GS	Sv	IP	H	R	BB	SO	HR
1990	4	5	4.28	17	17	0	96.2	108	49	33	44	10
Career	32	30	3.93	89	87	0	584.0	588	281	193	296	46

How Often He Throws Strikes

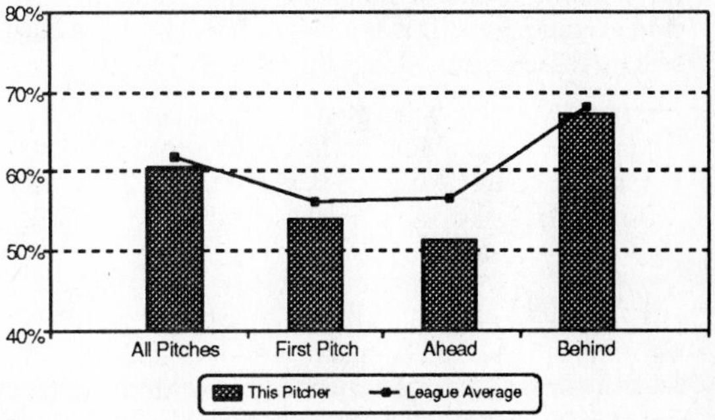

1990 Situational Stats

	W	L	ERA	Sv	IP		AB	H	HR	RBI	AVG
Home	1	2	3.54	0	28.0	LHB	205	57	4	23	.278
Road	3	3	4.59	0	68.2	RHB	172	51	6	21	.297
Day	3	2	3.53	0	35.2	Sc Pos	88	23	2	33	.261
Night	1	3	4.72	0	61.0	Clutch	19	10	0	3	.526

1990 Rankings (American League)

- Did not rank near the top or bottom in any category

HITTING:

Okay, so Felix (The Cat) Fermin isn't Jose Canseco. But never let it be said that this guy can't go deep. Babe Ruth and Lou Gehrig, now resting comfortably in baseball's happy hunting ground, had to crack a grin when Fermin hit his first and only home run as a pro last April 22 against Chicago. It ended a stretch of 2,915 homerless at-bats for Fermin. It also marked the beginning of Fermin's most productive season in the big leagues.

In 1989 Fermin set an American League record for the fewest RBI (21) by any player who appeared in 150 or more games. Last season Fermin finished with 40 RBI, 25 of them coming after the All-Star break. The difference was a weight training program that added muscle to Fermin's bat. Opposing outfielders still shaded him to right field -- Fermin's favorite place to hit -- but he was able to turn the tables on them from time to time by pulling the ball to left. His extra base hits increased from 10 in 1989 to 16 in 1990.

Fermin, who also benefitted from the instruction of hitting coach Jose Morales, hit .281 after the All-Star break. He is an excellent bunter and is extremely difficult to strike out. He's a dead fastball hitter. Pitches down and away will occasionally fool him.

BASERUNNING:

Fermin isn't fast and he hits into a lot of double plays because he usually makes hard contact. Although he's not swift, Fermin will try to take second on anything that resembles a double, and usually makes the right decision when it comes to taking the extra base. However, when he tries to get too aggressive, he often runs into an out. He's not much of a threat to steal.

FIELDING:

Fermin had a pretty good season offensively, but he's in the big leagues because he can play defense, and last year he kept the Indians' infield together. Fermin has good range and a strong arm that he uses only when needed. In 1989, he led the league in errors with 26. Last season, despite his usual post All-Star game slump, he made 16.

OVERALL:

Fermin fits very well into the Indians' revamped offense. Without a dominant home run hitter, they relied on speed, contact hitters and aggressive baserunning. He also gave them good defense up the middle. In fact, Fermin played so well that shortstop Mark Lewis, the Tribe's number one prospect, might be forced to spend another season in the minors. A key to Fermin's productive season was the rest given him by manager John McNamara. In 1989, he played 156 games and wore down.

FELIX FERMIN

Position: SS
Bats: R **Throws:** R
Ht: 5'11" **Wt:** 170

Opening Day Age: 27
Born: 10/9/63 in Mao, Valverde, Dominican Republic
ML Seasons: 4

Overall Statistics

	G	AB	R	H	D	T	HR	RBI	SB	BB	SO	AVG
1990	148	414	47	106	13	2	1	40	3	26	22	.256
Career	370	1053	112	262	22	5	1	67	12	79	68	.249

Where He Hits the Ball

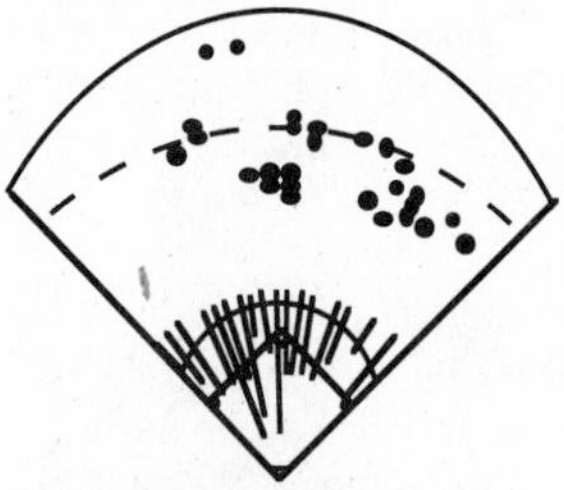

Vs. LHP

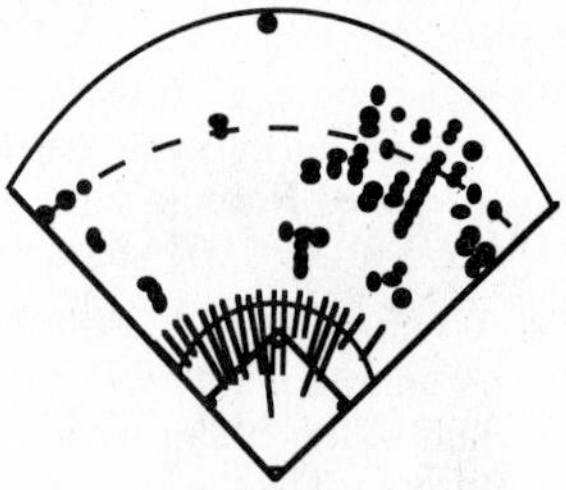

Vs. RHP

1990 Situational Stats

	AB	H	HR	RBI	AVG		AB	H	HR	RBI	AVG
Home	205	57	1	24	.278	LHP	130	34	0	15	.262
Road	209	49	0	16	.234	RHP	284	72	1	25	.254
Day	114	32	1	14	.281	Sc Pos	114	29	0	37	.254
Night	300	74	0	26	.247	Clutch	36	11	0	1	.306

1990 Rankings (American League)

- ➡ 2nd in batting average on a 3-2 count (.412) and batting average with 2 strikes (.277)
- ➡ 4th in sacrifice bunts (13)
- ➡ 7th lowest slugging percentage vs. left-handed pitchers (.285)
- ➡ 8th most GDPs per GDP situation (18.6%) and 8th highest batting average on a 0-2 count (.292)
- ➡ Led the Indians in sacrifice bunts, batting average on a 3-2 count, batting average with 2 strikes and percentage of extra bases taken as a runner (51.8%)
- ➡ Led AL shortstops in batting average on a 3-2 count and batting average with 2 strikes

KEITH HERNANDEZ

Position: 1B
Bats: L **Throws:** L
Ht: 6' 0" **Wt:** 205

Opening Day Age: 37
Born: 10/20/53 in San Francisco, CA
ML Seasons: 17

Overall Statistics

	G	AB	R	H	D	T	HR	RBI	SB	BB	SO	AVG
1990	43	130	7	26	2	0	1	8	0	14	17	.200
Career	2088	7370	1124	2182	426	60	162	1071	98	1070	1012	.296

Where He Hits the Ball

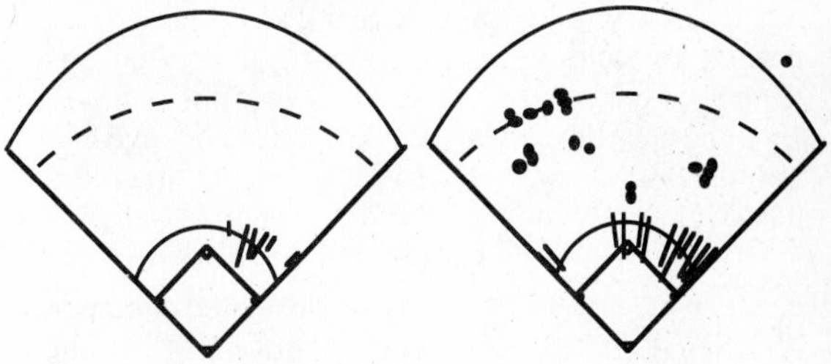

Vs. LHP   Vs. RHP

1990 Situational Stats

	AB	H	HR	RBI	AVG		AB	H	HR	RBI	AVG
Home	42	7	0	2	.167	LHP	27	4	0	2	.148
Road	88	19	1	6	.216	RHP	103	22	1	6	.214
Day	40	10	0	1	.250	Sc Pos	25	4	0	5	.160
Night	90	16	1	7	.178	Clutch	24	5	0	0	.208

1990 Rankings (American League)

- Did not rank near the top or bottom in any category

HITTING:

The Indians took a gamble on Keith Hernandez and lost twice. They lost on the field where Hernandez appeared in only 43 games. They lost even worse at the bargaining table, where they signed Hernandez to a two-year guaranteed deal worth $3.5 million.

Tribe President Hank Peters thought Hernandez could supply leadership and timely hitting to a young ball club. All Hernandez gave him was a headache. Injured much of the year, he batted only 130 times, and if he had five good at-bats among them, it was an upset. Starting from spring training, Hernandez had no bat speed. The left-handed hitter tried to go to left field on almost every pitch because he could no longer pull a major league fastball.

Even though Hernandez entered the year as a lifetime .295 hitter against lefties, manager John McNamara didn't let him face southpaws early in the season because they overmatched him. Later in the year, it didn't matter because Hernandez was always hurt. He had one homer and eight RBI. His swing looked as tired and old as his 37-year-old body.

BASERUNNING:

Hernandez is now one of the slowest men in the big leagues. Three consecutive seasons of leg injuries have reduced him to a slow jog. He couldn't even make it to second base to break up a double play. Hernandez was on the disabled list three times last year with pulled calf muscles, and never played again after the final injury on July 24. Hernandez last went on the DL under tense conditions. The Indians believed he could play, but Hernandez said he couldn't; he went to New York and obtained a second medical test that agreed with his own diagnosis. He went on the DL for the third and final time on Aug. 9.

FIELDING:

Amazingly, Hernandez could still play defense. He had no range, but he handled balls hit right at him and was a master at digging throws out of the dirt. It was easy to see why he won 11 Gold Gloves in the National League. However, that was the only part of his game that came anywhere close to equaling his storied past.

OVERALL:

Hernandez was an expensive disappointment to the Indians. Even before he was injured, it was obvious his skills had vanished. Hernandez' agent said that the first-sacker was moving to Florida last winter and hiring a personal trainer so he could get in top shape for the 1991 season. But all last year, Hernandez himself talked like an old athlete who couldn't wait to get his money and retire.

HITTING:

Brook Jacoby continued to remake himself as a hitter last season. When he first came to the Indians in 1984, Jacoby swung freely and often. He wanted to hit the ball as hard and as far as he could. Strikeouts didn't matter. Over the years, Jacoby has changed. He's shortened his swing, cut down on his strikeouts and become a much more consistent hitter. Hitting coach Jose Morales even got him to choke up with two strikes last season. Jacoby responded by hitting .293 with 75 RBI. The .293 was his highest average since 1987 (.300) and the 75 RBI were the most he's had since 1986 (80). Jacoby might never hit 32 home runs again like he did in 1987, but he has become a more dependable hitter.

He is a very coachable player. Since coming to Cleveland, Jacoby has had three hitting coaches -- Bobby Bonds, Charlie Manuel and Morales -- and he's had good seasons for all three of them. He's changed his stance from closed to wide open and everything in between. For the last two years, he's hit out of a straight-up stance. Fastballs high and inside give him trouble. But Jacoby has become one of the better breaking-ball hitters on the Indians. With two strikes, he tries to hit the ball to right field.

In the past, Jacoby has always disappeared at crunch time. In 1989, he hit .229 with runners in scoring position. Last season, though, he hit .293 in those situations.

BASERUNNING:

Jacoby isn't fast, although he always hustles, and he hits a lot of hard grounders. That explains why he grounded into 20 double plays, tops on the club last year. No stealing threat, he's a cautious baserunner with below average instincts. But Jacoby knows that and usually runs the bases under control.

FIELDING:

Jacoby had a Gold Glove year in 1990. There was only one problem. Gold Gloves are awarded to players who play one position. Jacoby split his time between third (102 games) and first (73 games). Jacoby's best position is third, but he made the switch to first without a whimper. He committed a career-low six errors while changing gloves and locations.

OVERALL:

Every winter there are rumors about the Indians trading Jacoby. But every spring, he's still an Indian. The same talk surfaced this winter, but no trade had yet occurred at press time. It appears Jacoby will start at first base this year because of Carlos Baerga's strong rookie season. But if Baerga can't handle third, Jacoby could easily move back to the hot corner.

BROOK JACOBY

Position: 3B/1B
Bats: R **Throws:** R
Ht: 5'11" **Wt:** 195

Opening Day Age: 31
Born: 11/23/59 in Philadelphia, PA
ML Seasons: 9

Overall Statistics

	G	AB	R	H	D	T	HR	RBI	SB	BB	SO	AVG
1990	155	553	77	162	24	4	14	75	1	63	58	.293
Career	1069	3810	477	1050	176	23	112	465	14	384	656	.276

Where He Hits the Ball

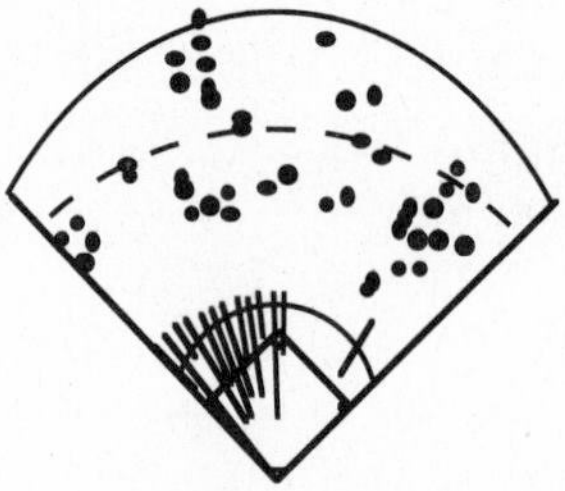

Vs. LHP

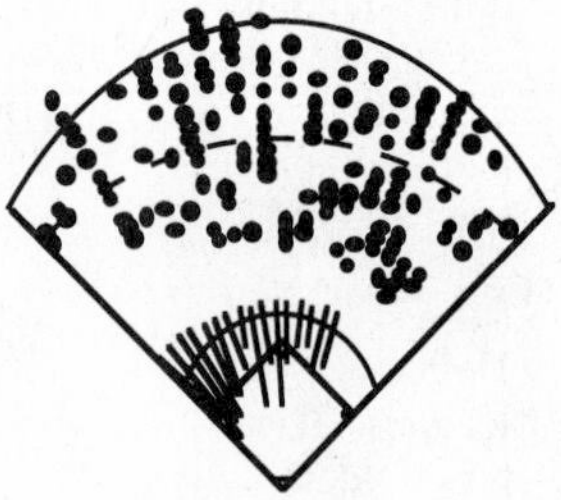

Vs. RHP

1990 Situational Stats

	AB	H	HR	RBI	AVG		AB	H	HR	RBI	AVG
Home	261	75	10	41	.287	LHP	158	50	3	18	.316
Road	292	87	4	34	.298	RHP	395	112	11	57	.284
Day	156	41	2	17	.263	Sc Pos	140	41	1	54	.293
Night	397	121	12	58	.305	Clutch	87	22	2	10	.253

1990 Rankings (American League)

- 4th in least pitches seen per plate appearance (3.18)
- 5th in GDPs (20)
- Led the Indians in hits (162), singles (120), intentional walks (6), times on base (227), GDPs, games (155), on-base average (.365) and on-base average vs. right-handed pitchers (.358)

CHRIS JAMES

Position: DH/LF
Bats: R **Throws:** R
Ht: 6' 1" **Wt:** 190

Opening Day Age: 28
Born: 10/4/62 in Rusk, TX
ML Seasons: 5

Overall Statistics

	G	AB	R	H	D	T	HR	RBI	SB	BB	SO	AVG
1990	140	528	62	158	32	4	12	70	4	31	71	.299
Career	553	1980	227	530	96	13	62	260	19	116	292	.268

Where He Hits the Ball

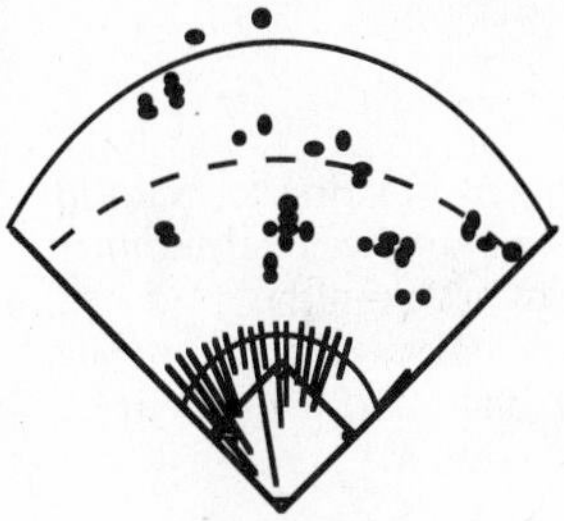

Vs. LHP

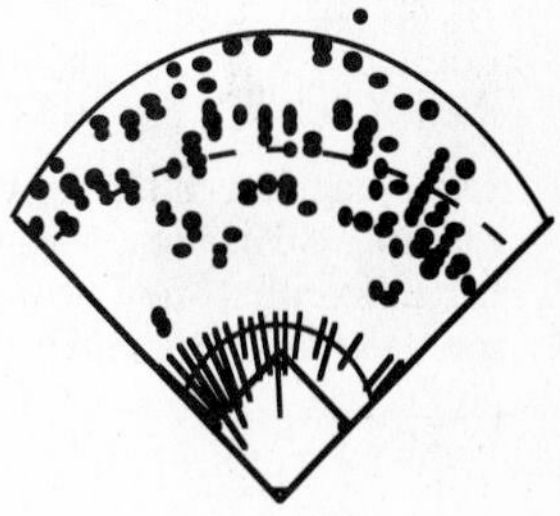

Vs. RHP

1990 Situational Stats

	AB	H	HR	RBI	AVG		AB	H	HR	RBI	AVG
Home	234	67	6	33	.286	LHP	162	49	4	22	.302
Road	294	91	6	37	.310	RHP	366	109	8	48	.298
Day	142	47	4	25	.331	Sc Pos	145	47	2	58	.324
Night	386	111	8	45	.288	Clutch	73	20	0	8	.274

1990 Rankings (American League)

- ➟ 6th in batting average on the road (.310)
- ➟ 9th in batting average (.299)
- ➟ Led the Indians in batting average, doubles (32), batting average with runners in scoring position (.324), batting average vs. right-handed pitchers (.298), slugging percentage vs. right-handed pitchers (.448) and batting average on the road
- ➟ Led designated hitters in batting average, doubles, triples (4), sacrifice bunts (3), batting average with runners in scoring position, batting average at home (.286), batting average on the road, bunts in play (5) and steals of third (3)

HITTING:

Last May 7, Chris James was hitting .113. At the time, it appeared that James, who came to Cleveland with a reputation of being a streak hitter -- he'd gone through an 0-for-38 slump in 1989 -- had started the season in a deep freeze. But then James broke the stereotype. He started hitting and never stopped until the last game of the season.

When talk turned to hot and cold streaks, James begged to differ. Last year's numbers backed him up. James hit .321 after May 7 and led the Indians with a .299 average, the ninth highest in the American League. (He needed one more hit in the last game of the season to finish at .300, but couldn't get it.) James spent most of the season at designated hitter. He had always been an everyday player in the National League with Philadelphia and San Diego, so it took the intense right-handed hitter a while to adjust to the new role.

James is not the typical power-hitting, slow-footed DH. He hit only 12 homers, but he drove in a career-high 70 runs by hitting singles and doubles in bunches. He was ninth in the league with 51 multi-hit games. A free swinger who would rather strike out than walk, he'll swing at any kind of fastball. But he showed much more patience against breaking balls than he did in the NL.

BASERUNNING:

James is extremely aggressive on the base paths. He'll gamble on turning a single into a double, and he almost always goes from first to third when the opportunity presents itself. Though not a great base stealer, he'll rattle an infielder's fillings going into second base to break up a double play.

FIELDING:

James made only 12 starts last year in the outfield, most of them in left field. He has a good arm and no fear of the fence. Yet he has some trouble judging fly balls. In 1991 he could be in for a lot more playing time depending on the fate of outfielders Candy Maldonado (free agent) and Cory Snyder (trade bait).

OVERALL:

James' aggressive attitude and style of play carried over to the rest of the Indians last season. In 1989, the team died early when they fell behind. Last year, James kept the Tribe's fires burning from the first inning to the last. James, who set career highs in hits, RBI and average, arrived in Cleveland with Sandy Alomar Jr. and Carlos Baerga from San Diego for Joe Carter. With James' help, the Indians won the first round in that trade.

DION JAMES

Position: 1B/LF
Bats: L **Throws:** L
Ht: 6' 1" **Wt:** 170

Opening Day Age: 28
Born: 11/9/62 in Philadelphia, PA
ML Seasons: 7

HITTING:

Dion James had the sweetest swing on the Indians. Yet he didn't produce a lot of runs, so the Indians released the left-handed hitter at the end of last year.

A line-drive hitter who produces singles and doubles, James should be able to help someone. He can't run very well and he's not going to drive the ball out of the park, but he can hit under difficult circumstances. He showed that last season in constructing a 16-game hitting streak, the longest of the season by an Indian. The streak started on July 17 and ended on Aug. 13. It lasted so long because Manager John McNamara rarely let James face a left- handed pitcher.

James also showed good survival instincts. McNamara got mad at him during the season after he inquired about his reduced playing time. Usually in those situations, McNamara buries the player. Yet James managed to hit and play himself out of the doghouse when the Indians grew short of first basemen.

Last year, James hit anywhere from first to ninth in the lineup. His most productive spot was the number-three hole, but the Indians didn't think he produced enough runs to take up permanent residence there. He showed a good eye at the plate and usually made contact.

BASERUNNING:

With the Indians retooling for speed, James didn't have much of a chance to stay with the club in 1991. James always hustled down to first base; he just didn't get there quickly enough. He did steal five bases last season, and he'll go from first to third on a single.

FIELDING:

James certainly isn't a Gold Glove candidate, but he gets the most out of his ability. Last season, he played left field, center field, first base and DH. He was a utility outfielder/infielder. He won't embarrass himself in the outfield, but it might be dangerous to let him play there for an extended period of time. He has a an average to below-average arm, but his lack of range keeps him from being a regular. At first base, he'll dive for balls and does a fine job making throws to other bases.

OVERALL:

Lack of speed and power cost James a job in Cleveland even though he's a .284 lifetime hitter. Another element factored into his release --money. The Indians have a lot of soft-hitting players who are switch- or left-handed hitters. It just happened that James, at 28, was making a lot more money than the rest of them. If James had batted .250-.260 and hit between 12-18 home runs a year, he'd still be with the Indians.

Overall Statistics

	G	AB	R	H	D	T	HR	RBI	SB	BB	SO	AVG
1990	87	248	28	68	15	2	1	22	5	27	23	.274
Career	644	1999	253	567	107	18	20	187	37	244	243	.284

Where He Hits the Ball

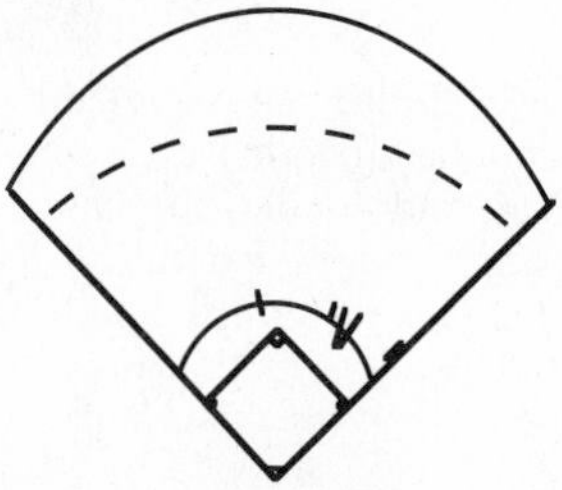

Vs. LHP

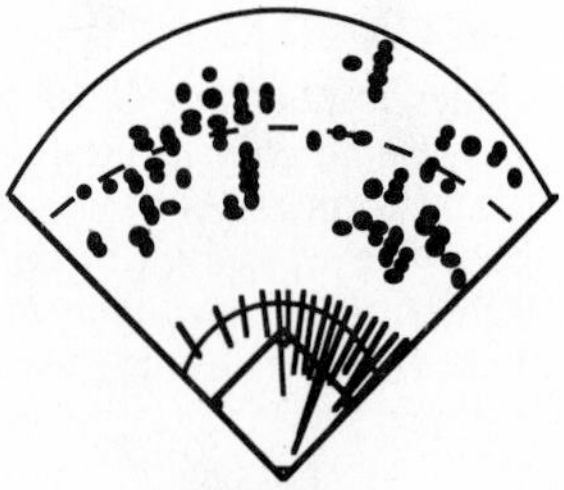

Vs. RHP

1990 Situational Stats

	AB	H	HR	RBI	AVG		AB	H	HR	RBI	AVG
Home	123	40	0	10	.325	LHP	9	1	0	1	.111
Road	125	28	1	12	.224	RHP	239	67	1	21	.280
Day	67	17	0	7	.254	Sc Pos	47	13	0	18	.277
Night	181	51	1	15	.282	Clutch	46	8	0	1	.174

1990 Rankings (American League)

- 10th worst batting average in the clutch (.174)

STOPPER

DOUG JONES

Position: RP
Bats: R **Throws:** R
Ht: 6' 2" **Wt:** 195

Opening Day Age: 33
Born: 6/24/57 in Covina, CA
ML Seasons: 6

PITCHING:

In the age of the hard-throwing, let-it-rip closer, Doug Jones keeps doing it his way. Jones stands on the mound throwing a decent fastball -- he may reach 88 MPH on a good night -- and a bewitching change-up. Hitters keep screwing themselves into the ground trying to hit either pitch and Jones keeps saving ball games. He saved a club record 43 games last season for a team that won only 77. In 1989, he saved 32. In 1988, he saved 37.

Last season Jones figured in 62 percent of the Tribe's victories, adding in his five wins. Dennis Eckersley, generally regarded as the best reliever in baseball, figured in 50 percent of Oakland's wins. Bobby Thigpen figured in 65 percent of the Chicago White Sox's victories which allowed him to break the major league save record with 57.

Jones, 33, has proven to be a durable, albeit late-arriving, closer. He learned his craft while spending nearly 10 years in the minors. As a minor league starter, he threw five or six pitches. Jones has economized, throwing just two pitches now. Yet by changing arm speed and deliveries, those two pitches look like five or six. Jones hides the ball well, coming toward home plate with his head, shoulder and body first. Then, at the last moment, his arm flashes from behind his body and the bottom drops out of the change-up.

Most relievers are subject to the dangers of overuse. This applies to Jones too. But inactivity may be an even greater threat to him. He slumped for a brief period in late August after going five days without working, taking several appearances to right himself. It wasn't the first time that had happened to Jones.

HOLDING RUNNERS AND FIELDING:

Jones usually doesn't worry about holding runners. That's because the American League hit only .218 against him and he walked just 22 batters in 84.1 innings. Jones isn't a great fielder, but he has improved. He has a thick build, but still gets off the mound quickly to cover first base.

OVERALL:

Attitude, more than anything, makes Jones a good closer. He isn't thrilled by a big win or crushed by a tough loss. Day in, day out, he's always the same -- a necessary trait for a closer. When Jones isn't pitching well, it's usually because his fastball and change-up start looking like the same pitch. The larger the difference in velocity between the two pitches, the more effective Jones will be. When he's tired, his fastball drops closer in speed to the change-up. And when he's overused, Jones tends to overthrow both pitches.

Overall Statistics

	W	L	ERA	G	GS	Sv	IP	H	R	BB	SO	HR
1990	5	5	2.56	66	0	43	84.1	66	26	22	55	5
Career	22	24	2.65	240	0	121	360.1	335	130	82	292	15

How Often He Throws Strikes

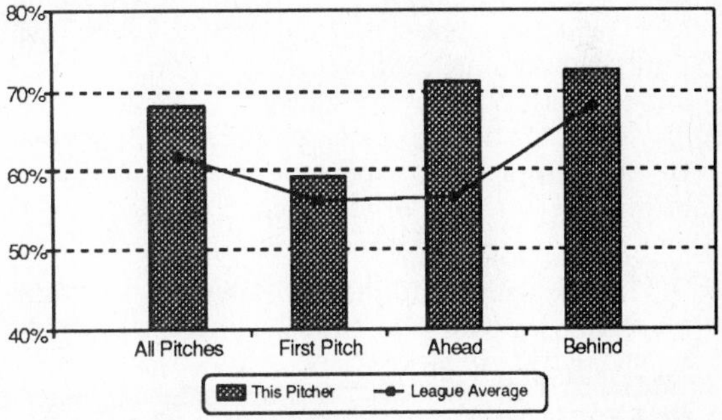

1990 Situational Stats

	W	L	ERA	Sv	IP		AB	H	HR	RBI	AVG
Home	4	4	3.11	23	46.1	LHB	165	33	3	18	.200
Road	1	1	1.89	20	38.0	RHB	138	33	2	16	.239
Day	0	0	0.62	16	29.0	Sc Pos	101	24	2	29	.238
Night	5	5	3.58	27	55.1	Clutch	229	52	2	26	.227

1990 Rankings (American League)

- 2nd in games finished (64), save opportunities (51) and lowest batting average vs. left-handed hitters (.200)
- 3rd in saves (43)
- 4th in blown saves (8)
- 6th in save percentage (84.3%)
- 8th in games pitched (66)
- Led the Indians in games pitched, saves, games finished, save opportunites, save percentage, blown saves, GDPs induced per GDP situation (17.8%) and batting average vs. left-handed hitters

CANDY MALDONADO

Position: LF/RF/DH
Bats: R **Throws:** R
Ht: 6' 0" **Wt:** 195

Opening Day Age: 30
Born: 9/5/60 in Humacao, Puerto Rico
ML Seasons: 10

HITTING:

They call Cleveland the Comeback City. Well, Candy Maldonado had a Comeback Year in the Comeback City. Given up for dead in San Francisco, Maldonado set career highs in home runs (22), runs batted in (95), hits (161), doubles (32), walks (49), strikeouts (134), runs (76) and at-bats (590).

In 1989, Maldonado had hit .217 with nine homers and 41 RBI. When he filed for free agency, people cheered. What fueled the comeback? It could have been Maldonado's desire to prove he could still play. It could have been the arrival of Jose Morales, Maldonado's personal hitting guru, as the Indians' hitting instructor. More than likely, it was a combination of both. In 1986 and 1987, Maldonado had his best years in the big leagues. Morales was there as the Giants' hitting coach. When Morales left to join the Indians as a roving minor league hitting instructor, Maldonado's numbers dropped suddenly. The two were finally reunited last year, and Maldonado started hitting again. Morales likes his hitters to move their hands through the strike zone as quickly as possible. He talks about hands staying behind and above the ball at all times. Maldonado listened.

Maldonado, who jumps all over left-handed pitching, has trouble with high fastballs. However, he'll hit a low fastball a long way. Off-speed pitches lengthen his swing and can make him look foolish at times.

BASERUNNING:

Maldonado has decent speed, but doesn't scare anyone as a base stealing threat. He runs to first hard, but last year he visibly wore down as the season progressed. Not afraid of contact, he'll break up a double play or bowl over a catcher to get where he's going.

FIELDING:

Maldonado came to Cleveland with the reputation of being a butcher masquerading as an outfielder. However, like the reports of Maldonado's sick bat, reports of his defensive demise were greatly exaggerated. Maldonado made the switch from right to left field and led the club in highlight-film catches. He had some problems going back on balls, but excelled at charging sinking line drives. When Cory Snyder struggled, Maldonado flip-flopped between right and left field and played well. He also displayed a surprisingly strong, if not always accurate, throwing arm.

OVERALL:

Maldonado filed for free agency at the end of the season. He's a good influence in the clubhouse, where the Indians have a lot of young Latin players. He carried himself well and set a good example. If the Indians don't re-sign him, he'll be missed.

Overall Statistics

	G	AB	R	H	D	T	HR	RBI	SB	BB	SO	AVG
1990	155	590	76	161	32	2	22	95	3	49	134	.273
Career	973	2826	336	723	159	12	92	427	26	221	537	.256

Where He Hits the Ball

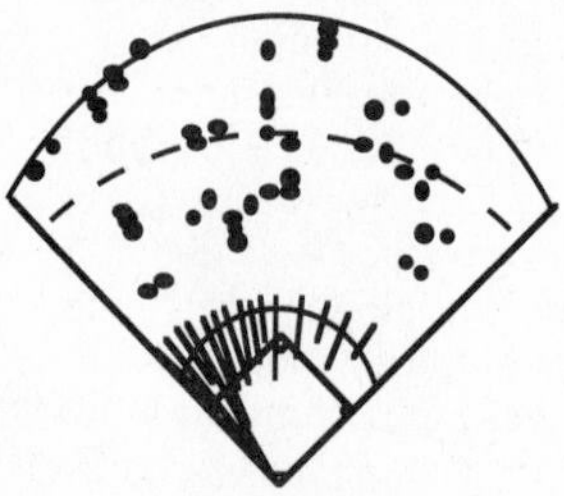

Vs. LHP

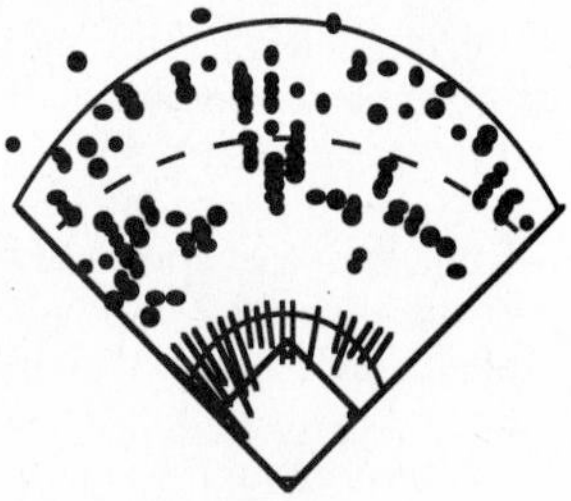

Vs. RHP

1990 Situational Stats

	AB	H	HR	RBI	AVG		AB	H	HR	RBI	AVG
Home	298	80	12	48	.268	LHP	175	58	10	34	.331
Road	292	81	10	47	.277	RHP	415	103	12	61	.248
Day	166	56	10	36	.337	Sc Pos	164	44	5	73	.268
Night	424	105	12	59	.248	Clutch	82	24	2	14	.293

1990 Rankings (American League)

- 6th in RBIs (95)
- 8th worst batting average on an 0-2 count (.045)
- Led the Indians in home runs (22), at-bats (590), doubles (32), total bases (263), RBIs, hit by pitch (5), strikeouts (134), pitches seen (2,444), plate appearances (651), games (155), slugging percentage (.446), HR frequency (26.8 ABs per HR), pitches seen per plate appearance (3.75) and slugging percentage vs. left-handed pitchers (.543)
- Led AL left fielders in RBIs, batting average vs. left- handed pitchers (.331) and fielding percentage (.995)

PITCHING:

Steve Olin became a big-league pitcher last season. He showed the ability to make adjustments, overcome slumps, handle disappointment and get batters out consistently. In spring training, Olin, a submarining right-handed pitcher, received good reviews from Dan Quisenberry, the high priest of submarining righties. "Out of all the submariners I've seen over the years, Olin looks like he has the best idea of how to pitch," Quisenberry said.

Olin broke camp with the Indians, but as in 1989, he couldn't get left-handed batters out. He was tough against righties, but lefties had a long time to pick up his underhand delivery and hurt him. Word soon spread and whenever Olin entered a game, the opposing manager was quick to counter with left-handed pinch hitters.

The problem earned Olin a trip to Class AAA on June 10. At Colorado Springs, Olin moved from the far left side of the pitching rubber to the far right side. This gave him a better angle to jam left-handed hitters with his slider and sinking fastball. Recalled on July 27, he became one of manager John McNamara's most dependable relievers. In his final nine appearances, he allowed two runs in 20.2 innings.

Olin pitched well in one start last year, but his future is in the bullpen. He's being groomed as the heir apparent to closer Doug Jones. Meanwhile, he'll serve as Jones' set-up man from the right side. He can also pitch long and middle relief. His arm is durable and, unlike so many other submariners, he is not a converted overhand pitcher. Olin has been throwing from down under since high school, so the style is natural to him. He has the ability to dominate right-handed lineups. He pitches inside and keeps the ball down.

HOLDING RUNNERS AND FIELDING:

Olin is a poor fielder. Slowly-hit balls frazzle him, and he's capable of throwing a double play ball into center field. He has a tough time holding runners because of his motion, but he doesn't ignore them.

OVERALL:

This is a pitcher to watch. Olin reached Cleveland rather quickly; he never spent a full season at Class AAA. He has shown the ability to make adjustments, and that, more than anything, may bring him major league success. But as with most righty submariners, Olin needs to work on getting out left-handed hitters. Despite his improvement, lefties batted .300 against him last year.

STEVE OLIN

Position: RP
Bats: R **Throws:** R
Ht: 6' 2" **Wt:** 185

Opening Day Age: 25
Born: 10/10/65 in Portland, OR
ML Seasons: 2

Overall Statistics

	W	L	ERA	G	GS	Sv	IP	H	R	BB	SO	HR
1990	4	4	3.41	50	1	1	92.1	96	41	26	64	3
Career	5	8	3.51	75	1	2	128.1	131	57	40	88	4

How Often He Throws Strikes

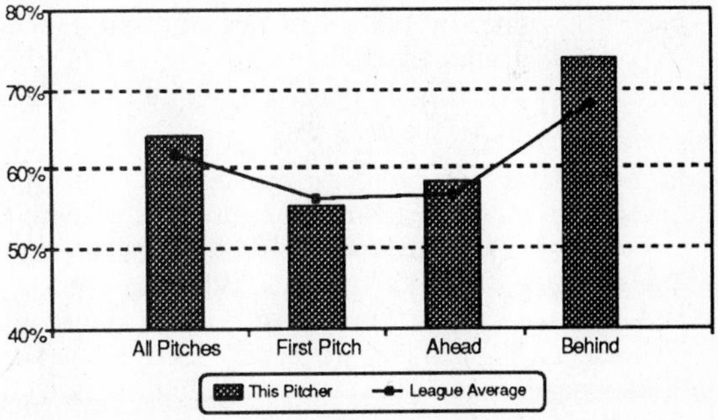

1990 Situational Stats

	W	L	ERA	Sv	IP		AB	H	HR	RBI	AVG
Home	1	0	5.50	0	36.0	LHB	140	42	1	15	.300
Road	3	4	2.08	1	56.1	RHB	215	54	2	36	.251
Day	1	1	5.40	0	30.0	Sc Pos	118	35	0	45	.297
Night	3	3	2.45	1	62.1	Clutch	52	12	1	4	.231

1990 Rankings (American League)

- Led the Indians in hit batsmen (6), holds (4) and errors by a pitcher (3)

JESSE OROSCO

Position: RP
Bats: R **Throws:** L
Ht: 6' 2" **Wt:** 185

Opening Day Age: 33
Born: 4/21/57 in Santa Barbara, CA
ML Seasons: 11

PITCHING:

After a strong season as Doug Jones' set-up man in 1989, Jesse Orosco had his problems last year. Manager John McNamara used him differently than former manager Doc Edwards did in 1989. Edwards would let Orosco work the seventh and eighth innings and then call on Jones in save situations. Johnny Mac had other ideas. When the Indians took the lead in the late innings, he went to Jones quickly. With Jones entering more games in the eighth inning, Orosco's role changed. Instead of pitching with leads, he started being used more and more in blowout situations. Orosco didn't respond well.

Part of Orosco's problem was control. After averaging only three walks per nine innings in 1989, he permitted 5.3 per nine last year. Mechanically, Orosco was having problems with his slider, his best pitch. He was dropping his arm and the ball was coming up in the strike zone. In 1989, American League hitters batted .198 against the lefthander. Last year, they hit .239, still a good figure but not as impressive when combined with all the walks.

Concentration was another problem. After spending most of his career pitching in tight spots, Orosco's concentration wandered when he entered games leading or trailing by wide margins. With the game no longer in the balance, Orosco tended to give up runs in bunches, which did severe damage to his ERA. The home run also hurt. He gave up nine homers in 64.2 innings.

Orosco, who has never been on the disabled list, continues to be a durable pitcher. He had the second most appearances on the Indians in 1990. In two years, he's appeared in 124 games for the Tribe, and he's appeared in 50 or more games for nine straight seasons.

HOLDING RUNNERS AND FIELDING:

Orosco, a good fielder, made only one error last year; it was his first miscue since 1985. He always hustles to cover first base. Since he's left-handed, not many runners get a good jump on him. He'll work to keep a runner close, too.

OVERALL:

Orosco is now a pitcher in search of a role. What's more, the Indians are going to have to find one for him because he's working on a guaranteed contract through the 1992 season. At 33, his career is on the downside. He's gone from being a top closer on a world champion (1986 New York Mets), to a sometimes closer, to a set-up man, to a mop-up reliever. He needs to apply the brakes and re-establish himself.

Overall Statistics

	W	L	ERA	G	GS	Sv	IP	H	R	BB	SO	HR
1990	5	4	3.90	55	0	2	64.2	58	35	38	55	9
Career	58	57	2.76	551	4	121	791.0	633	280	334	683	60

How Often He Throws Strikes

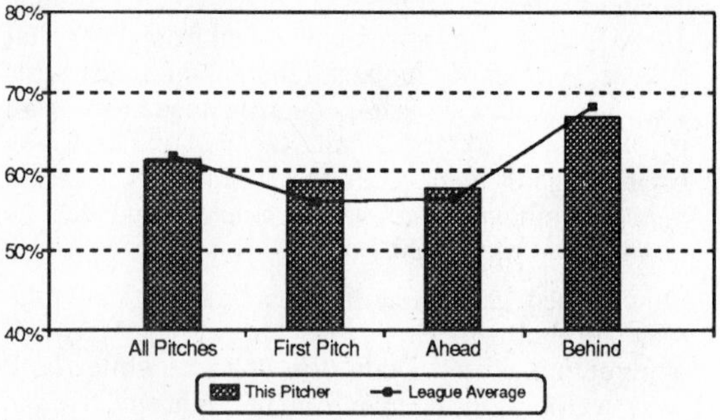

1990 Situational Stats

	W	L	ERA	Sv	IP		AB	H	HR	RBI	AVG
Home	3	3	3.00	2	39.0	LHB	67	15	2	12	.224
Road	2	1	5.26	0	25.2	RHB	176	43	7	26	.244
Day	2	2	4.95	2	20.0	Sc Pos	79	17	0	26	.215
Night	3	2	3.43	0	44.2	Clutch	90	20	2	9	.222

1990 Rankings (American League)

- Led the Indians in first batter efficiency (.200) and lowest percentage of inherited runners scored (26.0%)

HITTING:

Joel Skinner knew his playing time would be reduced considerably last year by the arrival of rookie catcher Sandy Alomar from San Diego. So Skinner economized, getting more out of less. Although he appeared in 30 fewer games than in 1989, Skinner hit for a higher average (.252-.230) and drove in more runs (16-13). In short, he did what a backup catcher is supposed to do -- play well when he's called on. When Alomar missed five games right after the All-Star break with a sore left thumb, Skinner stepped in and hit .294 (5- for-17) with four RBI and his only home run of the season, a three-run shot against California. He finished the year with a five-game hitting streak.

Skinner doesn't get cheated when he goes to the plate. In 139 at-bats last year, he struck out 44 times. He lived and died by baseball's golden rule for bench players: "Swing hard in case you hit something."

The 6'4" Skinner is a good fastball hitter. Breaking balls are a different story, although he did show some improvement against them last year. He generates a lot of power from his long, lean body, but he may have to be an everyday player before it ever surfaces. Until then, all he can do is show it off in batting practice.

BASERUNNING:

Skinner is slow. Very slow. He hustles, he strains, he pumps his legs up and down. He just doesn't go very fast. He does not shy away from contact on the bases, and he goes hard into second and home.

FIELDING:

Skinner arrived in Cleveland in the spring of 1989 with the reputation of being a defensive-oriented catcher with a good arm. That reputation took a beating in 1989; only 17 of 58 would-be base stealers (29 percent) were caught. Skinner improved last year by sending 39 percent (13 of 33) of the runners who attempted against him to the bench. With Alomar getting the majority of the playing time, Skinner came to the park early and worked hard on his throwing to stay sharp. Skinner is mobile behind the plate and does a nice job blocking low throws. He'll hang in there on tough plays at home even though it may mean a collision.

OVERALL:

Skinner had a solid season in 1990. Many teams consider him a starting catcher, but the Indians are reluctant to trade him. He gives them security and dependability in case something should happen to Alomar. His ability as a game-caller is still open to debate, however.

JOEL SKINNER

Position: C
Bats: R **Throws:** R
Ht: 6' 4" **Wt:** 205

Opening Day Age: 30
Born: 2/21/61 in La Jolla, CA
ML Seasons: 8

Overall Statistics

	G	AB	R	H	D	T	HR	RBI	SB	BB	SO	AVG
1990	49	139	16	35	4	1	2	16	0	7	44	.252
Career	465	1157	96	260	48	3	16	112	3	66	320	.225

Where He Hits the Ball

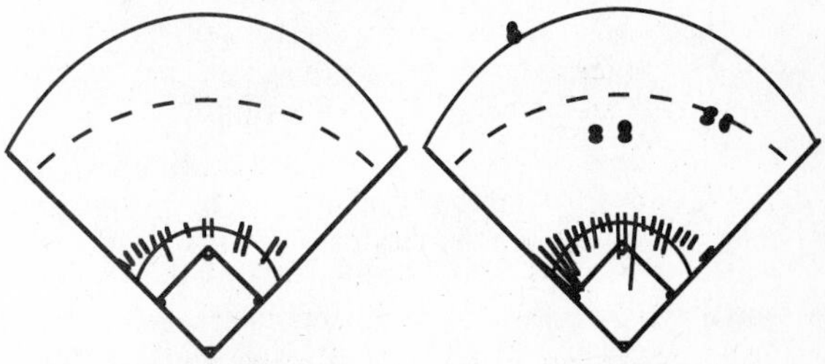

Vs. LHP   Vs. RHP

1990 Situational Stats

	AB	H	HR	RBI	AVG		AB	H	HR	RBI	AVG
Home	60	17	1	4	.283	LHP	47	11	0	4	.234
Road	79	18	1	12	.228	RHP	92	24	2	12	.261
Day	53	17	2	8	.321	Sc Pos	32	10	1	15	.313
Night	86	18	0	8	.209	Clutch	10	3	0	1	.300

1990 Rankings (American League)

- Did not rank near the top or bottom in any category

CORY SNYDER

Position: RF
Bats: R **Throws:** R
Ht: 6' 3" **Wt:** 185

Opening Day Age: 28
Born: 11/11/62 in Inglewood, CA
ML Seasons: 5

HITTING:

Cory Snyder's refusal to take instruction and adjust his hitting style resulted in his most frustrating year in the big leagues and, perhaps, a one-way ticket out of town. Manager John McNamara benched Snyder last Sept. 6, used him as a pinch hitter on Sept. 7, and then never wrote his name on the lineup card again.

After hitting .215 in 1989, the free-swinging Snyder attended Walt Hriniak's hitting school in Boston before the start of last year. Hriniak, who preaches contact, contact and more contact, seemed to reach Snyder. Snyder had an excellent spring and hit .329 in April. But his average quickly faded.

Why did Snyder regress after such a quick start? Several members of the Indians believe it had to do with the shortened spring training caused by the lockout. With pitchers having only three weeks of camp, they started the season throwing mostly fastballs to get their arms in shape. Snyder feasted on those pitches, but once the pitchers got in shape and began throwing breaking balls, he failed to adjust.

Snyder has always had trouble against breaking balls down and away. When he stopped trying to go to right field with that pitch, as Hriniak had instructed, he really had trouble. Three different hitting coaches worked with him and he didn't get along with any of them. Last season he and Jose Morales feuded. Morales suggested he choke up and try to go to right field. But Snyder refused, saying he didn't want to be a "Punch and Judy" hitter.

BASERUNNING:

Snyder has good to above-average speed, and he always hustles. But last year, as he struggled offensively, he made several errors on the bases that showed a lack of concentration. Never a base stealer, he swiped only one last year in five attempts.

FIELDING:

If Snyder is not the best right fielder in the American League, he's close. Yet even his defensive skills faltered last season as he made six errors in right and lost some of the accuracy on his lethal right arm. Still, not many runners dared to take an extra base against him.

OVERALL:

Right after the All-Star break, McNamara had a private meeting with Snyder. He told him he had to become more of a "team" player. Snyder thought being a "team" player meant hustling to first base. But McNamara was talking about advancing runners and other little things that make up a winning player. Instead, Snyder kept trying to hit home runs. Until he gets McNamara's message, he'll never be the player he should be.

Overall Statistics

	G	AB	R	H	D	T	HR	RBI	SB	BB	SO	AVG
1990	123	438	46	102	27	3	14	55	1	21	118	.233
Career	657	2431	298	595	113	9	115	340	19	133	642	.245

Where He Hits the Ball

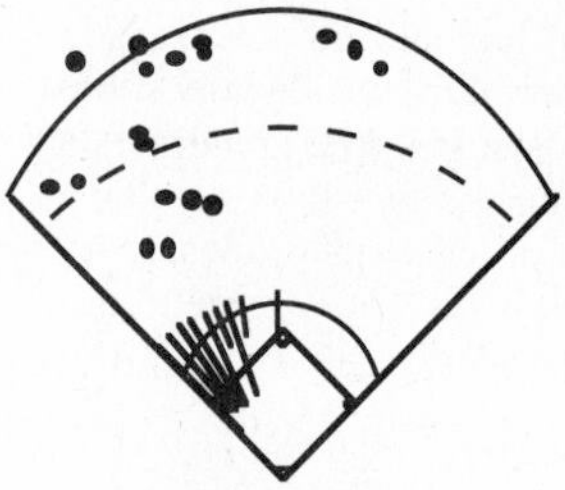

Vs. LHP

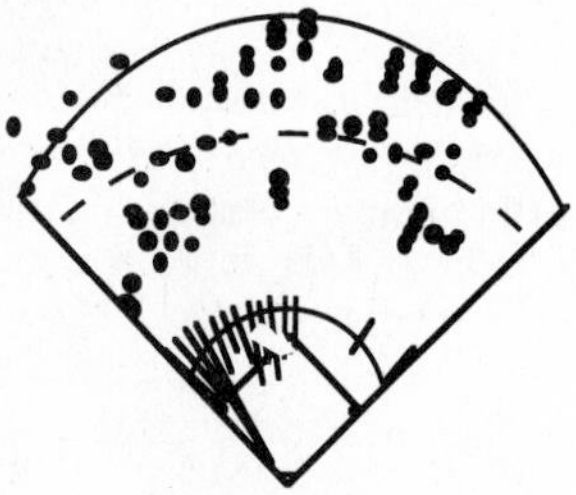

Vs. RHP

1990 Situational Stats

	AB	H	HR	RBI	AVG		AB	H	HR	RBI	AVG
Home	196	46	3	17	.235	LHP	135	30	4	14	.222
Road	242	56	11	38	.231	RHP	303	72	10	41	.238
Day	133	36	8	21	.271	Sc Pos	109	25	2	36	.229
Night	305	66	6	34	.216	Clutch	78	17	2	6	.218

1990 Rankings (American League)

- 2nd in lowest percentage of pitches taken (42.0%)
- 3rd in batting average on a 3-1 count (.750)
- Led the Indians in batting average on a 3-1 count (.750)
- Led AL right fielders in batting average on a 3-1 count

GREG SWINDELL

Position: SP
Bats: B **Throws:** L
Ht: 6' 3" **Wt:** 225

Opening Day Age: 26
Born: 1/2/65 in Fort Worth, TX
ML Seasons: 5

PITCHING:

Greg Swindell had two seasons last year. In his "first" season, he was absent without leave. He was so far gone, he may have been hanging out with Jimmy Hoffa. In his "second" season, Swindell finally started to pitch. The spring training lockout hurt the beefy lefthander. He was the club's player representative and attended several union meetings during contract negotiations. It hurt his workout schedule, and Swindell wasn't ready to pitch when the season opened after only three weeks of spring training.

There was another problem, a more chronic one. Swindell didn't want to throw his slider early in the season because he thought it would hurt his left elbow. He had good reason to hold such thoughts. Swindell has strained ligaments twice in his left elbow since joining the Indians in 1986. In 1987, it cost him more than half the season. In 1989, it ruined his chance at 20 victories. But without the slider, Swindell's best pitch, he wasn't the same. Swindell needed the slider to move right-handed hitters off the plate. Without it, he didn't have another pitch to throw inside, and batters were leaning out over the plate waiting for his fastball, change-up and curve.

Swindell began his turnaround on June 1, when he pitched well against Boston in a no-decision effort. From June 1 to August 26, he went 8-3. More importantly, the Indians went 13-5 in those 18 starts. Swindell was throwing more sliders, but not too many. He was also throwing his fastball inside more and more to keep the batters honest. On top of everything else, Swindell was in better shape physically. So when pitching coach Mark Wiley suggested that he work faster during his games -- in other words, to stop worrying about the last pitch while cutting down on his time between pitches -- he was able to do it.

HOLDING RUNNERS AND FIELDING:

Swindell keeps runners close at first and he has a good pickoff move. Only three of 15 runners were successful stealing against him in 1990. A decent fielder, he gets off the mound quickly despite his bulk.

OVERALL:

When the Indians selected Swindell as their number-one pick in the 1986 draft, they thought they were getting a pitcher they could build a staff around. So far, they've seen only flashes of that kind of talent. They're still waiting to get a complete season from Swindell, but they might never get it because of the fragile nature of his left elbow.

Overall Statistics

	W	L	ERA	G	GS	Sv	IP	H	R	BB	SO	HR
1990	12	9	4.40	34	34	0	214.2	245	110	47	135	27
Career	51	39	3.88	120	119	0	805.0	818	375	195	587	88

How Often He Throws Strikes

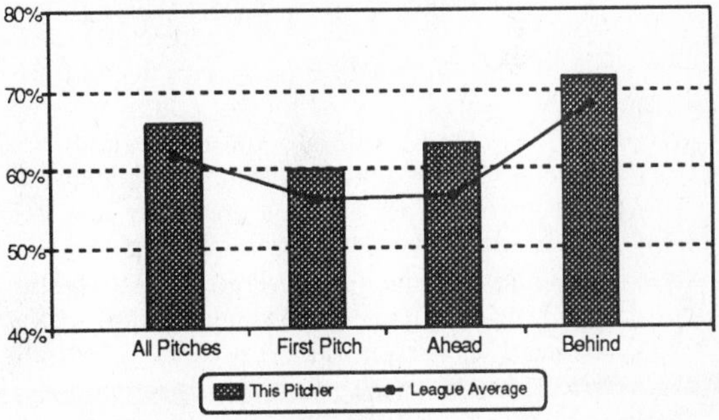

1990 Situational Stats

	W	L	ERA	Sv	IP		AB	H	HR	RBI	AVG
Home	7	4	4.67	0	113.2	LHB	126	37	4	15	.294
Road	5	5	4.10	0	101.0	RHB	724	208	23	84	.287
Day	5	3	4.03	0	67.0	Sc Pos	189	60	5	73	.317
Night	7	6	4.57	0	147.2	Clutch	59	17	2	6	.288

1990 Rankings (American League)

- 1st in lowest stolen base percentage allowed (20.0%)
- 2nd in hits allowed (245) and home runs allowed (27)
- 3rd highest batting average allowed (.288) and highest slugging average allowed (.451)
- 4th in strikeout/walk ratio (2.9), least pitches thrown per batter (3.49) and most HRS allowed per 9 innings (1.13)
- Led the Indians in games started (34), innings (214.2), hits allowed, batters faced (912), home runs allowed, strikeouts (135), runners caught stealing (12), strikeout/walk ratio, lowest stolen base percentage allowed and least pitches thrown per batter

SERGIO VALDEZ

Position: RP/SP
Bats: R **Throws:** R
Ht: 6' 1" **Wt:** 190

Opening Day Age: 25
Born: 9/7/65 in Elias Pina, Dominican Republic
ML Seasons: 3

PITCHING:

A late-season surge and an elbow injury to John Farrell have pushed Sergio Valdez into the forefront of the Indians' pitching plans for the 1991 season. The Indians claimed Valdez on waivers from Atlanta on April 30. The move paid fast returns when Valdez pitched seven strong innings to beat Minnesota, 7-3, in his first American League start on May 9.

Unfortunately, Valdez, pitching mostly out of the bullpen, won just one more game before being sent to Class AAA on July 12 with a 2-5 record and a 6.40 earned run average. In his last appearance before being farmed out, Valdez allowed four home runs -- including three in succession to Rickey Henderson, Carney Lansford and Jose Canseco. When he went to Colorado Springs, no one thought Valdez would be seen again in Cleveland.

Yet Valdez returned on August 25 and went 4-1 in his final eight starts of the season. In those eight starts, covering 50.1 innings, Valdez allowed only four homers and had a 3.04 ERA. What caused the transformation? At Colorado Springs, Valdez worked on a change-up and slider to go with his split-finger and straight fastballs. He also concentrated on his control. But those were not the only reasons for Valdez' success. While he was being hammered in his first start upon returning to Cleveland, Manager John McNamara noticed that Valdez was overthrowing and falling off to the side of the mound after his delivery. McNamara and pitching coach Mark Wiley suggested that he lengthen his stride and bend his body more during his delivery. It made Valdez' delivery smoother and helped his pitches stay in the strike zone. Success followed almost immediately.

HOLDING RUNNERS AND FIELDING:

Valdez is a decent fielder, but he doesn't pay much attention to baserunners. He's not very quick to the plate; baserunners can get a good jump on him.

OVERALL:

Valdez went into the off-season last year as the Indians' number three starter behind Greg Swindell and Tom Candiotti. That's quite a jump after being waived by the lowly Braves. Valdez has a strong, loose arm with the split-finger being his best pitch. However, he had a tendency to throw the split-finger too much and would leave it up in the strike zone and get hurt. By the end of the season, Valdez had confidence in his other pitches and was much more effective. The Indians hope the Valdez they saw in late August -- not the one they saw in May, June and July --returns this season.

Overall Statistics

	W	L	ERA	G	GS	Sv	IP	H	R	BB	SO	HR
1990	6	6	4.85	30	13	0	107.2	115	66	38	66	17
Career	7	12	5.39	54	19	0	165.1	185	110	66	112	24

How Often He Throws Strikes

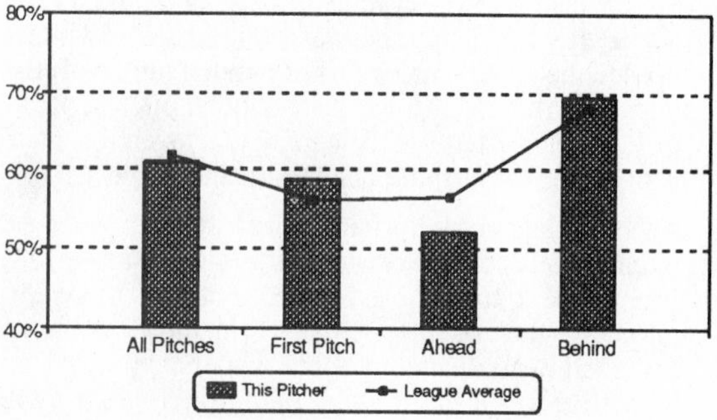

1990 Situational Stats

	W	L	ERA	Sv	IP		AB	H	HR	RBI	AVG
Home	3	2	3.49	0	56.2	LHB	192	40	6	19	.208
Road	3	4	6.35	0	51.0	RHB	225	75	11	40	.333
Day	1	2	7.30	0	24.2	Sc Pos	90	17	1	33	.189
Night	5	4	4.12	0	83.0	Clutch	48	16	1	6	.333

1990 Rankings (American League)

➠ 5th lowest batting average allowed vs. left-handed batters (.207)

MITCH WEBSTER

Position: CF/LF
Bats: B **Throws:** L
Ht: 6' 1" **Wt:** 185

Opening Day Age: 31
Born: 5/16/59 in Larned, KS
ML Seasons: 8

Overall Statistics

	G	AB	R	H	D	T	HR	RBI	SB	BB	SO	AVG
1990	128	437	58	110	20	6	12	55	22	20	61	.252
Career	799	2642	400	713	119	42	55	259	142	254	417	.270

Where He Hits the Ball

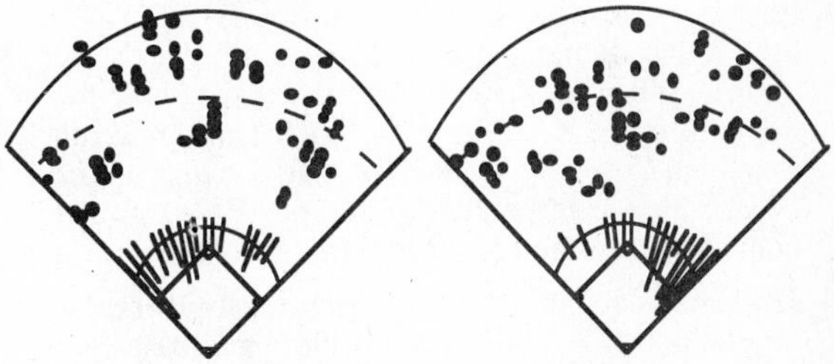

Vs. LHP Vs. RHP

1990 Situational Stats

	AB	H	HR	RBI	AVG		AB	H	HR	RBI	AVG
Home	231	57	6	35	.247	LHP	192	56	8	33	.292
Road	206	53	6	20	.257	RHP	245	54	4	22	.220
Day	127	28	0	14	.220	Sc Pos	94	25	4	42	.266
Night	310	82	12	41	.265	Clutch	72	16	2	13	.222

1990 Rankings (American League)

- 2nd in bunts in play (32)
- 7th in least GDPs per GDP situation (5.5%)
- 9th in sacrifice bunts (11) and steals of third (4)
- Led the Indians in triples (6), least GDPs per GDP situation and bunts in play
- Led AL center fielders in sacrifice bunts, least GDPs per GDP situation and bunts in play

HITTING:

Last year Mitch Webster had his most productive offensive season since 1987, but he has developed a disturbing habit. Wherever he goes, he loses his job to a hot-shot rookie. Webster started 1990 as the Indians' center fielder. He did well, too, until the arrival of Alex Cole on July 27. Suddenly Cole was the starting center fielder and Webster was on the bench.

In 1989, Webster opened the season as the Chicago Cubs' starting left fielder. He was hitting over .400 when he went on the disabled list. The Cubs called up a rookie named Dwight Smith, who went on to finish second in the Rookie of the Year balloting. Needless to say, Webster never got his job back.

In his return to the American League, Webster showed decent power. His 12 home runs -- eight from the right side of the plate -- were more than he hit in 1988 and 1989 combined. He usually hits home runs in bunches. The switch-hitting Webster is a much better hitter from the right side of the plate. In fact, at the beginning of the season manager John McNamara considered platooning him with Dion James in center field because Webster's left-handed swing looked so bad.

The Indians initially used Webster as their leadoff hitter, but he proved too impatient for the job. In 437 at-bats, he walked only 20 times. So the Indians moved Jerry Browne into the number-one spot and hit Webster second. Webster is much more comfortable hitting in the second spot. Throughout the season, he usually hit at the top or the bottom (eight or nine) of the lineup.

BASERUNNING:

Webster led the Indians in stolen bases until Cole arrived. He finished with 22 steals. He's aggressive and has more than enough speed to take the extra base.

FIELDING:

Webster was glad to leave the tricky winds of Wrigley Field after the Indians acquired him for Dave Clark. He played an excellent center field, charging the ball well and ranging far into the gaps. He has a below-average arm.

OVERALL:

Webster doesn't look like it, but he is an intense player. He may have set a new club record for breaking batting helmets after making outs; teammate Chris James nicknamed him "Norman Bates." Webster can play all three outfield positions and is expected to be the Tribe's fourth or fifth outfielder this year.

STAN JEFFERSON

Position: LF/CF
Bats: B **Throws:** R
Ht: 5'11" **Wt:** 175

Opening Day Age: 28
Born: 12/4/62 in New York, NY
ML Seasons: 5

Overall Statistics

	G	AB	R	H	D	T	HR	RBI	SB	BB	SO	AVG
1990	59	117	22	27	8	0	2	10	9	10	26	.231
Career	283	813	123	179	25	9	16	67	58	64	174	.220

HITTING, FIELDING, BASERUNNING:

The Indians claimed Stan Jefferson on waivers from Baltimore last May, but used him almost exclusively as a pinch runner before sending him back to the minors. When Jefferson returned in September, they decided to see if he could do more than pinch run. Benching Cory Snyder, they let Jefferson play almost every day. He responded by hitting .317 with two homers, 11 runs and seven RBI in 21 games.

Jefferson is a slap hitter with occasional power. His biggest asset is speed; it helps him steal bases and outrun his mistakes on defense. Jefferson has never been more than a part-time player with the Mets, Padres, Yankees and Orioles, but the Indians are intrigued by his speed. Manager John McNamara liked to hit Jefferson and Alex Cole back-to-back in the ninth and first spots, respectively, to give his offense a kick start.

Late in the year McNamara said Jefferson might indeed become an everyday player. That's debatable, but with the release of Dion James at the end of last season, it appears he'll at least get a chance to make the club. Defensively, Jefferson is average at best. He may have one of the weakest arms in the game.

OVERALL:

Jefferson is another switch-hitter that the Indians have added to give them a more versatile and up-tempo offense. He hits for a higher average from the right side, but he hit both his home runs left-handed. Look for him to be on the Tribe's roster this season.

JEFF MANTO

Position: 1B
Bats: R **Throws:** R
Ht: 6' 3" **Wt:** 210

Opening Day Age: 26
Born: 8/23/64 in Bristol, PA
ML Seasons: 1

Overall Statistics

	G	AB	R	H	D	T	HR	RBI	SB	BB	SO	AVG
1990	30	76	12	17	5	1	2	14	0	21	18	.224
Career	30	76	12	17	5	1	2	14	0	21	18	.224

HITTING, FIELDING, BASERUNNING:

Jeff Manto is a big, right-handed batter who hit 18 homers and drove in 82 runs at Class AAA Colorado Springs in only 96 games last year. It was a different story in Cleveland where he was summoned three times last year, but received only 76 at-bats. Manto hit just .224 for Cleveland.

Manto has a good eye at the plate, drawing 99 walks last year between AAA and Cleveland. When he did get some consistent playing time, Manto showed the ability to drive in runs for the Indians. Eight of his 17 hits went for extra bases and he had 14 RBI, six more than Keith Hernandez and 14 more than Ken Phelps -- two veteran hitters who received a lot more money for considerably less production.

Manto's speed is average at best. Third base is supposed to be his best position, but he didn't look comfortable there with the Indians. His future is probably at first. Manto offers a big target and can knock down most ground balls. After the season, he went to the Florida Instructional League to learn how to catch. It's believed the Indians would like to keep Manto as a bench player because of his power and are trying to improve his versatility. Manto says he can also play shortstop and outfield.

OVERALL:

If Manto hit left-handed, he'd have a spot on the Indians' roster under lock and key. But right now, he's just another right-handed hitter, and the Tribe already has plenty of them. However, Manto might have a chance as a bench player.

MARK McLEMORE

Position: 2B
Bats: B **Throws:** R
Ht: 5'11" **Wt:** 195

Opening Day Age: 26
Born: 10/4/64 in San Diego, CA
ML Seasons: 5

Overall Statistics

	G	AB	R	H	D	T	HR	RBI	SB	BB	SO	AVG
1990	28	60	6	9	2	0	0	2	1	4	15	.150
Career	280	833	117	192	29	6	5	73	45	85	136	.230

HITTING, FIELDING, BASERUNNING:

Mark McLemore came to the Indians from California last August as the player to be named later in a 1989 trade involving catcher Ron Tingley. The switch-hitting McLemore had been one of the Angels' brightest prospects, but he wore out his welcome through injuries and unproductive seasons.

McLemore's best position is second base, but he can play third and short. He's expected to receive a shot as the Tribe's utility infielder, especially with Tom Brookens -- who filled the role last year -- filing for free agency at the end of last season. McLemore is younger, faster and less expensive than Brookens, but his offense has always been suspect. In six games with the Tribe, he looked as if he had never swung a bat in his life. He had two hits, both singles. McLemore, who opened the season at shortstop for the Angels before injuring his wrist, has good range, especially at second base. He can turn the double play well.

OVERALL:

McLemore is yet another soft-hitting switch-hitter for manager John McNamara to fiddle with. He can run a little bit, having stolen 25 bases in 1987. McLemore could have become a free agent instead of reporting to the Indians, but they convinced him to join the club even though he had to report to Class AAA. Part of the deal was a guaranteed September call-up. The Indians kept their word, but certainly didn't overwork him when he arrived. From September 16 to the end of the season, McLemore had four at-bats.

AL NIPPER

Position: SP
Bats: R **Throws:** R
Ht: 6' 0" **Wt:** 194

Opening Day Age: 32
Born: 4/2/59 in San Diego, CA
ML Seasons: 7

Overall Statistics

	W	L	ERA	G	GS	Sv	IP	H	R	BB	SO	HR
1990	2	3	6.75	9	5	0	24.0	35	19	19	12	2
Career	46	50	4.52	144	124	1	797.2	846	452	303	381	97

PITCHING, FIELDING & HOLDING RUNNERS:

Al Nipper attempted the impossible last season. He tried to make the switch from a conventional pitcher who threw an occasional knuckleball to one who made his living throwing the knuckler. The experiment hasn't worked thus far.

Nipper started the season in the bullpen, but on April 28 the Indians sent him to Class AAA Colorado Springs and told him to start throwing the knuckleball full-time. It was a desperation move, but Nipper, who didn't pitch in 1989 because of knee and elbow injuries, went along with the idea because he was just as desperate.

Unfortunately, the Indians sent Nipper to the Rocky Mountains to remake himself. In the thin air, the knuckler didn't dance, but when he returned to Cleveland on June 22, the knuckleball moved so much Nipper couldn't control it. One day Nipper might learn to mix the knuckler with his assortment of other pitches, but it's difficult to go through on-the-job training in the big leagues. Nipper fields his position well and keeps runners close.

OVERALL:

Nipper is a good guy to have on a club. He's the first one out of the dugout to congratulate a teammate after a well pitched game or home run. He'd be an even bigger plus if he could still pitch. Injuries and a year's layoff have robbed him of much of his talent, which was marginal to begin with. That's why the Indians released him at the end of the season. Now he'll have to make it as a knuckleballer, which could take some time.

KEN PHELPS

Position: DH/1B
Bats: L **Throws:** L
Ht: 6' 1" **Wt:** 204

Opening Day Age: 36
Born: 8/6/54 in Seattle, WA
ML Seasons: 11

Overall Statistics

	G	AB	R	H	D	T	HR	RBI	SB	BB	SO	AVG
1990	56	120	10	18	2	0	1	6	1	22	21	.150
Career	761	1854	308	443	64	7	123	313	10	390	449	.239

HITTING, FIELDING, BASERUNNING:

The Indians purchased what remained of Ken Phelps' contract from Oakland last June 16. They needed a left-handed hitter who could drive the ball, and based on Phelps' track record, they thought they'd found one. They soon discovered, however, that all the juice had been squeezed from Phelps' once-lethal bat. All seven hits he had in an Indians' uniform were singles. He didn't drive in a run for Cleveland.

Phelps, who bounced from Seattle to the New York Yankees to Oakland and finally to the Indians from 1988-1990, just couldn't hit with power any more. He didn't even hit home runs during batting practice. Phelps entered the 1990 season averaging a home run in every 14.2 at-bats. He managed to hit one in 120 at-bats with the A's and Indians.

Immediately after obtaining Phelps, the Indians started him in nine straight games. He managed only six hits and the Tribe forgot about him. To make matters worse, during a West Coast trip after the All-Star break, Phelps complained about his role on the Indians. Manager John McNamara responded by saying, "He has no role." Phelps, who made his last appearance as an Indian on September 8, was officially buried. Defensively, Phelps did an adequate job at first base, but he mostly played DH for the Tribe. He has below-average speed.

OVERALL:

The Indians had an option on Phelps' contract for 1991, but they didn't pick it up. Phelps still thinks he can play, but at 36, it appears that his opinion is in the minority.

MIKE WALKER

Position: SP/RP
Bats: R **Throws:** R
Ht: 6' 1" **Wt:** 175

Opening Day Age: 24
Born: 10/4/66 in Brooksville, FL
ML Seasons: 2

Overall Statistics

	W	L	ERA	G	GS	Sv	IP	H	R	BB	SO	HR
1990	2	6	4.88	18	11	0	75.2	82	49	42	34	6
Career	2	7	5.12	21	12	0	84.1	90	56	52	41	6

PITCHING, FIELDING & HOLDING RUNNERS:

Mike Walker was one of several pitchers the Indians promoted from the minors to try and fill the hole in the bottom of their starting rotation. Walker's route was a little more curious than most. He struggled so much in the high altitude of Class AAA Colorado Springs that he lost confidence in his ability. To keep him sane, the Indians sent Walker to Class AA Canton-Akron, gave him a couple of games to steady himself, and then brought him to Cleveland.

After he'd pitched well in the bullpen, the Indians moved Walker into the rotation, but he won only one of 11 starts. Walker throws a decent forkball, but lack of control and an infatuation with strikeouts hurt him. He constantly tried to overthrow the ball and made almost every mistake a rookie pitcher could make. If there was one pitch Walker should not have thrown at a crucial part of a game, the righthander always seemed to throw it. Walker has good reflexes, and fielded his position well. But baserunners feasted on him because he was slow getting the ball to the plate.

OVERALL:

Walker's future with the Indians, if he has one, will probably be in the bullpen. He pitched well in relief, especially long relief, and that's a weak spot for the Tribe. Walker has a live arm, but needs to work on the mental part of his game. He also has to realize that a ground out is as good as a strikeout.

DAVE BERGMAN

Position: DH/1B
Bats: L **Throws:** L
Ht: 6' 2" **Wt:** 190

Opening Day Age: 37
Born: 6/6/53 in Evanston, IL
ML Seasons: 15

HITTING:

Always reliable, Dave Bergman proved once again to be a valuable utility player for the Tigers last year. Bergman can fill in defensively, is an excellent pinch hitter and is useful as a spot starter. He's best coming off the bench, although he did bat .322 in 40 games as a designated hitter.

Bergman rarely bats against lefthanders, seeing only 13 at-bats against southpaws last year. But he's the club's number-one pinch hitter against righthanders. His 31 career pinch hits rank Bergman seventh on the all-time Tiger list. A selective hitter, Bergman has a good eye at the plate. He drew 33 walks last year while striking out just 17 times in 205 at-bats. He has outstanding bat control and will foul off good pitches until he gets one he can hit, making him an excellent hit-and-run man.

Bergman likes the fastball, which means he often sees a steady diet of breaking stuff. But he's disciplined enough not to chase bad pitches, forcing pitchers to come in with the heater. Strictly a singles hitter, Bergman has accidental power. He usually manages to pull three or four balls a year into Tiger Stadium's short right field porch. A ground ball hitter, Bergman has always fared better on the road (.313) and on turf (.417) than at home (.248). Tiger Stadium's long infield grass turns potential base hits into ground outs, hampering Bergman's play there.

BASERUNNING:

Certainly not a speedster, Bergman managed to steal three bases last year. A good student of the game, he studies the pitcher's moves to help him get a better jump. Bergman won't hurt his team by getting greedy on the base paths.

FIELDING:

One of the great mysteries over the past few seasons in Detroit is why the club doesn't play Bergman more at first base. Although he made only 28 appearances there all season, Bergman is still considered one of the best defensive first basemen in baseball. He has soft hands, good range and a decent enough arm that the Tigers will still employ him in the outfield in a pinch. He made five appearances in left field last season.

OVERALL:

Nearly 38, Bergman shows no signs of slowing down. Long ago he accepted his spot as a utility player; perhaps because of that, he has thrived in the role. He remains a valuable asset, whether as a platoon player against righthanders, coming off the bench as a pinch hitter, or going in as a defensive replacement.

Overall Statistics

	G	AB	R	H	D	T	HR	RBI	SB	BB	SO	AVG
1990	100	205	21	57	10	1	2	26	3	33	17	.278
Career	1176	2304	272	602	87	15	46	250	17	325	288	.261

Where He Hits the Ball

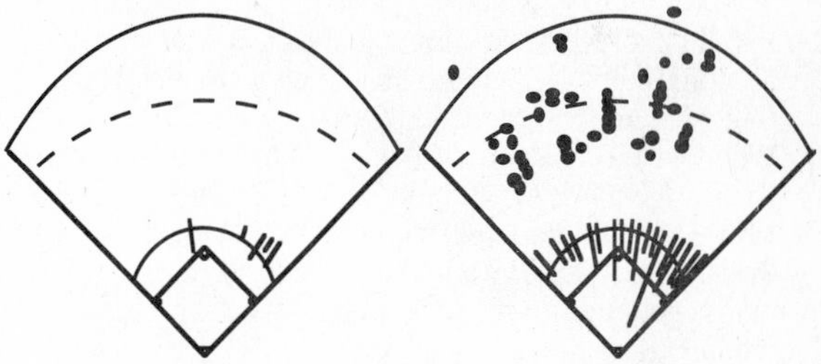

Vs. LHP Vs. RHP

1990 Situational Stats

	AB	H	HR	RBI	AVG		AB	H	HR	RBI	AVG
Home	109	27	1	13	.248	LHP	13	3	0	2	.231
Road	96	30	1	13	.313	RHP	192	54	2	24	.281
Day	76	23	0	12	.303	Sc Pos	59	14	0	23	.237
Night	129	34	2	14	.264	Clutch	36	7	0	5	.194

1990 Rankings (American League)

- 2nd in lowest percentage of extra bases taken as a runner (24.0%)
- Led the Tigers in batting average on a 3-2 count (.316)

HITTING:

His 51 homers got him all the attention, but Cecil Fielder is far more than just a home run hitter. Detroit gave Fielder a two-year, $3 million contract after he'd hit 38 homers in Japan, and there were some guffaws from other teams. It was the Tigers who had the last laugh, as Fielder had an awesome offensive season. Platooned during his Blue Jay days, Fielder did have some problems against right-handed pitching in 1990, batting only .235. But his power numbers against righties were outstanding, and his performance against lefties was simply devastating.

With his tremendous strength, Fielder doesn't need to swing for home runs. He likes the ball low and away, allowing him to extend his massive arms and drive the ball. Not just a one-dimensional pull hitter, Fielder will use the whole field, something he learned in Japan to take advantage of the smaller ballparks.

Fielder had two three-homer games last year, and like his long balls, his strikeouts come in streaks. He's a free swinger who fanned 182 times, obliterating Jake Wood's Detroit record of 141 and nearly toppling Rob Deer's AL mark of 189. Pitchers will try to climb the ladder with him and get him to chase fastballs out of the strike zone. He'll adjust, though, so the pitch which got him out the first time may land in the seats the next time around.

BASERUNNING:

When Fielder travels the base paths, he does so one base at a time. If he steals a base, there should be an investigation. He hasn't swiped one in seven years. He doesn't get down the line very well and grounded into a club high 15 double plays.

FIELDING:

Fielder may be built like a designated hitter, but surprisingly, he's a solid defensive first baseman. He has very soft hands, good reflexes and is very agile around the bag. He'll make diving stops and scoop throws out of the dirt as well as anyone. But Fielder has problems when he has to pursue a ball. Lack of speed hurts him on bunts and soft grounders, and he's very shaky chasing pop flies. Every pop-up behind first base is an adventure for him.

OVERALL:

What can Fielder do for an encore? He'll have trouble matching his 1990 totals, because teams will pitch him much more carefully. But 30 homers and 100 RBIs seem reasonable, and he has the talent to wallop 40 or more again. The Tiger organization would happily accept that sort of production.

CECIL FIELDER

Position: 1B/DH
Bats: R **Throws:** R
Ht: 6' 3" **Wt:** 230

Opening Day Age: 27
Born: 9/21/63 in Los Angeles, CA
ML Seasons: 5

Overall Statistics

	G	AB	R	H	D	T	HR	RBI	SB	BB	SO	AVG
1990	159	573	104	159	25	1	51	132	0	90	182	.277
Career	379	1079	171	282	44	3	82	216	0	136	326	.261

Where He Hits the Ball

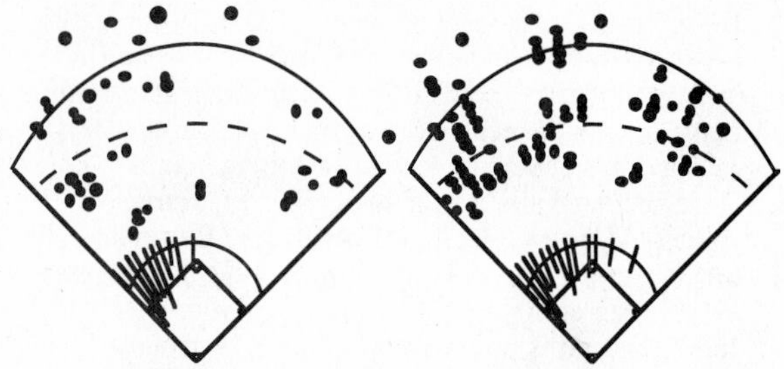

Vs. LHP Vs. RHP

1990 Situational Stats

	AB	H	HR	RBI	AVG		AB	H	HR	RBI	AVG
Home	271	76	25	60	.280	LHP	178	66	25	54	.371
Road	302	83	26	72	.275	RHP	395	93	26	78	.235
Day	165	35	15	38	.212	Sc Pos	151	40	11	74	.265
Night	408	124	36	94	.304	Clutch	85	19	3	9	.224

1990 Rankings (American League)

- 1st in home runs (51), total bases (339), RBIs (132), strikeouts (182), slugging percentage (.592), HR frequency (11.2 ABs per HR), slugging percentage vs. left-handed pitchers (.854) and on-base average vs. left-handed pitchers (.479)
- 2nd in runs (104), batting average vs. left-handed pitchers (.371), lowest percentage of swings put into play (31.1%)
- Led the Tigers in home runs, at-bats (573), runs, total bases, RBIs, intentional walks (11), hit by pitch (5), times on base (254), strikeouts, GDPs (15), games (159), slugging percentage and on-base average (.377)

HITTING:

As a hitter, Travis Fryman showed gradual improvement at each of his minor league stops. He improved even more when called to the majors last year. Fryman's Detroit success was all the more impressive because the Tigers asked him to play third base, a position he'd never played, even in little league.

Hitting 40 points above his 1990 minor-league average of .257, Fryman exhibited all the tools necessary to become a star in the major leagues. Showing remarkable consistency, he never went more than two consecutive games without a hit and had 23 multi-hit games in 66 games. He showed outstanding power, belting nine homers in only 232 at-bats. Fryman's .470 slugging percentage was second on the club to Cecil Fielder.

Fryman is an excellent fastball hitter, and much of his initial success was due to the fact that pitchers challenged him with hard stuff. But as teams began feeding him more breaking stuff, Fryman showed that he could adjust. Impressively, he batted .284 against teams seeing him for the second and third time.

Only 22, Fryman needs to work on his discipline at the plate. He fanned 51 times last year while drawing only 17 walks. Like many young hitters, he gets overanxious at times and starts chasing bad pitches. That was his problem in clutch situations. Fryman hit just .218 with runners in scoring position.

BASERUNNING:

Fryman won't be mistaken for Rickey Henderson, but he has decent speed and can steal a base. He gets out of the batter's box well and is tough to double up on a ground ball. Fryman shows good smarts on the base paths and doesn't make the baserunning mistakes normally associated with young players.

FIELDING:

As would be expected of one playing an unfamiliar position, Fryman struggled at third base. He had trouble positioning himself and often found himself trying to field balls between hops. At shortstop, his natural position, he looked much more sure of himself. When combined with Tony Phillips at second, Fryman gave Detroit a backup double play combination superior to some teams' number-one unit.

OVERALL:

Fryman hit much better as a major leaguer last year than he ever did in the minors, so he'll have to prove that his success last year wasn't a fluke. But he's convinced the Tigers, who consider him their best infield prospect since Howard Johnson. Fryman has the power stroke to hit 15-20 homers a year, whether he winds up at third base or shortstop.

TRAVIS FRYMAN

Position: 3B/SS
Bats: R **Throws:** R
Ht: 6' 2" **Wt:** 190

Opening Day Age: 22
Born: 3/25/69 in Lexington, Ky
ML Seasons: 1

Overall Statistics

	G	AB	R	H	D	T	HR	RBI	SB	BB	SO	AVG
1990	66	232	32	69	11	1	9	27	3	17	51	.297
Career	66	232	32	69	11	1	9	27	3	17	51	.297

Where He Hits the Ball

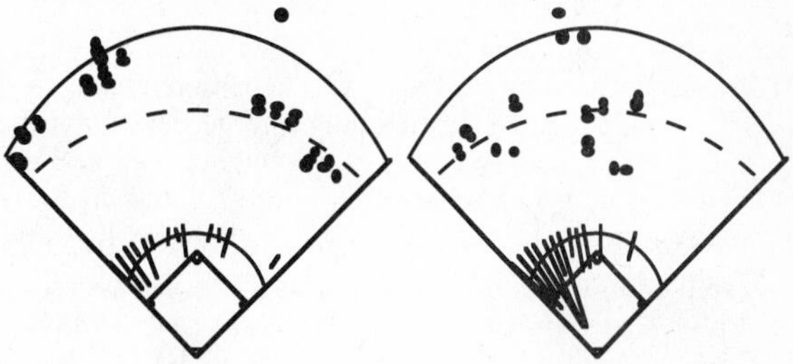

Vs. LHP Vs. RHP

1990 Situational Stats

	AB	H	HR	RBI	AVG		AB	H	HR	RBI	AVG
Home	108	28	5	8	.259	LHP	88	28	5	12	.318
Road	124	41	4	19	.331	RHP	144	41	4	15	.285
Day	64	24	4	6	.375	Sc Pos	55	12	2	17	.218
Night	168	45	5	21	.268	Clutch	22	8	0	2	.364

1990 Rankings (American League)

- Did not rank near the top or bottom in any category

PITCHING:

Paul Gibson doesn't do anything with flash, but he has quietly become a very valuable Detroit Tiger. A workhorse, he can give the club a lot of innings and is capable of working three or four days in succession. On the other hand, he won't complain -- and he'll stay effective -- if he has to sit around for five or six days.

Gibson made a career-high 61 appearances last year, working exclusively from the bullpen for the first time in his three-season career. Gibson has almost always been used as a middle man, and didn't earn his first major league save until last May 23 -- in his 87th career relief appearance. Gibson managed to save two more games last year, but don't be mistaken into thinking he's stopper material. He doesn't have overpowering stuff, although when he has an effective breaking ball he can surprise hitters and sneak the fastball past them.

Gibson yields a lot of hits (99 in 97.1 innings), and is prone to giving up the long ball. He has a tendency to give up homers in key situations, another reason why he'd make a poor late man. For a pitcher who needs good location to be effective, he still gives up too many walks.

Unlike most lefthanders, Gibson is far more successful at Tiger Stadium than on the road. He's 8-5 lifetime in Detroit, including a 4-2 mark with two saves and a 2.58 ERA at home last year. Probably the main reason for his success is that he's fairly tough to pull, and gets a lot of outs to Tiger Stadium's deep center field. Away from home, Gibson is far less successful, with a 5-9 career mark. He coughed up eight homers and 51 hits in 45 innings on the road last year.

HOLDING RUNNERS AND FIELDING:

His experience as a starter, both in the minors and the big leagues, makes Gibson very conscious of baserunners. He'll throw often to first base to try to hold a runner. His move to first is decent, but not especially tricky. Gibson works hard on his defensive play and while he may not be a great athlete, he'll make the routine plays and won't hurt himself in the field.

OVERALL:

Though no star, Gibson is a handy guy to have around. He'll start if he has to, pitch mop-up, set-up the closer, and finish an occasional game if need be. He's the ultimate jack of all trades, and the fact that he's a southpaw enhances his usefulness.

PAUL GIBSON

Position: RP
Bats: R **Throws:** L
Ht: 6' 0" **Wt:** 165

Opening Day Age: 31
Born: 1/4/60 in Southhampton, NY
ML Seasons: 3

Overall Statistics

	W	L	ERA	G	GS	Sv	IP	H	R	BB	SO	HR
1990	5	4	3.05	61	0	3	97.1	99	36	44	56	10
Career	13	14	3.67	146	14	3	321.1	311	140	135	183	27

How Often He Throws Strikes

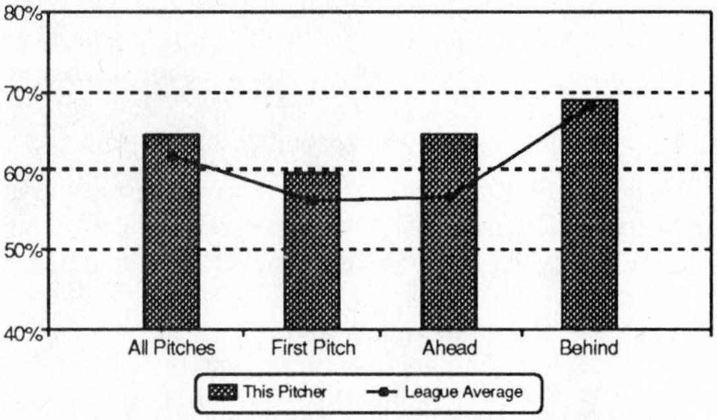

1990 Situational Stats

	W	L	ERA	Sv	IP		AB	H	HR	RBI	AVG
Home	4	2	2.58	2	52.1	LHB	118	31	2	15	.263
Road	1	2	3.60	1	45.0	RHB	250	68	8	31	.272
Day	1	0	2.00	2	27.0	Sc Pos	106	21	2	32	.198
Night	4	4	3.45	1	70.1	Clutch	106	32	3	10	.302

1990 Rankings (American League)

- 10th in lowest percentage of inherited runners scored (23.5%)
- Led the Tigers in holds (9)

JERRY DON GLEATON

Position: RP
Bats: L **Throws:** L
Ht: 6' 3" **Wt:** 210

Opening Day Age: 33
Born: 9/14/57 in Brownwood, TX
ML Seasons: 10

Overall Statistics

	W	L	ERA	G	GS	Sv	IP	H	R	BB	SO	HR
1990	1	3	2.94	57	0	13	82.2	62	27	25	56	5
Career	11	21	4.28	237	16	24	340.1	325	179	141	200	29

How Often He Throws Strikes

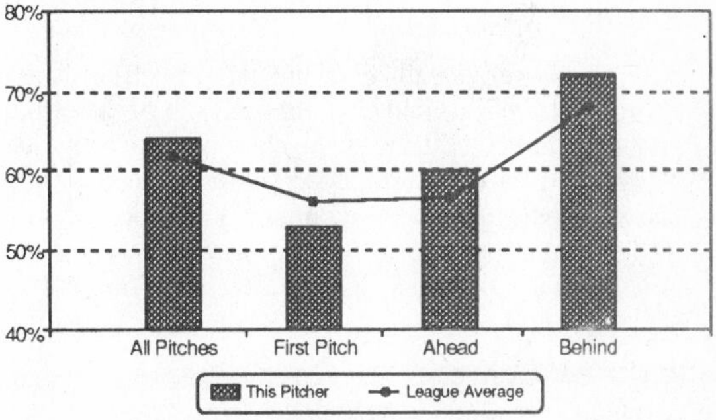

1990 Situational Stats

	W	L	ERA	Sv	IP		AB	H	HR	RBI	AVG
Home	1	2	3.73	5	41.0	LHB	91	22	1	16	.242
Road	0	1	2.16	8	41.2	RHB	200	40	4	22	.200
Day	0	1	3.77	4	28.2	Sc Pos	81	17	2	33	.210
Night	1	2	2.50	9	54.0	Clutch	86	19	2	12	.221

1990 Rankings (American League)

- Did not rank near the top or bottom in any category

PITCHING:

Although Jerry Don Gleaton didn't do what he was acquired to do, he was a very pleasant surprise for the Detroit Tigers in 1990. Picked up from Kansas City in spring training, Gleaton was supposed to be the southpaw reliever who would retire the tough left-handed hitters. But surprisingly, lefties hit him better, with a .242 average while righthanders hit only .200.

But Gleaton did succeed in an even bigger role: he emerged as the club's left-handed closer. Gleaton saved 13 games, two more than he'd saved in his previous nine big-league seasons combined. His timing couldn't have been better, as Detroit needed a lefty in the bullpen to replace Guillermo Hernandez. Gleaton blossomed just as Mike Henneman, Detroit's right-handed closer, went into a dreadful slump. Gleaton earned 12 of his saves after July 1.

The key to Gleaton's emergence was some early-season work with Tiger pitching coach Billy Muffett. Muffett got Gleaton to take a slightly higher leg kick and drive harder off his back foot, thus putting more zip and movement in Gleaton's heater. Mixed in with a sharp breaking ball, Gleaton became a very effective short man.

The success was unexpected. Though he'd pitched on and off in the majors since 1979, Gleaton was always the ninth or 10th pitcher on the roster. Before coming to Detroit, Gleaton had toiled in obscurity for the Rangers, Mariners, White Sox and Royals, entering 1990 with a lifetime ERA of 4.72. Turning his career around, Gleaton posted career-bests in appearances (57), earned run average (2.94) and strikeouts (56). He gave up only 12 extra-base hits in 82.2 innings. A devout physical fitness fanatic, Gleaton could often be seen working out on the Tiger Stadium playing surface long after his teammates had gone home.

FIELDING AND HOLDING RUNNERS:

Gleaton has a quick delivery to the plate, making it difficult for baserunners to get a good jump on him. His work ethic carries over to his defensive play. Gleaton is a sound fielder, but will occasionally get himself in trouble by trying to make a big play instead of taking the safe out.

OVERALL:

Last year, Gleaton finally lived up to the promise which made Texas draft him in the first round over a decade ago. He made a believer out of Detroit manager Sparky Anderson, who was fearless about going to Gleaton when Henneman was struggling. At age 33, the former bit-player will enter 1991 in a featured role as Detroit's number-one lefthander out of the bullpen.

MIKE HEATH

Position: C
Bats: R **Throws:** R
Ht: 5'11" **Wt:** 180

Opening Day Age: 36
Born: 2/5/55 in Tampa, FL
ML Seasons: 13

Overall Statistics

	G	AB	R	H	D	T	HR	RBI	SB	BB	SO	AVG
1990	122	370	46	100	18	2	7	38	7	19	71	.270
Career	1276	4073	458	1032	170	26	85	457	54	271	590	.253

Where He Hits the Ball

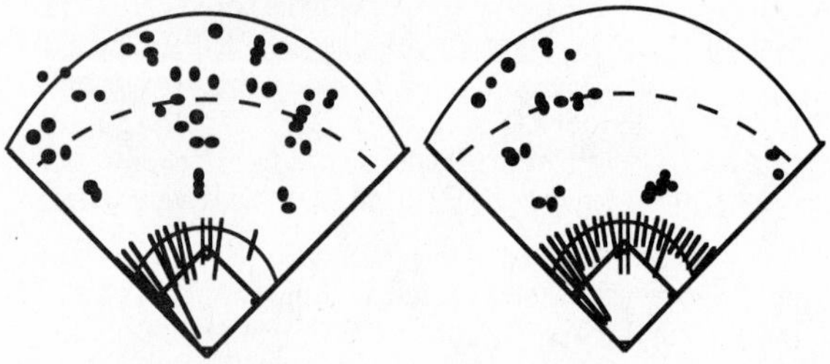

Vs. LHP Vs. RHP

1990 Situational Stats

	AB	H	HR	RBI	AVG		AB	H	HR	RBI	AVG
Home	169	46	3	15	.272	LHP	149	34	3	15	.228
Road	201	54	4	23	.269	RHP	221	66	4	23	.299
Day	105	28	4	13	.267	Sc Pos	100	21	2	29	.210
Night	265	72	3	25	.272	Clutch	58	12	2	5	.207

1990 Rankings (American League)

- 1st in lowest fielding percentage by a catcher (.980)
- 7th lowest on-base average vs. left-handed pitchers (.264)
- 9th lowest batting average with runners in scoring position (.210)

HITTING:

If Reggie Jackson was Mr. October, then Mike Heath is Mr. April. Always in top shape, Heath tried a new workout program before the 1990 season. Helped by that and the lockout's negative effect on pitchers, he hit a torrid .444 in April. After that, reality set in. Heath hit .318 in May, .304 in June and sunk to .181 in July. There were two reasons for this. First, Heath isn't a .300 hitter. Second, the strain of catching every day took a huge toll on Heath's 35-year-old, 5-foot-11, 180-pound body.

Heath is a hard-nosed competitor who plays through nagging injuries, another factor which always helps lower his batting average. He's basically a .250-.270 type, a singles hitter who can occasionally drive the ball for extra bases. A low-ball hitter, he draws most of his power from turning on inside pitches. Heath will spray the ball to all fields and take the outside pitch the opposite way.

A free swinger, Heath gets himself into trouble by being over-anxious and chasing balls out of the strike zone. He fanned 71 times last year while drawing just 19 walks. Heath also defied common baseball logic last year by hitting .299 against righthanders, while lefties limited him to a .228 average. Never a good RBI man, Heath hit a dismal .210 with runners in scoring position.

BASERUNNING:

A shortstop in the minor leagues, Heath still has above-average speed for a catcher and stole seven bases last year. He tends to be over-aggressive on the base paths, however. He'll always make a wide turn on singles to see if he has a shot at taking the extra base and will sometimes make ill-advised attempts to do just that. He goes into second hard on double play balls, without any thought for his own safety.

FIELDING:

Heath plays the game the only way he knows how -- all out. An aggressive receiver, he'll charge after every foul pop-up and isn't afraid to make a snap throw to a base if he thinks he can catch the runner napping. Heath has a strong arm, and though he didn't throw out many runners last year, that was more the fault of the Detroit pitchers. Very versatile, Heath has played every position except pitcher in his career.

OVERALL:

Heath's value to the club cannot be measured in mere numbers. His approach to the game rubs off on his teammates, as does the dedication he puts into keeping himself in shape. But at age 36 he will need more rest than he's been offered the past two seasons.

PITCHING:

Mike Henneman suffered through the first prolonged slump of his career in 1990, but emerged from it to again become a dominant reliever. The year began routinely for Henneman, as he started out 7-for-8 and 16-for-18 in save situations. It was the same sort of consistency Henneman had shown in his first three seasons, when he'd proven himself to be one of baseball's better relievers. But then trouble hit. Henneman went through a 6 appearance span where he allowed 13 earned runs in 7.2 innings.

Henneman's problems grew from the fact that the forkball, his money pitch, started hanging instead of dropping, allowing opposing hitters to jump all over it. Lefties were especially hard on Henneman, and that hindered him at Tiger Stadium, where lefty swingers have the advantage. Henneman continued to be a very effective pitcher on the road.

The struggles cost Henneman his role as Detroit's number-one closer, as manager Sparky Anderson opted to go to a stopper-by-committee formula. After picking up 18 of Detroit's first 26 saves, Henneman had only four of the remaining 19. Henneman got his act together again over the last two months of the season, allowing just four earned runs in his last 21 appearances, covering 31.1 innings. Even so, his 50 strikeouts were a career low, and the 90 hits he allowed were a career high.

Unlike most closers, Henneman doesn't possess an overpowering fastball. Instead he relies on keeping the ball down and away from hitters, producing numerous ground ball outs. Henneman has excellent stamina for a short reliever and is capable of working three or four innings in an outing. A determined competitor, he's extremely confident in his ability and doesn't let a bad outing rattle him. Henneman comes at hitters with a three-quarters/sidearm delivery, which keeps them off-balance. He's at his best when he pitches aggressively and goes right after hitters.

HOLDING RUNNERS AND FIELDING:

Henneman isn't blessed with a great pickoff move, but his unorthodox, quick delivery to the plate gives baserunners some trouble. Possessing great reflexes, Henneman fields his position extremely well. If a team tries to drop down a sacrifice bunt against him, it had better be a good one or he'll nail the lead runner.

OVERALL:

Although Anderson insists he'll continue with his stopper-by-committee plan in 1991, that doesn't mean Henneman won't still be Detroit's key man out of the bullpen. He's been too consistent over his career to be cast aside because of one bad month.

MIKE HENNEMAN

Position: RP
Bats: R **Throws:** R
Ht: 6' 4" **Wt:** 195

Opening Day Age: 29
Born: 12/11/61 in St. Charles, MO
ML Seasons: 4

Overall Statistics

	W	L	ERA	G	GS	Sv	IP	H	R	BB	SO	HR
1990	8	6	3.05	69	0	22	94.1	90	36	33	50	4
Career	39	19	2.90	249	0	59	372.1	332	141	138	252	23

How Often He Throws Strikes

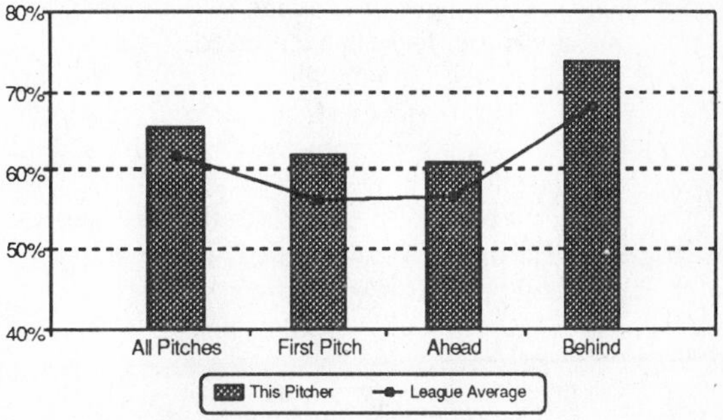

1990 Situational Stats

	W	L	ERA	Sv	IP		AB	H	HR	RBI	AVG
Home	5	3	3.72	8	48.1	LHB	144	40	0	10	.278
Road	3	3	2.35	14	46.0	RHB	212	50	4	24	.236
Day	2	3	4.78	8	32.0	Sc Pos	111	20	1	27	.180
Night	6	3	2.17	14	62.1	Clutch	209	52	3	19	.249

1990 Rankings (American League)

- 4th in games pitched (69)
- 5th worst save percentage (78.6%)
- 6th lowest percentage of inherited runners scored (19.4%)
- 8th in games finished (53) and most GDPs induced per GDP situation (18.8%)
- Led the Tigers in games pitched, saves (22), games finished, save opportunities (28), blown saves (6) and lowest percentage of inherited runners scored

CHET LEMON

Position: RF
Bats: R **Throws:** R
Ht: 6' 0" **Wt:** 190
Opening Day Age: 36
Born: 2/12/55 in Jackson, MS
ML Seasons: 16

Overall Statistics

	G	AB	R	H	D	T	HR	RBI	SB	BB	SO	AVG
1990	104	322	39	83	16	4	5	32	3	48	61	.258
Career	1988	6868	973	1875	396	61	215	884	58	749	1024	.273

Where He Hits the Ball

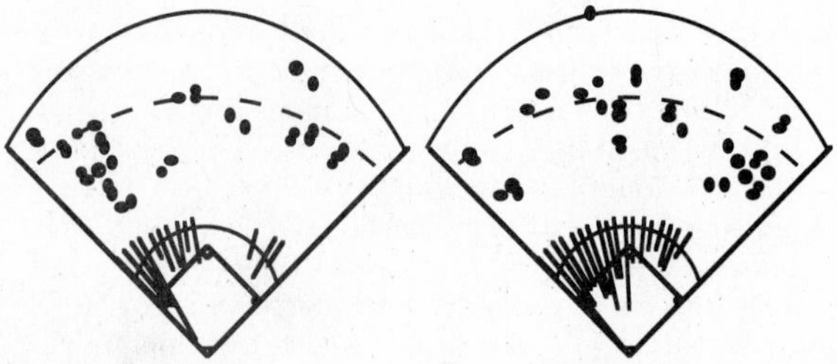

1990 Situational Stats

	AB	H	HR	RBI	AVG		AB	H	HR	RBI	AVG
Home	133	34	2	17	.256	LHP	138	39	3	12	.283
Road	189	49	3	15	.259	RHP	184	44	2	20	.239
Day	103	29	2	10	.282	Sc Pos	71	16	0	24	.225
Night	219	54	3	22	.247	Clutch	45	7	0	8	.156

1990 Rankings (American League)

- 3rd lowest batting average in the clutch (.156)

HITTING:

Like his infamous head first dives into first base, Chet Lemon's career is rapidly turning into a cloud of dust. Lemon appeared in only 104 games last year, the fewest he's played since reaching the majors in last 1975, except for the strike year of 1981. Lemon has had a variety of injuries the last two years, causing some members of the Tiger organization to question his desire.

There's no questioning the fact that this once consistent run-producer is no longer the player he once was. Lemon's home run and RBI totals dropped for the fourth successive year, hitting alarming lows of five homers and 32 RBI. Four of Lemon's five dingers came in a 25 at-bat span from April 28 to May 7, and he hit a dismal .225 with runners in scoring position.

Lemon is the active leader in being hit by pitches with 151, but he no longer crowds the plate and seldom gets hit any more. Righthanders used to tie him up with inside pitches, but now they get Lemon to chase outside stuff. He also takes a lot of called third strikes. Lemon has always had problems with righthanders, who fanned him 39 times in 184 at-bats last year. Once a decent bunter, he rarely uses this as a weapon anymore. He likes the ball up and struggles against breaking-ball pitchers.

BASERUNNING:

Despite decent speed, Lemon has never been a base stealing threat. He swiped three last year, giving him seven stolen bases since 1985. He might just be baseball's worst baserunner. Lemon gets overexcited on the base paths and will try and take the extra base even when he doesn't have a prayer of being safe. His aggressiveness does help him break up some double plays. Lemon's head- long slides into first are rarely successful, but they remain his trademark.

FIELDING:

Lemon is still a decent outfielder, although his skills are eroding in this area as well. He still goes after balls aggressively, but more are dropping in safely these days. He doesn't seem to be getting as good a read on the ball coming off the bat and consequently doesn't get the jump that he used to get. It's possible that lack of playing has dulled his edge. Lemon's arm remains the strongest in the Tiger outfield, but his throws tend to be erratic.

OVERALL:

Simply stated, the 36-year old Lemon is no longer the player he once was. Still, when he was healthy, the Tigers continued to employ Lemon as their everyday right fielder last year. That situation may change in 1991.

JACK MORRIS

Position: SP
Bats: R **Throws:** R
Ht: 6' 3" **Wt:** 200

Opening Day Age: 35
Born: 5/16/55 in St. Paul, MN
ML Seasons: 14

PITCHING:

For the second straight season, Jack Morris posted a losing record, and signs of erosion continued to appear in his numbers. The winningest pitcher of the 1980s with 162 victories, Morris was second in the American League in losses with 18 last year. And while he improved his ERA over 1989, it topped 4.50 for the second straight year.

Morris still continued to be a workhorse in 1990, never missing his turn in the rotation and firing 200+ innings for the eighth time in nine seasons. He also posted 11 of Detroit's 15 complete games, the 10th time in 11 years he's hit double-digits in that category. As usual, he was among the league leaders in strikeouts, fanning 162 in 249.2 innings, but his strikeout ratio was down for the fourth straight year. Morris hurled a complete game without striking out a batter on May 7 at Milwaukee, the first time that has happened to Morris since 1979.

Location, rather than lack of velocity, is Morris' problem these days. He can still blow the fastball by hitters. But he struggled with his control last year, uncorking a team high 16 wild pitches, and had difficulty finding the plate with his forkball. Morris also has an inconsistent straight change-up, a pitch he tends to rely on too much at times.

Home runs have always been a Morris problem. However, he used to have a knack for giving them up with the bases empty. That knack eluded him last year and his 26 homers allowed, many of them at critical times, ranked him among the AL leaders. At the same time, Morris was also victimized by unearned runs, all but one of them coming in his losses. No pitcher in the majors allowed as many unearned runs. When his defense lets down, Morris often lets his temper get the best of him, causing him to lose concentration.

HOLDING RUNNERS AND FIELDING:

A good athlete, Morris is an above-average fielder. He can make the difficult plays, but gets himself into trouble by aggressively going for the impossible play instead of taking the certain out. Morris has always taken an indifferent attitude towards baserunners, which didn't matter in the past when he wasn't allowing very many. But now runners are stealing him blind (45-for-51 last year) and he'll have to improve.

OVERALL:

Morris is still a workhorse, but he'll turn 36 in May and is no longer the ace he once was. He's 36-45 the past three seasons and can no longer be counted on to carry the club on his shoulders. Still, he's a good bet to win 13-15 games and pitch you 200+ innings.

Overall Statistics

	W	L	ERA	G	GS	Sv	IP	H	R	BB	SO	HR
1990	15	18	4.51	36	36	0	249.2	231	144	97	162	26
Career	198	150	3.73	430	408	0	3043.1	2767	1382	1086	1980	321

How Often He Throws Strikes

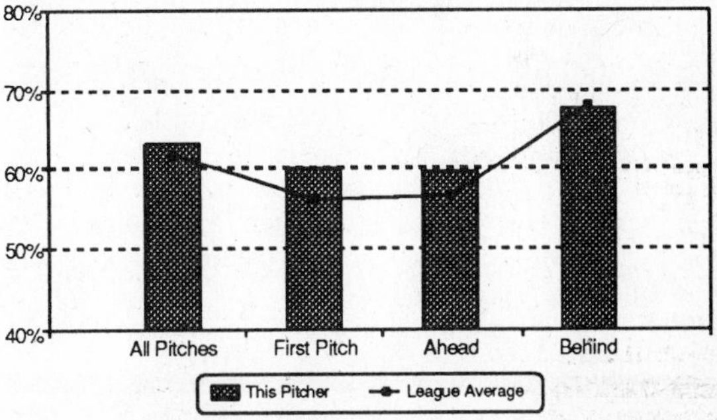

1990 Situational Stats

	W	L	ERA	Sv	IP		AB	H	HR	RBI	AVG
Home	8	8	4.06	0	113.0	LHB	466	125	13	60	.268
Road	7	10	4.87	0	136.2	RHB	487	106	13	64	.218
Day	6	5	3.95	0	82.0	Sc Pos	234	60	11	100	.256
Night	9	13	4.78	0	167.2	Clutch	109	30	2	14	.275

1990 Rankings (American League)

- 1st in games started (36), complete games (11), runs allowed (144), earned runs allowed (125), stolen bases allowed (45) and worst ERA on the road (4.87)
- 2nd in losses (18), innings (249.2), batters faced (1,073), wild pitches (16) and worst stolen base percentage allowed (88.2%)
- Led the Tigers in ERA (4.51), wins (15), losses, games started, complete games, shutouts (3), innings, hits allowed (231), batters faced (1,073), home runs allowed (26), walks (97), strikeouts (162), wild pitches (16), pitches thrown (3,753), stolen bases allowed and GDPs induced (23)

HITTING:

Once a star, Lloyd Moseby has become the perfect picture of mediocrity at the plate. He has now hit below .250 for three straight years, though his .248 batting average in 1990 was his best since 1987. After a fast start, Moseby's average hit .255 last May 25. From that point on, it never rose above .269 and never dipped below its final resting place of .248.

Moseby is a hard man to place in the batting order. He swings hard, which results in some monstrous home runs, but often means strikeouts and sharp ground outs. His power isn't quite good enough for him to bat in the middle of the lineup, yet is good enough that you don't want to bury him at the bottom. He doesn't make enough contact to bat second and isn't quite patient enough to hit leadoff, although that's where Toronto often used him. He'll draw a few walks, but with his low batting average, he simply doesn't reach base enough.

Like any Blue Jay product, Moseby doesn't know how to bunt. It's too bad, because with his speed, it could be an effective weapon. He likes high fastballs, especially ones that he can pull to right in Tiger Stadium. Never known as a clutch hitter, Moseby hit just .202 with runners in scoring position. He was also dismal against lefties, hitting a paltry .182.

BASERUNNING:

A bad back has slowed Moseby more than his 31 years have. He still swiped 17 bases, second-best on the slow-footed Tigers. Moseby is a smart baserunner who reads the pitcher well. He knows when it's time to take the extra base in hitting situations. He gets a lot of infield hits because of his quick acceleration out of the box.

FIELDING:

Moseby flatly refused to move out of center field in Toronto, but as a Tiger, he stepped aside for rookie Milt Cuyler last September. Unless Cuyler is a total flop in spring training, left field will be Moseby's home next year. He made 14 starts there last September, but struggled to make the adjustment. Accustomed to going back on fly balls in Tiger Stadium's spacious center field, Moseby found it difficult to adjust to the different view of the game in left field. He has an average arm which is probably more suited for left field than center.

OVERALL:

The Tigers unsuccessfully tried to deal Moseby during the stretch run last year. They'll likely continue to shop him in the off season. If he's back in Detroit, look for him to platoon in left, DH a bit and play center field on occasion.

LLOYD MOSEBY

Position: CF/LF
Bats: L **Throws:** R
Ht: 6' 3" **Wt:** 200

Opening Day Age: 31
Born: 11/5/59 in Portland, AR
ML Seasons: 11

Overall Statistics

	G	AB	R	H	D	T	HR	RBI	SB	BB	SO	AVG
1990	122	431	64	107	16	5	14	51	17	48	77	.248
Career	1514	5555	832	1426	258	65	163	702	272	595	1092	.257

Where He Hits the Ball

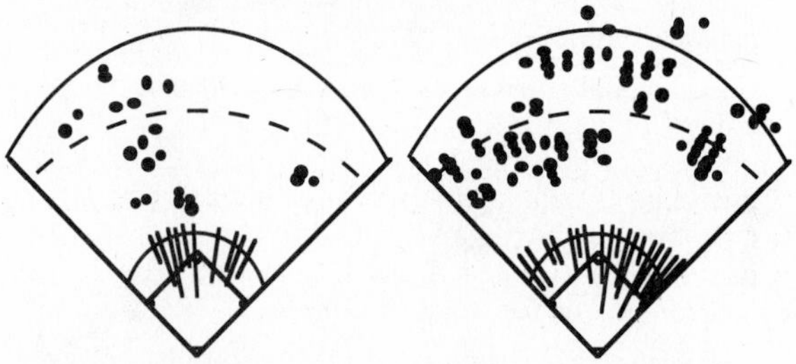

Vs. LHP Vs. RHP

1990 Situational Stats

	AB	H	HR	RBI	AVG		AB	H	HR	RBI	AVG
Home	221	53	8	25	.240	LHP	132	24	2	9	.182
Road	210	54	6	26	.257	RHP	299	83	12	42	.278
Day	125	25	3	9	.200	Sc Pos	114	23	2	37	.202
Night	306	82	11	42	.268	Clutch	73	20	1	11	.274

1990 Rankings (American League)

- 3rd lowest batting average vs. left-handed pitchers (.182) and lowest slugging percentage vs. left-handed pitchers (.242)
- 6th lowest batting average with runners in scoring position (.202), lowest on-base average vs. left-handed pitchers (.264)
- Led the Tigers in triples (5), hit by pitch (5), GDPs (15), stolen base percentage (77.3%) and percentage of extra bases taken as a runner (54.8%)

EDWIN NUNEZ

Position: RP
Bats: R **Throws:** R
Ht: 6' 5" **Wt:** 240

Opening Day Age: 27
Born: 5/27/63 in Humacao, Puerto Rico
ML Seasons: 9

PITCHING:

At age 27, Edwin Nunez regained his health last year and rediscovered the form which once made him such a promising prospect. Nunez had injured his right thumb in a fall late in the 1988 season, necessitating surgery to repair torn ligaments. He wasn't the same pitcher afterwards, earning his release from the New York Mets. The Tigers picked Nunez up, but he struggled in 1989.

The thumb finally healed after the '89 season, and Nunez was once more able to snap off his devastating split-finger pitch. By combining the splitter with his hard fastball, Nunez again became an effective strikeout pitcher. He fanned 66 in 80.1 innings and limited the opposition to 65 hits. He was no picnic to face for either lefties (.209) or righties (.223). While control is still a problem for him, Nunez improved his walks to innings pitched ratio.

Nunez started and finished last season slowly. After a so-so first month, he got hot. In a 36.2 inning span from May 4 to July 7, he checked the opposition on 21 hits and five earned runs. Nunez was 3-0 with two saves in that time. He was just earning a more prominent role in the Tiger bullpen when he caught a line drive hit by Kansas City's Pat Tabler, ripping the skin between the forefinger and thumb on his glove hand. Nunez spent the next six weeks on the disabled list and wasn't the same pitcher when he returned. He struggled for the rest of the season, posting a 6.21 ERA over the last month.

Nunez has pitched in virtually every role during his career. He's capable of coming in as a short man, but is equally at home working three or four innings in one stint. In 1985 at age 22, he was Seattle's closer working in 70 games. But ineffectiveness and injury followed, and Nunez is only now on the brink of coming all the way back.

HOLDING RUNNERS AND FIELDING:

Nunez has a big, slow delivery to the plate and doesn't have a great pickoff move, making him susceptible to the stolen base. The big man isn't too quick afoot and has difficulty fielding bunts and infield hits.

OVERALL:

Nunez has made himself a valuable part of the Detroit pitching staff. They learned this the hard way when they were without him for six weeks. Nunez picked the right year to put it all together. He's a free agent, and his 2.24 ERA should help make him a rich man before the 1991 season. Detroit will likely want to re-sign him, if the cost is not prohibitive.

Overall Statistics

	W	L	ERA	G	GS	Sv	IP	H	R	BB	SO	HR
1990	3	1	2.24	42	0	6	80.1	65	26	37	66	4
Career	22	26	3.83	284	14	42	477.0	460	235	206	362	58

How Often He Throws Strikes

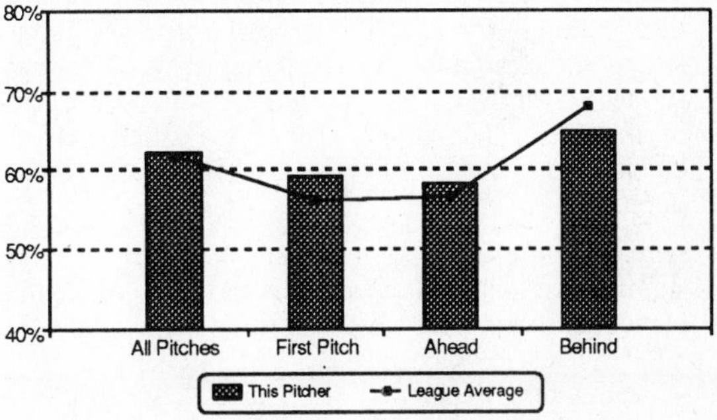

1990 Situational Stats

	W	L	ERA	Sv	IP		AB	H	HR	RBI	AVG
Home	0	0	2.95	4	42.2	LHB	110	23	2	10	.209
Road	3	1	1.43	2	37.2	RHB	188	42	2	18	.223
Day	1	0	1.31	1	20.2	Sc Pos	91	19	1	24	.209
Night	2	1	2.56	5	59.2	Clutch	73	21	2	15	.288

1990 Rankings (American League)

- 8th in lowest batting average allowed vs. left-handed batters (.209)
- Led the Tigers in batting average vs. left-handed batters and first batter efficiency (.200)

DAN PETRY

Position: SP/RP
Bats: R **Throws:** R
Ht: 6' 4" **Wt:** 215

Opening Day Age: 32
Born: 11/13/58 in Palo Alto, CA
ML Seasons: 12

<u>*PITCHING:*</u>

If it hadn't been for the arrival of Cecil Fielder, Dan Petry would have been the Detroit Tigers' 1990 comeback story. Unwanted by the other 25 major league clubs, Petry returned to the site of his greatest glories as a ballplayer, making the club after signing a minor league contract. Petry worked his way out of the bullpen into the starting rotation, hitting double digits in victories for the first time since 1985. His 4.45 earned run average, while not sensational, was the lowest of any Detroit starter with 100 innings.

Petry was a big winner for the Tigers during the first half of the eighties, averaging 17 wins per year from 1982 through 1985. In those days he had the stuff to overpower hitters, and his best pitch by far was a good, hard slider. But since 1986 elbow surgery, Petry had been unable to make the slider dive. Hitters could sit on it and tee off, sending Petry's ERA and opposition batting averages soaring. After five years of struggle, the pitch began moving again in 1990, and suddenly Petry was a winning hurler again. The return of the slider helped make Petry's fastball, which clocks in at about 88 MPH, more effective as a set-up pitch.

After pitching just 51 innings in 1989, Petry lacked stamina last year and faded badly in the second half. He was 5-2 with a 2.51 ERA on June 5, but went 5-7, 5.93 the rest of the way. He also pitched past the seventh inning in just four of 23 starts. Petry won just twice in 11 Tiger Stadium starts. He gave up a lot of hits, especially to right-handed hitters (.274) and walked more batters than he struck out. Arm problems again hampered Petry towards the end of the season, as a stiff shoulder forced him out of the rotation in September.

<u>*HOLDING RUNNERS AND FIELDING:*</u>

Petry takes pride in holding runners and will alter his delivery with men on base to try and prevent stolen bases. His pickoff move is decent enough to keep baserunners honest. He's also a solid, if unspectacular, fielder. Petry won't make any brilliant defensive plays, but is reliable on the routine balls.

<u>*OVERALL:*</u>

The Tigers will look to strengthen their starting pitching, which likely means Petry won't be back in the rotation in 1991. But the Tigers like his competitiveness. Petry, the ultimate team player, would be willing to go to the bullpen and work as a middle reliever and spot starter, because he wants to stay in Detroit.

Overall Statistics

	W	L	ERA	G	GS	Sv	IP	H	R	BB	SO	HR
1990	10	9	4.45	32	23	0	149.2	148	78	77	73	14
Career	123	101	3.89	330	294	0	1979.1	1868	956	807	1024	204

How Often He Throws Strikes

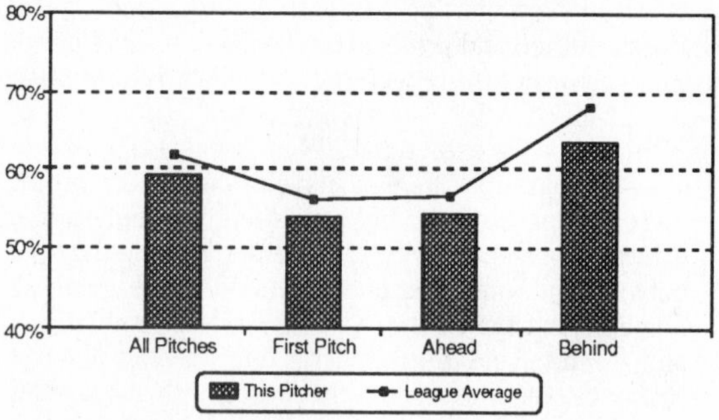

1990 Situational Stats

	W	L	ERA	Sv	IP		AB	H	HR	RBI	AVG
Home	4	5	5.49	0	62.1	LHB	245	61	3	24	.249
Road	6	4	3.71	0	87.1	RHB	318	87	11	41	.274
Day	4	2	3.80	0	45.0	Sc Pos	154	37	2	48	.240
Night	6	7	4.73	0	104.2	Clutch	41	11	1	5	.268

1990 Rankings (American League)

- → 10th in wild pitches (10)
- → Led the Tigers in winning percentage (.526), ERA on the road (3.71) and batting average allowed with runners in scoring position (.240)

TONY PHILLIPS

Position: 3B/2B/SS
Bats: B **Throws:** R
Ht: 5'10" **Wt:** 175

Opening Day Age: 32
Born: 4/15/59 in Atlanta, GA
ML Seasons: 9

Overall Statistics

	G	AB	R	H	D	T	HR	RBI	SB	BB	SO	AVG
1990	152	573	97	144	23	5	8	55	19	99	85	.251
Career	987	3161	451	793	130	30	41	314	75	441	575	.251

Where He Hits the Ball

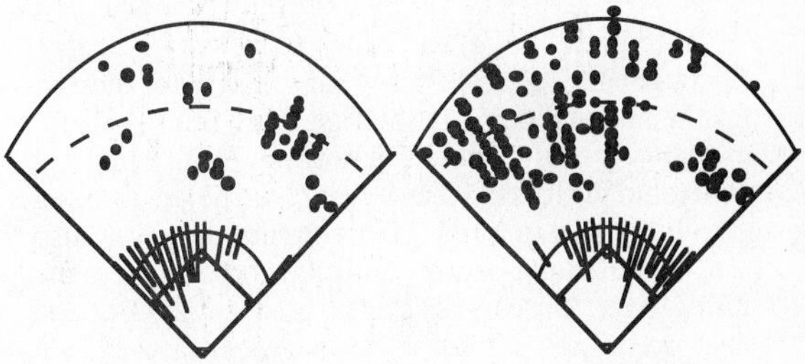

Vs. LHP Vs. RHP

1990 Situational Stats

	AB	H	HR	RBI	AVG		AB	H	HR	RBI	AVG
Home	286	69	4	23	.241	LHP	202	50	2	19	.248
Road	287	75	4	32	.261	RHP	371	94	6	36	.253
Day	170	40	2	15	.235	Sc Pos	113	32	3	46	.283
Night	403	104	6	40	.258	Clutch	76	20	1	4	.263

1990 Rankings (American League)

- 2nd in pitches seen (2,784)
- 3rd in walks (99)
- 5th in runs (97)
- 6th in highest percentage of pitches taken (62.9%)
- 7th in plate appearances (687)
- Led the Tigers in at-bats (573), triples (5), sacrifice bunts (9), stolen bases (19), walks, pitches seen, plate appearances, groundball/flyball ratio (1.42), bunts in play (23), highest percentage of pitches taken and steals of third (3)
- Led AL third basemen in runs, walks, bunts in play and steals of third

HITTING:

Given 500 at-bats for the first time in his nine year career, Tony Phillips responded to the challenge. His critics point to the fact that he hit only .251 last year, but batting average alone doesn't measure Phillips' contribution. Inserted as Detroit's permanent leadoff hitter on Aug. 7, Phillips hit .308 the rest of the way, scoring 39 runs in the final 49 games. He had a .364 on-base percentage for the season, with 97 runs scored and a club-leading 99 walks.

Phillips is a streak hitter. When he's slumping, Phillips tends to chase the high fastball. When he's in a groove, he lays off that pitch and works the count to his advantage. Phillips swings hard and has decent power, especially against low pitches when he's batting lefty. Six of Phillips' eight homers last year were off righthanders, in part due to Tiger Stadium's short right field porch.

Except for the extra power from the left side, Phillips hits righties and lefties about the same. He'll spray the ball around, showing occasional power to all fields. Phillips will bunt for base hits and produced a club-high nine sacrifice hits. His first full season as an everyday player helped him pick up career bests in at-bats (573), runs, bases on balls and hits (144). He's especially productive in key situations. Phillips batted .283 with runners in scoring position.

BASERUNNING:

Aggressive on the base paths, Phillips led the slow-footed Tigers with 19 steals. He has the speed to go from first to third on balls hit to right field. He'll also stretch a single into a double if an outfielder is nonchalant about getting to the ball.

FIELDING:

The versatile Phillips began last season as Detroit's everyday third baseman, and quickly had problems, with 14 errors by May 21. After getting positioning help from Alan Trammell and a new third baseman's glove, Phillips dramatically improved his third base play. He is better at second, however, playing it well enough to convince Sparky Anderson to sit Lou Whitaker against left-handed pitching. Phillips shows great range and he'll go a long way to make a play.

OVERALL:

Phillips quickly became a valuable member of the Tigers last year. He has great presence in the clubhouse and is popular with his teammates. A leader by example, Phillips never complains about the fact he's bounced all over the field. After all these years of part-time play, he's satisfied to see his name on the lineup card each day.

PITCHING:

Once considered the prize of the Detroit pitching staff, Jeff Robinson has become a giant enigma. After a 13-6 mark in 1988, Robinson looked ready to take over Jack Morris' role as Detroit's number-one starter. But then came two years of injuries. A circulation problem in his pitching hand ended Robinson's 1988 campaign in August. Then elbow and rib injuries limited him to 16 starts and 78 innings in 1989. He's never really recovered from the setbacks.

Robinson had a roller-coaster campaign in 1990. At times he was sensational, hurling a complete game shutout at Texas, eight shutout innings at Boston and pitching seven no-hit innings against Baltimore. But just as often he was dreadful. Robinson failed to retire a batter while surrendering seven runs at Boston, and twice couldn't last five innings for a win after being spotted five-run leads.

If you're going to get to Robinson, get to him early. He coughed up 25 first inning runs, and 57 of the 101 runs he allowed came in the first three innings. Robinson insists his injuries have not affected his pitching ability, but his forkball has never been the devastating out pitch it was in 1988. Likewise, his slider has also been inconsistent, darting into the dirt at times and sailing over the catcher's head to the backstop on other occasions. Robinson has a decent fastball, but gets behind in the count too often, making this pitch easier to hit.

Walks and the long ball were Robinson's chief shortcomings last year. He had more walks than strikeouts, and was pitching from behind too often. That helped him finish among the AL leaders in home runs allowed, with 23 dingers in 145 innings. He also shared the team lead with 16 wild pitches. Yet another injury, a stress fracture in his right forearm, ended Robinson's season prematurely in September, leaving another question mark about him heading into spring training.

FIELDING AND HOLDING RUNNERS:

A pure athlete in college, Robinson lettered in both baseball and basketball at Azusa Pacific. He uses that athletic ability to field his position well. He has good agility for a big man and will pounce on bunts and infield grounders. Robinson's jump pickoff move is above average and his quick delivery makes it difficult to steal on him.

OVERALL:

It's make or break time for Robinson in Detroit. The Tigers tried to unload him last year, but found no takers. It was another indication of how much this once-promising hurler's stock has fallen.

JEFF M. ROBINSON

Position: SP
Bats: R **Throws:** R
Ht: 6' 6" **Wt:** 210

Opening Day Age: 29
Born: 12/14/61 in Ventura, CA
ML Seasons: 4

Overall Statistics

	W	L	ERA	G	GS	Sv	IP	H	R	BB	SO	HR
1990	10	9	5.96	27	27	0	145.0	141	101	88	76	23
Career	36	26	4.65	96	87	0	522.1	470	295	260	328	68

How Often He Throws Strikes

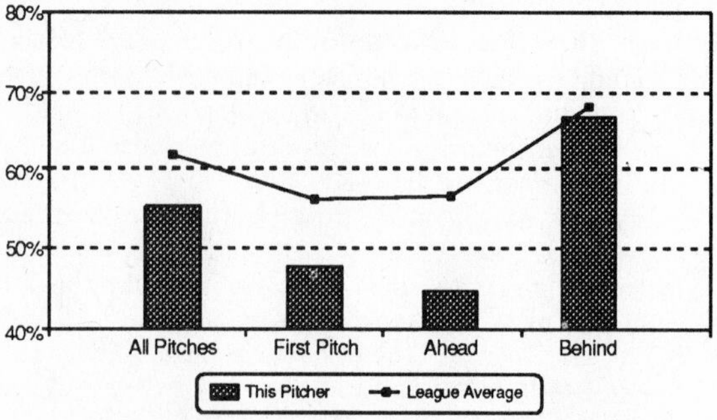

1990 Situational Stats

	W	L	ERA	Sv	IP		AB	H	HR	RBI	AVG
Home	6	4	5.63	0	86.1	LHB	254	62	10	32	.244
Road	4	5	6.44	0	58.2	RHB	298	79	13	54	.265
Day	0	3	7.83	0	23.0	Sc Pos	144	40	5	61	.278
Night	10	6	5.61	0	122.0	Clutch	17	6	1	4	.353

1990 Rankings (American League)

- 2nd in wild pitches (16) and worst ERA at home (5.63)
- 8th in most walks allowed (88)
- 9th in most home runs allowed (23)
- Led the Tigers in wild pitches and winning percentage (.526)

PITCHING:

Steve Searcy's latest stint as a Detroit Tiger still left more questions than answers. Called up after once again posting impressive numbers at AAA Toledo (10-5, 2.92), Searcy didn't show that he could consistently handle major league hitters. He surrendered more than a hit an inning, and was ineffective as both a reliever (4.22 ERA) and starter (4.73).

A left-handed power pitcher, Searcy has a fine fastball, along with a decent curveball and a change-up. When all his pitches are working, he can be plenty tough. He's piled up impressive strikeout numbers in the minor leagues, fanning nearly a batter an inning during his stints at Toledo over the last four years. Searcy continued to strike out hitters after his recall to Detroit last year (66 in 75.1 innings). But he simply wasn't able to control his pitches well enough to be successful. Searcy's only wins last year came against Texas and the New York Yankees, two teams not known for showing a lot of patience at the plate. He had problems against clubs who have discipline to lay off pitches out of the strike zone.

Searcy is most effective when he's aggressive and challenges the hitters. However, he tends to give big-league hitters too much credit and too often tries to nibble on the corners. Invariably he gets behind in the count and starts walking people. That's not a good situation for a fly ball pitcher who is prone to coughing up home runs of the moon-shot variety. Searcy has shown good stamina in the minors, where he's averaged nearly seven innings a start over his career. But because of his control problems, he averaged only 5.1 innings in his 12 starts last year for Detroit.

HOLDING RUNNERS AND FIELDING:

Searcy has an excellent pickoff move, which is further accentuated by the fact he's a southpaw. He's not a very good athlete, though and that hurts his defensive ability. He doesn't react well when the ball is hit; Searcy has difficulty snaring balls hit right up the middle.

OVERALL:

At 26, Searcy has been up with the Tigers three times, but has been given only 16 starts to show what he can do at the big-league level. Lack of control has held him back. Nonetheless, his minor league credentials are excellent, and he can throw hard. Before they give up on him, the Tigers might want to consider giving Searcy a longer look.

STEVE SEARCY

Position: SP
Bats: L **Throws:** L
Ht: 6' 1" **Wt:** 185

Opening Day Age: 26
Born: 6/4/64 in Knoxville, TN
ML Seasons: 3

Overall Statistics

	W	L	ERA	G	GS	Sv	IP	H	R	BB	SO	HR
1990	2	7	4.66	16	12	0	75.1	76	44	51	66	9
Career	3	10	5.03	26	16	0	105.2	111	66	67	82	15

How Often He Throws Strikes

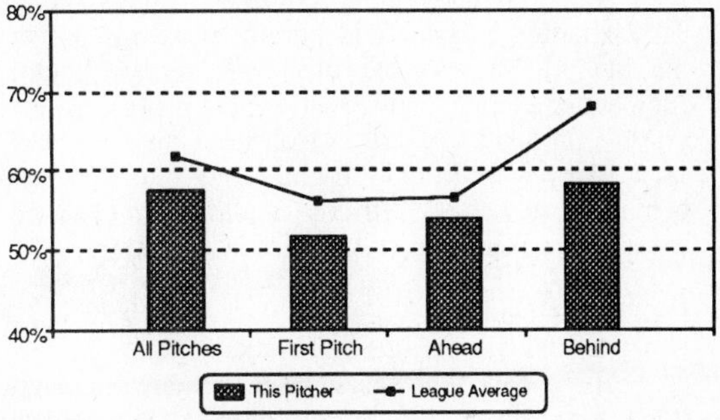

1990 Situational Stats

	W	L	ERA	Sv	IP		AB	H	HR	RBI	AVG
Home	2	2	4.65	0	40.2	LHB	46	15	1	9	.326
Road	0	5	4.67	0	34.2	RHB	236	61	8	32	.258
Day	2	2	2.78	0	35.2	Sc Pos	77	15	4	32	.195
Night	0	5	6.35	0	39.2	Clutch	12	6	0	1	.500

1990 Rankings (American League)

- Did not rank near the top or bottom in any category

HITTING:

Larry Sheets remains the victim of his own success. People continue to point to his 1987 numbers (.316, 31 HR, 94 RBI) and ask "What's wrong with this guy?" Simply put, he's not that good. That doesn't mean Sheets can't be a useful player. The Tigers discovered that fact last year after picking him up from Baltimore for a song.

Sheets likes the ball up and struggles to hit the breaking ball and the slider. He can hit the ball to all fields, but is most dangerous when he pulls the ball. He showed an alarming inability to do that for much of last year, with just four homers and 23 RBIs towards the end of July. Sheets then switched to a more open batting stance, and belted six homers and had 29 RBIs in the last two and one-half months of the season.

When he doesn't pull the ball, Sheets will go through long stretches where he becomes a singles hitter. Tiger Stadium's right field porch helped his power numbers. He hit seven of his ten homers there, but hit for a better average on the road (.276 to .246). Sheets doesn't show a lot of patience at the plate. He won't draw many walks and he'll chase bad pitches when behind in the count. Strictly a platoon player, he batted just 17 times against lefties last year.

BASERUNNING:

No speedster, Sheets has stolen exactly one base in each of the past four years. He's obviously slowed down some since 1986, because he swiped a career-high two that year. At the same time, Sheets is smart enough to know his limitations and won't get adventurous on the base paths. He doesn't take chances which might run his team out of an inning.

FIELDING:

One of only three American League players not to pick up his glove in 1989, Sheets got plenty of outfield time last year with Detroit. Despite his size and lack of speed, he's far from the worst outfielder in the game. Sheets lacks range, but he positions himself well. He won't throw to the wrong base or try and make an impossible play. Line drives give Sheets a lot of trouble, and he seems to have trouble picking up low-hit fly balls. His arm isn't great, but he's capable of making a good throw if he charges the ball.

OVERALL:

Sheets proved a useful addition to the Tigers, especially when you consider that the price was cheap. However, Sheets was a free agent after the season. Although Detroit would like him back in 1991, they aren't likely to give him much more than the $690,000 he earned last year.

LARRY SHEETS

Position: LF/RF/DH
Bats: L **Throws:** R
Ht: 6' 3" **Wt:** 236

Opening Day Age: 31
Born: 12/6/59 in Staunton, VA
ML Seasons: 7

Overall Statistics

	G	AB	R	H	D	T	HR	RBI	SB	BB	SO	AVG
1990	131	360	40	94	17	2	10	52	1	24	42	.261
Career	737	2267	273	605	97	5	94	338	6	173	350	.267

Where He Hits the Ball

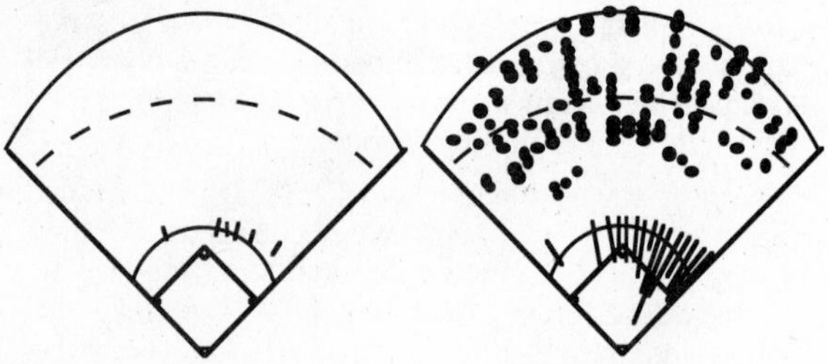

Vs. LHP   Vs. RHP

1990 Situational Stats

	AB	H	HR	RBI	AVG		AB	H	HR	RBI	AVG
Home	179	44	7	30	.246	LHP	17	4	0	1	.235
Road	181	50	3	22	.276	RHP	343	90	10	51	.262
Day	99	26	2	11	.263	Sc Pos	101	28	5	45	.277
Night	261	68	8	41	.261	Clutch	43	14	2	9	.326

1990 Rankings (American League)

➟ Did not rank near the top or bottom in any category

PITCHING:

Frank Tanana relies on pinpoint control to be successful, but he was out of control more often than not in 1990. Tanana is giving indications that time is running out on his 37-year-old arm. He hit bottom last year during a 10-start stretch in June and July, going 1-4 and allowing 46 earned runs in 40.1 innings for a 10.26 ERA. That earned Tanana banishment to the bullpen, and many people were speculating that his career was over.

But Tanana, who had been written off numerous other times during his career, fought his way back. He worked out some of his problems in the bullpen and even recorded the first save of his 18-season big-league career. Returning to the rotation late in the year, he posted a 4-1 mark with a 2.44 ERA over eight starts. Even that wasn't quite enough to salvage his season, however.

Tanana's dismal figures speak for themselves. His ERA of 5.31 was nearly two runs higher than his career average of 3.49. He hit a club-high nine batters, and his walk ratio (3.4 per nine innings) was a career high. His 176.1 innings pitched were the fewest he'd worked in seven seasons. With only nine wins, he failed to reach double figures for the first time since 1983. And his 114 strikeouts were his lowest total in that department since 1983.

Once a power pitcher who was only a step behind Angel teammate Nolan Ryan, Tanana lost his fastball at a young age due to arm problems. For over a decade he's had to out-think opposing hitters. He relies on his wide assortment of offspeed pitches to nibble at the corners and fool hitters, leaving himself little margin for error. Tanana uses these pitches to set up his weak fastball. But when his control deserted him last year, Tanana was easy pickings for the opposition. Right-handed hitters proved especially difficult, slugging 24 home runs and batting .290.

HOLDING RUNNERS AND FIELDING:

Tanana uses a variety of pickoff moves to try and freeze baserunners. These efforts compensate quite well for his slow delivery, allowing only nine of 24 base stealers to be successful. A superbly conditioned athlete, Tanana is still among baseball's best defensive pitchers. He hasn't made an error since 1988.

OVERALL:

Tanana still figures to help the Tigers, but he's no longer going to be the reliable starter he once was. He is likely to fill the role of a fourth or fifth starter. The club will just have to accept the fact that when he's off, they're in big trouble.

FRANK TANANA

Position: SP/RP
Bats: L **Throws:** L
Ht: 6' 3" **Wt:** 195

Opening Day Age: 37
Born: 7/3/53 in Detroit, MI
ML Seasons: 18

Overall Statistics

	W	L	ERA	G	GS	Sv	IP	H	R	BB	SO	HR
1990	9	8	5.31	34	29	1	176.1	190	104	66	114	25
Career	207	196	3.58	541	520	1	3580.0	3442	1600	1032	2459	372

How Often He Throws Strikes

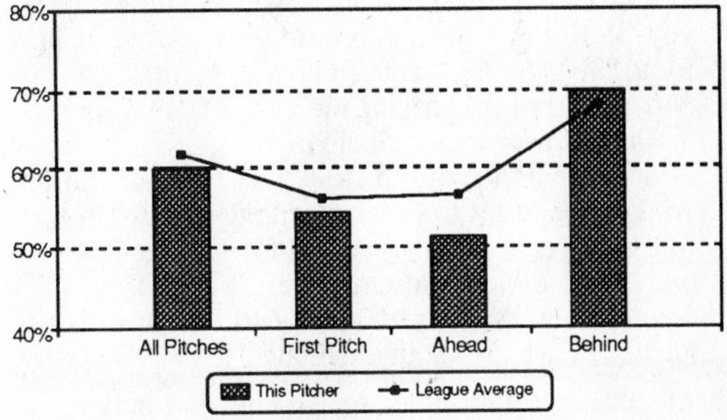

1990 Situational Stats

	W	L	ERA	Sv	IP		AB	H	HR	RBI	AVG
Home	4	6	6.00	0	99.0	LHB	113	26	1	10	.230
Road	5	2	4.42	1	77.1	RHB	565	164	24	89	.290
Day	2	2	6.91	1	41.2	Sc Pos	134	44	7	73	.328
Night	7	6	4.81	0	134.2	Clutch	60	12	2	3	.200

1990 Rankings (American League)

- 1st in worst ERA (5.31) and worst ERA at home (6.00)
- 2nd highest slugging percentage allowed (.453), highest on-base percentage allowed (.349) and most HRs allowed per 9 innings (1.28)
- 3rd in runners caught stealing (15), lowest stolen base percentage allowed (37.5%), most baserunners per 9 innings (13.5) and highest batting average allowed with runners in scoring position (.328)
- Led the Tigers in hit batsmen (9), pickoff throws (203), runners caught stealing, strikeout/walk ratio (1.73) and lowest stolen base percentage allowed

WALT TERRELL

Position: SP
Bats: L **Throws:** R
Ht: 6' 2" **Wt:** 205

Opening Day Age: 32
Born: 5/11/58 in Jeffersonville, IN
ML Seasons: 9

PITCHING:

Credit Billy Muffett with a save when it comes to Walt Terrell's career. Released by the Pirates last July, Terrell returned to Tiger Stadium, and pitching coach Muffett, with his career in tatters. Terrell had left the Tigers following the 1988 campaign, when Detroit traded him to San Diego. In a season and one-half without Muffett, Terrell had gone 13-25 with astronomical ERAs, while toiling for three different clubs.

Enter Muffett again. Almost immediately, he noticed that the righthander was delivering the ball with a three-quarters motion. That caused Terrell's money pitch, his sinking fastball, to hang out over the plate. The only sinking it did was into the bleachers after the batter gave it a wallop.

Muffett got Terrell to throw from directly over the top again, and the improvement was immediate. Not that Terrell suddenly was pitching like Cy Young, mind you. With the Tigers, opposition hitters tagged him for a .290 batting average and lefties hit him at a .314 clip, as Terrell coughed up more than 10 hits per nine innings. However, Terrell did improve in a number of areas. His ERA dropped from 5.88 to 4.54, and his wild pitches went from seven with the Pirates to zero for the Tigers. Terrell averaged 5.1 innings per start with Pittsburgh, 6.1 a start for the Tigers. His walks per nine innings dropped from 3.6 to 2.9. Most significantly, he was 2-7 with the Pirates, 6-4 for Detroit.

As someone who relies on ground ball outs to be successful, Terrell is much more at home in the American League, where there are just four artificial surface fields. Tiger Stadium, with its long infield grass, is ideally suited for him, to say the least: he's 39-14 lifetime there, 53-86 everywhere else. Terrell's only winning seasons as a big-league pitcher were his first three in a Detroit uniform, when he was a combined 47-32 from 1985-87. However, Terrell is 26-45 the past three seasons. As Muffett detected, his delivery is crucial to his success. When the ball doesn't sink for him, Terrell is sunk.

HOLDING RUNNERS AND FIELDING:

Terrell doesn't possess a great pickoff move, but his short leg kick and quick delivery to the plate make it difficult to steal on him. Terrell doesn't position himself well after delivery and has trouble fielding, especially on bunts and weak infield grounders.

OVERALL:

With Pittsburgh still paying Terrell's three-year, $3.7 million contract, Detroit will be happy to continue to rent Terrell for the major-league minimum of $100,000. Terrell's pitching late last year indicated that he can again be a capable fourth or fifth starter for the Tigers.

Overall Statistics

	W	L	ERA	G	GS	Sv	IP	H	R	BB	SO	HR
1990	8	11	5.24	29	28	0	158.0	184	98	57	64	20
Career	92	100	4.13	250	247	0	1631.1	1670	830	621	788	157

How Often He Throws Strikes

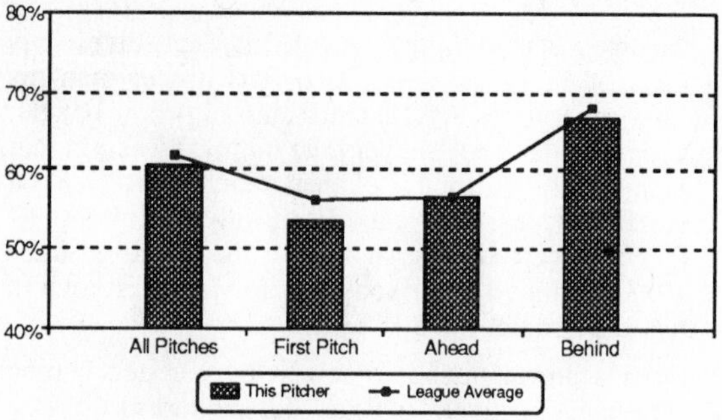

1990 Situational Stats

	W	L	ERA	Sv	IP		AB	H	HR	RBI	AVG
Home	5	4	4.58	0	78.2	LHB	341	110	16	53	.323
Road	3	7	5.90	0	79.1	RHB	288	74	4	26	.257
Day	2	1	3.15	0	40.0	Sc Pos	171	47	8	60	.275
Night	6	10	5.95	0	118.0	Clutch	39	9	1	2	.231

1990 Rankings (American League)

- 6th in hit batsmen (8)
- 9th in highest batting average allowed vs. left-handed batters (.314)

HITTING:

Alan Trammell placed himself in select company by hitting .304 last season. It was the sixth time he had batted above .300, making him only the sixth shortstop in baseball history to do so. The other five -- Luke Appling, Honus Wagner, Joe Sewell, Arky Vaughn and Joe Cronin -- are all in the Hall of Fame. More importantly, Trammell rebounded from his worst season to resume his place among the game's best hitters.

Two things helped Trammell once again become his old self. One was his return to health, as his chronic back problems forced him to miss only 16 games. The other was the arrival of Cecil Fielder to take over cleanup-hitting chores. When Trammell struggles at the plate, it's because he's trying to do things outside his capabilities. That was exactly what he'd been asked to do the past two seasons, as the departures of Kirk Gibson, Lance Parrish and Darrell Evans left him as Detroit's only power threat.

Trammell handles a bat about as well as anyone. He can hit for power, for average, or lay down a bunt. He absolutely kills inside pitches. Teams used to have success throwing him breaking balls away, but Trammell has adjusted and now covers the entire plate. Trammell is at his best in clutch situations. His compact swing keeps his strikeouts down and makes him an excellent hit-and-run man.

BASERUNNING:

Back woes have dramatically reduced Trammell's stolen base totals the past couple of years, but he's still one of baseball's best fundamental baserunners. Never blessed with great speed, Trammell has great instincts and knows when it's time to try and take the extra base or when to attempt a steal.

FIELDING:

Shoulder, elbow and forearm injuries in the mid-80s took a lot of zip out of Trammell's right arm, but he's learned to pace himself in the field. He'll only throw hard when he has to, and his quick release helps make up for the lack of arm speed. Trammell has lost some of his range, but again, through his instincts and knowledge of hitters' tendencies, he helps overcome the problem with better positioning.

OVERALL:

Trammell is still one of the steadiest, most reliable players in baseball. But at 33, he will need more rest from now on. With his heir apparent, Travis Fryman, now playing next to him at third base, the Tigers can afford to let Trammell DH more often. That should help prolong his career.

ALAN TRAMMELL

Position: SS
Bats: R **Throws:** R
Ht: 6' 0" **Wt:** 175

Opening Day Age: 33
Born: 2/21/58 in Garden Grove, CA
ML Seasons: 14

Overall Statistics

	G	AB	R	H	D	T	HR	RBI	SB	BB	SO	AVG
1990	146	559	71	170	37	1	14	89	12	68	55	.304
Career	1835	6702	1009	1929	329	50	152	810	199	707	712	.288

Where He Hits the Ball

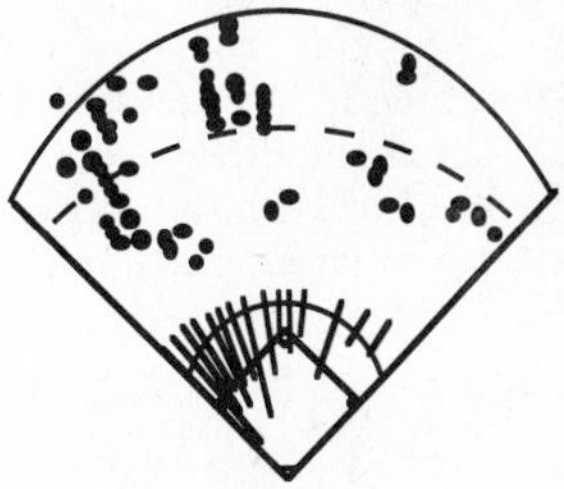

Vs. LHP

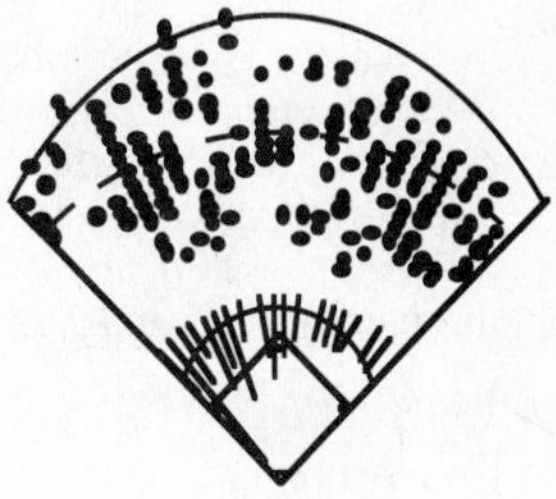

Vs. RHP

1990 Situational Stats

	AB	H	HR	RBI	AVG		AB	H	HR	RBI	AVG
Home	271	92	9	59	.339	LHP	173	50	7	27	.289
Road	288	78	5	30	.271	RHP	386	120	7	62	.311
Day	169	56	3	28	.331	Sc Pos	145	55	4	75	.379
Night	390	114	11	61	.292	Clutch	73	22	1	12	.301

1990 Rankings (American League)

- 1st in batting average with runners in scoring postion (.379)
- 4th in batting average (.304), batting average at home (.340) and highest percentage of swings put into play (56.9%)
- Led the Tigers in batting average, hits (170), singles (118), doubles (37), sacrifice flies (6), caught stealing (10), least GDPs per GDP situation (6.9%), batting average with runners in scoring position and batting average in the clutch (.301)
- Led AL shortstops in batting average, doubles (37), total bases (251), RBIs (89), slugging percentage (.449) and on-base average (.377)

HITTING:

In his prime, Gary Ward was a two-time All-Star, a .275-.280 hitter with 25 homers and 10-15 stolen bases a season. Those days are long gone for the 37-year-old Ward, but he can still do things to help a ball club.

Ward earns his keep by being a very good situational hitter. Always good off the bench, he batted .385 as a pinch hitter last season and hit .286 with runners in scoring position. Ward can hit the ball to all fields and he'll take the occasional outside pitch down the opposite-field line for extra bases. But most of his power comes when he pulls the ball. Ward doesn't possess the bat speed he once had and hard throwers can blow the ball by him. He showed better bat control last year, as his strikeouts were down, while his bases on balls increased.

Ward doesn't get a lot of playing time against righthanders. But he hit four of his nine homers off righthanders last year, the first time he'd gone deep off a righty since 1987. A streak hitter, he goes through hot and cold spells. Ward had 10, nine and eight-game hit streaks last year, but he also suffered through 1-for-25 and 2-for-29 skids.

BASERUNNING:

No longer a speedster, Ward had two stolen bases last year, doubling his total output of the two previous seasons. He doesn't have the acceleration he once had, making him a prime double-play candidate. But he's a smart baserunner who can still go from first to third on balls hit to right field. He isn't afraid to try for the extra base if an outfielder takes him for granted.

FIELDING:

The versatile Ward can handle five different defensive positions: all three outfield spots, first base and third base in a pinch. Left field is by far his best position. Ward has lost range and his arm is average at best. But he still gets a good jump on the ball and isn't afraid to crash into the wall to make a catch. Ward is much better when he's charging the ball. He tends to have judgement problems when going back on fly balls.

OVERALL:

The Tigers like the way this old pro comes off the bench. Ward's a good team man who doesn't complain to the media about his lack of playing time. He quietly works with the young players to help them improve. Ward will likely continue to platoon in left field and fill a utility role for the Tigers in 1991.

GARY WARD

Position: LF/RF/DH
Bats: R **Throws:** R
Ht: 6' 2" **Wt:** 202

Opening Day Age: 37
Born: 12/6/53 in Los Angeles, CA
ML Seasons: 12

Overall Statistics

	G	AB	R	H	D	T	HR	RBI	SB	BB	SO	AVG
1990	106	309	32	79	11	2	9	46	2	30	50	.256
Career	1287	4479	594	1236	196	41	130	597	83	351	775	.276

Where He Hits the Ball

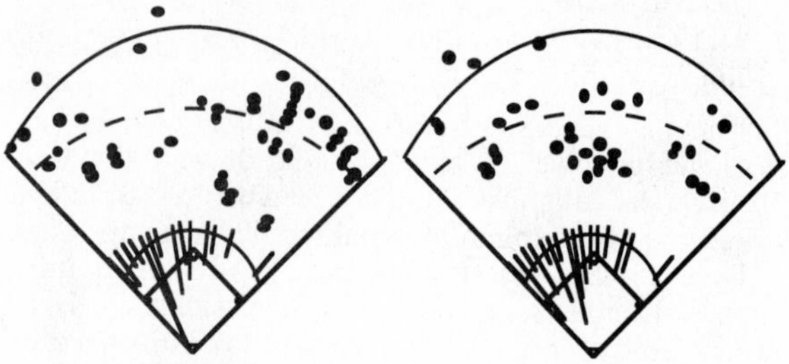

Vs. LHP **Vs. RHP**

1990 Situational Stats

	AB	H	HR	RBI	AVG		AB	H	HR	RBI	AVG
Home	131	34	2	17	.260	LHP	152	39	5	20	.257
Road	178	45	7	29	.253	RHP	157	40	4	26	.255
Day	109	31	0	9	.284	Sc Pos	70	20	3	39	.286
Night	200	48	9	37	.240	Clutch	43	11	0	8	.256

1990 Rankings (American League)

- 4th in batting average with the bases loaded (.539)
- Led the Tigers in batting average with the bases loaded and batting average on an 0-2 count (.238)
- Led AL left fielders in batting average with bases loaded

LOU WHITAKER

Position: 2B
Bats: L **Throws:** R
Ht: 5'11" **Wt:** 160

Opening Day Age: 33
Born: 5/12/57 in Brooklyn, NY
ML Seasons: 14

Overall Statistics

	G	AB	R	H	D	T	HR	RBI	SB	BB	SO	AVG
1990	132	472	75	112	22	2	18	60	8	74	71	.237
Career	1827	6693	1040	1831	301	60	167	781	124	876	874	.274

Where He Hits the Ball

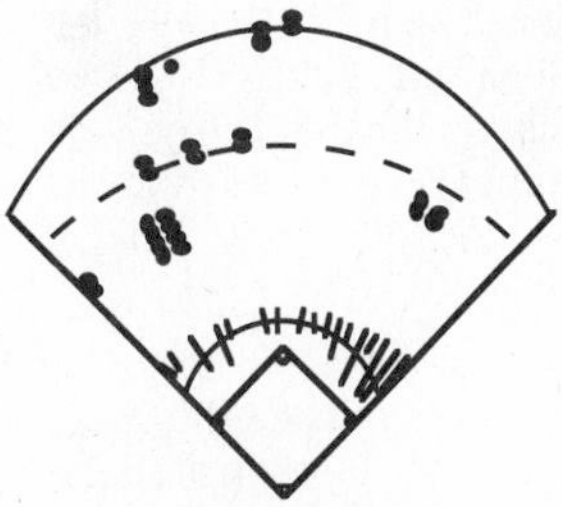

Vs. LHP

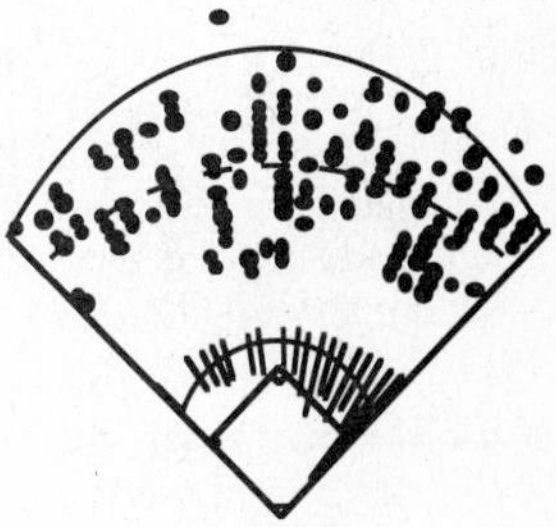

Vs. RHP

1990 Situational Stats

	AB	H	HR	RBI	AVG		AB	H	HR	RBI	AVG
Home	219	47	8	27	.215	LHP	99	16	2	7	.162
Road	253	65	10	33	.257	RHP	373	96	16	53	.257
Day	141	31	4	10	.220	Sc Pos	112	25	7	42	.223
Night	331	81	14	50	.245	Clutch	67	11	0	1	.164

1990 Rankings (American League)

- 3rd worst batting average at home (.215)
- 8th worst batting average (.237) and lowest groundball/flyball ratio (.88)
- Led the Tigers in steals of third (3)
- Led AL second basemen in home runs (18), intentional walks (7), slugging percentage (.407), HR frequency (26.2 ABs per HR), most pitches seen per plate appearance (3.87), least GDPs per GDP situation (8.2%) and slugging percentage vs. right-handed pitchers (.448)

HITTING:

After hitting a career-high 28 homers in 1989, Lou Whitaker spent the first two months of the 1990 season trying to pull the ball into the right field seats. It didn't take pitchers long to realize this, and they fed Whitaker a steady diet of outside pitches. Whitaker was batting a dismal .197 on May 29 when manager Sparky Anderson moved him from the number-three spot in the batting order to leadoff. Whitaker stopped thinking home run and started doing the things he does best: going with the pitch and using all three fields. Whitaker's hitting picked up, though he still turned in his lowest average in a decade.

Once he had his confidence back, Anderson dropped Whitaker into the number-two slot. Whitaker's a first-ball hitter who rarely tries to hit behind the runner, but he also has enough of an eye to walk more than he's struck out in each of the past three seasons.

Whitaker has never hit lefthanders well, and the arrival of Tony Phillips allowed Anderson to platoon Whitaker for the first time in his career. He made just 12 starts against southpaws and only six after May 6. The platooning was one more sign of the erosion in Whitaker's game. His batting average has been dropping steadily since peaking at .320 in 1983.

BASERUNNING:

When he's motivated, Whitaker is still a good base stealer. The trouble is, he isn't motivated all that often. Whitaker stole eight bases, four of them in July and three more in consecutive games in mid-August. The eight thefts equalled his total for the previous two seasons. Whitaker will use his own judgement on the base paths and will run through a coach's sign if he thinks he has a shot to make it.

FIELDING:

Defensively, Whitaker still has few peers at second base. He possesses a rifle arm, goes to his right on grounders as well as anyone and isn't afraid to take a beating to turn the double play. Whitaker's six errors were the fewest of any AL regular at second last year. His one weakness is a virtual refusal to go back on pop-ups to the outfield. He chases them with vague indifference, resulting in a lot of Texas League hits.

OVERALL:

If they could, the Tigers would probably trade the marketable Whitaker for some starting pitching. However, Whitaker has a $2 million contract and veto power over trades. He likes it in Detroit, so look for him to be back in Motown platooning with Phillips at second.

DARNELL COLES

Position: DH/3B/RF
Bats: R **Throws:** R
Ht: 6' 1" **Wt:** 185

Opening Day Age: 28
Born: 6/2/62 in San Bernardino, CA
ML Seasons: 8

Overall Statistics

	G	AB	R	H	D	T	HR	RBI	SB	BB	SO	AVG
1990	89	215	22	45	7	1	3	20	0	16	38	.209
Career	695	2239	261	545	108	10	60	291	18	192	348	.243

HITTING, FIELDING, BASERUNNING:

Darnell Coles made a surprise return to Detroit last year, and, unfortunately, picked up right where he left off. Acquired in a June trade from Seattle, Coles got off to a 3-for-21 start, and his work in the field quickly relegated him to a pinch-hitting/designated hitter role. Only a rash of late-season injuries allowed him to put on his glove again.

Coles gets himself out as much as the pitcher does. He'll swing wildly at two pitches outside the strike zone, then watch as the next one cuts through the heart of the plate. The next time up, he'll do exactly the opposite. Strictly a pull hitter, Coles was once a 20-homer man, but had just one homer and four RBIs in 108 at-bats with Detroit. Coles is just as erratic on the base paths, where he was 0-for-4 in steal attempts. Once Detroit's starting third baseman, he made just eight appearances there, all after September injuries to Lou Whitaker and Alan Trammell. He has the lowest fielding percentage of any active major league third baseman.

OVERALL:

Shuttled from team to team since 1985, including two stints with both the Mariners and Tigers, Coles is all screwed up. He's never really settled into a defensive position in the field, doesn't hit enough to be a DH and doesn't do enough things to be a valuable utility player. A free agent, Coles will be fortunate to get an offer from a major league club.

MILT CUYLER

Position: CF
Bats: B **Throws:** R
Ht: 5'10" **Wt:** 175

Opening Day Age: 22
Born: 10/7/68 in Macon, GA
ML Seasons: 1

Overall Statistics

	G	AB	R	H	D	T	HR	RBI	SB	BB	SO	AVG
1990	19	51	8	13	3	1	0	8	1	5	10	.255
Career	19	51	8	13	3	1	0	8	1	5	10	.255

HITTING, FIELDING, BASERUNNING:

If he proves he can hit major league pitching, Milt Cuyler will have a permanent home in Tiger Stadium's spacious center field. Possessing the type of blazing speed not seen in Detroit since the days of Ron LeFlore, Cuyler showed flashes of brilliance in 19 September games. While he stole only one base, Cuyler swiped 52 at Toledo last year, the second-best steal total in AAA ball.

That speed also makes it easy for Cuyler to cover center field in Detroit, where the fences are 440 feet away. He flat outruns fly balls, reminding people of Gary Pettis, the Detroit center fielder in 1988 and '89. Unlike Pettis, Cuyler is willing to listen to suggestions which will improve his hitting. A self-admitted fly ball hitter, Cuyler has put in a lot of time working on his swing, trying to learn to drive the ball into the ground. He's also not afraid to drop down a bunt and utilize his speed in that way.

Cuyler strikes out a lot, which makes him an unlikely candidate for the leadoff spot in the batting order. He doesn't have home run power, but can use his speed to turn singles into doubles and doubles into triples.

OVERALL:

The arrival of Cuyler and infielder Travis Fryman give Detroit two bona fide major league prospects. Cuyler enters 1991 as Detroit's center fielder and only a horrendous spring training will cost him that spot. His work ethic and willingness to listen make that seem unlikely.

LANCE McCULLERS

Position: RP
Bats: B **Throws:** R
Ht: 6' 1" **Wt:** 218

Opening Day Age: 27
Born: 3/8/64 in Tampa, FL
ML Seasons: 6

Overall Statistics

	W	L	ERA	G	GS	Sv	IP	H	R	BB	SO	HR
1990	2	0	3.02	20	1	0	44.2	32	19	19	31	4
Career	27	31	3.23	301	9	39	521.1	426	215	244	439	47

PITCHING, FIELDING & HOLDING RUNNERS:

A blood clot in his right shoulder has put a blot on the career of Lance McCullers. McCullers came to the Tigers in a midseason deal with the Yankees last year, and at first he struggled. He was just beginning to show the form which once made him such a promising prospect with San Diego when the clot was discovered in mid-July. The injury immediately ended McCullers' season and leaves his future in doubt.

The possessor of an overpowering fastball, McCullers gets into the bad habit of relying too much on his heater, instead of using the breaking ball to set up hitters. He doesn't walk a lot of hitters, but he'll get into slumps where his control simply eludes him. It's the same with home runs. McCullers won't serve up a bunch of them, but they always seem to come at the worst possible time. Two of the four round-trippers he surrendered in 1990 were grand slams.

McCullers moves well for a big man, but is an erratic fielder. He'll make a tough play look easy, then boot a routine grounder. He has an excellent pickoff move, however.

OVERALL:

McCullers arrived in Detroit a confused man. The Padres saw him as stopper material, while the Yankees used him as a set-up man. He doesn't possess the mental makeup necessary to be a short reliever, and the Tigers see him as an eventual member of their starting rotation. If there is no damage to the arm, McCullers should figure prominently in the Tigers' future plans.

CLAY PARKER

Position: RP/SP
Bats: R **Throws:** R
Ht: 6' 1" **Wt:** 185

Opening Day Age: 28
Born: 12/19/62 in Columbia, LA
ML Seasons: 3

Overall Statistics

	W	L	ERA	G	GS	Sv	IP	H	R	BB	SO	HR
1990	3	3	3.58	29	3	0	73.0	64	29	32	40	11
Career	7	8	3.90	54	21	0	200.2	202	92	67	101	25

PITCHING, FIELDING & HOLDING RUNNERS:

After obtaining Clay Parker from the Yankees in a June trade, the Tigers didn't exactly thrust him into a major role. At first they sent Parker to their Toledo farm club for a month. When they finally recalled him in July, they might well have advised him to bring along a mop. Parker made 18 of his 24 appearances when the Tigers were trailing. He finished seven games, all of them Tiger losses. Parker made only four relief appearances with the game on the line. To his credit, he did well in those games, going 1-1 with a 3.00 ERA.

Parker doesn't possess one dominant pitch, but relies on mixing his pitches. Lacking overpowering stuff, he needs to keep the ball down to be successful. When Parker keeps the ball down, he'll get a lot of ground ball outs. When he doesn't, he'll give up the long ball, as evidenced by the 11 home runs he coughed up in 73 innings.

Parker didn't exhibit much of a pickoff move last year, but then again, he didn't really need one. Teams don't steal a lot of bases when they have big leads. Parker is a better-than-average athlete and fields his position well.

OVERALL:

With the Tiger starting staff in disarray, Parker figures to get more of a chance to show his stuff in 1991. He doesn't own an overpowering pitch which would make him an effective short reliever, so his future is definitely as a starter or middle man.

MARK SALAS

Position: C
Bats: L **Throws:** R
Ht: 6' 0" **Wt:** 205

Opening Day Age: 30
Born: 3/8/61 in Montebello, CA
ML Seasons: 7

Overall Statistics

	G	AB	R	H	D	T	HR	RBI	SB	BB	SO	AVG
1990	74	164	18	38	3	0	9	24	0	21	28	.232
Career	476	1235	140	314	48	10	37	136	3	89	153	.254

HITTING, FIELDING, BASERUNNING:

Mark Salas had always hit well at Tiger Stadium as a visiting player, and he thrived while playing there on a daily basis in 1990. Signed to a minor league contract before the 1990 season, Salas got a chance to stay because of the lockout-produced 27-man roster. Hitting with good power, he quickly showed enough to allow the club to trade Matt Nokes to the Yankees. Salas ended up batting only .232, but his nine homers in only 164 at-bats made up for the low average. Eight of the nine dingers came at Tiger Stadium.

Once a free swinger, Salas has learned to take pitches up in the strike zone and draws a good number of walks. A pull hitter, he waits for the pitcher to make a mistake. Salas is slow afoot and will clog up the base paths. He's no threat to steal and a good candidate to ground into a double play. Defensively, he's an adequate backup receiver at best. He's a good handler of pitchers, but not very mobile behind the plate. His throwing arm is below average.

OVERALL:

The ultimate team player, Salas never complains about his lack of playing time. He's well liked by his teammates and a good clubhouse man. He should win a backup role again, but he's modeled enough uniforms to know a roster spot isn't guaranteed. Left-handed-hitting catchers are always in demand, and if he doesn't last in Detroit, Salas will probably find a job somewhere.

JOHN SHELBY

Position: CF/LF/RF
Bats: B **Throws:** R
Ht: 6' 1" **Wt:** 175

Opening Day Age: 33
Born: 2/23/58 in lexington, KY
ML Seasons: 10

Overall Statistics

	G	AB	R	H	D	T	HR	RBI	SB	BB	SO	AVG
1990	103	246	24	61	10	3	4	22	4	10	58	.248
Career	983	2947	370	717	120	23	67	305	98	174	648	.243

HITTING, FIELDING, BASERUNNING:

A new home has helped revitalize John Shelby's career -- again. Let go by the Dodgers, Shelby proved a welcome addition in Detroit, just as he had done when moving from Baltimore to Los Angeles in 1987. Filling in at all three outfield spots, the switch-hitting Shelby hit enough to make him a valuable utility outfielder.

Shelby likes the ball up when batting right-handed, but prefers inside pitches when batting left-handed, especially in Tiger Stadium. However, he's much more effective against right handers than against lefties. There's no secret to getting Shelby out -- feed him breaking balls until he starves. As one major league manager put it, Shelby "couldn't hit a breaking ball with 14 bats."

Shelby has good speed, but didn't steal many bases last year. He dropped down six sacrifice bunts, second-best on the Tigers, but rarely bunts for base hits, another area where his speed could be put to better use. Defensively, he was most effective in right field, where his above-average throwing arm helps.

OVERALL:

Shelby proved a useful player to the Tigers because of his switch-hitting and defensive versatility. His speed makes him handy as a pinch- runner and his outfield skills make him valuable as a late-inning defensive replacement. If he re-signs with Detroit, he'll see starting duty again in all three outfield spots. Quiet in the clubhouse and a professional on the field, Shelby has a future in a utility role.

PITCHING:

Kevin Appier emerged in 1990 as the Royals' most effective starting pitcher and one of the American League's top rookie pitchers. Appier was used sparingly out of the bullpen following his April 23rd recall from AAA Omaha, made his first start on May 7th, and eventually replaced ineffective Richard Dotson in the starting rotation in late May. Appier went on to win 12 of his remaining 23 starts and post a fine 2.59 ERA as a starter while striking out 127, second on the Royals staff to Tom Gordon.

Appier relies mainly on a fastball and also throws a hard slider. He throws hard, but has good control; Appier averaged just 2.6 walks per nine innings pitched in 1990 while striking out more than six per game. Appier displayed good durability as a starter, especially late in the season. His three shutouts were more than the total accomplished by all other Royals' pitchers combined; he tossed a one-hitter against Detroit on July 7th for his first career shutout and complete game. Appier was remarkably consistent as a starter -- he pitched six or more innings in 21 of his 24 starts.

Appier displayed good composure in tough situations, possibly because he is sometimes unaware of his surroundings -- he has a reputation as a flake. Called "Ape" by his teammates, Appier asked catcher Mike Macfarlane before a game against the Angels which way switch-hitter Johnny Ray would be batting against him. It probably didn't matter, since Appier has been effective against both left and right-handed batters. Lefties have hit for more power against Appier, however, slugging .363 versus a .311 slugging average by right-handed opponents.

HOLDING RUNNERS AND FIELDING:

Due to his lack of experience, Appier is an erratic fielder. In particular, he has had some trouble throwing to second base. But after receiving some tutoring from Frank White, Appier settled down and improved his throws to the bases. Appier does not have a great pickoff move to first and baserunners have been successful stealing against him; opponents stole 13 bases in 14 attempts versus Appier in 1990.

OVERALL:

Appier rose through the minors quickly and has proven himself a capable starting pitcher at a very young age (23). Along with Tom Gordon (age 23 in 1991), Bret Saberhagen (27) and Mark Gubicza (28), Appier will help round out one the best young pitching staffs in baseball next year. He is an important element in the immediate and long-term future success of the Royals.

KEVIN APPIER

Position: SP/RP
Bats: R **Throws:** R
Ht: 6' 2" **Wt:** 180

Opening Day Age: 23
Born: 12/6/67 in Lancaster, CA
ML Seasons: 2

Overall Statistics

	W	L	ERA	G	GS	Sv	IP	H	R	BB	SO	HR
1990	12	8	2.76	32	24	0	185.2	179	67	54	127	13
Career	13	12	3.43	38	29	0	207.1	213	89	66	137	16

How Often He Throws Strikes

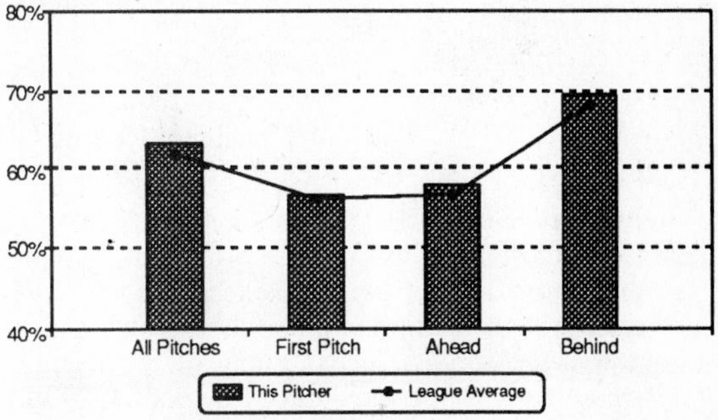

1990 Situational Stats

	W	L	ERA	Sv	IP		AB	H	HR	RBI	AVG
Home	7	4	2.77	0	84.1	LHB	311	81	7	32	.260
Road	5	4	2.75	0	101.1	RHB	399	98	6	27	.246
Day	3	1	1.91	0	28.1	Sc Pos	154	32	1	43	.208
Night	9	7	2.92	0	157.1	Clutch	57	14	1	7	.246

1990 Rankings (American League)

- 1st in worst stolen base percentage allowed (92.9%)
- 3rd in shutouts (3)
- 4th in ERA (2.76) and ERA on the road (2.75)
- 6th in GDPs induced per 9 innings (1.02) and lowest batting average allowed with runners in scoring position (.208)
- Led the Royals in ERA, shutouts, hit batsmen (6), GDPs induced (21), strikeout/walk ratio (2.35), lowest batting average allowed, lowest slugging percentage allowed (.334), lowest on-base average allowed (.307), groundball/flyball ratio (1.54) and GDPs induced per 9 innings

BOB BOONE

Position: C
Bats: R **Throws:** R
Ht: 6' 2" **Wt:** 207

Opening Day Age: 43
Born: 11/19/47 in San Diego, CA
ML Seasons: 19

Overall Statistics

	G	AB	R	H	D	T	HR	RBI	SB	BB	SO	AVG
1990	40	117	11	28	3	0	0	9	1	17	12	.239
Career	2264	7245	679	1838	303	26	105	826	38	663	608	.254

Where He Hits the Ball

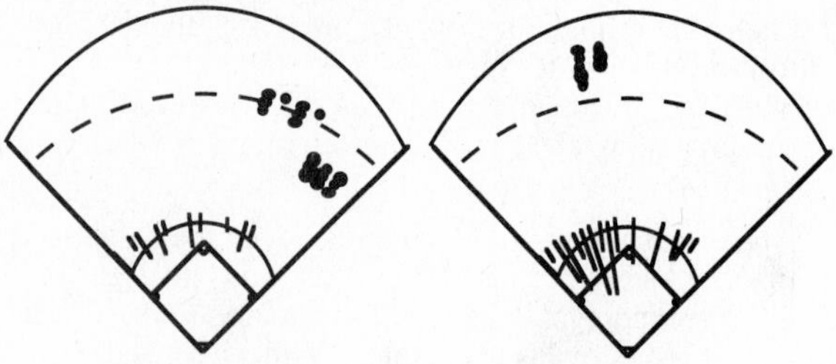

Vs. LHP   Vs. RHP

1990 Situational Stats

	AB	H	HR	RBI	AVG		AB	H	HR	RBI	AVG
Home	69	20	0	5	.290	LHP	40	10	0	3	.250
Road	48	8	0	4	.167	RHP	77	18	0	6	.234
Day	42	10	0	4	.238	Sc Pos	34	7	0	9	.206
Night	75	18	0	5	.240	Clutch	19	5	0	0	.263

1990 Rankings (American League)

- Did not rank near the top or bottom in any category

HITTING:

The disabled list finally caught up with Bob Boone last year. After 18 years of avoiding serious injury, a broken finger sidelined him for two months. Boone played in his fewest games since his rookie debut in 1972 and registered career lows in most offensive categories.

Boone's average has declined 56 points since 1988, and his offense now increasingly depends on the base on balls. Last year, his 17 walks in 134 plate appearances gave him a .336 on-base average despite hitting .239. Usually able to make contact, Boone struck out just 12 times in 1990. He has walked more often than striking out in five of his last six years. Boone is sometimes called on as a hit-and-run batter due to his contact hitting and slow baserunning.

A slap hitter, Boone takes a wide-open stance deep in the batter's box. That gives him time to punch fastballs to the opposite field, or wait for high breaking pitches to pull into left field. This produces few extra base hits; he has only 19 extra base hits in 522 at-bats since 1989. Boone failed to homer for the first time in his career and slugged just .265 in 1990.

Boone likes high breaking balls. Fastballs away give him the most trouble, and he often hits routine grounders on low breaking pitches. Pitchers with overpowering fastballs can make short work of him. For the second straight season, Boone hit much better at home than in opponents' parks; he batted .290 in Royals Stadium compared to a .167 average (with just eight hits) on the road.

BASERUNNING:

Boone runs like a 43-year-old catcher. Nevertheless, he runs the bases intelligently and doesn't take many chances which result in unnecessary outs. Boone succeeded in one of two steal attempts in 1990, embarrassing Toronto's Greg Myers.

FIELDING:

A seven-time Gold Glove winner (for three different teams), Boone is still among the best defensive catchers in the game. He has a strong and accurate arm and will throw to any base at any time. Boone has caught more games than anyone in major league history; that experience shows in his on- field leadership and handling of the young Royals pitchers.

OVERALL:

Mike Macfarlane's emergence as a competent major league catcher has diminished Boone's value to the Royals. A free agent, he will likely try to sign with another club. He feels he can still contribute in the majors and wants a chance to return to postseason play, where he's a career .327 hitter.

HALL OF FAMER

GEORGE BRETT

Position: 1B/DH
Bats: L **Throws:** R
Ht: 6' 0" **Wt:** 200

Opening Day Age: 37
Born: 5/15/53 in Glendale, WV
ML Seasons: 18

HITTING:

Reports of George Brett's demise as a hitter were premature. He rebounded from a dismal start to win his third batting title at age 37, becoming the first player ever to win titles in three different decades.

The Royals mirrored Brett's early struggles. Early in the season, Brett was struggling with a .220 average and mumbling about retirement while the Royals were buried in the AL West cellar. Near mid-season, Brett announced that he'd never played for a last place team and didn't care to in 1990. Brett went on a .395 tear for two months, boosting the Royals above .500 for the first time all year. The Royals didn't stay there, but Brett kept hitting.

Brett has a smooth swing and hits to all fields. He hits all kinds of pitches but primarily feasts on fastballs. Brett often takes a strike before swinging, although he likes to attack a reliever's first pitch. Brett displays fine strike zone judgement, but early in the year was pressing and not always swinging at strikes. Brett had more strikeouts than walks for the first time since '75, yet his .387 on base percentage still led the Royals.

A career .351 hitter in postseason play with 10 homers and a .662 slugging average, Brett is at his best under pressure. He hit .360 last year with men in scoring position; with the game on the line, Royals fans want Brett at the plate.

BASERUNNING:

Brett's advancing age may be cutting down on his speed, but he still runs the bases well. He stole nine bases in 11 attempts in 1990 and he has 37 steals in his last 46 attempts since 1988.

FIELDING:

Brett has lost some range in recent years, but he has become more adept at scooping low throws out of the dirt. He won a Gold Glove as a third baseman in 1985. His arm is the weakest part of his game and the shift to first base in 1987 de-emphasized his throwing. Due to his aggressive style of play, Brett is prone to making ill-advised throws and has sometimes been injured while trying to make difficult defensive plays. The Royals would like Brett to serve mainly as a designated hitter in the future, but Brett says he isn't ready to relinquish the first base job.

OVERALL:

A future Hall of Famer, Brett is the Royals' regular first baseman for 1991, but he will probably see increased time at designated hitter. This move should help him avoid injury and prolong his career for several more years. Brett needs only 293 more hits to reach 3000; that's less than two seasons away, if he keeps hitting and stays healthy.

Overall Statistics

	G	AB	R	H	D	T	HR	RBI	SB	BB	SO	AVG
1990	142	544	82	179	45	7	14	87	9	56	63	.329
Career	2279	8692	1382	2707	559	127	281	1398	184	964	697	.311

Where He Hits the Ball

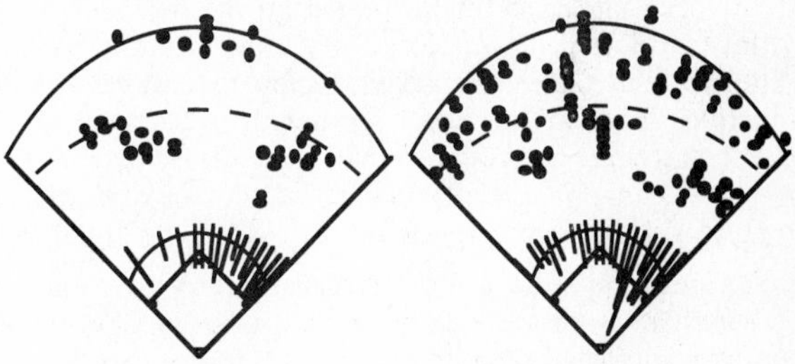

Vs. LHP   Vs. RHP

1990 Situational Stats

	AB	H	HR	RBI	AVG		AB	H	HR	RBI	AVG
Home	288	92	3	46	.319	LHP	187	59	5	28	.316
Road	256	87	11	41	.340	RHP	357	120	9	59	.336
Day	140	43	6	28	.307	Sc Pos	136	49	2	68	.360
Night	404	136	8	59	.337	Clutch	74	19	2	7	.257

1990 Rankings (American League)

- 1st in batting average (.329) and doubles (45)
- 2nd in batting average with runners in scoring position (.360) and batting average vs. right-handed pitchers (.336)
- 3rd in intentional walks (14), slugging percentage vs. right-handed pitchers (.529) and batting average on the road (.340)
- Led the Royals in batting average, hits (179), doubles, triples (7), total bases (280), RBIs (87), sacrifice flies (7), intentional walks (14), GDPs (17), slugging percentage (.515), on-base average (.387), HR frequency (38.9 ABs per HR) and batting average with runners in scoring position

STEVE CRAWFORD

Position: RP
Bats: R **Throws:** R
Ht: 6' 5" **Wt:** 225

Opening Day Age: 32
Born: 4/29/58 in Pryor, OK
ML Seasons: 9

PITCHING:

Steve Crawford resumed his long relief/set-up role in his first full season with Kansas City. Despite a month on the disabled list due to tendinitis, Crawford recorded his most major league innings (80) since 1985. Last season was a step back for Crawford, however; his ERA jumped from 2.83 in 1989 to 4.16 while he allowed 24 extra base hits and opponents slugged .379 against him.

On the bright side, Crawford regained a measure of his control, reducing his walks by more than half-a-walk per nine innings. He also recorded his first major league save since 1986, and won more games than in any year since 1985. Crawford struck out twice as many batters as he walked for the first time since 1985.

Crawford relies mainly on the fastball and throws offspeed pitches primarily to set up the heater. His fastball doesn't have a lot of movement, but he can throw it at different speeds to keep the batters off stride. Crawford has trouble throwing breaking balls for strikes and gets outs with his fastball. He tends to allow a lot of deep fly balls that can be tracked down in Royals Stadium's spacious outfield.

Unfortunately, those flies sometimes carry over the wall; Crawford allowed seven homers in just 80 innings. He was primarily used for no more than two innings, often entering the game in relief of a failed starter, or wielding a mop in a game already far out of reach. Crawford had far more success against right-handed hitters. While he held the righthanders to a .193 average, lefties lit him up at a .347 clip and slugged .524 with 15 extra base hits in 124 at-bats.

HOLDING RUNNERS AND FIELDING:

Crawford is an erratic fielder who has trouble throwing to the bases and fielding bunts quickly enough to provide opportunities to get a lead runner. He works slowly, especially when he has control difficulties, and is an excruciatingly slow worker with a runner on base. This tends to leave his fielders back on their heels, leading to more errors. Crawford has a slow delivery to the plate, but frequent throws to first help him do a reasonable job of holding runners.

OVERALL:

The Royals' bullpen is crowded, and Crawford has less of a future than other pitchers who have had better performances or longer contracts. Crawford will be 33 early in 1991 and the Royals will probably elect to use some of their younger guns if Crawford can't return to his 1989 form. Without a strong spring performance, Crawford will end up in AAA Omaha or be released.

Overall Statistics

	W	L	ERA	G	GS	Sv	IP	H	R	BB	SO	HR
1990	5	4	4.16	46	0	1	80.0	79	38	23	54	7
Career	27	21	4.01	244	16	18	516.0	583	267	168	282	51

How Often He Throws Strikes

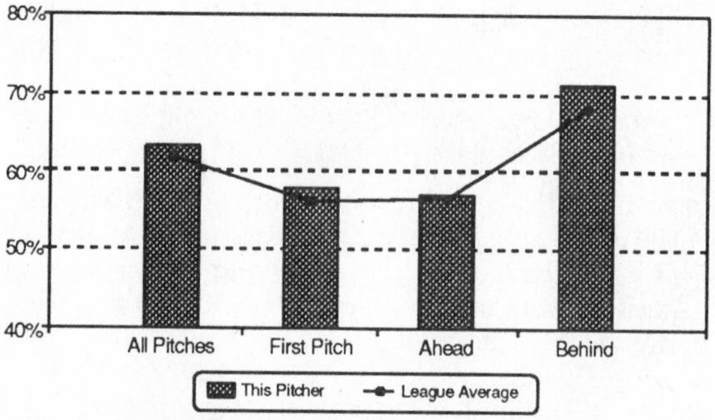

1990 Situational Stats

	W	L	ERA	Sv	IP		AB	H	HR	RBI	AVG
Home	4	1	4.09	1	50.2	LHB	124	43	3	20	.347
Road	1	3	4.30	0	29.1	RHB	187	36	4	23	.193
Day	2	3	5.85	0	20.0	Sc Pos	91	23	2	35	.253
Night	3	1	3.60	1	60.0	Clutch	86	25	1	11	.291

1990 Rankings (American League)

- 4th worst batting average allowed vs. left-handed batters (.347)
- Led the Royals in holds (7)

MARK DAVIS

Position: RP/SP
Bats: L **Throws:** L
Ht: 6' 4" **Wt:** 200

Opening Day Age: 30
Born: 10/19/60 in Livermore, CA
ML Seasons: 10

Overall Statistics

	W	L	ERA	G	GS	Sv	IP	H	R	BB	SO	HR
1990	2	7	5.11	53	3	6	68.2	71	43	52	73	9
Career	42	72	3.86	469	74	91	927.0	829	437	392	827	96

How Often He Throws Strikes

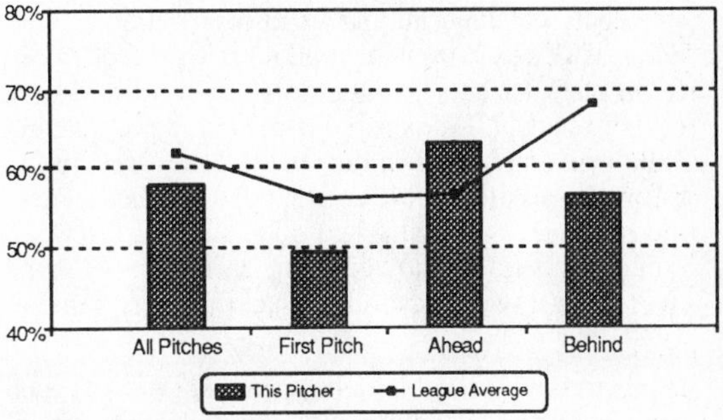

1990 Situational Stats

	W	L	ERA	Sv	IP		AB	H	HR	RBI	AVG
Home	2	1	4.46	5	38.1	LHB	55	11	0	7	.200
Road	0	6	5.93	1	30.1	RHB	219	60	9	42	.274
Day	1	2	6.66	2	24.1	Sc Pos	96	27	3	39	.281
Night	1	5	4.26	4	44.1	Clutch	106	33	4	22	.311

1990 Rankings (American League)

- → 4th worst percentage of inherited runners scored (40.0%)
- → Led the Royals in stolen bases allowed (15) and holds (7)

PITCHING:

One of the major questions about the 1990 Royals was: what happened to Mark Davis? Theories have been as plentiful as Davis' blown saves last year. But the most recent speculation has centered on a hairline fracture of a finger on his pitching hand that may have occurred in spring training. Royals management has been vague about the injury, but it would help explain the modest usage that Davis received early in the season. It would also partially explain Davis' poor performance, which was highlighted by control difficulties. Davis went on the disabled list August 10th with tendinitis and pitched better after his return on September 5th.

Davis had two major problems last year -- walks and homers. In addition to allowing an outrageous 52 walks in 68.2 innings pitched, he also coughed up nine homers, all to right-handed hitters. Righties hit .274 and had a .466 slugging average against Davis last year. However, he continued to be tough on lefties, who batted just .200 against him with only three extra base hits off him. Davis also struck out more than a batter per inning.

Unfortunately for Davis and the Royals, good control of his nasty curve was absent for most of the season. His early season failures mounted and he lost the confidence to blow away tough hitters with the game on the line. He eventually lost the stopper's job to Jeff Montgomery, then failed as a set-up man.

Rather than completely give up on Davis, the Royals tried him as a starter; that was a miserable failure, too. Later, when Davis returned from the disabled list, he posted a 2.18 ERA in his last 11 appearances. But he still walked 12 in 20.2 innings, proving that he was not yet back to Cy Young form.

HOLDING RUNNERS AND FIELDING:

Davis has a good move to first, but the results don't show it. Opposition base stealers were 15 for 15 with Davis on the mound. He is an average fielder who doesn't hurt himself with serious mistakes, and he throws accurately to all bases. Davis fields bunts well and quickly covers first on grounders to the right side.

OVERALL:

The Royals have signed ex-San Diego pitching coach Pat Dobson, who helped Davis emerge as one of the National League's top closers, to get him back on track. Davis should start 1991 sharing the closer's role in a left/right tandem with Jeff Montgomery. But he would be quickly upgraded to a full-time stopper if he regains his previous form.

STORM DAVIS

Position: SP
Bats: R **Throws:** R
Ht: 6' 4" **Wt:** 200

Opening Day Age: 29
Born: 12/26/61 in Dallas, TX
ML Seasons: 9

Overall Statistics

	W	L	ERA	G	GS	Sv	IP	H	R	BB	SO	HR
1990	7	10	4.74	21	20	0	112.0	129	66	35	62	9
Career	99	72	3.93	265	220	1	1431.0	1444	682	523	831	108

How Often He Throws Strikes

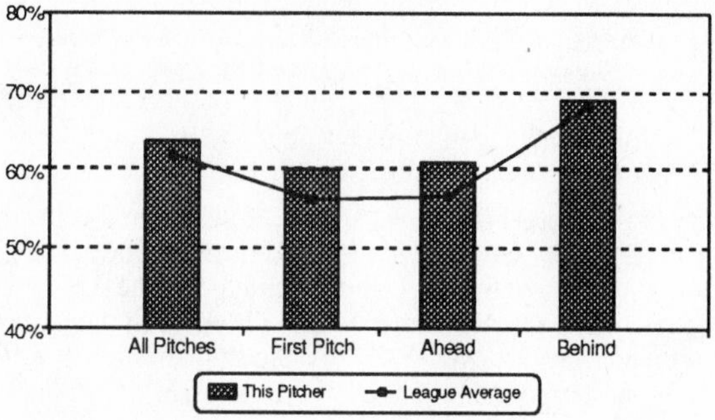

1990 Situational Stats

	W	L	ERA	Sv	IP		AB	H	HR	RBI	AVG
Home	5	7	4.50	0	80.0	LHB	235	69	4	29	.294
Road	2	3	5.34	0	32.0	RHB	224	60	5	26	.268
Day	1	1	4.35	0	10.1	Sc Pos	125	36	2	45	.288
Night	6	9	4.78	0	101.2	Clutch	12	4	0	1	.333

1990 Rankings (American League)

- 9th worst winning percentage (.412)

PITCHING:

Storm Davis pitched for the high-scoring Athletics in 1988 and '89, and the A's always seemed to have their bats blazing whenever he took the mound. Never a big winner before, he went 16-7 and then 19-7 for the A's despite relatively high ERAs. Ignoring the run support, a lot of people considered this proof that Davis was now a "winner," and the Royals eagerly signed him for big free agent dollars. But in 1990 for K.C., the run support disappeared, and so did Davis. Modest support and 40 days on the disabled list reduced his record to 7-10. On the Royals only Tom Gordon lost more often than Davis, and Gordon made 12 more starts. Davis' 4.74 ERA was the worst among Royals' starters.

Davis throws a fastball, overhand curve, and forkball; he is at his best when he keeps all of his pitches down in the strike zone. Evidenced by his fewer than five strikeouts per nine innings ratio in 1989 and 1990, Davis isn't a power pitcher and must work both sides of the plate. He gets into trouble when he doesn't have his best control. Davis is prone to hanging a breaking ball or getting behind in the count; that forces him to throw his less-than-blazing fastball over the heart of the plate. Davis usually had good control last year, reducing his walks allowed from nearly four per game over the last two years to less than three per game in 1990.

Davis missed the Athletic bullpen last year as much as he did Oakland's offense. He rarely lasted past the sixth inning and usually got into difficulty when he was allowed to pitch past the fifth. He often entered the fifth or sixth innings with a lead or with the score tied, then allowed the tying or go-ahead runs. Yet, when Davis got a quick hook, the Royals bullpen often couldn't hold the lead.

HOLDING RUNNERS AND FIELDING:

Davis is a good fielder who's quick to pounce on bunts and throws well to the bases. He holds runners well with a respectable move to first. Davis' set position appears to give baserunners trouble guessing whether he is throwing to first or to the plate; thus, base stealers don't get a great jump against him.

OVERALL:

Davis will probably be a spot starter for the Royals early this season. When a fifth starter is needed early in May, he'll begin taking a regular turn in the rotation. However, if Davis can't improve on his disappointing 1990 performance, he may go to the bullpen in a long relief role.

JIM EISENREICH

Position: LF/CF/RF
Bats: L **Throws:** L
Ht: 5'11" **Wt:** 195

Opening Day Age: 31
Born: 4/18/59 in St. Cloud, MN
ML Seasons: 7

HITTING:

After a fine 1989 campaign, Jim Eisenreich continued his steady play in 1990. Eisenreich began the season as the Royals' starting left fielder, but spent most of the year as a fill-in for one of the team's oft-injured outfielders. His starts were primarily in left or right field versus right-handed pitchers, against whom he batted .306. Eisenreich also saw duty in center field and as a late-inning defensive replacement. He mainly batted lower in the order -- fifth or sixth.

Eisenreich is a very aggressive hitter who will swing at any pitch near the plate. Nevertheless, he doesn't strike out a lot, with just 51 K's in 496 at- bats in 1990, similar to his 1989 totals of 44 strikeouts in 475 at-bats. Eisenreich prefers to hit low fastballs and can be overmatched by good breaking balls. He has the most trouble against finesse pitchers, especially lefties who nibble at the corners of the plate.

Eisenreich hits the ball up the middle and has power to the alleys. His power numbers were down somewhat from 1989, as he dropped from nine homers to five; Eisenreich is a line drive hitter and his homers come from pitcher mistakes. It's hard to hit the ball over the center field fence in Royals Stadium; Eisenreich batted .300 away from Kansas City. With his gap hitting and speed, Eisenreich is capable of regularly hitting near .290 with 30 doubles.

BASERUNNING:

Eisenreich is an aggressive baserunner who will occasionally run into an out. He is still learning opposing pitchers' moves, and after being caught stealing 14 times in 1990, he would help the team by running less often in the future.

FIELDING:

Eisenreich is a fine fielder who can play any outfield position well. He committed just one error in 268 chances, easily the best fielding percentage (.996) among Royals' outfielders. His arm is average, but he hits the cutoff man and throws accurately. Eisenreich gets a good jump on outfield hits and uses his above-average speed to keep balls in the alleys from reaching the fences. Right field is Eisenreich's best position, but he is better than average in left or center.

OVERALL:

One of the major league's best bargains (obtained via waivers for a dollar), Jim Eisenreich provides the Royals with a valuable left-handed bat and is a versatile and steady performer in the outfield. Unless Danny Tartabull is traded, Eisenreich is destined for a backup or platoon role in 1991. But, if injuries once again cut down the Royals' outfielders, Eisenreich is sure to step into the breach.

Overall Statistics

	G	AB	R	H	D	T	HR	RBI	SB	BB	SO	AVG
1990	142	496	61	139	29	7	5	51	12	42	51	.280
Career	450	1416	173	386	86	17	21	162	51	106	157	.273

Where He Hits the Ball

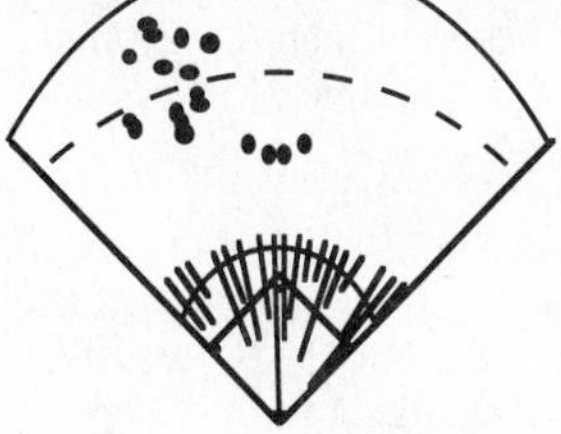

Vs. LHP

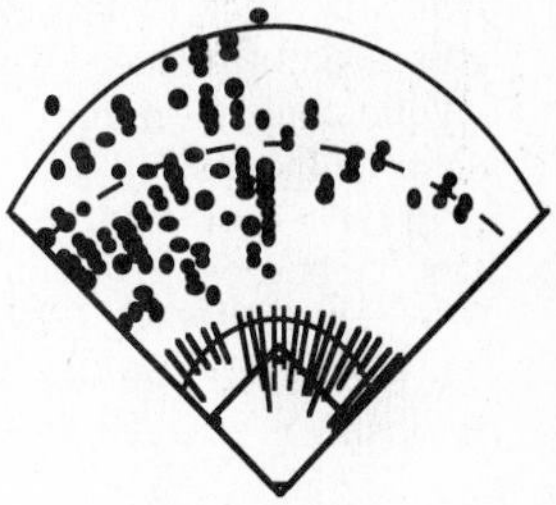

Vs. RHP

1990 Situational Stats

	AB	H	HR	RBI	AVG		AB	H	HR	RBI	AVG
Home	236	61	2	29	.258	LHP	156	35	1	16	.224
Road	260	78	3	22	.300	RHP	340	104	4	35	.306
Day	116	40	3	18	.345	Sc Pos	138	33	1	46	.239
Night	380	99	2	33	.261	Clutch	82	22	2	11	.268

1990 Rankings (American League)

- 3rd worst stolen base percentage (46.1%)
- 8th in triples (7) and caught stealing (14)
- 9th worst on-base average vs. left-handed pitchers (.268)
- Led the Royals in triples, caught stealing, groundball/flyball ratio (1.78) and batting average with the bases loaded (.417)
- Led AL left fielders in groundball/flyball ratio

PITCHING:

After returning to a set-up role in the Royals bullpen, Steve Farr posted his finest major league season. His 13 victories and 1.98 ERA led the Royals staff and were both career bests. Farr also recorded career highs in innings pitched and strikeouts.

Farr was mainly called on to pitch the seventh or eighth innings of close games, or to finish games that were already out of reach. He also made six spot starts to spare the Royals' injury-plagued staff, winning five with a 1.47 ERA, and also tossed a shutout. Despite his short-term success as a spot starter, Farr does better in a set-up role where he can rely primarily on a high-velocity fastball and face opposition batters no more than once through the order. Farr also throws a slider and a curve but uses the fastball to record outs.

Farr occasionally had control difficulties, walking 3.4 batters per nine innings. However, his control problems usually surfaced when the game was already beyond contention. Farr was more effective with the game on the line; he permitted just nine of 45 inherited runners to score. Opponents hit just .220 against Farr, the best on the Royals staff, and he allowed only six homers in 127 innings pitched. Farr can be particularly tough on right-handed hitters; he struck out 60 righthanders while allowing them only 53 hits in 247 at-bats. Farr also had great success at home, posting a 1.37 ERA in Royals Stadium.

As a spot starter in the minor leagues, as well as earlier in his major league career, Farr has usually produced mixed results. Because he doesn't have a large pitching repertoire, Farr tends to run into trouble by the third time through the order.

HOLDING RUNNERS AND FIELDING:

Farr is very adept as a fielder. He is quick to handle bunts and throws accurately to all bases. On several occasions in 1990, Farr was able to get out of an inning by fielding a grounder and beginning a double play. Farr helps himself with the glove. Although he lacks an outstanding pickoff move, he controls the running game with frequent throws to first. Also, Farr's reliance on the fastball gives his catcher a good chance to throw out base stealers.

OVERALL:

Steve Farr provided the Royals with an important ingredient -- a good set-up man in the bullpen. Although Farr is a versatile pitcher who can also be used as a spot starter or as a closer, the Royals would try to keep Farr in his preferred role of set-up man where he has been a solid performer. However, as a free agent, Farr may decide to test his versatility in another role for a different team in 1991.

STEVE FARR

Position: RP/SP
Bats: R **Throws:** R
Ht: 5'11" **Wt:** 200
Opening Day Age: 34
Born: 12/12/56 in Cheverly, MD
ML Seasons: 7

Overall Statistics

	W	L	ERA	G	GS	Sv	IP	H	R	BB	SO	HR
1990	13	7	1.98	57	6	1	127.0	99	32	48	94	6
Career	37	35	3.33	320	28	50	627.0	575	254	249	512	51

How Often He Throws Strikes

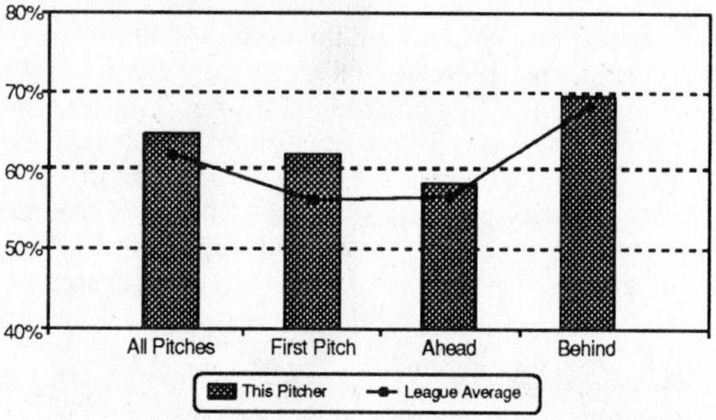

1990 Situational Stats

	W	L	ERA	Sv	IP		AB	H	HR	RBI	AVG
Home	9	2	1.37	1	65.2	LHB	204	46	2	14	.225
Road	4	5	2.64	0	61.1	RHB	247	53	4	24	.215
Day	2	4	2.64	0	44.1	Sc Pos	127	20	1	32	.157
Night	11	3	1.63	1	82.2	Clutch	130	33	1	15	.254

1990 Rankings (American League)

- 2nd in lowest batting average allowed with runners in scoring position (.157)
- 6th in first batter efficiency (.159)
- 7th in lowest percentage of inherited runners scored (20.0%)
- Led the Royals in wins (13), pickoff throws (97), holds (7), winning percentage (.650), batting average vs. left-handed batters (.226), first batter efficiency, lowest batting average allowed with runners in scoring position and lowest percentage of inherited runners scored

TOM GORDON

Position: SP
Bats: R **Throws:** R
Ht: 5' 9" **Wt:** 160

Opening Day Age: 23
Born: 11/18/67 in Sebring, FL
ML Seasons: 3

PITCHING:

Tom Gordon suffered a small sophomore slump in 1990, falling from 17 to 12 victories and increasing his ERA from 3.64 to 3.73. Most notably, Gordon's opponents batted .257 last year after hitting only .210 in 1989. The workhorse of the crippled Royals staff, he threw a team-leading 195.1 innings with six complete games. Gordon was the only member of the team's opening day starting rotation to make more than twenty starts in 1990.

A sharp breaking curve delivered in a whirling motion is Gordon's best weapon and he lives or dies by it. When he has it under control, he will throw it on any count for strikes and give both lefties and righties fits. If his control eludes him, Gordon has to come in to batters with a very hittable fastball.

Last year Gordon walked twice as many batters as any other Royals pitcher; he allowed more than 4.5 walks per nine innings after similar control problems in 1989. But the walk figure is a little deceiving, because Gordon will have fine control in about half his outings. The formula is pretty simple: when Gordon is controlling the curve, he won't issue many walks, and he's almost certain to pitch a strong game. But when he can't control it, the walks will be plentiful and he's likely to get hammered.

Royals' coaches were concerned that Gordon was tipping off his pitches by dropping his glove slightly before throwing a breaking ball. Several teams, particularly Detroit, seemed to know precisely what was coming, and hit him hard. Some adjustments were made in spring training to correct this flaw, but it later appeared that he was still tipping off the opposition. Gordon suffered a few shellackings before regaining control of his delivery later in the year.

HOLDING RUNNERS AND FIELDING:

Baserunners have a tough time against Gordon; they stole only eight bases in 18 attempts last year. His whirling motion is difficult for baserunners to decipher and he has developed a decent move to first base. Gordon has avoided many of the rookie fielding mistakes he made in 1989 and is now an average fielder. He works hard on his defense and should continue to improve with experience.

OVERALL:

With Bret Saberhagen and Mark Gubicza returning from arm problems, Gordon could be anything from the Royals' third starter to its ace. Whatever the case, they'll be depending on him heavily. At age 23, Gordon could be on the verge of becoming a big winner if he can get more consistent control of his curveball . . . and keep from tipping it off.

Overall Statistics

	W	L	ERA	G	GS	Sv	IP	H	R	BB	SO	HR
1990	12	11	3.73	32	32	0	195.1	192	99	99	175	17
Career	29	22	3.75	86	50	1	374.0	330	175	192	346	28

How Often He Throws Strikes

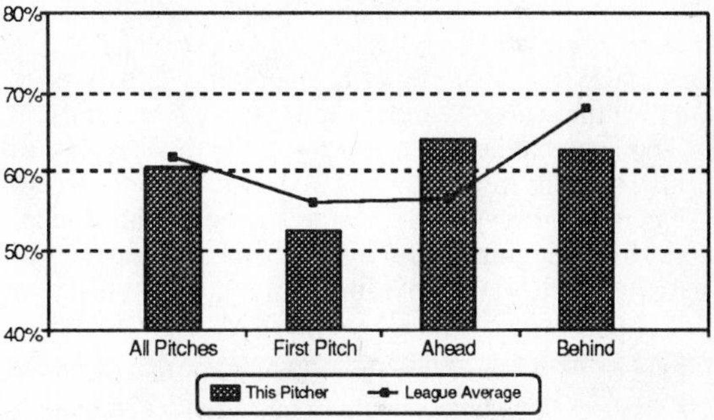

1990 Situational Stats

	W	L	ERA	Sv	IP		AB	H	HR	RBI	AVG
Home	7	5	3.10	0	93.0	LHB	365	92	6	30	.252
Road	5	6	4.31	0	102.1	RHB	381	100	11	49	.262
Day	3	2	2.57	0	42.0	Sc Pos	197	48	4	62	.244
Night	9	9	4.05	0	153.1	Clutch	30	9	1	4	.300

1990 Rankings (American League)

- 2nd most baserunners allowed per 9 innings (13.5)
- 3rd worst on-base average allowed (.346)
- 4th most strikeouts per 9 innings (8.1)
- 6th in walks allowed (99) and lowest stolen base perentage allowed (44.4)%)
- Led the Royals in losses (11), games started (32), complete games (6), innings (195.1), hits allowed (192), batters faced (858), home runs allowed (17), walks allowed, strikeouts (175), wild pitches (11), pitches thrown (3,215), runners caught stealing (10), lowest stolen base percentage allowed and strikeouts per 9 innings

PITCHING:

Mark Gubicza was another of the Royals' injured hurlers in 1990. He made his fewest career starts (16) and posted a career high 4.50 ERA. Gubicza struggled throughout the year before eventually being placed on the disabled list July 11th and later undergoing shoulder surgery.

When healthy, Gubicza relies mainly on fastballs and uses offspeed pitches to keep the hitters honest. He also throws a hard slider that is particularly tough on right-handed batters. There has never been any doubt that Gubicza has the raw talent to succeed in the big leagues, but he constantly battles his control. In 1990, Gubicza walked over 3.6 batters per nine innings after giving only 2.5 free passes per game in 1988 and 1989. He still managed a good strikeout rate, though, posting the second best ratio of strikeouts to innings pitched among the starting staff (behind Tom Gordon) at 6.8 per game.

Gubicza had trouble with right-handed batters in 1990; they hit .296 and slugged .407 while lefties hit .266 against him. One might surmise that because of his shoulder troubles, Gubicza wasn't able to throw hard enough, especially inside, to keep righty swingers from digging in. But his strikeout rate was higher, not lower, than in 1989. In '89, righthanders had also hit higher off him (by 25 points) than lefties did.

One of the hardest working pitchers in the American League, Gubicza has been among the league leaders in innings pitched, games started and complete games from 1987 through 1989. The heavy workload may be starting to exact a price, however. Gubicza missed his last start in 1989 due to a shoulder strain and had difficulty building complete arm strength far into the 1990 season before going on the disabled list.

HOLDING RUNNERS AND FIELDING:

Gubicza has some trouble holding runners close and he doesn't possess a great pickoff move. His height makes a quick release difficult and runners have a tendency to distract him. Gubicza has been prone to critical fielding mistakes in tight situations. He gets into trouble by trying too hard to make difficult defensive plays, sometimes throwing the ball away when hurried. He works hard to improve his fielding and has become less error-prone in recent years.

OVERALL:

Gubicza's shoulder injury was his second in less than two years and, although the surgery was deemed successful, the Royals must be concerned about his arm strength. If he is 100 percent healthy, Gubicza will be the number-two man in the rotation behind Bret Saberhagen and one of the American League's top starters.

MARK GUBICZA

Position: SP
Bats: R **Throws:** R
Ht: 6' 5" **Wt:** 220

Opening Day Age: 28
Born: 8/14/62 in Philadelphia, PA
ML Seasons: 7

Overall Statistics

	W	L	ERA	G	GS	Sv	IP	H	R	BB	SO	HR
1990	4	7	4.50	16	16	0	94.0	101	48	38	71	5
Career	88	74	3.57	215	203	0	1407.1	1308	611	540	921	79

How Often He Throws Strikes

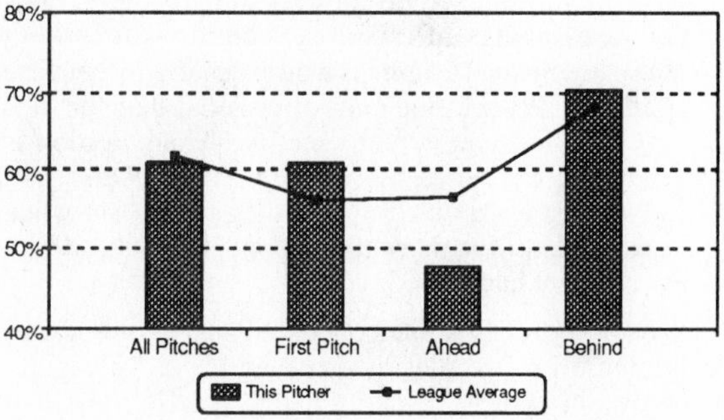

1990 Situational Stats

	W	L	ERA	Sv	IP		AB	H	HR	RBI	AVG
Home	3	2	5.45	0	38.0	LHB	158	42	3	11	.266
Road	1	5	3.86	0	56.0	RHB	199	59	2	30	.296
Day	1	2	2.94	0	33.2	Sc Pos	105	23	3	36	.219
Night	3	5	5.37	0	60.1	Clutch	23	6	0	2	.261

1990 Rankings (American League)

- Did not rank near the top or bottom in any category

HITTING:

Bo Jackson owns one of baseball's most powerful swings. He generates incredible bat speed and can hit the ball out of any ballpark to any field. Jackson became only the fourth Royals' player to hit 20 homers in four consecutive seasons and his power is important on a team that hit the fewest homers in the American League in 1990. Jackson also homered in four consecutive at-bats, the fourth coming after a five-week stint on the disabled list. Typical of Jackson's flair for the dramatic, it was a 460-foot blast to dead center.

Jackson prefers to swing at fastballs, especially on the outer half of the plate; he hits many of his home runs to center or to right field off outer half fastballs. He often hits singles to left or left-center on breaking pitches. Jackson's batting eye has improved, but he will still chase high fastballs and breaking balls in the dirt.

Last year Jackson displayed a knack for hitting home runs with runners in scoring position; he had 11 HRs and slugged .558 in such situations. Jackson usually hits for a good average in Royals Stadium; he batted .307 at home in 1990 and has a career .281 average at home. He displays more power on the road; 61 of his 109 career HRs have been hit in opposition parks.

BASERUNNING:

Jackson possesses blazing speed and seems able to steal a base at any time. However, he doesn't always have the best judgement about when to run. He was caught stealing nine times in 1990 and his aggressive baserunning occasionally led to costly outs.

FIELDING:

Jackson was moved from left field to center about a month into the season. However, after his injury, he moved back to left. Jackson is an erratic fielder capable of both incredible blunders and amazing catches or throws, often in the same game. His great speed allows him to run down some of his mistakes, and he has a cannon for a throwing arm. On the other hand, Jackson regularly misses the cutoff man, allowing runners to advance. There is still a lot of room for improvement in Jackson's defense; the Royals would certainly settle for more steady play.

OVERALL:

Jackson is one of the most exciting players in major league baseball. He is currently in the prime of his career and is capable of posting awesome offensive numbers if he avoids injury for an entire season. Jackson provides the Royals with a large part of their power game and will bat cleanup and play left or center field as long as he remains healthy.

BO JACKSON

Position: CF/LF
Bats: R **Throws:** R
Ht: 6' 1" **Wt:** 222

Opening Day Age: 28
Born: 11/30/62 in Bessemer, AL
ML Seasons: 5

Overall Statistics

	G	AB	R	H	D	T	HR	RBI	SB	BB	SO	AVG
1990	111	405	74	110	16	1	28	78	15	44	128	.272
Career	511	1837	278	460	66	14	109	313	81	145	638	.250

Where He Hits the Ball

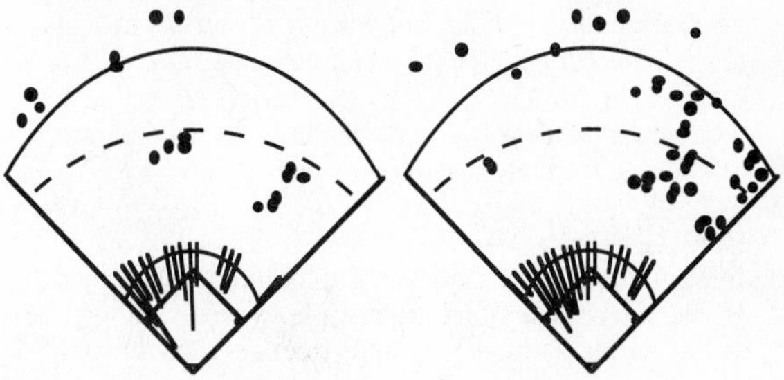

Vs. LHP　　Vs. RHP

1990 Situational Stats

	AB	H	HR	RBI	AVG		AB	H	HR	RBI	AVG
Home	192	59	12	37	.307	LHP	143	39	10	24	.273
Road	213	51	16	41	.239	RHP	262	71	18	54	.271
Day	105	29	9	17	.276	Sc Pos	113	27	11	55	.239
Night	300	81	19	61	.270	Clutch	66	19	6	13	.288

1990 Rankings (American League)

- 1st in lowest percentage of swings put into play (30.6%)
- 3rd in percentage of extra bases taken as a runner (60.5%)
- 5th lowest batting average with the bases loaded (.091)
- 6th in home runs (28)
- Led the Royals in home runs, strike outs (128), batting average on a 3-1 count (.571), slugging percentage vs. left-handed pitchers (.511) and percentage of extra bases taken as a runner
- Led AL center fielders in home runs and batting average on a 3-1 count

MIKE MACFARLANE

Position: C
Bats: R **Throws:** R
Ht: 6' 1" **Wt:** 200

Opening Day Age: 27
Born: 4/12/64 in STOCKTON, CA
ML Seasons: 4

HITTING:

Mike Macfarlane rewarded the Royals' patience by turning in his finest offensive year in 1990 while taking over the bulk of the catching chores for the first time in his career. Macfarlane set many personal offensive bests last year and gave the Royals steady RBI production from the lower part of the order. His 58 RBI more than doubled his career total, and he was among the Royals leaders in RBI per at-bat.

Primarily a fastball hitter, Macfarlane usually looks to swing at a first-pitch heater. He will try to pull most pitches down the line, often for doubles; Macfarlane collected 24 doubles in 1990 after having just 22 career doubles before last year. He has trouble with low breaking balls and pitches on the outer half of the plate. Pitchers who throw good off-speed stuff for strikes give Macfarlane fits.

Macfarlane has usually shown more success in Royals Stadium, where he was a career .272 hitter before last year. However, in 1990 Macfarlane fared better on the road, hitting five of his six homers and slugging .388 away from Kansas City.

BASERUNNING:

Despite his youth, Macfarlane runs like a catcher. He stole one base and hit four triples (career firsts) in 1990; he won't beat you with fleet feet. Macfarlane runs the bases conservatively and rarely tries for an extra base.

FIELDING:

An above-average catcher, Macfarlane has worked to improve his throwing game. However, he tossed out only 17 percent of opposing runners last year, which is a little worse than he did as a 1988 rookie. While he throws accurately, he doesn't possess a strong arm; Macfarlane has had reduced strength in his throwing arm since suffering a partial rotator cuff tear in 1986. Although his defensive fundamentals are generally very sound, Macfarlane must learn to shift his feet more quickly to better block pitches in the dirt.

OVERALL:

After his first full year behind the plate for the Royals, Macfarlane will probably continue to be the Royals' top catcher in 1991, with a little help from Bob Boone if the veteran returns. Macfarlane is in his prime and should be the team's starting backstop for the next few years. Expect steady, unspectacular offensive production and gradual defensive improvement from Macfarlane as long as he plays regularly.

Overall Statistics

	G	AB	R	H	D	T	HR	RBI	SB	BB	SO	AVG
1990	124	400	37	102	24	4	6	58	1	25	69	.255
Career	271	787	75	197	46	4	12	106	1	55	135	.250

Where He Hits the Ball

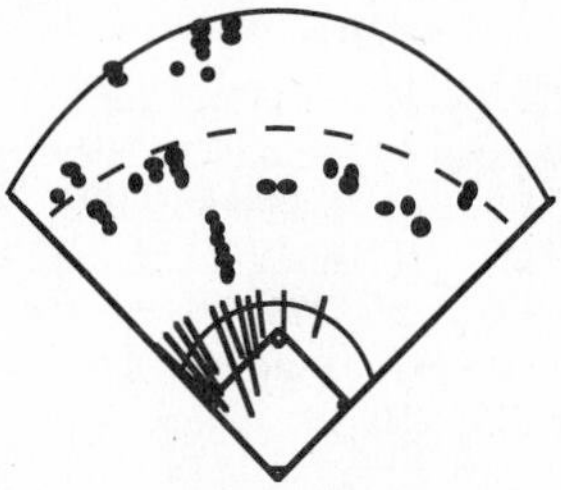

Vs. LHP

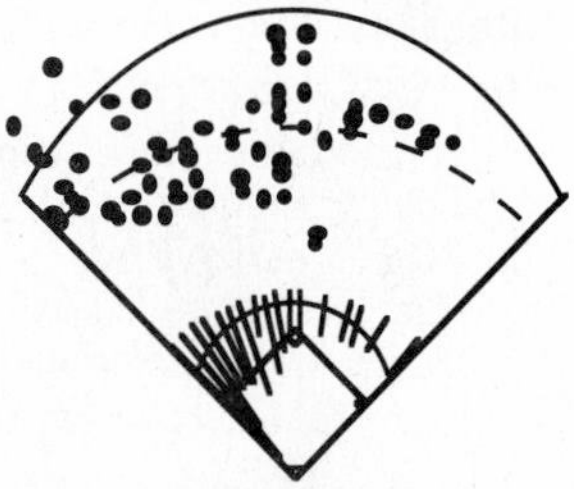

Vs. RHP

1990 Situational Stats

	AB	H	HR	RBI	AVG		AB	H	HR	RBI	AVG
Home	191	49	1	30	.257	LHP	147	36	2	12	.245
Road	209	53	5	28	.254	RHP	253	66	4	46	.261
Day	66	18	1	10	.273	Sc Pos	117	30	1	47	.256
Night	334	84	5	48	.251	Clutch	67	21	1	12	.313

1990 Rankings (American League)

- → 1st in worst caught stealing percentage by a catcher (17.1%)
- → 4th in hit by pitch (7)
- → Led the Royals in hit by pitch and batting average in the clutch (.313)
- → Led AL catchers in triples (4) and hit by pitch

PITCHING:

The Royals once again turned to Jeff Montgomery as their second-choice stopper in 1990. After stumbling slightly early in the year, Montgomery recovered to record a career high 24 saves after collecting 18 in 1989. Fine figures, but perhaps not quite fine enough to suit the Royals. Kansas City remembers the heyday of Dan Quisenberry, their stopper who would routinely record between 35 and 45 saves per season. They're not sure Montgomery can reach that level, which is why they signed Mark Davis a year ago.

In general, Montgomery's 1990 numbers were a close match to his 1989 totals. Montgomery continued to strike out nearly one batter per inning, while walking just three per nine innings pitched. He had a string of 23 games from May to July in which he struck out at least one batter per appearance. On the Royals staff, only Steve Farr had a better ERA than Montgomery's 2.39 mark.

Possessing a stopper's fireballing tenacity, Montgomery loves to rear back and fire; he often throws nothing but fastballs when entering the game to pitch the ninth inning. He sometimes loses control of his fastball, though; he has uncorked twelve wild pitches in 249 innings since 1988 and he hit five batters in 1990.

Montgomery's appearance in a game seems to serve as a spark plug for the Royals offense; he has been blessed with excellent offensive support. This has allowed him to post a 20-10 career record in less than three full seasons with the Royals to go along with his 43 career saves.

HOLDING RUNNERS AND FIELDING:

By relying on a fastball and throwing strikes, Montgomery does a good job of keeping opposing baserunners in check. He also possesses a good move to first, but will occasionally throw wildly when attempting a pickoff. While he is quick to field bunts, Montgomery doesn't always use good judgement regarding where to throw the ball. He has helped set up big innings for opponents by throwing wildly when trying to retire the lead runner.

OVERALL:

Montgomery will most likely begin the 1991 season in a left/right closer tandem with Mark Davis. It is no secret that the Royals would prefer to have Davis as the full-time stopper, though. Depending upon Davis' early season success next year, Montgomery may end up as a set-up man, or may again be called upon to be the team's relief ace. Much more than just a stopgap, he has the temperament and the tools to succeed in either role.

JEFF MONTGOMERY

Position: RP
Bats: R **Throws:** R
Ht: 5'11" **Wt:** 180

Opening Day Age: 29
Born: 1/7/62 in Wellston, OH
ML Seasons: 4

Overall Statistics

	W	L	ERA	G	GS	Sv	IP	H	R	BB	SO	HR
1990	6	5	2.39	73	0	24	94.1	81	36	34	94	6
Career	22	12	2.58	195	1	43	268.1	226	92	98	248	17

How Often He Throws Strikes

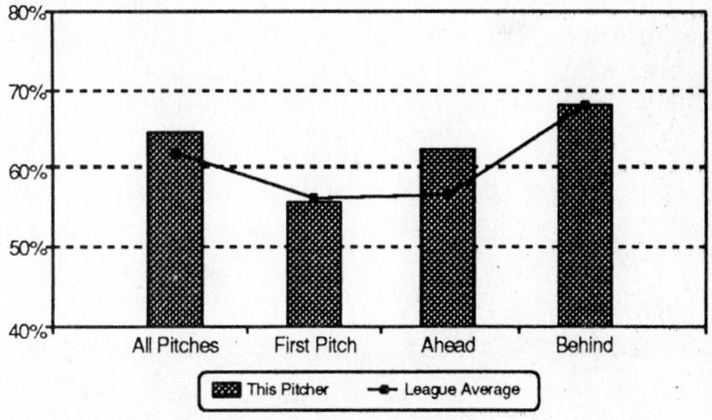

1990 Situational Stats

	W	L	ERA	Sv	IP		AB	H	HR	RBI	AVG
Home	3	1	1.20	14	52.2	LHB	176	49	4	22	.278
Road	3	4	3.89	10	41.2	RHB	179	32	2	20	.179
Day	2	2	2.05	5	26.1	Sc Pos	103	22	2	34	.214
Night	4	3	2.51	19	68.0	Clutch	215	51	4	28	.237

1990 Rankings (American League)

- 1st in blown saves (10)
- 2nd in games pitched (73) and worst save percentage (70.6%)
- 3rd in least GDPs induced per GDP situation (2.5%)
- 4th in games finished (59)
- 8th in save opportunities (34)
- 9th in first batter efficiency (.185)
- Led the Royals in games pitched, saves (24), games finished, save opportunities, holds (7) and blown saves

HITTING:

In his second full season with Kansas City, Bill Pecota showed marked improvement with increased playing time as the team's utility infielder. He set career marks in most offensive categories while fielding solidly at several defensive positions.

Pecota's improved batting was a pleasant surprise for the Royals. He had been an unimpressive hitter during most of his career and was coming off two consecutive weak seasons with the bat. Hitting coach John Mayberry helped Pecota learn to turn on pitches, resulting in the best power hitting of Pecota's career. He had 22 extra base hits in 240 at-bats and his 15 doubles were more than his career total prior to 1990.

Right-handed power pitchers seriously overmatch Pecota. Low fastballs and hard sliders away give him the most trouble. He prefers swinging at offspeed pitches and hits lefthanders far better than righthanders. Pecota batted just .207 against righthanders, slugging .314, compared to a .290 average and a .480 slugging average against lefties.

Pecota is a road warrior. He has always hit better away from Royals Stadium, and 1990 was no different. Pecota is a fine bunter; his six sacrifice hits led the team.

BASERUNNING:

Pecota runs well enough for frequent pinch runner usage by John Wathan. His stolen base success rate was down in 1990 (eight steals in 13 attempts) after he had previously succeeded 17 times in 21 career attempts. As a baserunner, Pecota does a good job of taking extra bases on outfield hits.

FIELDING:

Pecota's defensive versatility is the most important element of his game. He has spent time at all four infield positions and has also played in the outfield. Despite being fairly tall, Pecota is a smooth fielder and owns a strong and accurate arm. However, his defensive skills are geared more for second or third base; he lacks the range to be a good shortstop. He has been slow on double play pivots in the past, but has improved under Frank White's tutelage.

OVERALL:

Every team needs a "super sub" who can fill in anywhere on the field. Pecota played that role well in 1990 and will have the same job in 1991. His main use will be as Terry Shumpert's backup at second base. However, he will be 31 at the start of the 1991 season and his performance, in all likelihood, has already peaked. Pecota has little long-term future with the Royals but should play an important utility role over the next few seasons.

BILL PECOTA

Position: 2B/SS
Bats: R **Throws:** R
Ht: 6' 2" **Wt:** 190

Opening Day Age: 31
Born: 2/16/60 in Redwood City, CA
ML Seasons: 5

Overall Statistics

	G	AB	R	H	D	T	HR	RBI	SB	BB	SO	AVG
1990	87	240	43	58	15	2	5	20	8	33	39	.242
Career	320	686	114	161	29	8	12	56	25	76	110	.235

Where He Hits the Ball

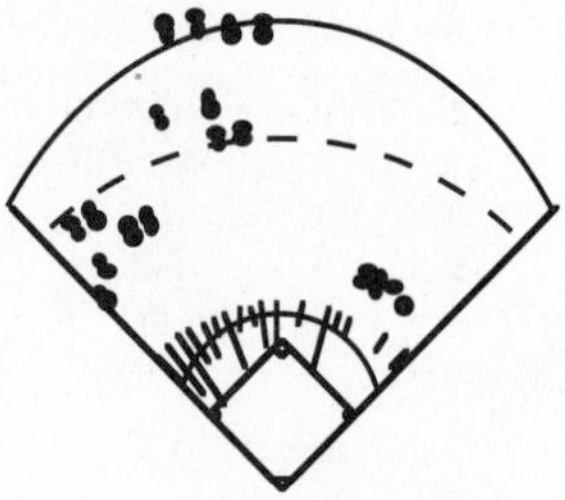

Vs. LHP

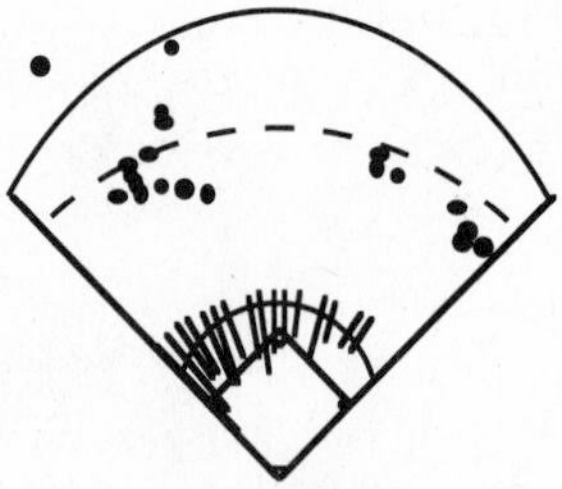

Vs. RHP

1990 Situational Stats

	AB	H	HR	RBI	AVG		AB	H	HR	RBI	AVG
Home	102	21	3	7	.206	LHP	100	29	2	6	.290
Road	138	37	2	13	.268	RHP	140	29	3	14	.207
Day	63	18	2	10	.286	Sc Pos	58	12	1	15	.207
Night	177	40	3	10	.226	Clutch	32	4	0	1	.125

1990 Rankings (American League)

→ Led the Royals in sacrifice bunts (6)

GERALD PERRY

Position: DH/1B
Bats: L **Throws:** R
Ht: 6' 0" **Wt:** 190

Opening Day Age: 30
Born: 10/30/60 in Savannah, GA
ML Seasons: 8

HITTING:

Gerald Perry's first year in the American League produced mixed results. He fulfilled most of the expectations for which the Royals dealt Charlie Leibrandt and Rick Luecken to Atlanta. He scored 57 runs and drove in 57 while connecting for eight homers and placed among the team's leaders in many offensive categories. Yet Perry's 1990 performance was something of a disappointment. He hit just .258 with runners in scoring position and failed to drive in runs while batting in the middle of the lineup. He was often impatient at the plate and failed to get on base regularly.

Perry is a line-drive hitter prone to streaks -- both good and bad. He hit .412 in a three week stretch after the All-Star break, but had several weeks during the year when he struggled in part-time play. Although Perry prefers swinging at fastballs, he hits all kinds of pitching and pitchers when he's on a tear. He had the most success against righthanders; Perry batted .272 and slugged .399 with 26 extra base hits (seven homers) against right-handed pitching. He managed only a .209 average against lefties. In 1989 Perry hit .337 vs. lefties, and only .198 vs. righties, but that appears to have been a fluke.

BASERUNNING:

Perry possesses great raw speed and is beginning to learn how to use it. He succeeded in 17 of 21 stolen base tries and reduced the serious baserunning mistakes for which he was notorious in Atlanta. Perry didn't run much early in the year while learning American League pitchers' moves; he succeeded in one of four attempts through May. Later, he ran more often and quite successfully. Expect more steal attempts and even more success in the future. Perry gives the Royals some much needed speed on the base paths.

FIELDING:

Perry is a poor fielder. He committed six errors in limited first base duty and could have easily been charged with another half dozen. While he is capable of making spectacular plays on occasion, Perry more often appears out of place with a glove on his hand.

OVERALL:

Perry provided a potent left-handed bat at times during 1990. He's one of the players the Royals wish to use at first base when George Brett is ready to take on full-time designated hitter chores. However, before Perry gets the starting first base job, he will have to carry a steadier glove and become a more consistent producer at the plate. In the meantime, Perry figures to be a part-time designated hitter who occasionally fills in for Brett at first base.

Overall Statistics

	G	AB	R	H	D	T	HR	RBI	SB	BB	SO	AVG
1990	133	465	57	118	22	2	8	57	17	39	56	.254
Career	776	2505	304	669	118	7	45	303	122	252	270	.267

Where He Hits the Ball

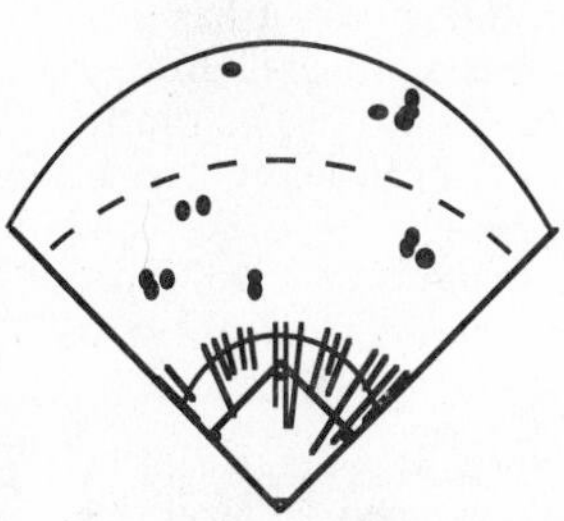

Vs. LHP

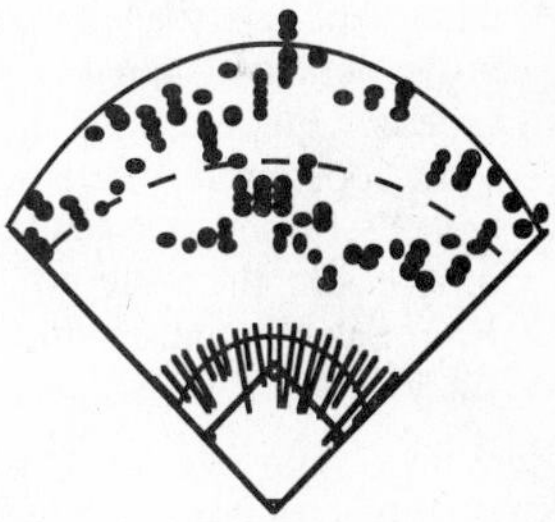

Vs. RHP

1990 Situational Stats

	AB	H	HR	RBI	AVG		AB	H	HR	RBI	AVG
Home	238	68	3	30	.286	LHP	134	28	1	14	.209
Road	227	50	5	27	.220	RHP	331	90	7	43	.272
Day	117	36	4	13	.308	Sc Pos	132	34	1	49	.258
Night	348	82	4	44	.236	Clutch	67	15	2	8	.224

1990 Rankings (American League)

- 4th in lowest on-base average vs. left-handed pitchers (.252)
- 6th in lowest batting average vs. left-handed pitchers (.209) and lowest slugging percentage vs. left-handed pitchers (.269)
- 8th in stolen base percentage (80.9%)
- Led the Royals in stolen base percentage and steals of third (3)
- Led designated hitters in stolen bases (17), groundball/flyball ratio (1.45), stolen base percentage and steals of third

BRET SABERHAGEN

Position: SP
Bats: R **Throws:** R
Ht: 6' 1" **Wt:** 185

Opening Day Age: 27
Born: 4/11/64 in Chicago Heights, IL
ML Seasons: 7

Overall Statistics

	W	L	ERA	G	GS	Sv	IP	H	R	BB	SO	HR
1990	5	9	3.27	20	20	0	135.0	146	52	28	87	9
Career	97	70	3.23	224	198	1	1464.0	1386	574	286	957	114

How Often He Throws Strikes

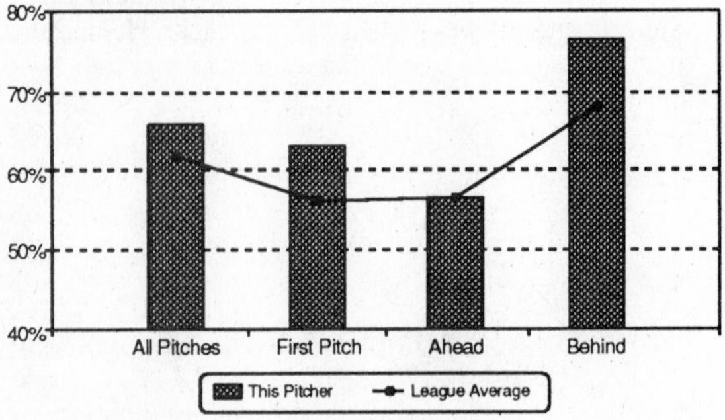

1990 Situational Stats

	W	L	ERA	Sv	IP		AB	H	HR	RBI	AVG
Home	3	5	3.42	0	73.2	LHB	222	61	5	25	.275
Road	2	4	3.08	0	61.1	RHB	302	85	4	23	.281
Day	1	2	3.26	0	47.0	Sc Pos	110	28	4	39	.255
Night	4	7	3.27	0	88.0	Clutch	53	15	2	7	.283

1990 Rankings (American League)

➟ 11th in complete games (5)

PITCHING:

In 1990, Bret Saberhagen again followed his pattern of poor seasons in even-numbered years after good odd-numbered seasons. If this pattern continues to hold true to form, 1991 will again see Saberhagen back among the American League's pitching elite. Saberhagen is 36-48 in even-numbered years and 61-22 in odd-numbered seasons.

After several poor outings in mid-season, Saberhagen went on the disabled list July 16th and had surgery to remove bone chips from his right elbow. At the time he was projected to miss the remainder of the season, but made two final starts after returning in late September. He lost both games, but appeared to have recovered most of his pitching strength.

Saberhagen has great control of an excellent fastball, a curve, a slider and a good change-up. The fastball is what sets Saberhagen apart, though, as it has good movement and can be thrown at several different speeds. Opponents rarely see the same pitch in the same location during a game; he can really wreck a batter's timing. He tends to get better as the game progresses; the hitters never know what to expect from Saberhagen. He has completed 41 of 123 starts since 1987.

With a high overhand delivery, Saberhagen throws hard but walks very few. He averaged 1.9 walks per nine innings in 1990 after giving up less than 1.5 walks per game in 1989. He strikes out a fair number of hitters, over six per game in the last four years. More important, Saberhagen has the ability to record a strikeout when it counts the most. Saberhagen has had a strikeout-to-walk ratio of three to one every year since 1985.

HOLDING RUNNERS AND FIELDING:

Saberhagen is one of the best fielding pitchers in the major leagues. He won a Gold Glove in 1989 and has always helped himself in the field. He pounces on bunts quickly, races into foul ground to grab soft pop-ups, throws accurately to all bases, and displays fine judgement about where to throw the ball. Saberhagen also possesses a fine pickoff move and regularly catches unsuspecting baserunners napping.

OVERALL:

Saberhagen's return to the starting rotation is vital to the Royals' success. If completely healthy, he will be the Royals number-one starter and be among the American League's best. He has already won two Cy Young awards (1985 and 1989) and, at age 27, will be entering his prime. This is an odd-numbered year; based on his past history, Saberhagen should be back in form again.

KEVIN SEITZER

Position: 3B
Bats: R **Throws:** R
Ht: 5'11" **Wt:** 180

Opening Day Age: 29
Born: 3/26/62 in Springfield, IL
ML Seasons: 5

Overall Statistics

	G	AB	R	H	D	T	HR	RBI	SB	BB	SO	AVG
1990	158	622	91	171	31	5	6	38	7	67	66	.275
Career	656	2515	380	747	117	21	32	240	46	340	305	.297

Where He Hits the Ball

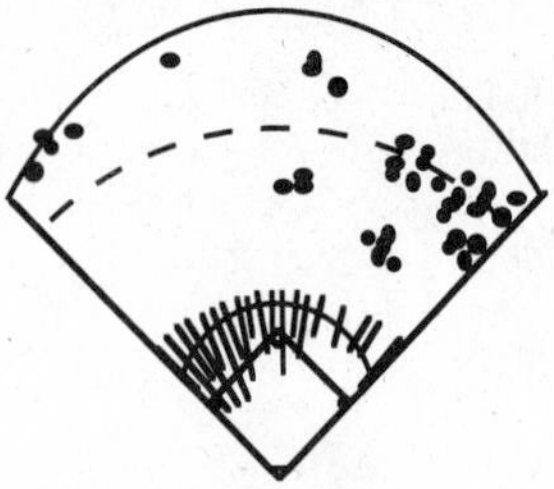

Vs. LHP

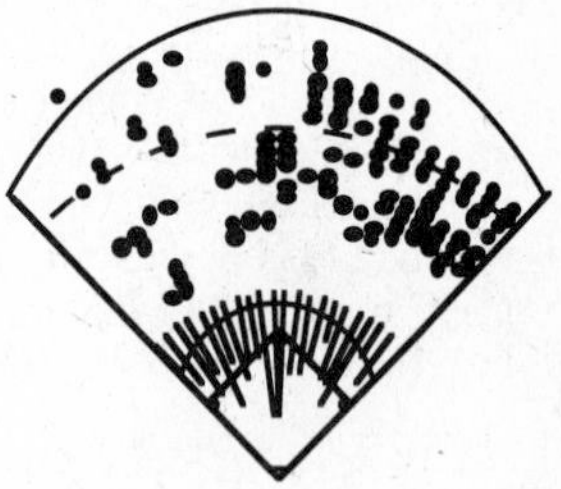

Vs. RHP

1990 Situational Stats

	AB	H	HR	RBI	AVG		AB	H	HR	RBI	AVG
Home	308	96	5	26	.312	LHP	209	58	4	23	.278
Road	314	75	1	12	.239	RHP	413	113	2	15	.274
Day	143	35	2	6	.245	Sc Pos	127	34	0	27	.268
Night	479	136	4	32	.284	Clutch	84	18	0	3	.214

1990 Rankings (American League)

- 4th in at-bats (622), plate appearances (697) and lowest slugging percentage vs. right-handed pitchers (.327)
- 7th in singles (129), batting average at home (.312) and lowest percentage of swings that missed (9.6%)
- Led the Royals in at-bats, runs (91), singles (129), walks (67), times on base (240), pitches seen (2,508), plate appearances (697), games (158), pitches seen per plate appearance (3.60) and runs scored per time reached base (37.9%)
- Led AL third basemen in at-bats and games

HITTING:

After three years of steady table-setting, Kevin Seitzer began last season as the Royals leadoff hitter. He led the team in runs scored (91), but failed to consistently reach base. Although Seitzer regained most of his power stroke in 1990, his offensive contribution fell off severely from previous seasons.

Seitzer is normally a patient hitter who will hit the ball where it's pitched. He is a line drive, gap hitter who prefers to swing at fastballs and spray hits to all fields. He showed less patience in 1990, though, and drew 35 fewer walks from the previous season while striking out at the same rate. He appeared to suffer from the pressure of being the team's leadoff batter, as he tried hard to ignite the Royals' sluggish offense.

Seitzer's offensive production has gradually diminished from his fine rookie season in 1987. In 1988, he lost much of his power and stopped driving in runs. In 1989, his batting average dipped sharply. Last year, Seitzer's on-base percentage fell off severely and he lacked his previous base stealing ability. The main bright spot for Seitzer was the return of his slugging, mostly against left-handed pitching; he slugged .455 versus lefties. Overall, he slashed 42 extra base hits in 1990 compared to just 23 the year before.

BASERUNNING:

A highly aggressive baserunner, Seitzer occasionally runs into outs by trying to stretch hits for extra bases or when going from first to third on base hits. He attempted fewer steals in 1990 and also had less success; Seitzer stole seven bases in twelve tries.

FIELDING:

Seitzer's fielding improved in 1990. He worked particularly hard on defense during spring training However, he is still prone to defensive slumps and had several in the latter part of the year, lowering his fielding average to a mediocre .953. Seitzer has a knack for sparkling plays, but he often allows routine grounders to play him rather than charging them aggressively. The Royals tried Seitzer at second base in September, giving him six starts there. He played the position well enough to effectively serve as emergency backup to rookie Terry Shumpert in 1991.

OVERALL:

Willie Wilson's inability to consistently reach base cost him his leadoff role in 1990, and the same fate may befall Seitzer in 1991. The Royals are considering Brian McRae for the leadoff role in 1991, so Seitzer may drop back to the second spot where he has seen the most success. He will also get better pitches hitting in front of Brett. The Royals need Seitzer to regain his 1987 rookie form.

TERRY SHUMPERT

Position: 2B
Bats: R **Throws:** R
Ht: 5'11" **Wt:** 190

Opening Day Age: 24
Born: 8/16/66 in Paducah, KY
ML Seasons: 1

HITTING:

Terry Shumpert's rapid rise through the minors landed him in Kansas City as the starting second baseman in late April last year. After a month of solid play he suffered a thumb injury and was out until the end of September, seeing only pinch running duty thereafter. But he showed enough that the Royals have released Frank White and made Shumpert the odds-on choice to be their second baseman in 1991.

A former number two draft choice, Shumpert has played only four seasons of professional ball since being drafted out of the University of Kentucky. In the minors he was never a high-average hitter -- in fact, he had only one year over .260 -- but he showed steady development. He jumped from Class A to AAA to the majors in two years without ever seeming overmatched, which is a good sign of his maturity.

Shumpert is a line-drive, singles hitter who drives the ball up the middle and prefers fastballs. He has doubles power to the gaps and led the league in doubles at Appleton in 1988. He's still over-matched by the better big league pitchers and struck out often toward the end of his one month stint. To succeed, Shumpert needs more patience at the plate; he fanned 17 times in 91 at-bats, but walked just twice.

BASERUNNING:

Shumpert has fine speed and good instincts on the bases. He stole 36 bases at Appleton in 1988 and 23 in Omaha in 1989, but what's more impressive are his outstanding success rates. He was 36 for 39 at Appleton in 1988, and 18 for 18 at Omaha this year. He was only three for six with the Royals, however, and will need time to learn the pitchers' moves before making frequent steal attempts.

FIELDING:

If Shumpert becomes the regular Royal second baseman, it will be primarily because of his glove. He showed good range while posting a decent fielding average (.977) for the Royals last year, and looked exactly like what they were hoping for. He has big shoes to fill at second base, though; Shumpert replaces eight-time Gold Glove winner Frank White.

OVERALL:

Impressed with his work last year, the Royals are ready to hand Shumpert the second base job; it is his to lose. He's just 24 years old and should continue to improve rapidly. If he can learn to hit major league pitching consistently, Shumpert could hold down second base for a many years to come.

Overall Statistics

	G	AB	R	H	D	T	HR	RBI	SB	BB	SO	AVG
1990	32	91	7	25	6	1	0	8	3	2	17	.275
Career	32	91	7	25	6	1	0	8	3	2	17	.275

Where He Hits the Ball

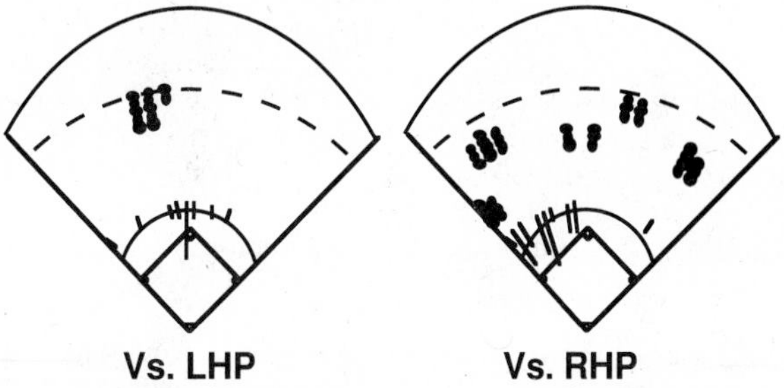

1990 Situational Stats

	AB	H	HR	RBI	AVG		AB	H	HR	RBI	AVG
Home	45	12	0	2	.267	LHP	30	11	0	3	.367
Road	46	13	0	6	.283	RHP	61	14	0	5	.230
Day	16	4	0	1	.250	Sc Pos	24	7	0	7	.292
Night	75	21	0	7	.280	Clutch	21	10	0	2	.476

1990 Rankings (American League)

- Did not rank near the top or bottom in any category

HITTING:

After five major league seasons, Kurt Stillwell is showing little improvement, and in some ways he moved backward last year. His batting average and slugging both fell off slightly, while his other hitting numbers remained about the same as they were in his first two years with the Royals.

Stillwell avoided his usual slow start by streaking to a .364 average in early May; he was virtually the only Royals' regular who was hitting early in the season. During his hot start Stillwell often swung at first pitches. Later, he began seeing fewer early strikes and started chasing bad pitches. Although he regained some patience later in the year, he couldn't reverse the downward trend; Stillwell hit .205 after July 1st.

Stillwell hits all pitches equally; fastballs by power pitchers bother him no more than finesse pitchers' curves. But, he's prone to sitting on just one pitch and can be fooled by a mixture of fastballs and offspeed stuff. Stillwell mainly hits the ball up the middle while displaying some power down the foul lines.

Reversing his previous trend of better road performance, Stillwell hit better at home last year (.268) than he did on the road (.230). But either at home or on the road, he didn't hit very well, certainly not as well as the Royals have been expecting.

BASERUNNING:

Baserunning was another area of regression for Stillwell. After swiping a career high nine bases in 1989, Stillwell had no steals last year. He has below average speed and doesn't take many chances. Stillwell is quick out of the batter's box, though, and will sometimes try for extra bases on outfield hits.

FIELDING:

Stillwell's fielding statistics are rather misleading. His range is better than his numbers would indicate (4.2 plays made per nine innings). The Royals pitching staff strikes out a large percentage of hitters and it's primarily a fly ball staff. Both circumstances result in fewer plays for the team's shortstop. Stillwell shows fine range going up the middle and has a strong, accurate arm. Yet, Stillwell is still just an average shortstop; he hasn't progressed much in the last two years. He doesn't turn the double play well and his .957 fielding average is below average.

OVERALL:

Stillwell is still quite young (25 on opening day, 1991) and has lots of major league experience for his age. However, his play appears to have leveled off. At least the Royals know what to expect; Stillwell's steadiness on both offense and defense should help the club as they break in a new second baseman.

KURT STILLWELL

Position: SS
Bats: B **Throws:** R
Ht: 5'11" **Wt:** 175

Opening Day Age: 25
Born: 6/4/65 in Glendale, CA
ML Seasons: 5

Overall Statistics

	G	AB	R	H	D	T	HR	RBI	SB	BB	SO	AVG
1990	144	506	60	126	35	4	3	51	0	39	60	.249
Career	637	2102	260	528	109	24	24	217	25	190	297	.251

Where He Hits the Ball

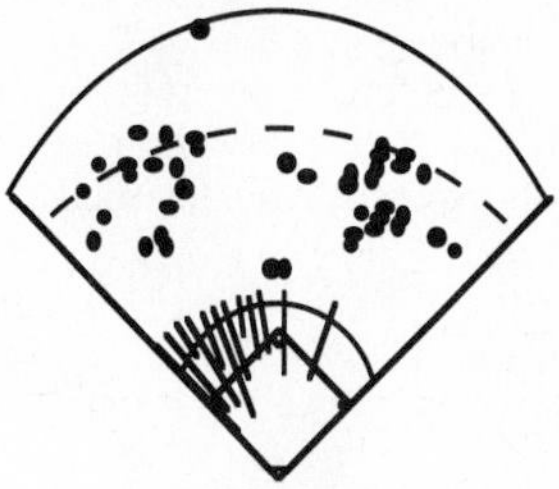

Vs. LHP

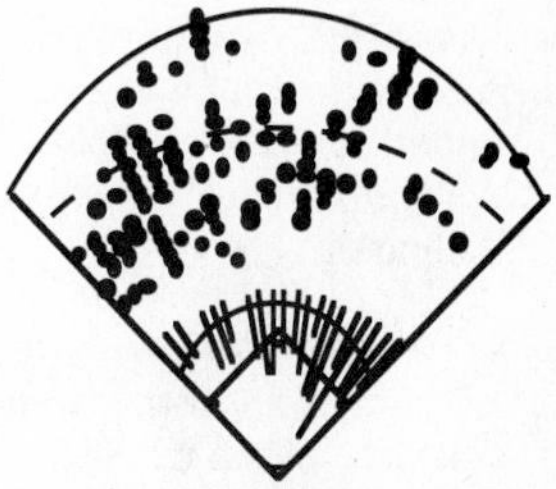

Vs. RHP

1990 Situational Stats

	AB	H	HR	RBI	AVG		AB	H	HR	RBI	AVG
Home	254	68	3	34	.268	LHP	128	27	0	20	.211
Road	252	58	0	17	.230	RHP	378	99	3	31	.262
Day	134	41	1	13	.306	Sc Pos	123	30	1	45	.244
Night	372	85	2	38	.228	Clutch	81	20	1	4	.247

1990 Rankings (American League)

- ➡ 4th lowest batting average on a 3-1 count (.063)
- ➡ 6th lowest HR frequency (168.7 ABs per HR) and worst on-base average vs. right-handed pitchers (.305)
- ➡ 7th worst on-base average (.304)
- ➡ 8th worst batting average vs. left-handed pitchers (.211)
- ➡ Led the Royals in sacrifice flies (7) and percentage of swings put into play (53.9%)
- ➡ Led AL shortstops in sacrifice flies and errors (24)

DANNY TARTABULL

Position: RF/DH
Bats: R **Throws:** R
Ht: 6' 1" **Wt:** 205

Opening Day Age: 28
Born: 10/30/62 in Miami, FL
ML Seasons: 7

Overall Statistics

	G	AB	R	H	D	T	HR	RBI	SB	BB	SO	AVG
1990	88	313	41	84	19	0	15	60	1	36	93	.268
Career	691	2435	357	685	139	13	121	435	27	331	645	.281

Where He Hits the Ball

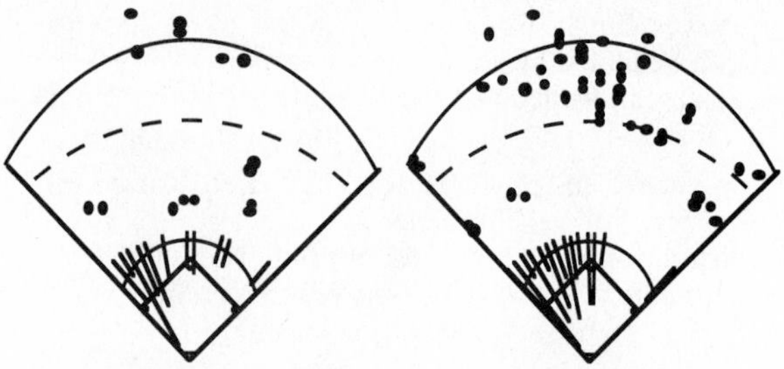

Vs. LHP Vs. RHP

1990 Situational Stats

	AB	H	HR	RBI	AVG		AB	H	HR	RBI	AVG
Home	142	33	5	25	.232	LHP	106	34	5	17	.321
Road	171	51	10	35	.298	RHP	207	50	10	43	.242
Day	71	21	7	21	.296	Sc Pos	100	26	3	42	.260
Night	242	63	8	39	.260	Clutch	44	14	3	9	.318

1990 Rankings (American League)

- ➟ 6th highest on-base average vs. left-handed pitchers (.426)
- ➟ Led the Royals in batting average vs. left-handed pitchers (.321) and on-base average vs. left-handed pitchers

HITTING:

Two disabled list stints cost Danny Tartabull half of the 1990 season and he posted career lows in most offensive categories. Yet Tartabull remained one of the Royals' top power hitters, trailing only Bo Jackson in homers with 15. He had one of the team's best rates of at-bats per RBI while providing solid offensive punch from the fifth spot in the order.

Being called upon to carry a large part of the team's RBI load, Tartabull has gradually changed his level swing into an uppercut as he tries to drive the ball out of cavernous Royals Stadium. As a result he often swings at bad pitches. His on-base percentage has dropped steadily since 1987, his first season with the Royals. His 1990 OBP of .341 is down from his career .371 OBP coming into last year.

In the past Tartabull had been steady both at home and on the road, but in 1990 he hit much better away from Kansas City. He hit just .232 at home, while batting .298 with 10 homers and a .561 slugging average in opponents' parks. That may be a result of his new uppercut swing, which works better in smaller road ballparks.

BASERUNNING:

Bad knees and other injuries have slowed Tartabull considerably in recent years. He used to have above-average speed, but was not a knowledgeable baserunner. Now he's a more intelligent baserunner, but lacks good speed. Tartabull stole just one base in two attempts last year and runs the bases cautiously.

FIELDING:

Tartabull is a below-average right fielder. He has trouble going back on deep fly balls, so he often plays very deep. Since Tartabull lacks the speed that most Royals' outfielders have, playing deep also lets him cut off balls in the gap or down the line. While this eliminates some extra-base hits, it does allow other runners to take extra bases on right field singles. Although Tartabull throws well enough, his deep positioning gives him little chance to cut down aggressive baserunners.

OVERALL:

Tartabull is one of the few power hitters in the Royals lineup, an important element for the league's worst power-hitting team. He would be sorely missed if traded, as is persistently rumored. His trade value has bottomed out after two straight injury-plagued, subpar seasons. Yet Tartabull is still in his prime and capable of having another superb year if he can remain healthy for more than a month at a time.

FRANK WHITE

Position: 2B
Bats: R **Throws:** R
Ht: 5'11" **Wt:** 190

Opening Day Age: 40
Born: 9/4/50 in Greenville, MS
ML Seasons: 18

HITTING:

In undoubtedly his last season with the Royals, Frank White struggled at the plate. His .216 average was his lowest ever and his seriously-reduced playing time resulted in other career lows. Meanwhile, White's starting second base job was given to rookie Terry Shumpert. All in all, 1990 was a forgettable year for White, who turned 40 in September.

White is a first-pitch fastball hitter who likes to pull the ball. He used to thrive on inner-half fastballs, driving them down the line for extra bases, but he now lacks the bat speed to get around on inside heaters. White still pulls most pitches, but hard throwing righthanders give him trouble, and he has always had problems against lefties who nibble at the corners with low breaking pitches. He tends to get impatient, falling behind in the count by chasing bad breaking balls. White is primarily a mistake hitter now.

White's batting value has always been in his extra-base hitting and his ability to drive in runs. However, his slugging average has dropped steadily in recent years, and he has managed just 57 RBI in the last two seasons combined. His .217 batting average with runners in scoring position didn't help his cause.

BASERUNNING:

Age and more than sixteen years of play on artificial turf have sufficiently eliminated the above-average speed White once possessed. Formerly capable of double-digit steal totals and a half-dozen triples each year, White now rarely attempts a stolen base and runs conservatively once on base.

FIELDING:

White is one of the finest fielding second basemen in baseball history and an eight-time Gold Glove winner. He remains among the top fielders in the American League despite losing a step from previous years. White is a student of opponent hitting tendencies and still makes a substantial number of plays due to adept positioning. He has served as fielding instructor to young Shumpert and to Kevin Seitzer during Seitzer's second base trial; White also helped pitcher Kevin Appier overcome some of his throwing difficulties. White's glove and experience will be missed in 1991.

OVERALL:

Although White believes he has one more season left, it won't be with the Royals. Kansas City wants to give Shumpert the second base job while White would like a chance to play more regularly. White should be long remembered by Royals fans for his 18-year career of fine play at second base and his deep commitment to community service in the Kansas City area. Shumpert has some giant shoes to fill.

Overall Statistics

	G	AB	R	H	D	T	HR	RBI	SB	BB	SO	AVG
1990	82	241	20	52	14	1	2	21	1	10	32	.216
Career	2324	7859	912	2006	407	58	160	886	178	412	1035	.255

Where He Hits the Ball

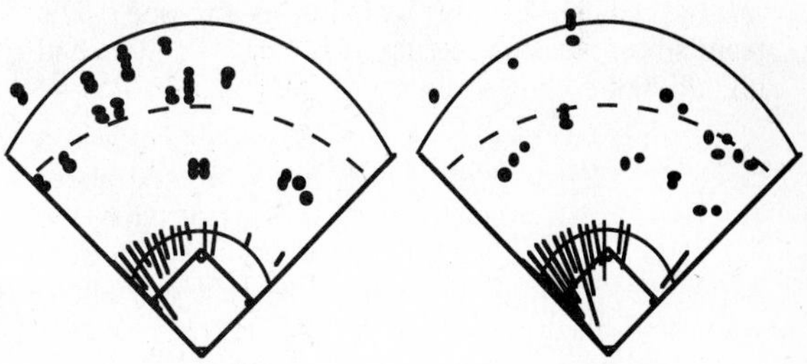

Vs. LHP Vs. RHP

1990 Situational Stats

	AB	H	HR	RBI	AVG		AB	H	HR	RBI	AVG
Home	145	36	2	15	.248	LHP	93	18	1	6	.194
Road	96	16	0	6	.167	RHP	148	34	1	15	.230
Day	36	8	1	4	.222	Sc Pos	60	13	1	18	.217
Night	205	44	1	17	.215	Clutch	33	3	0	1	.091

1990 Rankings (American League)

- 10th in batting average on a 3-2 count (.353)
- Led the Royals in batting average on a 3-2 count
- Led AL second basemen in batting average on a 3-2 count

WILLIE WILSON

Position: LF/CF
Bats: B **Throws:** R
Ht: 6' 3" **Wt:** 195

Opening Day Age: 35
Born: 7/9/55 in Montgomery, AL
ML Seasons: 15

HITTING:

For the first time since early 1979, Willie Wilson was not the Royals' every-day center fielder and leadoff hitter. Due to recent problems hitting right- handed pitching and a horrible on-base percentage, he was given a backup/platoon role and dropped to the bottom of the order. Wilson's reduced playing time resulted in a better batting average and OBP, but strikingly similar totals in other areas.

Wilson hacks away at almost any pitch. He has the most difficulty with pitches low or away and can be retired on pitches outside the strike zone. Wilson refuses to utilize his speed; he hits far too many fly balls by trying to pull nearly everything.

In 1990, Wilson's batting eye improved and he had a strikeout-to-walk ratio lower than two to one for the first time since 1984. He raised his OBP to .354 from an abysmal .300 in 1989. Wilson was also one of the team's best pressure hitters; he drove in 40 runs and hit .297 with runners in scoring position.

A part-time role was not to Wilson's liking and he did his best to let everyone know it. He pouted about being used as a substitute right fielder so much that Royals manager John Wathan eventually inserted left-handed hitting Jim Eisenreich against lefty pitchers and benched Wilson indefinitely.

BASERUNNING:

Wilson's 24 stolen bases in 1990 led the Royals and he now ranks 14th on the all-time stolen base list with 612. He runs less frequently now, but he still has a fine success rate; he was caught just six times in 1990 for a success rate of 80 percent. Once on base, Wilson is excellent at taking extra bases on outfield hits.

FIELDING:

Wilson is no longer among the league's top fielding center fielders. He can still run down the long fly balls in Royals Stadium's spacious outfield, but he has lost a step from earlier days. Wilson has one of the major league's weakest arms. Baserunners frequently take advantage of his rainbow throws, even moving up from first to second base after flies to medium-depth center field. Wilson also spent some time in left when Bo Jackson was shifted to center.

OVERALL:

Wilson has not adjusted to part-time play after such lengthy regular duty in center field. He has stated he won't return to Kansas City as the team's fifth outfielder; Royals management appears content to let him play elsewhere. Wilson's star is fading, but he might temporarily rejuvenate his career by signing with a weaker team for whom he can play every day.

Overall Statistics

	G	AB	R	H	D	T	HR	RBI	SB	BB	SO	AVG
1990	115	307	49	89	13	3	2	42	24	30	57	.290
Career	1787	6799	1060	1968	241	133	40	509	612	360	990	.289

Where He Hits the Ball

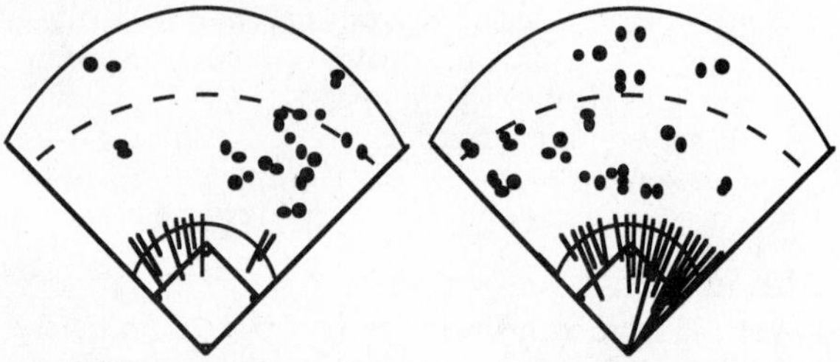

Vs. LHP Vs. RHP

1990 Situational Stats

	AB	H	HR	RBI	AVG		AB	H	HR	RBI	AVG
Home	166	55	1	22	.331	LHP	103	28	0	17	.272
Road	141	34	1	20	.241	RHP	204	61	2	25	.299
Day	65	16	0	7	.246	Sc Pos	101	30	1	40	.297
Night	242	73	2	35	.302	Clutch	53	11	1	8	.208

1990 Rankings (American League)

- 9th in stolen base percentage (80.0%)
- Led the Royals in stolen bases (24), least GDPs per GDP situation (6.3%), batting average with 2 strikes (.221) and steals of third (3)

LUIS AQUINO

Position: RP/SP
Bats: R **Throws:** R
Ht: 6' 1" **Wt:** 175

Opening Day Age: 25
Born: 5/19/65 in Rio Piedras, Puerto Rico
ML Seasons: 4

Overall Statistics

	W	L	ERA	G	GS	Sv	IP	H	R	BB	SO	HR
1990	4	1	3.16	20	3	0	68.1	59	25	27	28	6
Career	12	10	3.46	68	24	0	250.0	254	110	82	112	15

PITCHING, FIELDING & HOLDING RUNNERS:

Despite missing the last two months of the 1990 season, Luis Aquino had a successful summer for the Royals. As a long reliever and spot starter, he filled in for injured or failed starters. Aquino went on the disabled list July 27th with a muscle strain and didn't return until the last week of the season.

Aquino throws a slider and a curve, but mainly uses a surprisingly good fastball to record outs. He occasionally had control problems early in the year, walking more than 3.5 batters per nine innings for the year. Despite his good fastball, Aquino is not a strikeout pitcher; he struck out 3.7 batters per nine innings in 1990, a decline from his 1989 average of 4.3.

But Aquino is not easy to hit. He held opponents to a .237 batting average, behind only Steve Farr and Jeff Montgomery on the Royals staff. He was equally tough against right and left-handed hitters; righthanders hit .233 against Aquino and lefties batted .241. He did give up 20 extra base hits, and opponents slugged .365 against him.

OVERALL:

The Royals need a reliable long reliever/spot starter to step in when injuries strike, and Aquino can fill the role. He came to the majors at age 21 and is still only 25 years old. If he continues improving, Aquino may find a place in the rotation if one of the young Royals' starters falters or becomes injured again.

JEFF CONINE

Position: 1B
Bats: R **Throws:** R
Ht: 6' 1" **Wt:** 205

Opening Day Age: 24
Born: 6/27/66 in Tacoma, WA
ML Seasons: 1

Overall Statistics

	G	AB	R	H	D	T	HR	RBI	SB	BB	SO	AVG
1990	9	20	3	5	2	0	0	2	0	2	5	.250
Career	9	20	3	5	2	0	0	2	0	2	5	.250

HITTING, FIELDING, BASERUNNING:

After two solid seasons at Class A Baseball City, Jeff Conine had a fantastic 1990 season at AA Memphis. He was among the league leaders in most offensive categories, was named to Baseball America's AA All-Star team, and was chosen Southern League Most Valuable Player before earning a September call-up with the Royals.

Conine combines a keen batting eye with fine extra-base power and above-average speed. He hit .320 and slugged .522 for Memphis while drawing 94 walks -- compiling an impressive .425 on-base percentage. His 60 extra-base hits included 37 doubles as Conine led Memphis to the league championship. His home run total has increased each year (to 15 this season), and he's had at least 21 stolen bases in each of his three minor league seasons.

Primarily a pull hitter, Conine doesn't feast on any particular pitch, but hits lefties well. He had some trouble with good major league fastballs during his short September stint while hitting mostly fifth or sixth for the Royals. Conine is an above-average fielder at first base with a strong arm -- he was a pitcher at UCLA.

OVERALL:

The Royals' immediate plans for Conine depend on whether they re-sign free agent Gerald Perry. If so, Conine will spend most of 1991 at AAA Omaha. Otherwise he'll be the Royals' part-time designated hitter and backup first baseman. Either way, he's one of the team's hottest prospects. Conine should get the first base job when George Brett shifts permanently to DH.

STEVE JELTZ

Position: 2B/SS
Bats: B **Throws:** R
Ht: 5'11" **Wt:** 180

Opening Day Age: 31
Born: 5/28/59 in Paris, France
ML Seasons: 8

Overall Statistics

	G	AB	R	H	D	T	HR	RBI	SB	BB	SO	AVG
1990	74	103	11	16	4	0	0	10	1	6	21	.155
Career	727	1749	183	367	46	20	5	130	18	248	342	.210

HITTING, FIELDING, BASERUNNING:

Last season was a disaster for Steve Jeltz, a marginally-talented veteran just trying to survive in the major leagues. In his first year in the American League, Jeltz was well below the "Mendoza line" with a .155 mark, and he added few extras. His performance was a complete regression from 1989, in which he'd posted a very useful .356 on-base percentage. Last year, working as a backup for Kurt Stillwell and Frank White, Jeltz showed no skills that could be marginally considered as major league.

Jeltz is a switch-hitter who was completely overmatched by righthanders; he hit .113 with 19 strikeouts in 71 at-bats from the left side. Fastball pitchers had no trouble blowing Jeltz away, and he also had problems with low breaking pitches. He is usually a patient hitter who hits the ball up the middle. Jeltz will try to fight off fastballs while waiting for a curve to slap through the infield.

Jeltz displayed poor range in the infield and had difficulty turning double plays. He showed little speed and ran the bases tentatively when occasionally used as a pinch runner.

OVERALL:

Bill Pecota's versatility and Terry Shumpert's emergence have left Jeltz with no value to the Royals. Jeltz was acquired in exchange for Jose DeJesus prior to the 1990 season, and as DeJesus gets better for the Phillies, this trade looks worse for the Royals. With deteriorating defensive skills and a weak bat, Jeltz is unlikely to have much of a future in the big leagues.

ANDY McGAFFIGAN

Position: RP/SP
Bats: R **Throws:** R
Ht: 6' 3" **Wt:** 190

Opening Day Age: 34
Born: 10/25/56 in West Palm Beach, FL
ML Seasons: 10

Overall Statistics

	W	L	ERA	G	GS	Sv	IP	H	R	BB	SO	HR
1990	4	3	3.89	28	11	1	83.1	85	49	32	53	8
Career	38	33	3.37	359	62	24	825.1	759	346	292	607	55

PITCHING, FIELDING & HOLDING RUNNERS:

A well-traveled veteran of ten seasons, Andy McGaffigan effectively filled a void created by several injuries to Royals' starting pitchers last year. McGaffigan had been released earlier by the Giants before joining AAA Omaha. He pitched well there in limited relief duty, was recalled June 7th and soon entered the starting rotation. Exclusively a reliever since 1986, McGaffigan lasted past the sixth inning in only two of 11 starts. After returning to the bullpen when Storm Davis healed, McGaffigan was hammered in long relief.

McGaffigan uses a variety of offspeed pitches to keep batters off stride. Lacking an over-powering fastball, he must have good control to succeed; for the Royals, he walked 3.2 batters per nine innings. McGaffigan surrenders many fly balls and is well suited to large Royals Stadium, as he posted a 2.33 ERA in Kansas City.

An average fielder, McGaffigan lacks a great move to first. His frequent throws keep the runners close, but they run easily against his offspeed pitches. To counteract the running game, McGaffigan must stay ahead in the count.

OVERALL:

McGaffigan filled a hole for the Royals in 1990 similar to the way Larry McWilliams stepped into the breach in 1989. As was the case with McWilliams, McGaffigan's stay with the Royals may be short. Barring significant early season injuries to other pitchers, McGaffigan may be released or spend 1991 at Omaha.

BRIAN McRAE

Position: CF
Bats: B **Throws:** R
Ht: 6' 0" **Wt:** 180

Opening Day Age: 23
Born: 8/27/67 in Bradenton, FL
ML Seasons: 1

Overall Statistics

	G	AB	R	H	D	T	HR	RBI	SB	BB	SO	AVG
1990	46	168	21	48	8	3	2	23	4	9	29	.286
Career	46	168	21	48	8	3	2	23	4	9	29	.286

HITTING, FIELDING, BASERUNNING:

Switch-hitting rookie Brian McRae broke into the major leagues in style, tripling in his first left-handed plate appearance and singling in his first right-handed at-bat. Rapid progress by McRae at AA Memphis prompted his recall on August 7th when he took over in center field, usually batting second or leading off.

Like his father Hal, Brian McRae is a converted infielder. McRae occasionally appears unsure which way to run on fly balls hit his direction, but he uses his good speed to recover quickly. His speed also helps as a baserunner; McRae stole 20 or more bases in each of his six professional seasons. He ran the bases aggressively in his brief major league stint, often stretching hits for extra bases. McRae didn't attempt many steals, but may be running more freely once he learns to read the pitchers' moves.

McRae has a compact swing and often picks on the first or second pitch. He pounded lefties for a .361 average. McRae usually pulls the ball and hits for power to the alleys; his extra-base hits are line-drives that find outfield gaps.

OVERALL:

McRae has a fine chance to become the Royals future starting center fielder. He made excellent recent progress in the minors and showed great potential in his short 1990 major league tryout. Royals fans are happy to once again have a McRae in the lineup.

JEFF SCHULZ

Position: RF
Bats: L **Throws:** R
Ht: 6' 1" **Wt:** 190

Opening Day Age: 29
Born: 6/2/61 in Evansville, IN
ML Seasons: 2

Overall Statistics

	G	AB	R	H	D	T	HR	RBI	SB	BB	SO	AVG
1990	30	66	5	17	5	1	0	6	0	6	13	.258
Career	37	75	5	19	5	1	0	7	0	6	15	.253

HITTING, FIELDING, BASERUNNING:

Long-time minor leaguer Jeff Schulz got a quick look at the bigs in 1990. No kid at age 29, Schulz spent five long years at AAA Omaha before finally getting his chance. At the minor league level, he's always hit for a good average, but without home run punch or the ability to reach base via the walk. He's not a base stealer or a great glove man, either, and the result is the sort of incomplete package that makes a guy a career minor leaguer.

In 30 games last year, Schulz served the Royals fairly well as a left-handed pinch hitter and occasional outfielder, batting .258 before losing time with bruised ribs. He's strictly a fastball hitter who likes the ball down. He mainly tries to pull the ball along the right field line for extra bases.

Schulz is a below-average baserunner who stole just five bases in the previous four years at Omaha. He plays station-to-station ball once on base. Schulz appeared tentative in his few starts in right field late in the year. His best use is as a left-handed pinch hitter.

OVERALL:

Schulz did the same job in 1990 that Matt Winters handled the previous season and, like Winters, has little chance of a long-term future with the Royals. He will be 30 in 1991 and will no doubt begin the season in AAA Omaha. Schulz could see duty as a mid-season call-up if injuries strike the team's outfielders.

PITCHING:

Chris Bosio had a 3-0 record last April and appeared to be on the way to another outstanding season. Only 27, Bosio was taking over where he left off in 1989, when he posted career bests in both wins (15) and ERA (2.95). Bosio led Brewer starters in every significant category in 1989, and was widely regarded as one of the American League's best starting pitchers.

But after 1990's hot start, Bosio won only one more game, and his season ended on July 31 because of a knee problem that eventually needed surgery. The knee had been bothering him for months, and to compensate, he had altered his mechanics. That led to problems after his outstanding first month.

When he's healthy, Bosio has a good fastball that he can consistently throw in the 88-90 MPH range. He usually sinks it to try to get ground balls, but he also will throw a rising fastball. He also has an excellent slider and a good split-finger pitch. He needs to work on his change-up, which he tends to throw too hard. It then ends up looking like a batting-practice fastball, and hitters will drive it. He gave up 15 home runs last year, second on the team despite him making only 20 starts. The big righthander has good control and won't walk many hitters.

Bosio is big and strong and will pitch a lot of innings when he's healthy. But he weighs about 225, and the constant grind of pitching put a lot of strain on his knees last year. He's expected to be fully recovered, but only time will tell.

HOLDING RUNNERS AND FIELDING:

Bosio has made great improvement defensively. He moves well for a big man and fields his position adequately. The biggest improvement has been with his temperament. In his early seasons he would get so upset with himself that he would sometimes forget to cover first or get into position to back up a base. He still has to work on his move to first base. Baserunners have run fairly freely on Bosio throughout his career.

OVERALL:

Bosio has the ability and desire to be a big winner. He has learned to control his temper and not fight himself when he runs into trouble. He has had knee problems most of his career, however, and needs to stay healthy. Although he has also pitched effectively in short relief, he probably is best suited for a starting role because of his assortment of pitches and his durability. When he's right, he could be a number-one or two starter for almost any team.

CHRIS BOSIO

Position: SP
Bats: R **Throws:** R
Ht: 6' 3" **Wt:** 225

Opening Day Age: 28
Born: 4/3/63 in Carmichael, CA
ML Seasons: 5

Overall Statistics

	W	L	ERA	G	GS	Sv	IP	H	R	BB	SO	HR
1990	4	9	4.00	20	20	0	132.2	131	67	38	76	15
Career	37	46	3.94	147	98	8	754.0	774	366	187	512	71

How Often He Throws Strikes

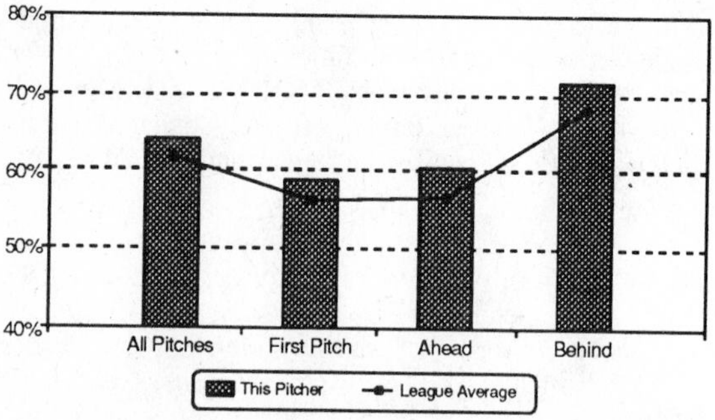

1990 Situational Stats

	W	L	ERA	Sv	IP		AB	H	HR	RBI	AVG
Home	2	7	5.11	0	81.0	LHB	273	78	10	37	.286
Road	2	2	2.26	0	51.2	RHB	235	53	5	23	.226
Day	2	3	1.92	0	51.2	Sc Pos	114	28	1	40	.246
Night	2	6	5.33	0	81.0	Clutch	37	7	0	2	.189

1990 Rankings (American League)

→ 4th worst ERA at home (5.11)

GREG BROCK

Position: 1B
Bats: L **Throws:** R
Ht: 6' 3" **Wt:** 205

Opening Day Age: 33
Born: 6/14/57 in McMinnville, OR
ML Seasons: 9

HITTING:

Earlier in his career, the Los Angeles Dodgers gave up on Greg Brock. Last year it was the Brewers' turn. Brock, who never became the power hitter he was expected to be, ended up on the bench when Paul Molitor was moved to first base during the last half of the season. Brock started only 20 of the last 63 games of the season.

At age 33 and after nine seasons in the big leagues, Brock's career has to be considered a big disappointment. He rolled up big power numbers as a minor leaguer, topped by a 44-home run season at Albuquerque in 1982. The Dodgers were so impressed that they let Steve Garvey go as a free agent, opening up their first base position for Brock. With the Dodgers he always batted for a low average, but averaged 18 homers a year from 1983 to 1986. The Brewers would have gladly settled for figures like that. But in four years with Milwaukee, Brock has averaged only 10 dingers per year, including just seven in 1990.

Brock is a line-drive hitter who will pull almost everything from lefthanders but will go to left center against righties. Brock likes the ball over the plate and up in the strike zone and has always had problems handling inside pitches.

Although Brock held his own against lefthanders in 1989, lefties have generally given him big problems; last year he slumped to a .209 mark against them. Brock's weakness against southpaws has kept him from becoming the hitting star he was projected to be.

BASERUNNING:

Brock is not blessed with speed and is rarely a threat to run. When he does, he picks the right spots and has a high success rate. He was successful in four of six attempts during the 1990 season. Because of his lack of speed, he can clog up the bases and is only a threat to go from first to third on balls which an outfielder has to run down.

FIELDING:

Brock is an excellent defensive first baseman who has good hands and a strong arm. He does a good job of digging throws out of the dirt and coming off the bag for an errant throw.

OVERALL:

Brock asked to be traded when he lost his starting position to Paul Molitor, but he doesn't have a lot of value on the trading market. He plays a power position and doesn't supply much power. With his problems against left-handed pitchers he is likely to spend the rest of his career as a platoon player.

Overall Statistics

	G	AB	R	H	D	T	HR	RBI	SB	BB	SO	AVG
1990	123	367	42	91	23	0	7	50	4	43	45	.248
Career	982	3142	411	777	137	6	109	456	40	420	460	.247

Where He Hits the Ball

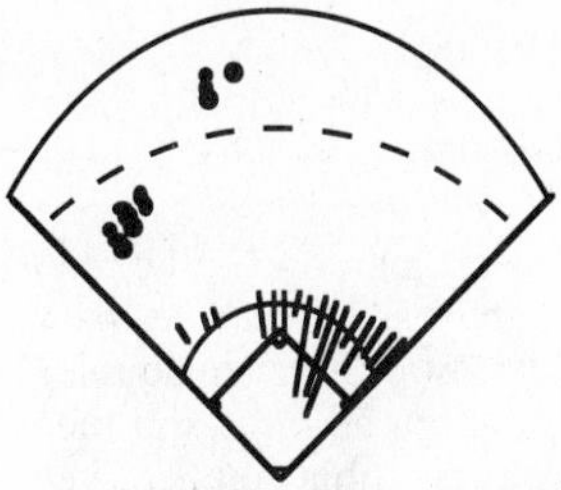

Vs. LHP

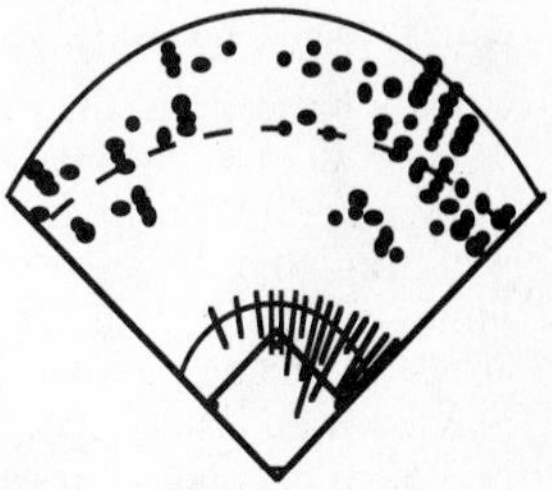

Vs. RHP

1990 Situational Stats

	AB	H	HR	RBI	AVG		AB	H	HR	RBI	AVG
Home	176	42	3	28	.239	LHP	86	18	2	17	.209
Road	191	49	4	22	.257	RHP	281	73	5	33	.260
Day	125	35	4	18	.280	Sc Pos	98	24	1	41	.245
Night	242	56	3	32	.231	Clutch	58	11	1	7	.190

1990 Rankings (American League)

- 5th worst percentage of extra bases taken as a runner (28.3%)
- 8th in sacrifice flies (8)
- Led AL first basemen in lowest percentage of swings that missed (11.6%)

PITCHING:

Chuck Crim led the Brewers' pitching staff in appearances for the third straight year in 1990, but there weren't a lot of other similarities. As the team's set-up man, Crim has been the pitcher the Brewers have used to keep things in line until Dan Plesac could come in and finish up. But the entire bullpen had problems last season, Crim and Plesac included.

Crim was ineffective in the first half of the season, failing at a time when the team still had a chance in the East Division race. He had a 4.29 earned run average before the All-Star Game, and had given up 56 hits in 50.1 innings. Opposing batters hit .275 against him in that span. He was much improved in the last half of the season with a 2.29 ERA in 27 games. Part of his earlier difficulties could be traced to a shoulder problem that forced him to go on the disabled list at midseason; it was the first time in his career he had been disabled.

Crim is basically a sinker/slider pitcher, although he will throw an occasional curve. He does not throw a change-up. He doesn't try to strike out a lot of hitters, preferring to use his sinker to get a ground ball or an inning-ending double play. In past seasons he has done that, but he was able to throw only seven double play balls all last season. Although he throws in the mid-80's, his biggest asset has been his competitive nature. He likes to pitch and challenges hitters.

He held left-handed hitters to a .252 batting average in 1990, but righthanders batted .267 against him. That statistic is crucial since a right-handed hitter is normally the first one he faces when he relieves.

HOLDING RUNNERS AND FIELDING:

Crim has good control when he pitches, but not when he throws to first base after fielding a ground ball. He has no problems covering his position or fielding a ball, but has a tendency to throw the ball away too often. His pickoff move is only average, so he throws to first a lot to keep the runners honest.

OVERALL:

A workhouse such as Crim is an important part of the bullpen when he is pitching well. In the last half of the season, he appeared to have regained his effectiveness and his confidence. It's possible that the wear and tear from pitching so often in his first three seasons caused the shoulder problem that contributed to his bad first half.

CHUCK CRIM

Position: RP
Bats: R **Throws:** R
Ht: 6' 0" **Wt:** 185

Opening Day Age: 29
Born: 7/23/61 in Van Nuys, CA
ML Seasons: 4

Overall Statistics

	W	L	ERA	G	GS	Sv	IP	H	R	BB	SO	HR
1990	3	5	3.47	67	0	11	85.2	88	39	23	39	7
Career	25	26	3.22	266	5	39	438.1	430	179	126	212	40

How Often He Throws Strikes

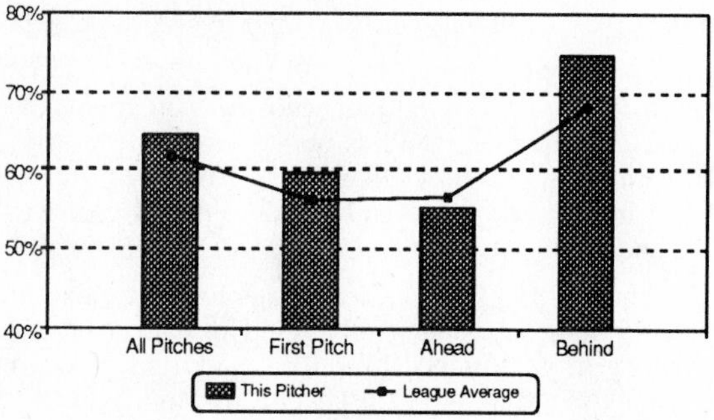

1990 Situational Stats

	W	L	ERA	Sv	IP		AB	H	HR	RBI	AVG
Home	0	3	3.10	6	40.2	LHB	131	33	1	15	.252
Road	3	2	3.80	5	45.0	RHB	206	55	6	26	.267
Day	0	2	2.63	2	24.0	Sc Pos	83	26	3	36	.313
Night	3	3	3.79	9	61.2	Clutch	219	55	5	27	.251

1990 Rankings (American League)

- 3rd in holds (19)
- 7th in games pitched (67)
- Led the Brewers in games pitched and holds

HITTING:

The 1990 season was a frustrating experience for Rob Deer. He led the Brewers in home runs for the fifth consecutive year, but he also spent more time on the bench than he liked. The reason for the frequent benchings was obvious to everyone except Deer, who complained about his lack of playing time. When you don't hit, you don't play. Righthanders continue to give Deer a lot of problems. He batted only .170 against them, and though he hit over .290 against lefties, Deer's overall average was only .209, his lowest mark since coming to Milwaukee in 1986.

Deer is a classic power hitter. He hits home runs in bunches, then cools off for long periods of time. But when he's hot, he's hot. The big right-handed hitter is strong and will hit the ball a long, long way when he connects. Too often, however, he doesn't connect. He led the team with 147 strikeouts -- the fifth straight time he has led in that category. Although he hit 27 home runs, he drove in only 69 runs, which points out his inability to hit in the clutch. He batted .218 with runners in scoring position and .233 in late-inning clutch situations.

Deer is a big swinger who tries to pull everything. He won't go to the opposite field. He is vulnerable to the high fastball, a pitch that he will often foul off. Although he has become a little more disciplined than in previous seasons, he will still chase a breaking ball thrown low and away.

BASERUNNING:

Though Deer has good speed for a big man and won't make a lot of mistakes on the base paths, he isn't a big threat to run. He's an aggressive player and will slide hard to break up a double play.

FIELDING:

Deer's defense may be the most consistent part of his game. Although he will often momentarily misjudge a ball, his hustle will make up for it and he will still make the play. So what if it isn't always pretty? He will crash into a fence or dive face first into the warning track to catch a ball. He has a strong, accurate arm, and runners won't take too many liberties with him.

OVERALL:

Deer was a free agent at season's end, and it might be best for him to get away from Milwaukee. Coaches and scouts like the way he plays hard all the time. He is, and always will be, a low average, high-strikeout hitter. But he's averaged 27 homers a year for the last five seasons, and that's bound to interest somebody.

ROB DEER

Position: RF/1B
Bats: R **Throws:** R
Ht: 6' 3" **Wt:** 210

Opening Day Age: 30
Born: 9/29/60 in Orange, CA
ML Seasons: 7

Overall Statistics

	G	AB	R	H	D	T	HR	RBI	SB	BB	SO	AVG
1990	134	440	57	92	15	1	27	69	2	64	147	.209
Career	758	2524	373	569	94	9	148	408	33	363	904	.225

Where He Hits the Ball

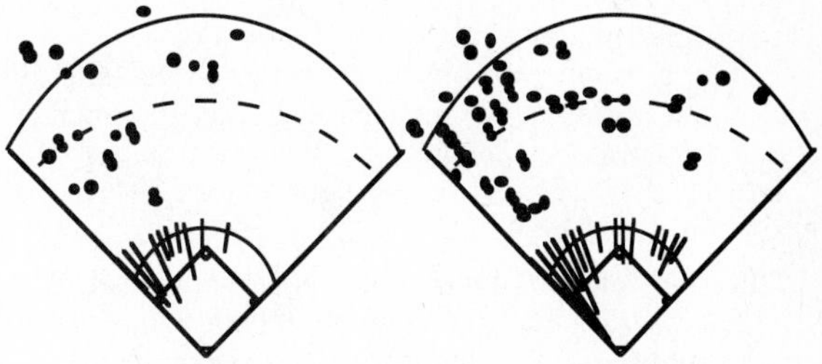

Vs. LHP   Vs. RHP

1990 Situational Stats

	AB	H	HR	RBI	AVG		AB	H	HR	RBI	AVG
Home	214	40	11	30	.187	LHP	140	41	16	34	.293
Road	226	52	16	39	.230	RHP	300	51	11	35	.170
Day	137	22	5	16	.161	Sc Pos	110	24	10	44	.218
Night	303	70	22	53	.231	Clutch	73	17	4	11	.233

1990 Rankings (American League)

- 1st in lowest batting average (.209), lowest batting average at home (.187) and least GDPs per GDP situation (0.0%)
- 2nd lowest groundball/flyball ratio (.542)
- 3rd highest slugging percentage vs. left-handed pitchers (.671)
- 5th in HR frequency (16.3 ABs per HR) and most pitches seen per plate appearance (4.12)
- Led the Brewers in home runs (27), strikeouts (147), HR frequency, pitches seen per plate appearance, least GDPs per GDP situation and batting average (.293)/slugging percentage/on-base average (.399) vs. left-handed pitchers

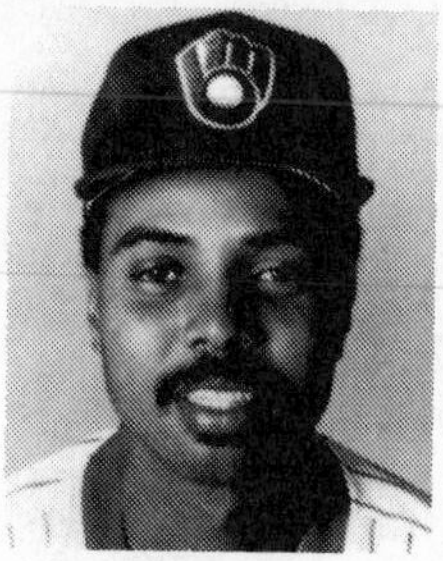

EDGAR DIAZ

Position: SS
Bats: R **Throws:** R
Ht: 6' 0" **Wt:** 160

Opening Day Age: 27
Born: 2/8/64 in Santurce, Puerto Rico
ML Seasons: 2

HITTING:

Edgar Diaz was supposed to be the Brewers' starting shortstop in 1987. At the time, he was only 23 and, coming off a .315 season at AAA Vancouver, looked to be one of Milwaukee's best prospects. But then the baseball fates interceded. After winning the shortstop job in spring training, Diaz dislocated his shoulder in an exhibition game. It took him three years to make it back to the major leagues.

When Diaz finally returned last year, it was as a utility infielder, not as a starter. In the minor leagues, Diaz earned the reputation as a defensive specialist whose hitting was suspect. His performance in his rookie year was just the opposite. While having problems defensively, Diaz batted a respectable .271 in 86 games.

Diaz is a slap hitter who makes good contact and pokes the ball to the opposite field. He is strictly a singles hitter. In eight seasons in the minor leagues, he hit only one home run, 18 triples and 44 doubles. His power didn't improve against big-league pitching. Diaz had two doubles and two triples in his 59 hits. He hit fairly well against both lefties (.284) and righties (.260).

Diaz' low total of 14 runs batted in reflected his lack of success in clutch situations. He batted just .138 with runners in scoring position and .143 in late-inning clutch situations. He was very successful with the bases loaded, however, batting .429.

BASERUNNING:

Diaz has stolen as many as 21 bases in the minors, but he's never been a big base thief. With the Brewers last year, he was fairly cautious, swiping three in five attempts. He has the potential to do a little better, but stealing is not a big part of his game. Diaz is fairly fast on the bases, but not very aggressive.

FIELDING:

Diaz made 17 errors in 1990, a lot for a part-time player who is supposed to be a defensive specialist. Still, he has outstanding range and a strong arm, and will make some unbelievable plays. His defensive problems could have been the result of rookie jitters.

OVERALL:

Don't be fooled by his defensive problems last season; Diaz has the ability to play much better. He could be a starting shortstop for a team that needs someone to play defense and not supply a lot of offense. Although the Brewers used him at second base at times, shortstop is his best position. He will likely be a utility player for Milwaukee once again.

Overall Statistics

	G	AB	R	H	D	T	HR	RBI	SB	BB	SO	AVG
1990	86	218	27	59	2	2	0	14	3	21	32	.271
Career	91	231	27	62	2	2	0	14	3	22	35	.268

Where He Hits the Ball

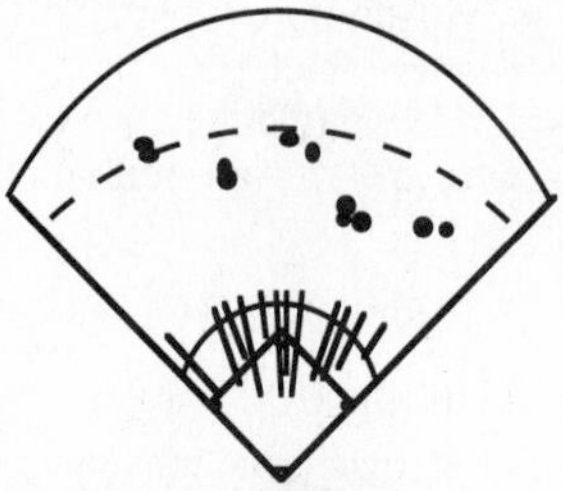

Vs. LHP

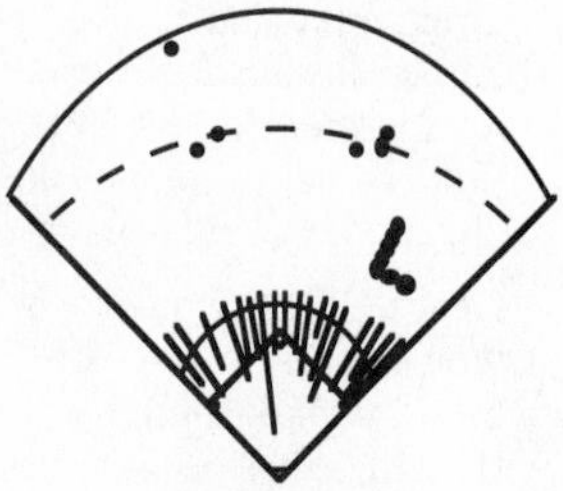

Vs. RHP

1990 Situational Stats

	AB	H	HR	RBI	AVG		AB	H	HR	RBI	AVG
Home	102	28	0	4	.275	LHP	95	27	0	2	.284
Road	116	31	0	10	.267	RHP	123	32	0	12	.260
Day	80	21	0	2	.262	Sc Pos	58	8	0	13	.138
Night	138	38	0	12	.275	Clutch	21	3	0	0	.143

1990 Rankings (American League)

- Did not rank near the top or bottom in any category

MIKE FELDER

Position: LF/CF/RF
Bats: B **Throws:** R
Ht: 5' 8" **Wt:** 160

Opening Day Age: 28
Born: 11/18/62 in Vallejo, CA
ML Seasons: 6

Overall Statistics

	G	AB	R	H	D	T	HR	RBI	SB	BB	SO	AVG
1990	121	237	38	65	7	2	3	27	20	22	17	.274
Career	455	1133	182	280	27	16	9	99	108	91	111	.247

Where He Hits the Ball

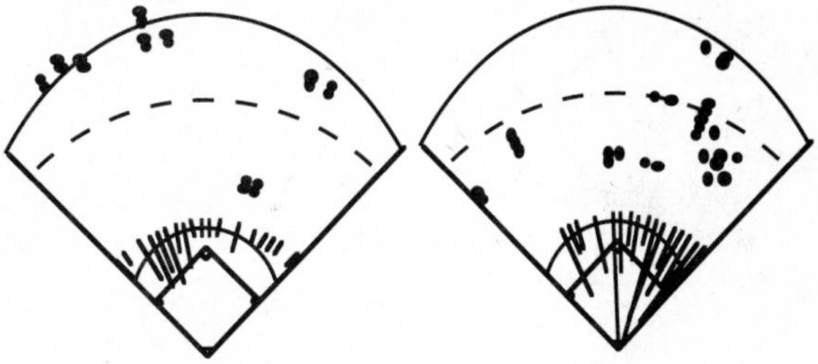

Vs. LHP **Vs. RHP**

1990 Situational Stats

	AB	H	HR	RBI	AVG		AB	H	HR	RBI	AVG
Home	110	29	1	10	.264	LHP	80	22	3	14	.275
Road	127	36	2	17	.283	RHP	157	43	0	13	.274
Day	87	21	2	6	.241	Sc Pos	68	19	0	23	.279
Night	150	44	1	21	.293	Clutch	50	13	0	8	.260

1990 Rankings (American League)

- 2nd in percentage of extra bases taken as a runner (61.5%)
- 9th in bunts in play (22)
- Led the Brewers in sacrifice bunts (8), bunts in play and percnetage of extra bases taken as a runner
- Led AL left fielders in bunts in play and percentage of extra bases taken as a runner

HITTING:

Mike Felder is strong for a little guy, but not strong enough to be swinging for the fences. When he remembers that, he can be an effective hitter. Felder's greatest asset is his speed, and he is learning to take advantage of it by bunting more and trying to hit the ball on the ground. Last year Felder batted .274, the highest average of his six-year career.

Felder was turned into a switch-hitter while he was in the minor leagues, and he had trouble getting used to batting left-handed. Apparently he's gotten the hang of it. He batted .275 right-handed and .274 left-handed in 1990. Felder is a contact hitter who doesn't strike out a lot. He should draw a lot of walks because of his size, but he doesn't show enough patience at the plate.

Because Felder gets the bat on the ball, he is adept at the hit-and-run. He will bunt a lot, and will often beat one out for a base hit when he is attempting to sacrifice. Although driving in runs isn't a big part of his game, he hit well in the clutch, batting .279 with runners in scoring position. Felder, who would be a big asset for a team that played its home games on artificial turf, had most of his success on the road, batting .283.

BASERUNNING:

Baserunning is Felder's specialty. He is often used as a pinch runner, especially when a stolen base is needed. Even when it's an obvious running situation, he's hard to throw out. Because of his speed, he will take chances on the base paths, challenging even the strongest arms. He is fast enough to be successful on most of those challenges.

FIELDING:

Defense is another one of Felder's specialties. He is used frequently as a defensive replacement. He can play all three outfield positions and play them well. Because of his great speed, he can run down almost anything. He has a strong, but sometimes erratic, arm. Felder was originally a second baseman and has been used there on occasion the last couple of seasons. He does an adequate job in the infield but has to learn how to turn a double play.

OVERALL:

Felder would like to play every day, but is probably more valuable on the bench because of his specialized talents. It's nice to have someone available to replace a slow runner on first base in a critical situation in the late innings.

JIM GANTNER

Position: 2B
Bats: L **Throws:** R
Ht: 5'11" **Wt:** 175
Opening Day Age: 37
Born: 1/5/54 in Eden, WI
ML Seasons: 15

<u>HITTING:</u>

Jim Gantner didn't hit a home run in 1990, which shouldn't surprise anyone. Gantner has now gone 1,395 at-bats without hitting a four bagger. The big surprise was that Gantner played at all. The scrappy second baseman suffered a career-threatening knee injury late in the 1989 season, and a lot of people didn't expect him to be back, especially at age 36. But Gantner underwent extensive surgery and was back in the lineup by mid-season. It was the same old Gantner, a pesky hitter and a hard-nosed player who has been the Brewers' on-field leader for years.

Gantner is a contact hitter who bats from a slight crouch with his weight on his back foot. Although he normally bats in the bottom of the batting order, he's been used successfully as a number-two hitter, especially against righthanders. Gantner hits to all fields but sometimes to tries to pull the ball too much, especially against righties. Gantner goes to the plate with the idea of swinging a bat. He doesn't walk very often, but doesn't strike out much, either. Pitchers can get him to chase balls high in the strike zone.

In 1990, Gantner batted over .300 against lefthanders and under .250 against righthanders, though for most of his career he has had equal success against righties and lefties. Gantner has never been a big RBI man and drove in only 25 runs last season, his lowest total since 1979.

<u>BASERUNNING:</u>

Despite the fact that he has undergone knee surgery three times in his career, Gantner still has good speed. He never ran a lot until the last three seasons, but since 1988 he's stolen 58 bases, including 18 in 21 attempts last year. He runs hard and slides hard. He isn't very big, but he isn't timid about barreling into someone twice his size.

<u>FIELDING:</u>

The Brewers, whose defense isn't great to begin with, suffer when Gantner isn't playing second base. Despite his age and his knee problems, he will hang in there as well as any second baseman to turn the double play. He has quick hands and a strong arm. His range is limited, but he's a smart player who knows how to play the hitter. Gantner originally was a third baseman and can play that position very well.

<u>OVERALL:</u>

Despite his age and knee problems, Gantner proved that he was still a valuable member of the Brewers last year. Although he won't be guaranteed a starting position when he reports to spring training in 1991, look for him to be the Brewers' second baseman on opening day.

Overall Statistics

	G	AB	R	H	D	T	HR	RBI	SB	BB	SO	AVG
1990	88	323	36	85	8	5	0	25	18	29	19	.263
Career	1560	5407	641	1484	223	33	44	503	127	344	450	.274

Where He Hits the Ball

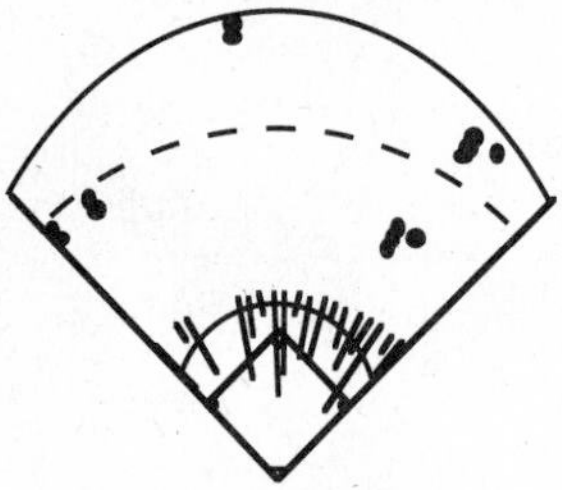

Vs. LHP

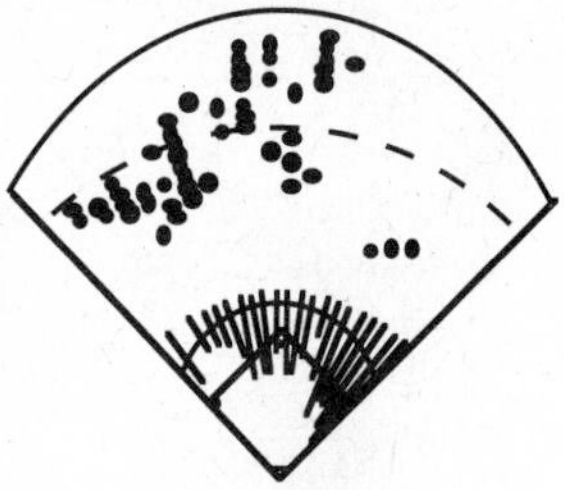

Vs. RHP

1990 Situational Stats

	AB	H	HR	RBI	AVG		AB	H	HR	RBI	AVG
Home	158	44	0	12	.278	LHP	88	27	0	9	.307
Road	165	41	0	13	.248	RHP	235	58	0	16	.247
Day	81	23	0	11	.284	Sc Pos	76	18	0	25	.237
Night	242	62	0	14	.256	Clutch	48	10	0	5	.208

1990 Rankings (American League)

- 3rd in stolen base percentage (85.7%)
- Led the Brewers in stolen base percentage
- Led AL second basemen in stolen base percentage

PITCHING:

For two straight seasons Teddy Higuera has been plagued with various injuries (back, ankle, hamstring, knee), and his reputation as the American League's best lefty has taken a beating. After averaging 17 wins a year in his first four seasons (1985-88), Higuera averaged only ten victories in 1989 and '90. His ERA has climbed from 2.45 in 1988 to 3.76 last year.

Last year Higuera pitched in only 27 games, and in eight of those starts he didn't last past the fifth inning. That's not the real Teddy Higuera. A healthy Higuera will be among the league leaders in innings pitched and complete games as well as strikeouts and victories. Higuera showed flashes of his old form last year, but he wasn't consistent. In most of his starts he had problems putting two good innings together. Going into the season, he had a lifetime record of 46-17 after the All-Star break. But last year he was 5-8 with a 4.75 earned run average in the second half.

The veteran lefthander throws a fastball in the high 80s and a nasty slider. He will also mix in an occasional curve, but his best pitch when he's throwing well is a super change-up that has been clocked as slow as 58-60 MPH. He mixes his speeds well and keeps the hitters off balance. He has excellent control and will often throw a breaking ball on a 3-2 count.

When he's healthy, Higuera will be tough on both lefthanders and righthanders. Higuera is aggressive and loves to pitch, but his temperament can cause problems. He has been known to lose his composure when he gets angry. When he does that, he also loses his effectiveness.

HOLDING RUNNERS AND FIELDING:

Higuera is one of the best at fielding his position. He has cat-like quickness off the mound and good instincts. During spring training he is as serious about the defensive drills as he would be if he was pitching in the seventh game of the World Series. One part of his defensive game that could use some improvement is his pickoff move. Fifteen of 19 runners were successful stealing against him last season.

OVERALL:

After being plagued by injuries for two straight seasons, there is reason for doubt about Higuera's future. Since he is eligible for free agency, the Brewers are left with a big decision. He would command big money as a free agent because of his past success, but how high do you want to bid to keep a pitcher that has just completed two injury-filled seasons? He's only 32, however, and may be worth a gamble.

TED HIGUERA

Position: SP
Bats: B **Throws:** L
Ht: 5'10" **Wt:** 180

Opening Day Age: 32
Born: 11/9/58 in Los Mochis, Mexico
ML Seasons: 6

Overall Statistics

	W	L	ERA	G	GS	Sv	IP	H	R	BB	SO	HR
1990	11	10	3.76	27	27	0	170.0	167	80	50	129	16
Career	89	54	3.34	181	179	0	1255.0	1108	511	381	986	112

How Often He Throws Strikes

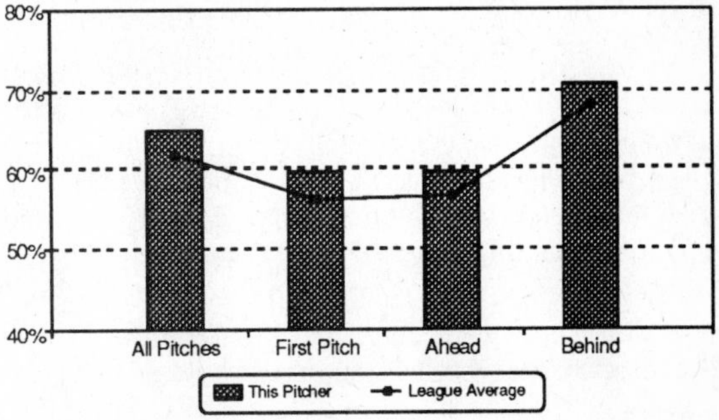

1990 Situational Stats

	W	L	ERA	Sv	IP		AB	H	HR	RBI	AVG
Home	7	4	3.36	0	96.1	LHB	126	31	1	12	.246
Road	4	6	4.28	0	73.2	RHB	527	136	15	61	.258
Day	2	3	2.66	0	47.1	Sc Pos	139	40	1	49	.288
Night	9	7	4.18	0	122.2	Clutch	76	19	1	5	.250

1990 Rankings (American League)

- 2nd in lowest groundball/flyball ratio (.813)
- 5th highest strikeout/walk ratio (2.6)
- 6th worst stolen base percentage allowed (78.9%)
- Led the Brewers in ERA (3.76), losses (10), games started (27), innings (170.0), batters faced (720), home runs allowed (16), strikeouts (129), pitches thrown (2,562), stolen bases allowed (15), strikeout/walks ratio and strikeouts per 9 innings (6.8)

PITCHING:

When injuries depleted the Milwaukee pitching staff, it appeared for a while as if Mark Knudson was going to be the Brewers' biggest winner. A shoulder problem of his own kept that from happening, and Knudson didn't last past the fourth inning in his last three starts. He missed his last three turns because of tendinitis in his shoulder, but Knudson did end up with 10 victories, third on the staff and just two fewer than Ron Robinson's leading total.

Despite the weak finish, it was Knudson's second straight successful season. The righthander had gone 8-5, 3.35 over 40 games in 1989, when he was used mainly as a reliever. Knudson's ERA (4.12) was up last year, but he set career marks in wins (10), innings (168.1), games started (27), complete games (four) and shutouts (two).

Knudson, who came to Milwaukee in the Danny Darwin deal back in 1986, isn't overpowering, but he can be effective if he sinks his fastball. He did that and was the most consistent pitcher on the Brewers' staff for the most of the season. He mixes his sinking fastball with an effective slider and an occasional curve. He does not throw a change-up. If he could develop one, he might be an even more effective pitcher.

Knudson has good control and will usually be around the plate. He won't walk many, yielding only 2.1 walks per nine innings last year, but he will give up a lot of hits (.282 opponents' average). He also has a tendency to give up home runs. Last year, he yielded 14 of them, third most on the team.

HOLDING RUNNERS AND FIELDING:

Knudson is a good athlete and fields his position very well. His delivery leaves him in a good position to field balls back to the mound, and he gets over to first base quickly on ground balls to the right side of the infield. He has an adequate pickoff move and will throw to first base a lot.

OVERALL:

Although he was the Brewers' best pitcher for a while last season, Knudson isn't likely to become the ace of anybody's staff. He can do a very good job as a dependable fourth of fifth starter, however. He also has been used in long relief, and although he prefers a starting role, his versatility is a great asset and should help lengthen his career. He's a good insurance policy on a club that has a lot of pitching question marks.

MARK KNUDSON

Position: SP
Bats: R **Throws:** R
Ht: 6' 5" **Wt:** 215

Opening Day Age: 30
Born: 10/28/60 in Denver, CO
ML Seasons: 6

Overall Statistics

	W	L	ERA	G	GS	Sv	IP	H	R	BB	SO	HR
1990	10	9	4.12	30	27	0	168.1	187	84	40	56	14
Career	23	26	4.24	105	52	0	441.1	493	232	108	169	49

How Often He Throws Strikes

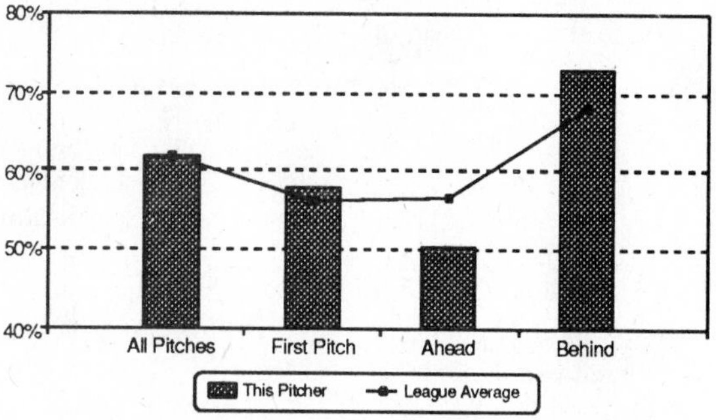

1990 Situational Stats

	W	L	ERA	Sv	IP		AB	H	HR	RBI	AVG
Home	5	3	3.55	0	78.2	LHB	340	95	6	29	.279
Road	5	6	4.62	0	89.2	RHB	324	92	8	39	.284
Day	4	4	4.86	0	63.0	Sc Pos	151	38	1	52	.252
Night	6	5	3.67	0	105.1	Clutch	54	14	0	3	.259

1990 Rankings (American League)

- 1st in least strikeouts per 9 innings (3.0)
- 4th in lowest strikeout/walk ratio (1.4) and highest batting average allowed (.282)
- 6th in shutouts (2) and highest slugging percentage allowed (.419)
- Led the Brewers in games started (27), shutouts, hits allowed (187), runners caught stealing (9), GDPs induced (16), highest groundball/flyball ratio (1.18), lowest stolen base percentage allowed (47.1%) and least HRs per 9 innings (.75)

JULIO MACHADO

Position: RP
Bats: R **Throws:** R
Ht: 5' 9" **Wt:** 160

Opening Day Age: 25
Born: 12/1/65 in Zulia, Venezuela
ML Seasons: 2

PITCHING:

Julio Machado, who was obtained from the New York Mets late last season, made an impressive debut with the Brewers. He joined them in September and had a 0.69 earned run average and three saves in 10 relief appearances. Opponents batted just .191 against him, and he struck out 12 in 13 innings of work.

Although he's only 25, Machado has been around. He pitched for a long time in the Phillies system, but was released in the spring of '89. The Mets signed him and Machado moved up fast, working his way from Class A to New York by the end of the year. He struck out 133 batters in 111.1 innings while playing for five different teams at every level of professional baseball. The Mets used him in middle relief for most of 1990, but felt Machado was unreliable with men on base. Eager to land catcher Charlie O'Brien from Milwaukee, they included Machado in the package.

Like a lot of hard throwers, Machado has had some control problems, especially when he was in the lower minor leagues. That continued in 1990 as he walked 25 batters in 47.1 innings. However, he looked tough against left-handed hitters, who were 0 for 14 against him in the American League. By the end of the season Manager Tom Trebelhorn was using Machado as his closer instead of the struggling Dan Plesac.

Machado has an unorthodox herky-jerky delivery that uses a lot of arm movement. Because he isn't likely to go through the lineup more than one time, hitters will have difficulty adjusting to his pitches. He's a two-pitch pitcher, throwing a fastball that reaches the low 90s, and a good slider. Scouts like him because he comes right in and challenges the hitters.

HOLDING RUNNERS AND FIELDING:

Machado has good reflexes and moves well off the mound. One observer said he moves like a cat. He has a good move to first, but doesn't throw there very often. In his brief stay with the Brewers, no runners attempted to steal against him, but he was in most games at a time when an errant baserunner would take the opposition out of the game.

OVERALL:

Machado all but assured himself a spot on the team with his performance after joining the Brewers. His ability to get out a tough left-handed hitter makes him a valuable guy to have around. His role in 1991 likely will be as a set-up man for closer Dan Plesac, but he showed the ability to move into that spot himself if Plesac struggles again. He appears to have the ability and the makeup to be an excellent closer in the not-too- distant future.

Overall Statistics

	W	L	ERA	G	GS	Sv	IP	H	R	BB	SO	HR
1990	4	1	2.47	37	0	3	47.1	41	14	25	39	4
Career	4	2	2.62	47	0	3	58.1	50	18	28	53	4

How Often He Throws Strikes

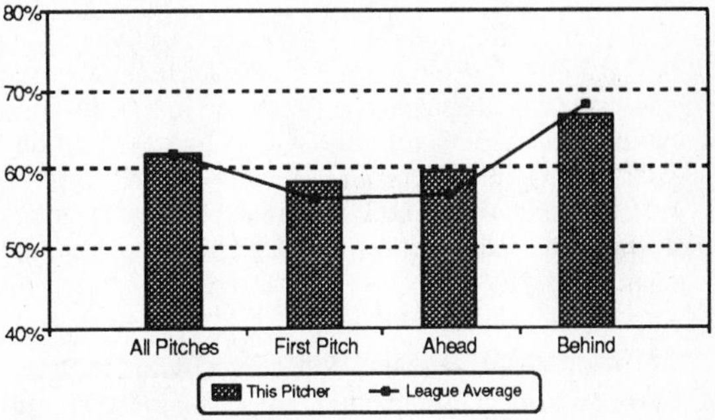

1990 Situational Stats

	W	L	ERA	Sv	IP		AB	H	HR	RBI	AVG
Home	1	0	0.86	2	21.0	LHB	77	15	1	11	.195
Road	3	1	3.76	1	26.1	RHB	99	26	3	15	.263
Day	1	1	2.35	1	15.1	Sc Pos	55	13	1	22	.236
Night	3	0	2.53	2	32.0	Clutch	52	16	1	12	.308

1990 Rankings (American League)

- 1st in lowest percentage of GDPs induced per GDP situation (0.0%)

PAUL MIRABELLA

Position: RP
Bats: L **Throws:** L
Ht: 6' 2" **Wt:** 185

Opening Day Age: 37
Born: 3/20/54 in Belleville, NJ
ML Seasons: 13

PITCHING:

Paul Mirabella is a well-travelled veteran who has lasted 13 seasons as a reliever, despite compiling a lifetime ERA of 4.45 and averaging exactly one save per year. With modest talent like Mirabella's, it helps to be left-handed, but it helps even more to keep your bags continually packed.

Mirabella has been assured of a spot on the opening-day roster only once in his career. That was after the 1988 season, when he had the finest performance of his career (1.65 ERA). So what happened? He injured his shoulder, the first injury of his long career, and spent most of the 1989 season on the disabled list. Now Mirabella is back to having to prove himself every spring. Somehow he keeps bouncing back. And he has done a lot of bouncing. He has pitched for six teams in the major leagues, and his career record reads like an Atlas.

Although he has been used as a starter, Mirabella is best suited for a role in middle relief. He is effective against lefthanders and often comes in to face just one batter. Lefthanders batted just .235 against him last year, but righthanders hit .299. He throws a good sinking fastball that he likes to keep under 86 miles an hour and also throws a slider and an occasional change-up. His control is good, and hitters can expect the ball to be around the plate.

Mirabella spent the entire 1990 season with the Brewers but was used infrequently, especially in the second half of the season. He pitched 49.2 innings in 24 games, compiling a 2-2 record and 3.93 earned run average before the All-Star break. He pitched in 20 games and compiled a 2-0 record in the second half but was only used in short stints to pitch to a batter or two.

HOLDING RUNNERS AND FIELDING:

As a veteran, Mirabella has developed good skills and won't embarrass himself fundamentally. He gets over to first base on ground balls to the right of the infield and always backs up the right base. His pickoff move isn't above average but being left-handed and facing first base keeps runners honest.

OVERALL:

Mirabella will be 37 years old when the 1991 season starts, and his career is nearing an end. He might be able to hang on another year or two simply because left-handed pitchers are always in demand. He is a hard worker and has learned how to pitch over the years, but has done little to distinguish himself.

Overall Statistics

	W	L	ERA	G	GS	Sv	IP	H	R	BB	SO	HR
1990	4	2	3.97	44	2	0	59.0	66	32	27	28	9
Career	19	29	4.45	298	33	13	500.0	526	284	239	258	43

How Often He Throws Strikes

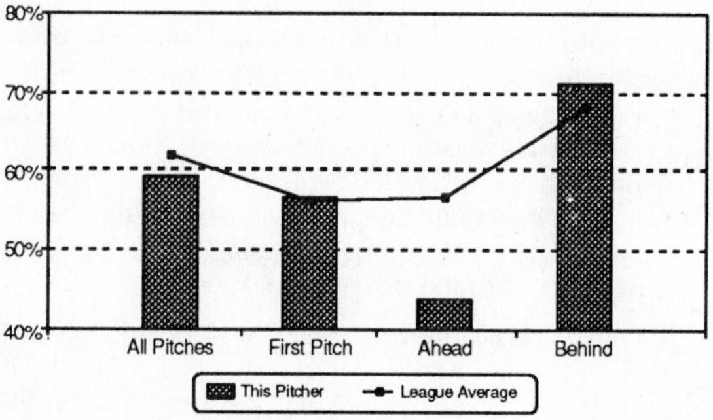

1990 Situational Stats

	W	L	ERA	Sv	IP		AB	H	HR	RBI	AVG
Home	2	1	3.72	0	29.0	LHB	68	16	0	8	.235
Road	2	1	4.20	0	30.0	RHB	167	50	9	30	.299
Day	3	2	3.68	0	29.1	Sc Pos	68	21	3	31	.309
Night	1	0	4.25	0	29.2	Clutch	37	8	1	1	.216

1990 Rankings (American League)

- 5th in worst first batter efficiency (.324)

HITTING:

The Brewers need Paul Molitor in their lineup to be successful. For injury-prone Molitor, that has been the big problem throughout his career. In 1990, after staying healthy for two straight seasons for only the second time in his career, Molitor was sidelined three times by three different injuries. He ended up playing in only 103 games, his fewest since 1984. The final injury, to his shoulder, resulted in a position switch to first base. The shoulder problem obviously affected Molitor's swing, dropping his average below .300 by the end of the season.

Molitor is an excellent leadoff hitter who bats from a slightly closed stance and uses the whole field. Although he doesn't have great power, he will hit 10-15 homers a season. He is the team's best bunter and has excellent speed -- he will often bunt for a base hit. Infielders on the corners have to be ready for the bunt.

Unlike a lot of leadoff hitters, Molitor goes to the plate with the idea of swinging a bat. He's a selective hitter but doesn't draw a lot of walks. He is always looking for a fastball on the first pitch and can be fooled by starting him out with a hard breaking ball. He will also chase fastballs high in the strike zone. Although Molitor has been one of the best hitters in baseball for years, he has never been a big run producer and has struggled in clutch situations. With Manager Tom Trebelhorn using him as a number three hitter on occasion, Molitor has improved greatly in the clutch. He batted .313 with runners in scoring position in 1990.

BASERUNNING:

The speedy Molitor is always a threat to run, and is a smart baserunner who has a high success rate. He is extremely alert and is always a threat to turn a single into a double. He has a knack for manufacturing runs.

FIELDING:

Because of his shoulder problems, Molitor ended up switching positions again in the last half of the season. This time, he was at first base, leaving pitching and catching the only positions he hasn't played regularly in the major leagues. Given his recent shoulder problems, it wouldn't be surprising to see him finish his career as a first baseman. A great athlete, he should eventually become a good fielder at the position.

OVERALL:

If it hadn't been for all of the injuries that have plagued him throughout his career, Molitor probably would be considered a leading candidate for the Hall of Fame. He is still an outstanding player and a frequent All-Star who always plays hard and contributes a lot.

PAUL MOLITOR

Position: 2B/1B
Bats: R **Throws:** R
Ht: 6' 0" **Wt:** 185

Opening Day Age: 34
Born: 8/22/56 in St. Paul, MN
ML Seasons: 13

Overall Statistics

	G	AB	R	H	D	T	HR	RBI	SB	BB	SO	AVG
1990	103	418	64	119	27	6	12	45	18	37	51	.285
Career	1540	6246	1053	1870	337	66	131	626	362	605	754	.299

Where He Hits the Ball

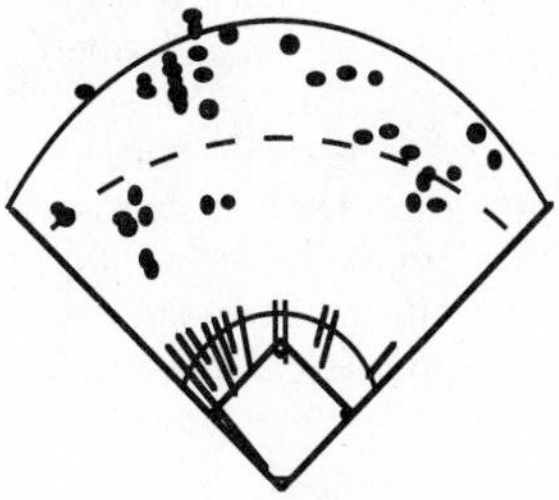

Vs. LHP

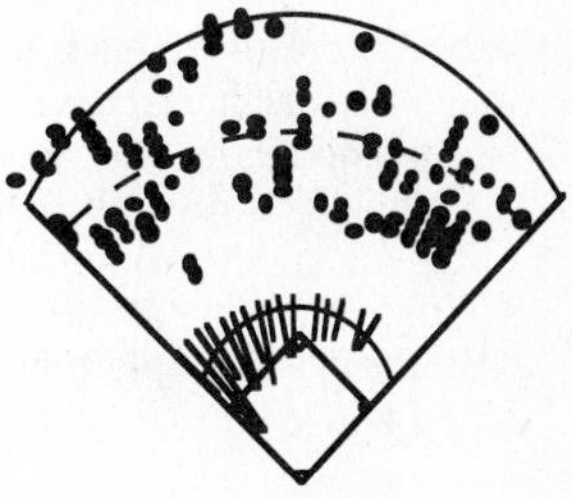

Vs. RHP

1990 Situational Stats

	AB	H	HR	RBI	AVG		AB	H	HR	RBI	AVG
Home	185	53	6	19	.286	LHP	112	35	5	14	.313
Road	233	66	6	26	.283	RHP	306	84	7	31	.275
Day	112	32	6	16	.286	Sc Pos	80	25	1	30	.313
Night	306	87	6	29	.284	Clutch	51	10	2	7	.196

1990 Rankings (American League)

- 3rd in stolen base percentage (85.7%)
- 7th in steals of third (5)
- Led the Brewers in triples (6), stolen base percentage and steals of third
- Led AL second basemen in stolen base percentage and batting average with runners in scoring position (.313)

JAIME NAVARRO

Position: SP/RP
Bats: R **Throws:** R
Ht: 6' 4" **Wt:** 210

Opening Day Age: 24
Born: 3/27/67 in Bayamon, Puerto Rico
ML Seasons: 2

Overall Statistics

	W	L	ERA	G	GS	Sv	IP	H	R	BB	SO	HR
1990	8	7	4.46	32	22	1	149.1	176	83	41	75	11
Career	15	15	3.89	51	39	1	259.0	295	130	73	131	17

How Often He Throws Strikes

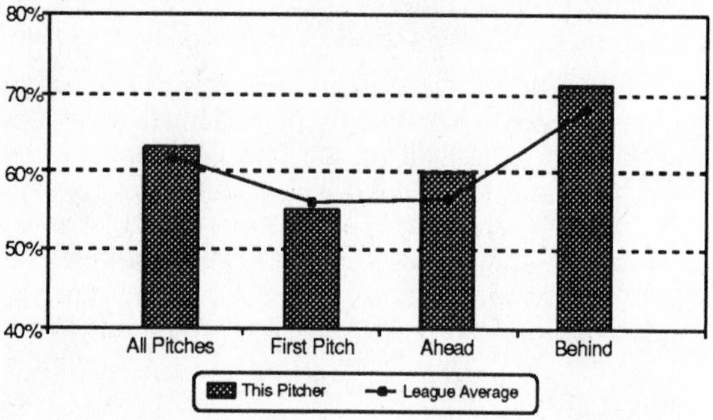

1990 Situational Stats

	W	L	ERA	Sv	IP		AB	H	HR	RBI	AVG
Home	4	4	4.09	1	72.2	LHB	321	96	4	33	.299
Road	4	3	4.81	0	76.2	RHB	279	80	7	32	.287
Day	2	2	4.69	0	48.0	Sc Pos	153	42	2	48	.275
Night	6	5	4.35	1	101.1	Clutch	47	19	1	9	.404

1990 Rankings (American League)

- 1st in balks (5)
- Led the Brewers in balks

PITCHING:

After an impressive rookie season, Jaime Navarro opened in 1990 as the Brewers' number-three starter. It turned out to be an up-and-down season -- or to be more accurate, down-and-up. Navarro was a major disappointment early in the season and was shipped to the minor leagues twice. But when he was recalled the last time at midseason, the Brewers finally saw what they were looking for from their young righthander.

Navarro started to doubt himself when he was struggling earlier in the season, but regained his confidence with some effective pitching in long relief. In his final stint, he was used out of the bullpen at first and had a 1.50 earned run average in 10 relief appearances. When he went back into the rotation, he was 5-2 with a 2.73 ERA in his last eight starts.

That's the sort of pitching the Brewers have been expecting from the big righty, who's the son of former major league hurler Julio Navarro. Young Navarro has a good arm and an excellent fastball that he consistently throws in the low 90s. He also has an excellent slider which he developed in his rookie season. He needs to work on his change-up, which he only throws a couple times a game. He seems to be afraid to use it.

Navarro was hit hard before the All-Star break, giving up 70 hits in 49.2 innings. At that point, opposing batters were hitting a whopping .330 against him. He lowered that in the second half, but overall, his opponents hit .293. Though he had a winning record last year, he's going to find it tough to be successful if he continues to be so easy to hit.

HOLDING RUNNERS AND FIELDING:

Although he has good hands, Navarro is a big guy and doesn't move around very well when he's coming off the mound. He has trouble fielding bunts and slow rollers back to the mound. Navarro's move to first needs some work.

OVERALL:

Navarro has a great arm and should develop into an excellent pitcher, although he will have to develop his change-up or some other third pitch. Two-pitch pitchers aren't very effective in a starting rotation. One of his major problems was that he was rushed up from the minor leagues when injuries caused a pitching shortage for the Brewers. Navarro was only starting his third season in professional baseball in 1989, pitching in Class AA, but ended up in the major leagues by midseason as a 21-year-old rookie.

DAVE PARKER

Position: DH
Bats: L **Throws:** R
Ht: 6' 5" **Wt:** 245

Opening Day Age: 39
Born: 6/9/51 in Jackson, MS
ML Seasons: 18

Overall Statistics

	G	AB	R	H	D	T	HR	RBI	SB	BB	SO	AVG
1990	157	610	71	176	30	3	21	92	4	41	102	.289
Career	2334	8856	1225	2592	500	73	328	1434	151	650	1439	.293

Where He Hits the Ball

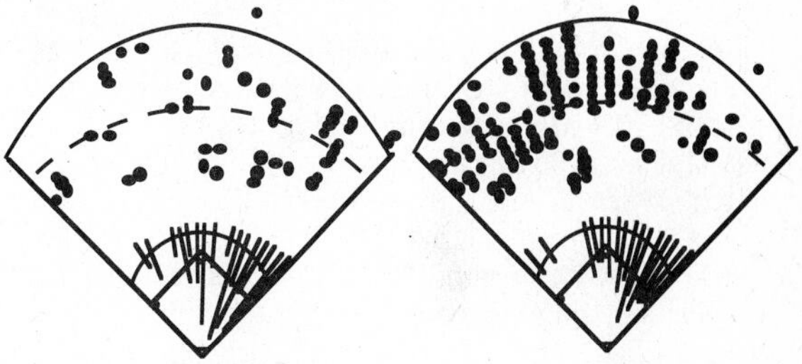

Vs. LHP   Vs. RHP

1990 Situational Stats

	AB	H	HR	RBI	AVG		AB	H	HR	RBI	AVG
Home	293	80	9	46	.273	LHP	185	48	6	24	.259
Road	317	96	12	46	.303	RHP	425	128	15	68	.301
Day	193	50	5	20	.259	Sc Pos	157	41	4	67	.261
Night	417	126	16	72	.302	Clutch	82	19	0	6	.232

1990 Rankings (American League)

- 1st in sacrifice flies (14)
- 3rd in lowest percentage of pitches taken (42.9%)
- 7th in at-bats (610), hits (176) and RBIs (92)
- 9th in total bases (275), intentional walks (11), least pitches seen per plate appearance (3.30), batting average vs. right-handed pitchers (.301) and slugging percentage vs. right-handed pitchers (.478)
- Led the Brewers in at-bats, hits, singles (122), doubles (30), total bases, RBIs, sacrifice flies, intentional walks, GDPs (18), slugging percentage (.451) and batting average/slugging average vs. right-handed pitchers

HITTING:

After passing up the free agent market for nine years, Brewers General Manager Harry Dalton finally went shopping last winter. He was looking for a left-handed hitter with some power, and he came back with Dave Parker, a 38-year-old designated hitter. It was a bargain. Although he isn't the dominating player he used to be because of age and chronic knee problems, Parker proved that he was still capable of hitting for a high average as well as driving in runs.

Parker certainly filled the Brewers' need. Despite a 3-for-44 slump at the end of the season that dropped his average to a final .289 after being over .300 all season, Parker led the team with 92 RBI and was second with 21 home runs. He is normally a pull hitter, although he will hit to all fields against righthanders. He can hit the ball a long way, and outfielders play him deep. He swings hard to generate power and is vulnerable to offspeed pitching and fastballs around the letters.

Despite his successful season, Parker's numbers in clutch situations weren't impressive. He batted only .232 in clutch situations and only .261 with runners in scoring position. Parker's production in clutch situations dropped drastically in the second half of the season. He batted .303 with runners in scoring position before the All-Star break but only .222 in the second half.

BASERUNNING:

Earlier in his career, Parker had excellent speed for a big man. Knee surgery has slowed him down, but he is still an excellent base runner with good instincts. He will take the extra base and still slides as hard as anyone to break up a double play. He stole only four bases in 11 attempts last year, but those were his first steals since 1987.

FIELDING:

Parker is rarely used on defense anymore. He has a strong throwing arm, but he no longer has a lot of range in the outfield. On the rare occasions when he was used defensively in 1990, he played first base and did an adequate job.

OVERALL:

Dalton wanted Parker for his leadership in the clubhouse as well as for his hitting. Parker's positive influence was a plus, but it wasn't enough to create a winning attitude on his new team. His on-field contributions weren't enough to turn the Brewers into winners, either, but it certainly wasn't his fault. The Oakland A's let him go because they were reluctant to give him more than a one-year contract at age 38. Parker showed that his age wasn't a problem.

DAN PLESAC

Position: RP
Bats: L **Throws:** L
Ht: 6' 5" **Wt:** 210

Opening Day Age: 29
Born: 2/4/62 in Gary, IN
ML Seasons: 5

PITCHING:

A one-pitch pitcher isn't going to get too many hitters out -- even if that pitch is a 95 MPH fastball. Dan Plesac found that out in 1990. For three years, Plesac had been one of the best relief pitchers in baseball. He pitched in three All-Star Games and saved 100 games in his first four seasons, breaking Rollie Fingers' team record of 97. In 1989, Plesac's 33 saves broke the team one-season mark set by Ken Sanders back in 1971, the Brewers' second year in Milwaukee.

He seemed primed for a big year in 1990, but it never happened. Plesac again led the team with 24 saves, but he also failed in 10 of 34 save opportunities. He had a 4.43 earned run average, the first time he had ever had an ERA over 3.00 in the majors, and opponents batted .257 against him, compared with .213 in 1989.

As a short reliever, Plesac had been able to rely on two pitches, a fastball and a wicked slider. Last year, his slider deserted him, and batters were able to sit on the fastball. Most of the time he had problems controlling the slider, but that wasn't the only problem with the pitch. When he did throw it for strikes, there were times when it came in flat and others when he forced it and threw it too hard. Either way, it often looked a lot like a batting-practice fastball to the hitters.

Plesac pitched a little better in the second half of the season, but by the end of September, rookie Julio Machado was getting most of the calls to warm up in the late innings. Despite his problems, Plesac did continue to pitch very well against lefthanders, holding them to a lowly .161 average. But righthanders pounded him for a .286 mark.

HOLDING RUNNERS AND FIELDING:

Because he's a hard thrower, Plesac's follow-through carries him to the third base side of the mound and leaves him in bad position to field a ball. Despite that, his defensive ability would rank about average. He has an average pickoff move but doesn't pay a lot of attention to runners on first. When he comes into a game, he's usually concentrating on striking out the man at the plate.

OVERALL:

Arms like Plesac's are rare, and nobody is going to give up on him after just one bad season, especially at age 29. He won't be successful with just the fastball, however. He will have to regain control of his slider or come up with another pitch. Plesac has been working on a change-up.

Overall Statistics

	W	L	ERA	G	GS	Sv	IP	H	R	BB	SO	HR
1990	3	7	4.43	66	0	24	69.0	67	36	31	65	5
Career	22	26	2.98	276	0	124	353.0	304	130	112	333	26

How Often He Throws Strikes

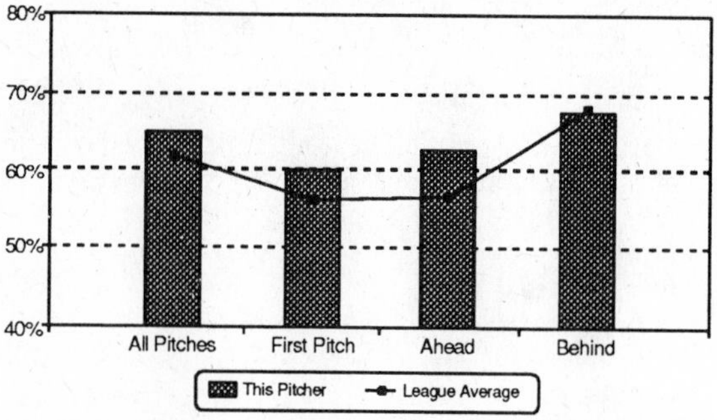

1990 Situational Stats

	W	L	ERA	Sv	IP		AB	H	HR	RBI	AVG
Home	2	3	6.03	11	31.1	LHB	62	10	0	13	.161
Road	1	4	3.11	13	37.2	RHB	199	57	5	34	.286
Day	1	4	4.13	6	28.1	Sc Pos	82	25	1	40	.305
Night	2	3	4.65	18	40.2	Clutch	177	51	4	39	.288

1990 Rankings (American League)

- 1st in blown saves (10)
- 2nd worst save percentage (70.6%)
- 8th in games pitched (66) and save opportunities (34)
- 9th in games finished (52)
- Led the Brewers in saves (24), games finished), save opportunites, blown saves (10), first batter efficiency (.228) and lowest percentage of inherited runners scored (31.3%)

PITCHING:

Faced with a pitching shortage, the Brewers sent Glenn Braggs and Billy Bates to the Cincinnati Reds in exchange for Ron Robinson with the 1990 season almost two months old. Braggs was an outfielder with a lot of potential who had been a disappointment with the Brewers. Robinson was a veteran righthander with a reputation as a five-inning pitcher. Robinson spent considerable time on the disabled list in both 1988 and '89, and wasn't pitching very well in 1990 (2-2, 4.88) at the time of the deal.

Bates and Braggs went on to World Series fame for the Reds, but it turned out to be an excellent trade for the Brewers as well. Robinson not only led the team with 12 victories, he also showed that he could go nine innings. As though taking the Cincinnati criticism as a personal challenge, he led the starting staff with seven complete games.

Robinson isn't a hard thrower anymore, but he's a smart pitcher who knows how to pitch. He throws four pitches: a fastball in the low 80s, an excellent curve, a slider and a change-up. He mixes speeds a lot and can throw his curve at three different speeds and three different locations to keep the hitters off balance.

Opponents hit .279 against him overall and he flirted with trouble a lot, but he had a knack for getting out of jams and posted a 2.91 earned run average with Milwaukee. Although he gave up a lot of hits, he didn't walk many batters, and he kept the ball in the ball park. He yielded only five homers in 148.1 innings. Surprisingly, he was more successful against lefthanders, who batted .265 against him. Righthanders batted .294.

HOLDING RUNNERS AND FIELDING:

Robinson is an excellent athlete and fields his position well. He has good range and good hands and knows his fundamentals. Although he has a good move to first base, runners were successful in 15 of 26 attempted steals while he was on the mound for Milwaukee and Cincinnati.

OVERALL:

Although he missed a chance to pitch for the World Champions when Cincinnati traded him to Milwaukee, Robinson couldn't have been happier. He gained a new lease on life in his new surroundings and ended up signing a big contract with the Brewers at the end of the season. He showed that he has come back from the elbow injury that threatened his career in 1988. He went from one team's junk heap to the ace of another team's staff in one season.

RON ROBINSON

Position: SP
Bats: R **Throws:** R
Ht: 6' 4" **Wt:** 230

Opening Day Age: 29
Born: 3/24/62 in Exeter, CA
ML Seasons: 7

Overall Statistics

	W	L	ERA	G	GS	Sv	IP	H	R	BB	SO	HR
1990	14	7	3.26	28	27	0	179.2	194	78	51	71	7
Career	47	34	3.52	223	93	19	760.1	762	347	236	461	58

How Often He Throws Strikes

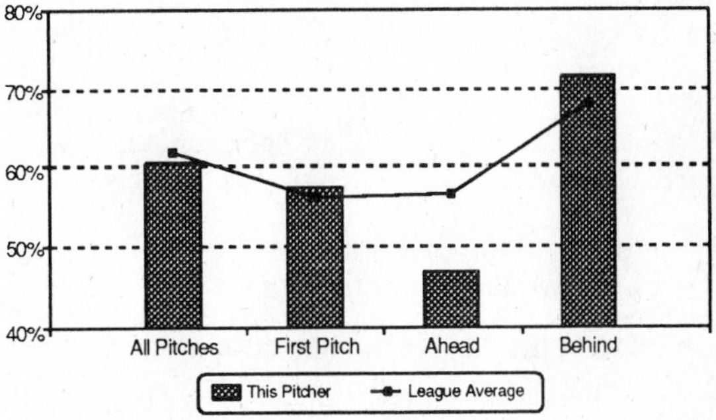

1990 Situational Stats

	W	L	ERA	Sv	IP		AB	H	HR	RBI	AVG
Home	6	3	2.40	0	86.1	LHB	370	98	4	31	.265
Road	8	4	4.05	0	93.1	RHB	326	96	3	37	.294
Day	1	3	7.16	0	32.2	Sc Pos	168	44	1	58	.262
Night	13	4	2.39	0	147.0	Clutch	42	10	1	5	.238

1990 Rankings (American League)

- 3rd in complete games (7)
- 6th in shutouts (2) and winning percentage (.706)
- Led the Brewers in wins (12), complete games, shutouts, hit batsmen (6) and winning percentage

GARY SHEFFIELD

Position: 3B
Bats: R **Throws:** R
Ht: 5'11" **Wt:** 190

Opening Day Age: 22
Born: 11/18/68 in Tampa, FL
ML Seasons: 3

HITTING:

The Gary Sheffield the Milwaukee Brewers saw in 1990 was the one they had been expecting all along. After making his major league debut in September of 1988, Sheffield was almost everybody's pre-season choice as AL Rookie of the Year in 1989. Instead, his play earned him a midseason demotion to the Brewers' Class AAA farm club until it was discovered he had been playing with a broken foot. When he returned to the Brewers, he was still hobbled and finished with only a .247 batting average. Sheffield, however, was only 20 years old, and the foot injury had an obvious effect both at bat and in the field.

Sheffield was healthy for most of 1990, and he hit well, batting .294 with excellent extra-base power. He was everything the Brewers hoped for with the bat, but the temperamental youngster continued to complain about not being used at shortstop, his original position. Late in the season he came down with a mysterious malady in Texas which put him on the shelf once again.

A great natural hitter, Sheffield has an unusual stance, slightly closed with the toes of his front foot turned toward his body, but his strange style doesn't make him susceptible to any particular pitch. Pitchers tried to challenge him with fastballs but didn't have a lot of success. He has a quick bat and hits a lot of line drives. He normally pulls the ball but will go to right field. He batted .336 with runners in scoring position.

BASERUNNING:

Pitchers and catchers have to pay attention when Sheffield is on base. He led the team with 25 stolen bases in 35 attempts. Although he will make some baserunning mistakes because of his inexperience, he is a smart baserunner who will go for the extra base and slide hard to break up a double play.

FIELDING:

Although Sheffield wants to return to shortstop, third base is his best position. He has an extremely strong arm and good hands, but doesn't have great range. Overall, his fielding still needs a lot of work. He makes a lot of errors and is prone to throw the ball away. He is quick, however, and makes a lot of highlight-film quality plays.

OVERALL:

There is no reason to doubt that Sheffield will be a big star in the near future, but it may not be in Milwaukee. In his two seasons with the Brewers, the talented young infielder has frequently complained about the way management has treated him. Unless the situation changes, Milwaukee may be forced to deal him rather than keep a very unhappy ballplayer.

Overall Statistics

	G	AB	R	H	D	T	HR	RBI	SB	BB	SO	AVG
1990	125	487	67	143	30	1	10	67	25	44	41	.294
Career	244	935	113	253	49	1	19	111	38	78	81	.271

Where He Hits the Ball

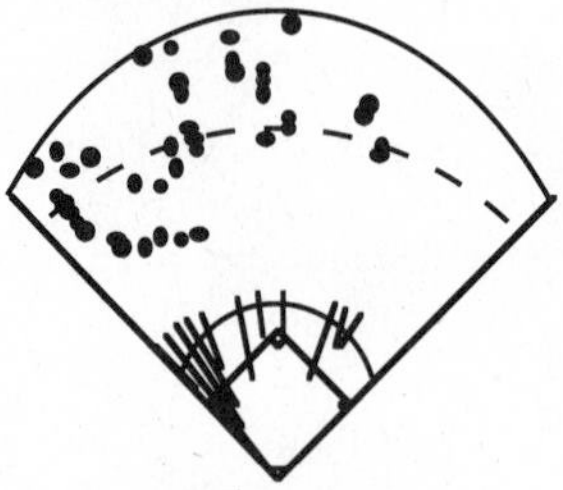

Vs. LHP

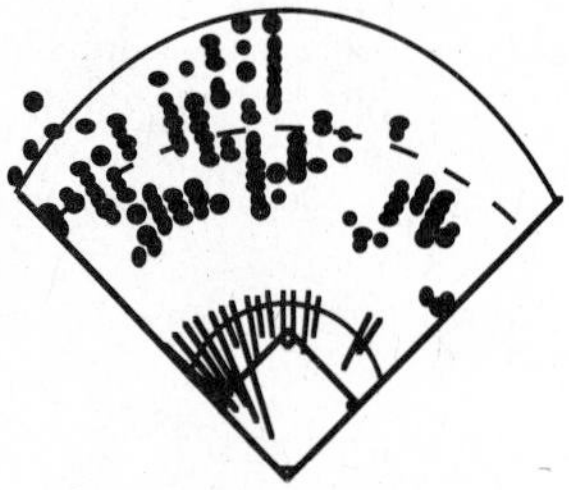

Vs. RHP

1990 Situational Stats

	AB	H	HR	RBI	AVG		AB	H	HR	RBI	AVG
Home	239	65	3	28	.272	LHP	135	37	3	18	.274
Road	248	78	7	39	.315	RHP	352	106	7	49	.301
Day	153	42	4	20	.275	Sc Pos	125	42	0	50	.336
Night	334	101	6	47	.302	Clutch	63	25	2	9	.397

1990 Rankings (American League)

- 3rd in batting average in the clutch (.397)
- 4th in batting average on an 0-2 count (.333)
- 5th in sacrifice flies (9), lowest batting average on a 3-2 count (.074) and batting average on the road (.315)
- 6th in batting average with runners in scoring position (.336)
- Led the Brewers in batting average (.294), doubles (30), stolen bases (25), caught stealing (10) and on-base average (.350)
- Led AL third basemen in stolen bases (25), sotlen base percentage (71.4%), batting average in the clutch, steals of third (3) and percentage of extra bases taken as a runner (47.6%)

BILL SPIERS

Position: SS
Bats: L **Throws:** R
Ht: 6' 2" **Wt:** 190
Opening Day Age: 24
Born: 6/5/66 in Orangeburg, SC
ML Seasons: 2

Overall Statistics

	G	AB	R	H	D	T	HR	RBI	SB	BB	SO	AVG
1990	112	363	44	88	15	3	2	36	11	16	45	.242
Career	226	708	88	176	24	6	6	69	21	37	108	.249

Where He Hits the Ball

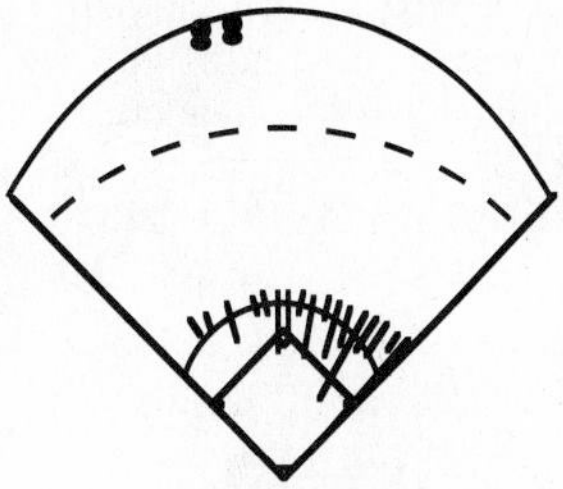

Vs. LHP

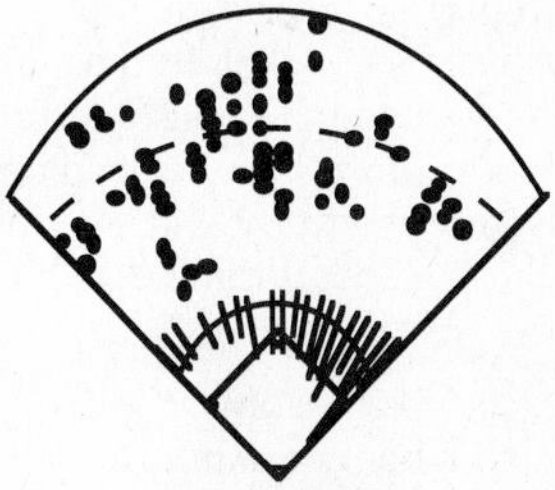

Vs. RHP

1990 Situational Stats

	AB	H	HR	RBI	AVG		AB	H	HR	RBI	AVG
Home	176	47	2	22	.267	LHP	81	19	0	7	.235
Road	187	41	0	14	.219	RHP	282	69	2	29	.245
Day	105	24	1	14	.229	Sc Pos	91	23	0	33	.253
Night	258	64	1	22	.248	Clutch	69	18	0	7	.261

1990 Rankings (American League)

- 3rd in batting average on a 3-2 count (.412)
- 7th in percentage of extra bases taken as a runner (57.4%)
- Led the Brewers in batting average on a 3-2 count
- Led AL shortstops in percentage of extra bases taken as a runner

HITTING:

Sheffield or Spiers? Shortstop Gary Sheffield was the Brewers' number one draft pick in 1986. Shortstop Bill Spiers was Milwaukee's first choice in 1987. Sheffield was considered the hotter prospect, however, and Spiers broke in at third when he made the Brewer roster in 1989; Sheffield was the opening day shortstop. But not for long. Sheffield got hurt, had some problems, and by year's end Spiers was the regular shortstop, while Sheffield was a very unhappy third baseman. That's how the Brewers still see their future -- with Spiers at short. People could be debating the choice for years.

Spiers had a fine rookie campaign in 1989, batting .255, but disappointed by slumping to .242 in 1990. Off-season shoulder surgery and a bone spur on his toe forced him to play hurt most of the season and could have affected his hitting. Spiers is a line-drive hitter who hits to all fields. He hit only two home runs but should be able to hit 7-12 homers a season when he matures.

Spiers drove in 36 runs in 363 at-bats last year, a decent total given that he normally batted either ninth or leadoff. A fair contact man, he doesn't strike out a lot but will still be fooled by a good breaking ball. Although he has good speed, Spiers grounded into 12 double plays, second on the team. Spiers had problems on the road last year, batting just .219 away from County Stadium. He hit much better at home in 1989 as well.

BASERUNNING:

Spiers has good speed and is a threat to run, but his success ratio was down from his rookie year, when he was caught only twice in 12 attempted steals. He plays hard and isn't afraid to break up a double play.

FIELDING:

Spiers is a good shortstop who has excellent range and can turn in a spectacular play. He goes to his left very well, cutting off balls hit over second base. Because he was recovering from off-season shoulder surgery, Spiers' arm wasn't at full strength until late in the year, but it is very strong and accurate. On slow ground balls hit in front of him, he is as good as anyone at making a strong throw while off balance or off the wrong foot.

OVERALL:

There are a lot of good shortstops in the major leagues, but Spiers has enough talent to become one of the better ones if he continues to develop. He works hard and should improve as a hitter. At times he seems to be a little too intense and will be a better player when he learns to relax.

HITTING:

The Brewer's selection of B.J. Surhoff over Will Clark as the number one draft pick in 1985 has drawn a lot of criticism, especially since Clark went on to stardom while Surhoff has struggled offensively and defensively. The complaints can still be heard, but Surhoff did something to silence his critics in 1990. Although he slumped slightly from his .296 average at midseason, Surhoff ended up with a respectable .276 batting average and drove in 59 runs, the most since his 68 RBI in his rookie season. Most importantly, he avoided the extensive slumps that had plagued him the previous two seasons.

Surhoff made some adjustments in his swing last year and the result was that he had more success against pitches low in the strike zone. A line-drive hitter with occasional power who hits to all fields, he makes good contact and doesn't strike out much. Surhoff is also an excellent bunter and will surprise a left-handed pitcher by pushing a bunt past him with a runner on third base. Although he bats left-handed, he was more successful against left-handed pitchers last year, batting .317. Against righthanders, he batted only .265. Surhoff also hit much better against lefties in 1989.

Unlike most Milwaukee hitters, Surhoff likes hitting in County Stadium, where his average was the only one on the team over .300. He had his problems on the road, batting .247. An improving clutch hitter, Surhoff was five for 11 with the bases loaded last year.

BASERUNNING:

Surhoff runs as well as any catcher in the game and is always a threat to steal. He was successful 18 times in 1990 and was caught seven times. He will challenge an outfielder's arm with his speed and will take the extra base.

FIELDING:

Surhoff made great improvements defensively, including the way he handled pitchers and called pitches. He has good reflexes and moves well behind the plate. His throwing still needs improvement. Although he has a strong arm, his mechanics need work, and runners can run on him. He threw out only 26 percent of the runners who attempted to steal against him last season.

OVERALL:

Surhoff is still a young player at 26 and will be a very good player if he keeps improving as he did last season. He has a way to go before he becomes an All-Star player, however, which was expected of him when he arrived in the major leagues as such a highly touted prospect.

B.J. SURHOFF

Position: C
Bats: L **Throws:** R
Ht: 6' 1" **Wt:** 190

Opening Day Age: 26
Born: 8/4/64 in Bronx, NY
ML Seasons: 4

Overall Statistics

	G	AB	R	H	D	T	HR	RBI	SB	BB	SO	AVG
1990	135	474	55	131	21	4	6	59	18	41	37	.276
Career	515	1798	194	478	81	11	23	220	64	133	145	.266

Where He Hits the Ball

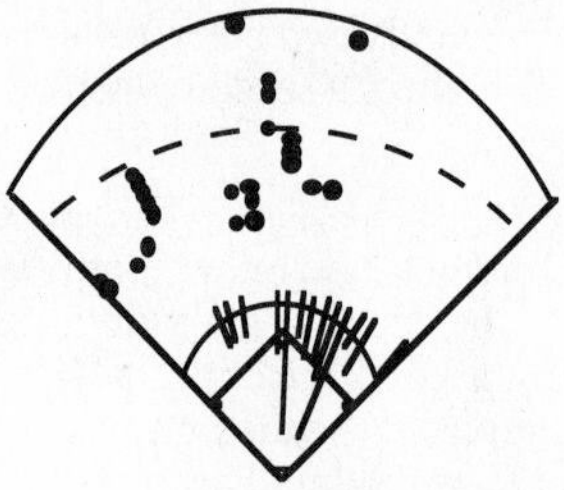

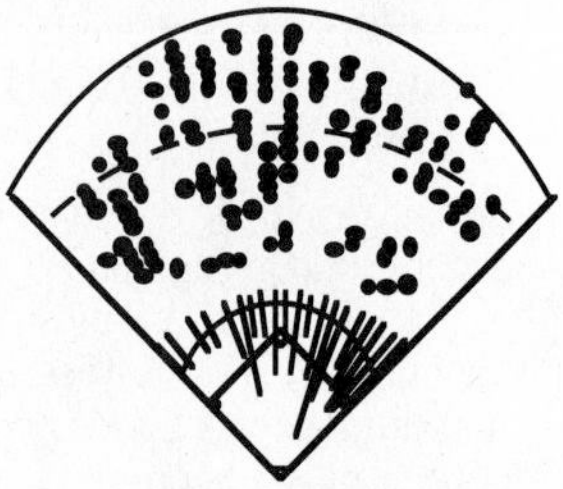

Vs. LHP   Vs. RHP

1990 Situational Stats

	AB	H	HR	RBI	AVG		AB	H	HR	RBI	AVG
Home	235	72	4	35	.306	LHP	104	33	2	17	.317
Road	239	59	2	24	.247	RHP	370	98	4	42	.265
Day	148	37	1	16	.250	Sc Pos	120	33	2	52	.275
Night	326	94	5	43	.288	Clutch	69	16	0	10	.232

1990 Rankings (American League)

- 2nd in highest percentage of swings put into play (57.5%) and worst caught stealing percentage for a catcher (25.8%)
- Led the Brewers in groundball/flyball ratio (1.46), batting average with the bases loaded (.454), batting average with 2 strikes (.238), highest percentage of pitches taken (57.9%), lowest percentage of swings that missed (9.9%) and highest percentage of swings put into play
- Led AL catchers in triples (4), sacrifice flies (7), stolen bases (18), caught stealing (7), batting average with 2 strikes, lowest percentage of swings that missed and highest percentage of swings put into play

HITTING:

Greg Vaughn was the latest in the long run of highly touted rookies to come out of the Brewers farm system. Like Glenn Braggs, Gary Sheffield and several others before him, the husky outfielder had a frustrating rookie season. Vaughn's 17 home runs last year tied the team record for a rookie, and his 61 runs batted in were impressive for a first-year player, but he also went through some long dry spells. After a stretch in which he went 10 for 21 with three home runs and 11 RBI in late July and early August, Vaughn fell into a 1-for-47 slump.

Vaughn has a short, compact swing when he's going good but has a tendency to lapse into a longer stroke. When he does that, he pulls off the ball and can't get around on pitches. That results in pop-ups on hard stuff inside and an inability to reach outside breaking stuff. When he's swinging right, Vaughn has a quick bat which allows him to wait on a pitch. He can then jump on a fastball and still be able to handle a breaking ball.

A slugger, Vaughn is a pull hitter who will be swinging the bat when he's at the plate; don't look for him to walk too often. Like most power hitters, he will strike out a lot. Although he batted just .220, he hit well in the clutch. Overall, he batted .283 with runners in scoring position, an excellent figure for a young player.

BASERUNNING:

Although he didn't run a lot in his rookie season, Vaughn has the speed and ability to steal 20 or more bases, which is what he did in the minors. He probably will be more aggressive at taking an extra base when he becomes more comfortable with playing in the major leagues.

FIELDING:

Vaughn came to the major leagues with the reputation of being a much improved defensive player. Either the reputation was wrong, or he regressed. Vaughn was a liability in left field, frequently misplaying balls and often getting a bad jump. His arm is weak, even for a left fielder.

OVERALL:

Although he had his problems, Vaughn still had a respectable rookie season. The long slump in July and August didn't prevent him from posting good numbers for a first-year player. Vaughn came up through the minor leagues in a hurry and he has the ability to become an above-average major leaguer. His weakest area is his defense, and he will have to work a lot harder than he did in his rookie year to overcome those shortcomings.

GREG VAUGHN

Position: LF
Bats: R **Throws:** R
Ht: 6' 1" **Wt:** 175

Opening Day Age: 25
Born: 7/3/65 in Sacramento, CA
ML Seasons: 2

Overall Statistics

	G	AB	R	H	D	T	HR	RBI	SB	BB	SO	AVG
1990	120	382	51	84	26	2	17	61	7	33	91	.220
Career	158	495	69	114	29	2	22	84	11	46	114	.230

Where He Hits the Ball

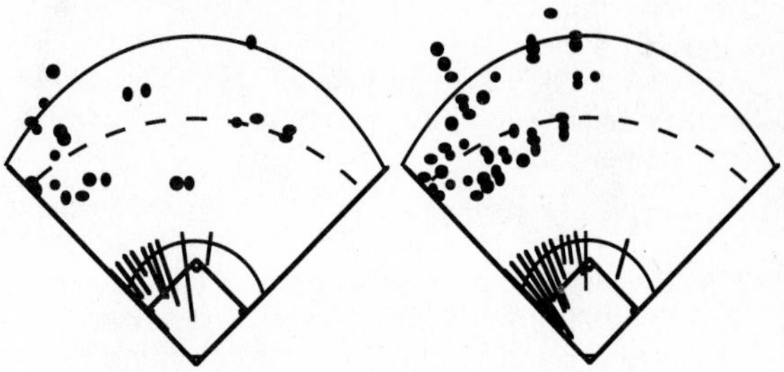

Vs. LHP Vs. RHP

1990 Situational Stats

	AB	H	HR	RBI	AVG		AB	H	HR	RBI	AVG
Home	193	42	9	32	.218	LHP	127	25	4	12	.197
Road	189	42	8	29	.222	RHP	255	59	13	49	.231
Day	91	15	3	11	.165	Sc Pos	92	26	4	43	.283
Night	291	69	14	50	.237	Clutch	39	5	1	7	.128

1990 Rankings (American League)

- 4th lowest batting average vs. left-handed pitchers (.197)
- 5th lowest on-base percentage vs. left-handed pitchers (.254)
- Led AL left fielders in errors (7)

HALL OF FAMER

HITTING:

What a difference a year makes. In 1989, Robin Yount won his second Most Valuable Player award after batting .318 with 103 RBI. It was Yount's fourth straight season over .300 and the sixth time he had topped the mark in his career. He also drove in more than 100 runs for the third time. It was a typically great season for Yount. But what followed was hardly typical. In 1990 Yount hit only .247, a career low, and managed to reach that plateau only because of a .327 binge after Aug. 31. His RBI total fell to 77.

What happened? Yount couldn't explain it, and neither could the Brewers' coaching staff. American League pitchers obviously found an answer, however. Although he can hit with power to all fields, Yount has always had his best success hitting line drives to right-center. Last season, pitchers fed him a steady diet of high and inside hard stuff. Still trying to go the opposite way, the result was a series of weak fly balls instead of line drives. Righthanders held him to a .239 average, and he wasn't much more successful against lefties, hitting .269.

Despite his problems, Yount still contributed to the Brewers' offense. He was still a selective hitter and drew a team-leading 78 walks and also led the team by scoring 98 runs. He batted just .228 with runners in scoring position and .233 in clutch situations. Perhaps putting pressure on himself, Yount had most of his problems at home, batting under .225 at County Stadium. On the road, he hit a respectable .272.

BASERUNNING:

Even at 35, Yount is one of the best baserunners in baseball. He has excellent speed and will invariably take the extra base. He is always a threat to steal in key situations. He is one of the fastest from the plate to first base and will run everything out.

FIELDING:

A former Gold Glove shortstop, Yount has become one of the best at chasing down fly balls. He has great instincts and speed and he very infrequently misses a ball hit over his head. Although shoulder problems forced his move to the outfield, his arm is again strong and accurate.

OVERALL:

Is Robin Yount washed up at age 35? That's doubtful. Everybody is entitled to an off year once in a while, and Yount's extensive struggles in 1990 were the first of his career. Yount plays hard all the time and wants to win. Look for him to bounce back with a good season in 1991.

ROBIN YOUNT

Position: CF
Bats: R **Throws:** R
Ht: 6' 0" **Wt:** 180

Opening Day Age: 35
Born: 9/16/55 in Danville, IL
ML Seasons: 17

Overall Statistics

	G	AB	R	H	D	T	HR	RBI	SB	BB	SO	AVG
1990	158	587	98	145	17	5	17	77	15	78	89	.247
Career	2449	9494	1433	2747	498	116	225	1201	241	815	1097	.289

Where He Hits the Ball

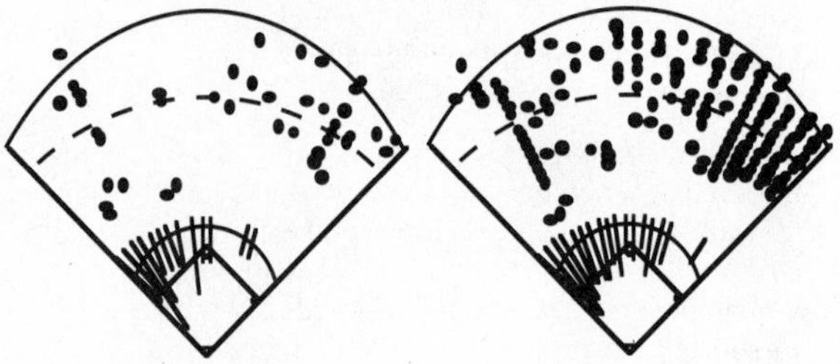

Vs. LHP Vs. RHP

1990 Situational Stats

	AB	H	HR	RBI	AVG		AB	H	HR	RBI	AVG
Home	293	65	8	35	.222	LHP	156	42	5	20	.269
Road	294	80	9	42	.272	RHP	431	103	12	57	.239
Day	188	37	5	17	.197	Sc Pos	167	38	7	62	.228
Night	399	108	12	60	.271	Clutch	86	20	1	16	.233

1990 Rankings (American League)

- 4th in runs (98)
- 5th lowest batting average at home (.222)
- 6th in runs scored per time reached base (42.8%)
- 8th in sacrifice flies (8) and lowest batting average vs. right-handed pitchers (.239)
- Led the Brewers in runs, walks (78), hit by pitch (6), times on base (229), pitches seen (2,488), plate appearances (683), games (158) and runs scored per time reached base
- Led AL center fielders in runs, sacrifice flies, walks and hit by pitch

TOM EDENS

Position: RP/SP
Bats: R **Throws:** R
Ht: 6' 3" **Wt:** 185

Opening Day Age: 29
Born: 6/9/61 in Ontario, OR
ML Seasons: 2

Overall Statistics

	W	L	ERA	G	GS	Sv	IP	H	R	BB	SO	HR
1990	4	5	4.45	35	6	2	89.0	89	52	33	40	8
Career	4	5	4.64	37	8	2	97.0	104	58	37	44	10

PITCHING, FIELDING & HOLDING RUNNERS:

Tom Edens spent most of seven seasons in the New York Mets' minor league system before the Brewers signed him as a minor-league free agent before the 1990 season. Though he'd never been a big winner in his years in the Mets system, Edens posted some fine ERAs and even started two games for the big club in 1987. Mostly, though, he was buried behind pitchers who were considered better prospects.

Edens finally got his chance with the pitching-poor Brewers last year, and he didn't do a lot to prove the Mets wrong, posting a 4-5 record and a 4.45 ERA in 35 appearances, most of them in long relief. Eden's repertoire is nothing special. He throws a very average fastball and a curve. He gave up exactly one hit an inning and was prone to the home run ball. He also had control problems, walking 33 hitters and consistently falling behind in the count. He doesn't hurt himself defensively and has an adequate move to first base.

OVERALL:

For the first time in his career, Edens was finally in the right place at the right time. He wouldn't have been in the major leagues without the Brewers' desperate need for pitching. He needs another pitch. His two pitches are marginal, and he doesn't have much of a chance to stick around unless the Brewers suffer more disasters in 1991.

DARYL HAMILTON

Position: LF/RF
Bats: L **Throws:** R
Ht: 6' 1" **Wt:** 180

Opening Day Age: 26
Born: 12/3/64 in Baton Rouge, LA
ML Seasons: 2

Overall Statistics

	G	AB	R	H	D	T	HR	RBI	SB	BB	SO	AVG
1990	89	156	27	46	5	0	1	18	10	9	12	.295
Career	133	259	41	65	9	0	2	29	17	21	21	.251

HITTING, FIELDING, BASERUNNING:

Darryl Hamilton is a good contact hitter and excellent defensive player who put together a very fine minor league record while moving through the Brewer system. Hamilton batted an eye-popping .391 in his debut at Helena in 1986, and hit well over .300 the next two years. He had a brief shot with the Brewers in 1988, but wasn't ready and hit only .184.

Hamilton got another chance last year, and he performed very well in a part-time role. Playing almost exclusively against righthanders, he batted over .300 for most of the season before winding up at .295, and he was a dependable hitter in clutch situations. He's a patient hitter who doesn't get fooled very often. He doesn't have any power but has good speed and could be used as a leadoff hitter.

Hamilton is an excellent outfielder with a good arm. He gets a good jump and has excellent range. He is also an excellent baserunner who is always a threat to run. He will take the extra base and isn't afraid to break up a double play.

OVERALL:

Hamilton might challenge someone for a starting position next season, but he has one big obstacle in his way. Although he can play all three outfield positions, center field is his best position. Somebody named Robin Yount has staked a claim to that spot in the Brewers' lineup. Hamilton may challenge for a platoon role in left or right, especially if he keeps hitting like he did in 1990.

BILL KRUEGER

Position: SP/RP
Bats: L **Throws:** L
Ht: 6' 5" **Wt:** 210

Opening Day Age: 32
Born: 4/24/58 in Waukegan, IL
ML Seasons: 8

Overall Statistics

	W	L	ERA	G	GS	Sv	IP	H	R	BB	SO	HR
1990	6	8	3.98	30	17	0	129.0	137	70	54	64	10
Career	36	41	4.35	162	89	4	670.1	714	394	318	326	52

PITCHING, FIELDING & HOLDING RUNNERS:

Veteran lefty Bill Krueger has been used as both a starter and reliever, but with the Brewers he has seemed best suited to start. Krueger throws an average fastball and a breaking ball, but he's smart and knows how to mix his pitches. As a reliever, however, his fastball can't blow hitters away, and if his breaking ball isn't working, he's in deep, deep trouble. "Forget it," said one scout, and that sums it up.

Krueger gives up a lot of hits and seems to be constantly pitching from the stretch, but he somehow managed to get out of trouble enough to have a decent season last year. Indeed, his two years in Milwaukee have been his best since his rookie season of 1983. Krueger is a fine fielder with good fundamentals. Although he has a good move to first, his big breaking ball gives runners an advantage. Only nine of 16 base stealers were successful against him last year, however.

OVERALL:

Although he is a fourth or fifth starter at best, Krueger has served the injury-plagued Brewers well in two seasons. A veteran on a rather shaky mound staff, he gives Tom Trebelhorn someone reliable to go to, particularly if one of his starters is shelved by injury. Krueger could be a very effective middle reliever if his breaking ball was more consistent, but even without it he seems to know how to survive in the majors.

DALE SVEUM

Position: 3B/2B
Bats: B **Throws:** R
Ht: 6' 3" **Wt:** 185

Opening Day Age: 27
Born: 11/23/63 in Richmond, CA
ML Seasons: 4

Overall Statistics

	G	AB	R	H	D	T	HR	RBI	SB	BB	SO	AVG
1990	48	117	15	23	7	0	1	12	0	12	30	.197
Career	421	1436	177	349	61	9	42	193	7	105	348	.243

HITTING, FIELDING, BASERUNNING:

Dale Sveum was a pleasant surprise for the Brewers when he had a 25 homer, 95 RBI season in 1987. Sveum came down to earth offensively in 1988, but he was still the Brewers' starting shortstop until he suffered a broken leg that September. More than two years later, he still hasn't made it back.

On the mend, Sveum missed all of the 1989 season and spent most of 1990 at Denver. He did get into 48 games with the Brewers last year, but his .197 average showed that he was overmatched in the major leagues. The Brewers would like to see him complete his comeback in 1991. Although he strikes out a lot, Sveum has always had a knack of getting a big hit or making a big play on defense when needed. He has good power and will drive in a lot of runs.

Defensively, Sveum makes a lot of errors but will still turn in the big play. He has an excellent arm but limited range at shortstop. Although he prefers short, third base is probably his best position. On the bases, he doesn't have a lot of speed and is not a threat to run.

OVERALL:

Sveum's future with the Brewers is cloudy and not just because he has to prove he has finally made a comeback from his broken leg. Although Manager Tom Trebelhorn is one of Sveum's biggest fans, finding a spot in the lineup for him isn't going to be easy. Gary Sheffield and Bill Spiers have taken over at third and short and Jim Gantner is a fixture at second base.

RANDY VERES

Position: RP
Bats: R **Throws:** R
Ht: 6' 3" **Wt:** 190

Opening Day Age: 25
Born: 11/25/65 in San Francisco, CA
ML Seasons: 2

Overall Statistics

	W	L	ERA	G	GS	Sv	IP	H	R	BB	SO	HR
1990	0	3	3.67	26	0	1	41.2	38	17	16	16	5
Career	0	4	3.78	29	1	1	50.0	47	22	20	24	5

PITCHING, FIELDING & HOLDING RUNNERS:

Randy Veres, a young righthander, split time between the Brewers and AAA Denver last year, as Milwaukee desperately searched for pitching help. Although Veres had been a starter for most of his minor-league career, the Brewers used him in middle relief during his 26 games. Veres had been pitching in the Brewer system since 1985, never winning a lot of games but always recording good ERAs and moving steadily up the ladder.

For the most part, Veres acquitted himself well in his Milwaukee stint, though he's still searching for his first major league win. He displayed a good arm, but his control is a major problem. He throws an above-average fastball and a good slider, but has trouble throwing either of them for strikes. Veres walked only 16 men in 41.2 innings, but that's deceptive because he was consistently behind in the count, forcing him to groove pitches that often ended up over the fence. The Brewers were impressed that Veres didn't give up a lot of hits, and by the fact that he was tough on righties, who batted just .237 against him. On defense, he fields his position adequately and will throw to first to keep runners honest.

OVERALL:

Nobody wants to give up on a good arm, and Veres has a good one. Unless he can throw more strikes, however, he isn't going to be an effective pitcher in the major leagues. The Brewers still consider him a prospect, and Veres could be destined for a future as a middle reliever.

BILL WEGMAN

Position: SP
Bats: R **Throws:** R
Ht: 6' 5" **Wt:** 200

Opening Day Age: 28
Born: 12/19/62 in Cincinnati, OH
ML Seasons: 6

Overall Statistics

	W	L	ERA	G	GS	Sv	IP	H	R	BB	SO	HR
1990	2	2	4.85	8	5	0	29.2	37	21	6	20	6
Career	36	44	4.63	123	112	0	720.2	776	410	176	321	102

PITCHING, FIELDING & HOLDING RUNNERS:

Bill Wegman is one of many young pitchers on the Brewers' staff whose future has been clouded by injuries. In his first three seasons, he was a dependable starter who could be expected to pitch a lot of innings and keep his team in the ball game. Wegman was 12-11 for the Brewers in 1987, and followed up with a 13-13 campaign in 1988, his best year.

Since then, Wegman's had nothing but trouble. He missed most of the 1989 season with a shoulder injury, but appeared to be on the way to a successful comeback last year when he pitched a shutout on May 18. But he re-injured his shoulder in that game and eventually needed surgery. He didn't win another game all year.

When healthy, Wegman is a good competitor who throws an average fastball and a good breaking ball. He also has a good change-up. He will get into trouble if he tries to overthrow his fastball. He is an exceptional athlete who played third base in college and fields his position very well. He has a quick move to first base and will throw over there a lot.

OVERALL:

Wegman remains an unknown quantity because of his shoulder problems. If he can come back, he can be a solid third or fourth starter and a dependable member of a pitching staff. He doesn't have the stuff to be a big winner but he is a competitor who will battle an opponent and keep his team in a game.

RICK AGUILERA

Position: RP
Bats: R **Throws:** R
Ht: 6' 5" **Wt:** 200

Opening Day Age: 29
Born: 12/31/61 in San Gabriel, CA
ML Seasons: 6

PITCHING:

When the Twins lost reliever Jeff Reardon to free agency, they quickly decided that Rick Aguilera would be the guy to replace him. The most experienced of the five pitchers acquired in 1989's Frank Viola deal, Aguilera wasn't thrilled by the prospect initially. But he put together a solid season and was rewarded midway through with a three-year contract. The Twins now have a proven closer who could always return to the starting rotation if they come up with another bullpen anchor.

Aguilera has a 90 MPH fastball that tends to rise and a good split-fingered fastball. He'll also mix in a slider and occasional curve, although the two fastballs are his money pitches. At first, Aguilera was tempted to adapt to his new role by trying to throw everything by the hitters. But he quickly realized that it would be silly not to use all the weapons he'd developed over the years. His slider is the kind of pitch that batters tend to chase out of the strike zone.

As a closer, Aguilera was more effective than ever against left-handed batters, which some folks expected to be his downfall. In fact, lefties touched him for only two extra-base hits -- and no homers -- last season. Mostly a middle reliever for the Mets, Aguilera showed that he could pitch several straight days in short relief. However, he suffered some shoulder stiffness that sidelined him for stretches during the second half of the season. Whether that was an adjustment problem from his new role, or a foreboding sign of things to come, remains to be seen. He also had shoulder troubles in 1987 and '88.

HOLDING RUNNERS AND FIELDING:

Aguilera has an unspectacular move to first, but has a quick enough delivery to keep his move from being a huge problem. Working late in close games prevents too many runners from testing him, in most cases. His fielding skills come from his college days as a third baseman. He finishes off in good position, handles bunts and grounders well and doesn't tarry when he needs to cover first base. His fielding is a part of his game from which other Twins' pitchers could learn.

OVERALL:

Some people think Aguilera could be a 15-game winner or better, if he stayed in the starting rotation for an entire season. Regardless, he proved last season that he can be a 30-save stopper. Not too many pitchers are as versatile as Aguilera, who established his value beyond much doubt in 1990, once given the opportunity he was looking for after he left New York.

Overall Statistics

	W	L	ERA	G	GS	Sv	IP	H	R	BB	SO	HR
1990	5	3	2.76	56	0	32	65.1	55	27	19	61	5
Career	45	35	3.44	181	70	39	614.0	601	270	173	469	50

How Often He Throws Strikes

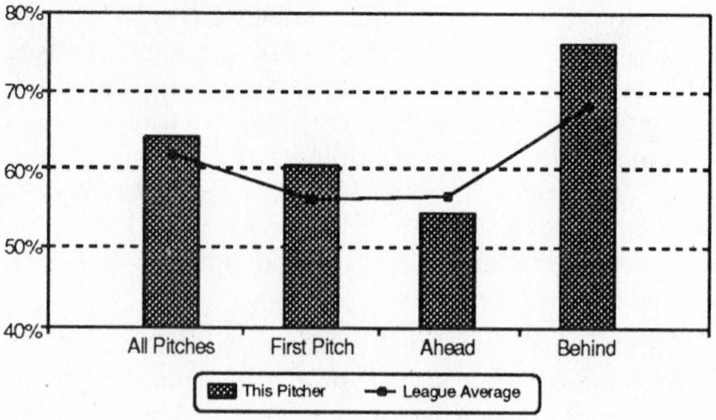

1990 Situational Stats

	W	L	ERA	Sv	IP		AB	H	HR	RBI	AVG
Home	3	2	3.44	16	34.0	LHB	114	25	0	5	.219
Road	2	1	2.01	16	31.1	RHB	131	30	5	21	.229
Day	3	2	2.81	12	25.2	Sc Pos	78	18	3	22	.231
Night	2	1	2.72	20	39.2	Clutch	175	39	5	21	.223

1990 Rankings (American League)

- → 5th in save opportunities (39)
- → 6th in saves (32)
- → 7th in games finished (54) and blown saves (7)
- → 8th in save percentage (82.1%) and lowest percentage of inherited runners scored (21.1%)
- → Led the Twins in games pitched (56), saves, games finished, save opportunites, blown saves, lowest batting average vs. left-handed batters (.219) and lowest percentage of inherited runners scored

ALLAN ANDERSON

Position: SP
Bats: L **Throws:** L
Ht: 6' 0" **Wt:** 194

Opening Day Age: 27
Born: 1/7/64 in Lancaster, OH
ML Seasons: 5

PITCHING:

Allan Anderson is a finesse pitcher who needs sharp control to be effective. The lefthander's problem isn't issuing walks -- he allowed just 39 free passes in 188.2 innings last year. Instead, he gets into trouble by throwing strikes that are simply too hittable. Lacking an overpowering fastball, Anderson needs to keep the ball low, hit the corners and mix his pitches -- fastball, curve and a better-than-average change-up -- to win consistently. In 1990 he couldn't do that until late in the year, and the result was a disastrous 7-18 campaign.

It was quite a comedown for the southpaw who had been counted on to succeed Frank Viola as the Twins' ace. Anderson had led the American League with a 2.45 ERA in 1988, and followed that with a solid 17-10 campaign in '89. The Twins even took to calling him "Little Frankie" because his style was similar to Viola's, particularly in his use of the change-up. When Viola was traded to the Mets on July 31, 1989, Anderson took up the slack, going 6-1 over the final two months of the season. But in 1990 it was a different story. Anderson floundered from the beginning, going 2-12 through mid-July, although a lack of offensive support was partly to blame. He didn't turn things around until his final eight starts, when he went 3-4 with a 3.11 ERA over 55 innings.

Even in his best years, Anderson hasn't had an impressive hits per inning ratio, and it's been getting worse: 199 hits in 202.1 IP in '88, 214 hits in 196.2 innings in '89, and 214 in 188.2 last year. He's been more effective pitching on natural grass the last two seasons, which is hardly a plus for a team that plays in a dome. In 1989 he was 9-4, 2.18 on grass, 8-6, 5.44 on turf; last year he was 2-5, 3.94 on grass, 5-13, 4.80 on turf.

HOLDING RUNNERS AND FIELDING:

Anderson is one of the Twins' best fielding pitchers, utilizing natural athletic quickness and smarts. He handled 44 chances flawlessly last year, including a team-high 37 assists. He's also excellent holding runners and has a good pickoff move that holds baserunners close. While Anderson was pitching, 11 of 21 would-be base stealers were caught in 1990.

OVERALL:

The Twins entered the 1990 off-season believing they needed to acquire a veteran starter to take the pressure off Anderson. Anderson handled his disappointing 1990 season admirably, enlisting the aid of a Twin Cities sports psychologist to aid in positive thinking. His pitching late last year indicated that, while he may not be in Viola's class, he is still a quality left-handed starter who could help any staff in the majors.

Overall Statistics

	W	L	ERA	G	GS	Sv	IP	H	R	BB	SO	HR
1990	7	18	4.53	31	31	0	188.2	214	106	39	82	20
Career	44	43	3.95	119	106	0	684.1	753	342	169	288	63

How Often He Throws Strikes

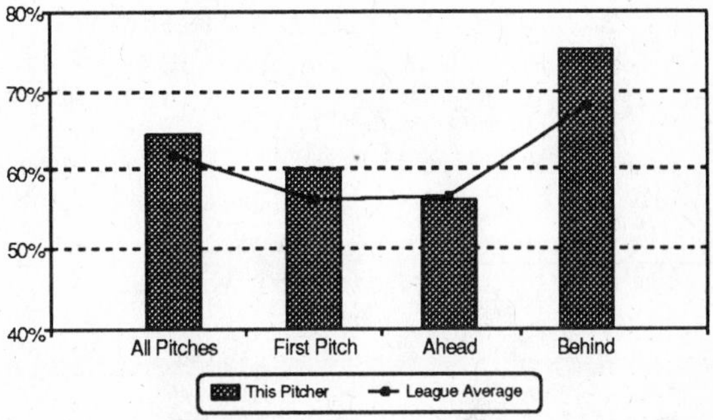

1990 Situational Stats

	W	L	ERA	Sv	IP		AB	H	HR	RBI	AVG
Home	4	12	4.77	0	111.1	LHB	109	28	2	13	.257
Road	3	6	4.19	0	77.1	RHB	632	186	18	84	.294
Day	2	5	4.79	0	56.1	Sc Pos	171	56	2	72	.327
Night	5	13	4.42	0	132.1	Clutch	53	16	2	4	.302

1990 Rankings (American League)

- ➡ 1st in lowest winning percentage (.280)
- ➡ 2nd in losses (18), highest batting average allowed (.289) and lowest run support per 9 innings (3.4)
- ➡ 3rd in least pitches thrown per batter (3.45) and highest batting average allowed vs. right-handed batters (.294)
- ➡ Led the Twins in losses (18), games started (31), complete games (5), innings (188.2), hits allowed (214), batters faced (797), hit batsmen (5), pitches thrown (2,750) and GDPs induced (19)

PITCHING:

Juan Berenguer is a hard-throwing middle reliever who needs a lot of work to be happy, and also apparently to be effective. He lost some innings to other pitchers last season and got off to a slow start. When the Twins relied on him more, sometimes out of necessity, he responded with his fourth straight solid season since coming to Minnesota as a free agent. He has a 33-13 record in that time, never winning fewer than eight games in a season.

At age 36, Berenguer still can throw a fastball at 93 or 94 MPH and, when he keeps it near the plate, can be as effective as anyone. He's the type of guy who can come in with a couple of runners on base and get out of a jam with strikeouts. On his bad days, though, walks often hurt him. He averaged over five walks per nine innings last year, despite sometimes going three or four innings without walking anyone. Teams that can stack lefties against Berenguer tend to do well, especially when they can sit on the fastball. Berenguer's No. 2 pitch is the forkball, and whether he can get it over is usually the deciding element between the good and bad days. "Wild enough to be effective," is the line often trotted out about Berenguer.

The Twins have learned to live with Berenguer's excitability. He'll frequently make an exaggerated gunfighter's motion after striking out an opponent or when a key play is turned behind him. Opposing players don't care much for this hot-dogging. But the Twins understand that's part of the package with Berenguer, and his enthusiasm counters some of the coolness that has come over the team in the last couple of unsuccessful seasons.

HOLDING RUNNERS AND FIELDING:

Berenguer doesn't finish in good position to field, yet fields more balls than one might expect. Still, there are plays he should make that aren't made. He's not the quickest guy to first base and sometimes is slow to back up plays. He has a high leg kick and is pretty easy to steal on. It's probably too late in his career to try making changes in this area.

OVERALL:

There will always be a place for someone who can throw hard and work 100 innings in relief. As long as Berenguer is happy and healthy, he can be a major contributor, keeping his team in close games until the offense can mount a comeback. As for his emotional nature, it's been suggested more than once that some of his teammates should follow his lead.

JUAN BERENGUER

Position: RP
Bats: R **Throws:** R
Ht: 5'11" **Wt:** 223

Opening Day Age: 36
Born: 11/30/54 in Aguadulce, Panama
ML Seasons: 13

Overall Statistics

	W	L	ERA	G	GS	Sv	IP	H	R	BB	SO	HR
1990	8	5	3.41	51	0	0	100.1	85	43	58	77	9
Career	63	54	3.88	394	93	14	1063.1	914	506	548	877	101

How Often He Throws Strikes

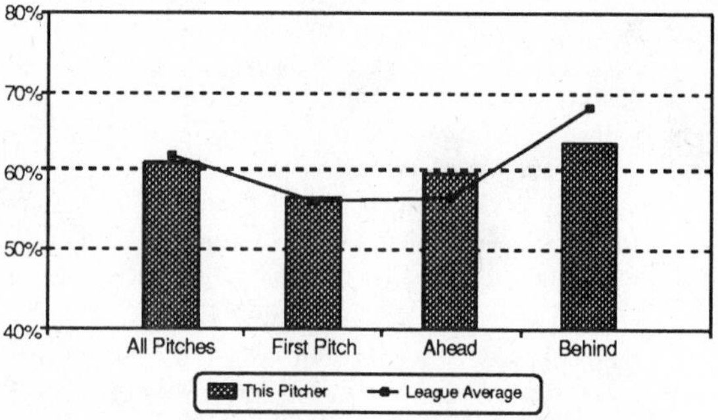

1990 Situational Stats

	W	L	ERA	Sv	IP		AB	H	HR	RBI	AVG
Home	4	2	3.54	0	48.1	LHB	159	42	3	19	.264
Road	4	3	3.29	0	52.0	RHB	208	43	6	21	.207
Day	3	1	2.16	0	33.1	Sc Pos	108	22	1	27	.204
Night	5	4	4.03	0	67.0	Clutch	159	35	3	9	.220

1990 Rankings (American League)

- 10th in first batter efficiency (.186)
- Led the Twins in holds (9)

RANDY BUSH

Position: RF/DH
Bats: L **Throws:** L
Ht: 6' 1" **Wt:** 184

Opening Day Age: 32
Born: 10/5/58 in Dover, DE
ML Seasons: 9

Overall Statistics

	G	AB	R	H	D	T	HR	RBI	SB	BB	SO	AVG
1990	73	181	17	44	8	0	6	18	0	21	27	.243
Career	991	2653	352	667	134	24	88	361	32	306	430	.251

Where He Hits the Ball

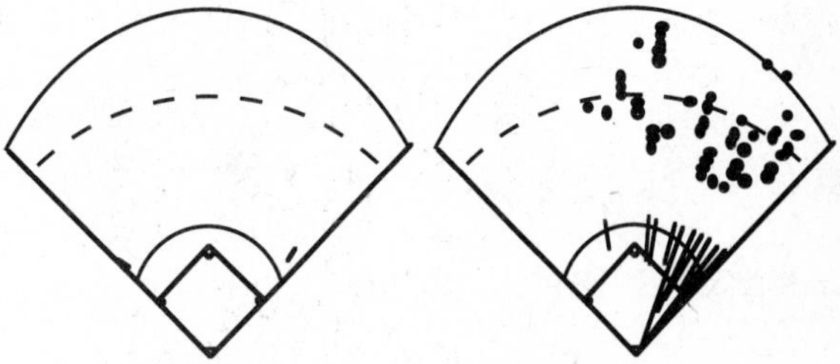

Vs. LHP Vs. RHP

1990 Situational Stats

	AB	H	HR	RBI	AVG		AB	H	HR	RBI	AVG
Home	98	29	4	12	.296	LHP	4	1	0	1	.250
Road	83	15	2	6	.181	RHP	177	43	6	17	.243
Day	41	8	3	7	.195	Sc Pos	40	6	1	9	.150
Night	140	36	3	11	.257	Clutch	31	8	2	6	.258

1990 Rankings (American League)

➡ Led AL right fielders in hit by pitch (6)

HITTING:

From the day he joined the Twins in 1982, Randy Bush has been labeled a platoon player, and his status still hasn't changed. Slowed by injuries, Bush had just four official at-bats last year against left-handed pitchers. He suffered a severe hamstring injury in mid-May that forced him to miss 58 games. An aggravation of the problem resulted in a second stint on the disabled list in August. As a result Bush, who started the year as the Twins right fielder against righties, batted only 181 times and hit just .243, his lowest average since 1985.

Although Bush's yearly numbers are consistently in the .240 to .260 range, he's a streaky hitter who blows hot and cold over the course of a season. He's usually a good fastball hitter, but he can be bothered at times by inside heat. He'll look foolish against off-speed pitches, but then he'll adjust to them. His main attribute is his home run power. Bush is a pull hitter, and when he's swinging well he provides the left-handed slugging that the Twins desperately need, since Kent Hrbek is their only other left-handed power threat. Though he's never hit more than 14 homers in a season, Bush has been consistently in double figures, and that's all the Twins require from him.

Once a free swinger, Bush has learned to lay off bad pitches and can take a walk. His on-base percentage has been in the .335-.365 range over the last five years -- respectable figures for a power hitter.

BASERUNNING:

The hamstring injury severely affected Bush's speed in 1990. He failed to steal a base after swiping five in 1989. Never blessed with great speed, Bush has been an adequate baserunner because of his intelligence.

FIELDING:

Bush's defense is similar to his baserunning. He's not blessed with great ability, but he's made himself a decent gloveman. He doesn't have great range, but his glove is solid and his arm adequate. The hamstring problem limited him to 32 games in the outfield last year; he didn't make an error in 53 chances.

OVERALL:

Bush is a solid veteran whose left-handed power makes him an asset in the Dome. The Twins, in dire need of his power, will certainly give him a chance to rebound from the 1990 injuries. His lengthy absence last season is considered by Twins officials to be part of the reason the club hit just 100 home runs, the team's lowest total for a full season since 1980. But the hamstring injury was severe enough -- a partially severed hamstring tendon -- that Bush's future is somewhat in question.

SCOTT ERICKSON

Position: SP
Bats: R **Throws:** R
Ht: 6' 0" **Wt:** 190

Opening Day Age: 23
Born: 2/2/68 in Long Beach, CA
ML Seasons: 1

PITCHING:

One year out of the University of Arizona, Scott Erickson made the jump from Class AA to the majors last summer. By the end of the season, he looked like a candidate to become one of the Twins' most important starters in the 90's. Erickson was asked to do a lot of learning on the fly, and made pretty good progress; he even appeared to learn from the times that he got knocked around. Whatever confidence he lost during some tough outings was regained by the end of the season.

Erickson has a good fastball, a forkball and a slider. All of his pitches have good, downward movement. After making the majors, Erickson confided that he didn't think he could pitch on artificial turf because he was giving up too many ground-ball hits that would have been routine grounders on grass. But by the end of the season, several strong outings at the Metrodome should have ended those fears.

Erickson also walked more batters because major-league hitters were apt to lay off pitches that minor-leaguers would chase out of the strike zone. The walks were probably his biggest single problem, and he needs to allow fewer in the future. Erickson's lack of control was more evident against lefties. He tended to sail along for a few innings and then run into a stretch of hits and walks which would put his opponents back in the game. But he showed a knack for pitching out of trouble, a sign that he's got some mental toughness.

HOLDING RUNNERS AND FIELDING:

Erickson is a good, natural athlete and his fielding was above average. He moved better toward third base than first, though, fielding bunts well but having some trouble covering on grounders to the right side. When his mastery of fundamentals matches that natural talent, he should gain a reputation as a pretty good fielding pitcher. His move to first is OK, and he pays attention to baserunners without overdoing it.

OVERALL:

The Twins have been worried about rushing some of their young pitchers to the majors. But they should have been comfortable with the way that Erickson made the jump. The starting rotation was pretty unsettled at the end of last season, and a good spring training could result in Erickson being the staff's number one or two starter. He put together a pretty good half-season in 1990.

Overall Statistics

	W	L	ERA	G	GS	Sv	IP	H	R	BB	SO	HR
1990	8	4	2.87	19	17	0	113.0	108	49	51	53	9
Career	8	4	2.87	19	17	0	113.0	108	49	51	53	9

How Often He Throws Strikes

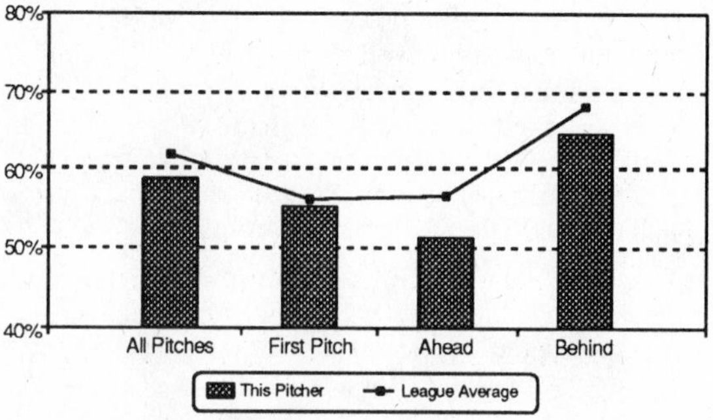

1990 Situational Stats

	W	L	ERA	Sv	IP		AB	H	HR	RBI	AVG
Home	7	2	3.45	0	78.1	LHB	224	55	4	27	.246
Road	1	2	1.56	0	34.2	RHB	198	53	5	17	.268
Day	3	0	1.83	0	39.1	Sc Pos	104	24	1	33	.231
Night	5	4	3.42	0	73.2	Clutch	18	3	1	2	.167

1990 Rankings (American League)

➟ Led the Twins in hit batsmen (5)

GARY GAETTI

Position: 3B
Bats: R **Throws:** R
Ht: 6' 0" **Wt:** 200

Opening Day Age: 32
Born: 8/19/58 in Centralia, IL
ML Seasons: 10

Overall Statistics

	G	AB	R	H	D	T	HR	RBI	SB	BB	SO	AVG
1990	154	577	61	132	27	5	16	85	6	36	101	.229
Career	1361	4989	646	1276	252	25	201	758	74	358	877	.256

Where He Hits the Ball

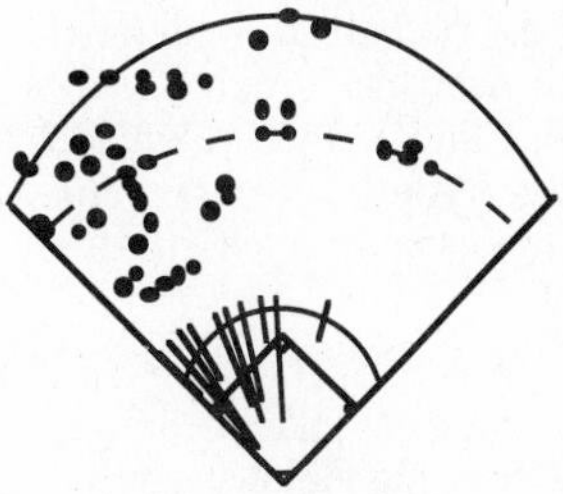

Vs. LHP

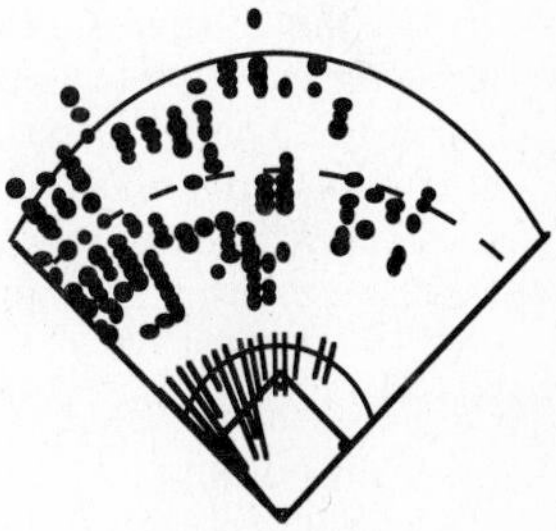

Vs. RHP

1990 Situational Stats

	AB	H	HR	RBI	AVG		AB	H	HR	RBI	AVG
Home	286	68	7	43	.238	LHP	166	37	5	18	.223
Road	291	64	9	42	.220	RHP	411	95	11	67	.231
Day	144	30	3	21	.208	Sc Pos	156	41	7	71	.263
Night	433	102	13	64	.236	Clutch	88	20	3	12	.227

1990 Rankings (American League)

- 1st in lowest on-base average (.274), lowest on-base average vs. right-handed pitchers (.270)
- 4th in lowest batting average (.229), GDPs (22), lowest batting average vs. right-handed pitchers (.231) and lowest percentage of pitches taken (43.8%)
- 7th lowest batting average on the road (.220)
- Led the Twins in at-bats (577), RBIs (85), sacrifice flies (8), strikeouts (101), GDPs, pitches seen (2,161), plate appearances (625) and games (154)
- Led AL third basemen in strikeouts and GDPs

HITTING:

Gary Gaetti suffered through his second straight sub-par year in 1990, and there are folks beginning to wonder if he's one of the Minnesota veterans who has seen better days. Gaetti stayed healthy last year, but he struggled to keep his average near the .230 mark and didn't show nearly as much power as was evident in some of his better years. Gaetti has never drawn many walks, a weakness that's even more glaring when his batting average dips.

Opposing pitchers have learned how to handle Gaetti, feeding him fastballs away and sliders that he'll chase in the dirt. He's had an unusual amount of trouble with left-handed pitchers in the last couple of years, and he was even benched against some lefties in 1990, the exact opposite of a typical platoon strategy. Gaetti did show enough flashes of power and clutch hitting, though, that nobody is giving much thought to replacing him. Instead, the Twins are hoping he can work through his offensive struggles in much the same way that he did when his power dropped in the mid-1980s.

Gaetti continued his pattern of grounding into a lot of double plays, many of them coming when he tried to pull outside pitches. In good times, Gaetti shows enough poise and discipline to hit outside pitches to right. Gaetti likes high fastballs and pulls the majority of his homers and extra-base hits.

BASERUNNING:

Gaetti could hand out a punishing collision in his younger years, but age and injuries have caused him to take greater care on the bases. He has become less of a threat to steal, but will still take the extra base when the chance comes up.

FIELDING:

Gaetti's fielding slipped a bit last season. He made more errors in 1990 than in the previous two years combined, most of them on misplayed grounders. He still moved toward the foul line as well as anyone, turning extra-base tries into spectacular outs, but he's weaker to his left and has trouble with balls that he has to charge. Gaetti still has a very good arm, and a career-long problem of sailing his throws high and wide wasn't evident last season.

OVERALL:

Gaetti still is among the better third baseman in the American League, but only time will tell if he can improve over the 1989 and 1990 seasons. The Twins would like to see him return to the 25-homer level he last reached in 1988. Gaetti did lead the Twins in runs batted in last season, a fact often lost among the things he didn't do well.

GREG GAGNE

Position: SS
Bats: R **Throws:** R
Ht: 5'11" **Wt:** 177

Opening Day Age: 29
Born: 11/12/61 in Fall River, MA
ML Seasons: 8

Overall Statistics

	G	AB	R	H	D	T	HR	RBI	SB	BB	SO	AVG
1990	138	388	38	91	22	3	7	38	8	24	76	.235
Career	855	2539	347	628	137	32	54	254	62	143	521	.247

Where He Hits the Ball

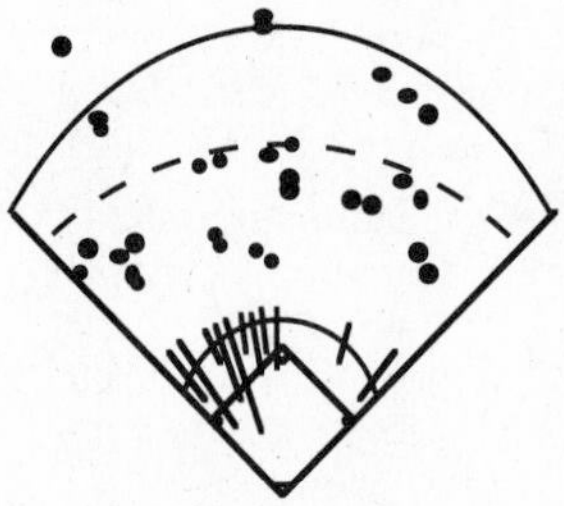

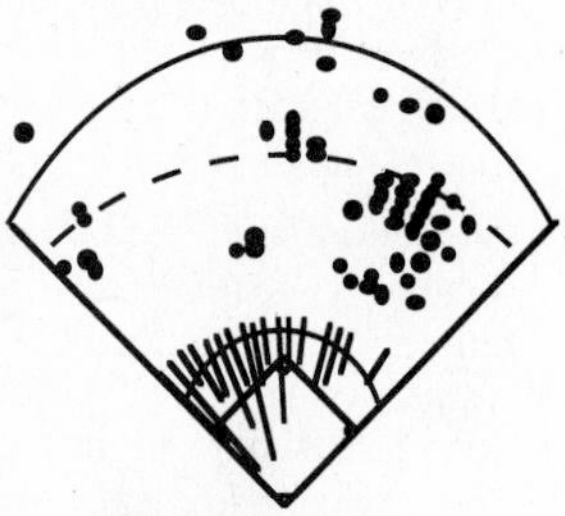

Vs. LHP   Vs. RHP

1990 Situational Stats

	AB	H	HR	RBI	AVG		AB	H	HR	RBI	AVG
Home	182	45	3	20	.247	LHP	124	37	3	18	.298
Road	206	46	4	18	.223	RHP	264	54	4	20	.205
Day	113	24	3	8	.212	Sc Pos	88	16	0	26	.182
Night	275	67	4	30	.244	Clutch	52	20	0	2	.385

1990 Rankings (American League)

- 3rd lowest batting average with runners in scoring position (.182)
- 4th highest batting average in the clutch (.385)
- Led the Twins in sacrifice bunts (8), least GDPs in GDP situations (7.0%) and highest batting average in the clutch
- Led AL shortstops in strikeouts (76), batting average vs. left-handed pitchers (.298) and batting average on a 3-1 count (.500)

HITTING:

Though he's led them to expect more, the Twins might have to realize that, more often than not, Greg Gagne is going to hit in the .235 to .250 range. There are times when Gagne makes progress at curing some of his bad habits. He batted .265 in 1987, and a career-high .272 just two years ago in 1989. He's hit as many as 14 homers in a season. But Gagne has never seemed able to sustain such efforts. He will show a little bit of power, but then frustrate his club with strikeouts and streaks in which it's probably better for him to be watching from the bench. Inevitably, he returns to chasing bad pitches, as would befit someone with a career on-base average that's below .300.

For a middle infielder, Gagne has pretty good power. But he doesn't get around as quickly as he should on pitches that others would drive. That turns potential home runs to left into harmless fly balls to center and left-center. Gagne seems to have that trouble more often against right-handed pitching. In fact, he's made substantial progress against lefties while slipping against righties. As a result, he spent increased time on the bench in 1990.

Gagne's bunting skills have improved, but he still has too many holes in his game. Pitchers take advantage of him with fastballs and sliders outside of the strike zone. It's almost as if the count is 0-and-1 or 0-and-2 before Gagne takes his at-bats seriously.

BASERUNNING:

Everyone seems to think that Gagne should steal about 20-25 bases per season because he's the fastest player on the Twins. But he's never mastered base-stealing techniques to the point of becoming a consistent threat. He takes the extra base whenever there's a chance, and he isn't afraid of contact.

FIELDING:

Gagne has learned the mental aspects of playing shortstop, especially positioning, and uses that in addition to having very good range in both directions. He gets rid of the ball quickly and turns the double play well. Gagne can't have been helped by the steady stream of second basemen he's been teamed with since 1987, but he hasn't complained.

OVERALL:

When Gagne's offense is compared to other shortstops, he does OK. He hasn't lived up to the Twins' expectations, but at this point they shouldn't expect much more than he's delivered the last few years. He'll fill a spot at the bottom of the order and help steady an infield that usually is a pretty solid unit.

DAN GLADDEN

Position: LF
Bats: R **Throws:** R
Ht: 5'11" **Wt:** 181

Opening Day Age: 33
Born: 7/7/57 in San Jose, CA
ML Seasons: 8

Overall Statistics

	G	AB	R	H	D	T	HR	RBI	SB	BB	SO	AVG
1990	136	534	64	147	27	6	5	40	25	26	67	.275
Career	867	3267	489	900	153	28	48	296	195	250	451	.275

Where He Hits the Ball

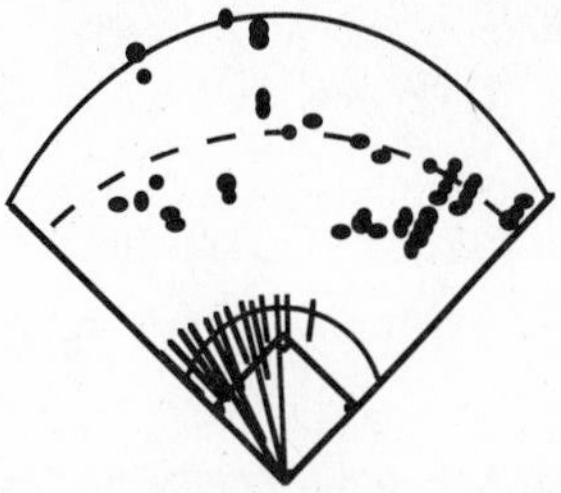

Vs. LHP

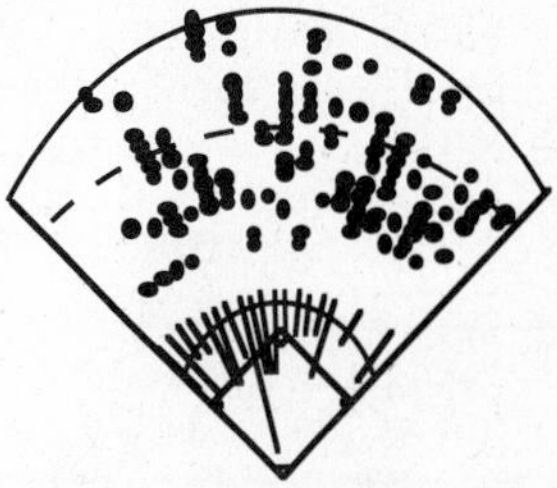

Vs. RHP

1990 Situational Stats

	AB	H	HR	RBI	AVG		AB	H	HR	RBI	AVG
Home	263	79	2	17	.300	LHP	163	44	2	16	.270
Road	271	68	3	23	.251	RHP	371	103	3	24	.278
Day	132	41	1	9	.311	Sc Pos	118	33	2	35	.280
Night	402	106	4	31	.264	Clutch	82	15	0	6	.183

1990 Rankings (American League)

- 1st in most GDPs per GDP situation (24.3%)
- 9th in steals of third (4)
- Led the Twins in singles (109), stolen bases (25), caught stealing (9), stolen base percentage (73.5%), most pitches seen per plate appearance (3.50) and steals of third

HITTING:

Dan Gladden has been used primarily in the leadoff position since coming to the Twins in 1987. But his days appear numbered -- if not with the Twins, then at least in the leadoff spot. Frustrated by Gladden's low on-base percentage, manager Tom Kelly auditioned several players, including veteran Shane Mack and rookie Pedro Munoz, at leadoff during the final weeks. Actually, it's surprising that it took Kelly and general manager Andy MacPhail four seasons to grow disenchanted. Gladden's on base percentages as a Twin -- .312, .325, .331, and .314 -- have always been well below those of the top leadoff men.

A very aggressive hitter, Gladden has struck out more than he's walked every year he's been in the majors. He compensates with some power, averaging eight home runs and 26 doubles per year with the Twins. Gladden likes the fastball up and can pull a pitch down the left field line, but has had his problems with offspeed pitches.

The self-confident Gladden has often been a top performer in pressure situations. He batted .350 against the Tigers in the '87 playoffs, and then hit .290, with four extra base hits including a home run, against the Cardinals in the World Series.

BASERUNNING:

By Twins' standards Gladden is a speedster, but by major league leadoff standards he's only average. He's stolen at least 23 bases in each of the last five years; his 25 led the team in 1990. A fiery competitor who lists Evil Knievel as his childhood hero, Gladden shows his fearless nature on the bases. He'll take out a catcher or second baseman with little regard for his own body. He's smart enough that his aggressiveness doesn't lead to many baserunning mistakes.

FIELDING:

Gladden goes full throttle after any ball hit his direction, and he's provided Twins fans with many memorable catches crashing against the fences. But he's no Gold Glover, and Twins officials are mildly concerned about his errors: six last year after committing nine in 1989. Gladden possesses a better-than-average arm, tying a career high with 12 assists last year, which gives him 41 in four seasons with the Twins.

OVERALL:

Gladden will be 33 in July and the Twins are concerned about how much longer he can be effective, given his all-out style. Based on last year's stats, there's no reason to believe he can't help somebody as an everyday player for a while longer. But the club will probably take a long look at Pedro Munoz as the left fielder in spring training.

PITCHING:

Mark Guthrie is similar in many respects to Allan Anderson, his fellow southpaw in the Twins' rotation. Neither has an overpowering fastball, and each requires command of all his pitches to be effective. Like Anderson, Guthrie is effective when he keeps the ball low in the strike zone and mixes his pitches; each can be lit up when his stuff is a little off. The main difference is that while Anderson's most effective pitch is his change-up, Guthrie's best is a forkball.

Guthrie was one of the Twins' most pleasant surprises in 1990. Only 24 when the season began, he'd had arm trouble early in his career and had made only 47 minor league starts before making his major league debut in mid-year 1989. He wasn't terribly effective in 13 appearances that year (2-4, 4.55), and when he started slowly in 1990, the Twins demoted him to Portland. Recalled in July, Guthrie proceeded to pitch his way into the starting rotation. From then on he was consistently good, pitching into the seventh inning in his last 11 starts, and recording a 2.49 ERA over his last 61.1 innings. Guthrie tied Kevin Tapani for the team lead in strikeouts with 101, and he walked just 39.

Lacking overpowering stuff, Guthrie is hittable, allowing 154 hits in 144.2 innings pitched last year. But he gave up only eight home runs, proof that he was keeping the ball low in the strike zone. Surprisingly, Guthrie had a tougher time with left-handed hitters (.343) than he did with righties (.262). Guthrie, like Anderson, appears to be a pitcher whose talents might be better suited to a different ball park. He was 5-3 with a 2.72 ERA on natural grass, 2-6 with a 4.55 ERA on artificial turf.

HOLDING RUNNERS AND FIELDING:

Guthrie has a superb move to first base. He needs the move, because he has a high leg kick that makes him a relatively easy target to steal on if a baserunner is allowed a good jump. His move is so lethal, however, that runners must be wary. Guthrie is not a polished fielder, a combination of his inexperience and some physical shortcomings. He lacks speed, and is sometimes slow to cover first base. His glove is adequate, evidenced by his making of just one error in 27 chances last year.

OVERALL:

Guthrie is being counted on to be an integral part of next year's starting rotation. That's a big jump, considering he started the 1989 season at Class AA Orlando. But he's been effective at every minor league stop, and with experience, figures to be a winner at the major league level.

MARK GUTHRIE

Position: SP
Bats: B **Throws:** L
Ht: 6' 4" **Wt:** 202

Opening Day Age: 25
Born: 9/22/65 in Buffalo, NY
ML Seasons: 2

Overall Statistics

	W	L	ERA	G	GS	Sv	IP	H	R	BB	SO	HR
1990	7	9	3.79	24	21	0	144.2	154	65	39	101	8
Career	9	13	4.01	37	29	0	202.0	220	97	60	139	15

How Often He Throws Strikes

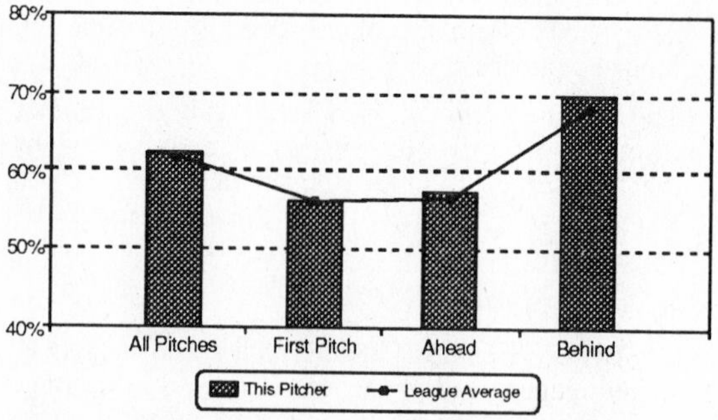

1990 Situational Stats

	W	L	ERA	Sv	IP		AB	H	HR	RBI	AVG
Home	2	4	3.93	0	68.2	LHB	99	34	1	10	.343
Road	5	5	3.67	0	76.0	RHB	458	120	7	40	.262
Day	1	2	3.79	0	35.2	Sc Pos	125	37	1	37	.296
Night	6	7	3.80	0	109.0	Clutch	57	20	1	8	.351

1990 Rankings (American League)

- ➟ 9th most runners caught stealing (12)
- ➟ Led the Twins in strikeouts (101), pickoff throws (143) and stolen bases allowed (17)

BRIAN HARPER

Position: C
Bats: R **Throws:** R
Ht: 6' 2" **Wt:** 195

Opening Day Age: 31
Born: 10/16/59 in Los Angeles, CA
ML Seasons: 11

HITTING:

In the summer of 1987 Brian Harper, who was being used as a reserve for Oakland's Class AAA Tacoma farm club, sat in a hotel room contemplating retirement. Instead, Harper decided to try a new batting style, hitting to all fields rather than pulling the ball. Presto. Since joining the Twins in mid-1988, Harper has been one of the major leagues' most consistent hitters. In 1990 he led the majors with a 25-game hitting streak, hit over .300 for most of the season, and finished with a .294 average after hitting .295 and .325 his first two seasons with the Twins.

The most amazing statistic about Harper is that he's struck out only 55 times in 1,030 at bats in his three years with the Twins.It's even more impressive given that Harper's not exactly a patient hitter, walking only 42 times in the last three years, including 19 last year. He has sound mechanics, and for a contact hitter, excellent power, with a career-high 42 doubles last season, the most by a major league catcher since Lance Parrish hit 42 in 1983.

An excellent fastball hitter, Harper helps himself considerably with his ability to use the whole field. He's yet to show any major weaknesses, and that would figure: in both the majors and the minors, Harper has always hit when given a chance to play.

BASERUNNING:

Suffice it to say speed is not a Harper asset. He was successful on three of five stolen base attempts last year, increasing his career stolen bases to six. Harper is a smart baserunner, but he did ground into 20 double plays last year, second on the team.

FIELDING:

Harper was a utility player, performing primarily at third base and the outfield while bouncing around the minor leagues for almost a decade. In 1987, the Twins were the first major league team to give him a shot at catcher, and he's improved steadily since then. He's still no Bob Boone, but his skills are adequate. Harper made 11 errors each of the last two seasons, but had only five passed balls in 1990. Base stealers were successful 63% of the time with Harper behind the plate, an average figure. Still, he's a smart player who works well with the inexperienced pitching staff.

OVERALL:

Harper has proven himself to be a quality major league hitter and at least an average defensive catcher. His batting average tailed off at the end of last year, but then so did almost every other Twin regular. Harper is the Twins' No. 1 catcher, and the position is one of the few in which the Twins have no qualms entering 1991.

Overall Statistics

	G	AB	R	H	D	T	HR	RBI	SB	BB	SO	AVG
1990	134	479	61	141	42	3	6	54	3	19	27	.294
Career	525	1420	152	406	92	5	28	181	6	55	96	.286

Where He Hits the Ball

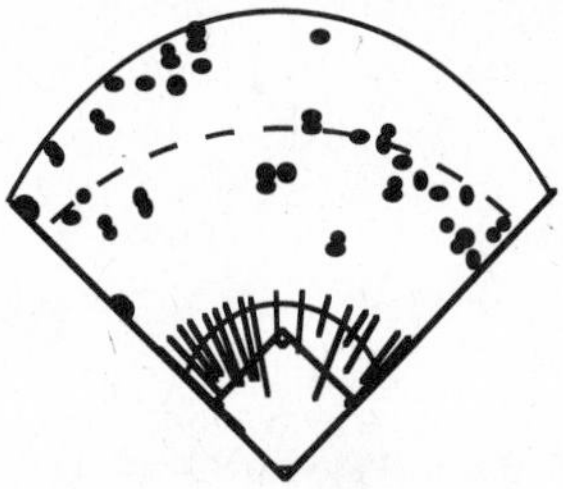

Vs. LHP

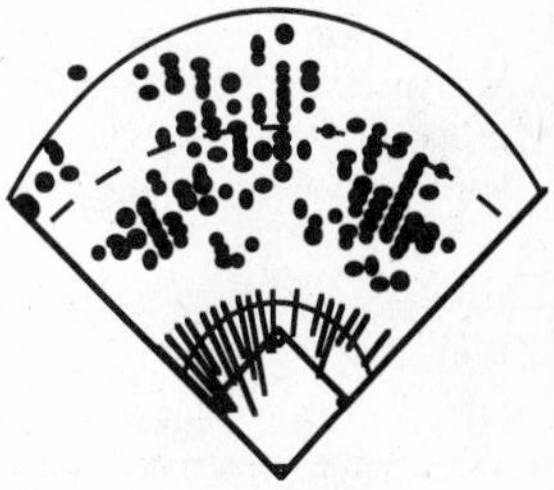

Vs. RHP

1990 Situational Stats

	AB	H	HR	RBI	AVG		AB	H	HR	RBI	AVG
Home	230	65	1	24	.283	LHP	146	46	4	20	.315
Road	249	76	5	30	.305	RHP	333	95	2	34	.285
Day	113	35	3	18	.310	Sc Pos	122	37	2	44	.303
Night	366	106	3	36	.290	Clutch	78	24	1	12	.308

1990 Rankings (American League)

- 4th in hit by pitch (7)
- 5th in doubles (42) and GDPs (20)
- 7th in least pitches seen per plate appearance (3.26)
- 8th in batting average on the road (.305)
- Led the Twins in doubles, hit by pitch, batting average on the road, lowest percentage of swings that missed (12.1%) and highest percentage of swings put into play (52.1%)
- Led AL catchers in batting average (.294), hits (141), doubles, hit by pitch, runs scored per time reached base (36.5%) and batting average on the road

HITTING:

Maybe hitting comes a little bit too easily for Kent Hrbek. He often goes into deep slumps, but when he emerges from them he can do well enough to finish the season with respectable totals. Hrbek sometimes hits from a wide open stance, but other times takes a more conventional approach. It that regard, he's something like Rod Carew, who was always tinkering with his stance, even when his average was well above .300. Unlike Carew, however, Hrbek can blast the ball a country mile. When he gets into one of his hot streaks, he can be almost impossible to retire.

Hrbek has never wanted to be classified as a dead-pull hitter and he isn't ... at least, not completely. Despite some defensive alignments that over-shift against him, Hrbek has hit home runs to center and left-center. And he isn't above dribbling a bunt toward third base if the opponents aren't looking for it. The best way to handle him is to move the ball around, finishing off with a fastball on the fists -- a pitch he doesn't handle as well as he used to. Hrbek was benched against some tough lefties last year, which didn't sit well with some fans. They didn't think a guy who just signed a five-year, $14 million contract should ever be over-matched.

Hrbek handles fastballs from the knee to the waist better than anything. He also doesn't strike out much for a slugger. He has a good eye, and has had more walks than strikeouts for four straight seasons.

BASERUNNING:

Hrbek has slowed substantially as his weight has ballooned into the 250-pound range. He'll steal a base when it isn't expected and he has average speed once he kicks into high gear, which takes longer than for most folks. He isn't a hard slider.

FIELDING:

Hrbek's extra weight has never hindered his fielding, and 1990 might have been his best season on defense. He saves infield teammates countless errors by digging throws out of the dirt and handling odd hops. He'll also dive in either direction and starts the 3-6-3 double play as well as anyone.

OVERALL:

Hrbek has been bothered by injuries for the last two seasons, ending 1990 early when he sprained an ankle while fooling around in the clubhouse. He did play 34 more games last year than in 1989 when a separated shoulder sidelined him. But the Twins are dependent on his power, and need him to be in the lineup 150-plus times.

KENT HRBEK

Position: 1B/DH
Bats: L **Throws:** R
Ht: 6' 4" **Wt:** 250

Opening Day Age: 30
Born: 5/21/60 in Minneapolis, MN
ML Seasons: 10

Overall Statistics

	G	AB	R	H	D	T	HR	RBI	SB	BB	SO	AVG
1990	143	492	61	141	26	0	22	79	5	69	45	.287
Career	1299	4670	685	1353	250	16	223	803	24	592	609	.290

Where He Hits the Ball

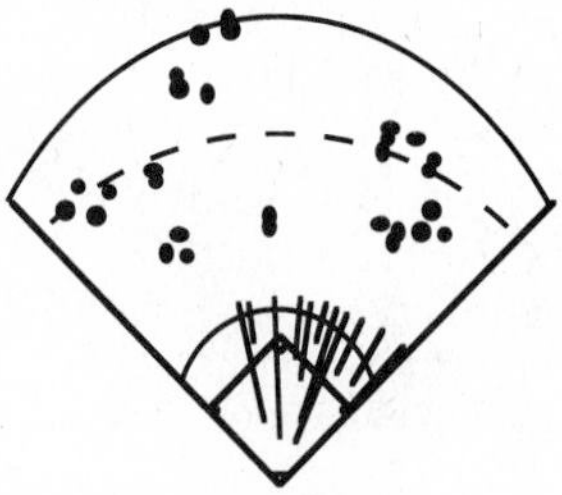

Vs. LHP

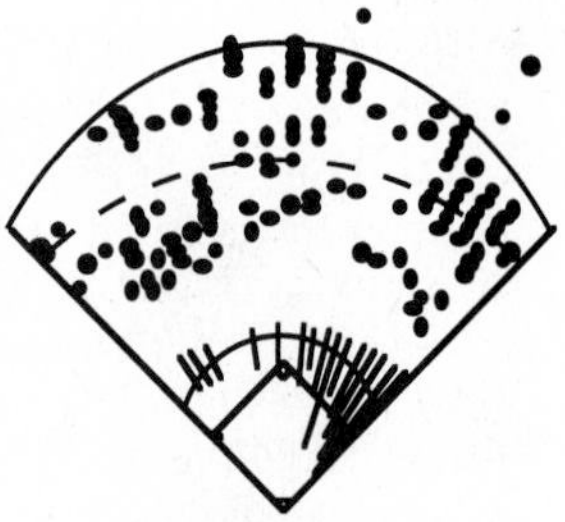

Vs. RHP

1990 Situational Stats

	AB	H	HR	RBI	AVG		AB	H	HR	RBI	AVG
Home	247	69	8	43	.279	LHP	129	37	2	17	.287
Road	245	72	14	36	.294	RHP	363	104	20	62	.287
Day	126	36	7	24	.286	Sc Pos	127	35	4	53	.276
Night	366	105	15	55	.287	Clutch	77	23	1	8	.299

1990 Rankings (American League)

- 4th in hit by pitch (7)
- 5th highest slugging percentage vs. right-handed pitchers (.515)
- 8th in sacrifice flies (8)
- Led the Twins in home runs (22), sacrifice flies, walks (69), hit by pitch, slugging percentage (.474), on-base average (.377) and HR frequency (22.4 ABs per HR)
- Led AL first basemen in hit by pitch, batting average on an 0-2 count (.238) and fielding percentage (.997)

HITTING:

In Gene Larkin, the Twins have a player who will consistently hit in the high .260's and drive in enough runs to be respectable. He won't ever be great, in all likelihood, but he won't be an automatic out, either. Larkin has a nice stroke from either side of the plate. Formerly a weak hitter from the left side, Larkin improved markedly last season.

Larkin's improvement batting lefty came when he stopped trying to pull everything. He has a little power from that side, but shouldn't be expected to hit more than a half-dozen homers per season. He's susceptible to being jammed from the left side, but batting righty he has enough bat speed to handle those pitches. As a righty he's more of a fastball hitter. From either side Larkin crowds the plate and usually is among the team leaders in getting hit by pitches. He is a pretty good bunter, although he doesn't have the speed to turn them into base hits.

That Larkin is a line drive and gap hitter is evidenced by the number of doubles that he gets. He also established a career high in triples during 1990. Larkin might never develop into the hitting machine that he was expected to be when he was called up during the 1987 season, but he's a useful offensive player who isn't one-dimensional.

BASERUNNING:

Larkin is an enthusiastic baserunner who will try to steal a base now and then. He rarely gets into trouble while advancing and he isn't timid about breaking up a double play or trying to jar an opposing catcher with a hard slide. He should have been blessed with more speed because he'd know how to use it.

FIELDING:

Seeing that Kent Hrbek had a stranglehold on first base, Larkin learned the outfield and has done a pretty good job in right. He has a better-than-average arm and has learned to get a pretty good jump on the ball. He's also a steady backup for Hrbek, with average range and acceptable hands. Most first basemen pale next to Hrbek, and Larkin suffers in that comparison as well.

OVERALL:

Larkin fits into the Twins plans as a guy who can do several things reasonably well. Being able to play the field increases his value, as does his improvement from the left side of the plate. Larkin is a known quantity, not someone to build the club around, but hardly a liability either.

GENE LARKIN

Position: RF/1B/DH
Bats: B **Throws:** R
Ht: 6' 3" **Wt:** 205

Opening Day Age: 28
Born: 10/24/62 in Astoria, NY
ML Seasons: 4

Overall Statistics

	G	AB	R	H	D	T	HR	RBI	SB	BB	SO	AVG
1990	119	401	46	108	26	4	5	42	5	42	55	.269
Career	489	1585	186	424	92	9	23	186	14	189	198	.268

Where He Hits the Ball

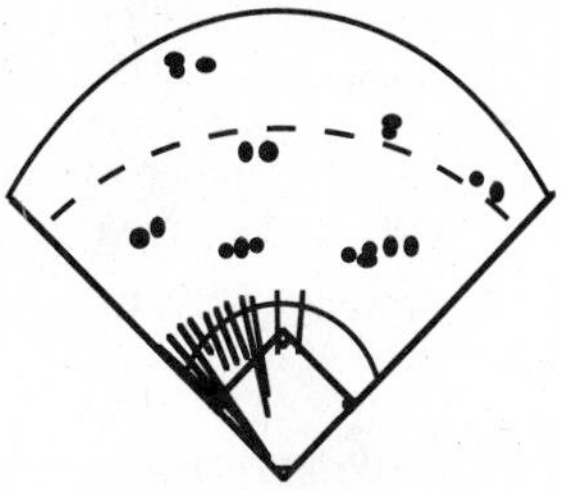

Vs. LHP

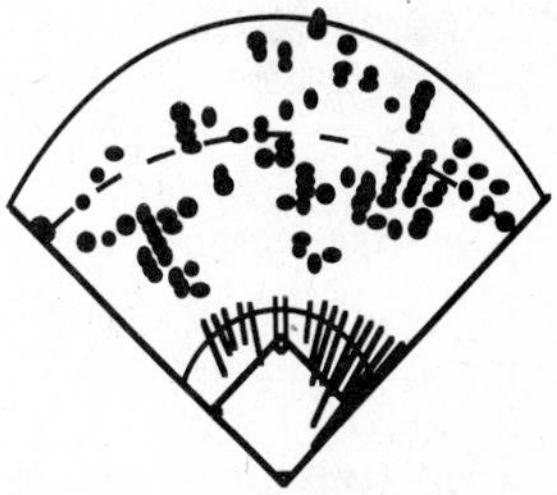

Vs. RHP

1990 Situational Stats

	AB	H	HR	RBI	AVG		AB	H	HR	RBI	AVG
Home	199	57	5	26	.286	LHP	121	30	0	12	.248
Road	202	51	0	16	.252	RHP	280	78	5	30	.279
Day	116	29	1	6	.250	Sc Pos	106	26	2	37	.245
Night	285	79	4	36	.277	Clutch	63	13	0	5	.206

1990 Rankings (American League)

- Led the Twins in percentage of pitches taken (56.4%)

TERRY LEACH

Position: RP
Bats: R **Throws:** R
Ht: 6' 0" **Wt:** 191

Opening Day Age: 37
Born: 3/13/54 in Selma, AL
ML Seasons: 8

PITCHING:

Terry Leach gave the Twins some quality innings last season, but seemed to lose his prowess as the year went on. Leach doesn't throw very hard, and needs to have pinpoint control and good movement on his submarine pitches in order to be effective. The ideal way to use Leach is against one or two right-handed batters, preferably free swingers, and then get him out of there before anyone gets too good of a look. Leach used to have good enough stuff to be a starter, but now you wouldn't want him to go more than once through a batting order.

Leach's main pitches are a sinking fastball and a curve, both of which he tries to get batters to chase in the dirt. Although lefties have usually given him more trouble during his career, he had about equal success against hitters on both sides of the plate in 1990. Against Leach, lefties tend to lay off the pitches in the dirt and attack the ones that stay over the plate. Not a power pitcher, Leach typically gets about one strike-out per two innings. His control last year was better than in '89, when he walked more batters than he struck out for the Kansas City Royals.

Leach also pitched better last season on grass, which probably follows for a guy who gets a lot of hard grounders. Leach has a rubber arm, and can work for several straight days. That strength came in handy early last season, when all of the Minnesota middle relievers were getting more work than they should have.

HOLDING RUNNERS AND FIELDING:

When Leach can get to a ball, he does a good job of getting rid of it. His throws are accurate, he's good on bunts and he throws to the right base. But his sidearm delivery usually puts him on the third base side of the mound, taking him out of position to field balls hit up the middle. Leach's odd delivery makes him successful, but his slow style also makes him pretty easy to steal against. His move to first doesn't fool people.

OVERALL:

Leach finally reached the 30-win mark for his career in his eighth season in the majors. He can help a team, as long as he isn't relied upon to carry a huge load, the kind of guy who can be a ninth or tenth pitcher on a staff. A team that needs Leach to save games or hold a lot of leads might be asking for too much at this stage of his career.

Overall Statistics

	W	L	ERA	G	GS	Sv	IP	H	R	BB	SO	HR
1990	2	5	3.20	55	0	2	81.2	84	31	21	46	2
Career	31	20	3.27	261	21	9	542.2	534	229	161	274	33

How Often He Throws Strikes

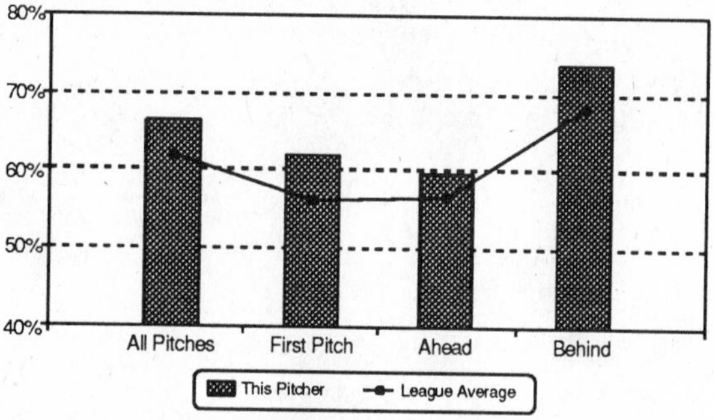

1990 Situational Stats

	W	L	ERA	Sv	IP		AB	H	HR	RBI	AVG
Home	0	0	3.53	1	43.1	LHB	126	34	0	11	.270
Road	2	5	2.82	1	38.1	RHB	187	50	2	28	.267
Day	1	2	5.01	0	23.1	Sc Pos	107	29	1	36	.271
Night	1	3	2.47	2	58.1	Clutch	119	37	1	20	.311

1990 Rankings (American League)

- 1st in first batter efficiency (.125)
- Led the Twins in first batter efficiency

HITTING:

The Twins picked up Nelson Liriano from Toronto with the hope that he'd finally answer the second base questions they've had since John Castino was forced to retire. Tim Teufel? Steve Lombardozzi? Tom Herr? Wally Backman? Fred Manrique? The Twins found problems with all of them. What they've been looking for is someone who can suffice in the field while filling one of the top two spots in the batting order. The jury may still be out on whether Liriano is the right guy, but they appear willing to give him every chance to succeed.

Liriano is a better hitter from the left side, although he's had some decent seasons batting righty. He's more of a line drive and pull hitter from the left. Batting righty he sometimes seems overmatched, hitting fly balls and weak grounders. Good pitchers seem to work him by getting ahead in the count with breaking balls and then offering a high fastball for him to chase. He could probably take more advantage of his speed by trying to slap more balls through turf infields.

Liriano probably is best known for his timely hits. A couple of years back, he broke up two no-hitters with extra-base hits in the ninth inning, and he's been a surprisingly good pinch hitter throughout his career. Liriano knows what he wants to do when he comes to the plate, and makes a quick study of his pitching opponent.

BASERUNNING:

Liriano is more of a stealing threat than he showed with the Twins last year. He has a good speed and usually gets a pretty good jump. He reads left-handers better than most runners. He also can be counted on to take an extra base.

FIELDING:

A mixed bag seems to be the most accurate assessment of Liriano's fielding skills. Liriano turns the double play well and isn't afraid to get a little banged-up in the process. At the same time, some Twins observers noticed that his first step is a bit slow, both on grounders and in covering second. He also has some trouble going back on pop-ups. But overall his defense is better than that of most folks the Twins have tried at second in recent years.

OVERALL:

If Liriano was that good, Toronto wouldn't have given up on him in favor of Manny Lee, who is hardly a head-turner. But if he can meet some modest expectations, the Twins will feel as if they made a good deal with his acquisition. Liriano won't fail for lack of effort.

NELSON LIRIANO

Position: 2B
Bats: B **Throws:** R
Ht: 5'10" **Wt:** 165

Opening Day Age: 26
Born: 6/3/64 in Puerto Plata, Dominican Republic
ML Seasons: 4

Overall Statistics

	G	AB	R	H	D	T	HR	RBI	SB	BB	SO	AVG
1990	103	355	46	83	12	9	1	28	8	38	44	.234
Career	371	1207	162	304	50	16	11	114	49	108	157	.252

Where He Hits the Ball

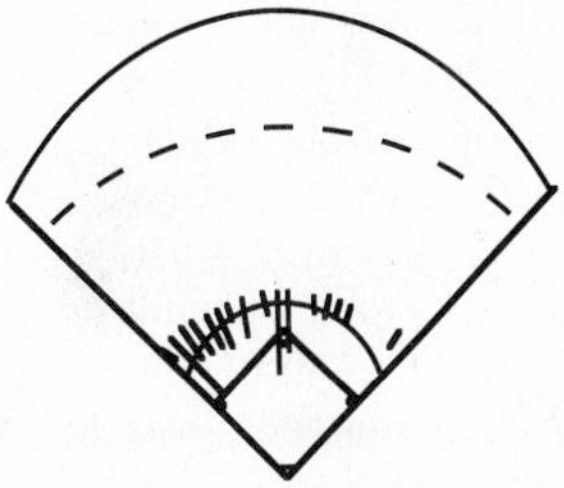

Vs. LHP

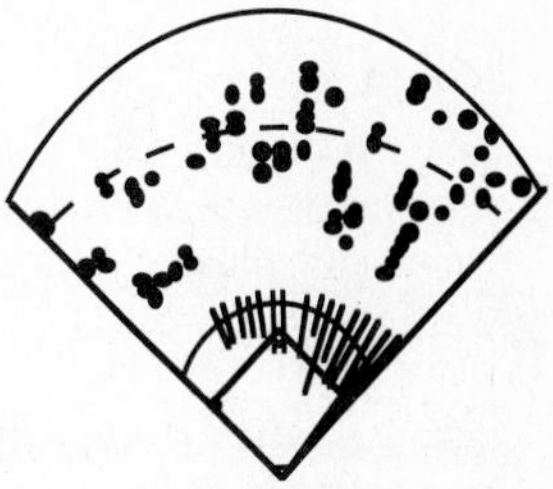

Vs. RHP

1990 Situational Stats

	AB	H	HR	RBI	AVG		AB	H	HR	RBI	AVG
Home	178	45	1	22	.253	LHP	67	13	0	6	.194
Road	177	38	0	6	.215	RHP	288	70	1	22	.243
Day	93	21	0	8	.226	Sc Pos	81	21	0	24	.259
Night	262	62	1	20	.237	Clutch	61	10	0	3	.164

1990 Rankings (American League)

- 3rd in triples (9)
- 7th lowest batting average in the clutch (.164)
- Led the Twins in triples (7 with the Twins)
- Led AL second basemen in triples (9)

HITTING:

After barely surviving spring training last year as the final outfielder on the Twins roster, Shane Mack enters 1991 expected to carry a heavy load for a rebuilding team. That's what happens when your average stays above .300 and you show yourself to be a talented all-around player. Mack went from being a platoon player, starting only against left-handed pitchers, to an everyday fixture in right or center field.

Mack missed most of the 1989 season following elbow surgery. Despite some impressive Triple-A statistics, the Padres left him off their 40-man roster, and the Twins gambled at the winter meeting draft. Many observers felt that Mack was overmatched by major league pitching and less than adequate in the field, but he proved the skeptics wrong. Mack showed good power to right field and right-center, hanging in there against good pitching. His strikeout total was fairly high, but he always seemed to get in good licks. Breaking pitches away did give him some trouble, though.

Mack attracted notice early in the season by coming off the bench and getting key hits. He was among the team batting leaders with runners in scoring position, often slapping key hits to the opposite field. While he was especially tough on lefties, Mack showed that he could hit righthanders pretty well, too.

BASERUNNING:

Mack isn't always a threat to steal, but makes the most of his opportunities. He runs the bases hard, taking extra bases and taking out second basemen if he's there in time to break up a double play. Mack is a hustler who makes the kind of plays on the bases that can inspire his team toward a big inning.

FIELDING:

When he didn't play regularly, Mack seemed to have trouble getting the jump on fly balls. With more playing time, that problem diminished. Manager Tom Kelly even used Mack in center field, feeling that Kirby Puckett would be better off covering less ground in right. Mack has good range and a good arm, although teams challenged it more than they did Puckett's arm.

OVERALL:

Mack is finally on the verge of becoming the solid regular the Padres envisioned when they made him their first pick in 1984. The Twins were hoping to get a serviceable player when they selected him, and they ended up with much more. It will be interesting to see if he can maintain the promising pace in 1991.

SHANE MACK

Position: RF/LF/CF
Bats: R **Throws:** R
Ht: 6' 0" **Wt:** 185

Opening Day Age: 27
Born: 12/7/63 in Los Angeles, CA
ML Seasons: 3

Overall Statistics

	G	AB	R	H	D	T	HR	RBI	SB	BB	SO	AVG
1990	125	313	50	102	10	4	8	44	13	29	69	.326
Career	286	670	91	188	24	7	12	81	22	61	137	.281

Where He Hits the Ball

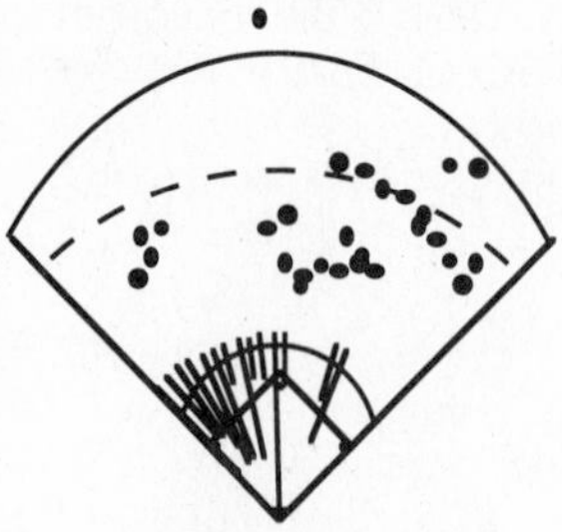

Vs. LHP

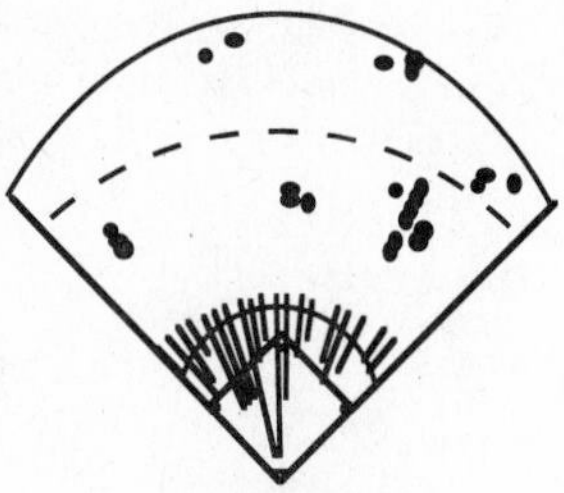

Vs. RHP

1990 Situational Stats

	AB	H	HR	RBI	AVG		AB	H	HR	RBI	AVG
Home	141	52	5	21	.369	LHP	146	54	5	27	.370
Road	172	50	3	23	.291	RHP	167	48	3	17	.287
Day	93	34	0	19	.366	Sc Pos	71	25	0	32	.352
Night	220	68	8	25	.309	Clutch	47	17	1	11	.362

1990 Rankings (American League)

- 3rd in batting average vs. left-handed pitchers (.370)
- 4th in on-base average vs. left-handed pitchers (.439)
- 7th in batting average in the clutch (.362)
- Led the Twins in batting average with the bases loaded (.444), batting average/on-base average vs. left-handed pitchers, slugging percentage vs. left-handed pitchers (.548)
- Led AL right fielders in batting average in the clutch, batting average with the bases loaded and batting average/on-base average vs. left-handed pitchers

AL NEWMAN

Position: 2B/3B/SS
Bats: B **Throws:** R
Ht: 5' 9" **Wt:** 183

Opening Day Age: 30
Born: 6/30/60 in Kansas City, Mo
ML Seasons: 6

Overall Statistics

	G	AB	R	H	D	T	HR	RBI	SB	BB	SO	AVG
1990	144	388	43	94	14	0	0	30	13	33	34	.242
Career	620	1615	214	375	58	7	1	125	78	179	165	.232

Where He Hits the Ball

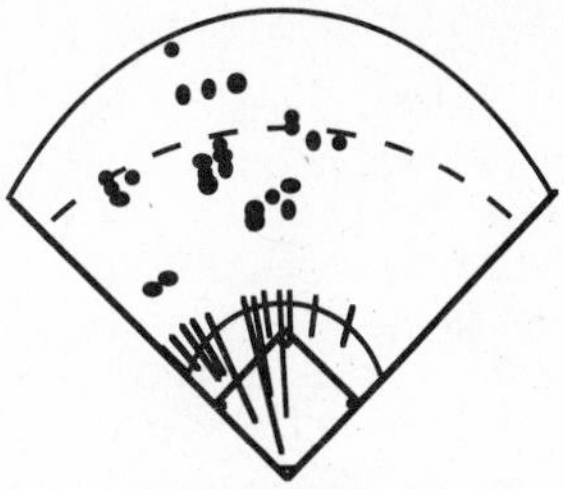

Vs. LHP

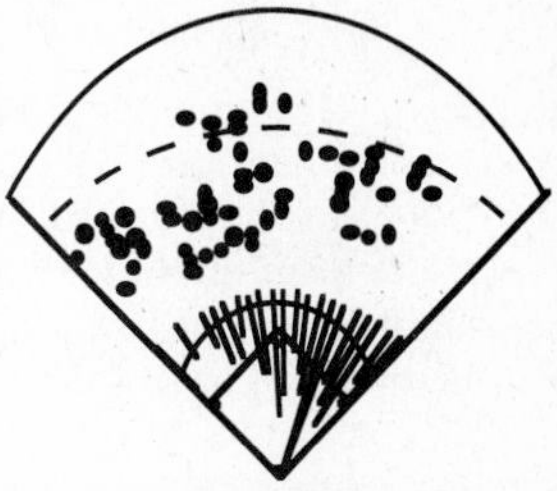

Vs. RHP

1990 Situational Stats

	AB	H	HR	RBI	AVG		AB	H	HR	RBI	AVG
Home	199	52	0	19	.261	LHP	123	31	0	6	.252
Road	189	42	0	11	.222	RHP	265	63	0	24	.238
Day	118	34	0	11	.288	Sc Pos	110	24	0	29	.218
Night	270	60	0	19	.222	Clutch	62	10	0	4	.161

1990 Rankings (American League)

- 5th worst batting average in the clutch (.161)
- 8th highest percentage of extra bases taken as a runner (57.1%)
- 9th worst batting average with the bases loaded (.100)
- Led the Twins in sacrifice bunts (8), bunts in play (15) and percentage of extra bases taken as a runner
- Led AL second basemen in percentage of extra bases taken as a runner

HITTING:

Al Newman has gone without a home run for longer than any non-pitcher currently in the majors. His only career homer came as an Expo on July 6, 1986, off Atlanta's Zane Smith. Bob Horner hit four homers for the Braves in that game. Toward the end of last season, Metrodome fans would chant "home run, home run" when Newman stepped to the plate. He took some mighty -- and mighty unsuccessful -- hacks. Newman would talk home runs but, most of the time, he was smart enough not to try doing anything about this shortcoming.

The switch-hitting Newman has a little more pop from the right side of the plate, but his average has been about equal from either side for the last couple of years. He's at his best when he tries to reach base by whatever means necessary -- bunting, slapping and poking the ball. Newman is one of those rare players with a higher on-base percentage than slugging percentage. He is usually among the team leaders in sacrifice bunts and, despite keeping the ball on the ground a lot, doesn't hit into many double plays. Newman needs to draw a lot of walks to be a valuable offensive player, and he slipped in that area in 1990.

BASERUNNING:

Newman is always a threat to run, but didn't steal as many bases last year as his career high of 25 in 1989. He never has had a great percentage in that area, and needs a few short, choppy strides to get started, a la Willie McGee. Despite his size, he's among the hardest sliders on the team, refusing to back down on the double play. He gets a good jump on balls hit to the outfield, too.

FIELDING:

Watching Twins' second basemen come and go, Newman would love to be the regular at that position. But the Twins think he's most valuable as a utility player who will usually be in the lineup in some capacity. Second base is his best position, but he also does a workmanlike job filling for Gary Gaetti at third and Greg Gagne at shortstop. He lacks great range, but has good hands and a quick release.

OVERALL:

Newman takes his utility role seriously. He has established increasing value by always being ready to play and filling whatever role is expected. He has played the outfield several times on an emergency basis, and has even volunteered to catch if the need arises. Newman has done a lot for the Twins in his four years with the team and is a very popular player.

JUNIOR ORTIZ

Position: C
Bats: R **Throws:** R
Ht: 5'11" **Wt:** 176

Opening Day Age: 31
Born: 10/24/59 in Humacao, Puerto Rico
ML Seasons: 9

Overall Statistics

	G	AB	R	H	D	T	HR	RBI	SB	BB	SO	AVG
1990	71	170	18	57	7	1	0	18	0	12	16	.335
Career	478	1191	91	319	44	3	5	122	6	78	150	.268

Where He Hits the Ball

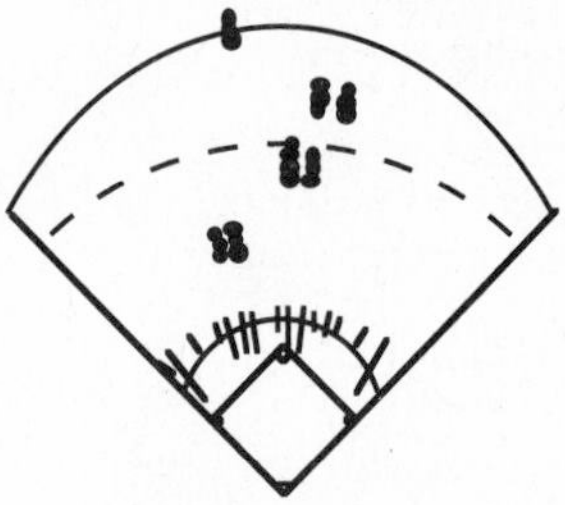

Vs. LHP

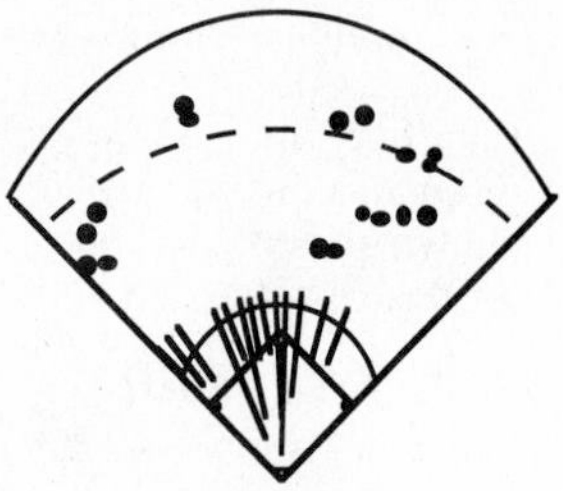

Vs. RHP

1990 Situational Stats

	AB	H	HR	RBI	AVG		AB	H	HR	RBI	AVG
Home	94	38	0	16	.404	LHP	50	18	0	7	.360
Road	76	19	0	2	.250	RHP	120	39	0	11	.325
Day	75	23	0	6	.307	Sc Pos	45	17	0	18	.378
Night	95	34	0	12	.358	Clutch	22	7	0	2	.318

1990 Rankings (American League)

- 6th in batting average with a 3-2 count (.375)
- Led the Twins in batting average with a 3-2 count
- Led AL catchers in batting average with a 3-2 count

HITTING:

When the Twins acquired Junior Ortiz at the start of last season, they envisioned him as a defensive replacement for Brian Harper, someone to work a game here and there or come in for the late innings of blowouts. With Tim Laudner suddenly and unexpectedly retired, they would have been happy to get anyone who knew how to put on the equipment. Ortiz had loftier goals, and established himself as a valuable player who performed well beyond those modest expectations.

Swinging a hot bat for most of the season, Ortiz looked nothing like the guy who had batted a lowly .217 for the '89 Pirates. In the press box, there was talk of Ortiz's "quest for .400," as his average stayed above the magic mark until late in the year. Ortiz will never be considered a serious offensive threat like Brian Harper, but he proved that he shouldn't be taken too lightly.

Ortiz is a pretty good fastball hitter who can turn on an inside pitch and poke others to the opposite field. Ortiz had several key hits in his limited service, leading the team in hitting with runners in scoring position, although he had only about 50 at-bats in those situations. He's good in hit-and-run situations and had pretty good pop against right-handers. All of this was unexpected because Ortiz finished 1989 with an 0-for-23 slump with Pittsburgh and didn't hit in his first 11 Minnesota at-bats.

BASERUNNING:

Ortiz isn't much of a stolen-base threat, even with the element of surprise on his side. He's a solid fundamental baserunner and doesn't make many mistakes. Also, Ortiz seems to have a good sense of where the ball is in the field and, despite his lack of speed, he'll go for the extra base if it's there for the taking.

FIELDING:

Twins pitchers appeared to enjoy working with Ortiz, who has a good arm and picked up quickly on staff strengths and weaknesses. At times, Ortiz's patience was tested by inexperienced pitchers who had trouble finding the plate, and he seemed to have more trouble blocking balls as the season progressed. Of course, once the Twins were committed to using young pitchers, there were that many more balls to block.

OVERALL:

Ortiz thought he was the best backup catcher in the National League and said he wanted to have that same reputation in the AL. He's probably not there yet, but could reach that status if 1991 mirrors 1990. He looks like a solid performer as long as he's not asked to do too much.

HITTING:

The American League batting champ in 1989, Kirby Puckett dropped to .298 in '90, with only 164 hits. Fine figures for most, but not for Puckett, who had hit at least .328 and recorded 207 or more hits every year since 1986. Equally surprising was Puckett's power drop-off during the '90 season; he had 12 home runs through July 15, then did not hit another in the final 74 games. Puckett's RBI totals the last three seasons have dropped from 121 to 85 to 80. What has happened to one of the game's greatest hitters?

Puckett, a notorious free swinger, believes the answer lies in his walks. He was issued 57 free passes in 1990; his previous major league high was 41. Puckett traces his decline to the reluctance of opposing pitchers to challenge him in the strike zone. Puckett will still chase bad pitches, and is particularly vulnerable to hard breaking balls low and away. Puckett struck out 73 times last year, 14 more than the previous year.

Although his home runs were off from his '86-'88 glory days, when he averaged 28 per year, Puckett had 40 doubles, the third straight year he has had at least that many. But for a number three hitter, Puckett dribbles too many grounders through the infield. Here's evidence: He batted only .245 on natural grass last year, compared to .330 on turf. That continued a career trend that saw him bat .372 and .370 on turf in '88 and '89, compared to .282 and .335 on grass.

BASERUNNING:

Puckett is a typical Twin, combining average speed with smarts on the bases. He was bothered by a nagging hamstring problem last year, netting a career-low five stolen bases in nine attempts. He also hit into 15 double plays.

FIELDING:

Puckett won four straight Gold Gloves between 1986-1989, but his reputation was enhanced by several leaping catches over the center-field wall. In truth, Puckett played a deep center, making it possible for him to get to the fence quickly, but allowing too many short flies to fall in front of him. Late last year the Twins experimented with Puckett in right and left fields, playing Shane Mack in center. The move was ostensibly made to save wear on Puckett's legs, but Mack may provide more range.

OVERALL:

No matter where he plays -- right, center or left -- Puckett remains an asset. He had an off-year at the plate in 1990, but there's no reason to believe that Puckett won't challenge for several more batting titles, and maybe even regain his power swing. He's a proven star, and one year shouldn't change that status.

KIRBY PUCKETT

Position: CF
Bats: R **Throws:** R
Ht: 5' 8" **Wt:** 210

Opening Day Age: 30
Born: 3/14/61 in Chicago, IL
ML Seasons: 7

Overall Statistics

	G	AB	R	H	D	T	HR	RBI	SB	BB	SO	AVG
1990	146	551	82	164	40	3	12	80	5	57	73	.298
Career	1070	4395	624	1407	237	41	108	586	89	244	561	.320

Where He Hits the Ball

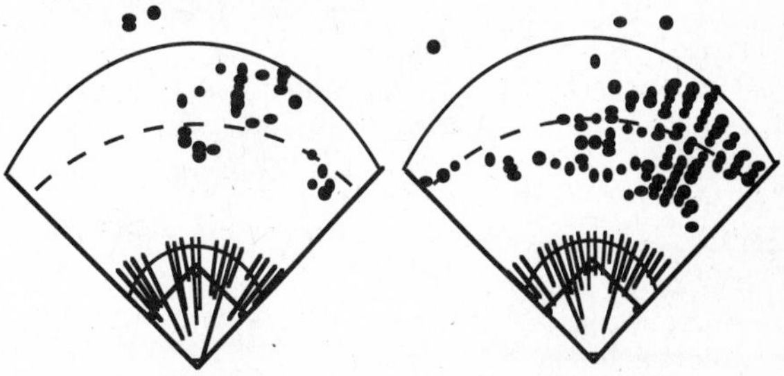

Vs. LHP | Vs. RHP

1990 Situational Stats

	AB	H	HR	RBI	AVG		AB	H	HR	RBI	AVG
Home	273	94	6	47	.344	LHP	164	49	4	22	.299
Road	278	70	6	33	.252	RHP	387	115	8	58	.297
Day	153	53	4	27	.346	Sc Pos	138	47	6	64	.341
Night	398	111	8	53	.279	Clutch	89	20	2	13	.225

1990 Rankings (American League)

- 2nd highest batting average at home (.344)
- 3rd in groundball/flyball ratio (2.38) and least pitches seen per plate appearance (3.17)
- 4th highest batting average with runners in scoring position (.341)
- Led the Twins in batting average (.298), runs (82), hits (164), singles (109), total bases (246), intentional walks (11), times on base (224), groundball/flyball ratio, runs scored per time reached base (36.6%) and batting average with runners in scoring position
- Led AL center fielders in doubles (40), grounball/flyball ratio and batting average at home

PITCHING:

If your idea of a pitcher is somebody who looks good on a radar gun, forget about Roy Smith. The righthander is a crafty veteran whose best pitch is a slow, tantalizing overhand curve. He combines the curve with a fastball that is just fast enough to keep the hitters honest, and depends on good control. It's a delicate mixture, and not one that figures to ever make him a star. After seven years, Smith's season high in victories is ten, and he's logged exactly one major league save.

Following a surprisingly good 1989 campaign, Smith began last year in the Twins' starting rotation, but things simply didn't work out. Finishing the season in the bullpen, his won-lost record was the Woolworth's special: 5-and-10. In 153.1 innings he allowed 191 hits, with opponents batting a gaudy .313. He also gave up 20 home runs, just one behind team-leader David West. Smith did have a respectable strikeout-walk ratio, fanning 87 while walking 47. His 1990 numbers, in short, were anything but great, but remember that Smith was effective in 1989, going 10-6 with a 3.92 ERA.

The Twins figure Smith might do well working in long relief, and the rationale is obvious. Left-handed batters had a .369 average against Smith last year, while righties hit only .262. The idea would be to use Smith in relief of lefthanders like Allan Anderson or Mark Guthrie, coming in to face lineups stacked with right-handed batters.

Smith might also be enticing to a National League team in a trade, because his curve is unique, and seems to work well against hitters who aren't used to it. That was the case in 1989, when he was used extensively for the first time in four years. In 1990 the element of surprise was gone, and Smith's work wasn't nearly as good.

HOLDING RUNNERS AND FIELDING:

Smith isn't a natural athlete and he'll never win a Gold Glove. But he's adequate defensively, seldom making a mistake (one error in 20 chances). He does have problems holding runners on because of this deadly combination: he's right-handed, has a high leg kick and lives on his slow overhand curve.

OVERALL:

Even after five seasons in Minnesota, Smith has to battle annually for a spot on the Twins staff. This season figures to be no exception, although with the Twins heavy on inexperienced pitchers, it's a good bet Smith's veteran status will earn him a spot in the bullpen. That is, if there's no trade.

ROY SMITH

Position: SP/RP
Bats: R **Throws:** R
Ht: 6' 3" **Wt:** 217

Opening Day Age: 29
Born: 9/6/61 in Mt. Vernon, NY
ML Seasons: 7

Overall Statistics

	W	L	ERA	G	GS	Sv	IP	H	R	BB	SO	HR
1990	5	10	4.81	32	23	0	153.1	191	91	47	87	20
Career	25	27	4.45	119	79	1	538.0	608	292	178	295	71

How Often He Throws Strikes

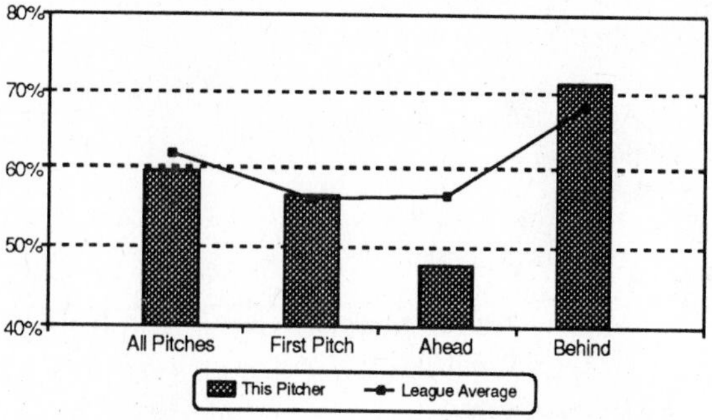

1990 Situational Stats

	W	L	ERA	Sv	IP		AB	H	HR	RBI	AVG
Home	4	5	4.30	0	73.1	LHB	287	106	9	47	.369
Road	1	5	5.29	0	80.0	RHB	324	85	11	38	.262
Day	1	3	5.58	0	30.2	Sc Pos	134	42	2	57	.313
Night	4	7	4.62	0	122.2	Clutch	18	9	1	1	.500

1990 Rankings (American League)

- 1st in highest batting average allowed vs. left-handed batters (.369)
- 6th worst winning percentage (.333)
- 7th most runners caught stealing (13) and highest batting average allowed with runners in scoring position
- Led the Twins in wild pitches (10) and runners caught stealing (13)

PITCHING:

Kevin Tapani was one of the few bright spots for the Twins in 1990. The right-hander, one of five pitchers obtained from the Mets in the Frank Viola deal, was 11-5 on Aug. 1 and appeared to be a leading candidate for AL Rookie Pitcher of the Year honors. But within a five-week span he suffered a bruised shin, a stiff right shoulder and a strained left rib cage muscle. As a result, Tapani didn't win his twelfth game until Oct. 1.

If he can stay healthy, Tapani looks to have a bright future. Mechanically, he's the most advanced of the Twins' young pitchers. Tapani throws strikes with four pitches -- fastball, slider, change-up and forkball. Although he's not overpowering, Tapani's fastball is certainly adequate, capable of reaching the high eighties. The only complaint Twins' officials had was with his consistency; even in his strong early-season showing, Tapani pitched five innings or less in six of his first 16 starts. Pitching coach Dick Such believes the solution could be no more complex than a more consistent warm-up routine prior to and between starts.

Since he pitched in both the Athletic and Met farm systems, it's no surprise that Tapani possesses solid mechanics. In 1990, that sound development showed up in his control stats: only 29 walks in 159.1 innings. Tapani benefitted from pitching in the Dome last year, going 8-2 with a 3.38 at home, 4-6, 4.68 on the road. Surprisingly, opponents batted .266 against Tapani at the Dome, .262 on the road. The key was that he allowed just one home run at home, 11 on the road, another evidence of his need to be more consistent.

HOLDING RUNNERS AND FIELDING:

Tapani entered 1990 about 15 pounds lighter than he had been during a late-season stint with the Twins in 1989. It showed in quickness that resulted in improved defensive work on the mound. Tapani made only one error in 35 chances and had 20 assists. He also showed improvement holding baserunners close. Even though he's right-handed, Tapani has a fluid pitching motion which makes it tough to steal bases on him.

OVERALL:

Tapani showed in 1990 that he can be a solid major league starter. For three months last year he was the Twins' ace. Minnesota won only twice during a 15-game span between June 7 and June 22; both wins were by Tapani. The question mark is his health. He also had shoulder problems while pitching in the Mets farm system in '88, so the Twins will be watching him closely this year.

KEVIN TAPANI

Position: SP
Bats: R **Throws:** R
Ht: 6' 0" **Wt:** 180

Opening Day Age: 27
Born: 2/18/64 in Des Moines, IA
ML Seasons: 2

Overall Statistics

	W	L	ERA	G	GS	Sv	IP	H	R	BB	SO	HR
1990	12	8	4.07	28	28	0	159.1	164	75	29	101	12
Career	14	10	4.02	36	33	0	199.1	203	93	41	124	15

How Often He Throws Strikes

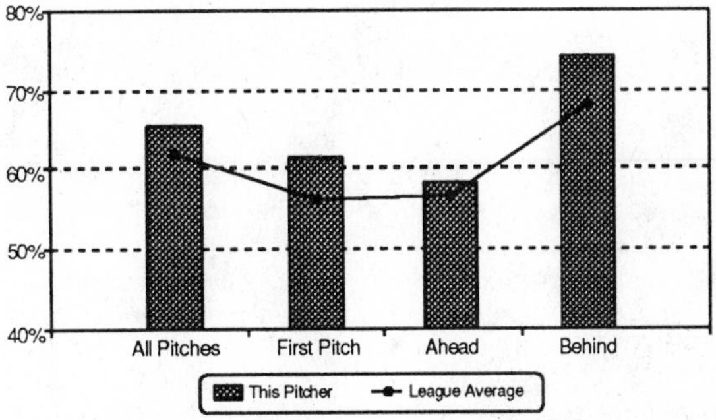

1990 Situational Stats

	W	L	ERA	Sv	IP		AB	H	HR	RBI	AVG
Home	8	2	3.38	0	74.2	LHB	317	90	6	30	.284
Road	4	6	4.68	0	84.2	RHB	304	74	6	32	.243
Day	4	1	2.38	0	45.1	Sc Pos	128	40	3	50	.313
Night	8	7	4.74	0	114.0	Clutch	37	12	0	6	.324

1990 Rankings (American League)

- 3rd highest ERA on the road (4.68)
- Led the Twins in wins (12), strikeouts (101) and winning percentage (.600)

PITCHING:

Two years ago, the Twins considered David West the key man among the five pitchers they received from the Mets for Frank Viola. Unfortunately, West has been nothing more than a 6-foot-6 enigma; he's gone 10-11 with a lofty 5.38 ERA in his year and a half in Minnesota. Compounding his ineffective pitching, West has been injured as well. His 1990 season was cut short by a hamstring injury on Sept. 4.

The Twins still contend that West has the physical tools -- in particular the live fastball -- to become the star he was always forecast to be. Minnesota pitching coach Dick Such believes the problems can be traced to mechanics. The theory is that West too often drops his arm on his delivery, pushing his pitches up in the strike zone. West also lacks a quality major league off- speed pitch, and that makes his offerings easier to time.

Last year's numbers offer a clear view of West's deficiencies. Although he limited opponents to a respectable .256 batting average, West walked 78 men in 146.1 innings and hung enough pitches to surrender a team-high 21 home runs. When his arm dropped, he became an easy target for right-handed hitters; of the 21 home runs he allowed, 20 were hit by righties. But when his mechanics were sound, West was tough. At times he looked like the overpowering minor leaguer who led the Texas League in strikeouts in 1987, and the International League in both winning percentage and ERA in '88.

HOLDING RUNNERS AND FIELDING:

West needs improvement in his defense. His problems are related to a lack of natural athletic ability. West often looks slow and awkward; that was reflected in his fielding percentage of .909 (two errors in 22 chances), the worst among Twins starters. However, base stealers had a tough time with West on the mound in 1990 as they were successful only five times in 10 attempts.

OVERALL:

West has reached a critical juncture. He's 26, and it's getting harder to swallow the contention that he is a young pitcher still learning his trade. Minnesota still believes he has a major league arm. But their patience is running out, and by the end of last season, younger pitchers like Guthrie and Scott Erickson had passed West. West will get a shot to win a starting job in spring training, but it's now-or-never time.

DAVID WEST

Position: SP
Bats: L **Throws:** L
Ht: 6' 6" **Wt:** 220

Opening Day Age: 26
Born: 9/1/64 in Memphis, TN
ML Seasons: 3

Overall Statistics

	W	L	ERA	G	GS	Sv	IP	H	R	BB	SO	HR
1990	7	9	5.10	29	27	0	146.1	142	88	78	92	21
Career	11	13	5.54	52	35	0	216.0	221	139	114	145	30

How Often He Throws Strikes

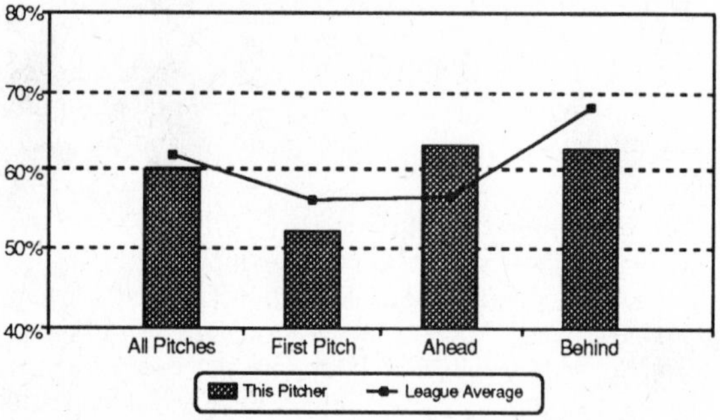

1990 Situational Stats

	W	L	ERA	Sv	IP		AB	H	HR	RBI	AVG
Home	2	4	6.03	0	62.2	LHB	90	22	1	13	.244
Road	5	5	4.41	0	83.2	RHB	464	120	20	70	.259
Day	2	2	6.38	0	36.2	Sc Pos	117	36	6	58	.308
Night	5	7	4.68	0	109.2	Clutch	14	8	0	2	.571

1990 Rankings (American League)

- 9th worst ERA on the road (4.41)
- Led the Twins in home runs allowed (21), walks allowed (78), GDPs induced per GDP situation (17.8%) and lowest batting average allowed vs. right-handed batters (.259)

PAUL ABBOTT

Position: SP
Bats: R **Throws:** R
Ht: 6' 3" **Wt:** 185

Opening Day Age: 23
Born: 9/15/67 in Van NUys, CA
ML Seasons: 1

Overall Statistics

	W	L	ERA	G	GS	Sv	IP	H	R	BB	SO	HR
1990	0	5	5.97	7	7	0	34.2	37	24	28	25	0
Career	0	5	5.97	7	7	0	34.2	37	24	28	25	0

PITCHING, FIELDING & HOLDING RUNNERS:

Paul Abbott was a stopgap measure, summoned to join the Twins last August because of injuries to other pitchers. Abbott had lost 14 of 19 decisions at Class AAA Portland, and proceeded to go 0-5 with a 5.97 ERA with the Twins. But during his six weeks in Minnesota, Abbott convinced Twins officials that he has a major league arm. He has a good fastball and a decent curve, the raw materials to be successful. His problem is control. The righthander walked 28 batters in 34.2 innings, and too many of his strikes were down the middle, rather than on the corners.

Although the overall figures don't show it, when Abbott was good last year, he was very good. He was especially impressive in his second major league start, allowing three hits in eight shutout innings; unfortunately the Twins couldn't score either, losing 1-0 after Abbott had left the game. When Abbott was bad, control was the culprit. He walked at least five batters in four of his seven starts. Abbott is no gazelle, and needs work both defensively and holding runners on.

OVERALL:

Abbott went to Venezuela over the winter to work on his control. It's likely that he'll start the 1991 season at Portland. But the Twins are convinced that Abbott has the repertoire to be a winner in the not-too-distant future.

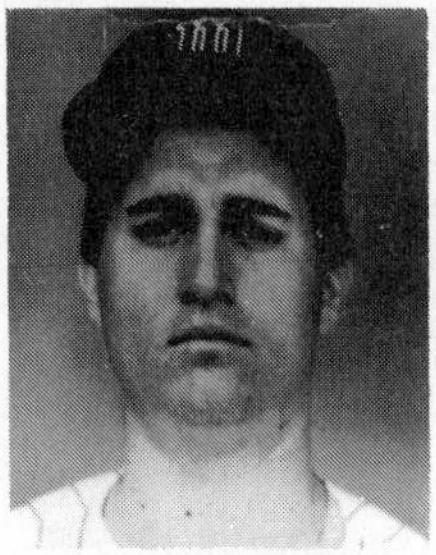

LARRY CASIAN

Position: SP
Bats: R **Throws:** L
Ht: 6' 0" **Wt:** 170

Opening Day Age: 25
Born: 10/28/65 in Lynwood, CA
ML Seasons: 1

Overall Statistics

	W	L	ERA	G	GS	Sv	IP	H	R	BB	SO	HR
1990	2	1	3.22	5	3	0	22.1	26	9	4	11	2
Career	2	1	3.22	5	3	0	22.1	26	9	4	11	2

PITCHING, FIELDING & HOLDING RUNNERS:

Larry Casian wasn't among the Twins' original September call-ups last year, but when David West was sidelined by a hamstring injury, Casian got his chance. The lefthander's stock had steadily dropped while he was posting ERAs of 4.52 and 4.48 at AAA Portland over the past two seasons. But in one month he pitched his way into 1991 consideration. Casian went 2-1 with a 3.22 ERA in 22.1 innings with the Twins. He looked once again like the hurler who'd posted sub-3.00 ERAs at Visalia and Orlando in 1987 and '88.

Casian was hardly unhittable in his September trial, with opponents posting a .306 average. But his control was solid. He enhanced his prospects by showing he could pitch in relief; his first major league victory came in two scoreless innings out of the bullpen. Casian has an adequate fastball and an excellent change-up. He has struggled periodically with his breaking ball, however. Casian is quick off the mound, and should prove an excellent fielder. Although he failed to pick off anyone with the Twins, he has an excellent pickoff move, nailing 27 runners in 18 games at Class A in 1987!

OVERALL:

Casian will get an opportunity to make the Twins staff in spring training as a long reliever. He's not overpowering, but his composure and control warrant consideration. If he doesn't make it, he's an excellent insurance policy at the AAA level.

CARMEN CASTILLO

Position: DH/RF
Bats: R **Throws:** R
Ht: 6' 1" **Wt:** 190

Opening Day Age: 32
Born: 6/8/58 in San Francisco de Macoris, Dominican Republic
ML Seasons: 9

Overall Statistics

	G	AB	R	H	D	T	HR	RBI	SB	BB	SO	AVG
1990	64	137	11	30	4	0	0	12	0	3	23	.219
Career	622	1507	190	381	71	7	55	197	15	90	289	.253

HITTING, FIELDING, BASERUNNING:

The Twins signed Carmen Castillo to a two-year contract before last season started, a move they couldn't help but regret as the season dragged on. Castillo went from being a platoon player in right field to a seldom-used reserve, clearly the 25th player on the roster. He went the entire 1990 season without a home run and didn't get his batting average over .200 until well into the season.

Castillo had always had success against hard-throwing pitchers, even some righthanders, but last year it seemed like his bat speed slowed and the pop disappeared. It was a blessing for the Twins, perhaps, because Castillo's problems resulted in Shane Mack being given the chance that he needed.

As much as anything else, Castillo dropped out of favor because of his defense. After misplaying a number of balls in the early part of the season, he saw less and less time in right field, and the Twins began to feel that the Indians were correct in giving up on Castillo because of his defensive liabilities. Castillo is an average baserunner. He's not especially fast and doesn't make many mistakes. He seems to understand his limitations on the bases.

OVERALL:

Castillo's effectiveness has always come because of his ability to hit lefties, and hit them for some power. Without that, there isn't much left in his overall game. Castillo's future in the majors, if he has one, is probably as a right-handed pinch hitter who plays defense only when absolutely necessary.

TIM DRUMMOND

Position: RP/SP
Bats: R **Throws:** R
Ht: 6' 3" **Wt:** 170

Opening Day Age: 26
Born: 12/24/64 in La Plata, MD
ML Seasons: 3

Overall Statistics

	W	L	ERA	G	GS	Sv	IP	H	R	BB	SO	HR
1990	3	5	4.35	35	4	1	91.0	104	46	36	49	8
Career	3	5	4.29	49	4	2	113.1	125	56	47	63	8

PITCHING, FIELDING & HOLDING RUNNERS:

Judging from the radar gun readings, Tim Drummond has a major league arm. But while his fastball has enough velocity, it's too straight. Drummond has been experimenting with different grips, trying to find one that yields more movement. He could also use a better change-up, although his forkball works as a decent off-speed pitch.

Originally signed by the Pirates, Drummond was dealt to the Mets and was pitching for AAA Tidewater when he became part of the package the Twins got for Frank Viola. In the minors he posted some impressive relief numbers, with good save and strikeout totals. But as a Twin last year Drummond didn't strike out many batters, and his control was only ordinary. His defense is adequate (one error, 13 chances), but like many inexperienced major league pitchers, he could use work holding runners on.

OVERALL:

The Twins have toyed with the idea of trying Drummond as a starter, but in four starts last year he was 0-3 with a 7.64 ERA. He stayed with the team last year primarily because the club feared he would be claimed on waivers if sent to the minors. Drummond will have to prove he belongs in 1991, and although the Twins still like his potential, he will have to work to win a job.

RICH GARCES

Position: RP
Bats: R **Throws:** R
Ht: 6' 1" **Wt:** 187

Opening Day Age: 19
Born: 5/18/71 in Maracay, VENEZUELA
ML Seasons: 1

Overall Statistics

	W	L	ERA	G	GS	Sv	IP	H	R	BB	SO	HR
1990	0	0	1.59	5	0	2	5.2	4	2	4	1	0
Career	0	0	1.59	5	0	2	5.2	4	2	4	1	0

PITCHING, FIELDING & HOLDING RUNNERS:

Rich Garces won the Rolaids Award for being the top statistical reliever in the minor leagues in 1990. He had a 1.81 ERA and 28 saves at Class A Visalia, then posted eight saves and a 2.08 ERA at Class AA Orlando. Given a September trial with the big club, Garces completed his memorable campaign by posting two more saves with a 1.59 ERA in five Twin appearances.

Those were impressive figures, but the biggest question about Garces has to do with a different number: his age, which is 19. Can one so young be a major league closer? The Twins believe he has all the physical tools. Garces' best pitch is a 90-plus mile per hour fastball, and he also has an adequate curveball. In his two minor league stops he struck out 97 and walked 30 in 72 innings. Although he saw only brief major league action at the end of the year, Garces looks like he'll be a handful for right-handed batters. He also looks adequate defensively, especially for one so young.

OVERALL:

While Garces is only a teenager, there's a chance he could win the job as Twins' closer in spring training. Team officials are enchanted by his power repertoire, and if he shows the necessary control and composure, the job could be his. That would allow the Twins to move veteran closer Rick Aguilera into the rotation, filling the need for another veteran starter.

JOHN MOSES

Position: RF/LF/CF
Bats: B **Throws:** L
Ht: 5'10" **Wt:** 170

Opening Day Age: 33
Born: 8/9/57 in Los Angeles, CA
ML Seasons: 9

Overall Statistics

	G	AB	R	H	D	T	HR	RBI	SB	BB	SO	AVG
1990	115	172	26	38	3	1	1	14	2	19	19	.221
Career	735	1680	239	434	67	17	11	143	97	136	215	.258

HITTING, FIELDING, BASERUNNING:

After two solid seasons, John Moses had a bad year, pure and simple, in 1990. Moses had been a steady role player for the Twins, batting .316 in '88 and .281 in '89, so his regression -- all the way down to .221 -- was a surprise. Moses, a contact hitter with limited power, doesn't walk very much, and he needs to hit for a high average to earn his keep.

Twins manager Tom Kelly originally considered Moses weak from the right side, batting him just nine times against lefthanders in 1988. Moses spent the next winter working to improve, and in 1989 batted .286 against lefthanders and .279 against righthanders. Last year Moses fell out of favor with Kelly in mid-season and played sparingly, batting just 21 times against southpaws. Moses, who stole 25 and 23 bases for Seattle in the mid-'80s, was successful on only two of five attempts last year. He also committed a couple of gaffes as a late-season pinch runner. Moses is an adequate fielder, although his arm is barely average. His value is enhanced by being able to play any of the outfield positions.

OVERALL:

Moses was a free agent after the 1990 season and the Twins made it clear they did not intend to re-sign him. Moses is 33, and last year's numbers will make it harder for him to find another major league home. Moses is strictly a role player, but he's proven in the past that he's capable of helping a good team.

PEDRO MUNOZ

Position: RF
Bats: R **Throws:** R
Ht: 5'11" **Wt:** 170

Opening Day Age: 22
Born: 9/19/68 in Ponce, Puerto Rico
ML Seasons: 1

Overall Statistics

	G	AB	R	H	D	T	HR	RBI	SB	BB	SO	AVG
1990	22	85	13	23	4	1	0	5	3	2	16	.271
Career	22	85	13	23	4	1	0	5	3	2	16	.271

HITTING, FIELDING, BASERUNNING:

Pedro Munoz was the "other player" in last summer's John Candelaria deal with Toronto, but he may eventually outshine the better-known Nelson Liriano. Munoz, a free-swinging outfielder, didn't look overmatched against major league pitching. He lined the ball to all fields, even though he didn't show any of the power that he had during his minor league years.

Munoz looks like a good fastball hitter who can be handled, at this point, with off-speed pitches and pitches low and away. He's a pretty good bet to swing at the first pitch and some teams took advantage of that fact. The Twins batted him leadoff at times, but he'll need to draw some walks to stay at the top. He's probably better suited, in the long run, to hitting sixth or seventh. The Twins feel that he can hit 10-15 homers per season if he continues to develop.

Munoz was a double-figure base stealer through the minors. He can break up the double play and isn't afraid to slide hard. Fielding could be his Achilles' heel. Munoz doesn't get a good jump on the ball, has an average arm, and doesn't have a quick release. He needs to improve.

OVERALL:

The Twins bring an unsettled outfield into 1991. If Munoz can play better defense and continue to hit, he might play a significant role. Otherwise, he stands to become a reserve player, part-time DH and pinch runner. The front office is hoping for more from Munoz.

PAUL SORRENTO

Position: DH/1B
Bats: L **Throws:** R
Ht: 6' 2" **Wt:** 195

Opening Day Age: 25
Born: 11/17/65 in Somerville, MA
ML Seasons: 2

Overall Statistics

	G	AB	R	H	D	T	HR	RBI	SB	BB	SO	AVG
1990	41	121	11	25	4	1	5	13	1	12	31	.207
Career	55	142	13	30	4	1	5	14	1	17	35	.211

HITTING, FIELDING, BASERUNNING:

Paul Sorrento has power, but like many young sluggers, he's an easy target for breaking balls and off-speed pitches. In 1990 Sorrento struck out in over one-fourth of his at-bats. He wasn't particularly patient, either, recording an anemic .281 on-base percentage. The most revealing statistic regarding Sorrento's weaknesses as a hitter was that he batted only .115 (3- for-26) with runners in scoring position. With runners in scoring position and two outs, he batted .053 (1-for-19).

The Twins considered Sorrento a platoon player, batting him just three times against left-handed pitchers. He showed flashes of power with five home runs, a ratio of one homer every 24.2 at bats. Twins' home run leader Kent Hrbek, by comparison, homered once every 22.4 at bats. Sorrento's defensive work at first base was a pleasant surprise. He was considered a liability at first base as recently as two seasons ago, but looked steady with the Twins, making just one error in 126 chances.

OVERALL:

Sorrento's future with the Twins is cloudy. Minnesota has Kent Hrbek at first base, and Gene Larkin, the regular designated hitter, is also a first baseman. Sorrento's left-handed power, though, is enticing to a team that experienced a power shortage in 1990. He'll get a look, but he has to hit better in the clutch to survive spring training.

GARY WAYNE

Position: RP
Bats: L **Throws:** L
Ht: 6' 3" **Wt:** 185

Opening Day Age: 28
Born: 11/30/62 in Dearborn, MI
ML Seasons: 2

Overall Statistics

	W	L	ERA	G	GS	Sv	IP	H	R	BB	SO	HR
1990	1	1	4.19	38	0	1	38.2	38	19	13	28	5
Career	4	5	3.61	98	0	2	109.2	93	47	49	69	9

PITCHING, FIELDING & HOLDING RUNNERS:

Gary Wayne has an unorthodox, herky-jerky delivery, and it serves him well against left-handed batters. Last year the southpaw reliever limited lefthanders to a .174 batting average (8-for-46). The problem was with righthanders, who batted .291 against Wayne. Effective as a rookie in 1989, Wayne had an up-and-down season in 1990, receiving a mid-season demotion to the minors. He returned in August to pitch respectably over the final six weeks.

Wayne's best pitch is his change-up, and he has a better-than-average curveball. His fastball is adequate, fitting into the "sneaky fast" classification. He had a decent strikeout-walk ratio last year, fanning 28 and walking 13 in 38.2 innings. It's hardly a good omen for the Twins that Wayne had a 5.63 ERA at the Dome, 3.18 on the road. Wayne looks to be standing too erect upon delivery, but pitching coach Dick Such said his mechanics are fundamentally sound. He follows through into a good fielding position, and appears to be solid defensively. He has a decent pickoff move, although he failed to nab a runner in 1990.

OVERALL:

Wayne is rather limited, but he could be an asset to a team that can afford to carry a short reliever capable of getting one or two left-handed hitters out per game. Whether the Twins can afford such a luxury remains to be seen. They may opt for more versatile left-handed relievers like Larry Casian, who can start or pitch in long relief.

OSCAR AZOCAR

Position: LF/RF
Bats: L **Throws:** L
Ht: 6' 1" **Wt:** 170

Opening Day Age: 26
Born: 2/21/65 in Caracas, VZ
ML Seasons: 1

HITTING:

Oscar Azocar never met a pitch he didn't like. He is a classic example of the impatient batter who will swing at almost anything and usually put it in play. It took him 100 major league at-bats to draw his first walk, which he finally received when the notoriously-wild Mike Jackson had a particularly wild outing. Azocar got only one more walk in 1990. When he steps to the plate, the Yankee coaches start flashing "take" signs, and they don't stop until they see some strikes.

Azocar never tries to hit a home run. He looks for the fastball and adjusts to breaking balls, trying to go with the pitch. He uses all fields, has good speed, and can bunt to get on base.

The obvious approach for pitchers is to keep the ball out of the strike zone against Azocar. By the end of 1990, with increased use of scouting information, Azocar was seeing more pitching to specific spots, with the defense carefully positioned. Azocar normally obliged the pitchers by hitting whatever they threw, and his batting average dropped accordingly.

Azocar will have to learn patience at the plate if he hopes to stick in the major leagues. His free swinging may have helped him arrive in the majors, but he will need to adjust now that he's there. His .248 batting average could drop sharply in 1991 if he continues to let the pitcher decide when and where the ball will be hit.

BASERUNNING:

Azocar uses his speed selectively, thanks to careful coaching by the Yankees. He has never been caught stealing in the major leagues. At Columbus in 1990, he was cut down in eight of 16 attempts, so the close supervision is a good idea at this stage of his career.

FIELDING:

Until 1987, Azocar was a pitcher, and a good one (lifetime 14-5, 2.30 ERA as a pro). He is a newcomer to the outfield, and this inexperience often shows. Although he was charged with only one error last year, he participated in some dramatic fielding adventures. Azocar's good speed and natural athletic ability raise expectations for the future, however. His rapid advancement in just three years is a good indication that he will become a fine fielder with more experience. He has all the tools.

OVERALL:

The Yankees have a crowded outfield for 1991. Lefty-hitting Azocar could offer some rest days to righties Hensley Meulens and Jesse Barfield, but there is no clearly-defined role for him, even as a platooner.

Overall Statistics

	G	AB	R	H	D	T	HR	RBI	SB	BB	SO	AVG
1990	65	214	18	53	8	0	5	19	7	2	15	.248
Career	65	214	18	53	8	0	5	19	7	2	15	.248

Where He Hits the Ball

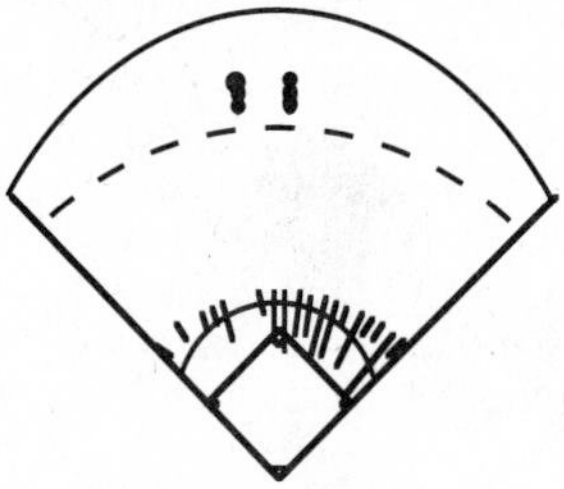

Vs. LHP

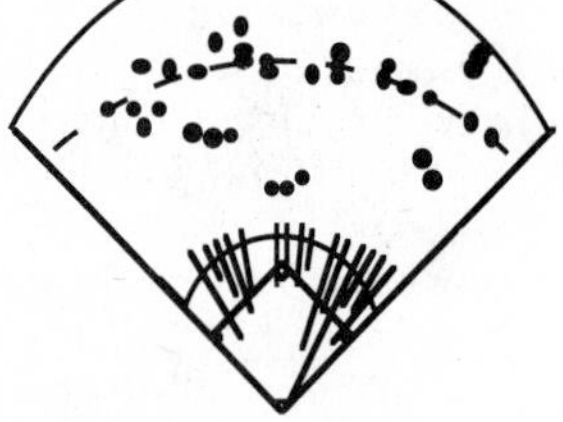

Vs. RHP

1990 Situational Stats

	AB	H	HR	RBI	AVG		AB	H	HR	RBI	AVG
Home	109	31	3	11	.284	LHP	60	12	1	7	.200
Road	105	22	2	8	.210	RHP	154	41	4	12	.266
Day	59	14	2	4	.237	Sc Pos	52	10	1	13	.192
Night	155	39	3	15	.252	Clutch	34	9	0	2	.265

1990 Rankings (American League)

- Did not rank near the top or bottom in any category

STEVE BALBONI

Position: DH/1B
Bats: R **Throws:** R
Ht: 6' 3" **Wt:** 225

Opening Day Age: 34
Born: 1/16/57 in Brockton, MA
ML Seasons: 10

Overall Statistics

	G	AB	R	H	D	T	HR	RBI	SB	BB	SO	AVG
1990	116	266	24	51	6	0	17	34	0	35	91	.192
Career	958	3115	351	711	127	11	181	495	1	273	854	.228

Where He Hits the Ball

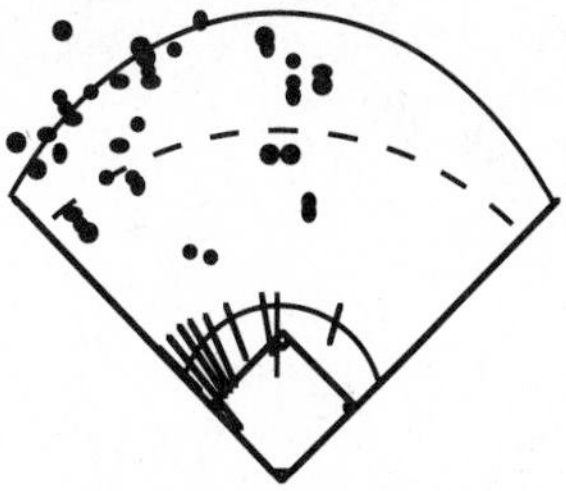

Vs. LHP

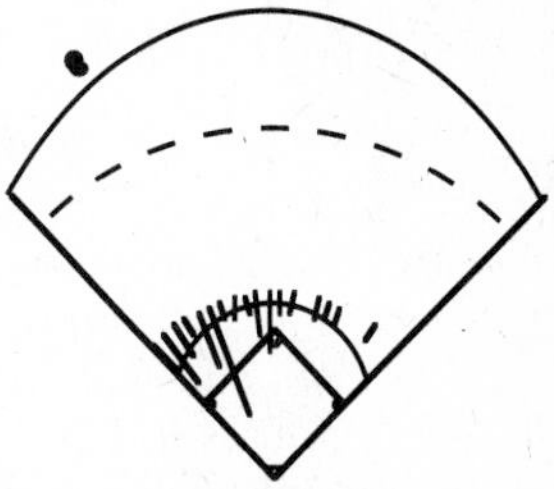

Vs. RHP

1990 Situational Stats

	AB	H	HR	RBI	AVG		AB	H	HR	RBI	AVG
Home	123	26	8	17	.211	LHP	161	34	14	27	.211
Road	143	25	9	17	.175	RHP	105	17	3	7	.162
Day	83	17	2	4	.205	Sc Pos	67	12	0	13	.179
Night	183	34	15	30	.186	Clutch	64	14	4	8	.219

1990 Rankings (American League)

- 5th lowest batting average on an 0-2 count (.038)
- 9th lowest batting average vs. left-handed pitchers (.211)
- Led the Yankees in batting average on a 3-1 count (.400)

HITTING:

Steve Balboni led the 1990 Yankees in homers and RBI against southpaws. Unfortunately, he specialized in solo homers. And when a player hits .192 at age 33, most people start wondering about his future, no matter how good his power stats may be. Dave Kingman left baseball after hitting 35 HR and 94 RBI, numbers that dwarf Balboni's 17 HR and 34 RBI.

Balboni likes to dig in and swing for the fences. In each of the past two years, almost half his hits have been for extra bases. In 1990, one third of his hits were homers. With a good knowledge of opposing pitchers, Balboni likes to guess what's coming, then pull the trigger. When he guesses right, the pitcher can suffer; when he guesses wrong, Balboni looks foolish. He looked foolish frequently during 1990, amassing 91 strikeouts in just 266 at bats.

Although hard-throwing righthanders are now able to blow the ball past Balboni, the safest approach is still to keep the ball away. Low breaking balls and fastballs off the outside part of the plate are the pitches he sees most often. For a veteran, Balboni has little inclination to go with the outside pitch. He is more likely to try and pull any pitch, even when it's barely within reach. With his great strength, he still succeeds on occasion.

BASERUNNING:

From a distance, you can see that Balboni is built for power, not speed. He has only one stolen base in his entire career, and will rarely try to advance an extra base. When speed is a critical factor, Balboni usually leaves the game for a pinch runner. Nonetheless, Balboni is an alert baserunner, and he always shows good effort running out ground balls.

FIELDING:

Since 1986, Balboni has been a designated hitter and pinch hitter in most of his appearances. With the injury to Don Mattingly during 1990, however, Steve got into 28 games at first. He is still an adequate first baseman despite his lack of mobility, capitalizing on good concentration and a knowledge of A.L. hitters. Balboni hasn't lost his old ability to dig out bad throws.

OVERALL:

Balboni's downward slide is most visible in his batting average against right-handed pitchers: .257 in 1988, .217 in 1989, and just .162 in 1990. The slump of 1990 got worse in the second half. Against all pitchers, Balboni hit a consistent .177 after the All-Star break. On a team that plans to emphasize youth, his outlook for playing time is poor, even if he succeeds in keeping a roster spot in 1991.

JESSE BARFIELD

Position: RF
Bats: R **Throws:** R
Ht: 6' 1" **Wt:** 200

Opening Day Age: 31
Born: 10/29/59 in Joliet, IL
ML Seasons: 10

Overall Statistics

	G	AB	R	H	D	T	HR	RBI	SB	BB	SO	AVG
1990	153	476	69	117	21	2	25	78	4	82	150	.246
Career	1314	4380	670	1142	202	30	222	661	64	506	1127	.261

Where He Hits the Ball

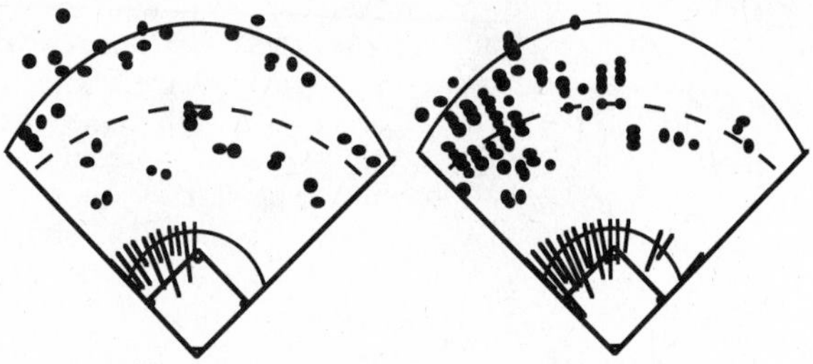

Vs. LHP **Vs. RHP**

1990 Situational Stats

	AB	H	HR	RBI	AVG		AB	H	HR	RBI	AVG
Home	239	52	12	35	.218	LHP	162	42	13	25	.259
Road	237	65	13	43	.274	RHP	314	75	12	53	.239
Day	112	27	4	13	.241	Sc Pos	110	29	4	49	.264
Night	364	90	21	65	.247	Clutch	90	19	3	11	.211

1990 Rankings (American League)

- 4th in strikeouts (150), most pitches seen per plate appearance (4.16) and lowest batting average at home (.218)
- 5th lowest percentage of swings put into play (33.4%)
- Led the Yankees in home runs (25), RBIs (78), walks (82), strikeouts, slugging percentage (.456), on-base average (.359), HR frequency (19.0 HRs per AB), most pitches seen per plate appearance and batting average with the bases loaded (.400)
- Led AL right fielders in walks, pitches seen (2,371) and pitches seen per plate appearance

HITTING:

Although he didn't hit 40 homers in 1990, Jesse Barfield feels that he is back to the peak of his hitting abilities. Barfield says he is fully recovered from the serious wrist injury of 1988, and has regained all his timing and rhythm at the plate.

The numbers generally support Barfield's optimism. For example, his 1990 on-base percentage of .359 was the best since he posted .368 in his great year of 1986, and better than that of many leadoff men. Barfield's strikeout to walk ratio of 1.82 remained near the level he reached in 1989, and was better than he had any year from 1984 through 1988.

Barfield is basically a pull hitter, usually hoping to hit the ball down the left field line or jerk it into the seats. He has proven power to right-center as well. Most pitchers simply throw breaking balls low and away and fastballs up and in, changing speeds frequently, hoping to keep him off balance and uncertain. When Jesse has his normal composure, anything over the middle of the plate, or inside and low, is likely to leave the ball park.

One weakness is Barfield's strikeout propensity. In 1990 he whiffed 150 times for the second consecutive year. Jesse simply refuses to give in to a pitcher by just trying to make contact. When he likes a pitch, he swings hard, no matter what the count.

BASERUNNING:

When Barfield first reached the major leagues, he had good speed and a desire to run, stealing 22 bases in 1985. Since then, he has grown less inclined to run, and less successful in steal attempts. He was caught in three of seven attempts last year. He still has enough speed that pitchers must keep an eye on him, and he will take an extra base whenever the game situation calls for aggressiveness.

FIELDING:

Barfield is arguably the best right fielder in the American League. Certainly he has the best arm in both strength and accuracy, as he proved for the second consecutive year by leading the league in outfield assists. Everyone respects Jesse's arm, but he continues to send optimistic baserunners back to the dugout, scratching their heads in amazement.

OVERALL:

Barfield is a quiet leader on a team that needs leadership desperately. He is an outgoing and stable personality on an unstable team. For some of the more tempestuous personalities like Mel Hall, Barfield was the only person able to exert any positive influence during 1990. On the field and off, the Yankees need more players like him.

PITCHING:

When the Yankees needed a starter to replace Chuck Cary in April and May, Greg Cadaret stepped into the rotation. When Lee Guetterman was unable to pitch in late July, Cadaret became the set-up man and number-two closer, capping this role with two saves on the same day against Cleveland on July 29. Cadaret's season peaked during July with a 1-0 record, two saves, and a 1.93 ERA for the month.

Obviously, the Yankees like to use Cadaret as a flexible role-player on a staff that changes pitchers' roles frequently. His pitching style shifts to fit the situation. In the role of a short reliever, Cadaret is a power pitcher; he loves to work inside. As a starter, he can roll out an assortment of pitches, including a curve and a forkball, that, theoretically, will keep hitters guessing when they face him a second or third time in the game.

In practice, however, Cadaret continues to struggle when thrown into starting situations. His fastball loses some velocity and movement after a few innings. More importantly, Cadaret does not have full command of his breaking pitches; he often gets behind in the count. His six starts in 1990 produced a 1-3 record with a 6.11 ERA. As a reliever he was 4-1 with 3 saves and a 3.57 ERA. The differential was just as clear in 1989, when Cadaret had a 2.70 ERA as a reliever before July 1, and then came unglued with a 4.57 ERA after the Yankees made him a starter in mid-season.

HOLDING RUNNERS AND FIELDING:

Don't try to run on Greg Cadaret. Last year 17 of 23 would-be base stealers were cut down, making a big contribution to the Yankees' overall 44% caught-stealing percentage. Cadaret has a good pickoff move that prevents runners from taking a big lead or getting a good jump, and he is very quick to the plate. Cadaret is also an excellent fielder who covers his position well. He ranked second in fielding assists among Yankee pitchers in 1990.

OVERALL:

The Yankees took an outstanding short reliever from Oakland, and have twice tried to make him into a starter. Both efforts failed, hiding Cadaret's true ability behind some unimpressive full-year numbers. The best Greg Cadaret is the one who makes the shortest appearances. In his nine briefest outings of 1990, Cadaret compiled 5.1 shutout innings and threw only 51 pitches to retire 16 hitters. If the Yankees want to get more of that kind of pitching, they will have to have to let him settle into a clearly-defined role as a short reliever.

GREG CADARET

Position: RP/SP
Bats: L **Throws:** L
Ht: 6' 3" **Wt:** 205

Opening Day Age: 29
Born: 2/27/62 in Detroit, MI
ML Seasons: 4

Overall Statistics

	W	L	ERA	G	GS	Sv	IP	H	R	BB	SO	HR
1990	5	4	4.15	54	6	3	121.1	120	62	64	80	8
Career	21	13	3.90	187	19	6	352.2	347	172	181	254	23

How Often He Throws Strikes

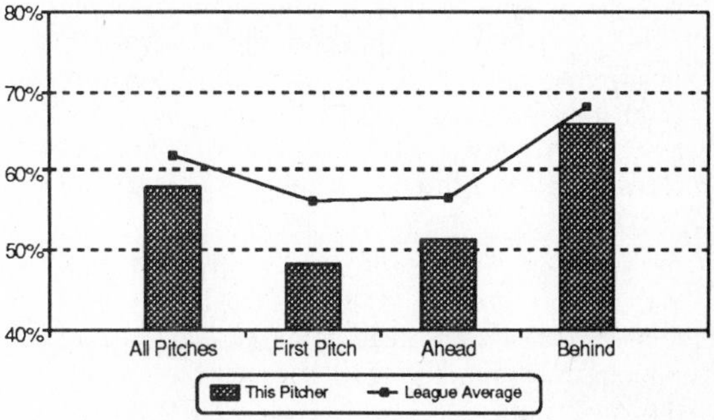

1990 Situational Stats

	W	L	ERA	Sv	IP		AB	H	HR	RBI	AVG
Home	3	0	2.78	0	58.1	LHB	119	30	3	15	.252
Road	2	4	5.43	3	63.0	RHB	328	90	5	42	.274
Day	3	2	4.28	2	67.1	Sc Pos	136	34	1	45	.250
Night	2	2	4.00	1	54.0	Clutch	101	28	0	7	.277

1990 Rankings (American League)

- 2nd most runners caught stealing (17)
- 5th in wild pitches (14)
- Led the Yankees in runners caught stealing

CHUCK CARY

Position: SP
Bats: L **Throws:** L
Ht: 6' 4" **Wt:** 210

Opening Day Age: 31
Born: 3/3/60 in Whittier, CA
ML Seasons: 6

PITCHING:

As the 1990 season began, Chuck Cary had emerged from a crowded field of candidates to earn a starting role. Bone chips in his left elbow sidelined Cary in April, however, and he never quite got back on track.

After a career of struggles, Cary had finally achieved some recognition in 1989, thanks to the development of a screwball that he could throw at two different speeds. Cary uses the scroogie mainly as a change-up against right-handed hitters. For the element of surprise, he'll also occasionally work it inside against some of the better lefty hitters. Cary's two main pitches, the fastball and slider, became more effective when hitters had to deal with a third possibility.

In 1990, however, Cary's slider sometimes didn't slide, and he sometimes "forgot" to mix in enough screwballs. His slider must move down and in to righties to be effective; too often in 1990 it was merely flat. As for neglect of the screwball, Cary won't mention it, but working with five different catchers during 1990 wasn't the best way to develop a regular repertoire and a set pattern. Plus, he was recovering from the elbow surgery for most of the season.

Cary had numerous hard-luck losses in 1990, but four bad outings really ruined his statistics. In those disasters, he gave up a total of 21 earned runs in 8.2 innings. Without these four bad games, his ERA for the year would have been 3.16, not 4.19.

HOLDING RUNNERS AND FIELDING:

For a lefty, Cary has never been among the best at holding runners, but he improved noticeably during 1990. Opposing runners were caught 10 times in 1990, compared to just once in 1989. Cary works hard on this aspect of his game, and he has been helped by Stump Merrill's propensity to signal for pickoff throws. Cary is a below-average fielder. He gets over to first base adequately, but he doesn't field many balls that are hit near him.

OVERALL:

Cary is obviously capable of producing quality starts, but he hasn't shown any real consistency since August 1989. The Yankees need him to be consistent; he doesn't have to be spectacular. Yankee Stadium is designed for left-handed pitchers to be successful, and Cary and Dave Lapoint were the only two lefty starters on the Yankee staff at the end of 1990. With the team openly searching for a lefty starter even before the season ended, and Steve Adkins possibly ready for the majors, Cary may have to earn his starting role again in 1991.

Overall Statistics

	W	L	ERA	G	GS	Sv	IP	H	R	BB	SO	HR
1990	6	12	4.19	28	27	0	156.2	155	77	55	134	21
Career	12	20	3.83	108	38	3	336.1	307	159	115	278	43

How Often He Throws Strikes

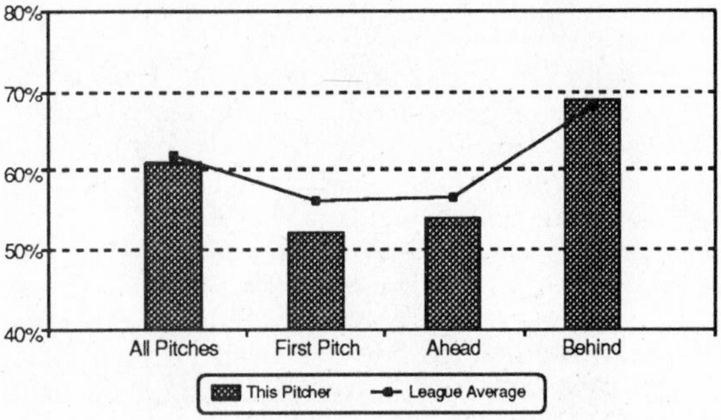

1990 Situational Stats

	W	L	ERA	Sv	IP		AB	H	HR	RBI	AVG
Home	4	3	3.04	0	91.2	LHB	113	33	4	12	.292
Road	2	9	5.82	0	65.0	RHB	484	122	17	58	.252
Day	0	2	5.56	0	22.2	Sc Pos	121	39	6	52	.322
Night	6	10	3.96	0	134.0	Clutch	37	10	0	1	.270

1990 Rankings (American League)

- 5th lowest winning percentage (.333)
- 7th in wild pitches (11)
- Led the Yankees in home runs allowed (21), ERA at home (3.04), lowest batting average allowed vs. right-handed batters (.252)

ALVARO ESPINOZA

Position: SS
Bats: R **Throws:** R
Ht: 6' 0" **Wt:** 170

Opening Day Age: 29
Born: 2/19/62 in Valencia, Venezuela
ML Seasons: 6

Overall Statistics

	G	AB	R	H	D	T	HR	RBI	SB	BB	SO	AVG
1990	150	438	31	98	12	2	2	20	1	16	54	.224
Career	369	1043	91	264	38	3	2	71	4	32	133	.253

Where He Hits the Ball

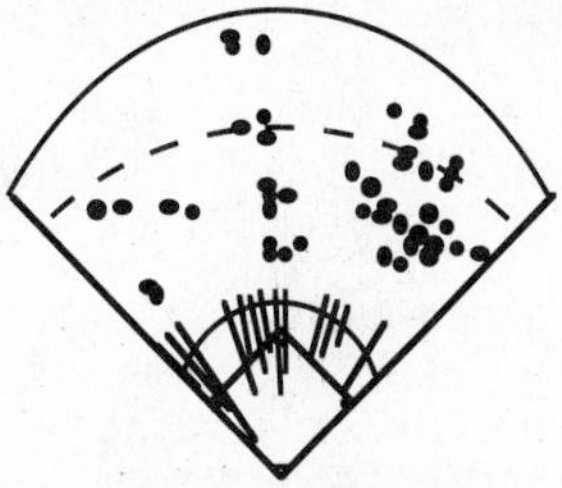

Vs. LHP

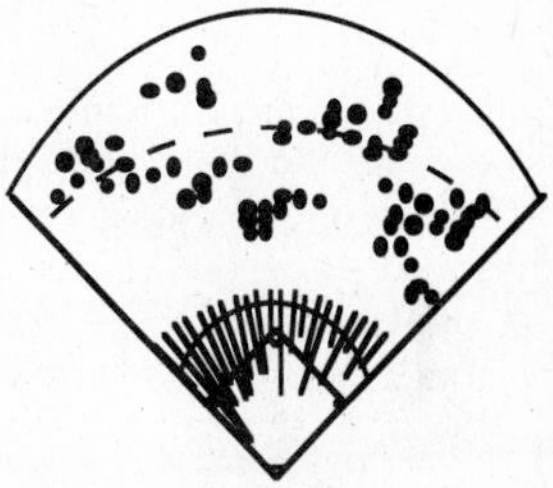

Vs. RHP

1990 Situational Stats

	AB	H	HR	RBI	AVG		AB	H	HR	RBI	AVG
Home	219	47	0	9	.215	LHP	144	36	1	9	.250
Road	219	51	2	11	.233	RHP	294	62	1	11	.211
Day	114	20	0	8	.175	Sc Pos	75	14	0	18	.187
Night	324	78	2	12	.241	Clutch	59	15	1	4	.254

1990 Rankings (American League)

- 9th in sacrifice bunts (11)
- Led the Yankees in sacrifice bunts (11), GDPs (13) and bunts in play (17)

HITTING:

A master of bat control, and certainly the Yankees' best bunter, Alvaro Espinoza had a disappointing season in 1990. He didn't lose his abilities, but the league's pitchers and defenses caught up with him. In 1989, Espinoza thrived by making contact, hitting pitches where they were thrown and going to right field extensively. The success evaporated in 1990, as pitchers learned to let him go the other way, with proper defensive positioning. Lefties, especially, quit pitching him inside, and Espinoza's average against southpaws dropped from .383 in 1989 to .250 in 1990.

Espinoza tried to adjust to the changes, but he never found the answer. His basic reaction was to try swinging harder, toward left field, but this approach just moved him away from his basic strength, the ability to go with the pitch. He never got his average much above .220 at any time during the season.

Never eager to take a walk (he drew just 14 in 1989 and 16 in 1990), Espinoza will have to learn to lay off the outside pitch. It does no good to hit a sharp bouncer between first and second if the second baseman is standing there waiting for it. Patience and selectivity are the keys to climbing out of the year-long slump that engulfed him last year.

BASERUNNING:

Possessing little speed for a shortstop, Espinoza was cut down in two of his three steal attempts last year. His main strength on the bases is a keen awareness of situations; he almost never makes a mistake or misses an opportunity. He knows the opposing pitchers well, gets a good lead, and takes the extra base when it matters.

FIELDING:

Espinoza positions himself exceptionally well. He has long been doing to the opposition what they did to him in 1990: taking away hits by being in the right place at the right time. With his good lateral mobility, he reaches hard-hit balls that would get through most American League infields. He teamed with Steve Sax as the league's number-two double play combination in 1990, and made only three errors after July 14.

OVERALL:

A gritty competitor who wants to play every day, Espinoza has played 296 games at shortstop in two years, the most since Phil Rizzuto played 297 for the Yankees in 1951-1952. Ironically, Espinoza was in the clubhouse on the last day of the season, with an injured foot contemplating his hitting woes. At age 29 he has little potential for major improvement (except for patience at the plate), but he has the ability to play better than he showed in 1990.

BOB GEREN

Position: C
Bats: R **Throws:** R
Ht: 6' 3" **Wt:** 205

Opening Day Age: 29
Born: 9/22/61 in San Diego, CA
ML Seasons: 3

HITTING:

After a remarkable season as an elderly rookie in 1989, Bob Geren fell back to earth in 1990 with a thud. Geren was hurt by a lack of playing time, as the Yankees assembled a roster that included five catchers by September. Geren's hitting was the part of his game that suffered. From 1989 to 1990, his batting average dropped from .288 to .213, and his slugging percentage from .454 to .325. What went wrong?

The only problem that Geren could identify was a lessened ability to hit the ball to right field. He never was much of an opposite field hitter, and feels that he needs to work more on going with the outside pitch.

One American League catcher who knows Geren well says that Geren has never learned how to hit a major league slider. Capitalizing on this weakness, pitchers have been working him more up and down, rather than in and out, with high fastballs and low breaking balls.

Despite these difficulties, Geren is a solid, but feared power hitter with a respectable total of 17 homers in less than 500 major league at-bats. Geren never enjoyed the "here comes my fastball" challenge that allows many rookies to amass impressive home run totals before the pitchers wise up. After ten years in the minors, the word preceded him: Geren can take you deep.

BASERUNNING:

Geren's speed is accurately reflected in his career stolen base record: zero for zero. Even in the minor leagues, he stole only three bases after 1985. Simply stated, he runs like a catcher. On the bases he is attentive and conservative, staying out of trouble.

FIELDING:

It was defensive skill that made Geren the Yankees number-one catcher in 1989. He has one of the best throwing arms in baseball, gunning down over 40% of all base stealers in both 1989 and 1990. Geren has quickly developed into an outstanding handler of pitchers. He feels his greatest strength in 1990 was pitch selection, as he showed more knowledge of opposing hitters' weaknesses and Yankee pitchers' strengths and preferences. The last-place Yankees were 17-14 in the last 31 games that Geren caught.

OVERALL:

Geren remained the Yankees' top catcher at the end of 1990. He is highly regarded by his manager, coaches and front office. But, in comparison to Geren, Matt Nokes is two years younger, has twice as much major league experience, and has the left-handed stroke for which Yankee stadium was designed. Geren will have to battle to win the number-one job again.

Overall Statistics

	G	AB	R	H	D	T	HR	RBI	SB	BB	SO	AVG
1990	110	277	21	59	7	0	8	31	0	13	73	.213
Career	185	492	47	119	12	1	17	58	0	27	120	.242

Where He Hits the Ball

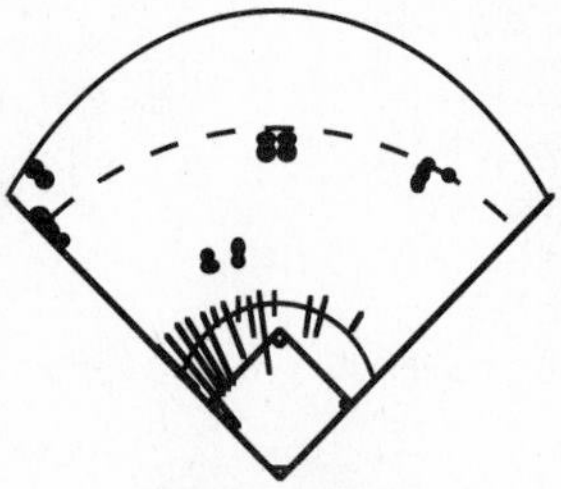

Vs. LHP

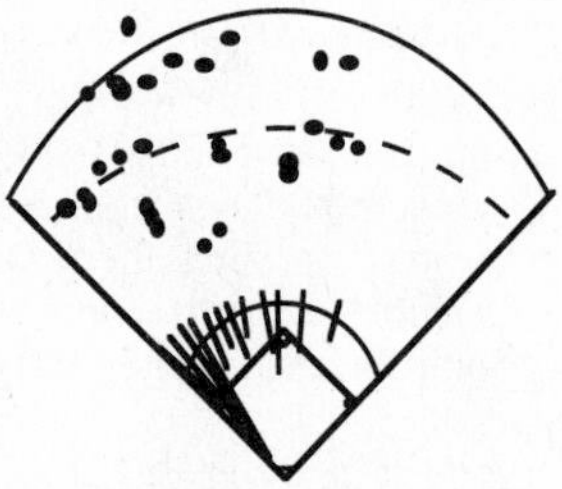

Vs. RHP

1990 Situational Stats

	AB	H	HR	RBI	AVG		AB	H	HR	RBI	AVG
Home	143	31	4	15	.217	LHP	114	29	4	10	.254
Road	134	28	4	16	.209	RHP	163	30	4	21	.184
Day	78	21	2	10	.269	Sc Pos	70	16	3	23	.229
Night	199	38	6	21	.191	Clutch	56	11	1	5	.196

1990 Rankings (American League)

- 1st in lowest percentage of extra bases taken as a runner (18.6%)
- 2nd in highest percentage of runners caught stealing by a catcher (43.3%)
- 3rd lowest batting average with an 0-2 count (.030)

LEE GUETTERMAN

Position: RP
Bats: L **Throws:** L
Ht: 6' 8" **Wt:** 225

Opening Day Age: 32
Born: 11/22/58 in Chattanooga, TN
ML Seasons: 6

PITCHING:

Lee Guetterman has enough different pitches to be a starter, but he doesn't have the stamina. The Yankees don't mind, because Guetterman has found his niche as a short reliever. In 1990, he achieved the distinction of leading all Yankee pitchers in wins, matching the 11 that he won for Seattle as a starter in 1987. He was the first Yankee reliever ever to lead the team in victories.

Guetterman is basically a sinker ball pitcher, but he can throw the fastball higher and harder when he wants to. He also has a curve, a slider and a straight change, but he uses the sinking fastball the most. He likes to throw strikes and doesn't nibble. His ratio of 14.7 pitches per inning was lowest among all Yankees last year.

Similar to the way in which he tires easily in each individual outing, Guetterman can wear down over the course of the season. He held up well in 1989, but in 1990 he finished the year by surrendering 11 earned runs, 16 hits, and 6 walks in his last 13 innings, raising his season ERA from 2.69 to 3.39. Guetterman's stats were also affected disproportionately by two very bad outings. He gave up 11 of his 35 earned runs in just 2.1 innings. In the other 62 of his 64 total appearances, his ERA was only 2.38.

Like many lefties, Guetterman loves pitching at Yankee Stadium. His home ERA in 1989 was 2.30, and 2.64 in 1990. Before the rough September last year, he had a 1.57 ERA in New York home games.

HOLDING RUNNERS AND FIELDING:

Guetterman is about average at holding runners, which means he is below average for a left-handed short reliever. The opposition does not run on him frequently, but they have a high success ratio. Last year, opposing runners got away with eight of 10 stolen base attempts. Guetterman is a former first baseman who knows how to field. He was credited with more assists (19) than some of the Yankee starters who worked more innings last year.

OVERALL:

Guetterman is a highly-effective short reliever. He has been overshadowed by Dave Righetti since coming to New York, and is likely to remain overshadowed as long as Righetti has the closer role. The Yankees have never indicated a willingness to let the popular Righetti get away via free agency. But there were hints late last year that if Righetti did escape from New York, the Yanks wouldn't consider it a disaster to have Guetterman and a much-improved Eric Plunk sharing the saves.

Overall Statistics

	W	L	ERA	G	GS	Sv	IP	H	R	BB	SO	HR
1990	11	7	3.39	64	0	2	93.0	80	37	26	48	6
Career	28	22	4.10	223	23	15	430.1	461	218	133	196	34

How Often He Throws Strikes

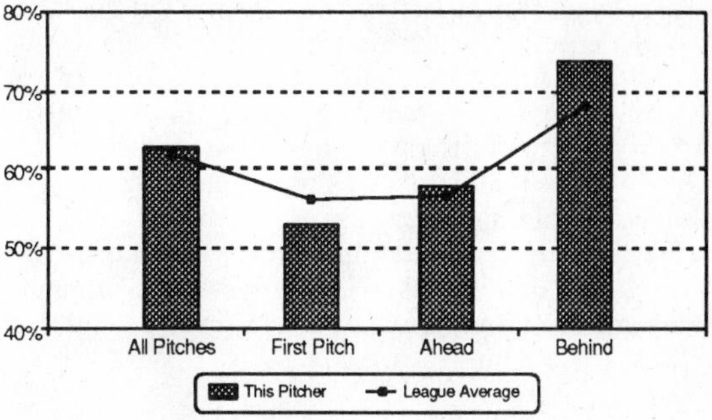

1990 Situational Stats

	W	L	ERA	Sv	IP		AB	H	HR	RBI	AVG
Home	9	4	2.64	1	58.0	LHB	99	25	1	11	.253
Road	2	3	4.63	1	35.0	RHB	240	55	5	31	.229
Day	3	1	1.90	0	23.2	Sc Pos	103	21	4	40	.204
Night	8	6	3.89	2	69.1	Clutch	211	53	5	30	.251

1990 Rankings (American League)

- 8th in holds (12)
- Led the Yankees in wins (11), games pitched (64), holds, winning percentage (.611) and blown saves (5)

MEL HALL

Position: DH/LF/RF
Bats: L **Throws:** L
Ht: 6' 1" **Wt:** 205

Opening Day Age: 30
Born: 9/16/60 in Lyons, NY
ML Seasons: 10

HITTING:

Mel Hall simply came unglued in 1990: physically and mentally, on the field and off. He suffered the ignominious distinction of producing a sixth consecutive season with a batting average lower than the year before. He struck out almost eight times as much as he walked. When he was dropped from the Yankee lineup in August, Hall expressed himself by slamming the door of manager Stump Merrill's office so hard that the doorknob fell off. Shortly after the season ended, he was in the news for illegally keeping wild animals in his home. Altogether, it was not a great year.

Hall's main function is to hit right-handed pitching. But his stats against righties in 1990 were mediocre at best. Hall's career average against lefties is .156, so unless he hits righthanders, he won't survive.

A dead pull hitter, Hall has no power to left field. His experience has not made him any wiser. He can be backed off the plate with inside heat, and then put away with outside breaking balls. He also chases curves in the dirt, having little ability to check his swing when fooled. His strike zone judgement is questionable, and he shows little interest in the count. He would rather chase high fastballs out of the strike zone than draw a walk. Hall's approach is simply to try and hit one out, and the pitchers (even the righties) have learned how to take advantage.

BASERUNNING:

Hall makes a good effort on the base paths, but he is often hurt by inappropriate optimism. His lack of attention to game situations is evident. He gets thrown out attempting extra bases when his team needs multiple runs. He has not attempted a stolen base in two seasons with the Yankees.

FIELDING:

For a good athlete with speed and a superior arm, Hall can look very bad in the outfield. He is capable of making great catches and strong throws, but he attracts more attention with his misjudged fly balls, poor jumps, and throws to wrong bases. The Yankees have half a dozen outfielders who are defensively better than Hall.

OVERALL:

Going back to his days with the Chicago Cubs, Hall has had a reputation as a slow learner who is difficult to coach. The Yankees have given him every opportunity to blossom as a platooner and designated hitter, but if 1990 is any indication, he isn't going to make the grade. The New York outfield is very crowded for 1991, and there is an adequate lefty DH somewhere among Don Mattingly, Kevin Maas and Matt Nokes.

Overall Statistics

	G	AB	R	H	D	T	HR	RBI	SB	BB	SO	AVG
1990	113	360	41	93	23	2	12	46	0	6	46	.258
Career	958	3137	431	865	170	20	100	454	27	211	478	.276

Where He Hits the Ball

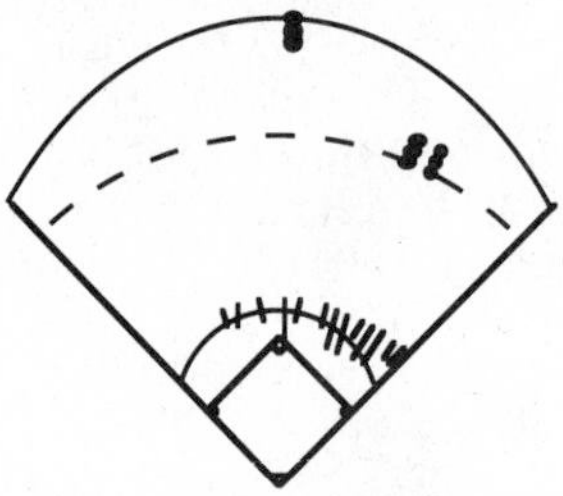

Vs. LHP

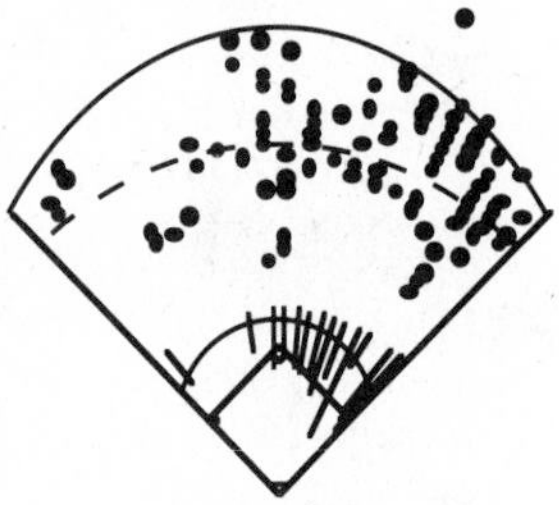

Vs. RHP

1990 Situational Stats

	AB	H	HR	RBI	AVG		AB	H	HR	RBI	AVG
Home	187	51	3	25	.273	LHP	58	12	1	5	.207
Road	173	42	9	21	.243	RHP	302	81	11	41	.268
Day	112	23	1	9	.205	Sc Pos	96	24	2	32	.250
Night	248	70	11	37	.282	Clutch	60	16	4	11	.267

1990 Rankings (American League)

- Led the Yankees in percentage of extra bases taken as a runner (52.9%)
- Led designated hitters in percentage of extra bases taken as a runner

ANDY HAWKINS

Position: SP
Bats: R **Throws:** R
Ht: 6' 3" **Wt:** 217

Opening Day Age: 31
Born: 1/21/60 in Waco, TX
ML Seasons: 9

PITCHING:

Andy Hawkins got off to a very slow start last year, pitched better as the weather got warmer --- including losing a no-hitter on July 1 -- and then faded late in the season. After September 12, Hawkins sat on the bench and watched younger arms show what they could do. The statistically-disastrous 1990 season was not as bad as the numbers indicate. Just like the no-hitter, which Hawkins lost when the White Sox scored four unearned runs, the year was filled with good pitches that produced poor results.

Hawkins became miscast in the role of "ace" in 1989, when he won twice as many games as any other Yankee pitcher. He is good enough as a third or fourth starter for a team that will score some runs, but all he did with the Yankees in 1990 was compile a pitiful .294 winning percentage.

Hawkins is a basic fastball/slider pitcher. He can augment his pitch selection with a cutter and a straight change, but his success depends on simply throwing strikes and letting the fielders do their work. He needs good location to be effective, but he cannot afford to nibble and fall behind in the count. Every time he takes the mound, his performance wavers on a fine line between success and failure.

In 1990, Hawkins fell behind the count too often, threw too many fat pitches that hitters were waiting to crush, and walked too many batters. For the first time since his rookie year of 1982, his walks exceeded his strikeouts, not a happy stat to contemplate at age 31.

HOLDING RUNNERS AND FIELDING:

Hawkins is clearly above average at holding runners. Over the past two years, fewer than 50% of attempted steals against him have been successful. He pays close attention to runners, and has a quick, smooth delivery. In the field he is a definite asset. He covers plenty of ground and is especially adept at covering first base.

OVERALL:

Unless Hawkins comes up with a new pitch or gets traded to a winning team soon, his best years are behind him. He has approached the star level in a couple of seasons, but never quite reached the status of a top quality starter. He is not exactly washed-up, however. With a tiny improvement in control, some good fielding behind him, a fair share of run support, and a little luck, Hawkins can be a winning pitcher. He should begin 1991 assured of a spot in the Yankee rotation, and will have to pitch very badly to lose it.

Overall Statistics

	W	L	ERA	G	GS	Sv	IP	H	R	BB	SO	HR
1990	5	12	5.37	28	26	0	157.2	156	101	82	74	20
Career	80	85	4.14	261	232	0	1468.2	1483	759	570	661	142

How Often He Throws Strikes

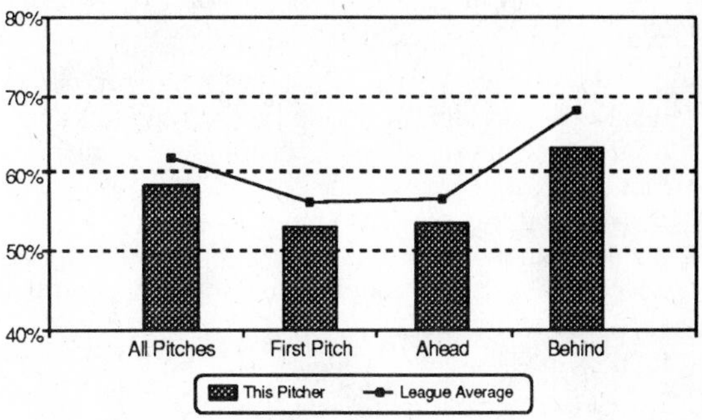

1990 Situational Stats

	W	L	ERA	Sv	IP		AB	H	HR	RBI	AVG
Home	2	8	5.44	0	89.1	LHB	313	92	8	37	.294
Road	3	4	5.27	0	68.1	RHB	286	64	12	45	.224
Day	1	5	4.60	0	43.0	Sc Pos	119	41	6	63	.345
Night	4	7	5.65	0	114.2	Clutch	63	9	1	4	.143

1990 Rankings (American League)

- 1st in highest batting average allowed with runners in scoring position (.345)
- 2nd in lowest winning percentage (.294)
- 3rd worst ERA at home (5.44)
- Led the Yankees in walks allowed (82)

ROBERTO KELLY

Position: CF/LF
Bats: R **Throws:** R
Ht: 6' 4" **Wt:** 185

Opening Day Age: 26
Born: 10/1/64 in Panama City, Panama
ML Seasons: 4

HITTING:

Roberto Kelly is living proof that the Yankees do not trade away all their best minor league talent. One must wonder, however, if the Yankees (or anyone else) ever knew how good Kelly would be. It took a long time for the New York fans and media to recognize Kelly as a star.

At age 26, Kelly put up numbers that indicate a career beginning to peak at the superstar level. Blossoming in the second half of 1990, Kelly was one of only two American League players who put up double digits in homers and steals after the All-Star break. The other: Rickey Henderson. Their second half numbers were remarkably similar. Kelly had a .285 average, 11 homers, 36 RBI, and 24 stolen bases after the break, while Henderson hit .313 with 11 homers, 26 RBI, and 26 steals. Comparable National Leaguers over this stretch included Eric Davis and Barry Bonds.

Kelly is a free swinger, with a long, whipping stroke. Many scouts peg him as a high fastball hitter, but in fact Kelly likes all fastballs, and actually prefers them to be low in the strike zone. The toughest pitches for him are breaking balls in the dirt and fastballs up and in or up and way outside. Kelly will swing at pitches that he cannot hit. He doesn't walk much, and strikes out excessively for a leadoff hitter. The Yankees often used him in the number-three slot while Don Mattingly was out of the lineup.

BASERUNNING:

Kelly has outstanding speed, and has been consistently above the 70% success rate in steal attempts since he first came up in 1987. He made big advances in reading the moves of opposing pitchers during 1989 and, although the numbers don't show it, he continued to improve this knowledge during 1990. He could easily steal 50 bases with an 80% success rate in 1991. Kelly is always a threat to take an extra base. He can really turn up the speed in clutch situations.

FIELDING:

In the Ponderosa-size outfield of Yankee Stadium, Kelly's speed is a huge asset. He gets a good jump on the ball, and pulls many drives that would be home runs in other parks, or extra-base hits with someone else playing center field. Kelly's arm is not especially strong, but he is good at hitting the cutoff man, and plays a heads-up game at all times.

OVERALL:

Kelly's star performance in 1989 was a surprise, and many New York observers remained unconvinced through much of 1990. But there's little doubt now that Kelly has arrived. He is the only Yankee outfielder assured of an everyday role in 1991.

Overall Statistics

	G	AB	R	H	D	T	HR	RBI	SB	BB	SO	AVG
1990	162	641	85	183	32	4	15	61	42	33	148	.285
Career	360	1211	171	349	57	8	26	123	91	82	267	.288

Where He Hits the Ball

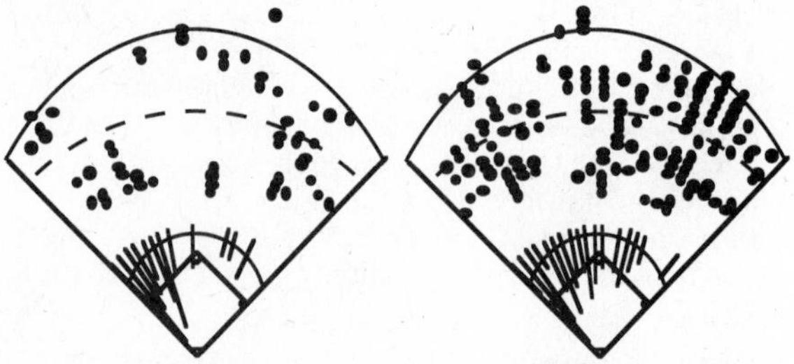

Vs. LHP　　Vs. RHP

1990 Situational Stats

	AB	H	HR	RBI	AVG		AB	H	HR	RBI	AVG
Home	315	96	5	25	.305	LHP	181	55	5	17	.304
Road	326	87	10	36	.267	RHP	460	128	10	44	.278
Day	180	55	5	21	.306	Sc Pos	122	30	1	39	.246
Night	461	128	10	40	.278	Clutch	111	29	4	15	.261

1990 Rankings (American League)

- 1st in games (162)
- 2nd in at-bats (641) and caught stealing (17)
- 3rd in hits (183), singles (132) and stolen bases (42)
- Led the Yankees in batting average (.285), at-bats, runs (85), hits, singles, doubles (32), triples (4), total bases (268), caught stealing (17), times on base (220), pitches seen (2,538), plate appearances (687) and games
- Led AL center fielders in at-bats, hits, singles, stolen bases, strikeouts (148), pitches seen, plate appearances and games

PITCHING:

Dave LaPoint is the prototypical junkballer. He is experienced, crafty, and (of course) left-handed. He throws a mediocre fastball, a very slow change of pace, and a slider. He relies on pinpoint control, deception, and a careful approach to every hitter each time through the lineup. After pitching for nine teams, LaPoint's accumulated knowledge of hitters and ballparks is an asset in his pitch selection. But like most junkballers, his pitching tends to be in tune with the strength of his team. LaPoint, 7-10 with a 4.11 ERA for the 1990 Yankees, was a little better than his last place ball club. But not much.

To succeed, LaPoint needs to change speeds, move the fastball around, and keep the ball away from right-handed hitters. He isn't going to overpower anybody. His fielding support is critical, because almost every hitter puts the ball in play. LaPoint gives up hits generously; he allowed the opposition a .311 batting average in 1989 and .292 in 1990. He has to avoid the base on balls to have any kind of success. In each of his seven wins last year, he gave up three walks or less.

It took LaPoint a long time, but he finally showed the ability to use Yankee Stadium's dimensions to his advantage in 1990. His home ERA was 3.13, compared to 5.60 on the road. In 1989 he allowed a home ERA of 4.60, with an opponents batting average of .313 -- not exactly the kind of numbers the Yankees have in mind when they acquire lefty pitchers.

HOLDING RUNNERS AND FIELDING:

When a pitcher lets opponents hit .300 against him, he must be pretty stingy with the stolen bases. LaPoint holds runners well, a skill that was a prerequisite to play three years for Whitey Herzog's Cardinals. LaPoint is also a good fielder. He is not especially mobile, but he is poised and alert around the mound, knows where to position himself on every conceivable play, and always throws the ball to the right base.

OVERALL:

LaPoint has been on the fringe of major league success for 11 years. His best year was a 14-13 record with a 3.25 ERA for the White Sox and Pirates in 1988, just before the Yankees made him a premium-priced free agent. He is a well-traveled journeyman whose real prime came and went with the Cardinals in 1983-84. Lefthanders often do well when they pitch for the Yankees, but there is a real question about what New York was expecting when they acquired LaPoint. He was a .500 pitcher when they signed him, and after two years in the Bronx, he isn't even that any longer.

DAVE LaPOINT

Position: SP
Bats: L **Throws:** L
Ht: 6' 3" **Wt:** 215

Opening Day Age: 31
Born: 7/29/59 in Glens Falls, NY
ML Seasons: 11

Overall Statistics

	W	L	ERA	G	GS	Sv	IP	H	R	BB	SO	HR
1990	7	10	4.11	28	27	0	157.2	180	84	57	67	11
Career	80	85	3.98	292	225	1	1482.0	1588	738	553	799	117

How Often He Throws Strikes

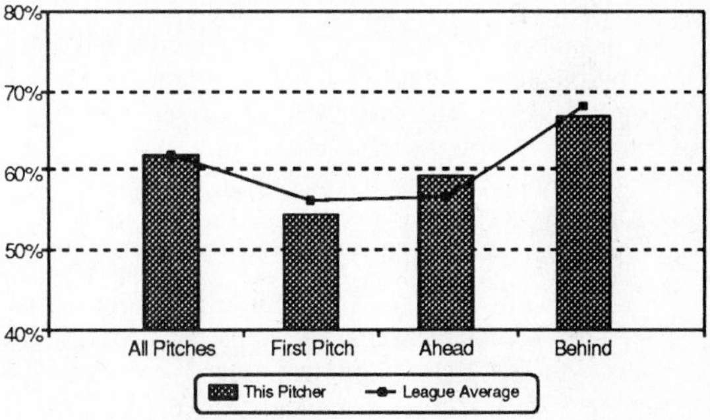

1990 Situational Stats

	W	L	ERA	Sv	IP		AB	H	HR	RBI	AVG
Home	6	3	3.13	0	95.0	LHB	95	28	2	9	.295
Road	1	7	5.60	0	62.2	RHB	522	152	9	61	.291
Day	0	4	4.70	0	46.0	Sc Pos	139	39	2	57	.281
Night	7	6	3.87	0	111.2	Clutch	50	12	1	2	.240

1990 Rankings (American League)

- ➟ 5th worst batting average allowed vs. right-handed batters (.291)
- ➟ 9th lowest winning percentage (.412)
- ➟ Led the Yankees in GDPs induced (21)

PITCHING:

The ace of the Yankee staff in 1990 had to be removed from the rotation in September to avoid the embarrassment of losing 20 games. You have to be a pretty good pitcher to get 20 losses in a season. Tim Leary was the best the Yankees had last year, but that's a dubious honor.

The Yankees have an uncanny knack for acquiring pitchers just after they have achieved success and are slipping back towards mediocrity. Leary soared to the top ranks of major league pitchers in 1988, after he developed a devastating forkball in the Mexican winter league. Unfortunately, he became tired in late 1988, succumbing to year-round work and Tommy Lasorda's tendency to overwork starting pitchers until they break down. Tim had become unimpressive again by 1989.

Leary has a good assortment of pitches to go with his split-finger pitch. He still has an average fastball, and he complements it with a curve and a slider. When he has good control, the slider is his out pitch. Leary can occasionally blow away a hitter to get out of a jam, but he is more dependent on control than power. He is a direct worker who likes to throw strikes, and averages very few pitches per inning.

Leary is acquiring the label, "Don't trade a potential star hitter for this pitcher." The Reds coughed up Kal Daniels to get their hands on Leary, and Daniels became a candidate for Comeback Player of the Year. The Yankees parted with International League batting champ Hal Morris for Leary, and Morris blossomed in Cincinnati. Now, if the Yanks could only find a team that wants to trade one of their fine young hitters...

HOLDING RUNNERS AND FIELDING:

One of the few Yankee pitchers who allowed opponents better than a 60% success rate in steal attempts, Leary is apparently never going to be very good at holding runners. He is a good fielder, however. In 1990 he was far ahead of all other Yankee pitchers in putouts and assists. Leary covers the mound area well and is adept at getting to first base quickly.

OVERALL:

On any good major league team, Leary could be a solid contributor as a number three-starter. He is no ace, but he can win when he gets run support. Early in 1990, Leary began to fulfill the Yankees' high expectations, posting a 2.53 ERA through June 1. This fine effort earned him only three wins in two months. Disappointment showed in the 4.87 ERA that he produced over the remainder of the season.

TIM LEARY

Position: SP
Bats: R **Throws:** R
Ht: 6' 3" **Wt:** 208

Opening Day Age: 32
Born: 12/23/58 in Santa Monica, CA
ML Seasons: 9

Overall Statistics

	W	L	ERA	G	GS	Sv	IP	H	R	BB	SO	HR
1990	9	19	4.11	31	31	0	208.0	202	105	78	138	18
Career	54	75	3.79	199	153	1	1039.1	1061	491	322	682	90

How Often He Throws Strikes

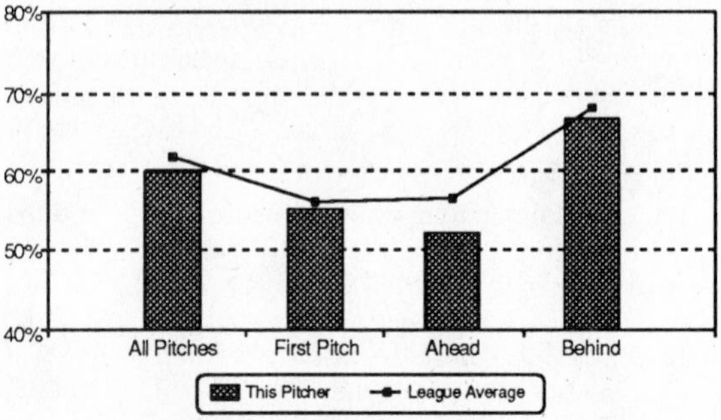

1990 Situational Stats

	W	L	ERA	Sv	IP		AB	H	HR	RBI	AVG
Home	1	9	4.73	0	83.2	LHB	408	106	10	47	.260
Road	8	10	3.69	0	124.1	RHB	377	96	8	37	.255
Day	2	5	5.53	0	53.2	Sc Pos	178	40	6	66	.225
Night	7	14	3.62	0	154.1	Clutch	74	20	2	5	.270

1990 Rankings (American League)

- 1st in losses (19), wild pitches (23) and lowest run support per 9 innings (3.07)
- 4th lowest winning percentage (.321) and highest groundball/flyball ratio (1.87)
- Led the Yankees in losses, games started (31), complete games (6), innings (208.0), hits allowed (202), batters faced (881), hit batsmen (7), strikeouts (138), wild pitches (23), pitches thrown (3,142), pickoff throws (173) and stolen bases allowed (18)

JIM LEYRITZ

Position: 3B
Bats: R **Throws:** R
Ht: 6' 0" **Wt:** 195

Opening Day Age: 27
Born: 12/27/63 in Lakewood, OH
ML Seasons: 1

Overall Statistics

	G	AB	R	H	D	T	HR	RBI	SB	BB	SO	AVG
1990	92	303	28	78	13	1	5	25	2	27	51	.257
Career	92	303	28	78	13	1	5	25	2	27	51	.257

Where He Hits the Ball

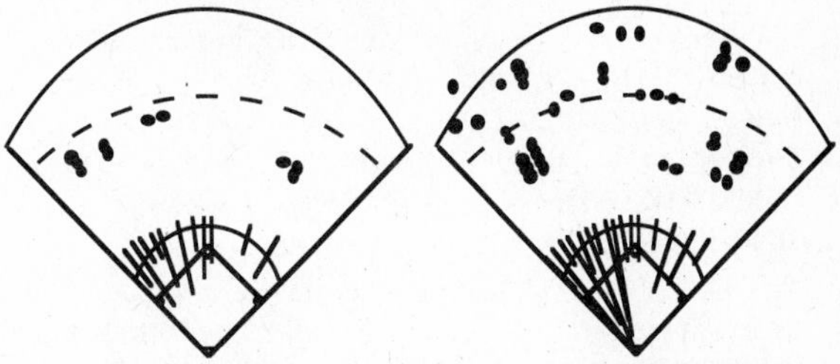

Vs. LHP   Vs. RHP

1990 Situational Stats

	AB	H	HR	RBI	AVG		AB	H	HR	RBI	AVG
Home	166	44	1	13	.265	LHP	103	30	2	7	.291
Road	137	34	4	12	.248	RHP	200	48	3	18	.240
Day	96	28	0	4	.292	Sc Pos	67	13	1	18	.194
Night	207	50	5	21	.242	Clutch	62	18	0	5	.290

1990 Rankings (American League)

- 4th in hit by pitch (7)
- 6th in most GDPs per GDP situation (19.3%)
- Led the Yankees in hit by pitch (7)

HITTING:

As a rookie last year, Jim Leyritz hit .313 in his first 96 major league at-bats, and then just .232 in his last 207. Obviously, there is still some question whether he can hit for a good average in the major leagues. Leyritz is unlikely to reach any dramatic new heights at age 27, but he has batted over .300 several times in the minor leagues.

Leyritz describes himself as a spray-type hitter who uses the whole field. He tries to hit the gaps, and emphasizes making contact and not striking out. Opposing pitchers and catchers give Leyritz credit for possessing good line drive power, and they fear him as a home run threat.

Most pitchers try to keep the ball away from Leyritz. He is a mistake-punisher who will jump on a weak heater down the middle. Leyritz looks for a fastball on almost every pitch, trying to adjust when he sees a breaking ball. He concentrates on zones rather than pitch types. Leyritz has the most trouble with the really hard flame-throwers. He names Roger Clemens and Nolan Ryan as the two pitchers that he least wants to face.

BASERUNNING:

Leyritz will try an occasional steal, but he needs to learn more about the league's pitchers and their moves. Leyritz was cut down in three of five steal attempts last year. He is never going to compile double-digit stolen base totals in any season, but he bears watching on the base paths.

FIELDING:

Leyritz is a catcher by trade, but he appeared mainly at third base and left field for New York last year. His strong arm is a big asset at all three positions. He can handle left field; when he is out there, runners are well-advised to be cautious. At the hot corner, Leyritz is still learning. In total, he made more errors than any Yankee except shortstop Alvaro Espinoza. Leyritz really wants to be a catcher, and is proud of his ability to throw out runners. But on the Yanks he rates behind both Bob Geren and Matt Nokes.

OVERALL:

For a player who hadn't appeared in even one game above the Double-A level before 1990, Leyritz has come a long way quickly. He brings an unusual combination of skills to the ball yard. The Yankees showed a willingness to try him at all three of his fielding positions, especially in September. Leyritz is a leading candidate for a third base platoon job or a major utility role in 1991.

KEVIN MAAS

Position: 1B/DH
Bats: L **Throws:** L
Ht: 6' 3" **Wt:** 205

Opening Day Age: 26
Born: 1/20/65 in Castro Valley, CA
ML Seasons: 1

HITTING:

In the never-ending battle between pitcher and hitter to adjust faster than the other, Kevin Maas finished behind the pitchers in 1990. Maas burst into the major leagues by hitting his first 11 homers faster than anyone in the history of the game. Within a few weeks, however, the pitchers had changed their approach. Going into 1991, Maas is the one who will have to be looking for adjustments.

On the Fourth of July, Maas provided his own fireworks by belting his first major league HR. More homers quickly followed. The experts said, "Let's see him hit lefties," so Maas homered off Greg Swindell and Paul Gibson. Throwing lefties at Maas was not the solution, at least not initially; throwing breaking balls from behind in the count WAS the way to get him out. It just took the opposing pitchers a while to find the answer.

Maas enjoyed his first tour around the league for two reasons: (1) he is an intelligent hitter who knows how to work the count and then look for a fastball, and (2) most major league pitchers like to challenge every rookie with their heater. Maas showed that he can hit anybody's fastball.

The latest book on Maas is the classic approach to every dangerous hitter: keep the ball away from him, work the outside corner, walk him if you have to, but don't give in to him. Throw only pitcher's pitches; one hitter's pitch is all he needs to beat you.

BASERUNNING:

Although he stole 14 bases in 1987, Maas suffered a knee injury in 1989 and was not a big threat to steal in 1990. Last year he was caught in two of four attempts at Columbus, and two of three in New York. For a youngster, Maas is advanced in his knowledge of situations, and usually makes appropriate decisions without hesitating.

FIELDING:

Maas in an adequate and self-confident first baseman, but he is still learning. He made nine errors in just 57 games last year at first. In two of his three minor league All-Star selections, he was chosen as the designated hitter, which tells you something. He can play a little outfield, too.

OVERALL:

The key to Maas' success will be mental toughness. Like many power hitters, he is streaky. We have seen one prolonged hot streak proving his potential. The question is: will he be able to bounce back from slumps and difficulties? Yankee hitting coach Darrell Evans is highly optimistic, saying that Maas will be among the premier power hitters of the 1990's.

Overall Statistics

	G	AB	R	H	D	T	HR	RBI	SB	BB	SO	AVG
1990	79	254	42	64	9	0	21	41	1	43	76	.252
Career	79	254	42	64	9	0	21	41	1	43	76	.252

Where He Hits the Ball

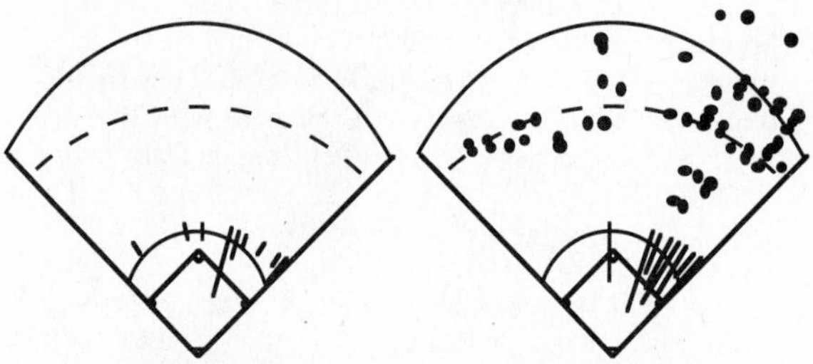

Vs. LHP　　Vs. RHP

1990 Situational Stats

	AB	H	HR	RBI	AVG		AB	H	HR	RBI	AVG
Home	135	38	12	27	.281	LHP	67	11	3	8	.164
Road	119	26	9	14	.218	RHP	187	53	18	33	.283
Day	69	18	8	15	.261	Sc Pos	58	12	2	18	.207
Night	185	46	13	26	.249	Clutch	42	7	3	5	.167

1990 Rankings (American League)

- → 2nd in least GDPs per GDP situation (3.8%)
- → 9th lowest batting average in the clutch (.167)
- → Led the Yankees in least GDPs per GDP situation
- → Led AL first basemen in least GDPs per GDP situation

DON MATTINGLY

Position: 1B/DH
Bats: L **Throws:** L
Ht: 6' 0" **Wt:** 175

Opening Day Age: 29
Born: 4/20/61 in Evansville, IN
ML Seasons: 9

Overall Statistics

	G	AB	R	H	D	T	HR	RBI	SB	BB	SO	AVG
1990	102	394	40	101	16	0	5	42	1	28	20	.256
Career	1117	4416	655	1401	288	15	169	759	9	342	258	.317

Where He Hits the Ball

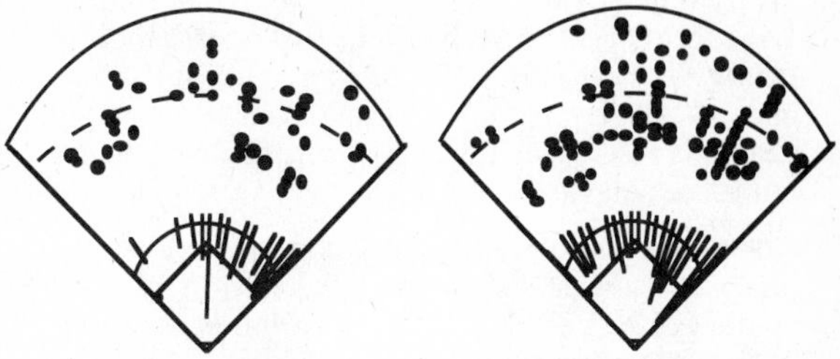

Vs. LHP   Vs. RHP

1990 Situational Stats

	AB	H	HR	RBI	AVG		AB	H	HR	RBI	AVG
Home	183	45	4	20	.246	LHP	126	33	0	17	.262
Road	211	56	1	22	.265	RHP	268	68	5	25	.254
Day	111	35	1	15	.315	Sc Pos	97	28	1	35	.289
Night	283	66	4	27	.233	Clutch	68	14	2	10	.206

1990 Rankings (American League)

- 4th in intentional walks (13)
- 5th in batting average on a 3-2 count (.381)
- Led the Yankees in intentional walks,GDPs (13), batting average with runners in scoring position (.289), batting average on an 0- 2 coutn (.227), batting average on a 3-2 count and batting average with 2 strikes (.242)
- Led AL first basemen in batting average on a 3-2 count and batting average with 2 strikes

HITTING:

At an age when most hitters are putting up their biggest offensive stats, Don Mattingly had his most disappointing season. He was disabled for seven weeks with pain in his lower back. One hopeful sign is that Mattingly hit .333 after returning from the disabled list on September 11, but pessimists can recite a longer list of disturbing numbers. One of the biggest concerns is that he finished the season by going 261 at-bats without a home run.

Mattingly has played through back pain in previous seasons, including 1989 when he finished with one of his best Septembers ever. But 1990 was almost all bad news. As late as May 21, he was hitting over .300, but in the next two months he went steadily downhill, hitting just .208 for over 200 at-bats, until he went on the disabled list July 25. His average stood at .245 at the time of the injury.

Mattingly is a thoughtful hitter with an excellent knowledge of the strike zone and what each pitcher can do with it. He likes to look at the first pitch just to get a feel for the pitcher's timing. A strike or two is no big deal, because he can hit almost any pitch to any field. He approaches every pitch as an individual project, with the goal of driving the ball hard, to a spot appropriate in the situation. His power extends to all fields, though his homers usually exit over right field.

BASERUNNING:

The back pain had no visible effect on Mattingly's running game, which features no speed whatsoever. He stole one base in 1990, as he does in most years. Mattingly is really aware of game situations when he is on the bases, just as he is at the plate. He rarely hurts the team, and seizes almost every possible opportunity.

FIELDING:

Mattingly is among the best at first base. His soft hands save many throwing errors over the course of a season. Most importantly, he has an excellent knowledge of opposing hitters and Yankee pitchers, and positions himself perfectly. He covers his territory so well that most observers have an inflated impression of his quickness and lateral movement.

OVERALL:

When he is healthy, Mattingly is arguably the best hitter in baseball. He is the very rare type of hitter who gets almost as many home runs as strikeouts, producing stats that haven't been seen in New York since Joe DiMaggio. The question for 1991 is whether he can recover from his injuries and resume his role as one of the game's greatest players.

MATT NOKES

Position: C/DH
Bats: L **Throws:** R
Ht: 6' 1" **Wt:** 185

Opening Day Age: 27
Born: 10/31/63 in San Diego, CA
ML Seasons: 6

Overall Statistics

	G	AB	R	H	D	T	HR	RBI	SB	BB	SO	AVG
1990	136	351	33	87	9	1	11	40	2	24	47	.248
Career	506	1539	175	402	54	3	71	226	5	112	222	.261

Where He Hits the Ball

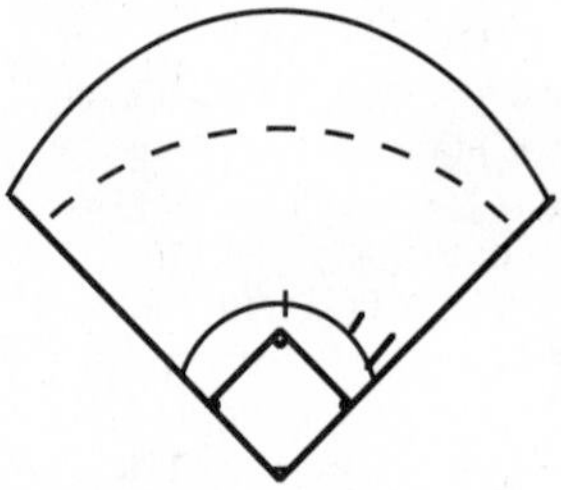

Vs. LHP

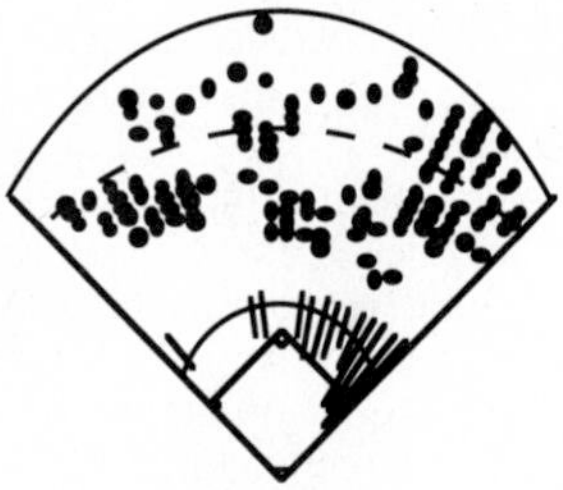

Vs. RHP

1990 Situational Stats

	AB	H	HR	RBI	AVG		AB	H	HR	RBI	AVG
Home	157	40	4	20	.255	LHP	14	2	0	2	.143
Road	194	47	7	20	.242	RHP	337	85	11	38	.252
Day	115	34	4	16	.296	Sc Pos	80	24	3	32	.300
Night	236	53	7	24	.225	Clutch	50	14	3	11	.280

1990 Rankings (American League)

- 10th in batting average on an 0-2 count (.273)

HITTING:

Matt Nokes showed his power potential by belting 32 home runs as a rookie in 1987. That was a tough act to follow, and Nokes hasn't been able to do it: he's totaled only 36 home runs in the three seasons since then. But Nokes remains a dangerous hitter while improving other aspects of his game.

Even before the '87 campaign ended, pitchers had learned that they would have to keep the ball away from Nokes. Now they approach him like they would any dangerous hitter, with fastballs off the plate or up and in, and many breaking balls. Nokes will never again see fastballs over the plate like he did in his first time around the league.

In 1990 Nokes was the Yankees' premier clutch hitter, hitting .333 with 27 RBI in 60 at-bats with men in scoring position. Nokes had a weak second half, however, compiling just a .217 average with three homers and 14 RBI after the All-Star break, compared to .274, eight homers and 26 RBI in the first half. Nokes also had a 60-point drop in his batting average in his big year of '87, dropping from .313 in the first half to .251 in the second that season.

Nokes gets little playing time against left-handed pitchers, but analysts must wonder why. In 1988-89 combined, Nokes hit better against lefties; in those two years he was .259 off the southpaws (21 for 81). He batted only 14 times against leftihanders in 1990.

BASERUNNING:

Nokes makes his offensive contributions with his bat, not with his legs. He has attempted only nine steals in his major league career, and failed in four of them. He is cautious on the base path, with good reason.

FIELDING:

Although the Yankee coaches like to think that Nokes has made big advances since coming to New York, Nokes himself feels that he made his greatest improvements before leaving the Tigers. For example, he was able to throw out only 18% of baserunners in 1987, but improved to 38% in 1988 and has stayed around 40% since then. Everyone now agrees that Nokes is a good defensive catcher. And he is gaining respect for his game-calling and ball-blocking abilities.

OVERALL:

Nokes is not the only player who had a big power year in 1987, then failed to duplicate it. Like Larry Sheets and several others, he created unrealistic expectations that year. Only 27, Nokes still has possibilities for the future, including a shot at the number-one catching job in 1991.

PITCHING:

The Yankees unveiled a new and improved Eric Plunk in 1990. Plunk has always been a good power pitcher, but last year he added a wide variety of pitches that elevated him to a new level. He became one of the few happy stories on a beleaguered pitching staff.

Working with bullpen coach Mark Connor, Eric experimented with a huge assortment of pitches. Getting up to throw two or three times in many games, Plunk developed confidence in his growing repertoire. By mid-season, he was truly comfortable with his curve for the first time in his career. He also improved his slider and straight change, and added a cutter and a forkball. Most important, he became convinced that he could rely on any of these pitches, especially the curve, no matter what the count.

Plunk had always been held back by the belief that he had to use his 90 MPH heater on all crucial pitches. Plunk's fastball has good velocity, but it lacks movement, and it's hittable when batters know it's coming. In 1990, Plunk showed true multi-pitch aggressiveness, and the results were outstanding. Eric finished the year pitching exceptionally well. In his last 18 appearances, he had a 1.53 ERA with 35 strikeouts in 29.1 innings.

HOLDING RUNNERS AND FIELDING:

Eight of 12 would-be base stealers were cut down when they tried to run on Plunk in 1990. He has improved his ability to hold runners, and he has benefitted from the Yankee practice of calling pickoff throws from the dugout. Plunk also showed significant improvement in his fielding during 1990, especially in moving to his right. He still needs to work on covering first base more quickly.

OVERALL:

Plunk's stock has really risen in the Yankee organization. Management now views him as being ready for a larger role, pitching in more critical game situations, and possibly sharing some of the closer duties. In a roundabout way, Plunk was helped by the Yankee experiments that made him a starter during the second half of 1989. He had to begin working on an assortment of pitches, including some that he hadn't used in years, and some that he had never tried. When he lacked confidence in these other pitches, they didn't help him much, but when he began to feel good about the larger repertoire, he became a dominant pitcher. For a late-inning short reliever, he now wields numerous weapons. Considering that he was regarded as a one-pitch pitcher just a year ago, he has come a long way in a short time.

ERIC PLUNK

Position: RP
Bats: R **Throws:** R
Ht: 6' 5" **Wt:** 210

Opening Day Age: 27
Born: 9/3/63 in Wilmington, CA
ML Seasons: 5

Overall Statistics

	W	L	ERA	G	GS	Sv	IP	H	R	BB	SO	HR
1990	6	3	2.72	47	0	0	72.2	58	27	43	67	6
Career	29	24	3.96	204	33	8	470.1	384	225	310	419	44

How Often He Throws Strikes

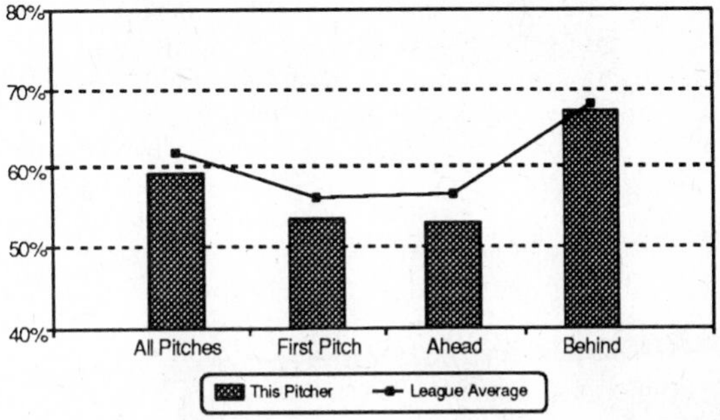

1990 Situational Stats

	W	L	ERA	Sv	IP		AB	H	HR	RBI	AVG
Home	4	0	3.71	0	26.2	LHB	91	26	1	9	.286
Road	2	3	2.15	0	46.0	RHB	167	32	5	27	.192
Day	3	1	1.62	0	16.2	Sc Pos	82	16	1	28	.195
Night	3	2	3.05	0	56.0	Clutch	75	21	1	10	.280

1990 Rankings (American League)

- ➟ Led the Yankees in balks (2)

STOPPER

DAVE RIGHETTI

Position: RP
Bats: L **Throws:** L
Ht: 6' 4" **Wt:** 210

Opening Day Age: 32
Born: 11/28/58 in San Jose, CA
ML Seasons: 11

PITCHING:

The Yankees did Dave Righetti an inadvertent favor last year by proposing to make him a starter, then changing their minds. Righetti worked on his third and fourth pitches during the off season, and arrived at spring training with a dusted-off starter's repertoire. As a result, he became a better relief pitcher.

Righetti had become a straightforward fastball/slider pitcher when he moved to the bullpen in 1984. For three years, this limited selection served him well, as the fastball hummed and the slider bit hard. But more recently, these two pitches had been wearing thin. His opponents batting average swelled gradually from .226 in 1986 to .277 in 1989. Righetti and his fans were pleased to note a dip to .238 in 1990. Dave credits the extra pitches, especially the change-up, for helping him in 1990.

The Yankees also helped Righetti in 1990 by using him more carefully. From 1987 through 1989, Righetti worked an average of 1.44 innings per appearance. In 1990, by design, the Yanks reduced his workload to exactly one inning per game. In 53 games last year, Righetti worked more than one inning only three times, and he threw more than 30 pitches only twice. Fresher and stronger, Righetti turned in a 92% (36 for 39) success ratio in save opportunities.

HOLDING RUNNERS AND FIELDING:

Righetti has a reputation for being easy on base stealers, but in 1990 no one even tried to steal. Dave will throw to first base to keep runners close, but his attention is always focused on the hitter first and foremost. Righetti is a below-average fielder. If he comes up with anything bunted or hit back through the middle, it is usually just a matter of luck. He made only two assists during 1990. The negative factors in his fielding are his single- minded concentration on the hitter, and a pitching motion that leaves him in poor position.

OVERALL:

After three consecutive years of so-so performance that had people questioning his status as a premier closer, Righetti gave his critics reason to pause and think during 1990. In addition to an outstanding single season, Dave also achieved a number of milestones. He passed Sparky Lyle (224 to 222) on the all-time save ranking. Righetti is now seventh on the all-time list, and number one among left-handed pitchers. He also became just the fifth pitcher in major league history to have 20 saves in seven consecutive seasons. Considering his improvement in 1990, the outlook for his future is indeed favorable.

Overall Statistics

	W	L	ERA	G	GS	Sv	IP	H	R	BB	SO	HR
1990	1	1	3.57	53	0	36	53.0	48	24	26	43	8
Career	74	61	3.11	522	76	224	1136.0	999	448	473	940	65

How Often He Throws Strikes

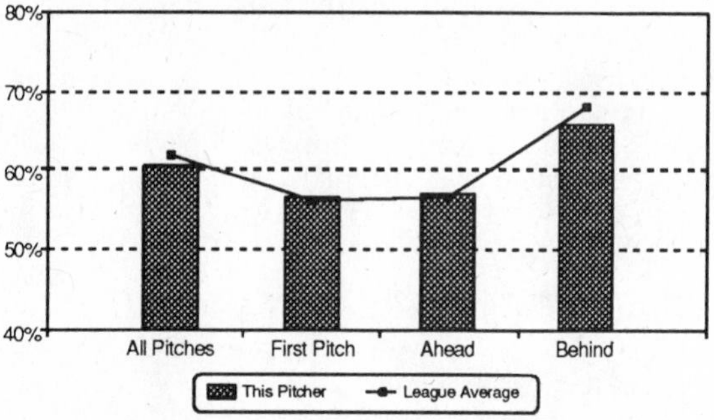

1990 Situational Stats

	W	L	ERA	Sv	IP		AB	H	HR	RBI	AVG
Home	1	1	2.60	21	27.2	LHB	41	10	2	8	.244
Road	0	0	4.62	15	25.1	RHB	164	38	6	18	.232
Day	1	1	6.60	7	15.0	Sc Pos	58	8	2	15	.138
Night	0	0	2.37	29	38.0	Clutch	146	31	7	18	.212

1990 Rankings (American League)

- 2nd in save percentage (92.3%)
- 5th in saves (36) and save opportunities (39)
- Led the Yankees in saves, games finished (47), save opportunities, save percentage and first batter efficiency (.191)

PITCHING:

Jeff Robinson has been somewhat of an enigma since he attempted to rise from the ranks of the National League's top set-up relievers. In 1989, Jim Gott's season-long injury gave Robinson the chance to become Pittsburgh's closer, but he failed miserably. The Pirates traded him to the Yankees after the '89 season, and Robinson went through a period of adjustment. After working briefly as a starter and swing man, Robinson seemed to find himself again last year. The Yankees have worked him back into the set-up role, although they did give him four starts when the rotation had a vacancy from July 16 to August 2.

In August and September, Robinson finally began re-emerging as a short reliever. In his final 18 appearances, he held the opposition scoreless 17 times. His 1.69 ERA during this streak would have been 0.00 but for one outing in Fenway Park when he faced 19 hitters over 3.2 innings and gave up four runs, not exactly a "short relief" appearance. Even with the Boston calamity included, he stranded 74% of inherited runners during the season.

Robinson had some adjustments to make when he came from the National League to the American. He found that A.L. hitters were generally less selective, and more likely to swing hard. In the National League, his two main pitches were a sinking fastball and a slider. In the junior circuit, he found that he had to re-learn the curveball, because, as Robinson says, "It's an American League pitch." He also throws a split-fingered fastball, a pitch he used more prominently during his best years with San Francisco.

HOLDING RUNNERS AND FIELDING:

Opponents stole only six bases against Robinson last year, and were caught five times. Robinson's success often depends on shutting down baserunners in crucial situations, and he works hard on this aspect of his game. As a fielder, Robinson has excellent range, but occasionally hurts himself with an errant throw. At age 30, he should really be showing a little more poise.

OVERALL:

From 1986 through 1988, Robinson was among the most successful and hardest working set-up relievers in baseball. With that solid track record of success, it's a mystery why he never graduated to the higher level of save artist. That question will likely remain unanswered during 1991, as Robinson is back in a set-up role, with other candidates in line ahead of him for the ace reliever job. If Robinson is comfortable with set-up work, he should have a good year in 1991, because that's how the Yankees plan to use him.

JEFF ROBINSON

Position: RP/SP
Bats: R **Throws:** R
Ht: 6' 4" **Wt:** 200

Opening Day Age: 30
Born: 12/13/60 in Santa Ana, CA
ML Seasons: 7

Overall Statistics

	W	L	ERA	G	GS	Sv	IP	H	R	BB	SO	HR
1990	3	6	3.45	54	4	0	88.2	82	35	34	43	8
Career	42	51	3.76	366	57	35	766.1	748	370	280	526	61

How Often He Throws Strikes

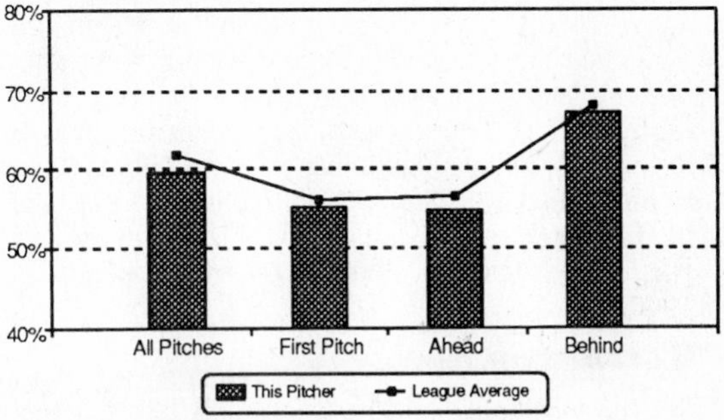

1990 Situational Stats

	W	L	ERA	Sv	IP		AB	H	HR	RBI	AVG
Home	1	3	3.02	0	44.2	LHB	140	31	3	13	.221
Road	2	3	3.89	0	44.0	RHB	191	51	5	26	.267
Day	0	1	3.91	0	25.1	Sc Pos	94	19	2	31	.202
Night	3	5	3.27	0	63.1	Clutch	90	22	1	14	.244

1990 Rankings (American League)

- 9th in holds (11)
- Led the Yankees in most GDPs induced per GDP situation (18.8%), lowest batting average allowed vs. left-handed batters (.221) and lowest percentage of inherited runners scored (25.8%)

HITTING:

Though somewhat below par in 1990, Steve Sax remains one of the top professional hitters in the game today. The book says to give him a mixture of breaking balls and fastballs away, and a few teams think he can be pitched down and in. The truth is, there is no safe way to pitch to Sax. He can adjust to any location and speed, and is an expert at driving the outside pitch to right field. He is an outstanding contact hitter with a fine sense of the strike zone. He uses the whole field, with an emphasis on hits up the middle and in the gaps. One of his greatest offensive weapons is the ability to read defenses and foresee the pitcher's approach.

Sax insists that his substandard season in 1990 was entirely due to bad luck. "Just one of those years," he says. Sax feels that last year, he made more outs hitting the ball directly at fielders than he did in 1988 and 1989 combined. Teammates and opponents all agree that Steve had more than his share of hard-hit outs in 1990, but some suggest that he may have reacted by pressing too hard, thereby losing some of his patience at the plate. Impatience is a difficult case to prove, however. Sax was not inclined to swing at the first pitch excessively, and he was one of the few A.L. hitters who got more walks than strikeouts in 1990.

BASERUNNING:

Sax had no slump on the base paths in 1990. Whether you look at total steals or success percentage, only Rickey Henderson was a better thief. Sax has achieved a 70% success rate every year since 1985, and posted his career best (83%) in 1990. Sax excels at every aspect of running the bases. He knows opposing pitchers and catchers, reads situations, gets a good jump, motors well, and slides expertly.

FIELDING:

The Dodgers organization has perpetuated a rap that Sax has fielding deficiencies, but the facts say otherwise. He has good range, positions himself well, and turns the double play as well as anyone. He ranked third in the A.L. in double plays turned in 1990 and made only ten errors all year.

OVERALL:

Sax is arguably the best overall second baseman in the American League. He has shown the ability to come back from off years with a bang, and his 1990 season wasn't all that bad. At age 31 he should produce another fine season in 1991.

STEVE SAX

Position: 2B
Bats: R **Throws:** R
Ht: 5'11" **Wt:** 185

Opening Day Age: 31
Born: 1/29/60 in Sacramento, CA
ML Seasons: 10

Overall Statistics

	G	AB	R	H	D	T	HR	RBI	SB	BB	SO	AVG
1990	155	615	70	160	24	2	4	42	43	49	46	.260
Career	1404	5578	732	1583	209	40	39	438	376	464	496	.284

Where He Hits the Ball

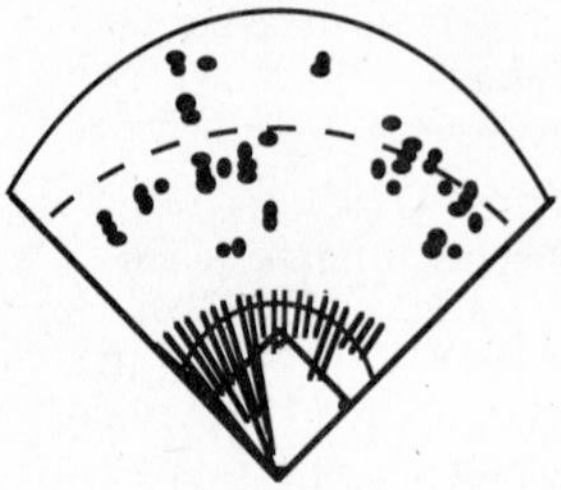

Vs. LHP

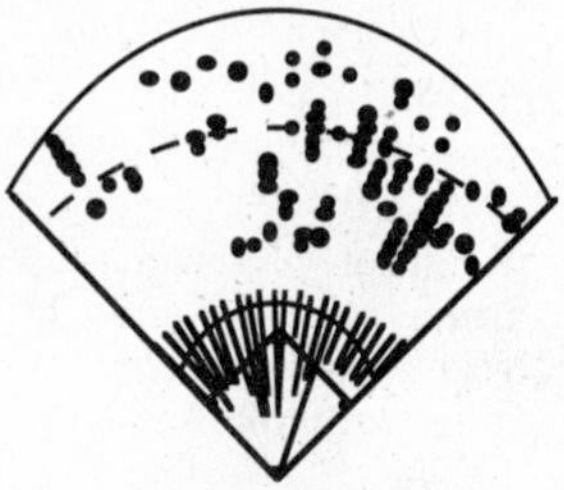

Vs. RHP

1990 Situational Stats

	AB	H	HR	RBI	AVG		AB	H	HR	RBI	AVG
Home	294	76	3	27	.259	LHP	177	44	0	11	.249
Road	321	84	1	15	.262	RHP	438	116	4	31	.265
Day	180	58	1	17	.322	Sc Pos	134	32	1	37	.239
Night	435	102	3	25	.234	Clutch	94	31	1	13	.330

1990 Rankings (American League)

- 1st in highest groundball/flyball ratio (2.84)
- 2nd in stolen bases (43) and steals of third (11)
- Led the Yankees in sacrifice flies (6), stolen bases, GDPs (13), highest groundball/flyball ratio, stolen base percentage (82.7%), batting average in the clutch (.330), highest percentage of pitches taken (58.3%), lowest percentage of swings that missed (9.3%), highest percentage of swings put into play (55.2%) and steals of third
- Led AL second basemen in stolen bases (43), hit by pitch (4), highest groundball/flyball ratio and steals of third

PITCHING:

Hear the name "Mike Witt," and you think "curve ball." At age 30, Witt still has one of the best curves in the game. He also has a 90 MPH fastball, and that's a formidable base for any pitcher. But Witt doesn't show much imagination beyond those two pitches. His nominal third pitch is a straight change, but Witt has never liked to throw it. He is more likely to use a soft curve when he wants to get a hitter off-balance. Witt doesn't like his offspeed pitches, however, and would happily work a whole game without using them.

The Angels gave up on Witt as a starter after the 1989 season, feeling that his curveball had become too predictable and too hittable. Witt started 1990 in the California bullpen, and worked effectively. He had a 1.77 ERA after ten appearances, including a shared no-hitter with Mark Langston on opening day. But then California traded Witt to the Yankees in exchange for Dave Winfield.

The Yankees immediately inserted Witt into their starting rotation. But as with the Angels in '89, Witt did little for New York. He worked his share of innings, but finished with a losing record and a 4.47 ERA. In a few short years, Witt has gone from being a top starter on a division champion to being just another starter on a poor team.

HOLDING RUNNERS AND FIELDING:

Witt is good at holding runners. Having a reputation for a good pickoff move is just as useful as several throws to first base; it makes the runners cautious and pessimistic. The opposition attempted 11 steals against Witt in 1990 and got caught four times. As a fielder, however, Witt is visibly reluctant to stab at balls hit through the middle, and has been rapped by press and management over the years for appearing over-cautious.

OVERALL:

After several outstanding seasons with low ERAs, a perfect game, two All-Star selections, and a part in leading the Angels to the brink of the 1986 World Series, Witt looked like a potential Hall of Famer. These days the notion seems far-fetched indeed. After ten seasons in the majors, Witt is still, basically, a two-pitch pitcher. Even Tom Seaver and Nolan Ryan had to develop a varied repertoire to remain effective. Witt will have to use his offspeed pitches more extensively, and develop with something new, if he wants to remain a solid major league contributor after age 30.

MIKE WITT

Position: SP/RP
Bats: R **Throws:** R
Ht: 6' 7" **Wt:** 198

Opening Day Age: 30
Born: 7/20/60 in Fullerton, CA
ML Seasons: 10

Overall Statistics

	W	L	ERA	G	GS	Sv	IP	H	R	BB	SO	HR
1990	5	9	4.00	26	16	1	117.0	106	62	47	74	9
Career	114	113	3.79	330	288	6	2062.0	2019	979	690	1343	175

How Often He Throws Strikes

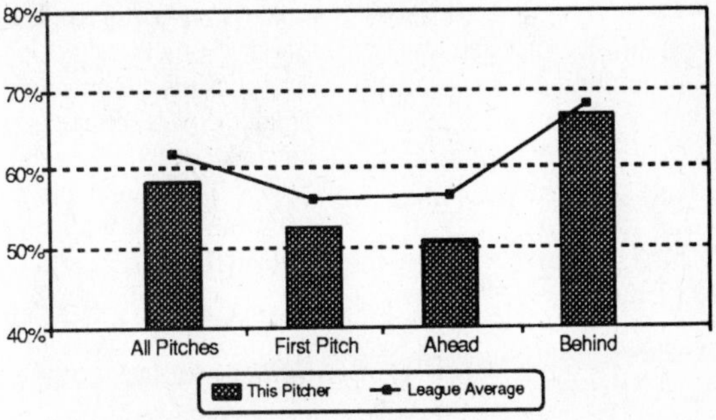

1990 Situational Stats

	W	L	ERA	Sv	IP		AB	H	HR	RBI	AVG
Home	2	5	3.29	1	52.0	LHB	217	58	3	28	.267
Road	3	4	4.57	0	65.0	RHB	222	48	6	25	.216
Day	2	3	4.24	0	34.0	Sc Pos	107	23	3	43	.215
Night	3	6	3.90	1	83.0	Clutch	64	17	3	13	.266

1990 Rankings (American League)

- Did not rank near the top or bottom in any category

STEVE ADKINS

Position: SP
Bats: R **Throws:** L
Ht: 6' 6" **Wt:** 200

Opening Day Age: 26
Born: 10/26/64 in Chicago, IL
ML Seasons: 1

Overall Statistics

	W	L	ERA	G	GS	Sv	IP	H	R	BB	SO	HR
1990	1	2	6.38	5	5	0	24.0	19	18	29	14	4
Career	1	2	6.38	5	5	0	24.0	19	18	29	14	4

PITCHING, FIELDING & HOLDING RUNNERS:

Even before Steve Adkins took the mound for his major league debut, the clubhouse talk was about umpire reactions to his pitching. Adkins' main pitch is a "knuckle curve," which breaks down so sharply that it really doesn't look like a strike until it hits the catcher's mitt. Adkins walked eight batters in his first 1.1 major league innings (leaving the game with no-hitter going). The trick pitch will take a little getting used to.

Adkins also throws a fastball and a good change-up. One coach compares Adkins to Jim Deshaies, because both are lefties with pitches that break sharply downward, enabling them to throw fastballs up in the strike zone without getting clobbered. When batters must guard against the likelihood of a big sinker, they cannot get too wide-eyed for a high fastball.

Adkins is extremely aware of situations. He watches runners closely and has a good move to first base. His defense reflects the same awareness and he has an ability to react quickly to batted balls.

OVERALL:

Although minor league win-loss marks are not the most meaningful stats, New York likes the fact that Adkins has been a consistent winner. He was 12-1 for AA Albany in 1989 and 15-7 last year for AAA Columbus. At age 26, he is mature enough for a major league role. The Yankees need left-handed starters in 1991. Undeterred by the 29 walks Adkins allowed in 24 innings last year, they will give him ample consideration.

RICK CERONE

Position: C
Bats: R **Throws:** R
Ht: 5'11" **Wt:** 195

Opening Day Age: 36
Born: 5/19/54 in Newark, NJ
ML Seasons: 16

Overall Statistics

	G	AB	R	H	D	T	HR	RBI	SB	BB	SO	AVG
1990	49	139	12	42	6	0	2	11	0	5	13	.302
Career	1206	3779	365	919	173	15	56	413	4	287	421	.243

HITTING, FIELDING, BASERUNNING:

After 15 years as a professional, Rick Cerone finally hit .300 in 1990. He was used sparingly by the Yankees, but performed well when given the chance. He reached base in 18 of his 19 starts, hitting .329. Cerone is a patient hitter who tries to make contact. He is not especially dangerous, but he will hit the ball where it is pitched, as evidenced by his ability to pull lefties who pitch him inside.

On the base paths, Cerone is a liability. He is alert but totally lacking in speed. Behind the plate, he is a defensive asset. He had one of his best seasons ever with 16 of 29 base stealers being caught with Cerone behind the plate, helping the Yankees lead the league in this category. He covers the ground around the plate very well, and is an aggressive, gutsy player on tag plays at home. Cerone has a reputation as a good game-caller, but the numbers show that his team's pitchers have better ERAs when someone else is catching.

OVERALL:

Cerone feels that the surgery which sidelined him from June 8 to August 11 was unnecessary. He is optimistic about a useful role in the coming year. The Yankees had five major league catchers at the end of 1990, however, and Cerone has been released twice in his career already. If he gets much playing time in 1991, it will probably not be in New York.

DAVE EILAND

Position: SP
Bats: R **Throws:** R
Ht: 6' 3" **Wt:** 210

Opening Day Age: 24
Born: 7/5/66 in Dade City, FL
ML Seasons: 3

Overall Statistics

	W	L	ERA	G	GS	Sv	IP	H	R	BB	SO	HR
1990	2	1	3.56	5	5	0	30.1	31	14	5	16	2
Career	3	4	5.00	14	14	0	77.1	90	48	22	34	13

PITCHING, FIELDING & HOLDING RUNNERS:

Dave Eiland is a basic sinker ball pitcher. In addition to the sinking fastball, he uses a curve, a straight change, and a slow curve/change. The key to his success is keeping the ball low and keeping it away from power hitters. When he is pitching well, he gives up a few scattered hits, walks no one, and keeps the score low.

Eiland is not an overpowering pitcher. He depends on good pitch location and fielding support. Eiland's control is outstanding. In the last two years at AAA Columbus, he has issued only 53 walks in 276 innings. A ratio of 1.73 walks per nine innings is excellent in any league.

A former defensive end for the University of Florida, Eiland is a superior athlete who covers the field well. He has good range and excellent decision-making ability. He is alert to baserunners, but he is still working on his pickoff move.

OVERALL:

The Yankees will be giving Eiland his fourth shot at their major league roster in 1991. He's only seen brief action in his previous trials, but he's lowered his earned run average each time. Although Eiland is still only 24, he should be mature enough now to fill a major league role if there is an opening. Eiland was 16-5 with a 2.87 ERA for Columbus last year, and was 9-4 for Columbus in 1989. The Yankees could use a winning pitcher in 1991.

HENSLEY MEULENS

Position: LF
Bats: R **Throws:** R
Ht: 6' 3" **Wt:** 190

Opening Day Age: 23
Born: 6/23/67 in Curacao, Netherlands Antilles
ML Seasons: 2

Overall Statistics

	G	AB	R	H	D	T	HR	RBI	SB	BB	SO	AVG
1990	23	83	12	20	7	0	3	10	1	9	25	.241
Career	31	111	14	25	7	0	3	11	1	11	33	.225

HITTING, FIELDING, BASERUNNING:

Giving him his first real major league trial, the Yankees put Hensley Meulens in their lineup on a regular basis last September. Meulens has compiled an impressive minor league power-hitting record over the last several seasons, and it was no great surprise that he handled major league pitching adequately. Meulens is a good fastball hitter, but he is over-anxious, strikes out frequently, and looks bad against crafty pitchers who use his aggressiveness against him. Meulens needs to be patient, and forget about home runs until he can hit singles more consistently.

Meulens is aggressive on the base paths, too. He attempted 10 steals at Columbus last year, and succeeded six times. He is not likely to run much in New York, however. Meulens had never played any position but third base at any level, but the Yankees used him in left field for most of the 1990 season. He looked better than anyone could expect from a novice, running down flies and throwing out runners. He has trouble reading hooks and slices off the bat, however, and is unaccustomed to tall stadiums.

OVERALL:

Meulens was the front-runner for the Yankees' left field job at the end of September. With an adequate performance in winter ball, he should become a starter. Many position players who reach the majors at age 23 are bound for stardom. Meulens looks like he may be one of them.

PASCUAL PEREZ

Position: SP
Bats: R **Throws:** R
Ht: 6' 3" **Wt:** 180

Opening Day Age: 33
Born: 5/17/57 in San Cristobal, Dominican Republic
ML Seasons: 10

Overall Statistics

	W	L	ERA	G	GS	Sv	IP	H	R	BB	SO	HR
1990	1	2	1.29	3	3	0	14.0	8	3	3	12	0
Career	65	64	3.45	193	179	0	1170.1	1099	515	320	781	100

PITCHING, FIELDING & HOLDING RUNNERS:

After signing a big contract, Pascual Perez delivered a small season. He pitched only three games before he was disabled with shoulder problems. Perez argued against surgery for months, but finally agreed to an operation on August 9. Surgeon James Andrews found a partially torn labrum, a bone spur in the shoulder, and a partially torn rotator cuff. It is not true that the Yankees are seeking "lemon law" remedies for used ballplayers, but they are disappointed.

When Perez is healthy, he can be phenomenally successful. His slider is among the best in baseball, he has pinpoint control, and his theatrical approach upsets hitters and sells tickets. From 1987 through 1989, Perez' overall 2.80 ERA was among the best of all major league starters.

Perez is an outstanding athlete whose appearance of inattention is pure pretense. He holds runners very closely, and fields his position as well as anyone.

OVERALL:

A healthy Perez could have helped the Yankees in 1990. Even if healthy, however, Perez has questions to answer. His success with Montreal included exceptional performances at home, in front of polite, supportive crowds. And his stats show an overwhelming preference to pitch on artificial turf rather than grass. These two factors are both absent in New York, so Perez must be regarded as a question mark for reasons beyond his injuries.

RANDY VELARDE

Position: 3B/SS
Bats: R **Throws:** R
Ht: 6' 0" **Wt:** 185

Opening Day Age: 28
Born: 11/24/62 in Midland, TX
ML Seasons: 4

Overall Statistics

	G	AB	R	H	D	T	HR	RBI	SB	BB	SO	AVG
1990	95	229	21	48	6	2	5	19	0	20	53	.210
Career	184	466	52	106	16	4	12	43	1	35	97	.227

HITTING, FIELDING, BASERUNNING:

Randy Velarde raised some high expectations by hitting .340 in 100 at-bats in 1989. His .245 career major league mark going into 1990 was more indicative of what to really expect. Even in the minor leagues, Velarde was a career .270 hitter. He can hit an occasional home run, but is more of a singles and gap-type hitter than a slugger.

As one opposing catcher described it, the American League's pitchers simply adjusted to Velarde in 1990. They realized that he is a good fastball hitter, stopped challenging him so directly, and shifted toward curves and offspeed pitches. They discovered that Velarde is particularly susceptible to a good change-up, because his hitting style keeps him leaning forward on his toes.

Velarde is a decent fielder with good range, and offers the value of versatility that is so important in a utility role. He is definitely error-prone, however, a symptom of never having settled into one position. He has good speed but only fair judgment on the base paths.

OVERALL:

Most utility infielders play one position for a number of years, and then learn the other positions to round out their skills. Velarde is attempting the difficult feat, at age 28, of becoming the Yankees' number-one infield backup. Despite batting only .210 last year, Velarde played in 34 of the Yankees final 46 games last year, and seems reasonably assured of a role for 1991.

HITTING:

Tony La Russa managed Harold Baines for six years with the Chicago White Sox, and coveted Baines for his A's until they finally swung a deal with Texas late last August. Baines' presence helped alleviate the righty-lefty imbalance that was created when Dave Parker left via free agency. Although his ravaged knees have taken away some of his weapons, he still gives the A's production as well as lineup balance.

Baines can hit the ball to all fields and hasn't lost any of his bat speed. He likes the ball low and in, and tends to try to pull that pitch. When he is pitched away, which most lefthanders try to do against him, he'll loop the bat and try to punch the ball to the opposite field. Consequently, teams tend to play him to pull in the infield and to spray in the outfield. He's not the power hitter he once was, but the A's, who have plenty of pop, don't need him to be.

Baines triggers his swing with his right leg, a la Darryl Strawberry. Like Strawberry, he can be made to look silly if he's guessing fastball and gets curveball. When that happens, his lower body is far out in front of his hands, and he gets little torque on his swing. Pitchers consequently go after him with breaking balls away, but not all the time because Baines is usually smart enough to stay back. Baines will probably have to start shortening up on the bat with two strikes and begin taking more pitches as his career progresses. He appears to be doing just that as he's walking more now than he ever has.

BASERUNNING:

Baines once had fair speed, but his battered knees make him virtually a station-to-station man on the bases. He's not a threat to steal. He plays hard all the time and still goes into take-out slides and collisions with alacrity.

FIELDING:

Baines played only two games in the outfield last season — both before he was traded to the A's. Oakland has an abundance of superior outfielders, and it's certain that Baines will be almost exclusively a designated hitter for the rest of his career because of his knees.

OVERALL:

Baines was picked up by the A's for their 1990 stretch drive, but he's only 32, and it's likely he'll be their designated hitter for at least the next few years. La Russa admires Baines for both his quiet leadership and his experienced bat. Baines' power output is down, but the A's are willing to live with that.

HAROLD BAINES

Position: DH
Bats: L **Throws:** L
Ht: 6' 2" **Wt:** 195

Opening Day Age: 32
Born: 3/15/59 in Easton, MD
ML Seasons: 11

Overall Statistics

	G	AB	R	H	D	T	HR	RBI	SB	BB	SO	AVG
1990	135	415	52	118	15	1	16	65	0	67	80	.284
Career	1563	5778	731	1665	291	45	205	900	29	516	889	.288

Where He Hits the Ball

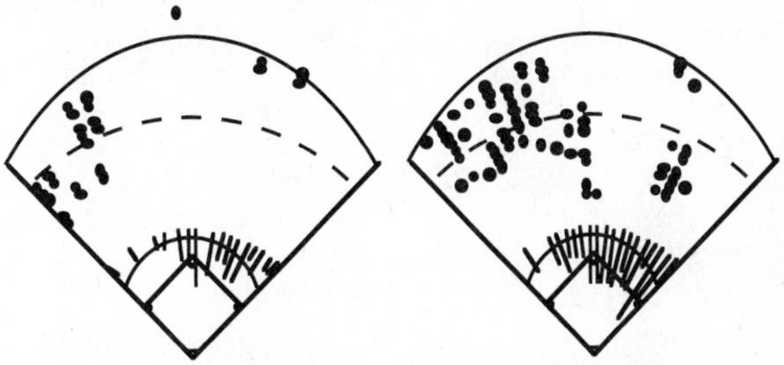

Vs. LHP　　Vs. RHP

1990 Situational Stats

	AB	H	HR	RBI	AVG		AB	H	HR	RBI	AVG
Home	200	56	9	40	.280	LHP	91	23	3	15	.253
Road	215	62	7	25	.288	RHP	324	95	13	50	.293
Day	98	28	6	15	.286	Sc Pos	122	32	2	49	.262
Night	317	90	10	50	.284	Clutch	59	22	3	11	.373

1990 Rankings (American League)

- 5th in batting average in the clutch (.373) and batting average on a 3-1 count (.647)
- 6th in on-base average vs. right-handed pitchers (.392)
- 9th most GDPs per GDP situation (18.5%)
- Led designated hitters in batting average in the clutch

PITCHING:

Oakland's starting pitchers take pride in their ability to pitch well into the late innings. That helps the club, but it hurts Todd Burns. On the deep A's staff, Burns is forced to work mostly as a middle reliever, coming in before set-up men Gene Nelson and Rick Honeycutt. Burns received plenty of work in 1989, especially when Eckersley was injured and Nelson and Honeycutt became replacement closers. But his workload decreased substantially in 1990, and he couldn't quite match the strong numbers he'd posted in his first two major league seasons. Often he sat around, waiting for the A's to use up their primary relievers. Burns also got a couple of starts late in the season, and pitched well.

It's too bad they can't find a more substantial role for him, because Burns is one of the A's most multi-faceted pitchers. As a starter, he mixes four solid pitches -- heavy fastball, curveball, forkball and change-up -- and does a good job of disguising his patterns so that hitters can't sit on a certain pitch. He has good velocity on his fastball, but the key to that pitch is its downward rotation. Burns is generally tough on left-handers, whom he usually tries to jam. But he missed inside more in 1990 and often had to pitch from behind, sometimes with unpleasant results.

While Burns will use location and pitch selection to set up hitters when he's starting, he's more of a power pitcher when used in short relief. If the fastball is working for him, he'll go after the hitters aggressively with it. Because he keeps the fastball down, he gets a lot of ground balls. In relief, he's usually around the plate and doesn't try to tease hitters, although his lack of work in 1990 hurt his control somewhat.

HOLDING RUNNERS AND FIELDING:

Burns doesn't have a tricky move, but is persistent and will make the runners respect him. He gets rid of the ball more quickly than he did when he first came up, and that has helped him hold runners better than in the past. Burns is an adequate but hardly spectacular fielder. He gets over to first quickly in most fielding situations.

OVERALL:

It's possible that the 27-year-old Burns won't attain his full potential until he gets regular work and a better-defined role. That's not likely to happen with the A's, who have the best-stocked bullpen in baseball. Burns has been mentioned in trade talks, and the A's might give him up for the right price.

TODD BURNS

Position: RP
Bats: R **Throws:** R
Ht: 6' 2" **Wt:** 186

Opening Day Age: 27
Born: 7/6/63 in Maywood, CA
ML Seasons: 3

Overall Statistics

	W	L	ERA	G	GS	Sv	IP	H	R	BB	SO	HR
1990	3	3	2.97	43	2	3	78.2	78	28	32	43	8
Career	17	10	2.79	110	18	12	277.2	237	93	94	149	19

How Often He Throws Strikes

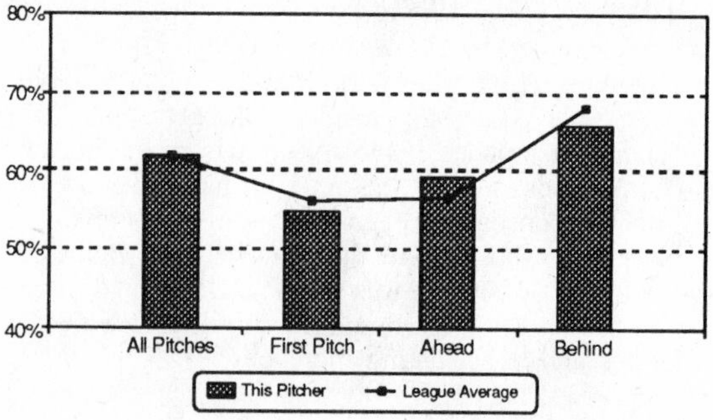

1990 Situational Stats

	W	L	ERA	Sv	IP		AB	H	HR	RBI	AVG
Home	2	1	2.85	2	41.0	LHB	127	34	3	13	.268
Road	1	2	3.11	1	37.2	RHB	170	44	5	23	.259
Day	2	2	2.45	1	33.0	Sc Pos	82	20	2	27	.244
Night	1	1	3.35	2	45.2	Clutch	80	17	2	3	.213

1990 Rankings (American League)

- 1st in worst first batter efficiency (.400)

JOSE CANSECO

Position: RF/DH
Bats: R **Throws:** R
Ht: 6' 3" **Wt:** 240

Opening Day Age: 26
Born: 7/2/64 in Havana, Cuba
ML Seasons: 6

Overall Statistics

	G	AB	R	H	D	T	HR	RBI	SB	BB	SO	AVG
1990	131	481	83	132	14	2	37	101	19	72	158	.274
Career	699	2644	425	715	124	7	165	525	96	292	718	.270

Where He Hits the Ball

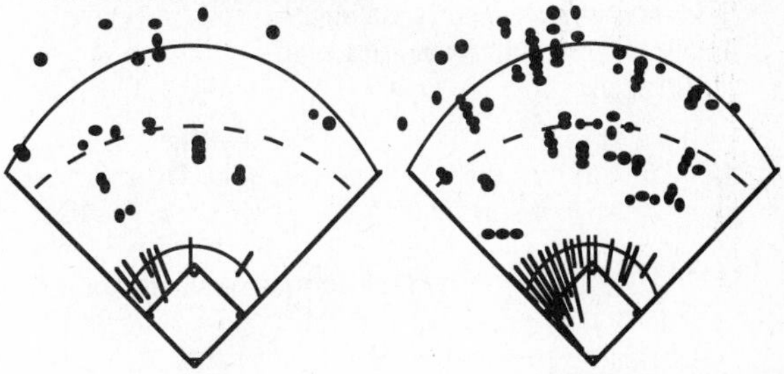

Vs. LHP   Vs. RHP

1990 Situational Stats

	AB	H	HR	RBI	AVG		AB	H	HR	RBI	AVG
Home	217	56	18	43	.258	LHP	123	34	12	28	.276
Road	264	76	19	58	.288	RHP	358	98	25	73	.274
Day	177	49	15	40	.277	Sc Pos	127	33	6	57	.260
Night	304	83	22	61	.273	Clutch	62	10	1	8	.161

1990 Rankings (American League)

- 2nd in HR frequency (13.0 ABs per HR)
- 3rd in home runs (37), strikeouts (158) and slugging percentage (.543)
- 4th in RBIs (101), lowest percentage of swings put into play (32.0%), slugging percentage vs. right-handed pitchers (.520) and worst batting average on a 3-2 count (.072)
- Led the A's in strikeouts and HR frequency
- Led AL right fielders in home runs, runs (83), total bases (261), RBIs, strikeouts, slugging percentage, on-base average (.371), HR frequency, slugging percentage/on-base average vs. right-handed pitchers

HITTING:

In 1990 Jose Canseco missed time because of several injuries: a protruding disc in his back, two wrist injuries and a jammed finger suffered when he slammed a refrigerator door on it. He hit only three home runs during the final two months of the regular season, and his bat disappeared at the worst possible time, during the World Series. For anyone else, we'd be talking a washout season. But Jose Canseco isn't anyone else. He still hit 37 homers and had his fourth 100-RBI season in five years. He also signed a contract to become the highest-paid player in baseball.

The problem for Canseco now is that, with the big contract, people tend to expect perfection. When he falls short -- as he did in the World Series -- the wolves come out. Canseco was playing hurt late last year, so he could have made excuses. For the most part, he simply took the heat, which is an encouraging sign of maturity.

When he's healthy -- and even when he isn't -- Canseco can hit a ball frightening distances to all fields. He's generally pitched away, and some teams use an exaggerated shift against him, daring him to hit the ball to right. For the most part, he took the dare last year, and it wouldn't be surprising to see such shifts become commonplace against him. A good low-ball hitter, he's still learning to lay off high sucker pitches.

BASERUNNING:

Canseco's back problems cut down on his base stealing last year, although he did manage to steal 19 bases in 29 tries. He's still a daring runner, looking to take the extra base any chance he gets. His instincts are good, although sometimes he'll run himself unnecessarily into an out.

FIELDING:

Despite his well-documented problems during the World Series, Canseco is a good outfielder when healthy. His arm remains one of the strongest in baseball, and few runners challenge him. He charges balls in front of him the same way he runs the bases: hard and fast. He still has problems on balls hit behind him (as in the Series), but his judgement continues to improve. He made only one error all season.

OVERALL:

The 1990 season reiterated the oft-expressed notion that Canseco's physique will make it difficult for him to avoid getting hurt. He seemed headed for a monster year at the end of May, but then came the injuries, which led to a long slump and a depressing postseason. Despite the sour finish, Canseco remains the most feared power hitter in the game, and one of its most multi-talented performers.

DENNIS ECKERSLEY

Position: RP
Bats: R **Throws:** R
Ht: 6' 2" **Wt:** 195

Opening Day Age: 36
Born: 10/3/54 in Oakland, CA
ML Seasons: 16

PITCHING:

A curious barrier stood between Dennis Eckersley and a season of 60 or more saves: his teammates went through a period when they were scoring too many runs. Eckersley still wound up with 48, the second-highest total ever in the majors. He blew only two save opportunities and had a 0.61 ERA, but the number that will endure in posterity is his walk total. Eckersley worked 73.1 innings and gave up only four walks -- two in one game. He has issued only six non-intentional walks in his past 131 innings. That's Christy Mathewson country.

Eckersley's masterful control is mainly related to the fact he almost never varies his delivery. An overthrower early in his career, he has learned that rhythm and a waste-free motion can generate the same velocity without straining the arm or diverting the pitch. Eckersley simply throws the ball the same way every time, and the result is that it usually winds up in the same place.

That isn't to say Eckersley simply throws the ball over the plate and lets the hitter take his cuts. He still has good velocity on his fastball, but he rides the fastball in on right-handed hitters and sails it away from lefties. He has a drop-down motion that makes his pitches heavy, and he doesn't toy with hitters; he makes his out pitch right away. Last year he threw his curveball more often than in the past, and hitters who usually look for hard stuff from him often couldn't react in time. Eckersley is not one to experiment as a rule, though; he tries to keep his job as simple as he can.

HOLDING RUNNERS AND FIELDING:

Eckersley isn't the best fielding pitcher in captivity, but he doesn't really have to be when he's pitching well. Because he almost never throws the ball directly over the middle of the plate, few batters hit comebackers against him. He had only one assist all season. Eckersley doesn't pay much attention to baserunners, but he has an adequate move.

OVERALL:

Eckersley, who has battled through a succession of problems in his personal life including alcoholism, exudes a sense of serenity in the clubhouse. That carries over into his work on the mound, where his incredible control is the direct product of self-control. At age 36, Eckersley is in the best shape of his life and is spotted perfectly by A's manager Tony La Russa. He had no arm trouble in 1990, and there's no reason to think he can't sustain his excellence indefinitely.

Overall Statistics

	W	L	ERA	G	GS	Sv	IP	H	R	BB	SO	HR
1990	4	2	0.61	63	0	48	73.1	41	9	4	73	2
Career	169	140	3.49	604	361	145	2815.1	2625	1181	659	1938	291

How Often He Throws Strikes

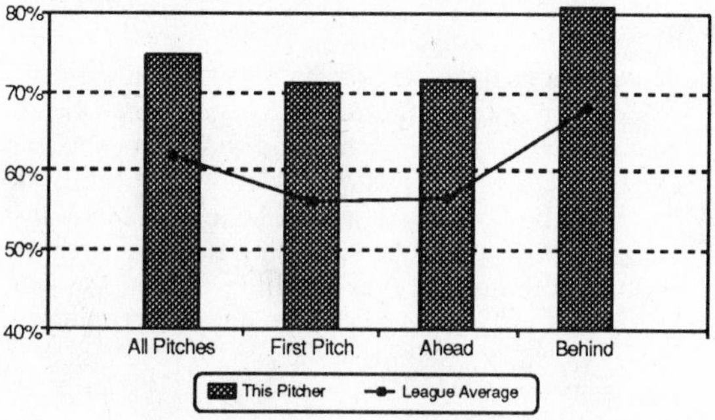

1990 Situational Stats

	W	L	ERA	Sv	IP		AB	H	HR	RBI	AVG
Home	3	2	1.02	22	35.1	LHB	119	20	1	10	.168
Road	1	0	0.24	26	38.0	RHB	138	21	1	2	.152
Day	3	2	1.04	20	34.2	Sc Pos	49	11	0	8	.224
Night	1	0	0.23	28	38.2	Clutch	192	32	2	12	.167

1990 Rankings (American League)

- 1st in save percentage (96.0%)
- 2nd in saves (48)
- 3rd in games finished (61) and save opportunities (50)
- Led the A's in games pitched (63), saves, games finished, save opportunities and save percentage

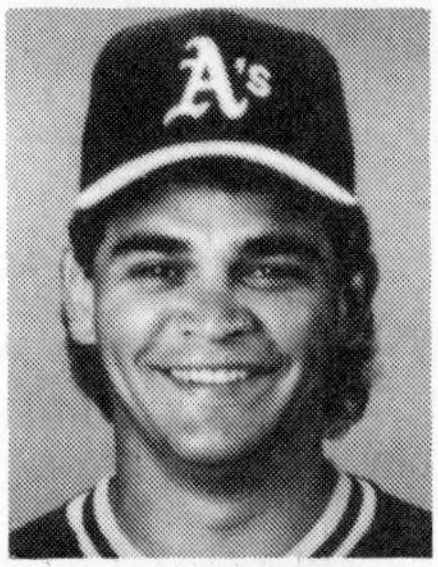

MIKE GALLEGO

Position: 2B/3B/SS
Bats: R **Throws:** R
Ht: 5' 8" **Wt:** 160

Opening Day Age: 30
Born: 10/31/60 in Whittier, CA
ML Seasons: 6

Overall Statistics

	G	AB	R	H	D	T	HR	RBI	SB	BB	SO	AVG
1990	140	389	36	80	13	2	3	34	5	35	50	.206
Career	570	1261	152	285	48	5	11	111	15	129	187	.226

Where He Hits the Ball

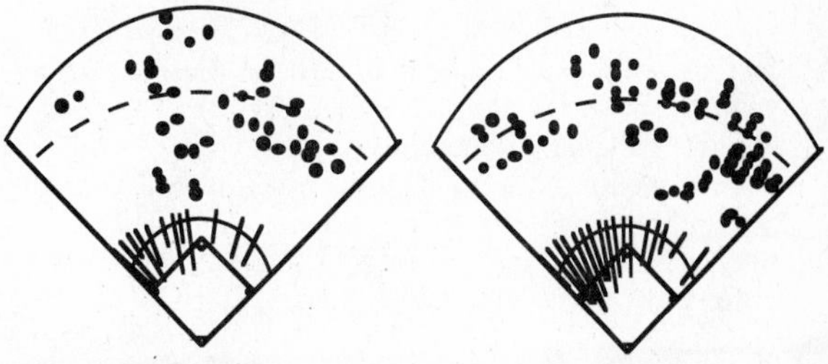

Vs. LHP Vs. RHP

1990 Situational Stats

	AB	H	HR	RBI	AVG		AB	H	HR	RBI	AVG
Home	187	40	1	14	.214	LHP	128	23	1	9	.180
Road	202	40	2	20	.198	RHP	261	57	2	25	.218
Day	155	32	1	15	.206	Sc Pos	94	19	0	27	.202
Night	234	48	2	19	.205	Clutch	44	11	0	5	.250

1990 Rankings (American League)

- 1st in sacrifice bunts (17)
- 2nd in worst batting average vs. left-handed pitchers (.180), worst slugging percentage vs. left-handed pitchers (.242) and worst on-base average vs. left-handed pitchers (.234)
- 7th worst batting average with runners in scoring position (.202)
- Led the A's in sacrifice bunts, GDPs (13) and bunts in play (20)
- Led AL second basemen in sacrifice bunts, hit by pitch (4) and batting average on a 3-1 count (.556)

HITTING:

A .252 hitter in 1989, Mike Gallego dropped off significantly to .206 in 1990. But though his average was low, he helped the A's attack in little ways. He went deep into counts, fouling off pitches that helped run up pitchers' delivery counts. He also was adept at hitting the ball to the right side with a runner at second base. That skill didn't improve his average, but helped the A's win some close games.

Gallego's main problem last year was that he was prone to chase breaking pitches outside the strike zone. His strikeout total was up over his 1989 season. Pitchers worked him away with sliders and other breaking balls more often last year, possibly because they respected him a little more after his .252 season.

Gallego can handle the fastball, even those in on him, and has some power for a small man. He moves up on the bat and controls it well. He did his best work on outside-corner pitches, taking them to the opposite field, sometimes with a little power. Gallego is perhaps the best bunter on the A's team, and was among the league leaders in sacrifice bunts. He will bunt for a hit on occasion.

BASERUNNING:

Gallego is an excellent baserunner who almost never makes a mistake on the bases. He's fearless in takeout and collision situations, and will take the extra base without hesitation on balls hit to right field. He doesn't steal much because he's the number-nine hitter most of the time, but gets a decent jump and can steal a base in a pinch.

FIELDING:

Gallego returned to second base, his natural position, last year, and his exceptional range got him considerable playing time even after the A's acquired Willie Randolph. He picks up the ball off the bat almost instantly, and because he's built so low to the ground, he can balance himself to throw even on difficult plays. Gallego played shortstop for an extended period in 1989 when Walt Weiss was injured, and again during the 1990 postseason. He's no Weiss at short, but compensates for his lack of arm strength with a quick release. He also can play third if needed.

OVERALL:

Though Gallego has had to function as a utility man with Weiss and Randolph on hand, he has never complained about his role, and has performed all his assignments admirably. He is perhaps the best example of Oakland's ability to find the right man for the right job, even if that job isn't always as a starter.

HITTING:

With his career in jeopardy, Ron Hassey lost 30 pounds before the 1990 season began. The weight loss didn't help Hassey's bat speed much at first, as he was hitting only .189 at the All-Star break. But the improved conditioning began to pay off in the second half. Hassey still wound up hitting a weak .213, but he was getting around much better on pitches that had been handcuffing him earlier.

Hassey, a left-handed hitter, became almost exclusively a wrong-field hitter in 1989 and the early part of 1990. Pitchers thus started to take liberties with him, trying to jam him. They were surprised when Hassey regained some of his pull-hitting ability, though he still goes more to the left-center field gap than anywhere else. Hassey's open stance helps him adjust to inside pitches, and he's still quick enough to flick the outside pitch to the opposite field.

Hassey faces very few left-handed pitchers, which is just as well because he's almost helpless against southpaws who work him outside. He doesn't swing at many bad pitches and likes to get deep into counts. Hassey won't chase the outside breaking ball much, but will swing at a pitch on his hands if he thinks the pitcher isn't too overpowering. Defenses usually play Hassey slightly around to left field.

BASERUNNING:

Ugh. Hassey did not attempt to steal a base in 1990, and has had only 13 steals in a 13-season career. His instincts on the bases are okay, but he's not aggressive and almost needs a triple to score from second. The weight loss helped him a bit in this respect, but age and the rigors of his position have taken away almost all his speed.

FIELDING:

Here's where the weight loss really showed, as Hassey had his best defensive season in many years. He's best known as Bob Welch's "personal catcher" and his handling of Welch had a lot to do with Welch's 27-victory season. Hassey remains an excellent handler of all pitchers, and with less bulk, he's a lot more mobile. Because he could get out of his crouch more quickly, he had better success against base stealers last year.

OVERALL:

Hassey was eligible for free agency after the 1990 season, but at age 38, he was not in a position to dictate terms to the A's. Even so, he's valuable to them because of his lefty bat and his ability to handle pitchers. Hassey may not be back with Oakland; if he is not, he'll probably find a job with a team looking for a smart veteran.

RON HASSEY

Position: C/DH
Bats: L **Throws:** R
Ht: 6' 2" **Wt:** 195

Opening Day Age: 38
Born: 2/27/53 in Tucson, AZ
ML Seasons: 13

Overall Statistics

	G	AB	R	H	D	T	HR	RBI	SB	BB	SO	AVG
1990	94	254	18	54	7	0	5	22	0	27	29	.213
Career	1140	3321	343	887	164	7	70	424	13	372	362	.267

Where He Hits the Ball

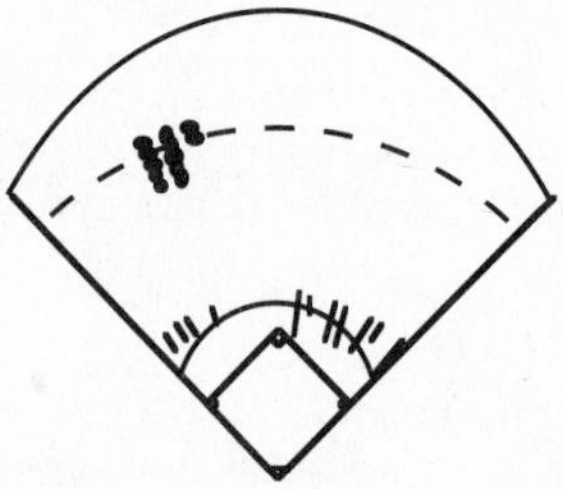

Vs. LHP

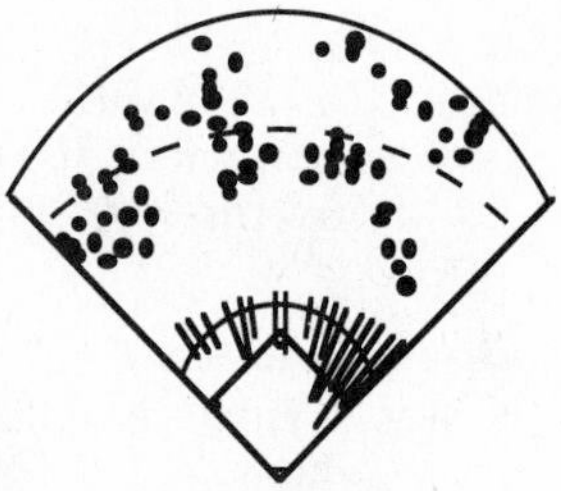

Vs. RHP

1990 Situational Stats

	AB	H	HR	RBI	AVG		AB	H	HR	RBI	AVG
Home	125	27	2	13	.216	LHP	33	3	0	1	.091
Road	129	27	3	9	.209	RHP	221	51	5	21	.231
Day	83	14	1	7	.169	Sc Pos	53	12	0	17	.226
Night	171	40	4	15	.234	Clutch	38	7	0	1	.184

1990 Rankings (American League)

➞ Did not rank near the top or bottom in any category

DAVE HENDERSON

Position: CF
Bats: R **Throws:** R
Ht: 6' 2" **Wt:** 210

Opening Day Age: 32
Born: 7/21/58 in Dos Palos, CA
ML Seasons: 10

HITTING:

Dave Henderson was on his way to approximating his career-season of 1988 when he suffered ligament damage to his right knee last August 21. He was out for most of the remainder of the regular season, but that didn't diminish the overall excellence of his performance.

While with Boston during parts of the 1986 and 1987 season, Henderson became a disciple of then-Red Sox batting coach Walt Hriniak. Henderson put Hriniak's top-hand-off-the-bat, head-down, use-the-whole-field techniques into practice during his .304 season with the A's in 1988. He seemed to deviate from that mind-set in 1989, when his average decreased to .250. But Henderson went much more frequently to right field last year and didn't seem as intent on pulling the ball; most of his 19 home runs whistled out of the park instead of arching out. He also adjusted to breaking balls better because he was able to one-hand such pitches to the opposite field.

Henderson batted cleanup much of the time after the All-Star break, and his power numbers went up after he and Mark McGwire were switched in the batting order. He seemed a lot more selective and went deeper into counts when he wasn't batting in the fifth slot. He doesn't bunt much, but he can if necessary.

BASERUNNING:

Henderson never has been a base stealing threat, but he was one of the A's most combative players in take-out situations. He has never feared contact, and he has become more opportunistic and ready to take the extra base as he has matured. This was his second knee operation, however, and his knees could slow him down in the future.

FIELDING:

Henderson is the linchpin of the A's outfield. He goes into the gaps so well that the other two outfielders can cheat toward the lines, and that saved the A's hurlers a number of hits last year. His arm strength is a little above average, but he is very accurate and doesn't miss many cutoff men. Henderson usually plays fairly shallow, but goes back on balls very well and has no fear of the outfield wall.

OVERALL:

When Henderson was injured last season, teammate Dave Stewart said it was the most costly loss the A's had suffered in three years. Henderson, once considered a showboat and an underachiever, has earned the respect and admiration of his teammates and manager. He may be the best clutch performer on the A's roster. Knees permitting, his best years still could be ahead of him.

Overall Statistics

	G	AB	R	H	D	T	HR	RBI	SB	BB	SO	AVG
1990	127	450	65	122	28	0	20	63	3	40	105	.271
Career	1205	3915	559	1024	219	16	147	537	42	357	835	.262

Where He Hits the Ball

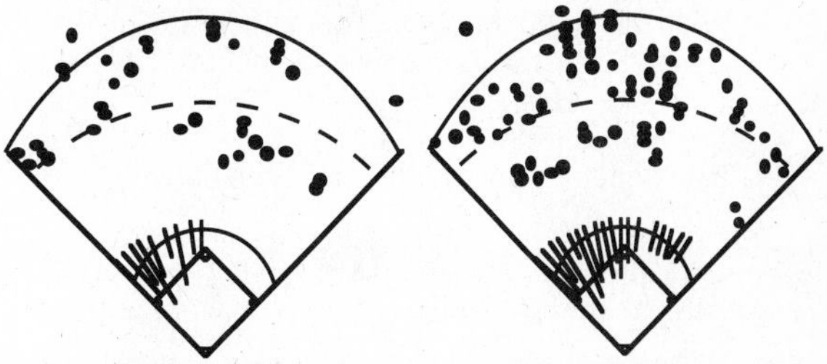

Vs. LHP   Vs. RHP

1990 Situational Stats

	AB	H	HR	RBI	AVG		AB	H	HR	RBI	AVG
Home	222	67	11	36	.302	LHP	133	47	11	23	.353
Road	228	55	9	27	.241	RHP	317	75	9	40	.237
Day	192	49	7	28	.255	Sc Pos	115	29	2	37	.252
Night	258	73	13	35	.283	Clutch	69	18	1	8	.261

1990 Rankings (American League)

- 4th highest batting average vs. left-handed pitchers (.353) and slugging percentage vs. left-handed pitchers (.654)
- 9th in least GDPs per GDP situation (5.7%)
- Led the A's in least GDPs per GDP situation and batting average/slugging percentage vs. left-handed pitchers
- Led AL center fielders in batting average with the bases loaded (.286), batting average/slugging percentage vs. left-handed pitchers and on-base average vs. left-handed pitchers (.400)

RICKEY HENDERSON

Position: LF/DH
Bats: R **Throws:** L
Ht: 5'10" **Wt:** 195

Opening Day Age: 32
Born: 12/25/58 in Chicago, IL
ML Seasons: 12

HITTING:

Rickey Henderson had the best offensive season of his brilliant career in 1990. He led the American League in hitting most of the season before George Brett overtook him in September. He tied his career high with 28 home runs. Most remarkably, he was second to Cecil Fielder in the American League in slugging percentage -- quite a feat for a leadoff man -- and he reached base via a hit or a walk in 125 of the 136 games he played.

As has been the case throughout his career, Henderson walked more often than he struck out. He doesn't go up looking to walk, though. He'll measure a pitcher and wait for his pitch, generally laying off teaser pitches. Although he has a long, pivoting stride from an open stance, Henderson stays back well and can handle the breaking ball. He likes to extend his arms, and generally is pitched inside. He can and does hit to all fields, although he sometimes was a trifle slow on inside fastballs and wound up lofting them to the right side. Henderson likes the ball low and generally hits grounders or line drives every time he pulls the ball, which he does more often than not.

Henderson almost never bunted in the past, but he laid down a couple of bunts for hits in 1990. His idea was to bring the third baseman in a little, opening up the infield.

BASERUNNING:

What are a pitcher and catcher to do? Henderson stole 65 bases last year despite leg trouble. He needs only three steals to break Lou Brock's career record, and has said he believes he can steal 1,500 before he's through. Henderson is just as enterprising on the bases. Twice last season he scored from third base on a sacrifice fly to an infielder. Another time, he scored from second on a ground ball to the shortstop.

FIELDING:

Almost overlooked because of Henderson's offense is his play in left field. Unlike most outfielders, he's at his best when he's moving to either side or retreating. His arm strength is good and his accuracy is outstanding. Rickey's only problem in the outfield is that he tends to be a trifle slow on balls hit in front of him.

OVERALL:

Henderson, 32, is the most complete player in the sport. The only worry the A's have about him has to do with the wear and tear his baserunning puts on his body. It's possible that he and manager Tony La Russa may both decide to reduce his base stealing because he is so valuable with the bat.

Overall Statistics

	G	AB	R	H	D	T	HR	RBI	SB	BB	SO	AVG
1990	136	489	119	159	33	3	28	61	65	97	60	.325
Career	1608	6013	1290	1762	294	50	166	622	936	1093	796	.293

Where He Hits the Ball

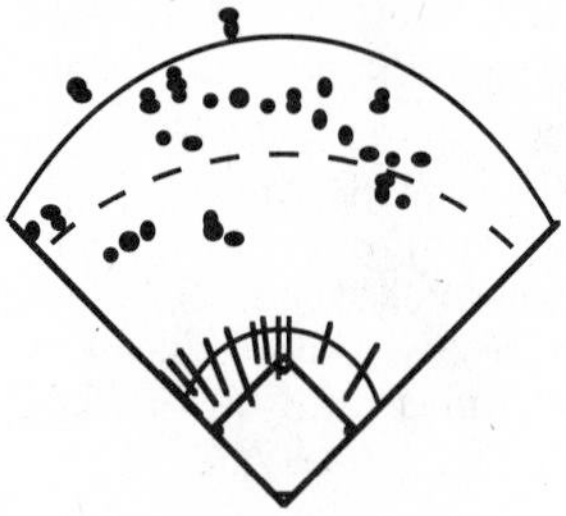

Vs. LHP

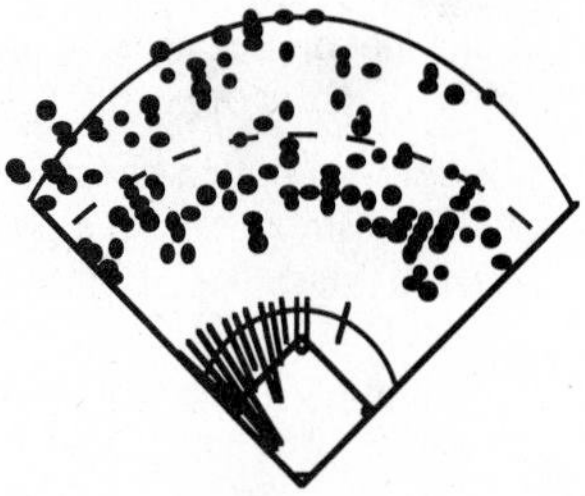

Vs. RHP

1990 Situational Stats

	AB	H	HR	RBI	AVG		AB	H	HR	RBI	AVG
Home	220	67	8	22	.305	LHP	134	42	9	17	.313
Road	269	92	20	39	.342	RHP	355	117	19	44	.330
Day	171	49	9	21	.287	Sc Pos	85	23	6	35	.271
Night	318	110	19	40	.346	Clutch	61	26	5	11	.426

1990 Rankings (American League)

- 1st in runs (119), stolen bases (65), on-base average (.439), runs scored per time reached base (45.8%), batting average in the clutch (.426), on-base average vs. right-handed pitchers (.446), batting average with 2 strikes (.310), percentage of pitches taken (66.3%) and steals of third (17)
- 2nd in batting average (.325), slugging percentage (.577) and stolen base percentage (86.7%)
- Led the A's in batting average, runs, hits (159), doubles (33), triples (3), total bases (282), stolen bases, times on base (260), GDPs (13), slugging percentage, on-base average and stolen base percentage

PITCHING:

As the only experienced lefthander in the Oakland bullpen, Rick Honeycutt is most valuable in specialty situations where he faces the opposition's most potent left-handed bat. But his success in such situations -- lefties batted only .163 against him last year -- tends to obscure his other talents.

A veteran of 14 seasons, Honeycutt possesses all the equipment to make life miserable for a lefty swinger. He goes about his business with the standard A's repertoire -- sinking fastball, slider, forkball. His best pitch against lefthanders, however, is his slider. He drops the angle of his arm when he throws the slider, and that often has left-handed hitters bailing out on him while he's working the outside corner.

Fooling lefties is Honeycutt's forte, but manager Tony La Russa has no qualms about using him against right-handed hitters, as well. Honeycutt uses a back-door breaking ball against righties, and can paint the corners with it. He walks righthanders occasionally by doing this, but he never seems to make the fatal pitch against righties because he has such outstanding location.

Most of Honeycutt's straight overhand pitches have a natural sinking motion to them, and he throws a lot of ground balls. The combination of the slow Coliseum infield and the excellent A's infielders usually takes care of the rest. Honeycutt isn't a strikeout pitcher, but he has evolved to the point where he realizes striking people out isn't needed for success.

HOLDING RUNNERS AND FIELDING:

Honeycutt has become one of the American League's scourges when it comes to giving up the stolen base. He never shows a baserunner the same technique twice; at a given juncture, he'll use a slide step, throw over until he tires the would-be base stealer, or go with the snap throw. He's very good at all three, and has reached the point where very few runners take liberties with him. Honeycutt fields his position acceptably, although he's somewhat slow coming off the mound and can be bunted on successfully. He even pinch hit twice last season, becoming the first A's pitcher to hit in more than three years.

OVERALL:

Honeycutt and Gene Nelson, the A's other prime setup man, both were given multi-year, seven-figure contracts last season. That's an indication of the regard in which they are held by La Russa and the A's organization. Even though he is 36, Honeycutt has a lot of resilience in his arm, and he can function in a variety of roles. He seems capable of remaining effective for the next several years.

RICK HONEYCUTT

Position: RP
Bats: L **Throws:** L
Ht: 6' 1" **Wt:** 190

Opening Day Age: 36
Born: 6/29/54 in Chattanooga, TN
ML Seasons: 14

Overall Statistics

	W	L	ERA	G	GS	Sv	IP	H	R	BB	SO	HR
1990	2	2	2.70	63	0	7	63.1	46	23	22	38	2
Career	97	127	3.73	491	268	27	1921.1	1952	926	580	888	165

How Often He Throws Strikes

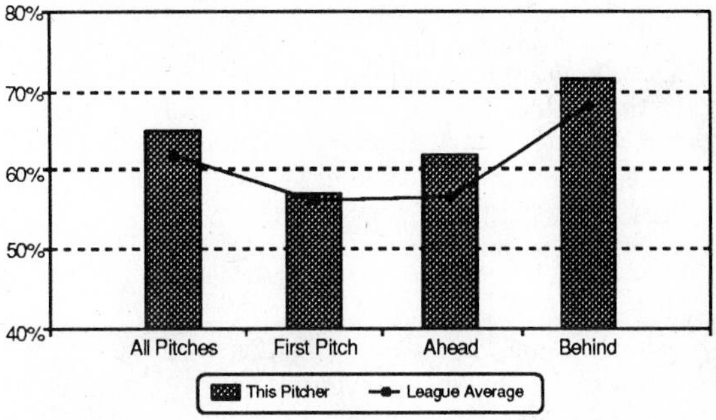

1990 Situational Stats

	W	L	ERA	Sv	IP		AB	H	HR	RBI	AVG
Home	2	0	1.80	6	30.0	LHB	86	14	1	7	.163
Road	0	2	3.51	1	33.1	RHB	139	32	1	18	.230
Day	1	1	1.48	4	30.1	Sc Pos	63	13	1	23	.206
Night	1	1	3.82	3	33.0	Clutch	149	23	1	12	.154

1990 Rankings (American League)

- 2nd in holds (27)
- 7th in first batter efficiency (.169)
- Led the A's in games pitched (63), holds, blown saves (3) and first batter efficiency

HITTING:

The 1990 season was a far cry from 1989 for Carney Lansford. In 1989, he made a run at the batting title, equaling his career high with a .336 average. Lansford has always been a smart hitter, and in '89 he used the whole field more than ever before. Hitting almost exclusively to the gaps and to dead center, he had his best season since winning the batting crown in 1981.

In 1990, however, Lansford got into the habit of trying to pull the ball too often. That wasn't entirely his fault. Lansford's gap-hitting style is ideally suited to the number-two spot in the batting order, but last year injuries to other players forced Tony La Russa to bat him lower in the order. Feeling that more power was expected of him, Lansford tried to pull more often. But the result was less power, not more, and a lower average as well. For the year, Lansford batted .290 when hitting first or second, .213 when batting third or lower.

Despite his subpar numbers, Lansford remained one of the tougher outs in the A's order. He has a quick bat, handles breaking balls and change-ups well and can take the outside pitch to right. At 34, he can still handle the high heat. Lansford is an excellent bunter, although he rarely tries to bunt for a hit.

BASERUNNING:

After stealing 37 bases in 1989, Lansford had nagging hamstring problems last year, stealing only 16 bases in 30 attempts. Nevertheless, he remains an excellent baserunner. Very aggressive, he takes a hard turn in situations where many players are nonchalant, and will knock over anybody in his way if need be.

FIELDING:

Lansford has led AL third basemen in fielding percentage four times in the last five years. He has outstanding reflexes and plays third base as if he were guarding a goalie's crease in hockey. His arm is only average, but he has a quick release. He sometimes gets in trouble when he sidearms the ball to first; these throws will sometimes tail away from their intended target.

OVERALL:

A total professional, Lansford remained one of the essential A's in 1990 despite having the second-lowest batting average of his career. He's a stabilizing influence in the clubhouse. His defense, his ability to provide a quality at-bat and his aggressive baserunning provide value beyond the numbers. Lansford has always been able to make adjustments throughout his career, and the thinking is that he still has several good years ahead of him.

CARNEY LANSFORD

Position: 3B
Bats: R **Throws:** R
Ht: 6' 2" **Wt:** 195

Opening Day Age: 34
Born: 2/7/57 in San Jose, CA
ML Seasons: 13

Overall Statistics

	G	AB	R	H	D	T	HR	RBI	SB	BB	SO	AVG
1990	134	507	58	136	15	1	3	50	16	45	50	.268
Career	1722	6646	942	1943	302	39	144	798	217	510	678	.292

Where He Hits the Ball

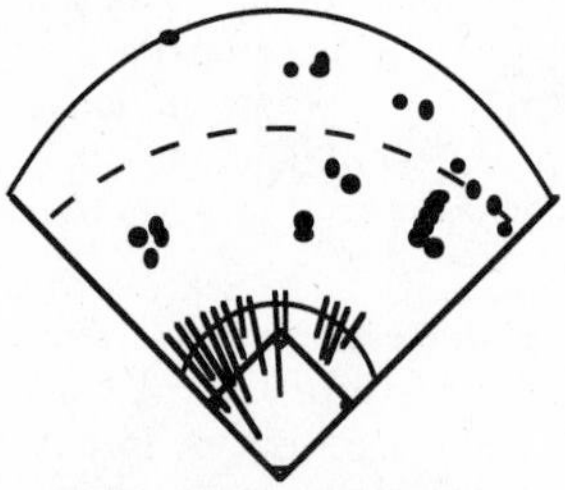

Vs. LHP

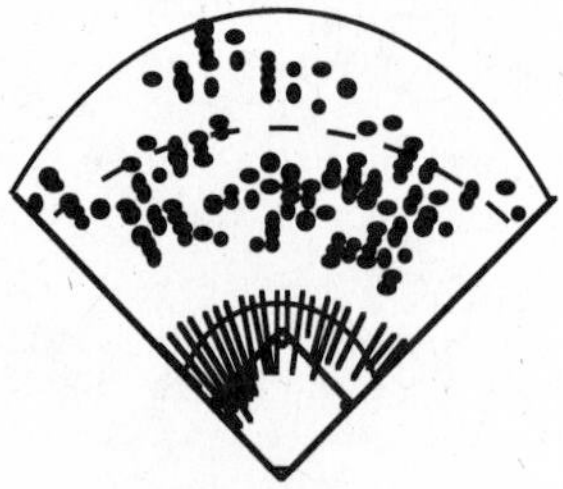

Vs. RHP

1990 Situational Stats

	AB	H	HR	RBI	AVG		AB	H	HR	RBI	AVG
Home	215	64	1	19	.298	LHP	119	41	1	11	.345
Road	292	72	2	31	.247	RHP	388	95	2	39	.245
Day	183	51	0	16	.279	Sc Pos	139	37	0	47	.266
Night	324	85	3	34	.262	Clutch	66	10	0	9	.152

1990 Rankings (American League)

- 2nd lowest batting average in the clutch (.152)
- 3rd lowest slugging percentage (.319)
- 4th lowest on-base average vs. right-handed pitchers (.298)
- Led the A's in singles (117), caught stealing (14), on-base average vs. left-handed pitchers (.439), lowest percentage of swings that missed (10.1%) and highest percentage of swings put into play (54.3%)
- Led AL third basemen in caught stealing, groundball/flyball ratio (1.65), batting average vs. left-handed pitchers, fielding percentage (.970) and steals of third (3)

HITTING:

In one of the more unique "rent-with-an-option-to-buy" arrangements in baseball history, Willie McGee spent the last month of 1990 with the Athletics while his .335 average for the Cardinals was winning the National League batting title by proxy. McGee's offensive work while filling in for Dave Henderson in center field did not indicate to the A's that he was an improvement over Henderson. McGee batted only .274 in 29 games for the A's, though he did give the A's a left-handed bat at the number-two spot, providing a screen on catchers for Rickey Henderson.

McGee has a Rod Carew-like stance with almost no stride, and he usually flicks at the ball, more often than not trying to take it the other way. With Oakland most pitchers jammed him, and he didn't show much ability to muscle balls into right. He didn't seem inclined to wait for pitches he could handle, and he was easily tempted by offerings high in the strike zone, even though his power is very limited.

As a hitter, McGee doesn't use his speed as well as he might. He doesn't bunt particularly well (or very often, either), and he doesn't get out of the box as quickly as one might expect.

BASERUNNING:

The A's got far less than they expected from a man who came to them with 274 career steals. McGee stole only three for Oakland. That may have been because he needed to learn American League pitchers, but his overall baserunning disappointed the A's as well. McGee was aggressive enough, but he made some strange mental mistakes. Once he failed to slide at home on a close play and was tagged out. He was also doubled off base in consecutive games.

FIELDING:

McGee was adequate for the A's in center field, but certainly not as good as Henderson. He had 17 errors during the season (16 of them with the Cardinals) and got a very slow start on several balls hit over his head. He charges the ball well and gets rid of it quickly, but his arm is only average and he occasionally missed cutoff men.

OVERALL:

The A's stated that they intended to negotiate with free agent McGee after the season. But they have a healthy Dave Henderson, who is one of manager Tony La Russa's favorite players, and a payroll larger than the gross national products of several countries. It seemed unlikely that they'd be willing to pay McGee the going rate for a batting champion, but stranger things have happened.

WILLIE McGEE

Position: CF
Bats: B **Throws:** R
Ht: 6' 1" **Wt:** 176

Opening Day Age: 32
Born: 11/2/58 in San Francisco, CA
ML Seasons: 9

Overall Statistics

	G	AB	R	H	D	T	HR	RBI	SB	BB	SO	AVG
1990	154	614	99	199	35	7	3	77	31	48	104	.324
Career	1193	4698	650	1393	207	78	52	560	277	252	716	.297

Where He Hits the Ball

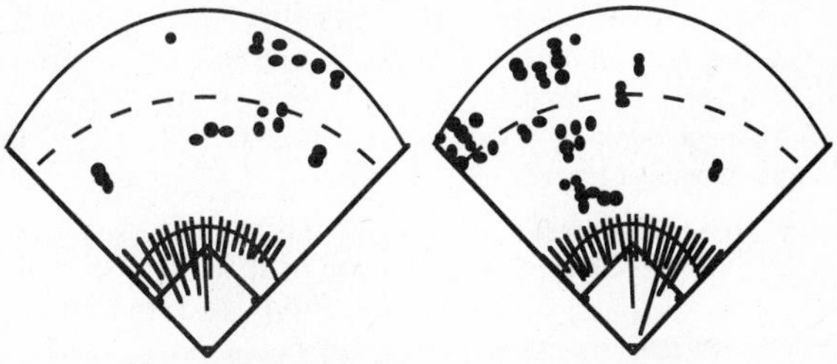

Vs. LHP   Vs. RHP

1990 Situational Stats

	AB	H	HR	RBI	AVG		AB	H	HR	RBI	AVG
Home	328	110	1	47	.335	LHP	225	73	2	27	.324
Road	286	89	2	30	.311	RHP	389	126	1	50	.324
Day	166	62	1	20	.373	Sc Pos	188	58	0	69	.309
Night	448	137	2	57	.306	Clutch	93	35	1	17	.376

1990 Rankings (American League)

- 1st (in the National League) in batting average (.335), groundball/flyball ratio (3.29) and errors in center field (16)

MARK McGWIRE

Position: 1B
Bats: R **Throws:** R
Ht: 6' 5" **Wt:** 225

Opening Day Age: 27
Born: 10/1/63 in Pomona, CA
ML Seasons: 5

Overall Statistics

	G	AB	R	H	D	T	HR	RBI	SB	BB	SO	AVG
1990	156	523	87	123	16	0	39	108	2	110	116	.235
Career	623	2173	355	550	84	5	156	429	4	344	476	.253

Where He Hits the Ball

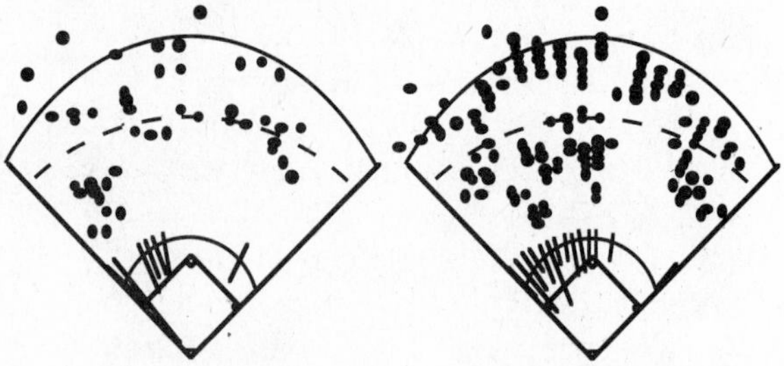

Vs. LHP   Vs. RHP

1990 Situational Stats

	AB	H	HR	RBI	AVG		AB	H	HR	RBI	AVG
Home	245	55	14	37	.224	LHP	132	34	11	38	.258
Road	278	68	25	71	.245	RHP	391	89	28	70	.228
Day	210	48	15	39	.229	Sc Pos	129	32	6	60	.248
Night	313	75	24	69	.240	Clutch	62	21	5	16	.339

1990 Rankings (American League)

- 1st in walks (110) and lowest groundball/flyball ratio (.54)
- 2nd in home runs (39)
- 3rd in RBIs (108), HR frequency (13.4 ABs per HR) and lowest batting average vs. right-handed pitchers (.228)
- 4th in hit by pitch (7)
- Led the A's in home runs, at-bats (523), RBIs, sacrifice flies (9), walks, intentional walks (9), hit by pitch, GDPs (13), plate appearances (650) and games (156)
- Led AL first basemen in sacrifice flies, walks, hit by pitch and batting average in the clutch (.339)

HITTING:

No other player in major league history has hit 30 home runs in each of his first four major league seasons, as Mark McGwire has done. Still, Tony La Russa demands a lot from his most talented players, and like Jose Canseco, McGwire was publicly criticized by his manager last year, especially about McGwire's low batting average, which had dropped into the .220s. McGwire said nothing, but clearly was disturbed by the criticism. He had some justification for being upset. McGwire ultimately led the team with 39 homers and 108 RBI, and his on-base percentage of .370 was third-best on the team. That was primarily because he led the major leagues with 110 walks -- an indication that he isn't the Dave Kingman clone many have accused him of being.

McGwire's problem is that, in going for home runs, he has developed an extreme uppercut swing. That serves him well on the road, where his home run rate surpasses even that of Babe Ruth. But in the spacious Oakland Coliseum, many of McGwire's drives simply become long fly outs. As a result, he's far less dangerous at home.

With his long swing, McGwire commits so early that he has been susceptible to change-ups. With his good strike zone judgement, he is learning to take those pitches for balls now. Most pitchers try to work him tight with fastballs, and lefties throw him lots of back-door sliders.

BASERUNNING:

McGwire is not as slow as he looks, but he's not fast by any means. He did steal the third and fourth bases of his career last season, and La Russa will occasionally start him on a hit-and-run. McGwire is pretty much a station-to-station guy on the bases, although he knows his own limitations and doesn't take many unwise chances.

FIELDING:

Once a mediocre glove man, McGwire has turned himself into an outstanding fielder at first base. He is particularly effective at handling low throws, but also has surprising range and does a fine job tracking foul balls in the Coliseum. He handles bunts well, and has a fine arm.

OVERALL:

McGwire's inability to approximate his rookie season batting average (.289) has frustrated La Russa. But it is hard to argue with 156 home runs and 429 RBI in only four full major league seasons. The A's may have to shrug off McGwire's batting average and look at his other numbers, along with his defense. It's a package that few players can match.

PITCHING:

The most startling aspect of Mike Moore's comedown 1990 season was his amazing drop in strikeouts. Always a power pitcher in the past, Moore had fanned 182 batters in 1988, his last season with Seattle, and 172 more in 1989, his first year with Oakland. But in 1990 Moore struck out only 73 men, a drop of nearly 100.

What happened? Nobody, including Moore and A's manager Tony La Russa, is exactly sure. But the number-one theory had to do with Moore's lack of aggressiveness on his first and second pitches. La Russa wanted Moore to go after hitters instead of trying to paint the corners, but Moore seemed more inclined to nibble. Falling behind frequently in the count, he either walked men or had to come in with pitches up the middle. Those pitches usually got clobbered.

Part of the problem was that Moore was having trouble with his forkball, the pitch that helped make him a 19-game winner in 1989. The forkball is Moore's best pitch against lefthanders because it breaks away from them. But he left it high in the strike zone on many occasions last season, and he appeared at times to lose confidence in it.

Nevertheless, Moore's pitching wasn't nearly as bad as some of his numbers might indicate, and he pitched well in many important games. He throws a sinking, high velocity fastball, and is proficient at running the ball in and out. His curveball and change also are well above average, although he had a tendency last year to open up his body too quickly when throwing the breaking ball. His arm would drag and his pitches would just miss the strike zone.

HOLDING RUNNERS AND FIELDING:

Moore's pickoff move and attention to baserunners have improved. He also has quickened his release. Nevertheless, opposing base stealers were 17 of 23 with Moore on the mound. He is a good fielder who uses his size and quickness to very good advantage.

OVERALL:

Manager Tony La Russa clearly was concerned by Moore's setback season, but he didn't show any lack of confidence in the man who was a 1989 All-Star. Moore stayed in the rotation all season, and while he couldn't sustain any winning streaks, neither did he string together more than two or three bad outings in a row. If he can regain his early-count aggression and fine-tune his mechanics so that he isn't high in the strike zone so often, it's possible that he could return to 1989 form next season.

MIKE MOORE

Position: SP
Bats: R **Throws:** R
Ht: 6' 4" **Wt:** 205

Opening Day Age: 31
Born: 11/26/59 in Eakly, OK
ML Seasons: 9

Overall Statistics

	W	L	ERA	G	GS	Sv	IP	H	R	BB	SO	HR
1990	13	15	4.65	33	33	0	199.1	204	113	84	73	14
Career	98	122	4.18	295	285	2	1898.0	1895	978	702	1182	174

How Often He Throws Strikes

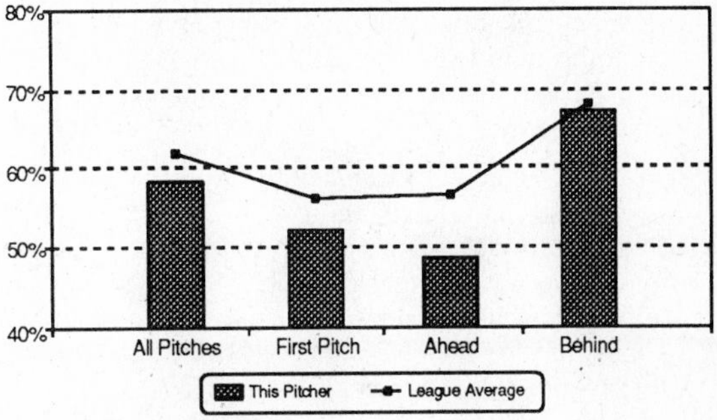

1990 Situational Stats

	W	L	ERA	Sv	IP		AB	H	HR	RBI	AVG
Home	7	10	4.66	0	119.2	LHB	404	105	5	53	.260
Road	6	5	4.63	0	79.2	RHB	360	99	9	43	.275
Day	6	6	4.82	0	89.2	Sc Pos	201	57	3	79	.284
Night	7	9	4.51	0	109.2	Clutch	47	11	1	3	.234

1990 Rankings (American League)

- 1st in lowest strikeout/walk ratio (.87)
- 2nd worst ERA (4.65) and least strikeouts per 9 innings (3.30)
- 5th highest on-base average allowed (.339) and most GDPs induced per 9 innings (1.04)
- Led the A's in losses (15), walks allowed (84), wild pitches (13), stolen bases allowed (17), groundball/flyball ratio (1.58) and most GDPs induced per 9 innings

PITCHING:

The A's bullpen was an octopus once again last season, and Gene Nelson remained one of its more important tentacles. Nelson's 1.57 ERA was a career low by a considerable margin; he'd never been below 3.00 previously in his career. He also recorded five saves, the second-highest total of his career. Opponents batted only .208 against him, and he walked only 17 in 74.2 innings. It was easily Nelson's best major league season, even though his workload decreased because the A's starters were so consistently good. Like left-handed set-up counterpart Rick Honeycutt, Nelson was rewarded with a long-term contract calling for a seven-figure salary.

As in his previous three seasons with the A's, Nelson depended mainly on his ability to keep the ball low and induce ground balls. He's a fastball/slider pitcher with good velocity that is enhanced by downward movement. He doesn't try to get cute with hitters and sometimes will leave the ball out over the middle of the plate, but that doesn't hurt him much in the spacious Coliseum.

The only change in Nelson's portfolio last season was his increased use of a change-up. Since hitters weren't looking for much offspeed stuff from him, the pitch worked well. No longer could batters simply sit on Nelson's fastball. He doesn't use the forkball as much as most of the other A's pitchers, but he'll occasionally mix one in to augment his other pitches.

HOLDING RUNNERS AND FIELDING:

Nelson improved in both of these respects in 1990. While he still isn't particularly mobile, he paid more attention to his defensive work last year, and it paid off. Nelson isn't as attentive to baserunners as he might be, but he used a slide step to help keep runners honest. His delivery is slightly slower than average, but not to the extent that it is a serious problem for him.

OVERALL:

The A's recognized Nelson's value by tendering him a contract far more lucrative than a set-up man might expect. Oakland has used Nelson in almost every role, including starter and closer and, at age 30, there's every reason to think he'll continue to be effective. Nelson has thrived under Tony La Russa, both in Oakland and in Chicago, and he has shown durability that bodes well for his future.

GENE NELSON

Position: RP
Bats: R **Throws:** R
Ht: 6' 0" **Wt:** 172

Opening Day Age: 30
Born: 12/3/60 in Tampa, FL
ML Seasons: 10

Overall Statistics

	W	L	ERA	G	GS	Sv	IP	H	R	BB	SO	HR
1990	3	3	1.57	51	0	5	74.2	55	14	17	38	5
Career	49	53	3.93	369	66	23	918.2	873	434	349	574	97

How Often He Throws Strikes

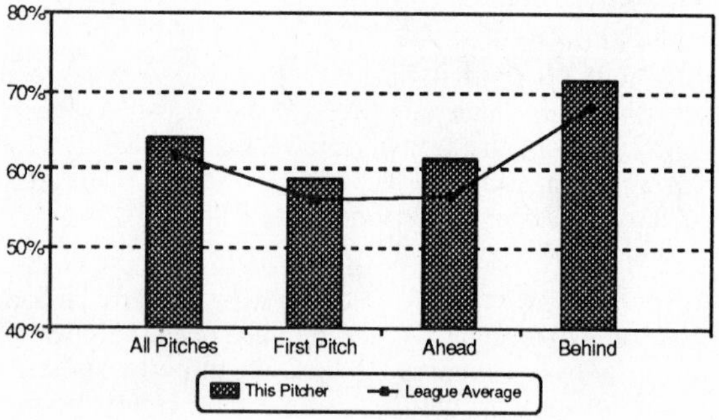

1990 Situational Stats

	W	L	ERA	Sv	IP		AB	H	HR	RBI	AVG
Home	1	2	1.91	3	28.1	LHB	110	26	2	8	.236
Road	2	1	1.36	2	46.1	RHB	155	29	3	11	.187
Day	0	1	1.74	2	20.2	Sc Pos	47	6	0	12	.128
Night	3	2	1.50	3	54.0	Clutch	114	28	2	11	.246

1990 Rankings (American League)

- 4th in holds (18) and most GDPs induced per GDP situation (20.4%)
- Led the A's in blown saves (3) and most GDPs induced per GDP situation

WILLIE RANDOLPH

Position: 2B
Bats: R **Throws:** R
Ht: 5'11" **Wt:** 163
Opening Day Age: 36
Born: 7/6/54 in Holly Hill, SC
ML Seasons: 16

Overall Statistics

	G	AB	R	H	D	T	HR	RBI	SB	BB	SO	AVG
1990	119	388	52	101	13	3	2	30	7	45	34	.260
Career	1988	7301	1150	1997	291	61	52	618	266	1128	603	.274

Where He Hits the Ball

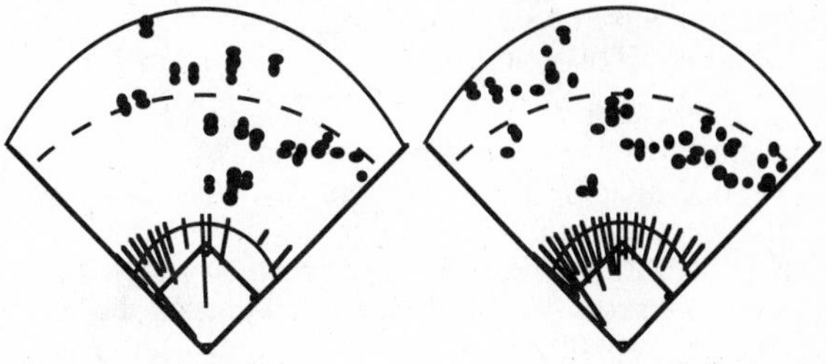

1990 Situational Stats

	AB	H	HR	RBI	AVG		AB	H	HR	RBI	AVG
Home	164	41	1	11	.250	LHP	116	41	0	12	.353
Road	224	60	1	19	.268	RHP	272	60	2	18	.221
Day	150	38	2	14	.253	Sc Pos	103	26	0	26	.252
Night	238	63	0	16	.265	Clutch	50	15	1	4	.300

1990 Rankings (American League)

- Led the A's in triples (3)

HITTING:

The A's obtained Willie Randolph last May with the idea that he could take over a second base position which had long been staffed by committee. As it turned out, Randolph struggled, and Mike Gallego wound up with just as much playing time, even though Gallego batted only .206. Randolph got his starting position back only when shortstop Walt Weiss was injured during the American League Championship Series, forcing Gallego to play shortstop. Randolph did finish well, batting .303 after September 1.

Randolph has a short, compact stroke that enables him to handle breaking balls and offspeed stuff as well as anybody on the club. However, his bat speed has decreased to the point where he has trouble getting around on a good fastball. The A's frequently used Randolph in the number-two spot in the batting order, but with Rickey Henderson so often on first, Randolph saw a lot of hard stuff. He batted only .206 when batting in the second slot, but hit better when moved farther down in the order.

Randolph still makes good contact, though, and had more walks than strikeouts for the 16th time in his 16-season career. Nobody knows the strike zone better than Randolph, even at age 36. It's best to pitch him down and in; he can be jammed. Randolph is an accomplished bunter, and it was somewhat surprising that he didn't try to bunt for hits more than he did in 1990 -- especially when he was struggling.

BASERUNNING:

Although he has slowed down, Randolph is still one of the smartest baserunners around. He doesn't steal much any more, but was successful six times in seven tries with the A's last year. Randolph isn't as aggressive as many of his teammates on the bases, but he doesn't shy from contact and almost never makes a mental mistake on the bases.

FIELDING:

At 36, Randolph no longer makes the plays he used to handle easily. But his range is still average, and he has a strong, accurate arm. He retains his extraordinary ability to turn the double play, which has long been his greatest strength. Randolph plays hitters well and reacts quickly when the ball leaves the bat.

OVERALL:

With Gallego emerging as a starter, it's possible that the A's could find Randolph expendable in 1991. Randolph has unquestionably slowed, but his instincts, his intelligence and his quiet dignity in the clubhouse make him a valued player in any case. Regardless of statistics, teams do not part with a Willie Randolph without losing something.

PITCHING:

The National League batters who saw Scott Sanderson throughout the 1980s probably wouldn't have recognized the pitcher American League batters faced in 1990. Signed by the A's as a free agent after six nondescript seasons with the Cubs, Sanderson had the best season of his 12-year career. A fly ball pitcher, Sanderson obviously benefitted by moving from tiny Wrigley Field to the spacious Oakland Coliseum. But the main reason for his success was his ability, at age 33, to transform himself into a complete pitcher.

In the past, Sanderson was a primarily a fastball pitcher who could be depended upon to throw the heater at crucial junctures. He began to diversify his approach during his final year with the Cubs, and A's pitching coach Dave Duncan accelerated the process. The result was that Sanderson went into 1990 with two offspeed pitches: a forkball that dropped, and a rainbow curve which was thrown so slowly that most hitters could only twitch.

The high fastball remained Sanderson's best pitch, and he got lots of long fly outs at the Coliseum. But he soon discovered that his forkball was extremely effective against hitters who were looking for the high hard one. The curve, though, was his most-improved pitch -- especially after he convinced himself that he could throw it for a strike almost any time he wanted. Sanderson's only problem with the curve was that he occasionally became too enamored with it, and threw it so often that the element of surprise was lost. When hitters did guess correctly on the slow curve, they hit it as if it were a batting-practice pitch.

HOLDING RUNNERS AND FIELDING:

Recovered from back problems at last, Sanderson is agile for his size and handles himself well around the mound. He moves quickly to cover first and to field bunts. His pickoff move is only average, but he has made his delivery more economical, so that runners can't get as much of a jump on him. He also throws to first often.

OVERALL:

Sanderson emerged as a complete pitcher last year and, like the man he replaced, Storm Davis, became arguably the best number-four starter in baseball. Given his new approach to his work, and given the success Duncan has had with previously average veterans, Sanderson looks to have a secure future with Oakland. He seems to have transformed himself from a spot-starter type into a solid member of the A's rotation.

SCOTT SANDERSON

Position: SP
Bats: R **Throws:** R
Ht: 6' 5" **Wt:** 198

Opening Day Age: 34
Born: 7/22/56 in Dearborn, MI
ML Seasons: 13

Overall Statistics

	W	L	ERA	G	GS	Sv	IP	H	R	BB	SO	HR
1990	17	11	3.88	34	34	0	206.1	205	99	66	128	27
Career	115	100	3.59	343	286	5	1826.1	1772	800	478	1209	189

How Often He Throws Strikes

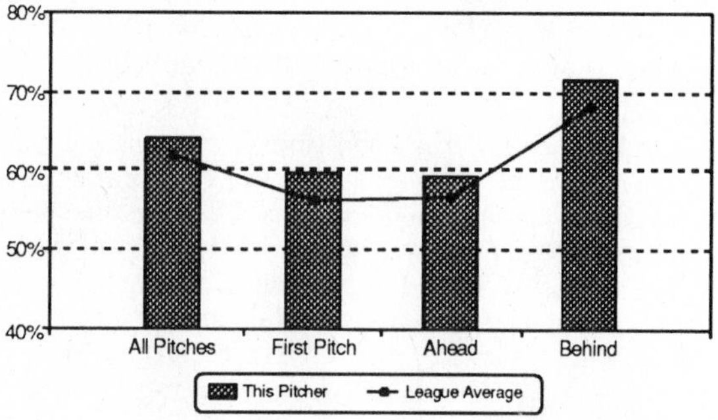

1990 Situational Stats

	W	L	ERA	Sv	IP		AB	H	HR	RBI	AVG
Home	6	7	3.17	0	96.2	LHB	402	94	13	46	.234
Road	11	4	4.51	0	109.2	RHB	401	111	14	45	.277
Day	4	5	3.50	0	69.1	Sc Pos	169	42	3	55	.249
Night	13	6	4.07	0	137.0	Clutch	20	3	0	0	.150

1990 Rankings (American League)

- 2nd in home runs allowed (27) and least GDPs induced per 9 innings (.26)
- 3rd most home runs allowed per 9 innings (1.18)
- 4th lowest groundball/flyball ratio (.87)
- 5th in games started (34), highest slugging percentage allowed (.422) and least GDPs induced per GDP situation (4.6%)
- Led the A's in home runs allowed

HITTING:

Though he's a two time All-Star catcher and a fine offensive performer, Terry Steinbach is a very streaky hitter. Last year was typical. Hitting only .186 on June 2, Steinbach rallied to bring his final average up to .251. The season mirrored 1988, when he came back from a slow start to hit .265. But it was the opposite of 1989, when he batted .313 in the first half, .229 in the second. Steinbach's average last year was a career low, but his 57 RBIs were a personal best.

Like teammate Mark McGwire, Steinbach is a back-foot lift hitter who hits a lot of fly balls when pitched high in the strike zone. He doesn't have McGwire's power or patience at the plate, but has a more compact swing and will shorten up when the situation calls for it. Steinbach, in fact, had a remarkable .579 average with the bases loaded last year, and his .297 average with runners in scoring position was the best among Oakland's regulars.

Steinbach has power to right-center field and tends to hit the ball up the middle; teams usually bunch him to the gaps. Most pitchers went inside with the fastball and outside with the breaking ball against him last year. Steinbach started to come on when he discerned that pattern and began laying off the pitches that were designed to set him up. Steinbach is a reliable bunter in sacrifice situations.

BASERUNNING:

Steinbach was caught in his only base stealing attempt last season; he's no threat to run even in a hit-and-run situation. His speed, though, isn't bad for a catcher, and he took the extra base occasionally when outfielders didn't pay attention to him. He's aggressive in collision and take-out situations.

FIELDING:

Steinbach slumped defensively last year. He threw out only 32 percent of base stealers after turning in a 41 percent success rate in 1989. Steinbach throws very well and has a quick release, but is only an average receiver and occasionally falls back into his old habit of reaching for pitches in the dirt instead of shifting his feet.

OVERALL:

With Cleveland's Sandy Alomar around, it's not likely that Steinbach will get his All-Star designation back, especially if he continues to be plagued by long slumps. Catching is one position where the A's aren't extremely talented, and it's possible the A's will shop for an addition there -- especially a lefty swinger. Still, Steinbach is more than adequate, and whatever shopping the A's do hardly falls into the urgent category.

TERRY STEINBACH

Position: C/DH
Bats: R **Throws:** R
Ht: 6' 1" **Wt:** 195

Opening Day Age: 29
Born: 3/2/62 in New Ulm, MN
ML Seasons: 5

Overall Statistics

	G	AB	R	H	D	T	HR	RBI	SB	BB	SO	AVG
1990	114	379	32	95	15	2	9	57	0	19	66	.251
Career	476	1590	180	428	63	7	43	210	5	115	245	.269

Where He Hits the Ball

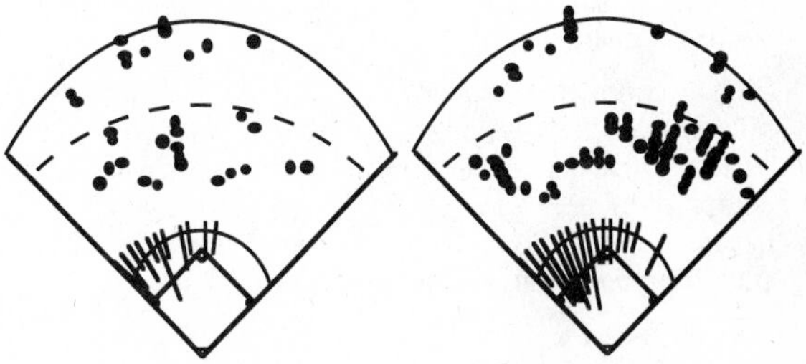

Vs. LHP   Vs. RHP

1990 Situational Stats

	AB	H	HR	RBI	AVG		AB	H	HR	RBI	AVG
Home	185	46	3	28	.249	LHP	109	31	3	16	.284
Road	194	49	6	29	.253	RHP	270	64	6	41	.237
Day	173	40	3	22	.231	Sc Pos	101	30	2	46	.297
Night	206	55	6	35	.267	Clutch	66	16	0	9	.242

1990 Rankings (American League)

- 2nd in batting average with the bases loaded (.579)
- Led the A's in batting average with runners in scoring position (.297) and batting average with the bases loaded
- Led AL catchers in batting average with the bases loaded

DAVE STEWART

Position: SP
Bats: R **Throws:** R
Ht: 6' 2" **Wt:** 200

Opening Day Age: 34
Born: 2/19/57 in Oakland, CA
ML Seasons: 11

PITCHING:

Only with a teammate like Dave Stewart around could Bob Welch win 27 games and not be his club's number-one starter when the postseason began. Last year Stewart, in winning a career-high 22 games, became the first pitcher since Jim Palmer in 1975-78 -- and only the twelfth since 1942 -- to win 20 or more games in four straight seasons. Even so, Stewart probably had his most difficult campaign since becoming Oakland's ace.

During midseason last year, Stewart went 5-6 and suffered some of the most thorough beatings of his Oakland career. His main problem was that he couldn't count on the riding fastball with which he moves right-handed hitters off the plate. The pitch was straying toward the middle of the plate, and the hitters were feasting on it. Righthanders, in fact, wound up hitting .253 against Stewart, while lefty swingers managed only a .207 average.

Stewart corrected the problem, which was mainly related to his release point, and won eight of his last 11 starts. He led the league in innings pitched and complete games, and kept intact his record of never having missed his scheduled turn since being installed in the starting rotation in 1986.

Stewart has two fastballs -- one the rider, the other a tailing pitch -- and a hard slider that he generally throws mostly to left-handed hitters. The pitch that made him a big winner was the forkball, which he learned from A's pitching coach Dave Duncan after arriving in Oakland; that's his standard offspeed pitch. Stewart is confrontational on his first pitch to almost every hitter, and because he's almost always near the plate, he gets ahead on most counts. He paces himself well and is at his best in the late innings; opponents had a .206 average against him after the seventh inning.

HOLDING RUNNERS AND FIELDING:

Stewart is a complete pitcher in every sense of the phrase. Still an excellent athlete at age 34, he fields his position at a Gold Glove-caliber level and almost never is caught off balance or out of position by a ball hit in his vicinity. He holds runners well, although his release from the stretch is a trifle slow, and he has a quick, though not deceptive, move to first.

OVERALL:

Despite a subpar World Series, Stewart's fourth straight 20-win season seemed to bring him closer, at long last, to recognition as the best pitcher in baseball. His career could well mirror that of Brooklyn Dodger Dazzy Vance, who won 197 games and was voted into the Hall of Fame even though he didn't win his first major league game until age 31.

Overall Statistics

	W	L	ERA	G	GS	Sv	IP	H	R	BB	SO	HR
1990	22	11	2.56	36	36	0	267.0	226	84	83	166	16
Career	123	85	3.52	393	218	19	1827.2	1681	788	677	1202	155

How Often He Throws Strikes

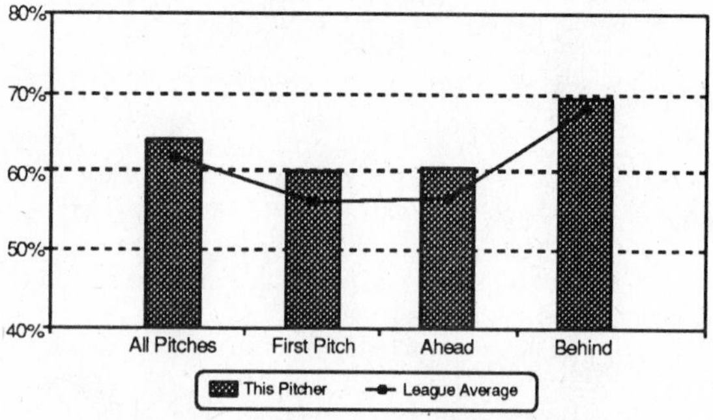

1990 Situational Stats

	W	L	ERA	Sv	IP		AB	H	HR	RBI	AVG
Home	11	4	1.74	0	145.0	LHB	478	99	8	39	.207
Road	11	7	3.54	0	122.0	RHB	502	127	8	43	.253
Day	10	3	2.18	0	115.1	Sc Pos	209	43	4	65	.206
Night	12	8	2.85	0	151.2	Clutch	99	23	2	6	.232

1990 Rankings (American League)

- 1st in games started (36), complete games (11), shutouts (4), innings (267.0), batters faced (1,088) and pitches thrown (3,977)
- 2nd in wins (2)
- 3rd in ERA (2.56) and ERA at home (1.74)
- 4th in hits allowed (226) and lowest slugging percentage allowed (.326)
- Led the A's in ERA, games started, complete games, shutouts, innings, hits allowed, batters faced, hit batsmen (5), strikeouts (166), pitches thrown, strikeout/walk ratio (2.0), lowest batting average allowed (.231), lowest slugging percentage allowed and lowest on-base average allowed (.291)

HITTING:

Walt Weiss was formerly considered a far better hitter from the left side than from the right, but it was difficult to tell in 1990. Last year Weiss had virtually identical numbers from either side of the plate, and the result was the best offensive season of his career.

Weiss attributes his newfound right-handed hitting prowess to the fact the A's saw more lefties than they did in 1989, thereby giving him more right-handed at-bats. Observers point instead to the fact he now seems to have the same mind-set right-handed as he does left-handed.

Weiss is a low-ball hitter whose best feature is the extension of his bat through the entire swing. That helps him get distance without impairing his ability to make contact, and it enables him to handle pitches in almost all areas. He isn't the most dangerous of the A's, but he's one of the toughest to pitch because he knows the strike zone. Weiss has the balance and timing to take offspeed pitches to the opposite field. He's one of the A's best bunters, and drag bunts for a hit frequently if he's in a slump.

BASERUNNING:

Weiss has above-average speed and extraordinary intelligence and instincts on the base paths. He doesn't steal much, but he's capable of 15-20 steals per year because he reads pitchers well and has very quick acceleration. Weiss goes in hard on take-outs, but is relatively conservative in terms of taking the extra base.

FIELDING:

Weiss holds his own with any shortstop in the American League. He isn't as flamboyant or acrobatic as Fernandez or Guillen, but he has a knack for reading the ball off the bat, his footwork is impeccable and he knows his own pitchers and the opposing hitters. Weiss' throwing arm isn't exceptional, but it's well above average, and his footwork is such that he can get more on an off-balance throw than most shortstops. He also covers a lot of ground on foul pop-ups, which is essential at the Coliseum.

OVERALL:

Their reputation for pitching and power notwithstanding, the A's defense is just as vital to their success, and Weiss is the linchpin of that defense. Weiss missed the World Series last year, and while the A's probably couldn't have beaten Cincinnati even if he had been in the lineup, they weren't nearly as good a team without him.

WALT WEISS

Position: SS
Bats: B **Throws:** R
Ht: 6' 0" **Wt:** 175

Opening Day Age: 27
Born: 11/28/63 in Tuxedo, NY
ML Seasons: 4

Overall Statistics

	G	AB	R	H	D	T	HR	RBI	SB	BB	SO	AVG
1990	138	445	50	118	17	1	2	35	9	46	53	.265
Career	385	1159	127	298	49	4	8	96	20	104	150	.257

Where He Hits the Ball

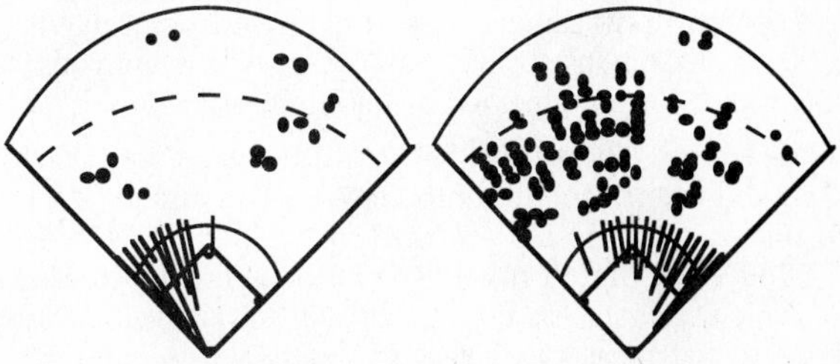

Vs. LHP Vs. RHP

1990 Situational Stats

	AB	H	HR	RBI	AVG		AB	H	HR	RBI	AVG
Home	235	58	1	16	.247	LHP	115	30	0	12	.261
Road	210	60	1	19	.286	RHP	330	88	2	23	.267
Day	192	54	2	17	.281	Sc Pos	98	22	0	32	.224
Night	253	64	0	18	.253	Clutch	74	30	0	10	.405

1990 Rankings (American League)

- 2nd highest batting average in the clutch (.405)
- 3rd lowest HR frequency (222.5 ABs per HR)
- 4th lowest slugging percentage (.321)
- 5th in lowest slugging percentage vs. right-handed pitchers (.327)
- Led the A's in groundball/flyball ratio (1.80) and percentage of extra bases taken as a runner (51.8%)
- Led AL shortstops in groundball/flyball ratio and batting average in the clutch

BOB WELCH

Position: SP
Bats: R **Throws:** R
Ht: 6' 3" **Wt:** 195

Opening Day Age: 34
Born: 11/3/56 in Detroit, MI
ML Seasons: 13

PITCHING:

Before 1990, Bob Welch had won 15 or more games five times, but he never had won more than 17. Welch's stuff last year wasn't radically different than it had been in the past -- in fact his ERA decreased only slightly, from 3.00 to 2.95. But Welch finally learned to conquer his biggest enemy, his tendency to rush and lose his concentration. Helped by this improvement -- and in no small measure by outstanding run support from his teammates -- Welch had a breakthrough season, and a Cy Young Award, at last. His 27 wins were the most in the majors since Steve Carlton won the same number in 1972.

One of the slowdown techniques Welch employed last season was to reach for the rosin bag, either on his own or on a signal from pitching coach Dave Duncan. It worked. Broken of his worst habits -- overthrowing and trying to make every pitch perfect -- Welch's superior stuff came to the fore. He also received improved defense behind him because his teammates were no longer unnerved by his edginess.

Welch still throws in the 90 MPH range, and his fastball tends to ride into right-handed hitters. He pitches to the inside part of the plate frequently and won't let plate-crowding hitters get a toehold. Welch's curve and cut fastball have become better now that he is making more extensive use of the forkball, which breaks away from left-handed hitters. His few poor outings largely were the result of his not using his forkball to set up his other pitches.

HOLDING RUNNERS AND FIELDING:

Along with everything else, Welch has improved the non-pitching aspects of his game. He is less prone to overreacting when a ball is hit to him, and he is athletic enough to range far from the mound to field bunts. His move to first is average, and so is his ability to hold runners; he throws over to check runners more often than in the past. He gets rid of the ball quickly and thus isn't easy to get a jump against.

OVERALL:

It was no secret throughout Welch's career that he had the talent to become a 20-game winner. His big 1990 season demonstrated the extent to which his mound personality kept him from making the jump to Cy Young Award level. Now that Welch has conquered that problem, it wouldn't be surprising if he wins 20 a few more times. Even though he is 34, he has had no major arm trouble since 1985, and he keeps himself in excellent shape. It will help, of course, if his teammates keep scoring runs for him as they did in 1990.

Overall Statistics

	W	L	ERA	G	GS	Sv	IP	H	R	BB	SO	HR
1990	27	6	2.95	35	35	0	238.0	214	90	77	127	26
Career	176	109	3.16	396	371	8	2512.1	2273	981	801	1714	194

How Often He Throws Strikes

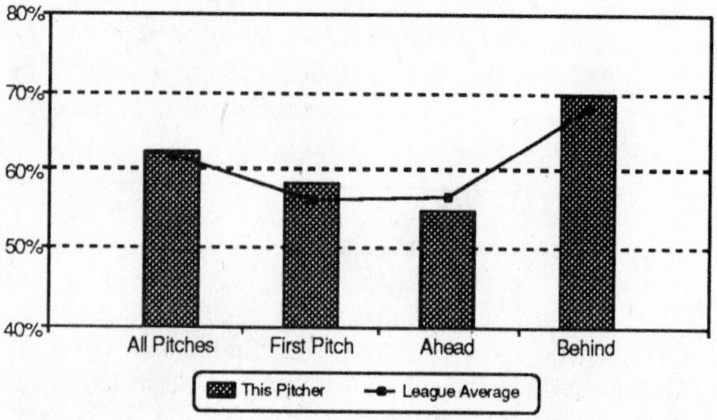

1990 Situational Stats

	W	L	ERA	Sv	IP		AB	H	HR	RBI	AVG
Home	14	2	1.92	0	117.0	LHB	465	120	12	39	.258
Road	13	4	3.94	0	121.0	RHB	421	94	14	42	.223
Day	10	2	2.28	0	83.0	Sc Pos	180	44	7	57	.244
Night	17	4	3.31	0	155.0	Clutch	76	12	1	4	.158

1990 Rankings (American League)

- 1st in wins (27), winning percentage (.818) and run support per 9 innings (5.9)
- 3rd in games started (35), innings (238.0), batters faced (979) and GDPs induced (25)
- 4th in home runs allowed (26)
- Led the A's in wins, hit batsmen (5), pickoff throws (96), GDPs induced, winning percentage, lowest stolen base percentage allowed (58.8%), least pitches thrown per batter (3.54), run support per 9 innings and lowest batting average vs. right-handed batters (.223)

CURT YOUNG

Position: SP/RP
Bats: R **Throws:** L
Ht: 6' 1" **Wt:** 175

Opening Day Age: 30
Born: 4/16/60 in Saginaw, MI
ML Seasons: 8

Overall Statistics

	W	L	ERA	G	GS	Sv	IP	H	R	BB	SO	HR
1990	9	6	4.85	26	21	0	124.1	124	70	53	56	17
Career	60	48	4.28	184	151	0	956.1	965	501	309	485	132

How Often He Throws Strikes

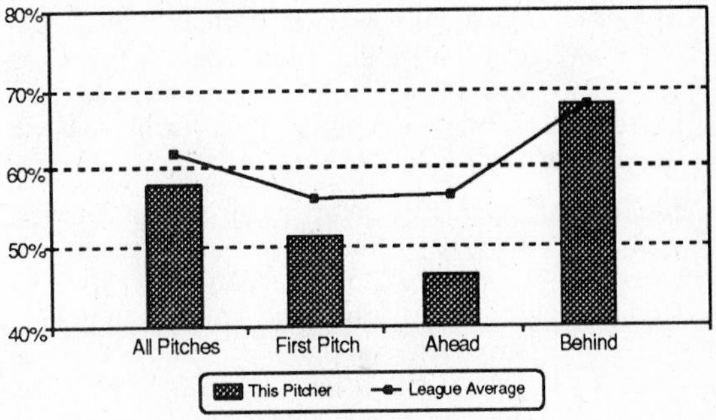

1990 Situational Stats

	W	L	ERA	Sv	IP		AB	H	HR	RBI	AVG
Home	5	2	3.18	0	70.2	LHB	96	25	1	12	.260
Road	4	4	7.04	0	53.2	RHB	370	99	16	45	.268
Day	5	2	4.77	0	77.1	Sc Pos	96	28	6	43	.292
Night	4	4	4.98	0	47.0	Clutch	18	2	0	0	.111

1990 Rankings (American League)

→ Led the A's in runners caught stealing (11)

PITCHING:

For two consecutive seasons, Curt Young has functioned in perhaps the most difficult role on the A's pitching staff -- that of fifth starter in what is normally a four-man rotation. Young's turn is usually skipped if the A's have an off-day in a given week, so maintaining sharpness is always a problem. Under those difficult circumstances, Young had a solid year in 1990, improving his record from 5-9 to 9-6. His earned run average went up, but that largely was the result of a few early exits that were more the exception than the rule.

Nearly 31, Young has evolved from a power pitcher into a location and change-of-speeds specialist. He works off the extreme right edge of the rubber and drops down to a three-quarter motion, thereby giving hitters an unfamiliar sight angle. He's not the sort of pitcher who will challenge right-handed hitters, mostly because he doesn't have that kind of velocity. Instead, he probes and teases. His control wavers occasionally when he isn't getting the border-line pitches, and he is hit hard when he has to come in with a fastball while behind in the count. More often, though, he has batters swinging at offspeed pitches or offerings outside of the strike zone.

Young sinks most of his pitches, especially his fastball and slider. His curve and forkball are improving, making it more necessary for hitters to respect his hard stuff. He showed more confidence last season in his offspeed pitches when he fell behind in the count. But he still must show more consistency in getting those secondary pitches over.

HOLDING RUNNERS AND FIELDING:

An improving fielder, Young has also developed a better-than-average move to first. Young's pickoff move doesn't look like much, but it becomes more deceptive because his laconic-looking motion is difficult to read. His big problem is that he uncoils slowly; if a baserunner can get a read on Young, he can usually get a steal as well.

OVERALL:

Young turned out to be the perfect number-five starting pitcher for the A's. He has shown that he can maintain his sharpness even with limited work, and being left-handed is a virtue because the A's other four starters are all righties. Young can pitch long relief if needed, he never complains about his status and always is looking to contribute. It would be a surprise if the A's were to alter a formula that has been successful, so look for Young to remain the number-five starter in 1991.

LANCE BLANKENSHIP

Position: 3B/2B/RF
Bats: R **Throws:** R
Ht: 6' 0" **Wt:** 185

Opening Day Age: 27
Born: 12/6/63 in Portland, OR
ML Seasons: 3

Overall Statistics

	G	AB	R	H	D	T	HR	RBI	SB	BB	SO	AVG
1990	86	136	18	26	3	0	0	10	3	20	23	.191
Career	154	264	41	55	8	1	1	14	8	28	55	.208

HITTING, FIELDING, BASERUNNING:

Lance Blankenship, 27, is an excitable type who tends to be overanxious at the plate. Pitchers figured that out early and go after him with offspeed breaking balls. Thus far Blankenship has chased them so frantically that it sometimes looks as if he's trying to bevel himself into the ground.

Blankenship has shown some line drive pop at times, especially on outside fastballs when he can extend his arms. But he won't be a major league hitter until he learns to stay back on the breaking ball. He knows the strike zone fairly well, and probably could draw even more walks if he could learn to judge the curve. Blankenship has the speed to steal a lot of bases, and the inclination to take chances. Again, his eagerness sometimes hurts him on the bases; he can be too aggressive.

Originally projected as the A's second baseman of the future, Blankenship has instead become a utility man, playing third base and the outfield as well as second. He doesn't have a great arm, but he handles all his defensive assignments steadily.

OVERALL:

Blankenship has the ability to be a solid major league player, but he needs playing time to overcome his urge to try to do too much with each at-bat. The A's are so loaded with talent at every position that Blankenship probably does not have a long-term future with them. Look for them to move him to a team that can offer him a chance to win a regular job.

REGGIE HARRIS

Position: RP
Bats: R **Throws:** R
Ht: 6' 1" **Wt:** 180

Opening Day Age: 22
Born: 8/12/68 in Waynesboro, VA
ML Seasons: 1

Overall Statistics

	W	L	ERA	G	GS	Sv	IP	H	R	BB	SO	HR
1990	1	0	3.48	16	1	0	41.1	25	16	21	31	5
Career	1	0	3.48	16	1	0	41.1	25	16	21	31	5

PITCHING, FIELDING & HOLDING RUNNERS:

The 1990 season was one of waiting, watching and learning for Reggie Harris. The A's can afford to let Harris, only 22, learn his trade gradually. Oakland drafted him out of the Boston organization with the idea that he could be a starting pitcher for them by mid-decade. That's an important consideration for a team whose youngest regular starter in 1990 was Curt Young at age 31.

Harris is a power pitcher with a lively fastball and a confrontational nature on the mound. He gave up only 25 hits in the 41 innings he worked, but did allow 21 walks. He has an adequate curve and a slider, but needs to develop an offspeed pitch; it can be expected that Dave Duncan will work with Harris on the forkball, the signature offspeed pitch of the Oakland staff.

Harris fields his position like a young Dave Stewart, although his decision-making isn't as sound as Stewart's. He needs work on his move to first, and doesn't give his catcher much help in terms of keeping tabs on baserunners.

OVERALL:

It appears that the A's picked up a valuable young pitcher when the Red Sox left Harris off their 40-man roster last winter. Harris didn't really pitch enough in 1990 to create a lasting impression, but the work he did turn in generally was of high quality. Once he learns the subtleties of pitching, he could turn out to be an excellent pitcher.

DOUG JENNINGS

Position: LF/RF
Bats: L **Throws:** L
Ht: 5'10" **Wt:** 165

Opening Day Age: 26
Born: 9/30/64 in Atlanta, GA
ML Seasons: 3

Overall Statistics

	G	AB	R	H	D	T	HR	RBI	SB	BB	SO	AVG
1990	64	156	19	30	7	2	2	14	0	17	48	.192
Career	139	261	28	51	13	2	3	29	0	38	78	.195

HITTING, FIELDING, BASERUNNING:

Doug Jennings is an impressive-looking 26-year-old prospect who so far hasn't produced at the major league level. Jennings has a graceful, controlled swing and is deft and agile in the field. His arm is such that he can impress a crowd with its strength.

Jennings batted .340 in 60 games with Class AAA Tacoma last year, the fourth time in five minor league seasons that he's hit at least .315. But after 261 major league at-bats, his average is below .200. With the A's, Jennings has looked quick enough to get around on the inside fastball -- most pitchers jam him -- but not strong enough to muscle the ball through the infield. He does extend well and seems able to hit the offspeed pitch. Jennings also needs better strike zone knowledge, having struck out at an appalling rate (48 times in 156 at-bats) in 1990. Pitchers use the inside fastball to set him up for the outside breaking ball, at which he lunges.

Jennings can play all three outfield positions and has very good range. His arm is strong, but not always accurate. He has good speed, but is a poor base stealer and a below-average baserunner.

OVERALL:

His outstanding minor league record would indicate that Jennings has major league talent. The A's don't have many left-handed hitters, so he will likely be kept around as a spare part. But he'll have to hit better off the bench if he wants to stick around with Oakland.

JOE KLINK

Position: RP
Bats: L **Throws:** L
Ht: 5'11" **Wt:** 175

Opening Day Age: 29
Born: 2/3/62 in Johnstown, PA
ML Seasons: 2

Overall Statistics

	W	L	ERA	G	GS	Sv	IP	H	R	BB	SO	HR
1990	0	0	2.04	40	0	1	39.2	34	9	18	19	1
Career	0	1	3.73	52	0	1	62.2	71	27	29	36	5

PITCHING, FIELDING & HOLDING RUNNERS:

Joe Klink was one of baseball's more intriguing against-all-odds stories last season. A non-roster player who'd saved 26 games in Class AA in 1989, Klink was a 28-year-old long shot who'd been roughed up in his previous major league trial with the '87 Twins. But he made the club in spring training and pitched very well, turning in a 2.04 earned run average.

Klink was valuable to the A's as a lefty-lefty specialist, freeing Rick Honeycutt for more wide-ranging duties. He's a curveballer who gets in trouble when he doesn't get downward action on his breaking ball. If he isn't throwing directly over the top, he's outside the strike zone and begins issuing walks, the only rap of consequence against him. From over the top, however, his breaking ball has a sweeping effect that makes it difficult for left-handed hitters to stand in against him.

Klink is persistent when it comes to holding runners, and that helps him compensate for a below-average move to first. He isn't particularly athletic and doesn't help himself defensively.

OVERALL:

Klink gave the A's exactly what they needed in 1990. His roster status for 1991 depends largely on whether the A's decide they can get a better lefty-lefty guy by spending more money. The low-salaried Klink gave the A's a lot for their money last year, so his chances look pretty good.

DARREN LEWIS

Position: CF
Bats: R **Throws:** R
Ht: 6' 0" **Wt:** 175

Opening Day Age: 23
Born: 8/28/67 in Berkeley, CA
ML Seasons: 1

Overall Statistics

	G	AB	R	H	D	T	HR	RBI	SB	BB	SO	AVG
1990	25	35	4	8	0	0	0	1	2	7	4	.229
Career	25	35	4	8	0	0	0	1	2	7	4	.229

HITTING, FIELDING, BASERUNNING:

The Athletics traded away two top outfield prospects --Stan Javier and Felix Jose -- during the 1990 season. One reason they felt comfortable doing so was the rapid development of Darren Lewis. Lewis, 23, made the major leagues in only his second full professional season. His playing time was curtailed after Willie McGee was acquired late in August, and he finished at .229 in 35 games. Nevertheless, the A's considered carrying him on their postseason roster.

Lewis has a graceful, controlled-yet-vigorous batting stroke. He seems to know the strike zone well, striking out only four times with the A's while drawing seven walks. He has hit for average since signing out of the University of California, but he hasn't shown much home run power. He does have some pop to the gaps, and seems to like extending his arms and taking the ball to the opposite field.

Lewis runs extremely well, with 37 steals in 50 minor league tries last year. He can play all three outfield positions, but seems most comfortable in right. He has a strong arm, although he had some problems with accuracy during his brief time with the A's.

OVERALL:

Lewis is perhaps the best young outfielder in the solid Oakland system. He seems to have all the ingredients for success except long-ball power, and is said to have excellent learning capacity. It's too bad that the A's are so well-stocked in the outfield, because Lewis has the talent to become a regular very soon.

JAMIE QUIRK

Position: C
Bats: L **Throws:** R
Ht: 6' 4" **Wt:** 200

Opening Day Age: 36
Born: 10/22/54 in Whittier, CA
ML Seasons: 16

Overall Statistics

	G	AB	R	H	D	T	HR	RBI	SB	BB	SO	AVG
1990	56	121	12	34	5	1	3	26	0	14	34	.281
Career	830	1886	164	452	89	6	40	219	5	145	379	.240

HITTING, FIELDING, BASERUNNING:

After a 1989 season during which he was released by three different organizations, Jamie Quirk somewhat surprisingly found a home with the A's in 1990. At age 36, his .281 average in 56 games as the A's third catcher and utility man was the second-highest of his 15-season career. Quirk also achieved a longtime dream by starting the fourth game of the World Series behind the plate. He had been on the Royals' World Series roster in both 1980 and 1985, but hadn't played.

The A's signed Quirk partly because he is a left-handed hitter on a team with a multitude of righties. Often a big-name right-handed hitter would be pitched around to face Quirk, and he responded by hitting .448 (13 for 29) with runners in scoring position. He also was 4-for-11 with three walks as a pinch hitter. Quirk likes the ball down and away from him, and he goes to left field fairly well.

Quirk did surprisingly well behind the plate, throwing out 10 of 20 would-be base stealers while handling pitchers well. He also played third, first and the outfield, but he's strictly a fill-in at those positions. He runs like a catcher.

OVERALL:

Quirk was a godsend to the A's in August when they were wracked by injuries. It would be easy to visualize him in 1991 as a third catcher. In fact, he played so well in 1990 that it's possible the A's may decide they like Quirk better than Ron Hassey because Quirk is more versatile.

SCOTT BRADLEY

Position: C
Bats: L **Throws:** R
Ht: 5'11" **Wt:** 185

Opening Day Age: 31
Born: 3/22/60 in Montclair, NJ
ML Seasons: 7

HITTING:

A consistently good hitter in the past, Scott Bradley suffered through a long 1990 season. Bradley batted only .223, a figure almost 50 points below his career average when the season began. Lack of use may have been a significant factor in the poor season. Bradley's 233 at-bats last year were his lowest total since 1986. After logging 342 ABs in 1987, Bradley has been given progressively less playing time.

Bradley has long been a great contact hitter, and one of the toughest players in baseball to strike out. But he has fanned 43 times in 503 at-bats, once every 12 at-bats, over the past two seasons after striking out only once every 20 at-bats in 1987-88. Last year Bradley showed much less bat control than in the past. Instead of spraying line drives to every part of the park, he tried to pull the ball more. The strategy didn't work, as he logged only one home run and ten extra-base hits, his lowest totals since 1985.

A fierce and intelligent competitor, Bradley always hangs tough on breaking balls. But last year his bat was slower and pitchers found that he had trouble handling fastballs in on the hands. For all his troubles, he remained a tough man in the clutch, hitting .300 with runners in scoring position.

BASERUNNING:

Bradley is a genuine student of the game who is considered superb material for coaching or managing; he studies the opposition more than most players do. Bradley knows on whom he can get an extra base or go from first to third. He does not steal bases.

FIELDING:

Bradley is below-average at both throwing and blocking balls in the dirt. When his mechanics are perfect, he has enough arm to catch most runners; unfortunately, his mechanics usually aren't perfect. Some Seattle pitchers, most notably lefthander Randy Johnson, prefer to throw to Bradley instead of front-liner Dave Valle. It's simply a matter of confidence since both call the same type of game.

OVERALL:

Over his four years with Seattle, Bradley's playing time has been gradually diminishing. At one time he was used as a versatile role player, playing third base and the outfield as well as catching, but lately, he's been primarily the second-string catcher. The Mariners intend to use Bradley more as a multi-position player in 1991, and sent him to the Arizona instructional league to polish his third base skills. By playing more, Bradley may return to his past form offensively.

Overall Statistics

	G	AB	R	H	D	T	HR	RBI	SB	BB	SO	AVG
1990	101	233	11	52	9	0	1	28	0	15	20	.223
Career	514	1470	138	387	68	6	18	172	3	83	90	.263

Where He Hits the Ball

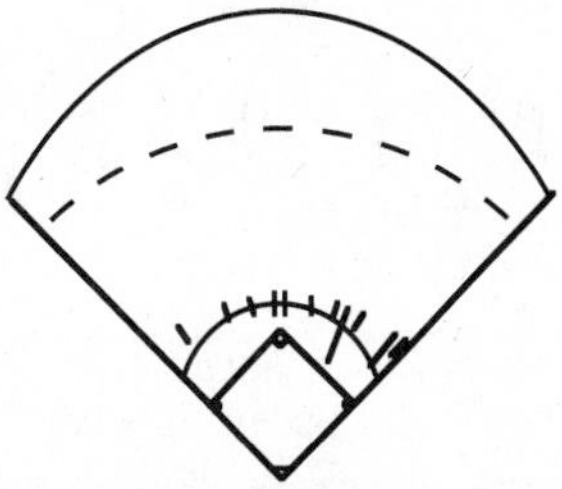

Vs. LHP

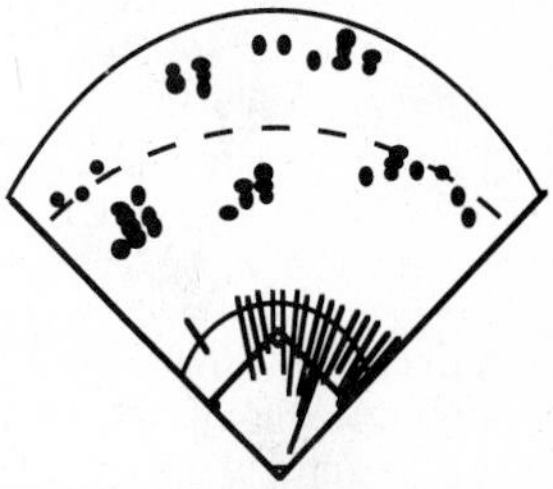

Vs. RHP

1990 Situational Stats

	AB	H	HR	RBI	AVG		AB	H	HR	RBI	AVG
Home	112	28	1	19	.250	LHP	25	4	0	4	.160
Road	121	24	0	9	.198	RHP	208	48	1	24	.231
Day	67	18	1	13	.269	Sc Pos	60	18	1	28	.300
Night	166	34	0	15	.205	Clutch	58	15	1	9	.259

1990 Rankings (American League)

- Did not rank near the top or bottom in any category

HITTING:

When Greg Briley first became a Mariner regular in 1989, club officials thought they had come up with another in a series of solid young players. Briley was not only talented, he was versatile: A converted infielder who did a fine job in both left and right after being shifted to the outfield. And he could hit.

However, after giving the Mariners a .351 average with five homers and 16 RBI in July of '89, Briley lost control of the hard but compact swing that had been compared to that of Hall of Famer Joe Morgan. Briley did not regain the swing in 1990. After belting 13 homers with 52 RBI as a rookie, Briley only managed five HR with 29 RBI in '90. His average dropped 20 points, from .266 to .246. He began to remind people of the other Joe Morgan, the Red Sox manager who was a lifetime .193 major league hitter.

Briley will chase a breaking ball out of the strike zone, but is a good low-ball hitter. Unlike many left-handed batters, he can also handle the pitch up and in but can be had up and away. Briley must work on going to the opposite field with those pitches.

BASERUNNING:

While most Mariner opponents pay more attention to Harold Reynolds and Henry Cotto, Briley quietly does a superb job on the base paths. If the club allowed more free-lancing, Briley would have swiped more, but his 16 steals in 20 tries is testimony to his ability. He combines good speed with a good jump, although he tends to be lazy in reading pitchers.

FIELDING:

A shortstop in college and a second baseman in his three minor league seasons with the Mariners, Briley was converted to the outfield at the major league level and has improved steadily in his two seasons in Seattle. His biggest area of improvement is his jump on fly balls; he already had the speed to cover a lot of ground. Briley must continue to work on going to the wall, and unfortunately, he has a second baseman's arm. Opponents take liberal use of the base paths on him.

OVERALL:

Insiders thought that Briley started last year with a chip on his shoulder after demanding -- and not getting -- a contract similar to that of his fellow rookie, Ken Griffey, Jr. However, they still regard Briley as a sleeper. The club figures that his level-headed approach will help him regain the sweet swing he showed after arriving in the majors, just as his good attitude has helped him learn the outfield. Should Briley work hard at second base, he would be even more valuable.

GREG BRILEY

Position: RF/LF
Bats: L **Throws:** R
Ht: 5' 8" **Wt:** 165
Opening Day Age: 25
Born: 5/24/65 in Greenville, NC
ML Seasons: 3

Overall Statistics

	G	AB	R	H	D	T	HR	RBI	SB	BB	SO	AVG
1990	126	337	40	83	18	2	5	29	16	37	48	.246
Career	254	767	98	197	42	6	19	85	27	81	136	.257

Where He Hits the Ball

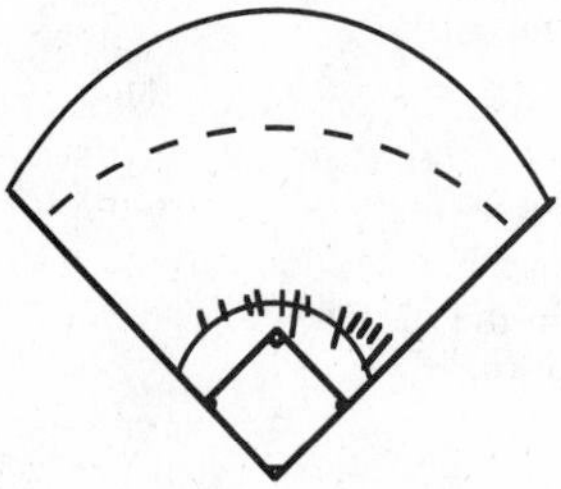

Vs. LHP

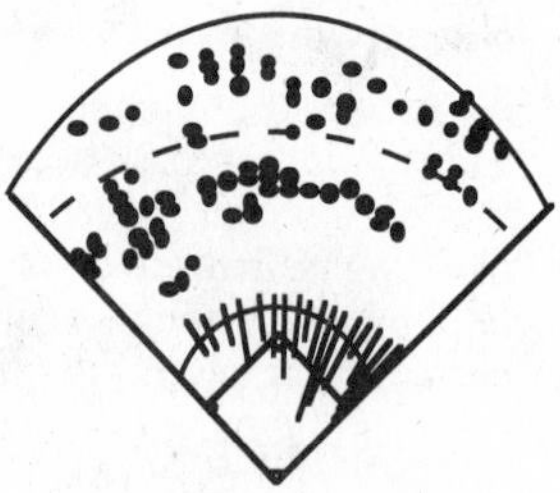

Vs. RHP

1990 Situational Stats

	AB	H	HR	RBI	AVG		AB	H	HR	RBI	AVG
Home	166	41	4	17	.247	LHP	33	7	0	3	.212
Road	171	42	1	12	.246	RHP	304	76	5	26	.250
Day	97	13	0	5	.134	Sc Pos	73	20	2	23	.274
Night	240	70	5	24	.292	Clutch	48	15	1	6	.313

1990 Rankings (American League)

- 1st lowest batting average on a 3-1 count (.000)
- 10th in stolen base percentage (80.0%)
- Led the Mariners in batting average in the clutch (.313)

JAY BUHNER

Position: RF
Bats: R **Throws:** R
Ht: 6' 3" **Wt:** 205

Opening Day Age: 26
Born: 8/13/64 in Louisville, KY
ML Seasons: 4

HITTING:

Jay Buhner says his injuries run in streaks. In high school Buhner was involved in three traffic accidents in one month; in the final mishap, he was tossed up in the air from the back of a pickup truck and landed on his feet. Unfortunately, Buhner hasn't landed on his feet yet in Seattle; the Mariners must be wondering what to expect next.

Buhner has given Seattle reason to expect big things if he could only end his current string of mishaps. But thus far he has never played even 100 games in a major league season. Last year, Buhner could only get into 51 games after suffering a torn-up ankle in spring training, then a broken right arm in June when hit by a pitch from Texas' Brad Arnsberg. Before the broken arm, Buhner had been a terror, belting five homers (including a grand slam in his first game) with 16 RBI in only 15 games. That was exactly the kind of production Seattle sorely needed for most of the season.

When Buhner came back late last year and again took his spot in right field, his numbers were not as spectacular, but they were plenty good enough. Buhner hit only two more homers, but batted .340 with men in scoring position for the year and wound up with a solid 33 RBI in his 51 games.

Buhner, the only right-handed batter ever to hit a ball into the center field seats in Yankee Stadium, is a typical power swinger. He is susceptible to fastballs in followed by breaking balls away. His strikeout ratio is nearly once every three at-bats. However, Buhner is not a dead-pull hitter and will take the fastball away to right.

BASERUNNING:

With his ankle problem, Buhner now has below-average speed. But his all-out approach makes him a threat to take an extra base whenever he can. He is a heady and intense player who could learn to steal occasionally.

FIELDING:

Buhner is an aggressive fielder who missed a month with a broken bone after crashing into a wall in Kansas City (and making the catch) in 1989. He gets a strong jump on the ball and has a solid arm. He makes the charge-and-throw play as well as anyone, often preventing runners from taking an extra base.

OVERALL:

The Mariners project Buhner as their right fielder in 1991, and the aggressive outfielder could well be a team leader. Should he stay healthy, he's a definite threat for a 100 RBI season. But given Buhner's injury-prone history, that's a very iffy proposition.

Overall Statistics

	G	AB	R	H	D	T	HR	RBI	SB	BB	SO	AVG
1990	51	163	16	45	12	0	7	33	2	17	50	.276
Career	201	650	79	162	42	2	29	105	4	65	204	.249

Where He Hits the Ball

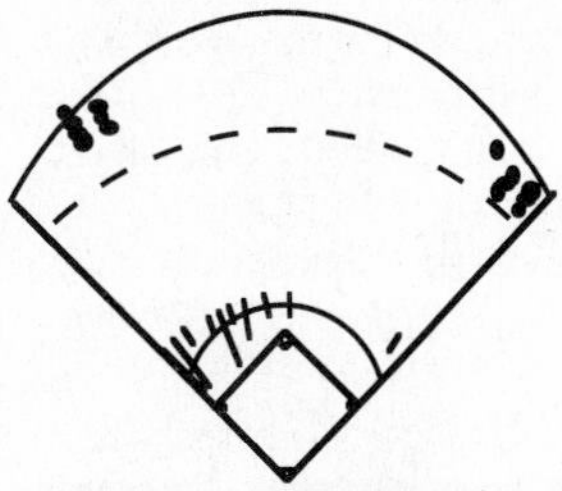

Vs. LHP

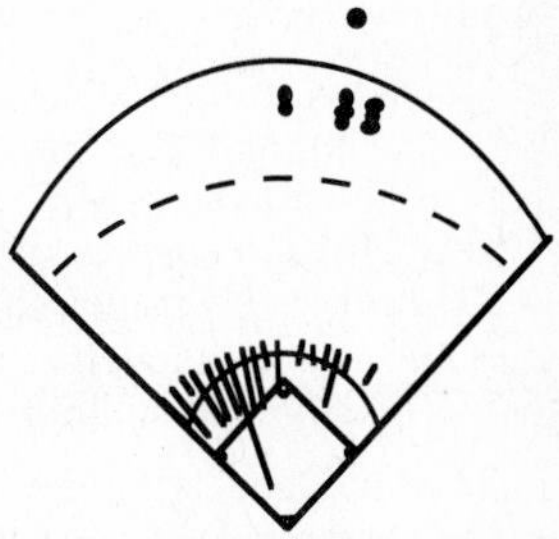

Vs. RHP

1990 Situational Stats

	AB	H	HR	RBI	AVG		AB	H	HR	RBI	AVG
Home	68	17	2	8	.250	LHP	56	20	4	15	.357
Road	95	28	5	25	.295	RHP	107	25	3	18	.234
Day	43	9	2	7	.209	Sc Pos	50	17	3	27	.340
Night	120	36	5	26	.300	Clutch	27	7	1	5	.259

1990 Rankings (American League)

- Did not rank near the top or bottom in any category

KEITH COMSTOCK

Position: RP
Bats: L **Throws:** L
Ht: 6' 0" **Wt:** 174

Opening Day Age: 35
Born: 12/23/55 in San Francisco, CA
ML Seasons: 5

Overall Statistics

	W	L	ERA	G	GS	Sv	IP	H	R	BB	SO	HR
1990	7	4	2.89	60	0	2	56.0	40	22	26	50	4
Career	10	7	3.95	143	0	3	152.2	132	72	74	142	14

How Often He Throws Strikes

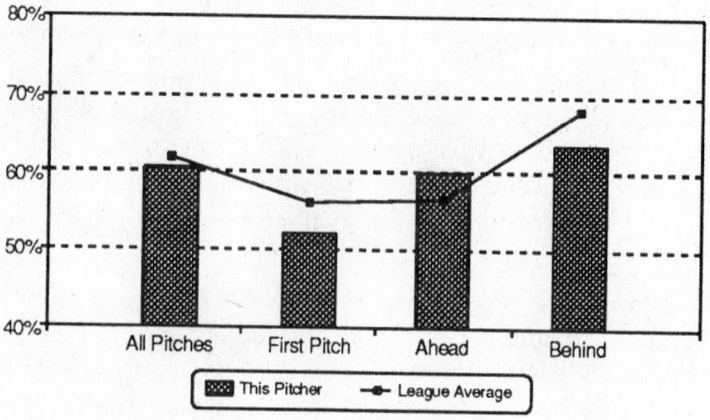

1990 Situational Stats

	W	L	ERA	Sv	IP		AB	H	HR	RBI	AVG
Home	4	2	2.40	2	30.0	LHB	72	18	0	11	.250
Road	3	2	3.46	0	26.0	RHB	122	22	4	20	.180
Day	2	0	4.15	0	8.2	Sc Pos	72	17	4	30	.236
Night	5	4	2.66	2	47.1	Clutch	93	22	1	14	.237

1990 Rankings (American League)

- 9th in lowest percentage of inherited runners scored (21.3%)
- Led the Mariners in lowest percentage of inherited runners scored

PITCHING:

In the past two years, it seems like the Mariners have gone through every living lefthander in their efforts to find southpaws for the bullpen. That's how they stumbled upon Keith Comstock, who has toiled for seven organizations, in 20 towns and three countries over the last decade and a half. Having worked for everyone from the Yomiuri Giants to the Toledo Mud Hens, Comstock wasn't about to blow the opportunity.

At last, the well-travelled Comstock got a complete chance to show what he could do. He made the most of it, joining righthander Mike Jackson as a set-up man for closer Mike Schooler. After recording just three wins and one save in pieces of four previous major league seasons, Comstock had seven wins and two saves in 1990. His earned run average ended at 2.89, but prior to having back pains for much of the last two months, he was under 2.00.

With one of the best screwballs in the majors, Comstock was more effective against right-handed batters than he was versus lefties. That worked in his favor, as opposing managers kept pinch hitting righthanders against him. Comstock continually screwballed righties into outs, although he did give up nine extra-base hits to them, including all four homers he allowed.

A canny and competitive pitcher, Comstock has learned how to survive the hard way. He has good movement on his fastball and has a slider to keep lefthanders honest. He is best in short stints, having averaged less than one inning per appearance last year. His hits-per-innings ratio and strikeouts-to-walks ratio were solid even though his back problem affected his control later in the season.

HOLDING RUNNERS AND FIELDING:

Comstock has not spent all this time in the game without learning how to field his position. He covers ground well in bunting situations, usually goes to first base rather than take risks, and makes good throws. He has a good move to first and average delivery time to the plate. It takes a better-than-average runner to be sure of stealing a base on him.

OVERALL:

The Mariners intended to spend the winter looking for another lefthander to help out Comstock. Russ Swan might be the answer, but ideally they would like another veteran like Comstock. A savvy competitor on a predominantly youthful staff, Comstock appears to have found a home at last.

HITTING:

Henry Cotto is the quintessential fourth outfielder. While he would like to play daily, he does not sulk when he sits. Cotto waits for his chance, sticks in a big hit or two, fields capably and runs well. He's been a steady player in his three Seattle seasons, hitting .259, .264 and .259. Though his power production was down last year, his bat has a little pop.

As often happens when a team is tempted to play a career backup in a regular role, the slender Cotto seems to wear down with regular duty. Last year, Jay Buhner was out for the first two months and Greg Briley was mired in a slump, so Seattle went to Cotto more than ever, giving him 206 at-bats in the first half of the season. Cotto responded by hitting over .300 and chipping in some key hits. But the exposure took its toll and as the club faded in August, Cotto faded with it. At one point he had two hits in 35 at-bats, the proverbial water finding its level. A career .258 hitter, he was right back at his level by season's end.

Cotto hits the fastball down and in, will hang tough on a breaking ball and can hit a mistake. He has trouble adjusting at times and can be had with a change of speed or fastballs up in the zone.

BASERUNNING:

Cotto is probably the best baserunner on the Seattle club. He has an ambling look to him and could be called "deceptively fast," but he knows how to steal bases. Last year he was 21 for 24, and his career success rate of 82 percent puts him in the company of players like Tim Raines, Willie Wilson and Rickey Henderson. Cotto just doesn't log enough playing time for people to notice.

FIELDING:

Being the basic handy man, Cotto can play all three outfield positions very well. He has an average arm but can go get a ball with anybody. Cotto committed only two errors last year and has made only seven miscues in the last four seasons.

OVERALL:

Cotto may be the one single player the Mariners hold up as an example of their efforts to be a good, deep team. While they were reminded again that he can't play full-time for long periods, they have turned down one request after another for him in a trade, reasoning that all good teams have dependable role players like him.

HENRY COTTO

Position: RF/LF/CF
Bats: R **Throws:** R
Ht: 6' 2" **Wt:** 180

Opening Day Age: 30
Born: 1/5/61 in New York, NY
ML Seasons: 7

Overall Statistics

	G	AB	R	H	D	T	HR	RBI	SB	BB	SO	AVG
1990	127	355	40	92	14	3	4	33	21	22	52	.259
Career	602	1467	194	379	62	6	28	139	75	78	236	.258

Where He Hits the Ball

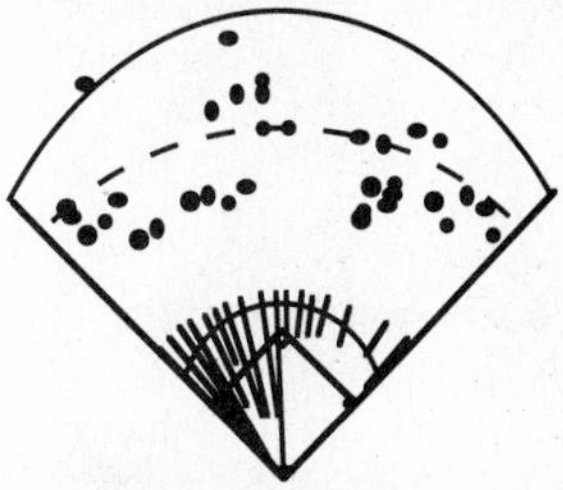

Vs. LHP

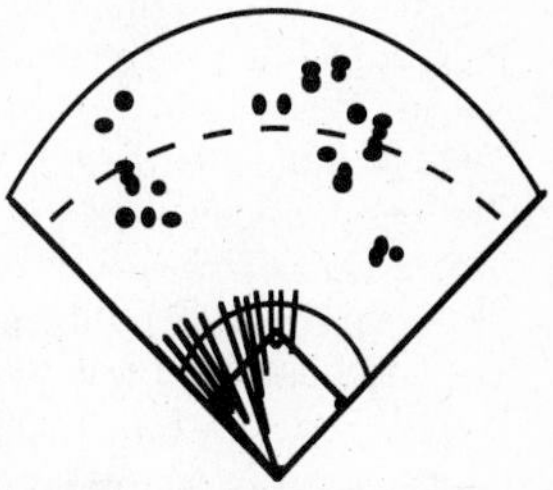

Vs. RHP

1990 Situational Stats

	AB	H	HR	RBI	AVG		AB	H	HR	RBI	AVG
Home	173	45	2	15	.260	LHP	192	50	2	19	.260
Road	182	47	2	18	.258	RHP	163	42	2	14	.258
Day	97	24	2	8	.247	Sc Pos	94	21	0	24	.223
Night	258	68	2	25	.264	Clutch	65	15	1	6	.231

1990 Rankings (American League)

- 1st in stolen base percentage (87.5%)
- 4th lowest batting average on a 0-2 count (.036)
- Led the Mariners in stolen base percentage and percentage of extra bases taken as a runner (55.0%)
- Led AL right fielders in stolen base percentage and percentage of extra bases taken as a runner

ALVIN DAVIS

Position: DH/1B
Bats: L **Throws:** R
Ht: 6' 1" **Wt:** 190

Opening Day Age: 30
Born: 9/9/60 in Riverside, CA
ML Seasons: 7

HITTING:

Regarded as one of the more consistent hitters and run producers in the American League, Alvin Davis slumped last year. A big finish, topped by two grand slams in the last week, brought him up to only 68 RBI. That was a career low for Davis, and a far cry from the 95 he knocked in during 1989.

Davis could have fingered his Mariner teammates, who didn't pose much of an offensive threat. Instead, he blamed his own troubles adjusting to the role of designated hitter after six seasons as the Mariners' regular first baseman. Watching Pete O'Brien play first, Davis hated the inaction between at-bats. He was just starting to settle into his new role when O'Brien was lost for five weeks, forcing Davis back onto the field again. He never really got settled in either role.

All season long, Davis couldn't hit effectively to the opposite field, something he'd done very well in the past. In addition, he swung at more first pitches than usual, although he is still known as one of the most patient hitters in the game. The combination of patience, confidence and an excellent batting eye has made Davis a man who must be thrown strikes. But last year his walk total was down from 101 to 85 and his strikeouts up from 49 to 68. Pitchers continue to avoid pitching him inside and had some success working away from Davis, who has good bat speed and is an excellent fastball hitter.

BASERUNNING:

After years of leg injuries, especially hamstring pulls, Davis has no speed whatsoever. He has stolen only one base since 1985 and is strictly a base-to-base runner; he may have the slowest first step in baseball. However, as a fly ball hitter he avoids grounding into many double plays.

FIELDING:

For years Davis has been regarded a steady fielder who holds on to what he reaches. His forte is handling the throw in the dirt with very soft hands. However, his range is very limited, especially to his left. Davis can fill in capably at first, but he's no Gold Glover.

OVERALL:

Davis is a proud man, a quiet, thoughtful sort used to leading by example, and he was hurt deeply by being relegated to designated hitting duties. Davis told those close to him that his plan is to come back in 1991 as the best DH in the league. There undoubtedly will be trade talk concerning him over the winter, but the Mariners went into the offseason feeling that Davis will come back and resume his role as a steady, productive hitter.

Overall Statistics

	G	AB	R	H	D	T	HR	RBI	SB	BB	SO	AVG
1990	140	494	63	140	21	0	17	68	0	85	68	.283
Career	1021	3674	524	1061	197	9	148	598	7	616	471	.289

Where He Hits the Ball

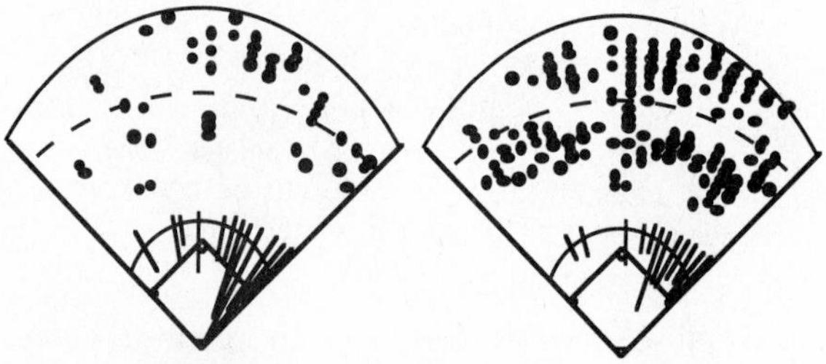

Vs. LHP Vs. RHP

1990 Situational Stats

	AB	H	HR	RBI	AVG		AB	H	HR	RBI	AVG
Home	252	70	12	40	.278	LHP	168	43	6	29	.256
Road	242	70	5	28	.289	RHP	326	97	11	39	.298
Day	121	34	1	9	.281	Sc Pos	126	35	4	53	.278
Night	373	106	16	59	.284	Clutch	85	23	3	10	.271

1990 Rankings (American League)

- 3rd least runs scored per time reached base (27.5%) and highest percentage of pitches taken (64.7%)
- 4th highest on-base average vs. right-handed pitchers (.400)
- 5th in sacrifice flies (9), on-base average (.387) and lowest groundball/flyball ratio (.84)
- Led the Mariners in sacrifice flies, walks (85), least GDPs per GDP situation (7.7%) batting average with the bases loaded (.417) and highest percentage of pitches taken
- Led designated hitters in walks, times on base (229), pitches seen (2,356) and on-base average

FUTURE MVP?

KEN GRIFFEY JR

Position: CF
Bats: L **Throws:** L
Ht: 6' 3" **Wt:** 195

Opening Day Age: 21
Born: 11/21/69 in Donora, PA
ML Seasons: 2

HITTING:

Arguably the best all-around player in the league at age 21, Ken Griffey, Jr. has a weakness: despite the candy bar which bears his name, he's allergic to chocolate. American League pitchers are frantically searching for some baseball-related allergies.

Last year the youngster scoffed at the sophomore jinx, hitting .300 (7th in the league) with 22 homers (12th) and 179 hits (tied for fifth). Griffey was the first Mariner ever voted to the starting lineup of the American League All-Star team, and the second-youngest starter ever, behind Al Kaline in 1955. Griffey led the league in hitting for 20 days in May and June and was among the league leaders in run production.

In each of his first two seasons, at ages 19 and 20, Griffey has fallen off late in the campaign. In 1989, he came off the disabled list and was out of shape the last six weeks. Last year, he wore down after playing every game in the first half and 155 in all. But he's still growing, and his second year numbers were an improvement in every significant category.

Griffey's only real problem is impatience, the curse of the young. Pitchers try to back him off the plate and then throw offspeed stuff away. At times Griffey will bite, although his great bat speed gives him the ability to look for the breaking ball and still hit the fastball. He improved markedly against lefthanders last year.

BASERUNNING:

If Griffey has a significant weakness, it is in this area. With his speed, he should steal more than 16 bases (his total in both 1989 and 1990). He also should not have been tossed out 11 times, as he was last year. The Mariners' conservative approach to running is one reason for this lack of success, and Griffey's own inexperience is another. Once he learns the value of reading pitchers, he should steal 30-plus easily.

FIELDING:

A good young hitter, Griffey is already a great fielder, without exaggeration. He can catch every reachable ball. He goes back on a ball better than any fielder in the league, with grace and courage near walls and great leaping ability. He does not charge balls quite as well, and he should learn to make more judicious throws with an arm that's rated well above average.

OVERALL:

One AL scout wrapped it up by stating simply: "He's going to be in the Hall of Fame." Griffey certainly has the talent. He'd do well to emulate two other notable natives of Donora, PA: his own father and the great Stan Musial.

Overall Statistics

	G	AB	R	H	D	T	HR	RBI	SB	BB	SO	AVG
1990	155	597	91	179	28	7	22	80	16	63	81	.300
Career	282	1052	152	299	51	7	38	141	32	107	164	.284

Where He Hits the Ball

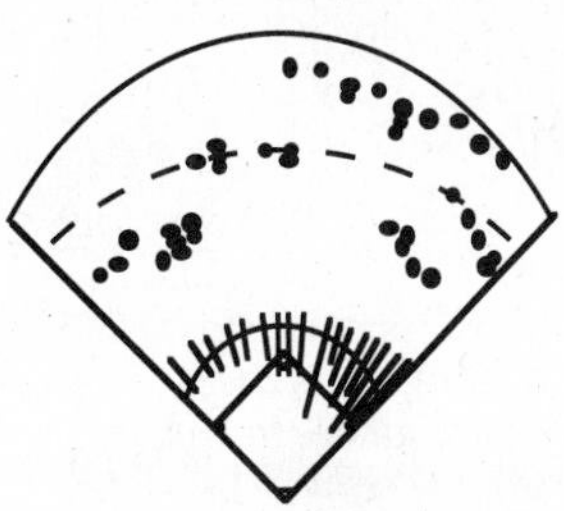

Vs. LHP

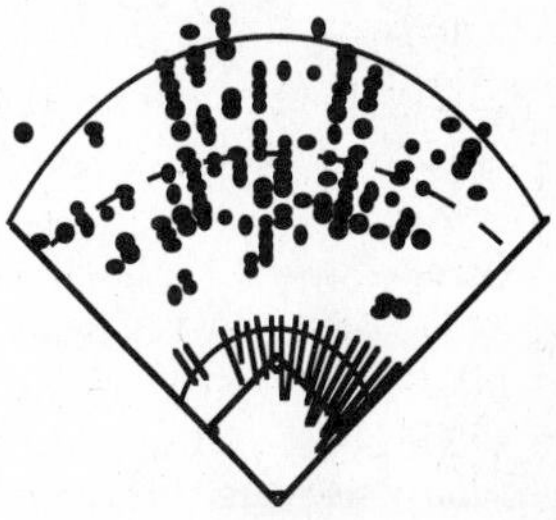

Vs. RHP

1990 Situational Stats

	AB	H	HR	RBI	AVG		AB	H	HR	RBI	AVG
Home	305	89	8	45	.292	LHP	219	67	5	22	.306
Road	292	90	14	35	.308	RHP	378	112	17	58	.296
Day	154	52	11	24	.338	Sc Pos	134	42	4	53	.313
Night	443	127	11	56	.287	Clutch	95	21	2	9	.221

1990 Rankings (American League)

- 4th in total bases (287)
- 5th in hits (179)
- 6th in intentional walks (12)
- Led the Mariners in home runs (22), hits, singles (122), triples (7), total bases, RBIs (80), intentional walks, slugging percentage (.481), HR frequency (27.1 ABs per HR), groundball/flyball ratio (1.30) and batting average with runners in scoring position (.313)
- Led AL center fielders in batting average (.300), total bases, intentional walks, times on base (244), on-base average (.366) and HR frequency

KEN GRIFFEY SR

Position: LF
Bats: L **Throws:** L
Ht: 6' 0" **Wt:** 210

Opening Day Age: 41
Born: 4/10/50 in Donora, PA
ML Seasons: 18

HITTING:

Ken Griffey Sr. has spent most of his career out of the spotlight, despite playing in three All-Star games, two World Series and recording well over 2,100 career hits. But Griffey finally made big news last August 31st. On that day, two days after signing a minimum salary contract with the Mariners, he started in left field for Seattle beside his son, center fielder Ken Griffey, Jr.

It was the first time a father had ever played with his son, and to extend the historic moment, the two hit back-to-back singles in the first inning. Two weeks later, they hit back-to-back home runs in California. But the most amazing part of this story was the play of man they called Senior around the Mariner clubhouse (they had always called his son Junior). After hitting just .206 with one HR and eight RBI as a little-used substitute with the Reds, Griffey got off to the hottest 10-game start in Mariner history. He hit .472 with three HR and 14 RBI and wound up as the American League Player of the Week for Sept. 3-9.

Thrilling more than a few people, Griffey scarcely cooled off. He wound up hitting .377 in 21 games as Manager Jim Lefebvre let him decide when he would play and when he would sit. Playing well, Griffey rarely chose to sit and played all 21 games in left field. The consensus is that his resurgence was no fluke. Griffey showed plenty of ability to turn on a fastball. He still has good power on low, inside pitches, and his spray-hitting style seems ideal for the increased dimensions of the Kingdome.

BASERUNNING:

A speed-burner in his prime, Griffey still moves pretty well for a man approaching his 41st birthday. He's no longer a base stealing threat, but he's a very intelligent baserunner.

FIELDING:

Griffey is forced to play left field with Seattle because of a logjam at first base and DH. He's never had a strong arm, and his range is nowhere near what it was in his younger days. He won't embarrass himself in the outfield, but he has to be considered a defensive liability.

OVERALL:

Griffey was a free agent at season's end, and the Mariners, who were delighted with his play, were expected to make a strong bid to re-sign him. At his age, he's best suited to role-playing. But if he keeps swinging a hot bat, he may end up with a surprising amount of playing time. A father figure to more people than his son, Griffey is an asset to a young ball club.

Overall Statistics

	G	AB	R	H	D	T	HR	RBI	SB	BB	SO	AVG
1990	67	140	19	42	4	0	4	26	2	12	8	.300
Career	2067	7144	1119	2119	357	77	151	850	200	706	885	.297

Where He Hits the Ball

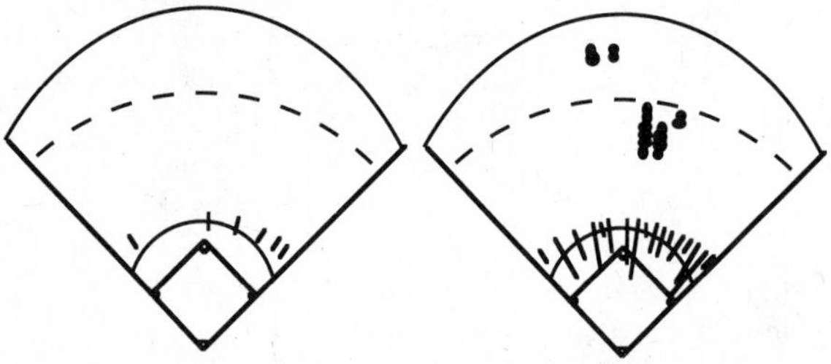

Vs. LHP Vs. RHP

1990 Situational Stats

	AB	H	HR	RBI	AVG		AB	H	HR	RBI	AVG
Home	50	13	2	7	.260	LHP	15	4	0	4	.267
Road	90	29	2	19	.322	RHP	125	38	4	22	.304
Day	37	13	0	3	.351	Sc Pos	42	10	1	22	.238
Night	103	29	4	23	.282	Clutch	32	8	0	3	.250

1990 Rankings (American League)

➟ Did not rank near the top or bottom in any category

CY YOUNG STUFF

ERIK HANSON

Position: SP
Bats: R **Throws:** R
Ht: 6' 6" **Wt:** 205

Opening Day Age: 25
Born: 5/18/65 in Kinnelon, NJ
ML Seasons: 3

PITCHING:

Many observers have commented on the excellence of Erik Hanson's three pitches, but the ultimate compliment may have come from an umpire. After the game of August 1, Rich Garcia, the plate ump and a veteran of 16 years, said, "Hanson has the best stuff I've ever seen." That particular day, Hanson would have traded much of that stuff for a simple win. He allowed only two hits in 10 innings, walked none and fanned 11 Athletics. But he wound up with a no-decision as Dave Stewart lasted 11 innings for a 1-0 win.

Despite that particular setback, there is little doubt that with health on his side, Hanson will be one of the American League's premier pitchers for years to come. Hanson has developed a much more competitive attitude, which had been the one reservation about him going into the 1990 season.

Hanson has three great pitches: a fastball in the 88-93 MPH range with good movement; a sharp, downward breaking 70-76 MPH curve on which he changes speeds; and a superb change of pace. He works both sides of the plate with outstanding control, keeping both right and left-handed batters off-balance.

Even with his abilities already established, Hanson keeps improving. Not only did he win all six of his September starts to wind up with 18 wins, but he had an ERA of 2.05 over his last 13 starts. His 211 strikeouts ranked third in the league behind Nolan Ryan (232) and Bobby Witt (221) of Texas. Hanson did pitch better on the road (11-3) than he did at home (7-6). But with the Kingdome's left field distance being increased another 12-15 feet in 1991, Hanson should be tougher at home in the future.

HOLDING RUNNERS AND FIELDING:

A former all-state high school basketball player who went on to play at Wake Forest, Hanson is a big man with good agility. He fields well, gets to bunts quickly and makes sure throws. His move to first still leaves something to be desired. He has quickened his time to the plate, but gives up too many stolen bases.

OVERALL:

The Mariners have only two players they consider to be "untouchable" in trade talks. One, obviously, is outfielder Ken Griffey, Jr. The other is Hanson, who can be expected to contend for the Cy Young Award in the near future. Still shy of his 26th birthday, he appears to have a boundless horizon.

Overall Statistics

	W	L	ERA	G	GS	Sv	IP	H	R	BB	SO	HR
1990	18	9	3.24	33	33	0	236.0	205	88	68	211	15
Career	29	17	3.22	56	56	0	391.0	343	149	112	322	26

How Often He Throws Strikes

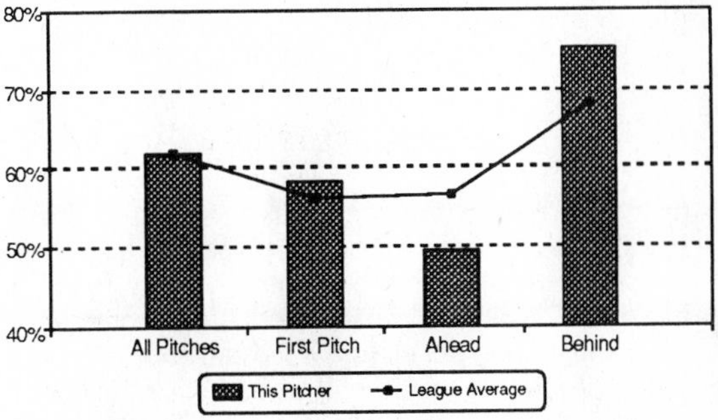

1990 Situational Stats

	W	L	ERA	Sv	IP		AB	H	HR	RBI	AVG
Home	7	6	3.56	0	111.1	LHB	465	103	5	33	.222
Road	11	3	2.96	0	124.2	RHB	418	102	10	42	.244
Day	1	3	3.72	0	38.2	Sc Pos	180	39	2	55	.217
Night	17	6	3.15	0	197.1	Clutch	78	15	1	6	.192

1990 Rankings (American League)

- 3rd in strikeouts (211) and strikeout/walk ratio (3.1)
- 4th in wins (18), innings (236.0), batters faced (236), lowest on-base average allowed (.287) and least baserunners per 9 innings (10.5)
- 5th in pitches thrown (3,739), strikeouts per 9 innings (8.0) and ERA on the road (2.96)
- Led the Mariners in ERA (3.24), wins, games started (33), innings, hits allowed (205), batters faced, strikeouts, pitches thrown, winning percentage (.667), strikeout/walk ratio, lowest on-base average allowed, least baserunners per 9 innings and most strikeouts per 9 innings

PITCHING:

When the Mariners acquired Brian Holman from Montreal in the Mark Langston deal in May, 1989, there were whispers that Holman was not a competitor. Rarely has anyone been described more inaccurately. If the club had any doubt about this gutty righthander, Holman dispelled it in August when he tried to pitch for weeks with a sore elbow. Seattle medical people finally pried the truth out of him, and in early September, Holman underwent surgery to remove bone chips.

Some people might be fooled by Holman's open and affable personality. But this is one tough kid, a reformed alcoholic who worked to help his mother support his brothers and sisters. Holman removed the few remaining doubts about him on April 20th, when he came within one out of throwing a perfect game against the then world champion Oakland Athletics. Former Mariner Ken Phelps spoiled his bid by homering; Phelps was the only Athletic batter to even come close to reaching base.

Holman was 11-7 with a 3.80 ERA when his elbow started to bother him in early August. He changed his delivery to relieve the pain, and as a result, his fastball straightened out and his various breaking balls flattened. He lost his last four decisions. Usually, Holman has a good sinking fastball, although he sometimes has a tendency to get on top of the ball and straighten it out. He will run the fastball away from lefthanders. Holman changes speeds well and as a breaking ball uses a slurve, a slider that breaks a bit more than usual. Against righthanders, he will drop his arm on the slurve and give it a sweeping, tough-to-reach break. At times, he rushes and gets too upright with his delivery.

More than anything, scouts like Holman's aggressiveness, the very thing that causes him to rush, and the way he goes after batters, the very thing that cost him his perfect game. He started Phelps out with a strike, and Phelps hit it for the homer.

HOLDING RUNNERS AND FIELDING:

Holman fields his position well, with few wasted motions. He is quick to cover first and field bunts, and he makes accurate throws. His move to first is not exceptional, but his delivery to the plate is quick, which can make him tough to run on.

OVERALL:

Holman is expected to come back from his surgery without problem. In fact, the only likely effect of the injury is that other teams will stop asking for him in trades. Last year Kansas City offered the M's slugger Danny Tartabull in exchange for Holman. Seattle refused.

BRIAN HOLMAN

Position: SP
Bats: R **Throws:** R
Ht: 6' 4" **Wt:** 185

Opening Day Age: 26
Born: 1/25/65 in Denver, CO
ML Seasons: 3

Overall Statistics

	W	L	ERA	G	GS	Sv	IP	H	R	BB	SO	HR
1990	11	11	4.03	28	28	0	189.2	188	92	66	121	17
Career	24	31	3.72	79	69	0	481.1	483	217	177	284	31

How Often He Throws Strikes

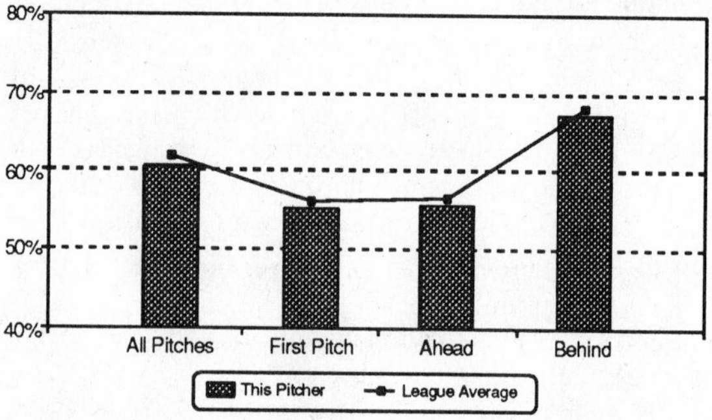

1990 Situational Stats

	W	L	ERA	Sv	IP		AB	H	HR	RBI	AVG
Home	4	6	4.04	0	104.2	LHB	379	106	10	37	.280
Road	7	5	4.02	0	85.0	RHB	345	82	7	42	.238
Day	1	4	4.89	0	38.2	Sc Pos	159	44	3	58	.277
Night	10	7	3.81	0	151.0	Clutch	66	22	1	8	.333

1990 Rankings (American League)

- ➡ 9th in least run support per 9 innings (4.3)
- ➡ Led the Mariners in pickoff throws (126), lowest stolen base percentage allowed (50.0%) and least pitches thrown per batter (3.63)

PITCHING:

If there is one pitcher the Mariners feel they can afford to give up before next season, it is Mike Jackson. Despite Jackson's failure to fill in for injured closer Mike Schooler in the final month last year, there is definite interest in the hard-throwing righthander.

There was even more interest in Jackson a year ago when he was coming off his second straight season of outstanding relief work. Atlanta, in need of a hard-throwing closer, was especially hot after Jackson, but the talks fell apart because the Braves felt Seattle was asking for too much in return. At the time, it did not appear the Mariners were being outrageous, and their position looked even better when Jackson got off to another strong start in 1990. At the All-Star break Jackson had a 2.96 ERA and had allowed only 29 hits in 46 innings with 46 strikeouts. It appeared all he needed to become a star was a chance to finish games.

Jackson got that chance when Schooler went down with shoulder troubles near the end of August. But his control deserted him and he recorded only one save in four opportunities. One possible explanation for this loss of control was that Jackson had undergone surgery on his right knee prior to the season. He claimed at the end of the year that the knee had bothered him at times in 1990.

A two pitch pitcher, Jackson has a fastball that has been clocked at 96 MPH, but he sometimes throws his slider too much. The heater alone makes some teams covet him as a closer, but Jackson's overall work leaves questions about his suitability for short relief. He has a tendency to first fall behind in the count, then give up walks or crucial hits. One scout describes him as a "top step" guy, meaning the manager always has to be poised to go out to the mound and yank him.

HOLDING RUNNERS AND FIELDING:

A former infielder, Jackson handles his position very well. He also does a good job of holding baserunners. He has a very quick move to first base.

OVERALL:

Despite his poor performance in 1990, Jackson has a quality arm. He's never proven himself as a closer, but a lot of teams, remembering a two-hit win over Montreal in 1987, think he could make a good starter. The Mariners can be expected to trade Jackson if Schooler proves to be sound in training camp -- sooner if the right deal comes along.

MIKE JACKSON

Position: RP
Bats: R **Throws:** R
Ht: 6' 0" **Wt:** 185

Opening Day Age: 26
Born: 12/22/64 in Houston, TX
ML Seasons: 5

Overall Statistics

	W	L	ERA	G	GS	Sv	IP	H	R	BB	SO	HR
1990	5	7	4.54	63	0	3	77.1	64	42	44	69	8
Career	18	28	3.59	254	7	15	398.2	319	182	201	335	44

How Often He Throws Strikes

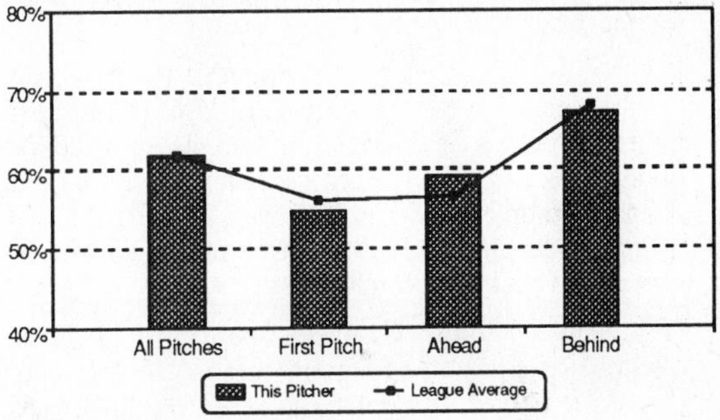

1990 Situational Stats

	W	L	ERA	Sv	IP		AB	H	HR	RBI	AVG
Home	3	4	4.95	0	40.0	LHB	105	27	5	18	.257
Road	2	3	4.10	3	37.1	RHB	174	37	3	31	.213
Day	0	2	3.04	2	23.2	Sc Pos	97	25	2	43	.258
Night	5	5	5.20	1	53.2	Clutch	169	39	2	33	.231

1990 Rankings (American League)

- 2nd in highest percentage of inherited runners scored (40.3%)
- 3rd in blown saves (9)
- 6th in holds (13)
- Led the Mariners in games pitched (63), holds and blown saves

RANDY JOHNSON

Position: SP
Bats: R **Throws:** L
Ht: 6'10" **Wt:** 225

Opening Day Age: 27
Born: 9/10/63 in Walnut Creek, CA
ML Seasons: 3

PITCHING:

A lot of baseball people have looked at Randy Johnson and proclaimed that if he ever puts it all together, look out. Last June 2 in the Kingdome, Johnson put it together and then some. He hurled a no-hitter, blanking Detroit 2-0; his final pitch was a 98 MPH heater to strike out Mike Heath. That performance, along with a 9-3 record and a 3.68 ERA at the break, earned Johnson selection to the American League All-Star team, where he joined teammate Ken Griffey, Jr. It was the first time Seattle ever placed two players on the team.

However, the other side of the big lefthander was also apparent on that no-hit night. Johnson walked six. Admirers later called him "constructively wild," meaning that the Tigers could not dig in at the plate. Maybe it worked that night, but most observers agree that Johnson's control is a big problem. His 120 walks led the majors.

Competitive but often temperamental, Johnson gets easily frustrated. Montreal grew tired of his temper tantrums, which included a broken hand when he punched a dugout wall in Indianapolis. Last year Johnson complained when Manager Jim Lefebvre got relievers up in the bullpen, eventually earning a closed-door session with his manager.

Any team would allow Johnson his few quirks if he pitched up to his immense promise. Certainly he's got the stuff: a high-90s fastball, a sharp, downward curveball and a change-up. At times, he hits all the spots with his pitches and fulfills his desire to be recognized as a pitcher, not just a hard thrower. But Johnson has trouble winning on days when he doesn't have his good stuff. The tallest pitcher in major league history, he finds that his long delivery can easily get out of sync. When that happens, he's prone to walks and home run balls. Last year Johnson gave up 26 dingers, fourth most in the league,

HOLDING RUNNERS AND FIELDING:

Tall and awkward on balls hit back toward the middle, Johnson is not a good fielder. His five errors were second to teammate Matt Young among AL pitchers. He does not hold runners well and takes a long time to deliver a pitch. The speed in which he gets the ball to the plate helps him a little.

OVERALL:

The young Mariner pitchers are highly sought after by other clubs, and rejecting offers for Johnson may be the hardest part for a club which would like to keep its rotation intact. Erik Hanson is untouchable, but Johnson could go in a whopper deal that brings a solid position player with right-handed power.

Overall Statistics

	W	L	ERA	G	GS	Sv	IP	H	R	BB	SO	HR
1990	14	11	3.65	33	33	0	219.2	174	103	120	194	26
Career	24	24	4.03	66	65	0	406.1	344	211	223	349	42

How Often He Throws Strikes

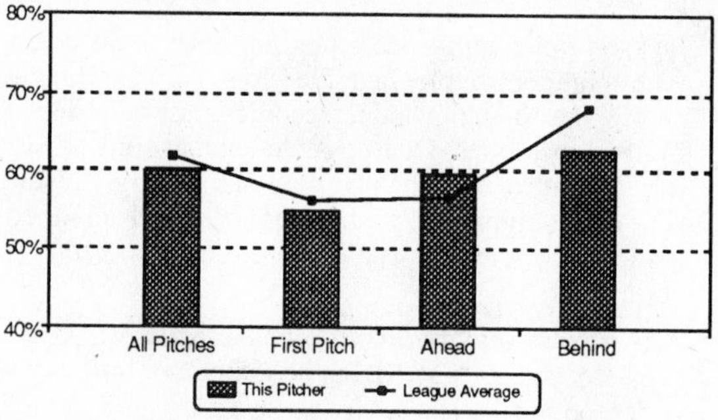

1990 Situational Stats

	W	L	ERA	Sv	IP		AB	H	HR	RBI	AVG
Home	8	4	2.90	0	102.1	LHB	82	16	0	4	.195
Road	6	7	4.30	0	117.1	RHB	724	158	26	76	.218
Day	4	2	3.51	0	66.2	Sc Pos	193	35	2	51	.181
Night	10	9	3.71	0	153.0	Clutch	67	10	2	3	.149

1990 Rankings (American League)

- 1st in walks allowed (120)
- 2nd in lowest batting average allowed (.216)
- 3rd in most pitches thrown per batter (3.96)
- 4th in home runs allowed (26), stolen bases allowed (28) and lowest batting average allowed with runners in scoring position (.181)
- Led the Mariners in games started (33), shutouts (2), home runs allowed, walks allowed, stolen bases allowed, lowest batting average allowed, most run support per 9 innings (4.6) and lowest batting average allowed with runners in scoring position

JEFF LEONARD

Position: LF/DH
Bats: R **Throws:** R
Ht: 6' 4" **Wt:** 200

Opening Day Age: 35
Born: 9/22/55 in Philadelphia, PA
ML Seasons: 14

Overall Statistics

	G	AB	R	H	D	T	HR	RBI	SB	BB	SO	AVG
1990	134	478	39	120	20	0	10	75	4	37	97	.251
Career	1415	5045	614	1342	223	37	144	723	163	342	1000	.266

Where He Hits the Ball

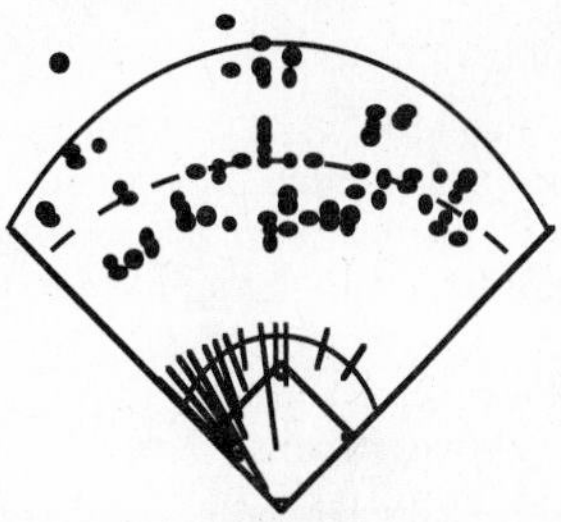

Vs. LHP

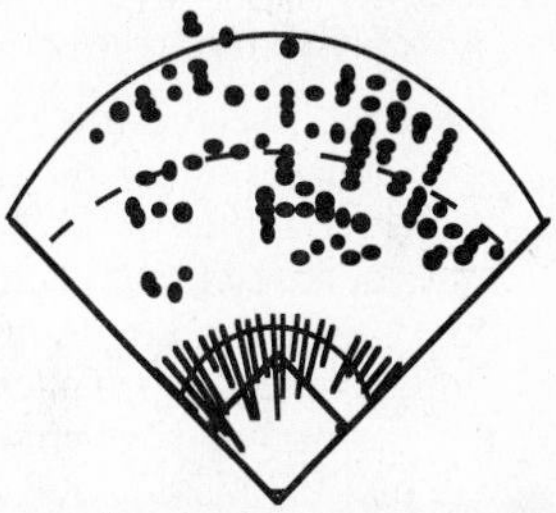

Vs. RHP

1990 Situational Stats

	AB	H	HR	RBI	AVG		AB	H	HR	RBI	AVG
Home	234	52	7	37	.222	LHP	175	54	6	40	.309
Road	244	68	3	38	.279	RHP	303	66	4	35	.218
Day	127	30	1	17	.236	Sc Pos	147	45	4	63	.306
Night	351	90	9	58	.256	Clutch	78	11	0	10	.141

1990 Rankings (American League)

- 1st in least runs scored per time reached base (24.4%) and lowest batting average in the clutch (.141)
- 5th in GDPs (20)
- 6th worst batting average at home (.222)
- Led the Mariners in strikeouts (97), GDPs and batting average vs. left-handed pitchers (.309)

HITTING:

Jeffrey Leonard may be one of the game's most misunderstood players. Loud, boisterous, and overbearing at times in his own clubhouse, Leonard gives it all he has on every play, every day when he's on the field. He played through pain as a designated hitter in 1989. When Manager Jim Lefebvre asked him to play right field two hours before game time on Opening Day last year, Leonard told him just to write his name in the lineup card at whatever position he was needed. He ended up playing most of the season in left.

Despite his all-out style and his 75 RBI last year, Leonard won't be back with Seattle. After a strong season in '89, he didn't provide the same production last year. His accusation that the club intentionally held him out of the lineup sealed his fate. Leonard felt the Mariners were trying to prevent him from reaching plate appearance levels which would have triggered automatic renewal of his $1.1 million contract.

Leonard insisted his RBI total would have equalled his 93 of 1989 had he continued to play regularly. He might have been right, even though he fell off significantly in the second half once again. Leonard went from 10 HR and 55 RBI in all 84 games before the break to no homers and 20 RBI in 50 games afterward. Leonard did finish strongly, going 14-for-23 in his last 10 games while wearing glasses.

Leonard is a basic power hitter, pulling almost all his home runs to left, but he will occasionally slap outside pitches to right. He sees a lot of those outside pitches, many off the plate. He often gets impatient, gearing himself only for the fastball.

BASERUNNING:

Limited by foot problems, Leonard has average speed at best, and is no longer much of a threat to steal. He is a smart and aggressive baserunner, however, always aware of the potential to take an extra base, and is outstanding at breaking up the double play.

FIELDING:

Leonard also rates as average in the outfield, with average coverage and an average arm. He rarely makes a mistake, but rarely comes up with big play, either. Having lost considerable speed, he's best suited to DH duty.

OVERALL:

Leonard has been released by Seattle, but could be worth a gamble by another club needing a veteran right-handed hitter. He'll probably have to accept a contract with lots of incentive clauses, however. Other clubs are now wary of Leonard's reputation, which was hurt again last year by a pushing incident with coach Rusty Kuntz before a game in Detroit.

EDGAR MARTINEZ

Position: 3B
Bats: R **Throws:** R
Ht: 5'11" **Wt:** 175

Opening Day Age: 28
Born: 1/2/63 in New York, NY
ML Seasons: 4

HITTING:

Edgar Martinez has had an unconventional life, and he's an unconventional third baseman. Martinez was born in New York City but returned with his mother to her native Puerto Rico when his parents separated. In Puerto Rico, Martinez learned how important quick hands are to both hitting and fielding. He applied those lessons well in his first chance to be an every day third baseman last year.

Martinez is the Mariners' best natural hitter, but unlike the classic third basemen, he is not a big run producer. Many were disappointed that he drove in only 49 runs last year, but that's not really being fair to Martinez. Though the shy third-sacker said nothing about it, he was hampered by leg problems much of the year, most notably a hamstring pull that lingered for months. Martinez had right knee surgery the day after the season was over. Given complete health, he probably would have been more productive.

But even if he doesn't drive in a lot of runs, Martinez is a valuable hitter. He can hit any pitch and put it anywhere on the field. He is an ideal number- two hitter, a contact man with patience and the ability to take a pitch to allow runners to steal. At times he is guilty of guessing on pitches and can be caught looking. But his good eye produces many walks. Martinez can pull the inside pitch and hit mistakes out of the park at a rate of 10-15 a year.

BASERUNNING:

Martinez is a capable man on the bases, methodical rather than daring. He won't make many mistakes but he won't get many extra bases, either. He stole only one base last year in five attempts.

FIELDING:

With 27 errors last year, Martinez shocked many who thought he was a much better fielder. Steady but limited in range, he made no excuses for his defensive problems. Some felt it was simply a case of nerves for a rookie who had been given his first full-time job.

OVERALL:

Martinez should be Seattle's regular third baseman again in 1991, and he's expected to play better in the field. The Mariners would also like him to drive in a few more runs. But with his ability to hit for average, draw walks and hit an occasional homer, Martinez can be an offensive asset even if he's not a big RBI guy.

Overall Statistics

	G	AB	R	H	D	T	HR	RBI	SB	BB	SO	AVG
1990	144	487	71	147	27	2	11	49	1	74	62	.302
Career	236	733	97	213	41	4	13	79	3	97	100	.291

Where He Hits the Ball

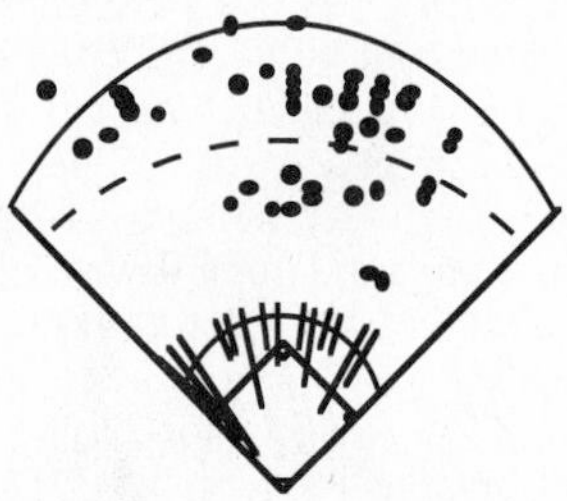

Vs. LHP

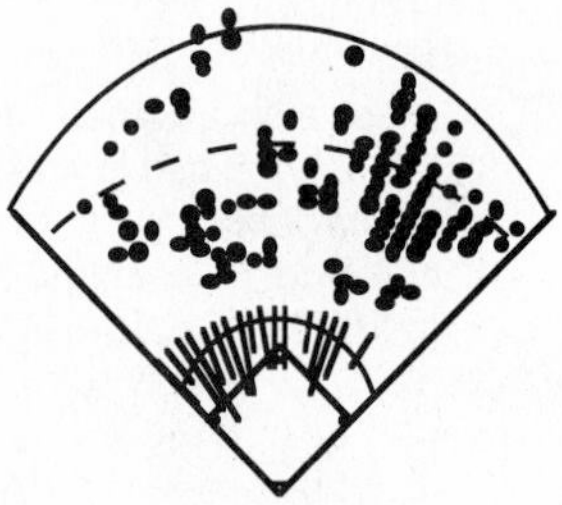

Vs. RHP

1990 Situational Stats

	AB	H	HR	RBI	AVG		AB	H	HR	RBI	AVG
Home	244	73	3	20	.299	LHP	156	48	6	24	.308
Road	243	74	8	29	.305	RHP	331	99	5	25	.299
Day	118	33	4	16	.280	Sc Pos	119	29	3	37	.244
Night	369	114	7	33	.309	Clutch	90	28	4	15	.311

1990 Rankings (American League)

- 3rd in on-base average (.397), highest batting average with 2 strikes (.270) and lowest percentage of swings that missed (8.3%)
- 4th in highest percentage of pitches taken (64.5%)
- 6th in batting average (.302)
- Led the Mariners in batting average, on-base average (.397), pitches seen per plate appearance (4.08), batting average vs. right-handed pitchers (.299), slugging percentage vs. left-handed pitchers (.487), on-base average vs. left-handed pitchers (.412), batting average on a 3-2 count (.314), batting average with 2 strikes and lowest percentage of swings that missed

PETE O'BRIEN

Position: 1B
Bats: L **Throws:** L
Ht: 6' 2" **Wt:** 205

Opening Day Age: 33
Born: 2/9/58 in Santa Monica, CA
ML Seasons: 9

HITTING:

Pete O'Brien signed a four-year, $7.6 million free-agent contract that made him the best-paid Mariner in history. Considering his annual salary became more than any entire Seattle club made until 1983, O'Brien started out as a focal point of the Mariners' 1990 season. The new owners, led by Jeff Smulyan, held O'Brien up as an example of their efforts to build a winner.

The fans expected $7.6 million worth of excellence from O'Brien, but they didn't get it. So hapless was his season that when he finally started to hit the ball with some authority after a horrendous April, he was hurt performing his forte: fielding a grounder. O'Brien broke his right thumb and missed five weeks.

When he came back, O'Brien hit the ball better than he had while he was earning the unhappy moniker "Popup Pete." Unfortunately, it seemed that nearly once a game -- at least -- he hit the ball hard at someone. O'Brien was batting only .191 at the break, with two homers and 12 RBI. He improved a little in the second half, hitting .247, but with only 15 RBI. Completing a dismal picture, he hit only .156 with men in scoring position for the season.

Most American League scouts feel that O'Brien is a better hitter than he showed in 1990. A typical left-handed low ball hitter, he can be had on hard pitches up and in or in on the hands.

BASERUNNING:

O'Brien is a normal Seattle player on the bases: good, but far from great. He makes few mistakes, but also gets few extra bases. He didn't attempt a stolen base in 1990, which is just as well; O'Brien is a career 41 percent base stealer.

FIELDING:

For years, as his run production has declined, O'Brien has maintained his reputation as one of the premier defensive first basemen in the game. His play in 1990 was one reason Seattle's pitching was so greatly improved. But the Mariners also have Alvin Davis and Tino Martinez at first, so O'Brien may wind up playing some left field in 1991. He figures to log some time as a defensive replacement at first base if nothing else.

OVERALL:

O'Brien drove in 92 runs in 1985, but his RBI total has declined every year since then. The Mariners expect better, and O'Brien, an earnest player, figures to be in shape and ready to give a better effort in 1991. But the Seattle first base position is crowded, and he's going to have to hit a lot better if he wants more playing time.

Overall Statistics

	G	AB	R	H	D	T	HR	RBI	SB	BB	SO	AVG
1990	108	366	32	82	18	0	5	27	0	44	33	.224
Career	1209	4271	526	1140	203	17	131	569	22	531	454	.267

Where He Hits the Ball

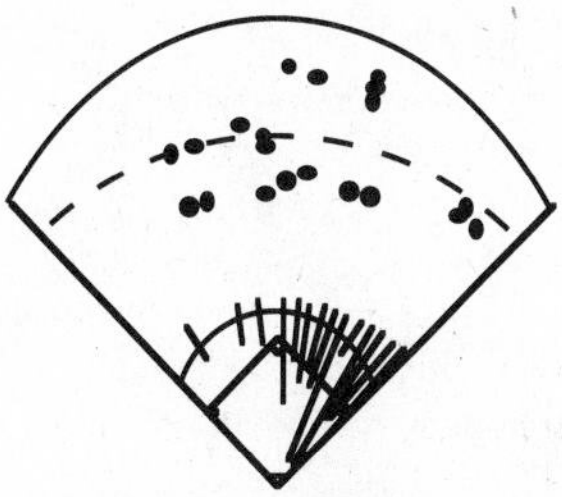

Vs. LHP

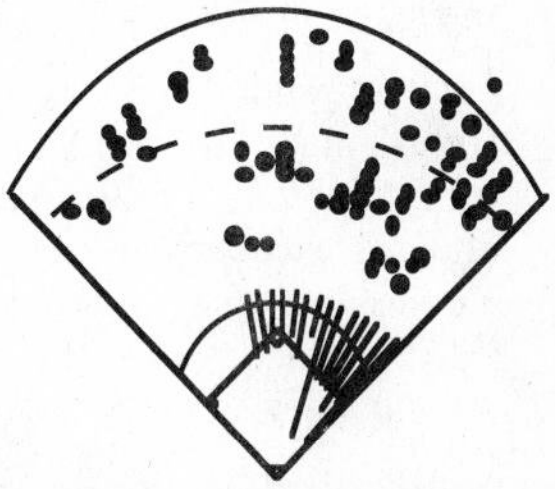

Vs. RHP

1990 Situational Stats

	AB	H	HR	RBI	AVG		AB	H	HR	RBI	AVG
Home	172	45	3	14	.262	LHP	130	26	1	12	.200
Road	194	37	2	13	.191	RHP	236	56	4	15	.237
Day	84	16	2	7	.190	Sc Pos	96	15	0	21	.156
Night	282	66	3	20	.234	Clutch	64	15	0	2	.234

1990 Rankings (American League)

- 1st in lowest slugging percentage vs. left-handed pitchers (.238)
- 2nd lowest batting average with runners in scoring position (.156)
- 3rd lowest batting average with the bases loaded (.056) and lowest percentage of extra bases taken as a runner (24.7%)
- 5th lowest batting average vs. left-handed pitchers (.200)

HAROLD REYNOLDS

Position: 2B
Bats: B **Throws:** R
Ht: 5'11" **Wt:** 165

Opening Day Age: 30
Born: 11/26/60 in Eugene, OR
ML Seasons: 8

HITTING:

The highlight of Harold Reynolds' 1990 season was literally becoming a highlight. At a White House ceremony in September, President George Bush named him one of his 1,000 Points of Light (No. 167, to be exact) and honored Reynolds for his work with black youths. Reynolds came back from that meeting to hit a grand slam home run in a win over the Orioles. But his season -- which featured a 48-point drop in batting average from .300 to .252 -- could have used about fifty more points of hits.

Reynolds halted his annual batting improvement of .222-.275-.283-.300 over the previous four seasons. But his season wasn't completely lost. He hit .301 with men in scoring position and set a mark for Seattle second basemen with 55 RBI. Drawing a career-high 81 walks, he was third in the league with 100 runs scored. Reynolds has shown increasing plate discipline since '86, when he drew only 29 walks.

A switch-hitter, Reynolds is considerably better as a right-handed hitter. Opposing pitchers concentrated on pitching Reynolds up in the strike zone last year and righthanders had a lot of success in that area. Reynolds swung at too many high offerings, flying into automatic outs much too often for a man who should hack and hustle. When he zones in on low pitches, Reynolds hits much better.

BASERUNNING:

Reynolds stole 60 bases in 1987, but since then he's yet to have a season in which he's been successful two-thirds of the time. Since that's generally considered the break-even point, manager Jim Lefebvre has given Reynolds the red light. Reynolds has both speed and quickness, but poor technique. Still, he goes from first to third as well as anyone . If he studied pitchers more, he would improve as a base stealer.

FIELDING:

Reynolds also had a strange year on defense in 1990. Always streaky with the glove, Reynolds gets to more balls than any other infielder in the league. But he also commits too many careless errors, and has led AL second basemen in miscues for four straight years.

OVERALL:

With a three-year contract he signed last winter, Reynolds has toughened over the years. No longer is he the wide-eyed kid with the mild demeanor; he has become a serious player, though one still prone to occasional lapses of concentration. When and if Reynolds closes these final gaps, he will take his place as one of the league's best players. The Mariners would love to see that, but they feel they have a pretty good player right now.

Overall Statistics

	G	AB	R	H	D	T	HR	RBI	SB	BB	SO	AVG
1990	160	642	100	162	36	5	5	55	31	81	52	.252
Career	854	3001	393	790	143	39	11	205	185	274	248	.263

Where He Hits the Ball

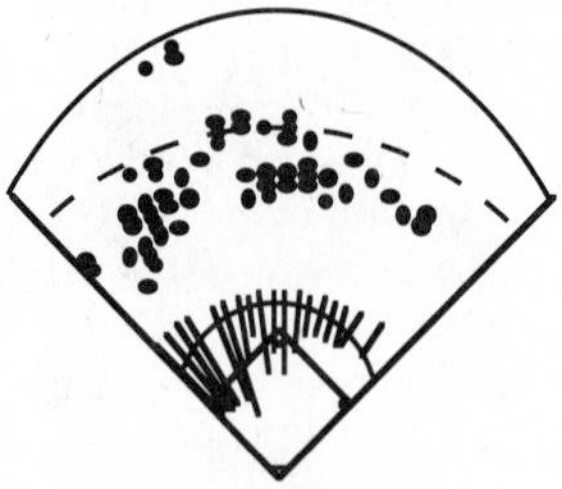

Vs. LHP

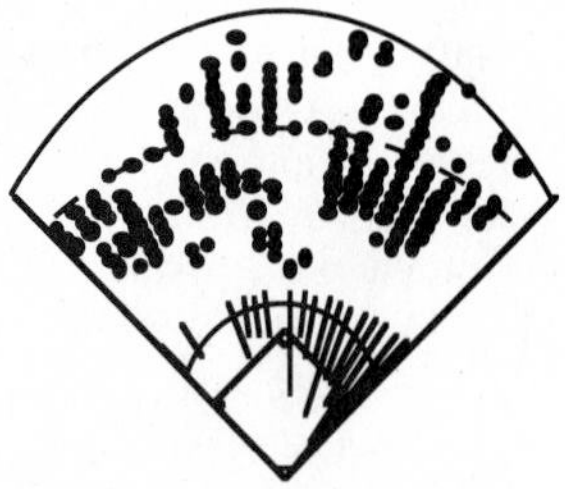

Vs. RHP

1990 Situational Stats

	AB	H	HR	RBI	AVG		AB	H	HR	RBI	AVG
Home	297	75	0	21	.253	LHP	207	59	1	22	.285
Road	345	87	5	34	.252	RHP	435	103	4	33	.237
Day	166	40	1	16	.241	Sc Pos	123	37	2	47	.301
Night	476	122	4	39	.256	Clutch	105	31	1	26	.295

1990 Rankings (American League)

- 1st in at-bats (642) and plate appearances (737)
- 3rd in runs (100) and lowest slugging percentage vs. right-handed pitchers (.326)
- Led the Mariners in at-bats, runs, doubles (36), stolen bases (31), caught stealing (16), times on base (246), pitches seen (2,686), plate appearances, games (160), runs scored per time reached base (40.7%), bunts in play (20), percentage of swings put into play (54.9%) and steal of third (3)
- Led AL second basemen in at-bats, runs, caught stealing, pitches seen, plate appearances, games and errors (19)

STOPPER

MIKE SCHOOLER

Position: RP
Bats: R **Throws:** R
Ht: 6' 3" **Wt:** 220

Opening Day Age: 28
Born: 8/10/62 in Anaheim, CA
ML Seasons: 3

PITCHING:

Even though Mike Schooler had 27 fewer saves -- and one more injury -- than Bobby Thigpen had in 1990, many baseball people draw close comparisons between the White Sox relief ace and his Seattle counterpart. Schooler is 11 months older, 30 pounds heavier and was drafted two rounds earlier in the 1985 draft than Thigpen. Both are married with one son. In the minors, both performed in the Midwest and Southern Leagues. However, they didn't oppose each other, because Seattle's policy was to bring players along more slowly than the White Sox.

Thigpen, a year ahead in experience, saved 16 games in 51 appearances in 1987; Schooler debuted with 15 saves in 40 appearances in 1988. In their first full major league seasons, Thigpen broke a White Sox record with 34 saves in 68 games in 1988 and Schooler set a Mariner record with 33 in 67 games in 1989. Thigpen saved 34 again in 1989, while Schooler had 30 in his injury-shortened 1990 season. Can Schooler (or anyone) match Thigpen's major league record 57 saves of 1990? That's a tall order; the Mariners would be pleased just to have Schooler healthy again.

Three days after Schooler recorded his 30th save last August 21, he went out for the year with what the Mariners' officially described as a "weakness" in his right shoulder. He was scheduled to come back after several weeks, but did not. The Mariners sorely missed him. Seattle was three games under .500 when Schooler went down, but were only 17-22 the rest of the way and made no real run at their first .500 season.

Schooler is known for his perfect relief demeanor. He wants the ball with the game on the line. He usually throws strikes with two outstanding pitches, a 90 MPH fastball and a vaunted hard slider. Only occasionally does he succumb to the constant pressure by trying to be too fine. When Schooler falls behind in the count, he can get into trouble, but that rarely happens. He had 30 saves in 34 opportunities last year, and retired 40 of 48 first batters.

HOLDING RUNNERS AND FIELDING:

Schooler is as poised when fielding as he is when pitching, an asset for a reliever who faces critical bunt situations. He has an average move to first, but it's good enough to keep most runners from hurting him.

OVERALL:

Schooler's health is critical to the Mariners in 1991. With Mike Jackson failing to adequately replace him in the last month, they have no proven back-up. Seattle didn't have a real relief ace between the departure of Bill Caudill (1983) and the arrival of Schooler in 1988.

Overall Statistics

	W	L	ERA	G	GS	Sv	IP	H	R	BB	SO	HR
1990	1	4	2.25	49	0	30	56.0	47	18	16	45	5
Career	7	19	2.83	156	0	78	181.1	173	66	59	168	11

How Often He Throws Strikes

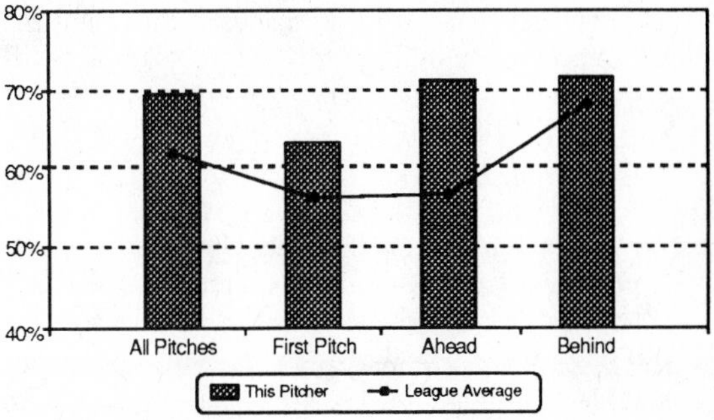

1990 Situational Stats

	W	L	ERA	Sv	IP		AB	H	HR	RBI	AVG
Home	0	3	1.72	16	31.1	LHB	110	23	2	15	.209
Road	1	1	2.92	14	24.2	RHB	97	24	3	6	.247
Day	1	2	3.10	5	20.1	Sc Pos	43	10	2	16	.233
Night	0	2	1.77	25	35.2	Clutch	154	37	4	18	.240

1990 Rankings (American League)

- 3rd in save percentage (88.2%)
- 4th in first batter efficiency (.130)
- 8th in saves (30) and save opportunities (34)
- 9th lowest batting average allowed vs. left-handed batters (.209)
- Led the Mariners in saves, games finished (45), save opportunites, save percentage, lowest batting average allowed vs. left-handed pitchers and first batter efficiency

PITCHING:

Occasionally a pitcher comes along who is so versatile that it hurts his own career. Bill Swift is one of those pitchers -- usually described as "rubber- armed" -- who can start, work middle relief and even work as the closer when necessary. For most of his Seattle tenure, Swift has pitched long relief and filled in when a starter went down. It's an undefined role, and Swift had only so-so results going into last season.

Through last year's All-Star break Swift was still in long relief, and was having his best season with a 2.29 ERA. Then, when Russ Swan went down with elbow trouble, Swift moved into the rotation. The entire starting staff promptly took off. From July 8 until August 24 -- when Swift went back to the bullpen after Mike Schooler was hurt -- Seattle starters posted a combined earned run average of 2.76. Swift himself was brilliant, dropping his own ERA to 1.81 at one point and leaving only two games earlier than the seventh. In one of those games, Gary Gaetti hit Swift on the forehead with a line drive. Showing his mettle, Swift didn't miss a start.

After Schooler went down, Swift went back to the bullpen, leading the team with five saves in the last five weeks. A ground ball pitcher who keeps the ball in play, Swift is not the classic closer, but he performed well nevertheless.

The key to Swift's improvement last year was better command of his sinking fastball, and a good slider. In the past, the sinker had straightened out when he brought it up in order to throw it for strikes; Swift was finally able to solve that problem. He still needs to run the sinker away from lefthanders better.

HOLDING RUNNERS AND FIELDING:

Swift is one of the best fielding pitchers in the game, and that helps a sinker ball pitcher immensely. He has an adequate move to first, with some deception, and delivers the ball quickly. He's not easy to run on, which also helps a sinker-baller.

OVERALL:

Swift is one of those pitchers who can be the key to a team's success: with his ability to do quality work in various roles, he's like a disaster-insurance policy. Other teams have asked about his availability, and to fill a larger need, Seattle could give him up. But it would take a pretty tempting offer. If Scott Bankhead, Rich DeLucia and/or Russ Swan don't make the starting rotation in camp, Swift might wind up back in there.

BILL SWIFT

Position: RP/SP
Bats: R **Throws:** R
Ht: 6' 0" **Wt:** 180

Opening Day Age: 29
Born: 10/27/61 in South Portland, ME
ML Seasons: 5

Overall Statistics

	W	L	ERA	G	GS	Sv	IP	H	R	BB	SO	HR
1990	6	4	2.39	55	8	6	128.0	135	46	21	42	4
Career	29	38	4.32	182	86	7	668.2	753	373	227	244	34

How Often He Throws Strikes

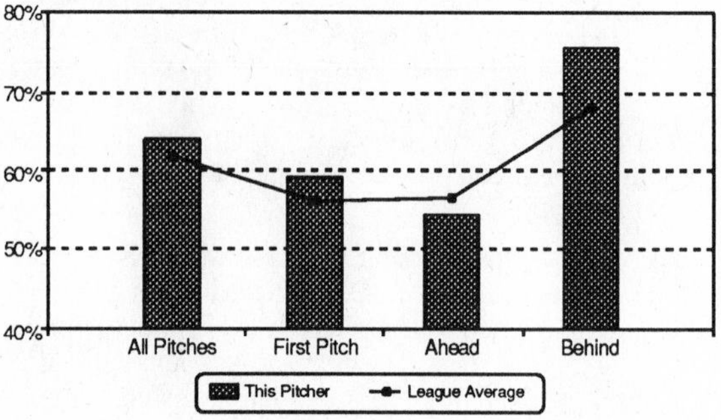

1990 Situational Stats

	W	L	ERA	Sv	IP		AB	H	HR	RBI	AVG
Home	3	1	1.34	2	53.2	LHB	216	62	4	27	.287
Road	3	3	3.15	4	74.1	RHB	280	73	0	27	.261
Day	4	1	1.50	1	36.0	Sc Pos	136	34	0	45	.250
Night	2	3	2.74	5	92.0	Clutch	129	36	2	14	.279

1990 Rankings (American League)

- 3rd in balks (3)
- 8th in hit batsmen (7)
- Led the Mariners in hit batsmen and balks

DAVE VALLE

Position: C
Bats: R **Throws:** R
Ht: 6' 2" **Wt:** 200

Opening Day Age: 30
Born: 10/30/60 in Bayside, NY
ML Seasons: 7

HITTING:

Signed as a second-round pick in 1978, when the Seattle franchise was in its second season, Dave Valle symbolizes the travails of the organization perfectly. Seemingly loaded with ability, Valle has simply never put it all together. The roadblock to progress has been his health.

Since his debut in '84, Valle has been on the disabled list seven times in seven years and has missed over a season (214 days) of playing time. He calls himself the living example of frustration, bristles at suggestions that he is brittle and wonders when, or if, he will ever get a clear chance to show what he can do.

Most scouts wonder the same. Valle is a fearless receiver, and that's great . . . but he's been injured four times in collisions at the plate. It always seems that he gets hurt when he's in a hot streak. Valle's worst break came in 1989, when a cheap shot from Milwaukee's Bill Spiers put him on the shelf just when he was off to a hot start, hitting .285. Last year, he was hitting .263 with 13 RBI in 30 games when he went out with a cracked rib in early May. When Valle came back, he stopped hitting, batting only .175 with 20 RBI in his final 77 games.

Over the years, Valle has become more aware of the need to control his swing, but it still has a pronounced hitch. He opens his front shoulder too much, and as a result, breaking balls away hurt him badly. When he connects, though, Valle has the power to hit mistakes a long way.

BASERUNNING:

Valle is a liability on the base paths. Not only is he slow, but he sometimes exhibits poor judgement and runs into outs. He has stolen only three bases in his seven-year major league career, but did log one in 1990. It took him three attempts.

FIELDING:

Valle can catch and throw with nearly anyone. His footwork is usually flawless and his arm is second to none. He annually ranks in the league's top three defensive catchers and deserves a large share of credit for helping develop Seattle's outstanding group of young pitchers.

OVERALL:

During organizational meetings late last season, the Mariners discussed the possibility of looking for more catching. However, since front-line catchers come to each organization about once a decade, it is most likely Valle will be back as the regular in 1991. He has a lot of tools, and when his intelligence finally controls his intensity, the talent may come out -- but he'll have to stay healthy.

Overall Statistics

	G	AB	R	H	D	T	HR	RBI	SB	BB	SO	AVG
1990	107	308	37	66	15	0	7	33	1	45	48	.214
Career	454	1388	154	328	61	8	42	193	3	116	193	.236

Where He Hits the Ball

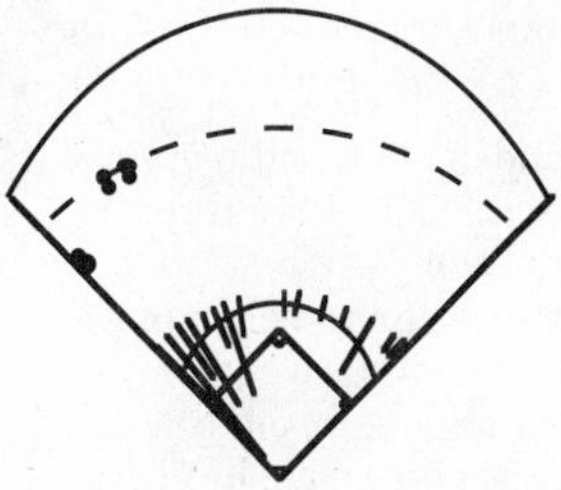

Vs. LHP

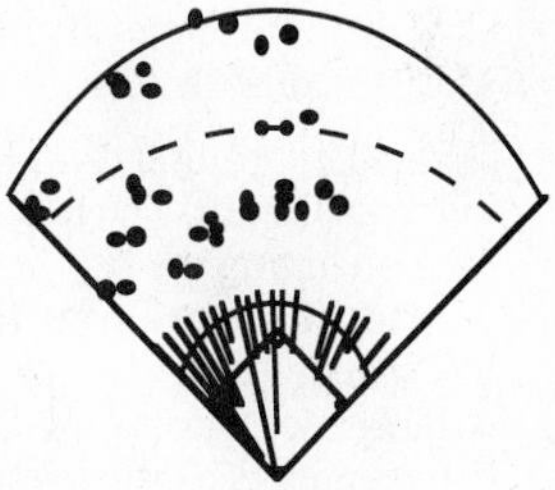

Vs. RHP

1990 Situational Stats

	AB	H	HR	RBI	AVG		AB	H	HR	RBI	AVG
Home	131	26	1	13	.198	LHP	104	21	2	10	.202
Road	177	40	6	20	.226	RHP	204	45	5	23	.221
Day	78	19	1	5	.244	Sc Pos	90	21	1	25	.233
Night	230	47	6	28	.204	Clutch	49	9	0	1	.184

1990 Rankings (American League)

- 1st lowest batting average with the bases loaded (.000)
- 4th in hit by pitch (7)
- Led the Mariners in hit by pitch
- Led AL catchers in hit by pitch and fielding percentage (.997)

HITTING:

Omar Vizquel missed the first three months of last season with a knee injury suffered in spring training, so it took a little while for people to notice how much stronger he had become. Vizquel is still no match for Cal Ripken or Alan Trammell, but gone are the days when pitchers could literally knock the bat out of his hands.

At 5-9 and 165 pounds (at most), Vizquel is built like fellow Venezuelan Luis Aparicio. The Mariners don't expect him to play like Aparicio, but they were pleased with how much more polished he was last year than in 1989, when he was rushed into service after Rey Quinones essentially quit the club. Vizquel, with greater endurance, raised his average by 27 points to .247; gone was the late-season fade which caused his average to plummet. A permanent ninth in the batting order, he drove in only 18 runs in his 255 at-bats. He'll have to improve that figure, and the Mariners think he can.

Vizquel is a natural right-handed hitter and is improving from the left. The feeling is that he should concentrate on hitting the ball in one zone, preferably on the ground; he hits too many fly balls for a small man who has speed. The M's think he can improve his hitting with men on base, which is often the result of confidence and concentration. But they wish Vizquel would show more patience at the plate. He drew 28 walks as a rookie, but only 18 a year ago.

BASERUNNING:

Vizquel is an intelligent runner who studies pitchers and can steal a base. He still doesn't run much, but he swiped four bases in five attempts last year after going only one-for-five as a rookie. The expectation is that he will work harder and become a better-than-average baserunner. Seattle does not hesitate to hit-and-run with him on base.

FIELDING:

Watching Vizquel take pre-game infield can be worth the price of admission. He does everything but juggle balls while exhibiting a wonderful pair of hands and superb glove and body control. The problem is that during games, he sometimes gets a little too flamboyant, and lapses into careless mistakes. But Vizquel made only seven errors a year ago, and he has steadily improved playing hitters.

OVERALL:

Two years ago, the Mariners almost dealt Vizquel to the Mets, and even at the start of last year, the club still wasn't sure if he was a major-league shortstop. But now they feel that Vizquel is a promising player who will continue his improvement with experience.

OMAR VIZQUEL

Position: SS
Bats: B **Throws:** R
Ht: 5' 9" **Wt:** 165

Opening Day Age: 23
Born: 4/24/67 in Caracas, Venezuela
ML Seasons: 2

Overall Statistics

	G	AB	R	H	D	T	HR	RBI	SB	BB	SO	AVG
1990	81	255	19	63	3	2	2	18	4	18	22	.247
Career	224	642	64	148	10	5	3	38	5	46	62	.231

Where He Hits the Ball

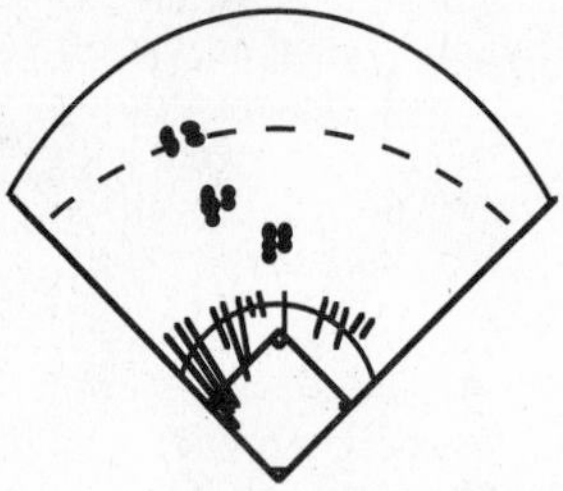

Vs. LHP

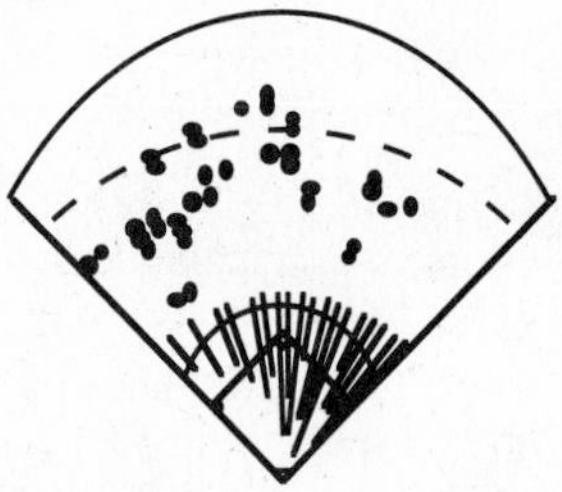

Vs. RHP

1990 Situational Stats

	AB	H	HR	RBI	AVG		AB	H	HR	RBI	AVG
Home	114	27	0	6	.237	LHP	81	19	1	8	.235
Road	141	36	2	12	.255	RHP	174	44	1	10	.253
Day	68	18	0	1	.265	Sc Pos	70	12	1	15	.171
Night	187	45	2	17	.241	Clutch	43	10	0	1	.233

1990 Rankings (American League)

➟ Led the Mariners in sacrifice hits (10)

MATT YOUNG

Position: SP
Bats: L **Throws:** L
Ht: 6' 3" **Wt:** 205

Opening Day Age: 32
Born: 8/9/58 in Pasadena, CA
ML Seasons: 7

PITCHING:

The Mariners spent a lot of time toward the end of last season figuring out if Matt Young deserved a three-year contract for $5-6 million. That is what Young was shooting for after a puzzling 1990 performance. Should his 8-18 record be the prime consideration, or his 3.51 ERA? Was the problem shaky support of three runs or less in 19 of his starts, or did he just pitch well enough to lose? Do you focus on his seven complete games or his league-leading nine errors and his team-record 15 wild pitches? His 107 walks (fourth in the league) or his 176 strikeouts (eighth)? How about Young's health? Do the Mariners worry about two years of elbow miseries in 1988-89 or do they look at his 225 innings in 1990?

Young's 1990 season was just good enough to tease potential suitors. Though apparently recovered from elbow troubles, he got off to a 2-9 start. Rust may have been the problem, as Young hadn't pitched much in two years. In the second half he improved greatly, turning in a 2.90 ERA after the All Star break. Still, he had his sixth losing season in seven major league years, and his lifetime record stands at 51-78.

After making the AL All-Star team as a Seattle rookie in 1983, Young has shown glimpses of his early promise. In a 1985 Sports Illustrated story, Wade Boggs and Don Mattingly agreed he was the toughest pitcher in the league for them to face. While he still sometimes falls victim to overthrowing, he throws a fastball that hits 87-92 on the slow gun. He also throws a curveball that is rated among the top three or four in the game -- that is, when Young is not bouncing it in the dirt. His good stuff is as good as anyone, but he often rushes and gets his pitches up in the zone at bad times.

HOLDING RUNNERS AND FIELDING:

Young is the worst fielding pitcher in baseball. Period. He often muffs grounders, and when he gets the ball there is no telling where his throw will go. He failed as a reliever largely because of his inability to deal with bunting situations. In holding runners, Young is better but still does not have a good enough move for a lefthander. He makes up some time by being quick to the plate.

OVERALL:

Every staff needs workhorses, but the Mariners have four starters who worked 189-plus innings last year. They need winners, pure and simple. Seattle was interested in re-signing Young, but given his consistent losing record, they weren't about to break the bank.

Overall Statistics

	W	L	ERA	G	GS	Sv	IP	H	R	BB	SO	HR
1990	8	18	3.51	34	33	0	225.1	198	106	107	176	15
Career	51	78	4.26	264	131	25	956.0	971	519	413	666	80

How Often He Throws Strikes

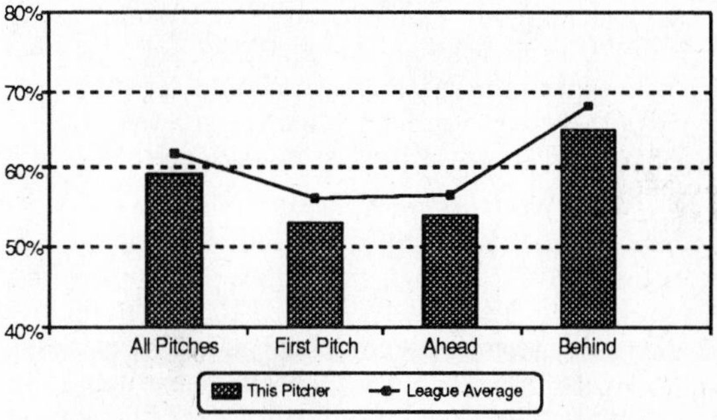

1990 Situational Stats

	W	L	ERA	Sv	IP		AB	H	HR	RBI	AVG
Home	4	10	2.69	0	134.0	LHB	101	16	0	7	.158
Road	4	8	4.73	0	91.1	RHB	735	182	15	79	.248
Day	5	5	3.09	0	78.2	Sc Pos	200	46	6	76	.230
Night	3	13	3.74	0	146.2	Clutch	73	27	4	9	.370

1990 Rankings (American League)

- 1st in GDPs induced (27) and most errors by a pitcher (9)
- 2nd in losses (18), wild pitches (16), groundball/flyball ratio (2.23) and worst ERA on the road (4.73)
- 3rd in complete games (7), lowest winning percentage (.308) and GDPs induced per 9 innings (1.08)
- 4th in walks allowed (107), runners caught stealing (14) and least run support per 9 innings (3.75)
- Led the Mariners in losses, games started (33), complete games, wild pitches, runners caught stealing, GDPs induced and lowest slugging percentage allowed (.328)

SCOTT BANKHEAD

Position: SP
Bats: R **Throws:** R
Ht: 5'10" **Wt:** 185

Opening Day Age: 27
Born: 7/31/63 in Raleigh, NC
ML Seasons: 5

Overall Statistics

	W	L	ERA	G	GS	Sv	IP	H	R	BB	SO	HR
1990	0	2	11.08	4	4	0	13.0	18	16	7	10	2
Career	38	34	4.18	109	100	0	628.2	609	315	182	441	78

PITCHING, FIELDING & HOLDING RUNNERS:

Scott Bankhead went into last year's short spring training as the Mariners' pitching ace, and came out of it with another in a series of shoulder problems. With the exception of four starts, only one of them good, Bankhead was lost for the season.

It was an old story for Bankhead. The Mariners got him from Kansas City in the Danny Tartabull deal before the 1987 season, and Bankhead arrived with a weakness in his shoulder. He had surgery to remove scar tissue after that season, but had more troubles in early 1988. Bankhead's only healthy year was 1989, and it was a good one. Succeeding Mark Langston as the staff leader, Bankhead went 14-6 with a 3.34 ERA. But once again he had to undergo surgery, this time to remove bone spurs.

Bankhead is known for his all-business approach to pitching during the seaon, even to the point of severely limiting his golf game, at which he excels. His basic stuff (fastball, breaking ball, change) is not exceptional. But Bankhead knows his limitations, most notably lack of movement on his fastball, and makes up for them with superb control and concentration. He fields his position extremely well, and has a good pickoff move.

OVERALL:

Bankhead is expected to be healthy again in 1991, but he can't really be counted on. He has worked over 150 innings only once in his five-year career; the Mariners would be thrilled if he fit into the number four or five slot in the rotation and stayed there all year.

RICH DELUCIA

Position: SP
Bats: R **Throws:** R
Ht: 6' 0" **Wt:** 180

Opening Day Age: 26
Born: 10/7/64 in Reading, PA
ML Seasons: 1

Overall Statistics

	W	L	ERA	G	GS	Sv	IP	H	R	BB	SO	HR
1990	1	2	2.00	5	5	0	36.0	30	9	9	20	2
Career	1	2	2.00	5	5	0	36.0	30	9	9	20	2

PITCHING, FIELDING & HOLDING RUNNERS:

Normally you discount September stats because they don't give a real indication of what a youngster can do. That may not be the case for Rich DeLucia, who started the 1990 season in A ball at San Bernardino, advanced through AA Williamsport and AAA Calgary, and finally made five starts for the Mariners. In those games DeLucia pitched against first-division clubs four times, including a strong debut against AL East champion Boston. He was lifted with a 2-1 seventh inning lead in that game, which Seattle went on to lose 10-2.

In his next start, DeLucia held California to a 1-1 tie in seven innings. Then he beat Texas and lost to Detroit, allowing only two earned runs in each game, and finally lost a complete game to the White Sox, 2-1. In that short time, DeLucia showed good command of his stuff that is generally a little weak. But to compensate for a fastball thrown about 85-86 MPH, DeLucia keeps the ball down and throws strikes to anyone. He's had a two-to-one or better strikeout-to-walk ratio at every stop in his career. His glove work appeared okay, and his move to first is decent enough.

OVERALL:

DeLucia, a sixth round pick out of Tennessee in 1986, made a strong impression in 1990 and may figure in the final makeup of the staff this spring. He figures to either start or possibly pitch in long relief, freeing Bill Swift for the rotation.

GENE HARRIS

Position: RP
Bats: R **Throws:** R
Ht: 5'11" **Wt:** 190

Opening Day Age: 26
Born: 12/5/64 in Sebring, FL
ML Seasons: 2

Overall Statistics

	W	L	ERA	G	GS	Sv	IP	H	R	BB	SO	HR
1990	1	2	4.74	25	0	0	38.0	31	25	30	43	5
Career	3	7	5.42	46	6	1	91.1	94	63	55	68	9

PITCHING, FIELDING & HOLDING RUNNERS:

For weeks before the Mariners sent Mark Langston to the Expos in 1989, there was no deal because Montreal flatly refused to part with young reliever Gene Harris. Desperate for Langston, the Expos finally said yes. But the Mariners heard that many of Montreal's player development people were very upset at letting Harris go.

Little wonder. Harris, a superb athlete, has tremendous promise. A former starting defensive back at Tulane, Harris is the fastest player on the Mariners and has been used as a pinch runner. His pitching abilities start with a fastball that has been regularly clocked in the mid to upper 90's, and a sharp breaking ball. The problem is earning a chance to work consistently. With the Mariners fighting to stay at or near .500, Manager Jim Lefebvre was reluctant to use Harris or his other young reliever, Brent Knackert.

Harris made 25 appearances before suffering a fractured right tibia last September. He was usually sharp when given regular work. He averaged over a strikeout per inning, but had control problems, perhaps due to lack of use. As would figure, the athletic Harris fields his position well. He also does a decent job of holding runners.

OVERALL:

Should there be any problem with closer Mike Schooler, Harris might be the first pitcher Seattle looks to as a replacement. He will undoubtedly be given regular work in the exhibition season to gauge his progress, especially his control. Much is expected of him.

TRACY JONES

Position: LF/DH
Bats: R **Throws:** R
Ht: 6' 3" **Wt:** 220

Opening Day Age: 30
Born: 3/31/61 in Inglewood, CA
ML Seasons: 5

Overall Statistics

	G	AB	R	H	D	T	HR	RBI	SB	BB	SO	AVG
1990	75	204	23	53	8	1	6	24	1	9	25	.260
Career	414	1128	143	312	48	5	24	140	60	82	118	.277

HITTING, FIELDING, BASERUNNING:

Almost two years removed from Cincinnati, Tracy Jones had mixed emotions watching his old teammates win the World Series last year. Jones was sad because he'd been through so many experiences with the Reds' players, but happy because he'd finally come to an organization which may finally give him playing time.

Of course, Jones has heard this story before, and the Mariners went into the off-season thinking hard about signing a right-handed power hitter for left field. Jones has been with five teams in the last four years, and is no longer the glittering prospect who batted .349 in his debut with the '86 Reds. Jones' once-outstanding speed has been reduced by three knee operations.

Last year, Jones was hitting well as a Mariner after arriving from Detroit for Darnell Coles. But then his right knee locked and he was forced to undergo surgery for torn cartilage. Before the injury, Jones impressed the club with his bat speed and plate discipline. His play seemed to spark the Mariners, who went 26-21 from the date they acquired him until the injury. Defensively, he needed more playing time.

OVERALL:

Barring a trade or free agent signing, Jones figures to share left field in '91 with Ken Griffey, Sr. The Mariners, who had wanted Jones for a long time before finally obtaining him, figure to give him some playing time. But there is a question about how much his third knee operation will affect his play.

BRENT KNACKERT

Position: RP
Bats: R **Throws:** R
Ht: 6' 4" **Wt:** 185

Opening Day Age: 21
Born: 8/1/69 in Los Angeles, CA
ML Seasons: 1

Overall Statistics

	W	L	ERA	G	GS	Sv	IP	H	R	BB	SO	HR
1990	1	1	6.51	24	2	0	37.1	50	28	21	28	5
Career	1	1	6.51	24	2	0	37.1	50	28	21	28	5

PITCHING, FIELDING & HOLDING RUNNERS:

Depending on which side you ask, there are conflicting stories on how the White Sox and Brent Knackert parted company. Whatever the case, the Sox, who had drafted Knackert in the second round in 1987, took him off their protected roster even though he was 24-15 in three seasons of A ball. The Mets promptly grabbed him in the Rule Five draft, meaning that they would have to keep him on their major league roster all season. New York wasn't quite willing to do that, but Seattle was, so the clubs made a waiver deal before the 1990 season started.

Knackert, who won't be 21 until August, struggled with inconsistent opportunities for work in Seattle. However, there were flashes of brilliance. After calling Knackert's pitches in a game late in May, umpire Terry Cooney said he had the best stuff he'd seen to that point in the season. Knackert's primary pitch is a fastball with outstanding movement. He also has a good curveball. Scouts say his biggest asset is fearlessness, but they are wary of his propensity to eat the wrong things and get out of shape.

OVERALL:

Barring the unforeseen, Knackert will start the 1991 season where he should have been last season -- in the minors, possibly Class AA. The Mariners showed a tremendous amount of faith in his ability by drafting him, keeping him on their roster all season and not letting him get too beaten up. Now they have to make up for the year of development he essentially lost.

TINO MARTINEZ

Position: 1B
Bats: L **Throws:** R
Ht: 6' 2" **Wt:** 205

Opening Day Age: 23
Born: 12/7/67 in Tampa, FL
ML Seasons: 1

Overall Statistics

	G	AB	R	H	D	T	HR	RBI	SB	BB	SO	AVG
1990	24	68	4	15	4	0	0	5	0	9	9	.221
Career	24	68	4	15	4	0	0	5	0	9	9	.221

HITTING, FIELDING, BASERUNNING:

According to everything one heard before Tino Martinez was called up last August, the former number-one draft choice couldn't miss. Star of the gold medal-winning team at the Seoul Olympics, Martinez was chosen USA Today's Minor League Player of the Year last year after batting .319 with 17 HR and 92 RBI at AAA Calgary. After recalling him, Seattle was so eager to see Martinez play first base that they moved Pete O'Brien to left field.

Martinez began sensationally, getting hits in his first two at-bats against Texas's Bobby Witt, and three more in his next game. But then he went into a one-for-16 slump, and Manager Jim Lefebvre stopped using him. Martinez suffered from lack of use, but he never looked overmatched. He showed plenty of bat speed, a good eye and ability to turn on a pitch inside. His biggest problem was adjusting to a major league strike zone. He displayed good footwork at first base and fielded exceptionally well, but had no better than average speed on the bases.

OVERALL:

If Martinez has a big spring, Seattle will be hard-pressed to find a reason to keep him at Triple A. This will cause a major logjam since O'Brien must play to justify his $7.6 million free agent contract, Alvin Davis is the DH and Ken Griffey, Sr. appears to be returning in left field. But if Martinez is ready, someone will have to step aside.

RUSS SWAN

Position: SP
Bats: L **Throws:** L
Ht: 6' 4" **Wt:** 210

Opening Day Age: 27
Born: 1/3/64 in Fremont, CA
ML Seasons: 2

Overall Statistics

	W	L	ERA	G	GS	Sv	IP	H	R	BB	SO	HR
1990	2	4	3.65	13	9	0	49.1	48	26	22	16	3
Career	2	6	4.50	15	11	0	56.0	59	36	26	18	7

PITCHING, FIELDING & HOLDING RUNNERS:

When the Mariners traded Gary Eave to San Francisco for Russ Swan, they were finally getting their man. The M's had drafted the lefthander from nearby Kennewick, WA, in the secondary phase of the June 1984 draft, but couldn't sign him. Swan went on to pitch at Texas A & M and finally signed with the Giants in 1986.

In obtaining Swan, Seattle reasoned that a southpaw with some ability was much more useful to them than a righthander of the same apparent level, like Eave. The reasoning proved true. While Eave never came back to the majors with the desperate-for-pitching Giants, Swan came up to Seattle and no-hit the Tigers for seven innings in his debut. Suffering from tendinitis all year, Swan was a different pitcher than he had been in the Giant organization. He threw mostly offspeed stuff with a good sinker. He later went on the disabled list twice and had surgery at the end of the season. Before he left for good, he threw harder, getting his fastball up to 90 MPH with good movement. He showed good break to his slider and an improved split-finger pitch. Slow to the plate, Swan will have to improve his move to first base.

OVERALL:

The left-handed Swan showed enough last year to warrant a long look as a lefty long man and spot starter. If healthy, he'll have to pitch his way off the staff in spring training in order to miss making the roster.

BRAD ARNSBERG

Position: RP
Bats: R **Throws:** R
Ht: 6' 4" **Wt:** 215

Opening Day Age: 27
Born: 8/20/63 in Seattle, WA
ML Seasons: 4

PITCHING:

Former Yankee prospect Brad Arnsberg has had an uphill struggle to establish himself as a major league pitcher, but he may finally have turned the corner last year. It hasn't been easy. Traded to the Rangers in the Don Slaught deal after the 1987 season, Arnsberg sat out the entire 1988 season after undergoing the "Tommy John" elbow surgery, which involved transplanting a tendon from his left wrist to his right elbow. After a so-so year in 1989, Arnsberg was released almost as soon as the 1990 season opened.

Arnsberg can credit the re-birth of his career to the re-birth of his breaking ball. Re-signed in May, he made two appearances that month, but from then on he was a busy man as he got into a total of 53 games, second on the club to Kenny Rogers. The injury to Jeff Russell contributed to his workload, but Arnsberg was due for a break.

Once he got the chance, Arnsberg pitched well. His 2.15 ERA was the best on the squad. He only recorded five saves, but that was a career high, and one of them was Nolan Ryan's 300th win. Going against the odds, the big righthander held lefties to a .225 batting average. Righties didn't fare much better, hitting .242. That was a big improvement from 1989, when Arnsberg struggled against lefties.

Arnsberg's basic stuff is pretty good. His fastball is in the high 80s, nothing exceptional, but he balances it with a curve and a forkball which he throws as an offspeed pitch. The curve is his best pitch, and it regained its bite as his arm got stronger last year. Arnsberg relies on keeping hitters off stride, but controlling his pitches has always been a problem. He gives up a good number of walks, which continued to be a problem in 1990.

HOLDING RUNNERS AND FIELDING:

In Arnsberg's 62.2 innings, there was only one attempted steal (it was successful), a telltale sign that he keeps close tabs on runners. Arnsberg is a good, sure-handed fielder who handles his position well.

OVERALL:

The Rangers showed their confidence in Arnsberg by the sheer number of times he came out of the pen. It is the unhappy lot of middle relievers to fall in the shadows of starters and stoppers, but Arnsberg's ERA must be welcome on a team with a bullpen ERA of 3.48. With his arm healed at last, his career may finally be on track.

Overall Statistics

	W	L	ERA	G	GS	Sv	IP	H	R	BB	SO	HR
1990	6	1	2.15	53	0	5	62.2	56	20	33	44	4
Career	9	5	3.39	77	4	6	138.0	136	62	69	87	16

How Often He Throws Strikes

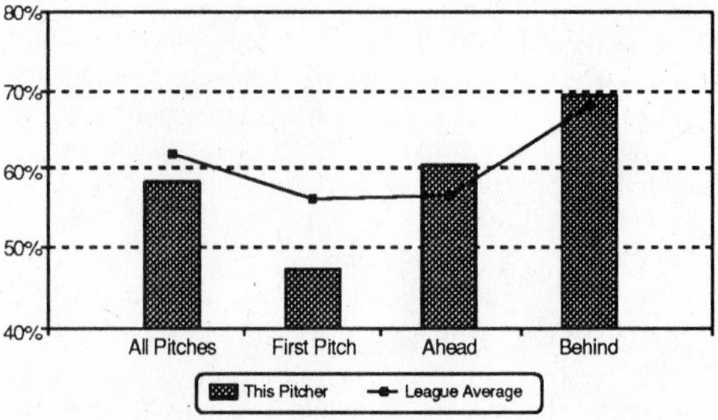

1990 Situational Stats

	W	L	ERA	Sv	IP		AB	H	HR	RBI	AVG
Home	4	0	2.02	2	35.2	LHB	89	20	2	12	.225
Road	2	1	2.33	3	27.0	RHB	149	36	2	17	.242
Day	3	1	0.77	0	11.2	Sc Pos	67	15	2	26	.224
Night	3	0	2.47	5	51.0	Clutch	133	33	1	13	.248

1990 Rankings (American League)

- 3rd in highest percentage of inherited runners scored (40.0%)
- 9th in holds (11)
- Led the Rangers in holds and first batter efficiency (.265)

PITCHING:

The fourth player picked in the 1986 draft -- behind Jeff King, Greg Swindell and Matt Williams -- Kevin Brown has turned in two steady seasons with the Rangers, going 12-9 and 12-10. The Rangers expect a little more from Brown, however, and he might be able to give it to them -- if he can stay healthy.

At midseason last year, Brown looked like he might be on his way to a 20-win campaign. On July 23rd, he was 12-7 with a 3.28 ERA. But then an inflamed right elbow began bothering him, and Brown wasn't able to win another game all season. He finished with an 0-3 streak during which he allowed a 4.93 ERA in his last six starts. Brown finally went on the shelf and did not pitch after September 4th. That was eerily reminiscent of 1989, when he went 1-3 with a 7.40 ERA in his last five starts and did not pitch after September 8.

Brown possesses a good fastball, but he's not a fireballer of the Nolan Ryan/Bobby Witt ilk. Instead, his fastball is a sinker, and he wins by making batters hit the ball on the ground. Does he ever! Brown led the American League in ground ball/fly ball ratio last year with an amazing 3.44; Matt Young of Seattle, the nearest pitcher to him, had a ratio of only 2.2. Not surprisingly, Brown also induces a lot of double play balls.

Durable when he's healthy, Brown was second on the club in complete games last year with six out of his 26 starts. He had a 3.60 ERA while batters hit a respectable .256; both these figures are above his three-season average, but of course, he was pitching in pain a good part of the time. Rangers' pitchers tossed five shutouts and Brown had two of those.

HOLDING RUNNERS AND FIELDING:

Brown was tied for third in the league with 209 throws to first base. He likes to make sure the runners stay honest, so he simply continues to remind them that he is watching. It worked, as only seven runners stole on him all year (four were caught). Brown gets himself into good position to field grounders, but is sometimes careless and committed three errors last year.

OVERALL:

Brown may finally be ready to become a big winner in 1991. If he's healthy, he'll certainly get more than 26 starts, and that's really all he needs to become a 15-18 game winner. Should he get exceptional support, he has the stuff to win 20. But his tender elbow will have to cooperate.

KEVIN BROWN

Position: SP
Bats: R **Throws:** R
Ht: 6' 4" **Wt:** 198

Opening Day Age: 26
Born: 3/14/65 in McIntyre, GA
ML Seasons: 4

Overall Statistics

	W	L	ERA	G	GS	Sv	IP	H	R	BB	SO	HR
1990	12	10	3.60	26	26	0	180.0	175	84	60	88	13
Career	26	20	3.52	59	59	0	399.1	381	182	138	208	25

How Often He Throws Strikes

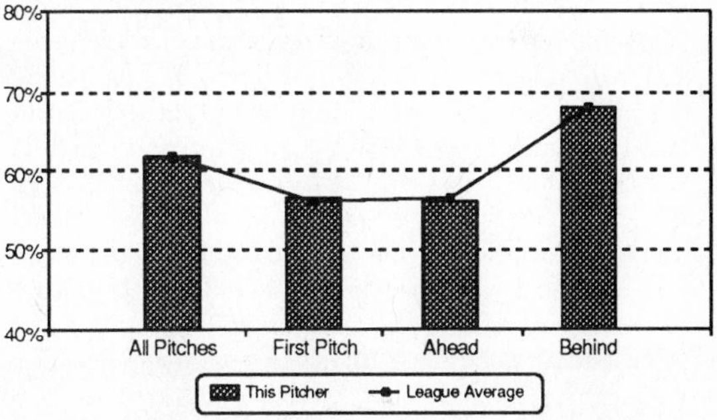

1990 Situational Stats

	W	L	ERA	Sv	IP		AB	H	HR	RBI	AVG
Home	6	4	2.58	0	87.1	LHB	337	84	6	35	.249
Road	6	6	4.56	0	92.2	RHB	348	91	7	36	.261
Day	4	2	4.66	0	48.1	Sc Pos	152	40	5	60	.263
Night	8	8	3.21	0	131.2	Clutch	93	25	5	12	.269

1990 Rankings (American League)

- ➟ 1st in groundball/flyball ratio (3.44),least pitches thrown per batter (3.40), and most GDPs induced per 9 innings (1.20)
- ➟ 3rd in pickoff throws (209)
- ➟ 5th in GDPs induced (24), ERA at home (2.58) and worst ERA on the road (4.57)
- ➟ Led the Rangers in shutouts (2), GDPs induced, groundball/flyball ratio, lowest stolen base percentage allowed (63.6%), least pitches thrown per batter (3.40), most run support per 9 innings (5.2), most GDPs induced per 9 innings and ERA at home

STEVE BUECHELE

Position: 3B
Bats: R **Throws:** R
Ht: 6' 2" **Wt:** 190

Opening Day Age: 29
Born: 9/26/61 in Lancaster, CA
ML Seasons: 6

Overall Statistics

	G	AB	R	H	D	T	HR	RBI	SB	BB	SO	AVG
1990	91	251	30	54	10	0	7	30	1	27	63	.215
Career	759	2283	279	540	98	11	76	272	14	205	451	.237

Where He Hits the Ball

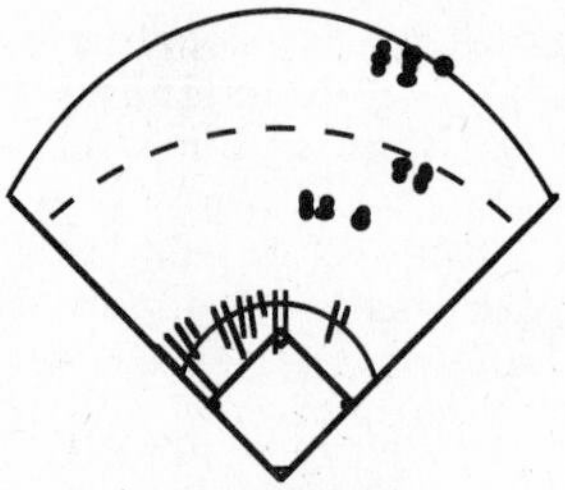

Vs. LHP

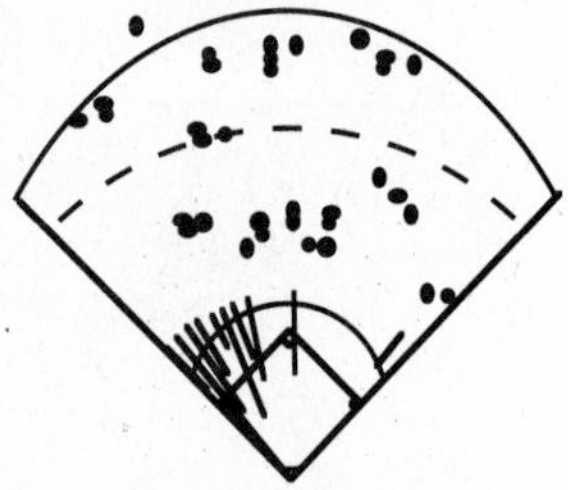

Vs. RHP

1990 Situational Stats

	AB	H	HR	RBI	AVG		AB	H	HR	RBI	AVG
Home	136	33	5	21	.243	LHP	80	22	4	12	.275
Road	115	21	2	9	.183	RHP	171	32	3	18	.187
Day	43	11	1	5	.256	Sc Pos	65	16	2	23	.246
Night	208	43	6	25	.207	Clutch	34	8	0	2	.235

1990 Rankings (American League)

- Did not rank near the top or bottom in any category

HITTING:

When Steve Buechele was hit on the left wrist by an Eric Plunk pitch last April 21, you may as well have stopped tracking his season. Buechele ended up missing a total of 71 games due to the broken wrist, plus a later bout with strained rib muscles. Before April 21, he was hitting .290 and had belted three homers in just 31 at-bats. For the remainder of the season Buechele managed only four more homers in 220 at-bats. As it turned out, all the Rangers' third basemen accounted for only 49 RBI for the year. Buechele had 59 by himself in 1989.

Prior to the injury, Buechele's lifetime batting average was .239, and while that's nothing to brag about, he could remain a regular because of his good glove. Replacement Jeff Kunkel will have a tough time keeping the position if he continues to hit .215, because he is not the glove-man that Buechele is.

Buechele is a good hitter against offspeed pitches, but has had much less success against fastballs. He doesn't have very good strike zone judgment and will chase all kinds of heat, often putting himself in a hole where pitchers can work on him. Buechele has been particularly susceptible to the inside fastball, and one must wonder if suffering the broken wrist has made him even more plate-shy. That would be a big problem for him, because he was weak against righthanders to begin with.

BASERUNNING:

Never a base stealing threat, this was the one area where Buechele managed to match his 1989 performance. He stole one base in each season. The strained rib cage muscles could not have made running comfortable, but when healthy, Buechele is a pretty good baserunner, though one without a lot of speed.

FIELDING:

Buechele's career fielding percentage has always been among the tops for third-sackers, and he retains his reputation as one of the best at his position -- not spectacular, but very solid. Buechele has also logged time at second. He looks like a natural at the position, and his hitting is more acceptable for a middle infielder. But Julio Franco's presence prevents him from getting a shot second base.

OVERALL:

After five seasons as their regular third baseman, the Rangers know pretty much what to expect from Buechele: a low average, some power and a good glove. Because he hasn't hit like the top third-sackers, Buechele is always in danger of losing his job, but he'll probably begin 1991 as the regular once more.

JACK DAUGHERTY

Position: LF/1B/DH
Bats: B **Throws:** L
Ht: 6' 0" **Wt:** 185

Opening Day Age: 30
Born: 6/3/60 in Hialeah, FL
ML Seasons: 3

HITTING:

A professional hitter, Jack Daugherty has intrigued the Rangers by turning in two straight .300 seasons. He batted only 106 times as a 29-year-old rookie in 1989, so most people withheld their judgement about him. But Daugherty continued to hit when given over 300 at-bats last year. He led the American League in pinch hit at-bats with a club record 45. Daugherty and Rafael Palmeiro were the only Rangers to have four four-hit games in 1990.

Daugherty's hitting shouldn't have been a great surprise. He's hit .300 at every level of professional baseball; he even topped .400 once, with Helena in the Rookie League in 1984. The problem is that Daugherty has been primarily a first baseman, and he lacks home run power. So he's been released by both the Oakland and Montreal organizations, and was labeled as a "career minor leaguer" until Texas finally gave him a chance.

The Rangers think he may be a little better than that. Daugherty has shown them good power to the gaps, with 20 doubles in only 310 at-bats last year. He's also demonstrated an ability to handle all kinds of pitches, not just the fastball. A left-handed thrower who became a switch hitter, he has much more power batting lefty. He's a decent hitter from the right side (.273 last year), but he's much more of a slap hitter batting righty.

BASERUNNING:

A fine baserunner, Daugherty has both good speed and judgement on the bases. He was always a high percentage base stealer in the minors, but in the majors he's been extremely cautious, not even attempting a steal last year. He's a threat to swipe a few, but it would be a surprise if he reached double figures.

FIELDING:

Daugherty is a sure-handed glove man who won't embarrass a club in the field. His best position is first base, but with Rafael Palmeiro there he won't get much playing time. In the outfield he doesn't have great range, but is quick and gets a decent jump on the ball. His arm is below average, but not to the extent that runners will go crazy on him.

OVERALL:

Daugherty gives the Rangers a happy dilemma -- he is too good to sit on the bench, but without a trade there is no regular slot for him in the field. His best role as it stands now would be at designated hitter, but he batted only .224 in 67 DH at-bats last year. Daugherty is a good enough glove man that the Rangers may make a trade to open up a position for him.

Overall Statistics

	G	AB	R	H	D	T	HR	RBI	SB	BB	SO	AVG
1990	125	310	36	93	20	2	6	47	0	22	49	.300
Career	188	426	52	126	25	4	7	58	2	33	73	.296

Where He Hits the Ball

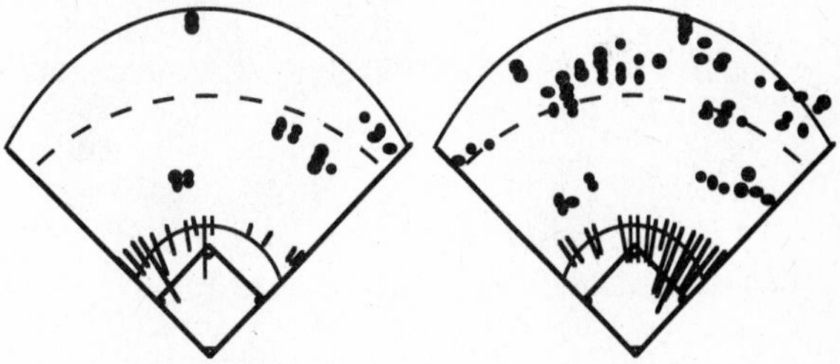

Vs. LHP　　Vs. RHP

1990 Situational Stats

	AB	H	HR	RBI	AVG		AB	H	HR	RBI	AVG
Home	164	51	5	25	.311	LHP	77	21	0	10	.273
Road	146	42	1	22	.288	RHP	233	72	6	37	.309
Day	76	22	2	12	.289	Sc Pos	81	22	0	32	.272
Night	234	71	4	35	.303	Clutch	64	16	2	6	.250

1990 Rankings (American League)

- 4th in batting average with 2 strikes (.261)
- Led the Rangers in least GDPs per GDP situation (7.0%) and batting average with 2 strikes

HITTING:

Julio Franco needed to go at least three-for-four in the final game of the 1990 season to hit .300 for the fifth consecutive year. He didn't make it, so he had to settle for a mere .296. Nonetheless he had another fine season, topped by becoming the first Ranger to be named Most Valuable Player in the All-Star game. Remarkably consistent, Franco hit .296 against left-handers and .295 against righties.

Most teams swing the outfield around to the right side when Franco is at the plate. He can spray the ball to all areas even though the last couple of fingers of his left hand are over the knob like a dead pull power hitter. That bat cocked over his helmet makes him appear to be unable to control it, but by the time the pitch is made, the bat is pretty much in the standard alignment for hitting.

Franco is tough on the high fastball, and will hit it where it's pitched. There is no secret about it when he decides to take a pitch. He is likely to stand there with the bat on his shoulder if he wants to look at one. More inclined to look these days, he led the team with a career-high 82 walks. But he also posted another career high with 83 strikeouts.

Franco drove in 69 runs last year. His RBI total was down considerably from 1989, when he had 92, but that figure had been his major league high. Franco's RBIs were down partly because he batted second a lot, and partly because he couldn't hope to match his 1989 average of .407 with men in scoring position.

BASERUNNING:

On the Rangers, only Gary Pettis had more steals than Franco's 31 (in 41 attempts). It was the third time that he had stolen more than 30. An aggressive baserunner, Franco will sometimes run himself into outs, but he also takes a lot of extra bases.

FIELDING:

Franco tied for first (with Harold Reynolds) for the dubious honor of committing the most errors by a second baseman with 19. Franco makes many excellent plays, but the more routine the hit, the more likely he will boot it. Franco has outstanding range, and watching him chase and catch a pop up at the foul line behind first base is a sheer joy.

OVERALL:

"The Three Amigos," Franco, Palmeiro, and Sierra, are a fixture on the right side of the Rangers' defensive alignment and Franco, the senior partner, has been a guiding figure for the whole team. How many people would have thought such a thing when he came over from Cleveland?

JULIO FRANCO

Position: 2B
Bats: R **Throws:** R
Ht: 6' 0" **Wt:** 165

Opening Day Age: 29
Born: 8/23/61 in San Pedro de Macoris, Dominican Republic
ML Seasons: 9

Overall Statistics

	G	AB	R	H	D	T	HR	RBI	SB	BB	SO	AVG
1990	157	582	96	172	27	1	11	69	31	82	83	.296
Career	1221	4720	680	1404	215	37	69	593	183	419	542	.297

Where He Hits the Ball

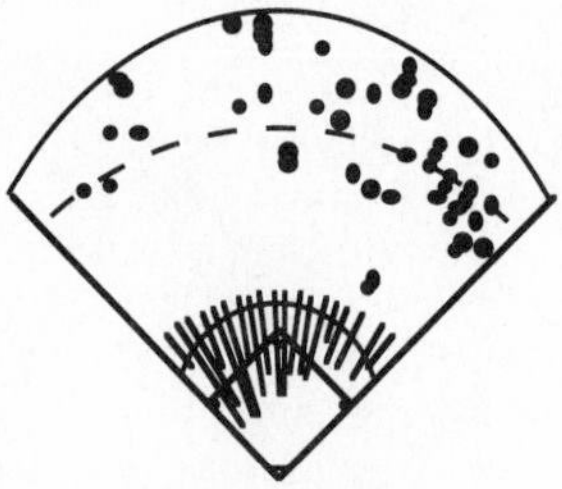

Vs. LHP

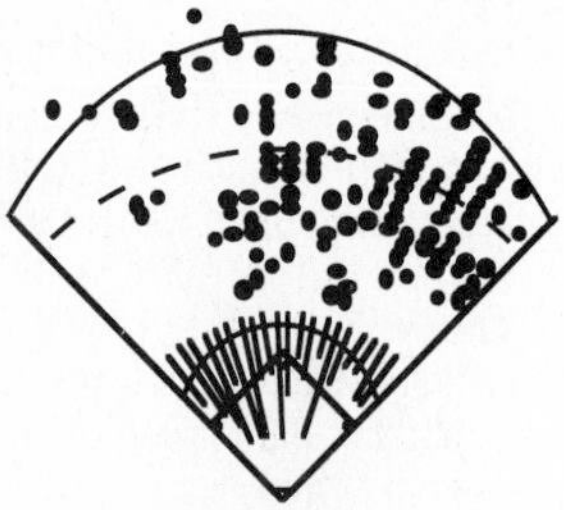

Vs. RHP

1990 Situational Stats

	AB	H	HR	RBI	AVG		AB	H	HR	RBI	AVG
Home	303	96	4	27	.317	LHP	179	53	3	19	.296
Road	279	76	7	42	.272	RHP	403	119	8	50	.295
Day	94	25	3	15	.266	Sc Pos	144	43	5	58	.299
Night	488	147	8	54	.301	Clutch	97	33	2	9	.340

1990 Rankings (American League)

- 2nd in singles (133)
- 4th in times on base (256)
- 6th in runs (96) and batting average at home (.317)
- Led the Rangers in runs, walks (82), times on base, pitches seen (2,558), plate appearances (670), on-base average (.383), groundball/flyball ratio (1.93), stolen base percentage (75.6%) and pitches seen per plate appearance (3.82)
- Led AL second basemen in batting average (.296), singles, total bases (234), RBIs (69), walks, times on base, on-base average and errors (19)

JUAN GONZALEZ

Position: CF
Bats: R **Throws:** R
Ht: 6' 3" **Wt:** 175

Opening Day Age: 21
Born: 10/16/69 in Vega Baja, Puerto Rico
ML Seasons: 2

HITTING:

Juan Gonzalez endeared himself to manager Bobby Valentine last year when he said he wanted to play and not to worry about limiting his number of at-bats. This was in reference to the very real possibility that Gonzalez, if he plays like he did at AAA Oklahoma City, could have been a contender for Rookie of the Year honors in 1991. Gonzalez preferred to get some major league experience last September, and because of that has logged too many at-bats (150 in 1989-90) to qualify as a rookie.

Rookie or not, Gonzalez is an outstanding prospect. At Oklahoma City, he had 29 homers, 101 RBI, and was named the American Association Most Valuable Player. Once he came up, he was hitless in his first 11 at-bats with the big club. But then he picked up the pace and recorded 12 extra-base hits, including four homers, for an excellent .522 slugging percentage.

Gonzalez batted only .258 at Oklahoma City, and hit over .265 only once during his five-year minor league career. If he's going to hit for a decent average in the majors, Gonzalez is going to have to cure his tendency to chase bad breaking balls. At Oklahoma City he drew only 32 walks (a career high) while striking out 109 times. He obviously needs work on his plate discipline, but then, he's still only 21.

BASERUNNING:

Gonzalez is not particularly fast and is not a base stealing threat. He has yet to reach double figures in steals, and at Tulsa in '89, was tossed out eight times in nine attempts. This part of his game needs work, as does his baserunning in general.

FIELDING:

A big man lacking great speed, Gonzalez has been able to play center field primarily because he has good instincts, an ability to play hitters and a strong arm. He may not be able to play center much longer because he's still growing. As he puts on size and weight, he may soon lack the range for the position. He would be a fine outfielder in left or right, however.

OVERALL:

Gonzalez is a tremendous power prospect, even more impressive than Ruben Sierra at the same age. But he'll likely hit for a low average until he gets more experience. One fact clouds the issue slightly -- Gonzalez missed the last few games of last season with bloated discs in his lower back. The word is that they are not serious.

Overall Statistics

	G	AB	R	H	D	T	HR	RBI	SB	BB	SO	AVG
1990	25	90	11	26	7	1	4	12	0	2	18	.289
Career	49	150	17	35	10	1	5	19	0	8	35	.233

Where He Hits the Ball

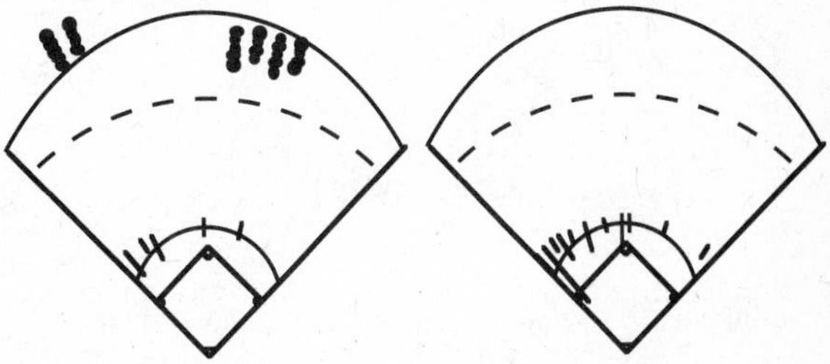

Vs. LHP   Vs. RHP

1990 Situational Stats

	AB	H	HR	RBI	AVG		AB	H	HR	RBI	AVG
Home	47	16	3	8	.340	LHP	24	7	1	3	.292
Road	43	10	1	4	.233	RHP	66	19	3	9	.288
Day	14	2	0	0	.143	Sc Pos	23	4	0	5	.174
Night	76	24	4	12	.316	Clutch	21	6	1	1	.286

1990 Rankings (American League)

- Did not rank near the top or bottom in any category

PITCHING:

After a decade of solid work in Texas, knuckleballer Charlie Hough finds himself apparently unwanted by the Rangers. It's difficult to figure out why. Hough will be 43 when the season opens, but he continues to be an effective pitcher, and 43 is not especially old for a knuckleballer. At the same age Phil Niekro went 17-4 for the Braves, and Niekro would continue to win in double figures through age 47. At 43, Hoyt Wilhelm was recording a 1.67 ERA for the White Sox, and Wilhelm, like Niekro, would continue to pitch effectively through age 47.

It is true that Hough is no longer as effective as he was a few years ago. His ERA has been over 4.00 for the last two years, after being under 3.80 for six straight seasons. And after winning at least 14 games for seven straight years, Hough has won only 10 and 12 the last two. Even so, Hough was a better pitcher in 1990 than he'd been in 1989. He made more starts, worked more innings, won more games (improving his record from 10-13 to 12-12) and lowered his ERA (from 4.35 to 4.07). He even allowed fewer home runs -- always a major problem for him.

Remarkably durable, Hough has started at least 30 games for nine straight seasons, pitched at least 200 innings in eight of them, and won in double figures in all nine. He has recorded 133 wins since Texas made him a starter in 1982, an average of 15 per year.

HOLDING RUNNERS AND FIELDING:

Hough covers the ground between the mound and first base as well as many younger players and he is not afraid to check the runners to keep them honest. His knuckleball has always been easy to run on, so Hough throws to first constantly. He led the American League in pickoff attempts last year with 368; Roger Clemens was a distant second with 269. This frustrates fans and writers, but it also bothers the hitter and the runner, which is the main idea. In one game against the Yankees last year, Hough made 11 pickoff attempts on Steve Sax, and finally nailed him.

OVERALL:

Hough was a free agent at season's end, and it appeared that the Rangers no longer wanted him. He hoped to catch on with the Dodgers or the Angels so that he could be near his California home. It seems unlikely that the Dodgers would re-sign him eleven years after giving up on him, so Hough may need to be willing to relocate.

CHARLIE HOUGH

Position: SP
Bats: R **Throws:** R
Ht: 6' 2" **Wt:** 190

Opening Day Age: 43
Born: 1/5/48 in Honolulu, HI
ML Seasons: 21

Overall Statistics

	W	L	ERA	G	GS	Sv	IP	H	R	BB	SO	HR
1990	12	12	4.07	32	32	0	218.2	190	108	119	114	24
Career	186	169	3.63	745	329	61	3106.2	2636	1438	1382	1988	306

How Often He Throws Strikes

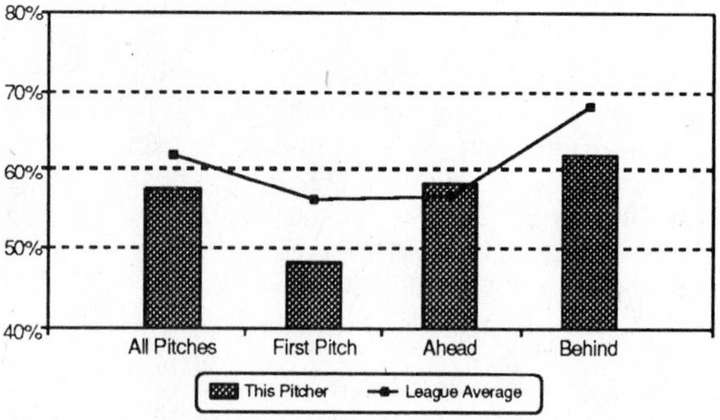

1990 Situational Stats

	W	L	ERA	Sv	IP		AB	H	HR	RBI	AVG
Home	5	8	4.47	0	96.2	LHB	349	84	7	34	.241
Road	7	4	3.76	0	122.0	RHB	458	106	17	60	.231
Day	2	2	3.09	0	43.2	Sc Pos	198	47	4	70	.237
Night	10	10	4.32	0	175.0	Clutch	54	12	0	4	.222

1990 Rankings (American League)

- ➡ 1st in hit batsmen (11) and pickoff throws (368)
- ➡ 2nd in walks allowed (119) and worst strikeout/walk ratio (.96)
- ➡ 3rd in stolen bases allowed (33) and highest stolen base percentage allowed (84.6%)
- ➡ 4th most baserunners per 9 innings allowed (13.2)
- ➡ 7th most home runs allowed per 9 innings (.99)
- ➡ Led the Rangers in losses (12), games started (32), home runs allowed (24), walks allowed, hit batsmen and pickoff throws

JEFF HUSON

Position: SS/3B
Bats: L **Throws:** R
Ht: 6' 3" **Wt:** 170

Opening Day Age: 26
Born: 8/15/64 in Scottsdale, AZ
ML Seasons: 3

HITTING:

Jeff Huson was acquired from the Montreal Expos before the 1990 season and pegged as a backup shortstop and utility infielder. But Huson soon showed himself to be a shortstop with the potential to play every day. Huson started the season hitting spectacularly, and soon began platooning with the regular shortstop, Jeff Kunkel, who was having problems getting his average above .150. By May 22nd, when Huson extended his hitting streak to seven games, his .330 batting average was the highest of any rookie in the major leagues with 100 or more at-bats.

It was a different story from then on, however. In 192 at-bats through June, Huson hit a respectable .281. By the end of July, he was still holding his own with a .268 average. The months of August and September killed him, though, as his offense fizzled and he went just 23 for 127 (.181) in his final 62 games.

The Rangers weren't completely discouraged because Huson has demonstrated good hitting in the past. In four minor league seasons he batted below .286 only once. Typical of a middle infielder, Huson has little power. Nearly 90% of his at-bats came against righthanders as he was platooned with Jeff Kunkel and Gary Green, but in his few shots at lefties, he hit .261. The big league breaking ball may still be his weak spot.

Huson usually batted either leadoff or in the ninth slot. His .199 batting average and .271 on-base average in the lead-off position need improvement. He looked much better at the bottom of the lineup where he hit .301 with a .373 on-base average.

BASERUNNING:

A fine base runner, Huson's 12 stolen bases in 16 attempts was the third best total on the team last year. Given regular duty and a chance to learn major league pitchers, he could easily swipe 30 or more. Huson has topped that figure several times in the minors, including 56 in the Southern League in 1988.

FIELDING:

Huson played shortstop, third base, and second base last season, but most of his time was at short. He had his problems there, recording a .961 fielding average and 17 errors, both figures among the worst in the league. He shows excellent range, but his throws are too often off the mark.

OVERALL:

If Huson can hit a little better and reduce his throwing errors this year, the Rangers will find themselves in the same boat as at the beginning of 1990. They will still need a reserve shortstop -- this time a right-handed hitter to back-up Huson.

Overall Statistics

	G	AB	R	H	D	T	HR	RBI	SB	BB	SO	AVG
1990	145	396	57	95	12	2	0	28	12	46	54	.240
Career	197	512	65	120	19	2	0	33	17	56	63	.234

Where He Hits the Ball

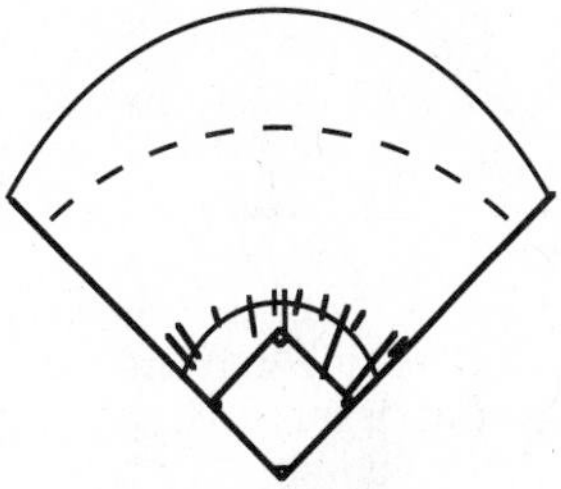

Vs. LHP

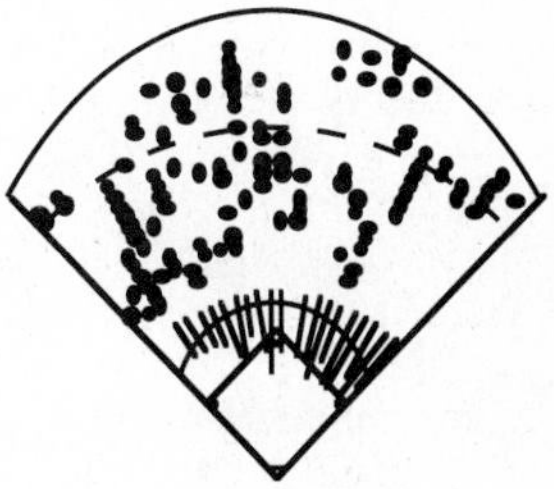

Vs. RHP

1990 Situational Stats

	AB	H	HR	RBI	AVG		AB	H	HR	RBI	AVG
Home	191	42	0	11	.220	LHP	46	12	0	3	.261
Road	205	53	0	17	.259	RHP	350	83	0	25	.237
Day	71	18	0	7	.254	Sc Pos	88	22	0	26	.250
Night	325	77	0	21	.237	Clutch	65	17	0	6	.262

1990 Rankings (American League)

- 1st in worst leadoff on-base average (.271) and worst slugging percentage vs. right-handed pitchers (.280)
- 7th worst batting average vs. right-handed pitchers (.237)
- 8th worst batting average with the bases loaded (.091)
- Led the Rangers in lowest percentage of swings that missed (12.3%) and highest percentage of extra bases taken as a runner (56.0%)

HITTING:

Pete Incaviglia is the first Texas Ranger to have five consecutive 20 home run seasons. In four of those years, he's driven in 80 or more runs. Incaviglia was one of only 10 American League players with 20 home runs and 85 RBI in 1990. He was 10th in the league in HR frequency, hitting one every 22 at-bats.

Despite that, Incaviglia's days in Texas may be numbered. Incaviglia continues to whale away at the ball, with increasingly modest results. His 146 strikeouts last year were only the sixth highest total in club history, but Incaviglia also ranks numbers one, two, and four on the list. Reggie Jackson once told Pete not to worry about striking out, and Incaviglia took the advice. The problem is that his batting average continues to decline -- .271, .249, .236 and .233 (a career low) -- the last four years. These days, Incaviglia is pretty much home run or nothing.

It has long been said that power hitters like to hit against power pitchers, but Incaviglia likes to swing for the downs against any pitcher and has had success against the curveballers. Unlike most righty power hitters, Incaviglia likes the ball away and hits a lot of homers to center and right. Pitchers know this, however, and tease him with outside breaking stuff that he can't handle. Then they'll get him leaning and bust him inside. If the pitchers miss he can hit it over the fence, but more often than not he takes another trip back to the bench.

BASERUNNING:

Incaviglia was caught stealing more times than he was successful for the second straight season last year, but no one expects a lot of steals from him. He moves quickly in the field and gets around the bases well for a big man.

FIELDING:

When Incaviglia began his career, every fly ball to left was an adventure. But he has developed the kind of hustle that wins fans (and they were rough on him at first). People now say that Pete Incaviglia would run through the fence to catch a fly ball. Manager Bobby Valentine had enough confidence in Inky's abilities that he played him in 27 games in center field last year. He had 12 assists, including five at the plate.

OVERALL:

At the end of last season, Incaviglia figured he was on the trading block. Since he was the team's closest approximation to a power hitter, the Rangers would be taking a risk by dealing him. But with Jack Daugherty's development as a left fielder and Juan Gonzalez' potential in center, one has to wonder how much longer the Inkman will remain in Texas.

PETE INCAVIGLIA

Position: LF/CF
Bats: R **Throws:** R
Ht: 6' 1" **Wt:** 220

Opening Day Age: 27
Born: 4/2/64 in Pebble Beach, CA
ML Seasons: 5

Overall Statistics

	G	AB	R	H	D	T	HR	RBI	SB	BB	SO	AVG
1990	153	529	59	123	27	0	24	85	3	45	146	.233
Career	694	2449	333	607	120	13	124	388	26	219	788	.248

Where He Hits the Ball

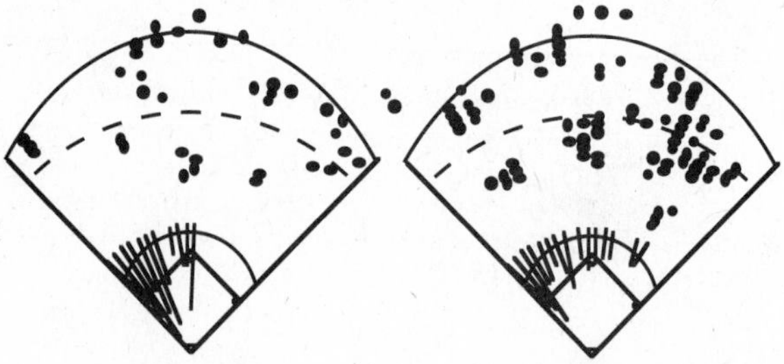

Vs. LHP   Vs. RHP

1990 Situational Stats

	AB	H	HR	RBI	AVG		AB	H	HR	RBI	AVG
Home	247	61	15	45	.247	LHP	169	42	8	30	.249
Road	282	62	9	40	.220	RHP	360	81	16	55	.225
Day	87	14	0	6	.161	Sc Pos	150	35	4	56	.233
Night	442	109	24	79	.247	Clutch	101	18	4	18	.178

1990 Rankings (American League)

- 1st in highest percentage of swings that missed (37.5%)
- 2nd in hit by pitch (9), lowest batting average with the bases loaded (.056), lowest batting average vs. right-handed pitchers (.225) and lowest on-base percentage vs. right-handed pitchers (.279)
- 5th in worst batting average (.233) and worst on-base percentage (.301)
- Led the Rangers in home runs (24), hit by pitch, strikeouts (146) and HR frequency (22.0 ABs per HR)
- Led AL left fielders in strikeouts and errors (7)

MIKE JEFFCOAT

Position: RP/SP
Bats: L **Throws:** L
Ht: 6' 2" **Wt:** 189

Opening Day Age: 31
Born: 8/3/59 in Pine Bluff, AR
ML Seasons: 7

PITCHING:

After several seasons toiling for the Rangers' AAA farm club at Oklahoma City, journeyman Mike Jeffcoat came up to the big club in midseason 1989 and made a strong impression. Jeffcoat went 9-6 with a 3.58 ERA in 22 starts with the Rangers, and looked like the lefty starter who could balance off righthanders Nolan Ryan, Bobby Witt, Charlie Hough and Kevin Brown.

It was a good plan, but things didn't work out for Jeffcoat. He strained his back working out during the offseason and did it again during a lockout workout. This unintentionally self-destructive activity contributed to reduced innings and starts in 1990. He ended up making only twelve starts for the Rangers and was hit hard, going 3-5 with a 5.91 ERA. Jeffcoat was finally moved back to the bullpen, where he was much more effective. Nonetheless, he finished the season with a 4.47 ERA over 44 appearances.

Jeffcoat wasn't a total disaster. He displayed excellent control, and his 2.3 walks per game were the best on the team. A finesse hurler, Jeffcoat needs good control to succeed. He throws both a curveball and split-fingered fastball, and has the ability to vary the speeds of those pitches. Jeffcoat's assortment was very effective against left-handed hitters, whom he held to a .233 average with only three extra-base hits, all doubles. But he's not a hard thrower, and his stuff came up a little short against righties who batted a hefty .296 against him and blasted 12 homers.

Jeffcoat is a 31-year-old veteran who first broke in with the Indians in 1983. He's had some major league success, especially in 1984, when he went 5-2 with a 2.99 ERA in 63 games out of the Cleveland bullpen. Dealt to the Giants in 1985, he couldn't retain his effectiveness and was eventually released and signed by the Rangers.

HOLDING RUNNERS AND FIELDING:

Jeffcoat has a natural and effective pickoff move. He throws to first a lot, holds runners close and is extremely tough to steal on. All six runners who tried to steal against him last year were caught. Jeffcoat is also a fine fielder who releases the ball in a balanced position and thus is ready for a come-backer.

OVERALL:

Though the Rangers would love Jeffcoat to start, his record last year strongly suggests that he's better in a relief role, especially coming in to pitch to lefties. He'll probably begin the year as a long man, and possibly get another shot at the rotation if he pitches well.

Overall Statistics

	W	L	ERA	G	GS	Sv	IP	H	R	BB	SO	HR
1990	5	6	4.47	44	12	5	110.2	122	57	28	58	12
Career	20	22	4.14	175	42	6	398.0	440	204	119	192	37

How Often He Throws Strikes

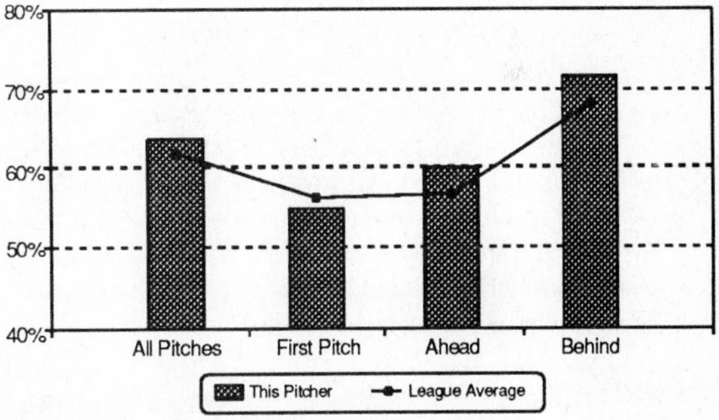

1990 Situational Stats

	W	L	ERA	Sv	IP		AB	H	HR	RBI	AVG
Home	3	1	3.03	3	65.1	LHB	90	21	0	10	.233
Road	2	5	6.55	2	45.1	RHB	341	101	12	44	.296
Day	1	1	5.63	0	16.0	Sc Pos	84	28	4	39	.333
Night	4	5	4.28	5	94.2	Clutch	91	25	2	13	.275

1990 Rankings (American League)

- Did not rank near the top or bottom in any category

JEFF KUNKEL

Position: SS/3B
Bats: R **Throws:** R
Ht: 6' 2" **Wt:** 190

Opening Day Age: 29
Born: 3/25/62 in West Palm Beach, FL
ML Seasons: 7

HITTING:

Opening day, 1990, found Jeff Kunkel right where he was supposed to be -- as the starting shortstop for the Texas Rangers. In 1989, Kunkel had hit a solid .270 with eight home runs in only 293 at-bats, and he finally seemed ready to live up the potential which made him the third player selected in the 1983 amateur draft.

Kunkel didn't hold the job for long. After two months, he was floundering with a .122 average; meanwhile his backup, Jeff Huson, was hitting a torrid .330. That was enough for the Rangers, who made Huson the shortstop and gave Kunkel a seat on the bench. Kunkel hit a little better the rest of the way, but his .170 average was a full 100 points under his 1989 figure. For the year, Kunkel managed to hit only .229 against lefties, but that was a nifty figure compared to his .085 average in 82 at-bats against righthanders. These numbers are particularly startling since Kunkel was given the chance to start because of his bat.

Kunkel takes a big swing and can look bad on a breaking pitch low and outside the strike zone. Even after seven seasons, he still swings at just about everything. He had 66 strikeouts in only 200 at-bats last year, giving him a worse strikeout ratio than even that well-known whiff machine, Pete Incaviglia. Meanwhile Kunkel drew only 11 walks.

BASERUNNING:

When running the bases, Kunkel looks taller and more gangly than his listed height and weight, which is 6-2 and 190. He stole only two bases in three tries and does not pose a big threat in taking the extra base. He is quick, but he is not fast.

FIELDING:

Kunkel played mostly at short, his original position, but he also spent time at third, second, left field and center. He has a powerful arm, one so strong that the Rangers toyed for awhile with making him a pitcher. The strong arm helps him in the outfield, but Kunkel still has the tendency to throw too many balls away. He made 11 errors last year.

OVERALL:

Kunkel has been around for seven seasons now, and while he's never been given a regular job for a full season, he hasn't shown a lot to indicate he could handle one. General Manager Tom Grieve stated last October that he thought Kunkel "has the ability to stay in the big leagues," but the Rangers' patience has about run out. The wild swings and errant throws are errors of commission rather than omission. Kunkel seems to be trying too hard.

Overall Statistics

	G	AB	R	H	D	T	HR	RBI	SB	BB	SO	AVG
1990	99	200	17	34	11	1	3	17	2	11	66	.170
Career	337	838	88	188	42	9	18	72	9	37	226	.224

Where He Hits the Ball

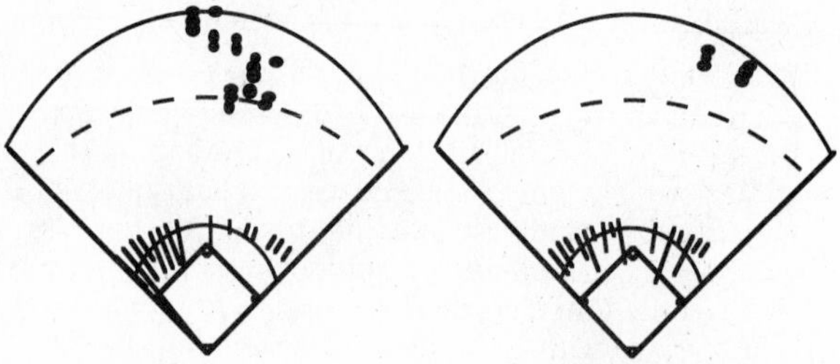

Vs. LHP   Vs. RHP

1990 Situational Stats

	AB	H	HR	RBI	AVG		AB	H	HR	RBI	AVG
Home	93	14	1	10	.151	LHP	118	27	2	14	.229
Road	107	20	2	7	.187	RHP	82	7	1	3	.085
Day	40	6	0	0	.150	Sc Pos	48	8	0	12	.167
Night	160	28	3	17	.175	Clutch	32	5	0	2	.156

1990 Rankings (American League)

- 5th lowest batting average with 2 strikes (.115)

GARY MIELKE

Position: RP
Bats: R **Throws:** R
Ht: 6' 3" **Wt:** 180
Opening Day Age: 28
Born: 1/28/63 in St. James, MN
ML Seasons: 3

Overall Statistics

	W	L	ERA	G	GS	Sv	IP	H	R	BB	SO	HR
1990	0	3	3.73	33	0	0	41.0	42	17	15	13	4
Career	1	3	3.56	79	0	1	93.2	97	37	41	42	10

How Often He Throws Strikes

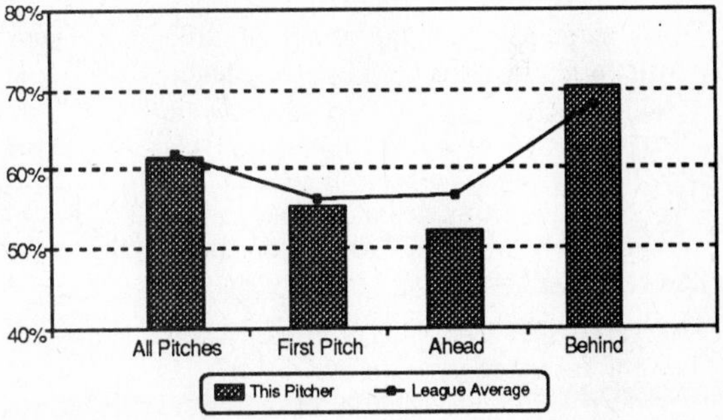

1990 Situational Stats

	W	L	ERA	Sv	IP		AB	H	HR	RBI	AVG
Home	0	1	6.06	0	16.1	LHB	48	14	2	7	.292
Road	0	2	2.19	0	24.2	RHB	107	28	2	17	.262
Day	0	0	4.35	0	10.1	Sc Pos	49	16	1	19	.327
Night	0	3	3.52	0	30.2	Clutch	33	12	2	6	.364

1990 Rankings (American League)

- 11th most GDPs induced per GDP situation (18.6%)

PITCHING:

After a promising rookie season in which he compiled a 3.26 ERA in 43 games out of the Ranger bullpen, Gary Mielke spent most of his second season wielding a mop. Mielke appeared in 33 games, 26 of them Rangers' losses, while compiling no wins and no saves. He didn't pitch badly, as his 3.73 ERA attests. Basically, he just didn't pitch, at least not in many contests of substance.

That wasn't really a reflection on Mielke's talents, or on what the Rangers thought of him; he just kind of got lost in the Ranger shuffle last year. Even after Jeff Russell went out with an elbow injury, the Texas pen was pretty stocked with Kenny Rogers, Brad Arnsberg, John Barfield, Mike Jeffcoat and sometimes Jamie Moyer and Craig McMurtry, all vying for pitching time. The Ranger starters led the American League in complete games, and pitchers like Nolan Ryan and Bobby Witt didn't get knocked out early very often. There wasn't enough work to keep the relievers sharp, which was one reason why the bullpen as a whole wasn't very effective. Mielke was just one of the victims.

Mielke mainly throws two pitches, a slider and a sinking fastball. His pitches move pretty well, and at most of his minor league stops he averaged more than a strikeout an inning. Mielke hasn't been able to blow away hitters at the major league level, but he has enough stuff to succeed. He's an aggressive pitcher, not afraid to work inside, and his stuff has been fairly effective against righties. He's had problems against lefties, however; last year they hit .292 against Mielke, with a whopping .563 slugging average.

HOLDING RUNNERS AND FIELDING:

Mielke doesn't have a great move to first, but he does a decent job of holding runners. He's also a pretty good fielder who helps himself with the glove. In one game against the Brewers, he came in with men on first and second with none out and handled three smashes up the middle to get out of the jam.

OVERALL:

Mielke had kind of a lost season in 1990, though it wasn't really a bad one. He might have figured on getting more work last year, especially with Russell out. Instead, he appeared in ten fewer games than in 1989. Mielke, though, is the kind of athlete who inspires armchair major leaguers. He isn't the superstar with all the muscles or the 95 MPH fastball, but he is a hard worker with a good attitude. He'll be back in 1991, hoping for a more substantial role.

JAMIE MOYER

Position: RP/SP
Bats: L **Throws:** L
Ht: 6' 0" **Wt:** 170

Opening Day Age: 28
Born: 11/18/62 in Sellersville, PA
ML Seasons: 5

PITCHING:

Troubled by arm problems and control difficulties the last couple of years, Jamie Moyer has gone from a promising young lefty to a marginal major leaguer. Moyer has now had four consecutive losing seasons, with a combined record of 27-45. His career ERA is 4.51, and it's been below that level only once in five seasons. Moyer is now 28, and it's getting to be put-up-or-shut-up time.

Moyer was exclusively a starter in 1989, but in 1990 he started just 10 of his 33 appearances. He began the season in the starting rotation, but after going 0-3 in three starts and five games in April, he did not start another game until July. Moyer doesn't have the stuff to be a late reliever -- he's never had a save at any professional level -- so if he's not used as a starter, long relief is the only alternative. He struggled in that role, also, in 1990.

Though he had a couple of decent strikeout seasons with the Cubs, Moyer is a finesse pitcher, and his best pitch is the change-up. When the change is working and he's throwing it for strikes, the change sets up his mediocre fastball and makes it work. When his control is off, however, he either gives up walks or has to come in with up-in-the-strike-zone fastballs that often end up over the fence.

Moyer was far from effective in 1990, but there were several encouraging signs in his work. His earned run average was down, slightly, from 4.86 to 4.66. More significantly, both his walk and home run ratios were down, indicating that his ability to throw strikes is returning. Moyer continued to be tough on lefties, holding them to a .222 average. But righties continued to torment him at a .308 clip. Moyer also induced 15 double plays, a sign that he can keep the ball down.

HOLDING RUNNERS AND FIELDING:

Moyer is a good fielder. He is almost always in good position to field balls up the middle, and that's essential for pitchers of his style. His move to first is not the greatest, especially for a lefty, but Moyer was much more successful at controlling the running game last year than he was in 1989.

OVERALL:

The Rangers have a need for left-handed starting pitching, but apparently Jamie Moyer didn't fit the bill, as he was released in November. Moyer's pitching the last few years makes him a marginal bet to fill a left-handed spot-starter's role elsewhere; he'll be fighting for a job in the majors during spring training.

Overall Statistics

	W	L	ERA	G	GS	Sv	IP	H	R	BB	SO	HR
1990	2	6	4.66	33	10	0	102.1	115	59	39	58	6
Career	34	49	4.51	133	104	0	668.2	728	373	266	415	74

How Often He Throws Strikes

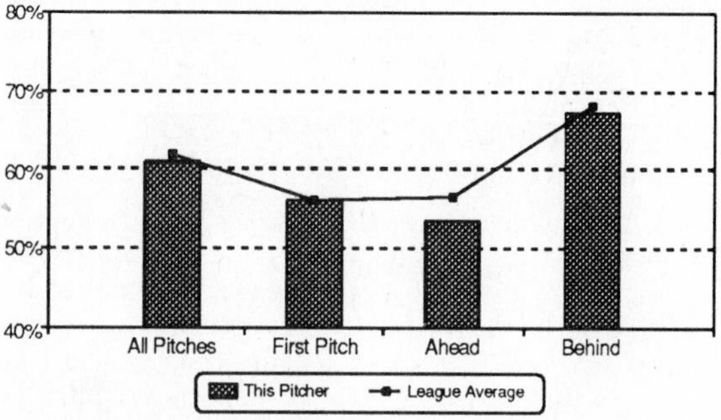

1990 Situational Stats

	W	L	ERA	Sv	IP		AB	H	HR	RBI	AVG
Home	2	2	3.77	0	59.2	LHB	81	18	1	12	.222
Road	0	4	5.91	0	42.2	RHB	315	97	5	39	.308
Day	0	0	13.97	0	9.2	Sc Pos	108	32	1	43	.296
Night	2	6	3.69	0	92.2	Clutch	23	5	1	2	.217

1990 Rankings (American League)

- 14th most GDPs induced per GDP situation (18.5%)

HITTING:

After a somewhat disappointing first season in Texas, Rafael Palmeiro has regained his reputation as one of the best young hitters in baseball. Palmeiro contended for the batting title up until the final five games of last season, when he went four for his last 22. Even so, Palmeiro's .319 average was good enough for third in the league. He led the American League with 191 hits.

For Palmeiro, probably the most satisfying part of his season was his improvement in power production. In '89, he belted 23 doubles, four triples and only eight homers, mediocre figures for a first baseman. But in 1990 his figures were 35 doubles, six triples and 14 homers. Even more significant was his improved RBI count, from 64 to 89. Palmeiro produced those figures while continuing to be handicapped by his home ballpark. In '89, Palmeiro hit .291 on the road, only .259 in Arlington. In 1990, he batted a robust .350 on the road, .288 at home.

Palmeiro uses the whole ballpark. He likes the fastball, hitting it where it's pitched, and he was a more aggressive hitter in 1990. His walks were down, his strikeouts up. He still struck out only 59 times, and, in a big turnaround from 1989, actually hit lefties better than righties. With his good concentration, Palmeiro was an exceptional hitter last year both with runners on (.362) and in scoring position (.324). Palmeiro hits the ball hard on the ground a lot, and as a result grounded into 24 double plays.

BASERUNNING:

Most first basemen are not threats to steal and Palmeiro fit that mold by successfully stealing only 3 bases in 6 attempts. Palmeiro is not very big, but he isn't a fast runner. He does run intelligently and will take the extra base whenever he can.

FIELDING:

Palmeiro had appeared at first base only 23 times prior to coming to the Rangers in 1989. He has played there exclusively now for two years and finally seems comfortable. Like other players, his offense may have suffered while he concentrated on the defensive conversion. In 1990, he had just seven errors.

OVERALL:

Palmeiro was the best of Texas' Three Amigos (Palmeiro, Franco, and Sierra) in 1990, and that's saying a lot. The Rangers will have take his pay upa notch in the future, especially if he contunues to produce as well as he did in 1990. A potential All-Star and batting champion like Palmeiro is hard to find and harder to replace.

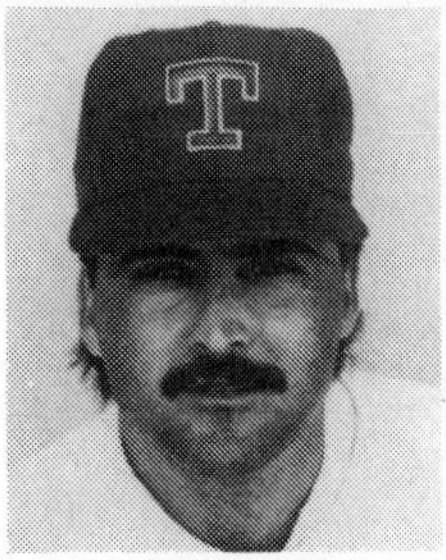

RAFAEL PALMEIRO

Position: 1B
Bats: L **Throws:** L
Ht: 6' 0" **Wt:** 180

Opening Day Age: 26
Born: 9/24/64 in Havana, Cuba
ML Seasons: 5

Overall Statistics

	G	AB	R	H	D	T	HR	RBI	SB	BB	SO	AVG
1990	154	598	72	191	35	6	14	89	3	40	59	.319
Career	568	2031	264	602	118	16	47	248	22	165	173	.296

Where He Hits the Ball

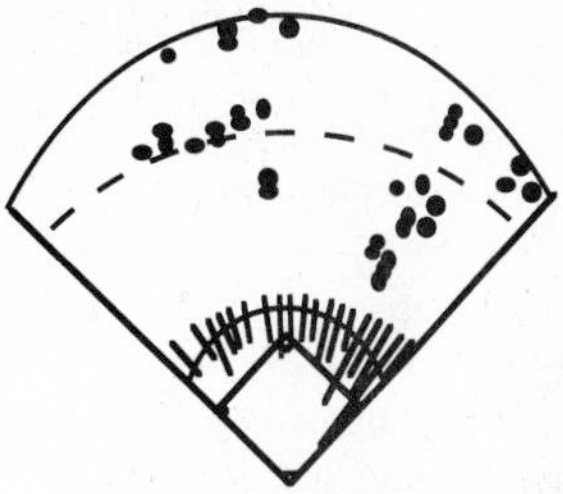

Vs. LHP

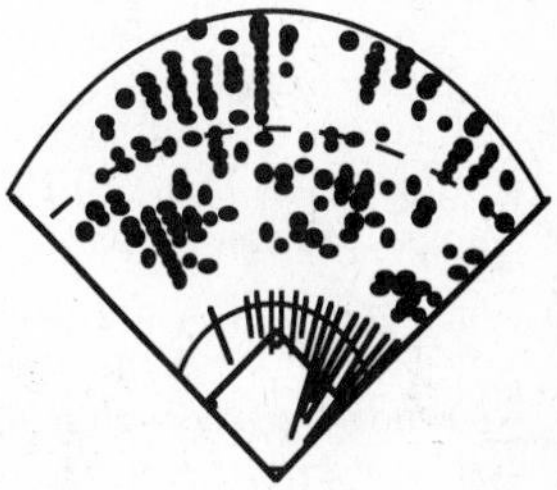

Vs. RHP

1990 Situational Stats

	AB	H	HR	RBI	AVG		AB	H	HR	RBI	AVG
Home	295	85	9	46	.288	LHP	189	64	5	32	.339
Road	303	106	5	43	.350	RHP	409	127	9	57	.311
Day	108	34	2	23	.315	Sc Pos	148	48	1	65	.324
Night	490	157	12	66	.320	Clutch	111	32	3	14	.288

1990 Rankings (American League)

- 1st in hits (191), singles (136) and batting average on the road (.350)
- 2nd in GDPs (24)
- 3rd in batting average (.319)
- 7th in total bases (280)
- Led the Rangers in batting average, hits, singles, total bases, sacrifice flies (8), GDPs, slugging percentage (.468), batting average with runners in scoring position (.324) and highest percentage of swings put into play (53.6%)
- Led AL first basemen in at-bats (598), hits, singles, GDPs, batting average on the road and highest percentage of swings put into play

GENO PETRALLI

Position: C
Bats: L **Throws:** R
Ht: 6' 1" **Wt:** 180

Opening Day Age: 31
Born: 9/25/59 in Sacramento, CA
ML Seasons: 9

HITTING:

In his first eight years in the majors, Geno Petralli had a combined .287 average, so his .255 showing in 1990 needs to be put into perspective. Petralli broke the big toe on his right foot while warming up Nolan Ryan on May 12th. He missed only a few games before a protective cap was put on his shoe and he got back into the fray. He was probably rushing himself back into action, and he paid for it: Petralli hit just .205 during June and July after starting with a .289 average in April. He hit better after that, but the injury obviously affected him.

The lefty-swinging Petralli used to be a switch-hitter, but he always had problems against southpaws, and he's now strictly a platoon man against right-handed pitching. He's generally fared very well in that role. In 1989 Petralli hit .314 against righties, but, hampered by the injury, he slumped to .252 against them last year. This was one of the reasons that the Rangers were 54-54 against right-handed starters. Petralli did hit .300 against lefties last year, but he batted only 20 times against them. In 1989 Petralli batted only nine times against left-handed pitching, with a single hit.

Petralli is a spray hitter who goes the opposite way a lot. He can drive the low pitch, but he's sometimes overpowered by high heat. Petralli has never been a real power hitter, but it was unusual that he did not have even one home run last year. His 21 RBIs were a major drop from 1989, when he had 23 RBI in 141 fewer at-bats.

BASERUNNING:

A broken toe would really slow down most runners, but in Petralli's case, there was no discernible difference. He couldn't run even before the injury, and hasn't stolen a base since 1986. Petralli grounded into more than his fair share of double plays (12).

FIELDING:

Petralli has been rapped for his defense, mostly because he holds the major league record for passed balls with 35 in 1987. But that was mostly because he was catching knuckleballer Charlie Hough so often. If Hough is gone this year, as expected, Petralli will look a lot better. He doesn't have much mobility, but he has a decent arm.

OVERALL:

If he can stay healthy, Petralli should continue to be the Rangers' number-one catcher. Besides the toe, he has had a tender left knee, but since he sits down against lefties, he should be able to rest enough to get back to pre-1990 consistency. What the Rangers need from Petralli is a steady bat and a few more RBIs.

Overall Statistics

	G	AB	R	H	D	T	HR	RBI	SB	BB	SO	AVG
1990	133	325	28	83	13	1	0	21	0	50	49	.255
Career	569	1350	136	377	58	8	20	141	4	153	187	.279

Where He Hits the Ball

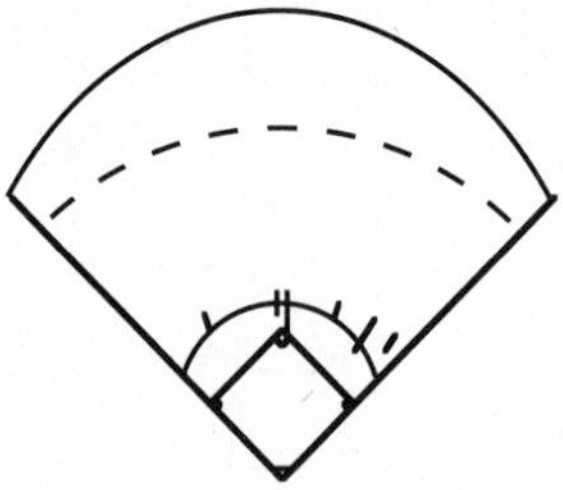

Vs. LHP

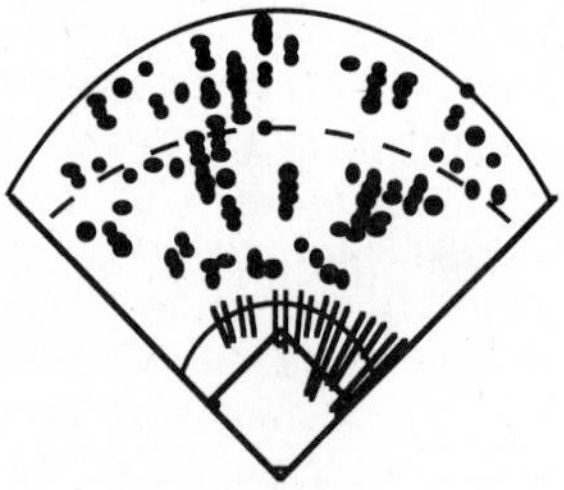

Vs. RHP

1990 Situational Stats

	AB	H	HR	RBI	AVG		AB	H	HR	RBI	AVG
Home	170	45	0	11	.265	LHP	20	6	0	3	.300
Road	155	38	0	10	.245	RHP	305	77	0	18	.252
Day	58	17	0	5	.293	Sc Pos	61	14	0	20	.230
Night	267	66	0	16	.247	Clutch	58	13	0	2	.224

1990 Rankings (American League)

→ 4th most GDPs per GDP situation (20.7%)

HITTING:

When Gary Pettis was signed as a free agent in November 1989, the Rangers might have hoped for more, but they knew they were getting a .239 lifetime hitter with great defensive skills and the ability to steal bases. Pettis didn't surprise, hitting exactly .239. In fact, Pettis performed pretty much exactly as he has throughout his major league career. That means he had some pluses, but he also had all the other minuses that have kept him from becoming a star.

Pettis is a patient hitter, taking a lot of pitches and getting on base frequently via the walk. The downside is that he also strikes out a lot, more than once every four at-bats in his major league career. Pettis has been constantly coached to hit the ball on the ground to take advantage of his speed, and he's done that, becoming a pretty good low-ball hitter. But pitchers have always been able to overpower him with high fastballs, and that's probably never going to change.

Because of his speed and his ability to draw some walks, Pettis is usually used in the leadoff spot. He was a flop in that role, hitting only .234 with a .319 on-base average when batting first. Perhaps he was pressing after signing the free agent contract, because when Pettis batted in the number nine slot, he was much better, hitting .273 with a .390 on-base average. A switch-hitter, Pettis hit much better against righties, whom he tended to take to left field.

BASERUNNING:

Speed is Pettis' game, and he didn't disappoint the Rangers; his 38 stolen bases ranked fifth in the American League. He remains an outstanding baserunner, and he grounded into just six double plays last year.

FIELDING:

More than anything, it was Pettis's Gold Glove defense which attracted the Rangers. He was as good as advertised. Always playing shallow, his speed allows him to go back on the deep ones while compensating for a somewhat weak throwing arm. The beauty of being able to play in close is that he can, and does, snag the liners that would fall in front of anyone else.

OVERALL:

Pettis remains, as he has always been, an outstanding defensive player and baserunner whose hitting has never developed. Both Jack Daugherty and Juan Gonzalez pack more punch at the plate, and Pettis may find himself coming off the bench in 1991, logging time as a defensive replacement and role player.

GARY PETTIS

Position: CF
Bats: B **Throws:** R
Ht: 6' 1" **Wt:** 160

Opening Day Age: 33
Born: 4/3/58 in Oakland, CA
ML Seasons: 9

Overall Statistics

	G	AB	R	H	D	T	HR	RBI	SB	BB	SO	AVG
1990	136	423	66	101	16	8	3	31	38	57	118	.239
Career	968	3188	504	762	97	41	20	228	311	438	822	.239

Where He Hits the Ball

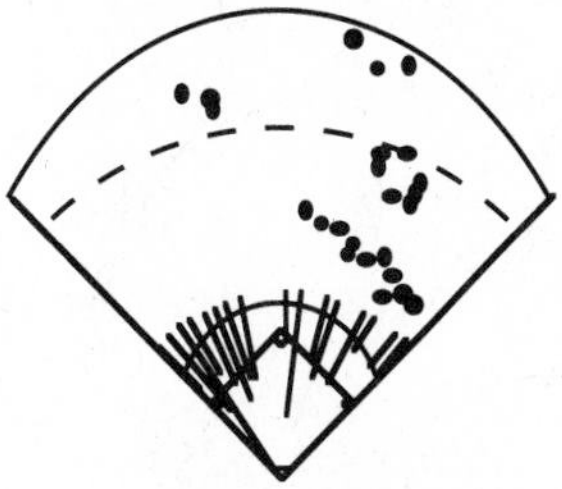

Vs. LHP

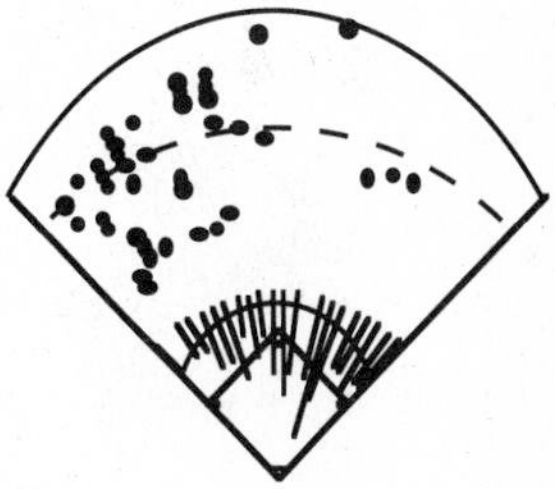

Vs. RHP

1990 Situational Stats

	AB	H	HR	RBI	AVG		AB	H	HR	RBI	AVG
Home	221	56	3	21	.253	LHP	152	33	0	7	.217
Road	202	45	0	10	.223	RHP	271	68	3	24	.251
Day	80	24	0	7	.300	Sc Pos	77	17	0	24	.221
Night	343	77	3	24	.224	Clutch	65	18	1	3	.277

1990 Rankings (American League)

- 5th in stolen bases (38)
- 6th in triples (8) and bunts in play (24)
- 7th in caught stealing (15)
- Led the Rangers in triples, sacrifice bunts (11), stolen bases, caught stealing and bunts in play
- Led AL center fielders in sacrifice bunts and highest percentage of pitches taken (60.7%)

PITCHING:

What is Kenny Rogers' role? Is he a stopper, a middle man, or a starter? In 1990, Rogers proved to be the fourth busiest pitcher in the American League, appearing in 69 games. The reason, of course, is that he was called upon to act as the stopper in the absence of Jeff Russell. Rogers did a very acceptable job, recording 15 saves while compiling 10 wins and just 6 losses in the new role.

Rogers is used to a heavy workload. In 1989, his first year in the bigs, he appeared in 73 games while being used primarily in middle relief. That year, though, Rogers was much more of a lefty specialist, often seeing only one or two batters as he averaged about one inning per outing. Rogers pitched more innings last year, but, demonstrating his durability, got stronger as the year progressed. In September he appeared in nine games. He won five and got three saves while holding the opposition to a 1.93 ERA.

While he lacks the fastball of a blow-em-away closer, Rogers possesses good stuff. His fastball reaches the low 90s, and he also throws a good slider. Rogers gets a respectable number of strikeouts, but his control is not outstanding. He generally keeps the ball low in the strike zone, and thus does not allow very many homers. The home run ball was, however, more of a problem for Rogers last year than it was in 1989, as he worked to get more velocity on his fastball.

In an interesting experiment, Rogers started three games last year, including his last two, and pitched so well that the Rangers are now thinking that he might work out as the fifth man, a much needed lefthander, in their 1991 rotation. His work as a starter was promising, with a 2.35 ERA and only one earned run allowed in his final twelve innings. Rogers would certainly help the club as a starter if Charlie Hough leaves, as expected.

HOLDING RUNNERS AND FIELDING:

Baserunners managed to steal only six bases while Rogers was pitching. He has a good move to first and his follow-through allows him to be quick off the mound either to field the ball or to cover the bag.

OVERALL:

Rogers is fun to watch as he stalks determinedly behind the mound getting psyched before each pitch. He probably wouldn't be able to do that throwing 100 or more pitches as a starter. But with two successful major league seasons behind him, Rogers is willing to try his luck in a starter's role. If he fails, he can always go back to the bullpen.

KENNY ROGERS

Position: RP/SP
Bats: L **Throws:** L
Ht: 6' 1" **Wt:** 200

Opening Day Age: 26
Born: 11/10/64 in Savannah, GA
ML Seasons: 2

Overall Statistics

	W	L	ERA	G	GS	Sv	IP	H	R	BB	SO	HR
1990	10	6	3.13	69	3	15	97.2	93	40	42	74	6
Career	13	10	3.05	142	3	17	171.1	153	68	84	137	8

How Often He Throws Strikes

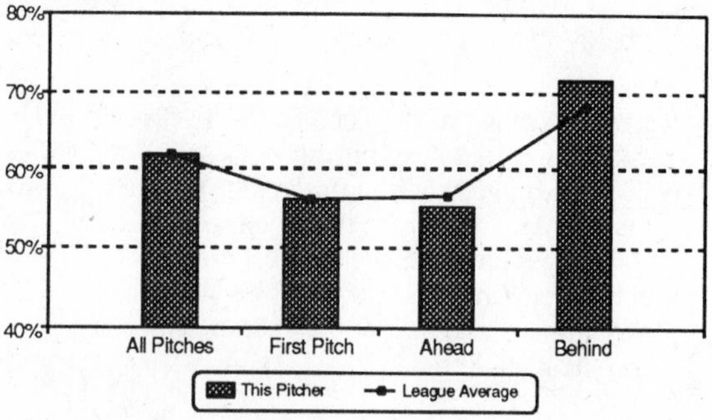

1990 Situational Stats

	W	L	ERA	Sv	IP		AB	H	HR	RBI	AVG
Home	9	1	2.01	8	53.2	LHB	96	21	1	10	.219
Road	1	5	4.50	7	44.0	RHB	278	72	5	36	.259
Day	0	2	5.06	4	16.0	Sc Pos	142	32	2	40	.225
Night	10	4	2.76	11	81.2	Clutch	198	48	3	27	.242

1990 Rankings (American League)

- 1st in worst save percentage (65.2%)
- 4th in games pitched (69) and blown saves (8)
- Led the Rangers in games pitched, saves (15), games finished (46), save opportunities (23), blown saves and lowest percentage of inherited runners scoring (33.3%)

JEFF RUSSELL

Position: RP
Bats: R **Throws:** R
Ht: 6' 3" **Wt:** 210

Opening Day Age: 29
Born: 9/2/61 in Cincinnati, OH
ML Seasons: 8

PITCHING:

After missing most of the 1990 season with bone chips in his right elbow, Jeff Russell will enter the '91 campaign as something of a question mark. Russell was one of the top relief aces in baseball in 1989, but he was able to post only ten saves in 27 appearances last year.

A veteran righty who'd pitched for seven seasons without overwhelming success, Russell hit the jackpot in '89. Taking over as the Rangers' relief ace early in the season, Russell racked up 38 saves, posting a 1.98 ERA and giving up only 45 hits in 72.2 innings. Russell parlayed that success into a big multi-year contract before the start of the 1990 season.

The Rangers expected Russell to take over where he left off last year, but instead he got off to a slow start. After a ragged April and May, Russell decided he'd had enough after taking the loss in a May 28 appearance against Boston. Russell chose to have the bone chips in his right elbow removed immediately, even though that meant he would probably miss the remainder of the season. As it turned out Russell didn't miss all of it, but he was out for three and a half months. At the time of his surgery, on May 30th, Russell had posted one win, five losses, eight saves and a 4.71 ERA. During the rest of the year, he threw only 65 pitches but picked up two more saves.

While Russell owns a change-up and a slider, as a short reliever he depends primarily on his outstanding fastball. Unofficially, Russell has the fastest timed pitch on the Rangers' radar gun -- 98 MPH, Ryan included. Russell used the fastball to devastating effect in 1989, striking out more than one batter per inning. Bothered by the bone chips in 1990, he recorded only 16 Ks in 25.1 innings. Russell punished lefties last year, holding 39 lefties to a .128 batting average, but the 52 righties punched back at a .346 clip.

HOLDING RUNNERS AND FIELDING:

Russell doesn't have a great move to first, but he did a effective job of controlling the running game last year; all five runners who attempted to steal on him were caught. He gets around smoothly enough on grounders and in covering the bag.

OVERALL:

Some folks are still wondering about the timing of Russell's surgery last year. It was common knowledge that he had the bone chips at the end of the '89 season. Russell appeared recovered when he came back in September, and the Rangers, with no viable alternatives, need him to resume his role as stopper desperately.

Overall Statistics

	W	L	ERA	G	GS	Sv	IP	H	R	BB	SO	HR
1990	1	5	4.26	27	0	10	25.1	23	15	16	16	1
Career	40	53	4.03	277	79	53	778.0	763	400	303	476	72

How Often He Throws Strikes

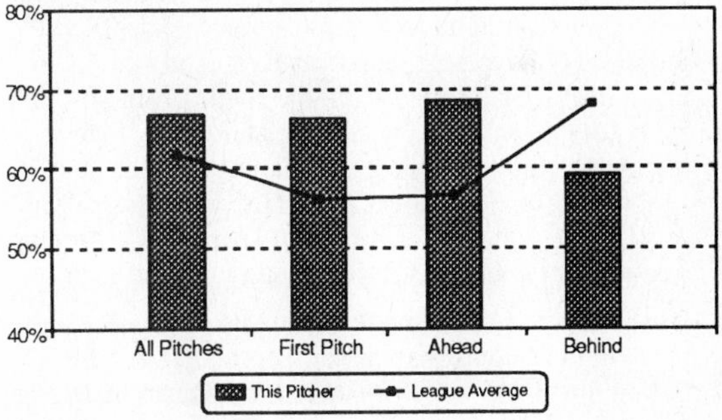

1990 Situational Stats

	W	L	ERA	Sv	IP		AB	H	HR	RBI	AVG
Home	0	4	5.54	6	13.0	LHB	39	5	1	4	.128
Road	1	1	2.92	4	12.1	RHB	52	18	0	12	.346
Day	0	1	1.80	1	5.0	Sc Pos	42	11	0	14	.262
Night	1	4	4.87	9	20.1	Clutch	63	18	1	13	.286

1990 Rankings (American League)

- Did not rank near the top or bottom in any category

HALL OF FAMER

NOLAN RYAN

Position: SP
Bats: R **Throws:** R
Ht: 6' 2" **Wt:** 220

Opening Day Age: 44
Born: 1/31/47 in Refugio, TX
ML Seasons: 24

Overall Statistics

	W	L	ERA	G	GS	Sv	IP	H	R	BB	SO	HR
1990	13	9	3.44	30	30	0	204.0	137	86	74	232	18
Career	302	272	3.16	740	706	3	4990.1	3629	1998	2614	5308	295

How Often He Throws Strikes

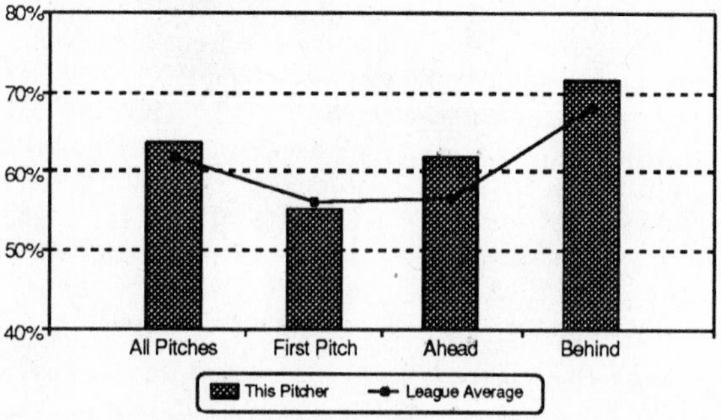

1990 Situational Stats

	W	L	ERA	Sv	IP		AB	H	HR	RBI	AVG
Home	8	5	3.32	0	130.0	LHB	362	79	8	31	.218
Road	5	4	3.65	0	74.0	RHB	367	58	10	41	.158
Day	1	1	3.22	0	22.1	Sc Pos	140	22	3	45	.157
Night	12	8	3.47	0	181.2	Clutch	76	12	1	6	.158

1990 Rankings (American League)

- 1st in strikeouts (232), lowest batting average allowed (.188), most piches thrown per batter (4.04), least baserunners per 9 innings (9.6), least GDPs induced per 9 innings (.22), most strikeouts per 9 innings (10.2), lowest batting average allowed vs. right-handed batters (.158) and lowest batting average allowed with runners in scoring position (.157)
- 2nd in strikeout/walk ratio (3.1)
- Led the Rangers in shutouts (2), strikeouts, runners caught stealing (9), batting average/slugging percentage (.322)/on-base average allowed (.268), least baserunners per 9 innings and most strikeouts per 9 innings

PITCHING:

In his 24th season, Nolan Ryan seemed to be intent on doing the few remaining things he hadn't done in the previous 23. On April 24, he pitched the twelfth one-hitter of his career, an awesome 16-strikeout performance against the White Sox in which the only hit was a check-swing single by Ron Kittle. Six weeks later, on June 11, Ryan threw his sixth no-hitter (no one else has thrown five) against the Oakland Athletics. He got his long-awaited 300th victory on July 31 at Milwaukee. He won his fourth consecutive strikeout crown with 232; Ryan has now led his league in Ks 11 different times. And of course, every Ryan strikeout further insures that the career strikeout record will be his forever. As of the end of 1990, Ryan has 5308 of them.

Even at 44, it's hard to find many signs of age creeping up on Ryan. He suffered from back spasms early in the season and had to be placed on the disabled list in late May; it was the first time Ryan had been on the DL since 1986. Because of the back problems, his ERA rose a bit last year, to 3.44, and his victory total fell from 16 to 13, but he still compiled the second best record on the team at 13-9. His strikeout-to-walk ratio, however, was a super 3.14. In the American League, only Rogers Clemens topped that figure.

Ryan threw five complete games last year, only the third highest total on the Rangers staff, but he undoubtedly could have thrown more. During the first six innings he held hitters to a .190 average, and from the seventh on they hit just .177.

HOLDING RUNNERS AND FIELDING:

Never a particularly strong fielder, Ryan did not improve in that department in 1990. Bear in mind that he was playing with a bad back for much of the season. The high leg-kicking Ryan has always been among the easiest pitchers to steal on. His best defense is not allowing many baserunners.

OVERALL:

How does he do it year after year? Conditioning is one key. In 1989, following the game in which he got his 5000th career strikeout, one sportscaster walked through the clubhouse after nearly all the players had left. Ryan was still there, riding the stationary bicycle just like he had done after the other 700-plus games. Though his back is a concern and he will be 44 when the season opens, Ryan seems capable of making more history in 1991.

HITTING:

In 1989 Ruben Sierra led the American League in slugging, triples, RBI, games, and total bases. In 1990 he was in the top ten only in RBI and doubles; those, plus games played, were the only categories in which he even led the Rangers. Still, there can be no denying that Sierra is an offensive player to be reckoned with. Although he did not finish strongly enough to get his third 100 RBI season, Sierra is one of only five major leaguers to have four consecutive 90-plus RBI years.

Sierra has more power from the left side than from the right, but his hitting has gotten more consistent from the right. In 1990, he hit 69 points higher from the right and for the first time, opposing managers might have thought about switching pitchers to get him to the left side, where his .255 average wasn't so scary. Sierra still hits with power to all fields, and is an excellent clutch hitter, with a .320 average last year with men in scoring position.

The fact of the matter is, Ruben Sierra suffered a long term power outage in 1990. He scored 31 fewer runs, had 24 fewer hits, 12 less triples, 13 fewer homers, 23 less RBI, and lowered his batting average by 26 points.

BASERUNNING:

An excellent percentage stealer, Sierra was nine for nine last year and is 35 for 41 the last three years; the real question is why he doesn't run more often. The dramatic drop off in his number of triples (from 14 to two) and runs scored (101 to 70) may not say as much about his speed as about his determination.

FIELDING:

Often referred to as "The Golden One," Sierra reminded fans that his nickname came from his jewelry, and not from his glove. He was second among right fielders, and third among all outfielders, in number of errors committed with 10. He can make the spectacular sliding catch and follow it one pitch later by mis-judging a routine fly. This type of inconsistency can only be due to lack of concentration. Sierra has an excellent arm.

OVERALL:

Going into 1990, Sierra was on everyone's soon-to-be-MVP and future Hall of Famer lists. But in Texas he is now number-one only on the boo-bird list. There's nothing wrong with a .280 average, 16 homers, and 96 RBI. A lot of clubs, and fans, would be more than happy with figures like that. Except when people think you can do better.

RUBEN SIERRA

Position: RF
Bats: B **Throws:** R
Ht: 6' 1" **Wt:** 175

Opening Day Age: 25
Born: 10/6/65 in Rio Piedras, Puerto Rico
ML Seasons: 5

Overall Statistics

	G	AB	R	H	D	T	HR	RBI	SB	BB	SO	AVG
1990	159	608	70	170	37	2	16	96	9	49	86	.280
Career	748	2882	395	790	152	32	114	470	58	197	438	.274

Where He Hits the Ball

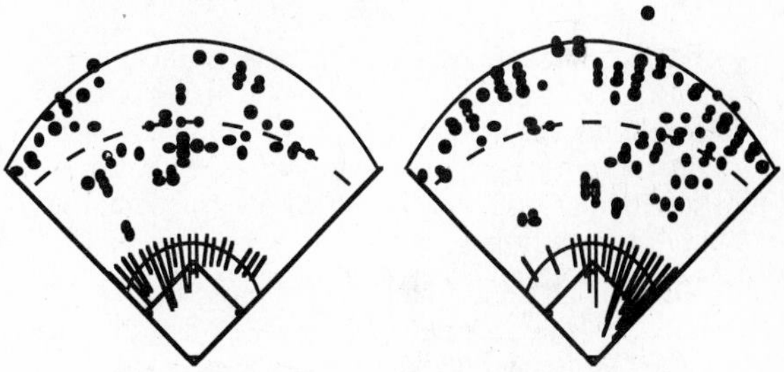

Vs. LHP Vs. RHP

1990 Situational Stats

	AB	H	HR	RBI	AVG		AB	H	HR	RBI	AVG
Home	301	80	10	46	.266	LHP	216	70	3	31	.324
Road	307	90	6	50	.293	RHP	392	100	13	65	.255
Day	112	29	2	18	.259	Sc Pos	169	54	6	82	.320
Night	496	141	14	78	.284	Clutch	98	29	5	21	.296

1990 Rankings (American League)

- 2nd most errors in right field (10)
- 4th in intentional walks (13)
- 5th in RBIs (96)
- Led the Rangers in at-bats (608), doubles (37), RBIs, sacrifice flies (8), intentional walks (13) and games (159)
- Led AL right fielders in batting average (.280), at-bats, hits (170), singles (115), doubles, sacrifice flies, intentional walks, times on base (220), plate appearances (666), games and batting average with runners in scoring position (.319)

MIKE STANLEY

Position: C/DH
Bats: R **Throws:** R
Ht: 6' 0" **Wt:** 185

Opening Day Age: 27
Born: 6/25/63 in Ft. Lauderdale, FL
ML Seasons: 5

Overall Statistics

	G	AB	R	H	D	T	HR	RBI	SB	BB	SO	AVG
1990	103	189	21	47	8	1	2	19	1	30	25	.249
Career	357	806	89	203	30	3	13	95	6	113	171	.252

Where He Hits the Ball

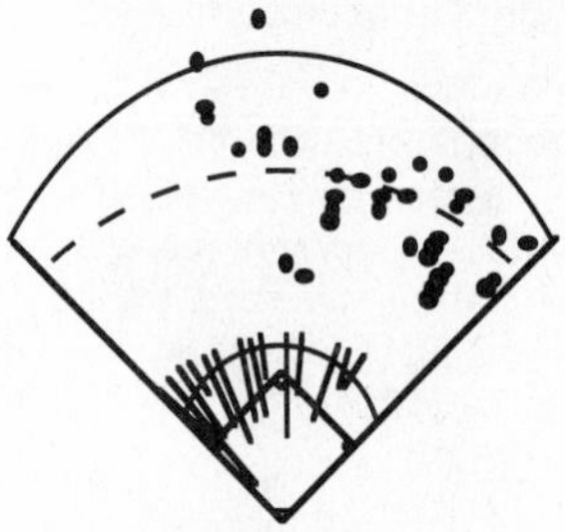

Vs. LHP

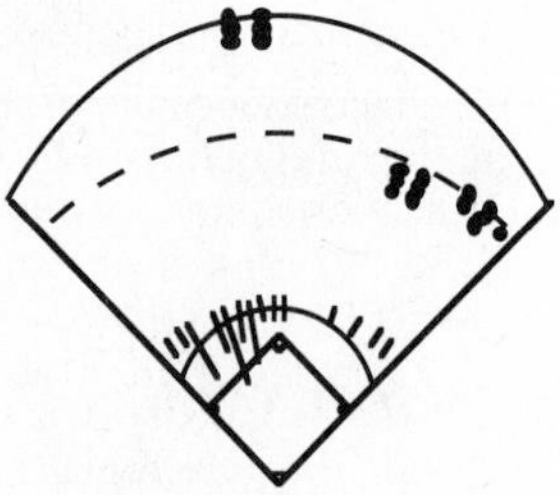

Vs. RHP

1990 Situational Stats

	AB	H	HR	RBI	AVG		AB	H	HR	RBI	AVG
Home	85	24	1	10	.282	LHP	137	38	2	17	.277
Road	104	23	1	9	.221	RHP	52	9	0	2	.173
Day	39	9	1	4	.231	Sc Pos	49	14	1	15	.286
Night	150	38	1	15	.253	Clutch	24	6	1	4	.250

1990 Rankings (American League)

- Did not rank near the top or bottom in any category

HITTING:

For the past couple of years Mike Stanley seemed to devote so much of his energy to the task of being a good catcher that his hitting suffered. In 1990, he started to look comfortable at the plate again. That's an encouraging sign, because, coming through the Ranger system, Stanley had always had outstanding credentials as a hitter.

Stanley was one of two Rangers who drew more walks than strikeouts last year. He maintained his career average of .252 by hitting .249 and following a familiar pattern of the slow start and a strong finish. After going just 19 for 96 (.198) in the first three months, Stanley finished with a 28-for-93 (.301) tear, including a red-hot 23-for-63 (.365) in July and August. Stanley had a .513 on-base percentage and .526 slugging percentage in August. Overall, his 1990 OBP of .350 was fourth on the team.

A righty swinger, Stanley hit 104 points higher against lefties than from the other side of the plate and thus is a perfect match with the other main Ranger catcher, Geno Petralli. Stanley hit .286 with runners in scoring position, but has little power and contributed just 11 extra-base hits.

Stanley can hit the fastball, as evidenced by his only two grand slams coming in 1987 off Jeff Reardon and Cecilio Guante, neither known for their finesse. He's a definite high fastball hitter, and pitchers can have a lot of success against him if they keep the ball down.

BASERUNNING:

This is not one of Stanley's tools. He did have a perfect one for one theft record in 1990 which gives him a major league total of six stolen bases in 357 games. He has never been caught stealing in the big leagues.

FIELDING:

Stanley is now used primarily as the right-handed hitting side of the Rangers' catching platoon. At this point, he's in the lineup mainly for his bat. Stanley made four errors and threw out only seven of 45 baserunners last year. The pitching staff had a 4.15 ERA while he was behind the plate as compared to 3.85 overall. Pitchers like working with him, however, and he's still young enough to improve his defensive work.

OVERALL:

Although Stanley does not figure to supplant Geno Petralli as the number-one catcher on the Rangers, he contributes a useful bat and an improving hand behind the plate. When not catching, he can play first and occasionally, third base. He's no star, but he's a very useful player.

PITCHING:

It would appear that as Bobby Witt goes, so go the Texas Rangers. Last year, Texas started with 21 wins and 32 losses through May, while Witt was struggling with a 2-6 record. Then Witt got himself together, going 15-4 the rest of the way, including a team record 12 straight victories. The Rangers turned things around at the same time, going 62-47 from June 1 on to wind up with a winning record at 83-79.

At 26, Witt may have finally completed the maturing process that began during the second half of 1988, when he shed his reputation as a "six inning pitcher" by hurling nine consecutive complete games. Witt backslid somewhat in 1989, when his ERA rose to 5.14. But even then he was winning a career-high 12 games, and last year he finally seemed to get his emotions -- and his pitches -- under control. Gone is the kid who used to agonize over an umpire's missed call or a miscue in the field. Now Witt simply goes on to the next pitch. Manager Bobby Valentine says Witt had been "a victim of too much coaching," and he's probably right.

Along with his emotions, Witt has gotten more control over his exploding 95 MPH fastball. He's finally able to throw inside strikes to right-handed hitters; as a result, he gave up just six home runs in his last 20 starts last year. Witt also has a slider and a curve ball, but it is the heater that does the job. With 221 K's, Witt was second in strikeouts in the American League to his teammate, Nolan Ryan.

HOLDING RUNNERS AND FIELDING:

Witt seems to be getting this part of his game together as well. While he still doesn't check runners very often, lowering his leg kick has quickened his delivery and should cut into the base thefts. Witt had five errors, which tied him for second in the league, but it was not all bad. For example, on August 4, against Toronto, in a span of ten outs, Witt had four putouts and an assist. It looked like he and first baseman Rafael Palmeiro were running pitcher-covers-first-base drills in spring training. Each play was routine and textbook smooth, a far cry from Witt's early days.

OVERALL:

Is Witt finally for real? The Rangers thought he finally had it together in 1988, but it turned out that he had another year of struggling ahead of him. This time, success looks more certain. Witt might very well be the staff ace for years to come.

BOBBY WITT

Position: SP
Bats: R **Throws:** R
Ht: 6' 2" **Wt:** 205

Opening Day Age: 26
Born: 5/11/64 in Arlington, VA
ML Seasons: 5

Overall Statistics

	W	L	ERA	G	GS	Sv	IP	H	R	BB	SO	HR
1990	17	10	3.36	33	32	0	222.0	197	98	110	221	12
Career	56	52	4.48	143	141	0	891.1	757	490	608	869	67

How Often He Throws Strikes

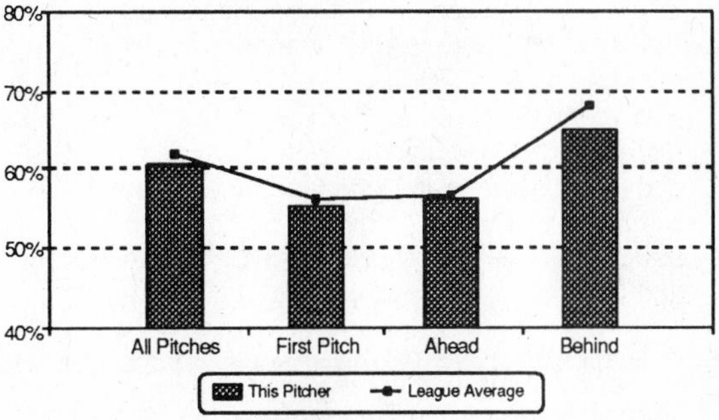

1990 Situational Stats

	W	L	ERA	Sv	IP		AB	H	HR	RBI	AVG
Home	7	5	3.40	0	100.2	LHB	396	92	5	42	.232
Road	10	5	3.34	0	121.1	RHB	433	105	7	41	.242
Day	2	3	3.55	0	45.2	Sc Pos	200	49	0	65	.245
Night	15	7	3.32	0	176.1	Clutch	84	19	0	9	.226

1990 Rankings (American League)

- 2nd in strikeouts (221), pitches thrown (3,780), stolen bases allowed (36) and strikeouts per 9 innings (9.0)
- 3rd in complete games (7) and walks allowed (110)
- 4th highest stolen base percentage allowed (83.7%)
- Led the Rangers in ERA (3.37), wins (17), games started (32), complete games, innings (222.0), hits allowed (197), batters faced (954), wild pitches (11), pitches thrown, stolen bases allowed, winning percentage (.630) and least home runs allowed per 9 innings (.49)

JOHN BARFIELD

Position: RP
Bats: L **Throws:** L
Ht: 6' 1" **Wt:** 185

Opening Day Age: 26
Born: 10/15/64 in Little Rock, AR
ML Seasons: 2

Overall Statistics

	W	L	ERA	G	GS	Sv	IP	H	R	BB	SO	HR
1990	4	3	4.67	33	0	1	44.1	42	25	13	17	2
Career	4	4	4.98	37	2	1	56.0	57	35	17	26	2

PITCHING, FIELDING & HOLDING RUNNERS:

Left-handed hitters had no problems hitting John Barfield last year, as they compiled a .340 batting average. He held righties to a more subdued .236. The oddity in those numbers is that Barfield is left-handed. Since his lot in life is to be a long reliever (he had two six-inning appearances), he will have to learn to handle batters on both sides of the plate. Barfield thus far has shown some reluctance to crowd lefties and bring the heater inside.

One problem is that his fastball is not that great. Barfield is primarily a finesse pitcher, relying on keeping the ball low. He gets a good number of double play balls because of his style, and he displayed fine control last year. He also fielded his position in fine fashion and did a good job of controlling the running game.

Only 26, Barfield has been a starter through most of his professional career. He has a strong arm and a record that indicates he could be successful at the major league level. But he'll have to work on becoming more effective against lefties.

OVERALL:

The Rangers need long relief and Barfield may be the man to do the job. His 4.67 ERA is not acceptable but he didn't get much work last year. With another year or two at the big league level, he should be throwing inside to lefties and getting those double plays.

SCOTT CHIAMPARINO

Position: SP
Bats: L **Throws:** R
Ht: 6' 2" **Wt:** 195

Opening Day Age: 24
Born: 8/22/66 in San Mateo, CA
ML Seasons: 1

Overall Statistics

	W	L	ERA	G	GS	Sv	IP	H	R	BB	SO	HR
1990	1	2	2.63	6	6	0	37.2	36	14	12	19	1
Career	1	2	2.63	6	6	0	37.2	36	14	12	19	1

PITCHING, FIELDING & HOLDING RUNNERS:

Scott Chiamparino is one of two pitchers the Rangers received in the Harold Baines deal. Both Chiamparino and Joe Bitker came up to the Rangers last September and acquitted themselves well, taking some heat off Texas for their trading of the popular Baines. Bitker, a reliever, unveiled a good forkball and looked good in five bullpen appearances. Chiamparino, a starter, won only one game for the Rangers, but he turned in a 2.63 ERA in six starts and averaged more than six innings an outing. That was no real surprise, as Chiamparino has pitched well at every level during his professional career.

Chiamparino, a former fourth round draft choice for the A's, was considered one of Oakland's brightest prospects until 1989, when a shoulder injury limited him to half a season. In the lower minors he'd averaged more than a strikeout an inning, but it took him some time to regain the pop on his fastball after the injury. He now looks fully recovered, and impressed the Rangers with his professionalism and his aggressive attitude. He fields his position well and did a good job of controlling the running game.

OVERALL:

With Charlie Hough probably not coming back, the Rangers have a spot open in their rotation. Ideally they'd like a lefty to fill it, but Chiamparino showed enough last year to give him a fighting chance at the job. He's still only 24, however, and might well end up back in AAA to get a little more experience.

SCOTT COOLBAUGH

Position: 3B
Bats: R **Throws:** R
Ht: 5'11" **Wt:** 185

Opening Day Age: 24
Born: 6/13/66 in Binghampton, NY
ML Seasons: 2

Overall Statistics

	G	AB	R	H	D	T	HR	RBI	SB	BB	SO	AVG
1990	67	180	21	36	6	0	2	13	1	15	47	.200
Career	92	231	28	50	7	0	4	20	1	19	59	.216

HITTING, FIELDING, BASERUNNING:

Before the 1991 season opened, Scott Coolbaugh was being touted as the new third baseman for the Rangers. It didn't turn out that way. Instead, Coolbaugh went back and forth between Texas and AAA Oklahoma City no less than three times, twice in attempts to fill the injured Steve Buechele's slot. He couldn't do it, but came back again when the rosters expanded in September. If Coolbaugh is to get the third-sacker's job, he will have to improve his fielding, as he had two more errors in far fewer games than did Buechele.

Coolbaugh batted only .200 last year, but he wasn't a total disaster. He batted .315 against lefties, but righthanders tied him up badly with a .151 average. He struck out in nearly one-third of his at-bats against righties. In the minors, Coolbaugh had looked like a power hitter with good patience, but last year, possibly because he was anxious, he swung at too many bad offerings. He seemed particularly vulnerable to the fastballs on the fists from righties. Coolbaugh is built like Ron "The Penguin" Cey and is not much of a baserunner.

OVERALL:

Despite his rough season in 1990, Coolbaugh is still only 24 and remains a prospect. His problem is that Steve Buechele, the man he has to beat out, also bats righty and is a much better fielder. Coolbaugh's numbers in the minors hint that he can hit 10-15 homers and bat in the .260 range. If he can improve his hitting against righties this year, the competition will get interesting.

CRAIG McMURTRY

Position: RP/SP
Bats: R **Throws:** R
Ht: 6' 5" **Wt:** 195

Opening Day Age: 31
Born: 11/5/59 in Temple, TX
ML Seasons: 7

Overall Statistics

	W	L	ERA	G	GS	Sv	IP	H	R	BB	SO	HR
1990	0	3	4.32	23	3	0	41.2	43	25	30	14	4
Career	28	41	4.03	201	79	4	657.1	635	330	327	345	54

PITCHING, FIELDING & HOLDING RUNNERS:

In 1983, The Sporting News named Craig McMurtry their Rookie Pitcher of the Year. That year, McMurtry was 15-9 with a 3.08 ERA for the Atlanta Braves. Since then, it's been pretty much downhill. McMurtry has had flashes of success while pitching for the Rangers over the last three years -- just enough to keep the club from completely giving up on him -- but he's never really been able to get back to his '83 form.

McMurtry started last year with the Rangers, but after getting hammered in his first two appearances, he was given his release on April 25th. But he signed with the Rangers' AAA club in Oklahoma City on May 4, and was picked up again by the big club on June 1. McMurtry's 3.34 ERA after returning gave a ray of hope, but he was used only five times in the final 57 games.

When he is on, McMurtry has a good fastball and change-up. His stuff is decent, but he's had control problems throughout his career, and last year it was worse than ever, with 30 walks in only 41.2 innings. The righthander also had problems with lefties, who hit him for a .326 average.

OVERALL:

The Rangers always need middle relievers and last year they were still hoping that McMurtry would regain his 1988 form, when he had a 2.25 ERA and a 3-3 record for them. He didn't. At age 31, it seems unlikely that he will see many more chances.

KEVIN REIMER

Position: DH
Bats: L **Throws:** R
Ht: 6' 2" **Wt:** 215

Opening Day Age: 26
Born: 6/28/64 in Macon, GA
ML Seasons: 3

Overall Statistics

	G	AB	R	H	D	T	HR	RBI	SB	BB	SO	AVG
1990	64	100	5	26	9	1	2	15	0	10	22	.260
Career	79	130	7	29	9	1	3	17	0	10	29	.223

HITTING, FIELDING, BASERUNNING:

Kevin Reimer was listed in the Rangers' 1990 Media Guide as an outfielder-designated hitter. It still seems strange that DH would be a "position" for a young player. But Reimer was the Rangers' Minor League Player of the Year in 1988 and that bodes well for the future.

Reimer got into 64 games in 1990, and while he batted only .260, 12 of his 26 hits went for extra bases. He did well off the bench, coming to bat as a pinch hitter 40 times and tying a club record with 12 hits. Reimer had eight RBI in pinch roles and a .475 slugging percentage -- signs that he could be a very tough clutch hitter. A left-handed batter, his average against lefties was a fat .000, but he was only allowed to face them five times.

Reimer is not a base stealer, but he is a good, aggressive baserunner who has always bagged a lot of doubles and triples. His glove is a big question mark, however. It is hard to imagine how Reimer earned two errors when he played in the outfield so little. He wants to play -- the day after the season ended he had arthroscopic surgery on his right elbow.

OVERALL:

Reimer looks like a fine young power hitter. Thus far he's been limited to bench duty, and has been impressive in that limited role. He's still a little too young to be pegged a career DH/pinch hitter, and may get a chance to break out of that mold this year.

JOHN RUSSELL

Position: C/DH
Bats: R **Throws:** R
Ht: 6' 0" **Wt:** 195

Opening Day Age: 30
Born: 1/5/61 in Oklahoma City, OK
ML Seasons: 7

Overall Statistics

	G	AB	R	H	D	T	HR	RBI	SB	BB	SO	AVG
1990	68	128	16	35	4	0	2	8	1	11	41	.273
Career	401	1028	108	236	49	3	33	123	3	80	334	.230

HITTING, FIELDING, BASERUNNING:

John Russell will forever be a trivia question answer as the man who caught Nolan Ryan's sixth no-hitter. Historians will forget -- but Russell will remember -- that he did not catch any of the Rangers' final 55 games of the 1990 season. The main reason for that was that Russell managed to throw out only one of 25 base runners.

Russell did pinch hit and play several other positions, however, and all-in-all he had a fairly successful year, hitting 91 points higher than in 1989. His .273 batting average was 50 points over his previous career average. Although Russell was used mostly against lefties, he hit .308 off righthanders. Russell remains a hitter with very poor strike zone judgement. He fanned 41 times in 128 at-bats last year, a fairly typical performance for him, while drawing only 11 walks. He runs very slowly, though he did manage to steal a base last year. It was Russell's first stolen base in five years.

OVERALL:

Russell's hitting last year figures to secure him a place as a Ranger bench player this year. His catching isn't good enough to make him more than a number-three man at the position, but he's bound to see some action as a designated hitter and pinch swinger. The fact that he hits righties as well as lefties gives him added value.

JIM ACKER

Position: RP
Bats: R **Throws:** R
Ht: 6' 2" **Wt:** 212
Opening Day Age: 32
Born: 9/24/58 in Freer, TX
ML Seasons: 8

Overall Statistics

	W	L	ERA	G	GS	Sv	IP	H	R	BB	SO	HR
1990	4	4	3.83	59	0	1	91.2	103	49	30	54	9
Career	30	44	3.78	396	28	29	785.1	796	375	281	427	62

How Often He Throws Strikes

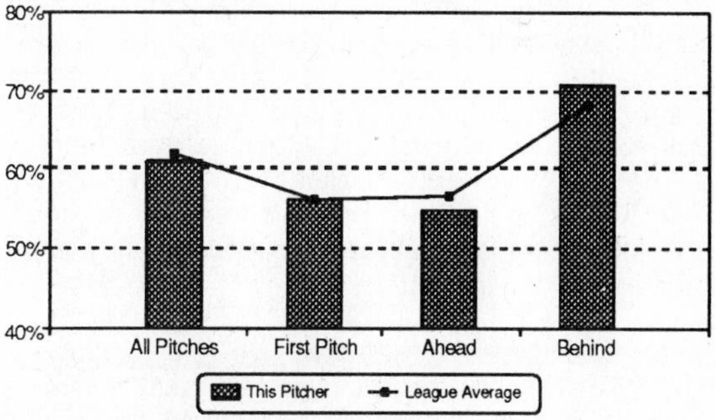

1990 Situational Stats

	W	L	ERA	Sv	IP		AB	H	HR	RBI	AVG
Home	2	3	3.76	1	52.2	LHB	149	43	2	16	.289
Road	2	1	3.92	0	39.0	RHB	217	60	7	37	.276
Day	2	0	3.67	1	34.1	Sc Pos	108	29	5	45	.269
Night	2	4	3.92	0	57.1	Clutch	100	32	1	11	.320

1990 Rankings (American League)

- 2nd worst first batter efficiency (.382)

PITCHING:

The Jays re-acquired Jim Acker from Atlanta in 1989 and he's been able to fulfill the main expectation that people have for him -- doing whatever is necessary. Acker doesn't get as much notice as the other relievers, especially Tom Henke and Duane Ward, but he pitched in 59 games, mostly in set-up roles for the closers. That's been his primary job through eight major league seasons.

Acker can pitch several days in a row when the team needs him, and holds his own against left-handed batters. In fact, righties were more of a threat to hit homers off him last season. That betrays his reputation of being a tough target for righties. But, at the same time, his ability to handle lefties will improve his stock as a middle reliever who can work two or three innings to replace a shaky starter or in extra innings. When Acker's stuff is working, he doesn't get a lot of strikeouts, but he gets a good number of ground balls and double plays.

Acker's main pitch is a fastball that stays down in the strike zone. His slider is average and he's developed a change-up that has improved with age. In other words, Acker beats you -- or gets beat -- with basic stuff. He sometimes goes through periods when he'll be as effective as anyone, and others when there's little mystery at all to his pitches. Acker averaged about one walk every three innings last season, a slight improvement over his career totals.

Acker had some elbow problems during his stint with Atlanta, but has been pitching often enough that he must be considered to be in good health. While he isn't likely to evolve into a closer, his style should allow him to keep contributing to a deep bullpen.

HOLDING RUNNERS AND FIELDING:

Acker's defense has also improved with time. He handles bunts well and is usually in good position to field ground balls. He doesn't spend an extraordinary amount of time worrying about baserunners, but he has a good enough move to keep them from running too often.

OVERALL:

Acker will never be a standout, but he should have several years left as a significant contributor in the bullpen. Acker is the kind of pitcher who has the potential to rack up victories by keeping his team in the game in middle relief. He's had a couple of those seasons despite a career record that's under .500. Judge his effectiveness by appearances and innings pitched.

GEORGE BELL

Position: LF/DH
Bats: R **Throws:** R
Ht: 6' 1" **Wt:** 202

Opening Day Age: 31
Born: 10/21/59 in San Pedro de Macoris, Dominican Republic
ML Seasons: 9

HITTING:

In 1991, George Bell will be coming back from an off year that would look pretty good to most players. Bothered by an eye injury, he went six late-season weeks without a home run and didn't have an extra base hit for more than a month. Still, Bell has a well-earned reputation for being a solid clutch player.

Bell has excellent bat speed and will take a hack at high fastballs, regardless of whether they're inside or out. He'll also go after pitches that might be headed for the dirt. But he's a guy whose average seems to climb with the game on the line, relishing the power pitcher versus power hitter matchup that comes his way in the eighth or ninth inning.

One thing Bell doesn't like is the off-speed pitch. He wants to be challenged, and can be frustrated by a pitcher who changes speeds and throws junk his way. Pitchers have known success against him by getting Bell to chase breaking-balls down and away. He also takes it personally when a pitcher comes inside on him, and some teams have gotten the better of him by doing so. But his wrists are so quick that the pitcher who doesn't jam him enough is a pitcher likely to give up the long ball. While he doesn't draw a lot of walks, Bell seems to have a better eye -- and slightly more patience -- against lefthanders.

BASERUNNING:

It has taken Bell the last five seasons combined to steal as many bases as the 21 he captured in 1985. He has been bothered by a sore left knee for several years, and that has cut his speed considerably. He still has good instincts, and will try for an extra base or break up a double play when the opportunity arises.

FIELDING:

Once furious when used as a DH, Bell now accepts the role more willingly. That makes sense, given his limitations as an outfielder. Bell has a good arm when it is sound, but his range is limited and he especially has trouble going back on balls. Sometimes he seems lazy in the outfield, which invites opponents to get aggressive with him. He's definitely not a Gold Glove candidate.

OVERALL:

Though Bell's power stats have been down the last few years, one shouldn't assume that his best days are behind him. He's a competitor who has successfully adjusted to physical limitations, and he has an intense desire to win. If he can recapture his health for an entire season, he could easily hit 30 homers and drive in more than 100 runs.

Overall Statistics

	G	AB	R	H	D	T	HR	RBI	SB	BB	SO	AVG
1990	142	562	67	149	25	0	21	86	3	32	80	.265
Career	1181	4528	641	1294	237	32	202	740	59	255	563	.286

Where He Hits the Ball

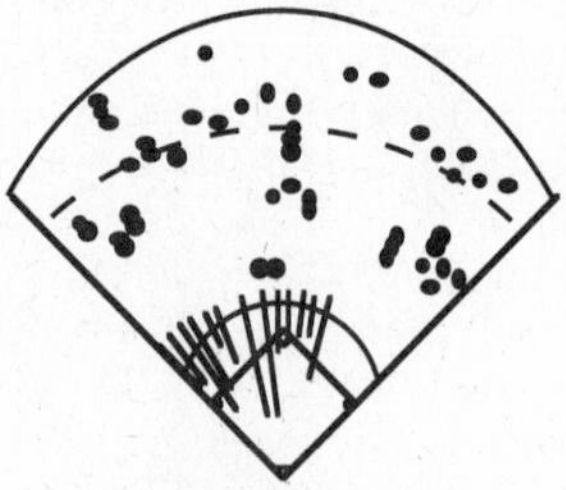

Vs. LHP

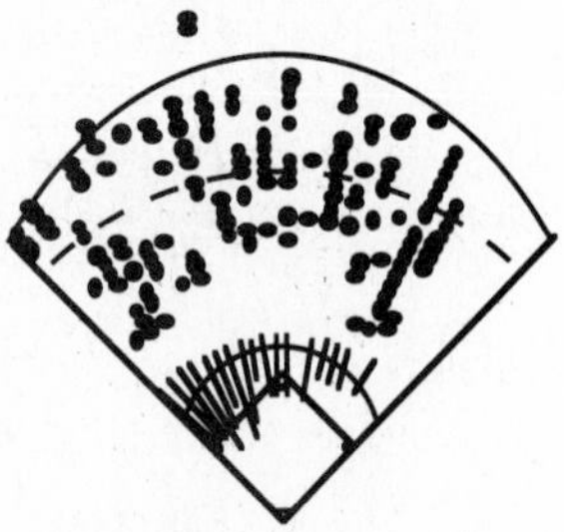

Vs. RHP

1990 Situational Stats

	AB	H	HR	RBI	AVG		AB	H	HR	RBI	AVG
Home	274	70	11	41	.255	LHP	149	37	5	22	.248
Road	288	79	10	45	.274	RHP	413	112	16	64	.271
Day	165	51	6	22	.309	Sc Pos	149	41	6	67	.275
Night	397	98	15	64	.247	Clutch	89	17	5	14	.191

1990 Rankings (American League)

- → 3rd in sacrifice flies (11) and lowest on-base average vs. right-handed pitchers (.298)
- → 4th lowest groundball/flyball ratio (.76)
- → 6th lowest on-base average (.303)
- → Led AL left-fielders in sacrifice flies

PITCHING:

After spending most of last season with Cleveland, Bud Black was traded to the Jays for the stretch drive. A free agent at season's end, he signed with San Francisco in November. Black is 33 years old, and has been through some of the downturns that usually happen to older pitchers. He was among the AL's most effective pitchers a few years back, with Kansas City, only to fall on hard times and find himself working out of the bullpen. Black rediscovered himself a couple of years ago, regaining his prowess and returning to a starting role.

Black's records have been in the .500 range for the past two seasons, but they would have looked much better if he'd gotten more offensive support. He keeps his defense hustling, keeping the ball in play as opposed to giving up walks and striking out many. The elbow problems that hindered him a couple of years ago seem to have cleared up.

Black has five different pitches, including two fastballs, the standard, sinking variety and a cut fastball with which he can jam right-handed batters. The latter pitch is important, as teams tend to load their lineups with righties because he's been so tough on lefties during most of his ten-year career. He also throws a slider, curve and change-up. Sometimes, the problem for a pitcher with that many pitches -- and Black is no exception -- is to find out what's working on a given day and stay away from the stuff that isn't.

Black has good movement on his pitches, which can sometimes make for a tough day for his catcher. He can throw a slow, looping curve that messes with the minds of power hitters and can then back them off the plate with his high-80s fastball.

HOLDING RUNNERS AND FIELDING:

One interesting thing about Black is that he's very aggressive -- and very successful -- at going after the lead runner on bunt plays. He's quick off the mound and you'll never see him get lazy about covering first base on grounders to the right side. He pays a lot of attention to base runners, both at first and second base, and does a pretty good job of keeping them close.

OVERALL:

Black should have several more productive years because he's made a habit of relying on his wits instead of strictly on physical ability. He's the sort of stable influence, a consummate professional, who could have a positive effect on younger pitchers as well.

BUD BLACK

Position: SP
Bats: L **Throws:** L
Ht: 6' 2" **Wt:** 185

Opening Day Age: 33
Born: 6/30/57 in San Mateo, CA
ML Seasons: 10

Overall Statistics

	W	L	ERA	G	GS	Sv	IP	H	R	BB	SO	HR
1990	13	11	3.57	32	31	0	206.2	181	86	61	106	19
Career	83	82	3.70	299	198	11	1466.2	1397	673	428	746	139

How Often He Throws Strikes

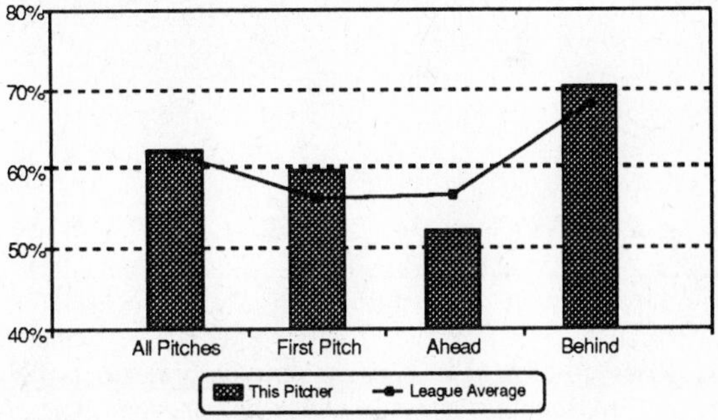

1990 Situational Stats

	W	L	ERA	Sv	IP		AB	H	HR	RBI	AVG
Home	8	5	3.13	0	103.2	LHB	145	41	7	20	.283
Road	5	6	4.02	0	103.0	RHB	633	140	12	49	.221
Day	3	2	2.33	0	46.1	Sc Pos	153	32	3	48	.209
Night	10	9	3.93	0	160.1	Clutch	69	13	1	4	.188

1990 Rankings (American League)

- 4th least GDPs induced per 9 innings (.39)
- 5th lowest on-base average allowed (.290)
- 6th in shutouts (2), least baserunners allowed per 9 innings (10.8) and lowest batting average allowed vs. right-handed batters (.221)
- 7th lowest batting average allowed (.233) and lowest batting average allowed with runners in scoring position (.209)
- 8th lowest run support per 9 innings (4.3)

PAT BORDERS

Position: C
Bats: R **Throws:** R
Ht: 6' 2" **Wt:** 205

Opening Day Age: 27
Born: 5/14/63 in Columbus, OH
ML Seasons: 3

HITTING:

Pat Borders bulled his way into being the number one Blue Jay catcher last season. Proving that he could hit right-handed pitching, he finally broke out of the platoon role he'd been sharing with Greg Myers.

Borders has evolved from a hitter who could be counted on to chase a first-pitch fastball into a free swinger who doesn't appear to be overmatched by anything. That's one difference between playing only against lefties and then getting more than half of the catching at-bats. After struggling against righthanders for years, Borders's average was virtually identical against lefties and righties in 1990.

Borders still doesn't draw enough walks, especially against right-handers, but that's a flaw to be worked on with experience. Pitchers take advantage of his tendency to chase sliders in the dirt. Borders was also among the team leaders at grounding into double plays, even though he didn't have that many at-bats. Borders seemed anxious in the clutch last season, as his average dropped markedly with runners in scoring position. But he struck out less frequently than in his first two seasons.

Borders was among those who favored the SkyDome for power. He hit a disproportionate number of homers at home, while hitting for a higher average on the road. Whatever the case, those who were worried about the dropoff in Borders's production from 1988 to 1989 -- both seasons in which he was very much a part-time player -- had to be satisfied that he recaptured his offensive abilities. Maybe all he needed was enough playing time to get into a groove.

BASERUNNING:

This guy is strictly a chugger. Borders goes from base-to-base and doesn't think about taking an extra one. He isn't much of a factor around second base, or barreling into a catcher at home, because he rarely gets there in time to break up a play.

FIELDING:

Originally a third baseman who switched to catching to better his chances of making the majors, Borders is still learning the mechanics of the position. He's doing so without a veteran catcher on the team for guidance, and that hasn't helped. He's adequate, but still has a lot to learn.

OVERALL:

The Jays would probably have been satisfied if Borders had turned out to be a platoon player. Instead, they're getting much more, especially on offense. If his batting eye and his defense improve, Borders could take his place as one of the three or four best all-around catchers in the league.

Overall Statistics

	G	AB	R	H	D	T	HR	RBI	SB	BB	SO	AVG
1990	125	346	36	99	24	2	15	49	0	18	57	.286
Career	275	741	73	203	41	6	23	99	2	32	126	.274

Where He Hits the Ball

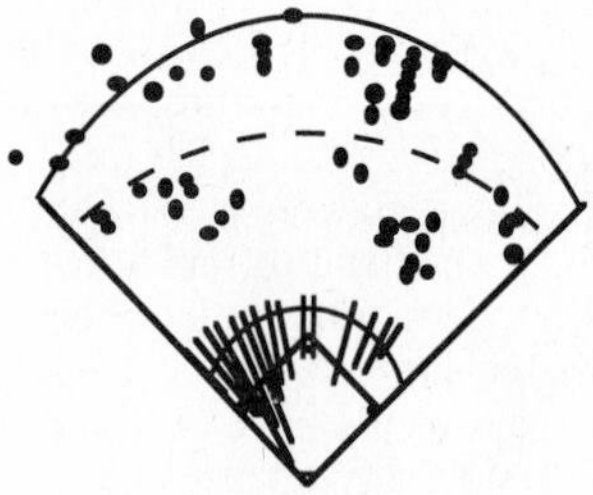

Vs. LHP

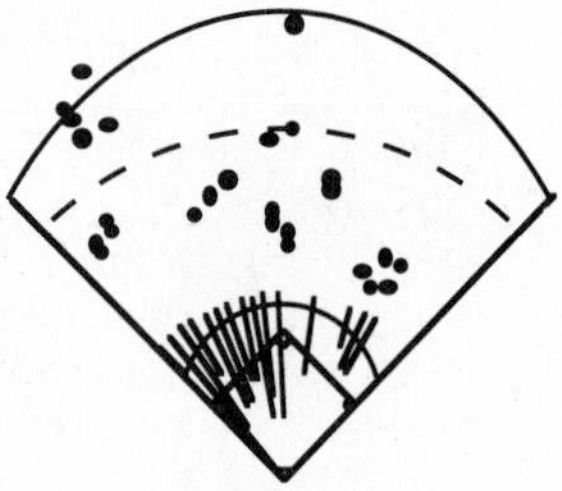

Vs. RHP

1990 Situational Stats

	AB	H	HR	RBI	AVG		AB	H	HR	RBI	AVG
Home	164	45	10	28	.274	LHP	186	53	10	27	.285
Road	182	54	5	21	.297	RHP	160	46	5	22	.287
Day	114	35	6	15	.307	Sc Pos	89	20	2	28	.225
Night	232	64	9	34	.276	Clutch	67	17	2	9	.254

1990 Rankings (American League)

- 2nd most GDPs per GDP situation (21.5%)
- 3rd most runners caught stealing by a catcher (42.6%)
- 9th highest slugging percentage vs. left-handed pitchers (.554)
- Led the Blue Jays in GDPs (17)
- Led AL catchers in highest slugging percentage vs. left-handed pitchers

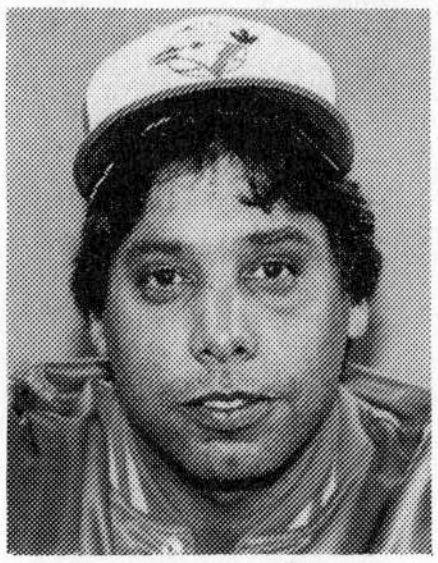

JOHN CANDELARIA

Position: RP/SP
Bats: R **Throws:** L
Ht: 6' 6" **Wt:** 225

Opening Day Age: 37
Born: 11/6/53 in Brooklyn, NY
ML Seasons: 16

PITCHING:

John Candelaria was a late-season acquisition for the Jays, and could fit into their future plans if he finds a niche. After being an effective starting pitcher in his younger years, Candelaria seems more at home as a reliever. He can go three or four effective innings, but there are questions about whether he could last longer than that on a regular basis. Still, in a game where good lefties are tough to find, there should be a place for him somewhere in the majors.

Candelaria is very tall and has an unusual, slingshot delivery that is especially tough on lefties. Yet he couldn't be an effective long reliever without being able to get righthanded batters out, and they, too, seem to have trouble with him. Candelaria has good control and can still put the ball wherever he wants. Throughout his career, he has sometimes frustrated managers by wanting to use the outside corner too much instead of busting hitters inside. It's a sign of self-confidence, through, that Candelaria feels he can be effective while using the outside half of the plate.

Depending on the situation, Candelaria can throw a fastball that seems to explode -- his strikeout pitch -- or a sinking fastball that can get ground balls and double plays. He has become more susceptible to the home run ball in recent years, and has never been one to rely much on off-speed pitches. He also was a streaky pitcher in 1990, picking up several saves by taking over in the middle innings and looking good enough that the manager didn't think of taking him out.

HOLDING RUNNERS AND FIELDING:

Candelaria has a motion that's slow to unfold in the stretch and, as a result, a good baserunner can study and take advantage of him. It's a problem shared by many tall pitchers. Candelaria fields grounders well, especially balls hit in front of him and bunts near home plate. But he sometimes is late to first base because his delivery takes him in the other direction.

OVERALL:

At this stage of his career, Candelaria wants to work out of the bullpen -- a change from earlier days when he was miffed about being yanked from the Pittsburgh rotation. He still can be a fill-in starter, if the need exists. Candelaria has been plagued by knee, back and arm problems that have cut into his playing time over the years. He's seemed to bounce back and, if healthy, should have a couple of more years to contribute.

Overall Statistics

	W	L	ERA	G	GS	Sv	IP	H	R	BB	SO	HR
1990	7	6	3.95	47	3	5	79.2	87	36	20	63	11
Career	174	113	3.29	467	356	21	2447.2	2323	994	559	1595	239

How Often He Throws Strikes

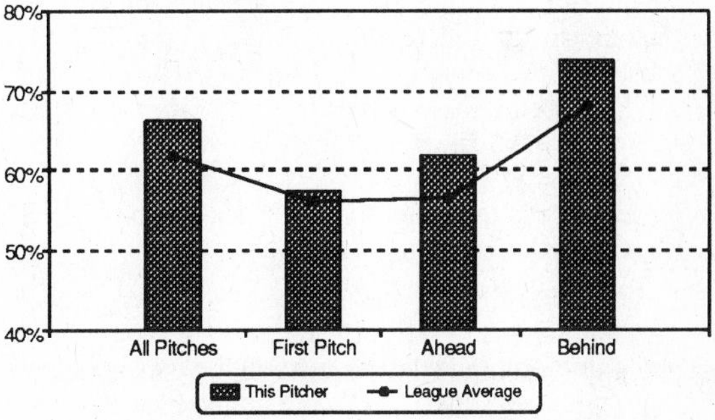

1990 Situational Stats

	W	L	ERA	Sv	IP		AB	H	HR	RBI	AVG
Home	2	2	3.66	5	39.1	LHB	79	20	0	7	.253
Road	5	4	4.24	0	40.1	RHB	236	67	11	34	.284
Day	2	0	1.71	3	21.0	Sc Pos	88	17	2	28	.193
Night	5	6	4.76	2	58.2	Clutch	90	25	2	18	.278

1990 Rankings (American League)

- Did not rank near the top or bottom in any category

PITCHING:

After 1989, John Cerutti seemed on the verge of establishing himself as a regular member of the Jays rotation. That seems in doubt now, in part because 1990 brought a couple of new lefties into that role and, in larger part, because Cerutti didn't have a very good season. He started 23 games, and was working from the bullpen down the stretch drive.

Cerutti is a finesse pitcher who needs to have pinpoint control to be effective. He has an above-average curveball and slider, which allows him to get away with a fastball that is clocked no faster than the 84-86 MPH range. When the breaking pitches aren't working, batters can sit on the fastball and have a field day. In his younger days, Cerutti kept the ball high in the strike zone, but he's since come up with a sinking fastball.

Despite his mediocre statistics, Cerutti led Toronto pitchers in ground ball double plays, averaging almost one and a half per nine innings. The downside was that Cerutti also allowed more homers than any of his teammates, even though he was only fifth on the team in innings pitched. That's an inconsistency that he needs to overcome, or at least control, if he hopes to make a return to the rotation.

Cerutti doesn't walk many batters, so hitters tend to dig in against him. He's never been a strikeout pitcher and didn't dominate lefties in 1990 the way he's done in previous seasons. He also seemed to have a disproportionate amount of trouble pitching at the SkyDome, the Jays' new stadium, in which he had an ERA well over five.

HOLDING RUNNERS AND FIELDING:

Cerutti gets enough ground balls that he had better be a good fielding pitcher -- and he is. He has a good sense of timing on his throws to second base, and he's quick off the mound on bunts and to cover first base. He's always had a good move to first that seems to keep even the top baserunners off balance, which makes up for a slower-than-average delivery. He makes a lot of throws to first.

OVERALL:

There's some question about what the future holds for Cerutti. If he has a solid spring, he could return to the rotation. Otherwise, he could become a swingman, a sixth starter who gets most of his work in long relief. He's made adjustments to different situations throughout his career, so the uncertainty won't be anything new.

JOHN CERUTTI

Position: SP/RP
Bats: L **Throws:** L
Ht: 6' 2" **Wt:** 200

Opening Day Age: 30
Born: 4/28/60 in Albany, NY
ML Seasons: 6

Overall Statistics

	W	L	ERA	G	GS	Sv	IP	H	R	BB	SO	HR
1990	9	9	4.76	30	23	0	140.0	162	77	49	49	23
Career	46	37	3.87	191	108	2	772.1	800	378	254	369	110

How Often He Throws Strikes

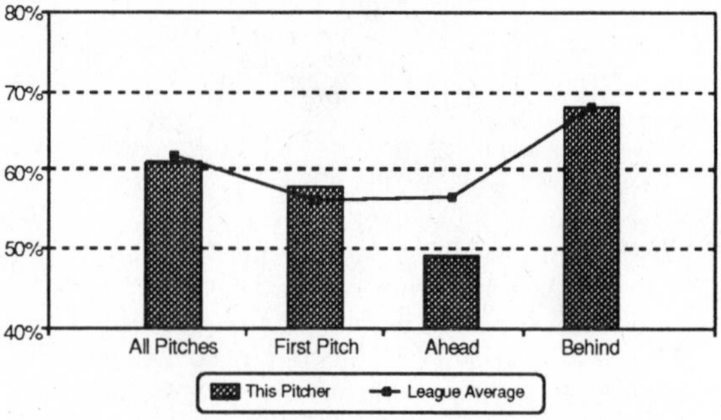

1990 Situational Stats

	W	L	ERA	Sv	IP		AB	H	HR	RBI	AVG
Home	5	5	5.32	0	71.0	LHB	112	31	3	14	.277
Road	4	4	4.17	0	69.0	RHB	434	131	20	59	.302
Day	2	1	3.94	0	32.0	Sc Pos	107	29	4	45	.271
Night	7	8	5.00	0	108.0	Clutch	39	14	2	7	.359

1990 Rankings (American League)

- 1st in highest batting average allowed vs. right-handed batters (.302)
- 9th in home runs allowed (23)
- Led the Blue Jays in home runs allowed and GDPs induced (22)

JUNIOR FELIX

Position: RF/CF
Bats: B **Throws:** R
Ht: 5'11" **Wt:** 165

Opening Day Age: 23
Born: 10/3/67 in Laguna Sabada, Dominican Republic
ML Seasons: 2

Overall Statistics

	G	AB	R	H	D	T	HR	RBI	SB	BB	SO	AVG
1990	127	463	73	122	23	7	15	65	13	45	99	.263
Career	237	878	135	229	37	15	24	111	31	78	200	.261

Where He Hits the Ball

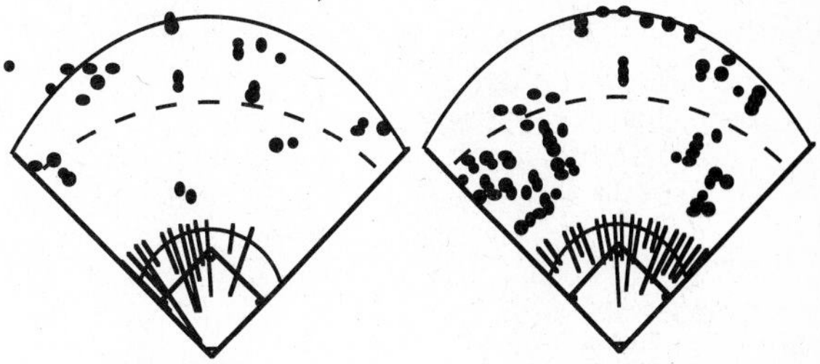

1990 Situational Stats

	AB	H	HR	RBI	AVG		AB	H	HR	RBI	AVG
Home	236	58	7	29	.246	LHP	152	32	9	22	.211
Road	227	64	8	36	.282	RHP	311	90	6	43	.289
Day	156	41	6	20	.263	Sc Pos	106	31	3	48	.292
Night	307	81	9	45	.264	Clutch	75	12	1	7	.160

1990 Rankings (American League)

- 3rd worst leadoff on-base average (.288)
- 4th least GDPs per GDP situation (4.9%) and worst batting average in the clutch (.160)
- 5th most runs scored per time reached base (43.2%)
- 7th lowest batting average vs. left-handed pitchers (.211)
- 8th in triples (7)
- Led the Blue Jays in least GDPs per GDP situation

HITTING:

A speedy switch-hitter, Junior Felix has shown that he can help the Jays in any number of ways. Batting at the top of the order, he can reach and cause commotion on the bases. But Felix has shown more power than you'd expect from a slim 165-pounder, and can bat lower in the lineup. He's still very young, only 23 years old, and has the potential to be among baseball's elite players if he continues to improve.

As with most switch hitters, Felix has one side from which he's been considerably stronger -- the left side. Felix had more homers in fewer at-bats swinging right-handed last year, but he also battled to keep his average at .200 from that side of the plate. He tends to take the ball up the middle and toward left-center from the right, while spraying the ball to all fields from the left. Teams can bunch their outfielders when they use a left-handed pitcher, but must play him more honestly otherwise.

Felix uses a very open stance and, as a result, suffers when pitchers work the outside half of the plate. He also has a tendency to fall behind in the count, although his walk total indicates increased patience. Felix likes fastballs from both sides of the plate and has trouble with breaking pitches. He also could take better advantage of his speed by slapping more grounders, especially on artificial turf. The discipline of knowing when to swing away, and when to try to get on base, is difficult for a young power hitter like Felix.

BASERUNNING:

Felix has a lot of speed but still hasn't learned how to use it to his advantage. He's too aggressive on the bases, a habit that other Toronto players have, and sometimes runs himself out of good situations. He doesn't always get a good lead off first and steals more on sheer talent than technique. He's fast from first to third.

FIELDING:

Felix can get to balls that other players can't, but he still needs to get a better jump on the ball. He isn't afraid of outfield walls or colliding with teammates, but he sometimes risks injury taking needless chances. You can't fault Felix for his enthusiasm, however, or his strong throwing arm.

OVERALL:

Nobody in Toronto seems to miss Jesse Barfield, who was traded to the Yankees in 1989. That indicates how well Felix is performing. It isn't difficult to imagine that he'll hit .290 with 30 steals and 15 homers on a regular basis.

HITTING:

After two injury-plagued seasons, Tony Fernandez may be headed toward regaining recognition as the best all-around shortstop in the American League. Last year Fernandez showed unprecedented restraint, drawing more walks than ever before while remaining a contact hitter with the ability to spray line drives to all fields. His .276 average didn't approach his 1987 high of .322, but it was a big step up from the career low of .257 to which Fernandez tumbled in '89.

A switch-hitter, Fernandez was tougher against righthanders last season, after being tougher against lefties the year before. He favors low pitches from the left and high fastballs from the right. Batting left-handed, he gets jammed a lot; batting right, Fernandez usually gets worked down and away. Fernandez grounds into more double plays that you would expect from someone with his speed.

Fernandez has occasional power, especially from the right side, although his homer total was down markedly from the 11 he hit in 1989. He's had a reputation throughout his eight-year career for hitting in the clutch. Unlike a lot of contact hitters, Fernandez can come to the plate wanting to pull the ball and do it effectively. He isn't the sort to overswing and hit 250-foot fly balls. From either side of the plate, with a runner on first, he's good at using the gap in the right side of the infield, an excellent hit-and-run man.

BASERUNNING:

Fernandez had the lowest stolen base percentage of his career in 1990, which was odd considering that he was 22-for-28 the year before and thought to be fully recovered from the badly injured left knee he suffered in '87. That he still has speed, though, was demonstrated beyond doubt by his league leadership in triples. He was stealing well late in the year, and he isn't afraid to make a hard slide into second base.

FIELDING:

The AL version of Ozzie Smith, Fernandez has Ozzie's knack for making impossible plays look easy. Totaling only 15 errors over the last two seasons, he's different from the guys who don't make miscues because they don't have any range. Fernandez is one of the handful of baseball players worth watching for their defensive skills alone.

OVERALL:

Fernandez is still young -- only 28 -- and should have a number of good years ahead of him. With 100 percent health, he should be able to put up the same numbers as he had a few years back and be a cornerstone for whatever success Toronto has in the coming seasons.

TONY FERNANDEZ

Position: SS
Bats: B **Throws:** R
Ht: 6' 2" **Wt:** 170

Opening Day Age: 28
Born: 6/30/62 in San Pedro de Macoris, Dominican Republic
ML Seasons: 8

Overall Statistics

	G	AB	R	H	D	T	HR	RBI	SB	BB	SO	AVG
1990	161	635	84	175	27	17	4	66	26	71	70	.276
Career	1028	3952	510	1142	192	61	40	404	138	285	344	.289

Where He Hits the Ball

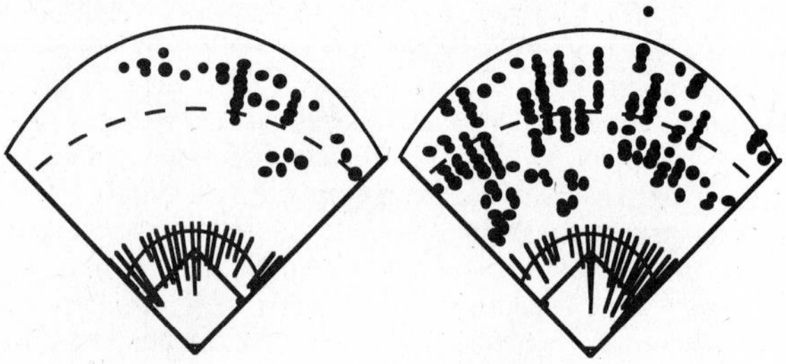

Vs. LHP   Vs. RHP

1990 Situational Stats

	AB	H	HR	RBI	AVG		AB	H	HR	RBI	AVG
Home	321	99	2	38	.308	LHP	202	48	1	13	.238
Road	314	76	2	28	.242	RHP	433	127	3	53	.293
Day	200	58	2	18	.290	Sc Pos	151	47	3	60	.311
Night	435	117	2	48	.269	Clutch	85	28	0	5	.329

1990 Rankings (American League)

- 1st in triples (17)
- 2nd in plate appearances (721) and games (161)
- 3rd in at-bats (635)
- Led the Blue Jays in at-bats, hits (175), singles (127), triples, stolen bases (26), caught stealing (13), GDPs (17), pitches seen (2,578), plate appearances, games and batting average in the clutch (.329)
- Led AL shortstops in at-bats, runs (84), hits, singles, triples, stolen bases, hit by pitch, times on base (253), GDPs, pitches seen, plate appearances, games and stolen base percentage (66.7%)

KELLY GRUBER

Position: 3B
Bats: R **Throws:** R
Ht: 6' 0" **Wt:** 185

Opening Day Age: 29
Born: 2/26/62 in Bellaire, TX
ML Seasons: 7

HITTING:

Last year Kelly Gruber emerged as one of the AL's most dangerous power hitters. He made the transformation from a guy who could hit the occasional homer to a guy who now hits them frequently -- a perfect right-handed complement to first baseman Fred McGriff. Gruber started last season quickly and finished just as strongly, adding more than 30 RBIs to his previous single-season best.

The secret? Well, Gruber was the player who seemed to take best to the new SkyDome. Thought to be a pitcher's park when it opened in 1989, Gruber showed that the initial returns were somewhat misleading. Most of his power has traditionally been to left and left-center, but Gruber added some healthy opposite-field homers last year. He was also able to cut down on his swing at times and put line drives up the gap. Gruber's strikeout total mushroomed from the previous season, but it was worth the extra output.

Gruber is a high fastball hitter who appeared to have better success against breaking pitches in '90 than in years past. He's also different from many sluggers in that he doesn't get frustrated by lollipop curves and other offspeed gimmicks. He simply waits for a pitch to drive or, failing that, shortens his swing accordingly. Gruber can be a bad-ball hitter and doesn't draw many walks. With McGriff and George Bell in the lineup, teams don't often have the luxury of pitching around him.

BASERUNNING:

Gruber can make a second baseman or catcher pay for hanging in there with a hard slide, but he's also hurt himself more than once by coming in head first. He'll take the extra base at every opportunity and is an efficient stealer, one who studies the opposing pitcher and makes the most of his speed and quickness.

FIELDING:

Gruber has a strong but erratic arm. He cut down his error total from 1989 to 1990 and might not be as much of a test for Toronto first basemen in the future. He has good range, and has sent more than a few batters back to the dugout muttering after taking away what looked like extra-base hits into the corner. He can also play the outfield if the Jays need him there.

OVERALL:

This volume last year stated: "Kelly can only get better. He's capable of hitting .300 with 25 homers and 100 RBIs." Well, three out of four (everything but the .300 part) isn't bad, and nobody should rule that out for the future. Gruber probably took over last year as the best all-around third baseman in the American League.

Overall Statistics

	G	AB	R	H	D	T	HR	RBI	SB	BB	SO	AVG
1990	150	592	92	162	36	6	31	118	14	48	94	.274
Career	688	2219	321	590	111	19	83	326	61	138	351	.266

Where He Hits the Ball

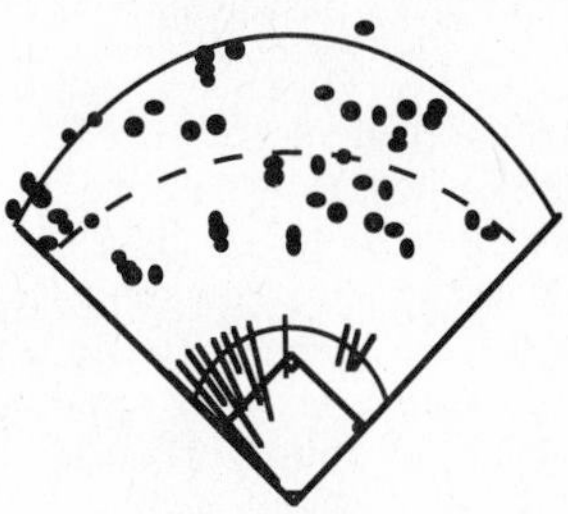

Vs. LHP

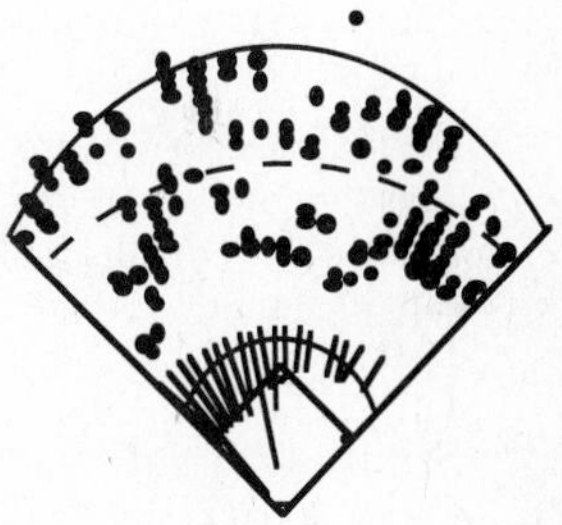

Vs. RHP

1990 Situational Stats

	AB	H	HR	RBI	AVG		AB	H	HR	RBI	AVG
Home	305	89	23	62	.292	LHP	166	49	8	34	.295
Road	287	73	8	56	.254	RHP	426	113	23	84	.265
Day	182	43	13	38	.236	Sc Pos	150	47	13	93	.313
Night	410	119	18	80	.290	Clutch	97	25	3	24	.258

1990 Rankings (American League)

- 2nd in total bases (303), RBIs (118) and sacrifice flies (13)
- 3rd in hit by pitch (8)
- 5th in home runs (31) and lowest percentage of pitches taken (54.9%)
- Led the Blue Jays in runs (92), doubles (36), total bases, RBIs, sacrifice flies, hit by pitch and batting average with runners in scoring position (.313)
- Led AL third basemen in home runs, triples (6), total bases, RBIs, sacrifice flies, hit by pitch, slugging percentage (.512), HR frequency (19.1 ABs per HR) and runs scored per time reached base (42.2%)

STOPPER

TOM HENKE

Position: RP
Bats: R **Throws:** R
Ht: 6' 5" **Wt:** 225

Opening Day Age: 33
Born: 12/21/57 in Kansas City, MO
ML Seasons: 9

PITCHING:

The last few years, many folks have been waiting to give up on Tom Henke as the Toronto closer. But he's shown those thoughts to be unwise. Manager Cito Gaston was willing to acknowledge Henke as a slow starter and brought him along cautiously last season, using Duane Ward and David Wells for some early-season saves and guarding Henke from overuse over the entire year.

Gaston and the Jays were rewarded for their patience, as Henke was untouchable for much of the season. He doesn't have many secrets. He throws a monster fastball that is clocked in the mid-90s when he's sharp. By comparison, at the start of the 1989 season (when there was the most concern about his future), Henke was clocked in the high-80s and without much movement. He loves to throw the fastball high, giving batters a good-looking pitch that's past them before they know it.

Henke has also developed a forkball over the past few seasons, and is at his best when it is working in concert with the fastball -- batters swinging above the dirt-breaking forkball and below the shoulder-high fastball. When the forkball isn't working, Henke is vulnerable, especially to the home run ball. Henke also throws a slider once in a while, mostly when he's ahead in the count and looking to waste a pitch.

With Henke, it doesn't seem to matter if he's facing lefties or righties. Both have the same success (or lack of it) with him. In 1989, his statistics were down significantly in day games, causing some to wonder if batters merely needed a better look at his stuff, but his day-time ERA in 1990 was around one. So don't get the idea that the secret to beating Henke is waiting until Sunday afternoon.

FIELDING AND HOLDING RUNNERS:

Henke doesn't get many ground balls, which negates the fact that he has some problems fielding them. He doesn't get off the mound well and is only average at getting to first base. His pickoff move isn't great, but his fastball makes up for much of that. Also, runners aren't often willing to test him with the game on the line.

OVERALL:

With the right understanding -- some would call it "TLC" -- Henke should stay a factor for years to come. Developing the forkball showed that he won't give up when things get a little tough, but Henke is a soft-spoken and sensitive guy who needs an understanding manager. He appears to have a good situation in Toronto.

Overall Statistics

	W	L	ERA	G	GS	Sv	IP	H	R	BB	SO	HR
1990	2	4	2.17	61	0	32	74.2	58	18	19	75	8
Career	29	26	2.72	381	0	154	517.0	404	168	165	596	40

How Often He Throws Strikes

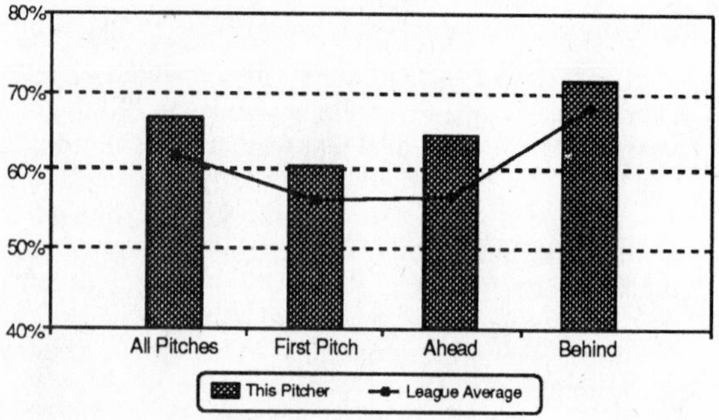

1990 Situational Stats

	W	L	ERA	Sv	IP		AB	H	HR	RBI	AVG
Home	2	0	2.39	16	37.2	LHB	138	29	4	17	.210
Road	0	4	1.95	16	37.0	RHB	134	29	4	7	.216
Day	0	1	1.33	8	20.1	Sc Pos	77	10	0	12	.130
Night	2	3	2.48	24	54.1	Clutch	176	39	6	22	.222

1990 Rankings (American League)

- 5th in games finished (58) and lowest percentage of inherited runners scored (18.8%)
- 6th in saves (32)
- 7th in save opportunities (38) and save percentage (84.2%)
- Led the Blue Jays in saves, games finished, save opportunities, save percentage, lowest batting average allowed vs. left-handed pitchers (.210) and lowest percentage of inherited runners scored

GLENALLEN HILL

Position: RF/LF/DH
Bats: R **Throws:** R
Ht: 6' 2" **Wt:** 210

Opening Day Age: 26
Born: 3/22/65 in Santa Cruz, CA
ML Seasons: 2

HITTING:

Back in 1985, it would have been hard to imagine Glenallen Hill making it to the majors. He connected for 20 home runs that season at Kingston of the Class A Carolina League, but he batted only .210 and struck out 211 -- yes, 211 -- times in 466 at-bats. Over the years, the holes in Hill's swing have gotten smaller, and some have disappeared altogether. In fact, with some teams which aren't as deep in outfielders as the Jays, Hill would probably be seeing regular action instead of part-time service.

Hill got a peek at the majors in 1989, hitting a grand slam in his first game. He showed some power last season -- surprisingly, showing more against right-handed pitchers than lefties. He's in a tough situation because the Jays have a number of talented outfielders, and many of his at-bats came as a designated hitter. He shared the job with another rookie, John Olerud, but each would have benefitted from increased playing time.

For much of his minor league career, Hill seemed to think that if he could reach it, he should swing at it -- an act that major-league pitchers would have loved. But now he's learned that he can get better swings if he's ahead in the count and that a single to right field can have some value, too. His average was lower than what was expected last season, but the lack of steady playing time kept him from getting into a groove.

BASERUNNING:

Hill is a big guy who runs well and isn't afraid to take out a second baseman. He's been stealing bases on pure speed and should be a threat to steal between 20 and 30, providing he gets enough playing time in the future.

FIELDING:

Hill was often used to spell George Bell in left field when the veteran was out of the lineup or moved to DH for a day. He isn't the kind of player you'd think of as a defensive replacement. His arm and range are average, and scouts have noticed that he takes too long to get rid of the ball. That's a problem that can be corrected if Hill wants to work on it.

OVERALL:

Hill went through some tough times in the minors, including a demotion from Class AAA to Class AA. But his attitude has improved and he apparently understands that the Jays aren't a team that's likely, right now, to give him 500 at-bats. There are several other players on the team who got their starts as bench players before moving into significant roles. Hill could well become another.

Overall Statistics

	G	AB	R	H	D	T	HR	RBI	SB	BB	SO	AVG
1990	84	260	47	60	11	3	12	32	8	18	62	.231
Career	103	312	51	75	11	3	13	39	10	21	74	.240

Where He Hits the Ball

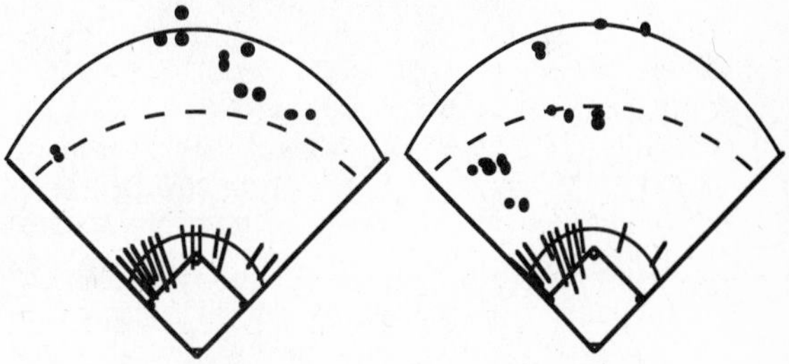

Vs. LHP   Vs. RHP

1990 Situational Stats

	AB	H	HR	RBI	AVG		AB	H	HR	RBI	AVG
Home	140	33	7	17	.236	LHP	143	32	5	12	.224
Road	120	27	5	15	.225	RHP	117	28	7	20	.239
Day	87	17	2	9	.195	Sc Pos	56	14	2	20	.250
Night	173	43	10	23	.249	Clutch	37	9	0	0	.243

1990 Rankings (American League)

- 2nd worst batting average with 2 strikes (.093)
- 9th lowest batting average with an 0-2 count (.045)

PITCHING:

Jimmy Key showed signs in 1990 that he can come back from the arm and shoulder problems that have hindered him for the past several seasons. While putting together a winning record, Key was less consistent than in past years, finishing with an ERA higher than four for the first time since his rookie season of 1984. Key, though, has never been a hard thrower, and has the ability to compensate for whatever has been taken away by the surgeon's knife. The Jays have had enough pitching depth that they've resisted the temptation to rush him along.

Key uses the entire plate and isn't afraid to throw any pitch on any count. He uses the fastball most of the time, backing batters away from the plate while maintaining excellent control. He's usually been good at keeping the ball down in the strike zone and knowing when he can challenge batters. His fastball is usually in the mid-80s, but has better movement than most. He has three other pitches, and uses the curve as a set-up pitch. It will break in on the fists of a righthander, allowing Key to work him away with the fastball or change-up later on. He remembers how he works hitters, changing his patterns to keep them from getting comfortable.

Opposing managers tend to give their lefty batters a rest against Key, and he's held those who've remained in the lineup to under a .200 average over the last three seasons while only allowing three homers. His health problem seems to have taken a toll, as much as anything, on his abilities against right-handers.

HOLDING RUNNERS AND FIELDING:

Other pitchers would do well to watch Key in action. His fundamentals are sound and he winds up in perfect position to field grounders and bunts. As a result, he gets 1-3 putouts on grounders that might otherwise turn into singles to center. He also gets to first base as quickly as anyone. Key doesn't fool baserunners. He has the kind of move that doesn't result in pickoffs but keeps most runners from trying to steal.

OVERALL:

If Key can stay healthy -- 225-innings healthy -- he has the stuff to win 20 games. With Dave Stieb, Toronto could have a lefty-righty combination as good as any, with a good supporting cast. Whatever the case, there are enough accomplished pitchers on the team that Key doesn't have to feel undue pressure.

JIMMY KEY

Position: SP
Bats: R **Throws:** L
Ht: 6' 1" **Wt:** 190

Opening Day Age: 29
Born: 4/22/61 in Huntsville, AL
ML Seasons: 7

Overall Statistics

	W	L	ERA	G	GS	Sv	IP	H	R	BB	SO	HR
1990	13	7	4.25	27	27	0	154.2	169	79	22	88	20
Career	87	56	3.47	251	184	10	1269.2	1212	538	301	702	129

How Often He Throws Strikes

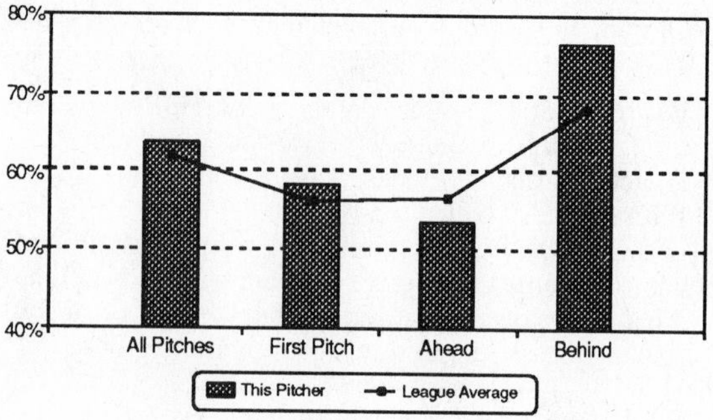

1990 Situational Stats

	W	L	ERA	Sv	IP		AB	H	HR	RBI	AVG
Home	7	3	4.47	0	88.2	LHB	88	16	0	5	.182
Road	6	4	3.95	0	66.0	RHB	514	153	20	61	.298
Day	5	6	5.57	0	74.1	Sc Pos	101	28	3	43	.277
Night	8	1	3.02	0	80.1	Clutch	12	3	0	0	.250

1990 Rankings (American League)

- 2nd highest batting average allowed vs. right-handed batters (.298)

MANNY LEE

Position: 2B
Bats: B **Throws:** R
Ht: 5' 9" **Wt:** 161

Opening Day Age: 25
Born: 6/17/65 in San Pedro de Macoris, Dominican Republic
ML Seasons: 6

HITTING:

Last season marked only the second time that Manny Lee had 400 plate appearances in a season. He was hardly brilliant, but it appears that the second base job will be his, unless Lee does something to ruin his standing. More than anything else, Lee is a guy who'll fill a spot at the bottom of the order, playing strong defense to make up for the fact that he won't be a consistent offensive contributor.

Lee has traditionally been stronger against left-handed pitchers and was platooned with Nelson Liriano until Liriano was traded to Minnesota last summer. Given the chance to play more often, Lee's average was about the same from both sides of the plate -- and lower than any season since 1985 and '86, when he was used mostly as a defensive replacement.

Primarily an opposite-field hitter from either side of the plate, Lee is vulnerable both to hard fastballs and breaking pitches. In other words, he can simply be outclassed by good pitching. He'd never hit more than three homers in a season until 1990, but the Jays would probably trade those longball swings for a better eye and more contact. Lee struck out about 23 percent of the time, a marked increase for him.

To his credit, Lee took advantage of the home field's artificial turf and hit much better at home and on fake grass. It's a skill on which he should concentrate more. While some players found the SkyDome a home-run haven, Lee hit his homers on the road.

BASERUNNING:

Lee's speed is only average, and he has never learned the finer points of stealing. He saves his quickness for playing defense. He's a cautious guy on the bases who will take the extra base when the chance comes up, but won't unsettle the defense with his daring. With his slight build, he isn't a terror when it comes to breaking up the double play.

FIELDING:

Shortstop is Lee's natural position, but as long as Tony Fernandez is around, he'll only be a backup there. He's made steady progress at second base and turns the double play reasonably well. He has a quick first step, something that Liriano lacked, and soft hands. Lee can make the spectacular play.

OVERALL:

The Jays haven't had a standout second baseman since the days of Damaso Garcia. Lee will probably never hit the way Garcia could, but if he can make some improvement at the plate and play solid defense, his team won't ask for much more. Should he falter, though, the Jays probably wouldn't wait long before looking elsewhere.

Overall Statistics

	G	AB	R	H	D	T	HR	RBI	SB	BB	SO	AVG
1990	117	391	45	95	12	4	6	41	3	26	90	.243
Career	487	1311	141	339	39	13	13	131	13	84	246	.259

Where He Hits the Ball

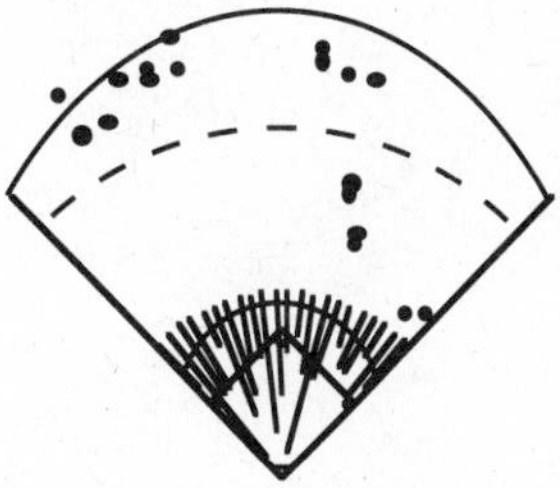

Vs. LHP

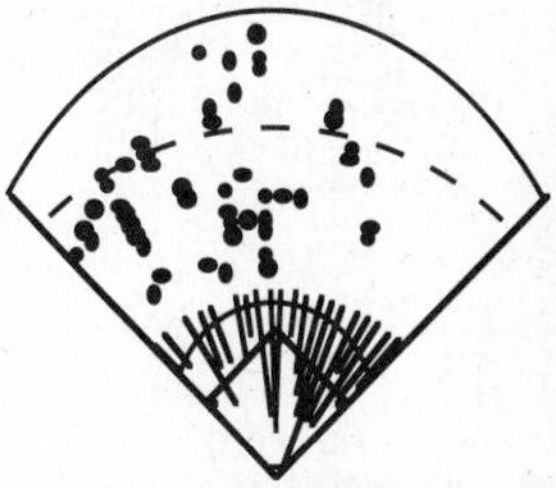

Vs. RHP

1990 Situational Stats

	AB	H	HR	RBI	AVG		AB	H	HR	RBI	AVG
Home	190	50	2	19	.263	LHP	178	43	6	20	.242
Road	201	45	4	22	.224	RHP	213	52	0	21	.244
Day	125	34	4	17	.272	Sc Pos	101	25	1	35	.248
Night	266	61	2	24	.229	Clutch	65	14	0	5	.215

1990 Rankings (American League)

- 8th lowest on-base average vs. left-handed pitchers (.265)
- Led AL second basemen in strikeouts (90) and fielding percentage (99.3%)

FUTURE MVP?

FRED McGRIFF

Position: 1B
Bats: L **Throws:** L
Ht: 6' 3" **Wt:** 208

Opening Day Age: 27
Born: 10/31/63 in Tampa, FL
ML Seasons: 5

Overall Statistics

	G	AB	R	H	D	T	HR	RBI	SB	BB	SO	AVG
1990	153	557	91	167	21	1	35	88	5	94	108	.300
Career	578	1944	348	540	99	8	125	305	21	352	495	.278

Where He Hits the Ball

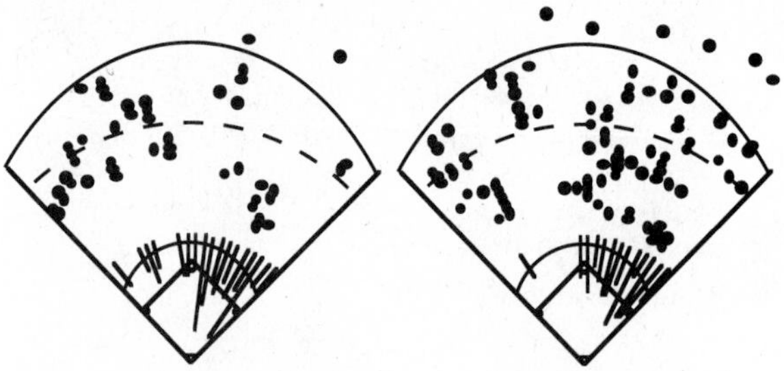

Vs. LHP　　Vs. RHP

1990 Situational Stats

	AB	H	HR	RBI	AVG		AB	H	HR	RBI	AVG
Home	264	73	14	38	.277	LHP	202	52	8	30	.257
Road	293	94	21	50	.321	RHP	355	115	27	58	.324
Day	181	53	12	35	.293	Sc Pos	129	34	5	48	.264
Night	376	114	23	53	.303	Clutch	87	20	4	11	.230

1990 Rankings (American League)

- 1st in slugging percentage vs. right-handed pitchers (.597)
- 2nd in on-base average (.400) and on-base average vs. right-handed pitchers (.440)
- 3rd in total bases (295)
- Led the Blue Jays in batting average (.300), home runs (35), walks (94), intentional walks (12), times on base (263), strikeouts (108), slugging percentage (.530), on-base average, HR frequency (15.9 ABs per HR), batting average (.324)/slugging percentage/on-base average vs. right-handed pitchers

HITTING:

Fred McGriff is one of the best left-handed sluggers in baseball, and he put together another solid year in 1990. He has been the everyday first baseman for three seasons, and has bettered the 30-homer mark in all of them. McGriff is a terror against right-handed pitchers and isn't overmatched against lefties. He's a student of hitting, and isn't shy about hitting the ball to the opposite field. He doesn't get frustrated when he's pitched away, unlike some "pull-everything" types whose weakness in that area is manifested in weak grounder after weak grounder.

In addition to being a 30-homer guy, McGriff will draw about 100 walks per season. He'd rather walk than swing wildly, a wise thing with the solid lineup that the Jays usually field. He has good power to left field and left-center, in addition to the upper-deck strength that you'd expect when he pulls the ball.

The one thing that can slow McGriff down is an inside fastball. Some teams try to do nothing but jam him, which works until a pitch doesn't get inside enough. He has always been a good low fastball hitter, and has learned with more experience not to chase high heaters. He has good bat speed, and also has become a solid breaking-ball hitter.

McGriff has gone into slumps at times when he's lapsed in one or two of those fundamentals. But he's one of the manager's best pupils -- Cito Gaston was the batting instructor before he became manager -- and finds a way to beat his problems, as well as the opposition.

BASERUNNING:

No Rickey Henderson, McGriff steals a base now and then, not because of his speed as much as that opponents aren't expecting him to try. He sometimes misses an extra base now and then when he watches his long drives bang off the wall. But they don't pay McGriff to leg out triples, so that's a minor flaw.

FIELDING:

McGriff has pretty good range, especially toward second base, and can handle errant throws. Sometimes he seems to let up on plays that he should make, and that's the main reason for a good number of his errors. But he's far from being a guy who needs a late-inning defensive caddy.

OVERALL:

Despite hitting more than 100 homers the past three seasons, McGriff can still improve. He often presses in clutch situations, which is one reason he's yet to drive in 100 runs. McGriff, still young at 27, takes his place with Jose Canseco and Cecil Fielder, a former teammate, as a contestant for the home run crown.

GREG MYERS

Position: C
Bats: L **Throws:** R
Ht: 6' 2" **Wt:** 200

Opening Day Age: 25
Born: 4/14/66 in Riverside, CA
ML Seasons: 3

Overall Statistics

	G	AB	R	H	D	T	HR	RBI	SB	BB	SO	AVG
1990	87	250	33	59	7	1	5	22	0	22	33	.236
Career	111	303	34	65	9	1	5	23	0	24	45	.215

Where He Hits the Ball

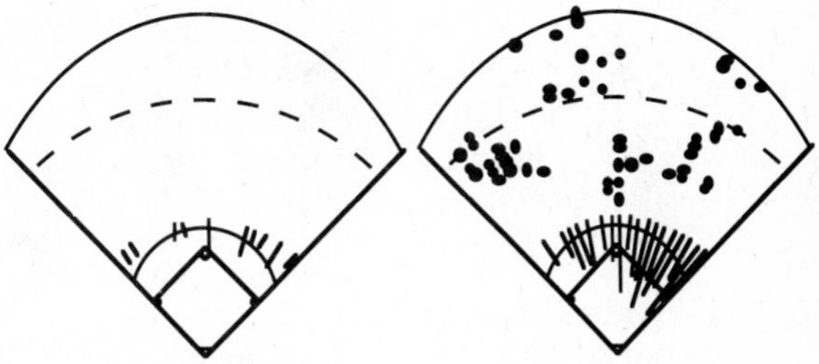

Vs. LHP **Vs. RHP**

1990 Situational Stats

	AB	H	HR	RBI	AVG		AB	H	HR	RBI	AVG
Home	122	29	3	13	.238	LHP	23	4	0	2	.174
Road	128	30	2	9	.234	RHP	227	55	5	20	.242
Day	66	14	2	5	.212	Sc Pos	71	12	2	19	.169
Night	184	45	3	17	.245	Clutch	31	13	1	3	.419

1990 Rankings (American League)

➟ 3rd most GDPs per GDP situation (21.1%)

HITTING:

When the Jays decided that Ernie Whitt didn't fit into their plans, it was partially because they felt Greg Myers could take his place as the left-handed batting half of a catching platoon. Myers did fairly well in that regard in 1990, especially for a youngster who had only 24 games of major league experience going into last season. As the season went on, though, Pat Borders ended up doing most of the catching. Manager Cito Gaston seemed to limit Myers to playing in the spots where he felt that the youngster wouldn't be overmatched.

Myers had respectable offensive numbers, although he did nothing to prove that he could hit lefties. Myers had one season in Class A in which he hit 20 homers, but he never came close to that total again, and is considered more of a contact hitter. He doesn't strike out much but needs to develop a better eye at the plate, as he has a tendency to chase low pitches. He hit into an unhealthy number of double plays last year, especially for a lefty.

Myers may yet develop into a solid offensive threat; he may even pick up some extra punch in his bat with more experience. Good catching platoons are hard to come by. Toronto will probably do its best to nurture the Myers/Borders combination, and hope that it can eventually put forth the quality once exhibited by Whitt and Buck Martinez.

BASERUNNING:

Myers is about average for a catcher, which means he's not a threat to steal or take an extra base. He'll slide into second hard when the situation presents itself, but Myers doesn't get there in enough time on grounders to be much of a factor when it comes to breaking up a double play. He also doesn't get out of the batter's box quickly after making contact.

FIELDING:

Myers has had a history of shoulder and elbow problems which keep him from throwing as well as you'd like to see from a young catcher. He doesn't have a weak arm, however, and opponents don't steal an overt number of bases when he's behind the plate. Myers has good hands and handles balls hit around home plate pretty well.

OVERALL:

The Jays could be worse off than having the Borders/Myers combination. It will be interesting to see if it evolves more toward a pure platoon. For that to happen, Myers is going to have to show more with the bat and probably improve his defense a touch. Otherwise, he'll become more of a second-stringer.

JOHN OLERUD

Position: DH/1B
Bats: L **Throws:** L
Ht: 6' 5" **Wt:** 205

Opening Day Age: 22
Born: 8/5/68 in Seattle, WA
ML Seasons: 2

HITTING:

John Olerud came to the Jays as a two-position player last year, a pitcher/first baseman. Well, he didn't pitch, and he didn't play much first base, for that matter. Most of his service came as a designated hitter, starting mostly against right-handers, despite the fact that he hit lefties at a .342 clip. He handled himself well, making the transition directly from college baseball to the majors, and he showed signs that he's ready for increased playing time.

Olerud is a line drive hitter who has good power. He can hit singles and go deep to all fields, depending on where the ball is pitched, and doesn't seem to be overmatched by anything. He gets good swings at tough pitches and, although he struck out a fair amount, it wasn't from chasing pitches well outside of the strike zone. Much of his power comes from his discipline and excellent eye-hand coordination. While Olerud is tall, he doesn't give the physical appearance of the slugger that he can become.

Olerud's statistics showed a better average and a better eye with runners in scoring position, although he was less inclined to hit for power in those situations. That trade-off isn't unusual for a rookie and was nothing to complain about. Olerud could probably hit for a higher average if he'd sacrifice the home runs, but nobody is asking him to do that because he might be able to do both.

BASERUNNING:

Olerud isn't fast and hasn't yet learned what it takes to steal bases, but that's clearly a secondary concern for him. He's an intelligent baserunner, though. He understands his limitations and knows when an extra base is there for the taking.

FIELDING:

The Jays haven't seen enough of Olerud to make a good evaluation of his defense. But he came to them with a reputation for having an especially good reach and an ability to make all the plays that could be expected. He hasn't done anything to prove the scouting reports inaccurate. He's supposed to have a good move to first which will probably never be seen because his pitching days seems to be over.

OVERALL:

The Jays resisted the gimmick of using Olerud as a mop-up pitcher despite the 26-4 record he compiled playing for Washington State University. The Jays have too much respect for his potential, and Olerud could turn out to be a full-time DH for years to come. Remember that in limited service against left-handed pitchers, Olerud batted well over .300 and had several homers.

Overall Statistics

	G	AB	R	H	D	T	HR	RBI	SB	BB	SO	AVG
1990	111	358	43	95	15	1	14	48	0	57	75	.265
Career	117	366	45	98	15	1	14	48	0	57	76	.268

Where He Hits the Ball

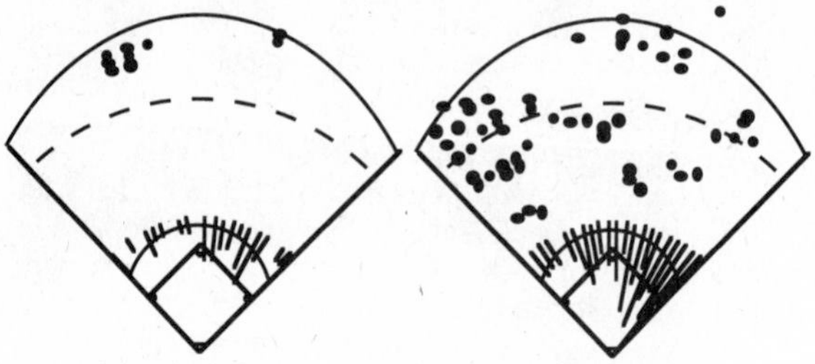

Vs. LHP

Vs. RHP

1990 Situational Stats

	AB	H	HR	RBI	AVG		AB	H	HR	RBI	AVG
Home	187	51	11	26	.273	LHP	73	25	3	15	.342
Road	171	44	3	22	.257	RHP	285	70	11	33	.246
Day	100	19	2	9	.190	Sc Pos	85	25	2	27	.294
Night	258	76	12	39	.295	Clutch	68	22	3	15	.324

1990 Rankings (American League)

- 5th least GDPs per GDP situation (5.2%)
- 8th highest percentage of pitches taken (61.9%)
- Led the Blue Jays in highest percentage of pitches taken
- Led designated hitters in least GDPs per GDP situation

PITCHING:

Someday, Dave Stieb will win 20 games and get the recognition he deserves as one of baseball's most effective pitchers. His consolation prize for 1990 was finally getting the no-hitter that he'd come close to so many times in previous seasons. Stieb also had the winningest season of his career, another fact that will probably be lost because the Jays fell short once again in the Eastern Division race.

At first glance, Stieb seems to be a power pitcher. His fastball has good movement and is in the 90-MPH range. But what sets Stieb apart is his slider, a vicious pitch that has a natural down-and-away drop. Stieb tried to move away from the pitch a few years ago, thinking it was wearing out his arm, but his lack of success caused him to reconsider. Stieb throws the slider as well as anyone, and still uses it about one-third of the time. He also has a curve and a change-up, but those pitches take a back seat when the game is on the line. These days Stieb sometimes throws the curve from a three-quarters motion after throwing it overhand earlier in his career. Righthanders are lucky to get a good swing against him.

Stieb is one of the most competitive pitchers in the game, and that sometimes works against him. He allows himself to get rattled, and sometimes has to battle with that lack of composure. The proud Stieb use to love going nine innings, and turned in 19 complete games back in 1982. To his credit, he's learned to go all out for seven innings, rather than pace himself for the benefit of a statistic that doesn't always translate into wins.

HOLDING RUNNERS AND FIELDING:

A converted outfielder, Stieb has no problems with bunts, comebackers or getting to first. He's an aggressive fielder who rarely makes a misplay. He has an odd-looking, but effective, pivot-and-hop move toward first base that usually keeps runners honest -- as long as he remembers to use it and doesn't get into a predictable pattern that allows for a big jump. The move doesn't look natural, but it works.

OVERALL:

Stieb doesn't overpower hitters the way he used to, but he's come up with other ways to maintain his effectiveness. He figures to be a standout pitcher for at least a few more years. With the exception of one bad year (1986) in a 12-year career, he's been one of baseball's most consistent performers.

DAVE STIEB

Position: SP
Bats: R **Throws:** R
Ht: 6' 0" **Wt:** 195

Opening Day Age: 33
Born: 7/22/57 in Santa Ana, CA
ML Seasons: 12

Overall Statistics

	W	L	ERA	G	GS	Sv	IP	H	R	BB	SO	HR
1990	18	6	2.93	33	33	0	208.2	179	73	64	125	11
Career	166	123	3.34	390	382	1	2667.0	2337	1097	937	1557	205

How Often He Throws Strikes

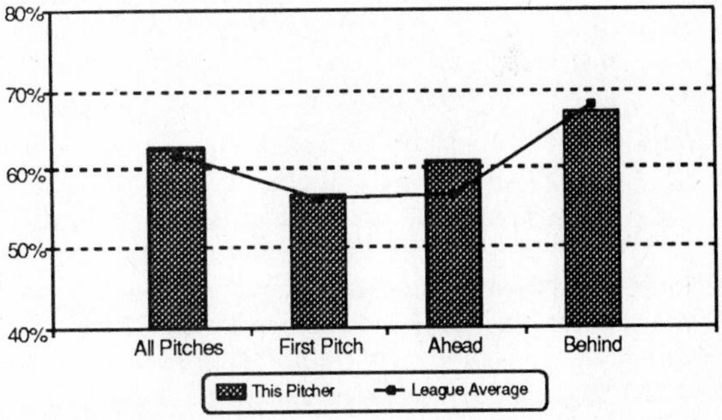

1990 Situational Stats

	W	L	ERA	Sv	IP		AB	H	HR	RBI	AVG
Home	9	5	3.15	0	103.0	LHB	403	102	8	39	.253
Road	9	1	2.73	0	105.2	RHB	375	77	3	29	.205
Day	7	2	3.31	0	73.1	Sc Pos	171	43	0	54	.251
Night	11	4	2.73	0	135.1	Clutch	72	14	0	2	.194

1990 Rankings (American League)

- 2nd in hit batsmen (10), lowest slugging percentage allowed (.320) and lowest batting average allowed vs. right-handed batters (.205)
- 3rd in winning percentage (.750) and least GDPs induced per 9 innings (.30)
- 4th in wins (18), lowest batting average allowed (.230) and least HRs allowed per 9 innings (.47)
- Led the Blue Jays in ERA (2.93), wins, games started (33), shutouts (2), innings (208.2), hit batsmen, strikeouts (125), pitches thrown (3,181), winning percentage and lowest stolen base percentage allowed (42.9%)

TODD STOTTLEMYRE

Position: SP
Bats: L **Throws:** R
Ht: 6' 0" **Wt:** 190

Opening Day Age: 25
Born: 5/20/65 in Yakima, WA
ML Seasons: 3

PITCHING:

After two half-seasons in the majors, 1990 was Todd Stottlemyre's first complete year with the Jays. He established himself as a guy who would take the ball every fifth day and put out a workman-like, if unspectacular, effort. Stottlemyre, a second-generation major leaguer, has a lot of poise with his 25 years, and that started to serve him well last year. He led the Jays in complete games, although you should consider that going start-to-finish is an endangered species owing to the deep Toronto bullpen.

Stottlemyre's poise is most noticeable in the way he uses his three pitches -- fastball, curve and slider. He'll change speeds on all of them while maintaining relative command. Stottlemyre's fastball is usually clocked in the low 90s and it tends to be a riser, when he doesn't overthrow it. The Jays would like him to show a bit better control, and one of his continuing problems is falling behind in the count. When he does, like most youngsters, he tends to rely on his fastball. He doesn't strike out as many batters as you would expect, either.

Stottlemyre still has difficulty with left-handed hitters, who batted .300 against him. The cure for that may be for him to pitch inside more often to back them off the plate. Stottlemyre was second to Dave Stieb in hit batsman last year, but unlike with Stieb, that's wildness more than intimidation. Jimmy Key would be a good model, a pitcher who busts 'em inside and then works the outside corner effectively.

Stottlemyre also was a much better pitcher on grass last season, with an ERA about one run below his turf ERA. When his ball is moving well, off-balance opponents are beating it into the ground.

HOLDING RUNNERS AND FIELDING:

Here's another area where Stottlemyre could learn from Key. Stottlemyre has the moves of a true athlete, but often seems flustered once the ball is in his glove. He needs work in that area, mainly with pickoff throws. His entire move to first still needs work. Opponents have found him a pretty easy target, and sometimes he responds by making a lot of throws to keep them close. (As close as he can, anyway.)

OVERALL:

Stottlemyre seems certain of a place in the Toronto rotation. His faults on the mound, none of them particularly mysterious, seem to be the sort of things that will be worked out with time. Being in pennant races for the last two seasons has helped him mature, too. Stottlemyre's best years are most definitely ahead.

Overall Statistics

	W	L	ERA	G	GS	Sv	IP	H	R	BB	SO	HR
1990	13	17	4.34	33	33	0	203.0	214	101	69	115	18
Career	24	32	4.51	88	67	0	428.2	460	227	159	245	44

How Often He Throws Strikes

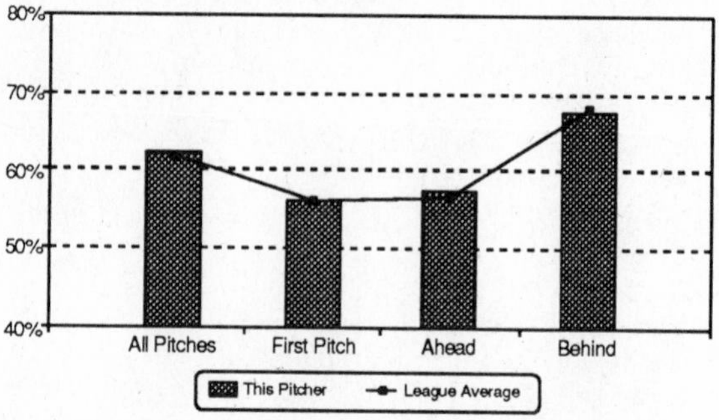

1990 Situational Stats

	W	L	ERA	Sv	IP		AB	H	HR	RBI	AVG
Home	7	8	4.28	0	103.0	LHB	393	118	8	52	.300
Road	6	9	4.41	0	100.0	RHB	388	96	10	44	.247
Day	3	7	4.35	0	62.0	Sc Pos	185	57	6	74	.308
Night	10	10	4.34	0	141.0	Clutch	35	5	0	1	.143

1990 Rankings (American League)

- 2nd in most run support per 9 innings (5.8)
- 5th in losses (17)
- 6th in hit batsmen (8) and stolen bases allowed (23)
- Led the Blue Jays in losses (17), games started (33), complete games (4), hits allowed (214), walks allowed (69), pickoff throws (162), stolen bases allowed, runners caught stealing (13), least pitches thrown per batter (3.63),most run support per 9 innings and most GDPs induced per 9 innings (.58)

PITCHING:

It's been tough on Duane Ward. He's a workhorse for the Blue Jays, but his role does not give him a chance to run up gaudy statistics. This combination seems to give his detractors more opportunities to criticize. As the set-up man, Ward has the role of holding leads so that starters get wins and Tom Henke, most of the time, gets the save. What does Ward get? Boos from the home folks when he doesn't do the job.

Ward has one of the best fastballs in the game, a heavy pitch that's hard to drive. He also has a slider with good movement. Often in the past, those pitches had too much movement for his catcher as well as the batter. But Ward cut down on both wild pitches and walks in 1990, while still getting as much work as in the past.

Ward doesn't take complete advantage of his 92-to-94 MPH fastball, sometimes trying to finesse hitters when he should be challenging them. But he's a better pitcher than many fans are willing to recognize, and all of the work he gets keeps others in the Toronto pen from being overexposed.

Early last season, with Henke being brought along slowly, Ward was occasionally used in save situations. He did reasonably well, but he'll probably continue in the set-up role. Some scouts wonder how Ward can work as often as he does because, they say, his odd motion makes him a candidate for arm problems. At the same time, it can be said that his motion may be the key to getting so much movement on the ball, and tinkering with it may be injurious to the Jays' health.

HOLDING RUNNERS AND FIELDING:

Ward has a high leg kick, and therefore is fairly easy to steal against. His move to first isn't much better than average, and it's not a natural-looking move, either. Ward's follow-through sometimes take him out of position for grounders, but he doesn't make mistakes with the ones he can reach.

OVERALL:

Ward is a tough competitor and probably fancies himself a successful closer. He won't get that chance with the Jays as long as Henke is effective. But the workload he handles is impressive, and he's almost untouchable when he's on top of his game. Imagine how the Red Sox might have fared against Oakland in the ALCS last year if Ward had been in their bullpen. Those late-inning bust-outs by the Athletics might not have happened.

DUANE WARD

Position: RP
Bats: R **Throws:** R
Ht: 6' 4" **Wt:** 205

Opening Day Age: 26
Born: 5/28/64 in Parkview, NM
ML Seasons: 5

Overall Statistics

	W	L	ERA	G	GS	Sv	IP	H	R	BB	SO	HR
1990	2	8	3.45	73	0	11	127.2	101	51	42	112	9
Career	16	23	3.82	227	2	41	383.2	335	178	184	344	20

How Often He Throws Strikes

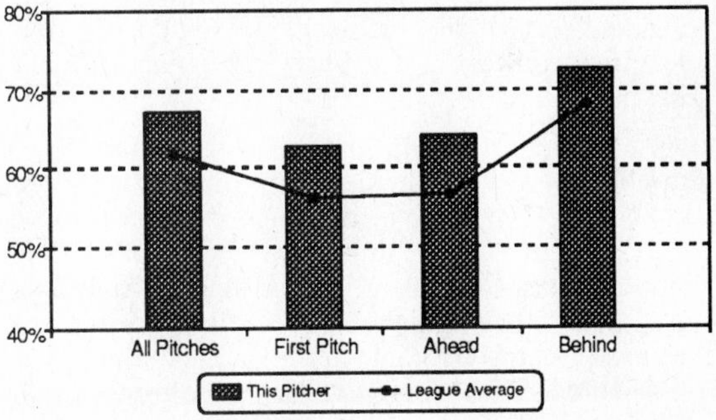

1990 Situational Stats

	W	L	ERA	Sv	IP		AB	H	HR	RBI	AVG
Home	0	4	3.02	5	65.2	LHB	189	49	5	26	.259
Road	2	4	3.92	6	62.0	RHB	268	52	4	27	.194
Day	1	1	2.53	2	32.0	Sc Pos	103	30	4	44	.291
Night	1	7	3.76	9	95.2	Clutch	229	59	5	32	.258

1990 Rankings (American League)

- 2nd in games pitched (73)
- 3rd in first batter efficiency (.129)
- 7th in blown saves (7)
- 9th in holds (11)
- Led the Blue Jays in games pitched, holds, blown saves, most GDPs induced per GDP situation (17.7%) and first batter efficiency

PITCHING:

David Wells never really got the chance he deserved in the deep Toronto bullpen. So Manager Cito Gaston did the lefthander a favor: he experimented by moving Wells into the starting rotation and was rewarded with quality and consistency. Though Wells had averaged less than two innings per appearance in his three previous seasons, the Jays didn't need him to go nine innings, or even seven, because of their deep bullpen.

While he'd been primarily a fastball and curveball pitcher as a reliever, Wells used a change-up more often as a starter. He paced himself by challenging batters to hit the ball instead of going after strikeouts all the time, and that showed in a lowered strikeout-to-innings ratio. At the same time, Wells continued to allow less than one hit per inning and had acceptable, if not pinpoint, control. He has pitched from behind in the count less often as he's gotten more experience, and he's reaped the benefits by giving up home runs less frequently and not pitching with runners in scoring position as often.

As a youngster, Wells seemed to get himself into trouble and then bail himself out, which he did often enough to keep his statistics good. He seems to be over that, but Wells continues to be been bothered by another unusual problem: he has more trouble with lefty batters than righties. Perhaps this is true because he hasn't learned to come inside on them as often as he should. Lefties seem to wait and take his pitches to the opposite field.

HOLDING RUNNERS AND FIELDING:

Wells is a power pitcher with a slow motion and high leg kick. Good thing he's left-handed, or opponents might steal until there was nothing left to take. He fields ground balls relatively well, but there are times when he is slow getting to first base. As a starter, he should get more chances to work on those fundamentals, and has already shown a little bit of improvement.

OVERALL:

Wells was the Jays' most consistent and effective lefty in 1990, and he'll be pressed by some veterans to keep that role. He's especially valuable, though, because he provides a different look -- a hard-throwing look -- than Jimmy Key. The Jays took a risk by removing their best lefty from the bullpen, but it seems to have paid dividends, and could continue to do so for years to come.

DAVID WELLS

Position: SP/RP
Bats: L **Throws:** L
Ht: 6' 4" **Wt:** 225

Opening Day Age: 27
Born: 5/20/63 in Torrance, CA
ML Seasons: 4

Overall Statistics

	W	L	ERA	G	GS	Sv	IP	H	R	BB	SO	HR
1990	11	6	3.14	43	25	3	189.0	165	72	45	115	14
Career	25	18	3.29	156	27	10	369.0	333	147	116	281	31

How Often He Throws Strikes

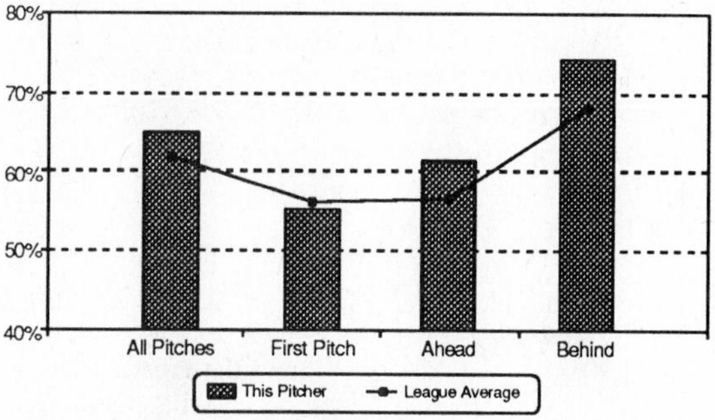

1990 Situational Stats

	W	L	ERA	Sv	IP		AB	H	HR	RBI	AVG
Home	3	2	2.61	2	82.2	LHB	110	29	2	15	.264
Road	8	4	3.55	1	106.1	RHB	591	136	12	50	.230
Day	2	2	3.05	1	44.1	Sc Pos	146	34	1	43	.233
Night	9	4	3.17	2	144.2	Clutch	83	21	2	7	.253

1990 Rankings (American League)

- 3rd in lowest on-base average allowed (.283) and least baserunners allowed per 9 innings (10.1)
- 5th lowest groundball/flyball ratio (.87) and least GDPs induced per 9 innings (.43)
- 6th in ERA at home (2.61)
- 7th in ERA (3.14)
- Led the Blue Jays in wild pitches (7), strikeout/walk ratio (2.6), lowest on-base average allowed, least baserunners allowed per 9 innings, strikeouts per 9 innings (5.5), ERA at home and lowest batting average allowed with runners in scoring position (.233)

FRANK WILLS

Position: RP/SP
Bats: R **Throws:** R
Ht: 6' 2" **Wt:** 200

Opening Day Age: 32
Born: 10/26/58 in New Orleans, LA
ML Seasons: 8

Overall Statistics

	W	L	ERA	G	GS	Sv	IP	H	R	BB	SO	HR
1990	6	4	4.73	44	4	0	99.0	101	54	38	72	13
Career	22	25	4.95	150	35	6	431.1	430	246	193	279	48

How Often He Throws Strikes

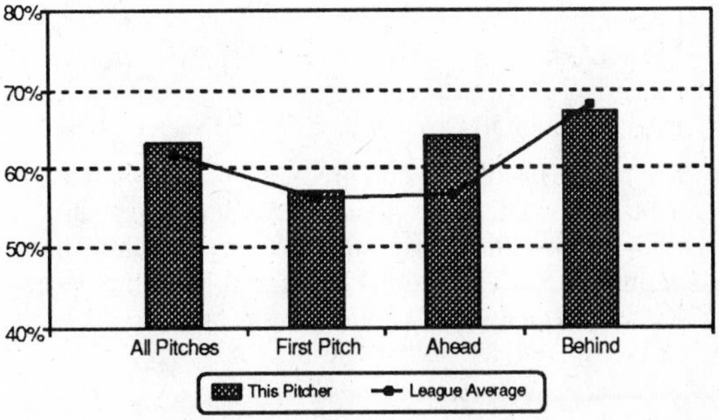

1990 Situational Stats

	W	L	ERA	Sv	IP		AB	H	HR	RBI	AVG
Home	3	4	4.50	0	62.0	LHB	172	43	4	14	.250
Road	3	0	5.11	0	37.0	RHB	208	58	9	39	.279
Day	1	3	6.84	0	26.1	Sc Pos	98	33	4	41	.337
Night	5	1	3.96	0	72.2	Clutch	70	21	4	9	.300

1990 Rankings (American League)

- Did not rank near the top or bottom in any category

PITCHING:

Frank Wills does not lead the glamourous life. As often as not, his job is to pitch leftover innings in games that have been decided, take over when a Toronto starter is kayoed, or fill in as an emergency starter. Wills puts forth an honest effort, and he had a better-than-.500 record to show for his work in 1990. Wills doesn't have great stuff and he doesn't have great stamina, but every pitching staff needs a guy who can do the low-profile work without complaining.

Wills was a first-round draft choice 11 years ago by Kansas City and was considered a good prospect because he threw the ball very hard. He had a 94 MPH fastball in his younger days, but had struggles with control that continue to this day. He's lost something from the fastball, but it's still his number-one pitch, mixed in with an occasional change-up or curve. When he falls behind in the count, he's a mark for the home run ball.

Wills has usually been more effective working out of the bullpen during his career, probably because hitters get used to his stuff after seeing him once or twice. He also has more success than you might suspect with lefties, who tend to find his stuff better than they're expecting. He also tends to have better control against them, cutting fastballs that come in on their wrists. Right-handers get better swings against him, and his delivery doesn't do anything to keep them off balance.

HOLDING RUNNERS AND FIELDING:

Wills is a sound fundamental defensive player. He won't hurt his team with the glove and won't beat himself with wild throws and bad decisions. He has an average move to first, but is very careful to check runners. A cynic might say that he's put enough runners on base during his career that he'd better have mastered those skills fur survival's sake.

OVERALL:

Other pitchers on the Jays staff get more attention than Wills, who has kept plugging away and pitching well enough to keep his place on the club. The team has enough depth, though, that his future may be in doubt. Scouts have always been impressed with his live arm, which is why he's been given a chance with four organizations. Down the road, if he doesn't stay with Toronto, someone will likely take the chance that he will become a late bloomer.

MOOKIE WILSON

Position: CF
Bats: B **Throws:** R
Ht: 5'10" **Wt:** 170

Opening Day Age: 35
Born: 2/9/56 in Bamberg, SC
ML Seasons: 11

HITTING:

Mookie Wilson does some things pretty well. He's a good singles hitter and has enough speed to turn singles into doubles with his hustle. He can leg out infield hits. He isn't overmatched from either side of the plate, even though his former team, the New York Mets, used him most often from the right side, in platoon with Lenny Dykstra. There's no such thing as a fastball that he can't handle, and he can show surprising power from the left side when a pitch is in his wheelhouse.

When Wilson came to the Jays in 1989, he was the sparkplug they needed at the top of the order and a veteran influence in the clubhouse. Last season, despite the fact that he still played almost every day, some of the flaws in his game showed through. His batting average dropped and his on-base percentage hovered near the .300 mark, too low for anyone, and especially for someone billed as a leadoff hitter. He reached the 100-strikeout mark for the first time since the early 1980s, when he was offsetting that by stealing more than 50 bases a year for the Mets.

Wilson has problems with breaking pitches, and tends to be at his weakest against hard sliders and curves, pitches that come down-and-in. Veteran pitchers have taken advantage of that weakness over the years. Wilson has never been much for bunting and it's probably too late for him to start.

BASERUNNING:

This is where Wilson shines. He doesn't need much leeway to take an extra base, and will try going from first to third, or second to home, as often as he can. He is a good slider who avoids several outs per season with that prowess, and his base stealing percentage is still high even though he doesn't go as often as in younger days.

FIELDING:

Wilson's natural position is center field, but he's played all three outfield spots for the Jays. He has good range from side to side, but doesn't go back for balls as well as you'd expect. In addition, he has the sort of arm that invites opponents to take an extra base. Mookie on the bases would probably take the gamble against Mookie in the outfield 99 times out of 100.

OVERALL:

Wilson probably has seen his best years, but he can still play an important role for the Jays, whether or not he continues as an everyday player. There will be pressure from younger folks, but Wilson won't give in without spirited competition.

Overall Statistics

	G	AB	R	H	D	T	HR	RBI	SB	BB	SO	AVG
1990	147	588	81	156	36	4	3	51	23	31	102	.265
Career	1317	4853	705	1339	215	67	65	410	316	274	831	.276

Where He Hits the Ball

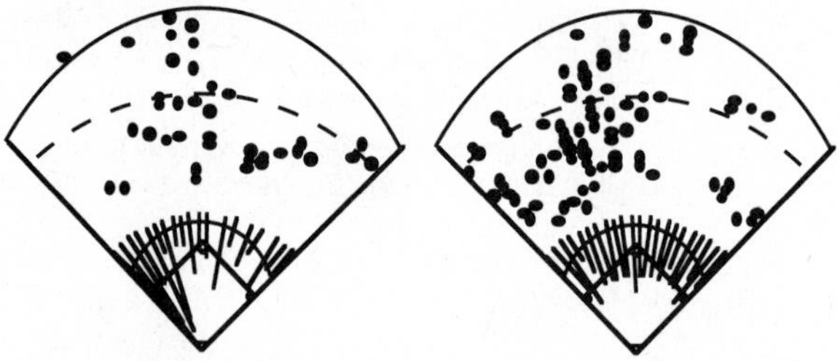

Vs. LHP Vs. RHP

1990 Situational Stats

	AB	H	HR	RBI	AVG		AB	H	HR	RBI	AVG
Home	271	67	0	20	.247	LHP	188	46	2	21	.245
Road	317	89	3	31	.281	RHP	400	110	1	30	.275
Day	174	41	0	17	.236	Sc Pos	136	35	0	46	.257
Night	414	115	3	34	.278	Clutch	97	30	1	12	.309

1990 Rankings (American League)

- 4th in lowest on-base average (.300), lowest HR frequency (196 ABs per HR), most runs scored per time reached base (43.3%) and highest percentage of extra bases taken as a runner (60.0%)
- Led the Blue Jays in doubles (36), sacrifice bunts (6), groundball/flyball ratio (2.2), stolen base percentage, (85.2%), most runs scored per time reached base, bunts in play (10) and highest percentage of extra bases take as a runner
- Led AL center fielders in stolen base percentage, runs scored per time reached base, batting average in the clutch (.309) and batting average on an 0-2 count (.235)

ROB DUCEY

Position: LF
Bats: L **Throws:** R
Ht: 6' 2" **Wt:** 175

Opening Day Age: 25
Born: 5/24/65 in Toronto, Canada
ML Seasons: 4

Overall Statistics

	G	AB	R	H	D	T	HR	RBI	SB	BB	SO	AVG
1990	19	53	7	16	5	0	0	7	1	7	15	.302
Career	121	231	39	58	14	1	1	26	6	29	57	.251

HITTING, FIELDING, BASERUNNING:

The Jays have called up Rob Ducey for parts of the past four seasons -- small enough parts that he has only about two years of actual major league service. Ducey was born in Toronto and, at one time, appeared to have all the makings of a favorite son. He was thought to have the best chance of breaking up the Bell-Moseby-Barfield outfield that led the Jays through the second half of the 1980s. It didn't turn out that way, though. Ducey hurt his knee twice in 1989, which seems to have hurt his stock.

But Ducey played pretty well after being called up toward the end of last season and could either challenge Mookie Wilson in center field or spell George Bell and Junior Felix in left and right. Ducey has shown some power throughout his minor-league career, but is more of a contact hitter who can spray line drives to all fields. He has better than average speed, but has never been much of a base-stealing threat. He is a fine defensive player with a good arm.

OVERALL:

Ducey could help the Jays with left-handed bench strength and as a backup to the current outfield. Even though they might have expected more from him when he was a hotter prospect, Ducey may have value as a role player for the Jays, or as trade bait if another team is willing to take a chance.

RICK LUECKEN

Position: RP
Bats: R **Throws:** R
Ht: 6' 6" **Wt:** 210

Opening Day Age: 30
Born: 11/15/60 in McAllen, TX
ML Seasons: 2

Overall Statistics

	W	L	ERA	G	GS	Sv	IP	H	R	BB	SO	HR
1990	1	4	5.83	37	0	1	54.0	75	37	31	35	6
Career	3	5	5.10	56	0	2	77.2	98	46	44	51	9

PITCHING, FIELDING & HOLDING RUNNERS:

A veteran minor leaguer who turned 30 last winter, Rick Luecken has toiled for the Royals, Braves and Blue Jays during the last two seasons. Luecken got most of his work with pitching-poor Atlanta, but he didn't impress many people with his 5.77 ERA. He was dealt to Toronto in time to get into one September game, but the Blue Jays took him off their 40-man roster over the winter.

Luecken's minor league record continues to interest people. Pitching in relief for Memphis, Omaha and Richmond during the last two seasons, he has posted good save totals and ERAs under 2.50. He has only a mediocre fastball, but he also throws a knuckleball which could be a good pitch if he could master it. The Braves' master knuckleballer, Phil Niekro, worked with Luecken last year, but after some initial success, he couldn't control it well enough to rely on it. Luecken doesn't hurt himself as a fielder and lands from his delivery in good position to field the ball. He is adequate at holding runners close at first and rarely batted for the Braves.

OVERALL:

Though Luecken is getting too old to be considered a prospect, knuckleball pitchers are notorious for maturing late. He'll probably be back in the minors at the start of this year, but if he can get the pitch over, some club desperate for pitching will probably give him a chance.

RANCE MULLINIKS

Position: 3B
Bats: L **Throws:** R
Ht: 6' 0" **Wt:** 175

Opening Day Age: 35
Born: 1/15/56 in Tulare, CA
ML Seasons: 14

Overall Statistics

	G	AB	R	H	D	T	HR	RBI	SB	BB	SO	AVG
1990	57	97	11	28	4	0	2	16	2	22	19	.289
Career	1225	3327	417	911	214	16	71	411	15	415	511	.274

HITTING, FIELDING, BASERUNNING:

Rance Mulliniks became a bit part of the Jays scene last season, as Kelly Gruber stayed healthy all season at third base and John Olerud took most of the at-bats for a left-handed DH. That reduced Mulliniks to mostly pinch hitting duty, and he did well despite limited service. Mulliniks has been a platoon player for most of his career, a low fastball hitter who's always done a lot of his damage to the opposite field.

Mulliniks is patient at the plate and can handle breaking balls and change-ups, sometimes fouling off a number of pitches until getting one that looks more hittable. Age may have caught up with him somewhat in that he doesn't get around very well against good fastballs. He is also content with going from station-to-station on the base paths these days. His range in the field has been decreasing for several seasons. It's still acceptable, but there is a noticeable difference between what Mulliniks could do in his prime and what he's taken to the field since Gruber became the regular third baseman.

OVERALL:

If Mulliniks stays with the Jays, it would probably be as a pinch hitter and little more. If Toronto dumps him to go with younger players, though, there would probably be a team willing to take him on. Guys who are fluid, intelligent hitters tend to find work somewhere and Mulliniks has certainly earned the respect of opponents over the years.

LUIS SOJO

Position: 2B
Bats: R **Throws:** R
Ht: 5'11" **Wt:** 174

Opening Day Age: 25
Born: 1/3/66 in Barquisimeto, Venezuela
ML Seasons: 1

Overall Statistics

	G	AB	R	H	D	T	HR	RBI	SB	BB	SO	AVG
1990	33	80	14	18	3	0	1	9	1	5	5	.225
Career	33	80	14	18	3	0	1	9	1	5	5	.225

HITTING, FIELDING, BASERUNNING:

Another one of their young, midseason call-ups, Luis Sojo filled a role as a utility infielder for the Jays, and took on an expanded role after Nelson Liriano was traded. Sojo's natural position is shortstop, but nobody is expecting him to replace Tony Fernandez, except in emergency situations. Sojo has very limited power and doesn't draw many walks, but he's a contact hitter. He strikes outs infrequently, especially for someone who made a habit of falling behind in the count during his minor league days. Sojo doesn't hit many fly balls, and knows that he has to be careful not to go chasing high fastballs.

Sojo has good range and a good arm for a shortstop, and may get a chance to compete for the starting second base job based on his defensive potential. It will be interesting to see if he can learn the double-play pivot from that side of the base, after showing quick hands and slick moves at short. He has average speed, and has never been a very successful base stealer.

OVERALL:

Sojo could be Manny Lee's main competition at second base, with the loser taking a utility role. The Jays were happy with the versatility he showed after being called up and see him as a part of their future, even if it takes another season for him to begin making larger contributions.

MARK WHITEN

Position: RF
Bats: B **Throws:** R
Ht: 6' 3" **Wt:** 215

Opening Day Age: 24
Born: 11/25/66 in Pensacola, FL
ML Seasons: 1

Overall Statistics

	G	AB	R	H	D	T	HR	RBI	SB	BB	SO	AVG
1990	33	88	12	24	1	1	2	7	2	7	14	.273
Career	33	88	12	24	1	1	2	7	2	7	14	.273

HITTING, FIELDING, BASERUNNING:

Mark Whiten was chosen the number one prospect in the International League by one baseball newspaper at the end of last season. He has put up good statistics during his six years in the minors, and didn't look overmatched when he was called up by the Jays last season. At this point, he is thought to be a player whose minor-league statistics might not convey the expectations that are held for him at a major-league level. He had 14 home runs and 14 stolen bases for Class AAA Syracuse, with a .290 average.

Whiten's been called a "Bo Jackson type," in that he has the potential to excel at every aspect of the game. He has good range in the outfield and a terrific throwing arm. As a hitter he has learned to cut down his swing with two strikes and go to the opposite field when he isn't being challenged. When he was younger, Whiten had trouble making contact, but he didn't strikeout an unusual number of times during his stint in the majors. He still needs to do more with breaking pitches and make better use of his speed on the bases, skills that should come with experience.

OVERALL:

Whiten is another one of the talented young Jays who will be bucking for playing time; he may possibly even be fighting for a spot on the major league roster. He'll be battling Rob Ducey and Glenallen Hill for a backup role, and it would be no surprise if he has to go back to Syracuse.

KEN WILLIAMS

Position: RF/LF/CF/DH
Bats: R **Throws:** R
Ht: 6' 1" **Wt:** 187

Opening Day Age: 27
Born: 4/6/64 in Berkeley, CA
ML Seasons: 5

Overall Statistics

	G	AB	R	H	D	T	HR	RBI	SB	BB	SO	AVG
1990	106	155	23	25	8	1	0	13	9	10	42	.161
Career	404	1055	120	227	35	6	26	115	46	49	263	.215

HITTING, FIELDING, BASERUNNING:

Ken Williams joined the Jays midway through last season as a backup outfielder and didn't do anything to warrant more playing time. He struggled at the plate and was used mostly as a late-inning defensive replacement. The Jays had some rookies and second-year players who got much of the playing time that Williams might have gotten if he'd shown a little bit more.

An outstanding athlete, Williams once showed promised as a hitter, but has never been the same since an ill-fated move by the White Sox to shift him to third base. He still hasn't learned the strike zone, and can be had by a pitcher who moves the ball around and doesn't groove a fastball. He falls behind in the count too often and doesn't draw walks. In the outfield, Williams uses his sprinter's speed to great advantage. He gets a good jump on the ball and has a quick and accurate arm. He'd be a constant threat to steal bases, except that he doesn't reach often enough to be worried about.

OVERALL:

At this point of his career, Williams seems doomed to a role as a defensive replacement and pinch runner. He's been inconsistent at best in recent years and probably doesn't fit into Toronto's plans, given the number of youngsters lined up for playing time. It's doubtful that another team would give him much of a look, except in a limited role.

National League Players

PITCHING:

Enormously talented, Steve Avery is one of those players for whom sketches of his Hall of Fame plaque were drawn up long before he threw a major league pitch. Avery may yet become a baseball immortal, but he looked very human as a 20-year-old rookie last year. Instead of putting up Doc Gooden numbers, Avery pitched more like expansion-hopeful teammate Marty Clary. The young lefty's 3-11 record and 5.64 ERA made for a truly humbling debut.

Perhaps the problem was that people were simply expecting too much. Recently, the only other pitcher so young to make an immediate impact was Gooden, who could simply blow his fastball past hitters. While Avery's fastball can reach the low 90s, he does not have the speed of a young Gooden and needs to rely more on his curveball and change, which are excellent but still-developing pitches. Last year he was forced to live or die with the fastball, to the point that he suffered from blisters on his pitching hand, probably from trying to throw too hard. When Avery puts his game together (1991 or 1992 at the latest), he will be the dominant pitcher the Braves have been looking for.

During his first two years in the minors (1988-89) Avery compiled an imposing record of 19-8 with a 1.94 ERA and 245 strikeouts in 237 innings. Promoted to Richmond for the start of the 1990 campaign, he was good but not awesome with a 5-5 record, 3.50 ERA and 69 Ks in 82.1 innings. The Braves brought him up not because he was dominating the International League, but because they were struggling and needed to give their fans some hope. It might not have been the wisest move.

HOLDING RUNNERS, FIELDING AND HITTING:

It used to be easy to excuse Avery's inability to hold runners close because he never had many runners on base. That's no longer the case, and he'll need to improve. Avery is a fairly strong fielder and showed some signs of life with the bat late in the season.

OVERALL:

It is no accident that Steve Avery was one of only two players named to Baseball America's list of the ten people who would influence baseball in the '90s. However nightmarish last year was for the 20 year old, he is strong enough to learn from it. Avery may well be an All-Star by age 22.

STEVE AVERY

Position: SP
Bats: L **Throws:** L
Ht: 6' 4" **Wt:** 180

Opening Day Age: 20
Born: 4/14/70 in Trenton, MI
ML Seasons: 1

Overall Statistics

	W	L	ERA	G	GS	Sv	IP	H	R	BB	SO	HR
1990	3	11	5.64	21	20	0	99.0	121	79	45	75	7
Career	3	11	5.64	21	20	0	99.0	121	79	45	75	7

How Often He Throws Strikes

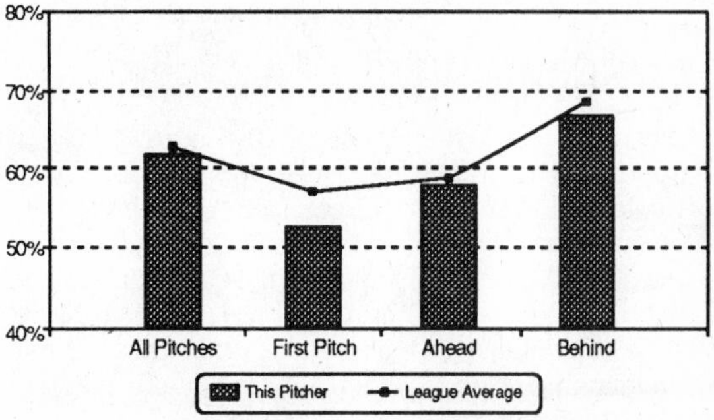

1990 Situational Stats

	W	L	ERA	Sv	IP		AB	H	HR	RBI	AVG
Home	3	4	4.25	0	59.1	LHB	61	16	0	12	.262
Road	0	7	7.71	0	39.2	RHB	340	105	7	55	.309
Day	0	4	8.26	0	28.1	Sc Pos	136	42	2	55	.309
Night	3	7	4.58	0	70.2	Clutch	34	10	0	5	.294

1990 Rankings (National League)

- 1st in highest batting average allowed vs. right-handed batters (.309)
- 3rd highest batting average allowed with runners in scoring position (.309)

JEFF BLAUSER

Position: SS/2B
Bats: R **Throws:** R
Ht: 6' 0" **Wt:** 170

Opening Day Age: 25
Born: 11/8/65 in Los Gatos, CA
ML Seasons: 4

Overall Statistics

	G	AB	R	H	D	T	HR	RBI	SB	BB	SO	AVG
1990	115	386	46	104	24	3	8	39	3	35	70	.269
Career	326	1074	127	283	57	9	24	107	15	93	216	.264

Where He Hits the Ball

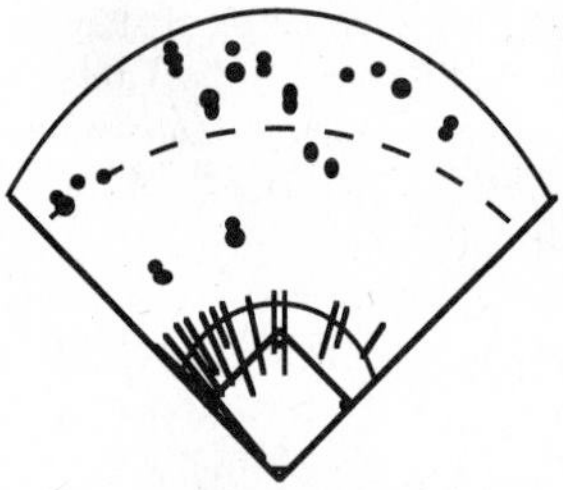

Vs. LHP

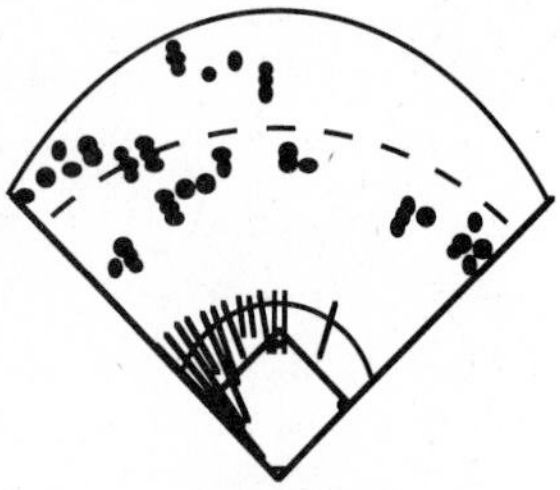

Vs. RHP

1990 Situational Stats

	AB	H	HR	RBI	AVG		AB	H	HR	RBI	AVG
Home	172	51	3	21	.297	LHP	136	40	3	17	.294
Road	214	53	5	18	.248	RHP	250	64	5	22	.256
Day	93	25	2	10	.269	Sc Pos	79	19	1	25	.241
Night	293	79	6	29	.270	Clutch	61	11	4	10	.180

1990 Rankings (National League)

- 4th lowest batting average with 2 strikes (.135)
- 6th lowest batting average in the clutch (.180)
- Led NL shortstops in least GDPs per GDP situation (4.9%), batting average vs. left-handed pitchers (.294) and on-base average vs. left-handed pitchers (.373)

HITTING:

For a while in 1988, Chicago was abuzz over the impending trade with Atlanta of Shawon Dunston for Jeff Blauser. That deal never came off. In 1989, the talk was that Blauser would become a Yankee. Once again a deal couldn't be worked out. Now Blauser has had two straight good years with the Braves, and the club is starting to feel glad that they didn't trade him after all.

Like Andres Thomas, the man he has often replaced as the Braves shortstop, Blauser takes a good cut and has fine power for a middle infielder. Given full-time duty, each is capable of 10-15 home runs. But while occasional power is basically all Thomas supplies as a hitter, Blauser presents a much more complete package. He's a much more selective hitter than Thomas, and not nearly as prone to chase bad breaking stuff. As a result he's a much tougher out. Blauser looks like a consistent .260-.270 hitter with pop in his bat and the patience to take an occasional walk. All in all, he's a very valuable hitter for a shortstop.

Blauser was able to make some key improvements in 1990 even while playing three different infield positions. He lowered his strikeout rate while increasing his walk percentage. He was more aggressive on inside pitches, popping many of them for doubles and getting hit by a few offerings as well. A switch-hitter, he improved his work as a right-handed hitter while maintaining respectable totals from the left side.

BASERUNNING:

The Atlanta baserunning attack is pretty much the exclusive domain of Ron Gant. Blauser ran well in the minor leagues, stealing 76 bases in 484 games. However, with the Braves, he has stolen only 15 in 326 contests. The Braves would do well to encourage him to become more aggressive on the bases.

FIELDING:

Shifted between second, third and short, Blauser committed 16 errors last year, all at short. He'd probably cut down on his errors if he stuck to one position, and shortstop is his best spot. He lacks Thomas' great range, but he has an excellent arm and is much steadier overall than Thomas. He can handle the position as a regular, though he'll never be a star glove man.

OVERALL:

At 25, Blauser seems more than ready for regular duty. He's hit well and proven himself adept enough with the glove to handle shortstop comfortably. Given 150 games or more at the position, he could turn in some impressive numbers.

FRANCISCO CABRERA

Position: 1B
Bats: R **Throws:** R
Ht: 6' 4" **Wt:** 195

Opening Day Age: 24
Born: 10/10/66 in Santo Domingo, Dominican Republic
ML Seasons: 2

HITTING:

One of two minor leaguers the Braves received in the 1989 Tom Acker trade, Francisco Cabrera has long been an intriguing power hitting prospect. A catcher throughout most of his professional career, Cabrera made the Braves as a first baseman last year and saw considerable playing time after Dave Justice was shifted to right field in August. Cabrera batted only 137 times, but his power stats and .277 average impressed the Braves very much.

Still only 24, Cabrera began drawing attention from scouts in 1987, when he belted 14 home runs at Class A Myrtle Beach. He slugged 20 more at AA Knoxville a year later, and was hitting .299 at AAA Syracuse in '89 when the Braves acquired him in the Acker deal. Like many young Latins, Cabrera doesn't draw many walks, but he's no wild swinger, either; he's never had a 100 strikeout season at any level of play. Over one third of his hits with the Braves went for extra bases, and he impressed even more with his seven home runs and 20 RBI. He displayed good power to all fields.

The most encouraging sign of all to the Braves was Cabrera's production with runners in scoring position. He led the Braves with an average over .400 in his limited opportunities and was nearly 150 points higher than the team as a whole. Cabrera was used mostly against lefties last year; he didn't hit righties in brief action against them, but it's hard to say whether he can or can't handle them on the basis of 28 at-bats.

BASERUNNING:

Like almost everybody else on the Braves, Cabrera does not have a history of either speed or stolen bases. However, he is fast enough to take an extra base once he learns the league. Until that happens he will probably remain cautious on the base paths.

FIELDING:

Former catcher Cabrera is inexperienced at first base, and he looked uncomfortable at the position, making three errors in limited action. He showed flashes of brilliance at times and will undoubtedly improve with more work. The Braves could also use Cabrera behind the plate again. He was an All-Star receiver in the minors, despite leading three leagues in errors.

OVERALL:

Much of the talk about Cabrera's future with the Braves hinges on his ability to play the outfield. The idea is that he could take over for Lonnie Smith, who is a trade candidate. Cabrera may wind up there, but given his impressive record to date, the Braves might consider handing him the first base job if Nick Esasky still can't play.

Overall Statistics

	G	AB	R	H	D	T	HR	RBI	SB	BB	SO	AVG
1990	63	137	14	38	5	1	7	25	1	5	21	.277
Career	70	163	15	43	8	1	7	25	1	6	27	.264

Where He Hits the Ball

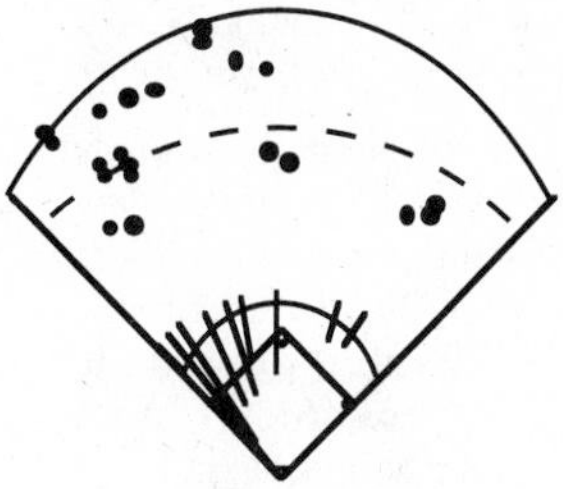

Vs. LHP

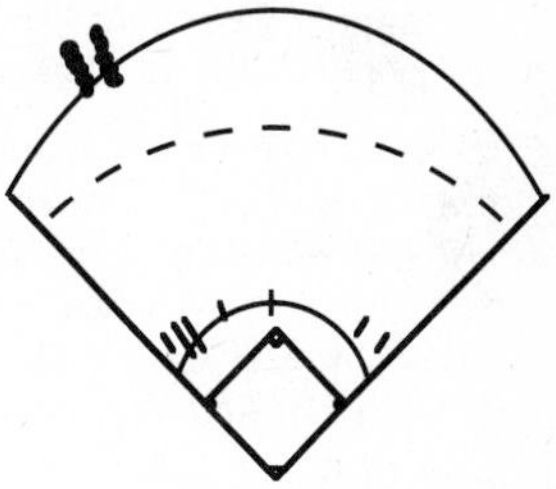

Vs. RHP

1990 Situational Stats

	AB	H	HR	RBI	AVG		AB	H	HR	RBI	AVG
Home	79	23	4	17	.291	LHP	109	32	6	21	.294
Road	58	15	3	8	.259	RHP	28	6	1	4	.214
Day	32	11	1	6	.344	Sc Pos	34	14	2	18	.412
Night	105	27	6	19	.257	Clutch	29	4	0	2	.138

1990 Rankings (National League)

- Did not rank near the top or bottom in any category

MARTIN CLARY

Position: RP/SP
Bats: R **Throws:** R
Ht: 6' 4" **Wt:** 190

Opening Day Age: 29
Born: 4/3/62 in Detroit, MI
ML Seasons: 3

Overall Statistics

	W	L	ERA	G	GS	Sv	IP	H	R	BB	SO	HR
1990	1	10	5.67	33	14	0	101.2	128	72	39	44	9
Career	5	14	4.48	58	32	0	225.0	251	132	74	81	17

How Often He Throws Strikes

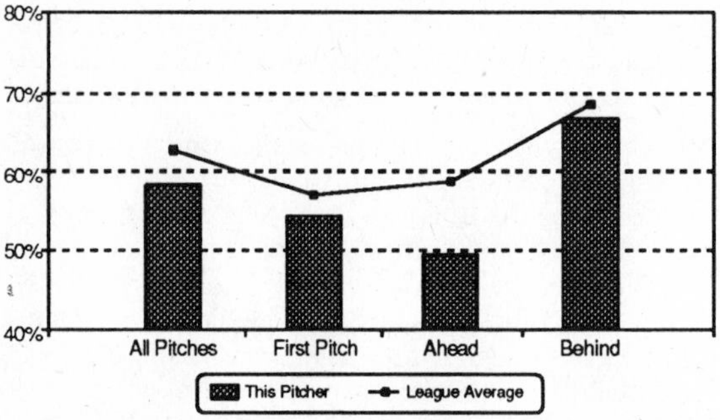

1990 Situational Stats

	W	L	ERA	Sv	IP		AB	H	HR	RBI	AVG
Home	0	5	5.01	0	46.2	LHB	240	78	7	29	.325
Road	1	5	6.22	0	55.0	RHB	176	50	2	22	.284
Day	0	2	4.18	0	28.0	Sc Pos	123	32	4	43	.260
Night	1	8	6.23	0	73.2	Clutch	24	9	1	4	.375

1990 Rankings (National League)

→ 9th worst batting average allowed vs. left-handed batters (.325)

PITCHING:

After putting in nearly five full seasons with the Braves' AAA farm club at Richmond, Marty Clary got his first real chance with the big club during the second half of 1989. He made the most of it, going 4-3 and turning in a very nice 3.15 ERA in 17 starts. Last year Clary hoped to take it from there, but instead he looked very much like a minor league pitcher. Clary's 1-10 record and 5.67 ERA were the worst figures on a very bad Braves pitching staff.

Only marginally talented, Clary has to get out hitters with very basic stuff. He has an average fastball, a good change-up and a fine curve. He's the type who "paints the corners," relying on pinpoint control and depending on his fielders to make the plays behind him. He's sort of a right-handed Charlie Leibrandt, and like Leibrandt with the '89 Royals, Clary suffers when his control is off just a little. Last year his walks were up, and he was behind on way too many counts. As a result he got hit hard. It didn't help that he was pitching for a team with a very shaky defense.

Clary split his first two decisions, then lost his last nine. With his precise control intact, Clary had held left-handed hitters to a .237 average in '89. Last year that control was off, and lefties dug in and belted Clary for a .325 mark. His statistics were very similar to those of the Braves' golden boy, Steve Avery. Unfortunately for Clary, he's not going to be given as many chances as Avery to straighten himself out.

HOLDING RUNNERS, FIELDING & HITTING:

Clary is a good defensive player and ends his delivery in position to field balls hit through the middle. He has an adequate move to first and keeps runners close with looks and frequent pickoff throws. Clary does himself absolutely no good with a bat in his hands. His last hit was on August 16, 1989 and he's gone 0-for-39 since then.

OVERALL:

Clary has been released by the Braves, capping his thoroughly forgettable 1990 season. He is still young enough to latch on with another team, and may get a trial in someone's spring camp. If not, he can probably go back to pitch for Richmond again; he is now about as well known there as Robert E. Lee.

RON GANT

Position: CF/LF
Bats: R **Throws:** R
Ht: 6' 0" **Wt:** 172

Opening Day Age: 26
Born: 3/2/65 in Victoria, TX
ML Seasons: 4

HITTING:

Back from the dead, Ron Gant survived a 1989 campaign in which he batted .177, fielded .915 and suffered the humiliation of being farmed out to the Class A South Atlantic League. Returning as a center fielder, Gant looked like a different person as he hit .303 and was a 30/30 man in home runs and stolen bases. He became only the third player in Braves history to reach the 30/30 level, joining the select company of Henry Aaron and Dale Murphy.

Gant has always been a talented player, but after a solid rookie campaign in 1988 (.259, 19 homers), he got all messed up in '89. A switch from second base to third didn't help as Gant couldn't handle the new position and committed 16 errors in 53 games. Like a lot of players, he took his fielding problems to the plate and soon lost his strike zone judgement. Farming him out and letting him get comfortable as an outfielder was probably the best thing the Braves could have done. It also didn't hurt him to have Aaron as his minor league tutor.

Last year Gant arrived for spring training bulked up by an off season conditioning program and with a new attitude about the game. He regained his patience at the plate and soon replaced the slumping Oddibe McDowell in center field. Gant's extra strength helped him drive the ball even better than he had as a rookie, and his improved plate discipline gave him the patience to lay off pitches in the dirt. Ahead on the count more often, he got fastballs to hit. That was all he needed.

BASERUNNING:

Atlanta has a name for baserunning: Ron Gant. With his great speed, Gant stole over a third of all the bases the Braves swiped in 1990. Next year, especially with Dave Justice hitting behind him, Gant should try to pick his spots better, as he was thrown out 16 times. His overall baserunning judgement needs to improve.

FIELDING:

Gant in the outfield was a big improvement over Gant in the infield, but he still needs some polish before he'll be a good center fielder. He has the speed to cover a lot of ground, but needs work in playing hitters and getting a better jump on the ball. That will undoubtedly come with experience. Gant has a very strong, but not completely accurate, throwing arm.

OVERALL:

TBS broadcasters Pete Van Wieren, Skip Caray and Don Sutton all like to emphasize that Gant should look for a house in Atlanta. With his great play in 1990 and the strong promise of an even better career, maybe the Braves should buy that house for him.

Overall Statistics

	G	AB	R	H	D	T	HR	RBI	SB	BB	SO	AVG
1990	152	575	107	174	34	3	32	84	33	50	86	.303
Career	394	1481	227	388	74	14	62	178	65	117	278	.262

Where He Hits the Ball

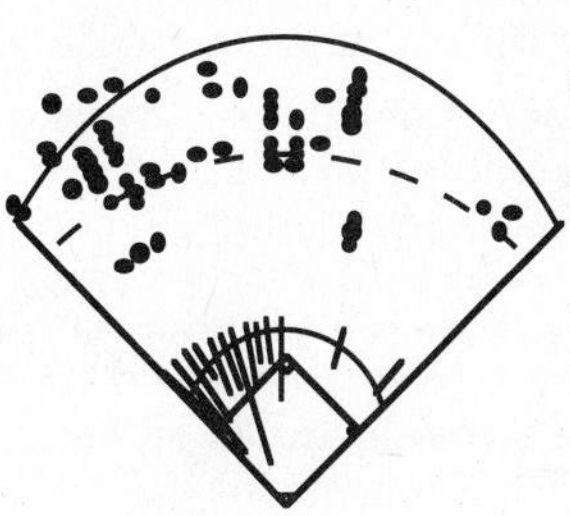

Vs. LHP

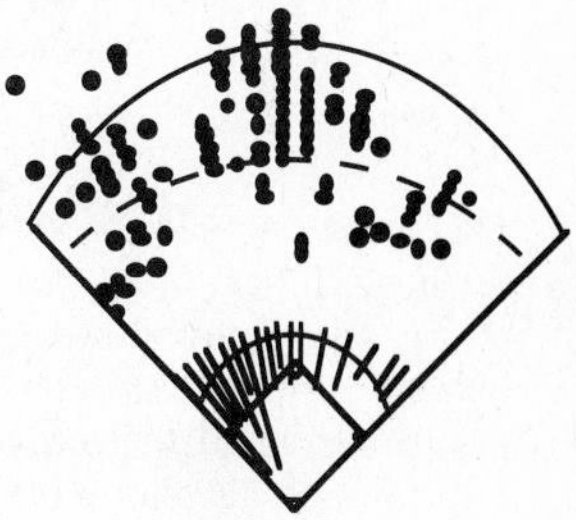

Vs. RHP

1990 Situational Stats

	AB	H	HR	RBI	AVG		AB	H	HR	RBI	AVG
Home	288	90	18	47	.313	LHP	204	61	10	32	.299
Road	287	84	14	37	.293	RHP	371	113	22	52	.305
Day	143	42	8	23	.294	Sc Pos	144	37	3	47	.257
Night	432	132	24	61	.306	Clutch	77	18	4	8	.234

1990 Rankings (National League)

- 1st lowest batting average with the bases loaded (.000)
- 3rd in total bases (310) and runs scored per time reached base (47.6%)
- 4th in runs (107) and slugging percentage (.539)
- Led the Braves in home runs (32), at-bats (575), runs, hits (174), singles (105), doubles (34), total bases, RBIs (84), stolen bases (33), caught stealing (16), plate appearances (631), games (152) and slugging percentage
- Led NL center fielders in home runs, total bases, slugging percentage and runs scored per time reached base

PITCHING:

After a trying rookie season in 1988 (7-17) and an excellent year in 1989 (14-8), Atlanta had high expectations for Tom Glavine in 1990. Unfortunately, before you could say Cy Young Award, he was buried with a sub-.500 record and an ERA over one-half run higher than in 1989. Glavine ended the year with a mediocre record of 10-12 but with the promise of pulling it together for 1991. He is, after all, only 25.

Glavine is a very strong pitcher who relies on a great fastball to get batters out. He also has a good change-up, and a developing curve and slider. But the fastball is his primary pitch, and perhaps he uses it too often. Glavine has been very effective against left-handed hitters, but too often righties hit his fastball over the fence. Last year he allowed 16 of his 18 homers to righties, and they belted him around for a .296 average. He needs to mix in his other pitchers against right handers, and come inside on them a little more.

Last year Glavine seemed intent on returning to his days in the low minors, when he was blowing away a man an inning. He did strike out more batters, but in the process he almost doubled his walk total, from 40 to 78, and grooved too many pitches when he was behind in the count. Glavine's poor record could be partly attributed to lack of run support, but he had only himself to blame for the rise in his ERA, from 3.68 to 4.28. After allowing only 10 baserunners per nine innings in 1989, he permitted 13 in 1990 -- far too many for a pitcher with his stuff.

HOLDING RUNNERS, FIELDING & HITTING:

Glavine is a good athlete who was drafted by the Los Angeles Kings of the National Hockey League, and he fields his position well. When there is a runner on first, he will often throw the ball over to keep the runners close, but he does not have a great move. As a batter, Glavine is strictly a .100 hitter with occasional extra-base pop. He is a very competent bunter.

OVERALL:

Glavine is one pitcher whose name is engraved in stone in the Braves' 1991 starting rotation. Like most of the pitchers on the staff, he is quite young, and his 1990 problems may simply have been part of his maturing process. If he can learn to mix his pitches a little better, Glavine may become a big winner in the very near future.

TOM GLAVINE

Position: SP
Bats: L **Throws:** L
Ht: 6' 0" **Wt:** 175

Opening Day Age: 25
Born: 3/25/66 in Concord, MA
ML Seasons: 4

Overall Statistics

	W	L	ERA	G	GS	Sv	IP	H	R	BB	SO	HR
1990	10	12	4.28	33	33	0	214.1	232	111	78	129	18
Career	33	41	4.29	105	105	0	646.0	660	344	214	323	55

How Often He Throws Strikes

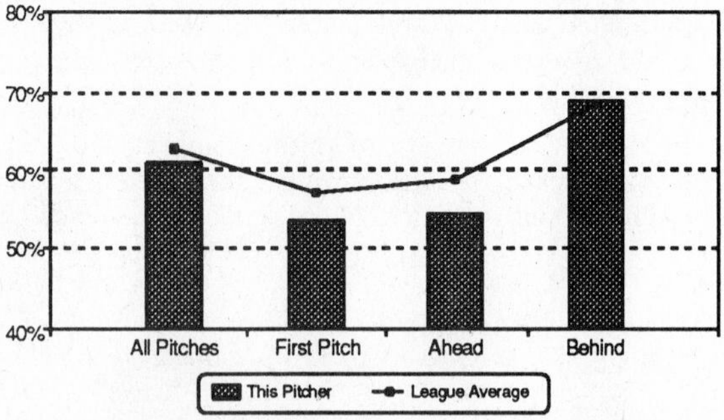

1990 Situational Stats

	W	L	ERA	Sv	IP		AB	H	HR	RBI	AVG
Home	5	8	4.86	0	103.2	LHB	151	32	2	11	.212
Road	5	4	3.74	0	110.2	RHB	676	200	16	83	.296
Day	1	3	5.02	0	57.1	Sc Pos	210	57	3	77	.271
Night	9	9	4.01	0	157.0	Clutch	72	30	1	8	.417

1990 Rankings (National League)

- 2nd worst ERA at home (4.86)
- 3rd in hits allowed (232), pickoff throws (272), GDPs induced (23) and highest on-base average allowed (.343)
- 4th highest batting average allowed (.280)
- 5th in walks allowed (78)
- Led the Braves in losses (12), hits allowed, pickoff throws, GDPs induced, groundball/flyball ratio (1.58), ERA on the road (3.74) and lowest batting average allowed with runners in scoring position (.271)

PITCHING:

The trade that brought Mark Grant to the Braves for Derek Lilliquist was a classic case of two teams trading problems. Both were number one draft picks who never had the type of seasons that their organizations expected. Lilliquist at least had failed only one club, the Braves; Grant had been a flop for both the Giants and the Padres. Grant's acquisition was a last ditch effort to save the Braves' bullpen after the likes of Lilliquist, Charlie Kerfeld and Joe Boever couldn't stop the flood of runs. Unlike Jeff Parrett, who was able to turn his season around after arriving in Atlanta, Grant stayed on the same course and put up poor numbers for both San Diego and Atlanta.

Grant throws a less than impressive fastball in conjunction with a good change-up and breaking ball. When he is at his best, opposing batters will foul off or pop up pitches. He pitches in many ways like teammate Charlie Leibrandt, but without Leibrandt's savvy. Grant will get more strikeouts than Leibrandt, and had some success in middle relief with the Padres. He was 8-2 with a 3.33 ERA for San Diego in '89, and he's had other periods of effectiveness. Basically, though, he's struggled throughout his career.

The Braves need to be careful about the way Grant is used. Excluding his last outing of the year, when he went four innings against the Giants, he was ineffective when pitching more than two innings. He seems to tire easily and has failed when tried as a starter.

HOLDING RUNNERS, FIELDING & HITTING:

Grant has an adequate move to first that will keep the lesser base stealing threats from running. He is also a decent fielder and lands from his delivery in a good fielding position. Grant has only batted a handful of times in his career, with no real success. The way he pitched last year for the Braves, he probably should not have gotten even one at-bat.

OVERALL:

Grant is like a lot of the Braves hurlers -- long on promise, short on results. He's still only 27, so he'll probably be kept around this year to see if he can get his act together. But unless he improves, he cannot realistically be considered part of the Braves' next five year plan.

MARK GRANT

Position: RP
Bats: R **Throws:** R
Ht: 6' 2" **Wt:** 205

Opening Day Age: 27
Born: 10/24/63 in Aurora, IL
ML Seasons: 6

Overall Statistics

	W	L	ERA	G	GS	Sv	IP	H	R	BB	SO	HR
1990	2	3	4.73	59	1	3	91.1	108	53	37	69	9
Career	20	27	4.23	190	48	7	532.1	542	271	202	326	62

How Often He Throws Strikes

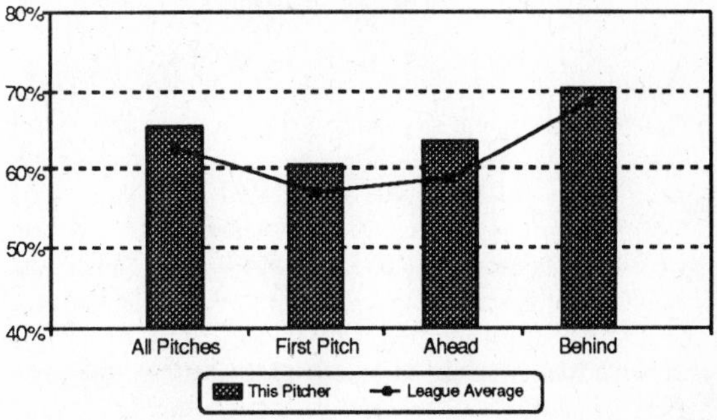

1990 Situational Stats

	W	L	ERA	Sv	IP		AB	H	HR	RBI	AVG
Home	1	0	5.70	2	47.1	LHB	199	62	4	29	.312
Road	1	3	3.68	1	44.0	RHB	163	46	5	38	.282
Day	1	1	6.04	0	25.1	Sc Pos	121	37	3	54	.306
Night	1	2	4.23	3	66.0	Clutch	56	20	1	11	.357

1990 Rankings (National League)

- 4th highest percentage of inherited runners scored (48.1%)

TOMMY GREGG

Position: 1B/RF
Bats: L **Throws:** L
Ht: 6' 1" **Wt:** 190

Opening Day Age: 27
Born: 7/29/63 in Boone, NC
ML Seasons: 4

Overall Statistics

	G	AB	R	H	D	T	HR	RBI	SB	BB	SO	AVG
1990	124	239	18	63	13	1	5	32	4	20	39	.264
Career	261	567	50	145	26	1	12	62	7	41	92	.256

Where He Hits the Ball

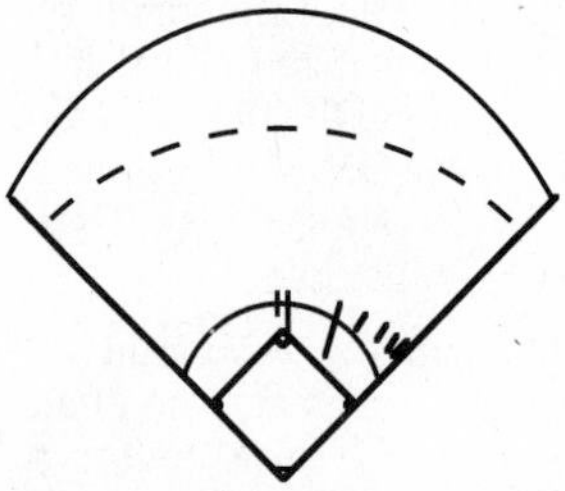

Vs. LHP

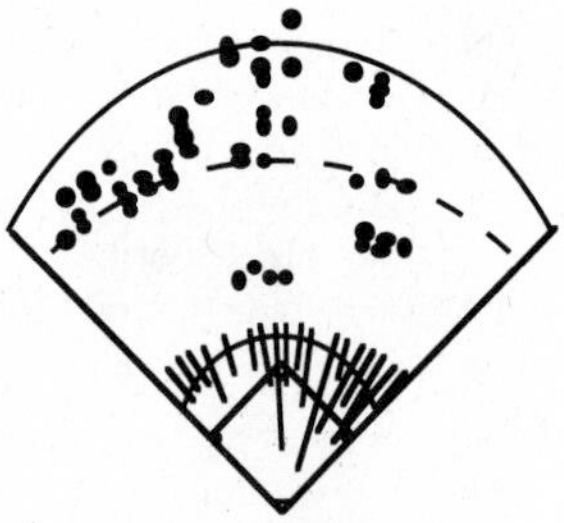

Vs. RHP

1990 Situational Stats

	AB	H	HR	RBI	AVG		AB	H	HR	RBI	AVG
Home	122	30	2	19	.246	LHP	19	2	0	0	.105
Road	117	33	3	13	.282	RHP	220	61	5	32	.277
Day	54	19	1	8	.352	Sc Pos	70	20	3	30	.286
Night	185	44	4	24	.238	Clutch	42	10	2	8	.238

1990 Rankings (National League)

- Did not rank near the top or bottom in any category

HITTING:

If Tommy Gregg could take back his first 33 at-bats of 1990, he would be a very happy man. Gregg managed only one hit in that span and was buried under the Mendoza line. After that stretch, Gregg batted .301 (62 for 206), bringing his season average to a very respectable .264.

A valuable bench player, Gregg was also the premier pinch hitter in the National League with four of his five home runs coming off the bench. Though he wasn't playing full-time, he put together his finest season in the majors.

Gregg reached career highs in doubles, walks and RBI even though he batted 37 fewer times than in 1989. Gregg improved by 30 points against right-handed pitchers, batting .277. However, his two-for-19 performance against lefties will probably guarantee that Gregg won't be seeing too many south-paws in 1991.

Because of Nick Esasky's season-long illness, Gregg saw a lot of time at first base last year, especially after Dave Justice replaced the traded Dale Murphy in right field. Gregg was usually platooned with Francisco Cabrera, and the two may end up sharing the position in 1991. But Gregg's lack of power -- only 12 homers in 567 career at-bats -- is hardly what the Braves would like from the man who gets most of the at-bats at first base. Gregg is a line drive hitter, and even playing in Atlanta hasn't helped his power numbers.

BASERUNNING:

The broken foot Gregg suffered in 1989 has put his running game on hold. He was a legitimate base stealing threat in the minor leagues but stole only four bases in seven attempts in 1990. He runs the bases well and rarely makes a blunder on the base paths.

FIELDING:

Gregg shifted between the outfield and first base last year and handled the switches well, committing only six errors. He is only an average outfielder at best, and his weak arm is a liability. He is a much stronger glove man at first base and is very good at picking up throws in the dirt. Also, at first base, his lack of speed is less of a liability.

OVERALL:

However he's used, Gregg should be a valuable member of the 1991 Braves. His work in 1990 indicates that he'd be best used as a bench player, filling in at first and the outfield and making frequent pinch hitting appearances. Gregg may end up with a lot of time at first, however, especially if Cabrera is shifted to the outfield.

DAVE JUSTICE

Position: 1B/RF
Bats: L **Throws:** L
Ht: 6' 3" **Wt:** 195

Opening Day Age: 25
Born: 4/14/66 in Cincinnati, OH
ML Seasons: 2

Overall Statistics

	G	AB	R	H	D	T	HR	RBI	SB	BB	SO	AVG
1990	127	439	76	124	23	2	28	78	11	64	92	.282
Career	143	490	83	136	26	2	29	81	13	67	101	.278

Where He Hits the Ball

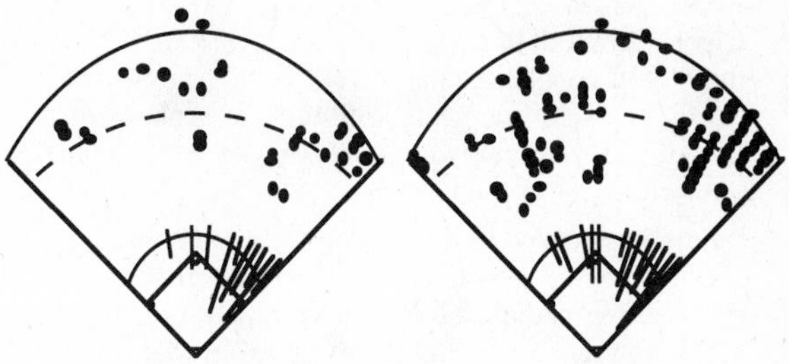

Vs. LHP **Vs. RHP**

1990 Situational Stats

	AB	H	HR	RBI	AVG		AB	H	HR	RBI	AVG
Home	225	72	19	48	.320	LHP	131	48	10	32	.366
Road	214	52	9	30	.243	RHP	308	76	18	46	.247
Day	104	24	6	16	.231	Sc Pos	113	36	7	50	.319
Night	335	100	22	62	.299	Clutch	62	18	4	10	.290

1990 Rankings (National League)

- 1st in least GDPs per GDP situation (2.7%) and slugging percentage while batting cleanup (.565)
- 2nd in slugging percentage vs. left-handed pitchers (.656) and on-base percentage vs. left-handed pitchers (.443)
- 3rd highest batting average vs. left-handed pitchers (.366)
- Led the Braves in walks (64), HR frequency (15.7 ABs per HR), most pitches seen per plate appearance (3.94) and batting average at home (.320)
- Led NL first basemen in home runs (28), slugging percentage (.535) and runs scored per time reached base (40.4%)

HITTING:

In a touching move, Dale Murphy, the longtime Atlanta Brave, placed an ad in the August 12 edition of the Atlanta Journal and Constitution last year. Murphy thanked the fans of Atlanta for their support during his 15-year career with the Braves, which had ended with an August 3 trade to Philadelphia. But by the time the ad appeared, the fans might have asked "Dale who?" In the eight games played by Dave Justice in right field after Murphy was traded, Justice batted .394 with six homers and 11 RBI. The performance won Justice National League Player of the Week honors, and he was later chosen Player of the Month for August. When the season ended, Justice added the NL Rookie of the Year award. A new franchise player may have been found.

Batting .282 with 28 homers and 78 RBI, Justice shocked more than a few people with his performance. Though the Braves had always considered him a fine prospect and probably the best athlete in their system, even they were a bit surprised. As a minor leaguer Justice had never belted more than 22 homers in a season, but moved steadily up the ladder and always displayed excellent plate discipline.

Justice generates great bat speed with a beautiful line drive stroke. His swing has been compared to two great Williamses (Ted and Billy). Justice took full advantage of Fulton County Stadium last year, hitting 19 of his 28 homers there, and the lefty swinger batted an amazing .366 against left-handed pitching.

BASERUNNING:

Swiping 11 bases, Justice came within one stolen base of tieing his professional high (12 with Richmond in 1989). He is a fast runner and should improve. He is very smart on the bases and knows when he can take an extra base.

FIELDING:

Justice broke in at first base last year, serving on the Nick Esasky relief corps. He never felt comfortable there but did an adequate job. He was moved to right field, his natural position, after Murphy was traded. He displayed a very strong defensive game which should only improve. Justice has great speed in right field and has a strong arm. He needs to improve the accuracy of his throws, however.

OVERALL:

Early last year, baseball card collectors were using Dave Justice's 1990 rookie baseball card for a bookmark. By the end of the season, they were hoarding them at $5.00 each (if they could find them at all). Justice looks like the real thing, and his value, like that of his cards, should continue to go up.

PITCHING:

In "Bull Durham," Crash Davis remarked that strikeouts are un-American and not at all democratic. The wealth of outs should be shared by all the defensive players. Charlie Leibrandt is certainly a follower of this philosophy. In his entire career, Leibrandt has gotten batters out by frustrating them with underwhelming stuff. Leibrandt simply coaxes hitters to put the ball in play and lets the seven men behind him take care of the rest. While 21% of his runs last year were unearned, compliments of Atlanta's poor defense, Leibrandt continued to be an effective pitcher.

Leibrandt had great success last year after starting the season on the disabled list with a slight tear in his left rotator cuff. In his 24 starts, he averaged 6.8 innings and completed five games; that helped cut down the workload of the beleaguered bullpen. A year after the worst season of his career (5-11, 5.14 for Kansas City), Leibrandt had a team low ERA of 3.16. Despite moving to a hitters' park in Atlanta, that was his lowest mark in five years. Leibrandt was also stingy in issuing walks, allowing only two per nine innings, easily the best of the Braves' starters.

Leibrandt is now 34, but it doesn't matter; he never could throw very hard. He relies on changing speeds, mixing his fastball, slider, curve and change-up to perfection. His slider has always been his out pitch.

Leibrandt might also be a good mentor for the young Atlanta pitching staff. The common thread the young pitchers have is that they are hard throwers who rely on the strikeout, but haven't yet learned how to pitch. Leibrandt might be there to remind them that baseball is a democratic game and that they should spread the outs around -- even with the woeful Atlanta defense.

HOLDING RUNNERS, FIELDING AND HITTING:

For Leibrandt, baserunners are a way of life. He has survived by incorporating a good move to first base to keep runners close. However, his slow delivery and velocity give the baserunner an extra step. Leibrandt is a capable fielder who comes off the mound in good position to field a ball hit through the box. Five years in the American League did not diminish his skills as a batter, as he was one of the best hitters on the Braves' staff.

OVERALL:

Leibrandt has been granted free agency by the Collusion III arbitration decision, and the services of this heady veteran should be in demand. The Braves will no doubt want to keep him, because Leibrandt's consistency is important to a young and erratic pitching staff.

CHARLIE LEIBRANDT

Position: SP
Bats: R **Throws:** L
Ht: 6' 3" **Wt:** 200

Opening Day Age: 34
Born: 10/4/56 in Chicago, IL
ML Seasons: 11

Overall Statistics

	W	L	ERA	G	GS	Sv	IP	H	R	BB	SO	HR
1990	9	11	3.16	24	24	0	162.1	164	72	35	76	9
Career	101	89	3.71	300	253	2	1735.0	1818	801	513	800	130

How Often He Throws Strikes

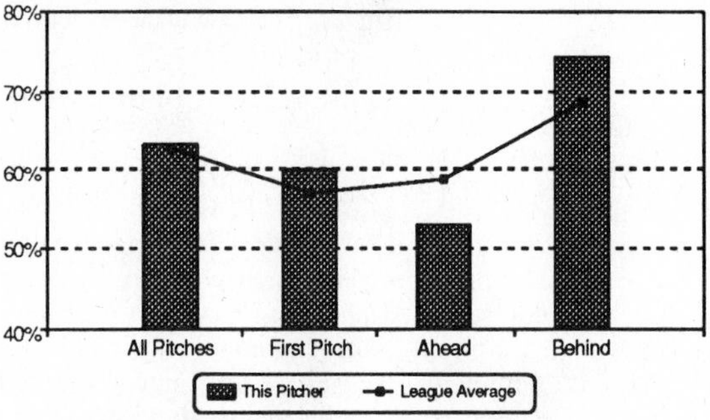

1990 Situational Stats

	W	L	ERA	Sv	IP		AB	H	HR	RBI	AVG
Home	6	5	2.59	0	87.0	LHB	99	21	3	14	.212
Road	3	6	3.82	0	75.1	RHB	529	143	6	51	.270
Day	2	4	3.08	0	49.2	Sc Pos	161	44	4	54	.273
Night	7	7	3.20	0	112.2	Clutch	45	8	0	1	.178

1990 Rankings (National League)

- 2nd highest stolen base percentage allowed (87.5%)
- 6th least strikeouts per 9 innings (4.2)
- 7th least HRs allowed per 9 innings (.50)
- Led the Braves in ERA (3.16), shutouts (2), hit batsmen (4), balks (3), strikeout/walk ratio (2.2), lowest on-base average allowed (.302), least pitches thrown per batter (3.63), least baserunners allowed per 9 innings (11.3), least HRs allowed per 9 innings and ERA at home (2.59)

ODDIBE McDOWELL

Position: CF/LF
Bats: L **Throws:** L
Ht: 5' 9" **Wt:** 160

Opening Day Age: 28
Born: 8/25/62 in Hollywood, FL
ML Seasons: 6

Overall Statistics

	G	AB	R	H	D	T	HR	RBI	SB	BB	SO	AVG
1990	113	305	47	74	14	0	7	25	13	21	53	.243
Career	771	2646	424	667	120	27	73	251	155	266	511	.252

Where He Hits the Ball

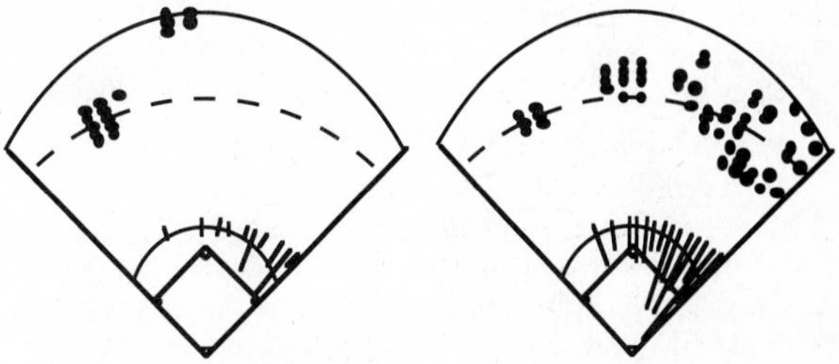

Vs. LHP Vs. RHP

1990 Situational Stats

	AB	H	HR	RBI	AVG		AB	H	HR	RBI	AVG
Home	150	41	4	14	.273	LHP	39	4	0	1	.103
Road	155	33	3	11	.213	RHP	266	70	7	24	.263
Day	57	13	1	6	.228	Sc Pos	50	17	3	21	.340
Night	248	61	6	19	.246	Clutch	43	8	1	3	.186

1990 Rankings (National League)

- 2nd worst leadoff on-base average (.299)
- 7th in bunts in play (25)
- Led the Braves in bunts in play

HITTING:

When the Braves acquired Oddibe McDowell from Cleveland halfway through the 1989 season, he proceeded to put up great numbers. McDowell batted .304 for Atlanta, showed power to the gaps and added strong run production with 56 runs scored in only 76 games. The Braves were McDowell's third team in less than a year, but Atlanta seemed to be a safe place to call home. A year later, after a lackluster 1990 campaign in which he batted .243 and lost his center field job to Ron Gant, McDowell is keeping his bags packed again.

A former number one draft choice, McDowell was once an outstanding prospect who won the 1984 Golden Spikes Award as the top amateur in the country. He has had some major league success, particularly in 1986, his first full season, when he hit 18 homers and scored 105 runs for the Rangers. But McDowell never really developed after that, and in most areas, he's regressed. He's still never batted more than .266 in a full season, and his 1986 figures remain his career highs in most significant categories.

McDowell remains a good fastball hitter, particularly on balls out over the plate. He provides good extra-base power, especially for a little man, and he's a fine bunter. But he has never handled off speed stuff very well, and he's helpless against breaking pitches from lefties; last year he batted only .103 against southpaws, with no extra-base hits. McDowell has cut down on his swing -- his strikeout rate has declined every year since 1986 -- and he did very well in the clutch last year, batting .340 with runners in scoring position.

BASERUNNING:

McDowell stole only 13 bases last year, a career low, but he hasn't lost his touch; lack of playing time limited him to 15 attempts. He has not lost a step on the base paths and he continues to be a smart, aggressive base runner.

FIELDING:

McDowell is not an exceptional fielder but he gets to the ball quickly, often saved by his great speed. He does not have a strong arm and will allow runners to take an extra base. He is probably best suited to left field, though he has mostly played center in his career.

OVERALL:

McDowell is still looking for the type of year he had in 1986. He has a chance with the Braves, but he'll only play regularly if they trade Lonnie Smith. His best chance would be yet another trade, particularly to a club who could use him as a platoon player against righties.

KENT MERCKER

Position: RP
Bats: L **Throws:** L
Ht: 6' 1" **Wt:** 175

Opening Day Age: 23
Born: 2/1/68 in Dublin, OH
ML Seasons: 2

PITCHING:

Being the closer on the Atlanta Braves is comparable to being a peacemaker in the Middle East; while the role is important, a man has very little chance of making an impact. Lefthander Kent Mercker was thrust in the role of closer last year when Mike Stanton went down with an injury, and both Joe Boever and Charlie Kerfeld proved ineffective. Considering his lack of experience in the role, Mercker handled himself very well, recording seven saves and a 3.17 ERA in 36 games.

Prior to the 1990 season, Mercker had been used almost exclusively as a starting pitcher, with excellent results. His career minor league record was 27-21 with a very respectable 3.05 ERA, and he had averaged over a strikeout per inning. Opening the season at AAA Richmond, Mercker was typically strong, with a 5-4 record, a 3.55 ERA and a hefty total of 69 strikeouts in only 58 innings. After his recall to Atlanta, he continued to pitch well, though he did taper off at the end of the season with six straight losses after August 15. Fatigue was probably the reason.

Mercker uses a slow delivery for his great fastball. He also has strong command of his change-up, but his curveball was on and off in 1990. Mercker needs more than one pitch, because when he only has command of his fastball, he is very hittable. As he has progressed through the Braves organization, his strikeout-to-walk ratio has been consistently better than two-to-one. But as he has faced more patient hitters, the ratio has declined, and it was down to 1.6 to one with Atlanta last year. Struggling to control his curve, Mercker walked a batter every two innings with the Braves last year, and behind on counts, yielded six homers in only 48.1 innings.

HOLDING RUNNERS, FIELDING AND HITTING:

Mercker is a heads-up fielder and a valuable asset to an otherwise weak Atlanta infield. He keeps runners close by constantly looking over to first, even offering a glance during his move to the plate. Should Mercker be placed in the starting rotation in 1991, he is a good enough athlete to be a successful batter and bunter. He rarely got to hit as Atlanta's closer in 1990.

OVERALL:

Even though Mercker is a fierce competitor, he is probably not a closer the Braves can ride to a championship (let alone .500). His proper role is starting, but the Braves' rotation is crowded. Mercker may be used in middle relief if Mike Stanton can resume his closer's role. Otherwise Mercker may be asked to be the stopper again.

Overall Statistics

	W	L	ERA	G	GS	Sv	IP	H	R	BB	SO	HR
1990	4	7	3.17	36	0	7	48.1	43	22	24	39	6
Career	4	7	3.93	38	1	7	52.2	51	28	30	43	6

How Often He Throws Strikes

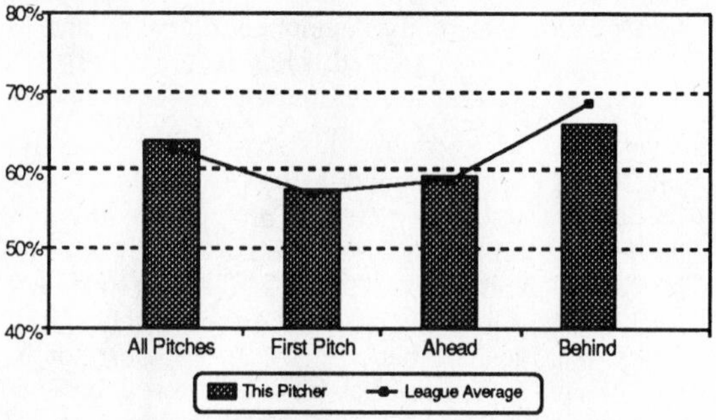

1990 Situational Stats

	W	L	ERA	Sv	IP		AB	H	HR	RBI	AVG
Home	3	2	2.53	5	21.1	LHB	48	12	1	2	.250
Road	1	5	3.67	2	27.0	RHB	134	31	5	20	.231
Day	1	4	5.59	0	9.2	Sc Pos	46	9	0	15	.196
Night	3	3	2.56	7	38.2	Clutch	114	27	5	14	.237

1990 Rankings (National League)

- Led the Braves in games finished (28)

GREG OLSON

Position: C
Bats: R **Throws:** R
Ht: 6' 0" **Wt:** 200

Opening Day Age: 30
Born: 9/6/60 in Marshall, MN
ML Seasons: 2

HITTING:

A long-time minor leaguer who'd toiled for eight years in the Met and Twin systems without exciting many people, Greg Olson had a 1990 season which even he had trouble believing. Winning a job on the Braves almost by default, Olson was a National League All-Star at mid-season and finished the year batting a very respectable .262.

Drafted out of the Twins system as a six-year free agent, Olson began last spring rated far behind Ernie Whitt, Jody Davis and Phil Lombardi on the Braves catching charts. But Davis couldn't cut it and got released, Lombardi unexpectedly retired, and Whitt first got hurt and then couldn't find his stroke. Olson took full advantage of his chance to play, and his .289 average at the break earned him a richly deserved job as an All-Star reserve. Even then, Olson had to deal with the fates of baseball. Whitt returned from the disabled list, and All-Star or not, Olson found himself sharing time. In reality, a platoon role made sense for Olson, who batted .312 vs. lefties, but only .208 against righties.

Even though Olson's batting average dropped during the second half, he batted higher than his minor league average of .248 and showed fair power. He has always shown good plate discipline, and he's a good contact hitter. Olson looked very weak against right-handed breaking ballers He hit the fastball well enough to stay in the lineup against lefties.

BASERUNNING:

Only once in Olson's eight year minor league career did he steal more than one base. Last year was certainly no different. Like most of his teammates, he is a very cautious runner on the base paths.

FIELDING:

With the offense-minded Mets, the weak-hitting Olson had no real shot at making the major league club. While his offensive production picked up with Atlanta, he maintained his defensive skills. Olson does not have the type of arm that a Vince Coleman or Rickey Henderson should worry about, but he does throw well enough to cut down the mere mortals on the base path. In 1989 he threw out over 50% of the runners in AAA Portland.

OVERALL:

For the next couple of years, Olson will be the Tom Brookens of the Braves, winning the catching job over the highly touted prospects in the organization (Kelly Mann, Jim Kremers and Tyler Houston). Like Brookens, who held off a series of third base challengers in Detroit for years, he will not be spectacular or flashy, but simply get the job done very solidly.

Overall Statistics

	G	AB	R	H	D	T	HR	RBI	SB	BB	SO	AVG
1990	100	298	36	78	12	1	7	36	1	30	51	.262
Career	103	300	36	79	12	1	7	36	1	30	51	.263

Where He Hits the Ball

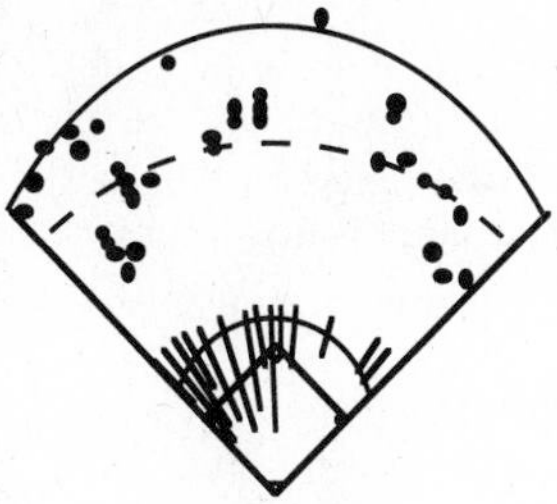

Vs. LHP

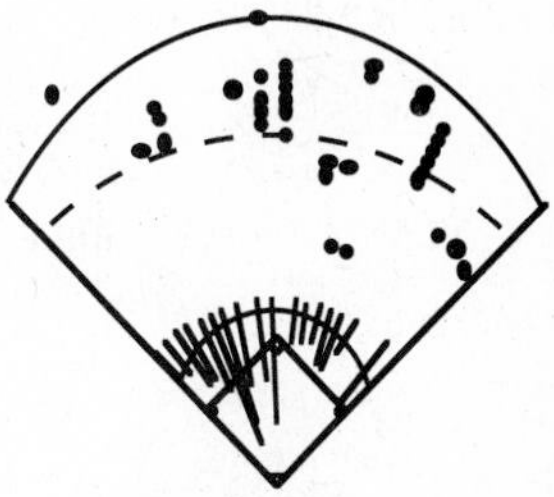

Vs. RHP

1990 Situational Stats

	AB	H	HR	RBI	AVG		AB	H	HR	RBI	AVG
Home	151	43	4	21	.285	LHP	154	48	5	25	.312
Road	147	35	3	15	.238	RHP	144	30	2	11	.208
Day	74	21	1	8	.284	Sc Pos	74	16	3	27	.216
Night	224	57	6	28	.254	Clutch	50	11	0	6	.220

1990 Rankings (National League)

- 4th lowest batting average with the bases loaded (.091)
- Led NL catchers in slugging percentage vs. left-handed pitchers (.481)

JEFF PARRETT

Position: RP/SP
Bats: R **Throws:** R
Ht: 6' 3" **Wt:** 200

Opening Day Age: 29
Born: 8/26/61 in Indianapolis, IN
ML Seasons: 5

PITCHING:

In 1988 for Montreal and in 1989 for Philadelphia, Jeff Parrett was one of the best middle relief pitchers in baseball. Parrett was remarkably consistent both years, as he won 12 games, saved six and posted an ERA under 3.00 in each season. He slumped badly at the start of the 1990 season, however, and the Phillies included him in the package they offered the Braves for Dale Murphy. Parrett pitched much better for the Braves, and looks capable of resuming his role as a top middle man.

While Parrett's overall statistics last year were very poor, he put up improved numbers with the Braves. After getting hammered for a 5.18 ERA and going 4-9 with the Phils, he split two decisions and posted an ERA of 3.00 in 20 games for Atlanta. More encouraging was his improvement in keeping the ball down; Parrett gave up 10 homers in 47 games for the Phils, but allowed only one dinger for the Braves. Parrett did spend much of his Atlanta time pitching from the stretch after giving up 27 hits and 19 walks in only 27 innings, but by pitching well with men on base, he was successful in keeping those runners from scoring.

Parrett throws a great fastball that is often clocked at over 90 MPH. When his fastball has movement, he is usually successful and doesn't need to worry about his other pitches. When the heater isn't working, he turns to his slider or split-finger pitch, which is his change-up. The breaking pitches induce ground balls, but they also drop out of the strike zone a lot. Parrett needs better control of those pitches if he's going to return to his '88-'89 form.

HOLDING RUNNERS, FIELDING & HITTING:

Parrett changes his move to first base, using both a slow and a quick move in an effort to keep runners off balance. He generally succeeds. Parrett's delivery does not throw him to either side and leaves him in good position to field the balls hit back at him. He is inexperienced at bat and would have to work on his hitting if he ever became a starting pitcher.

OVERALL:

Like Mark Grant, his fellow middle reliever in the Braves' bullpen, Parrett had a rough 1990 season. But unlike Grant, he pitched much better after his trade to Atlanta. If Parrett can regain his control, he should be a valuable set-up man in 1991.

Overall Statistics

	W	L	ERA	G	GS	Sv	IP	H	R	BB	SO	HR
1990	5	10	4.64	67	5	2	108.2	119	62	55	86	11
Career	36	27	3.66	257	5	20	388.1	347	178	187	323	36

How Often He Throws Strikes

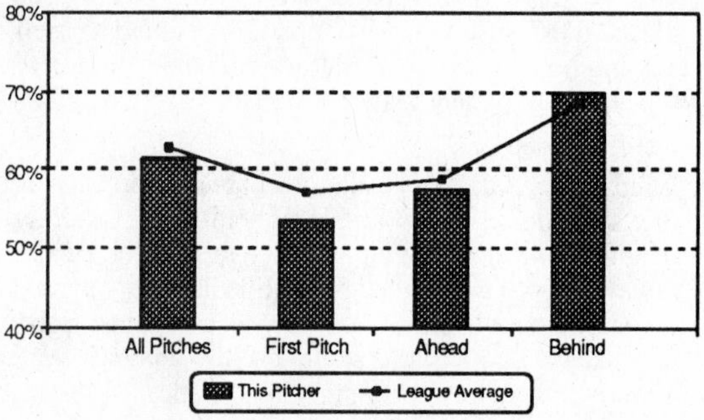

1990 Situational Stats

	W	L	ERA	Sv	IP		AB	H	HR	RBI	AVG
Home	2	5	5.06	2	58.2	LHB	213	57	7	32	.268
Road	3	5	4.14	0	50.0	RHB	197	62	4	28	.315
Day	0	4	5.35	1	33.2	Sc Pos	123	32	1	43	.260
Night	5	6	4.32	1	75.0	Clutch	149	47	3	24	.315

1990 Rankings (National League)

- 4th in pickoff throws (213) and worst winning percentage (.333)
- 5th in holds (11) and blown saves (6)
- 8th in games pitched (67)

JIM PRESLEY

Position: 3B/1B
Bats: R **Throws:** R
Ht: 6' 1" **Wt:** 190

Opening Day Age: 29
Born: 10/23/61 in Pensacola, FL
ML Seasons: 7

Overall Statistics

	G	AB	R	H	D	T	HR	RBI	SB	BB	SO	AVG
1990	140	541	59	131	34	1	19	72	1	29	130	.242
Career	939	3487	410	867	181	14	134	490	9	206	843	.249

Where He Hits the Ball

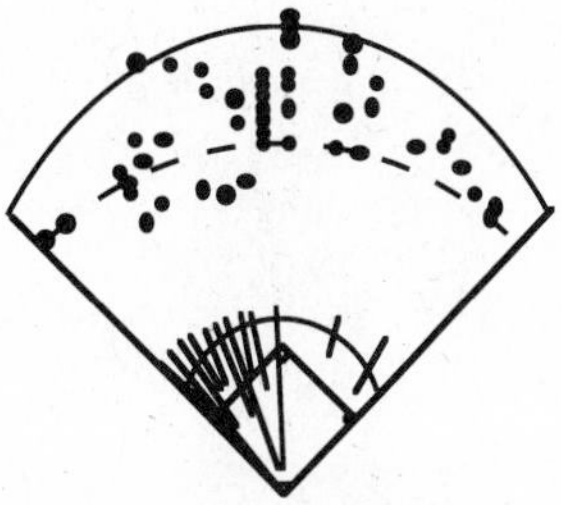

Vs. LHP

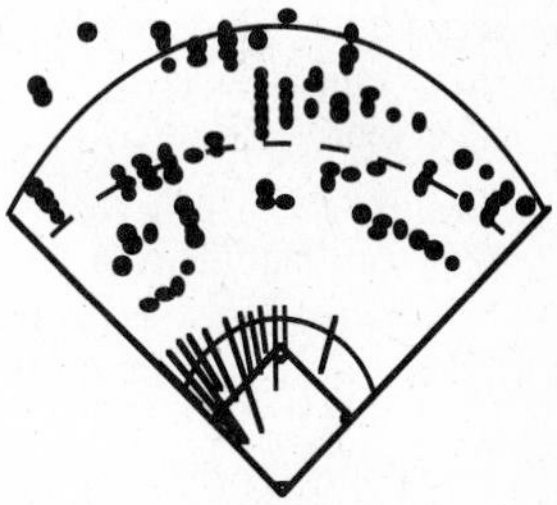

Vs. RHP

1990 Situational Stats

	AB	H	HR	RBI	AVG		AB	H	HR	RBI	AVG
Home	288	75	10	38	.260	LHP	180	48	6	28	.267
Road	253	56	9	34	.221	RHP	361	83	13	44	.230
Day	124	28	5	19	.226	Sc Pos	149	32	1	47	.215
Night	417	103	14	53	.247	Clutch	84	15	3	11	.179

1990 Rankings (National League)

- 1st in lowest on-base average vs. right-handed pitchers (.257), highest percentage of swings that missed (32.2%) and lowest percentage of extra bases taken as a runner (24.7%)
- 2nd lowest batting average vs. right-handed pitchers (.230) and highest batting average on a 3-1 count (.667)
- 3rd in strikeouts (130) and lowest on-base average (.282)
- Led the Braves in doubles (34), strikeouts, batting average with the bases loaded (.364) and batting average on a 3-1 count
- Led NL third basemen in batting average on a 3-1 count and errors (25)

HITTING:

Going into the 1990 season, Jim Presley was a veteran in decline. Once a fine power hitter, Presley's homer output had dropped for four straight seasons, from 28 all the way down to 12, and his RBI count had tumbled from 107 in 1986 to 41 in 1989. Desperate for an established third baseman after Ron Gant failed there in 1989, the Braves traded two prospects to Seattle for Presley. The Braves weren't expecting miracles, but they did want better production at third, and Presley provided that. While he did not challenge Barry Bonds for Most Valuable Player, he put together a solid year that might have saved his career.

Presley did not benefit from the small park in Atlanta as much as he did from the hard throwing pitchers in the National League. Early in the year, he got a lot of the over-the-plate fastballs he loves to hit, and his average was over .300 for two months. But pitchers soon learned that Presley was weak against off speed pitches, low-and-away breaking balls and hard stuff high and inside. Presley's average ultimately fell to .242, but that was still his best mark in three years, and he was able to maintain strong run production. In many ways, his 1990 season resembled his 1987 campaign, when he batted .247, hit 24 home runs and drove in 88 runs.

However, Presley continued to have a terrible strikeout-to-walk ratio, always a major weakness of his. Last year he struck out 130 times in 140 games while drawing only 29 walks. Presley has fanned over 100 times every year since 1985 while drawing over 40 walks only once.

BASERUNNING:

When Presley's on first, the opponent should not even bother holding him on. He had one stolen base in two attempts last year, and that represents normal output for him. Presley knows he is not a speed demon and is rightfully cautious on the base paths.

FIELDING:

Presley has good instincts and average range at third, but his arm is erratic and leads to frequent throwing errors. His 25 errors easily led the league at his position. Presley has usually been able to provide enough offense to make you accept the errors.

OVERALL:

The Braves have a policy not to negotiate contracts during the season. However, they broke that rule last year and set out to sign their rejuvenated third baseman. They failed and Presley was a free agent at season's end. His better numbers in 1990 figure to get him a few offers, including one from Atlanta.

HITTING:

Lonnie Smith was one of the great comeback stories of 1989 when he came back from years of drug problems and declining production to hit .315 with 21 homers for the Braves. Following the season, Smith put on too much weight -- giving up smoking was a factor -- and reported to training camp out of shape in 1990. A lot of people gave up on Smith once more when he got off to a sluggish start, hitting .221 for his first 44 games. Proving the skeptics wrong yet again, Smith brought his average up to .305 by season's end.

Even at 35, Smith can still turn on a fastball, and with his incredibly quick wrists, he can drive the ball to all fields. Smith's home run total was down last year from 21 to nine, but that was still the second highest total of his career, and he belted a personal best nine triples. A patient hitter, Smith drew 58 walks and posted an excellent .384 on-base percentage. He crowds the plate and pitchers tend to work him inside; as a result he was hit by 11 pitches in '89 and six more last year.

Smith's work last year did have some negatives. His RBI production was way down, from 79 to 42. He also looked careless at times, which is almost understandable for a longtime veteran now playing for a chronic loser. There's not much excuse, however, for reporting to camp 15 pounds overweight.

BASERUNNING:

Since Smith had 337 lifetime stolen bases going into the 1990 season, the Braves were expecting speed from their left fielder. However, he appeared to have slowed down (the early extra weight was a factor) and stole only 10 bases in 20 attempts. However, he is still smart enough to know when to take the extra base.

FIELDING:

Known as "Skates" for his skittish defensive ways, Smith proved that his low total of two errors in 1989 was a fluke. Returning to his old ways, he booted 12 balls last year and made flies to left field a nightmare for Braves' pitchers. Smith also lacked hustle at times and allowed a number of catchable hits to drop in front of him or between him and center fielder Ron Gant. His arm is not really weak, but very inaccurate.

OVERALL:

A veteran of three World Championship teams, Smith did not seem happy playing for the downtrodden Braves last year, and sometimes it showed in his work. He has played very well in Atlanta, but would undoubtedly prefer to play for a contending team. Still productive, Smith might be a good 1991 pickup for a team that is one player from a title.

LONNIE SMITH

Position: LF
Bats: R **Throws:** R
Ht: 5' 9" **Wt:** 170

Opening Day Age: 35
Born: 12/22/55 in Chicago, IL
ML Seasons: 13

Overall Statistics

	G	AB	R	H	D	T	HR	RBI	SB	BB	SO	AVG
1990	135	466	72	142	27	9	9	42	10	58	69	.305
Career	1269	4377	772	1278	237	51	77	427	347	494	678	.292

Where He Hits the Ball

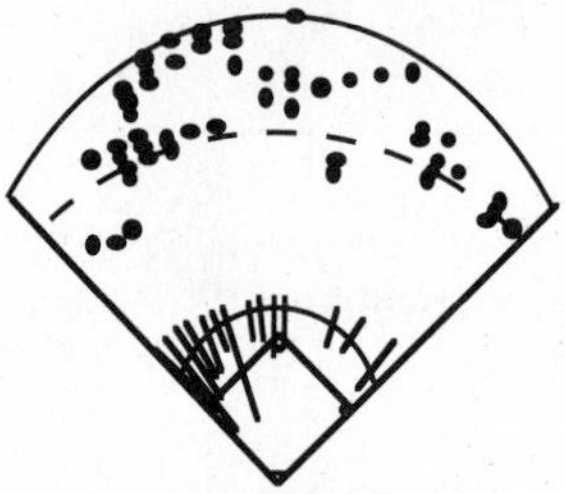

Vs. LHP

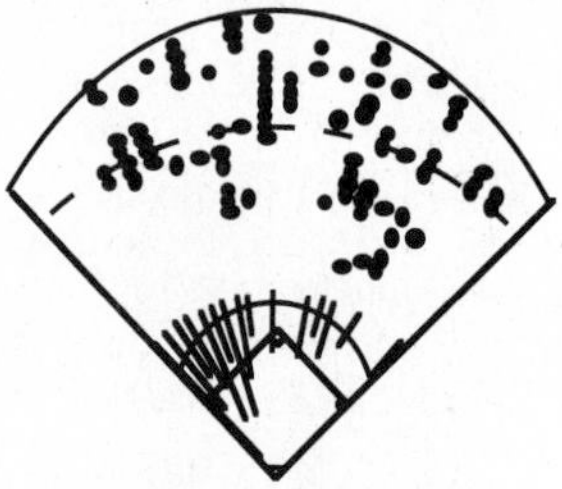

Vs. RHP

1990 Situational Stats

	AB	H	HR	RBI	AVG		AB	H	HR	RBI	AVG
Home	231	72	2	16	.312	LHP	197	58	6	18	.294
Road	235	70	7	26	.298	RHP	269	84	3	24	.312
Day	123	41	3	7	.333	Sc Pos	90	21	0	28	.233
Night	343	101	6	35	.294	Clutch	61	20	2	4	.328

1990 Rankings (National League)

- 1st in lowest stolen base percentage (50.0%)
- 2nd in least GDPs per GDP situation (2.7%), batting average on an 0-2 count (.381) and on-base average while batting leadoff (.419)
- 3rd in triples (9)
- Led the Braves in batting average (.305), triples, sacrifice flies (6), hit by pitch (6), on-base average (.384), batting average in the clutch and batting average with 2 strikes (.254)
- Led NL left fielders in triples, hit by pitch, least GDPs per GDP situation, errors (12) and percentage of extra bases taken as a runner (54.1%)

PITCHING:

After two rocky seasons in which he turned in records of 7-15 and 5-14, Pete Smith entered 1990 expecting to find pitching maturity at age 24. Smith did match his 1989 total of five wins, but had a very depressing season nonetheless. An abbreviated one, also: Smith's year ended on June 24 when he left a game against San Diego with a sore right shoulder. At the time Smith was expected to return late in the year, but it eventually became apparent that the shoulder would not heal without surgery. With a few days left in the season, Smith underwent surgery to repair a partial tear in his right rotator cuff.

Smith has reason to feel optimistic about recovery because he had the same kind of surgery several years ago when he was still pitching in the Braves' minor league system. After that operation, Smith was able to regain his impressive fastball which has been clocked at over 90 MPH. He will need the fastball to become a successful major league pitcher because his other pitches, which include a hard slider, curve and a circle change picked up in 1989, are not strong enough to carry him in the majors.

Before the injury last year, Smith was pitching about as he had in the past -- which is to say he was struggling. His won-lost record was much improved at 5-6, and his control was a little better, but those were about the only positives. He continued to allow a hit an inning while compiling a very high ERA of 4.79. Most depressing of all, he'd allowed a whopping 11 home runs in only 77 innings after permitting 13 in 142 innings in '89. Smith did show more stamina in 1990, pitching nearly six innings a start and turning in three complete games. But after the surgery, he'll have to rebuild the arm for '91.

HOLDING RUNNERS, FIELDING & HITTING:

Often plagued by base stealers, Smith committed seven balks in 1989. He reduced that figure to one last year, but his move to first still needs plenty of improvement. Smith remains a steady fielder with good range from the mound. His hitting satisfies the normally low expectations of a NL pitcher.

OVERALL:

Even if he should recover from his surgery, Smith is still not guaranteed a spot in the starting rotation. With the emergence of Paul Marak, among others, Smith might be relegated to middle relief where the Braves are desperate for help.

PETE SMITH

Position: SP
Bats: R **Throws:** R
Ht: 6' 2" **Wt:** 185

Opening Day Age: 25
Born: 2/27/66 in Abington, MA
ML Seasons: 4

Overall Statistics

	W	L	ERA	G	GS	Sv	IP	H	R	BB	SO	HR
1990	5	6	4.79	13	13	0	77.0	77	45	24	56	11
Career	18	37	4.30	79	78	0	446.0	443	238	183	306	42

How Often He Throws Strikes

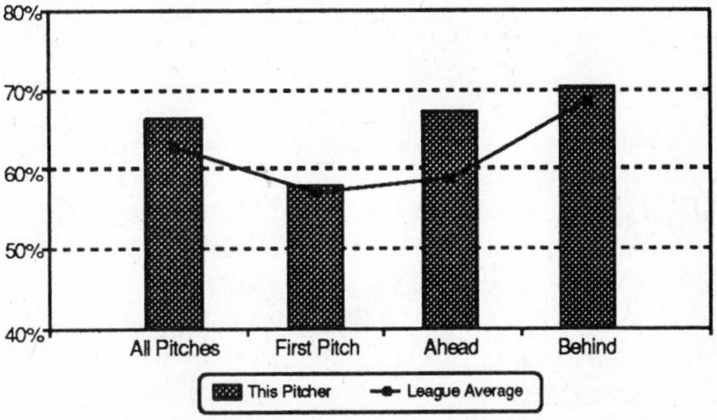

1990 Situational Stats

	W	L	ERA	Sv	IP		AB	H	HR	RBI	AVG
Home	3	3	6.35	0	39.2	LHB	166	49	3	18	.295
Road	2	3	3.13	0	37.1	RHB	130	28	8	19	.215
Day	1	2	7.08	0	20.1	Sc Pos	57	17	3	26	.298
Night	4	4	3.97	0	56.2	Clutch	21	5	0	2	.238

1990 Rankings (National League)

➟ Did not rank near the top or bottom in any category

STAFF ACE

JOHN SMOLTZ

Position: SP
Bats: R **Throws:** R
Ht: 6' 3" **Wt:** 185

Opening Day Age: 23
Born: 5/15/67 in Detroit, MI
ML Seasons: 3

PITCHING:

At the 1990 All-Star break, John Smoltz was probably wondering what went wrong. Smoltz had been Atlanta's representative in the 1989 summer classic with a 11-6 record and a great 2.10 ERA. But for the year since that game, he'd had a record of 8-11 with an ERA of 4.62. Smoltz finally found his game once again and became the dominant pitcher he had not been in a year. After the All-Star game, he was 8-5 with a respectable ERA of 3.06. That allowed Smoltz to put the cap on a second productive major league season.

A workhorse, Smoltz has pitched over 200 innings in each of the last two years, and in 1990 was tied with Cy Young winner Doug Drabek for fifth in the NL with 231.1 innings pitched. He averaged an impressive 6.8 innings a start last year, and led the club with six complete games. When he slumped in mid-year 1989, some wondered whether the heavy workload had given Smoltz a tired arm. If that was the problem, he now seems fully recovered.

Smoltz's bread and butter pitch is a fastball that travels over 90 MPH. He also throws a slider, a change and a curve that often drops out of the strike zone. When Smoltz does not have command of his curve, he will throw it in the dirt, resulting in a league-high 14 wild pitches. At the end of the year he was working on improving his change-up, a pitch which was not very effective in 1990. With some work, it could prove to be a more valuable part of his repertoire. Smoltz still prefers the fastball, however. He loves to strike out batters and ranked sixth in the National League with 170.

HOLDING RUNNERS, FIELDING & HITTING:

Part of the success Smoltz had in 1990 comes from his ability to do more than throw the ball. He has a good move to first but he struggled in '90 allowing 31 opposition stolen bases. Unlike many power pitchers, he does not flop off the mound, but lands in a position to field balls hit through the box. He had a decent year at the plate (for a pitcher) and has shown good bunting ability.

OVERALL:

With all their emphasis on drafting pitchers in the early rounds of the draft, it is ironic that the finest pitcher on the Braves came in a trade. The 1987 deal that brought Smoltz over to the Braves for Doyle Alexander will be remembered as the crowning achievement in the regime of ex-general manager (and current manager) Bobby Cox.

Overall Statistics

	W	L	ERA	G	GS	Sv	IP	H	R	BB	SO	HR
1990	14	11	3.85	34	34	0	231.1	206	109	90	170	20
Career	28	29	3.68	75	75	0	503.1	440	228	195	375	45

How Often He Throws Strikes

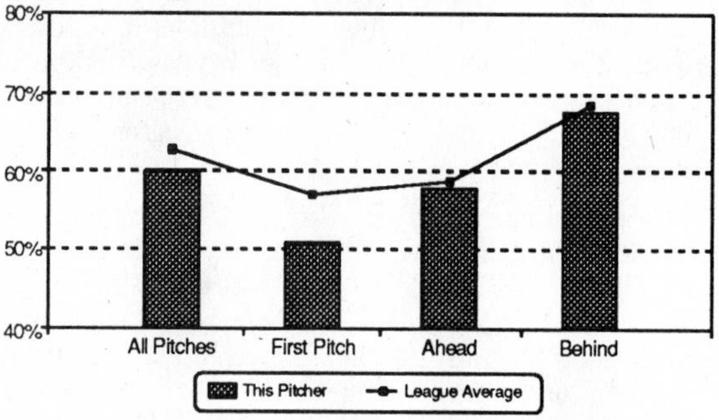

1990 Situational Stats

	W	L	ERA	Sv	IP		AB	H	HR	RBI	AVG
Home	9	4	2.76	0	124.0	LHB	510	137	10	51	.269
Road	5	7	5.11	0	107.1	RHB	348	69	10	44	.198
Day	2	3	4.63	0	35.0	Sc Pos	180	49	5	73	.272
Night	12	8	3.71	0	196.1	Clutch	67	12	0	9	.179

1990 Rankings (National League)

- 1st in walks allowed (90) and wild pitches (14)
- 2nd lowest batting average allowed vs. right-handed batters (.198)
- 3rd in most stolen bases allowed (31)
- Led the Braves in wins (14), games started (34), complete games (6), shutouts (2), innings (231.1), batters faced (966), home runs allowed (20), walks allowed, strikeouts (170), wild pitches, pitches thrown (3,611), most stolen bases allowed and most run support per 9 innings (5.1)

HITTING:

At age 27, Andres Thomas has apparently lost his job as the Braves shortstop. Thomas has always committed a boatload of errors, and to remain a regular he needs to hit as he did in 1988 when he batted .252 and drove in 68 runs. In the last two years Thomas has hit .213 and .219, and that's simply not going to cut it.

If he is to continue at the major league level, Thomas needs to learn his limitations and stop trying to hit everything out of the park. He does have some pop in his bat, and given full-time work, he'd probably reach double figures in home runs and drive in 60 runs or so. The downside is that he has terrible plate discipline, routinely swinging at the first offering, wherever it is. While he's never struck out more than 95 times in a season, he's also never drawn more than 14 walks. After six years, Thomas has a career on-base percentage of only .255, a ridiculously low figure.

Thomas can hit the fastball, which is why he jumps on the first pitch so often; once he gets behind in the count, he'll probably never see another one. But pitchers won't offer him hittable fastballs unless they have to, and they can make him look helpless against breaking stuff.

BASERUNNING:

In every possible infield combination put together last year by Russ Nixon or Bobby Cox, three factors ring true of every player: shaky defense, medium power and no speed. Thomas certainly fits right in to the limited speed category, although he is more likely to challenge an outfield arm than any other Braves infielder.

FIELDING:

Thomas is often derided for his defense, but in all fairness, his great range at shortstop is often his undoing. He frequently boots balls that other shortstops would never get to. On those plays, he lacks the patience to regain his balance and make a clean throw to first. Even though Thomas recorded only 10 errors in 1990 (a career low), he was injured or benched for much of the season. Thomas made his share of great plays in 1990, but unfortunately, the adventure began after he reached the ball.

OVERALL:

Thomas' injury at the end of the 1990 season could not have helped him keep the shortstop job for 1991. The only possible edge he has over Jeff Blauser and Mark Lemke is that he is more experienced at shortstop. That probably won't be enough, and a trade seems his only chance of continuing as a major league regular.

ANDRES THOMAS

Position: SS
Bats: R **Throws:** R
Ht: 6' 1" **Wt:** 185

Opening Day Age: 27
Born: 11/10/63 in Boca Chica, Dominican Republic
ML Seasons: 6

Overall Statistics

	G	AB	R	H	D	T	HR	RBI	SB	BB	SO	AVG
1990	84	278	26	61	8	0	5	30	2	11	43	.219
Career	577	2103	182	493	76	4	42	228	22	59	301	.234

Where He Hits the Ball

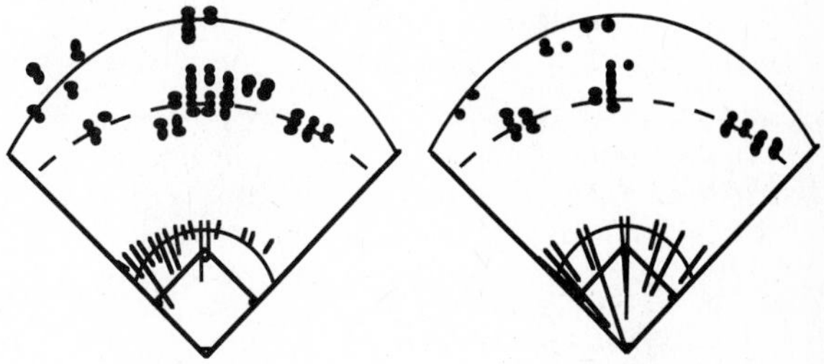

Vs. LHP Vs. RHP

1990 Situational Stats

	AB	H	HR	RBI	AVG		AB	H	HR	RBI	AVG
Home	157	36	1	12	.229	LHP	102	23	4	15	.225
Road	121	25	4	18	.207	RHP	176	38	1	15	.216
Day	69	12	1	6	.174	Sc Pos	73	19	1	26	.260
Night	209	49	4	24	.234	Clutch	46	12	1	5	.261

1990 Rankings (National League)

- 5th most GDPs per GDP situation (18.9%)

HITTING:

While Manager Bobby Cox continually changed the makeup of his infield after taking over from Russ Nixon last year, Jeff Treadway remained a constant. One of the most productive players on the Braves, Treadway is not yet an All- Star, but he has improved his output each year while putting together three consecutive solid seasons.

Treadway can hit. He had a career .313 average in the minors and never batted below .300 in five years in the Reds' system. He had a solid rookie year with Cincinnati in 1988 (.252), but Pete Rose soured on him, and the Reds sold him to the Braves in the spring of '89. Atlanta is happy they did, because Treadway has proven himself to be a steady .280 hitter. Last year he raised his average (from .277 to .283), homers (eight to 11) and RBI totals (40 to 59). After hitting only .198 against lefties in 1989, he batted .303 against them last year, eliminating the need to be platooned. He also hit .341 with men in scoring position.

Treadway is a contact hitter who does not walk or strike out much and can be used for the hit-and-run play (if the Braves ever decide to use it). A good fastball hitter, he likes the ball inside and can hit with some power to all fields. He improved against breaking balls last year, particularly against lefties. Treadway certainly has the offensive edge over Mark Lemke in any battle for second base.

BASERUNNING:

Treadway will never threaten Vince Coleman for the stolen base crown having swiped just nine bases in just over three years. He has not been gifted with great speed and is very easy to double up. Treadway is a very conservative runner who knows the limitations of his speed.

FIELDING:

While Treadway is no Jose (Lind or Oquendo) at second, he is a scrappy fielder who makes the routine plays with high accuracy and is very comfortable turning the double play. His range is limited, however, and he lets many balls get past him for hits. He's competent, unspectacular, and in the lineup primarily because of his bat.

OVERALL:

A Georgia native, Treadway has made a home for himself in Atlanta. He's only 28, and given his improvement against lefties, should finally be an every day player this year. He's a solid young veteran on a club which could use a lot more guys just like him.

JEFF TREADWAY

Position: 2B
Bats: L **Throws:** R
Ht: 5'11" **Wt:** 170

Opening Day Age: 28
Born: 1/22/63 in Columbus, GA
ML Seasons: 4

Overall Statistics

	G	AB	R	H	D	T	HR	RBI	SB	BB	SO	AVG
1990	128	474	56	134	20	2	11	59	3	25	42	.283
Career	388	1332	153	369	61	9	23	126	9	84	116	.277

Where He Hits the Ball

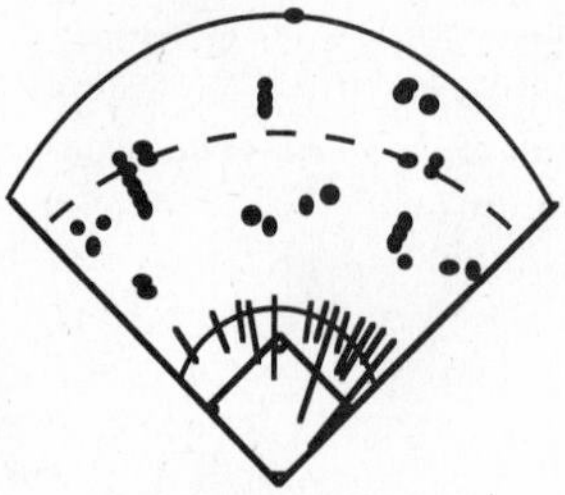

Vs. LHP

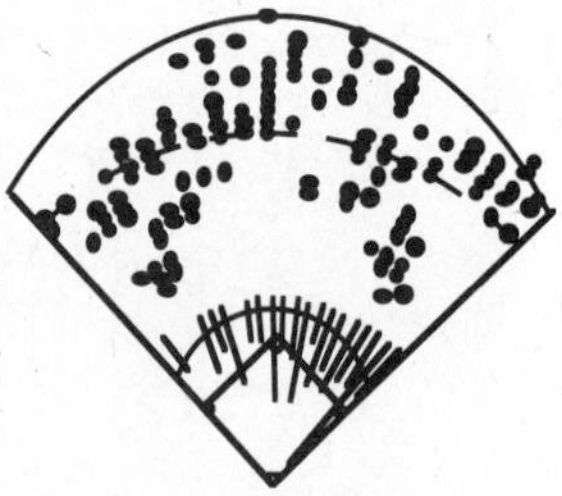

Vs. RHP

1990 Situational Stats

	AB	H	HR	RBI	AVG		AB	H	HR	RBI	AVG
Home	219	66	5	27	.301	LHP	119	36	4	20	.303
Road	255	68	6	32	.267	RHP	355	98	7	39	.276
Day	113	34	3	16	.301	Sc Pos	123	42	3	47	.341
Night	361	100	8	43	.277	Clutch	62	18	1	14	.290

1990 Rankings (National League)

- 4th highest batting average with runners in scoring position (.341)
- 5th least pitches seen per plate appearance (3.23)
- Led the Braves in batting average with runners in scoring position, batting average on a 3-2 count (.286), lowest percentage of swings that missed (9.5%) and highest percentage of swings put into play (50.3%)
- Led NL second basemen in batting average with runners in scoring position

ERNIE WHITT

Position: C
Bats: L **Throws:** R
Ht: 6' 2" **Wt:** 200

Opening Day Age: 38
Born: 6/13/52 in Detroit, MI
ML Seasons: 14

Overall Statistics

	G	AB	R	H	D	T	HR	RBI	SB	BB	SO	AVG
1990	67	180	14	31	8	0	2	10	0	23	27	.172
Career	1293	3712	442	923	174	15	134	531	22	428	479	.249

Where He Hits the Ball

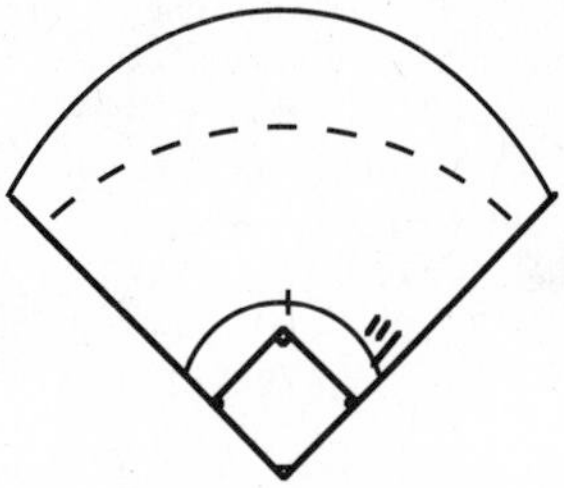

Vs. LHP

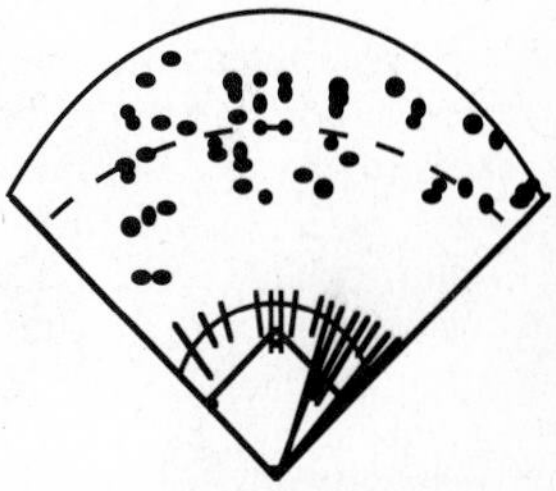

Vs. RHP

1990 Situational Stats

	AB	H	HR	RBI	AVG		AB	H	HR	RBI	AVG
Home	86	14	2	8	.163	LHP	17	2	0	2	.118
Road	94	17	0	2	.181	RHP	163	29	2	8	.178
Day	35	11	0	2	.314	Sc Pos	37	5	0	8	.135
Night	145	20	2	8	.138	Clutch	32	9	0	2	.281

1990 Rankings (National League)

- Did not rank near the top or bottom in any category

HITTING:

After 12 solid seasons with the Blue Jays, Ernie Whitt was traded to Atlanta last year, joining his former Blue Jay manager, Bobby Cox. Playing in Atlanta's "launching pad," Whitt hoped to regain some of his glory days. Instead he batted .172, hit two homers, and mostly reminded Atlantans of Cox's last catching import, Jody Davis.

If Whitt had been more of a hitting threat, Braves' opponents might have considered using an exaggerated shift by placing the third baseman, second baseman and the left fielder behind the first baseman. Even at his advanced age, Whitt has shown no desire to use the whole field and is perfectly happy to try to pull everything down the right field line. He can still hit the fastball up and over the plate, but pitchers can retire him pretty easily by jamming him with breaking stuff and change-ups. Whitt might be more successful if he went to the opposite field once in a while, but it's hard to change your style at age 38.

In fairness to Whitt, he was beset by injuries and forced to play catch-up after missing most of the first half. He did hit well for a while when Cox placed him in the number two spot in the line up, where he tended to see more fastballs. But Whitt looked nothing like the hitter who'd had double figures in home runs for eight straight years. And maybe he never will look like that again.

BASERUNNING:

Four years after Steve Avery was born, Ernie Whitt stole 12 bases while playing for AA Bristol. That was his career high. Needless to say, Whitt has stayed in baseball by being a wise baserunner who will rarely get thrown out trying to take an extra base.

FIELDING:

For all Whitt's problems with the bat, he was one of the defensive bright spots for the Braves last year. He had great success in throwing runners out and continued to show a lot of poise behind the plate. He also won some praise for handling the young Brave pitchers.

OVERALL:

What's the future for a 38-year-old player coming off a .172 season? Zilch -- except maybe if he's a left-handed hitting catcher. Like Jamie Quirk, who found himself catching in the World Series a year after he'd batted .176, Whitt will probably find someone interested in his services if he's willing to accept a role as a low-salaried backup.

TONY CASTILLO

Position: RP/SP
Bats: L **Throws:** L
Ht: 5'10" **Wt:** 177

Opening Day Age: 28
Born: 3/1/63 in Lara, Venezuela
ML Seasons: 3

Overall Statistics

	W	L	ERA	G	GS	Sv	IP	H	R	BB	SO	HR
1990	5	1	4.23	52	3	1	76.2	93	41	20	64	5
Career	7	3	4.40	95	3	2	118.2	134	65	36	93	7

PITCHING, FIELDING, HITTING & HOLDING RUNNERS:

Tony Castillo put together a strong season last year, and very quietly became one of the bright spots for the beleaguered Atlanta bullpen. Early in the year, Castillo had a good stint at AAA Richmond, where he was 3-1 with a 2.52 ERA and 27 strikeouts in 25 innings while being used mainly as a starter. When he was promoted to the Braves, Castillo became a swing man for Bobby Cox. He started three games with good success, but was primarily used out of the bullpen, where Atlanta's needs were more critical.

Throughout his career, Castillo has been a good strikeout pitcher. He employs a high leg kick (the only such delivery on the Braves) and is primarily a fastballer. Castillo's fastball is not quite up to the speed of Steve Avery's or John Smoltz's, but it's effective and works well with his good curveball, which he often slows down to use as a change-up. Castillo likes to throw around the plate and had 64 strikeouts and only 20 walks in 76.2 innings last year. However, concentrating on keeping the ball in the strike zone, he allowed a high opponent's batting average of .302. The high leg kick both hampers Castillo's fielding and makes him easy to run on.

OVERALL:

Castillo will probably serve the 1991 Braves the same way he did in 1990. He will be used as a left-handed set-up man, probably with Kent Mercker. At Castillo's age, he probably won't develop into a star, but he could provide a steady hand in the bullpen.

NICK ESASKY

Position: 1B
Bats: R **Throws:** R
Ht: 6' 3" **Wt:** 215

Opening Day Age: 31
Born: 2/24/60 in Hialeah, FL
ML Seasons: 8

Overall Statistics

	G	AB	R	H	D	T	HR	RBI	SB	BB	SO	AVG
1990	9	35	2	6	0	0	0	0	0	4	14	.171
Career	810	2703	336	677	120	21	122	427	18	314	712	.250

HITTING, FIELDING, BASERUNNING:

While Nick Esasky was not as big a financial flop as the Goodwill Games, Braves owner Ted Turner has to be cursing his luck. Turner brought the Florida native to the Braves with a three year $5.7 million contract, and so far no one can even figure out the cost per RBI; Esasky did not have one in the nine games he played.

While sports reporters were running to their video store to rent "Vertigo" (the reason given for Esasky's year long stay on the disabled list), it was determined that he had Lyme disease. Whatever his ailment, Braves fans were never able to see the player that put up career numbers at Boston in 1989 (.277, 30 homers, 108 RBI & 79 runs in 154 ball games). Esasky has power to all fields and figured to thrive in Atlanta -- where he'd always been a devastating slugger as a visiting player -- even more than he did at Fenway Park. While he never added stolen bases to his power attack, Esasky played solid first base and has compiled a lifetime fielding percentage of .995.

OVERALL:

If Esasky ever plays for the Braves, he should do well, but the emphasis is on should. His illness has kept him out of the game for so long that it will take him a while to get back into shape. Even with Tommy Gregg and Francisco Cabrera willing and able to play first, a healthy Esasky is definitely needed to help pull this club out of the cellar

DWAYNE HENRY

Position: RP
Bats: R **Throws:** R
Ht: 6' 3" **Wt:** 205

Opening Day Age: 29
Born: 2/16/62 in Elkton, MD
ML Seasons: 7

Overall Statistics

	W	L	ERA	G	GS	Sv	IP	H	R	BB	SO	HR
1990	2	2	5.63	34	0	0	38.1	41	26	25	34	3
Career	5	8	5.43	100	0	5	116.0	115	74	84	106	9

PITCHING, FIELDING, HITTING & HOLDING RUNNERS:

In each season since 1984, Dwayne Henry has played for both a major league and minor league team. Henry has put up some impressive numbers in the minor leagues -- 50-38 with 689 strikeouts in 696 innings through 1990. He has been especially effective for the Braves' AAA Richmond farm team the last two years, going 12-6 with a 2.42 ERA and 137 strikeouts in 111.2 innings, while holding opponents to a batting average of .141. But despite those imposing figures, Henry has never been a successful hurler in the major leagues. Last year he posted an Atlanta ERA of 5.63, just a little above his career average in the major leagues.

Henry is a large man who throws a fastball that rarely drops below the belt. His fastball is not overpowering, but he mixes it well with a change and slider and often gets batters to strike out while waiting on his fastball. Control has always been his problem -- he has walked 6.5 batters per nine innings in his major league career. He is aware of runners but does not throw very often to first base to keep them close. Henry is a strong fielder for a relatively large man, but has almost no professional batting experience.

OVERALL:

There is no reason to think that Henry will break his string of seven straight seasons of both major and minor league play, especially since the Braves have released him. He has a good enough arm -- and just enough talent -- to interest another team.

MARK LEMKE

Position: 2B/3B
Bats: B **Throws:** R
Ht: 5' 9" **Wt:** 165

Opening Day Age: 25
Born: 8/13/65 in Utica, NY
ML Seasons: 3

Overall Statistics

	G	AB	R	H	D	T	HR	RBI	SB	BB	SO	AVG
1990	102	239	22	54	13	0	0	21	0	21	22	.226
Career	132	352	34	77	19	1	2	33	0	30	34	.219

HITTING, FIELDING, BASERUNNING:

Mark Lemke has two advantages going into the 1991 season. He is a switch hitter, and he is the only member of the Atlanta infield who might someday be a candidate for a Gold Glove. However, the value in Lemke ends there. He is very weak against right-handed pitchers and he has thus far shown little power from either side of the plate.

The Braves expected more from Lemke. A small man, he nonetheless showed fine power in the minors averaging 18 homers and 71 RBI from 1986 to 1988. Lemke has a nice line drive stroke but has not been able to put up good numbers with Atlanta; he has yet to demonstrate an ability to hit the major league fastball. Lemke is not blessed with great speed and made a few blunders on the base paths in 1990. But if he sticks with the Braves, it will be defense that gets him the job. He committed only four errors while playing second and third base last year and is clearly the finest fielder on the team.

OVERALL:

Lemke was learning to play shortstop over the winter. But his best chance at a job might be if the Braves can't re-sign Jim Presley, if they trade Jeff Treadway, or if new GM John Schuerholz decides that the team needs Lemke's glove in the lineup. Given a chance to play, his minor league record suggests he will hit respectably.

PAUL MARAK

Position: SP
Bats: R **Throws:** R
Ht: 6' 2" **Wt:** 180

Opening Day Age: 25
Born: 8/2/65 in Lakenheath, England
ML Seasons: 1

Overall Statistics

	W	L	ERA	G	GS	Sv	IP	H	R	BB	SO	HR
1990	1	2	3.69	7	7	0	39.0	39	16	19	15	2
Career	1	2	3.69	7	7	0	39.0	39	16	19	15	2

PITCHING, FIELDING, HITTING & HOLDING RUNNERS:

Before the 1990 season, Paul Marak had never been on a major league roster and had found limited success in the minors. Marak really didn't get himself together until this year, but when he did, he wound up with a ticket to Atlanta.

Marak began his professional career as a less-than-promising starter. But after two dismal seasons in short-season play in 1985 and 1986, Marak was moved to long relief and began to prosper. When he was called up to the Braves late last year, he had compiled a 9-8 record with AAA Richmond with a league-best ERA of 2.49.

Marak throws a good sinker ball and only gave up two home runs while with the Braves. His average of only one gopher ball per 18.5 innings is considerably better than that of his hard-throwing teammates, Glavine (11.9), Smoltz (11.6) and Pete Smith (7.0). He's not a strikeout pitcher, but he's not afraid to pitch inside: he hit three batters in only 39 innings. His defensive instincts looked good -- essential to a pitcher who gets a lot of ground balls -- and he did a decent job of holding runners.

OVERALL:

New Braves' General Manager John Schuerholz put up a "help wanted" sign early in the off season for the Braves' pitching staff. Unless he is able to sign Bob Welch and Ted Higuera, look for Marak to become one of the fixtures in the Braves bullpen in 1991.

MIKE STANTON

Position: RP
Bats: L **Throws:** L
Ht: 6' 1" **Wt:** 190

Opening Day Age: 23
Born: 6/2/67 in Houston, TX
ML Seasons: 2

Overall Statistics

	W	L	ERA	G	GS	Sv	IP	H	R	BB	SO	HR
1990	0	3	18.00	7	0	2	7.0	16	16	4	7	1
Career	0	4	5.23	27	0	9	31.0	33	20	12	34	1

PITCHING, FIELDING, HITTING & HOLDING RUNNERS:

Mike Stanton's season ended very early last year. An inflamed left rotator cuff on April 28 put Stanton on the disabled list, and when the pain in his shoulder persisted during a short rehabilitation stint at AA Greenville, the Braves scrapped plans for him to come back to Atlanta. Stanton's left arm was considered too valuable to risk, so the Braves sent him home to rest.

Entering the season, Stanton figured to be Atlanta's relief ace. The hard throwing left hander had averaged over a strikeout an inning coming through the Braves system, and got a trial in late relief at the end of the 1989 season. Stanton responded brilliantly, with 27 strikeouts in only 24 innings, seven saves and an ERA of only 1.50. Stanton got hammered at the start of the '90 campaign, but his shoulder problems may have been the reason.

When healthy, Stanton possesses a fastball which reaches the low 90s, and he can keep hitters off balance with his fine curveball. Stanton does a good job of holding runners, but he's a poor fielder. He seldom gets to hit.

OVERALL:

A healthy Stanton in the bullpen would allow Kent Mercker to join the Braves' starting rotation in 1991. Mercker has been primarily a starting pitcher throughout his career, and Stanton has the better credentials for late relief. If fully recovered, he could become a star closer.

PAUL ASSENMACHER

Position: RP
Bats: L **Throws:** L
Ht: 6' 3" **Wt:** 200
Opening Day Age: 30
Born: 12/10/60 in Detroit, MI
ML Seasons: 5

PITCHING:

Paul Assenmacher is a solid left-handed relief pitcher who was thrust into the role of closer late last season by the Cubs. Assenmacher's work didn't make anyone forget Dennis Eckersley, but he continued to establish himself as a solid major league reliever.

Assenmacher's out pitch is a curveball which he can bring at differing speeds. He has pretty good control and can paint the corners. What is amazing is that while Assenmacher has only an average fastball, his tantalizing variety of curves, changes and "pseudo heat" is enough to pile up strikeout totals rivaling those of Randy Myers and other hard-throwing relievers.

Don Zimmer pegged Assenmacher as his closer towards the end of the season after Mitch Williams had failed in the role. Assenmacher did a decent job, recording ten saves, but he got the job mainly because the Cubs had nobody else. His stuff is best suited for a middle relief/set-up role. With his excellent curve, Assenmacher is very tough against lefties. He's no slouch against righthanders, either, but righties get a better look at his stuff and are much more likely to take him deep. In the past two years, Assenmacher has yielded 13 homers, 12 of them to righties. That's another reason why he's best suited for middle relief. He can come in to pitch specifically to lefties, and get them out.

Assenmacher is a very durable pitcher. He worked in 74 games last year, the second-most in the National League, and has averaged 67 appearances a year since 1988. The fact that he can retain his effectiveness while handling such a heavy workload makes him even more valuable.

HOLDING RUNNERS, FIELDING, HITTING:

Assenmacher has a decent move, and because of this and the Cubs' catchers, an impressive 40 percent of the runners trying to steal off him were caught. As a fielder, he is nothing special. He can cover the bag on a bunt and knows which base to throw to in most situations. He almost never gets to touch a bat.

OVERALL:

Assenmacher has pitched in poor pitchers' parks in his career (Wrigley and Fulton County Stadium in Atlanta), yet his career numbers remain good. He looks like a decent bet to continue his success, especially if used in middle relief. He'll make a competent closer if given the role, but probably not a great one.

Overall Statistics

	W	L	ERA	G	GS	Sv	IP	H	R	BB	SO	HR
1990	7	2	2.80	74	1	10	103.0	90	33	36	95	10
Career	26	17	3.37	314	1	24	382.0	355	162	146	340	30

How Often He Throws Strikes

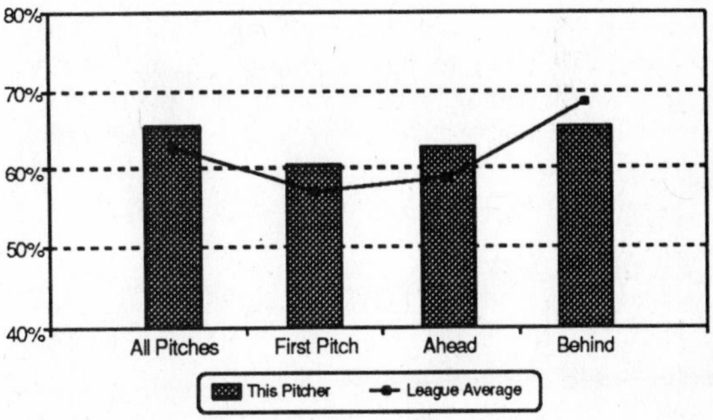

1990 Situational Stats

	W	L	ERA	Sv	IP		AB	H	HR	RBI	AVG
Home	6	1	3.46	3	52.0	LHB	121	27	1	19	.223
Road	1	1	2.12	7	51.0	RHB	255	63	9	23	.247
Day	5	1	2.67	4	60.2	Sc Pos	104	20	2	28	.192
Night	2	1	2.98	6	42.1	Clutch	190	47	5	22	.247

1990 Rankings (National League)

- 1st in worst save percentage (50.0%) and blown saves (10)
- 2nd in games pitched (74)
- 6th in holds (10)
- 7th in first batter efficiency (.194)
- Led the Cubs in games pitched, save opportunities (20), holds, blown saves, first batter efficiency and lowest percentage of inherited runners scored (29.1%)

DAMON BERRYHILL

Position: C
Bats: B **Throws:** R
Ht: 6' 0" **Wt:** 205

Opening Day Age: 27
Born: 12/3/63 in South Laguna, CA
ML Seasons: 4

Overall Statistics

	G	AB	R	H	D	T	HR	RBI	SB	BB	SO	AVG
1990	17	53	6	10	4	0	1	9	0	5	14	.189
Career	215	724	64	181	37	1	13	89	2	41	129	.250

Where He Hits the Ball

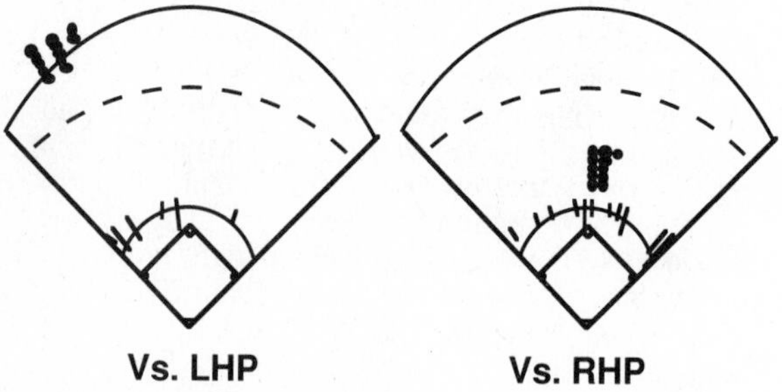

1990 Situational Stats

	AB	H	HR	RBI	AVG		AB	H	HR	RBI	AVG
Home	26	4	1	8	.154	LHP	16	4	1	3	.250
Road	27	6	0	1	.222	RHP	37	6	0	6	.162
Day	29	7	0	6	.241	Sc Pos	13	4	1	9	.308
Night	24	3	1	3	.125	Clutch	9	1	0	1	.111

1990 Rankings (National League)

- Did not rank near the top or bottom in any category

HITTING:

Tabbed as one of the best young catchers in the National League after his fine performances in 1988 and '89, Damon Berryhill missed most of last season while recovering from rotator-cuff surgery. It's a scary injury for a player dependent on his throwing, and Berryhill must now demonstrate that he can recover.

Berryhill is a switch-hitter, but during the past two years he's been far more effective from the right side. Before he was injured in 1989, he was hitting .340 batting righty, only .224 batting lefty. He likes to sit on the fastball, but from the left side he's more prone to chase bad pitches. Batting righty he likes the ball up and has a little power. Batting lefty, he prefers low pitches and is much more of slap hitter.

The basic problem Berryhill faces with the Cubs is that Joe Girardi, his rival for the catching job, matches his strengths and weaknesses. Neither is a very disciplined hitter, neither has much power, and each does most of his damage against left-handed pitching. Little wonder that the Cubs have contemplated trading Berryhill, and were considering dealing him even before he was hurt.

BASERUNNING:

Not exactly Craig Biggio, Berryhill has always been slow, and squatting behind the plate isn't going to make him any faster. He only has two major league stolen bases, and would probably crack out the champagne if he swiped two in one year. Obviously, he's a conservative runner who'll go one base at a time.

FIELDING:

Damon's excellent ability to call a game has not been damaged by his injury. He's pretty mobile behind the plate and does a fine job of blocking pitches. His strength, however, has always been his great throwing arm, which was one of the best in the business before the rotator cuff injury. Last year was too early to tell whether he can fully recover. It would be surprising if he hasn't lost at least a little arm strength.

OVERALL:

The Cubs' number-one catcher in their division winning year of 1989, Berryhill is now a big question mark. Only playing time will answer the question, but unfortunately for him, Girardi stands in his way. A trade might be the best thing for Berryhill, but what's the market value for a non-slugging catcher whose throwing strength is suspect?

MIKE BIELECKI

Position: SP/RP
Bats: R **Throws:** R
Ht: 6' 3" **Wt:** 195

Opening Day Age: 31
Born: 7/31/59 in Baltimore, MD
ML Seasons: 7

Overall Statistics

	W	L	ERA	G	GS	Sv	IP	H	R	BB	SO	HR
1990	8	11	4.93	36	29	1	168.0	188	101	70	103	13
Career	38	37	4.12	143	109	1	673.0	671	343	293	414	54

How Often He Throws Strikes

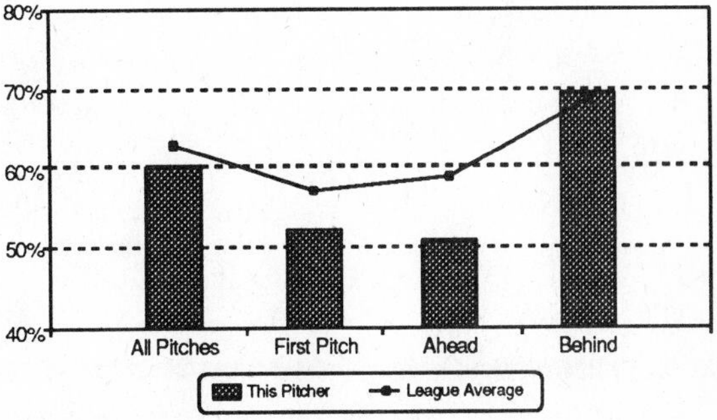

1990 Situational Stats

	W	L	ERA	Sv	IP		AB	H	HR	RBI	AVG
Home	2	7	4.88	0	75.2	LHB	403	111	8	51	.275
Road	6	4	4.97	1	92.1	RHB	251	77	5	36	.307
Day	2	5	5.04	1	69.2	Sc Pos	163	49	3	69	.301
Night	6	6	4.85	0	98.1	Clutch	42	8	2	5	.190

1990 Rankings (National League)

- 1st in worst ERA (4.93), higest on-base average allowed (.359) and most baserunners allowed per 9 innings (14.1)
- 3rd in wild pitches (11) and highest slugging percentage allowed (.428)
- 5th worst ERA on the road (4.97) and highest batting average allowed with runners in scoring position (.301)
- 6th lowest strikeout/walk ratio (1.5)
- Led the Cubs in wild pitches, pickoff throws (148), stolen bases allowed (17), runners caught stealing (9) and strikeouts per 9 innings (5.5)

PITCHING:

What a difference a year makes. Last season Mike Bielecki made the sad regression from an effective 18-game winner to an in-game batting practice pitcher. The Cubs gave him every chance last year, leaving him in the rotation for most of the year. But Bielecki went two months without a win at one point, and never came close to recovering his '89 form. He won only eight games, and his ERA rose from 3.14 to 4.93.

It was obvious to those who observed Bielecki in 1990 that he did not have the same control over his pitches that he possessed in 1989. He's the sort of pitcher who's very dependent on throwing strikes, and last year his borderline pitches missed the mark way too often. Bielecki not only gave up more walks, but got behind in too many counts. He had to come in with a lot of fat pitches, and the hitters took full advantage. The numbers tell the story: In 1989, Bielecki allowed 11.4 baserunners per nine innings; in 1990 he allowed 14.1. Additionally, hitters slugged .428 against Mike in 1990, while in 1989, they slugged only .362 when facing him.

Bielecki throws four pitches: a fastball that tops off at around 87 MPH, a curveball, a change-up, and a split-finger pitch. Of the four, however, Mike has no definite out pitch. He spent the season mixing his pitches and trying to find the successful formula he had in 1989. His quest was unsuccessful and he was lucky to end up with a 8-11 record.

Bielecki did pitch effectively in spots last year; for example, his performance against the World Champion Reds was excellent. But with righthanders hitting .307 against him and lefties getting on base 35% of the time, opposition hitters spent 1990 waving "bye bye" to Bielecki instead of the other way around.

HOLDING RUNNERS, FIELDING, HITTING:

Bielecki's pickoff move is good. Only 17 of 26 runners gambled correctly against him in 1990. Unfortunately, he had more of a chance to practice it last year than he would have liked. As a fielder, Bielecki is major league average. He is pretty nimble around the mound and can pounce on bunts quite well.

OVERALL:

Now 31, Bielecki has had two careers. In 1989, he was splendid, with the 18-7 record; for the other six years his record is 20 wins, 30 losses. Don Zimmer likes Bielecki's stuff, and given the Cubs' shortage of pitching, he'll probably give Bielecki every chance to recover his '89 form. But Bielecki will need much sharper control than he had in 1990.

HITTING:

After years of bouncing between the Cleveland Indians and their various AAA farm clubs, minor league slugger Dave Clark was traded to the Cubs last year for Mitch Webster. Clark was tabbed mostly for bench duty and pinch hitting, but when Dwight Smith slumped in the early going, he received some playing time in left field. Clark's bat cooled off after a hot start, and he eventually returned to his part-time role. But he managed to hit five homers, and his .275 average was his best since he'd batted one point higher in his 58 at-bat debut in 1986.

Long a promising prospect, Clark had a 30-homer, .340 season at AAA Buffalo in 1987. He hit well at Wrigley last year, and playing there every day, he'd have the potential to be a 25-homer man. Clark has never shown much ability to hit lefties, but he's never really been given a chance to play against them: he's had only 34 at-bats against southpaws in five seasons, with seven hits.

Clark will draw an occasional walk, but he chases a lot of bad pitches and struck out in nearly one-fourth of his at-bats last year. He's a good low-ball hitter, and pitchers generally throw him high fastballs along with breaking pitches. When given regular duty he tends to become too anxious, swinging for the longball in an effort to prove himself as a slugger.

BASERUNNING:

Though he doesn't have a lot of speed, Clark is a pretty good baserunner. Before he put on weight he stole as many as 27 bases in a season in the minors. Running intelligently, he was seven-for-eight last year; he'll have trouble doing better than that. He's aggressive in taking the extra base and in breaking up double plays.

FIELDING:

As a left fielder, Clark is a cut below-average. He doesn't have a lot of range or great instincts. He's fairly sure-handed, however, and has committed only three errors in the majors (none last year). Clark does possess a strong throwing arm, but didn't get much of a chance to display it last year.

OVERALL:

At 28, Clark still yearns to be a regular and show that his big minor league numbers were no fluke. He has a small chance with the Cubs, who would like more guys in the lineup who can hit the ball out of Wrigley, but chances are that he'll be working off the bench again. He seems like one of those players who gets sold to the Japanese League and hits 35 homers.

DAVE CLARK

Position: LF
Bats: L **Throws:** R
Ht: 6' 2" **Wt:** 200

Opening Day Age: 28
Born: 9/3/62 in Tupelo, MS
ML Seasons: 5

Overall Statistics

	G	AB	R	H	D	T	HR	RBI	SB	BB	SO	AVG
1990	84	171	22	47	4	2	5	20	7	8	40	.275
Career	296	725	75	182	26	3	22	88	9	64	166	.251

Where He Hits the Ball

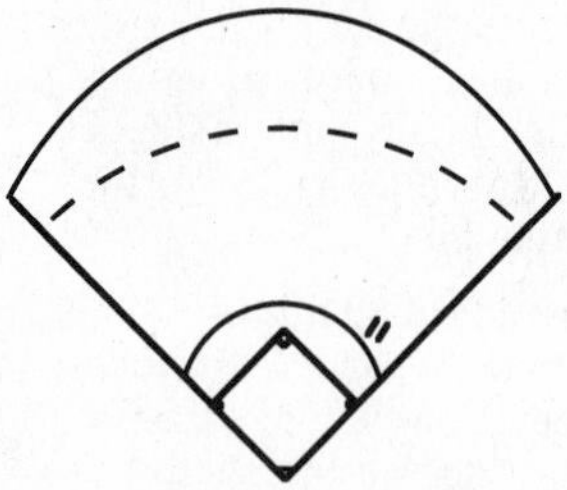

Vs. LHP

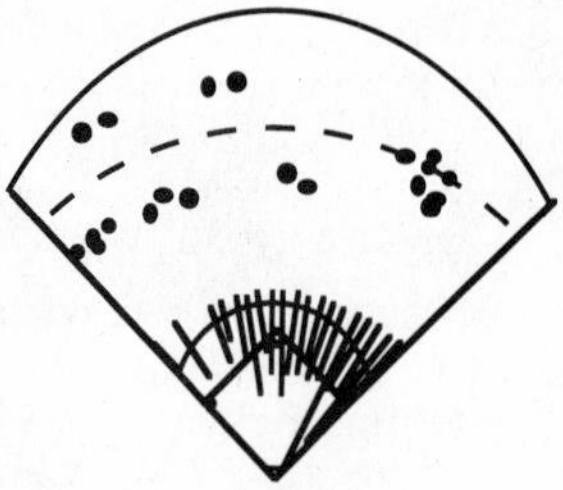

Vs. RHP

1990 Situational Stats

	AB	H	HR	RBI	AVG		AB	H	HR	RBI	AVG
Home	100	29	3	14	.290	LHP	5	1	0	0	.200
Road	71	18	2	6	.254	RHP	166	46	5	20	.277
Day	94	28	3	14	.298	Sc Pos	49	12	0	13	.245
Night	77	19	2	6	.247	Clutch	35	10	0	5	.286

1990 Rankings (National League)

➟ Did not rank near the top or bottom in any category

DOUG DASCENZO

Position: CF/LF/RF
Bats: B **Throws:** L
Ht: 5' 8" **Wt:** 160

Opening Day Age: 26
Born: 6/30/64 in Cleveland, OH
ML Seasons: 3

Overall Statistics

	G	AB	R	H	D	T	HR	RBI	SB	BB	SO	AVG
1990	113	241	27	61	9	5	1	26	15	21	18	.253
Career	186	455	56	100	13	5	2	42	27	43	35	.220

Where He Hits the Ball

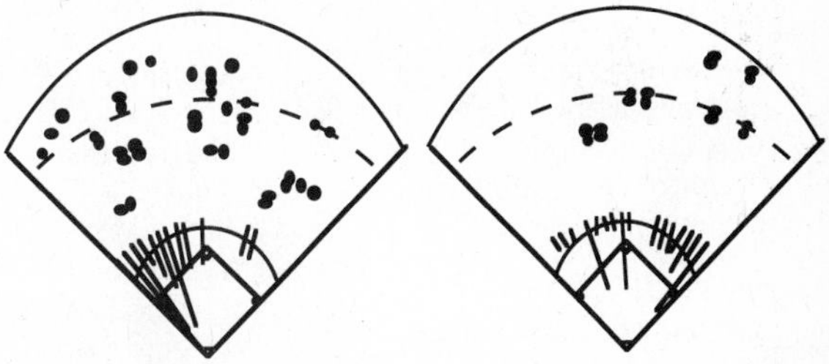

Vs. LHP Vs. RHP

1990 Situational Stats

	AB	H	HR	RBI	AVG		AB	H	HR	RBI	AVG
Home	119	33	1	13	.277	LHP	136	38	1	19	.279
Road	122	28	0	13	.230	RHP	105	23	0	7	.219
Day	127	32	1	15	.252	Sc Pos	47	15	0	22	.319
Night	114	29	0	11	.254	Clutch	30	8	0	8	.267

1990 Rankings (National League)

- 1st in lowest batting average with a 3-1 count (.000)

HITTING:

Doug Dascenzo is a scrapper, the kind of hustling player that fans love to watch. Dascenzo doesn't have the most natural hitting talent in the world, but he makes the best out of his modest skills. Given more playing time last year, Dascenzo batted .253, his best performance in three major league seasons.

Dascenzo has a few pluses as a hitter. He makes excellent contact, striking out only 18 times in 241 at-bats last year. He's an excellent bunter, one who can get on base that way or help his club with a sacrifice. He has excellent speed, so he can beat out some leg hits and stretch doubles into triples. A switch-hitter, he's become a pretty tough out from the right side. And he's performed very well in the clutch.

Unfortunately, Dascenzo had just as many negatives. At 5-9 and 160 pounds, he's not capable of hitting the ball very far. Only 20 percent of his hits have gone for extra bases, and he's produced only two major league homers. He's a very weak hitter batting lefty. He looks like he'll never be able to hit for a high average. And, lacking patience, he hasn't learned to use his small stature to draw walks.

Dascenzo looks like the kind of guy a pitcher could overpower, but he's actually a very good fastball hitter. In one memorable game last year, he ripped fireballer Rob Dibble for a single and a triple in consecutive at-bats. His ability to handle fastballs has helped Dascenzo in clutch situations, where pitchers usually fire heat, but breaking stuff and offspeed pitches give him a lot of trouble.

BASERUNNING:

Dascenzo has fine speed, and he's a good base stealer who was 15-for-21 last year. He sometimes gets caught napping, however, and was picked off twice. Possibly the most aggressive runner on a very aggressive team, he sometimes lacks judgement and will occasionally run his team out of an inning.

FIELDING:

Dascenzo has won plaudits for his fielding, and he's often brought in for defense in the late innings. He has good range, is unafraid to crash into walls, and he never stops hustling. Dascenzo doesn't have much of an arm, though, and runners can take advantage of him.

OVERALL:

Dascenzo uses his constant hustle to make the most of his ability. His enthusiasm is a positive influence on a team. He could probably only be a regular on a pretty bad club, but he has value as a substitute, pinch hitter and defensive replacement.

ANDRE DAWSON

Position: RF
Bats: R **Throws:** R
Ht: 6' 3" **Wt:** 195

Opening Day Age: 36
Born: 7/10/54 in Miami, FL
ML Seasons: 15

Overall Statistics

	G	AB	R	H	D	T	HR	RBI	SB	BB	SO	AVG
1990	147	529	72	164	28	5	27	100	16	42	65	.310
Career	2018	7785	1130	2201	396	88	346	1231	300	500	1199	.283

Where He Hits the Ball

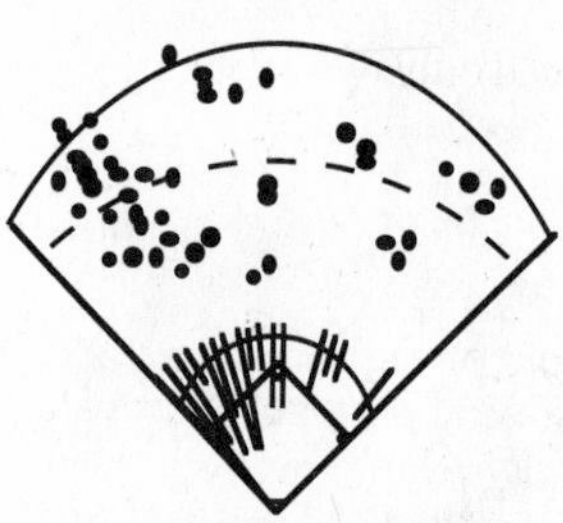

Vs. LHP

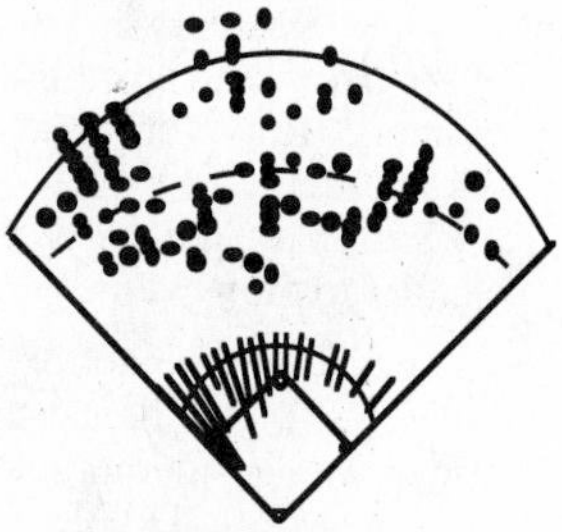

Vs. RHP

1990 Situational Stats

	AB	H	HR	RBI	AVG		AB	H	HR	RBI	AVG
Home	266	84	14	51	.316	LHP	181	54	8	25	.298
Road	263	80	13	49	.304	RHP	348	110	19	75	.316
Day	270	88	15	56	.326	Sc Pos	145	43	4	69	.297
Night	259	76	12	44	.293	Clutch	87	27	4	13	.310

1990 Rankings (National League)

- 1st in intentional walks (21)
- 5th in batting average (.310) and slugging percentage vs. right-handed pitchers (.549)
- 6th in RBIs (100) and slugging percentage (.535)
- 7th in least pitches seen per plate appearance (3.25) and batting average vs. right-handed pitchers (.316)
- Led the Cubs in batting average, RBIs, intentional walks, batting average with the bases loaded (.385) and batting average with 2 strikes (.250)
- Led NL right fielders in batting average, slugging percentage (.535), batting average in the clutch (.310) and intentional walks

HITTING:

A year ago this spring, a lot of people were saying Andre Dawson was washed up. His knees, as always, were a problem, and Dawson was coming off a season in which he'd batted .252, his second lowest average in 14 full seasons, and in which he played only 118 games, his fewest (except for the 1981 strike year) since his 35-game debut in 1976. Was Dawson finished? He answered his critics by belting 27 homers, driving in 100 runs and hitting a career-high .310.

Pitchers still threw Dawson high fastballs, and he proved he can still get around on them. He's deadly on pitches from the middle half of the plate inward. He's smart enough to foul off pitches he can't pull and whack away at those he can. The Braves managed to make Dawson look bad by giving him a combination of hard curves outside and harder fastballs at eye-level, but in reality, there's no way to consistently retire him.

Though he's apt to swing at just about anything, Dawson usually makes contact. He struck out only 65 times last year and has fanned more than 100 times only three times in his career. The underside is that he's too impatient to draw a walk. Dawson did walk 42 times last year, the second-highest total of his career, but half of them were intentional. The Reds' Lou Piniella ordered five intentional walks to Dawson in one game, which tells you a lot about Dawson's reputation, and a lot about the hitters who bat behind him.

BASERUNNING:

A very smart baserunner, Dawson was 16-for-18 stealing last year, the best success rate of his career. He joined Willie Mays and Bobby Bonds as the only players with both 300 homers and 300 steals. He's not as fast as he once was, but he remains an excellent baserunner who is rarely thrown out.

FIELDING:

No longer a Gold Glove right fielder, Dawson has lost range due to age and knee problems. His range is still good, however, and he plays hitters extremely well. His arm is still one of the best at his position.

OVERALL:

Dawson is now 36. He still has those bad knees, and it's unrealistic to expect him to have another year like he did in 1990. But he remains an outstanding offensive and defensive player and an ideal role model for the younger Cubs. This spring, people won't be writing his epitaph.

SHAWON DUNSTON

Position: SS
Bats: R **Throws:** R
Ht: 6' 1" **Wt:** 175

Opening Day Age: 28
Born: 3/21/63 in Brooklyn, NY
ML Seasons: 6

HITTING:

It's amazing that Shawon Dunston wasn't born in San Pedro de Marcoris because he embodies almost all the traits of a fine Dominican shortstop: he swings at everything and he catches everything. As a hitter, Dunston has shown that he can hit for power and a respectable average, though with no patience whatsoever. Dunston has also demonstrated that he can carry or bury a team with his bat. When he is hot, he can hit any pitch anywhere. When he is cold, he'll swing at a pickoff throw to first.

Dunston remains the quintessential first-pitch fastball hitter. Pitchers don't really have to throw him strikes, so they work the corners, often opening with a breaking pitch. If Dunston doesn't put one of the first two pitches in play, he's in big trouble, but he usually makes hard contact enough to be a very dangerous hitter. Last year, he was the hardest hitting shortstop in the National League. His 17 homers and 8 triples led all NL shortstops. A line drive hitter, he's never been able to take full advantage of Wrigley because he doesn't hit enough wind-blown fly balls. Only seven of his 17 homers came at home last year.

Dunston not only doesn't draw many walks (15 last year); he hardly ever even gets to three balls. His career on-base percentage is a meager .287. But he doesn't strike out all that much, either. He's up there to hit, and he usually makes contact.

BASERUNNING:

Very aggressive, Dunston is one of the best baserunners in the business. He will take the extra base whenever possible and is almost never gunned down. He has also become a good base stealer, with 25 thefts in 30 attempts in 1990.

FIELDING:

Maybe the hardest-throwing shortstop ever, Dunston has been clocked at 91 MPH on his throws to first. (Cub pitchers should throw that hard). He sometimes relies on the arm too much, laying back on grounders and then just nipping the runner. He needs to charge the ball a little more, especially on the slow grass at Wrigley. But his range is outstanding, and he's a wizard on liners and pop flies. Once error-prone, he made 20 last year, which is good but not great.

OVERALL:

At 28, Dunston is in his prime, and rates just below Barry Larkin among National League shortstops. Despite his noted impatience and his tendency to go into long slumps, he's a dangerous hitter and one of the best defensive shortstops around. A 20-homer season is in reach.

Overall Statistics

	G	AB	R	H	D	T	HR	RBI	SB	BB	SO	AVG
1990	146	545	73	143	22	8	17	66	25	15	87	.262
Career	758	2768	340	712	132	30	61	290	110	111	505	.257

Where He Hits the Ball

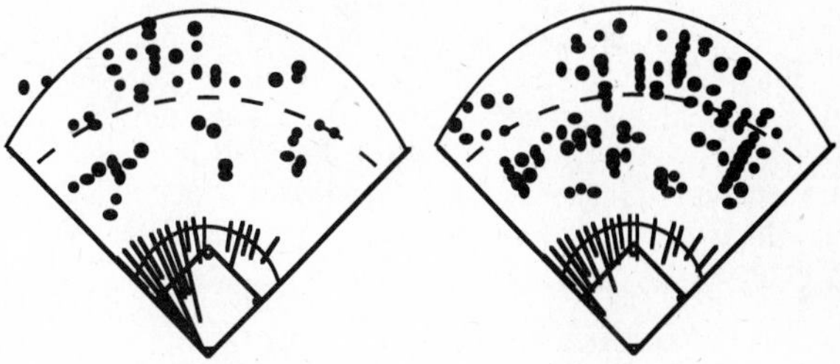

Vs. LHP Vs. RHP

1990 Situational Stats

	AB	H	HR	RBI	AVG		AB	H	HR	RBI	AVG
Home	268	67	7	25	.250	LHP	188	54	9	23	.287
Road	277	76	10	41	.274	RHP	357	89	8	43	.249
Day	284	77	11	34	.271	Sc Pos	122	28	5	48	.230
Night	261	66	6	32	.253	Clutch	92	25	3	14	.272

1990 Rankings (National League)

- 2nd lowest batting average on a 3-2 count (.048)
- 3rd in least pitches seen per plate appearance (3.19), worst on-base average vs. right-handed pitchers (.277) and lowest percentage of pitches taken (41.4%)
- 4th lowest on-base percentage (.283)
- Led the Cubs in triples (8), stolen bases (25), strikeouts (87), stolen base percentage (83.3%) and steals of third (6)
- Led NL shortstops in home runs (17), triples, slugging percentage (.426), most runs scored per time reached base (45.3%) and highest percentage of extra bases taken as a runner (53.5%)

HITTING:

Late in 1989, Joe Girardi took full advantage of Damon Berryhill's rotator-cuff injury to finish the year as the number-one catcher for the division-winning Cubs. With Berryhill sidelined almost the whole season in 1990, Girardi had the job to himself last year and acquitted himself very well, batting a solid .270.

A righty swinger, Girardi is not much of a power hitter, with only one homer last year. But he belted 24 doubles, a fine total. Primarily a fastball hitter, he's been very tough against lefties thus far in his career, but is a much easier out against righty breakingballers. Against lefties, he has excellent bat control and is very hard to strike out; versus righties, he is a little more prone to fanning, but he can still put wood on the ball with consistency. In either situation, Girardi will almost never walk, and because of this has a poor on-base percentage.

Very steady, Girardi was consistent in almost every batting breakdown except for left/right last year. Be it day, night, home or road, Girardi hit a consistent .270. The only other time he really geared up was in clutch situations. Managers should note the consistency with which Girardi breaks up games with a sharp single at exactly the right time.

BASERUNNING:

No leadfoot, Girardi stole eight bases and was caught stealing three times last year, an outstanding success rate for a catcher. He may be the second- best running catcher in the NL, behind only Craig Biggio of Houston. Girardi is an aggressive baserunner with good judgement and a cross-blocking style when going into second.

FIELDING:

There is no question that Girardi controls the running game as well as anyone playing today. He allowed 80 steals and gunned down 47 runners last year, a ratio that is murderous to the opposition. Girardi is also very intelligent, and pitchers like working with him. But he is certainly not sure-handed. He committed 11 errors and 16 passed balls, an extremely high miscue rate.

OVERALL:

Girardi may face a battle for his job this year with Berryhill, who finally appears to be healthy again. They have many of the same strengths and weaknesses (good throwing, low power, good average vs. lefties). Berryhill is more sure-handed, but otherwise Girardi is just as good if not better. He looks capable of winning the number-one job again.

JOE GIRARDI

Position: C
Bats: R **Throws:** R
Ht: 5'11" **Wt:** 195

Opening Day Age: 26
Born: 10/14/64 in Peoria, IL
ML Seasons: 2

Overall Statistics

	G	AB	R	H	D	T	HR	RBI	SB	BB	SO	AVG
1990	133	419	36	113	24	2	1	38	8	17	50	.270
Career	192	576	51	152	34	2	2	52	10	28	76	.264

Where He Hits the Ball

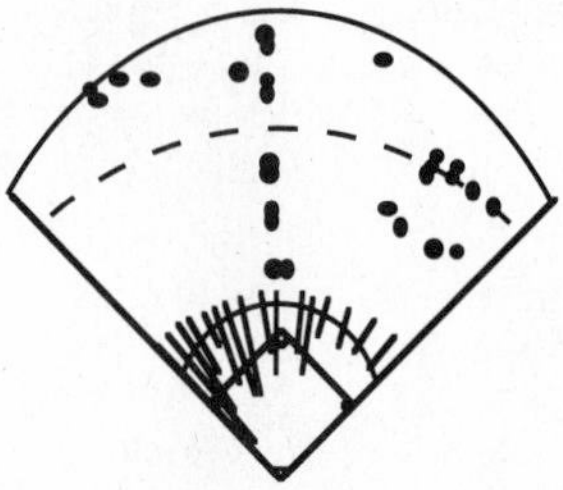

Vs. LHP

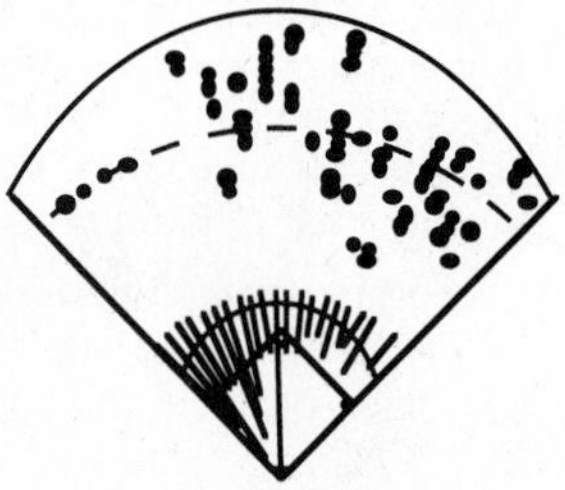

Vs. RHP

1990 Situational Stats

	AB	H	HR	RBI	AVG		AB	H	HR	RBI	AVG
Home	202	55	1	25	.272	LHP	141	46	1	16	.326
Road	217	58	0	13	.267	RHP	278	67	0	22	.241
Day	208	55	1	24	.264	Sc Pos	105	29	1	34	.276
Night	211	58	0	14	.275	Clutch	70	24	0	6	.343

1990 Rankings (National League)

- → 2nd highest runners caught stealing percentage among catchers (37.0%)
- → 8th highest batting average vs. left-handed pitchers (.326)
- → 9th most GDPs per GDP situation (17.1%)
- → Led the Cubs in GDPs (13), batting average in the clutch (.343) and batting average vs. left-handed pitchers
- → Led NL catchers in hit by pitch (3), GDPs and batting average vs. left-handed pitchers

HITTING:

Though he ended up in the right place, Mark Grace spent his 1990 season mixing slumps that pushed the edge of the Mendoza Line with streaks that made him look like a young Stan Musial. The net result is that Grace is about where he was in 1989 as a hitter: hitting for a good average, but continuing to adjust his strike zone.

When Grace was slumping, the usually crisp liners to all fields were replaced by fly outs and easy grounders. His normally excellent strike-zone judgement was poor and his ability to reach base was undermined during these times. Normally, Grace will hit any ball where it's pitched. Give him an outside pitch and it may go down the line; a pitch down the middle will end up creamed into one of the gaps. With an inside pitch Grace is sometimes able to hit one out. Grace got anxious at times in 1990, and let the pitcher control too many at-bats.

With experience, Grace has learned to hang in better against lefthanders' breaking balls, and as a result his average against southpaws improved by 44 points last year. His home run total declined back into single figures, however, which is not what you expect from a strong young first-sacker who plays in Wrigley Field. Grace is sometimes compared to Musial, but Musial never had a single-digit home run season.

BASERUNNING:

With maturity, Grace has improved his stolen base percentage each year. He is better at picking his spots and has learned the moves of the league's hurlers. He's a situational baserunner who takes the extra base when needed and exercises sound judgement.

FIELDING:

Very smooth, Grace makes playing first base look effortless. He has good range, evidenced by his enormous assist total. His arm is decent if the 3-6-3 needs turning, and his ability to snare line drives continues to frustrate the opposition. Grace's ability to scoop bad throws prevents Shawon Dunston and his scattershot cannon from challenging for the league lead in errors.

OVERALL:

Grace's up-and-down 1990 campaign was part of his maturing process, and he'll probably be a better hitter this year because of it. But exactly what kind of hitter he'll be is an interesting question. In similar circumstances the young Don Mattingly, who also came up as a high-average, non-home run hitting first-sacker, learned to use his ball park and hit the ball into the seats. Will Grace do the same, or maintain the status quo?

MARK GRACE

Position: 1B
Bats: L **Throws:** L
Ht: 6' 2" **Wt:** 190

Opening Day Age: 26
Born: 6/28/64 in Winston-Salem, NC
ML Seasons: 3

Overall Statistics

	G	AB	R	H	D	T	HR	RBI	SB	BB	SO	AVG
1990	157	589	72	182	32	1	9	82	15	59	54	.309
Career	433	1585	211	486	83	8	29	218	32	199	139	.307

Where He Hits the Ball

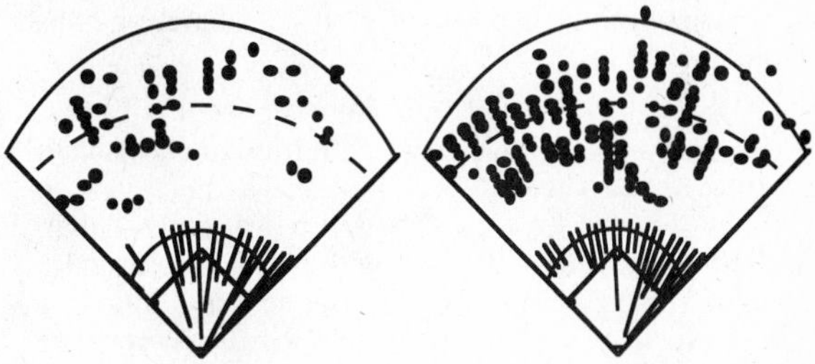

Vs. LHP Vs. RHP

1990 Situational Stats

	AB	H	HR	RBI	AVG		AB	H	HR	RBI	AVG
Home	308	102	4	46	.331	LHP	185	57	3	33	.308
Road	281	80	5	36	.285	RHP	404	125	6	49	.309
Day	314	101	7	48	.322	Sc Pos	170	56	0	72	.329
Night	275	81	2	34	.295	Clutch	98	31	1	13	.316

1990 Rankings (National League)

- 4th in singles (140)
- 5th in most times on base (246)
- 6th in batting average at home (.331)
- Led the Cubs in singles, doubles (32), walks (59), hit by pitch (5), times on base, games (157), on-base average (.372), groundball/flyball ratio (1.59), batting average with runners in scoring position (.329), lowest percentage of swings that missed (11.9%) and highest percentage of swings put into play (52.4%)
- Led NL first basemen in singles, doubles, caught stealing (6), games, groundball/flyball ratio and steals of third (2)

PITCHING:

Brilliant but brittle, Mike Harkey was again plagued by injuries in 1990. Harkey was battling hard for Rookie of the Year and was in the middle of a 7-3 stretch with a 2.38 ERA when arm woes finished him for the season. Harkey's visits to the DL in 1989 and 1990 have outside observers wondering if he will be able to have a long, successful major league career. Some feel he will end up like Jose Rijo: pitching well while missing big parts of each season.

Harkey has all the tools the great power pitchers have. He has a 90 MPH fastball that overpowers hitters and has good movement. To the heat he adds a hard breaking curveball, a slider, and a change-up that shows some promise. Though his strikeout total wasn't too high for the season, Harkey's stuff is such that it could place him comfortably among the leaders in K's over a full season. Additionally, his control was very good and he allowed only 3.1 bases on balls per nine innings.

Harkey is excellent at squelching opposition hitters. He held both righthanders and lefties in check with averages well under .240, and he was not prone to giving up the longball. Though not a sinker-baller, Harkey thrived at Wrigley with a 5-2 record and a sparkling 2.43 ERA. On the road, he was a little less consistent, going 7-4 with a 4.08 ERA. But if you take away an appearance in St. Louis where Harkey was knocked out after getting just one out while giving up 8 earned runs, his ERA on the road sinks to a very respectable 3.27.

HOLDING RUNNERS, FIELDING, HITTING:

Even though Harkey is a good athlete, he is not yet a good fielding pitcher. His range is below-average, and despite his ability to field bunts well, he doesn't lay his hands on enough come-backers or balls hit into his general area. His ability to cut off the running game is excellent, however. He also looks like a terrific young hitter with a .250 average, four doubles and eight sacrifice hits.

OVERALL:

Harkey has been compared to the great Bob Gibson both in appearance and makeup, as well as in the tools he brings to the mound. This is a comparison Harkey probably doesn't deserve yet, but it shows how much talent he has. If he stays healthy, he can be one of the best in the league, but that's a big if.

MIKE HARKEY

Position: SP
Bats: R **Throws:** R
Ht: 6' 5" **Wt:** 220

Opening Day Age: 24
Born: 10/25/66 in San Diego, CA
ML Seasons: 2

Overall Statistics

	W	L	ERA	G	GS	Sv	IP	H	R	BB	SO	HR
1990	12	6	3.26	27	27	0	173.2	153	71	59	94	14
Career	12	9	3.15	32	32	0	208.1	186	85	74	112	14

How Often He Throws Strikes

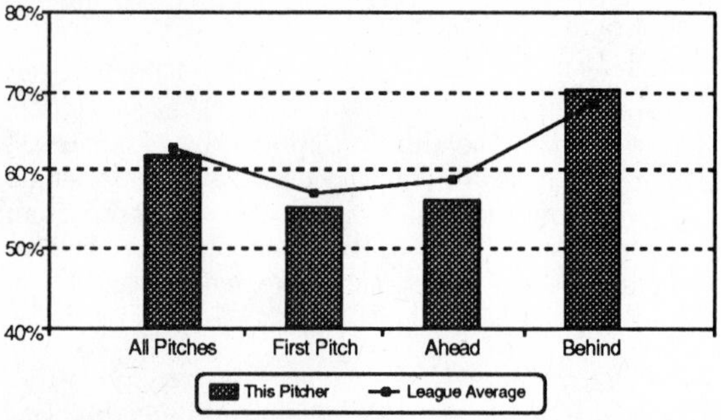

1990 Situational Stats

	W	L	ERA	Sv	IP		AB	H	HR	RBI	AVG
Home	5	2	2.43	0	85.1	LHB	411	98	7	35	.238
Road	7	4	4.08	0	88.1	RHB	242	55	7	26	.227
Day	9	3	2.80	0	122.0	Sc Pos	140	33	1	45	.236
Night	3	3	4.35	0	51.2	Clutch	61	15	1	4	.246

1990 Rankings (National League)

- 4th in hit batsmen (7)
- 6th in ERA at home (2.43)
- 7th in winning percentage (.667) and lowest stolen base percentage allowed (57.1%)
- Led the Cubs in ERA (3.27), hit batsmen, winning percentage, lowest batting average allowed (.234), lowest on-base average allowed (.303) and lowest stolen base percentage allowed, least baserunners allowed per 9 innings (11.3), most run support per 9 innings (4.6) and lowest batting average allowed with runners in scoring position (.236)

LES LANCASTER

Position: RP/SP
Bats: R **Throws:** R
Ht: 6' 2" **Wt:** 200

Opening Day Age: 28
Born: 4/21/62 in Dallas, TX
ML Seasons: 4

PITCHING:

Les Lancaster came undone before the sad eyes of Cub fans in 1990. The good news is that Lancaster is a good candidate to bounce back in 1991. Switched between starting and relieving, he had problems finding his rhythm last year. But late in the season he settled for good in the bullpen and looked like the Lancaster who posted a 1.36 ERA in 1989.

Lancaster started strongly in the bullpen last year, with an April ERA of 2.13, though his ratio of hits and walks indicated problems. At that point Don Zimmer inserted Lancaster into his starting rotation, and he continued to pitch well, reeling off three excellent starts. On May 24, LA clobbered him, scoring eight runs in 2.1 innings, and that began his undoing. Soon after, Lancaster was pulled from the rotation and, strangely enough, given the closer's role. After a nine earned run bludgeoning at the hands of the Mets on June 13, Les' stock plummeted. With his ERA threatening the sound barrier, Lancaster was demoted to the minors in August.

The move did Lancaster some good as he returned to the big club and posted a 2.05 ERA in September giving up only four walks and 12 hits in 22 innings. Lancaster's problem early in the season was control. In 1989, he allowed only 15 walks and struck out 56 in 73 innings. In 1990, he gave up 40 free passes and struck out 65 in 109 innings. Lancaster spent the early part of the season trying to nibble the corners with his fastball and slider against lefties (lefties had a .362 opposition OBP), the middle part grooving the change-up and fastball to the first hitter he faced (.304 BA with .543 slugging by first batters), and finished the season by mixing his pitches in an unhittable pattern like he did in 1989.

HOLDING RUNNERS, FIELDING, HITTING:

Lancaster is a good fielder with a quick delivery to the plate; he usually leaves himself in good fielding position. He throws to the right base and plays a conservative game, going for the sure out whenever possible. He also has a quick move and keeps the runners extremely close. He was one-for-20 as a hitter, and is not a threat.

OVERALL:

Lancaster is likely to be much better than he was in 1990. Late in the season, he re-established his dominating control and was painting the black with his fastball and slider as in 1989. If he can keep using the change effectively with his above-average fastball, he will keep the hitters off-balance and have a fine season.

Overall Statistics

	W	L	ERA	G	GS	Sv	IP	H	R	BB	SO	HR
1990	9	5	4.62	55	6	6	109.0	121	57	40	65	11
Career	25	16	3.94	168	27	19	399.2	408	187	140	235	31

How Often He Throws Strikes

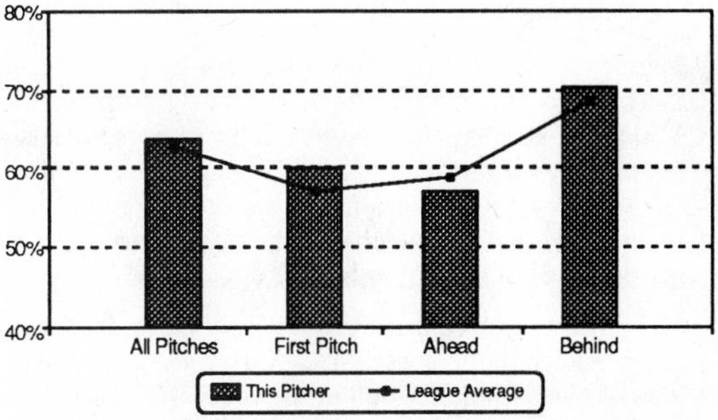

1990 Situational Stats

	W	L	ERA	Sv	IP		AB	H	HR	RBI	AVG
Home	4	3	5.37	3	57.0	LHB	227	64	3	23	.282
Road	5	2	3.81	3	52.0	RHB	200	57	8	39	.285
Day	6	5	5.98	3	55.2	Sc Pos	122	34	4	53	.279
Night	3	0	3.21	3	53.1	Clutch	136	41	3	24	.301

1990 Rankings (National League)

- 11th in blown saves (5)

BILL LONG

Position: RP
Bats: R **Throws:** R
Ht: 6' 0" **Wt:** 185

Opening Day Age: 31
Born: 2/29/60 in Cincinnati, OH
ML Seasons: 5

PITCHING:

Several late season trouncings made a good season look like a bad one for Bill Long. Long rolled into September with a 6-0 record and a 3.27 ERA. After giving up eight runs in his last five appearances (14.40 ERA), Long was saddled with an overall ERA of 4.55.

Long is quite a bit like Jeff Pico in that he is a nibbler with middling stuff. In Long's case, he has a below-average fastball and a big-breaking curveball that either hits the right spot or is yanked out of the ball yard. Long is the distance the ball travels if a hitter gets good wood on one of Bill's pitches. He allowed 10 homers in 61.1 innings.

Long works up in the strike zone, and Wrigley Field absolutely kills him. In 1990 he had a 2.59 ERA on the road and a 6.17 ERA at Wrigley. He also has major problems with lefties who ripped him for a .328 average with a .533 slugging percentage. Long stays in the majors by allowing most of his extra-base hits with the bases empty and by holding down righthanders. You could also say that he stays in the majors because he wants to: Long is extremely tenacious, and after spending six full seasons in the minors before getting his first real big league chance, he does everything in his power to avoid going back.

Long was not good at getting the first batter he faced upon entering the game. Despite this, he stranded almost every runner he inherited (only 16% of inherited runners scored, best on the Cubs). He is a gamer, and by working through lineups carefully, he keeps his team in the game until the big boys can come in to finish the game. He is probably unsuited for any job other than long relief.

HOLDING RUNNERS, FIELDING, HITTING:

Long has a good move to first, and the good-throwing Cub catchers help him control the running game. He is also a fine fielder, not incredibly sure-handed but with a great ability to get to the ball. He never hit in the major leagues before last year, and it showed.

OVERALL:

Long has little natural ability, yet he keeps his team in the game by playing the role of the crafty veteran. He should be able to hold his job this year because of his thorough professionalism, but he'll continue to be the ninth or tenth pitcher on the staff.

Overall Statistics

	W	L	ERA	G	GS	Sv	IP	H	R	BB	SO	HR
1990	6	2	4.55	46	0	5	61.1	72	34	23	34	10
Career	27	27	4.35	156	52	9	517.0	564	274	136	247	63

How Often He Throws Strikes

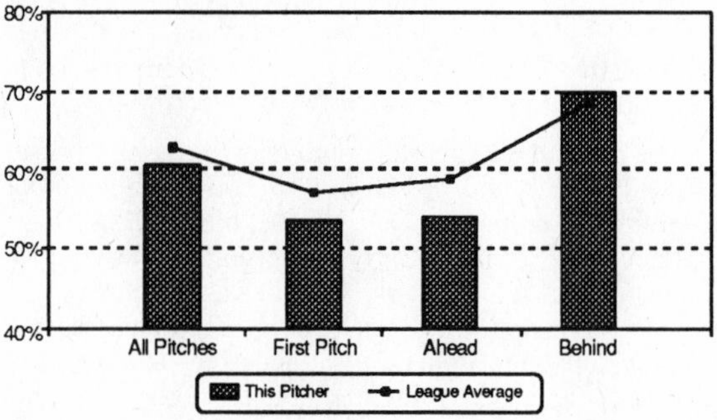

1990 Situational Stats

	W	L	ERA	Sv	IP		AB	H	HR	RBI	AVG
Home	4	2	6.41	1	26.2	LHB	122	40	5	14	.328
Road	2	0	3.12	4	34.2	RHB	120	32	5	21	.267
Day	4	1	6.83	2	29.0	Sc Pos	64	11	2	18	.172
Night	2	1	2.51	3	32.1	Clutch	94	25	2	5	.266

1990 Rankings (National League)

- 3rd highest batting average allowed vs. left-handed batters (.354)

PITCHING:

With Greg Maddux, what you see is not always what you get. Starting with his breakthrough season in 1988, Maddux has neatly sliced each season into two halves. Each year, in one portion he looks like Christy Mathewson, and in the other the opposition hits like a collective Will Clark. The end result is a fine season, but observers are left expecting more. Maddux was only 15-15 in 1990, a decline from 1989's 19-12 mark, but he was also pitching for a much worse ball club.

Maddux has three pitches with good movement: a good fastball that he can put a sink on, a change-up, and a good slider. He also has a curve, but it's pretty hittable and Maddux would be better off if he junked it. Maddux uses the "circle" grip on his change. It's an effective pitch because it drops; at the release point it looks like hard stuff to the batter.

Maddux has all the tools to be an effective pitcher and he is one, but his attitude might be working against him. From the pressbox, it's common to hear Maddux swearing after releasing a hanging curve or to see him seething after a bad call. Don Zimmer has also ripped Maddux for not using his head in game situations. Also, Maddux is prone to getting beaten up early in the game. His ERA in the first inning is over 7.50, and good teams are able to knock him out of the box. Still, with 52 wins from 1988-1990, there isn't too much to find fault with.

HOLDING RUNNERS, FIELDING, HITTING:

As a fielder, Maddux has no peer in the National League and maybe none in baseball. A great all-around athlete, his range is tremendous and he makes all the plays. He's got a solid move to first for a righty and occasionally pulls a devastating pickoff play with a runner on second. As a batsman, Maddux is one of the best hitting pitchers in the National League.

OVERALL:

In 1990, an awful lot of things went wrong for the Cubs, and also for Maddux, who had a miserable first half (4-8, 4.57 at the All-Star break). The Cubs didn't turn around their season, but Maddux certainly turned around his. His next goal is to get his emotions under control and then put together two good halves. He should continue to be the ace of the Cubs staff for many years to come.

GREG MADDUX

Position: SP
Bats: R **Throws:** R
Ht: 6' 0" **Wt:** 170

Opening Day Age: 25
Born: 4/14/66 in San Angelo, TX
ML Seasons: 5

Overall Statistics

	W	L	ERA	G	GS	Sv	IP	H	R	BB	SO	HR
1990	15	15	3.46	35	35	0	237.0	242	116	71	144	11
Career	60	53	3.68	140	136	0	911.0	919	434	319	540	57

How Often He Throws Strikes

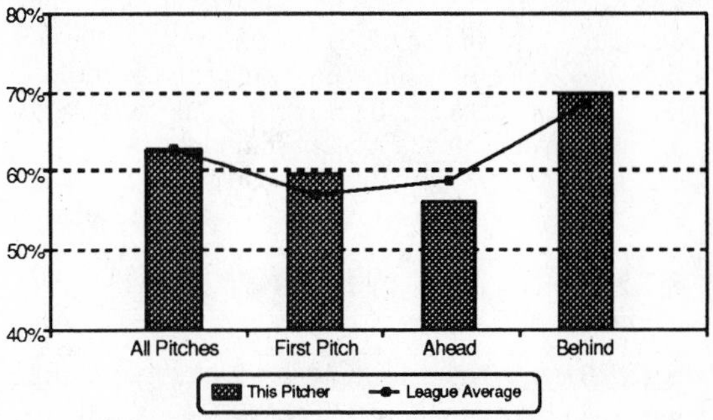

1990 Situational Stats

	W	L	ERA	Sv	IP		AB	H	HR	RBI	AVG
Home	8	6	3.58	0	115.2	LHB	564	164	6	70	.291
Road	7	9	3.34	0	121.1	RHB	349	78	5	28	.223
Day	7	5	4.04	0	100.1	Sc Pos	209	59	5	86	.282
Night	8	10	3.03	0	136.2	Clutch	98	28	1	10	.286

1990 Rankings (National League)

- 1st in games started (35), hits allowed (242) and runs allowed (116)
- 2nd in innings (237.0), batters faced (1,011), GDPs induced (27), groundball/flyball ratio (2.59), least HRs allowed per 9 innings (.42)
- Led the Cubs in wins (15), losses (15), games started, complete games (8), shutouts (2), innings, hits allowed, batters faced, walks allowed (71), strikeouts (144), pitches thrown (3,433), GDPs induced, strikeout/walk ratio (2.0), lowest slugging percentage allowed (.354), least HRs allowed per 9 innings and groundball/flyball ratio

LUIS SALAZAR

Position: 3B/LF
Bats: R **Throws:** R
Ht: 5' 9" **Wt:** 180

Opening Day Age: 34
Born: 5/19/56 in Barcelona, Venezuela
ML Seasons: 11

HITTING:

Nearly 35, Luis Salazar is no star, but he's a very useful ballplayer. Salazar is versatile, he has some pop in his bat, and he always hustles. But he probably shouldn't be a regular third baseman any more, and the fact that the Cubs gave him 410 at-bats last year indicates the weakness of the 1990 ball club.

Salazar did his best last year, as always, knocking a dozen homers while batting .254. He continued to be a good contact hitter, striking out only 59 times, but an impatient one as well, walking only 19. His on-base percentage was a very weak .293, and he hit only 13 doubles. His run production was also poor, with only 47 RBI batting primarily from the 5th slot in the lineup. All in all, his performance probably made the Cubs yearn for their glory years, when they still had Vance Law.

The successful way to pitch Salazar is with junk outside. All of his power is basically down the left field line. Give him some hard stuff inside and it'll leave the park or rattle off the ivy. It's Salazar's ability to hit the inside pitch that keeps him in the majors. He can occasionally "lean" his body and cue a shot up the middle or to right field (usually in a clutch situation where the RBI is needed), but the common result of a Salazar ball hit to the right side is an easy chance for the fielder.

BASERUNNING:

Salazar is still an aggressive baserunner, but he has lost almost all the speed that made him a good-percentage base thief. He will run occasionally, but he's smart enough not to try to steal very often. Salazar will take the extra base if the opportunity arises and has decent, if not great, judgement.

FIELDING:

Very versatile, Salazar has played all over the field in his career, and once kept the Tigers in a pennant race by filling in at short for Alan Trammell. Third base is still his best position. He has lost range there, but he plays hitters well and has a strong arm. At this stage of his career, he would have to be considered below-average for the position.

OVERALL:

Salazar's career is winding down, and at his age he would be best suited for a utility role. He still has a little power, and his versatility and hustle are always a plus. It would be unfortunate if the Cubs made him their regular third baseman again, but if given the job, Salazar will give it his absolute best.

Overall Statistics

	G	AB	R	H	D	T	HR	RBI	SB	BB	SO	AVG
1990	115	410	44	104	13	3	12	47	3	19	59	.254
Career	1101	3513	384	931	123	30	75	392	116	153	574	.265

Where He Hits the Ball

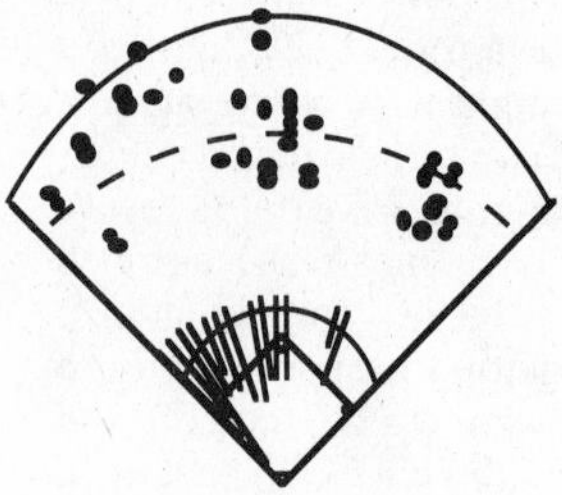

Vs. LHP

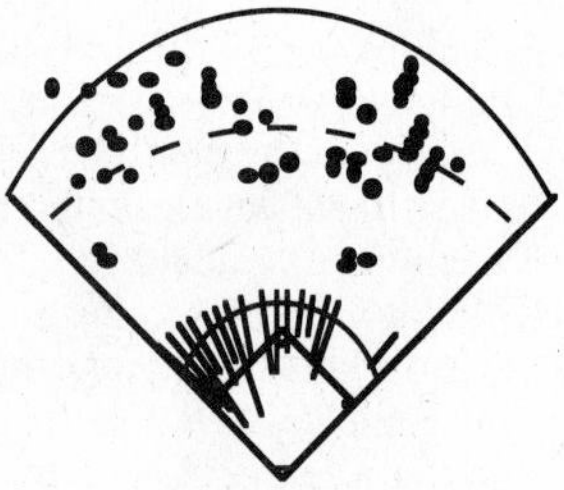

Vs. RHP

1990 Situational Stats

	AB	H	HR	RBI	AVG		AB	H	HR	RBI	AVG
Home	218	64	7	20	.294	LHP	157	46	6	22	.293
Road	192	40	5	27	.208	RHP	253	58	6	25	.229
Day	221	58	7	26	.262	Sc Pos	115	28	4	37	.243
Night	189	46	5	21	.243	Clutch	60	20	2	11	.333

1990 Rankings (National League)

- Led the Cubs in least GDPs per GDP situation (5.5%)
- Led NL third basemen in least GDP per GDP situation and batting average in the clutch (.333)

HITTING:

Like a fine wine, Ryne Sandberg improves with age. Sandberg was All-World in 1990 as he led the league in homers, becoming the first second baseman to top the NL since Rogers Hornsby in 1925. He also scored 116 runs, drove in 100, both career highs, and batted .306, his best average since his MVP year of 1984. It was another MVP-type performance, even though Sandberg didn't take home the trophy.

In waging war against NL pitchers, Sandberg changed his tune from 1989. In '89 he hammered lefthanders and was as big a threat on the road as he was at home. In 1990, Sandberg went berserk in Wrigley, slugging .679 and hitting over .350. He also crushed righthanders with a .616 slugging percentage. Sandberg's power remained very good on the road, with 15 homers; he had a personal-best 25 at home.

Against Sandberg, a pitch coming from the middle of the plate on in is suicide. He seldom homers to the opposite field, but anything that can be pulled is likely to end up in the seats. Sandberg doesn't jerk many homers down the line; most of them go to left-center.

Sandberg would seem like the classic number-three hitter, but he feels much more comfortable, and has been a lot more effective, batting second. The Cubs undoubtedly have considered switching Sandberg with number-three hitter Mark Grace, whose style (high on-base percentage, not many homers) would be well suited to the second slot. But Sandberg likes hitting second, and the Cubs are understandably reluctant to move him.

BASERUNNING:

Sandberg is a great baserunner who is very judicious in every aspect. If aggressiveness is called for, he will run with abandon; if conservatism is required, he'll show restraint. He never makes mistakes. His 25 stolen bases last year were a normal total for him.

DEFENSE:

The highlight of Sandberg's season, defensively, was breaking the record for consecutive errorless games at second base. The streak finally ended on May 18, at 123 games. Sandberg wound up the season with eight miscues. His range has diminished a little, and Jose Lind is threatening his Gold Glove domination. But if he's no longer the best, he's very, very close to it.

OVERALL:

Long one of the greatest players in baseball, Sandberg has made himself even greater over the last two years by increasing his power stroke and belting first 30, then 40 homers. He may not be able to top his 1990 figure, but he will undoubtedly stay on the road to the Hall of Fame in 1991.

RYNE SANDBERG

Position: 2B
Bats: R **Throws:** R
Ht: 6' 2" **Wt:** 180

Opening Day Age: 31
Born: 9/18/59 in Spokane, WA
ML Seasons: 10

Overall Statistics

	G	AB	R	H	D	T	HR	RBI	SB	BB	SO	AVG
1990	155	615	116	188	30	3	40	100	25	50	84	.306
Career	1389	5508	872	1583	256	57	179	649	275	464	786	.287

Where He Hits the Ball

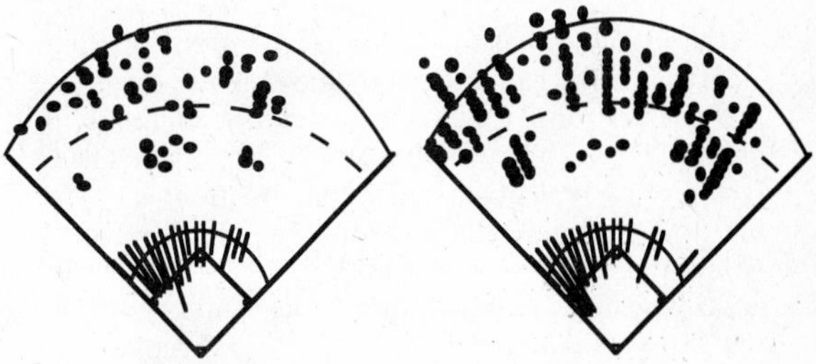

Vs. LHP Vs. RHP

1990 Situational Stats

	AB	H	HR	RBI	AVG		AB	H	HR	RBI	AVG
Home	305	109	25	62	.357	LHP	214	54	10	23	.252
Road	310	79	15	38	.255	RHP	401	134	30	77	.334
Day	320	102	22	57	.319	Sc Pos	124	37	9	56	.298
Night	295	86	18	43	.292	Clutch	96	31	6	19	.323

1990 Rankings (National League)

- 1st in home runs (40), runs (116), total bases (344), slugging percentage vs. right-handed pitchers (.616) and batting average at home (.357)
- 2nd in slugging percentage (.559) and runs scored per time reached base (48.5%)
- Led the Cubs in home runs, at-bats (615), runs, hits (188), total bases (344), RBIs (100), sacrifice flies (9), stolen bases (25), caught stealing (7), plate appearances (675) and slugging percentage
- Led NL second basemen in batting average (.306), home runs, at-bats, runs, hits, total bases, RBIs, sacrifice flies, plate appearances and slugging percentage

DWIGHT SMITH

Position: LF/RF
Bats: L **Throws:** R
Ht: 5'11" **Wt:** 175

Opening Day Age: 27
Born: 11/8/63 in Tallahassee, FL
ML Seasons: 2

Overall Statistics

	G	AB	R	H	D	T	HR	RBI	SB	BB	SO	AVG
1990	117	290	34	76	15	0	6	27	11	28	46	.262
Career	226	633	86	187	34	6	15	79	20	59	97	.295

Where He Hits the Ball

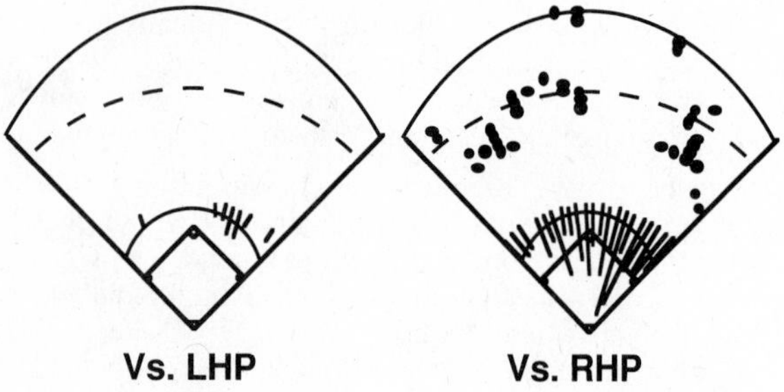

1990 Situational Stats

	AB	H	HR	RBI	AVG		AB	H	HR	RBI	AVG
Home	131	33	3	12	.252	LHP	36	8	1	3	.222
Road	159	43	3	15	.270	RHP	254	68	5	24	.268
Day	153	40	2	15	.261	Sc Pos	76	20	0	20	.263
Night	137	36	4	12	.263	Clutch	52	15	2	8	.288

1990 Rankings (National League)

- 3rd highest batting average on a 3-2 count (.444)
- Led NL left fielders in batting average on a 3-2 count

HITTING:

A Rookie of the Year contender in 1989 when he batted a very solid .325, Dwight Smith suffered through a long sophomore campaign. Smith's average plummeted all the way to .262 and his RBI count was almost cut in half, to a skimpy 27. Smith spent long stretches of the season on the bench, watching Dave Clark and Doug Dascenzo play left field.

After a season in which some people questioned his dedication, Smith finds himself needing to prove himself to the Cubs once again. A terror against righties as a rookie -- Smith has always been platooned -- he sometimes looked overmatched even by mediocre pitchers last year. Don Zimmer tried various things to get him going, even moving Smith to leadoff for a while. But when he failed to flash his '89 form, Zimmer benched him, giving Smith only 88 at-bats after the All-Star break.

Certainly Smith has the talent to hit better than .262. He's a good fastball hitter, with most of his power low in the strike zone, and pitchers tend to work him with breaking stuff away or try to jam him with inside fastballs. They kept the ball up on him more last year, but Smith's outstanding minor league hitting record would indicate that he has no big, exploitable weakness. No wild swinger, Smith struck out at a similar rate last year than he did as a rookie, and walked at a higher clip. For whatever reason, he simply didn't hit the ball as hard.

BASERUNNING:

Smith has excellent speed, but bad judgement when he reaches base. He stole 11 bases, but he was caught six times and picked off once. He was also caught napping several times on the bases. In an early season series against the Reds, he cost the Cubs one game and possibly another with his blunders. That was one reason Zimmer soured on him.

FIELDING:

Smith's bat will keep him in the majors; his glove will not. His range is mediocre at best. He is not the best judge of fly balls, and he does not position himself well. His arm is also not very good and runners can take advantage of him.

OVERALL:

Smith finished last season in Don Zimmer's doghouse, and when the year ended, the Cubs were talking about trading for a power-hitting left fielder like Pete Incaviglia or signing free agent George Bell. Smith is too valuable to waste on the bench, and it would be no shock if the Cubs dealt him. Whatever his problems were last year, he's never going to solve them sitting on the bench.

RICK SUTCLIFFE

Position: SP
Bats: L **Throws:** R
Ht: 6' 7" **Wt:** 215

Opening Day Age: 34
Born: 6/21/56 in Independence, MO
ML Seasons: 14

PITCHING:

Long the ace of the Cub staff, Rick Sutcliffe begins 1991 as one of the team's big question marks. Sutcliffe missed most of the 1990 season with shoulder trouble, and didn't make his first appearance until August 29. He pitched well in his fist two starts, but was belted around unmercifully after that. He finished the year without a win, and at season's end, Manager Don Zimmer said he had lost faith in Sutcliffe's ability to get people out.

Sutcliffe will be 35 in June, and he's already past the age when most power pitchers lose their stuff. Stubborn to the point of bull-headedness, he's done a lot of hard pitching in his time. Sutcliffe is a "wrist wrapper," starting his motion with his wrist cocked to give his pitches extra movement. The motion puts added strain on his arm, and he's now paying the price. Sutcliffe freely admits that he's often pitched with arm pain, and he wants to go nine innings every time out. Last year all that abuse finally caught up with him, and it's an open question as to how many innings his arm has left in it.

Sutcliffe has three main pitches, a fastball, curve, and slider, and mixes in an occasional change-up. His fastball used to come in at 90+ MPH and the slider used to be his out pitch. In 1990, the fastball had little velocity, which is understandable because he was still trying to build up his arm. His major problem was the slider, however. Flat sliders fool only the worst major leaguers and Sutcliffe's had no break at all. The end result was that the league batted .305 against him.

HOLDING RUNNERS, FIELDING, HITTING:

Though Sutcliffe has an excellent pickoff move to first base, his delivery is herky-jerky and very slow to the plate. Once a runner realizes a throw is not coming to first, Sutcliffe is easy to run on. He is, however, an excellent athlete, and he fields his position very well. He's also a talented left-handed hitter who belted a homer in the '84 playoffs, certainly one of the more memorable moments in his outstanding career.

OVERALL:

The big question for Sutcliffe in 1991 is whether his arm will be healthy. The hitters will provide the answer; Sutcliffe's the type who will go out and pitch without saying a word, even if the arm is about to fall off. He's such a competitor that, if his right arm is too sore to pitch, you expect him to come back as a lefty, or a third baseman.

Overall Statistics

	W	L	ERA	G	GS	Sv	IP	H	R	BB	SO	HR
1990	0	2	5.91	5	5	0	21.1	25	14	12	7	2
Career	133	105	3.83	357	296	6	2130.1	2010	984	856	1412	178

How Often He Throws Strikes

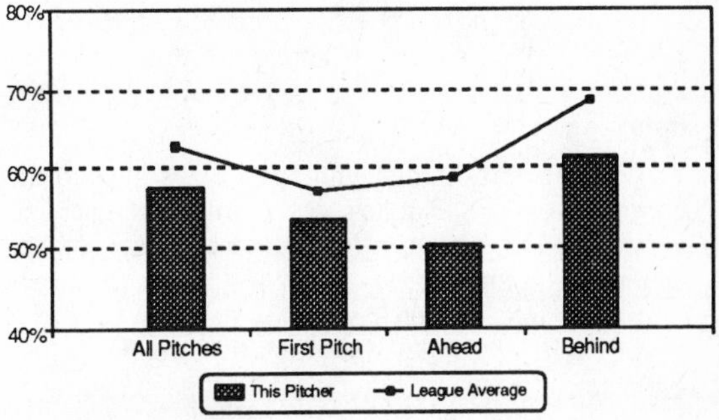

1990 Situational Stats

	W	L	ERA	Sv	IP		AB	H	HR	RBI	AVG
Home	0	1	9.58	0	10.1	LHB	47	15	0	7	.319
Road	0	1	2.45	0	11.0	RHB	35	10	2	5	.286
Day	0	1	7.16	0	16.1	Sc Pos	22	7	0	10	.318
Night	0	1	1.80	0	5.0	Clutch	1	1	0	0	.000

1990 Rankings (National League)

- Did not rank near the top or bottom in any category

JEROME WALTON

Position: CF
Bats: R **Throws:** R
Ht: 6' 1" **Wt:** 175

Opening Day Age: 25
Born: 7/8/65 in Newnan, GA
ML Seasons: 2

HITTING:

The National League's Rookie of the Year in 1989, Jerome Walton was one more Cub who had a long 1990 season. Walton got off to a slow start last year, then suffered a broken left hand when hit by a pitch in Philadelphia. Walton's hand continued to plague him after coming off the disabled list, and he wound up batting only .263, a 30-point drop from his rookie mark.

Despite his sinking average, Walton showed improvement in a key area last year. With increased plate discipline, he drew 23 more walks in 73 fewer at-bats, and his on-base percentage rose from .335 to .350. That made Walton a better leadoff man; he scored only one less run than in '89, while playing 15 fewer games. On the negative side, Walton's RBI count dropped by an enormous amount, from 46 to 21, and his power production was off. Walton was no slugger as a rookie, but he did belt five homers and record 31 extra-base hits. Last year his power figures were two homers and 20 extra-base hits. Of course, the hand injury was a big factor.

Walton is a spray hitter who specializes in hard-hit grounders and line singles and doubles. He uses his good speed to leg out a fair number of hits, but in general his main tactic is to hit a sharp ground ball into either hole. Walton has a tendency to dive into the pitch -- that's how he was injured last year -- and many teams try to jam him. Since he can lean out over the plate better against lefties, he hits them much better. Walton is an excellent bunter, and is always a threat to lay one down.

BASERUNNING:

Walton is blessed with very good speed. His stolen base total declined from 24 to 14 last year, but he was probably trying to protect his hand; he stole only four after the injury. Like most of the Cubs, he's a very aggressive baserunner, and will take an extra base whenever he can.

FIELDING:

Walton has very good range and is quite comparable to Andy Van Slyke in this regard. He usually plays at moderate depth and can come in on Texas Leaguers very well. He shies away a bit from walls, and his arm is not strong.

OVERALL:

Though his average dropped last year, Walton was hampered by the hand injury, and he figures to rebound this year. His increased patience makes him a better leadoff man, and the other parts of his game are basically sound. He should have a better season in 1991.

Overall Statistics

	G	AB	R	H	D	T	HR	RBI	SB	BB	SO	AVG
1990	101	392	63	103	16	2	2	21	14	50	70	.263
Career	217	867	127	242	39	5	7	67	38	77	147	.279

Where He Hits the Ball

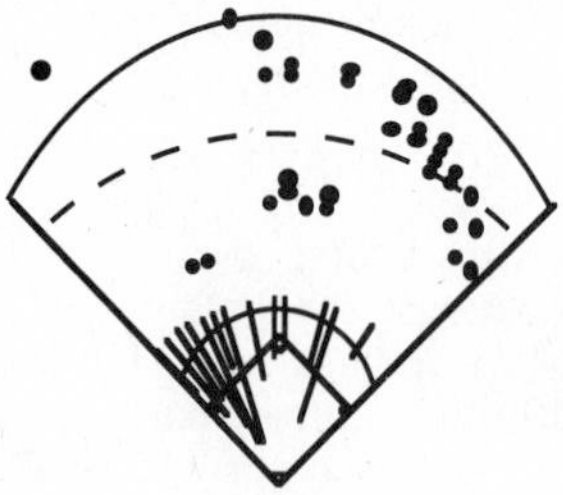

Vs. LHP

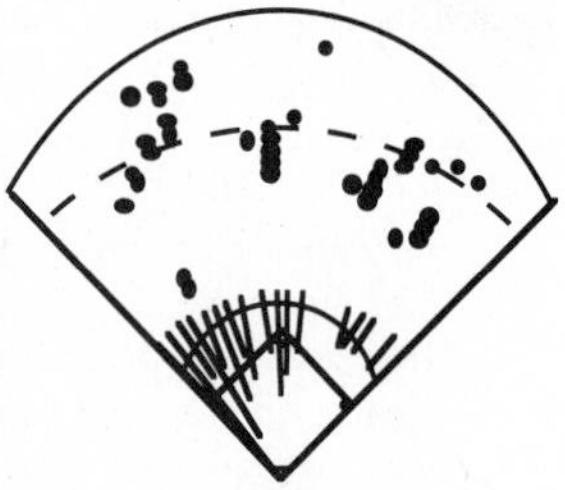

Vs. RHP

1990 Situational Stats

	AB	H	HR	RBI	AVG		AB	H	HR	RBI	AVG
Home	200	58	2	8	.290	LHP	146	42	1	12	.288
Road	192	45	0	13	.234	RHP	246	61	1	9	.248
Day	203	55	1	13	.271	Sc Pos	73	17	0	19	.233
Night	189	48	1	8	.254	Clutch	57	15	0	3	.263

1990 Rankings (National League)

- 10th in worst stolen base percentage (66.7%)
- Led the Cubs in caught stealing (7), bunts in play (16) and highest percentage of pitches taken (58.7%)

CURT WILKERSON

Position: 3B/2B
Bats: B **Throws:** R
Ht: 5' 9" **Wt:** 160

Opening Day Age: 29
Born: 4/26/61 in Petersburg, VA
ML Seasons: 8

HITTING:

A weak hitter when he first came to the major leagues, Curtis Wilkerson seemed to be improving during his last years with the Texas Rangers. Wilkerson batted .237, .268 and .293 from 1986 to 1988, then came to the Cubs in the Mitch Williams/Rafael Palmeiro deal. The Cubs didn't expect Wilkerson to hit .300, but they have to be disappointed in his performance.

In his two seasons in Chicago, Wilkerson's career has gone in the wrong direction, as he's batted .244 and then .220. That's not good for a guy with no power. Wilkerson has hit only four major league homers (none in 1990), and though he's batted as many as 484 times in a season, his career high in doubles is 12. Last year with the Cubs, Wilkerson had only six extra-base hits in 186 at-bats. In 1989, he had seven.

Wilkerson remains an extremely undisciplined hitter. His career high in walks is 26, and in two seasons with the Cubs he has drawn 15 bases on balls in 154 games. Wilkerson's career on-base percentage is a very weak .292. He's not a good contact man either, striking out at same rate as a lot of power hitters. Last year he fanned about once every five at-bats.

A switch-hitter, Wilkerson likes the ball high as a right-handed hitter and low when he's batting lefty. He's had years when he's batted much better from the left side (as in 1989) and others when he's been better righty (as in 1990). From either side he doesn't do much damage, though he is a good bunter.

BASERUNNING:

Despite a lack of speed and a very poor base stealing record -- he was only two-for-four last year -- Wilkerson is a good baserunner in non-steal situations.

FIELDING:

Wilkerson played primarily at third and second last year. He came up as a shortstop, but has rarely played there with the Cubs. He has a shortstop's arm, however, and that helps at both third and second. He's only average as a third baseman, but he has good range at second. Wilkerson lacks soft hands, however, and makes more than his share of errors.

OVERALL:

Wilkerson's ability to play respectably at second, short and third gives him some value. He doesn't need to hit that much to keep a major league job, and that's just as well. But if his average continues to sink, even his versatility may not save him. His position with the Cubs is hardly assured for 1991.

Overall Statistics

	G	AB	R	H	D	T	HR	RBI	SB	BB	SO	AVG
1990	77	186	21	41	5	1	0	16	2	7	36	.220
Career	764	1937	224	486	59	21	4	132	59	104	310	.251

Where He Hits the Ball

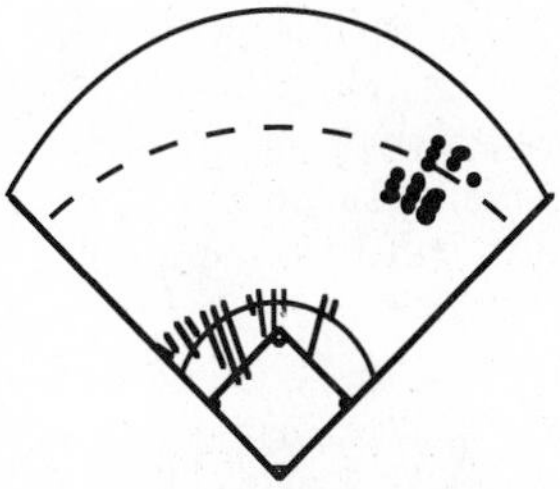

Vs. LHP

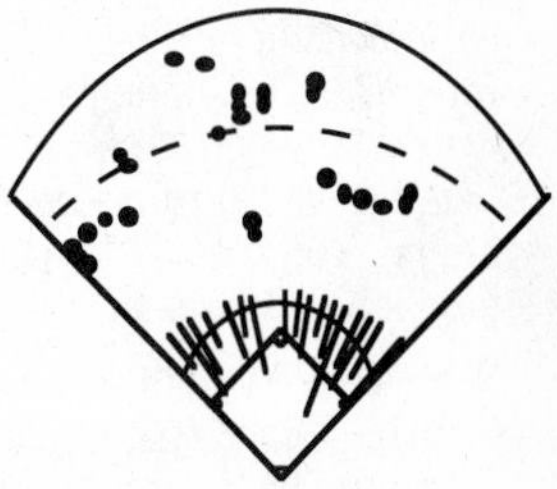

Vs. RHP

1990 Situational Stats

	AB	H	HR	RBI	AVG		AB	H	HR	RBI	AVG
Home	81	24	0	11	.296	LHP	58	14	0	7	.241
Road	105	17	0	5	.162	RHP	128	27	0	9	.211
Day	84	21	0	9	.250	Sc Pos	54	11	0	16	.204
Night	102	20	0	7	.196	Clutch	29	8	0	3	.276

1990 Rankings (National League)

- Did not rank near the top or bottom in any category

PITCHING:

Mitch Williams makes his living on the edge: he always says that if there isn't a clutch situation to pitch in, he doesn't want the ball. While Williams can be as dominating as any reliever, the reality is that in 1990, he was one of the National League's poorer closers. Williams' inability to get the ball over the plate directly led to his 1-8 win-loss record and 3.93 ERA.

Williams used to throw only the hard stuff: a fastball, a slider and a split-finger pitch. Last year in spring training, he unveiled a hard-breaking curve. He also showed a new command of the strike zone which made it seem certain that an even better season was imminent. It didn't happen that way.

In fairness to Williams, he suffered an injury in mid-season. But even that was his own fault. It doesn't take much observation to notice that Williams' horrible mechanics are murder on his driving leg. Therefore, it hardly came as a surprise to most Williams' watchers when four-and-a-half years of grinding, twisting and turning on that leg resulted in a knee injury. You can bet that this won't be the last one, unless he changes his motion.

Williams could not get anyone out after coming back from the injury, so Don Zimmer put him in the starting rotation. His performance as a starter amplified the fact that Williams' "new-found control" in spring training was just an illusion. He got battered in both his starts and then was relegated to long relief.

HOLDING RUNNERS, FIELDING, HITTING:

Williams has a great move to first, and runners have to worry about being picked off. But when they go, they're almost always safe because of his slow delivery. Williams is one of the worst fielders at any position in major league baseball. He finishes his wind-up so off balance that he's defenseless; he was skulled by a line drive in 1989, and it could happen again at any time. Needless to say, this leaves him in an inferior position to field the ball. Williams hit a memorable homer in 1989; he's not an automatic out at the plate.

OVERALL:

Even when he was successful in 1989, a lot of people thought Williams was lucky. They felt he couldn't keep walking the bases loaded and then striking out the side. That argument gained credibility last year. Williams finished 1990 watching Paul Assenmacher close games, and the Cubs spent the offseason looking for another late reliever. Williams will have to work to get his job back.

MITCH WILLIAMS

Position: RP
Bats: L **Throws:** L
Ht: 6' 4" **Wt:** 200

Opening Day Age: 26
Born: 11/17/64 in Santa Ana, CA
ML Seasons: 5

Overall Statistics

	W	L	ERA	G	GS	Sv	IP	H	R	BB	SO	HR
1990	1	8	3.93	59	2	16	66.1	60	38	50	55	4
Career	23	31	3.53	367	3	84	422.2	311	189	322	402	31

How Often He Throws Strikes

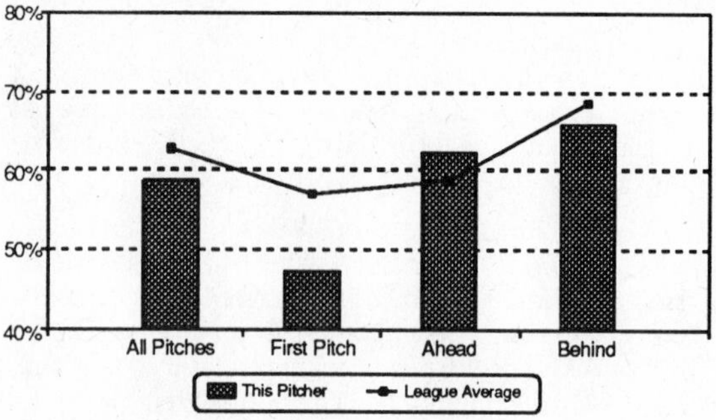

1990 Situational Stats

	W	L	ERA	Sv	IP		AB	H	HR	RBI	AVG
Home	1	1	3.78	4	33.1	LHB	66	15	2	14	.227
Road	0	7	4.09	12	33.0	RHB	185	45	2	30	.243
Day	0	1	3.38	6	29.1	Sc Pos	93	24	2	36	.258
Night	1	7	4.38	10	37.0	Clutch	105	26	1	16	.248

1990 Rankings (National League)

- 6th in save percentage (80.0%)
- 9th in games finished (39)
- 10th in saves (16)
- Led the Cubs in saves, games finished, save opportunities (20), and save percentage

PITCHING:

After a so-so rookie season in 1989, Steve Wilson took a step backwards in 1990. Wilson was no great shakes as a rookie, going 6-4 with a 4.20 ERA, but last year the numbers were a lot worse: 4-9, 4.79. The Cubs gave Wilson plenty of chances, using him as both a starter and a reliever. But he could never get untracked.

Wilson's two main pitches are a fastball and a change-up. The fastball has good movement and the change provides a significant difference in speeds. Neither pitch is really outstanding, however, and Wilson often gets crushed when he goes through the lineup for the second or third time. That's because hitters are able to get a look at both pitches and sit on the one they can handle. Last year Wilson was 2-7 with a 5.67 ERA as a starter, but 2-2, 3.62 in relief.

Though the Cubs used him in a variety of roles last year, Wilson is probably best suited for middle relief. He was by far the most effective pitcher on the team against lefties, holding them to a .219 average. Righties, however, really teed off on Wilson, belting him for 14 homers and a .273 average. If Wilson's going to be a successful starter, he'll have to find some pitches that can move righthanders off the plate. Even without changing, however, he can be effective coming in to pitch to a lineup stacked with lefty swingers. He allowed only 23 percent of his inherited runners to score last year.

HOLDING RUNNERS, FIELDING, HITTING:

Wilson is a solid fielder with decent range but with a somewhat alarming tendency to go after the lead runner when fielding a grounder. His move to the bases is impeccable, and like most Cub pitchers he allowed very few runners to steal. He allowed only six steals and eight were thrown out trying to run on him. Wilson hit .162 with little power, but he did get down five sacrifice hits.

OVERALL:

After 101 major league appearances, Wilson has a lifetime ERA of 4.61. He's allowed less than a hit an inning, however, has shown good control and has struck out more than twice as many batters as he's walked. That indicates he has good stuff. If he's used more carefully -- and if he can keep the ball in the park against righties -- his ERA will improve.

STEVE WILSON

Position: RP/SP
Bats: L **Throws:** L
Ht: 6' 4" **Wt:** 195

Opening Day Age: 26
Born: 12/13/64 in Victoria, BC
ML Seasons: 3

Overall Statistics

	W	L	ERA	G	GS	Sv	IP	H	R	BB	SO	HR
1990	4	9	4.79	45	15	1	139.0	140	77	43	95	17
Career	10	13	4.61	101	23	3	232.1	230	125	78	161	24

How Often He Throws Strikes

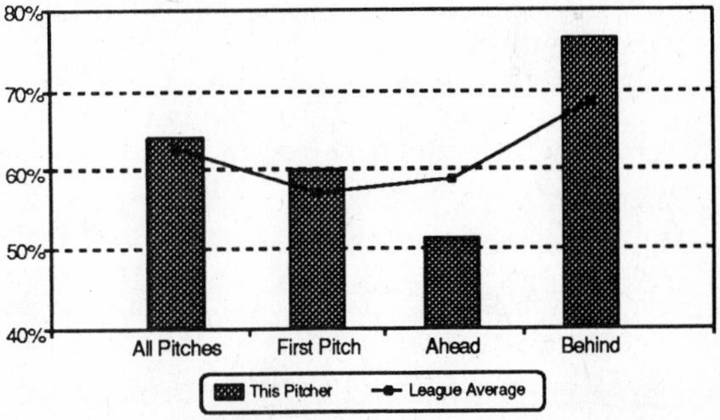

1990 Situational Stats

	W	L	ERA	Sv	IP		AB	H	HR	RBI	AVG
Home	2	5	5.40	1	71.2	LHB	137	30	3	20	.219
Road	2	4	4.14	0	67.1	RHB	403	110	14	52	.273
Day	2	5	5.45	1	76.0	Sc Pos	128	41	1	49	.320
Night	2	4	4.00	0	63.0	Clutch	60	20	1	8	.333

1990 Rankings (National League)

- 7th worst batting average allowed vs. right-handed batters (.273)
- Led the Cubs in most home runs allowed (17) and lowest batting average allowed vs. left-handed batters (.219)

SHAWN BOSKIE

Position: SP
Bats: R **Throws:** R
Ht: 6' 3" **Wt:** 205

Opening Day Age: 24
Born: 3/28/67 in Hawthorne, NV
ML Seasons: 1

Overall Statistics

	W	L	ERA	G	GS	Sv	IP	H	R	BB	SO	HR
1990	5	6	3.69	15	15	0	97.2	99	42	31	49	8
Career	5	6	3.69	15	15	0	97.2	99	42	31	49	8

PITCHING, FIELDING, HITTING & HOLDING RUNNERS:

The Cubs are desperate for pitching help, and young righty Shawn Boskie showed enough last year to give them some hope. Boskie's record was only 5-6 in 15 starts last year, but he kept the Cubs in most of the games, and his earned run average was very respectable at 3.69.

Only 24, Boskie appears to have excellent stuff. He is primarily a power pitcher with an excellent fastball, a sharp curveball, and a fine change-up that balances the fastball very nicely. He didn't strike out a lot of batters last year, but his strikeout totals in the minors were excellent. With the Cubs he displayed excellent control, averaging only 2.9 walks per nine innings.

One problem for Boskie is that he's primarily a fly ball pitcher. A lot of those long flies left Wrigley Field last year; he allowed eight home runs, seven of them at home. He'll need to work more carefully when working at home. Boskie did an excellent job of holding runners last year and displayed good range in fielding his position. He also showed off a fine bat, hitting .222 with three doubles. His bunting still needs a little work.

OVERALL:

Boskie had some arm trouble late last year and will need to demonstrate that he's recovered in spring training. If he is healthy, he will probably be able to grab a spot in the Cubs' starting rotation.

DERRICK MAY

Position: LF
Bats: L **Throws:** R
Ht: 6' 4" **Wt:** 210

Opening Day Age: 22
Born: 7/14/68 in Rochester, NY
ML Seasons: 1

Overall Statistics

	G	AB	R	H	D	T	HR	RBI	SB	BB	SO	AVG
1990	17	61	8	15	3	0	1	11	1	2	7	.246
Career	17	61	8	15	3	0	1	11	1	2	7	.246

HITTING, FIELDING, BASERUNNING:

The Cubs are excited about Derrick May, a young outfielder who's the son of former big league fly-chaser Dave May. In five minor league seasons May has batted .320, .298, .305, .295 and .296 while moving up through the club's minor league system. He has been very consistent the last three years, hitting 29, 26 and 27 doubles; eight, nine and eight home runs; and recording 65, 70 and 69 RBI.

After his fine season at AAA Iowa this year, May was called up to the big club in September. He performed respectably, hitting .246 and belting his first major league homer. May looks like a doubles-type hitter with power to the gaps and the capability to hit for a decent average in the bigs. He hasn't hit for home run power yet, but he's 6'4", 210 and only 22 years old. Playing in Wrigley Field, he could blossom.

Despite his size, May has good speed and stole in double figures three times during his minor league career. He was only five-for-11 at Iowa, but he should be able to swipe a few in the majors. Defensively, May showed very good range and instincts in left. He is reputed to have a below-average arm, but didn't get a chance to display it very often last year.

OVERALL:

May has a chance to make the Cub roster this spring, but only if he can play regularly. His best chance would come if the Cubs trade Dwight Smith. They'd like more power out of left field, though, so May would do well to try to develop more of a home run stroke.

JOSE NUNEZ

Position: RP/SP
Bats: R **Throws:** R
Ht: 6' 3" **Wt:** 185

Opening Day Age: 27
Born: 1/13/64 in Jarabocoa, Dominican Republic
ML Seasons: 4

Overall Statistics

	W	L	ERA	G	GS	Sv	IP	H	R	BB	SO	HR
1990	4	7	6.53	21	10	0	60.2	61	47	34	40	5
Career	9	10	5.05	77	22	0	197.2	188	118	111	171	20

PITCHING, FIELDING, HITTING & HOLDING RUNNERS:

Righthander Jose Nunez was long considered a promising prospect while advancing through the Toronto system. Nunez developed slowly, in part because the Jays had to keep him on their major league roster in 1987 after drafting him from the Royals. Nunez finally seemed to have it together in 1989, when he led the International League in ERA (2.21) while striking out 122 men in 134 innings. Nunez also pitched well for Toronto that September, fanning 14 and walking only two in 10.2 innings. When the Cubs obtained Nunez for Paul Kilgus before the 1990 season, they had a few expectations for the young hurler.

Nunez didn't satisfy those expectations in 1990, going 4-7 for the Cubs with a hefty 6.53 ERA. His control was a big problem, with 34 walks in 60.2 innings. But there were encouraging signs. He displayed a tough "rolling" fastball, and returned from a midseason demotion with a tight-breaking curve that could give hitters fits in 1991. He fielded his position well and did an average job of holding runners. He's a good athlete, so he could learn to hit.

OVERALL:

While Nunez is no youngster at age 27, he has good stuff, and pitchers often develop late. The Blue Jays thought highly enough of him to claim him in the Rule 5 draft, the method they used to snare George Bell and Kelly Gruber, among others. That shows how promising they thought he was, but it probably set him back. The Cubs certainly need pitching, and if Nunez can find home plate, he may be working a lot at Wrigley Field this season.

JEFF PICO

Position: RP/SP
Bats: R **Throws:** R
Ht: 6' 2" **Wt:** 170

Opening Day Age: 25
Born: 2/12/66 in Antioch, CA
ML Seasons: 3

Overall Statistics

	W	L	ERA	G	GS	Sv	IP	H	R	BB	SO	HR
1990	4	4	4.79	31	8	2	92.0	120	53	37	37	7
Career	13	12	4.24	113	26	5	295.1	327	153	105	132	21

PITCHING, FIELDING, HITTING & HOLDING RUNNERS:

Strictly a finesse hurler, Jeff Pico needs to control the black of the plate to achieve success. He has only average stuff and has to disrupt hitters with good location and changes in velocity. Pico has the two basic pitches: fastball and curve. Neither is impressive, but if Pico is on, he locates his pitches well and lets the hitters get themselves out.

Pico couldn't do that in 1990, and the result were very poor, including a 4.79 ERA. His big problem was pitching to left-handed hitters: they destroyed him to the tune of a .372 average. Used as both a starter and reliever, he was far more effective in starting roles. In his eight starts, Pico had a 3.83 ERA and allowed a lot fewer hits and walks while adding more strikeouts.

Pico's peripheral skills are all excellent. He has a fine move to first, and all four runners who tried to steal off him last year were retired. He's a good fielder with fine range, and he's an excellent hitter, batting .273 last year. Pico's a right-handed swinger, but if he batted against himself, he'd probably want to hit lefty.

OVERALL:

Pico had a tough year in 1990, but he pitched fairly well for the Cubs in both 1988 and 1989. He won't be successful, however, until he can become more effective against left-handed hitters. He may need to develop another pitch.

DOMINGO RAMOS

Position: 3B/SS
Bats: R **Throws:** R
Ht: 5'10" **Wt:** 154

Opening Day Age: 33
Born: 3/29/58 in Santiago, Dominican Republic
ML Seasons: 11

Overall Statistics

	G	AB	R	H	D	T	HR	RBI	SB	BB	SO	AVG
1990	98	226	22	60	5	0	2	17	0	27	29	.265
Career	507	1086	109	261	34	2	8	85	6	92	138	.240

HITTING, FIELDING, BASERUNNING:

Utility players have to learn to accept modest rewards, and for Domingo Ramos, 1990 was a career year. With the Cubs suffering a meltdown after their '89 division title, Ramos found himself in the lineup more than ever before. He played in 98 games, a career high, and finally logged more than 200 at-bats for the first time in his 11 big league seasons. Ramos didn't exactly tear the cover off the ball, but he batted a respectable .265.

It probably helps Ramos that Don Zimmer, his manager, spent a lot of his own career in the very same utility role. Ramos has played more in his two years under Zimmer than he ever had before, and as a result he's kept his modest bat skills sharp. Zimmer uses Ramos as a spot player at short and third, giving his regulars a rest. Ramos has very little power, but he handles the bat well and draws an occasional walk. He was very effective against lefties in 1989, but that success didn't continue in 1990.

Defensively, Ramos is better at short than he is at third. He plays hitters well, but he lacks the quick reflexes of a good third-sacker. He's a slow runner who won't steal and is accustomed to getting the stop sign from his coaches.

OVERALL:

Ramos has had an up-and-down career with the bat, but he has thrived under Zimmer's handling. He lacks the hitting and fielding skills to be a regular, but as a utility man, he has definite value.

HECTOR VILLANUEVA

Position: C/1B
Bats: R **Throws:** R
Ht: 6' 1" **Wt:** 210

Opening Day Age: 26
Born: 10/2/64 in San Juan, Puerto Rico
ML Seasons: 1

Overall Statistics

	G	AB	R	H	D	T	HR	RBI	SB	BB	SO	AVG
1990	52	114	14	31	4	1	7	18	1	4	27	.272
Career	52	114	14	31	4	1	7	18	1	4	27	.272

HITTING, FIELDING, BASERUNNING:

Hector Villanueva will hit major league pitching if given a chance. In the pitching (and Jerome Walton) dominated Eastern League of 1988, Villanueva quietly was the league's best hitter. He led the league with a .408 on-base percentage and backed it up with a .314 batting average which was third in the league. He also had 37 extra-base hits in 436 at-bats. Given his first major league shot last year, Villanueva showed a penchant for delivering the longball: he had seven homers and an impressive .509 slugging percentage in limited duty. Villanueva had been a patient hitter in the minors, but he walked only four times with the Cubs. Now that he's made an impression, he should be a little more selective.

At 6-1 and at least 210 pounds, Villanueva is built for comfort, not for speed. He actually stole as many as six bases in a minor league season, but that was in his younger, slimmer days. Call him a "cautious" baserunner. Villanueva has been mostly a catcher during his career, but he's not a very good one. He lacks mobility and is only a fair thrower. Villanueva has also played some first base, but he's not very good there, either. Unfortunately for him, he's a DH-type in a non-DH league.

OVERALL:

Villanueva is a professional hitter, one who could probably turn in some decent power numbers if used every day. That's unlikely, given his defensive shortcomings. But players with his hitting skill tend to stick around, and Villanueva figures to be a valuable bench player for the Cubs this year.

JACK ARMSTRONG

Position: SP
Bats: R **Throws:** R
Ht: 6' 5" **Wt:** 220

Opening Day Age: 26
Born: 3/7/65 in Englewood, NJ
ML Seasons: 3

PITCHING:

Jack Armstrong won a spot in the Reds' starting rotation with an impressive spring training and, for the first half of the season, was one of the game's most dominating pitchers. At the All-Star break, Armstrong was 11- 3 with a 2.28 ERA and was also the National League's starting pitcher in the mid-summer classic at Chicago's Wrigley Field.

But the second half was a disaster. Armstrong lost all four of his July starts after the break, allowing 19 runs in 22 innings. He was inconsistent in August and finally was placed on the disabled list on August 25 with a sore right elbow -- perhaps because he was unaccustomed to pitching so many innings. He didn't pitch again until a relief stint on September 19. Armstrong's second-half numbers: a 1-6 record with a 5.96 ERA. He pitched 114.2 innings in the first half and just 51.1 innings in the second half.

Armstrong has an excellent fastball and slider, along with a good change-up. He had superb control (31 walks in 114.2 IP) in the season's first half; in the second half, he lost velocity on his fastball and his control suffered (28 walks in 51.1 IP).

Armstrong is a physical-fitness freak. During the season, it's not unusual for him to run five or six miles a day, swim hundreds of laps in a pool and lift weights. No one knows if that strenuous workload -- "I want to be known as an athlete rather than just a pitcher," Armstrong says -- contributed to his breakdown last season. Some Cincinnati people thought so and wanted him to lighten the routine. But they can't deny that the righthander has the potential to develop into one of the game's premier pitchers.

HOLDING RUNNERS, FIELDING, HITTING:

Armstrong worked diligently on quickening his delivery to the plate -- which helped him keep runners close. In addition to a good pickoff move, he also contributes in the field. He has quick feet and is always in position to field a ball hit his way. As a hitter, he batted only .106 and didn't make much contact, striking out 21 times in 47 at-bats.

OVERALL:

Even a world championship club can't have too much pitching, and the Reds are counting on Armstrong to be one of the mainstays of their starting staff in 1991. If he stays healthy, he has the potential to develop into a consistent 15-game winner. At least.

Overall Statistics

	W	L	ERA	G	GS	Sv	IP	H	R	BB	SO	HR
1990	12	9	3.42	29	27	0	166.0	151	72	59	110	9
Career	18	19	4.17	52	48	0	274.0	254	140	118	178	22

How Often He Throws Strikes

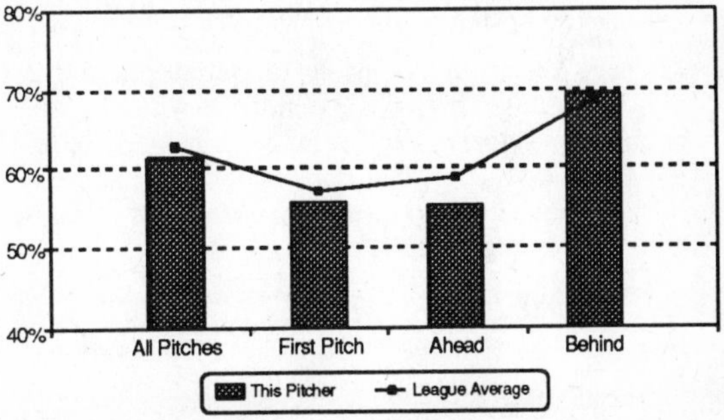

1990 Situational Stats

	W	L	ERA	Sv	IP		AB	H	HR	RBI	AVG
Home	6	4	3.93	0	71.0	LHB	386	99	6	46	.256
Road	6	5	3.03	0	95.0	RHB	238	52	3	18	.218
Day	2	3	3.92	0	41.1	Sc Pos	162	42	3	52	.259
Night	10	6	3.25	0	124.2	Clutch	38	8	0	3	.211

1990 Rankings (National League)

- 1st in balks (5)
- 5th in least HRs allowed per 9 innings (.49)
- 7th in hit batsmen (6)
- Led the Reds in losses (9), hit batsmen, balks, pickoff throws (196), most run support per 9 innings (4.7) and most GDPs per 9 innings (.49)

HITTING:

Early last season, Todd Benzinger's Cincinnati teammates began calling him "Todd Pipp," as in Wally Pipp, the man who was replaced by Lou Gehrig. In early June, Benzinger was replaced by Hal Morris, who was promoted from AAA Nashville and went on a hitting tear with the Reds. At first, Benzinger, who had been the everyday first baseman, was platooned with the left-handed hitting Morris. But Benzinger, who hit .339 in April and was still hitting .301 in early June, began getting fewer starts at first as the season progressed. He did play several games in left field, his first outfield duty since 1988 with Boston.

Benzinger, a switch-hitter, could work his way into a platoon situation at first or in left field this year. He sprays the ball to all fields from both sides. He hit .285 right-handed and .225 left-handed. His at-bats dropped significantly from the previous year (628 to 376) as did his home runs (17 to five).

Pitchers like to throw inside to Benzinger and not allow him to get his arms extended -- which is when he displays some power. From the right side, Benzinger feasts on pitches belt high or above. He's a low-ball, fastball hitter from the left side. Low breaking balls give him problems.

BASERUNNING:

Benzinger has average speed, at best. He is conservative on the base paths and doesn't have great instincts. Last year, he stole three bases in seven attempts after going three for 10 the previous season. He has stolen just 13 bases in 472 career games, while getting tossed out 18 times. Ricky Henderson he is not.

FIELDING:

Benzinger is an average fielder at both first base and in the outfield. He is adequate, but not outstanding, at scooping balls out of the dirt at first. He has made strides at first base during the last two seasons, particularly in fielding grounders. In the outfield, Benzinger has limited range with a very average arm.

OVERALL:

Benzinger, whose name has surfaced in trade talks, is a solid veteran; he is particularly valuable as a role player for a quality team. He will probably spend time at both first and left field and accumulate about 300 at-bats. If someone goes down with an injury or slumps, Benzinger is a steady, though not spectacular, replacement.

TODD BENZINGER

Position: 1B
Bats: B **Throws:** R
Ht: 6' 1" **Wt:** 190

Opening Day Age: 28
Born: 2/11/63 in Dayton, KY
ML Seasons: 4

Overall Statistics

	G	AB	R	H	D	T	HR	RBI	SB	BB	SO	AVG
1990	118	376	35	95	14	2	5	46	3	19	69	.253
Career	472	1632	197	414	81	7	43	235	13	107	310	.254

Where He Hits the Ball

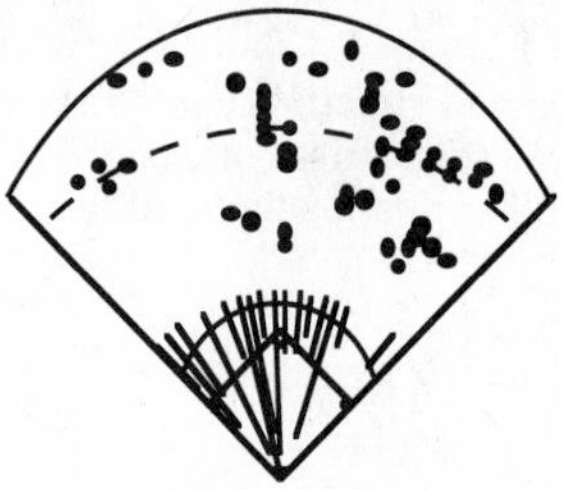

Vs. LHP

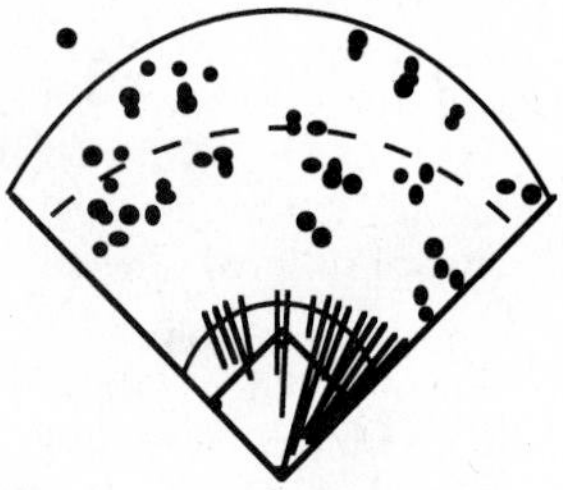

Vs. RHP

1990 Situational Stats

	AB	H	HR	RBI	AVG		AB	H	HR	RBI	AVG
Home	190	49	4	23	.258	LHP	172	49	2	17	.285
Road	186	46	1	23	.247	RHP	204	46	3	29	.225
Day	107	30	1	6	.280	Sc Pos	115	29	1	40	.252
Night	269	65	4	40	.242	Clutch	62	13	1	7	.210

1990 Rankings (National League)

- 3rd in least GDPs per GDP situation (3.9%)
- 4th highest batting average on an 0-2 count (.310)
- Led the Reds in sacrifice flies (7), least GDPs per GDP situation and batting average on an 0-2 count
- Led NL first basemen in batting average on an 0-2 count

HITTING:

The Milwaukee Brewers, frustrated with Glenn Braggs' inability to reach his enormous potential, dealt the outfielder to Cincinnati last June 9. For Braggs, the change of scenery was immediately beneficial. He hit safely in his first eight games (12 for 30, .400) with the Reds, during which time he slammed two homers and collected seven RBI. Braggs was often platooned in right field with Paul O'Neill, and also saw considerable time in left. Though he slumped in August, Braggs had a productive season. He finished strongly, batting .326 in September as the Reds held off their NL West challengers.

The muscular Braggs is a fastball hitter with good power to left and left-center. If a pitch is on the middle of the plate, or away, Braggs is a power threat. He can be handled with fastballs on the inside corner and by breaking balls down and away. Righthanders give him particular problems with off speed pitches. Braggs hit righties for a respectable average last year, batting .273, but he hit lefties with much more power.

BASERUNNING:

Braggs has above-average speed but makes his share of mistakes on the base paths. Braggs stole just eight bases in 15 attempts last year. He isn't the successful baserunner he was in the minors, where he stole at least 20 bases in three of four seasons.

FIELDING:

Braggs is not rated as a good fielder. That said, it should be noted that, years from now, when someone mentions Braggs' name, it will probably conjure up one thought: the sensational, over-the-fence catch he made to rob Pittsburgh's Carmelo Martinez of a two-run, ninth-inning homer in Game Six of the NL championship series. The grab saved the Reds' title-clinching 3-2 win. It was ironic that Braggs made the catch. Twice during the season he dropped fly balls that led to Cincinnati defeats. Braggs doesn't have much range and doesn't have sure hands, but he does have a quality arm. He's better in right field than in left.

OVERALL:

Braggs will probably partially platoon in right with O'Neill. He also figures to see action in left. He could make it difficult for manager Lou Piniella to take him out of the lineup. Braggs has the physical tools to develop into a 20-homer guy. Based on his production last year, he may have found a permanent home in Cincinnati.

GLENN BRAGGS

Position: RF/LF
Bats: R **Throws:** R
Ht: 6' 3" **Wt:** 210

Opening Day Age: 28
Born: 10/17/62 in San Bernardino, CA
ML Seasons: 5

Overall Statistics

	G	AB	R	H	D	T	HR	RBI	SB	BB	SO	AVG
1990	109	314	39	88	14	1	9	41	8	38	64	.280
Career	515	1820	232	473	76	13	51	244	44	152	378	.260

Where He Hits the Ball

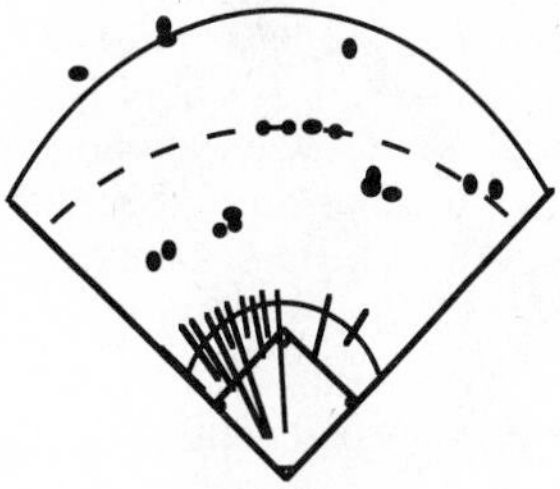

Vs. LHP

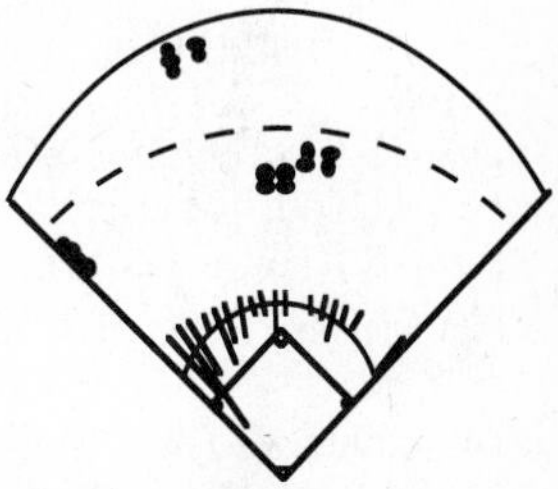

Vs. RHP

1990 Situational Stats

	AB	H	HR	RBI	AVG		AB	H	HR	RBI	AVG
Home	161	45	5	25	.280	LHP	149	43	6	19	.289
Road	153	43	4	16	.281	RHP	165	45	3	22	.273
Day	92	23	4	14	.250	Sc Pos	70	21	0	26	.300
Night	222	65	5	27	.293	Clutch	54	16	0	5	.296

1990 Rankings (National League)

- 4th highest on-base average vs. left-handed pitchers (.437)
- 5th highest batting average vs. left-handed pitchers (.339)
- Led the Reds in batting average on a 3-1 count (.500)
- Led NL right-fielders in batting average/on-base average vs. left-handed pitchers

TOM BROWNING

Position: SP
Bats: L **Throws:** L
Ht: 6' 1" **Wt:** 190

Opening Day Age: 30
Born: 4/28/60 in Casper, WY
ML Seasons: 7

Overall Statistics

	W	L	ERA	G	GS	Sv	IP	H	R	BB	SO	HR
1990	15	9	3.80	35	35	0	227.2	235	98	52	99	24
Career	93	61	3.73	220	219	0	1439.0	1376	650	389	774	173

How Often He Throws Strikes

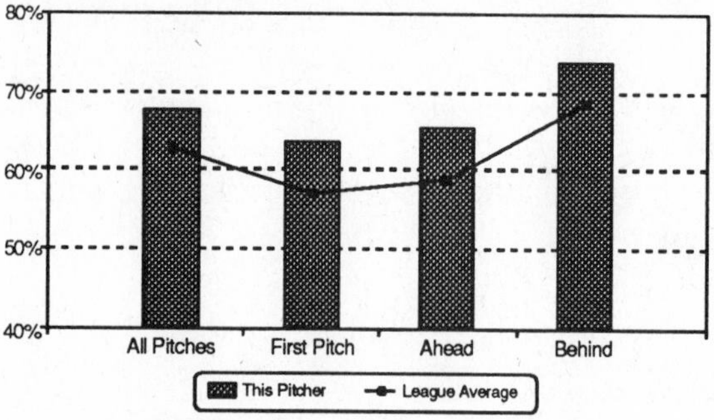

1990 Situational Stats

	W	L	ERA	Sv	IP		AB	H	HR	RBI	AVG
Home	8	8	4.64	0	128.0	LHB	162	41	5	15	.253
Road	7	1	2.71	0	99.2	RHB	720	194	19	73	.269
Day	3	3	4.03	0	60.1	Sc Pos	169	40	2	58	.237
Night	12	6	3.71	0	167.1	Clutch	101	28	2	7	.277

1990 Rankings (National League)

- 1st in games started (35)
- 2nd in hits allowed (235), least pitches thrown per batter (3.21) and least GDPs induced per 9 innings (.24)
- 3rd in home runs allowed (24), lowest stolen base percentage allowed (54.5%), least strikeouts per 9 innings (3.9) and worst ERA at home (4.64)
- Led the Reds in wins (15), losses (9), innings (227.2), batters faced (957), home runs allowed, pitches thrown (3,076), runners caught stealing (10), lowest stolen base percentage allowed, least pitches thrown per batter and lowest ERA on the road (2.71)

PITCHING:

Tom Browning put together his third straight solid season in 1990. He led the Reds in several categories, including wins (15) and innings pitched (227.2). He also led the team in a dubious department -- most home runs allowed (24). Browning is a fly ball pitcher, but his tendency to give up the longball hasn't ruined his effectiveness. He has won at least 15 games in five of his six full season with the Reds.

Browning, who reminds folks of Jim Kaat with his rapid-fire pitching style, didn't have the best of luck last season. On August 17, he strained ligaments in his left ankle while batting against Pittsburgh. It was 11 days before he was able to pitch again and, when he returned, he had some difficult moments. He lost three of his next four decisions, allowing 27 earned runs in 27.2 innings.

When healthy, Browning possesses great location and control. His fastball is just average, at best, and his curve isn't dazzling. But he has an outstanding change-up -- one he isn't afraid to throw even when he's behind in the count. He also has an excellent screwball, one of his money pitches. He constantly moves the ball in and out, keeping the hitters off-stride.

Browning, who likes to use the inside part of the plate, works more quickly than anyone in the league. He keeps his infielders in the game with his quick delivery, and his rhythm throws hitters out of sync. Last year, however, Browning allowed more hits (235, the league's second-highest total) than innings pitched (227.2) for the first time since 1987 when he had a 5.02 ERA. Attribute some of his problems to the fact that he was overcompensating because of his ankle injury.

HOLDING RUNNERS, FIELDING, HITTING:

Browning has a less-than-average pickoff move, but his quick delivery hinders would-be base thieves. The lefthander is a very good fielder and an above-average (and aggressive) baserunner. In fact, the Reds use him as a pinch-runner. At the plate, Browning batted a Bob Buhl-like .093 last year and is a .141 career hitter. However, he is regarded as a better-than-average hitting pitcher.

OVERALL:

Browning obviously hasn't returned to his rookie form of 1985 (20-9). But, the fact is, there aren't many lefthanders that have shown the consistency that Browning has displayed during the last three years. For this reason and the loss of Danny Jackson to the Cubs, the Reds desperately wanted to re-sign him and keep the free-agent sharks away. There was no guarantee that they could.

PITCHING:

Norm Charlton established himself as one of the three "Nasty Boys" in the Reds' bullpen during the first half of last season. In the second half, he showed that he also might have a promising future as a starter -- a role not unfamiliar to the lefthander. Charlton was a starter during his five minor league seasons (1984-88), and he led the American Association in strikeouts in 1988.

In last season's first half, Charlton was primarily a set-up man for fellow "Nasty Boys" Randy Myers and Rob Dibble. There wasn't a better trio of relievers in the majors. However, because of injuries to Red's starting pitchers, Charlton moved out of the bullpen, where he was 6-4 with a 3.02 ERA, and into the starting rotation. He had not started since 1988, ending a string of 108 consecutive relief appearances. No matter, Charlton developed into one of the Reds' most consistent starters. As a starter, he was 6-5 with a 2.60 ERA before moving back to the bullpen for the NL championship series.

Charlton throws a fastball in the low 90s, and has an outstanding breaking pitch. He uses a back-door curve that frustrates right-handed hitters by painting the outside part of the plate. And his forkball contributes heavily to his success. When he's behind in the count, he usually throws his fastball, which is hittable.

Charlton has a tendency to be somewhat wild; he walked 70 in 154.1 innings. He also tossed nine wild pitches.

HOLDING RUNNERS, FIELDING, HITTING:

Charlton displayed an average pickoff move in 1990, but he made strides in this area from the previous season. As a fielder, Charlton has good range and is better than adequate. On the base paths, he has average speed, but is extremely daring. Know any other pitchers who crashed into Dodgers' catcher Mike Scioscia with their shoulder and knocked the ball loose last year? Charlton wasn't as feisty at the plate, hitting .135 -- he batted .200 (in 10 at-bats) from the right side and .111 (in 27 at-bats) from the left side.

OVERALL:

The Reds have an interesting dilemma: Do they keep the National League's best bullpen intact by using Charlton as a set-up man, or do they shift him into the starter's role that he seems more than capable of handling? The odds are that Charlton will find himself in the starting rotation.

NORM CHARLTON

Position: RP/SP
Bats: B **Throws:** L
Ht: 6' 3" **Wt:** 195

Opening Day Age: 28
Born: 1/6/63 in Fort Polk, LA
ML Seasons: 3

Overall Statistics

	W	L	ERA	G	GS	Sv	IP	H	R	BB	SO	HR
1990	12	9	2.74	56	16	2	154.1	131	53	70	117	10
Career	24	17	3.04	135	26	2	311.0	258	118	130	254	21

How Often He Throws Strikes

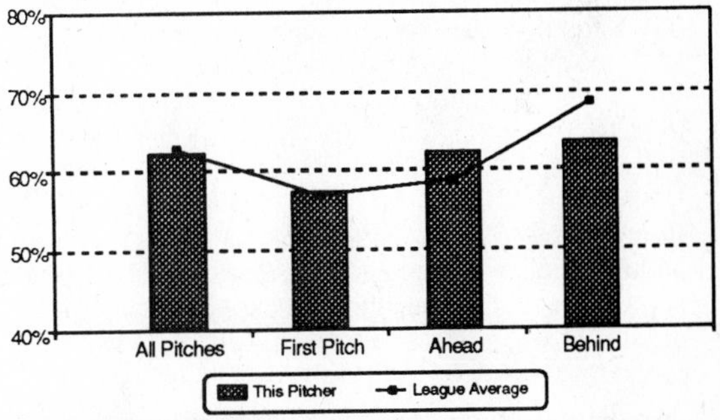

1990 Situational Stats

	W	L	ERA	Sv	IP		AB	H	HR	RBI	AVG
Home	6	4	3.09	1	75.2	LHB	116	26	4	19	.224
Road	6	5	2.40	1	78.2	RHB	451	105	6	27	.233
Day	3	3	2.03	1	48.2	Sc Pos	152	34	1	33	.224
Night	9	6	3.07	1	105.2	Clutch	123	28	3	8	.228

1990 Rankings (National League)

- 6th in GDPs induced (19) and most GDPs induced per GDP situation (17.3%)
- 7th in wild pitches (9) and lowest batting average allowed vs. right-handed batters (.233)
- 9th in holds (9)
- Led the Reds in losses (9), wild pitches, GDPs induced, lowest batting average allowed vs. right-handed batters and lowest batting average allowed with runners in scoring position (.224)

ERIC DAVIS

Position: CF/LF
Bats: R **Throws:** R
Ht: 6' 3" **Wt:** 185

Opening Day Age: 28
Born: 5/29/62 in Los Angeles, CA
ML Seasons: 7

HITTING:

Injuries caused Eric Davis to have a sub-par season in 1990. Then again, most players would have gladly settled for the number of homers (24) and RBI (86) that Davis produced. Davis, who sprained the medial collateral ligament in his right knee early last season, was hitting just .224 on August 21. However, during the pennant drive from August 22 until he was injured again on September 27, Davis batted .357 (45 for 126) with nine homers and 29 RBI.

When healthy, Davis, who waves his bat like a conductor's baton, is one of the game's best all-around players. When he's in a hitting groove, he rips the ball to all fields. When he gets in a hitting rut, he's usually trying to pull most of the pitches. Davis, whose bat speed may be the quickest in the majors, will hit the long ball when he gets a high breaking pitch, or when he gets a fastball on the middle or outside part of the plate. He can be retired on inside fastballs and breaking balls that are down and away. When he gets behind in the count, he has a tendency to chase high pitches that are out of the strike zone.

BASERUNNING:

Injuries slowed Davis on the base paths last year, but he has excellent speed and is usually extremely daring. He excels at taking the extra base on a teammate's hit. Davis, who stole 21 bases in 24 attempts last year, probably won't ever return to his 1986 form on the base paths (80 steals), but if his knees recover, he should be able to at least double last year's stolen base total.

FIELDING:

Normally a center fielder with great range, Davis spent considerable time in left field last year because knee problems reduced his mobility. When healthy, he is one of baseball's best at making leaping catches at the fence. Davis has a very good arm, and had 11 assists last year.

OVERALL:

Davis, who also suffered a partial tear in his kidney in the World Series, is hopeful of a successful response to off season surgery to his right knee. If he does, he will probably move back to his customary spot in center. The Reds were in first place every day last year despite a less-than-sensational year by Davis. If Davis returns to good health, it will be difficult for a team to dethrone the Reds.

Overall Statistics

	G	AB	R	H	D	T	HR	RBI	SB	BB	SO	AVG
1990	127	453	84	118	26	2	24	86	21	60	100	.260
Career	767	2572	515	700	109	18	166	499	233	376	661	.272

Where He Hits the Ball

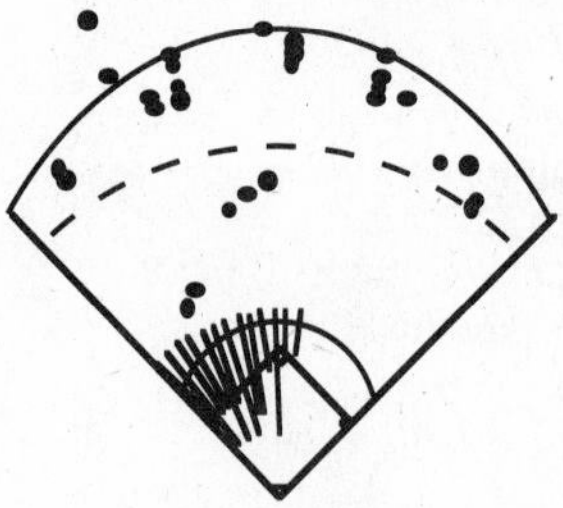

Vs. LHP

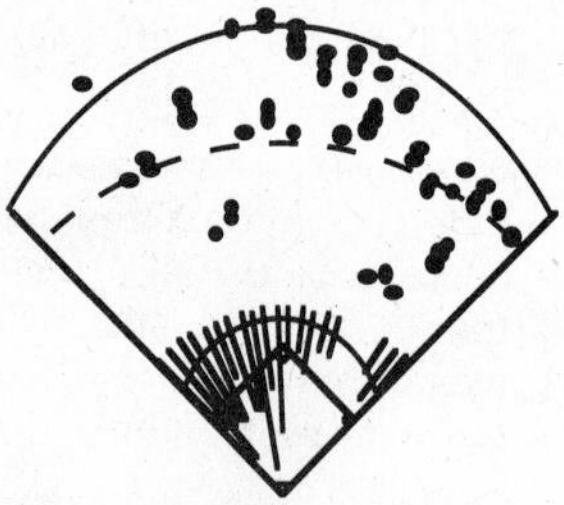

Vs. RHP

1990 Situational Stats

	AB	H	HR	RBI	AVG		AB	H	HR	RBI	AVG
Home	193	45	13	34	.233	LHP	150	43	8	36	.287
Road	260	73	11	52	.281	RHP	303	75	16	50	.248
Day	125	36	7	20	.288	Sc Pos	131	33	6	61	.252
Night	328	82	17	66	.250	Clutch	75	18	3	13	.240

1990 Rankings (National League)

- 3rd in stolen base percentage (87.5%)
- 4th most runs scored per time reached base (46.7%)
- 7th in steals of third (7)
- Led the Reds in RBIs (86), slugging percentage (.486), HR frequency (18.9 ABs per HR), stolen base percentage, most pitches seen per plate appearance (3.79), highest percentage of pitches taken (56.7%) and percentage of extra bases taken as a runner (53.6%)
- Led NL center fielders in stikeouts (100) and slugging percentage vs. left-handed pitchers (.520)

ROB DIBBLE

Position: RP
Bats: L **Throws:** R
Ht: 6' 4" **Wt:** 235

Opening Day Age: 27
Born: 1/24/64 in Bridgeport, CT
ML Seasons: 3

Overall Statistics

	W	L	ERA	G	GS	Sv	IP	H	R	BB	SO	HR
1990	8	3	1.74	68	0	11	98.0	62	22	34	136	3
Career	19	9	1.90	179	0	13	256.1	167	57	94	336	9

How Often He Throws Strikes

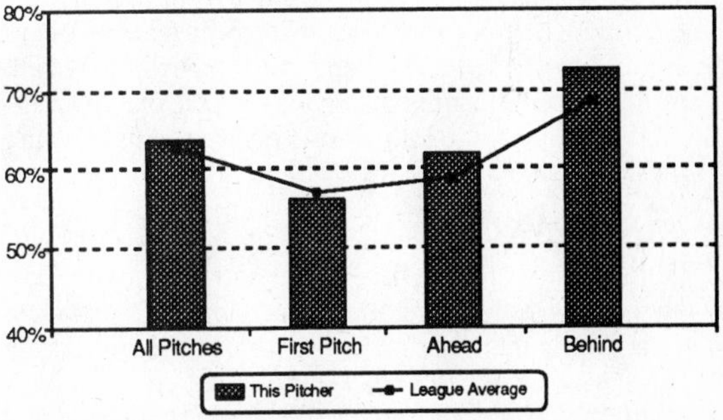

1990 Situational Stats

	W	L	ERA	Sv	IP		AB	H	HR	RBI	AVG
Home	4	1	2.15	6	46.0	LHB	173	32	1	19	.185
Road	4	2	1.38	5	52.0	RHB	166	30	2	19	.181
Day	3	1	2.76	2	29.1	Sc Pos	109	19	0	34	.174
Night	5	2	1.31	9	68.2	Clutch	224	50	1	28	.223

1990 Rankings (National League)

- 1st in holds (17)
- 3rd in lowest batting average allowed vs. left-handed batters (.185)
- 5th in blown saves (6)
- 6th in games pitched (68) and first batter efficiency (.191)
- Led the Reds in games pitched, most stolen bases allowed (20), holds, blown saves, lowest batting average allowed vs. left- handed batters and first batter efficiency

PITCHING:

Rob Dibble, perhaps the hardest thrower in the big leagues, was a major reason why the Reds were in first place from opening day last season. For the second straight year, Dibble was one of the majors' premier relievers. Batters hit only .183 against him, and he struck out 12.5 hitters per nine innings. He also walked only 3.1 batters and allowed just 5.7 hits per nine innings. Nasty.

Dibble, primarily a set-up man for Randy Myers, didn't do it with finesse. He did it with an exploding fastball; it was clocked at 101 MPH three times during an August 28 game in Pittsburgh. Dibble did not allow an earned run until his sixteenth outing. He was amazingly consistent throughout the season. Dibble's workload increased down the stretch; he worked two or more innings in five straight outings in late August and early September.

In addition to his awesome fastball, Dibble possesses a terrific slider, which he throws in the 85-88 MPH range. When he is getting both pitches over the plate, he is virtually unhittable. It is not unusual for hitters to chase bad pitches with Dibble on the mound.

Dibble's control has improved in the majors. In the minors, he walked 157 in 338.2 innings (4.2 walks per 9 innings.) In his last three major league seasons, however, Dibble has averaged 3.3 walks per nine innings. He has walked 95 (19 of those intentional) and struck out 336 in 256.1 innings.

HOLDING RUNNERS, FIELDING, HITTING:

Dibble has a poor pickoff move. With his big leg-kick and his long-arm motion, he has difficulty keeping runners close. Only his velocity gives his catcher a chance to throw out a base stealer. Dibble is also a below-average fielder. He puts so much effort into firing the ball that he is frequently out of position to field it -- not that opponents hit many pitches. As a hitter, Dibble is still searching for his first major league hit. He was 0-for-7 last season, but he did make contact six times, and is 0-for-17 in his career.

OVERALL:

He may not get many saves because of the way he is used, but Dibble -- who last year frequently whined about his salary -- is clearly one of the game's most dominating players. If you were building a team and had a chance to pick any reliever, you couldn't go wrong by choosing this fearsome, colorful righthander.

HITTING:

When the 1990 season started, Bill Doran, then playing with Houston, had to prove that his miserable second half performance in 1989, .131 after the All-Star break, was a fluke. The switch-hitting Doran showed that there was still life in his bat last year, hitting .300 overall, including a .373 mark in 59 at-bats after he was traded to the Reds on August 31.

But as the 1991 season approaches, Doran must once again prove himself. He must prove that, at age 32, he can recover from the injury that caused him to miss the playoffs and World Series. Doran had surgery on a herniated disk in his back. While full recovery is expected, the proof will be in the playing.

Doran is a better low-ball hitter from the left side, where he hit .385. He is a better high-ball hitter from the right side. Doran is a good fastball hitter but sometimes has problems handling low breaking balls from both sides of the plate. A spray hitter with occasional power, he has had an excellent strikeout-walk ratio in his eight-plus major league seasons, averaging 74 walks and 63 strikeouts per year. His lifetime on-base percentage is a splendid .356.

BASERUNNING:

Doran is an excellent baserunner and very aggressive on the base paths. He stole 23 bases in 32 attempts last year. Doran has averaged 24 steals during each of his full seasons in the majors. He grounded into just three double plays in 1990.

FIELDING:

Doran is steady at second base. Though his range is diminishing somewhat, it is still above average. He is excellent at turning the double play. Doran has sure hands; he committed just six errors at second last year. As a third baseman, he had his problems with the Reds, committing two errors in just six chances.

OVERALL:

Doran, a free agent after the World Series, has always wanted to play in Cincinnati, his birth place. It is where he lives and where he hopes to finish his career. With Mariano Duncan having problems hitting righthanders, Doran could work his way into a semi-platoon at second base. He is also insurance for Chris Sabo at third.

BILLY DORAN

Position: 2B
Bats: B **Throws:** R
Ht: 6' 0" **Wt:** 175

Opening Day Age: 32
Born: 5/28/58 in Cincinnati, OH
ML Seasons: 9

Overall Statistics

	G	AB	R	H	D	T	HR	RBI	SB	BB	SO	AVG
1990	126	403	59	121	29	2	7	37	23	79	58	.300
Career	1182	4323	621	1161	188	35	70	409	196	593	518	.269

Where He Hits the Ball

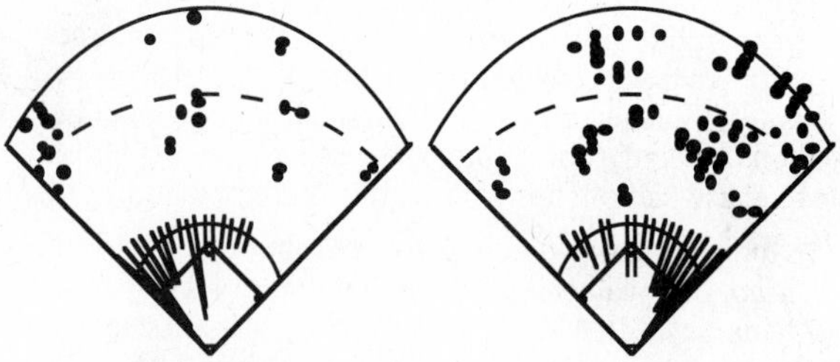

Vs. LHP   Vs. RHP

1990 Situational Stats

	AB	H	HR	RBI	AVG		AB	H	HR	RBI	AVG
Home	199	66	4	18	.332	LHP	142	38	2	12	.268
Road	204	55	3	19	.270	RHP	261	83	5	25	.318
Day	129	51	2	17	.395	Sc Pos	93	21	2	28	.226
Night	274	70	5	20	.255	Clutch	52	13	0	3	.250

1990 Rankings (National League)

- 7th in walks (79) and on-base average vs. left-handed pitchers (.408)
- 9th in least GDPs per GDP situation (4.5%)
- Led NL second basemen in walks and least GDPs per GDP situation

MARIANO DUNCAN

Position: 2B/SS
Bats: R **Throws:** R
Ht: 6' 0" **Wt:** 185

Opening Day Age: 28
Born: 3/13/63 in San Pedro de Macoris, Dominican Republic
ML Seasons: 5

HITTING:

Mariano Duncan, a .235 career hitter before last season, made a stunning turnaround in 1990, batting .306 and collecting more extra-base hits than Von Hayes, Mark Grace and Harold Baines, among others. Duncan used to be a fastball hitter. Period. But last year he learned how to hit the breaking ball. He can still be retired with breaking pitches, provided they are down in the strike zone.

Primarily a pull hitter for most of his career, Duncan improved his strength with an offseason workout program prior to the 1990 campaign. When the season started, he displayed much more patience at the plate than in previous seasons and with a shorter, quicker swing, learned to hit to right field. Manager Lou Piniella and coach Tony Perez taught him to wait on the ball. Duncan made another change: he held the bat back further and higher, and didn't dip as much at the plate. Consequently, neither did his average. Duncan destroyed lefthanders, hitting them at a .410 clip, the highest in the majors. He batted just .227 against righthanders. The 183-point disparity in his left-right average was the biggest in the majors.

BASERUNNING:

Duncan has good speed and is aggressive on the bases, as evidenced by his league-leading 11 triples. Since he frequently batted towards the bottom of the lineup, Duncan didn't run as much as he is capable, stealing 13 bases in 20 attempts. If he picks his spots better, those figures should improve. Duncan once stole 38 and 48 bases in consecutive seasons with the Dodgers. Prior to 1989, Duncan had an 82 percent success rate in career steals. In the last two years, it's been 65 percent.

FIELDING:

Duncan is an average fielder, at best. He played shortstop with the Dodgers and has a strong arm, but he has to learn when not to make unnecessary throws, particularly on double play balls in which he has little (if any) chance to retire the runner at first. Hold the ball, Mariano, and save yourself some grief. Duncan's fielding percentage (.973) ranked 11th among NL second baseman last year. Enough said.

OVERALL:

Was last year a fluke? Is Duncan really a .300 hitter? We'll see. Duncan will probably have to improve against righthanders if he is going to keep his full-time job. He made a superb turnaround last year but sometimes reverted back to his free-swinging style, especially when he got behind in the count.

Overall Statistics

	G	AB	R	H	D	T	HR	RBI	SB	BB	SO	AVG
1990	125	435	67	133	22	11	10	55	13	24	67	.306
Career	546	1923	251	483	76	20	33	163	119	117	371	.251

Where He Hits the Ball

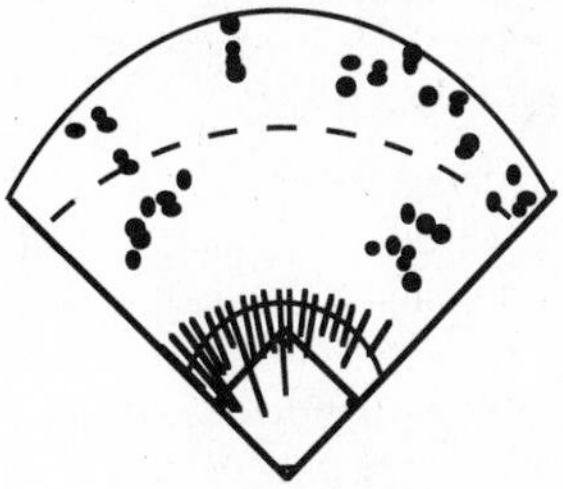

Vs. LHP

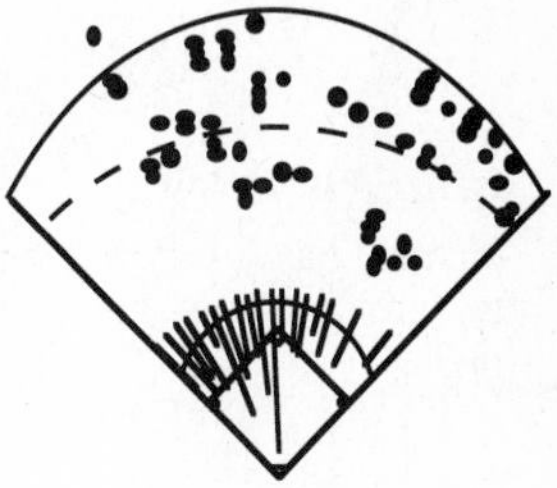

Vs. RHP

1990 Situational Stats

	AB	H	HR	RBI	AVG		AB	H	HR	RBI	AVG
Home	230	71	5	30	.309	LHP	188	77	4	27	.410
Road	205	62	5	25	.302	RHP	247	56	6	28	.227
Day	125	34	3	18	.272	Sc Pos	105	27	1	40	.257
Night	310	99	7	37	.319	Clutch	68	17	0	6	.250

1990 Rankings (National League)

- 1st in triples (11), lowest batting average with the bases loaded (.000) and highest batting average vs. left-handed pitchers (.410)
- 3rd in highest on-base average vs. left-handed pitchers (.437)
- 4th in highest slugging percentage vs. left-handed pitchers (.606)
- Led the Reds in triples and batting average/on-base average/slugging percentage vs. left-handed pitchers
- Led NL second basemen in triples and batting average/on- base average/slugging percentage vs. left-handed pitchers

HITTING:

When spring training started last year, Billy Hatcher was regarded as an excellent fourth outfielder. About eight months later, he was a World Series hero, hitting a remarkable .750.

Traded from the outfield-rich Pirates just before last season, Hatcher made an immediate impact. With the Reds, he was projected as a platoon player in left field. but he began the season with an eight-game hitting streak (16 for 40, .400) and became a regular. When Eric Davis went on the disabled list in late April, Hatcher was shifted to center. After a sub-par 1989 season (.231), Hatcher bounced back and hit .276 overall.

Hatcher, who used to try to pull most pitchers, is a fastball hitter. He frequently chases breaking balls out of the strike zone, particularly when he's behind in the count. When he's in a hitting groove -- the World Series is a good example -- Hatcher sprays the ball to all fields. He has greatly improved as a contact hitter, striking out only 42 times last year.

BASERUNNING:

Hatcher has excellent speed -- and good instincts -- on the base paths. A gambler, he frequently attempts to take an extra base on a teammate's hit. In addition, he is adept at pushing a bunt down the first base side and using his speed to beat it out. Hatcher, who occasionally will be caught napping and get picked off, has averaged 35 steals per year during the last five seasons. Hatcher grounded into a double play every 126 at-bats; he was the league's fourth-toughest player to double-up. He had 29 infield hits last year.

FIELDING:

When injuries reduced Davis' mobility and forced him to play primarily left field, Hatcher moved to center. He filled in admirably and led the league with a .997 fielding percentage. Hatcher has excellent speed and covers a lot of ground. His arm is average, though he had a key assist in the NL Championships Series against the Pirates. He is adept at charging singles and making quick pick-ups. He seems more comfortable charging than he does drifting back for balls.

OVERALL:

Hatcher, provided Davis is healthy, will probably begin the year as the Reds' regular left fielder. He also figures to see action in center. Hatcher isn't a superstar, but he does a lot of things well. Plus, he is an excellent influence in the clubhouse. His acquisition, for a pair of unspectacular minor leaguers, ranks as one of the shrewdest moves the Reds made last year.

BILLY HATCHER

Position: LF/CF
Bats: R **Throws:** R
Ht: 5' 9" **Wt:** 175

Opening Day Age: 30
Born: 10/4/60 in Williams, AZ
ML Seasons: 7

Overall Statistics

	G	AB	R	H	D	T	HR	RBI	SB	BB	SO	AVG
1990	139	504	68	139	28	5	5	25	30	33	42	.276
Career	748	2670	382	708	127	20	35	237	181	173	294	.265

Where He Hits the Ball

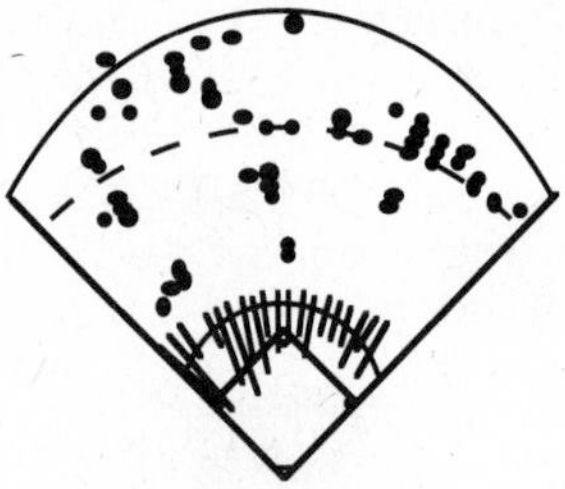

Vs. LHP

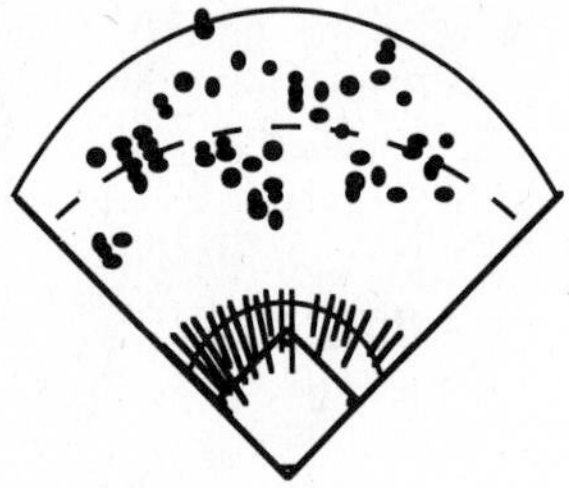

Vs. RHP

1990 Situational Stats

	AB	H	HR	RBI	AVG		AB	H	HR	RBI	AVG
Home	246	65	2	11	.264	LHP	207	51	1	8	.246
Road	258	74	3	14	.287	RHP	297	88	4	17	.296
Day	123	28	3	8	.228	Sc Pos	106	21	0	18	.198
Night	381	111	2	17	.291	Clutch	76	17	0	1	.224

1990 Rankings (National League)

- 4th lowest batting average with runners in scoring position (.198)
- 6th in hit by pitch (6)
- 7th in steals of third (7) and lowest slugging percentage vs. left-handed pitchers (.319)
- Led the Reds in stolen bases (30) and bunts in play (19)
- Led NL left fielders in hit by pitch (6) and lowest perdcentage of swings that missed (12.3%)

PITCHING:

Danny Jackson spent a large part of the 1990 season visiting doctors. He went on the disabled list three times for a total of 54 days. It was the second straight frustrating season for Jackson, who in 1989 (6-11, 5.60) spent nearly half the season on the DL. He's only 12-17 over the last two seasons after going 23-8 in 1988.

In 1989, Jackson had shoulder, toe and wrist injuries. In 1990, he was sidelined for about three weeks after a liner struck his left forearm. When he returned to action on May 20, he allowed two earned runs or less in 10 of his next 11 starts. Then his shoulder problems resurfaced. Twice.

Jackson, who gets so low on his follow-through that his left knee is usually filthy from hitting the ground, recovered late in the season and showed flashes of his old self. He allowed just three hits in eight innings against the Padres on September 28, and was a 6-3 winner against the Pirates in the NL Championship Series.

When healthy, Jackson throws one of the league's best sliders. His fastball has good movement but is just a little above average, and his hard slider, his money pitch, breaks at the last instant and is deceptive. When Jackson can't get his slider over the plate, he becomes a very hittable pitcher. Opponents hit .266 against him last year and socked 11 homers in 117.1 innings. That's an average of one homer every 10.7 innings. Before last year, he had allowed just one homer every 18.5 innings.

HOLDING RUNNERS, FIELDING, HITTING:

Jackson has one of the better pickoff moves on the Reds' staff. As a fielder, he is better than adequate. He's always on his toes and very alert. At the plate, Jackson batted .054 last year with 21 strikeouts in 34 at-bats. That was a sharp decline from his .167 career average before the season.

OVERALL:

At 29, Jackson should be in the prime of his career. But consecutive injury-plagued seasons have left lingering questions. When healthy, Jackson is one of the league's most respected lefthanders. The Chicago Cubs, who signed Jackson in November, are confident that they'll get what they bargained for, despite his recent medical history.

DANNY JACKSON

Position: SP
Bats: R **Throws:** L
Ht: 6' 0" **Wt:** 205

Opening Day Age: 29
Born: 1/5/62 in San Antonio, TX
ML Seasons: 8

Overall Statistics

	W	L	ERA	G	GS	Sv	IP	H	R	BB	SO	HR
1990	6	6	3.61	22	21	0	117.1	119	54	40	76	11
Career	72	74	3.66	196	183	1	1206.1	1162	563	473	737	70

How Often He Throws Strikes

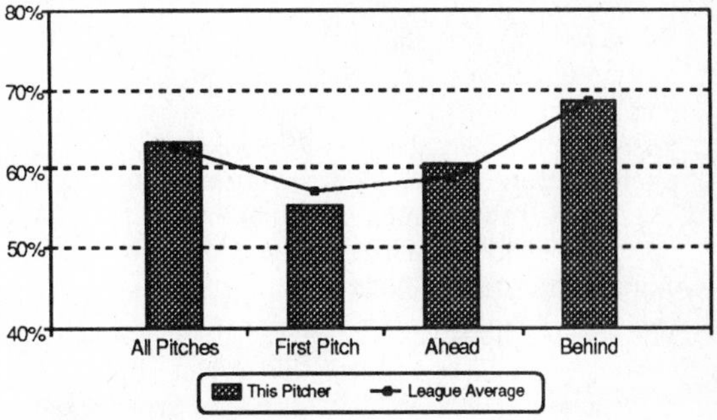

1990 Situational Stats

	W	L	ERA	Sv	IP		AB	H	HR	RBI	AVG
Home	2	3	3.83	0	54.0	LHB	79	19	2	5	.241
Road	4	3	3.41	0	63.1	RHB	369	100	9	44	.271
Day	1	2	2.25	0	44.0	Sc Pos	112	28	1	31	.250
Night	5	4	4.42	0	73.1	Clutch	35	10	2	5	.286

1990 Rankings (National League)

- 8th in highest batting average allowed vs. right-handed batters (.271)

BARRY LARKIN

Position: SS
Bats: R **Throws:** R
Ht: 6' 0" **Wt:** 185

Opening Day Age: 26
Born: 4/28/64 in Cincinnati, OH
ML Seasons: 5

HITTING:

In 1989, a freak injury to his right elbow suffered during the skills competition as part of the All-Star game festivities put Barry Larkin on the shelf for almost the entire second half of the season. Larkin ended up batting .342, but played only 97 games.

Last year, Larkin wasn't stopped by an injury, or by National League pitchers. He solidified his reputation as one of the game's premier shortstops as he hit .301 and had career-highs in hits (185), RBIs (67), triples (six) and at-bats (614). Larkin, who hit .311 with runners in scoring position, was a model of consistency. He had four hitting streaks of 10 games or longer and he went hitless in more than two straight games only twice. Amazingly, he has gone hitless more than two consecutive games only three times in three years.

Larkin hits to all fields and is difficult to defense. When he is in a rare slump, he is trying to pull the ball. More often, he regularly slices balls into the gaps. He displays great discipline at the plate -- he struck out just 49 times (and also had 49 walks) -- and makes pitchers throw strikes. A terrific fastball hitter, Larkin likes the ball away from him and high. When a pitcher got ahead in the count, Larkin had a tendency to chase extra-high fastballs and breaking balls in the dirt.

With Larkin, however, it's not easy to get ahead in the count. He fanned once every 13.9 at-bats, making him the league's fifth most-difficult player to strike out.

BASERUNNING:

An excellent baserunner, Larkin stole 30 bases in 35 attempts last year. He has an outstanding career success rate of 83 percent. Despite his speed, Larking did ground into 14 double plays, the league's seventh-highest total.

FIELDING:

You can make a case for calling Larkin the best-fielding shortstop in baseball. A great athlete, he can field balls on the run, whirl and make stunningly accurate throws. His arm isn't overpowering, but it is accurate. On balls hit in the hole, Larkin has become adept at using the Astroturf to throw a one-hop strike, la Dave Concepcion, to first base. He is also superb at charging slow-hit balls and making on-target throws on the run.

OVERALL:

He can run, hit and field with the best of them. He has even mastered Ozzie Smith's famous flip. Acrobatic Barry Larkin is an MVP in the making.

Overall Statistics

	G	AB	R	H	D	T	HR	RBI	SB	BB	SO	AVG
1990	158	614	85	185	25	6	7	67	30	49	49	.301
Career	572	2125	314	622	91	20	38	221	109	155	169	.293

Where He Hits the Ball

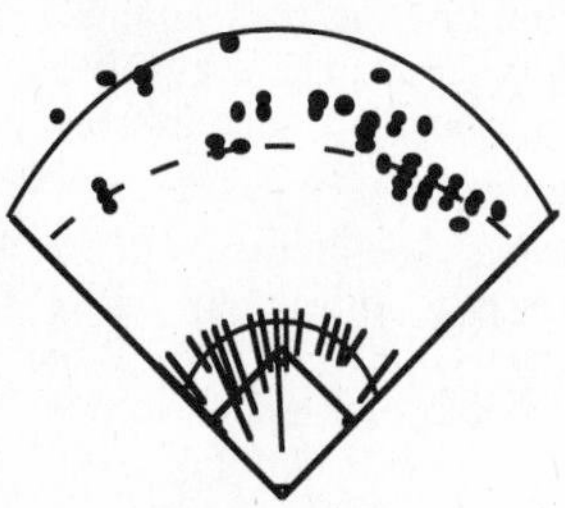

Vs. LHP

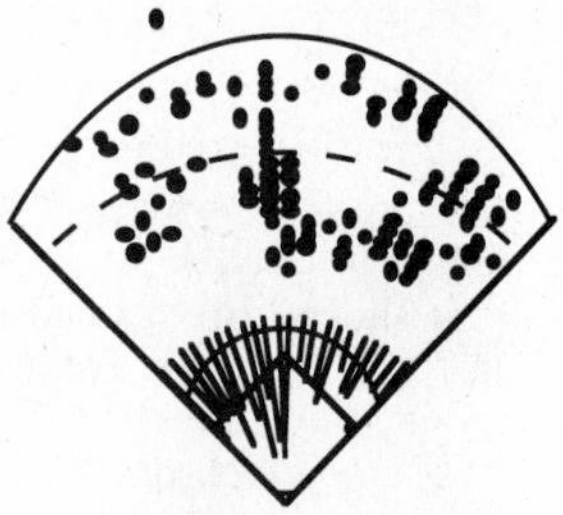

Vs. RHP

1990 Situational Stats

	AB	H	HR	RBI	AVG		AB	H	HR	RBI	AVG
Home	286	78	4	26	.273	LHP	203	54	4	21	.266
Road	328	107	3	41	.326	RHP	411	131	3	46	.319
Day	164	48	0	18	.293	Sc Pos	161	50	1	59	.311
Night	450	137	7	49	.304	Clutch	94	29	1	15	.309

1990 Rankings (National League)

- 2nd in singles (147) and hit by pitch (7)
- 3rd in batting average on the road (.326)
- 4th in hits (185) and steals of third (10)
- 5th in stolen base percentage (85.7%)
- Led the Reds in batting average (.301), at-bats (614), hits, singles, stolen bases (30), hit by pitch, times on base (241), GDPs (14), plate appearances (681), games (158), on-base average (.358) and steals of third
- Led NL shortstops in batting average, at-bats, hits, singles, total bases (243), RBIs (67), hit by pitch, times on base, on-base average, stolen base percentage and steals of third

PITCHING:

Tim Layana developed into a valuable, though unsung, middle reliever last year and is a pitcher who definitely fits into the Reds' future plans. Drafted from the Yankees in December 1989, Layana made the jump from Class AA to the big leagues. As a Rule 5 free agent, the Reds had to keep him on their roster for the entire season or they would have had to offer him back to the Yankees. But Layana made a quick impression, making such thoughts unnecessary. He pitched a scoreless inning on opening night, then pitched two scoreless innings the next night and defeated Houston for his first big-league win. As the season progressed, he continued to contribute, compiling a 5-3 record and 3.49 ERA in 55 appearances, all in relief.

Layana depends mostly on his knuckle-curve, a rare pitch made famous in the seventies by Burt Hooton, the former Dodger. Layana's knuckle-curve drops sharply and confuses hitters. He has an average fastball, and his location could use some improving. Layana spent four seasons with the Yankees' organization, the first three as a starter. He was switched to the bullpen in 1989 and enjoyed great success at Albany (7-4, 1.73), where he struck out 48, walked 15 and allowed just 53 hits in 67.2 innings. Layana's strikeout/walk ratio wasn't as impressive with the Reds: he struck out 53 while walking 44 in 80 IP.

Used primarily as a set-up man last year, Layana improved as the season progressed. He's effective when not overworked. However, he wasn't at his best when he entered the game in a jam. He allowed 10 of 25 inherited runners to score -- not exactly comparable to, say, Randy Myers, who permitted just three of 32 inherited runners to cross home plate.

HOLDING RUNNERS, FIELDING, HITTING:

Layana's pickoff move is barely adequate. In the field he made the routine play but didn't show any outstanding ability. His hitting is a question. Layana probably wishes the NL offered the DH; he was 0-for-5 last season, striking out twice.

OVERALL:

Layana made strides last season but still demonstrated his inexperience, as evidenced by his four balks. But when you consider that Layana had struggled mightily in the minors in 1988 and 1989, you realize just how much progress he has made. Layana has a good chance to be a middle or long-reliever with Cincinnati again this season.

TIM LAYANA

Position: RP
Bats: R **Throws:** R
Ht: 6' 2" **Wt:** 195

Opening Day Age: 27
Born: 3/2/64 in Inglewood, CA
ML Seasons: 1

Overall Statistics

	W	L	ERA	G	GS	Sv	IP	H	R	BB	SO	HR
1990	5	3	3.49	55	0	2	80.0	71	33	44	53	7
Career	5	3	3.49	55	0	2	80.0	71	33	44	53	7

How Often He Throws Strikes

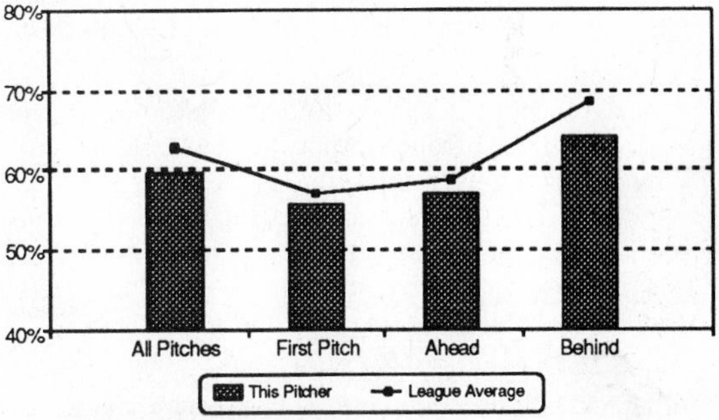

1990 Situational Stats

	W	L	ERA	Sv	IP		AB	H	HR	RBI	AVG
Home	4	2	3.77	1	45.1	LHB	133	34	3	17	.256
Road	1	1	3.12	1	34.2	RHB	158	37	4	17	.234
Day	0	1	3.26	1	19.1	Sc Pos	87	19	3	28	.218
Night	5	2	3.56	1	60.2	Clutch	54	16	0	3	.296

1990 Rankings (National League)

- 3rd in worst first batter efficiency (.356)
- 5th most GDPs induced per GDP situation (17.8%)
- 6th in balks (4)
- Led the Reds in most GDPs induced per GDP situation

PITCHING:

Rick Mahler pitched in 38 or more games for six straight seasons -- until 1990. At 37 years of age, Mahler still feels he can pitch regularly in a starting rotation. The Reds, however, only seem to have room for a middle or long reliever.

Mahler, who had a winning record (7-6) for the first time since 1985, had physical problems at the beginning of last season, straining a quadriceps muscle in his left thigh on May 1 against the Phillies. Eventually, he went on the disabled list for the first time in his career. When he returned in early June, he had mixed success as a starter. All told, he allowed 16 homers in 134.2 innings, but was a solid contributor out of the bullpen. In five straight relief appearances from July 4 to August 2, Mahler pitched 10.2 shutout innings, allowing just four hits in that span. In late August, when a rash of injuries plagued Reds starters, Mahler briefly went into the rotation and won three straight games.

The righthander throws a fastball, slider and curve. His fastball is far from overpowering, which explains why he has allowed more hits (1,999) than innings pitched (1,885.1) in his career. But because he has hitters looking for his other pitches, his fastball is sneaky-fast. Mahler is excellent at changing speeds and hitting spots.

Mahler's control has improved with age. He allowed only 2.6 walks per nine innings last season. In the last three seasons, he has yielded just 1.97 walks per nine innings.

HOLDING RUNNERS, FIELDING, HITTING:

Mahler has an above-average pickoff move, one that he has perfected during his 12 seasons. He is rated as an adequate fielder, though his foot speed is s-l-o-o-o-o-w. At the plate, he hit only .114 last year, but, remarkably, struck out just four times in 35 at-bats. In his career, he has a .180 average, which is pretty good for a pitcher.

OVERALL:

Mahler, who became a free agent after the World Series, must have pondered his fate a little last season. For years he got all the work he wanted, but he was pitching for the usually miserable Braves. Finally with a World Champion, he had to settle for a minor part in the success. Despite being with the Reds, Mahler isn't happy in his role as a long reliever. He wants to be a starter, a role he has filled since 1981 in Atlanta. He may get his wish, but not with the Reds.

RICK MAHLER

Position: RP/SP
Bats: R **Throws:** R
Ht: 6' 1" **Wt:** 202

Opening Day Age: 37
Born: 8/5/53 in Austin, TX
ML Seasons: 12

Overall Statistics

	W	L	ERA	G	GS	Sv	IP	H	R	BB	SO	HR
1990	7	6	4.28	35	16	4	134.2	134	67	39	68	16
Career	94	107	3.98	369	263	6	1885.1	1999	935	578	925	161

How Often He Throws Strikes

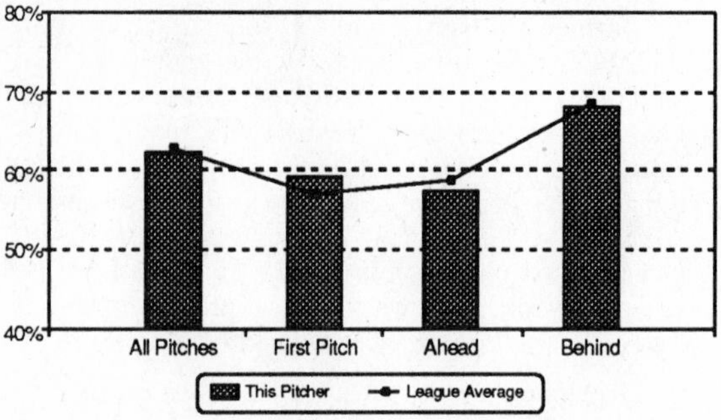

1990 Situational Stats

	W	L	ERA	Sv	IP		AB	H	HR	RBI	AVG
Home	3	1	4.45	1	56.2	LHB	295	82	9	34	.278
Road	4	5	4.15	3	78.0	RHB	219	52	7	25	.237
Day	2	1	3.46	1	39.0	Sc Pos	111	30	4	47	.270
Night	5	5	4.61	3	95.2	Clutch	29	7	2	7	.241

1990 Rankings (National League)

➞ Did not rank near the top or bottom in any category

HITTING:

Hal Morris blossomed into one of the Reds' most pleasant surprises last year. He seemed ticketed for platoon duty in left field until the Reds made a deal for Billy Hatcher on the eve of the season opener. Morris got just 27 at-bats in the season's first two months and was sent to AAA Nashville to sharpen his batting stroke. At Nashville, he hit .344 in 16 games and returned to the Reds on June 18. Morris platooned at first base with Todd Benzinger and, by the middle of July, became the regular.

A spray hitter in the Dave Magadan mold, Morris would have contended for the batting title had he received enough at-bats last year. He combines both aggressiveness and discipline at the plate as he struck out just 32 times in 309 at-bats. Teams try to throw Morris off speed stuff, because he **loves** hitting the fastball. He occasionally turns on an inside pitch, with power, to right field. As he gains experience, Morris should learn to pull more pitches and hit with more power. He is capable of hitting 15-20 homers.

Morris has an unusual approach to hitting. As a pitch is being delivered, he moves both feet, making sort of a stutter-step toward the pitcher. Most hitters move just the front foot. Morris hit .340 last year. Maybe he's started a new trend.

BASERUNNING:

Morris has average speed but seems to pick the right times to attempt to a stolen base. He stole nine bases in 12 tries last year. In his minor league career, he never stole more than eight bases. Last year, Morris grounded into 12 double plays, making him one of the league's easiest players to double up.

FIELDING:

Morris is an average fielder at first base. He is adequate at digging throws out of the dirt while his arm and range are nothing spectacular. He has good hands -- balls that he reaches, he usually gloves. Morris committed just three errors in 642 chances at first base last year. He is an average left fielder.

OVERALL:

Morris established himself as an everyday player last year and has the ability to challenge for the batting crown. He will probably he rested against certain lefthanders but is likely to accumulate close to 500 at-bats. For what it's worth, Morris is one of three Reds' infielders (Barry Larkin and Chris Sabo are the others) who played at the University of Michigan.

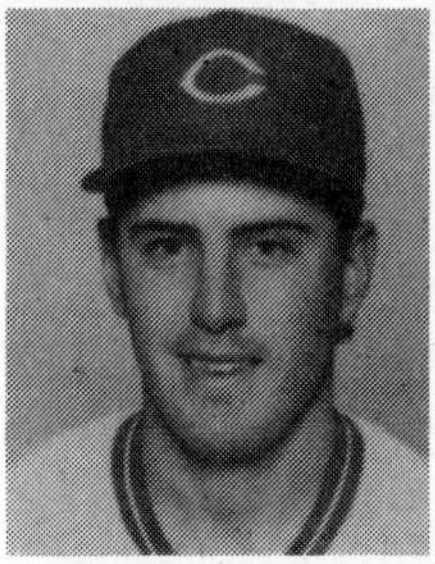

HAL MORRIS

Position: 1B
Bats: L **Throws:** L
Ht: 6' 4" **Wt:** 200

Opening Day Age: 26
Born: 4/9/65 in Fort Rucker, AL
ML Seasons: 3

Overall Statistics

	G	AB	R	H	D	T	HR	RBI	SB	BB	SO	AVG
1990	107	309	50	105	22	3	7	36	9	21	32	.340
Career	137	347	53	112	22	3	7	40	9	22	45	.323

Where He Hits the Ball

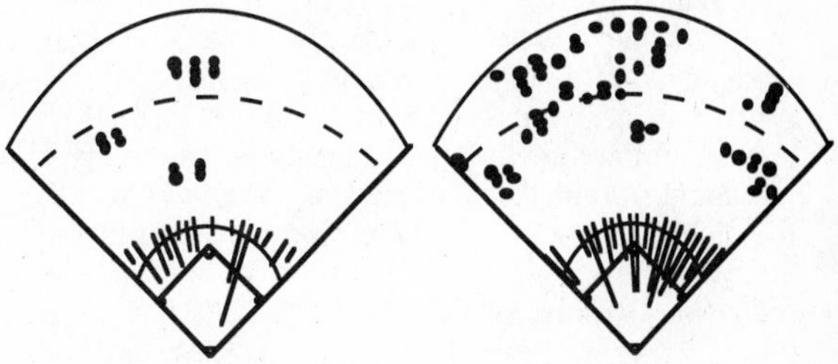

Vs. LHP　　Vs. RHP

1990 Situational Stats

	AB	H	HR	RBI	AVG		AB	H	HR	RBI	AVG
Home	148	50	3	20	.338	LHP	76	17	0	5	.224
Road	161	55	4	16	.342	RHP	233	88	7	31	.378
Day	103	34	3	12	.330	Sc Pos	83	28	1	27	.337
Night	206	71	4	24	.345	Clutch	53	13	0	2	.245

1990 Rankings (National League)

- 1st in highest batting average on a 3-2 count (.526)
- 8th in highest batting average with 2 strikes (.255)
- Led the Reds in batting average on a 3-2 count and batting average with 2 strikes
- Led NL first basemen in batting average on a 3-2 count

STOPPER

RANDY MYERS

Position: RP
Bats: L **Throws:** L
Ht: 6' 1" **Wt:** 208

Opening Day Age: 28
Born: 9/19/62 in Vancouver, WA
ML Seasons: 6

PITCHING:

In a fascinating swap of relief aces, the Mets' Randy Myers came to the Reds a year ago in exchange for John Franco. It'll take a few years to evaluate the trade, which thus far looks pretty even. In 1990, Franco had 33 saves, Myers 31. Franco's save percentage was 85%, Myers' 84%. Give Franco a slight advantage, but the Reds are thrilled with Myers, who teamed with Rob Dibble to form the most feared lefty/righty bullpen combo in the majors. And Myers, not Franco, is wearing the championship ring.

Myers, one of the few pitchers in baseball who can prevent Dibble from wresting away the closer's role, continued his amazing strikeout pace last year. He fanned 10.2 batters per nine innings. In his major league career, he has struck out 362 in 326.2 innings, also 10 per nine innings.

Like Dibble, Myers is overpowering. Unlike Dibble, Myers' slider is below average. It hangs and has a tendency to get him in trouble. Thus he doesn't throw it that much. Myers throws his 90+ MPH fastball 75 percent of the time; he uses the slider -- which gives lefthanders problems when he keeps the ball away -- the other 25 percent. Opponents hit just .193 off him last year. He allowed just one run in 15 appearances (covering 19 innings) from April 28 to June 3, recording eight saves in that span. Shortly thereafter, he went on another brilliant streak, yielding just one run over his next 14 games, a span of 20.1 innings. He had two wins and nine saves during that streak. He wasn't as dominating the rest of the year, but he was effective. Throughout the year he displayed fine control, yielding just 30 unintentional walks in 86.2 innings.

HOLDING RUNNERS, FIELDING, HITTING:

Myers has a strong pickoff move, with good deception. Because of the energy he uses while heaving his fastballs, Myers isn't always in a great fielding position after he delivers a pitch. He is rated as an average fielder. As a hitter, Myers rarely gets a chance to show his ability. He was 1-for-4 last season and is a .200 (4-for-20) career hitter.

OVERALL:

Myers, Dibble and Charlton give the Reds arguably the hardest-throwing bullpen in major league history. Having Dibble as a set-up man will save Myers some wear and tear. There's no reason to believe that he won't continue to be one of the game's most dominating closers.

Overall Statistics

	W	L	ERA	G	GS	Sv	IP	H	R	BB	SO	HR
1990	4	6	2.08	66	0	31	86.2	59	24	38	98	6
Career	21	19	2.56	251	0	87	326.2	238	103	135	362	22

How Often He Throws Strikes

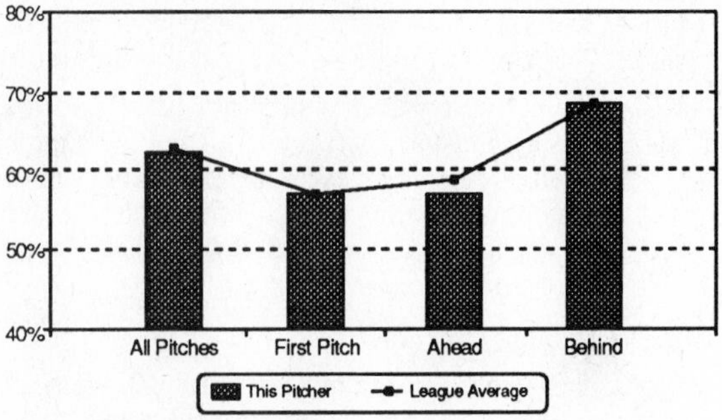

1990 Situational Stats

	W	L	ERA	Sv	IP		AB	H	HR	RBI	AVG
Home	2	2	0.62	15	43.1	LHB	72	13	2	5	.181
Road	2	4	3.53	16	43.1	RHB	234	46	4	21	.197
Day	0	2	2.59	7	24.1	Sc Pos	84	12	2	22	.143
Night	4	4	1.88	24	62.1	Clutch	210	38	5	20	.181

1990 Rankings (National League)

- 1st in lowest percentage of inherited runners scored (9.4%)
- 2nd in saves (31), games finished (59) and save opportunities (37)
- 3rd in save percentage (83.8%)
- 5th in blown saves (6)
- Led the Reds in saves, games finished, save opportunities, save percentage, blown saves and lowest percentage of inherited runners scored

PAUL O'NEILL

Position: RF
Bats: L **Throws:** L
Ht: 6' 4" **Wt:** 210

Opening Day Age: 28
Born: 2/25/63 in Columbus, OH
ML Seasons: 6

Overall Statistics

	G	AB	R	H	D	T	HR	RBI	SB	BB	SO	AVG
1990	145	503	59	136	28	0	16	78	13	53	103	.270
Career	499	1590	191	421	92	6	54	254	43	156	264	.265

Where He Hits the Ball

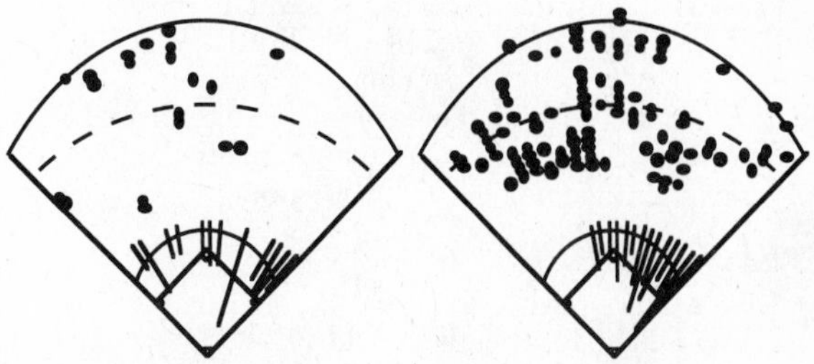

Vs. LHP **Vs. RHP**

1990 Situational Stats

	AB	H	HR	RBI	AVG		AB	H	HR	RBI	AVG
Home	241	70	10	36	.290	LHP	143	37	3	25	.259
Road	262	66	6	42	.252	RHP	360	99	13	53	.275
Day	148	36	5	23	.243	Sc Pos	144	42	6	64	.292
Night	355	100	11	55	.282	Clutch	86	23	2	9	.267

1990 Rankings (National League)

- 2nd worst stolen base percentage (54.2%)
- 5th worst batting average with an 0-2 count (.067)
- Led the Reds in caught stealing (11), strikeouts (103), slugging percentage vs. right-handed pitchers (.428) and batting average at home (.290)
- Led NL right fielders in caught stealing and fielding percentage (.993)

HITTING:

"Consistent" is the word that best describes Paul O'Neill. He hit .270 with 16 homers and 78 RBIs last year. That was strikingly similar to his 1989 (.276-15-74) and 1988 (.252-16-73) numbers. Consistency also marked the early part of O'Neill's 1990 season. He hit .283 in April, .281 in May and .287 in June. O'Neill started 128 games in right field, where he was platooned with Glenn Braggs during the last few weeks of the season.

For the second straight year, even O'Neill's slumps were consistent. In 1989, he had 12 homers and 56 RBI at the All Star break, but produced just three homers and 18 RBIs during an injury-shortened second half, in which he had 121 at-bats. Last year O'Neill was off to another hot start, with 11 homers and 46 RBI at the break. Perhaps worn down by the season's long grind, he hit only .252 with five homers and 32 RBIs in the second half.

O'Neill is a great fastball hitter. He pulls the ball more frequently than he did when he broke into the majors, and has good power to right; he can also hit the longball to left-center and center. O'Neill is vulnerable to off speed pitches that are low and away. His strikeouts jumped to 103 last season, by far his highest total in the majors. Obviously, not every pitcher treated him as well as Don Robinson, who O'Neill pounded for 5 of his 16 home runs.

BASERUNNING:

O'Neill has slightly above-average speed and is not an exceptional base stealer. Last year, he stole 13 bases, a respectable figure. He also was caught stealing 11 times, a not-too-respectable figure. O'Neill's stolen-base percentage was 54 percent last year, a sharp decline from his 80 percent rate in 1989.

FIELDING:

Teams don't run that often on O'Neill's strong, accurate arm. Still, he managed 12 assists last year. O'Neill, who will forever be remembered for drop-kicking the ball back into the infield (and saving a run) two years ago in Philadelphia, has slightly above-average range, but has improved since he first entered the league. He ranked second in the league with a .993 fielding percentage last year.

OVERALL:

If he can ever put together a strong second half, O'Neill has the potential to be a star, especially in the Reds' lineup. Batting primarily fifth behind a group of high-powered offensive players, O'Neill could be a 100-RBI man. Because of his problems against lefties, however, O'Neill may be platooned in right with Braggs.

JOE OLIVER

Position: C
Bats: R **Throws:** R
Ht: 6' 3" **Wt:** 215

Opening Day Age: 25
Born: 7/24/65 in Memphis, TN
ML Seasons: 2

HITTING:

Joe Oliver established himself as an everyday catcher in 1990. Despite batting mostly out of the number-eight spot in the order, Oliver knocked in 52 runs during his first full season in the majors. He batted .274 with runners in scoring position. Oliver had problems hitting both the low-and-away breaking ball and inside fastballs. Primarily a pull hitter, he has decent power if he gets a fastball out over the plate. He likes the ball down. Oliver is a below-average breaking ball hitter, though he is improving.

Oliver became a regular in August, 1989. During his brief '89 stint, he had a poor strikeout (28) to walk (six) ratio. Last year, he made strides in that area, fanning 75 times and drawing 37 walks.

The well-constructed, 6-foot-3, 215-pounder started 63 of the team's 79 games in the first half of the season when he hit .242 with 29 RBIs. In the second half, Oliver slumped to .214 with 23 RBIs as he and Jeff Reed divided the catching duties evenly. Oliver must learn how to hit the breaking pitch to the opposite field. He has good extra-base potential, and fifteen homers are not out of the question.

BASERUNNING:

Oliver is a typical catcher on the base paths: slow. He's no threat to steal, though he did swipe one when no one was looking last year. It was his first steal since 1986, when he played for AA Vermont where sap runs out of maple trees faster than Oliver goes from first to second. He is extremely conservative (a wise choice) on the bases.

FIELDING:

Oliver is an above-average catcher with a quick release and strong arm. He is adequate at blocking balls in the dirt. When Oliver was catching, only 59.8% (64 of 107) of base-stealers were successful, a league leading figure. His .992 fielding percentage ranked number one among starting National League catches. That accomplishment, however, is diminished somewhat when you consider that he committed a whopping 16 passed balls.

OVERALL:

Oliver, a take-charge type, calls a good game and has a solid rapport with his pitching staff. He had some decent hitting stats in the minors, and should hit better than .231 in the future. He has power potential and a good arm. The Reds have been very happy with his work thus far; Oliver is a very valuable commodity.

Overall Statistics

	G	AB	R	H	D	T	HR	RBI	SB	BB	SO	AVG
1990	121	364	34	84	23	0	8	52	1	37	75	.231
Career	170	515	47	125	31	0	11	75	1	43	103	.243

Where He Hits the Ball

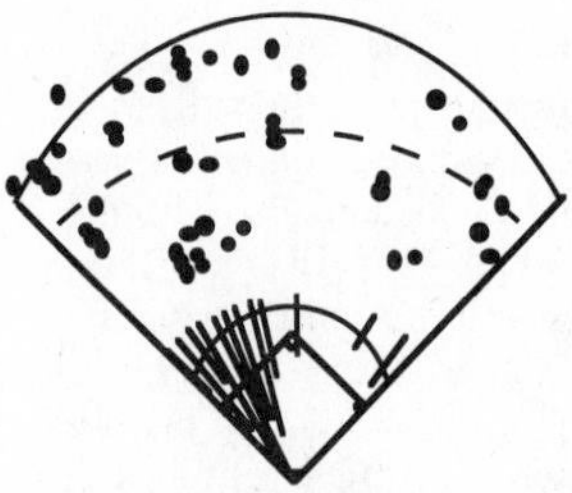

Vs. LHP

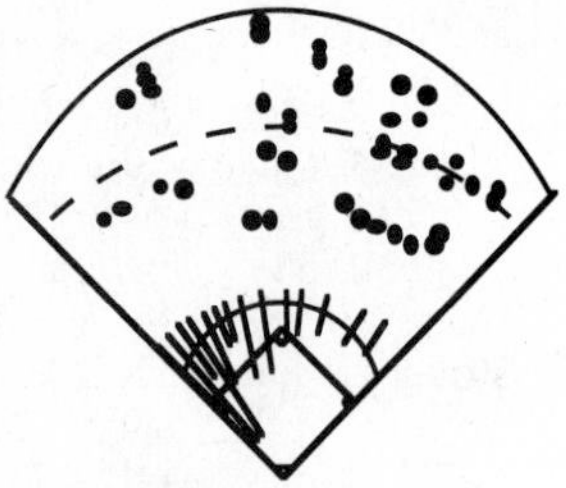

Vs. RHP

1990 Situational Stats

	AB	H	HR	RBI	AVG		AB	H	HR	RBI	AVG
Home	172	38	3	25	.221	LHP	180	51	5	28	.283
Road	192	46	5	27	.240	RHP	184	33	3	24	.179
Day	85	28	3	16	.329	Sc Pos	106	29	3	45	.274
Night	279	56	5	36	.201	Clutch	50	11	2	7	.220

1990 Rankings (National League)

- 3rd in lowest batting average with 2 strikes (.131)
- 9th in intentional walks (15)
- Led the Reds in intentional walks
- Led NL catchers in intentional walks, highest percentage of runners caught stealing (40.2%), batting average on a 3-1 count (.444) and fielding percentage (.992)

CY YOUNG STUFF

PITCHING:

Jose Rijo began last year with a sub-.500 career record and an ERA near 4.00. He ended the season as the staff ace and the World Series MVP. Rijo won a career-high 14 games -- he now has a 53-52 career mark -- and had an ERA below 3.00 (at 2.70) for the third straight season.

Rijo has been frequently injured in his career, and last year was no exception, as an ailing right shoulder sidelined him from June 29 until July 21. Rijo lacked consistency in his next few starts, then put together a spectacular finish. In his nine starts from Aug. 22 to Sept. 30, Rijo went 6-2 and posted a 1.27 ERA in 71 innings. In the World Series, he was 2-0 with a 0.59 ERA. During the regular season, Rijo allowed just 151 hits in 197 innings and held opponents to a .212 average; that was second in the NL to the Mets' Sid Fernandez (.200). In addition, Rijo averaged 6.9 strikeouts per nine innings, the league's sixth-best figure among starting pitchers.

Rijo, who likes to use the inside part of the plate, has a lively fastball which was clocked at 97 MPH during the World Series. He also throws a quality slider and forkball. His fastball, slider and change-up are outstanding when he gets them over the plate, and are the keys to his success. Rijo is adept at disguising his change-up, throwing it with the same motion as his fastball, making the pitch hard to decipher. To beat Rijo, you have to score early. He generally gets stronger as the game progresses.

HOLDING RUNNERS, FIELDING, HITTING:

Rijo had difficulty holding runners last year with 83% of opposition base stealers enjoying success. He has quick feet in the field and is skilled at stabbing balls hit up the middle. At the plate, Rijo likes to do the unusual. It's not rare for him to attempt to bunt for a base hit with two strikes on him. Rijo had 10 hits in 1990, batting .188, a good performance for a pitcher; he is a career .146 hitter.

OVERALL:

Rijo credits his father-in-law, Hall of Famer Juan Marichal, with teaching him how to get mentally prepared for each start and how to shake off setbacks during games. Earlier in his career, Rijo was known to allow a bad break to affect his concentration. Now, Rijo is one of the National League's most dependable pitchers, just like his father-in-law used to be.

JOSE RIJO

Position: SP
Bats: R **Throws:** R
Ht: 6' 2" **Wt:** 200

Opening Day Age: 25
Born: 5/13/65 in San Cristobal, Dominican Republic
ML Seasons: 7

Overall Statistics

	W	L	ERA	G	GS	Sv	IP	H	R	BB	SO	HR
1990	14	8	2.70	29	29	0	197.0	151	65	78	152	10
Career	53	52	3.60	193	121	3	872.0	781	400	399	753	68

How Often He Throws Strikes

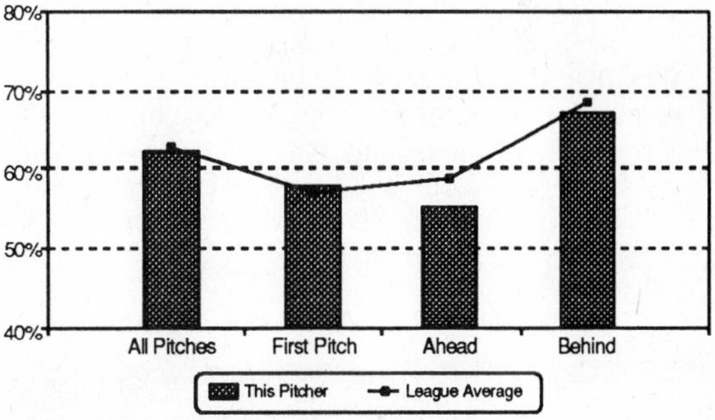

1990 Situational Stats

	W	L	ERA	Sv	IP		AB	H	HR	RBI	AVG
Home	8	4	2.24	0	108.1	LHB	409	89	7	32	.218
Road	6	4	3.25	0	88.2	RHB	303	62	3	21	.205
Day	4	1	2.21	0	40.2	Sc Pos	161	38	1	39	.236
Night	10	7	2.82	0	156.1	Clutch	49	13	0	3	.265

1990 Rankings (National League)

- 1st in balks (5) and lowest slugging percentage allowed (.313)
- 2nd in lowest batting average allowed (.212)
- 3rd in ERA at home (2.24)
- 4th in least HRs allowed per 9 innings (.46)
- 5th in ERA (2.70), complete games (7), walks allowed (78) and highest stolen base percentage allowed (82.6%)
- Led the Reds in ERA, complete games, walks allowed, strikeouts (152), balks, winning percentage (.636), strikeout/walk ratio (1.9), least HRs allowed per 9 innings and most strikeouts per 9 innings (6.9)

CHRIS SABO

Position: 3B
Bats: R **Throws:** R
Ht: 6' 0" **Wt:** 185

Opening Day Age: 29
Born: 1/19/62 in Detroit, MI
ML Seasons: 3

Overall Statistics

	G	AB	R	H	D	T	HR	RBI	SB	BB	SO	AVG
1990	148	567	95	153	38	2	25	71	25	61	58	.270
Career	367	1409	209	378	99	5	42	144	85	115	143	.268

Where He Hits the Ball

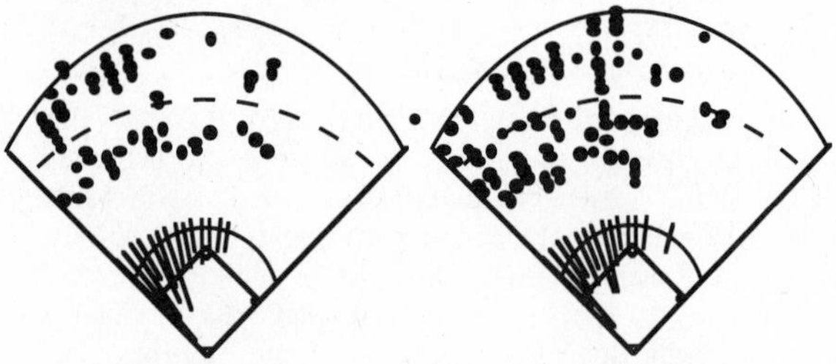

Vs. LHP Vs. RHP

1990 Situational Stats

	AB	H	HR	RBI	AVG		AB	H	HR	RBI	AVG
Home	275	77	15	45	.280	LHP	214	70	14	33	.327
Road	292	76	10	26	.260	RHP	353	83	11	38	.235
Day	138	32	7	21	.232	Sc Pos	136	33	5	47	.243
Night	429	121	18	50	.282	Clutch	89	22	5	11	.247

1990 Rankings (National League)

- 3rd in doubles (38) and lowest batting average vs. right-handed pitchers (.235)
- Led the Reds in home runs (25), runs (95), doubles, total bases (270) and walks (61)
- Led NL third basemen in runs, doubles, caught stealing (10), on-base average (.343), batting average vs. left-handed pitchers (.327), batting average on an 0-2 count (.294), slugging percentage vs. left-handed pitchers (.589), on-base average vs. left-handed pitchers (.408), fielding percentage (.966) and steals of third (5)

HITTING:

After a disappointing sophomore year, Chris Sabo came of age last season as he put together some stunning power totals. Sabo, who had hit 17 homers in his previous 842 major league at-bats, slammed 25 homers and 38 doubles last year. The Reds made a change in Sabo's hitting style last year, getting him to take his bat out of a "set" position. Instead, he waved it slightly as the pitcher was delivering, generating more bat speed -- and more power. And, while his home run production soared, Sabo showed plenty of discipline at the plate, striking out just 58 times and drawing 61 walks. The 61 walks surpassed his totals for 1988 and '89 combined.

Sabo, a pull hitter, helped trigger the Reds' fast start last year, hitting .391 with five homers in April. He was voted as the starting third baseman in the All-Star game, a reward for his totals at the break: .299 average, 16 homers and 42 RBIs.

Sabo, who played in 148 games despite knee problems that plagued him throughout the season, is an excellent fastball hitter. He generates most of his power on fastballs that are out over the plate. Low-and-away breaking balls and extra-hard inside fastballs give Sabo problems. Sabo has a tendency to get out in front of a lot of pitches. He hits a lot of long fouls to left.

BASERUNNING:

Fast and aggressive on the base paths, Sabo stole 25 bases in 35 attempts last year. Sabo can sometimes be **too** daring. It's not unusual for him to try to stretch a single into a double, with mixed results.

FIELDING:

Sabo, who was spectacular in the World Series, displayed sure hands, good range and a strong, accurate arm. He had good range to his left, and also excelled at making diving stops behind the third base bag. For the second time in three years, Sabo led the league in fielding percentage. He fielded at a .966 clip last season.

OVERALL:

Which is the real Chris Sabo? Is he the player who took a .312 average into the 1988 All-Star break? Is he the player who struggled mightily during the second half of '88, and for most of '89? Or is he the player who was one of the game's best all-around third baseman last year? The Reds are hoping Sabo improves with age, but will settle for the status quo.

HERM WINNINGHAM

Position: CF
Bats: L **Throws:** R
Ht: 5'11" **Wt:** 175

Opening Day Age: 29
Born: 12/1/61 in Orangeburg, SC
ML Seasons: 7

Overall Statistics

	G	AB	R	H	D	T	HR	RBI	SB	BB	SO	AVG
1990	84	160	20	41	8	5	3	17	6	14	31	.256
Career	665	1485	168	359	55	24	17	129	95	136	324	.242

Where He Hits the Ball

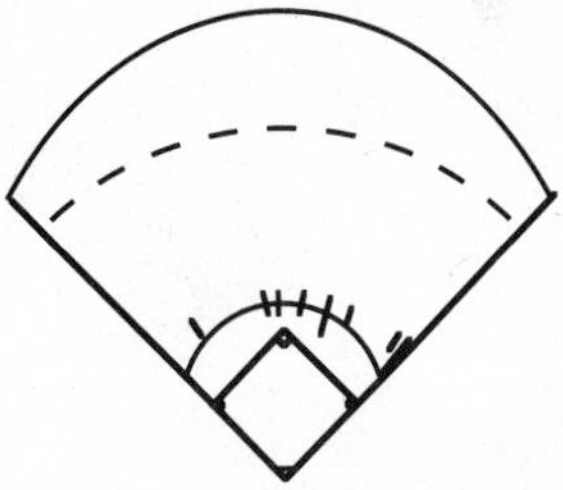

Vs. LHP

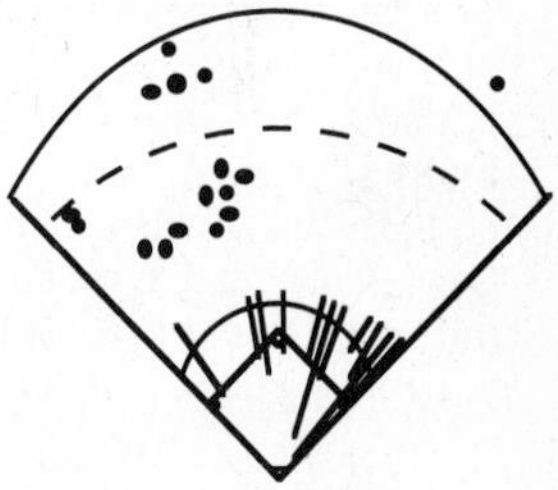

Vs. RHP

1990 Situational Stats

	AB	H	HR	RBI	AVG		AB	H	HR	RBI	AVG
Home	82	16	0	5	.195	LHP	28	4	1	3	.143
Road	78	25	3	12	.321	RHP	132	37	2	14	.280
Day	65	17	1	6	.262	Sc Pos	36	11	0	12	.306
Night	95	24	2	11	.253	Clutch	30	9	1	5	.300

1990 Rankings (National League)

- Did not rank near the top or bottom in any category

HITTING:

Herm Winningham was once a promising prospect in the New York Mets farm system. He hit .354 one season in the minors, and stole 50 bases in another. But Winningham, a former number-one draft pick in three separate drafts, isn't going to reach stardom. His job description is role player, and he's turning out to be a good one. In limited playing time, Winningham hit a career-high .256 last year, highlighted by an NL record-tying performance in St. Louis, when he hit three triples in a game on August 15.

A somewhat wild swinger, Winningham doesn't make enough contact and frequently chases pitches out of the strike zone. He can't help swinging at fastballs and breaking pitches that are at eye level, and because of that, he's never developed into an outstanding hitter. Winningham can usually be retired on inside fastballs. He likes to spray the ball around, though he had a respectable 16 extra-base hits (including five triples) in 160 at-bats last year.

Winningham would probably be more effective if he hit more balls on the ground to take advantage of his excellent speed. He doesn't do that enough, but he's skilled at dragging bunts down the first base side. His eighth-inning bunt single in the World Series keyed the game-winning rally in the title clincher. Winningham scored the winning run as the Reds completed their shocking sweep of the A's.

BASERUNNING:

Winningham, who early in his career said he planned to match Tim Raines' steal totals, has excellent speed and is a good baserunner. Last year, however, he wasn't as aggressive on the bases; he had only six steals in 10 attempts.

FIELDING:

Speed comes in handy when you play center field which is where Winningham made his 31 starts in 1990. Winningham has good range and decent hands. His arm is average, at best. Winningham handled 92 chances last year without making an error.

OVERALL:

Winningham has never fulfilled his promise, but he is a valuable role player. He supplies the Reds with good defense and speed off the bench. He would enhance his worth if he could improve his strikeout-walk ratio, but at 29 it's getting late to expect him to change his style. Winningham is ticketed for duty as a fill-in outfielder once again this year.

TIM BIRTSAS

Position: RP
Bats: L **Throws:** L
Ht: 6' 7" **Wt:** 240

Opening Day Age: 30
Born: 9/5/60 in Pontiac, MI
ML Seasons: 5

Overall Statistics

	W	L	ERA	G	GS	Sv	IP	H	R	BB	SO	HR
1990	1	3	3.86	29	0	0	51.1	69	24	24	41	7
Career	14	14	4.08	138	30	1	328.2	324	168	170	231	37

PITCHING, FIELDING, HITTING & HOLDING RUNNERS:

Tim Birtsas appeared in 29 games (all in relief) last year and, despite an adequate 3.86 ERA, was not very effective, particularly against righthanders. Birtsas **looks** imposing -- he stands 6'-7" and weighs 240 pounds. But his fastball and curve are below average. Opponents hit .326 off him, collecting a whopping 69 hits and slamming seven homers in just 51.1 innings. Righties walloped Birtsas for a .356 average.

Birtsas, who was acquired with Jose Rijo in the deal that sent Dave Parker to Oakland in 1987, hasn't pitched horribly on the big league level, but in five years he's yet to post an ERA below 3.75. Home runs have been his biggest problem -- he allowed 37 in only 328.2 career innings.

Birtsas allows a lot of baserunners, but he isn't very good at holding them to first. He has a slow-developing move, and runners get big jumps off him. He is a below-average fielder. He was 0-for-4 at the plate last year and is a .056 hitter (one for 18, with a homer) in his career.

OVERALL:

Birtsas will have a difficult time earning a spot on the Reds' roster this year. If he does, he can be used as a spot starter or long reliever because his arm is fairly resilient. Birtsas figures to be battling for the final pitching spot on the roster.

CHRIS HAMMOND

Position: SP
Bats: L **Throws:** L
Ht: 6' 1" **Wt:** 190

Opening Day Age: 25
Born: 1/21/66 in Atlanta, GA
ML Seasons: 1

Overall Statistics

	W	L	ERA	G	GS	Sv	IP	H	R	BB	SO	HR
1990	0	2	6.35	3	3	0	11.1	13	9	12	4	2
Career	0	2	6.35	3	3	0	11.1	13	9	12	4	2

PITCHING, FIELDING, HITTING & HOLDING RUNNERS:

Chris Hammond spent most of the 1990 season in the minors and was far from impressive in his three starts with the Reds (0-2, 6.35). But Hammond was spectacular in the American Association (15-1, 2.17) and his future appears bright. In 149 innings at AAA Nashville, Hammond struck out 149, walked 63 and allowed just 118 hits.

Signed as a sixth-round draft choice out of the University of Alabama in 1986, Hammond has moved quickly through the Reds' organization. He's been successful wherever he's pitched; the last three seasons -- one at AA Chattanooga, two at Nashville -- his record is an imposing 42-13.

Hammond has an outstanding change-up that he throws with an extremely deceptive motion. He has a sneaky-fast fastball and his curve and slider are rated as average. Hammond seems to have decent fielding instincts, though he made two errors in just 11.1 innings with Cincinnati; he has a decent pickoff move and a quick delivery to the plate. The jury is still out on Hammond as a hitter. He was 0-for-3, with a strikeout, in his three games with the Reds.

OVERALL:

A great competitor, Hammond could battle Scott Scudder for a spot in the starting rotation. After two outstanding seasons at Nashville, he's got nothing more to prove in the minor leagues. His future is promising.

RON OESTER

Position: 2B
Bats: B **Throws:** R
Ht: 6' 2" **Wt:** 190

Opening Day Age: 34
Born: 5/5/56 in Cincinnati, OH
ML Seasons: 13

Overall Statistics

	G	AB	R	H	D	T	HR	RBI	SB	BB	SO	AVG
1990	64	154	10	46	10	1	0	13	1	10	29	.299
Career	1276	4214	458	1118	190	33	42	344	40	369	681	.265

HITTING, FIELDING, BASERUNNING:

Despite limited playing time, Ron Oester put together a productive season in 1990. The switch-hitter batted .299 -- .300 right-handed and .298 left-handed. He saw most of his action from mid-May to early June, when second baseman Mariano Duncan was injured. Though he appeared in only 64 games, Oester earned his season's salary for his work in that period alone.

Oester hits to the opposite field from both sides of the plate. A line drive hitter, he feasts on fastballs. He can be retired on low breaking balls. Oester, who began playing with Cincinnati in 1978, has below-average speed, and stole only one base in three attempts last year. However, he is a smart, aggressive baserunner who will use his hustle to take an extra base.

A fine fielder, Oester has good hands, a quick release and is excellent at turning the double play. His fielding is his strong point. He can play short (his original position) or third in a pinch, but second base is by far his best position.

OVERALL:

Though he's still a hard-nosed player, Oester's days as a starter are over. The Reds declined to pick up the option on Oester's contract, presumably ending their 13-year association. But the 34-year-old infielder is still a valuable backup, and may find employment elsewhere. If not, the Cincinnati native has his 1990 ring to show for a solid career.

LUIS QUINONES

Position: 3B/2B
Bats: B **Throws:** R
Ht: 5'11" **Wt:** 175

Opening Day Age: 28
Born: 4/28/62 in Ponce, Puerto Rico
ML Seasons: 6

Overall Statistics

	G	AB	R	H	D	T	HR	RBI	SB	BB	SO	AVG
1990	83	145	10	35	7	0	2	17	1	13	29	.241
Career	342	786	87	179	32	8	15	85	8	54	123	.228

HITTING, FIELDING, BASERUNNING:

Switch-hitting Luis Quinones, a super-sub, played all four infield positions last year. He was also the team's emergency catcher, but never had to be used in that role. Quinones, who is Barry Larkin's backup at shortstop, made his biggest contributions as a pinch hitter. He had 13 pinch hits, matching the most for a Reds player since 1983. He hit .471 (8-for-17) with a homer and eight RBIs as a right-handed pinch hitter, including the game-winning RBI that gave the Reds the pennant.

A high fastball hitter, Quinones pulls the ball more frequently from the right side. He's a straightway hitter from the left side. He hit .266 right-handed, .222 left-handed last year. Quinones showed surprising power in 1989, belting 12 homers in only 340 at-bats. Most people considered that a fluke, and Quinones did nothing to dispel the notion last year when he managed only two homers in 145 at-bats. He does have some gap power, however, especially from the right side, and he's a threat to knock one for extra bases.

Quinones has below-average speed and is conservative on the base paths. He has only eight lifetime steals in 15 attempts. Quinones is a decent fielder with an accurate arm. He lacks range at all three of his primary positions -- second, short and third.

OVERALL:

Because of his versatility and pinch hitting ability, Quinones fills an important role with the Reds. He has more pop in his bat than most utility infielders, and that gives him added value.

CINCINNATI REDS

JEFF REED

Position: C
Bats: L **Throws:** R
Ht: 6' 2" **Wt:** 190

Opening Day Age: 28
Born: 11/12/62 in Joliet, IL
ML Seasons: 7

Overall Statistics

	G	AB	R	H	D	T	HR	RBI	SB	BB	SO	AVG
1990	72	175	12	44	8	1	3	16	0	24	26	.251
Career	434	1130	81	256	48	4	10	86	2	116	161	.227

HITTING, FIELDING, BASERUNNING:

Jeff Reed was used infrequently in the first half of last season, and he showed the effects of his inactivity, batting only .170 (9 for 53). After the All-Star break, however, the lefty-swinging Reed started about half the games, giving Joe Oliver a frequent break against righthanders, and batted a solid .287 (35 for 122). Reed's overall .251 average was easily the highest of his career -- his career average going into the season was only .222. Reed wasn't a big part of the Reds' championship drive last year, but he made a contribution.

A line drive hitter who sprays the ball without much power, Reed had a respectable 12 extra-base hits in 175 at-bats. Reed is a fastball hitter and played mostly against righties, but in 25 at-bats against southpaws he had nine hits (.360 average), including two doubles and two homers. Don't expect that to continue; Reed batted .171 against lefties in 1989.

As a catcher, Reed is only average. Though the Reds' pitchers must share some of the blame for not holding runners close, he threw out just 12 of 82 (14.6 percent) base stealers. Reed calls a decent game but has a less-than-overpowering arm. He is a slow runner.

OVERALL:

The left-handed hitting Reed seems destined to have a career as a number-two catcher, especially with Oliver around. Reed, who in 1980 was the Minnesota Twins' number-one draft selection, will probably get about 40 starts, and the Reds would be pleased if he approached his 1990 form.

SCOTT SCUDDER

Position: RP/SP
Bats: R **Throws:** R
Ht: 6' 2" **Wt:** 180

Opening Day Age: 23
Born: 2/14/68 in Paris, TX
ML Seasons: 2

Overall Statistics

	W	L	ERA	G	GS	Sv	IP	H	R	BB	SO	HR
1990	5	5	4.90	21	10	0	71.2	74	41	30	42	12
Career	9	14	4.66	44	27	0	172.0	165	95	91	108	26

PITCHING, FIELDING, HITTING & HOLDING RUNNERS:

Only 23, Scott Scudder is a prize prospect who has had a fine minor league record. Last year he finally had some major league success as well. Scudder has had ERAs of 2.02, 2.96, 2.68 and 2.34 for various Reds' farm clubs, but until late last year, he'd been roughed up in his Cincinnati appearances.

Scudder spent the first part of last season with AAA Nashville, where he was typically excellent (7-1, 2.34). He returned to the Reds on June 30 and was used as a spot starter and reliever. The going was rough for a while, but Scudder turned in some fine performances late in the season when he allowed one run in five relief appearances that spanned 11.1 innings. In one of those games, a Sept. 16 contest against the contending Dodgers, he entered a bases loaded, no-out situation and escaped without any runs scoring. Scudder went on to pitch two more shutout innings and recorded the win.

Scudder throws a 90 MPH fastball and a sometimes-effective curve; he also uses a still-developing slider and change-up. He has an average (but improving) pickoff move and is rated as a good fielder with quick feet. As a hitter, Scudder batted .056 (1-for-18).

OVERALL:

Scudder has a lively arm and has been much sought-after by other clubs, but thus far the Reds have resisted moving him. If an opening arises, he could battle Chris Hammond for a starting job this year. More than likely, he seems destined to fill a long and middle relief role.

JUAN AGOSTO

Position: RP
Bats: L **Throws:** L
Ht: 6' 2" **Wt:** 190

Opening Day Age: 33
Born: 2/23/58 in Rio Piedras, Puerto Rico
ML Seasons: 10

PITCHING:

The most active pitcher in the major leagues since 1988 has been Juan Agosto: 228 appearances, all in relief. The Houston Astros' veteran lefthander averaged 76 outings a year in that span, working a total of 267 innings. That's a lot of work for one guy, but Agosto is a durable pitcher who seems to be blessed with a rubber arm. No matter how much he is used, he keeps bouncing back out of the bullpen.

Agosto has been an excellent situation pitcher for the Astros and he even served as a closer for a short spell when Dave Smith became overworked. The Astros signed him as a free agent in late April, 1987, after he had worn out his welcome with both the White Sox and Twins. Agosto was only 9-10 in the American League, but found his bearings once he reached the National. He is 24-16 with 11 saves as an Astro, including a 10-2 record in 1988.

Several scouts refer to Agosto as a junkball pitcher. "If he doesn't get you out with that big breaking ball," says one, "then he's in trouble." That's not completely accurate. Agosto depends a lot on his sinker ball, also. One opposing manager says, "He's tough on left-handed hitters. He gets a lot of ground balls for outs with that sinker he throws. It's a good sinker, too." Indeed, both the curve and sinker are very difficult for lefties to handle, and Agosto generally holds them to a very low average; he's not nearly as tough against righties. Agosto also needs good control to be effective.

Agosto gives the Astros what every ball club wants: a lefthander out of the bullpen who can pitch often. Agosto rarely gets hurt by the long ball, going 91 innings at one point without allowing a home run. He yielded four homers in '90.

HOLDING RUNNERS, FIELDING, HITTING:

Agosto is quick fielding his position. He didn't commit an error last season. He does a good job holding runners at first and has a nice pickoff move. He rarely goes to bat more than five times a season, so he and the bat rack are pretty much strangers.

OVERALL:

After pitching in 75 games in '88, Agosto wasn't as effective the next year, and in 1990 his ERA shot up to 4.29. Is fatigue finally getting to him? It's an important question for clubs interested in signing Agosto, who was a free agent after the 1990 season. Without his ability to effectively work in a lot of games, Agosto is not nearly as desirable.

Overall Statistics

	W	L	ERA	G	GS	Sv	IP	H	R	BB	SO	HR
1990	9	8	4.29	82	0	4	92.1	91	46	39	50	4
Career	33	26	3.62	426	1	27	484.2	473	221	197	245	23

How Often He Throws Strikes

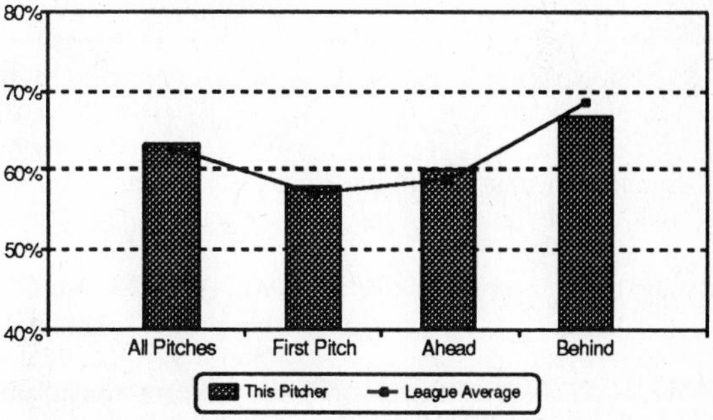

1990 Situational Stats

	W	L	ERA	Sv	IP		AB	H	HR	RBI	AVG
Home	6	4	2.47	3	43.2	LHB	110	25	1	15	.227
Road	3	4	5.92	1	48.2	RHB	239	66	3	24	.276
Day	2	2	3.80	0	21.1	Sc Pos	94	25	3	36	.266
Night	7	6	4.44	4	71.0	Clutch	180	51	2	21	.283

1990 Rankings (National League)

- 1st in games pitched (82)
- 2nd in holds (16) and lowest percentage of inherited runners scored (16.9%)
- 4th in hit batsmen (7)
- Led the Astros in games pitched, holds and lowest percentage of inherited runners scored

ERIC ANTHONY

Position: RF/LF
Bats: L **Throws:** L
Ht: 6' 2" **Wt:** 195

Opening Day Age: 23
Born: 11/8/67 in San Diego, CA
ML Seasons: 2

HITTING:

Eric Anthony can hit the ball a mile -- when he hits it. A Rookie of the Year candidate when the 1990 season began, the young outfielder found himself back in AAA ball at Tucson. Anthony was in a 1-for-33 slump and batting .193 when the Astros sent him down "to work on some things." Anthony got himself together at Tucson, hitting .286, but questions remain about whether he's ready for the majors. Last year much was expected of him, and the pressure seemed to bother him.

Anthony gave the Astros flashes of brilliance from his thunderous bat. He hit one of the longest home runs in Astrodome history, a blast to the right field upper deck. Everyone in the dugout agreed the ball soared at least 500 feet. With 10 homers in 239 at-bats, Anthony showed he has big league power. The ball jumps off his bat and he can hit them out to all fields.

At present, however, Anthony is the supreme tease. His power is unquestioned, but will he hit for a high enough average to stay in the lineup? He uppercuts the ball and is a deadly low ball hitter. Pitchers have found they handle him best by working him from the belt up. He has a big, looping swing and lunges at the ball a lot, resulting in frequent strikeouts: 78 in only 239 at-bats last year. Still, Anthony is only 23, and has but 109 big league games under his belt. What excites the Astros are his 14 homers in 300 major league at-bats and the fact that his 57 hits have produced 36 RBI.

BASERUNNING:

Anthony has better than average speed on the base paths, and he was successful in all five of his stolen base attempts. The more he gains experience, the more likely he is to boost that total. He's a good athlete who should get more aggressive as he matures.

FIELDING:

Anthony started out in left field and appeared tentative at times. His arm is best suited for left, but he is most comfortable in right field. When he switched to right, his confidence and his performance improved. He's still learning the position, however.

OVERALL:

Anthony is a rare talent, but must make adjustments at the plate. Says one scout, "He's got Reggie Jackson power. When he connects, the ball leaves in a hurry." Now he'll have to work at connecting more often. He's still only played 52 games of AAA ball, and it would be no great shock if he went back to Tucson again this year.

Overall Statistics

	G	AB	R	H	D	T	HR	RBI	SB	BB	SO	AVG
1990	84	239	26	46	8	0	10	29	5	29	78	.192
Career	109	300	33	57	10	0	14	36	5	38	94	.190

Where He Hits the Ball

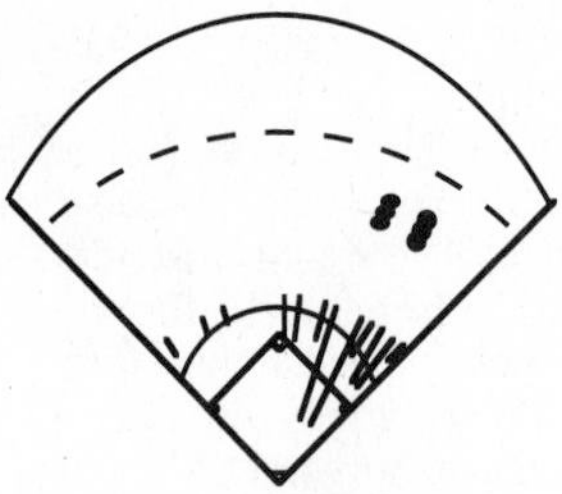

Vs. LHP

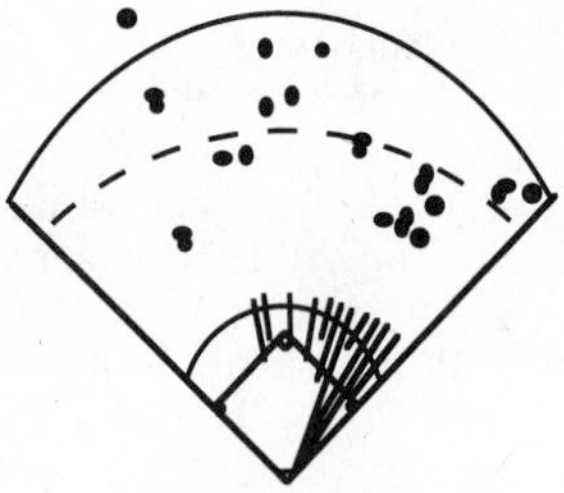

Vs. RHP

1990 Situational Stats

	AB	H	HR	RBI	AVG		AB	H	HR	RBI	AVG
Home	110	24	5	14	.218	LHP	84	18	3	10	.214
Road	129	22	5	15	.171	RHP	155	28	7	19	.181
Day	65	11	2	8	.169	Sc Pos	50	9	2	19	.180
Night	174	35	8	21	.201	Clutch	43	12	2	4	.279

1990 Rankings (National League)

- 1st in lowest batting average with 2 strikes (.112)
- 3rd lowest batting average on a 3-2 count (.061)
- Led the Astros in sacrifice flies (6)

CRAIG BIGGIO

Position: C/LF/CF
Bats: R **Throws:** R
Ht: 5'11" **Wt:** 180

Opening Day Age: 25
Born: 12/14/65 in Smithtown, NY
ML Seasons: 3

HITTING:

One valuable lesson the Astros learned last season is not to tamper with success. In Craig Biggio, they have one of the best hitting young catchers in the National League, who also has excellent speed for the position. With the idea of preserving those legs from the rigors of catching, the Astros moved him to the outfield -- left and center. Talk of Biggio being their future second baseman cropped up, too. If the NFL Oilers had called, one had the feeling the Astros would have lent them Biggio to play middle linebacker.

Biggio wants to catch, and made his feelings known after almost 50 games in the outfield. Despite this confusion, Biggio remained steady at the plate, although his homer and RBI numbers dropped. His .276 batting average was tops on the club and he also led the team in hits (153), doubles (24) and multi-hit games (38). Biggio also displayed patience at the plate with 53 walks.

"I think he's going to hit enough as a catcher," says one veteran NL scout. "He's not a weak hitter. He's got some pop in his bat. I look for him to hit for more power." Biggio needs to match his '89 numbers (13 HR, 60 RBI), not those of '90 (four HR, 42 RBI). He has made a good adjustment to breaking balls, raising his batting average almost 20 points. Pitchers have learned not to feed him a steady diet of fastballs.

BASERUNNING:

With his speed and quickness, Biggio stole more bases (25) last year, but he also was thrown out more times (11). He has excellent athletic instincts and what the scouts call "quick feet." Biggio owns 52 stolen bases in a little over two seasons; not many catchers can make that claim. His numbers will probably decline, however, as the constant squatting behind the plate begins to take its toll.

FIELDING:

Aggressive behind the plate, Biggio blocks balls very well and is agile in his movements. He improved his percentage of throwing out runners, but needs to work on his mechanics and develop a quicker release. Fielding is a part of his game that still needs a lot of work.

OVERALL:

Biggio is a cornerstone for a rebuilding ball club. He is durable, having made 111 starts in the Astros' first 119 games. Says one scout: "You have only five number-one catchers, guys like Santiago, Alomar, Scioscia. The others are number-two types. Biggio can be a number-one in time." That's true, but he'll have to improve his throwing to truly reach the ranks of the top catchers.

Overall Statistics

	G	AB	R	H	D	T	HR	RBI	SB	BB	SO	AVG
1990	150	555	53	153	24	2	4	42	25	53	79	.276
Career	334	1121	131	293	51	5	20	107	52	109	172	.261

Where He Hits the Ball

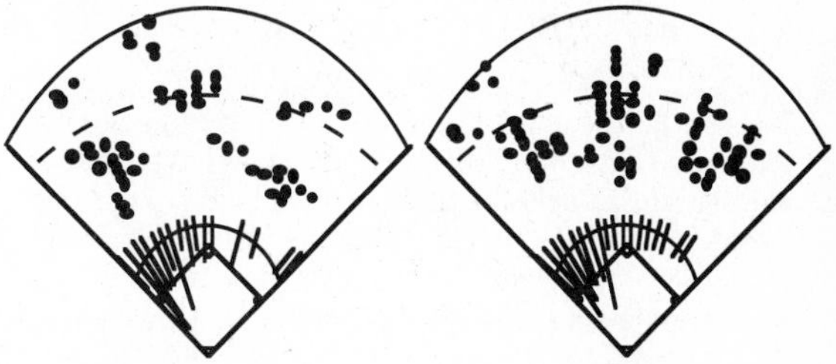

Vs. LHP Vs. RHP

1990 Situational Stats

	AB	H	HR	RBI	AVG		AB	H	HR	RBI	AVG
Home	277	76	2	21	.274	LHP	218	50	2	13	.229
Road	278	77	2	21	.277	RHP	337	103	2	29	.306
Day	136	53	1	17	.390	Sc Pos	138	41	1	35	.297
Night	419	100	3	25	.239	Clutch	109	21	0	5	.193

1990 Rankings (National League)

- 3rd in bunts in play (31)
- 4th in least runs scored per time reached base (25.4%) and lowest slugging percentage vs. left-handed pitchers (.294)
- Led the Astros in batting average (.276), at-bats (555), hits (153), singles (123), doubles (24), sacrifice bunts (9), plate appearances (621), slugging percentage (.348), on-base percentage (.342) and bunts in play
- Led NL catchers in batting average, at-bats, hits, singles, sacrifice hits, stolen bases (25), caught stealing (11), hit by pitch (3), strikeouts (79), plate appearances, games (150), bunts in play and steals of third (4)

KEN CAMINITI

Position: 3B
Bats: B **Throws:** R
Ht: 6' 0" **Wt:** 200

Opening Day Age: 27
Born: 4/21/63 in Hanford, CA
ML Seasons: 4

Overall Statistics

	G	AB	R	H	D	T	HR	RBI	SB	BB	SO	AVG
1990	153	541	52	131	20	2	4	51	9	48	97	.242
Career	407	1412	138	345	60	6	18	153	13	116	252	.244

Where He Hits the Ball

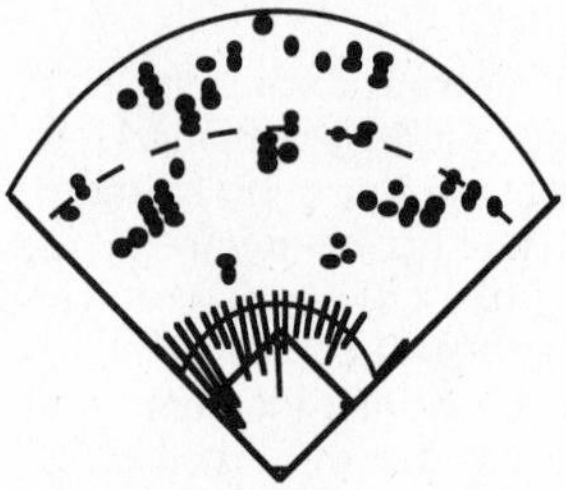

Vs. LHP

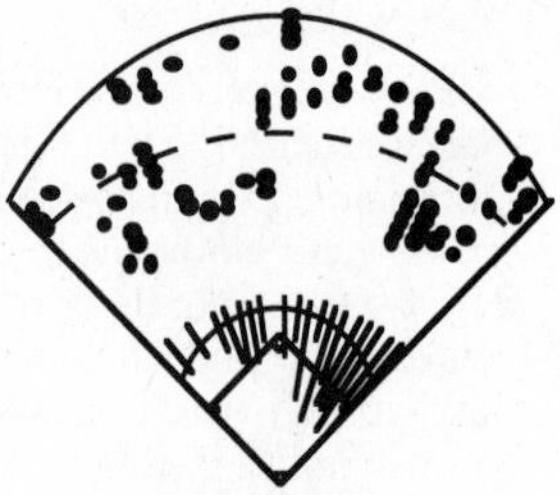

Vs. RHP

1990 Situational Stats

	AB	H	HR	RBI	AVG		AB	H	HR	RBI	AVG
Home	285	82	2	31	.288	LHP	240	59	2	23	.246
Road	256	49	2	20	.191	RHP	301	72	2	28	.239
Day	131	33	2	14	.252	Sc Pos	143	37	2	45	.259
Night	410	98	2	37	.239	Clutch	100	28	0	9	.280

1990 Rankings (National League)

- 1st in lowest batting average on the road (.191)
- 4th lowest slugging percentage (.309) and lowest batting average with the bases loaded (.533)
- 5th lowest batting average (.242)
- 6th lowest slugging percentage vs. left-handed pitchers (.317)
- Led the Astros in games (153), batting average with the bases loaded (.533) and batting average at home (.288)
- Led NL third basemen in GDPs (14), batting average with the bases loaded and batting average at home

HITTING:

In 1989, his first full season in the major leagues, Ken Caminiti slugged 10 homers and left the promise of more to come. He drove in 72 runs that year and felt that total could be raised, too. He batted .255 and was unsatisfied with that figure as well. Thus, 1990 was to be the year of progress. Instead, it turned out to be one of regression.

Last year, Caminiti went some 90 games without homering and ended up with only four homers and 51 RBI. He also grounded into 14 double plays, two short of the team lead. Nobody knows why he stopped hitting for power. Caminiti is big and strong, and should pop 15 a year by accident. He has good bat speed, but needs to generate more power. The Astros say Caminiti needs to work on his left-handed stroke, but he hit two homers from each side of the plate. The switch-hitting third baseman collected 23 RBI right-handed and 28 RBI left- handed, where he had 61 more at-bats.

"Guys who don't grow up switch-hitting and go to the left side," says one NL scout, "usually have trouble with a righthander's breaking ball and are going to be overmatched for a while. Caminiti just hasn't come along that strong as a lefty hitter. The thing is, he makes contact and I think he's going to have a chance to be a pretty good player." The scout rates Caminiti as an above-average talent. Another scout familiar with Caminiti says: "He's only a kid in experience. He's got power from both sides."

BASERUNNING:

An average runner at best, Caminiti stole nine bases in 13 attempts. He is aggressive on the base paths and will go hard to break up the double play. He comes to play.

FIELDING:

Caminiti has the tools to be an outstanding third baseman. He has great hands in the field, good reactions and a strong, but inconsistent, arm. He has made 21 and 22 errors the last two seasons, too much for a glove man with his talent.

OVERALL:

This could be the season for Caminiti to fulfill his promise. With 407 big-league games behind him at age 27, he is entering his prime. He should know his way around the league now, and he's certainly capable of hitting .275 with 15 homers and 80 RBI.

CASEY CANDAELE

Position: 2B/LF
Bats: B **Throws:** R
Ht: 5' 7" **Wt:** 165

Opening Day Age: 30
Born: 1/12/61 in Lompoc, CA
ML Seasons: 4

HITTING:

With the trade of Billy Doran, the second base sweepstakes began for the Houston Astros. Little Casey Candaele was the fellow who took the early lead, earning the starting role during the final month of 1990 with his hustle in the field and his surprisingly good bat. Candaele flirted with the .300 mark before finishing at .286, the highest average of his up-and-down four year career.

People tend to underrate Candaele because of his size (5'7", 165), but he is a good ballplayer who spent most of the season as a reserve before earning his starting spurs. He hits for a better average from the right side of the plate (.341) but has a tad more pop as a lefty swinger, with 10 of his 17 extra-base hits coming of righthanders. Candaele also hit for a much better average batting righty during his previous major league season as a regular, 1987, and he will need to improve his hitting from the left side if he wants to remain a regular.

Candaele drove in 22 runs, showing a knack for delivering with men in scoring position. He also led the team in triples with six and in pinch hits with 10. He has four career homers -- three versus Los Angeles, two off Fernando Valenzuela. An aggressive player who comes to the ballpark to win, Candaele won two games in two nights with hits (a homer and a triple) after entering the contest for defensive purposes. The next day, the Astros hung a sign beyond the right field fence with a star, Candaele's uniform number, 1, and the slogan, "The Little Bopper."

BASERUNNING:

Everything Candaele does is in high gear, and his play on the base paths included. He has good speed, with six triples in 262 at-bats, but was successful on only seven of 12 stolen base attempts. Despite his speed, he has a terrible lifetime stolen base percentage of 46 percent, which he'll need to improve. He's a smart player and quick to take the extra base.

FIELDING:

Candaele made only three errors in 1990, two while playing second base. He goes after every ball, has a good arm for the position and turns the double play pretty well. The question is, can he hold up under the grind of regular duty this season?

OVERALL:

A year ago, Candaele was the team's best player off the bench. For the rebuilding Astros, Candaele, an overachiever, can be a stopgap player for the team until the second baseman of the future arrives in another year or two.

Overall Statistics

	G	AB	R	H	D	T	HR	RBI	SB	BB	SO	AVG
1990	130	262	30	75	8	6	3	22	7	31	42	.286
Career	355	962	112	246	43	12	4	56	18	85	102	.256

Where He Hits the Ball

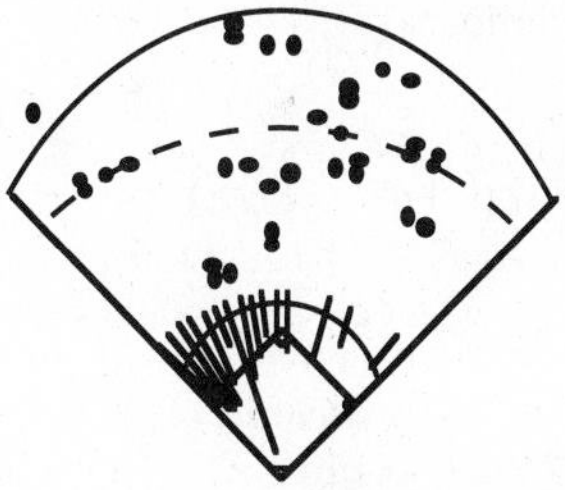

Vs. LHP

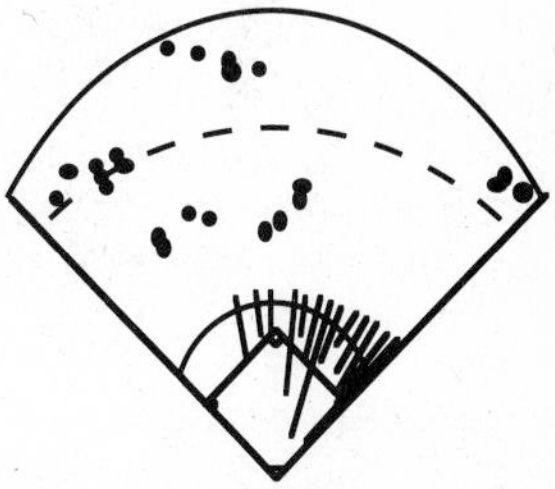

Vs. RHP

1990 Situational Stats

	AB	H	HR	RBI	AVG		AB	H	HR	RBI	AVG
Home	126	36	1	12	.286	LHP	126	43	2	10	.341
Road	136	39	2	10	.287	RHP	136	32	1	12	.235
Day	59	15	1	8	.254	Sc Pos	66	20	1	19	.303
Night	203	60	2	14	.296	Clutch	64	16	1	9	.250

1990 Rankings (National League)

- 4th highest batting average vs. left-handed pitchers (.341)
- 8th highest on-base average vs. left-handed pitchers (.407)
- Led the Astros in triples (6) and batting average vs. left-handed pitchers

JIM CLANCY

Position: RP/SP
Bats: R **Throws:** R
Ht: 6' 4" **Wt:** 220

Opening Day Age: 35
Born: 12/18/55 in Chicago, IL
ML Seasons: 14

PITCHING:

One of the Astros' great mysteries is Jim Clancy. Since signing with Houston as a free agent before the 1989 season, it's been nothing but a blizzard of misery for the big righthander. He has toiled long and hard to regain the form he'd had with his previous team, Toronto, but nothing seems to work. Clancy endured another season of pain this year, even accepting demotion to the minors. Since joining the Astros, he's gone 9-22 -- 4-16 since the All-Star break of '89 when everything began to blow up in his face.

The burning question: Is the decline the result of poor mechanics in his pitching motion, or can he no longer do the job? With AAA Tucson, coaches drilled Clancy on extending his right arm to keep the ball down in the strike zone and to get more movement on the ball. They worked on his change-up and his slider. Clancy went 3-2 with a 2.98 ERA in 42.1 innings with Tucson, and pitched out of the bullpen on his return to the Astros.

The hometown fans have tired of Clancy's act and boo his entry into the game. The batters feast on him, as all his pitches seem to travel about the same rate of speed. Without any variety of speeds, it wouldn't matter if he threw 90 MPH. A bad sign for any pitcher is giving up base hits on his best pitches. This happened to Clancy with breaking balls down and away. In 33 games with the Astros this year, it was more bad news: a 2-8 record with a 6.51 ERA. That figures out to 55 earned runs in 76 innings. To paraphrase a popular TV commercial -- it doesn't get much worse than this.

HOLDING RUNNERS, FIELDING, HITTING:

Clancy has created so much action on the base paths that he must feel a bit shell-shocked. Runners have taken liberties with him, and his fielding has been shaky at times. He did avoid being charged with an error after committing seven in the same number of games (33) the previous year. He batted .214 in limited plate appearances.

OVERALL:

As an Astro, Clancy has been one of those pitchers that everyone can hit. He needs to give hitters a different look -- drop down with his pitching motion, throw sidearm, something. Right now, hitters have drawn a good bead on him. His best bet for a comeback this year appears to be in the bullpen. Clancy needs a measure of success to regain his confidence, but when and from where will it come?

Overall Statistics

	W	L	ERA	G	GS	Sv	IP	H	R	BB	SO	HR
1990	2	8	6.51	33	10	1	76.0	100	58	33	44	4
Career	137	162	4.24	418	381	2	2429.0	2440	1262	913	1372	236

How Often He Throws Strikes

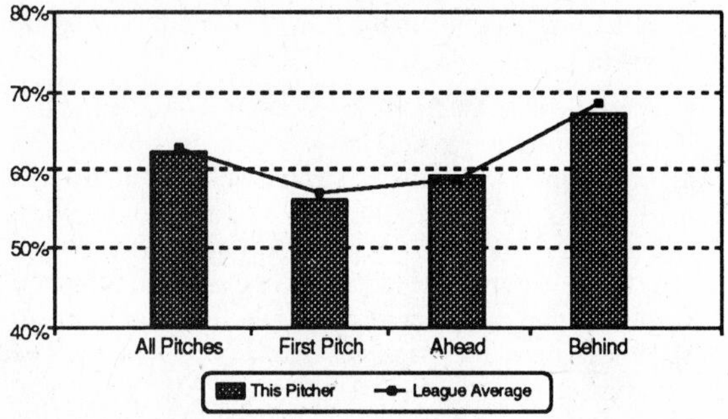

1990 Situational Stats

	W	L	ERA	Sv	IP		AB	H	HR	RBI	AVG
Home	1	2	6.67	1	29.2	LHB	166	60	1	32	.361
Road	1	6	6.41	0	46.1	RHB	145	40	3	26	.276
Day	0	0	0.00	1	5.2	Sc Pos	98	34	1	50	.347
Night	2	8	7.04	0	70.1	Clutch	31	8	1	4	.258

1990 Rankings (National League)

- 2nd highest batting average allowed vs. left-handed batters (.361)

DANNY DARWIN

Position: RP/SP
Bats: R **Throws:** R
Ht: 6' 3" **Wt:** 190

Opening Day Age: 35
Born: 10/25/55 in Bonham, TX
ML Seasons: 13

PITCHING:

Danny Darwin underwent a mid-life change in his baseball career last season. At his age, 35, most pitchers move from starting pitcher to the bullpen. Darwin did just the opposite -- with outstanding results.

In past seasons, Darwin's versatility has been something of a curse to him, though being a pitcher who could start, close or pitch middle relief has been a blessing to his teams. Last year, with his starting rotation in shambles, Astros' Manager Art Howe yanked Darwin out of the bullpen and started him for the first time after 111 consecutive relief appearances dating back to August 28, 1988. The number-five spot in the rotation was a shambles at that point -- Jim Clancy and Dan Schatzeder were a combined 2-9.

Darwin turned number-five into number-one, clipping off a nine-game winning streak and finishing at 11-4. As a bonus, his 2.21 ERA was good enough to lead the National League. This comes after Darwin had gone 18-8 with 12 saves and a 2.34 ERA over nearly two seasons in the Astro bullpen.

Darwin's fastball and slider are his best pitches, but he threw more curveballs once he became a starter again. One NL scout believes Darwin's problem as a starter in the past was a matter of consistency. "When you see his stuff," he said, "you think, Gee, this guy's got as good a stuff as anybody in baseball. He'll show you good winning stuff -- good tailing fastball, good sinking fastball, good hard slider. You'd see him again a month later and he's not the same pitcher." In 1990, Darwin put all that behind him. He became the fourth player in club history to win the ERA title, joining J.R. Richard (2.71 in 1979), Nolan Ryan (1.69 in 1981 and 2.76 in 1987) and Mike Scott (2.22 in 1986). Ryan's first ERA title came in the '81 split season and he pitched fewer than 162 innings, so Darwin's 2.21 stands as the club record.

HOLDING RUNNERS, FIELDING, HITTING:

Darwin made just one error in 48 games and handles fielding his position well. He has a strong pickoff throw to first base, but rates as only average at holding runners. He was just five-for-38 at bat, but drove in three runs.

OVERALL:

On a team in need of starting pitching, Darwin has emerged as the Astros' number one man, succeeding Mike Scott in the role. They'll have to sign him first, however, as Darwin was declared a "new look" free agent as part of the collusion settlement. Dependable and solid either as a starter or reliever, Darwin should find his services very much in demand.

Overall Statistics

	W	L	ERA	G	GS	Sv	IP	H	R	BB	SO	HR
1990	11	4	2.21	48	17	2	162.2	136	42	31	109	11
Career	111	109	3.40	488	208	29	1913.1	1776	820	581	1265	161

How Often He Throws Strikes

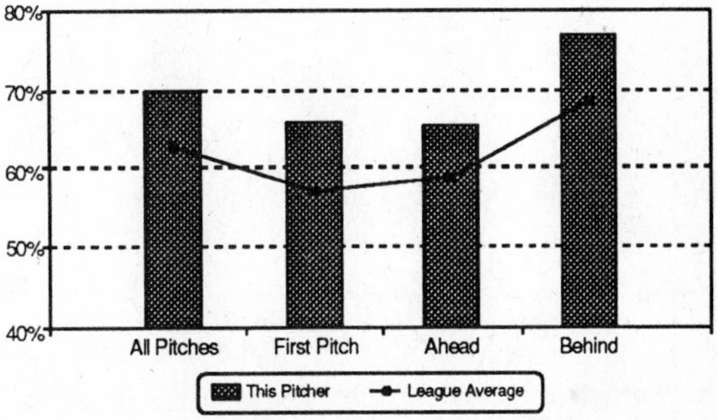

1990 Situational Stats

	W	L	ERA	Sv	IP		AB	H	HR	RBI	AVG
Home	6	2	2.42	1	78.0	LHB	363	96	7	24	.264
Road	5	2	2.02	1	84.2	RHB	242	40	4	20	.165
Day	5	2	2.91	0	46.1	Sc Pos	140	28	3	35	.200
Night	6	2	1.93	2	116.1	Clutch	111	26	2	4	.234

1990 Rankings (National League)

- 1st in ERA (2.21), lowest on-base average allowed (.266), least baserunners allowed per 9 innings (9.5) and ERA on the road (2.02)
- 2nd highest strikeout/walk ratio (3.5) and lowest slugging percentage allowed (.331)
- 3rd lowest groundball/flyball ratio (.74) and lowest batting average allowed with runners in scoring position (.200)
- Led the Astros in ERA, wins (11), winning percentage (.733), strikeout/walk ratio, lowest batting average allowed (.225), lowest on-base average allowed, lowest slugging percentage allowed and least HRs allowed per 9 innings (.61)

GLENN DAVIS

Position: 1B
Bats: R **Throws:** R
Ht: 6' 3" **Wt:** 210

Opening Day Age: 30
Born: 3/28/61 in Jacksonville, FL
ML Seasons: 7

Overall Statistics

	G	AB	R	H	D	T	HR	RBI	SB	BB	SO	AVG
1990	93	327	44	82	15	4	22	64	8	46	54	.251
Career	830	3032	427	795	150	10	166	518	23	310	490	.262

Where He Hits the Ball

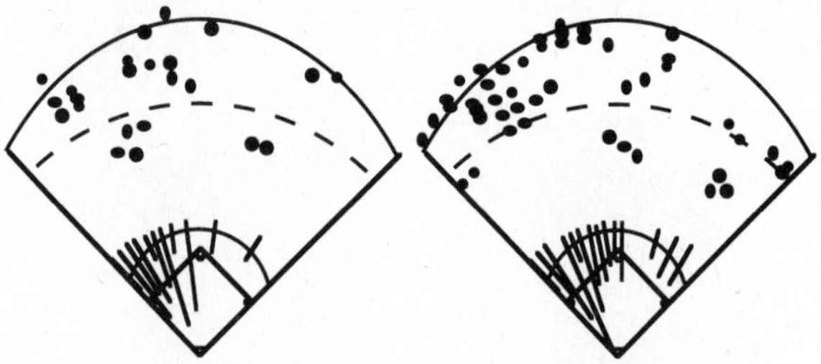

Vs. LHP Vs. RHP

1990 Situational Stats

	AB	H	HR	RBI	AVG		AB	H	HR	RBI	AVG
Home	175	38	4	22	.217	LHP	123	31	11	27	.252
Road	152	44	18	42	.289	RHP	204	51	11	37	.250
Day	89	24	6	22	.270	Sc Pos	99	26	6	43	.263
Night	238	58	16	42	.244	Clutch	60	16	3	11	.267

1990 Rankings (National League)

- 1st in hit by pitch (8)
- 6th in intentional walks (17)
- 7th in slugging percentage vs. left-handed pitchers (.569)
- 8th in highest percentage of extra bases taken as a runner (57.8%)
- Led the Astros in intentional walks, hit by pitch and slugging percentage vs. left-handed pitchers
- Led NL first basemen in hit by pitch and highest percentage of extra bases taken as a runner

HITTING:

Glenn Davis has a picture-perfect swing for a power hitter. It is a thing of beauty when the slugging first baseman is in the groove and clearing distant fences. A year ago, Davis was headed for his biggest season ever, with 19 homers and 48 RBI as the All-Star break approached. Then his world -- and that of the Astros -- caved in. Davis suffered a pulled rib cage muscle that cost him two months playing time. The injury forced him out of the lineup on other occasions and limited him to a career low 93 games. Yet he still concluded the season with 22 homers, 64 RBI and a .251 average.

Davis is a strong pull hitter and pitchers will work him with breaking pitches low and away, which he'll chase. Still, he's one of the game's premier sluggers, despite playing in the Astrodome, which hurts any power hitter's production. Davis hit only four of his 22 homers at home last year, and his career totals are 72 homers in Houston, 94 on the road. Says one NL scout: "Any time you can hit as many home runs as he does in this ballpark (Astrodome), you have sheer ability. You put him in some other ballpark -- Boston, Philadelphia, Atlanta -- and he might hang some real big numbers up there. I'm not saying he has Jose Canseco power, but he's in that category."

Davis will go for the hit with men in scoring position, but he's a big, free swinger. As he has learned patience, his walk total has gone up, and he's struck out over 100 times only once in his career -- very unusual for a big slugger.

BASERUNNING:

Davis has steadily improved his baserunning mechanics. In only 93 games, he stole a career high eight bases and was caught only three times. Davis runs well enough for his size, and is almost as aggressive on the base paths as he is when swinging at pitches.

FIELDING:

Davis has made himself into an above-average fielding first baseman. He works at defense, scoops balls up well, and has improved on making throws to other bases. He was charged with only four errors in 91 games at first base.

OVERALL:

Unless the Astros get a bundle of talent in return, they are unlikely to trade Davis, despite the fact that they could lose him to free agency after the season. He remains the Big Bopper and the team's lone proven run producer in his five-and-a-half seasons as a regular.

JIM DESHAIES

Position: SP
Bats: L **Throws:** L
Ht: 6' 4" **Wt:** 222

Opening Day Age: 30
Born: 6/23/60 in Massena, NY
ML Seasons: 7

Overall Statistics

	W	L	ERA	G	GS	Sv	IP	H	R	BB	SO	HR
1990	7	12	3.78	34	34	0	209.1	186	93	84	119	21
Career	56	48	3.50	155	152	0	948.0	818	398	358	638	95

How Often He Throws Strikes

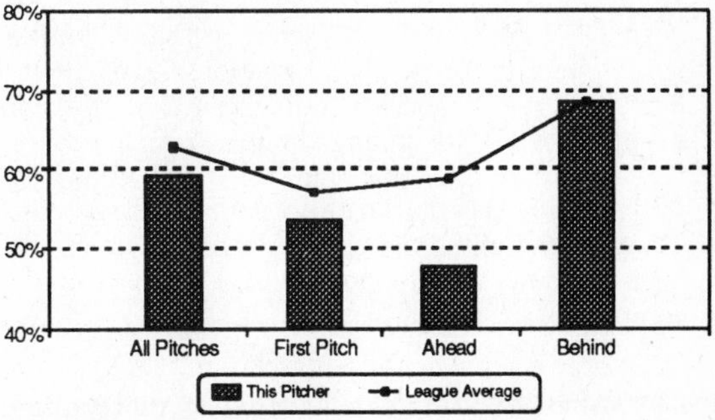

1990 Situational Stats

	W	L	ERA	Sv	IP		AB	H	HR	RBI	AVG
Home	4	3	2.75	0	98.1	LHB	115	35	1	14	.304
Road	3	9	4.70	0	111.0	RHB	645	151	20	69	.234
Day	1	1	4.40	0	47.0	Sc Pos	180	46	3	60	.256
Night	6	11	3.60	0	162.1	Clutch	51	8	1	1	.157

1990 Rankings (National League)

- 1st in pickoff throws (341)
- 2nd in hit batsmen (8)
- 3rd in least GDPs induced per 9 innings (.34)
- 4th in games started (34)
- 5th in home runs allowed (21), lowest winning percentage (.368), lowest strikeout/walk ratio (1.4) and lowest groundball/flyball ratio (.78)
- Led the Astros in games started, innings (209.1), batters faced (881), walks allowed (84), hit batsmen, pitches thrown (3,285), pickoff throws and runners caught stealing (9)

PITCHING:

As the lone lefthander in the Houston Astros' starting rotation, Jim Deshaies carries a heavy burden for the team. The load became too heavy last year. After four seasons of winning in double figures, the former New York Yankee saw his victory total dwindle to less than half that of '89. Deshaies went from 15-10 in 1989 to 7-12 in 1990. His earned run average rose from 2.91 to 3.78, and his complete games fell from six to two in the same number of starts (34).

Some who have closely observed Deshaies believe he has lost something on his fastball. "It doesn't look like he's throwing as hard, like he's lost four or five miles on his fastball," says one baseball veteran. "He seems to be short-arming the ball more than ever." Many times in 1990, Deshaies' problems arose in the first few innings. It appeared he couldn't get good and loose with his pitches. Walks often set up those big innings. "He is one of those pitchers," says one rival manager, "that if you don't get to him early, you don't get to him. I've never understood why he never throws hard the first couple of innings."

Deshaies comes over the top and throws a high-riding fastball. He gets a lot of fly balls with the pitch, but if it isn't working, it's tough for him to win. He has come up with an effective change-up, but he tried to compensate for the lost zip on his fastball by throwing more breaking balls and offspeed pitches. Considering the loss in velocity, as well as his low run support, Deshaies' slump, perhaps, was inevitable. He pitched in some close games, and usually made one mistake which cost him the decision. Deshaies served up 21 home runs and allowed 15 more earned runs in 16 fewer innings than 1989.

HOLDING RUNNERS, FIELDING, HITTING:

Deshaies works at holding runners and will make repeated throws to first when a steal situation arises. His move to first is slightly above-average for a lefty. He was charged with two errors in the field, but handles balls hit back to the mound well. Deshaies threatened no one with the bat, going four-for-63 for an .063 average. He had nine hits in '89.

OVERALL:

His seven wins were the fewest for Deshaies since joining the Astros full-time in 1986. He must recapture his '89 form in order to remain the number-two man in the rotation. Last year, he was no better than number-four. The Astros need a strong comeback from him this season.

PITCHING:

After spending two years in Japan, Bill Gullickson needed to prove himself in the major leagues once again last season. He did in part, recording his seventh consecutive season with double-figures in wins by going 10-14 with the Astros. Gullickson's ERA wasn't great at 3.82, but it was respectable enough.

For Gullickson, last year became a re-learning process in which he found out all over again what kinds of pitches he could throw to get out big-league hitters. In his earlier years, before he went to Japan, Gullickson owned an above-average fastball which had a sinking motion that he augmented with a good, hard slider. Now he's become much more of a breaking ball pitcher. Says one National League scout, "He's completely changed now. He throws a curveball, lots of change-ups. He throws the fastball, but it's not a sinker any more. He's coming over the top."

No longer a staff ace, Gullickson is best suited for the number-four or five spot in the rotation. He makes the best of what he's got. He is durable (32 starts) and dependable (193.1 innings) but not spectacular. Gullickson will throw the home run ball (21 this past season) and he is not going to intimidate anybody. The veteran righthander changes speeds a lot on his pitches, knows how to work a hitter and is a tough competitor.

Once a power pitcher who struck out 18 Cubs in a game, Gullickson is now a finesse hurler who must be able to hit his spots. He yielded 100 runs in 1990, second only to Mike Scott's 102 on the Astros' staff. "If I had him," says one NL manager, "I would make him have a better rotation in his delivery. It could help him throw the ball harder than he does."

HOLDING RUNNERS, FIELDING, HITTING:

Gullickson is aggressive in all of his actions. He pounces on balls off the mound, covers the bag well and rates about average in holding runners at first base. He batted for the most total bases among Astro pitchers, a total pumped up by the staff's lone homer.

OVERALL:

The Astros announced they wouldn't try to re-sign Gullickson, but he'll undoubtedly find work somewhere. He's a tough guy and a bulldog as a competitor. He likes to pitch and gives his best; he doesn't give in to the hitter. However, if you have to win a big game, Bill Gullickson doesn't have the stuff that you could count on with confidence.

BILL GULLICKSON

Position: SP
Bats: R **Throws:** R
Ht: 6' 3" **Wt:** 220

Opening Day Age: 32
Born: 2/20/59 in Marshall, MN
ML Seasons: 10

Overall Statistics

	W	L	ERA	G	GS	Sv	IP	H	R	BB	SO	HR
1990	10	14	3.82	32	32	0	193.1	221	100	61	73	21
Career	111	100	3.64	280	274	0	1837.0	1833	825	459	989	173

How Often He Throws Strikes

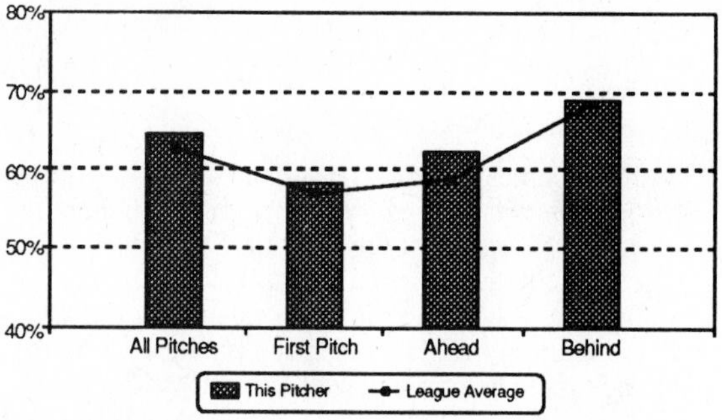

1990 Situational Stats

	W	L	ERA	Sv	IP		AB	H	HR	RBI	AVG
Home	8	7	3.94	0	114.1	LHB	471	149	12	55	.316
Road	2	7	3.65	0	79.0	RHB	298	72	9	35	.242
Day	4	1	1.69	0	58.2	Sc Pos	189	49	5	66	.259
Night	6	13	4.75	0	134.2	Clutch	32	12	2	3	.375

1990 Rankings (National League)

- 1st in least strikeouts per 9 innings (3.4)
- 2nd lowest strikeout/walk ratio (1.2) and highest slugging percentage allowed (.441)
- 3rd highest batting average allowed (.287), least pitches thrown per batter (3.31) and most HRs allowed per 9 innings (.98)
- Led the Astros in losses (14), hits allowed (221), runners caught stealing (9), GDPs induced (18), least pitches thrown per batter and most GDPs induced per 9 innings (.84)

XAVIER HERNANDEZ

Position: RP
Bats: L **Throws:** R
Ht: 6' 2" **Wt:** 185

Opening Day Age: 25
Born: 8/16/65 in Port Arthur, TX
ML Seasons: 2

PITCHING:

Xavier Hernandez spent most of 1990 pitching in meaningless games out of the Houston Astros bullpen. He yearned for something more, and a late-season spurt may have put him in the thick of things for this season. So could the development of another pitch: Hernandez spent the winter trying to polish a forkball to complement his other pitches.

Until now, Hernandez has been a two pitch pitcher -- a sinker and slider man toiling in middle-inning relief. Coming up through the Toronto system, Hernandez was always a starting pitcher, and a fairly successful one, but two pitches don't get a hurler very far in the majors. Thus the forkball is important to the continued development of his promising career. He used the pitch in 1986, but more or less abandoned it after he hurt his arm. He took it off the shelf late in the '90 season and although he used it sparingly, the forkball could give him the edge he needs to stay in the big leagues.

Hernandez pitched in 34 games last year, compiling a 2-1 record -- both wins came in the final month -- and a hefty 4.62 ERA. A disaster versus the Phillies early in the year (1.2 innigs, 8 earned runs) created the high ERA, but he pitched exceptionally well in the Astrodome. He drew a start in the season's final series, losing at Cincinnati 3-2, and hadn't allowed a run in the previous 10 games covering 15 innings leading up to that start. He throws only an 84 MPH fastball, so he depends on control and good location. When Hernandez puts the ball in the zone where he wants to throw it, he gets people out. Infrequent use out of the bullpen worked against his effectiveness, but Hernandez showed his staying power by sticking with the role and making the best out of a difficult situation.

HOLDING RUNNERS, FIELDING, HITTING:

As a reliever, Hernandez knows the value of holding runners close to the bag. He fields his position well and is accurate on throws to first base. He was not charged with an error in the field last season. He went one-for-three in his limited trips to the plate.

OVERALL:

This is an important year for Hernandez. He may be the ninth or tenth pitcher on the major league staff or find himself back in the minors. The ability to harness the forkball and throw it for strikes will probably dictate whether he can handle a more substantial role with the big club. He's only 25 and still has some time to develop.

Overall Statistics

	W	L	ERA	G	GS	Sv	IP	H	R	BB	SO	HR
1990	2	1	4.62	34	1	0	62.1	60	34	24	24	8
Career	3	1	4.66	41	1	0	85.0	85	49	32	31	10

How Often He Throws Strikes

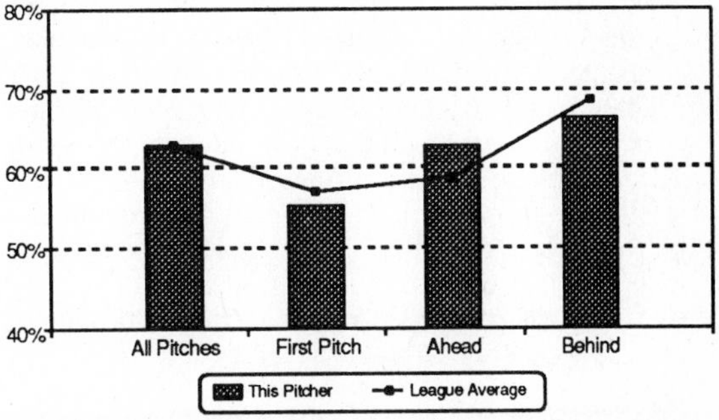

1990 Situational Stats

	W	L	ERA	Sv	IP		AB	H	HR	RBI	AVG
Home	2	0	0.64	0	28.0	LHB	114	33	4	15	.289
Road	0	1	7.86	0	34.1	RHB	120	27	4	18	.225
Day	0	0	6.00	0	9.0	Sc Pos	58	14	2	24	.241
Night	2	1	4.39	0	53.1	Clutch	14	3	0	5	.214

1990 Rankings (National League)

- Led the Astros in wild pitches (6)

HITTING:

The Houston Astros had a specific role in mind for Ken Oberkfell when they signed him as a free agent last year -- left-handed pinch hitter off the bench. It's an assignment Oberkfell has handled expertly since his playing days as a regular ended a few years ago. He had proven to be one of the best pinch swingers for the Giants in 1989, leading the league with 18 pinch hits and batting .360 in the role.

With the Astros in 1990, though, the hits stopped falling for the veteran infielder. Oberkfell flopped in the pinch role, going four-for-30 (.133) off the bench while driving in just two runs. Overall, Oberkfell batted only .207 in 77 games, with only eight extra-base blows among 31 hits. He had one homer and 12 RBI. At 34, Oberkfell looked a lot like a washed-up veteran.

Oberkfell now has little power, and his bat speed has declined substantially even from 1989. In particular, he seems to have trouble getting around on the good fastball, fouling a lot of pitches off to the left side last year, an indication that the lefty swinger was dragging his bat through the strike zone. Pitchers work Oberkfell low and away, and he needs the snap in his stroke to drive the ball to left field. He hit only .167 with men in scoring position last season, a very bad sign for a pinch hitter who must deliver in the clutch. He also went only 1-for-17 vs. lefties.

BASERUNNING:

With his many years in the game, Oberkfell knows how to size up situations on the base paths, but he has no speed. As a result, he rarely attempts to steal a base. He stole one base and was thrown out once in 1990. He's a tough man to score from second base.

FIELDING:

Oberkfell can play first, second, or third, but he can no longer play them very well. Even in his prime, he didn't have a lot of range, and now he has less than ever. Oberkfell did most of his playing at third base last year (24 games), but he lacks the arm for the position. He retains his quick hands around the bag.

OVERALL:

The asset that has kept Oberkfell in the big leagues the past two years is his ability to produce as a late-inning, left-handed pinch hitter. There's certainly a use for his talents as long as he can hit, but he'll have to prove he still can in 1991.

KEN OBERKFELL

Position: 3B/2B
Bats: L **Throws:** R
Ht: 6' 1" **Wt:** 210

Opening Day Age: 34
Born: 5/4/56 in Maryville, IL
ML Seasons: 14

Overall Statistics

	G	AB	R	H	D	T	HR	RBI	SB	BB	SO	AVG
1990	77	150	10	31	6	1	1	12	1	15	17	.207
Career	1508	4713	545	1314	232	44	29	422	62	524	343	.279

Where He Hits the Ball

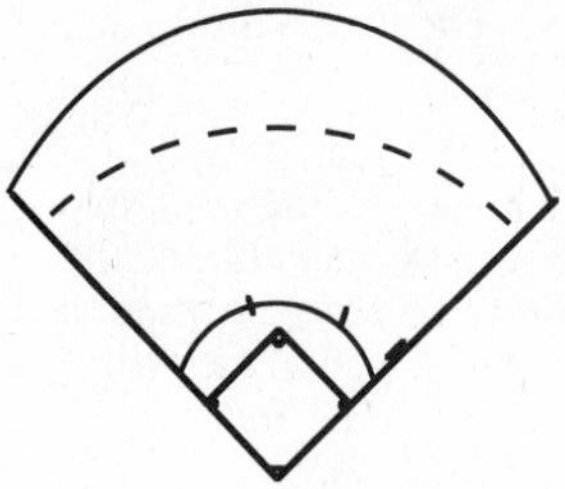

Vs. LHP

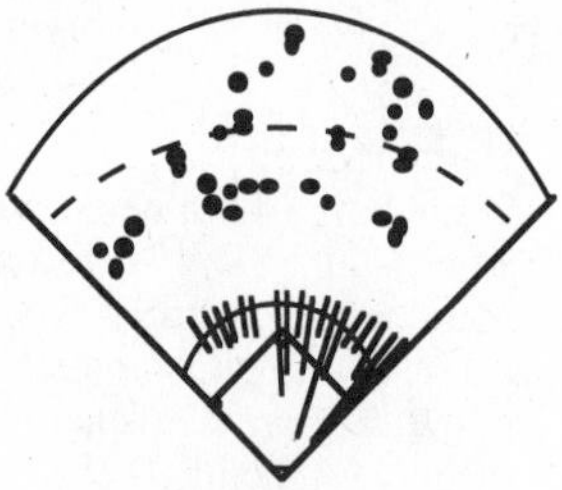

Vs. RHP

1990 Situational Stats

	AB	H	HR	RBI	AVG		AB	H	HR	RBI	AVG
Home	59	8	0	3	.136	LHP	17	1	0	0	.059
Road	91	23	1	9	.253	RHP	133	30	1	12	.226
Day	43	10	0	4	.233	Sc Pos	42	7	1	10	.167
Night	107	21	1	8	.196	Clutch	33	6	0	2	.182

1990 Rankings (National League)

➟ Did not rank near the top or bottom in any category

JAVIER ORTIZ

Position: LF
Bats: R **Throws:** R
Ht: 6' 4" **Wt:** 220

Opening Day Age: 28
Born: 1/22/63 in Boston, MA
ML Seasons: 1

HITTING:

Knock on wood, Javier Ortiz just wants to stay healthy this season. Ortiz labored in the minor leagues for eight years before getting his break last year with the Astros, but then an injury ruined his big chance. His offensive production after he was called up from AAA Tucson in mid-June was encouraging to Manager Art Howe, though. Says Howe, "He swings the bat like he means it."

Ortiz jumped off to a quick start after his recall from AAA, then settled down. He was still hitting .273 with one HR and 10 RBI in 30 games when a knee injury sidelined him for the season. In his brief action Ortiz made a strong impression on Howe and the Astros brass, and he placed himself firmly in the outfield picture in 1991.

Ortiz' determination to prove himself worthy of major league status was obvious in his play. He is very aggressive at the plate, takes a good healthy cut and has good power to the alleys. He is strong enough to produce 12-15 home runs a year once he gains some experience at the big league level. With his hard-work ethic, Ortiz has given indications that he may be able to make adjustments as a hitter and do whatever is necessary to remain with the Astros. He showed good plate discipline, walking 12 times and striking out only 11 times in 77 at-bats.

BASERUNNING:

A big man, Ortiz is no great threat to steal bases, but he doesn't clog up the base paths, either. He stole 15 bases in the minors in his best season, and was one for two last year for Houston. Ortiz is an alert runner, and aggressive. His knee injury came in a home plate collision with San Diego's Mark Parent.

FIELDING:

Not a great glove man, Ortiz is primarily a left fielder; he committed one error last year, while in right field. His arm is adequate for left field. If he gets to the ball, he can catch it. He covers adequate ground for a player his size, which is 6'4", 220 pounds.

OVERALL:

With the Astros' outfield situation wide open, Ortiz has a definite chance to stick. He opened enough eyes in his trial period a year ago to put himself in the middle of the left field roll call. He's gotten a taste of big-league life and likes it. He is a hungry ballplayer.

Overall Statistics

	G	AB	R	H	D	T	HR	RBI	SB	BB	SO	AVG
1990	30	77	7	21	5	1	1	10	1	12	11	.273
Career	30	77	7	21	5	1	1	10	1	12	11	.273

Where He Hits the Ball

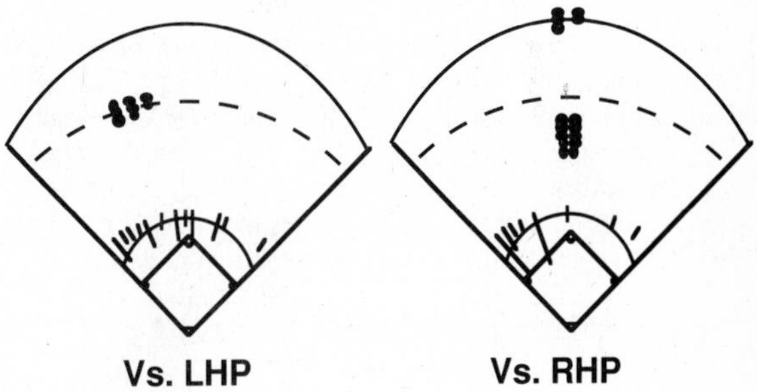

1990 Situational Stats

	AB	H	HR	RBI	AVG		AB	H	HR	RBI	AVG
Home	38	9	1	9	.237	LHP	39	13	1	5	.333
Road	39	12	0	1	.308	RHP	38	8	0	5	.211
Day	12	4	0	2	.333	Sc Pos	24	6	0	8	.250
Night	65	17	1	8	.262	Clutch	14	5	0	2	.357

1990 Rankings (National League)

- Did not rank near the top or bottom in any category

MARK PORTUGAL

Position: SP
Bats: R **Throws:** R
Ht: 6' 0" **Wt:** 200

Opening Day Age: 28
Born: 10/30/62 in Los Angeles, CA
ML Seasons: 6

PITCHING:

Mark Portugal needs to start the 1991 season in reverse. For whatever reasons, the second half of the baseball season has been the most productive part for Portugal in his two years with the Houston Astros. In 1989, the veteran righthander went 7-0 after July 15. Last season, Portugal followed the same winning script, posting an 8-2 mark after the All-Star game. That makes Portugal 15-2 in the second half of the past two campaigns. The reverse side? Portugal is 3-9 (combined) the first half.

Portugal's 1990 surge allowed him to tie Danny Darwin for the team lead in wins (11), and he topped all Astro pitchers with 136 strikeouts in 196.2 innings. Portugal is unable to explain the differences in the two halves of the campaign. He seems to have better control and location of his pitches, however, once the year wears on; he gets into a rhythm and stays in it.

Since his acquisition from Minnesota, Portugal has put up winning numbers in Houston (18-11). "I never liked him in the American League," admits one scout, "but he came up with that curveball and that's his best pitch. Before, he had trouble getting it over the plate." There's no doubt that Portugal has matured since his days as a Twin. In four seasons with Minnesota, his record was only 11-19, and he never posted an ERA below 4.30.

These days he's a much more complete pitcher. Portugal throws all the pitches -- a tailing fastball, curve, slider, change-up. It's a good repertoire and when the pitches are all working, he's very tough to beat. Just ask San Francisco. Portugal owns a 6-1 career record against the Giants (he's 12-10 vs. the rest of the league) with an ERA under 2.00. "Every time we see him he looks like Walter Johnson or Cy Young," says Giants manager Roger Craig. "He's got good stuff and when we face him, he throws it for good location."

HOLDING RUNNERS, FIELDING, HITTING:

Portugal is all business on the mound, and that extends to fielding his position and keeping runners close to the bag. He tied Bill Gullickson for most hits (nine) and RBI (five) by Astro pitchers in '90. He is competitive in all that he does on the field.

OVERALL:

With his good stuff and two years of experience as an Astro, Portugal could be on the verge of blossoming into a 15-game winner. He wants the ball, loves the challenge, and has the pitches to become a consistent winner. All he needs to do is to put two good halves together.

Overall Statistics

	W	L	ERA	G	GS	Sv	IP	H	R	BB	SO	HR
1990	11	10	3.62	32	32	0	196.2	187	90	67	136	21
Career	29	30	4.11	124	73	4	543.1	532	266	209	360	65

How Often He Throws Strikes

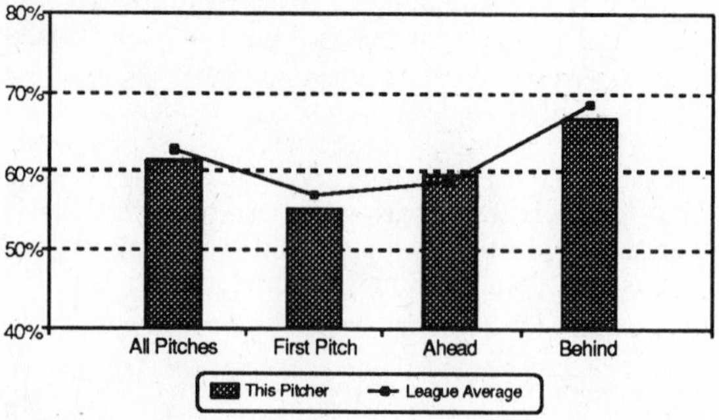

1990 Situational Stats

	W	L	ERA	Sv	IP		AB	H	HR	RBI	AVG
Home	8	2	1.78	0	101.1	LHB	427	97	10	41	.227
Road	3	8	5.57	0	95.1	RHB	320	90	11	39	.281
Day	3	5	3.84	0	68.0	Sc Pos	162	40	6	59	.247
Night	8	5	3.50	0	128.2	Clutch	54	17	1	4	.315

1990 Rankings (National League)

- 1st in ERA at home (1.78)
- 2nd worst ERA on the road (5.57)
- 4th most HRs allowed per 9 innings (.96)
- 5th in home runs allowed (21) and least run support per 9 innings (3.5)
- Led the Astros in wins (11), strikeouts (136), wild pitches (6), runners caught stealing (9), groundball/flyball ratio (1.58), most strikeouts per 9 innings (6.2), ERA at home and lowest batting average allowed vs. left-handed batters

RAFAEL RAMIREZ

Position: SS
Bats: R **Throws:** R
Ht: 5'11" **Wt:** 190

Opening Day Age: 32
Born: 2/18/59 in San Pedro de Macoris, Dominican Republic
ML Seasons: 11

HITTING:

The bloom is beginning to fade on Rafael Ramirez. His three-year reign as the Houston Astros' starting shortstop, following his 1988 acquisition from Atlanta, appears to be over. Young Eric Yelding is expected to take the 32-year-old veteran's job this season.

Ramirez has given the Astros some good years, especially with his bat in run-scoring situations. However, his errors continue to be prolific (25 in 1990) despite playing more than half his games on carpet. Though he hit .311 with runners in scoring position, he only knocked in 37 runs, his lowest RBI total as a regular player since gathering 33 with Atlanta in 1986. Without run production, the other weaknesses in Ramirez' game -- especially his tendency to swing at everything -- become more obvious.

Ramirez seldom pulls the ball; instead, he takes the pitch to center or right field. He has no home run power (two in '90), though he's usually in the 20's in doubles. A good contact man despite his free-swinging style, Ramirez fanned only 46 times last year. Ramirez is also a good guy to have on a team. "When he's going good, when he's going bad, you never can tell," says ex-teammate Bill Doran. "He's a happy-go-lucky guy, always smiling and fun to be around."

A guy who starts swinging the bat from the moment he leaves the dugout, Ramirez rarely walks, drawing just 15 unintentional passes in '90. Last year Ramirez kept alive his unenviable record of having more errors than walks in every season of his 11-year career. He made it close this time, with 25 errors and 24 total walks. At least he's never short-changed on an at-bat.

BASERUNNING:

Ramirez usually bats in the lower part of the batting order and doesn't get much chance to run. He did succeed on 10 of 15 theft attempts in '90 and is aggressive in taking the extra base. He still possesses fine speed.

FIELDING:

Ramirez hustles and enjoys the game, but his fielding has always been erratic. His arm is starting to weaken a little bit and his range in the field has decreased. He appears to be a step slower. Ramirez is always among the leaders in errors, but at least he stayed under 30 last year.

OVERALL:

Ramirez must battle for his starting job in 1991 as the Astros rebuild with youth. The speedy Yelding is the heir-apparent, but Ramirez is a wise veteran who will give it his best shot. He's looking at long odds this time and might end up being dealt away.

Overall Statistics

	G	AB	R	H	D	T	HR	RBI	SB	BB	SO	AVG
1990	132	445	44	116	19	3	2	37	10	24	46	.261
Career	1365	5085	528	1333	208	31	51	451	109	244	557	.262

Where He Hits the Ball

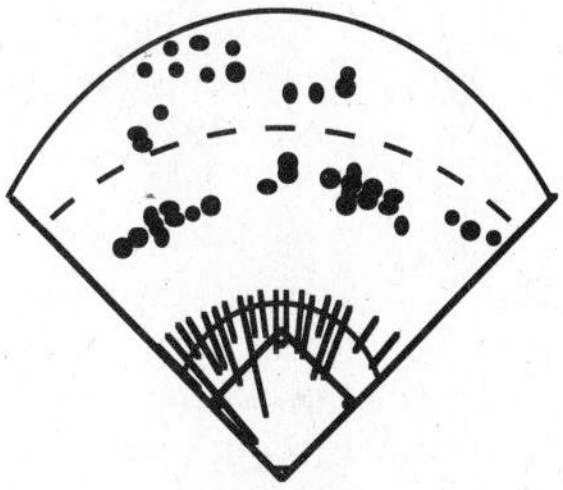

Vs. LHP

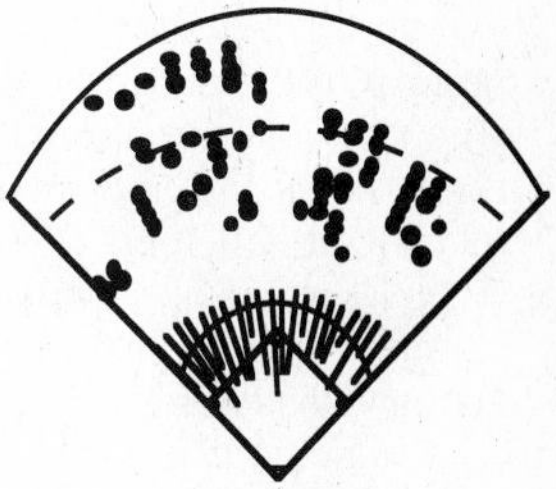

Vs. RHP

1990 Situational Stats

	AB	H	HR	RBI	AVG		AB	H	HR	RBI	AVG
Home	206	55	1	20	.267	LHP	192	50	1	15	.260
Road	239	61	1	17	.255	RHP	253	66	1	22	.261
Day	118	31	2	17	.263	Sc Pos	103	32	1	33	.311
Night	327	85	0	20	.260	Clutch	78	21	0	9	.269

1990 Rankings (National League)

- 1st in worst fielding percentage at shortstop (.953)
- 3rd highest batting average on an 0-2 count (.314)
- Led the Astros in sacrifice bunts (9), batting average with runners in scoring position (.311), batting average on an 0-2 count, batting average with 2 strikes (.228) and highest percentage of swings put into play (51.3%)
- Led NL shortstops in batting average with runners in scoring position and batting average on an 0-2 count

PITCHING:

After averaging 17 wins a year for the previous five seasons, Mike Scott hit the skids in 1990. He didn't even reach double figures, stalling out at 9-13. The dramatic no-hitter, the '86 division title, even the 20 wins in '89 are things of the past. "Ancient history," says Scott. Which begs the question: is Scott ancient history as a dominant pitcher in the National League?

All of Scott's important numbers declined last year. He rebounded from a 1-5 start (6.33 ERA) and had several winning spurts, but basically he struggled. He served up 27 home runs -- the second-worst total in the league -- and finished with a 3.81 ERA. It was his fewest wins and highest ERA since 1984, when he went 5-11 with a 4.68 ERA. Scott did lead the staff in shutouts (two) and complete games (four).

Management wondered about Scott's physical conditioning last season, but a drop-off in velocity was at the heart of his problems. He also had some mechanical problems with his delivery. "He's not the devastating pitcher he was before," says one NL scout, "but who can hold that form as long as he did? If you're not striking out guys as much as before, as long as they hit the ball, they've got a chance to get base hits." At his age (36 in April), Scott can be expected to continue to lose a little speed on his pitches. For him, losing velocity on the pitch that made him a star -- the split-fingered fastball -- was more important than losing it on the fastball. Even after dropping just a little velocity, the split-finger simply wasn't as effective. It was no longer the sinking, darting pitch that overwhelmed batters in the past. Without that extra zip, Scott became a mere mortal like other pitchers.

HOLDING RUNNERS, FIELDING, HITTING:

With his slow leg kick, Scott is the most susceptible of Astro pitchers to stolen bases. Almost 32 percent of the thefts against the team came with him on the mound. Runners were 53-for-60 with Scott pitching. He fields his position well, but is slow running the bases. A decent hitter, he averages 7 to 9 hits per season.

OVERALL:

Though not as dominating as in past years, Scott nonetheless remains a good, solid major league pitcher. His age works against him in Houston, as the club begins to reshape the staff for the future. The Astros will look at his age and his salary and then decide. He could prove a positive influence on a young pitching staff, but he would also be tempting to a contending club needing a veteran starter.

MIKE SCOTT

Position: SP
Bats: R **Throws:** R
Ht: 6' 3" **Wt:** 215

Opening Day Age: 35
Born: 4/26/55 in Santa Monica, CA
ML Seasons: 12

Overall Statistics

	W	L	ERA	G	GS	Sv	IP	H	R	BB	SO	HR
1990	9	13	3.81	32	32	0	205.2	194	102	66	121	27
Career	124	106	3.51	345	317	3	2061.0	1847	898	623	1466	171

How Often He Throws Strikes

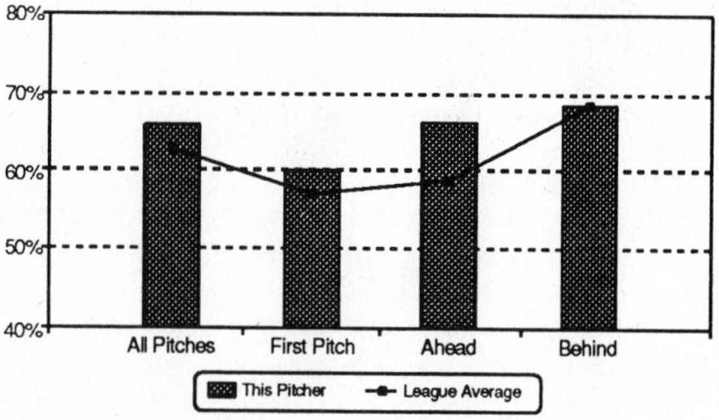

1990 Situational Stats

	W	L	ERA	Sv	IP		AB	H	HR	RBI	AVG
Home	5	4	2.42	0	130.0	LHB	450	108	11	52	.240
Road	4	9	6.19	0	75.2	RHB	339	86	16	41	.254
Day	2	4	4.91	0	55.0	Sc Pos	193	44	5	62	.228
Night	7	9	3.40	0	150.2	Clutch	63	10	0	2	.159

1990 Rankings (National League)

- 1st in highest stolen base percentage allowed (88.3%)
- 2nd in home runs allowed (27), stolen bases allowed (53) and most HRs allowed per 9 innings (1.2)
- 3rd least run support per 9 innings (3.1)
- 5th best ERA at home (2.42)
- Led the Astros in complete games (4), shutouts (2), home runs allowed and stolen bases allowed

DAVE SMITH

Position: RP
Bats: R **Throws:** R
Ht: 6' 1" **Wt:** 195

Opening Day Age: 36
Born: 1/21/55 in San Francisco, CA
ML Seasons: 11

PITCHING:

Old Man River has nothing on Dave Smith. The Astros' long-time reliever keeps rolling along, too. Just think of the wear and tear on his right arm over 11 seasons with Houston: 563 games, 762 innings, 53 wins (and 47 losses) and 199 saves. He was the team's save leader for the sixth consecutive year in 1990. His 200th save will make Smith only the third pitcher in baseball history to record that total with one club. He was also the Astros' lone player on the All-Star squad last year.

Still, Smith has pitched in relative anonymity during the course of his lengthy career, in part because he's had only one 30-save season. In his youth, Smith's fastball topped out at 94 MPH and he threw heat like most closers. Now, he's in the mid-80s, but he's a better pitcher because he knows how to set up the hitter for his two varieties of fastball, his curveball and his forkball. "I wish I knew in 1980 what I know now," says Smith. "It would have been much easier." Smith is also a student of body language, watching the batter at the plate to see where he wants the ball or where he wants to hit it. Then, Smith keeps it away from that zone.

For those reasons, Smith keeps piling successful season upon successful season. The trouble is, few people know it. One problem is his name: he should have a colorful nickname or call himself "D.K." Smith. That's not his style, though. He comes to the ballpark, keeps his mouth shut, does his job and goes home. He has pitched through 11 years of pressure-packed situations and his 23 saves in 1990 once again show that not many people do it better.

HOLDING RUNNERS, FIELDING, HITTING:

Smith has made one error in the past two seasons covering 101 games, most of which he appeared in with the outcome on the line. He works at holding runners on base and is good at covering the bag on balls hit toward first. He's not much of a hitter, but then, he doesn't hit very often, batting just three times in two years.

OVERALL:

Count on Smith trotting out to the hill some 50 times this year and winning most of the battles. The question is who he'll win the battles for. As a "new look" free agent, Smith has been given the chance to negotiate with any club. Smith may not be famous, but by the time the 1991 season starts, he figures to be rich.

Overall Statistics

	W	L	ERA	G	GS	Sv	IP	H	R	BB	SO	HR
1990	6	6	2.39	49	0	23	60.1	45	18	20	50	4
Career	53	47	2.53	563	1	199	762.1	646	254	260	529	28

How Often He Throws Strikes

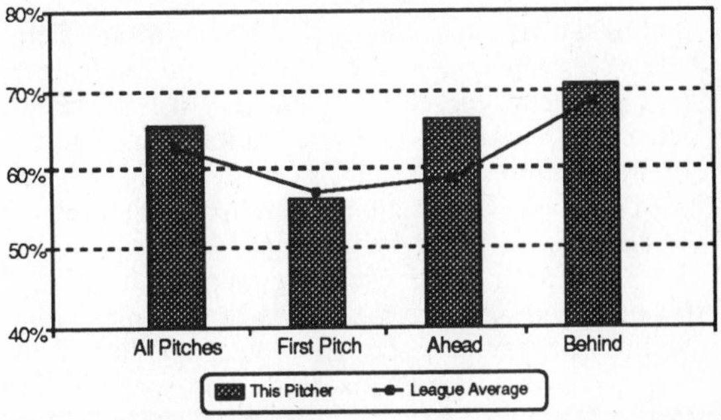

1990 Situational Stats

	W	L	ERA	Sv	IP		AB	H	HR	RBI	AVG
Home	3	4	2.25	13	32.0	LHB	113	26	1	8	.230
Road	3	2	2.54	10	28.1	RHB	101	19	3	12	.188
Day	2	2	3.57	7	17.2	Sc Pos	58	12	3	17	.207
Night	4	4	1.90	16	42.2	Clutch	152	32	3	17	.211

1990 Rankings (National League)

- 1st in balks (5)
- 4th in saves (23) and save percentage (82.1%)
- 5th in save opportunities (28)
- 7th in games finished (42)
- Led the Astros in saves, games finished, balks, save opportunities, save percentage and blown saves (5)

FRANKLIN STUBBS

Position: 1B/LF
Bats: L **Throws:** L
Ht: 6' 2" **Wt:** 218

Opening Day Age: 30
Born: 10/21/60 in Laurinburg, NC
ML Seasons: 7

HITTING:

On April Fool's Day, 1990, the Houston Astros acquired Franklin Stubbs. He turned out be no joke. They swapped minor league pitcher Terry Wells to Los Angeles for Stubbs, a reserve outfielder/first baseman who, they thought, might hit a few home runs off the bench. What they obtained, instead, was a 23-homer, 71-RBI man who batted .261 and slugged his way into the starting lineup. With Glenn Davis injured much of the year, Stubbs became the Astros' main power threat and led the team in home runs.

Always searching for power, Houston was grateful to have Stubbs when their only other proven home run threat, Davis, went on the disabled list for two months with a rib cage injury. Pressed into regular duty, Stubbs proved he could hit consistently and with power, that he could handle left-handed pitching and that he could drive in clutch runs.

Stubbs did an outstanding job, moving to left field when Davis returned to the lineup. The ex-Dodger broke the club record for homers by a left-handed hitter in a season. He also wrested the team HR and RBI titles from Davis and just missed a 20-20 year with 19 stolen bases. Call it a career year, the result of being more patient at the plate and not trying to pull too many pitches. He also hung tough against lefty pitching, hitting .258, a knock against him in LA. Stubbs still hammers fastballs, but has adjusted to offspeed pitches. He hit six of his 23 homers vs. the Dodgers.

BASERUNNING:

The 30-year-old Stubbs trimmed down some 10 pounds because he knew he would have to play in the outfield. A side-effect was a career high 19 stolen bases in 25 attempts. Stubbs also grounded into just four double plays in 146 games. He shows good speed for his age and size.

FIELDING:

Stubbs has improved his outfield play to where he is slightly above-average. Lighter, he covers more ground than in his LA years. Stubbs' arm proved strong enough to handle left field, but he's still a better first baseman than outfielder. He made five errors in his first regular duty in three years.

OVERALL:

Stubbs could form a pretty good one-two power punch with Davis, which would be a real rarity for the Astros. The only trouble is that he's a free agent and the club might not be able to sign him. After years of being unwanted, Stubbs was of a mind to test his market value.

Overall Statistics

	G	AB	R	H	D	T	HR	RBI	SB	BB	SO	AVG
1990	146	448	59	117	23	2	23	71	19	48	114	.261
Career	688	1825	225	430	71	9	82	249	50	179	460	.236

Where He Hits the Ball

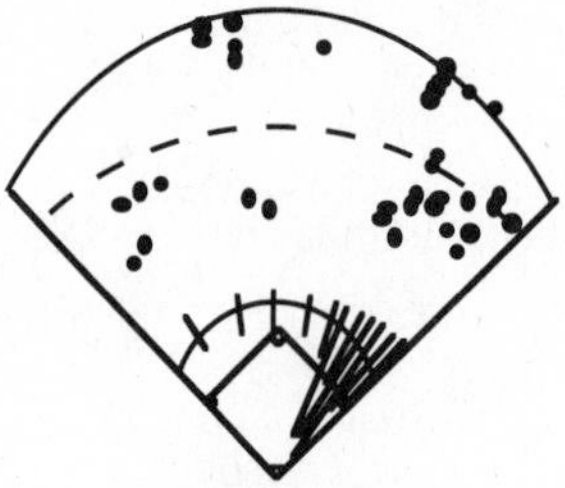

Vs. LHP

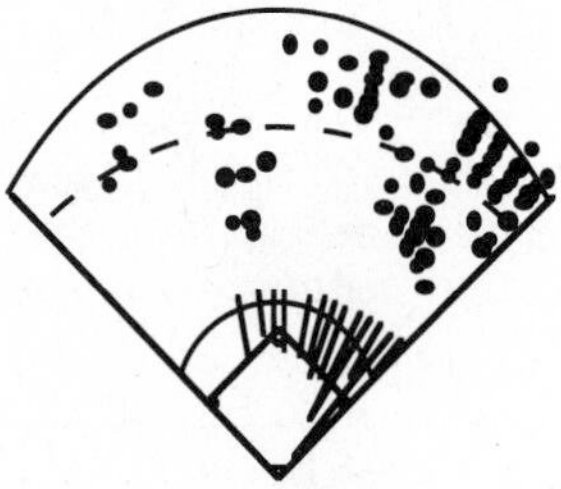

Vs. RHP

1990 Situational Stats

	AB	H	HR	RBI	AVG		AB	H	HR	RBI	AVG
Home	229	58	9	39	.253	LHP	159	41	7	23	.258
Road	219	59	14	32	.269	RHP	289	76	16	48	.263
Day	125	28	5	19	.224	Sc Pos	118	26	7	45	.220
Night	323	89	18	52	.276	Clutch	86	31	7	18	.360

1990 Rankings (National League)

- 3rd highest batting average on a 3-1 count (.636)
- 5th least GDPs per GDP situation (4.1%) and lowest percentage of swings put into play (37.3%)
- Led the Astros in home runs (23), total bases (213), RBIs (71), strikeouts (114), stolen base percentage (76.0%), batting average in the clutch (.361) and batting average on a 3-1 count
- Led NL first basemen in stolen bases (19), caught stealing (6), stolen base percentage (76.0%) and batting average on a 3-1 count

HITTING:

Glenn Wilson has had a well-travelled career, but one place he didn't want to visit was the disabled list. Unfortunately, that is where Wilson finished the 1990 season. He grounded into a team-high 16 double plays before undergoing knee surgery when the pain became too much. Wilson hung in there long enough to club 10 homers and drive in 55 runs in 118 games in what he hoped would be his first full campaign as an Astro. Wilson bowed out with a .245 batting average, his lowest mark since hitting .240 in 1984, his first year with Philadelphia.

Wilson's career average is only .265, but he retains a reputation for driving in big runs. His RBI production last year -- 55 in 368 at-bats -- was excellent. He uses the whole ballpark and has a good stroke to center and right field. Make a mistake with him and Wilson will pull the ball to deep left. He loves to hit with men on base and will chase some bad pitches at times in his zeal to drive in runs. That's especially true when he falls behind in the count. Because of his anxiety, he's never drawn many walks, and never hits for a high average.

"You've got to be careful pitching to him," says a National League scout. "He's a high-ball-hitting son-of-a-gun. If you make a mistake, if you don't get that ball far enough in, he'll hurt you." Wilson did just that in pinch hitting roles last year, knocking in seven runs in 15 at-bats. Whatever his role, he takes great pride in his work.

BASERUNNING:

His bad knee kept Wilson from doing much on the base paths last year, and he was thrown out on all three stolen base attempts. Wilson has never stolen more than seven bases in a season, even in his youth. His baserunning is aggressive for a man without much speed, but he usually doesn't get himself thrown out.

FIELDING:

Wilson has always been very solid in the field, with one of the strongest arms in the game in right field. Says club assistant GM Bob Watson, "I've only seen four guys with arms I think better than Glenn's -- Reggie Smith, Ollie Brown, Ellis Valentine and Roberto Clemente." That's high praise.

OVERALL:

As he has grown older, Wilson has become more of a role player. He moved from right field to left in '90 to clear the way for young Eric Anthony. If the Astros' more youthful talent doesn't measure up, look for Wilson to re-establish a claim to a starting spot.

GLENN WILSON

Position: RF/LF
Bats: R **Throws:** R
Ht: 6' 1" **Wt:** 190

Opening Day Age: 32
Born: 12/22/58 in Baytown, TX
ML Seasons: 9

Overall Statistics

	G	AB	R	H	D	T	HR	RBI	SB	BB	SO	AVG
1990	118	368	42	90	14	0	10	55	0	26	64	.245
Career	1191	4137	451	1096	209	26	98	521	27	253	663	.265

Where He Hits the Ball

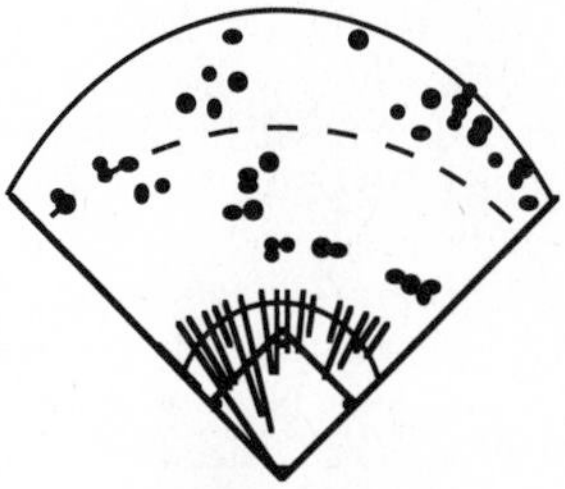

Vs. LHP

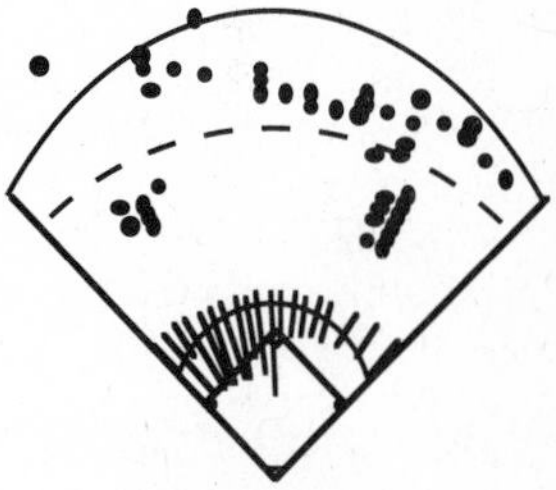

Vs. RHP

1990 Situational Stats

	AB	H	HR	RBI	AVG		AB	H	HR	RBI	AVG
Home	174	45	5	33	.259	LHP	164	43	2	25	.262
Road	194	45	5	22	.232	RHP	204	47	8	30	.230
Day	88	27	3	16	.307	Sc Pos	105	30	3	46	.286
Night	280	63	7	39	.225	Clutch	62	14	2	14	.226

1990 Rankings (National League)

- 2nd in most GDPs per GDP situation (22.2%)
- 5th in GDPs (16)
- 7th lowest batting average with the bases loaded (.111)
- Led the Astros in GDPs

ERIC YELDING

Position: CF/SS
Bats: R **Throws:** R
Ht: 6' 1" **Wt:** 170

Opening Day Age: 26
Born: 2/22/65 in Montrose, AL
ML Seasons: 2

Overall Statistics

	G	AB	R	H	D	T	HR	RBI	SB	BB	SO	AVG
1990	142	511	69	130	9	5	1	28	64	39	87	.254
Career	212	601	88	151	11	5	1	37	75	46	106	.251

Where He Hits the Ball

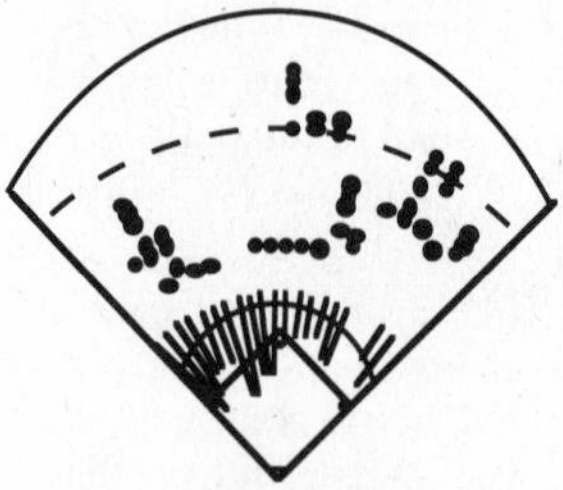

Vs. LHP

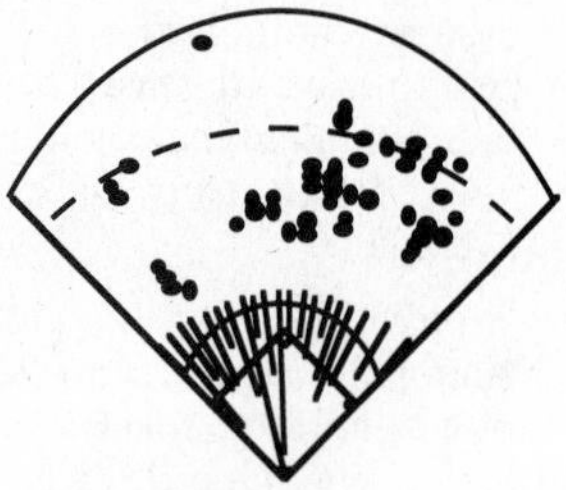

Vs. RHP

1990 Situational Stats

	AB	H	HR	RBI	AVG		AB	H	HR	RBI	AVG
Home	245	62	0	13	.253	LHP	235	66	0	16	.281
Road	266	68	1	15	.256	RHP	276	64	1	12	.232
Day	141	35	0	7	.248	Sc Pos	101	23	0	25	.228
Night	370	95	1	21	.257	Clutch	78	19	0	4	.244

1990 Rankings (National League)

- 1st in caught stealing (25)
- 2nd in stolen bases (64) and lowest slugging percentage (.298)
- 3rd lowest HR frequency (511 ABs per HR) and highest percentage of extra bases taken as a runner (64.4%)
- Led the Astros in runs (69), stolen bases, caught stealing, groundball/flyball ratio (1.77), runs scored per time reached base (40.8%), lowest percentage of swings that missed (13.5%), steal of third (9) and highest percentage of extra bases taken as a runner (64.4%)
- Led NL center fielders in stolen bases, caught stealing and GDPs (12)

HITTING:

For much of 1990, Eric Yelding looked like an infielder playing the outfield, and for good reason. Although considered the Astros' shortstop of the future, Yelding spent more time in the outfield (94 games) than at his chosen position (40). He even played 10 games at second base and three at third. Sometimes versatility can be a curse.

Despite all this moving about, Yelding hit .254, improving on his rookie average by 21 points, and stole 64 bases. He missed the club record by one theft and finished second in the National League. At times, though, he had to be a confused young man. Asked about Yelding's play, one scout replied, "It's hard to tell. I saw him play short one game, center field the next and then go back to short. They need to make a decision on where he's going to play and go with it."

The Astros expect to do so this season. With the switch to youth, it means out with the old (Rafael Ramirez) and in with the new (Yelding) at shortstop. Yelding's hitting is better than some baseball people expected. Mainly a singles hitter, he yanks an occasional hard-hit ball down the line, but had only 15 extra-base blows in his 130 base hits. Yelding's game is singles and speed, but with his limited bat skill, he'll have to reach base more often to be effective. He drew only 39 walks last year and had an on-base percentage of only .305, far too low for a guy tabbed for the top spot in the lineup.

BASERUNNING:

Karl Rhodes, one of Yelding's teammates, was asked about Yelding's great speed. "I've got speed, but not Eric Yelding speed," Rhodes said. Although Yelding stole 64 bases, at least 10 of his 25 caught stealings resulted from him being picked off the bag and trying to high-tail it to the next base. He refers to his pick-offs as "brain cramps" and had far too many of them the last part of the season.

FIELDING:

Yelding is not yet fluid at shortstop, but his arm is above-average and he covers a lot of ground. He made 17 errors while splitting time between the infield and outfield. The true test will come when he settles into one position.

OVERALL:

Among the league's swiftest players, Yelding is a showpiece for the Astros' franchise. He is working at building strength and stamina for his slim frame. After his two-year apprenticeship, 1991 could be the big year for Yelding.

HITTING:

The once-promising career of Gerald Young continues to travel in reverse. Once part of a trio of young players thought to be the cornerstone of the Astros' future, he found himself back in the minor leagues in 1990. The promise of a .321 rookie year has been washed out by dwindling returns at the plate and on the base paths ever since. His batting average shrank to .257 in '88 and then .233 in '89, his stolen bases from 65 to 34. In 1990, it only got worse.

Told to snap out of his slump and concentrate on things aimed to revive his game, Young instead hit only .175 with one home run, four RBI and six steals in 57 games. In late May, he drew a ticket to Tucson, Arizona, and AAA ball. There, he missed six weeks with a broken index finger on his left hand, but hit .337 and stole 13 bases in 48 games to prompt his recall. Once again, however, he failed to hit.

After his worst year ever, Young's career is at the crossroads. He needs to stop balking at instructions and learn to utilize his speed as a hitter. "They tell me he doesn't listen," one NL scout says of the former New York Mets farmhand. "He's got to listen and learn when they tell him things. Gerald must learn to use the bat -- bunt, drag, slap the ball and run. Use that great speed to his advantage." When Young begins to do these things - - fake a bunt, draw the infield in and slap the ball by them -- he may put his career in the right direction again.

BASERUNNING:

Once Young regains his old desire and hustle, he may regain his stature as one of the game's rising stars. He can steal 60 bases again by becoming a student of the game. He cannot do it by just depending on his speed. He stole six bases in nine attempts, hardly the measure of his ability.

FIELDING:

Young has loads of talent in the field. He can run and go get the ball. He also has the quickness to recover and make the catch even on a misjudged ball. He covers a lot of real estate with his speed, and he has a fine arm.

OVERALL:

Young must change his attitude, adjust his swing, take the bunt when it's there and really use his speed. Says one National Leaguer, "If he hits leadoff, takes his bases on balls and hits .260, he's worth millions of dollars the way he plays center field." Will that day ever come?

GERALD YOUNG

Position: CF
Bats: B **Throws:** R
Ht: 6' 2" **Wt:** 185

Opening Day Age: 26
Born: 10/22/64 in Tele, Honduras
ML Seasons: 4

Overall Statistics

	G	AB	R	H	D	T	HR	RBI	SB	BB	SO	AVG
1990	57	154	15	27	4	1	1	4	6	20	23	.175
Career	423	1537	209	387	51	15	2	94	131	186	176	.252

Where He Hits the Ball

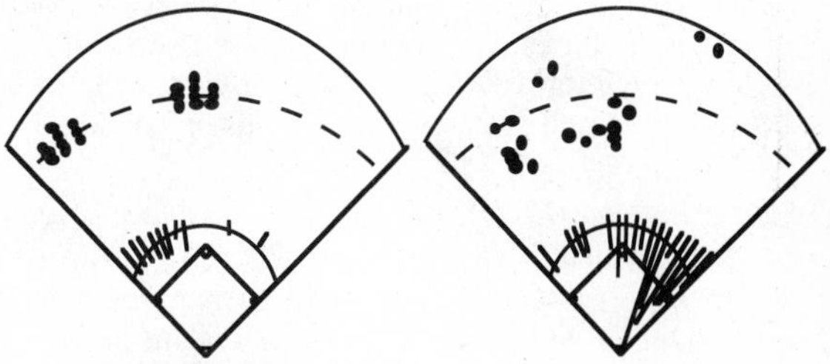

Vs. LHP Vs. RHP

1990 Situational Stats

	AB	H	HR	RBI	AVG		AB	H	HR	RBI	AVG
Home	93	17	1	3	.183	LHP	46	8	1	4	.174
Road	61	10	0	1	.164	RHP	108	19	0	0	.176
Day	34	4	0	0	.118	Sc Pos	33	3	0	3	.091
Night	120	23	1	4	.192	Clutch	35	3	0	0	.086

1990 Rankings (National League)

- 10th highest batting average on a 3-2 count (.350)

MARK DAVIDSON

Position: RF/LF
Bats: R **Throws:** R
Ht: 6' 2" **Wt:** 190

Opening Day Age: 30
Born: 2/15/61 in Knoxville, TN
ML Seasons: 5

Overall Statistics

	G	AB	R	H	D	T	HR	RBI	SB	BB	SO	AVG
1990	57	130	12	38	5	1	1	11	0	10	18	.292
Career	328	519	78	122	21	3	4	42	15	46	100	.235

HITTING, FIELDING, BASERUNNING:

If the Houston Astros' outfield remains open to all contenders, Mark Davidson may have a shot at either cracking the lineup or being one of the reserve outfielders. An impressive late-season showing with the bat in '90 opened some eyes, as Davidson wound up hitting a career-high .292.

Davidson needs only to continue to hit big-league pitching to stick with the Astros. He does a lot of things well, offering the complete package of running, fielding and throwing. He is excellent on defense, but prior to 1990 had always been a low average hitter. After a good campaign at AAA Tucson, he continued to hit when recalled to the big club.

Davidson gives no indication of power, though he's 6-2 and 190. Although he hits the ball hard, his best shots carry to the track, not beyond the fences. Davidson appears to have shortened his swing, making him a better contact hitter, and he goes with the pitch. He struck out 18 times in 130 official at-bats, not bad for a player who spent much of his time in a reserve role. Though swift, he was caught stealing on all three stolen base attempts.

OVERALL:

A lack of power is Davidson's biggest drawback in his bid to nail down a regular job. The Astros are hurting for power and have more than their share of singles hitters. If no one steps forward, he could squeeze into the outfield picture and at least earn one of the substitute spots.

RICH GEDMAN

Position: C
Bats: L **Throws:** R
Ht: 6' 0" **Wt:** 215

Opening Day Age: 31
Born: 9/26/59 in Worcester, MA
ML Seasons: 11

Overall Statistics

	G	AB	R	H	D	T	HR	RBI	SB	BB	SO	AVG
1990	50	119	7	24	7	0	1	10	0	20	30	.202
Career	946	2960	319	762	171	12	84	366	3	221	472	.257

HITTING, FIELDING, BASERUNNING:

With his best years behind him, Rich Gedman wants to salvage something of his fading career this season. His trade from Boston to Houston last year did not energize his batting skill, and a change of scenery failed to re-establish his starting status. The original intent of the deal was to spring the speedy Craig Biggio from behind the plate for outfield duty. Biggio didn't like the outfield, however, and Gedman couldn't shake off the rust. After failing to prove he could hit, he finished the '90 season on the bench.

As an Astro, Gedman batted .202 in 40 games and his production included only one homer. He also struck out an average of once every four trips to the plate. After having played so little for two years, his confidence has dropped. Gedman hasn't known success since his All-Star days of the mid-1980s. He hasn't batted higher than .231 since 1986.

Gedman runs hard, but has no speed on the base paths. He is a fine catcher with a good arm who unexplainably can no longer gun down runners. He works well with pitchers, calls a good game, blocks balls in the dirt well and has a veteran's touch behind the plate.

OVERALL:

Once Biggio returned to catching last year, Gedman became virtually an invisible man. He went weeks without playing. A free agent at season's end, he'll probably have to work cheap if he wants to find another club. It's hard to believe Gedman is only 31, because his bat looks so much older.

CARL NICHOLS

Position: C
Bats: R **Throws:** R
Ht: 6' 0" **Wt:** 192

Opening Day Age: 28
Born: 10/14/62 in Los Angeles, CA
ML Seasons: 5

Overall Statistics

	G	AB	R	H	D	T	HR	RBI	SB	BB	SO	AVG
1990	32	49	7	10	3	0	0	11	0	8	11	.204
Career	76	135	13	28	5	0	0	17	0	13	32	.207

HITTING, FIELDING, BASERUNNING:

Still trying to squeeze his foot inside the major league door, Carl Nichols has spent parts of five seasons in the majors and 11 years in the minors. His early experience came with Baltimore, and Houston acquired him in a trade at the minor league level. Manager Art Howe seems to like Nichols because he can catch or fill in at first base and the outfield. He caught in 15 games, played the outfield in one and first base in three others before being injured.

Nichols tries to hit the ball hard each trip to the plate and he has good power to the alleys. His best shots usually go for doubles. Nichols batted .204 in 32 games, but his 10 hits produced 11 RBI for the Astros. He runs the bases well and has all the tools of the catching trade. Possessor of a strong arm, Nichols cut down 16 of 30 runners at AAA Tucson and picked five more off first base; he also hit .253 there, with four HR and 33 RBI. The knock against him in the Baltimore system was that he needed to be more motivated. For this reason, he welcomed the trade that sent him to the Houston organization and a fresh start.

OVERALL:

Nichols could be a sleeper, one of those players who comes around late in his career. Since the Astros want backup help behind Craig Biggio and Rich Gedman following the release of Alex Trevino, Nichols may find a spot on the roster. Once a good prospect, Nichols fell off the pace in the past. This year, he may show enough ability to stick around.

TERRY PUHL

Position: LF
Bats: L **Throws:** R
Ht: 6' 2" **Wt:** 197

Opening Day Age: 34
Born: 7/8/56 in Melville, Saskatchewan
ML Seasons: 14

Overall Statistics

	G	AB	R	H	D	T	HR	RBI	SB	BB	SO	AVG
1990	37	41	5	12	1	0	0	8	1	5	7	.293
Career	1516	4837	676	1357	226	56	62	432	217	502	505	.281

HITTING, FIELDING, BASERUNNING:

Even with his advanced years, Canadian-born Terry Puhl remains a valuable member of the Houston Astros. Some people tend to think Puhl is no longer a factor because he has been around for so long, but he hit .301 in 60 games with the club in 1977, and .293 thirteen seasons later in 1990.

Puhl's problem hasn't been age (34), but staying away from injuries. The 1990 season was no exception. He fractured his right shoulder in May, spent seven weeks on the disabled list, came back briefly, then went out again when the problem failed to clear up. When healthy, Puhl is an excellent asset to the club. He stays in good shape and retains his skills in the field where he has decent range and a good arm when it's healthy. He's lost running speed, however, and stole only one base last year.

Never much of a power threat, Puhl had just one extra-base hit, a double, among his 12 hits. He was 8-for-20 as a pinch swinger. "Puhl can't play like he used to," says one NL scout, "but he's still a valuable player in case someone gets hurt and you need him to play a few days. Play him two, three days, then pinch hit him, and he does a good job for you."

OVERALL:

If Puhl's arm comes around as expected, he is likely to be the Astros' fourth outfielder again. He can still hit for average, he is solid in the field, and his experience off the bench is invaluable to a team committed to rebuilding with youth.

KARL RHODES

Position: LF
Bats: L **Throws:** L
Ht: 5'11" **Wt:** 170

Opening Day Age: 22
Born: 8/21/68 in Cincinnati, OH
ML Seasons: 1

Overall Statistics

	G	AB	R	H	D	T	HR	RBI	SB	BB	SO	AVG
1990	38	86	12	21	6	1	1	3	4	13	12	.244
Career	38	86	12	21	6	1	1	3	4	13	12	.244

HITTING, FIELDING, BASERUNNING:

Karl Rhodes is a young player who has a load of confidence in his ability to play the game and hit the baseball. His first exposure to major league ball didn't dim his optimism. Rhodes plays the running game, although he doesn't possess blinding speed. His game consists of getting on base, stealing, and scoring runs.

Rhodes has a short, quick stroke at the plate and he is a contact hitter. Although he hit only .244 in 39 games for Houston, he gave no signs of being intimidated by big-league pitching. The Astros promoted him from AAA Tucson when Terry Puhl went on the disabled list. A lefty swinger, Rhodes batted .275 with 3 homers, 59 RBI and 24 stolen bases (in 28 attempts) at Tucson. He has line drive power and won't reach the fences too often. He's a good doubles and triples man, however, with 11 three baggers in only 107 games at Tucson.

Rhodes is a smart baserunner who has stolen as many as 65 bases in the minors. He was four-for-five in 1990 with the Astros. He can cover a lot of territory in the field and he has a good arm.

OVERALL:

Rhodes can be an explosive type of player and is improving his game with experience. His playing time with the Astros last season should help him challenge for a spot in the outfield in 1991. Someone else must carry the power load in the outfield. He can handle the rest.

DAVID ROHDE

Position: 2B
Bats: B **Throws:** R
Ht: 6' 2" **Wt:** 182

Opening Day Age: 26
Born: 5/8/64 in Los Altos, CA
ML Seasons: 1

Overall Statistics

	G	AB	R	H	D	T	HR	RBI	SB	BB	SO	AVG
1990	59	98	8	18	4	0	0	5	0	9	20	.184
Career	59	98	8	18	4	0	0	5	0	9	20	.184

HITTING, FIELDING, BASERUNNING:

Dave Rohde drew the first crack at Bill Doran's old job at second base last September. The hitting numbers didn't fall right for him, as he batted only .184 in 98 at-bats. Now Rohde is looking for a second chance and, if that fails, he will set his sights on an infield utility spot. After five years in the minors, Rohde, 26, has the necessary experience for a reserve role.

Rohde hit decently when first promoted from AAA Tucson last year, and his audition for replacing Doran began well. He even had back-to-back three-hit games in July. He was never able to get untracked after being reduced to spot duty, however, and he finished the season on an 0-for-24 streak.

The switch-hitting Rohde can play second, short and third, making him a strong utility player candidate. He has the arm to make the throws from each position and looks like he has sufficient range. He played errorless ball in 59 games with the Astros. Rohde has excellent running speed and is a definite base stealing threat.

OVERALL:

The University of Arizona product has hit well at each minor league level, especially in 1990, when he hit .353 in 170 at-bats at Tucson. Rohde is no power hitter, but he uses his speed to good advantage. If he proves he can hit a little in the big leagues, the Astros have a spot for him on the roster.

TIM BELCHER

Position: SP
Bats: R **Throws:** R
Ht: 6' 3" **Wt:** 210

Opening Day Age: 29
Born: 10/19/61 in Sparta, OH
ML Seasons: 4

Overall Statistics

	W	L	ERA	G	GS	Sv	IP	H	R	BB	SO	HR
1990	9	9	4.00	24	24	0	153.0	136	76	48	102	17
Career	40	29	3.12	105	86	5	596.2	491	233	186	477	47

How Often He Throws Strikes

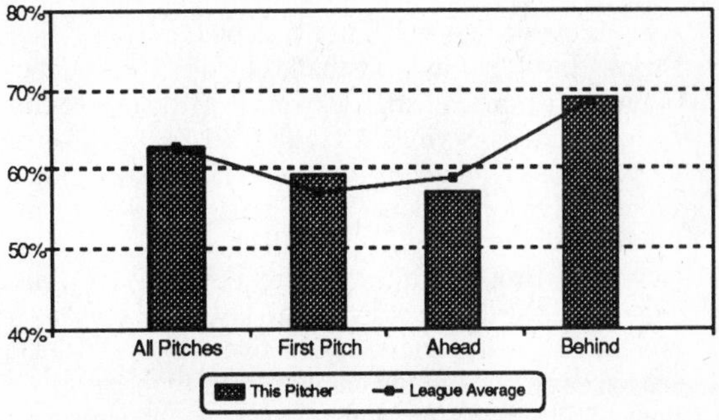

1990 Situational Stats

	W	L	ERA	Sv	IP		AB	H	HR	RBI	AVG
Home	6	3	2.77	0	74.2	LHB	302	68	8	27	.225
Road	3	6	5.17	0	78.1	RHB	264	68	9	40	.258
Day	1	2	5.70	0	36.1	Sc Pos	104	27	3	46	.260
Night	8	7	3.47	0	116.2	Clutch	36	7	0	2	.194

1990 Rankings (National League)

- 9th in shutouts (2)
- Led the Dodgers in sacrifice bunts as a batter (9)

PITCHING:

After leading the majors with eight shutouts in 1989, Tim Belcher picked up where he left off, tossing a three-hit shutout April 10 in San Diego. As it turned out, that was one of the few highlights of Belcher's season. Bothered by shoulder problems, he made only 24 starts. His 9-9 record and 4.00 ERA were a far cry from his 1989 figures of 15-12 and 2.82.

Although he didn't go on the disabled list until August, Belcher was pitching hurt for months before that, and was never able to take over as staff ace for Orel Hershiser, who went down in April with his own (more serious) shoulder problems. Belcher took himself out of a game May 28 in Pittsburgh, battled insufficient shoulder strength in subsequent starts, and received his first ever cortisone shot at the All-Star break.

Though he pitched a one-hit shutout in which he faced the minimum 27 batters on his next trip to Pittsburgh, Belcher's troubles continued, and he was placed on the disabled list August 17 due to "acute tendinitis" in his shoulder. Rest didn't help his condition, and arthroscopic surgery in September revealed a piece of loose cartilage floating in his shoulder capsule. Trainers compared the situation to "a pebble in your shoe," and Belcher should be ready to again stomp on opposing hitters.

When he's 100 percent, Belcher overpowers batters with a 95 MPH fastball and hard slider. The absence of a "strikeout pitch" with two-strike counts last season forced Belcher to learn more about pitching. His finesse pitches include a split-finger fastball and occasional curve.

HOLDING RUNNERS, FIELDING, HITTING:

Belcher is a good fielder and tries to hold runners on base, but his high leg kick makes it easy for opposing runners to steal. Belcher's bat sometimes is his own best friend. In just 24 games, he led the entire club with nine sacrifice hits.

OVERALL:

A perfectionist on the mound, Belcher's biggest problem is his temper. If something unexpected occurs in a game, he can lose his concentration for a few moments. Belcher also needs to get off to a good start. Prior to last season's disappointing second half (2-3, 4.46 ERA), Belcher had a career 21-8 record and 2.25 ERA after the All-Star break. Things should be better for Belcher in 1991, especially with a clean bill of health. Look for Belcher to blossom into a Cy Young Award candidate and regain his place among the National League strikeout leaders.

HITTING:

The Dodgers paid $6 million to import veteran Hubie Brooks from the Montreal Expos, and they weren't disappointed. Brooks overcame a sore wrist and sore knee last year to drive in 91 runs while matching his career high with 20 homers. A consistent medium-level power hitter, Brooks has averaged 16 homers for the last seven seasons, never hitting less than 13 or more than 20. He's also averaged 79 RBI per year over that span.

Batting in the number-five slot last year, Brooks provided protection for cleanup hitter Eddie Murray. In bases-loaded situations, he went 8-for-17 with 24 RBI and just one double play. That was a welcome sight, especially after the 1989 Dodgers hit just .222 overall with runners in scoring position -- the worst in the National League. Brooks batted .286 after July 31 with eight homers and 38 RBI.

An aggressive first-ball hitter with power to all fields, Brooks loves the high fastball, but offspeed pitches often cause him to swing awkwardly. Brooks loses his bat on countless swings, including a 140-foot propeller toss in San Diego that landed in the lap of Dodger executive vice president Fred Claire, who was sitting in the third base box seats. Because of that wild swinging, Brooks strikes out frequently -- he's had exactly 108 strikeouts each of the last three seasons -- and rarely walks. He's drawn over 40 walks in a season only once in his career. More than anything, lack of discipline has kept Brooks as a dangerous hitter instead of a great one.

BASERUNNING:

At 34, Brooks is slowing down. He was two-for-seven stealing in 1990 and is a combined eight-for-24 over the last two seasons. With figures like that, the Dodgers might consider nailing him to first base. Brooks isn't afraid to take the extra base, but his judgement isn't the greatest.

FIELDING:

A converted third baseman and shortstop, Brooks was second out of all NL right fielders with 10 errors in 1990. His most embarrassing moment came August 4 in San Francisco when he caught a ball and started to run toward the dugout. Unfortunately there were only two outs, and Brett Butler scored from second. Brooks does possess a strong throwing arm.

OVERALL:

Brooks contributes to the Dodgers' clubhouse harmony in a quiet manner. He works hard, doesn't complain and stays out of controversy. Brooks has never played in a postseason game, but that hasn't been his fault. He can hit, and he can help a ball club.

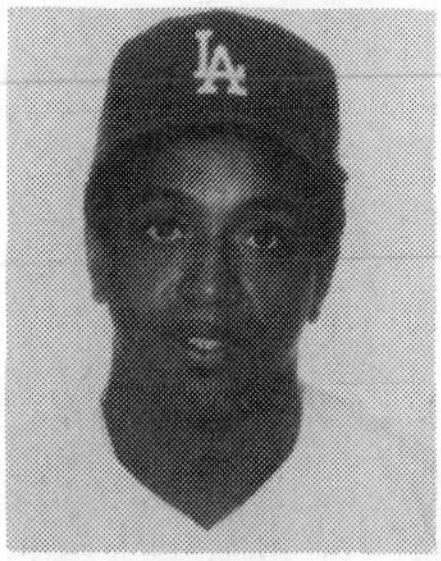

HUBIE BROOKS

Position: RF
Bats: R **Throws:** R
Ht: 6' 0" **Wt:** 205

Opening Day Age: 34
Born: 9/24/56 in Los Angeles, CA
ML Seasons: 11

Overall Statistics

	G	AB	R	H	D	T	HR	RBI	SB	BB	SO	AVG
1990	153	568	74	151	28	1	20	91	2	33	108	.266
Career	1351	5082	561	1395	252	30	123	700	57	318	860	.274

Where He Hits the Ball

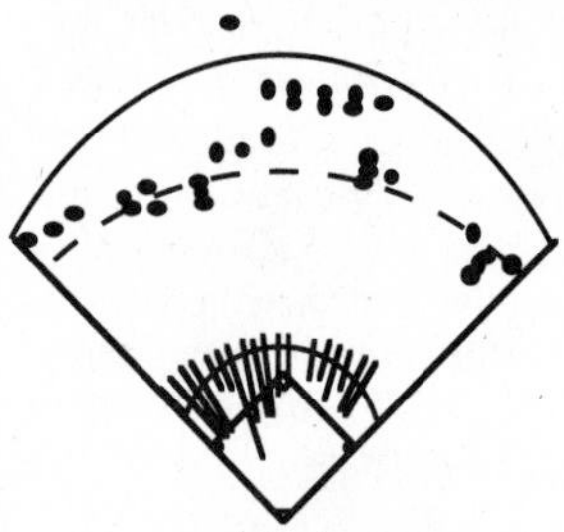

Vs. LHP

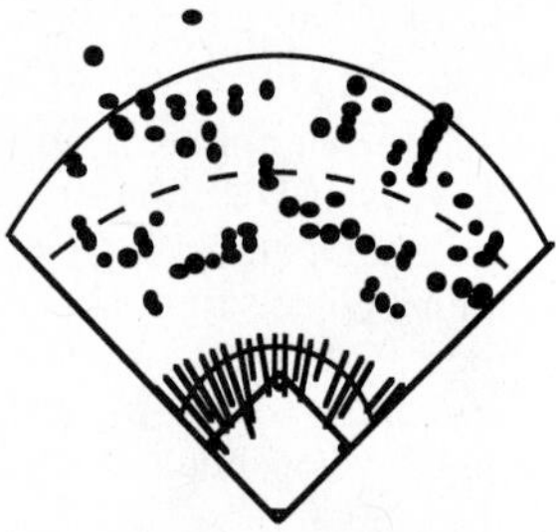

Vs. RHP

1990 Situational Stats

	AB	H	HR	RBI	AVG		AB	H	HR	RBI	AVG
Home	275	69	9	44	.251	LHP	217	52	9	34	.240
Road	293	82	11	47	.280	RHP	351	99	11	57	.282
Day	144	39	7	20	.271	Sc Pos	150	40	6	72	.267
Night	424	112	13	71	.264	Clutch	83	25	4	16	.301

1990 Rankings (National League)

- 1st in batting average on a 3-1 count (.750)
- 3rd in sacrifice flies (11)
- 6th in hit by pitch (6) and batting with the bases loaded (.471)
- Led the Dodgers in at-bats (568), doubles (28), sacrifice flies, hit by pitch, batting average with the bases loaded and batting average on a 3-1 count
- Led NL right fielders in hit by pitch and batting average on a 3-1 count

PITCHING:

The Dodgers were able to pry lefty Dennis Cook from Philadelphia last September for catcher Darrin Fletcher when the Phillies were concerned about Darren Daulton's impending free agency. Cook has been with three teams in two years, but the Dodgers couldn't resist a left-handed pitcher who might be able to replace their own free agent, Fernando Valenzuela, in the starting rotation. Cook might also be able to help the Dodger bullpen, which received only one save from a lefthander last year.

Switched between starting and relieving last year, Cook was off and on. In his first six starts with the Phillies, Cook went 5-0 with a 1.35 ERA, but he cooled off considerably and was eventually moved to the bullpen where he never really found his niche. Cook says he doesn't care whether he starts or relieves. "My preference is keeping my name on the back of a uniform," he said. An admirable attitude, but a fixed role probably would help Cook's career.

Cook mixes his fastball with a hard slider and split-finger sinker. He occasionally drops sidearm against left-handed hitters, but gets in trouble with an inconsistent leg kick. Cook's fastball isn't overpowering, and he needs good control to succeed. He can get rattled on the mound, and sometimes leaps into the air in disgust after a mistake. He is also very prone to the home run ball. In the last two seasons, Cook has allowed 38 homers in only 277 innings.

Cook started three games for the Dodgers last September, but looked good only once. In his final start, against the Padres, he gave up four homers including three in one inning. Obviously, he'll have to do better to earn a spot in the rotation.

HOLDING RUNNERS, FIELDING, HITTING:

Cook has an outstanding move to first base, but too often throws pickoff attempts in the dirt. A former All-Southwest Conference outfielder at the University of Texas, Cook fields his position well and swings a mean stick. He batted .306 in 1990 with one homer and four RBI and even pinch hit five times.

OVERALL:

Cook becomes the latest project for Dodgers' pitching coach Ron Perranoski, who helped Mike Morgan's floundering career three years ago. If he doesn't fit into the rotation, Cook might become a set-up man/spot-starter like Cincinnati's Norm Charlton. A simple tune-up of Cook's mechanics, mixed with a little maturity, might unlock his potential.

DENNIS COOK

Position: RP/SP
Bats: L **Throws:** L
Ht: 6' 3" **Wt:** 185

Opening Day Age: 28
Born: 10/4/62 in Lamarque, TX
ML Seasons: 3

Overall Statistics

	W	L	ERA	G	GS	Sv	IP	H	R	BB	SO	HR
1990	9	4	3.92	47	16	1	156.0	155	74	56	64	20
Career	18	13	3.76	74	38	1	299.0	274	141	105	144	39

How Often He Throws Strikes

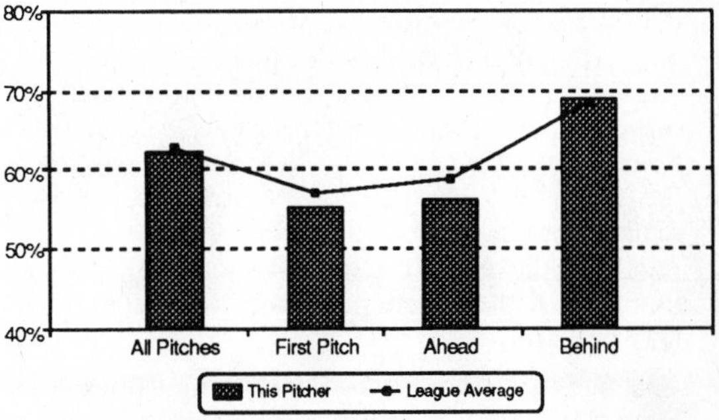

1990 Situational Stats

	W	L	ERA	Sv	IP		AB	H	HR	RBI	AVG
Home	5	3	3.65	1	98.2	LHB	135	40	4	20	.296
Road	4	1	4.40	0	57.1	RHB	456	115	16	56	.252
Day	2	0	2.73	0	33.0	Sc Pos	124	34	5	57	.274
Night	7	4	4.24	1	123.0	Clutch	44	18	1	6	.409

1990 Rankings (National League)

- 3rd highest percentage of inherited runners scored (48.6%)
- 10th most home runs allowed (20) and highest batting average allowed with runners in scoring position (.274)

TIM CREWS

Position: RP
Bats: R **Throws:** R
Ht: 6' 0" **Wt:** 190

Opening Day Age: 30
Born: 4/3/61 in Tampa, FL
ML Seasons: 4

PITCHING:

Last year the Dodgers found out just how valuable Tim Crews was after injuries sidelined Jay Howell and Jim Gott. Scheduled for mop-up chores, Crews gradually received some save opportunities. He led the club with 66 appearances and saved five, second on the club to Howell. He stranded 25 of 38 inherited runners, and he held first batters he faced to a collective .203 average (12-for-59). A steady and reliable reliever, Crews has a lifetime ERA of 2.94 in 172 appearances, all but two out of the pen.

With a decent fastball and effective breaking pitch, Crews is not an overpowering hurler. He gets his share of strikeouts, but the key to his success is control. He recorded 76 strikeouts and 18 unintentional walks in 107 innings last year. His brightest moment occurred September 17 in a 5-2 victory at Atlanta. Trailing by 5 1/2 games with 16 remaining, the Dodgers called on Crews to make an emergency start after Mike Hartley suffered a pulled muscle. Crews took a one-hit shutout into the sixth inning before his triceps muscle stiffened up. After the game, catcher Mike Scioscia called Crews the most valuable pitcher on the staff. "He's so versatile," Scioscia said. "He's really kept our ball club together, whether it's short relief, middle relief, long man, set-up man. . . You just don't realize the importance of a Tim Crews until you take him away."

That's quite a compliment, considering Crews' track record. In 1988, Crews was knocked off the postseason roster hours before the August 31 deadline after the Dodgers traded for White Sox reliever Ricky Horton. When John Tudor made his abbreviated comeback into the starting rotation in 1989, the Dodgers moved Tim Belcher to the bullpen and sent Crews to AAA Albuquerque.

HOLDING RUNNERS, FIELDING, HITTING:

Crews is a good fielder and maintains his composure in bunt situations. Although his pickoff move to first is decent, he is a fairly easy target for opposing baserunners. Crews fanned in five of his seven at-bats in 1990, but drove in a run on a sacrifice fly.

OVERALL:

Although a starter in the Milwaukee organization from 1981 to 1986, Crews has established himself as a handyman in the Dodger bullpen. Tom Lasorda won't be afraid to try Crews again in a spot start or save situation. He might be anonymous to many fans, but a good season from Crews is critical to the Dodgers' success.

Overall Statistics

	W	L	ERA	G	GS	Sv	IP	H	R	BB	SO	HR
1990	4	5	2.77	66	2	5	107.1	98	40	24	76	9
Career	9	7	2.94	172	2	9	269.2	274	105	71	197	21

How Often He Throws Strikes

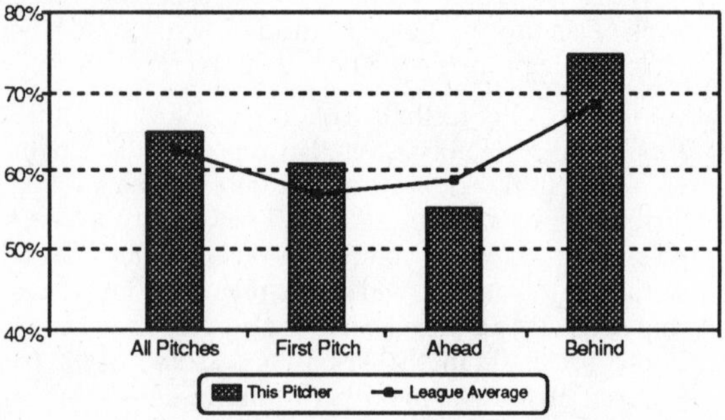

1990 Situational Stats

	W	L	ERA	Sv	IP		AB	H	HR	RBI	AVG
Home	0	4	3.04	2	50.1	LHB	220	57	3	15	.259
Road	4	1	2.53	3	57.0	RHB	191	41	6	22	.215
Day	3	2	1.62	2	39.0	Sc Pos	91	18	2	27	.198
Night	1	3	3.42	3	68.1	Clutch	115	29	3	17	.252

1990 Rankings (National League)

- 10th in first batter efficiency (.203)
- Led the Dodgers in games pitched (66), first batter efficiency and lowest percentage of inherited runners scored (34.2%)

HITTING:

A history of five knee operations and an irregular heartbeat discovered in spring training left the Dodgers wondering if Kal Daniels could play on a regular basis in 1990. Next question. Although he missed 32 games due to various ailments, Daniels resumed his old role as one of the most feared offensive threats in the National League. Posting career highs with 27 homers and 94 RBI, he ranked second in the NL in at-bats per RBI (4.8), and sixth in at-bats per homer (16.7).

Still only 27, Daniels has battled injuries throughout his career. After a trade brought him over from Cincinnati for Tim Leary in July of '89, he played only 11 games with the Dodgers (batting .342) before going out with season-ending knee surgery. Last year he strained the oblique muscle in his side on August 8, then twice aggravated the injury on swings, each time forcing him to leave games in the middle of at-bats. Later, on September 28, he crashed into the left-field wall at Candlestick Park and suffered a partially collapsed lung that ended his season.

Daniels has great power to all fields, and he owns the fourth highest active slugging percentage in the league. He is a great fastball hitter, so pitchers usually work him with breaking stuff, but he has great discipline at the plate, and usually ends up with a hittable pitch. Often weak against lefthanders in the past, Daniels batted .285 against southpaws last year. "My biggest problem as a hitter is facing somebody I've hit hard in the past," Daniels said. "I get overanxious at the plate because I know I can hit him." This group of pitchers continues to grow.

BASERUNNING:

The gimpy-legged Daniels stole just four bases in seven attempts last year, a far cry from the 27 he stole for Cincinnati in 1988. Daniels has lost considerable speed, and while he'll go for the extra base, he won't force anything unless it's a high-percentage play.

FIELDING:

Daniels has limited range in left field. Opponents usually tested his arm, and he responded with 13 assists. Daniels had trouble with backhanding long flies on the dead run, but he often sacrificed his body in pursuit of the ball.

OVERALL:

The key for Daniels is staying healthy. A move to the American League for designated hitter duties might lengthen his career, but he's such a valuable hitter that the Dodgers won't give him up for a small price. Dangerous power hitters with a lifetime .300 batting average are hard to find.

KAL DANIELS

Position: LF
Bats: L **Throws:** R
Ht: 5'11" **Wt:** 195

Opening Day Age: 27
Born: 8/20/63 in Vienna, GA
ML Seasons: 5

Overall Statistics

	G	AB	R	H	D	T	HR	RBI	SB	BB	SO	AVG
1990	130	450	81	133	23	1	27	94	4	68	104	.296
Career	507	1665	316	500	99	7	81	262	81	280	323	.300

Where He Hits the Ball

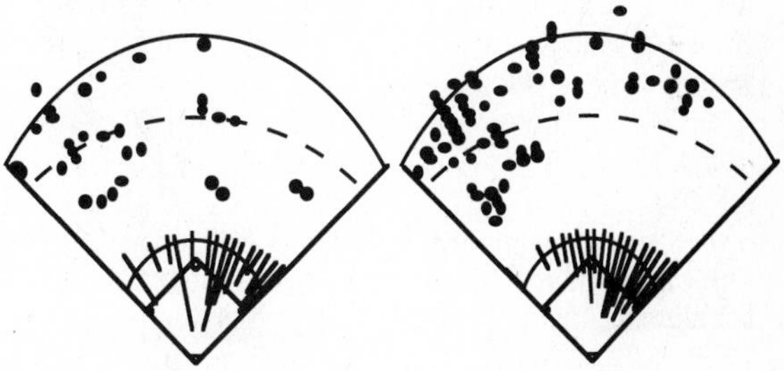

Vs. LHP Vs. RHP

1990 Situational Stats

	AB	H	HR	RBI	AVG		AB	H	HR	RBI	AVG
Home	231	67	12	43	.290	LHP	151	43	6	30	.285
Road	219	66	15	51	.301	RHP	299	90	21	64	.301
Day	112	31	7	25	.277	Sc Pos	130	38	10	69	.292
Night	338	102	20	69	.302	Clutch	52	16	3	12	.308

1990 Rankings (National League)

- 1st in most pitches seen per plate appearance (4.09)
- 6th in on-base average (.389) and HR frequency (16.7 ABs per HR)
- 7th in slugging percentage (.531)
- Led the Dodgers in home runs (27), slugging percentage, HR frequency, groundball/flyball ratio (1.52), most pitches seen per plate appearance, most runs scored per time reached base (39.7%) and highest percentage of pitches taken (59.6%)
- Led NL left fielders in strikeouts (104) and most pitches seen per plate appearance

KIRK GIBSON

Position: CF/LF
Bats: L **Throws:** L
Ht: 6' 3" **Wt:** 215

Opening Day Age: 33
Born: 5/28/57 in Pontiac, MI
ML Seasons: 12

HITTING:

Three years after his heroic MVP season of 1988, Kirk Gibson appears to be on his way out of Los Angeles. Gibson's 1990 campaign was highlighted not by fireworks with his bat, but by a July shouting match with Dodger executive Fred Claire. The veteran was upset about playing center field (he preferred left) and by a published report that said he had demanded a trade. Claire could have dumped Gibson and played Stan Javier in center, but he knew even a hobbled Roy Hobbs could still be a catalyst.

Indeed, Gibson was a model citizen after the All-Star break and helped spark the Dodgers to a second-half charge. Just when the Dodgers had moved back into contention though, Gibson lapsed into a deep September slump. He batted .159 (11-for-69) with no homers, four RBI and 17 strikeouts over the last month, and was benched for six games after a one-for-27 slump. At one point, Gibson went 20 days without a hit against a left-handed pitcher.

A dangerous low-ball hitter, Gibson still displays power to all fields, but not as much as in the past. His eight homers last year were his lowest total since he posted the same number in 1982. Lefthanders gave him big problems at times last year, though his .255 average against them was 129 points higher than 1989.

BASERUNNING:

The former Michigan State wide receiver still is one of the smartest and most aggressive baserunners around. Gibson stole 26 bases in 28 attempts last year, and his 93 percent success rate was the best in baseball. Gibson needs eight more homers to join Robin Yount and Andre Dawson as the only active major leaguers with at least 200 homers and 200 stolen bases.

FIELDING:

Gibson has only 34 career assists in 1,061 games, the lowest assist rate among active outfielders. Runners on third base take advantage of his weak arm, even on shallow flies to center. Gibson wasn't comfortable playing center last year, but he made the best of the situation. His speed allowed him to catch balls hit into the gap, and he usually got a proper jump on balls.

OVERALL:

It's hard to believe Gibson will turn 34 on May 28, and, unless the Dodgers trade Kal Daniels, it's even more difficult imagining a future for him in Los Angeles. A free agent, he expressed a desire to return to the Tigers, and other teams figured to have some interest. Used properly, he could help a lot of ball clubs.

Overall Statistics

	G	AB	R	H	D	T	HR	RBI	SB	BB	SO	AVG
1990	89	315	59	82	20	0	8	38	26	39	65	.260
Career	1203	4320	728	1178	196	38	192	641	235	527	953	.273

Where He Hits the Ball

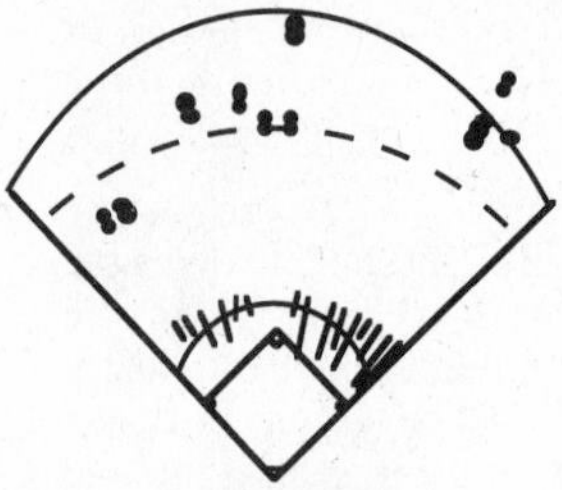

Vs. LHP

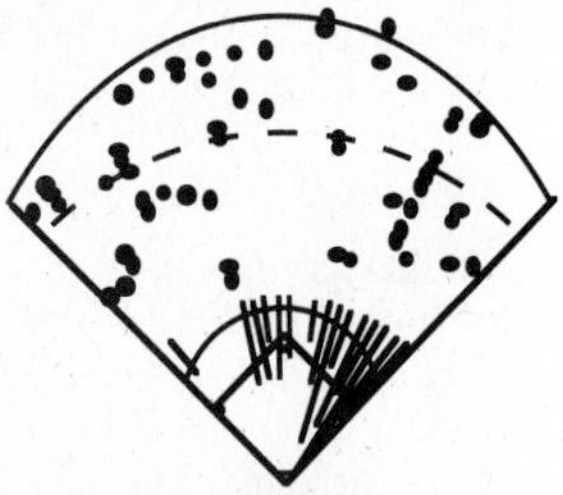

Vs. RHP

1990 Situational Stats

	AB	H	HR	RBI	AVG		AB	H	HR	RBI	AVG
Home	157	39	2	19	.248	LHP	102	26	3	15	.255
Road	158	43	6	19	.272	RHP	213	56	5	23	.263
Day	92	22	5	17	.239	Sc Pos	62	18	2	28	.290
Night	223	60	3	21	.269	Clutch	54	17	0	9	.315

1990 Rankings (National League)

- 1st in stolen base percentage (92.9%)
- 3rd worst batting average on an 0-2 count (.038)
- 6th in steals of third (8)
- Led the Dodgers in stolen base percentage, least GDPs per GDP situation (5.1%) and steals of third
- Led NL center fielders in stolen base percentage

JIM GOTT

Position: RP
Bats: R **Throws:** R
Ht: 6' 4" **Wt:** 220

Opening Day Age: 31
Born: 8/3/59 in Hollywood, CA
ML Seasons: 9

Overall Statistics

	W	L	ERA	G	GS	Sv	IP	H	R	BB	SO	HR
1990	3	5	2.90	50	0	3	62.0	59	27	34	44	5
Career	38	53	4.07	307	96	53	810.2	791	418	344	574	65

How Often He Throws Strikes

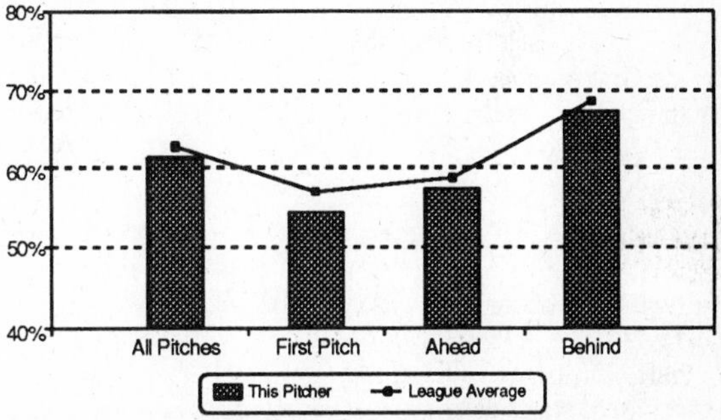

1990 Situational Stats

	W	L	ERA	Sv	IP		AB	H	HR	RBI	AVG
Home	2	3	2.88	1	34.1	LHB	134	39	1	9	.291
Road	1	2	2.93	2	27.2	RHB	96	20	4	16	.208
Day	0	1	2.63	1	13.2	Sc Pos	67	15	2	21	.224
Night	3	4	2.98	2	48.1	Clutch	98	22	3	11	.224

1990 Rankings (National League)

➟ Led the Dodgers in holds (6)

PITCHING:

A Pittsburgh television station turned Jim Gott's reconstructive elbow surgery on May 12, 1989 into a medical documentary. A follow-up film hasn't been planned, but based on 1990, it would be a story with a happy ending. After pitching only one game for the Pirates in 1989, Gott signed with the Dodgers last year and made a fine comeback, turning in a 2.90 ERA in 50 relief appearances.

It wasn't easy. A Hollywood native, Gott was excited to be returning to his hometown, but the short spring training hurt him more than any pitcher on the staff. Afraid to cut loose on his curveball because of scar-tissue adhesions in his elbow, Gott opened the season on the disabled list. A rehabilitation assignment to Class A Bakersfield still didn't convince the Dodgers that he was ready, especially after he walked off the mound in frustration because he wasn't sharp during a simulated game with the big club.

Gott finally returned May 27, but his early work was so bad that after a disappointing appearance on June 8, he was so upset that he walked from San Diego's Jack Murphy Stadium to the team's hotel two miles away. That was Gott's turning point, however. Pitching coach Ron Perranoski credited Gott's success to increased arm speed and the confidence to use his slider and curve in conjunction with his 92 MPH fastball. Gott also got some encouragement from Tommy John, who missed over a year after rupturing a ligament in his left elbow in 1974. "It took about 18 months for Tommy to pitch without thinking he might get hurt," Gott said. "Getting your mind set is the biggest thing. It's almost like you have to retrain everything." Gott's work during the rest of the campaign indicated that he had crossed both his mental and physical hurdles.

HOLDING RUNNERS, FIELDING, HITTING:

Gott is a fairly good fielder, but no more than adequate at holding runners. A former high school batting phenom, he has belted four big-league home runs. Unfortunately, Gott's bullpen role limited him to only one at-bat last year.

OVERALL:

Gott, who has now come back twice from major arm problems, gives the Dodger bullpen inspiration, enthusiasm and leadership. He pitched well in the second half last year, and his good work figures to carry over into 1991. He provides valuable insurance in case of injury to incumbent closer Jay Howell.

ALFREDO GRIFFIN

Position: SS
Bats: B **Throws:** R
Ht: 5'11" **Wt:** 165

Opening Day Age: 34
Born: 3/6/57 in Santo Domingo, Dominican Republic
ML Seasons: 15

HITTING:

Alfredo Griffin struggled in silence during a disappointing 1990 season. Lower back pains plagued the veteran, who refused to complain about his physical condition. Griffin was also sidelined for a week due to an eye injury suffered during a July 21 nightclub altercation in Pittsburgh. Griffin had missed just four innings all season up until that point, and he never again got on track. He wound up batting only .210, his second-lowest full-season mark since becoming a big league regular in 1979.

Bothered by his injuries and the mental distraction caused by the notification that his mother had suffered a stroke in his native Dominican Republic, Griffin hit only .167 in the second half of last season. He didn't have an extra-base hit from August 15 through September 19, a span of 67 at-bats.

Griffin, who walked just four times with Toronto in 1984, is a slash hitter with no power. He loves to chase the first pitch and usually isn't around long enough in the count to walk or strike out. He walked 29 times in 1990, to go along with 65 strikeouts, but 11 of those walks were intentional.

Though he is a consumate professional, Griffin's career is clearly winding down, and his future with the Dodgers appears to be as caddy to Jose Offerman, the 1989 Class AAA Player of the Year. Griffin's second-half slump gave Offerman and Mike Sharperson occasional starts at shortstop last year.

BASERUNNING:

Griffin stole a career high 33 bases with Oakland in 1986, but has slowed down on the base paths since then. He stole six bases in nine attempts last year, his lowest total since becoming a big-league regular. Griffin has always lacked sound judgement in running the bases, and gets thrown out far more often than a veteran should.

FIELDING:

Griffin made a team-high 26 errors in 1990, but just two in his final 33 starts. He still possesses fine range, and most of his problems occur on backhanded plays that require a long throw to first base.

OVERALL:

Griffin can become a free agent after this season, and 1991 will probably be his final year with the Dodgers. As the 1988 World Championship team slowly breaks up, it's important to remember that Griffin stabilized one of the league's worst infields. At 34, he provides insurance in case Offerman isn't ready to play every day.

Overall Statistics

	G	AB	R	H	D	T	HR	RBI	SB	BB	SO	AVG
1990	141	461	38	97	11	3	1	35	6	29	65	.210
Career	1744	6185	696	1548	229	76	24	487	184	304	583	.250

Where He Hits the Ball

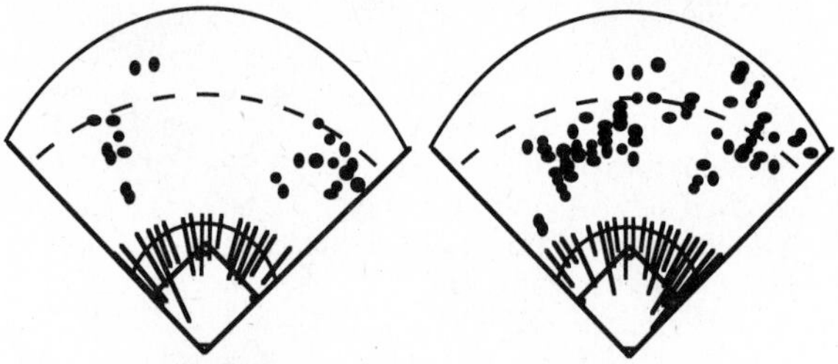

Vs. LHP Vs. RHP

1990 Situational Stats

	AB	H	HR	RBI	AVG		AB	H	HR	RBI	AVG
Home	218	48	0	22	.220	LHP	169	35	1	12	.207
Road	243	49	1	13	.202	RHP	292	62	0	23	.212
Day	134	23	0	9	.172	Sc Pos	122	26	0	34	.213
Night	327	74	1	26	.226	Clutch	63	10	0	2	.159

1990 Rankings (National League)

- → 1st in lowest batting average (.210), lowest slugging percentage (.254), lowest on-base average (.258)
- → 2nd in least pitches seen per plate appearance (3.15), lowest slugging percentage vs. left-handed pitchers (.237) and lowest batting average on the road (.202
- → 3rd in lowest on-base average vs. left-handed pitchers (.257)
- → Led the Dodgers in bunts in play (22)
- → Led NL shortstops in errors (26)

HITTING:

Lenny Harris established himself as a major leaguer last season, but only after a couple of breaks. First, Dodgers' third baseman Jeff Hamilton didn't play after mid-April due to tendon problems in his right shoulder, and Harris found himself platooning at the position with Mike Sharperson. Later, he got a lot of playing time at second after the Dodgers traded Willie Randolph, and Juan Samuel failed to take over the position. Harris wound up playing in 137 games and batted a solid .304, though he drove in only 29 runs.

Harris spent much of the season in the leadoff spot, receiving his chance on May 23 when Manager Tom Lasorda dropped the struggling Samuel into the number-seven slot. For the year, Harris batted .315 (101-for-321) with 23 RBI and 55 runs scored when batting first. He drew only 29 walks all year, however, and will probably have to do better than that if he wants to remain at the top of the lineup.

Harris is an aggressive hitter who loves to chase the first pitch, especially a high fastball. He tried to pull the ball too much in 1989, but learned to become a spray hitter to all fields last year. Left-handed pitchers with a good breaking ball give Harris the most trouble. He batted only .238 in 42 at-bats against southpaws last year.

BASERUNNING:

Harris is an aggressive base stealer, but he doesn't have the speed to match his style. He was caught stealing 10 times last year, and is only 33-for-53 lifetime. He challenges opposing outfielders on a daily basis, and will rarely make a glaring mistake on the base paths.

FIELDING:

Juggled between third base and second last year, Harris made nine errors in 74 starts at third and only two in 29 starts at second. He has soft hands, but sometimes rushes his throws. If Samuel doesn't return and the Dodgers can't acquire a Bill Doran-type free agent, Harris probably will play second base this year.

OVERALL:

Harris isn't afraid to reveal his true feelings to the media, which sometimes got him into trouble last season. Toward the end of the campaign, Harris questioned whether some players had already called it a season. He apologized to his teammates the next day, but the incident revealed Harris' competitive fire. If the Dodgers don't have a full-time position for him, Harris will provide valuable insurance.

LENNY HARRIS

Position: 3B/2B
Bats: L **Throws:** R
Ht: 5'10" **Wt:** 195

Opening Day Age: 26
Born: 10/28/64 in Miami, FL
ML Seasons: 3

Overall Statistics

	G	AB	R	H	D	T	HR	RBI	SB	BB	SO	AVG
1990	137	431	61	131	16	4	2	29	15	29	31	.304
Career	268	809	104	226	27	5	5	63	33	54	68	.279

Where He Hits the Ball

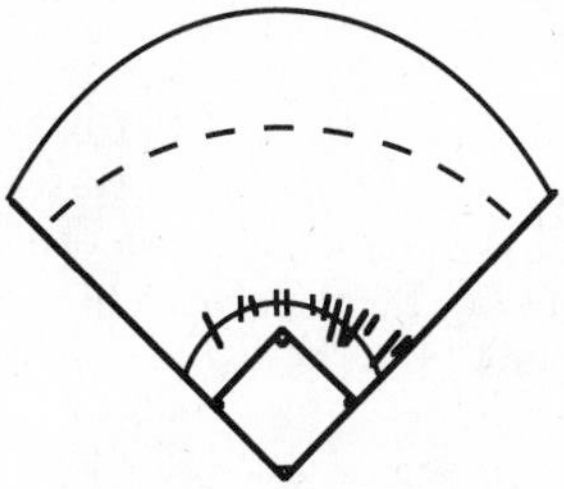

Vs. LHP

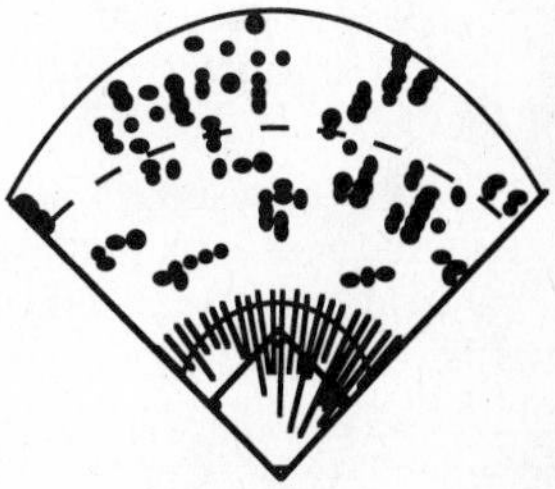

Vs. RHP

1990 Situational Stats

	AB	H	HR	RBI	AVG		AB	H	HR	RBI	AVG
Home	217	60	0	9	.276	LHP	42	10	0	6	.238
Road	214	71	2	20	.332	RHP	389	121	2	23	.311
Day	115	37	2	13	.322	Sc Pos	73	22	0	27	.301
Night	316	94	0	16	.297	Clutch	54	14	0	2	.259

1990 Rankings (National League)

- → 3rd in batting average with 2 strikes (.275)
- → 4th lowest stolen base percentage (60.0%) and highest percentage of swings put into play (56.3%)
- → Led the Dodgers in triples (4) and batting average with 2 strikes
- → Led NL third basemen in caught stealing (10), batting average vs. right-handed pitchers (.311), on-base average vs. right-handed pitchers (.353), batting average with 2 strikes, lowest percentage of swings that missed (11.6%), highest percentage of swings put into play (56.3%) and highest percentage of extra bases taken as a runner (55.3%)

MIKE HARTLEY

Position: RP/SP
Bats: R **Throws:** R
Ht: 6' 1" **Wt:** 192

Opening Day Age: 29
Born: 8/31/61 in Hawthorne, CA
ML Seasons: 2

PITCHING:

A rash of injuries to teammates gave rookie Mike Hartley the biggest break of his nine-year professional career in 1990. Hartley, best known for his great high school wrestling record, jumped into the rotation during the pennant race and body-slammed his way to success. He went 6-3 with a 2.95 ERA in 32 games.

Hartley barely made the team's 27-man roster out of spring training, but flashed potential on April 30 when he fanned five consecutive Giants -- Will Clark, Kevin Mitchell, Kevin Bass, Matt Williams, and Terry Kennedy. Optioned to AAA Albuquerque on May 25, he concentrated on his mechanics, working on his offspeed pitches with coach Claude Osteen. He returned June 10 when Pat Perry went on the disabled list, determined to stick around. "I'm coming back to stay and show I can get people out," he said. "I know I make some mistakes when I get ahead in the count. I try to be aggressive, and that's why you might see a lot of 0-2 hits."

Though he went through a period of inactivity, Hartley eventually got his chance after another injury to a Dodger pitcher, this time Tim Belcher. Given his first major league start August 14 in New York, he hurled six scoreless innings in front of 46,000 at Shea Stadium, and the Dodgers won 2-1. It was his first professional start since 1986, but he was successful enough to stay in the rotation. Hartley's biggest highlight was a three-hit shutout September 6 against Atlanta. The performance was a big one, because it came after the Dodgers had used 17 pitchers in their previous three games. Hartley suffered a pulled ribcage muscle in his next start and missed his final four starts, but he'd already made an impression.

Hartley's best pitch is a two-seam fastball, and he's learning to throw a sinker. He also throws a split-finger fastball and added a curveball prior to the 1990 season.

HOLDING RUNNERS, FIELDING, HITTING:

Hartley's rapid promotion into the starting rotation didn't give him enough time to polish the rough edges. He is a good fielder, but his biggest weakness is holding runners on base. Hartley also needs practice at the plate. He went one-for-13, including eight strikeouts and three sacrifice hits.

OVERALL:

At 29, Hartley suddenly has a future in the majors. Like Tim Crews, he gives the Dodgers several options. The only question about him is his endurance. Hartley's career high in innings pitched is 139.1 with the Cardinals' Class A St. Petersburg affiliate in 1984.

Overall Statistics

	W	L	ERA	G	GS	Sv	IP	H	R	BB	SO	HR
1990	6	3	2.95	32	6	1	79.1	58	32	30	76	7
Career	6	4	2.85	37	6	1	85.1	60	33	30	80	7

How Often He Throws Strikes

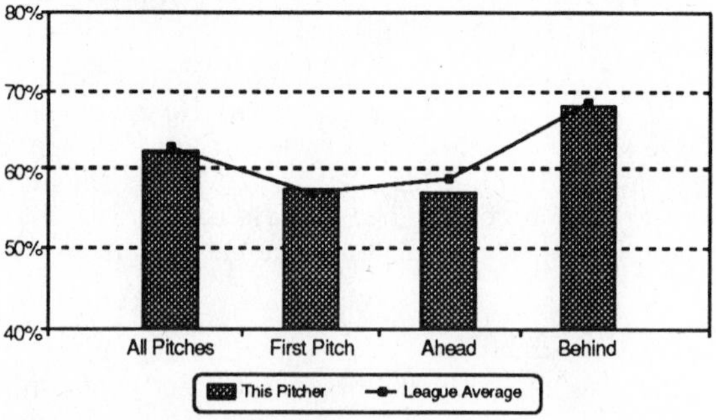

1990 Situational Stats

	W	L	ERA	Sv	IP		AB	H	HR	RBI	AVG
Home	4	1	1.45	1	43.1	LHB	155	33	2	10	.213
Road	2	2	4.75	0	36.0	RHB	135	25	5	19	.185
Day	2	0	2.35	1	23.0	Sc Pos	64	14	2	19	.219
Night	4	3	3.20	0	56.1	Clutch	11	6	1	2	.545

1990 Rankings (National League)

- 8th lowest batting average allowed vs. left-handed batters (.213)
- Led the Dodgers in lowest batting average allowed vs. left-handed batters

PITCHING:

Last year Orel Hershiser went from Cy Young Award Candidate to $7.9 million guinea pig after shoulder surgery on April 27. Hershiser had been off to a slow start in 1990, but most people, including Orel himself, thought the shortened spring training was to blame. It turned out that his problems were a lot more complicated.

The surgical procedure performed on Hershiser was unique, and no one knows whether it's going to work. Team physician Dr. Frank Jobe used retractors to separate Hershiser's muscles before reconstructing the anterior capsule and tightening the ligaments. "What we can't rate, what we don't know enough yet, is how he's going to be in a year," Jobe said. The original muscle-bone relationship still was intact, and that may have saved Hershiser's career. Jobe said Hershiser's labrum, the cartilage lining of the shoulder capsule, looked like it had been struck repeatedly with a hammer.

The damage came after Hershiser averaged 252 innings per year over the previous five seasons (309.2 innings in 1988, including postseason). Hershiser was effective in the early innings of his four 1990 starts, but couldn't get past the seventh. After the surgery, Hershiser didn't watch games in the dugout because he feared his competitive juices would interfere with his physical therapy. He began lobbing a ball in August, and took a two week "mental break" after the season before beginning his push to be ready for spring training.

When healthy, Hershiser's strengths are a sinking fastball and a hard-breaking curveball. Hershiser also studies charts of opposing hitters. In case Hershiser forgets anything, he can read his autobiography, "Out of the Blue." The chapters on pitching and preparation are considered a textbook by other pitchers.

HOLDING RUNNERS, FIELDING, HITTING:

Prior to the injury, Hershiser was an outstanding fielder and hitter. Opponents stole only 11 bases against him in 1989. A career .189 hitter, Hershiser has always been able to help himself with the stick. He went three-for-three in the second game of the 1988 World Series.

OVERALL:

Hardly anyone expected Hershiser to pitch as he did during his magical 1988 season, which included a record 59 consecutive scoreless innings streak. Now, hardly anyone expects Hershiser to fully recover from his complicated shoulder surgery. But don't bet against his comeback at age 32. His determination might make Hershiser the Tommy John of the 1990s.

OREL HERSHISER

Position: SP
Bats: R **Throws:** R
Ht: 6' 3" **Wt:** 190

Opening Day Age: 32
Born: 9/16/58 in Buffalo, NY
ML Seasons: 8

Overall Statistics

	W	L	ERA	G	GS	Sv	IP	H	R	BB	SO	HR
1990	1	1	4.26	4	4	0	25.1	26	12	4	16	1
Career	99	65	2.71	235	195	5	1482.1	1266	520	438	1027	76

How Often He Throws Strikes

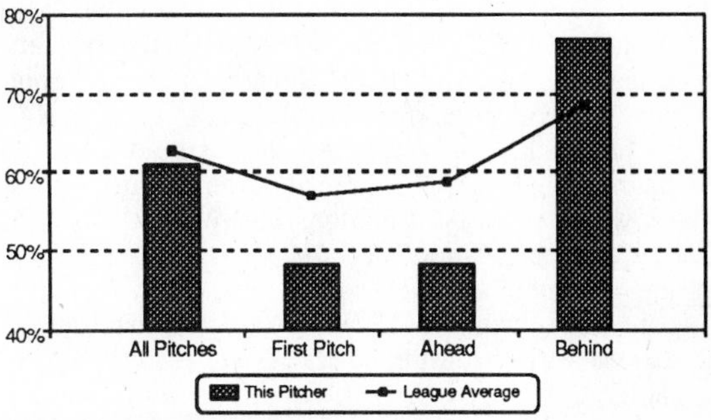

1990 Situational Stats

	W	L	ERA	Sv	IP		AB	H	HR	RBI	AVG
Home	1	1	4.19	0	19.1	LHB	53	10	1	3	.189
Road	0	0	4.50	0	6.0	RHB	47	16	0	5	.340
Day	0	0	3.00	0	12.0	Sc Pos	18	7	0	7	.389
Night	1	1	5.40	0	13.1	Clutch	3	2	0	1	.667

1990 Rankings (National League)

- Did not rank near the top or bottom in any category

JAY HOWELL

Position: RP
Bats: R **Throws:** R
Ht: 6' 3" **Wt:** 205

Opening Day Age: 35
Born: 11/26/55 in Miami, FL
ML Seasons: 11

PITCHING:

No Nasty Boy, Jay Howell has never answered to a fancy nickname. A blue-collar closer, he has overcome injuries to record at least 15 saves in each of the last six seasons. His ERAs the last three years have been 2.08, 1.58 and 2.18. Howell was hurting for much of last year, though, and a full season of health is essential if the Dodgers expect to contend this season in the National League West.

In his final spring training appearance of 1990, Howell looked brilliant, striking out the side against the Braves. It turned out to be the worst thing Howell could have done. "Jay tried to get ready too soon after the lockout," pitching coach Ron Perranoski said. "I cringed when he struck out the side, because I knew it was going to catch up with him. Jay usually is a slow starter, but he felt good at the beginning of camp. Maybe too good."

Perranoski was right. Howell soon began feeling pain in his left knee, and finally underwent arthroscopic surgery to repair a partial cartilage tear on April 24. He returned in only three weeks, without a minor league rehab assignment, and immediately was thrown into pressure situations. Howell finally had to ask Manager Tommy Lasorda for some middle-inning assignments to perfect his mechanics. "I didn't want to be in the position of hurting the ball club," Howell said, admitting he wasn't yet ready to close games.

Howell eased into the late relief role, finally overcoming the nagging tenderness in his left knee. In the second half, Howell was 2-1 with a 1.45 ERA in 37.1 innings. As in the past, he mixed his fastball, curve and slider with great effectiveness, and the Dodgers heaved a sigh of relief.

HOLDING RUNNERS, FIELDING, HITTING:

Howell is a good fielder, but sometimes has trouble getting a quick jump on bunts. He does his best to hold runners on base, but he's one of the easiest relievers to steal against because of his high leg kick. Howell went hitless in two cameo at-bats in 1990, dropping his career mark to zero-for-nine.

OVERALL:

People may look back in 10 years and wonder why the Dodgers let Bob Welch get away, but Howell helped the Dodgers win a World Series. If teammate Jim Gott becomes a dependable set-up man, Howell might be able to avoid further strain and stay injury-free this year.

Overall Statistics

	W	L	ERA	G	GS	Sv	IP	H	R	BB	SO	HR
1990	5	5	2.18	45	0	16	66.0	59	17	20	59	5
Career	44	41	3.43	389	21	133	645.0	610	262	230	531	39

How Often He Throws Strikes

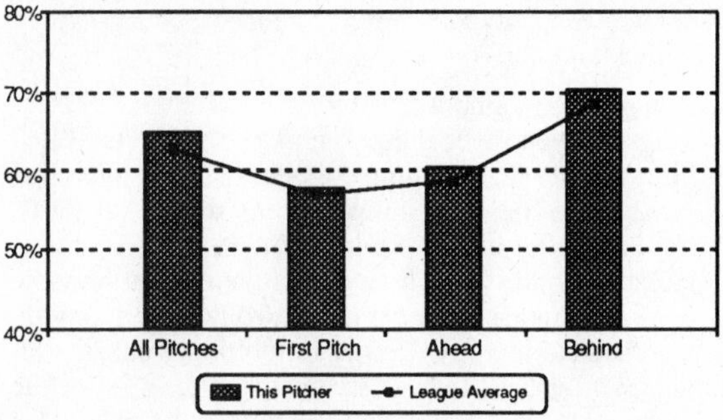

1990 Situational Stats

	W	L	ERA	Sv	IP		AB	H	HR	RBI	AVG
Home	1	3	2.91	8	34.0	LHB	153	36	3	14	.235
Road	4	2	1.41	8	32.0	RHB	91	23	2	11	.253
Day	1	2	1.15	5	15.2	Sc Pos	68	17	0	19	.250
Night	4	3	2.50	11	50.1	Clutch	173	47	5	24	.272

1990 Rankings (National League)

- 2nd in lowest save percentage (66.7%), blown saves (8) and worst first batter efficiency (.359)
- 7th in hit batsmen (6)
- 8th in save opportunities
- Led the Dodgers in saves (16), game finished (35), hit batsmen, save opportunities and blown saves

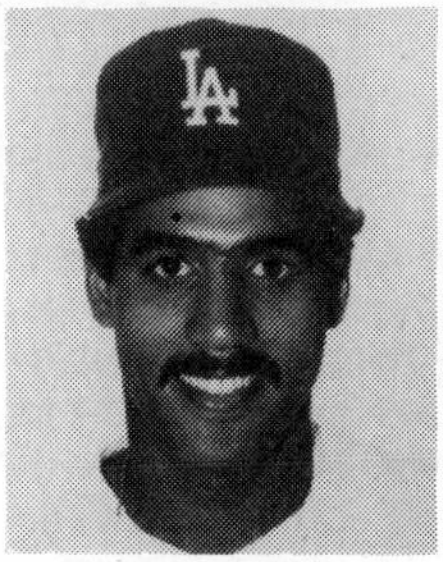

STAN JAVIER

Position: CF/RF
Bats: B **Throws:** R
Ht: 6' 0" **Wt:** 185

Opening Day Age: 25
Born: 9/1/65 in San Francisco de Macoris, Dominican Republic
ML Seasons: 6

HITTING:

Stan Javier didn't need much time to adjust to National League pitchers after the May 12 trade from Oakland for second baseman Willie Randolph. The Dodgers welcomed Javier because the trade allowed them to move Juan Samuel from center field to second base. Javier welcomed the trade, also. The son of former major league infielder Julian Javier figured he'd get more playing time in LA. He was right, but only for a while.

Javier struggled for a few weeks after his arrival in LA, but then a hot streak lifted his average above the .300 mark. Surprising more than a few people, he kept it there for the rest of the season. Even so, his numbers didn't win Javier the center field job, because the Dodgers needed a place for Kirk Gibson in their crowded outfield. So, .300 or not, Javier returned to part-time duty. When the season ended, he'd batted 309 times; he'd played more than that in each of his last two seasons in Oakland.

Javier isn't a flashy player, but is solid in every aspect of the game. He is a patient hitter who loves the fastball and can hit it from either side of the plate. Javier is considered better as a righthander because he pulls the ball more often, but from either side, he's not much of a home run threat. Javier's .259 average with two out and runners in scoring position for LA wasn't overwhelming, but it represented a 100-point rise from his previous career average in such situations.

BASERUNNING:

Prior to his departure from Oakland, Javier had 43 career stolen bases in 48 attempts. The 89.6% success rate was the highest among active players with at least 40 steals. Javier didn't enjoy immediate success in the National League (15-for-22) because he was learning the pitchers. He should be better with a year's experience. Javier is a smart runner, and seldom makes careless mistakes.

FIELDING:

Platooning with Kirk Gibson in center field would make anybody look like Willie Mays by comparison, but Javier is nevertheless terrific on defense. He rarely gets the wrong jump on line drives, and he has enough range to track down balls hit into the alley. His arm is not strong, but it's accurate.

OVERALL:

Javier, who was lost behind the Henderson-Henderson-Canseco trio in Oakland, now finds himself pencilled in as the backup for the Dodgers' new outfield of Daniels-Strawberry-Brooks. Chances are they'll be needing his glove before too long.

Overall Statistics

	G	AB	R	H	D	T	HR	RBI	SB	BB	SO	AVG
1990	123	309	60	92	9	6	3	27	15	40	50	.298
Career	507	1288	187	323	45	13	8	107	58	138	219	.251

Where He Hits the Ball

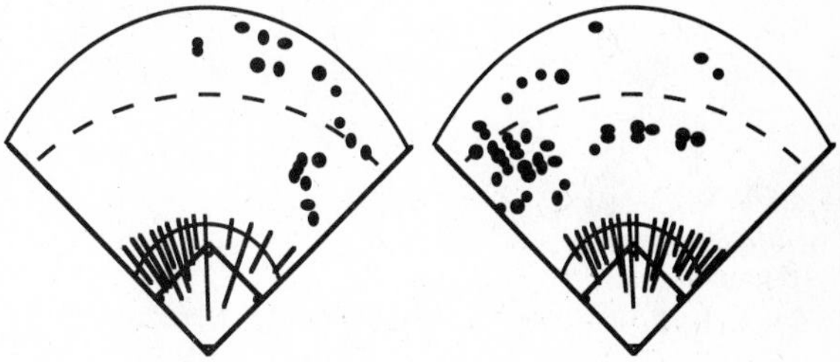

1990 Situational Stats

	AB	H	HR	RBI	AVG		AB	H	HR	RBI	AVG
Home	161	46	1	16	.286	LHP	124	39	1	10	.315
Road	148	46	2	11	.311	RHP	185	53	2	17	.286
Day	99	30	1	10	.303	Sc Pos	68	20	0	22	.294
Night	210	62	2	17	.295	Clutch	63	14	0	6	.222

1990 Rankings (National League)

- 2nd in highest percentage of extra bases taken as a runner (64.6%)
- 9th in on-base average vs. left-handed pitchers (.401)
- Led the Dodgers in triples (4), on-base average vs. left-handed pitchers, batting average on a 3-2 count (.325) and percentage of extra bases taken as a runner
- Led AL center fielders in on-base average vs. left-handed pitchers

CY YOUNG STUFF

PITCHING:

At age 22, Ramon Martinez became the youngest Dodger to win 20 games since Ralph Branca in 1947. He struck out 223 batters, the second highest total in the league next to David Cone's 233. He fanned 18 batters in a game on June 4, and might easily have had 20 or more that night. He held opponents to a .221 batting average, third best behind Sid Fernandez and Jose Rijo. His .769 winning percentage was second only to Cy Young winner Doug Drabek. He led the league in complete games with 12. Plus, he kept the club in contention after season-ending injuries to Orel Hershiser and Tim Belcher. What can Martinez do for an encore?

Just six years ago, when Martinez signed with the Dodgers as a free agent, he was a skinny kid who weighed 150 pounds. A member of the Dominican Republic's 1984 Olympic team that played at Dodger Stadium, Martinez gradually worked his way to the majors. He finally made it on Aug. 10, 1988, when, in a move that was eerily symbolic, the Dodgers released 324-game winner Don Sutton. Even a career like Sutton's doesn't seem beyond Martinez now.

In 1990, Martinez perfected the release point of his slingshot delivery, and an improved change-up complemented his 94 MPH fastball. He also learned subtle lessons, such as how to prepare for a start after a rain delay (he was roughed up in one such outing in Philadelphia). There is not much more he needs to learn. "(Martinez) had a lot of things thrown at him," first baseman Eddie Murray said late last year, "and he handled it all."

HOLDING RUNNERS, FIELDING, HITTING:

Martinez is a good fielder, but his pitching motion makes him vulnerable to a bunt along the third base line. He is conscious of runners on base, but his only pickoff at first occurred in the eighth inning of his final start. Martinez batted only .125 last year, but he helped himself with nine sacrifice hits.

OVERALL:

If Martinez perfects a curveball, he could become the first Dominican pitcher to win a Cy Young Award. However, the Dodgers ought to be careful with his precious right arm. Two of Martinez' league-high 12 complete games required pitch counts of 148 and 149, and from June 16 to July 5, he threw 617 pitches in a five-start span. Having lost Sandy Koufax, Don Drysdale and now possibly Orel Hershiser to arm problems, LA doesn't want to lose yet another ace starter.

RAMON MARTINEZ

Position: SP
Bats: R **Throws:** R
Ht: 6' 4" **Wt:** 172

Opening Day Age: 23
Born: 3/22/68 in Santo Domingo, Puerto Rico
ML Seasons: 3

Overall Statistics

	W	L	ERA	G	GS	Sv	IP	H	R	BB	SO	HR
1990	20	6	2.92	33	33	0	234.1	191	89	67	223	22
Career	27	13	3.08	57	54	0	368.2	297	145	130	335	33

How Often He Throws Strikes

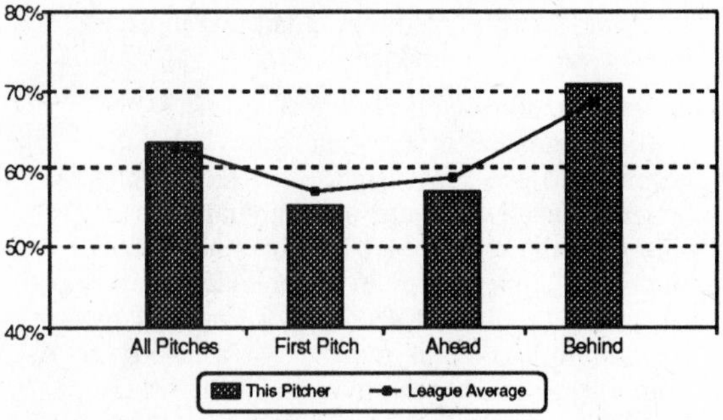

1990 Situational Stats

	W	L	ERA	Sv	IP		AB	H	HR	RBI	AVG
Home	12	2	2.71	0	129.2	LHB	515	127	13	56	.247
Road	8	4	3.18	0	104.2	RHB	350	64	9	29	.183
Day	6	2	2.89	0	74.2	Sc Pos	178	39	4	59	.219
Night	14	4	2.93	0	159.2	Clutch	96	20	2	6	.208

1990 Rankings (National League)

- 1st in complete games (12), pitches thrown (3,802) and most pitches thrown per batter (4.00)
- 2nd in wins (20), strikeouts (223) and winning percentage (.769)
- 3rd in shutouts (3), innings (234.1), strikeout/walk ratio (3.3) and lowest batting average allowed (.221)
- Led the Dodgers in ERA (2.92), wins, games started (33), complete games, innings, batter faced (950), strikeouts, stolen bases allowed (22), runners caught stealing (13), winning percentage, strikeout/walk ratio and batting average/slugging percentage/on-base average allowed

MIKE MORGAN

Position: SP
Bats: R **Throws:** R
Ht: 6' 2" **Wt:** 215

Opening Day Age: 31
Born: 10/8/59 in Tulare, CA
ML Seasons: 10

PITCHING:

After toiling for a string of cellar-dwellers, Mike Morgan's hard-luck stories continued during his first pennant race with the Dodgers. Morgan tied Bruce Hurst for the league lead in shutouts (four) while notching 11 wins, only one less than his career best. When all was said and done, though, Morgan's win-loss record was 11-15. After 10 seasons, he has yet to have a season over .500, and his lifetime mark is 53-94.

A strong-armed hurler, Morgan got upset with the media toward the end of last season. He doesn't like people dwelling on his career record, which is the worst among active pitchers with at least 20 decisions. He also bristles when people call him a first-half pitcher, even though that's exactly what he's been with the Dodgers. Last year he was 7-7 at the All-Star break, 4-8 afterward.

Morgan is a finesse pitcher, depending on his ability to change speeds to keep hitters off guard. His main pitches are a four-seam fastball and a sinking fastball. He also throws a slider and uses a split-finger fastball for a change-up. Control is the key to Morgan's success because he relies on ground ball outs. Last year he had the highest ground ball-to-fly ball ratio in the National League, but he still served up enough fat pitches to allow 19 homers.

Morgan's biggest game in 1990 was a two-hitter July 30 against Cincinnati. The clutch performance convinced the Dodgers they had a chance in the division. Two months later, Morgan lasted just 15 pitches in a crucial start at Houston, and was charged with three runs in one-third of an inning in a 10-1 defeat. That's typical of Morgan's unreliable mound work.

HOLDING RUNNERS, FIELDING, HITTING:

Morgan's smooth delivery leaves him in a perfect position for sharp grounders up the middle, but he isn't nimble off the mound, and bunts along the third-base line give him trouble. He has a decent pickoff move and is tough to run on. He is no hitting threat, with a .113 average last year.

OVERALL:

Now 31, Morgan is no one's idea of an ace, but he can be useful to a rotation. His arm, which he doesn't ice after games, has been pain-free his entire career, and he can log the 200+ innings that take pressure off a staff. One of these years, he might even break through with a winning record.

Overall Statistics

	W	L	ERA	G	GS	Sv	IP	H	R	BB	SO	HR
1990	11	15	3.75	33	33	0	211.0	216	100	60	106	19
Career	53	94	4.37	230	171	2	1149.0	1251	615	406	520	111

How Often He Throws Strikes

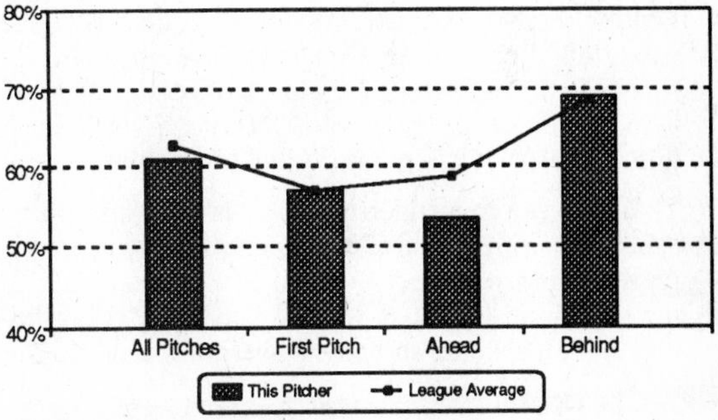

1990 Situational Stats

	W	L	ERA	Sv	IP		AB	H	HR	RBI	AVG
Home	5	6	3.77	0	105.0	LHB	461	133	9	46	.289
Road	6	9	3.74	0	106.0	RHB	350	83	10	40	.237
Day	3	3	3.88	0	53.1	Sc Pos	186	44	4	67	.237
Night	8	12	3.71	0	157.2	Clutch	64	22	2	8	.344

1990 Rankings (National League)

- 1st in shutouts (4) and groundball/flyball ratio (2.65)
- 3rd in losses (15)
- 4th in lowest stolen base percentage allowed (55.2%)
- 5th in runners caught stealing (13) and least pitches thrown per batter (3.38)
- Led the Dodgers in losses (15), games started (33), shutouts, pickoff throws (152), runners caught stealing, GDPs induced (19), groundball/flyball ratio, lowest stolen base percentage allowed, least pitches thrown per batter, least HRs allowed per 9 innings (.81) and most GDPs induced per GDP situation (13.3%)

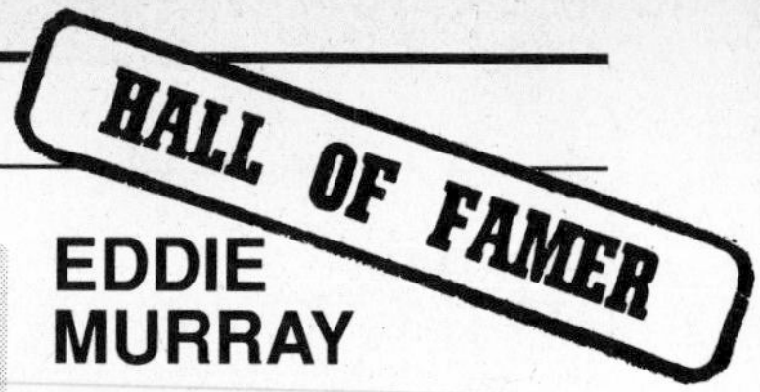

HITTING:

Don't expect invitations to Eddie Murray's retirement party in the near future. Last year, at age 34, Murray raised his average 83 points and almost won his first batting title. Batting .330, a career high, Murray knocked home 95 runs, his best total in five years. And as was so often the case during his Baltimore years, Murray was at his best late in the year, when his torrid hitting got the Dodgers back into the pennant race. In the second half, Murray batted .361, with 15 homers and 54 RBI.

Murray appeared more comfortable in his second National League season for several reasons. He was finally used to Dodger Stadium, upping his home run total there from four in 1989 to 12 in 1990. Unlike 1989, when he was the only threat in the Dodger lineup for much of the season, Murray got some help last year from the likes of Kal Daniels and Hubie Brooks. Perhaps because of that, he didn't feel the need to pull everything, especially when he was batting righty. The difference was astonishing. Murray, who had batted a career low .210 as a right-handed hitter in 1989, hit .316 batting righty in 1990.

Though a power swinger, Murray has great discipline, especially with two strikes. He can fight pitches off until getting one he can handle. His discipline is reflected in his totals of 82 walks and only 64 strikeouts in 588 at-bats, an amazing ratio for a home run hitter.

BASERUNNING:

Murray doesn't run much any more, but his eight stolen bases in 1990 marked the third-highest total of his 14-year career. Murray isn't afraid to take extra bases on a hit to the outfield, but he was hampered at times last season due to hamstring injuries.

FIELDING:

Murray is the only first baseman in the last seven decades to lead both leagues in fielding. Those who take Murray's good glove for granted were shocked on a couple of two-out grounders in September. In each case, Murray forgot the number of outs and threw to an unoccupied second base to start a double play.

OVERALL:

Murray has been the catalyst Dodgers' executive vice president Fred Claire hoped for when he rescued the veteran from a difficult situation in Baltimore after the 1988 season. Murray's composure on the field gives some fans the mistaken impression that he's not giving 100 percent. Anyone who's watched Murray carry a club in a pennant race knows just how wrong that impression is.

EDDIE MURRAY

Position: 1B
Bats: B **Throws:** R
Ht: 6' 2" **Wt:** 224

Opening Day Age: 35
Born: 2/24/56 in Los Angeles, CA
ML Seasons: 14

Overall Statistics

	G	AB	R	H	D	T	HR	RBI	SB	BB	SO	AVG
1990	155	558	96	184	22	3	26	95	8	82	64	.330
Career	2135	7997	1210	2352	402	29	379	1373	76	1026	1076	.294

Where He Hits the Ball

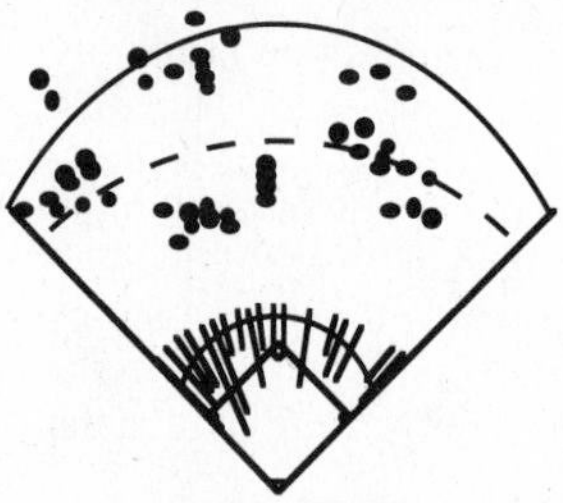

Vs. LHP

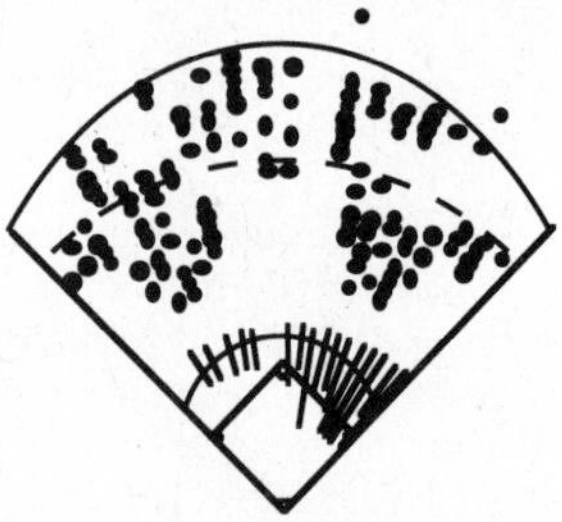

Vs. RHP

1990 Situational Stats

	AB	H	HR	RBI	AVG		AB	H	HR	RBI	AVG
Home	271	93	12	43	.343	LHP	206	65	8	36	.316
Road	287	91	14	52	.317	RHP	352	119	18	59	.338
Day	151	48	7	24	.318	Sc Pos	150	49	9	73	.327
Night	407	136	19	71	.334	Clutch	78	25	1	9	.321

1990 Rankings (National League)

- → 1st in intentional walks (21)
- → 2nd in batting average (.330), batting average vs. right-handed pitchers (.338) and on-base average vs. right-handed pitchers (.429)
- → 3rd in times on base (267), GDPs (19), on-base average (.414), slugging percentage vs. right-handed pitchers (.551) and batting average at home (.343)
- → Led the Dodgers in batting average, runs (96), hits (184), singles (133), total bases (290), RBIs (95), walks (82), intentional walks, times on base, GDPs, pitches seen (2,260), plate appearances (645), games (155) and on-base average

JIM NEIDLINGER

Position: SP
Bats: B **Throws:** R
Ht: 6' 4" **Wt:** 180

Opening Day Age: 26
Born: 9/24/64 in Vallejo, CA
ML Seasons: 1

Overall Statistics

	W	L	ERA	G	GS	Sv	IP	H	R	BB	SO	HR
1990	5	3	3.28	12	12	0	74.0	67	30	15	46	4
Career	5	3	3.28	12	12	0	74.0	67	30	15	46	4

How Often He Throws Strikes

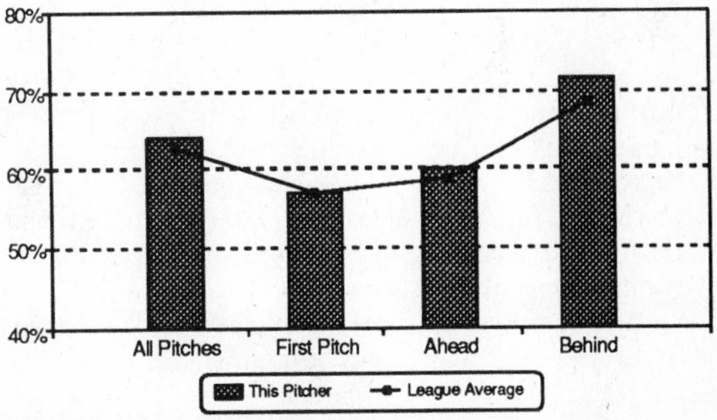

1990 Situational Stats

	W	L	ERA	Sv	IP		AB	H	HR	RBI	AVG
Home	2	1	3.34	0	29.2	LHB	172	47	1	14	.273
Road	3	2	3.25	0	44.1	RHB	106	20	3	11	.189
Day	1	2	6.63	0	19.0	Sc Pos	47	11	2	21	.234
Night	4	1	2.13	0	55.0	Clutch	22	5	0	3	.227

1990 Rankings (National League)

→ Did not rank near the top or bottom in any category

PITCHING:

The Dodgers' fifth choice to replace Orel Hershiser in the starting rotation turned out to be the best. After 10 weeks of drama with John Wetteland, Tim Crews, Mike Maddux and Terry Wells, Jim Neidlinger walked into a pennant race and pitched like a veteran. Neidlinger was a big part of the Dodgers' late-season surge, winning five games even though he only made 12 starts.

Neidlinger's July 30 promotion from AAA Albuquerque came at the crossroads of his career. Though he'd turned in some fine seasons, he was buried in Pittsburgh's minor league system for five seasons until a trade brought him to the Dodgers for pitcher Bill Krueger in October '88. Neidlinger compared his situation to former teammate Dave Johnson, another good righty who pitched for seven seasons in Pittsburgh's chain before finally getting a chance with Baltimore.

Neidlinger got his first major league victory August 12 at Atlanta. From then on he was very tough, going eight consecutive starts without a loss in the heat of the pennant race. He wasn't overpowering, but kept hitters guessing with a sinking fastball, curve and change-up. Neidlinger also wasn't afraid to throw offspead pitches behind in the count. "If Neidlinger strikes a guy out on a 3-2 curveball, it makes them think it could come on any count," manager Tom Lasorda said. "Consequently, it makes his fastball look like it got shot out of a cannon." Like Mike Morgan, the key to Neidlinger is control. He walked only 15 in 74 innings, the best ratio in the rotation.

HOLDING RUNNERS, FIELDING, HITTING:

Neidlinger keeps runners reasonably close with a decent move to first, but his slow delivery gives them a good jump against catchers. He showed good defensive reactions while playing errorless ball last year. Neidlinger managed three hits in 25 at-bats, but he was the only Dodger starter without a sacrifice hit. He'll have to learn to bunt better.

OVERALL:

Pressure? What pressure? Neidlinger's first trip to the majors proved he can handle on-the-job stress. When his wife was in an Albuquerque hospital about to deliver the couple's first child, he didn't miss his scheduled start. With Orel Hershiser's status uncertain, Neidlinger will get a good shot this spring at making the rotation. He's come a long way in two years, when he was driving a UPS truck in the off season for extra money.

HITTING:

Jose Offerman isn't known for power, but nobody will ever forget his major league debut August 19 at Dodger Stadium. Batting leadoff, Offerman homered on an 0-2 pitch against Montreal's Dennis Martinez. No Dodger had homered in his first career plate appearance since Brooklyn pitcher Dan Bankhead on August 26, 1947. Offerman finished that day 3-for-5, and added an over-the-shoulder catch in shallow left field.

With veteran Alfredo Griffin struggling at .224, it looked like Offerman might take over for good, but Offerman quickly found out that one good day doesn't make a career. He stopped hitting, was eventually dropped to the number-eight slot, and ended the season in a 5-for-49 slump.

Rated the number one prospect in the Pacific Coast League last year, Offerman is definitely considered the club's shortstop of the 1990s. "He's going to be an impact player in the big leagues," says his Albuquerque manager, Kevin Kennedy, and most observers agree. The question is whether, at 22, Offerman will be ready this year. At AAA Albuquerque, Offerman batted .326 in 117 games, but with no homers and only 27 extra-base hits. He showed unusual discipline for a young player, drawing 71 walks. With great speed -- some people have compared him to Willie Wilson -- Offerman needs to bunt more, especially from the left side of the plate. His lack of power will force Offerman to concentrate on hitting line drives.

BASERUNNING:

Offerman's speed should guarantee him a spot on the major league roster this season. Offerman, who stole 60 in only 117 games at Albuquerque, will get plenty of opportunities to run.

FIELDING:

Offerman has great range and a strong arm, but needs to smooth out his rough edges. He's been extremely error-prone during his brief career, with 104 errors in only 307 minor league contests. Offerman committed four errors in 27 games with Los Angeles, including a pair in the ninth inning August 21 that sparked Philadelphia's infamous nine-run rally and 12-11 comeback victory.

OVERALL:

Despite his problems, Offerman never acted like an overmatched rookie during the pressure of the pennant race, but replacing Griffin this year isn't guaranteed. The Dodgers figure to be contenders, and if Offerman can't settle down both offensively and defensively, he might not claim the shortstop job just yet. His day is coming, however -- very soon.

JOSE OFFERMAN

Position: SS
Bats: B **Throws:** R
Ht: 6' 0" **Wt:** 160

Opening Day Age: 22
Born: 11/8/68 in San Pedro de Macoris, Dominican Republic
ML Seasons: 1

Overall Statistics

	G	AB	R	H	D	T	HR	RBI	SB	BB	SO	AVG
1990	29	58	7	9	0	0	1	7	1	4	14	.155
Career	29	58	7	9	0	0	1	7	1	4	14	.155

Where He Hits the Ball

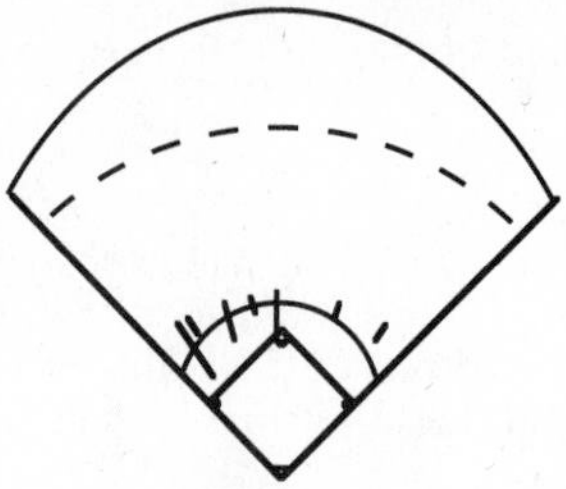

Vs. LHP

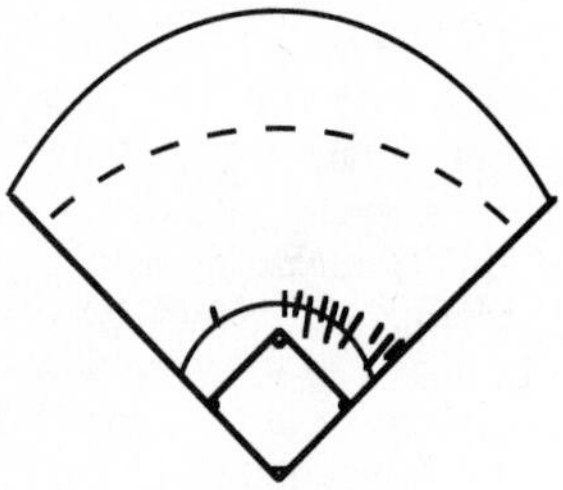

Vs. RHP

1990 Situational Stats

	AB	H	HR	RBI	AVG		AB	H	HR	RBI	AVG
Home	35	5	1	3	.143	LHP	26	5	0	2	.192
Road	23	4	0	4	.174	RHP	32	4	1	5	.125
Day	9	4	1	2	.444	Sc Pos	16	3	0	6	.188
Night	49	5	0	5	.102	Clutch	7	0	0	0	.000

1990 Rankings (National League)

- Did not rank near the top or bottom in any category

JUAN SAMUEL

Position: 2B/CF
Bats: R **Throws:** R
Ht: 5'11" **Wt:** 170

Opening Day Age: 30
Born: 12/9/60 in San Pedro de Macoris, Dominican Republic
ML Seasons: 8

HITTING:

How the mighty have fallen! Juan Samuel was once a feared slugger with great speed, capable of belting as many as 80 extra-base hits in a season (1987). These days, however, he's a .240 hitter who can blast an occasional longball. Given Samuel's defensive shortcomings, that just isn't enough production.

Last year Samuel tried his best to satisfy the Dodgers' need for a center fielder who could hit with power and steal bases. He failed miserably and soon had to be moved back to his original position, second base. For a while he was reduced to platoon status. Samuel finally improved late in the year, batting .386 with five homers and 18 RBI in his last 23 games, but even that couldn't salvage his season.

A good low fastball hitter, Samuel has always leaned over the plate and looked for hard stuff to whack. He has always lacked discipline and will chase outside breaking stuff. Pitchers will then bust him inside with high fastballs. With that style, he's continued to be very effective against lefties, batting .289 and slugging .524 against them last year, but he's been completely ineffective against righties, hitting for neither average (.213) nor power (three homers in 305 at-bats). Samuel has the talent and bat speed to make adjustments, but over the last few years he simply hasn't done so.

BASERUNNING:

Still a fine base stealer, Samuel swiped 38 bases last year. But he was also caught a career-high 20 times, negating most of the value of his successes. He's not always the most attentive runner. During a memorable game last September, Samuel, who was trying to steal, slid into second base instead of advancing to third; he hadn't realized the batter had blooped a single to right. The blunder cost the Dodgers the game.

FIELDING:

Samuel wasn't a butcher in center field, but he lacked instinct and didn't always get the proper jump on routine fly balls. Moved back to second, he made 13 errors in 108 games. He has good range at the position, but has difficulty backhanding grounders and is not smooth on the double play.

OVERALL:

The Dodgers had a difficult decision about whether to re-sign Samuel, who became a free agent after the 1990 season. Was his September hot streak just an illusion, or a return to his old form? Samuel has to hit to have value, because he's a liability as a defensive player.

Overall Statistics

	G	AB	R	H	D	T	HR	RBI	SB	BB	SO	AVG
1990	143	492	62	119	24	3	13	52	38	51	126	.242
Career	1081	4328	622	1116	213	75	116	493	318	283	1026	.258

Where He Hits the Ball

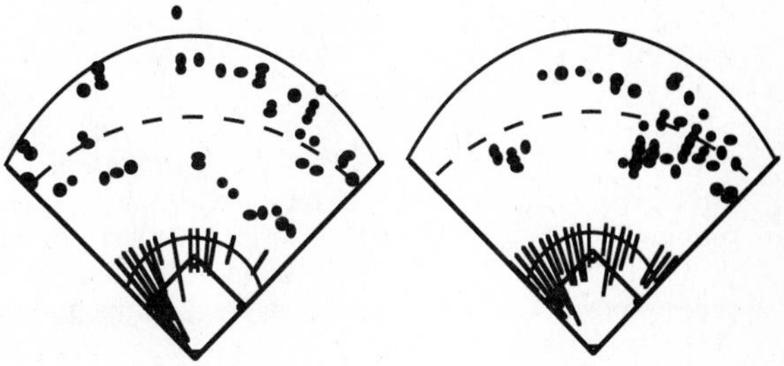

Vs. LHP Vs. RHP

1990 Situational Stats

	AB	H	HR	RBI	AVG		AB	H	HR	RBI	AVG
Home	224	55	6	26	.246	LHP	187	54	10	25	.289
Road	268	64	7	26	.239	RHP	305	65	3	27	.213
Day	133	30	1	6	.226	Sc Pos	126	26	2	36	.206
Night	359	89	12	46	.248	Clutch	69	20	4	15	.290

1990 Rankings (National League)

- 1st in lowest leadoff on-base average (.249)
- 2nd in lowest percentage of swings put into play (34.8%)
- 3rd in caught stealing (20)
- 4th in lowest batting average (.242)
- Led the Dodgers in stolen bases (38), caught stealing, strikeouts (126) and slugging percentage vs. left-handed pitchers (.524)
- Led NL second basemen in strikeouts, batting average with the bases loaded (.467) and steals of third (6)

HITTING:

Mike Scioscia doesn't have an intimidating presence in the batter's box, yet his statistics are always among the leaders at catcher. The steady Scioscia had one of his best seasons with the bat last year, reaching career highs with 12 homers and 66 RBI while batting a solid .264. Those figures don't seem very exciting -- until you look at how other catchers are doing.

Scioscia has always been a high fastball hitter, but he's changed his style a little over the last couple of years. Noticing that many of his drives to left and left-center just died on the warning track, he became more of a pull hitter. The result was more power production, without a loss of his ability to hit for a decent average. Very steady, Scioscia has hit between .250 and .265 each of the last five seasons.

One of Scioscia's unheralded qualities is his excellent discipline at the plate. He's had more walks than strikeouts during each of his 11 seasons, and usually many more: over his career, he has exactly twice as many walks as strikeouts. A great contact hitter, Scioscia simply cuts down on his swing when he needs to put the ball in play. That bat control allows Tom Lasorda to use Scioscia on hit-and-run plays, even with two-strike counts. Scioscia has also improved in the clutch. He hit only .204 with runners in scoring position in 1989, but his average jumped to .311 last season.

BASERUNNING:

Don't ask how, but Scioscia stole four bases in five attempts in 1990 after recording no stolen bases in his previous two seasons. Scioscia has no speed on the base paths, but he is a smart runner and knows his limitations.

FIELDING:

Scioscia's road blocks in front of home plate have become his trademark. He still isn't afraid of a collision, and most runners prefer a hook slide rather than attempting to knock Scioscia over. He's an excellent handler of pitchers and retains his fine throwing arm, though he wasn't helped much by his pitchers last year.

OVERALL:

When a journeyman like Alex Trevino floats between three teams in a one-month span, it makes you appreciate the work of a Scioscia. At 32, he ranks behind only San Diego's Benito Santiago in most National League catching polls. Scioscia's durability and longevity help the consistency of a pitching staff, especially a young pitcher like Ramon Martinez.

MIKE SCIOSCIA

Position: C
Bats: L **Throws:** R
Ht: 6' 2" **Wt:** 219

Opening Day Age: 32
Born: 11/27/58 in Upper Darby, PA
ML Seasons: 11

Overall Statistics

	G	AB	R	H	D	T	HR	RBI	SB	BB	SO	AVG
1990	135	435	46	115	25	0	12	66	4	55	31	.264
Career	1205	3680	340	963	176	7	57	382	22	488	244	.262

Where He Hits the Ball

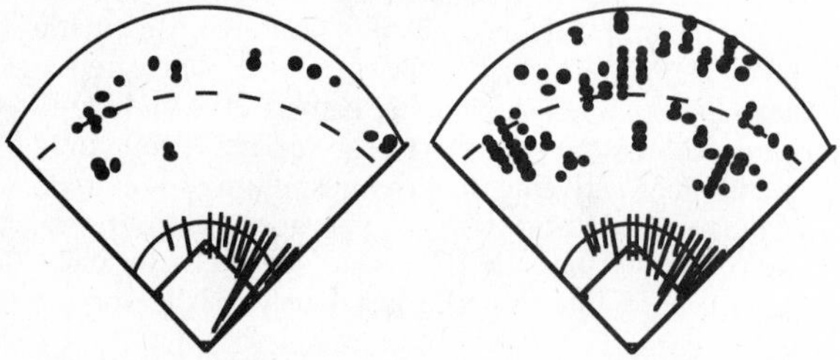

Vs. LHP   Vs. RHP

1990 Situational Stats

	AB	H	HR	RBI	AVG		AB	H	HR	RBI	AVG
Home	208	58	5	32	.279	LHP	119	28	2	18	.235
Road	227	57	7	34	.251	RHP	316	87	10	48	.275
Day	120	33	4	18	.275	Sc Pos	119	37	1	54	.311
Night	315	82	8	48	.260	Clutch	58	12	1	1	.207

1990 Rankings (National League)

- → 3rd in highest percentage of swings put into play (57.5%)
- → 7th in lowest percentage of swings that missed (9.4%)
- → Led the Dogers in lowest percnetage of swings that missed and highest percentage of swings put into play
- → Led NL catchers in RBIs (66), hit by pitch (3), batting average with runners in scoring position (.311), batting average with the bases loaded (.412), batting average on an 0-2 count (.207), batting average with 2 strikes (.245), lowest percentage of swings that missed and highest percentage swings put into play

MIKE SHARPERSON

Position: 3B/SS
Bats: R **Throws:** R
Ht: 6' 3" **Wt:** 185

Opening Day Age: 29
Born: 10/4/61 in Orangeburg, SC
ML Seasons: 4

Overall Statistics

	G	AB	R	H	D	T	HR	RBI	SB	BB	SO	AVG
1990	129	357	42	106	14	2	3	36	15	46	39	.297
Career	244	573	63	158	24	3	3	55	17	62	78	.276

Where He Hits the Ball

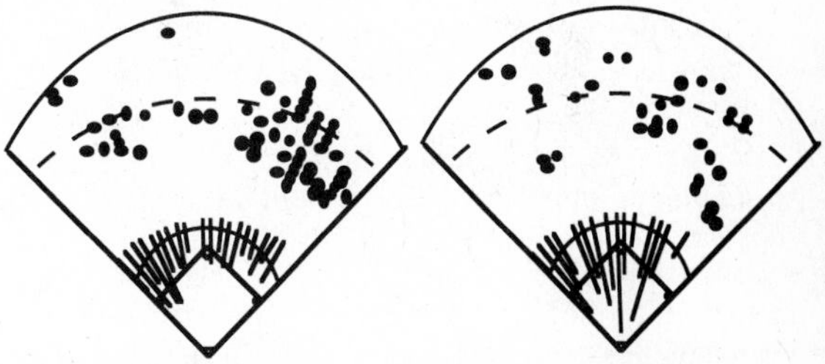

Vs. LHP   Vs. RHP

1990 Situational Stats

	AB	H	HR	RBI	AVG		AB	H	HR	RBI	AVG
Home	195	60	1	19	.308	LHP	208	67	1	17	.322
Road	162	46	2	17	.284	RHP	149	39	2	19	.262
Day	100	35	2	18	.350	Sc Pos	88	24	0	30	.273
Night	257	71	1	18	.276	Clutch	52	13	1	8	.250

1990 Rankings (National League)

- 9th highest batting average vs. left-handed pitchers (.322)
- 10th highest on-base average vs. left-handed pitchers (.296)
- Led the Dodgers in batting average vs. left-handed pitchers
- Led NL third basemen in sacrifice bunts (8) and bunts in play (16)

HITTING:

Mike Sharperson, along with teammate Lenny Harris, made the Dodgers forget about losing third baseman Jeff Hamilton last spring. With no every-day replacement for Hamilton, who went out early with a severe shoulder injury, the club settled on a platoon of Sharperson and Harris. The measure worked well enough to turn a potential trouble spot into one of the steadiest positions on the club.

Sharperson, the right-handed part of the platoon, batted a career-high .297 in his first extended shot in the major leagues. Sharperson had been Toronto's opening day second baseman in 1987, but the Jays sent him down after 32 games and a .208 average. He never got another chance, and the Jays traded him to Los Angeles that September for pitcher Juan Guzman.

As an emergency replacement during times of injury, Sharperson shuttled seven times between Triple-A Albuquerque and Los Angeles in 1988-89. He made the Dodgers last season primarily because the club's number-one utility infielder, Dave Anderson, signed with the Giants. Then came the injury to Hamilton. Sharperson took full advantage of it by showing a fine ability to reach base. His .373 on-base percentage was third on the club to Eddie Murray and Kal Daniels among players with at least 300 at-bats.

Sharperson is a high-ball spray hitter. Opposing pitchers try and keep him off-balance with offspeed pitches around the knees. He's always lacked power, and his three homers last year were his first in the majors. They all came in a 20-day span between August 14 and September 2.

BASERUNNING:

Sharperson, who'd had only two stolen bases in 115 major league games before last season, proved he was a base stealing threat last year by swiping 15 in 21 attempts. He also grounded into just five double plays in 357 at-bats.

FIELDING:

Sharperson isn't a spectacular fielder, but sometimes versatility is just as important. In 1990, he became the only player in the 32-year history of the LA Dodgers to start at least one game at every infield position over a season. Sharperson committed 12 of his 15 errors at third, and second base remains his best and most natural position.

OVERALL:

Sharperson might have too many holes to play on a regular basis, but nobody will know until he gets a chance. If he fails to make it as a regular, however, he has the skills to have a long career as a utility player.

PITCHING:

Fernando Valenzuela's June 29 no-hitter against St. Louis capped a long comeback from career-threatening shoulder problems. It was a triumphant moment, but last year Valenzuela alternated brilliant outings with terrible ones. In an off-and-on season, he won 13 games, his highest total since 1987, but he was easier to hit than ever before, and his 4.59 ERA was easily the highest of his career. He led the league in earned runs allowed (104), and was second in wild pitches (13).

For the veteran lefty, it was a strange and inconsistent year. Belying the high ERA, Valenzuela allowed two earned runs or less in 16 of his 33 starts. His longest losing streak was two games, and the club was 10-3 in games in which Valenzuela pitched seven or more innings. The Dodgers couldn't depend on good work from him, though, and he blew up just when they needed him most. Valenzuela's effectiveness plunged from August (4-2, 3.79 ERA) to September (1-3, 8.40).

Once a pitcher who dominated hitters with his good fastball and outstanding screwball, Valenzuela has become a nibbler. Last year he worked on improving his cut fastball, which kept right-handed hitters off the plate. Control of the inside fastball set up Valenzuela's screwball and curve. The repertoire worked reasonably well against righties, but he lacked the weapons to retire lefthanders, who batted .315 against him. He just couldn't seem to count on having good stuff from one outing to the next.

HOLDING RUNNERS, FIELDING, HITTING:

Valenzuela has a slick pickoff move, and despite his chunkiness, he fields his position very well. Where he really helps himself is with the bat. His 21 hits last year were the most among National League pitchers, and he set career highs with five doubles and 11 RBI. Valenzuela, who posted a whopping .420 slugging percentage, sometimes needled other pitchers about their hitting. It was good-natured fun, but the bottom line was that teammates began to take their batting more seriously.

OVERALL:

Valenzuela was a free agent at season's end, and the Dodgers, weary of his recent inconsistency, seemed of a mind to let him go. Despite his problems, Valenzuela is a survivor. He's no longer the brilliant lefty who can blow away hitters, but he can still win. Given the shortage of quality lefties, his services figure to be somewhat in demand.

FERNANDO VALENZUELA

Position: SP
Bats: L **Throws:** L
Ht: 5'11" **Wt:** 202

Opening Day Age: 30
Born: 11/1/60 in Navajoa, Mexico
ML Seasons: 11

Overall Statistics

	W	L	ERA	G	GS	Sv	IP	H	R	BB	SO	HR
1990	13	13	4.59	33	33	0	204.0	223	112	77	115	19
Career	141	116	3.31	331	320	2	2348.2	2099	981	915	1759	152

How Often He Throws Strikes

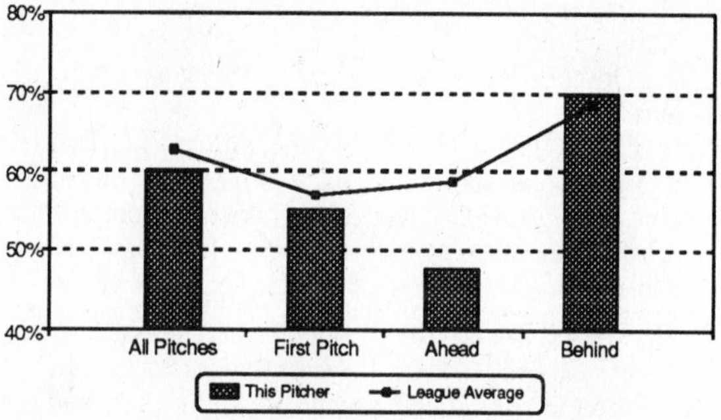

1990 Situational Stats

	W	L	ERA	Sv	IP		AB	H	HR	RBI	AVG
Home	8	5	3.75	0	117.2	LHB	130	41	4	18	.315
Road	5	8	5.73	0	86.1	RHB	678	182	15	86	.268
Day	2	2	6.00	0	24.0	Sc Pos	210	58	5	79	.276
Night	11	11	4.40	0	180.0	Clutch	54	14	0	5	.259

1990 Rankings (National League)

- 1st in earned runs allowed (104) and worst ERA on the road (5.73)
- 2nd in worst ERA (4.59) and wild pitches (13)
- 3rd most baserunners allowed per 9 innings (13.2)
- 4th worst slugging percentage allowed (.412), most pitches thrown per batter (3.82) and most run support per 9 innings (5.65)
- 5th in pitches thrown (3,440) and highest batting average allowed (.276)
- Led the Dodgers in games started (33), hits allowed (223), walks allowed (77), wild pitches (13) and run support per 9 innings

RICK DEMPSEY

Position: C
Bats: R **Throws:** R
Ht: 6' 0" **Wt:** 184

Opening Day Age: 41
Born: 9/13/49 in Fayetteville, TN
ML Seasons: 22

Overall Statistics

	G	AB	R	H	D	T	HR	RBI	SB	BB	SO	AVG
1990	62	128	13	25	5	0	2	15	1	23	29	.195
Career	1697	4536	508	1058	218	12	92	450	20	567	715	.233

HITTING, FIELDING, BASERUNNING:

Rick Dempsey's four-decade career may finally be over. Certainly his career with the Dodgers is in jeopardy following LA's signing of right-handed catcher Barry Lyons. Dempsey, 41, batted just .167 after the All-Star break last year and managed one hit in 17 at-bats as a pinch-hitter.

Those numbers were a little deceptive because Dempsey went 12-for-38 (.316) with runners in scoring position, and drove in 15 runs in 128 at-bats. He remained valuable on defense, and proved he hadn't lost any intensity. While arguing a called strike August 20 at Dodger Stadium, Philadelphia's Lenny Dykstra told Dempsey to quit "brown nosing" the home plate umpire. Dempsey wound up slugging Dykstra in the face with his catcher's glove, then followed with a right hook. The brawl cost Dempsey a one-game suspension and a $1,000 fine. If he could have swung his bat as potently as he did his fists, Dempsey wouldn't have been looking for work this winter.

OVERALL:

Dempsey isn't a Hall of Fame candidate, but his 22-year career behind the plate is a tribute to his work ethic. Only one other catcher has lasted four decades -- Carlton Fisk (Tim McCarver also played in four decades, but played first base his last year). Dempsey figured to be a long shot to earn a contract this winter, and might accept a non-roster invitation to spring training. The Dodgers might still give him a shot if they decide to keep three catchers.

JOSE GONZALEZ

Position: LF/CF/RF
Bats: R **Throws:** R
Ht: 6' 2" **Wt:** 196

Opening Day Age: 26
Born: 11/23/64 in Puerto Plata, Dominican Republic
ML Seasons: 6

Overall Statistics

	G	AB	R	H	D	T	HR	RBI	SB	BB	SO	AVG
1990	106	99	15	23	5	3	2	8	3	6	27	.232
Career	337	504	76	121	26	6	7	33	25	40	124	.240

HITTING, FIELDING, BASERUNNING:

It took 10 years and five trips between AAA Albuquerque and Los Angeles for outfield prospect Jose Gonzalez to find an everyday position with the Dodgers. Unfortunately, it was the bench. Center field is Gonzalez' best position, but he spent most of 1990 watching Juan Samuel, Stan Javier and Kirk Gibson handle the position. Gonzalez did see frequent work as a defensive replacement. He wound up appearing in 106 games, but batted only 99 times.

Gonzalez started only 15 games last year. He did well, going 15-for-50 with five RBI, but he couldn't hit off the bench and batted only .143 (3-for-21) as a pinch hitter, with eight strikeouts and no walks. A good fastball hitter, he has had consistent problems with offspeed pitches.

On the base paths, Gonzalez is always a threat to steal. He stole 44 for Albuquerque in 1988, and is 25 for 33 in his major league career. His reserve role sometimes causes him to get overanxious and become vulnerable to a pickoff play. He is a good outfielder with great range and a strong arm.

OVERALL:

Gonzalez has maintained his sanity and sense of humor during his inactive career. Manager Tom Lasorda said before one game last year that he had put Juan Samuel in the leadoff slot because he'd dreamed Samuel would have a good game. When given a start of his own a few days later, Gonzalez said, "Tommy must have had a bad dream." At 26, Gonzalez still dreams of regular duty, but he'll have a hard time getting it if he remains with the Dodgers this year.

CHRIS GWYNN

Position: LF
Bats: L **Throws:** L
Ht: 6' 0" **Wt:** 200

Opening Day Age: 26
Born: 10/13/64 in Los Angeles, CA
ML Seasons: 4

Overall Statistics

	G	AB	R	H	D	T	HR	RBI	SB	BB	SO	AVG
1990	101	141	19	40	2	1	5	22	0	7	28	.284
Career	162	252	30	65	7	2	5	31	1	11	46	.258

HITTING, FIELDING, BASERUNNING:

Call him the kid brother of San Diego's four-time National League batting champion, but don't label Chris Gwynn a bench player -- at least, not yet. Gwynn is now 26, and has compiled a fine minor league batting record. Given his most extensive major league usage last year, Gwynn responded by hitting a very solid .284. He also belted five homers in 141 at-bats, showing home run ability for the first time in his career. With Kal Daniels, Hubie Brooks and now Darryl Strawberry around, Gwynn seems to have little chance to prove he can make it as an everyday outfielder.

Gwynn used to be known strictly as a high fastball hitter, but scouts noticed that he adjusted his swing in 1990, and pulled low fastballs with surprising ease. Gwynn's highlight came on August 29 in Philadelphia, when, subbing for the injured Kal Daniels, he hit two homers, including a grand slam. It was only his third start in two months, and he was back on the bench again the next night.

Gwynn, who has very thick thighs, isn't a threat on the base paths. In 162 career games, he has stolen one base in two attempts. He is a solid outfielder who has yet to make a big league error.

OVERALL:

Gwynn has a good batting stroke, but he might be in the same situation as former teammate Franklin Stubbs -- that is, he might need a trade to get into a major league lineup. Gwynn's market value will soar if his homers continue.

JEFF HAMILTON

Position: 3B
Bats: R **Throws:** R
Ht: 6' 3" **Wt:** 214

Opening Day Age: 27
Born: 3/19/64 in Flint, MI
ML Seasons: 5

Overall Statistics

	G	AB	R	H	D	T	HR	RBI	SB	BB	SO	AVG
1990	7	24	1	3	0	0	0	1	0	0	3	.125
Career	375	1111	107	261	57	3	23	110	0	39	190	.235

HITTING, FIELDING, BASERUNNING:

Once considered the Dodgers' third baseman of the future, Jeff Hamilton's career is in jeopardy due to a severe shoulder injury. Hamilton, who had appeared in a career high 151 games while serving as the club's regular third sacker in 1989, appeared in only seven contests in 1990.

Hamilton first felt pain last year during spring training. The situation shocked Hamilton because his strong arm, which had fired a 95 MPH fastball during an emergency pitching stint in 1989, was the cornerstone of his athletic career. Hamilton tried to play, but it was hopeless. He underwent arthroscopic surgery May 4 to repair a tear in the posterior labrum of his right shoulder. At first he was expected to miss just six weeks, but the injury quickly proved too serious, and he couldn't return.

During the summer, Hamilton pondered whether to have further surgery to correct a tendon problem in the front of the shoulder. That might have reduced his throwing velocity, so Hamilton vetoed the procedure with the hope that the condition would heal naturally by spring training. Hamilton wishes to return to his 1989 form, when he belted 12 homers and 35 doubles. He possesses no speed, and has never stolen a base in 375 major league games.

OVERALL:

Remember the trade rumors at the end of the 1989 season that had LA sending Hamilton and pitcher John Wettleland to the Pirates for Barry Bonds? That deal never came off, and now Hamilton will have to rebuild his career. The Dodgers will give him his shot and hope for the best.

MICKEY HATCHER

Position: 1B
Bats: R **Throws:** R
Ht: 6' 2" **Wt:** 202

Opening Day Age: 36
Born: 3/15/55 in Cleveland, OH
ML Seasons: 12

Overall Statistics

	G	AB	R	H	D	T	HR	RBI	SB	BB	SO	AVG
1990	85	132	12	28	3	1	0	13	0	6	22	.212
Career	1130	3377	348	946	172	20	38	375	11	164	246	.280

HITTING, FIELDING, BASERUNNING:

The final curtain is coming down on one of baseball's most appealing goodwill ambassadors. Mickey Hatcher had a chance for more playing time in 1990 after third baseman Jeff Hamilton's season-ending shoulder injury in mid-April, but he had a couple shaky games on defense, and he gradually stepped aside for the successful Lenny Harris-Mike Sharperson platoon. Hatcher did fill in at first base and the outfield, but he batted only 132 times and hit an anemic .212, the worst average of his 12-year career. Hatcher is a lifetime .280 hitter, and needs to hit in order to stay in the majors. He's a slow runner, and he's always been a weak defensive player.

Hatcher batted .298 with 10 RBI as a pinch swinger last year, and his 14 hits off the bench were within one of the club record. However, he hit only .155 in the second half, and could no longer jump on the fastball, the pitch he used to feast on. His bat sometimes appeared painfully slow.

Hatcher's final hit of the season on October 2 was a classic, and maybe his swan song. With the Dodgers trailing 7-6 in the eighth inning against San Diego, Hatcher looped a two-run single into center field. As the throw sailed home, Hatcher belly-flopped into second base to the delight of 22,883 at Dodger Stadium.

OVERALL:

The Dodgers might invite Hatcher back in 1991 as a pinch hitter. His enthusiasm for the game is contagious, and he remains the prototype of how men should take pleasure playing a kid's game.

JOHN WETTELAND

Position: RP/SP
Bats: R **Throws:** R
Ht: 6' 2" **Wt:** 195

Opening Day Age: 24
Born: 8/21/66 in San Mateo, CA
ML Seasons: 2

Overall Statistics

	W	L	ERA	G	GS	Sv	IP	H	R	BB	SO	HR
1990	2	4	4.81	22	5	0	43.0	44	28	17	36	6
Career	7	12	4.08	53	17	1	145.2	125	74	51	132	14

PITCHING, FIELDING, HITTING & HOLDING RUNNERS:

Just two years ago, Ramon Martinez and John Wetteland were considered the untouchable rookie bookends of the Dodgers. Wetteland's name even surfaced during the 1989 winter meetings in trade talks involving Pittsburgh's Barry Bonds and Philadelphia's Lenny Dykstra. As Martinez zoomed to stardom in 1990, Wetteland's career headed south.

Wetteland looked bad from the start of spring training last year. He blamed his sluggish form on a 100-day winter ball stint in the Dominican Republic, saying that it drained his mental approach and enthusiasm for the game. He began the year in the bullpen, but when Orel Hershiser was lost for the year in late April, Wetteland was the first choice to take Hershiser's spot in the rotation. He couldn't handle it, and eventually had to be demoted to AAA Albuquerque. After missing six weeks with a cracked rib, he came back in September and pitched a little better.

Wetteland still possesses the tools to be a star, a 93 MPH fastball among them. He needs some other pitches, though, and his attitude needs work. He's a good fielder, but one who sometimes rushes a bunt play in tight situations. Opposing runners also have an easy time stealing bases against Wetteland.

OVERALL:

Wetteland needs to get command of his exceptional stuff. In two years he's struck out 132 batters in 145.2 innings, but he's also uncorked the ridiculous total of 24 wild pitches. It's important to remember that he's just 24 years old, and could well be a late bloomer like Orel Hershiser and Dave Stewart.

DENNIS BOYD

Position: SP
Bats: R **Throws:** R
Ht: 6' 1" **Wt:** 160

Opening Day Age: 31
Born: 10/6/59 in Meridian, MS
ML Seasons: 9

Overall Statistics

	W	L	ERA	G	GS	Sv	IP	H	R	BB	SO	HR
1990	10	6	2.93	31	31	0	190.2	164	64	52	113	19
Career	70	62	3.96	183	176	0	1207.1	1231	584	311	684	145

How Often He Throws Strikes

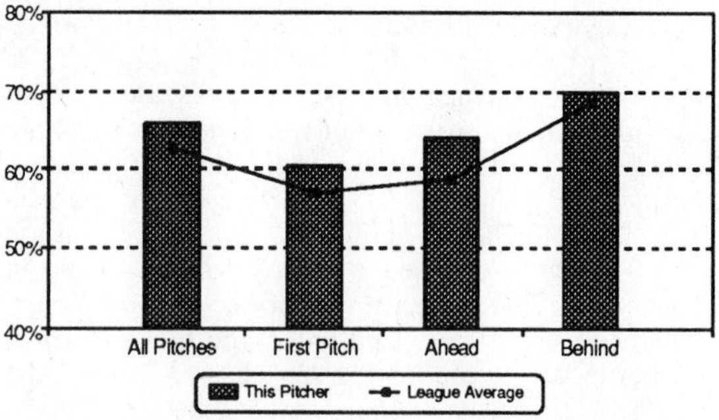

1990 Situational Stats

	W	L	ERA	Sv	IP		AB	H	HR	RBI	AVG
Home	6	3	2.91	0	89.2	LHB	432	98	10	33	.227
Road	4	3	2.94	0	101.0	RHB	271	66	9	27	.244
Day	3	4	3.29	0	65.2	Sc Pos	172	29	4	38	.169
Night	7	2	2.74	0	125.0	Clutch	13	3	1	2	.231

1990 Rankings (National League)

- 1st in lowest batting average allowed with runners in scoring position (.169) and lowest fielding percentage for a pitcher (.909)
- 3rd in shutouts (3)
- 6th in most stolen bases allowed (25) and least pitches thrown per batter (3.38)
- 7th in lowest groundball/flyball ratio (.88) and highest stolen base percentage allowed (80.7%)
- Led the Expos in ERA (2.93), shutouts, home runs allowed (19), least pitches thrown per batter, most run suppport per 9 innings (4.20), ERA at home (2.91) and lowest batting average allowed with runners in scoring position

PITCHING:

Dennis "Oil Can" Boyd was the surprise story of the unpredictably strong Expos pitching staff in 1990. Coming out of spring training, the Expos expected little from the 30-year-old righthander, who had spent much of 1989 on the disabled list. But by the end of the season, Boyd had become the team's most consistent starter.

Boyd was cut loose by the Boston Red Sox after blood clots in his right shoulder had sidelined him for 120 days in 1989. Boyd reported to spring training with a 70 MPH fastball and a right arm that had lost much of its strength to the blood clotting. But following his prescribed treatment religiously, Boyd missed only one start in 1990, finishing the year with a 2.93 earned-run average. He was second on the team in starts with 31 and in innings pitched with 190.2.

"We were very fortunate with our pitching," Expos manager Buck Rodgers said after his team finished with the league's best ERA at 3.37. "Who would have believed that 'The Can' would be our most consistent pitcher? I certainly wouldn't have, especially after watching him the first few weeks of spring training."

Boyd, who was once considered somewhat of a power pitcher, has always had a vast repertoire, but the eight-year veteran completed the transition to a finesse pitcher last season. In his bag of tricks, Boyd lists a sinking fastball, an "extra-sinking" fastball, slider, curve, straight change, screwball and a split-finger fastball. Boyd can also throw any of these pitches from over-the-top, three-quarters or sidearm. Boyd, who has a tremendous feel for changing speeds, varies his out pitch from game to game.

HOLDING RUNNERS, FIELDING, HITTING:

Last year was Boyd's first in the National League, and it showed, as he had only three hits in 59 at-bats. He did, however, sacrifice 12 times. Boyd also will have to improve his move to first base. With only 160 pounds covering his 6-foot-2 frame, Boyd is quick around the mound, but he made three errors in only 33 changes last year.

OVERALL:

Boyd has re-established himself as a solid major league starter, though his lack of stamina keeps the bullpen busy. His pitching intelligence and his innate ability to know when and why to change speeds make him a valuable commodity. The Expos expect him to be one of their primary starters in 1991 and hope that an extra year of medication and strengthening exercises will build up his endurance.

PITCHING:

Tim Burke's numbers don't tell the tale of his 1990 season. While his 2.52 earned run average and 20 saves appear to the casual observer as a fine season, Burke actually was horrible for much of the year. But the right-handed reliever salvaged his season with a spectacular September, a month during which he lowered his ERA by almost a full run. Burke didn't allow a run in 13 appearances covering 19.1 innings during the month. He sparked a late-season bid by the Expos to get back into the National League East pennant race.

Signed to a three-year, $6-million contract before the start of the 1990 season, Burke responded with the most inconsistent season of his six-year career. Burke's ERA was hovering around 5.00 when he broke his leg May 30 and subsequently missed more than a month of play. He finished among the league leaders in blown saves with five.

More a power pitcher than finesse, Burke has a sinking fastball, slider and change-up. His inconsistent slider is the pitch which often gets him in trouble. Though he has proven to be an effective reliever in his career, Burke is more suited to a bullpen-by-committee situation than as the lone closer on a team. He is subject to lengthy bad streaks and has always had problems against left-handed batters.

Burke, who had limited right-handed batters to a .199 batting average prior to 1990, was hit at an overall .247 clip. He continued to stifle righties in 1990 as he held them to a .210 average. Lefties, on the other hand, ripped him for a .285 average. Burke is also missing the one dominating pitch that most closers have.

HOLDING RUNNERS, FIELDING, HITTING:

Burke, whose broken leg occurred during a fielding play in Atlanta, is actually a good fielder, quick off the mound to snare balls or to cover first. He has a good move to first base and can pick off a napping baserunner. As a late-inning reliever, Burke rarely gets the opportunity to hit.

OVERALL:

Burke, whose career ERA is the lowest among active pitchers with more than 350 innings pitched, is an outstanding reliever, but needs left-handed help in the bullpen. The Expos will be trying to work a new pitch into Burke's repertoire this spring, possibly a split-fingered fastball for use against lefties.

TIM BURKE

Position: RP
Bats: R **Throws:** R
Ht: 6' 3" **Wt:** 200

Opening Day Age: 32
Born: 2/19/59 in Omaha, NE
ML Seasons: 6

Overall Statistics

	W	L	ERA	G	GS	Sv	IP	H	R	BB	SO	HR
1990	3	3	2.52	58	0	20	75.0	71	29	21	47	6
Career	40	22	2.48	388	2	96	554.1	476	176	175	370	38

How Often He Throws Strikes

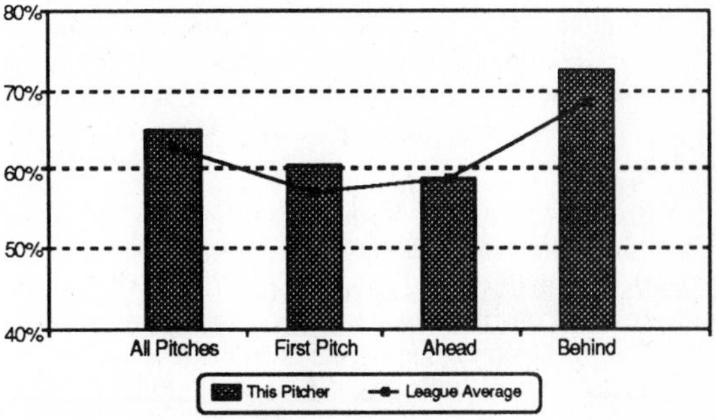

1990 Situational Stats

	W	L	ERA	Sv	IP		AB	H	HR	RBI	AVG
Home	2	2	2.87	8	31.1	LHB	144	41	3	18	.285
Road	1	1	2.27	12	43.2	RHB	143	30	3	20	.210
Day	0	2	1.82	7	29.2	Sc Pos	93	25	2	32	.269
Night	3	1	2.98	13	45.1	Clutch	204	49	5	31	.240

1990 Rankings (National League)

- 5th in save percentage (80.0%)
- 7th in saves (20) and save opportunities (25)
- Led the Expos in saves, games finished (35), save opportunities, holds (6), save percentage, blown saves (5) and lowest percentage of inherited runners scored (27.1%)

DELINO DeSHIELDS

Position: 2B
Bats: L **Throws:** R
Ht: 6' 1" **Wt:** 170

Opening Day Age: 22
Born: 1/15/69 in Seaford, DE
ML Seasons: 1

HITTING:

Although Dave Justice has the award, voters could have done a lot worse than pick Delino DeShields as National League Rookie of the Year. Sure, home run hitters get most of the attention, but DeShields played a starring role for the surprising Expos while playing a tough defensive position to boot. After hitting only .270 at AA Jacksonville and .260 at AAA Indianapolis in 1989, the 21-year-old DeShields figured to have a tough time with major league pitching in 1990. But this talented young athlete opened a lot of eyes.

DeShields flirted with .300 for most of the season before winding up with a solid .289 batting average. He tied for the team lead in runs scored (69) with Tim Wallach and his 144 hits ranked behind only Wallach and Andres Galarraga. DeShields was third on the team in doubles with 28, and third in stolen bases with 42. He was caught stealing 22 times, but that can be chalked up to his overall lack of baseball experience, at any level. And the young left-handed hitter even showed an ability to hang in there against lefties, hitting .264 against them (he hit .304 against right-handers).

A line drive singles and doubles hitter who uses the whole field, DeShields showed a good eye at the plate even though he is an aggressive swinger. His 69 walks were third on the team and gave him an impressive .375 on-base percentage. Like most hitters, DeShields likes to see fastballs but he doesn't appear to be overmatched against any type of pitching. DeShields also showed the makings of a good clutch hitter, hitting .283 with runners in scoring position and .359 with runners on third.

BASERUNNING:

The speed is there but the experience is missing. With a little more work, DeShields could develop into one of the top base stealers in the National League.

FIELDING:

DeShields' play in the field was equally impressive. Playing second base for the first time (he was a shortstop in the minors), he showed great range, moving to his left and his right gracefully. He completes plays with a strong, accurate arm. A gifted athlete -- he was offered a basketball scholarship to play point guard for Villanova but turned it down to sign with the Expos -- DeShields is outstanding when peeling back to shallow outfield to catch soft pops.

OVERALL:

DeShields figures to be a mainstay in the Expos infield for a long time to come and will almost certainly develop into one of the best second basemen in the NL.

Overall Statistics

	G	AB	R	H	D	T	HR	RBI	SB	BB	SO	AVG
1990	129	499	69	144	28	6	4	45	42	66	96	.289
Career	129	499	69	144	28	6	4	45	42	66	96	.289

Where He Hits the Ball

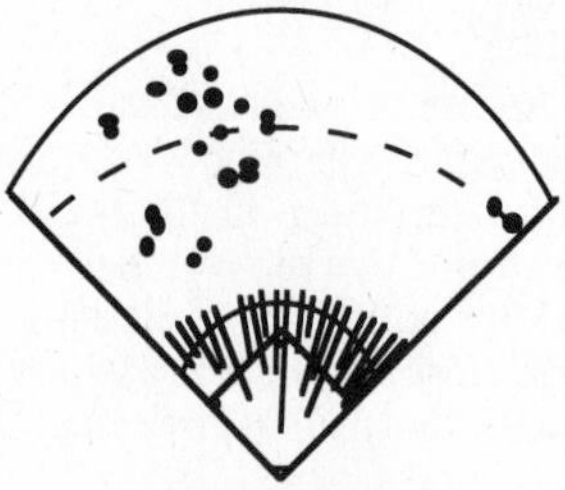

Vs. LHP

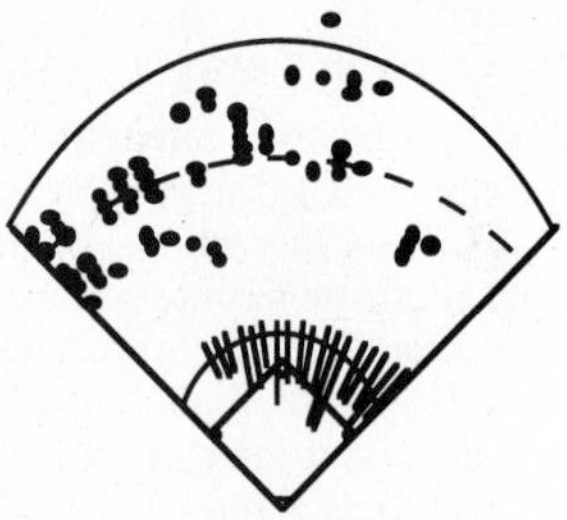

Vs. RHP

1990 Situational Stats

	AB	H	HR	RBI	AVG		AB	H	HR	RBI	AVG
Home	226	71	3	27	.314	LHP	193	51	2	17	.264
Road	273	73	1	18	.267	RHP	306	93	2	28	.304
Day	134	38	0	14	.284	Sc Pos	106	30	0	40	.283
Night	365	106	4	31	.290	Clutch	101	23	0	7	.228

1990 Rankings (National League)

- 2nd in caught stealing (22)
- 3rd in groundball/flyball ratio (2.15) and most pitches seen per plate appearance (4.01)
- Led the Expos in runs (69), triples (6), caught stealing, groundball/flyball ratio, most pitches seen per plate appearance, batting average on a 3-1 count (.450), batting average at home (.314) and highest percentage of pitches taken (62.2%)
- Led NL second basemen in stolen bases (42), caught stealing, on-base average (.375), groundball/flyball ratio, most pitches seen per plate appearance, bunts in play (20) and steals of third (6)

MIKE FITZGERALD

Position: C
Bats: R **Throws:** R
Ht: 5'11" **Wt:** 190

Opening Day Age: 30
Born: 7/13/60 in Long Beach, CA
ML Seasons: 8

HITTING:

Mike Fitzgerald has completed his long road back from a career-threatening injury, justifying manager Buck Rodgers' faith in the veteran catcher. The oft-injured Fitzgerald suffered his worst injury on August 1, 1986, fracturing a finger on his right hand while trying to scoop a pitch out of the dirt. Subsequent surgery left Fitzgerald with a badly misshapen finger. It made throwing so painful that Fitzgerald had trouble getting the ball back to the pitcher and made throwing out base stealers all but impossible.

Fitzgerald lost his starting job and hit bottom when he was the team's 25th player and third-string catcher coming out of spring training in 1989. He became the full-time catcher last year when Nelson Santovenia was injured. The 30-year-old hit .243 with 18 doubles, nine homers and 41 RBI in only 313 at-bats.

Fitzgerald is a line drive hitter with extra-base power who looks for the fastball. He has been working on hitting the ball up the middle, with some success, but he is still a slight pull hitter, especially against left-handers. Though he hit only .225 against lefties last season, he did show some power with five homers against them. Fitzgerald often hacks away at the first pitch but he does have a good eye at the plate, drawing 60 walks last season. Fitzgerald is considered one of the team's most dependable hitters in the clutch. Last season, he hit .277 with runners in scoring position.

BASERUNNING:

With a typical catcher's speed, Fitzgerald is a conservative baserunner, going station to station. He does pull off the occasional surprise steal and last season was very successful in that department, stealing eight bases while being caught only once.

FIELDING:

Fitzgerald still has trouble throwing out baserunners but manager Rodgers, himself a major league catcher for nine seasons, contends that the seven-year veteran has an uncanny knack for handling pitchers. Fitzgerald is one of only two catchers with a winning record as a starting catcher in each of the past seven seasons. His record last season was 49-35 and is 294-232 for his career, including his rookie season with the Mets in 1984.

OVERALL:

Rodgers considers the handling of pitchers to be the most important element of a catcher's game. That means that, barring injury, Fitzgerald will almost certainly be the team's starting catcher come opening day. His offensive production, though modest, is more than adequate considering the dearth of catching at the major league level.

Overall Statistics

	G	AB	R	H	D	T	HR	RBI	SB	BB	SO	AVG
1990	111	313	36	76	18	1	9	41	8	60	60	.243
Career	682	1929	184	465	88	7	38	248	25	248	363	.241

Where He Hits the Ball

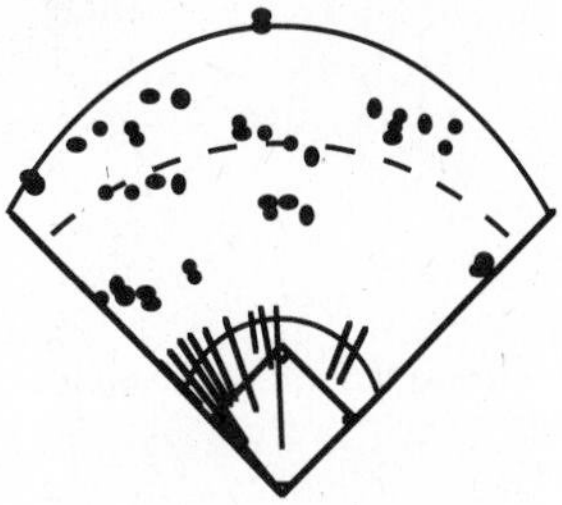

Vs. LHP

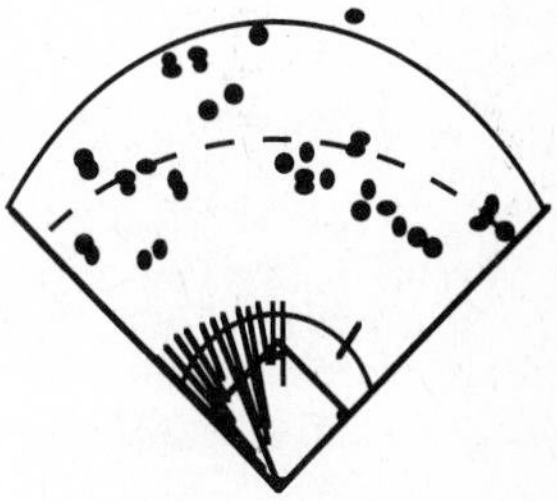

Vs. RHP

1990 Situational Stats

	AB	H	HR	RBI	AVG		AB	H	HR	RBI	AVG
Home	134	33	2	14	.246	LHP	138	31	5	20	.225
Road	179	43	7	27	.240	RHP	175	45	4	21	.257
Day	96	30	5	18	.313	Sc Pos	83	23	1	29	.277
Night	217	46	4	23	.212	Clutch	88	19	0	11	.216

1990 Rankings (National League)

- 2nd lowest percentage of runners caught stealing (20.2%)
- 4th lowest percentage of extra bases taken as a runner (27.5%)
- Led the Expos in on-base average vs. left-handed pitchers (.359)

TOM FOLEY

Position: SS/2B
Bats: L **Throws:** R
Ht: 6' 1" **Wt:** 180

Opening Day Age: 31
Born: 9/9/59 in Columbus, GA
ML Seasons: 8

Overall Statistics

	G	AB	R	H	D	T	HR	RBI	SB	BB	SO	AVG
1990	73	164	11	35	2	1	0	12	0	12	22	.213
Career	794	2084	196	523	100	17	26	204	26	184	288	.251

Where He Hits the Ball

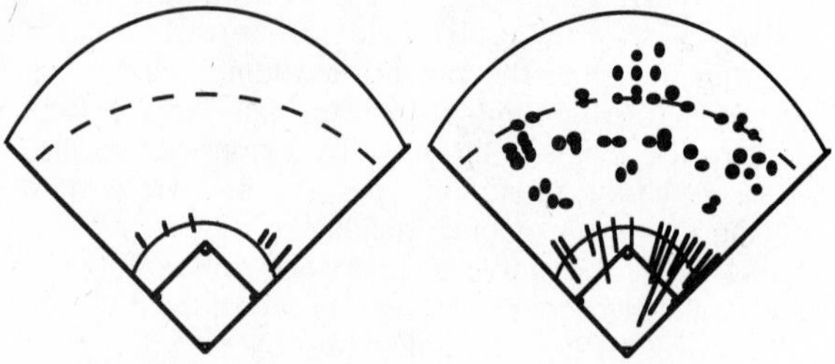

Vs. LHP **Vs. RHP**

1990 Situational Stats

	AB	H	HR	RBI	AVG		AB	H	HR	RBI	AVG
Home	84	16	0	6	.190	LHP	18	5	0	1	.278
Road	80	19	0	6	.237	RHP	146	30	0	11	.205
Day	46	14	0	3	.304	Sc Pos	42	11	0	12	.262
Night	118	21	0	9	.178	Clutch	44	8	0	3	.182

1990 Rankings (National League)

- 7th lowest batting average in the clutch (.182)

HITTING:

The emergence of Delino DeShields as an outstanding second baseman doesn't bode well for Tom Foley's future with the Expos. Foley, the Expos' starting second baseman against right-handed pitching for two-and-one-half seasons, posted his lowest at-bat total since his first year in the majors, with just 164.

The subject of trade rumors throughout most of last summer -- the Oakland Athletics were the most frequently mentioned destination -- Foley now finds himself as a utility infielder with the Expos. His reduced playing time seemed to affect him at the plate as he hit only .158 and didn't drive in a run in 95 at-bats after July 4. Pinch hitting didn't seem to suit him either since he had only one hit in 10 at-bats.

Foley is somewhat of a contradiction at the plate -- a pull hitter with little power (seven homers in a season is his career high). Most of his hits are between center field and the right-field line. Foley is a contact hitter with good bat control and is often called upon to hit-and-run by manager Buck Rodgers. Although he rarely plays against left-handed pitching, Foley has posted better batting averages against lefties than against righties in each of the past two seasons (.278 against lefthanders, .205 against righthanders in 1990; .261 and .227 in 1989).

BASERUNNING:

With his penguin-like gait, Foley is not a quick runner. His 0-for-1 in stolen bases last season marked the fourth straight year he was thrown out more often than he was successful in steal attempts (10 for 30 in his three previous years). The eight-year veteran, however, is an intelligent base runner and doesn't clog up the bases.

FIELDING:

Foley is among the best fielding second basemen in the game. In 1989 when he played in 108 games at second, Foley averaged 5.49 chances per nine innings, ranking second in the National League at his position. A converted shortstop, Foley has good range to either side but seems to go to his right a little more naturally.

OVERALL:

Foley won't be getting much playing time with the Expos next season. As the backup at third base, shortstop and second base, Foley has the unfortunate fate of playing behind iron man Tim Wallach, durable Spike Owen, and DeShields, who played in 129 games last season and figures to start more in 1991. However, a veteran middle infielder with a decent bat is a marketable commodity and Foley may find himself playing elsewhere come opening day.

PITCHING:

Steve Frey figures to play a big role in the Expos' pitching plans for the 1991 season. And that's a far cry from the way the team looked at him last spring. Acquired from the Mets' organization in a minor league trade two seasons ago, Frey spent part of 1989 with the Expos, but made the wrong kind of impression. He was sent down after allowing 29 hits and 11 walks in 21 innings.

Not much was expected from the little lefthander in spring training last season, but Frey fooled the coaching staff. After playing winter ball in the Dominican Republic, Frey reported in tip-top shape. The short spring training proved to be a blessing as he caught the eyes of the Expos' brass immediately. "We knew we needed help in the bullpen," pitching coach Larry Bearnarth said. "Because of the short camp we knew we were going to have to make decisions quickly. We gave Frey a lot of key assignments. He passed all of them, and, what's even more important, he carried the good work into the regular season."

The 27-year-old finished at 8-2 with nine saves and a minuscule earned-run average of 2.10. Frey was particularly effective following a week in the hospital because of a staph infection. From his return on August 6 to the end of the season, Frey was 4-1 with four saves in 19 appearances and a stingy 0.98 ERA.

Frey is a finesse pitcher who's best pitch is a sharply breaking curveball. He also has a cut fastball and a change-up. Frey's control is relatively good, though he pitches too carefully at times and loses batters. However, the Expos feel he has proven his toughness in clutch situations. Though he broke down once, his stamina was good in his first full year in the majors.

HOLDING RUNNERS, FIELDING, HITTING:

Frey needs to improve his pickoff move to first base. He is only fair at holding runners close. He is, however, a good fielder. Judging Frey as a hitter is hardly fair since he only had his first at-bat August 31 in his 62nd major league game.

OVERALL:

If the Expos don't land an established closer during the off season, Frey will certainly get a shot at sharing the role with right-handed reliever Tim Burke. However, he will have to prove that he can get lefthanders out consistently, a weakness of his in 1990.

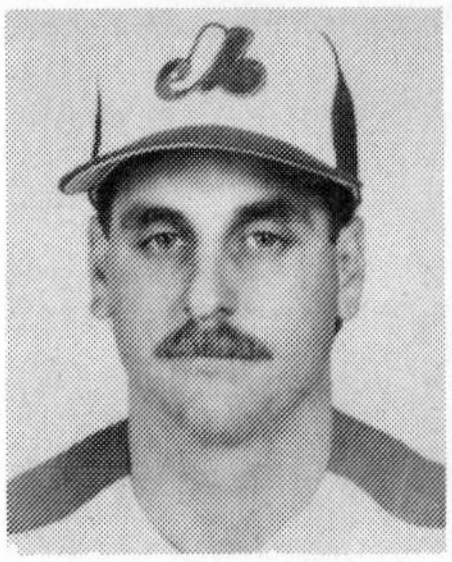

STEVE FREY

Position: RP
Bats: L **Throws:** L
Ht: 5' 9" **Wt:** 170

Opening Day Age: 27
Born: 7/29/63 in Meadowbrook, PA
ML Seasons: 2

Overall Statistics

	W	L	ERA	G	GS	Sv	IP	H	R	BB	SO	HR
1990	8	2	2.10	51	0	9	55.2	44	15	29	29	4
Career	11	4	3.04	71	0	9	77.0	73	30	40	44	8

How Often He Throws Strikes

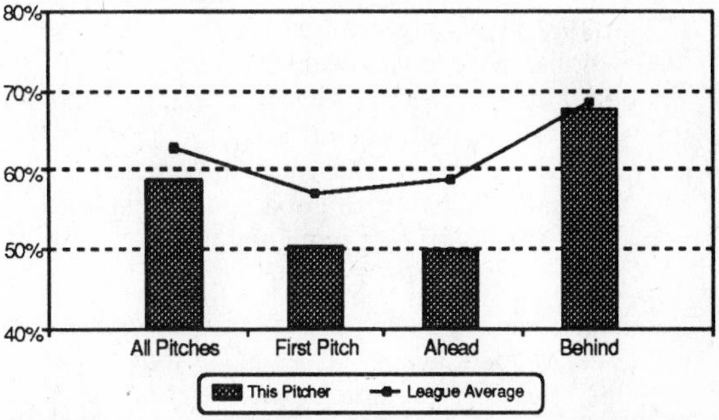

1990 Situational Stats

	W	L	ERA	Sv	IP		AB	H	HR	RBI	AVG
Home	4	0	0.59	7	30.1	LHB	62	17	2	8	.274
Road	4	2	3.91	2	25.1	RHB	139	27	2	6	.194
Day	3	1	3.63	4	22.1	Sc Pos	59	10	0	9	.169
Night	5	1	1.08	5	33.1	Clutch	141	31	4	9	.220

1990 Rankings (National League)

➟ Led the Expos in first batter efficiency (.250)

ANDRES GALARRAGA

Position: 1B
Bats: R **Throws:** R
Ht: 6' 3" **Wt:** 235

Opening Day Age: 29
Born: 6/18/61 in Caracas, Venezuela
ML Seasons: 6

HITTING:

Andres Galarraga's 1990 season had Expos general manager Dave Dombrowski mumbling that the team should lower its expectations for the slick-fielding first baseman. For the second consecutive season, the "Big Cat" failed to live up to the impressive standard he set in his first two full seasons in the majors (.305, 13 homers, 90 RBIs in 1987 and .302, 29 homers, 92 RBIs in 1988). Galarraga last season hit .256 with 20 homers, 29 doubles and 87 RBIs, almost a mirror image of his 1989 season, when he hit .257 with 23 homers, 30 doubles and 85 RBIs. The number are still not too shabby and, the Expos concede that they are probably a more realistic reflection of his talents.

Galarraga's big weakness, and it's a big one, is his selectivity at the plate. For the third straight season, Galarraga led the National League in strikeouts, racking up 169 after striking out 158 times in 1989 and 153 in 1988. Galarraga can be made to look absolutely foolish with low, outside breaking pitches and can be set up to chase eye-high fastballs. Though he feasts on both fastballs and breaking pitches over the plate, hitting some of the longest homers in the league, smart pitchers with good control exploit his impatience and don't give him good pitches to hit.

The big right-handed hitter tailed off dramatically against left-handed pitching last year. After compiling a .322 career mark against lefties in his four previous seasons, the highest among active NL players, Galarraga slumped to .226 last year, though he still slugged lefties at a good pace, hitting nine homers and driving in 35 runs in only 217 at-bats.

BASERUNNING:

Galarraga is aggressive on the bases with surprising speed for a 6-foot-3, 235-pounder. Though it takes him a few steps to get his frame into high gear, Galarraga can be counted on to steal 10-15 bases. Last season, he stole 10 bases and was caught only once.

FIELDING:

This is where the Venezuelan earned his "Cat" nickname. Galarraga doesn't take a back seat to anyone as a defensive first baseman, whether he's scooping up infielder's bouncing throws, fielding tough chances before leading pitchers with soft throws to first, or starting 3-6-3 double plays. He is equally adept at going either to his right or his left.

OVERALL:

An excellent fielder who can hit in the .260-.270 range with 20 homers, 30 doubles and 85 RBIs is nothing to scoff at. Even without any improvement, Galarraga makes a tremendous contribution. A little more discipline could make him an MVP candidate.

Overall Statistics

	G	AB	R	H	D	T	HR	RBI	SB	BB	SO	AVG
1990	155	579	65	148	29	0	20	87	10	40	169	.256
Career	740	2707	360	748	155	12	97	400	49	201	704	.276

Where He Hits the Ball

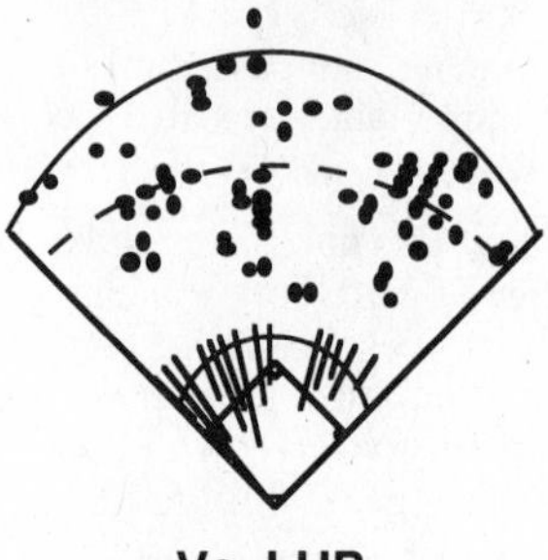

Vs. LHP

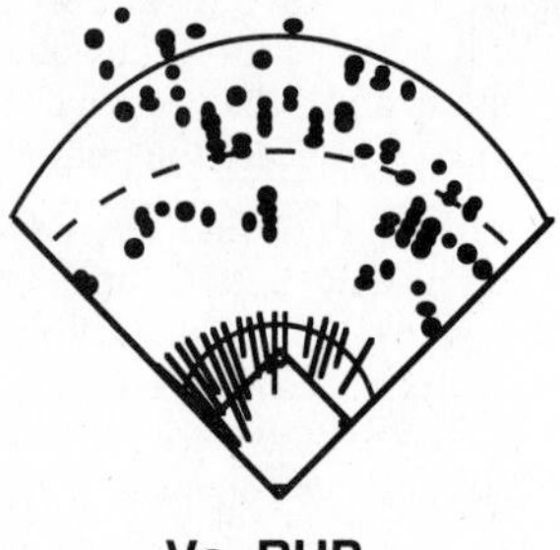

Vs. RHP

1990 Situational Stats

	AB	H	HR	RBI	AVG		AB	H	HR	RBI	AVG
Home	286	76	6	42	.266	LHP	217	49	9	35	.226
Road	293	72	14	45	.246	RHP	362	99	11	52	.273
Day	164	34	7	23	.207	Sc Pos	169	45	7	69	.266
Night	415	114	13	64	.275	Clutch	119	31	2	17	.261

1990 Rankings (National League)

- → 1st in strikeouts (169) and lowest percentage of swings put into play (34.1%)
- → 2nd in highest percentage of swings that missed (30.1%)
- → 5th lowest on-base average vs. left-handed pitchers (.260)
- → 7th in GDPs (14)
- → Led the Expos in strikeouts, GDPs, HR frequency (29.0 ABs per HR), most runs scored per time reached base (33.8%), batting average with the bases loaded (.333) and on-base average vs. right-handed pitchers (.333)
- → Led NL first basemen in strikeouts and batting average with the bases loaded

PITCHING:

Mark Gardner had a potential Rookie of the Year season ruined by a tired arm in August. His season-ending stats of 7-9 with an earned run average of 3.42 don't begin to tell the story. For four months, the 28-year-old righthander was among the most effective starters in the league. In fact, Gardner was the league leader in ERA in early August. But Gardner, not used to being a regular starter in the majors, wore out. After weeks of ineffectiveness, Gardner was put through a series of tests by several doctors. The reports were always similar. There was no structural damage. His arm simply got tired.

The premature end to his season has whetted the appetite of Expos management, who predict that Gardner will be a reliable member of the rotation for years to come. Last season Gardner pitched three shutouts and held the opposition scoreless on three other occasions in which he wasn't involved in the decision. Overall, he limited opposing batters to a .230 average, which ranked ninth among National League starters last season.

Though Gardner can't be considered a power pitcher, he is definitely a strikeout pitcher. He struck out 135 batters in 152.2 innings last season. Most of those strikeouts came on Gardner's best pitch, which is an outstanding curveball. He also throws a fastball, which is only average, and a split-finger change-up. Gardner walked 61 batters last season, but the best measure of his control involves the sharpness of his curveball. When the curve is working, Gardner is capable of throwing shutouts and striking out batters in bunches.

HOLDING RUNNERS, FIELDING, HITTING:

With a lot of work, Gardner has become respectable at keeping runners close at first base, a necessity since most of his pitches are curves. His delivery often puts him in a poor fielding position. Gardner is a poor batter, hitting .114 in his first year in the majors, though he did have one double and one triple among his five hits. He laid down eight sacrifice bunts.

OVERALL:

In 1989 Gardner served notice that he would be a factor in the majors when he led all of Class AAA in strikeouts, posted a 12-4 record with a 2.37 ERA, and was named playoff MVP. Now, the Expos hope that off season work will build up Gardner's arm to the point where he can stretch his four-month brilliance of 1990 over a whole season.

MARK GARDNER

Position: SP
Bats: R **Throws:** R
Ht: 6' 1" **Wt:** 190

Opening Day Age: 29
Born: 3/1/62 in Los Angeles, CA
ML Seasons: 2

Overall Statistics

	W	L	ERA	G	GS	Sv	IP	H	R	BB	SO	HR
1990	7	9	3.42	27	26	0	152.2	129	62	61	135	13
Career	7	12	3.67	34	30	0	179.0	155	78	72	156	15

How Often He Throws Strikes

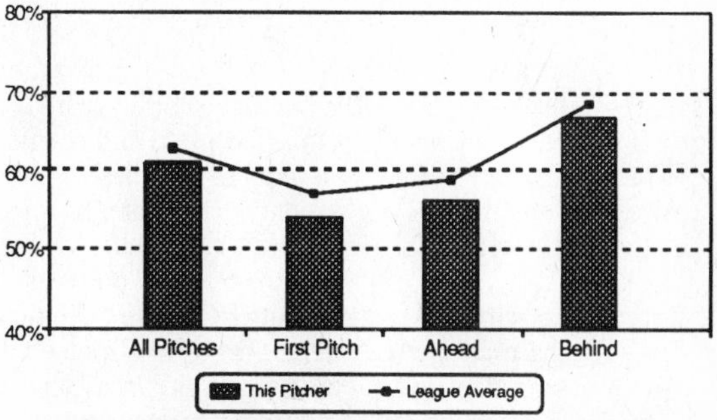

1990 Situational Stats

	W	L	ERA	Sv	IP		AB	H	HR	RBI	AVG
Home	5	3	1.91	0	80.0	LHB	321	74	9	33	.231
Road	2	6	5.08	0	72.2	RHB	240	55	4	23	.229
Day	1	4	6.19	0	36.1	Sc Pos	127	33	2	40	.260
Night	6	5	2.55	0	116.1	Clutch	37	11	0	4	.297

1990 Rankings (National League)

- → 1st in hit batsmen (9)
- → 3rd in shutouts (3)
- → Led the Expos in shutouts, hit batsmen and balks (4)

MARQUIS GRISSOM

Position: RF/LF/CF
Bats: R **Throws:** R
Ht: 5'11" **Wt:** 190

Opening Day Age: 23
Born: 4/17/67 in Atlanta, GA
ML Seasons: 2

HITTING:

Despite a mediocre rookie season, Expos management feels that Marquis Grissom proved during the 1990 season that he can play in the major leagues. Grissom, one of three Expos' rookies who started last season as an everyday player, was forced onto the disabled list May 28 when he fractured a bone in his hand while sliding into second base in a game in Atlanta. He didn't return until June 30, and by that time had lost his starting job to Dave Martinez. Grissom was used mostly as a fourth outfielder for the remainder of the season.

Despite the inauspicious debut (.257 batting average), the Expos feel that Grissom was a steal in the third round of the 1988 draft. A three-letter athlete in College Park, Georgia, Grissom was a standout at Florida A&M. In his junior year, Grissom was 9-3 with a 2.40 earned run average on the mound while hitting .448 with 12 homers.

Grissom is mostly a line drive hitter but he has enough power to hit 10-15 homers a year. He's a free swinger who likes to whale away at the first pitch and seems to have a knack for finding a gap (14 doubles in 288 at-bats). Though he is not patient at the plate, hitting coach Hal McRae, for one, doesn't consider that a weakness in a young hitter with Grissom's potential. Grissom has shown an early ability to handle fastballs out over the plate but has been all but overmatched with breaking stuff away -- the type of pitch the Expos hope he will learn to lay off with experience.

BASERUNNING:

Grissom showed no signs of rookie jitters on the base paths. Working with base running coach Tommy Harper, Grissom showed speed and an ability to read pitchers as he stole 22 bases while being caught only twice.

FIELDING:

During the early part of the season Grissom had problems going back on balls hit to center, but he overcame that difficulty with playing time. His speed allows him to cover lots of ground in the outfield and he has an above-average arm.

OVERALL:

The Expos consider Grissom to be a potential star who will hit for average and for some power and who already flies on the base paths. However, the team will have to resolve a glut in the outfield (Tim Raines, Dave Martinez, Larry Walker, Otis Nixon) if Grissom is to play every day.

Overall Statistics

	G	AB	R	H	D	T	HR	RBI	SB	BB	SO	AVG
1990	98	288	42	74	14	2	3	29	22	27	40	.257
Career	124	362	58	93	16	2	4	31	23	39	61	.257

Where He Hits the Ball

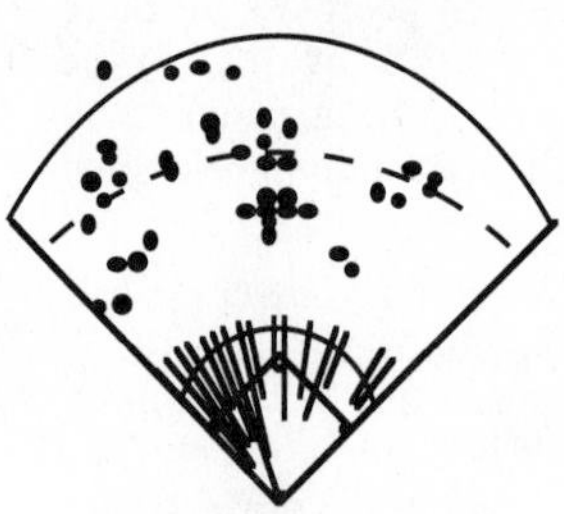

Vs. LHP

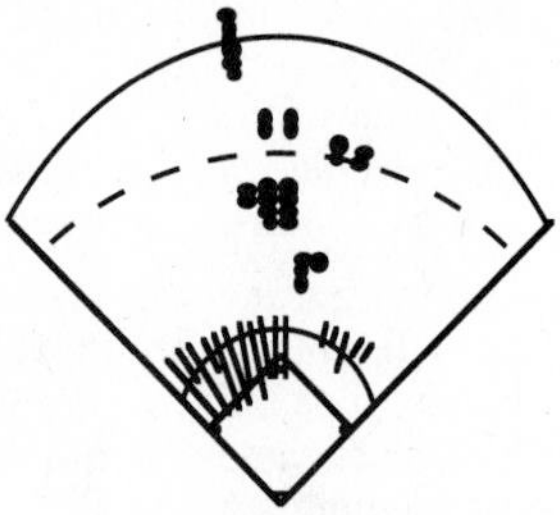

Vs. RHP

1990 Situational Stats

	AB	H	HR	RBI	AVG		AB	H	HR	RBI	AVG
Home	146	36	2	17	.247	LHP	181	44	2	16	.243
Road	142	38	1	12	.268	RHP	107	30	1	13	.280
Day	85	20	1	6	.235	Sc Pos	74	19	1	24	.257
Night	203	54	2	23	.266	Clutch	66	20	2	11	.303

1990 Rankings (National League)

- 2nd in stolen base percentage (91.7%)
- 9th highest batting average on an 0-2 count (.280)
- Led the Expos in stolen base percentage, least GDPs per GDP situation (5.9%) and batting average on an 0-2 coutn
- Led NL right fielders in stolen base percentage and steals of third (5)

PITCHING:

For Kevin Gross, the pot of gold was snatched away by a finger tip -- a broken finger tip, that is. The veteran righthander was off to a sizzling start with the Expos last season with an 8-4 record, and was well on his way to another season with 200-plus innings. He was playing out his option and discussing a multi-year, multi-million dollar contract when disaster struck at Wrigley Field June 27. Attempting to bunt against Jeff Pico, Gross suffered a fracture on the tip of the middle finger on his pitching hand.

The hurt lasted much longer than the recuperation period. Gross and his agent had turned down a lucrative two-year deal from the Expos, insisting on a three-year pact and the big bucks that his consistent contributions as a workhorse (30 starts in five consecutive seasons heading into last year) appeared to warrant. But Gross could not regain his form upon return to duty. After six straight losing decisions, Gross was relegated to the bullpen. Though he did straighten out somewhat, Gross was never inserted back into the rotation, working as a reliever and spot starter. An obviously disappointed Gross took several shots at Expos management as the season wound down. He didn't win another game until October 1, the second-to-last game of the season, and finished with a 9-12 record and an earned-run average of 4.57.

Gross has a varied repertoire of pitches and can change his game from power to finesse. He throws a fastball, sinking fastball, slider, curve, change and cut fastball. However, Gross doesn't always change speeds as effectively as he should. His below-average control doesn't show in his walk total (65 walks in 163.1 innings) but rather in bad pitches which have him behind in the count much too often.

HOLDING RUNNERS, FIELDING, HITTING:

Gross' high leg kick and mediocre move to first base make him vulnerable to the stolen base. His delivery also often puts him in a poor fielding position. Gross, who has spent his entire major league career in the National League, is a decent hitting pitcher. He hit .200 last season, with four doubles and one homer.

OVERALL:

Gross made it clear at the end of last season that he would only return to Montreal in a visiting team's uniform. The Expos, for their part, said they didn't want him back. A fresh start in a new environment may be the tonic Gross needs to get back on track.

KEVIN GROSS

Position: SP/RP
Bats: R **Throws:** R
Ht: 6' 5" **Wt:** 215

Opening Day Age: 29
Born: 6/8/61 in Downey, CA
ML Seasons: 8

Overall Statistics

	W	L	ERA	G	GS	Sv	IP	H	R	BB	SO	HR
1990	9	12	4.57	31	26	0	163.1	171	86	65	111	9
Career	80	90	4.02	265	221	1	1469.1	1447	712	583	996	133

How Often He Throws Strikes

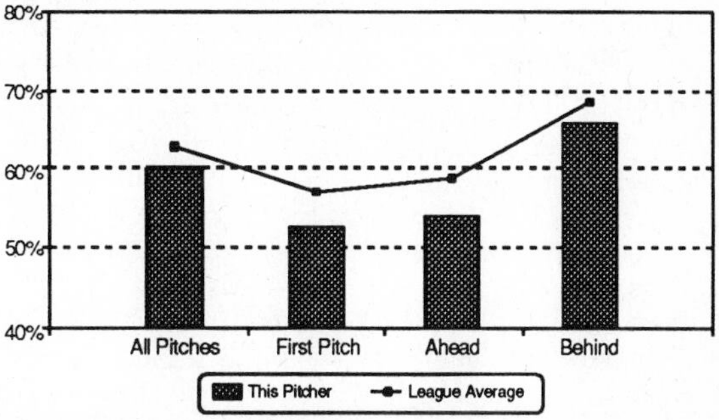

1990 Situational Stats

	W	L	ERA	Sv	IP		AB	H	HR	RBI	AVG
Home	3	5	4.43	0	69.0	LHB	371	110	7	52	.296
Road	6	7	4.67	0	94.1	RHB	257	61	2	21	.237
Day	3	3	3.52	0	53.2	Sc Pos	171	44	2	64	.257
Night	6	9	5.09	0	109.2	Clutch	33	12	1	5	.364

1990 Rankings (National League)

- 3rd worst ERA (4.57) and most stolen bases allowed (31)
- 4th worst on-base average allowed (.340), highest stolen base percentage allowed (86.1%) and most baserunners allowed per 9 innings (13.2)
- 5th least GDPs induced per 9 innings (.39)
- Led the Expos in losses (12), walks allowed (65), wild pitches (4), stolen bases and least HRs allowed per 9 innings (.50)

DAVE MARTINEZ

Position: CF/RF
Bats: L **Throws:** L
Ht: 5'10" **Wt:** 150

Opening Day Age: 26
Born: 9/26/64 in New York, NY
ML Seasons: 5

Overall Statistics

	G	AB	R	H	D	T	HR	RBI	SB	BB	SO	AVG
1990	118	391	60	109	13	5	11	39	13	24	48	.279
Career	577	1766	235	471	61	27	29	155	79	152	317	.267

Where He Hits the Ball

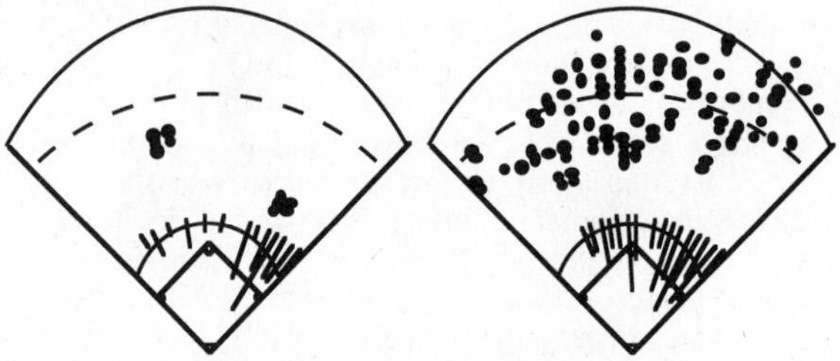

Vs. LHP   Vs. RHP

1990 Situational Stats

	AB	H	HR	RBI	AVG		AB	H	HR	RBI	AVG
Home	204	56	5	18	.275	LHP	78	19	1	11	.244
Road	191	54	6	21	.283	RHP	317	91	10	28	.287
Day	103	25	4	11	.243	Sc Pos	91	21	3	28	.231
Night	292	85	7	28	.291	Clutch	67	14	0	10	.209

1990 Rankings (National League)

- 2nd worst stolen base percentage (54.2%)
- Led the Expos in batting average on a 3-2 count (.350)

HITTING:

Dave Martinez took full advantage of his opportunity last year, and in the process made strides toward proving that he can be an everyday player. Martinez, who in his four previous seasons had been used as a platoon player, found himself on the bench for most of the early going last year while the Expos experimented with rookie Marquis Grissom in center field. But Martinez got a chance to start and play against both lefthanders and righthanders after Grissom broke his hand May 28.

Martinez responded with a solid season, playing fine defense and hitting a respectable .279. Martinez, who has long said that he can hit lefthanders if given the chance, had a career average of .193 in limited opportunities against lefties. But he answered the challenge last season, hitting .244 against southpaws and cutting down his strikeout ratio (15 Ks in 78 at-bats against lefties after striking out 10 times in 30 at-bats in 1989). Martinez hit .287 against righthanders.

After much pleading and cajoling from the Expos coaching staff, Martinez has become aggressive at the plate, often swinging at the first pitch. He finally has broken his habit of waiting for the perfect pitch. A singles hitter who showed surprising power (11 homers, 13 doubles in 391 at-bats), Martinez likes the fastball but can be fooled by offspeed pitches. He is also starting to earn a reputation as a clutch hitter. With men in scoring position and less that two outs, Martinez hit .279, driving home 17 runs with 12 hits. In '89, Martinez hit .300 with men in scoring position.

BASERUNNING:

Martinez has the tools but maybe not the passion to be a consistently good base stealer. After leading the team in stolen base percentage in 1989 (23 out of 27), Martinez slumped badly last season, getting nailed 11 of 24 times. It was his first bad year on the bases, however, and he should recover.

FIELDING:

Martinez, with his excellent speed, is an outstanding defensive center fielder who goes back well on the ball. He has an above-average arm in both strength and accuracy.

OVERALL:

The relatively young Martinez has become a solid center fielder who could start for many teams. He could also be an immensely valuable fourth outfielder because he can play left, center and right fields. However, if Tim Raines isn't used in a major trade, Martinez becomes the Expos' next most marketable commodity, and may find himself on a new team when the season starts.

PITCHING:

Dennis Martinez hogged the headlines again in 1990. Unfortunately, it wasn't always his outstanding pitching that did the talking. The veteran righthander remains one of the most outspoken players in the game, and always says what's on his mind. Despite the tenuous position Martinez puts himself in with his critique of teammates, management or whatever might irk him on a particular day, Martinez is an invaluable talent.

Martinez had another superb season last year, finishing among the league leaders in earned run average (ninth at 2.95), innings pitched (ninth with 226), complete games (fifth with seven), strikeouts (ninth with 156), fewest walks per nine innings (fourth with two) and opponents' batting average (seventh at .228). However, poor run support hurt Martinez as he finished with a 10-11 record.

Martinez relies more on power than finesse, with both a fastball and a sinking fastball. But his out pitch is often his devastating hard curve, which is considered among the best in the National League. Martinez also mixes in a straight change occasionally. Martinez is an intelligent pitcher; he rarely follows any set pattern against a hitter and will rely more on what is working for him on a particular day than what a scouting report says is a hitter's weakness. Martinez is equally effective against lefthanders (.226 batting average) and righthanders (.229) -- 1989 was the only season since 1980 when lefties (.283) hit for a higher average than righthanders (.224) off Martinez.

A consistent, durable pitcher, Martinez can be counted on for 200-plus innings and more than 30 starts -- most of them good. In spite of his outspoken nature, Martinez is not only a winner on the mound but serves as an example for others on how to compete. His work on the mound and his work habits between starts are models for younger pitchers on the team.

HOLDING RUNNERS, FIELDING, HITTING:

Martinez has a good move to first base and pays particular attention to baserunners, throwing to first base often. He is quick off the mound, has soft hands and is a decisive fielder. He is not a threat at bat.

OVERALL:

Called the toughest righthander in the National League by Will Clark, Martinez is a proven winner. As a "new look" free agent, Martinez would have a chance to discover how much his ability is worth to other clubs. He could be the number-one or number-two starter in a lot of rotations.

DENNIS MARTINEZ

Position: SP
Bats: R **Throws:** R
Ht: 6' 1" **Wt:** 183

Opening Day Age: 35
Born: 5/14/55 in Granada, Nicaragua
ML Seasons: 15

Overall Statistics

	W	L	ERA	G	GS	Sv	IP	H	R	BB	SO	HR
1990	10	11	2.95	32	32	0	226.0	191	80	49	156	16
Career	163	134	3.82	460	379	5	2711.1	2691	1272	804	1423	265

How Often He Throws Strikes

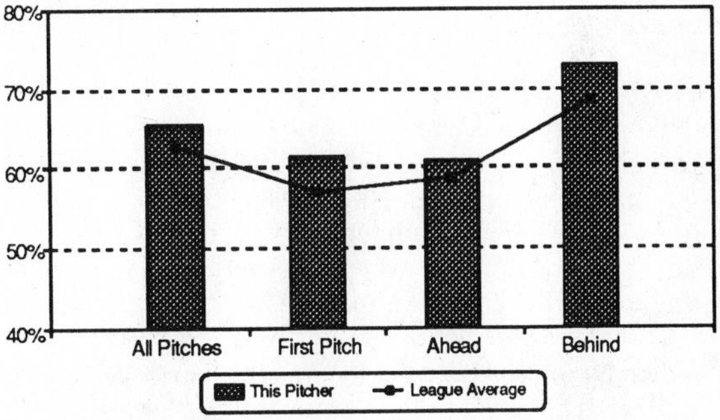

1990 Situational Stats

	W	L	ERA	Sv	IP		AB	H	HR	RBI	AVG
Home	6	10	3.41	0	134.2	LHB	499	113	9	46	.226
Road	4	1	2.27	0	91.1	RHB	340	78	7	30	.229
Day	3	4	3.24	0	66.2	Sc Pos	191	40	3	53	.209
Night	7	7	2.82	0	159.1	Clutch	90	27	6	17	.300

1990 Rankings (National League)

- 2nd in ERA on the road (2.27)
- 3rd lowest on-base average allowed (.274) and least baserunners allowed per 9 innings (9.8)
- 5th in complete games (7), strikeout/walk ratio (3.2), lowest slugging percentage allowed (.335), groundball/flyball ratio (1.77) and lowest batting average allowed with runners in scoring position (.209)
- Led the Expos in game started (32), complete games, innings (226.0), hits allowed (191), strikeouts (156), pitches thrown (3,189), strikeout/walk ratio, lowest batting average (.228)/slugging percentage/on-base average allowed and groundball/flyball ratio

OTIS NIXON

Position: CF/LF
Bats: B **Throws:** R
Ht: 6' 2" **Wt:** 180

Opening Day Age: 32
Born: 1/9/59 in Evergreen, NC
ML Seasons: 8

HITTING:

Otis Nixon couldn't scare anybody with a bat, even in a dark alley. But his speed can kill once he gets on the bases. Nixon's game is built entirely on his speed, which, as the saying goes, never goes into a slump. Manager Buck Rodgers has said that Nixon, who had a career average of .222 entering last season, could be of great value to the team if he could just hit .230 or so. Nixon exceeded the Expos' expectations last year by hitting .251.

Strictly a singles hitter, Nixon hit his first National League homer last season -- 1,708 days after hitting his previous major league homer as a member of the Cleveland Indians on September 4, 1985. Nixon now has four career home runs. He is a patient hitter (28 walks in his limited playing time) who continually must remind himself to hit the ball on the ground. His biggest improvement last year was in his handling of breaking balls.

BASERUNNING:

Nixon earns his money on the base paths. On a team which doesn't score a lot of runs and depends on pitching and defense, Nixon becomes an effective weapon as a pinch runner in close games. Nixon's at-bats are secondary when determining his value to the team. He becomes important after somebody else has parlayed an at-bat into a life on the bases; that's when Nixon can take a game into his hands as a pinch runner. That he led the team in stolen bases with 50 and scored 46 runs in only 231 at-bats will attest to his importance. Nixon set a record of sorts last season -- 50 stolen bases in the fewest number of at-bats. Nixon, who was caught stealing only 13 times, has learned to read pitchers' moves and to take advantage of every opportunity.

FIELDING:

Nixon obviously can cover a lot of ground in the outfield. He is a superior outfielder with soft hands, good instincts and a better-than-average arm. A natural center fielder, Nixon can start in a pinch or can fill any outfield role in the late innings.

OVERALL:

A valuable bench player and spare outfielder, the 32-year-old Nixon has put personal problems behind him and has become an important member of the team both on and off the field. Nixon lives in Montreal during the off season, preaching the value of clean living to students.

Overall Statistics

	G	AB	R	H	D	T	HR	RBI	SB	BB	SO	AVG
1990	119	231	46	58	6	2	1	20	50	28	33	.251
Career	625	1139	221	260	29	7	4	75	192	122	170	.228

Where He Hits the Ball

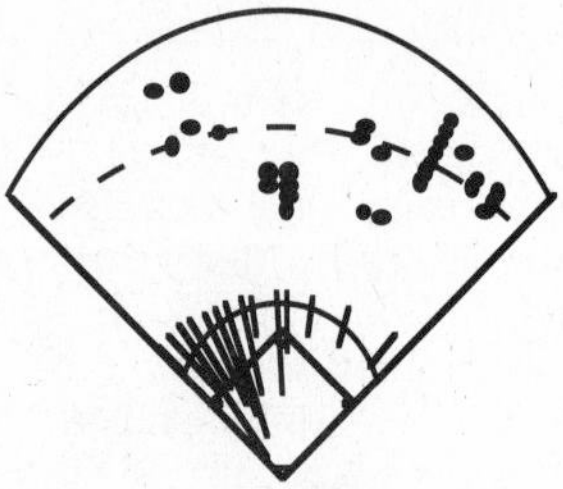
Vs. LHP

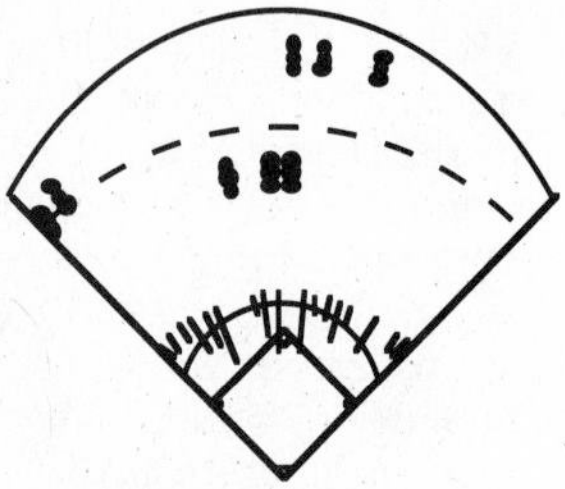
Vs. RHP

1990 Situational Stats

	AB	H	HR	RBI	AVG		AB	H	HR	RBI	AVG
Home	108	26	0	8	.241	LHP	151	36	1	11	.238
Road	123	32	1	12	.260	RHP	80	22	0	9	.275
Day	73	18	0	8	.247	Sc Pos	56	15	0	16	.268
Night	158	40	1	12	.253	Clutch	63	22	0	5	.349

1990 Rankings (National League)

- 1st in lowest batting average on a 3-1 count (.000)
- 2nd in steals of third (13)
- 5th in stolen bases (50) and lowest slugging percentage vs. left-handed pitchers (.305)
- 6th in bunts in play (26)
- 8th in caught stealing (13)
- 9th in batting average in the clutch (.349)
- Led the Expos in stolen bases, batting average in the clutch, bunts in play and steals of third
- Led NL center fielders in steals of third

SPIKE OWEN

Position: SS
Bats: B **Throws:** R
Ht: 5'10" **Wt:** 165

Opening Day Age: 29
Born: 4/19/61 in Cleburne, TX
ML Seasons: 8

Overall Statistics

	G	AB	R	H	D	T	HR	RBI	SB	BB	SO	AVG
1990	149	453	55	106	24	5	5	35	8	70	60	.234
Career	1016	3300	408	788	135	41	30	288	63	381	359	.239

Where He Hits the Ball

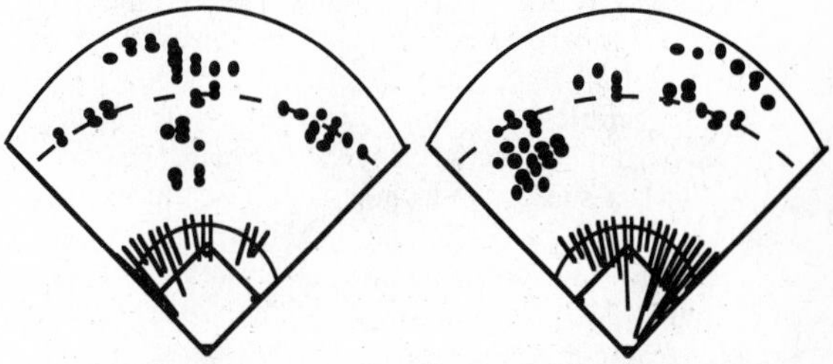

Vs. LHP Vs. RHP

1990 Situational Stats

	AB	H	HR	RBI	AVG		AB	H	HR	RBI	AVG
Home	215	49	2	16	.228	LHP	201	52	3	17	.259
Road	238	57	3	19	.239	RHP	252	54	2	18	.214
Day	128	31	2	13	.242	Sc Pos	100	17	0	27	.170
Night	325	75	3	22	.231	Clutch	91	22	3	11	.242

1990 Rankings (National League)

- 2nd worst batting average with runners in scoring position (.170) and worst batting average at home (.228)
- 3rd worst batting average (.234)
- 5th highest percentage of pitches taken (61.7%)
- 7th worst slugging percentage (.342)
- Led the Expos in walks (70), intentional walks (12) and highest percentage of swings put into play (50.9%)
- Led NL shortstops in walks, most pitches seen per plate appearance (3.92), fielding percentage (.989) and highest percentage of pitches taken

HITTING:

Expos' pitchers know that they're in good hands with Spike Owen, the reliable shortstop who set a National League record last season with 63 consecutive errorless games at short. Owen, who had a career .240 batting average entering last season, was acquired by the Expos after the 1988 season for his steady defense and not for his offense. However, the little shortstop has proven more than adequate as a hitter out of the number-eight spot in the lineup.

Owen hit .234 last season and showed some decent power, working in 24 doubles, five triples and five homers among his 106 hits. The secret to his success, however, has been his patience at the plate. Owen drew 70 walks last season (12 intentional), giving him a respectable .333 on-base percentage. The walks are an important element for an eighth-place hitter in the NL since they bring the pitcher to the plate and allow the offense to start the next inning at the top of the order.

A switch-hitter, Owen is much more effective from the right side of the plate, hitting .259 right-handed and .214 left-handed. Owen generally has trouble with offspeed pitches and inside fastballs, pitches he tries to pull too much. Owen also had trouble with runners on base last season, hitting .170 with runners in scoring position, .238 with runners on third and .200 with the bases loaded. Another disturbing trend is that for the second consecutive year, Owen has faded in the second half, leading to speculation that the 165-pounder needs more rest during the season.

BASERUNNING:

With ordinary speed, Owen is not much of a threat on the base paths -- he was caught six times in 14 tries last season. However, the eight-year veteran runs the bases intelligently and aggressively.

FIELDING:

Though Owen doesn't have the flash or the range of a Shawon Dunston, he consistently handles all balls he gets to and makes uncannily accurate throws to first base, as only six errors in 148 games at short will attest. His .989 fielding percentage led NL shortstops, the second consecutive year he has finished atop that category.

OVERALL:

A hard-nosed competitor, Owen quickly established himself as a leader in the Expos clubhouse and helped smooth rookie Delino DeShields' transition to second base. With the team relying heavily on pitching and defense, Owen appears to be solidly entrenched at his position.

TIM RAINES

Position: LF
Bats: B **Throws:** R
Ht: 5' 8" **Wt:** 180

Opening Day Age: 31
Born: 9/16/59 in Sanford, FL
ML Seasons: 12

Overall Statistics

	G	AB	R	H	D	T	HR	RBI	SB	BB	SO	AVG
1990	130	457	65	131	11	5	9	62	49	70	43	.287
Career	1405	5305	934	1598	273	81	96	552	634	775	563	.301

Where He Hits the Ball

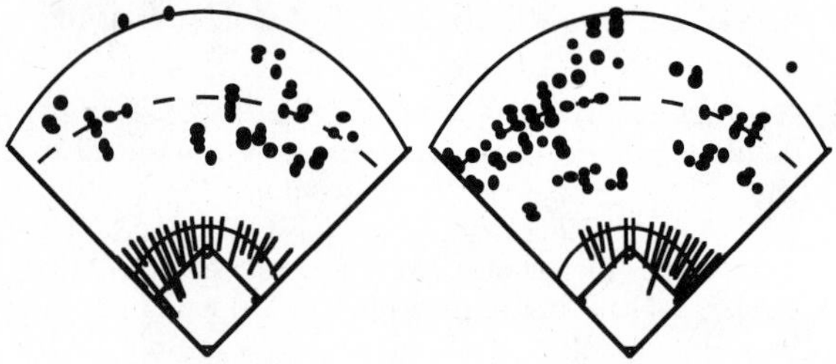

Vs. LHP Vs. RHP

1990 Situational Stats

	AB	H	HR	RBI	AVG		AB	H	HR	RBI	AVG
Home	202	62	6	28	.307	LHP	180	52	3	27	.289
Road	255	69	3	34	.271	RHP	277	79	6	35	.285
Day	132	36	3	15	.273	Sc Pos	125	39	3	54	.312
Night	325	95	6	47	.292	Clutch	91	29	2	15	.319

1990 Rankings (National League)

- 6th in stolen bases (49) and caught stealing (16)
- 7th in steals of third (7)
- Led the Expos in sacrifice flies (8), walks (70), on-base average (.379), batting average with runners in scoring position (.312), batting average with 2 strikes (.235) and lowest percentage of swings that missed (12.8%)
- Led NL left fielders in sacrifice flies

HITTING:

Tim Raines wants the Expos to cut out the charade. After three seasons of being juggled in the batting order, Raines wants to return to the leadoff spot permanently. "I'm taking too much heat for the team's lack of offense," Raines said after the 1990 season. "People look at my numbers and say they aren't good enough for a number-three hitter. They forget that I'm hitting third because that's where the team wants me to play. I'm paid $2 million a year to bat leadoff but I'm doing other jobs because they needed me."

The switch-hitting Raines hit .287 last season (.289 right-handed, .285 left-handed), his third straight sub-.290 season, coinciding with the three years Raines has been shuffled around the top four spots in the lineup. Raines had four successive seasons hitting between .309 and .334 before 1988.

The compact Raines hits for some power (nine homers last season) and is a patient fastball hitter who hits the ball all over the field. Good offspeed stuff gives him problems. Though he often swings at the first pitch, Raines has a keen eye at the plate (he drew 70 walks last season and ranked 10th in the league with a .379 on-base percentage) and is tough to strike out, fanning only once every 12.5 at-bats, seventh-best in the NL. Raines, who had hit 29 or more doubles seven of his previous eight seasons, suddenly lost the touch last season, hitting a ridiculously-low total of 11 for a player with his speed. A great clutch hitter, Raines hit .312 with runners in scoring position last season after hitting .325 or better in each of his five previous seasons.

BASERUNNING:

Raines' 49 steals were up from the past two seasons when he had 41 and 33. But it's still a far cry from the 70-or-more steals he had in six straight seasons. He's still outstanding at running the bases, however.

FIELDING:

Raines can cover a lot of ground in left field, and, though he sometimes looks shaky on line drives, is actually a good outfielder. His arm, however, is weak.

OVERALL:

Though still an outstanding player, Raines has lost the superstar status he once enjoyed. "He used to be compared to Tony Gwynn," said manager Buck Rodgers. "If you did that now, people would laugh." However, he remains the Expos' most marketable commodity and may find himself elsewhere when the season begins. A change in scenery may help him regain the desire he appears to have lost.

PITCHING:

Scott Ruskin has a more immediate challenge than finding ways of getting major league hitters out: Ruskin is still learning how to pitch. Less than two years away from being a minor league outfielder, Ruskin has displayed enormous potential at the major league level. Acquired from the Pirates Aug. 8 along with Moises Alou and Willie Greene for left-handed pitcher Zane Smith, Ruskin will certainly be the first of the trio to make his presence felt. His final numbers with the Expos were impressive, as he posted a 1-0 record with a 2.28 earned run average over 27.2 innings. For the year, Ruskin was 3-2 with a 2.75 ERA and two saves over 75.1 innings. He was eighth in the league in appearances, pitching in 67 games.

Ruskin possesses an outstanding curve and a decent fastball, but like many curveball pitchers out of the bullpen, he walked too many hitters (38). With the Expos, Ruskin also had trouble against left-handed hitters, giving up 15 hits in 44 at-bats (.341 average), but the Expos are confident that Ruskin will improve once he learns how to pitch. Ruskin was much more effective against righthanders, limiting them to a minuscule .170 batting average with Montreal.

Ruskin pitched and played outfield during a four-year career with the University of Florida. When he hit .355 with Rookie League Bradenton in 1986, he decided to concentrate on being an everyday player. Ruskin hit .294 with 12 homers and 53 RBI in 104 games at Class-A in 1987 but decided to switch back to pitching during the 1988 season. "The decision was easy," Ruskin said. "When you hit .233 in Double-A that tells you to try some other way to make a living."

HOLDING RUNNERS, FIELDING, HITTING:

Ruskin obviously still has a lot to learn about pitching, including how to hold runners and field his position. But he is an all-around athlete and should be able to pick up those things quickly. His experience as an outfielder should make him a better-than-average hitter for a pitcher.

OVERALL:

The Expos plan to have Ruskin work on another pitch, probably another type of fastball with more movement, in the off season. The fact he already owns a major league curve and has the durability to pitch three or four times a week has team officials thinking about him eventually becoming a closer. But he'll get at least another year of experience as a middle reliever before that happens.

SCOTT RUSKIN

Position: RP
Bats: R **Throws:** L
Ht: 6' 2" **Wt:** 185

Opening Day Age: 27
Born: 6/8/63 in Jacksonville, FL
ML Seasons: 1

Overall Statistics

	W	L	ERA	G	GS	Sv	IP	H	R	BB	SO	HR
1990	3	2	2.75	67	0	2	75.1	75	28	38	57	4
Career	3	2	2.75	67	0	2	75.1	75	28	38	57	4

How Often He Throws Strikes

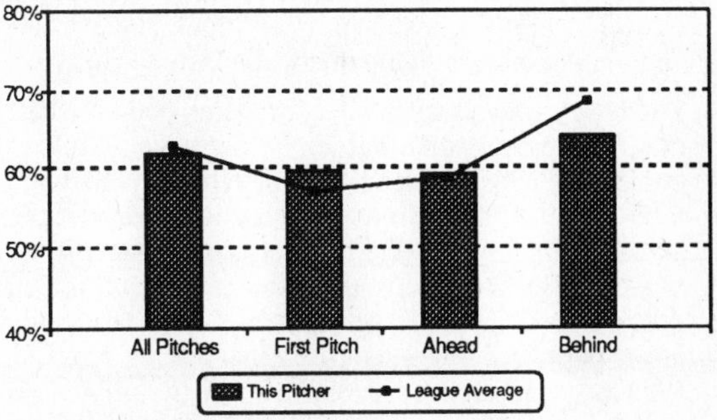

1990 Situational Stats

	W	L	ERA	Sv	IP		AB	H	HR	RBI	AVG
Home	2	0	1.31	2	41.1	LHB	114	32	3	13	.281
Road	1	2	4.50	0	34.0	RHB	175	43	1	14	.246
Day	1	1	2.14	1	21.0	Sc Pos	83	16	1	21	.193
Night	2	1	2.98	1	54.1	Clutch	141	43	3	16	.305

1990 Rankings (National League)

- 3rd in holds (15)
- 5th in blown saves (6)
- 8th in games pitched (67)
- Led the Expos in holds

PITCHING:

Bill Sampen may have been the prototypical Expos pitcher of 1990, the most unrecognizable of names on a no-name pitching staff that led the National League in earned run average. Prior to the 1990 season, Sampen was a household name only in the Sampen household. But the Expos plucked him out of the lower ranks of the Pirates organization at the December 1989 draft, converted him from a starter to a reliever -- and watched him become the team's top winner.

The 27-year-old Sampen had never won more than 11 games in five years at rookie, Class A and Class AA ranks, yet he finished last season with a 12-7 record for the Expos. At AA Harrisburg in 1989, Sampen led the Eastern League with 26 starts and was second in strikeouts with 134 in 165 innings. He was 11-9 with an earned run average of 3.21. Someone in scouting director Gary Hughes' department noticed his work, and the Expos reaped the dividends last season.

The surprise in Sampen's record stems from the fact that he does not stand out in any one area. A power pitcher -- the fastball is his best pitch by far -- Sampen falls considerably short with his change-up and slider and needs work on his control. Despite the fact that he racked up so many wins, the Expos feel that Sampen doesn't have the stuff yet to be a clutch performer either out of the bullpen or from the starting rotation. Pitching coach Larry Bearnarth spent the off season with Sampen in the Instructional League to work on improving Sampen's breaking ball.

HOLDING RUNNERS, FIELDING, HITTING:

Another of Bearnarth's priorities in the Instructional League was to help Sampen improve his weak move to first base. Sampen is a pretty good fielder, though he, like many of the Expos' young pitchers, is still learning to cope with the speed of the game at the major league level. As a middle reliever, Sampen gets few opportunities at the plate.

OVERALL:

Despite the fact that Sampen led the team in wins as a reliever, the Expos feel Sampen has the mental makeup of a starting pitcher. A decision on how to use him will depend on developments over the winter and at spring training. A little short on equipment to be either a closer or a top member of the starting rotation, Sampen nevertheless looms large in the Expos' plans.

BILL SAMPEN

Position: RP/SP
Bats: R **Throws:** R
Ht: 6' 1" **Wt:** 185

Opening Day Age: 28
Born: 1/18/63 in Lincoln, IL
ML Seasons: 1

Overall Statistics

	W	L	ERA	G	GS	Sv	IP	H	R	BB	SO	HR
1990	12	7	2.99	59	4	2	90.1	94	34	33	69	7
Career	12	7	2.99	59	4	2	90.1	94	34	33	69	7

How Often He Throws Strikes

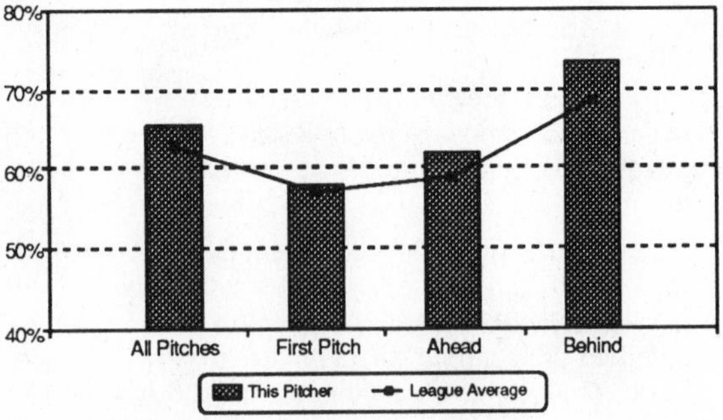

1990 Situational Stats

	W	L	ERA	Sv	IP		AB	H	HR	RBI	AVG
Home	7	4	2.96	0	45.2	LHB	177	45	1	19	.254
Road	5	3	3.02	2	44.2	RHB	174	49	6	20	.282
Day	3	1	3.74	0	21.2	Sc Pos	104	27	1	31	.260
Night	9	6	2.75	2	68.2	Clutch	148	36	3	17	.243

1990 Rankings (National League)

- 9th highest winning percentage (.632)
- Led the Expos in wins (12), games pitched (59), wild pitches (4) and winning percentage

NELSON SANTOVENIA

Position: C
Bats: R **Throws:** R
Ht: 6' 3" **Wt:** 220

Opening Day Age: 29
Born: 7/27/61 in Pina del Rio, Cuba
ML Seasons: 4

Overall Statistics

	G	AB	R	H	D	T	HR	RBI	SB	BB	SO	AVG
1990	59	163	13	31	3	1	6	28	0	8	31	.190
Career	250	777	69	180	37	4	19	100	4	56	145	.232

Where He Hits the Ball

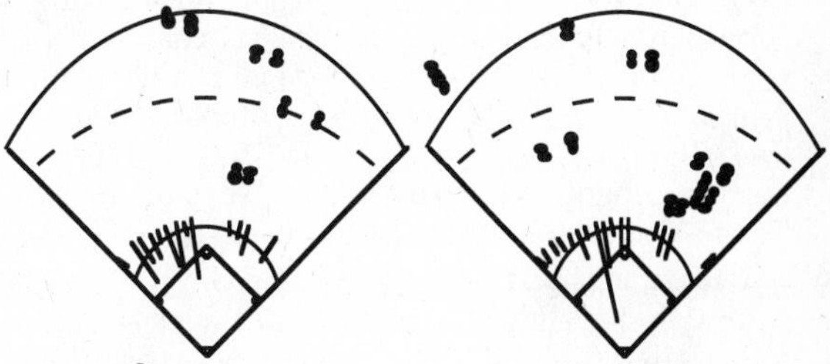

Vs. LHP **Vs. RHP**

1990 Situational Stats

	AB	H	HR	RBI	AVG		AB	H	HR	RBI	AVG
Home	81	21	4	20	.259	LHP	67	11	1	7	.164
Road	82	10	2	8	.122	RHP	96	20	5	21	.208
Day	39	10	2	8	.256	Sc Pos	50	13	3	25	.260
Night	124	21	4	20	.169	Clutch	33	10	0	6	.303

1990 Rankings (National League)

→ Did not rank near the top or bottom in any category

HITTING:

The 1990 season was a nightmare for Nelson Santovenia, who now must rebuild what had been the beginning of a promising career. After a fine 1989 season,Santovenia entered the year as the Expos' number-one catcher and was rated the third-best at his position in a poll of National League managers. In '89 he raised his batting average to .250 and cut his strikeouts in half. But the Cuban-born right-handed hitter fell flat on his face as soon as the season began and was demoted to AAA Indianapolis on May 14.

Things didn't get any better for Santovenia when he was recalled two weeks later. He showed no signs of snapping out of his batting funk and then was forced to undergo knee surgery on July 21. He didn't return until September 1. For the season, the big catcher batted .190 with six home runs and 28 runs batted in. Though the number of RBIs in his 163 at-bats seems impressive, most of them came in bunches -- he had six in a June 8 game against the Cardinals. The majority of the time his bat fired blanks.

Santovenia is a line-drive hitter with extra-base power -- 10 of his 31 hits were for extra bases last season, 20 of 76 in 1989. He's mostly a pull hitter and is extremely undisciplined at the plate. He can hit fastballs and breaking balls but can be set up to chase pitches far out of the strike zone. Santovenia, who had entered the season with a career batting average of .279 with runners on base and .213 with the bases empty, was still a good clutch hitter last year despite his poor season, hitting .260 with runners in scoring position.

BASERUNNING:

Santovenia is agonizingly slow. He was caught all three times he attempted to steal last season, and is four-for-11 lifetime. Obviously, he's strictly a station-to-station runner.

FIELDING:

Santovenia has a strong, accurate arm, and under the tutelage of manager Buck Rodgers, a former catcher, is improving at calling games. He still needs to work on blocking pitches in the dirt and blocking the plate with his 6-foot-3, 220-pound frame.

OVERALL:

Santovenia can be a solid starting catcher if he can regain his 1989 form. However, he will spend the spring in a battle for the backup catching job behind Mike Fitzgerald. The fact that both are right-handed may be an advantage to the left-hand hitting Jerry Goff. Because of his string of injuries, Santovenia will have to prove he is not jinxed.

PITCHING:

Dave Schmidt is certainly a competitor. Last year, he proved to be one of those proverbial pitchers who "pitched their arms off" for the cause. The 33-year-old veteran gave everything he had to the team during a critical stage of the Expos' season -- and may very well have jeopardized his future.

When right-handed reliever Tim Burke -- the team's closer -- went down with a broken bone in his leg May 30 in Atlanta, Schmidt, whom the Expos took a gamble on in the off season, stepped into the breach. Schmidt saved 12 games and earned two of his three wins during the five weeks that Burke was out. He was the Expos' player of the month in June, when he kept the Expos within range of the division leaders.

But Schmidt also blew out his arm during that stretch. Eligible to become a free agent after the 1990 season, Schmidt was forced to undergo major shoulder surgery in August and may have lost his chance at a lucrative contract. "When everyone else in the bullpen broke down with broken legs, tiredness, whatever, Schmidt came to the forefront," pitching coach Larry Bearnarth said. "He actually kept us in the league. The duty proved to be a little too much."

Definitely a finesse pitcher, Schmidt has a slider, curveball, sinking fastball and a palm ball. The palm ball is often his out pitch. Schmidt has excellent control, a necessity since he allows a lot of hits (58 in 48 innings last year, 946 in 894.2 innings over his career). Schmidt's stamina, which has often been called into question, proved to be his undoing last year. Despite having worked as a starter occasionally in his career, Schmidt's career high in innings pitched is 156.2 in 1989.

HOLDING RUNNERS, FIELDING, HITTING:

A good athlete, Schmidt gets the job done around the pitching mound. Though he has a high leg kick, he is fairly good at keeping runners close to the bag. Schmidt is not asked to do anything with the bat except hold it.

OVERALL:

The Expos would be glad to have the right-handed veteran back at the right price. They feel Schmidt has tremendous value not only as a set-up man, occasional closer and spot starter, but also simply because he knows how to pitch. Schmidt has also proven to be a leader by action rather than words.

DAVE SCHMIDT

Position: RP
Bats: R **Throws:** R
Ht: 6' 1" **Wt:** 194

Opening Day Age: 33
Born: 4/22/57 in Niles, MI
ML Seasons: 10

Overall Statistics

	W	L	ERA	G	GS	Sv	IP	H	R	BB	SO	HR
1990	3	3	4.31	34	0	13	48.0	58	26	13	22	3
Career	54	54	3.79	369	63	50	894.2	946	422	232	475	82

How Often He Throws Strikes

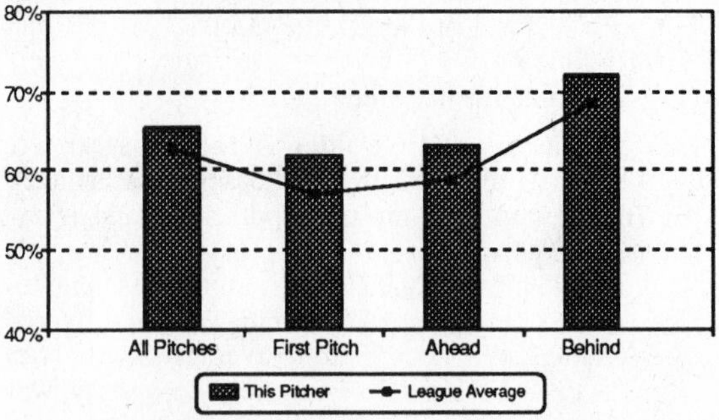

1990 Situational Stats

	W	L	ERA	Sv	IP		AB	H	HR	RBI	AVG
Home	0	0	3.52	7	23.0	LHB	110	34	2	14	.309
Road	3	3	5.04	6	25.0	RHB	83	24	1	9	.289
Day	1	1	5.63	2	8.0	Sc Pos	60	19	1	21	.317
Night	2	2	4.05	11	40.0	Clutch	140	44	2	18	.314

1990 Rankings (National League)

- 10th in most GDPs induced per GDP situation (16.1%)

HITTING:

Though it may be hard to consider a .241 hitter as untouchable, Larry Walker falls into that category with the Expos. Walker fits two glaring needs for the Expos -- a left-handed hitter with power and, as a Canadian, much-needed help for the marketing department.

Hidden in the long shadow cast by fellow rookie Delino DeShields, Walker had a fine inaugural season himself. The 24-year-old outfielder, who missed the entire 1988 season with a knee injury, tied an Expos rookie record for homers with 19, a mark set by Andre Dawson in 1977. And Walker did it in only 419 at-bats. Forty of Walker's 101 hits went for extra bases as he also stroked 18 doubles and three triples for a more-than-respectable .434 slugging percentage.

But Walker is still a raw talent. Perhaps because of inexperience, he was a streak hitter in the extreme. The aggressive Walker struck out far too much last season (112 times, more than once every four at-bats), usually chasing high fastballs or low and away curves. The flip side is that Walker drew 49 walks, a high number for a young power hitter. Walker, a pull hitter who likes to swing at the first pitch, can pull the trigger on pitchers' mistakes -- fastballs out over the plate and high breaking balls. Though he batted only .207 against lefthanders, Walker showed signs of being able to hit southpaws for power, cranking six homers and six doubles in 116 at-bats. He was ineffective in clutch situations (.194 with runners in scoring position) but hitting coach Hal McRae writes that off to inexperience.

BASERUNNING:

The serious knee injury didn't rob Walker of any of his speed. He stole 21 bases in 28 attempts, and he's a smart, alert baserunner.

FIELDING:

Still learning at the plate, Walker has completed his defensive schooling. Manager Buck Rodgers claims Walker is already the best defensive right fielder in the National League and deserved to win the Gold Glove. Walker covers a lot of ground in the outfield, gets a good jump on balls and has one of the best throwing arms around.

OVERALL:

The Expos will give Walker, who has the rare combination of power and speed, all the time he needs to work out the kinks in his game. His emergence as a bona-fide home-grown star could go a long way toward lifting the Expos' image in their domestic battle with the Blue Jays for Canadian supremacy.

LARRY WALKER

Position: RF
Bats: L **Throws:** R
Ht: 6' 2" **Wt:** 185

Opening Day Age: 24
Born: 12/1/66 in Maple Ridge, BC
ML Seasons: 2

Overall Statistics

	G	AB	R	H	D	T	HR	RBI	SB	BB	SO	AVG
1990	133	419	59	101	18	3	19	51	21	49	112	.241
Career	153	466	63	109	18	3	19	55	22	54	125	.234

Where He Hits the Ball

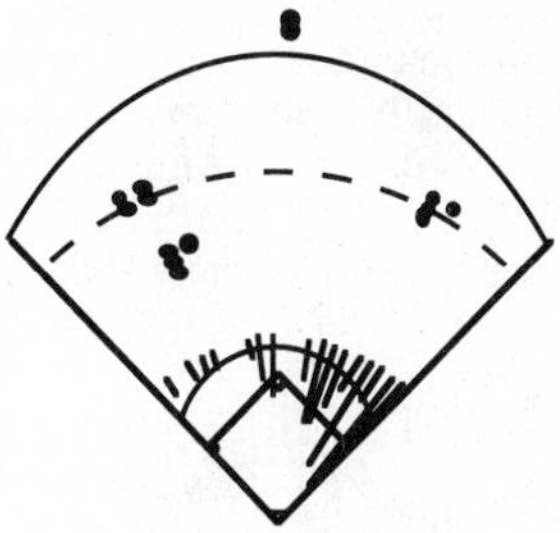

Vs. LHP

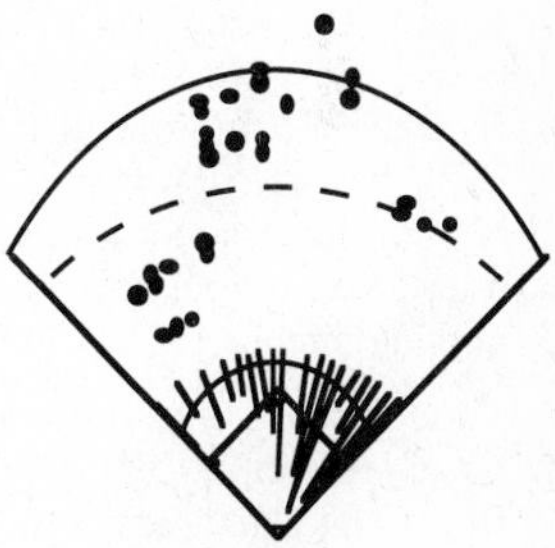

Vs. RHP

1990 Situational Stats

	AB	H	HR	RBI	AVG		AB	H	HR	RBI	AVG
Home	196	50	9	27	.255	LHP	116	24	6	18	.207
Road	223	51	10	24	.229	RHP	303	77	13	33	.254
Day	116	25	6	17	.216	Sc Pos	108	21	4	32	.194
Night	303	76	13	34	.251	Clutch	87	21	2	7	.241

1990 Rankings (National League)

- 1st lowest batting average on an 0-2 count (.000)
- 3rd lowest batting average with runners in scoring position (.194) and lowest batting average vs. left-handed pitchers (.207)
- 4th in lowest percentage of swings put into play (36.6%)
- 5th lowest batting average on the road (.229) and highest percentage of swings that missed (28.7%)
- Led the Expos in hit by pitch (5) and highest percentage of extra bases taken as a runner (58.7%)

TIM WALLACH

Position: 3B
Bats: R **Throws:** R
Ht: 6' 3" **Wt:** 200

Opening Day Age: 33
Born: 9/14/57 in Huntington Park, CA
ML Seasons: 11

Overall Statistics

	G	AB	R	H	D	T	HR	RBI	SB	BB	SO	AVG
1990	161	626	69	185	37	5	21	98	6	42	80	.296
Career	1466	5415	624	1444	309	29	182	773	46	414	819	.267

Where He Hits the Ball

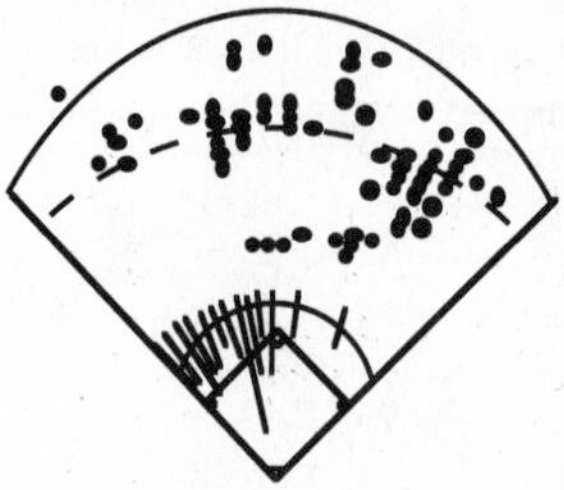

Vs. LHP

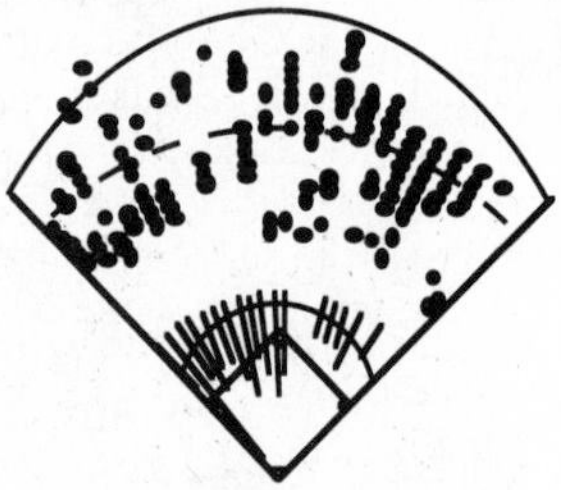

Vs. RHP

1990 Situational Stats

	AB	H	HR	RBI	AVG		AB	H	HR	RBI	AVG
Home	301	83	9	46	.276	LHP	204	59	6	29	.289
Road	325	102	12	52	.314	RHP	422	126	15	69	.299
Day	179	60	8	33	.335	Sc Pos	175	49	8	76	.280
Night	447	125	13	65	.280	Clutch	129	37	3	16	.287

1990 Rankings (National League)

- 2nd in at-bats (626) and games (161)
- 4th in hits (185) and doubles (37)
- 5th in total bases (295)
- Led the Expos in batting average (.296), home runs (21), at- bats, runs (69), hits, singles (122), doubles, total bases, RBIs (98), times on base (230), pitches seen (2,443), plate appearances (678), games and slugging percentage (.471)
- Led NL third basemen in batting average, at-bats, hits, singles, triples (5), times on base, pitches seen, plate appearances, games, most pitches seen per plate appearance (3.60) and batting average on the road (.314)

HITTING:

If there was any doubt that Tim Wallach belongs alongside Graig Nettles, Ron Cey, Buddy Bell and other recent third basemen one notch below Mike Schmidt, the 11-year veteran laid them to rest in 1990. Wallach was named Expos' player of the year for the third time in four years. He led the team in batting average (.296), hits (185), home runs (21), runs batted in (98), doubles (37) and slugging percentage (.471) and tied for the team lead in runs scored (69) with Delino DeShields. After two mediocre seasons, Wallach rejoined the league's offensive elite for the first time since 1987, when he drove in 123 runs. He was first in the National League in multi-hit games (58), eighth in RBIs, fourth in hits, fifth in total bases (295), fourth in doubles and sixth in extra-base hits (63).

The best gap hitter in the league, Wallach leads all National Leaguers with 300 doubles over the past nine years. An aggressive hitter to a fault, he likes to go after his favorite fastballs and hanging breaking balls on the first pitch. This tends to see him fall behind in the count a little too often. Wallach can be over-anxious when he's in a slump and will chase low, outside pitches.

Though he is a right-handed hitter, Wallach shows little preference for which side the pitcher throws from. His career average is .274 against lefthanders (one homer every 28 at-bats) and .264 against righthanders (one homer every 29 at-bats). Wallach, however, has been hurt playing in cavernous Olympic Stadium. He has hit 111 of his 182 career home runs on the road (12 on the road, nine at home last season).

BASERUNNING:

Wallach is a conservative baserunner, mostly because he is slow, but the veteran knows the game and isn't too big a hazard on the bases. Though he stole six times last year, he was caught nine times.

FIELDING:

A three-time Gold Glove winner, Wallach is still arguably the best fielding third baseman in the NL. He is excellent at charging bunts and slow hoppers and at diving to his left or right. He makes tough chances on foul pop-ups down the line look easy with over-the-shoulder catches.

OVERALL:

Wallach is easily the Expos' most valuable player. He is solid offensively, stellar defensively and a leader by example. Wallach, who played 161 games last season, is also extremely durable -- he has played less than 153 games only once over the past nine years (134 games in 1986).

MIKE ALDRETE

Position: LF/1B
Bats: L **Throws:** L
Ht: 5'11" **Wt:** 185

Opening Day Age: 30
Born: 1/29/61 in Carmel, CA
ML Seasons: 5

Overall Statistics

	G	AB	R	H	D	T	HR	RBI	SB	BB	SO	AVG
1990	96	161	22	39	7	1	1	18	1	37	31	.242
Career	521	1259	155	343	66	7	16	156	15	188	210	.272

HITTING, FIELDING, BASERUNNING:

Mike Aldrete appears to be getting comfortable with his role as an Expo. After hitting .325 and .267 with the San Francisco Giants in 1987 and 1988, Aldrete thought he deserved something more than backup duty with the Expos. The obviously unhappy outfielder hit only .221 in 1989. But Aldrete bounced back somewhat with a .242 average last season and continued to produce as a pinch hitter.

Aldrete, who had a career .302 mark as a pinch hitter entering last season, was nine-for-36 with one homer off the bench, good for six runs batted in. The left-handed batter is used almost exclusively against righthanders, against whom he hit .257 in 152 at-bats. A statistical oddity saw Aldrete go hitless in nine at-bats against lefties yet manage to score three runs as a result of his three walks against the southpaws. Aldrete is a singles, spray hitter who tends to be too patient and sometimes finds himself behind in the count quickly. He is basically a fastball hitter who is rarely overmatched, though he is vulnerable to hard stuff inside.

The Expos value Aldrete defensively because of his versatility. Last season, he started 35 games -- 11 at first base, 20 in left field and seven in right. He has also seen some duty in center field. The five-year veteran gets a good jump on the ball in the outfield and has a decent arm.

OVERALL:

With the Expos' emphasis on youth and speed, Aldrete is not going to win a starting job. But his defensive versatility along with an ability to hit off the bench can make him a valuable asset.

BRIAN BARNES

Position: SP
Bats: L **Throws:** L
Ht: 5' 9" **Wt:** 170

Opening Day Age: 24
Born: 3/25/67 in Roanoke Rapids, NC
ML Seasons: 1

Overall Statistics

	W	L	ERA	G	GS	Sv	IP	H	R	BB	SO	HR
1990	1	1	2.89	4	4	0	28.0	25	10	7	23	2
Career	1	1	2.89	4	4	0	28.0	25	10	7	23	2

PITCHING, FIELDING, HITTING & HOLDING RUNNERS:

The impressive strikeout totals painted the picture of an imposing pitcher with a blazing fastball. But Brian Barnes is just the opposite. A smallish 5-foot-9, 170-pounder, Barnes throws a devastating change-up and a much-better than average curveball. In fact, while the lefthander was on his way to becoming the top strikeout pitcher in all of professional baseball in 1990, the Expos didn't once consider moving him from AA Jacksonville, reasoning that his fastball wasn't good enough to keep major league hitters off-balance.

Only after Barnes struck out 213 batters in 201 innings and the AA season was over did the Expos call up Barnes. The Expos' fears proved to be unfounded as Barnes posted a 1-1 record and struck out 23 batters in 28 innings in four late-season starts. He limited opposing batters to a .234 batting average and showed good control, walking only seven in his 28 innings. A winter project was planned by the Expos to get Barnes some more movement on his fastball. He was also tutored on keeping runners close during the Instructional League. If his nine major league at-bats are an accurate reflection, then Barnes is in trouble at the plate -- he went hitless in the nine trips, striking out seven times.

OVERALL:

Though he's had less than two full seasons of minor league experience, Barnes has made a strong impression on the Expos. Odds are that Barnes' excellent offspeed pitch will earn him a spot in the Expos' starting rotation, especially if he improves his fastball.

JERRY GOFF

Position: C
Bats: L **Throws:** R
Ht: 6' 3" **Wt:** 205

Opening Day Age: 27
Born: 4/12/64 in San Rafael, CA
ML Seasons: 1

Overall Statistics

	G	AB	R	H	D	T	HR	RBI	SB	BB	SO	AVG
1990	52	119	14	27	1	0	3	7	0	21	36	.227
Career	52	119	14	27	1	0	3	7	0	21	36	.227

HITTING, FIELDING, BASERUNNING:

Jerry Goff's .227 batting average last year didn't make many people sit up and take notice, but he did impress the one person who counts -- Expos manager Buck Rodgers. Goff is a catcher, a position in which Rodgers has considerable expertise. He is also a left-handed hitter with potential for power hitting, a commodity the Expos have been trying to obtain for years.

Goff made a good first impression on Rodgers during spring training. "Goff has as much raw power as anyone on this club," Rodgers said shortly after the unhappy Mariner was secured in exchange for minor-league pitcher Pat Pacillo. Nevertheless, Goff started the season at AAA Indianapolis. He had two stints with the Expos, during which he hit three homers in 119 at-bats. Two of the homers were monstrous clouts.

Goff is a pull hitter who rarely swings at the first pitch and has trouble with offspeed stuff. He showed a good eye at the plate, drawing 21 walks. With typical catcher's speed, Goff is no threat on the bases. Goff showed a strong arm behind the plate but allowed far too many passed balls (12). Then again, Goff is still learning the position. A star third baseman at the University of California, Goff was converted to catching in the minor leagues.

OVERALL:

Goff enters spring training as the third-string catcher, but he could move up soon enough. He could work himself into a platoon behind the plate if his defensive work improves.

DREW HALL

Position: RP
Bats: L **Throws:** L
Ht: 6' 4" **Wt:** 220

Opening Day Age: 28
Born: 3/27/63 in Louisville, KY
ML Seasons: 5

Overall Statistics

	W	L	ERA	G	GS	Sv	IP	H	R	BB	SO	HR
1990	4	7	5.09	42	0	3	58.1	52	35	29	40	6
Career	9	12	5.21	125	4	5	195.1	184	122	95	148	20

PITCHING, FIELDING, HITTING & HOLDING RUNNERS:

Last season was a lost campaign for Drew Hall, who spent part of the year on the disabled list and who pitched ineffectively when off it. The Expos gambled on the big lefthander, trading infielder Jeff Huson to the Texas Rangers for Hall one day before the start of the season.

The Expos felt that the 6-foot-4 Hall, who had posted a 3.70 ERA and had limited left-handed batters to a .159 batting average in 1989, would help right-handed reliever Tim Burke in the bullpen. But that never worked out. Hall has lost some of the pop on his fastball and is trying to convert from being a power pitcher to a finesse pitcher. And because his slider is not up to par, he seems to have lost his advantage against lefthanders, who hit .270 against him last year.

Hall, who's repertoire consists of a fastball, slider and split-fingered fastball, has poor control, making him a bad risk to bring in to the game to retire one key batter. Indecisiveness, which could stem from a lack of confidence, makes him an extremely slow worker with men on base. He spends a lot of time looking runners back to the bag, making numerous throws to first.

OVERALL

A pleasant man who is willing to work and is coachable, Hall appears to lack the drive to be a consistent major leaguer. He'll get another shot -- maybe his last at age 28 -- to win a left-handed role in the bullpen, but the odds are against him.

DALE MOHORCIC

Position: RP
Bats: R **Throws:** R
Ht: 6' 3" **Wt:** 220

Opening Day Age: 35
Born: 1/25/56 in Cleveland, OH
ML Seasons: 5

Overall Statistics

	W	L	ERA	G	GS	Sv	IP	H	R	BB	SO	HR
1990	1	2	3.23	34	0	2	53.0	56	21	18	29	6
Career	16	21	3.49	254	0	33	363.2	378	163	99	174	37

PITCHING, FIELDING, HITTING & HOLDING RUNNERS:

Despite a decent season in 1990, a future in the major league looks bleak for Dale Mohorcic. But that won't stop the 35-year-old righthander from trying. Mohorcic, who spent nine years in the minors before finally cracking the big leagues, is used to adversity. He is a finesse pitcher who relies mostly on a sinking fastball, a pitch he doesn't throw very hard. His repertoire also includes a slider and a forkball.

Mohorcic is a game competitor who can be counted on to deliver his best in tough situations. Despite the fact that opponents hit .286 off him and hit six home runs in only 53 innings, Mohorcic somehow posted an earned run average of 3.23. Lefthanders found it a treat to hit off the veteran, as they pounded him for a .320 batting average, with five homers in 97 at-bats. Mohorcic has good stamina and needs a lot of work to keep his sinker sharp and low. He works hard at holding runners close, frequently throwing to first, though he is average at best in protecting against a stolen base. He fields his position cleanly if not gracefully.

OVERALL:

Mohorcic spent much of his career in the minors so he isn't in awe of the need to scramble to keep a job in the majors. Though he is a marginal major league pitcher, he can be of use as a 10th or 11th pitcher on a staff, particularly in a mop-up role where he can rack up innings while keeping the rest of the bullpen rested.

CHRIS NABHOLZ

Position: SP
Bats: L **Throws:** L
Ht: 6' 5" **Wt:** 210

Opening Day Age: 24
Born: 1/5/67 in Harrisburg, PA
ML Seasons: 1

Overall Statistics

	W	L	ERA	G	GS	Sv	IP	H	R	BB	SO	HR
1990	6	2	2.83	11	11	0	70.0	43	23	32	53	6
Career	6	2	2.83	11	11	0	70.0	43	23	32	53	6

PITCHING, FIELDING, HITTING & HOLDING RUNNERS:

When the Expos traded left-handed pitcher Zane Smith to the Pirates Aug. 8 for Scott Ruskin, Moises Alou and Willie Greene, they were dealing the present for the future. The future arrived much quicker than anticipated in the form of Chris Nabholz, who was called up from AAA Indianapolis to take Smith's place in the rotation.

Though he had been outstanding at AA Jacksonville earlier in the season (7-2 3.03), Nabholz had struggled at Indianapolis, where he was 0-6 with a 4.83 ERA. But the big lefthander found his groove with the Expos, reeling off six straight wins before finishing with a 6-2 record and a superb 2.83 ERA. Nabholz, a 6-foot-5, 210-pounder, reported with a good sinking fastball and an excellent curve. He is learning a change-up and used it well against good hitting clubs like the Pirates and Mets. He showed remarkable composure in clutch situations.

Like most young pitchers adjusting to the majors, the 23-year-old was short on stamina and was prone to wild streaks (32 walks in 70 innings). Though he can be better, Nabholz improved on his fielding and at holding runners to the point where his work is acceptable. He is an atrocious hitter, going hitless in 21 at-bats.

OVERALL:

Simply put, Nabholz was dominating in his two-month tryout. He limited opposing batters to a meager .176 batting average and was absolute murder on lefties, who could only manage a weak .116 against him (righthanders fared marginally better, hitting .188). The trade of Smith means the Expos won't have to spend the spring assessing Nabholz -- he is assured a spot in the starting rotation.

JUNIOR NOBOA

Position: 2B
Bats: R **Throws:** R
Ht: 5' 9" **Wt:** 160

Opening Day Age: 26
Born: 11/10/64 in Azua, Dominican Republic
ML Seasons: 5

Overall Statistics

	G	AB	R	H	D	T	HR	RBI	SB	BB	SO	AVG
1990	81	158	15	42	7	2	0	14	4	7	14	.266
Career	185	309	32	75	9	3	0	22	6	11	26	.243

HITTING, FIELDING, BASERUNNING:

Junior Noboa can do in a pinch. The Expos found many ways to use the little Dominican last season and he didn't let them down. In fact, Noboa was the team's leading pinch hitter with a 11-for-37 contribution (.297 batting average). Though he had only five runs batted in as a pinch hitter, Noboa starts rallies and sets the table for the run producers. Overall, the 26-year-old Noboa, who made his major league debut with Cleveland as a 19-year-old in 1984, hit .266 in 158 at-bats.

An aggressive singles hitter with excellent bat control, Noboa led Class AAA in batting in 1989 with a .340 mark. A good bunter, he's primarily a spray hitter who tries to hit the ball on the ground. He is a good fastball hitter but has trouble with any pitch on the outside corner or off the plate. Though Noboa is a good baserunner and stole four bases in five attempts, he doesn't have the speed to be a consistent threat on the bases.

Noboa was used as a utility fielder at numerous positions last year, playing 31 games at second base, eight at third, seven at shortstop and nine in the outfield. He even pitched once, shutting out the Astros over two-thirds of an inning. His natural position is second base, where he was the 1989 league leader in Triple-A with a .986 fielding percentage.

OVERALL:

Though he won't crack the Expos' starting lineup, Noboa has the potential to be a solid bench player who can give infielders and outfielders an occasional rest.

DARYL BOSTON

Position: CF
Bats: L **Throws:** L
Ht: 6' 3" **Wt:** 203

Opening Day Age: 28
Born: 1/4/63 in Cincinnati, OH
ML Seasons: 7

Overall Statistics

	G	AB	R	H	D	T	HR	RBI	SB	BB	SO	AVG
1990	120	367	65	100	21	2	12	45	19	28	50	.272
Career	615	1717	244	423	84	15	50	168	70	137	290	.246

Where He Hits the Ball

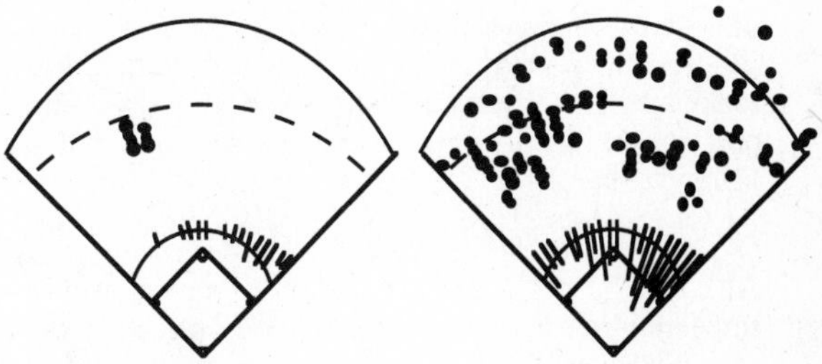

Vs. LHP   Vs. RHP

1990 Situational Stats

	AB	H	HR	RBI	AVG		AB	H	HR	RBI	AVG
Home	186	50	4	17	.269	LHP	60	15	0	8	.250
Road	181	50	8	28	.276	RHP	307	85	12	37	.277
Day	118	31	2	16	.263	Sc Pos	98	27	4	33	.276
Night	249	69	10	29	.277	Clutch	61	17	1	7	.279

1990 Rankings (National League)

- 1st in percentage of extra bases taken as a runner (66.7%)
- 9th worst batting average on an 0-2 count (.083)
- Led the Mets in percentage of extra bases taken as a runner
- Led NL center fielders in percentage of extra bases taken as a runner

HITTING:

The Mets knew that Daryl Boston wasn't washed up at age 27 when the White Sox let him go. He was an all-state high school athlete, a first round pick (the seventh player taken in 1981), and he had risen quickly through the minors. In 1984, he stole 40 bases while hitting .312 with 15 homers and 82 RBI in Class AAA. While waiting for a full-time role in the White Sox lineup, he hit 15 HR in just 281 at-bats in 1988. But Boston was never able to win a regular position in Chicago, and, being loaded with outfielders, the White Sox released him early in the 1990 season. The Mets, who needed outfield help, took a chance, and they're glad they did.

Boston hadn't hit for high average since the minors, but he held his own in the National League (.273) and produced double-digit homers and steals. Last year, the Mets generally kept him away from lefty pitchers, but he did all right with those he faced.

Boston is a big swinger by nature, but he has been visibly influenced by Walt Hriniak. He now uses all fields. He can turn on the inside pitch and pull it over the right field fence, or he can line a single to left. The most common approach by pitchers is to work him up and in with fastballs, and low and away with breaking pitches. Boston is a good student of opposing pitchers, knowing what to look for.

BASERUNNING:

Boston uses his speed to good advantage, legging out base hits and taking bases when the opportunity exists. His 72% success rate on steal attempts reflects a good jump and great raw speed. Boston runs hard and slides hard.

FIELDING:

Boston's speed is a great asset in the roomy Shea Stadium outfield. His range is above average, and though he had only three assists last year, he has a strong and accurate arm. With more time in the National League, Boston will get a better jump on balls hit near him, and he will have more opportunities to show his throwing ability.

OVERALL:

The Mets had a number of holes in their lineup last year, and Boston filled one of them very nicely. He compares favorably with any platoon outfielder with his overall combination of speed, power, and defense. He was also a positive influence in the clubhouse. At age 28, he could be ready for his biggest year yet.

HITTING:

Mark Carreon helped clinch a spot on the Mets 1990 roster by hitting four pinch hit home runs in 1989, and by finishing the year with a 14-for-29 streak that raised his average from .260 to .308. Despite that mark, Carreon is really more like a .260 hitter, which is about where he finished in 1990. His strength is hitting for power and hitting in the clutch. Whatever the numbers may say, there is an overwhelming perception in New York that the Mets need better clutch hitting. Carreon offered that promise, and delivered with a .286 average with runners in scoring position in 1990.

Carreon had produced 10 to 14 homers three times in the minor leagues, but no one expected him to clout 10 dingers in just 188 at-bats last year. If his season hadn't been cut short, he could easily have hit 15 or more. Carreon is a hard swinger who strikes out almost twice as often as he walks. He has made progress at taking pitches and waiting for pitchers to make mistakes. He understands game situations well, and can shorten his swing to make contact when that is appropriate.

BASERUNNING:

Although he stole 30-plus bases in the minor leagues three times, Carreon is not a serious threat in the major leagues. He is overmatched by major league pickoff moves and catchers' throwing arms. Last year he stole just one base in one attempt. Carreon can turn on a little extra speed in crucial situations, however.

FIELDING:

Carreon is on the roster for his bat, not for his glove. He has poor range, and last year he made just one assist in 385 innings in the outfield. Carreon is capable of spectacular misplays on easy fly balls, and will rarely be found playing the field late in a close game. His one defensive asset is that he can play all three outfield positions with equal levels of adventure.

OVERALL:

Just when he had established himself as the Mets utility outfielder and number-one pinch hitter, Carreon tore a ligament in his right knee on August 21, and was out for the season. Practically speaking, he will have to reestablish himself to some extent in 1991, depending on how much talent the Mets succeed in retaining or acquiring. Carreon's main contribution is power hitting, not speed or defense. Unless the Mets' needs change dramatically, Carreon will have the opportunity to pick up his career where it left off.

MARK CARREON

Position: CF/LF/RF
Bats: R **Throws:** L
Ht: 6' 0" **Wt:** 194

Opening Day Age: 27
Born: 7/19/63 in Chicago, IL
ML Seasons: 4

Overall Statistics

	G	AB	R	H	D	T	HR	RBI	SB	BB	SO	AVG
1990	82	188	30	47	12	0	10	26	1	15	29	.250
Career	166	342	55	96	20	0	17	44	3	30	48	.281

Where He Hits the Ball

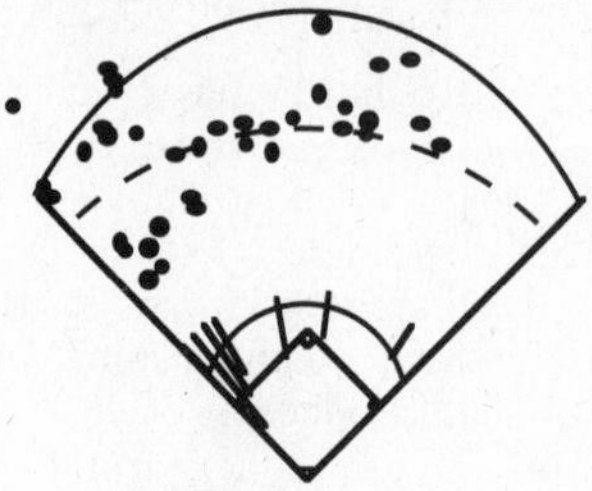

Vs. LHP

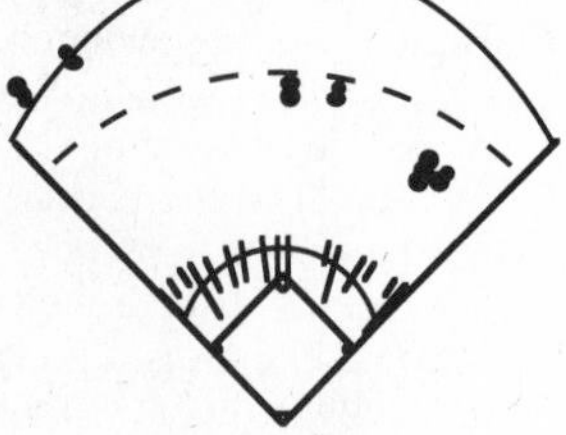

Vs. RHP

1990 Situational Stats

	AB	H	HR	RBI	AVG		AB	H	HR	RBI	AVG
Home	87	20	1	7	.230	LHP	116	30	7	17	.259
Road	101	27	9	19	.267	RHP	72	17	3	9	.236
Day	73	17	4	10	.233	Sc Pos	49	14	2	16	.286
Night	115	30	6	16	.261	Clutch	42	9	1	3	.214

1990 Rankings (National League)

- 6th in batting average on a 3-2 count (.389)
- Led the Mets in slugging percentage vs. left-handed pitchers (.517) and batting average with a 3-2 count
- Led NL center fielders in batting average with a 3-2 count

CY YOUNG STUFF

PITCHING:

Last year David Cone had ERAs of 6.65 in April and 5.59 in May. Then on June 9 he held Pittsburgh to six hits, and in his next outing he shut out the Cardinals. Cone had begun another one of his streaks. His ERA was 2.63 in June, 2.70 in July, and 2.27 in August. By year-end, his ERA had dropped to 3.23.

Pitching coach Mel Stottlemyre says that Cone was hurt by the short spring training of 1990 because he didn't work much during the winter. In 1989, however, Cone had the same type of surge in July and August. The Mets don't like the word "streaky" to describe Cone's game, but they allude to a tendency to "hold his game at a high level" once he gets himself going.

Cone believes his key is working with his defense. He has to pitch to spots, letting hitters put the ball in play where the fielders can generate outs. When he tries to be overpowering, he gets into trouble. You wouldn't expect such a broad view from the major league strikeout leader, but Cone has an excellent understanding of the interrelationship between pitches and defensive positioning.

Cone's repertoire is frequently mentioned by opposing hitters and managers as one of the toughest in the league. He has a sharp fastball with good movement, a biting slider, a major league curveball, and a devious change-up. Cone likes to use a sidearm delivery against righties.

HOLDING RUNNERS, FIELDING, HITTING:

Baserunners have an easy time against Cone. They stole 23 bases in 32 attempts last year, and had 27 steals the year before. Cone is easily rattled when he starts thinking about runners, and has been most successful when he concentrates on getting the hitters out. He is, however, a decent fielder, and he has become one of the NL's best hitting pitchers, as well as a good bunter.

OVERALL:

"Being able to command himself" is the requisite quality for Cone's success, according to one coach. He is superstitious, tempestuous, and always in danger of faltering if he loses his focus. If he can start the season with his concentration intact and his confidence level high, he is a Cy Young candidate. Every year, it is just a question of how long it takes for him to find his groove and stay in it.

DAVID CONE

Position: SP
Bats: L **Throws:** R
Ht: 6' 1" **Wt:** 185

Opening Day Age: 28
Born: 1/2/63 in Kansas City, MO
ML Seasons: 5

Overall Statistics

	W	L	ERA	G	GS	Sv	IP	H	R	BB	SO	HR
1990	14	10	3.23	31	30	0	211.2	177	84	65	233	21
Career	53	27	3.14	132	104	1	784.2	654	303	276	725	64

How Often He Throws Strikes

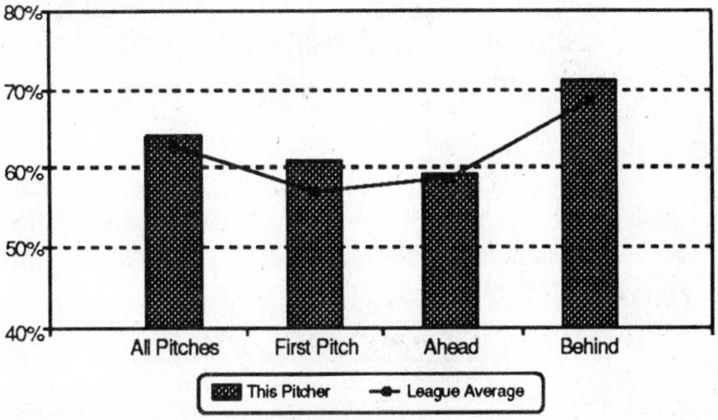

1990 Situational Stats

	W	L	ERA	Sv	IP		AB	H	HR	RBI	AVG
Home	7	6	3.85	0	107.2	LHB	473	101	14	36	.214
Road	7	4	2.60	0	104.0	RHB	311	76	7	33	.244
Day	3	3	3.25	0	61.0	Sc Pos	186	34	5	44	.183
Night	11	7	3.23	0	150.2	Clutch	75	15	2	8	.200

1990 Rankings (National League)

- 1st in strikeouts (233), strikeout/walk ratio (3.6) and strikeouts per 9 innings (9.9)
- 2nd in most pitches thrown per batter (4.00) and lowest batting average allowed with runners in scoring position (.183)
- 4th in least GDPs induced per 9 innings (.38)
- 5th in most home runs allowed (21) and ERA on the road (2.60)
- Led the Mets in home runs allowed, strikeouts, balks (4), pickoff throws (208), strikeout/walk ratio, strikeouts per 9 innings, ERA on the road, lowest batting average allowed vs. left-handed pitchers and lowest batting average allowed with runners in scoring position

RON DARLING

Position: SP/RP
Bats: R **Throws:** R
Ht: 6' 3" **Wt:** 195

Opening Day Age: 30
Born: 8/19/60 in Honolulu, HI
ML Seasons: 8

PITCHING:

Ron Darling lost his spot in the rotation to a raw rookie in the heat of a pennant race last year. He was understandably unhappy. Darling never got on track in 1990. He lost two of three games in April, had an 8.35 ERA in May, and although he pitched well in June and July, his full-year numbers never looked good.

Darling remains basically a fastball, power pitcher, despite the fact that his fastball has neither the velocity nor the movement that it had three or four years ago. Even in his troubled campaign of 1990, he averaged over seven strikeouts per nine innings. In recent years, he has made increasing use of a forkball to keep hitters off balance, adding to his curve, change-up and slider. Controlling the accessory pitches is the key to success for Darling.

Darling is a thinking man's pitcher. A Yale alumnus and a student of Zen, he is keenly aware of the mental components in pitching. Darling is especially comfortable pitching at Shea Stadium. He has always had favorable home differentials, but in 1990 they were really pronounced. Ron had a 5.23 ERA on the road, 3.52 in New York. His inability to pitch well on the road has been detrimental to the Mets' efforts to trade him for a power hitter.

HOLDING RUNNERS, FIELDING, HITTING:

Darling is reputed to have the best pickoff move on the Mets staff, and he caught five runners last year. Because of his good move, scouts have long overrated Darling's ability to shut down the running game. He gave up 26 steals in 1989 and 24 in 28 attempts last year, not good numbers. He is adequate in the field, however, and above average when it comes to making offensive contributions. He can hit for power, bunt, and run the bases well.

OVERALL:

Darling would like to forget 1990. For six years, he was a stalwart member of the Mets staff, always pitching 200-plus innings and never having a losing record. He was only the second Mets pitcher to win ten or more games in six consecutive seasons. Last year he pitched only 126 innings, lost more than he won, and failed to get 100 strikeouts for the first time in his career. At year end, he was facing the possibility of elbow surgery. If he returns to the ranks of effective starters in 1991, it will be an accomplishment. Darling was a dominant pitcher as recently as 1988, however, and there should be a number of teams willing to give him a chance if the Mets don't.

Overall Statistics

	W	L	ERA	G	GS	Sv	IP	H	R	BB	SO	HR
1990	7	9	4.50	33	18	0	126.0	135	73	44	99	20
Career	94	64	3.48	240	224	0	1517.2	1377	666	586	1090	146

How Often He Throws Strikes

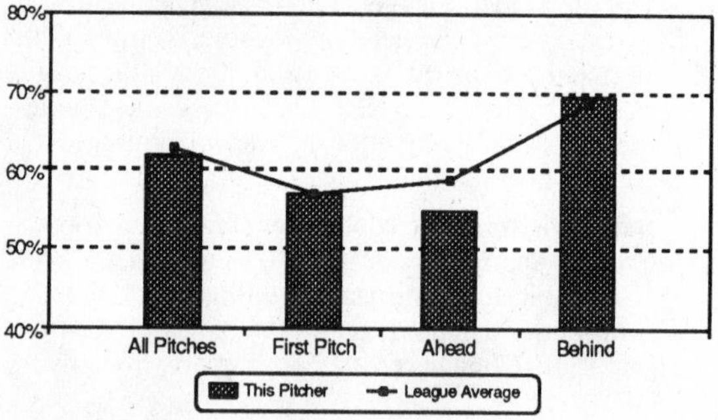

1990 Situational Stats

	W	L	ERA	Sv	IP		AB	H	HR	RBI	AVG
Home	4	2	3.52	0	53.2	LHB	288	75	9	40	.260
Road	3	7	5.23	0	72.1	RHB	207	60	11	27	.290
Day	3	2	3.89	0	34.2	Sc Pos	125	28	3	43	.224
Night	4	7	4.73	0	91.1	Clutch	41	9	1	5	.220

1990 Rankings (National League)

- 8th in most stolen bases allowed (24)
- 10th in most home runs allowed (20) and hit batsmen (5)

KEVIN ELSTER

Position: SS
Bats: R **Throws:** R
Ht: 6' 2" **Wt:** 195

Opening Day Age: 26
Born: 8/3/64 in San Pedro, CA
ML Seasons: 5

HITTING:

Kevin Elster is a hard swinger with good power. When his season was cut short on August 4, Elster was second only to Shawon Dunston for most homers among NL shortstops. Unfortunately, Elster doesn't offer the contact hitting and on-base ability that a team normally gets from their shortstop. Elster improved his strikeout/walk ratio a little last year, but his batting average dropped from .231 to .207.

In three years as a major leaguer, Elster has had remarkably consistent offensive stats. If he was older, that would be good news. However, most players show dramatic improvement in their mid-20s, and Elster hasn't really advanced. He has developed in specific areas like turning on inside fastballs and pulling them to left field, but in general, the pitchers have been figuring out Elster faster than he's been figuring them out. Outside breaking balls give him as much trouble as they ever have.

Elster has a history of good second-half numbers. Since his 1990 season was cut short, it's not possible to tell what he would have done in August and September. It's also not possible to know the impact of his shoulder tendinitis on his hitting; it certainly didn't help.

BASERUNNING:

Elster is not one of the faster shortstops in the National League. He stole only two bases last year, and has a career high of only 13, way back in A-ball. The best aspect of Kevin's running game is that he is realistic about his limits, and doesn't waste any outs on optimistic dashes.

FIELDING:

Elster holds the National League record for consecutive errorless games by a shortstop. Three things contributed to that record: one, Elster has a nice, soft glove and an accurate throwing arm; two, his range is unspectacular; and three, he plays behind a pitching staff that generates a lot of fly balls and strikeouts. Elster is certainly a solid defensive shortstop, but he is not a great one.

OVERALL:

Elster could have trouble winning back his job in 1991 if the Mets decide to start Howard Johnson at shortstop. Previous experiments along these lines have failed because Johnson just couldn't make the grade as a middle infielder. But Johnson looked very good at short in late 1990, and he is miles ahead of Elster offensively. Spring training 1991 will be interesting for Elster, and possibly unpleasant.

Overall Statistics

	G	AB	R	H	D	T	HR	RBI	SB	BB	SO	AVG
1990	92	314	36	65	20	1	9	45	2	30	54	.207
Career	416	1218	133	267	59	4	28	138	8	102	187	.219

Where He Hits the Ball

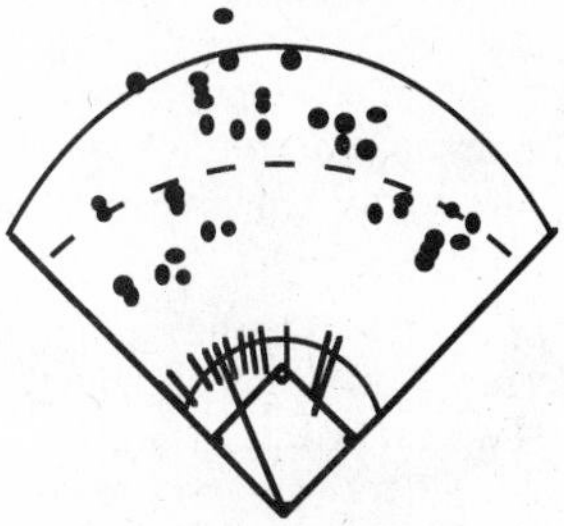

Vs. LHP

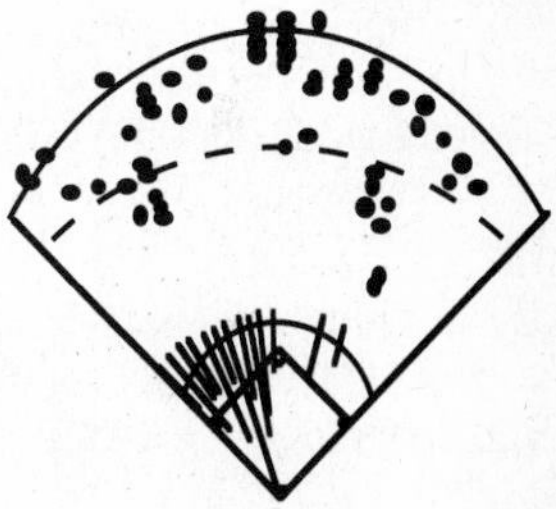

Vs. RHP

1990 Situational Stats

	AB	H	HR	RBI	AVG		AB	H	HR	RBI	AVG
Home	163	32	2	24	.196	LHP	119	27	2	8	.227
Road	151	33	7	21	.219	RHP	195	38	7	37	.195
Day	102	14	2	15	.137	Sc Pos	78	20	2	36	.256
Night	212	51	7	30	.241	Clutch	48	6	1	7	.125

1990 Rankings (National League)

- 2nd lowest batting average in the clutch (.125)
- 5th lowest percentage of extra bases taken as a runner (29.1%)
- 9th lowest on-base percentage vs. left-handed pitchers (.282)

PITCHING:

Sid Fernandez has been among the premier pitchers in the National League for several years; certainly he has been the toughest to hit. Fernandez held opposing batters to a .200 average in 1990, and a .198 mark in 1989. Fernandez has an occasional wild day, but most of his walks come on carefully-thrown pitches that just barely miss the strike zone. His poor record in 1990 (9-14) was due, more than anything, to lack of support from his teammates. The Mets scored only 14 runs for Fernandez in his 14 losses last year.

Fernandez uses his fastball extensively, generating fly balls and strikeouts. He is sneaky-fast, and mixes in a change-up and curve expertly. The change-up is his equalizer against righties. At his best, he throws the change for strikes on the outside corner, keeps his fastball away, and drops the curve in for strikes. At such times, he is unhittable. Against lefties, Fernandez likes to set up the hitter with inside hard stuff, especially throwing sidearm, and then switch to outside fastballs and curves. The best approach for hitters is to stay back, look for the outside fastball, and try to adjust to the outside curve or inside heater.

Most hitters are so frozen by his curve that they don't swing at it. A few guess hitters in 1990 started looking for telegraphed curveballs. Two theories circulated: one that Fernandez exaggerates the rocking motion of his windup when he intends to throw a curve; the other was that his arm motion is higher (three-quarters to overhand) when the curve is coming. Adherents of both theories had uneven results at best.

HOLDING RUNNERS, FIELDING, HITTING:

Fernandez worked really hard at holding runners during 1990, practicing a slide-step motion to quicken his delivery. Nonetheless, runners got away with 20 of 26 steal attempts. He is an adequate (but not outstanding) fielder. At the plate, he is genuinely dangerous.

OVERALL:

Fernandez is a premier pitcher who has never gotten premier recognition. He gets much more respect from opposing teams than he does from New York fans and media. He has even been maligned at times by his own management, especially during Davey Johnson's tenure. One big season would change all these perceptions, and Fernandez has been on the verge of that big season for a long time.

SID FERNANDEZ

Position: SP
Bats: L **Throws:** L
Ht: 6' 1" **Wt:** 230

Opening Day Age: 28
Born: 10/12/62 in Honolulu, HI
ML Seasons: 8

Overall Statistics

	W	L	ERA	G	GS	Sv	IP	H	R	BB	SO	HR
1990	9	14	3.46	30	30	0	179.1	130	79	67	181	18
Career	78	59	3.26	199	193	1	1212.1	894	478	491	1153	105

How Often He Throws Strikes

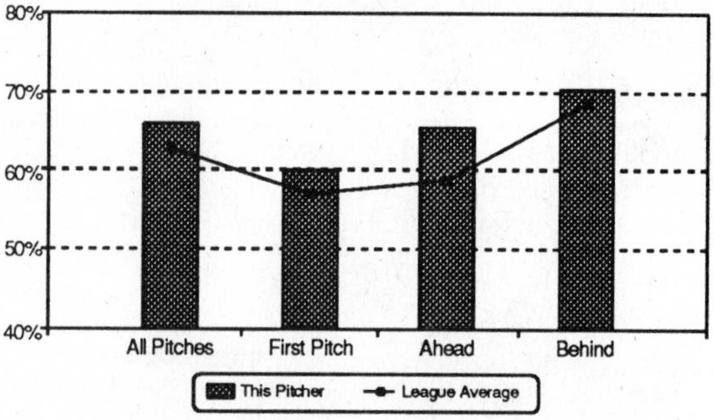

1990 Situational Stats

	W	L	ERA	Sv	IP		AB	H	HR	RBI	AVG
Home	8	5	2.41	0	104.2	LHB	126	28	3	22	.222
Road	1	9	4.94	0	74.2	RHB	524	102	15	46	.195
Day	2	6	4.41	0	67.1	Sc Pos	127	28	4	45	.220
Night	7	8	2.89	0	112.0	Clutch	22	7	0	2	.318

1990 Rankings (National League)

- 1st in lowest batting average allowed (.200), lowest groundball/flyball ratio (.58), least GDPs induced per 9 innings (.20) and lowest batting average allowed vs. right-handed batters (.195)
- 2nd most strikeouts per 9 innings (9.1)
- 3rd most pitches thrown per batter (3.92)
- 4th lowest on-base average allowed (.278) and lowest ERA at home (2.41)
- Led the Mets in losses (14), lowest batting average allowed, lowest on-base average allowed, least baserunners per 9 innings (10.1), ERA at home and lowest batting average allowed vs. right-handed batters

STOPPER

PITCHING:

When the Mets traded for John Franco, they said he would eliminate the need for a righty set-up reliever. They acquired Alejandro Pena anyway, but Franco proved he didn't need much help last year. Though he had some rough moments late in the race, Franco led the National League in both saves with 33 and save percentage (85%). Over the last five seasons, he has averaged 33 saves per year, and that's exactly what he got in 1990.

Although he is tougher on lefties, Franco is indeed effective against righties. He is renowned for a wicked screwball that moves like a righthander's slider. Franco gave *The Scouting Report* an exclusive insight about this pitch: "No, it's not a screwball. Everybody thinks it's a screwball, but it's just a change-up that fades away." Whatever you call it, Franco has a nice weapon to go with his fastball and slider. He also began throwing a cut fastball in 1990, but hasn't used it extensively.

Franco's greatest asset is the wide variety of speeds, locations and motions that he can use. He almost always knows exactly where the ball is going, where it will cross the plate, and where it will be hit (if it's hit). Franco's main goal is to get the ball into play, on the ground, near a fielder. He can reach back for a strikeout, but his most dramatic saves are built around ground ball double plays.

HOLDING RUNNERS, FIELDING, HITTING:

Runners don't steal very many bases on Franco. He gave up six steals in 1990. In the field, Franco helps his double play strategy by covering his position extremely well; he made just one error last year. Like most ace relievers, Franco is rarely concerned with swinging a bat or running the bases, but he can hold his own at both when called upon.

OVERALL:

Franco had some questions to answer after his weak performance in the second half of 1989. Had he lost his control? Was his "screwball" suddenly flattening out? Had he lost the killer instinct and the will to win? The answer to all these questions was a resounding no. Franco remains one of the few National League pitchers who can be assured of getting almost all of his team's saves in 1991. He is a genuine ace reliever, and will be for the foreseeable future.

JOHN FRANCO

Position: RP
Bats: L **Throws:** L
Ht: 5'10" **Wt:** 185

Opening Day Age: 30
Born: 9/17/60 in Brooklyn, NY
ML Seasons: 7

Overall Statistics

	W	L	ERA	G	GS	Sv	IP	H	R	BB	SO	HR
1990	5	3	2.53	55	0	33	67.2	66	22	21	56	4
Career	47	33	2.49	448	0	181	595.2	526	196	231	423	31

How Often He Throws Strikes

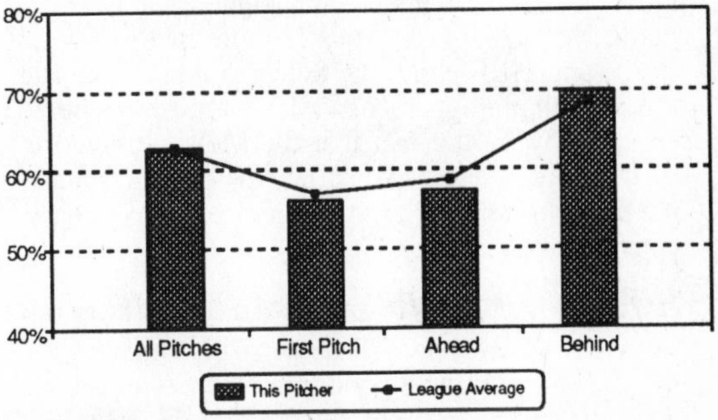

1990 Situational Stats

	W	L	ERA	Sv	IP		AB	H	HR	RBI	AVG
Home	4	2	2.82	17	38.1	LHB	57	13	0	9	.228
Road	1	1	2.15	16	29.1	RHB	205	53	4	19	.259
Day	3	1	2.67	11	27.0	Sc Pos	92	20	0	23	.217
Night	2	2	2.43	22	40.2	Clutch	202	50	4	22	.248

1990 Rankings (National League)

- 1st in saves (33), save opportunities (39) and save percentage (84.6%)
- 4th in games finished (48)
- 5th in blown saves (6)
- 1st in games pitched (55), saves, games finished, save opportunities, save percentage, blown saves and first batter efficiency (.216)

PITCHING:

If Dwight Gooden has control of his curveball when he takes the mound, OR if his fastball is crackling and moving, he will hold the opposition to one or two runs. If both pitches are working, he simply cannot be scored upon. Even when he has trouble getting the curve in for strikes, and his fastball is below par (say "only" 89 MPH), Gooden is still a tough, competitive pitcher who can beat any team.

Most opposing hitters cite control as the one factor that makes Gooden successful. When he can hit spots with either of his two big pitches, he will be very tough. In 1990 he was also throwing a change-up and a cut fastball to keep hitters off balance.

Although he won 19 games in 1990, Gooden was not at his best. His 3.83 ERA was, by far, his worst ever. The .258 batting average that he allowed opposing hitters was more than 40 points higher than his career mark. He gave up four runs or more in 13 of his 34 starts, and in 10 games he failed to make it through the seventh inning. Gooden's 19-7 record was helped enormously by the fact that the Mets averaged 6.8 runs per nine innings when he was on the mound -- the best run support for any major league starter, by a considerable margin.

HOLDING RUNNERS, FIELDING, HITTING:

Gooden has always had difficulty with a high leg kick that lets runners get a good jump. Opposing runners amassed 60 stolen bases against him last year, with only 16 caught trying. Gooden has worked on this problem at times during his career, but let up some last year. Gooden believes that some opposing runners have been successful stealing signs from Mets' catchers, a problem that he can fix with a little effort. Fielding is a particular strength for Gooden. He led Mets pitchers in assists (35) in 1990, and was just one behind David Cone for most putouts. He takes his hitting very seriously and enjoys swinging the bat, even if he isn't the Mets best hitting pitcher.

OVERALL:

In many ways, 1990 was a growth year for Gooden. Many times it was obvious that he didn't have good command of either his fastball or his curveball, but he was able to battle and keep his team in the game. All great pitchers have had to go through periods of adjustment. The victories that carried Gooden through the adversity of 1990 may provide the foundation for his future development.

DWIGHT GOODEN

Position: SP
Bats: R **Throws:** R
Ht: 6' 3" **Wt:** 210

Opening Day Age: 26
Born: 11/16/64 in Tampa, FL
ML Seasons: 7

Overall Statistics

	W	L	ERA	G	GS	Sv	IP	H	R	BB	SO	HR
1990	19	7	3.83	34	34	0	232.2	229	106	70	223	10
Career	119	46	2.82	211	209	1	1523.2	1282	529	449	1391	75

How Often He Throws Strikes

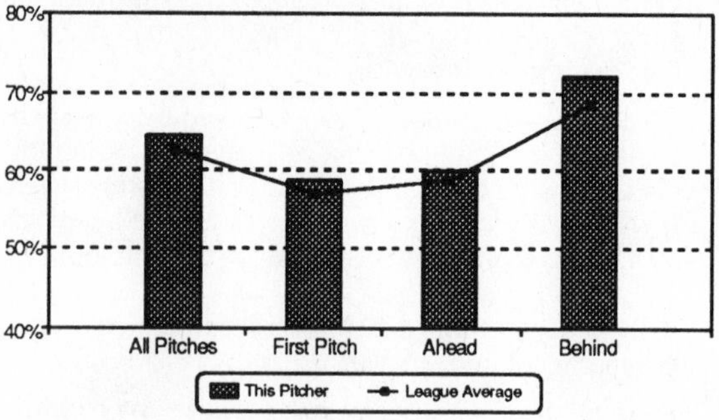

1990 Situational Stats

	W	L	ERA	Sv	IP		AB	H	HR	RBI	AVG
Home	9	3	3.56	0	126.1	LHB	520	135	6	58	.260
Road	10	4	4.15	0	106.1	RHB	367	94	4	36	.256
Day	5	5	4.40	0	86.0	Sc Pos	254	61	3	81	.240
Night	14	2	3.50	0	146.2	Clutch	73	16	1	7	.219

1990 Rankings (National League)

- 1st in stolen bases allowed (60), runners caught stealing (16), run support per 9 innings (6.8) and least HRs allowed per 9 innings (.39)
- 2nd in strikeouts (223) and pitches thrown (3,690)
- 3rd in batters faced (983) and strikeouts per 9 innings (8.6)
- Led the Mets in hits allowed, walks allowed (70), hit batsmen (7), pitches thrown, stolen bases allowed, runners caught stealing, winning percentage (.731), groundball/flyball ratio (1.88), run support per 9 innings and least HRs allowed per 9 innings

TOMMY HERR

Position: 2B
Bats: B **Throws:** R
Ht: 6' 0" **Wt:** 185

Opening Day Age: 35
Born: 4/4/56 in Lancaster, PA
ML Seasons: 12

HITTING:

Tommy Herr had his career year in 1985, hitting .302 with 110 RBI. Herr had a unique experience in 1985, batting third behind Vince Coleman and MVP Willie McGee, and he'll probably never come close to 100 RBI again. The Mets are more concerned with Herr's batting average -- in the five seasons since 1985, he's batted higher than .263 only once.

Herr is an intelligent, slap-type hitter with a good eye and quick hands. He knows the pitchers well, and concentrates on every pitch. He has a remarkable ability to foul off pitches that aren't to his liking, and to hit to a specific location when he sees a pitch that he does like. His doubles and triples include many carefully placed shots over the heads of first and third basemen. At age 35, however, Herr is finding that his hands are not always as quick as his eyes.

Considering that Herr spent most of 1990 batting second for Philadelphia behind Len Dykstra, his .261 batting average was a disappointment. He frequently saw gaping holes between the first and second basemen, but couldn't hit the ball into this area often enough. While his extra-base hit total was about the same as in 1989, he looked less sure about where the ball was going. The loss of bat speed has had a visible impact on his hitting game.

BASERUNNING:

Herr has only fair speed, but he is excellent at reading situations and knowing when he should steal or take an extra base. He picks his spots, and last year he maintained an 88% success rate (7-for-8). He will probably never again steal 20 bases, but pitchers need to be concerned with him.

FIELDING:

Even when he was much younger, Herr depended on positioning and knowledge of situations to be a superior fielder. At this stage of his career, he is a crafty veteran. His range was never great and is now diminished, but he can make up a full two steps by being in the right place at the right time.

OVERALL:

Herr should be an asset for the Mets in 1991. He is a veteran middle infielder who can help the less experienced players. He is a switch-hitter who offers the promise of potent offense against lefty pitchers, the Mets' nemesis. And finally (despite some backbiting in Philadelphia) Herr offers the promise of both field and clubhouse leadership. At the end of 1990, he was the only Met who had been to the World Series three times.

Overall Statistics

	G	AB	R	H	D	T	HR	RBI	SB	BB	SO	AVG
1990	146	547	48	143	26	3	5	60	7	50	58	.261
Career	1412	5134	653	1405	246	40	27	553	179	582	556	.274

Where He Hits the Ball

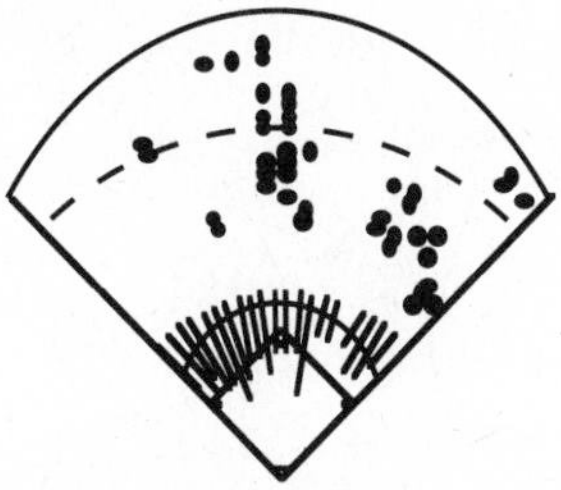

Vs. LHP

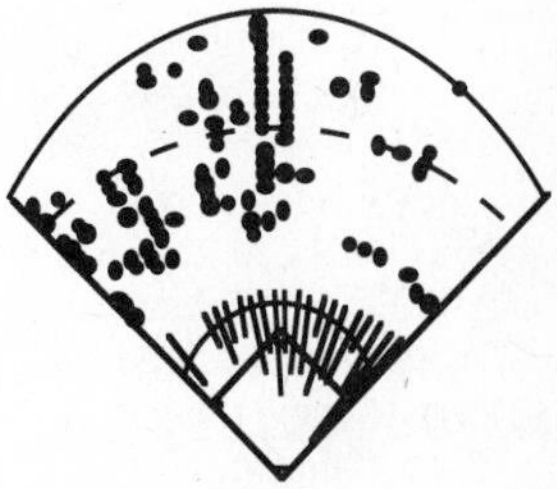

Vs. RHP

1990 Situational Stats

	AB	H	HR	RBI	AVG		AB	H	HR	RBI	AVG
Home	265	72	4	38	.272	LHP	208	55	1	20	.264
Road	282	71	1	22	.252	RHP	339	88	4	40	.260
Day	139	34	1	12	.245	Sc Pos	153	36	1	48	.235
Night	408	109	4	48	.267	Clutch	90	19	1	9	.211

1990 Rankings (National League)

- 3rd lowest percentage of runs scored per time reached base (24.6%)
- 6th lowest percentage of swings that missed (8.9%)
- 8th lowest slugging percentage (.347)
- 9th highest groundball/flyball ratio (1.79)
- Led NL second basemen in lowest percentage of swings that missed (8.9%)

GREGG JEFFERIES

Position: 2B/3B
Bats: B **Throws:** R
Ht: 5'10" **Wt:** 175

Opening Day Age: 23
Born: 8/1/67 in Burlingame, CA
ML Seasons: 4

HITTING:

Gregg Jefferies got his first two seasons reversed. He had his sophomore slump in 1989, then had his Rookie of the Year type season in 1990. Jefferies started hitting .280 in June 1989, and hasn't stopped since. He is one of the great young hitting talents in the game today. Still developing at age 23, Jefferies hits for average and power. He has a picture-perfect, compact swing from both sides of the plate. He has the potential to lead the league in batting average.

There is no safe way to pitch to Jefferies. He has an outstanding knowledge of the strike zone and is an expert at hitting any pitch where it's thrown. Don't give him anything he can pull, especially when he is batting lefty. Any fastball or breaking ball inside could quickly fly over the right field fence. Jefferies turns on the ball smoothly and generates more power than many larger, stronger hitters.

As a switch-hitter in a lineup that has trouble against lefties, Jefferies is counted upon to deliver punch from the right side of the plate. He was equally successful against righties and lefties in 1989, but like most Mets, he couldn't do much against southpaws in 1990. Gregg likes hitting at Shea Stadium, even though it's a pitcher's ballpark. He enjoys the visual consistency and familiarity, especially with sunlight during day games; he doesn't particularly like the West Coast stadiums. If Jefferies has a general weakness, it is a tendency to let slumps get the best of him and last longer than necessary.

BASERUNNING:

Jefferies has good speed and excellent knowledge of situations. He reads pitchers well, knows the league's catchers, picks his spots carefully, and gets a good jump, all reflected in his 85% success rate on steal attempts last year, and 78% in 1989.

FIELDING:

Considering that he has been shuffled from shortstop to third base, over to second, and back to third again, Jefferies has remained remarkably solid in the field. He was just becoming proficient at turning the double play at second base when moved. He has good range at third, fair range at second, and a good throwing arm from either position.

OVERALL:

Jefferies is the only untouchable among Mets' position players going into 1991. The world has not yet seen Gregg Jefferies on a long hot streak; if he can stay hot for as long as he stays cold in slumps, baseball fans nationwide are going to be hearing plenty about this rising young star.

Overall Statistics

	G	AB	R	H	D	T	HR	RBI	SB	BB	SO	AVG
1990	153	604	96	171	40	3	15	68	11	46	40	.283
Career	329	1227	187	340	77	7	33	143	37	93	96	.277

Where He Hits the Ball

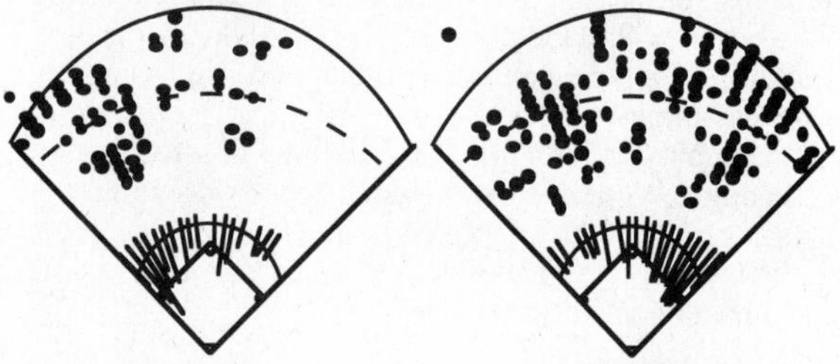

1990 Situational Stats

	AB	H	HR	RBI	AVG		AB	H	HR	RBI	AVG
Home	311	99	9	41	.318	LHP	222	59	5	23	.266
Road	293	72	6	27	.246	RHP	382	112	10	45	.293
Day	208	66	3	25	.317	Sc Pos	144	39	0	45	.271
Night	396	105	12	43	.265	Clutch	98	28	0	11	.286

1990 Rankings (National League)

- 1st in doubles (40)
- 5th in batting average with an 0-2 count (.308)
- 6th highest percentage of swings put into play (55.3%)
- 7th in batting average with 2 strikes (.269)
- Led the Mets in at-bats (604), runs (96), hits (171), singles (113), doubles, hit by pitch (5), GDPs (13), runs scored per time reached base (43.2%), batting average on an 0-2 count and batting average at home (.318)
- Led NL second basemen in doubles, batting average on an 0-2 count, batting average with 2 strikes and highest percentage of swings put into play

HITTING:

Howard Johnson's move to shortstop highlighted his offensive value. His stats can now be compared to Shawon Dunston and Dickie Thon, rather than Tim Wallach and Chris Sabo, and Johnson looks even better than he did before. Johnson is one of the great multidimensional players in the game today. Even hitting .244, as he did in 1990, the range of his skills give him considerable offensive value.

Johnson is a switch-hitter who likes to pull the ball from either side of the plate. He made dramatic improvement as a hitter when he started looking for curveballs, and began to use his quick wrists to adjust to fastballs. The curve used to be his nemesis; now it is his friend. He must be approached like any power hitter: keep the ball away from him, even if it means giving up a walk.

The Mets had a great deal of trouble beating lefty starters last year. They looked to Johnson, a switch-hitter, to provide punch against southpaws. Johnson came to work early many days and worked on hitting lefties, but in real games, he hit just .208 against them. Otherwise, however, Johnson is one of the better clutch hitters on the Mets, as evidenced by last year's .297 average with men in scoring position.

BASERUNNING:

Johnson is always a threat to steal, and is usually successful. Last year he nabbed 34 bases with an 81% success rate. He is a little too aware of his stats, however. Although he didn't hurt the team badly in 1990, he often ran when it wasn't appropriate.

FIELDING:

When the Mets put HoJo at shortstop to fill in for Kevin Elster, they were holding their breath as Johnson had been shaky enough at third base. He performed surprisingly well at short, however. He has always had poor range, but is developing sure hands as he gets older. His arm is fine, if he just doesn't stop to think about throwing. Johnson credits Bud Harrelson for working with him extensively at shortstop, before Harrelson became manager. Progress was most visible in his improved turning of the double play.

OVERALL:

The two main criticisms of Johnson before 1990 were that he was an unreliable fielder, and that he made inappropriate comments which indicated that he put his personal goals ahead of the team. Both problems seemed to just disappear last year. It may be that Howard Johnson simply grew up.

HOWARD JOHNSON

Position: 3B/SS
Bats: B **Throws:** R
Ht: 5'10" **Wt:** 195

Opening Day Age: 30
Born: 11/29/60 in Clearwater, FL
ML Seasons: 9

Overall Statistics

	G	AB	R	H	D-	T	HR	RBI	SB	BB	SO	AVG
1990	154	590	89	144	37	3	23	90	34	69	100	.244
Career	1023	3395	516	868	172	13	159	512	161	443	692	.256

Where He Hits the Ball

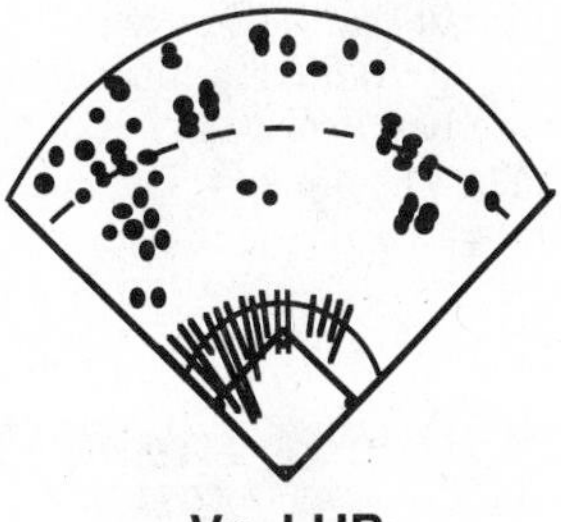

Vs. LHP

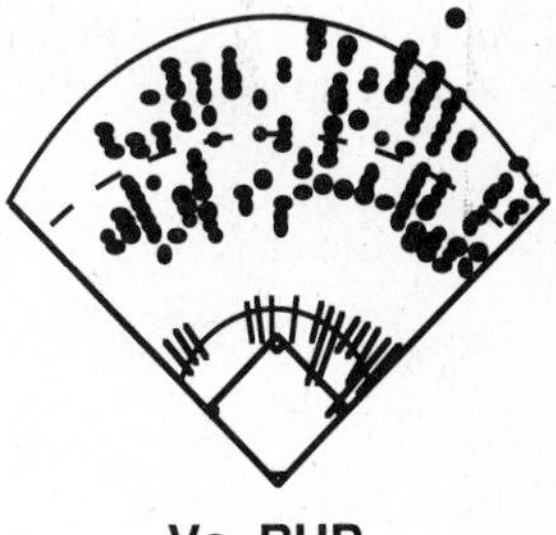

Vs. RHP

1990 Situational Stats

	AB	H	HR	RBI	AVG		AB	H	HR	RBI	AVG
Home	291	68	13	45	.234	LHP	221	46	6	23	.208
Road	299	76	10	45	.254	RHP	369	98	17	67	.266
Day	217	58	9	38	.267	Sc Pos	138	41	5	66	.297
Night	373	86	14	52	.231	Clutch	111	28	4	20	.252

1990 Rankings (National League)

- 1st in lowest groundball/flyball ratio (.61)
- 4th in doubles (37), lowest batting average at home (.234)
- 5th lowest batting average vs. left-handed pitchers (.208)
- 7th in lowest batting average (.244)
- Led the Mets in stolen bases (34), caught stealing (8), plate appearances (668), games (154) and stolen base percentage (80.9%)
- Led NL third basemen in sacrifice flies (9), stolen bases, walks (69), intentional walks (12), stolen base percentage, slugging percentage vs. right-handed pitchers (.488) and highest percentage of pitches taken (54.3%)

HITTING:

When Dave Magadan finally got a full-time job last year, he challenged for the National League batting crown. Magadan is a line drive, singles hitter. He can hit doubles down the lines and into the gaps, but when he hits a home run, it's not by design. Magadan has an outstanding knowledge of the strike zone, and is extremely patient. The Mets wish he wouldn't be quite so patient. Lacking big guns, they depend on line drive hitters like Magadan to swing more freely with men on base. Magadan is making progress in this area. He walked less, and had a higher batting average with men in scoring position last year than in '89.

There is no safe way to pitch to Magadan, although sending out a lefty hurler will help. Magadan hit just .256 against southpaws last year, compared to .371 against righties. Against lefties, Magadan is an up-the-middle hitter; most teams give him the lines. If there is any pitch that Magadan doesn't like, it is the fastball up and in. The safest way to pitch to him in crucial situations is to keep the ball out of the strike zone because his patience can be a handicap when the game is on the line.

BASERUNNING:

When Magadan steals a base, it's an event. Within the population of first basemen, he is below-average, and that's a slow bunch of players. Magadan's two stolen bases in 1990 increased his career total to three. He may be slow, but he's not foolish.

FIELDING:

Following in the footsteps of a Gold-Glover and potential Hall of Famer can lead to unfair comparisons, but Magadan has held his own in the field. When you play a season at first base and make only two errors, no one can accuse you of bad fielding. Magadan is short on range, but his glove is soft enough, and his arm is as strong as you would expect from a former third baseman.

OVERALL:

In 1987, Dave Magadan had the Mets third base job nailed down until he got hurt in spring training. Howard Johnson's 30/30 year kept Magadan out of the lineup. Then for two more years, Magadan waited behind Keith Hernandez at first. In 1990, it looked like Magadan would be stuck again, behind Mike Marshall, but one day in Chicago, Marshall got back spasms, which led to Wally Pipp disease. Magadan will be a fixture in 1991, although his left/right differential means that platooning is still an open issue.

DAVE MAGADAN

Position: 1B/3B
Bats: L **Throws:** R
Ht: 6' 3" **Wt:** 195

Opening Day Age: 28
Born: 9/30/62 in Tampa, FL
ML Seasons: 5

Overall Statistics

	G	AB	R	H	D	T	HR	RBI	SB	BB	SO	AVG
1990	144	451	74	148	28	6	6	72	2	74	55	.328
Career	478	1349	184	411	78	10	14	175	3	208	154	.305

Where He Hits the Ball

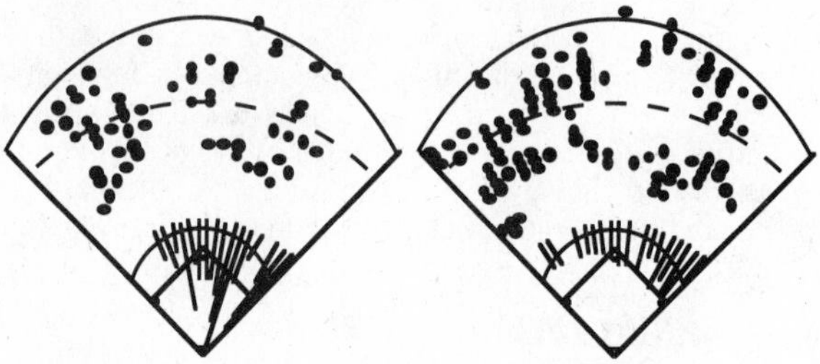

Vs. LHP Vs. RHP

1990 Situational Stats

	AB	H	HR	RBI	AVG		AB	H	HR	RBI	AVG
Home	212	59	2	34	.278	LHP	168	43	2	27	.256
Road	239	89	4	38	.372	RHP	283	105	4	45	.371
Day	141	43	4	25	.305	Sc Pos	110	42	2	63	.382
Night	310	105	2	47	.339	Clutch	69	27	1	8	.391

1990 Rankings (National League)

- 1st in batting average on the road (.372), batting average with 2 strikes (.309) and highest percentage of pitches taken (65.9%)
- 2nd in on-base average (.417), most pitches seen per plate appearance (4.07) and highest batting average with runners in scoring position (.382)
- 3rd in batting average (.328) and batting average in the clutch (.391)
- Led the Mets in batting average, triples (6), sacrificie flies (10), walks (74), times on base (224), on-base average, grounball/flyball ratio (1.51), batting average with runners in scoring position and batting average in the clutch

HITTING:

A lot of New Yorkers will tell you that Kevin McReynolds had a lousy year in 1990. He let the team down: only 24 homers, only 82 RBI, and a paltry .269 batting average. The truth is, McReynolds stacks up fine against every left fielder in the league except Barry Bonds and Kevin Mitchell, even in his "off year" of 1990. His on-base average (.353) was just shy of his career high and he hit .295 with runners in scoring position. The Mets had problems in 1990, but McReynolds wasn't one of them.

At 31, McReynolds may be playing a notch lower than his peak years of '86 to '88, but no one stays 27 forever. McReynolds remains a dangerous power hitter capable of driving the ball over any fence. As the stats indicate, he is a good clutch hitter who becomes more aggressive when the situation calls for it.

Pitching to McReynolds requires the normal approach to any dangerous power hitter: keep the ball away from him, use breaking balls low and away, and never give him anything inside that he can pull. McReynolds is always willing to swing at the first or second pitch if he sees what he likes.

BASERUNNING:

Crossing the age barrier from age 29 to 30 has affected McReynolds' speed more than his hitting. He stole 21 bases (in 21 attempts, setting an all-time record) in 1988, 15 bases in 1989, and just 9 last year. Kevin maintained an 82% success ratio in 1990, however. He may be slower, but he's just as smart as ever. McReynolds doesn't miss opportunities to take extra advances, either.

FIELDING:

McReynolds is among the best left fielders in baseball. His abilities to get to a batted ball quickly and fire an accurate throw to any base are as good as anyone's. He tied Barry Bonds for most outfield assists (14) in the National League last year. Although coaches warn their runners to respect McReynolds, he keeps surprising people year after year.

OVERALL:

The national media love to praise underrated players by saying, "If this guy played in New York or Los Angeles, he would be a superstar." Kevin McReynolds proves that statement isn't always true. The big media markets do blow things out of proportion, but sometimes they do it with a negative twist. McReynolds' production as he has advanced in age from 28 to age 30 has been portrayed as a major collapse, when the numbers just don't support such a notion. Kevin Mac is just fine, and has many good years left.

KEVIN McREYNOLDS

Position: LF
Bats: R **Throws:** R
Ht: 6' 1" **Wt:** 215

Opening Day Age: 31
Born: 10/16/59 in Little Rock, AR
ML Seasons: 8

Overall Statistics

	G	AB	R	H	D	T	HR	RBI	SB	BB	SO	AVG
1990	147	521	75	140	23	1	24	82	9	71	61	.269
Career	1089	3997	550	1080	194	28	167	621	76	349	523	.270

Where He Hits the Ball

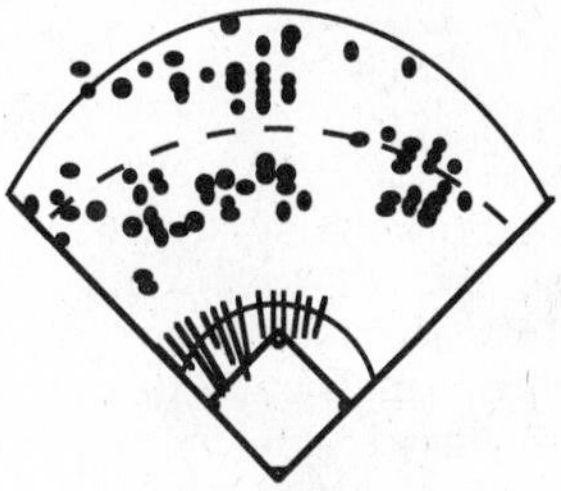

Vs. LHP

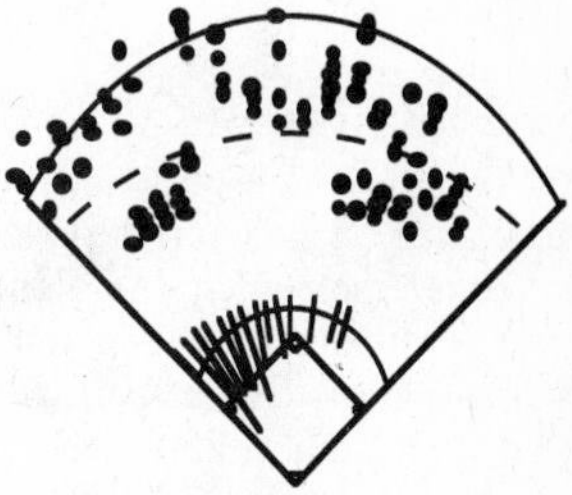

Vs. RHP

1990 Situational Stats

	AB	H	HR	RBI	AVG		AB	H	HR	RBI	AVG
Home	244	63	11	39	.258	LHP	194	45	4	15	.232
Road	277	77	13	43	.278	RHP	327	95	20	67	.291
Day	171	51	11	30	.298	Sc Pos	132	39	6	58	.295
Night	350	89	13	52	.254	Clutch	97	28	4	18	.289

1990 Rankings (National League)

- 1st in batting average with the bases loaded (.800)
- 2nd in lowest groundball/flyball ratio (.72)
- 6th in batting average with 2 strikes (.273)
- Led the Mets in batting average with the bases loaded and on-base average vs. left-handed pitchers (.358)
- Led NL left fielders in sacrifice flies, batting average with the bases loaded, batting average with 2 strikes, fielding percentage (.988) and highest percentage of swings put into play (51.3%)

<u>*HITTING:*</u>

Keith Miller's offense is built around the smaller aspects. He doesn't hit for high average, and he doesn't hit for power, but he gets on base just as frequently as Billy Hatcher or Eric Yelding (for example), and his purpose is to make things happen. He is a spray hitter who likes to go with a pitch. He can bunt for a hit, bunt for a sacrifice, and hit behind the runner.

Miller is a good judge of the strike zone, but pitchers are not afraid to challenge him, so he doesn't walk much. He likes the ball on the outside part of the plate, or even a little off the outside corner. Because he often leans that way, he is susceptible to inside pitches, both hard stuff and breaking balls. He often gets caught looking at a called strike three on the inside corner. The most popular approach by pitchers is to work Miller in and out, showing him an occasional fastball out off the plate, and a large number of curves and sliders.

<u>*BASERUNNING:*</u>

The Mets have touted Miller as the type of player who can win a game on the base paths, but he is no Rickey Henderson or Vince Coleman. He is, however, a good base stealer, proven by his 16 steals (and 84% success rate) in just 233 at-bats. Miller is still learning to read pitchers and situations. In the minor leagues, he never stole more than 23 bases in a season, but is now clearly capable of 35 to 40 steals per year with enough playing time.

<u>*FIELDING:*</u>

Versatility is Miller's main asset. He can play second, short, and all three outfield positions, which he did in 1990. He is a converted infielder who was once slated to play second base every day. Miller had some adventures in the outfield last year, beginning with a wind-blown fly ball on opening day, but his great range will become evident with experience. His arm is more than adequate for the outfield.

<u>*OVERALL:*</u>

Miller handled all the diverse duties that the Mets gave him during 1990. He played five different positions, appeared in six different places in the batting order, and was a prolific pinch runner and pinch hitter. He was most often used as the righty-hitting half of a center field platoon, and that's his best hope for regular duty in 1991. It is more likely he'll be an all-purpose utility man.

KEITH MILLER

Position: CF
Bats: R **Throws:** R
Ht: 5'11" **Wt:** 180

Opening Day Age: 27
Born: 6/12/63 in Midland, MI
ML Seasons: 4

Overall Statistics

	G	AB	R	H	D	T	HR	RBI	SB	BB	SO	AVG
1990	88	233	42	60	8	0	1	12	16	23	46	.258
Career	210	497	80	127	18	3	3	25	30	36	89	.256

Where He Hits the Ball

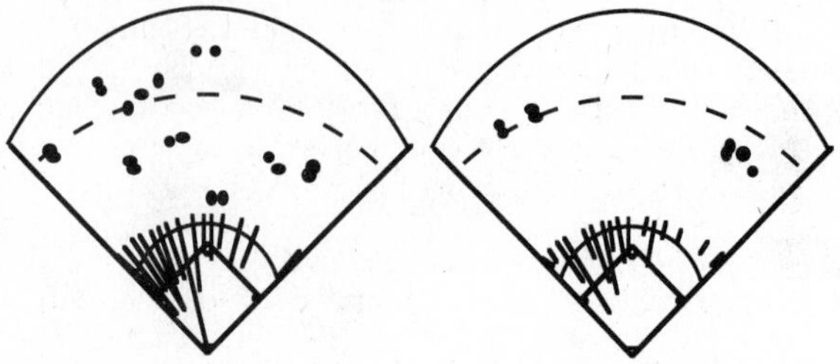

Vs. LHP Vs. RHP

1990 Situational Stats

	AB	H	HR	RBI	AVG		AB	H	HR	RBI	AVG
Home	107	25	1	9	.234	LHP	149	43	0	8	.289
Road	126	35	0	3	.278	RHP	84	17	1	4	.202
Day	99	28	1	5	.283	Sc Pos	35	7	0	10	.200
Night	134	32	0	7	.239	Clutch	41	10	0	1	.244

1990 Rankings (National League)

- 4th in percentage of extra bases taken as a runner (64.1%)
- Led the Mets in batting average vs. left-handed pitchers (.289) and steals of third (3)

CHARLIE O'BRIEN

Position: C
Bats: R **Throws:** R
Ht: 6' 2" **Wt:** 190

Opening Day Age: 29
Born: 5/1/61 in Tulsa, OK
ML Seasons: 5

Overall Statistics

	G	AB	R	H	D	T	HR	RBI	SB	BB	SO	AVG
1990	74	213	17	38	10	2	0	20	0	21	34	.178
Career	202	565	56	118	30	3	8	65	0	54	68	.209

Where He Hits the Ball

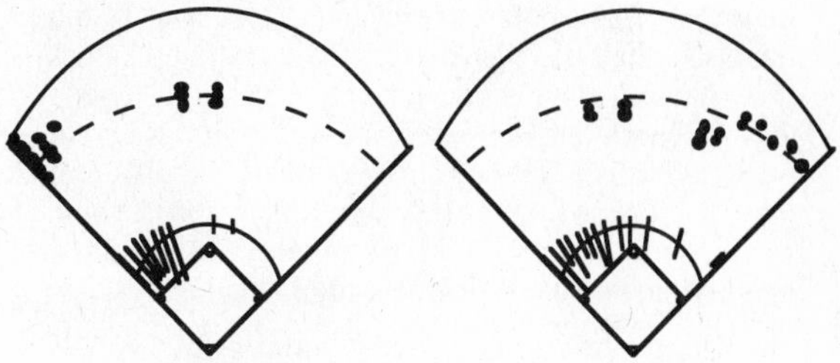

Vs. LHP Vs. RHP

1990 Situational Stats

	AB	H	HR	RBI	AVG		AB	H	HR	RBI	AVG
Home	88	15	0	11	.170	LHP	112	16	0	7	.143
Road	125	23	0	9	.184	RHP	101	22	0	13	.218
Day	80	13	0	3	.162	Sc Pos	50	12	0	20	.240
Night	133	25	0	17	.188	Clutch	30	7	0	1	.233

1990 Rankings (National League)

- Did not rank near the top or bottom in any category

HITTING:

The Mets didn't acquire Charlie O'Brien for offense. O'Brien had his career year in 1989, and it wasn't much: .234 BA, six homers, 35 RBI. He was hitting only .186 with 11 RBI when the Mets took him from the Brewers late last summer. With New York, he did even worse, batting .162 in 28 games.

O'Brien has a little power, shown by the 15 homers he hit five years ago in the Texas League, but he doesn't usually swing for the fences. His basic approach is to make contact and hope the ball drops in. If you throw him a fat pitch inside, however, he will try to pull it.

The best approach for pitchers is to keep the ball on the outside half of the plate, or way inside. A good mixture of fastballs and curveballs will usually keep him off balance. It is safer to challenge O'Brien than to risk walking him. He has a good eye, and will take advantage of pitchers who can't get the ball over the plate.

BASERUNNING:

O'Brien is very slow (no attempted steals in two years), cautious to a fault, and he doesn't seem to know how to slide. His next major league stolen base will be the first of his career.

FIELDING:

Defense is the reason O'Brien is a major league ballplayer. He joined the Mets in the heat of a pennant race, and immediately began handling a seasoned pitching staff as if he had been in the National League working with these same pitchers for years. O'Brien is a quick study who can call a good game in any league, and he is adept at all the physical skills of catching. He can throw out runners, block pitches in the dirt, field bunts, and make tag plays at home.

OVERALL:

Charlie O'Brien is the kind of player who was helped by the DH rule. When the pitcher doesn't have to hit, a team can afford to have one weak bat in the lineup, a defensive specialist. The Mets were happy to get O'Brien; their top catcher was hurt, and their backup was straight from Double-A. The situation isn't going to be so favorable for O'Brien in 1991, but until Todd Hundley matures, O'Brien will be an asset on the Mets roster.

PITCHING:

Bob Ojeda was displaced from the Mets' starting rotation in 1990. He accepted the reliever's role, and performed well, much better in fact than he did during a mid-season return to the rotation. For the year, Ojeda was 3-1 with a 2.19 ERA in 49 innings working out of the pen. As a starter, he compiled a 4.72 ERA and a 4-5 record in 69 innings. Shifting between starting and relieving is never easy, but Ojeda made the best of a difficult situation. Always the subject of trade rumors, he did nothing to decrease his marketability.

Ojeda has been the subject of much curiosity since slicing through one finger of his pitching hand in a freak run-in with a hedge-trimmer. The most practical question was the impact on his change-up, which he throws tightly squeezed back in his palm. In 1989, Ojeda found that his change-up didn't have the movement that it had before the accident. He also found that his fastball had increased velocity, but with a loss of its natural downward movement. In 1990, Ojeda got the benefit of extensive work with John Franco in the Mets bullpen. Franco showed him some different grips, and Ojeda found a tiny shift that restored a nice running motion to the change-up. He also regained the good downward movement to his fastball.

Ojeda likes pitching at Shea Stadium. In fact, he calls his home ballpark "our feeding ground." Last year, he had an overall ERA of 3.50 at Shea, and 3.86 on the road. In 1989 the difference was 2.95 at home vs. 3.88 on the road.

HOLDING RUNNERS, FIELDING, HITTING:

Ojeda showed genuine progress at holding runners during 1990. The opposition got away with only 14 steals, while being cut down 11 times. In 1989, he gave up 28 steals in 38 attempts. As a lefty reliever often working with men on base, Ojeda concentrates on runners better than he did as a starter. He is a good fielder who led all Mets pitchers in assists per inning last year. He has good athletic ability and sharp presence of mind. His hitting is nothing to brag about.

OVERALL:

At age 33, many pitchers are clearly heading downhill. But Ojeda, who had elbow surgery in 1987 and the clipper accident in 1988, has shown the ability to keep working and to keep learning. Ojeda held lefty hitters to a meager .168 batting average last year, a sign that he can adjust to the role of specialist. He should continue to be effective either starting or relieving, whatever his role may be in 1991.

BOB OJEDA

Position: RP/SP
Bats: L **Throws:** L
Ht: 6' 1" **Wt:** 195

Opening Day Age: 33
Born: 12/17/57 in Los Angeles, CA
ML Seasons: 11

Overall Statistics

	W	L	ERA	G	GS	Sv	IP	H	R	BB	SO	HR
1990	7	6	3.66	38	12	0	118.0	123	53	40	62	10
Career	95	79	3.65	280	222	1	1482.1	1424	668	498	884	116

How Often He Throws Strikes

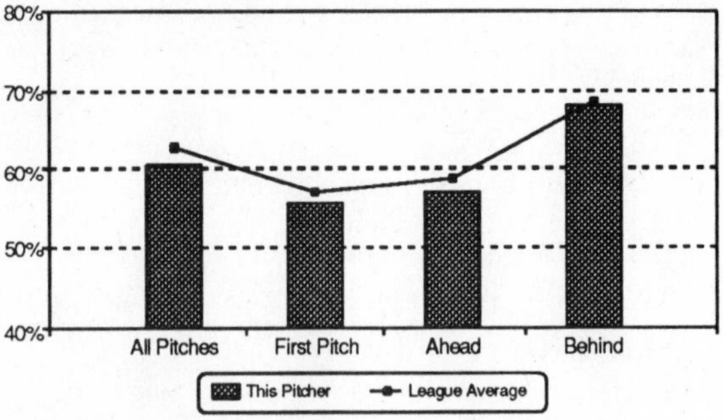

1990 Situational Stats

	W	L	ERA	Sv	IP		AB	H	HR	RBI	AVG
Home	4	2	3.50	0	64.1	LHB	113	19	1	7	.168
Road	3	4	3.86	0	53.2	RHB	339	104	9	42	.307
Day	2	0	2.51	0	32.1	Sc Pos	113	25	2	38	.221
Night	5	6	4.10	0	85.2	Clutch	72	13	0	4	.181

1990 Rankings (National League)

- 2nd highest batting average allowed vs. right-handed batters (.307)
- 9th in runner caught stealing (11)
- Led the Mets in most GDPs induced per GDP situation (13.1%)

PITCHING:

Alejandro Pena is an uncomplicated, hard-throwing righty set-up reliever. A stoic worker, he is always cool under pressure. The baseball world has seen Pena enjoying both the thrill of victory and the agony of defeat, but his facial expression never changes. Pena fell short of expectations in his first few months with the Mets last year (ERAs of 5.00 in April and 6.92 in June, for example), but he just kept working, and was New York's most reliable reliever during the pennant stretch.

Pena's pitching game is built around velocity and movement on the fastball. He uses a slider as a complement, and he has a decent change-up that he mixes in mainly against lefty hitters. Pena has been reported to be throwing a forkball and a curve, but he denies having such pitches. Pena still gets his heater into the high 80s, but control is the keystone for his success. When he can hit spots, his three pitches work together to keep hitters off balance. When he is just trying to throw strikes, the hitters can look for the number-one, and drive it every time.

Pena has a history of shoulder problems. Back in 1984 he was a premier starter, leading the National League in ERA and shutouts. Like so many Dodger pitchers, however, he succumbed to overwork, and missed almost all of the 1985 season after surgery. When he was ineffective in 1986, most people thought Pena was finished. His comeback in 1987-88 was a thrilling surprise.

HOLDING RUNNERS, FIELDING, HITTING:

When it comes to fielding and holding runners, Pena is hurt by a lack of concentration and a general disinterest in all the aspects of the game that don't involve throwing the ball to the catcher. All 11 steal attempts against him were successful last year, and he participated in only six fielding plays during 1990 -- by far the lowest of any Mets' pitcher with at least 50 innings. As a hitter, Alejandro swings hard but is rarely an offensive factor.

OVERALL:

One of the little-noticed comeback stories of 1990 was the re-emergence of Pena late in the season. After August 12, the opposition scored only one run on him in 23.1 innings (a 0.39 ERA), and he walked only one batter in September. If Pena can pick up where he left off in 1990, the Mets will have solved the problem that has existed ever since they traded Roger McDowell.

ALEJANDRO PENA

Position: RP
Bats: R **Throws:** R
Ht: 6' 1" **Wt:** 205

Opening Day Age: 31
Born: 6/25/59 in Cambiaso, Dominican Republic
ML Seasons: 10

Overall Statistics

	W	L	ERA	G	GS	Sv	IP	H	R	BB	SO	HR
1990	3	3	3.20	52	0	5	76.0	71	31	22	76	4
Career	41	41	2.95	333	72	37	845.0	764	332	266	647	48

How Often He Throws Strikes

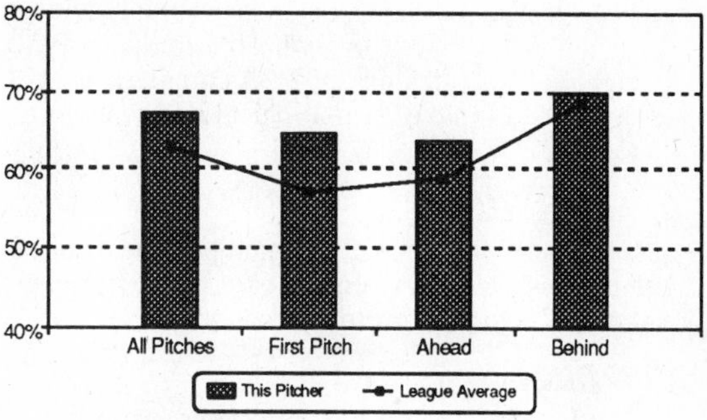

1990 Situational Stats

	W	L	ERA	Sv	IP		AB	H	HR	RBI	AVG
Home	1	0	3.19	2	31.0	LHB	133	33	1	16	.248
Road	2	3	3.20	3	45.0	RHB	157	38	3	17	.242
Day	0	1	5.13	4	26.1	Sc Pos	79	20	0	27	.253
Night	3	2	2.17	1	49.2	Clutch	102	21	1	15	.206

1990 Rankings (National League)

- Led the Mets in holds (6)

HITTING:

Since joining the Mets in 1988, Mackey Sasser has always hit well, never batting lower than .285. Davey Johnson always used Sasser sparingly, however, never batting him more than 182 times in a season. When Bud Harrelson took over in mid-season last year, one of his first moves was to put Sasser into the lineup. Sasser responded by batting a career-high .307, and might have posted some very impressive batting totals if he hadn't been sidelined with late-season injuries.

Sasser is a free swinger who would rather put the ball in play than try to work the count and draw a walk. He makes good contact, though, and last year he had the fewest strikeouts of any Met with 120 or more at-bats. Sasser uses the whole ballpark, and has no big holes in his swing. He is a fastball hitter who can adjust to a curve unless it really catches him by surprise.

The best way to get Sasser out is to put a lefty pitcher on the mound. Sasser's overwhelming propensity to hit right-handed pitching (.332 BA compared to .208 vs. lefties) still makes him a logical candidate to be platooned.

BASERUNNING:

Sasser is very slow. He did not attempt to steal during 1990. He is no dummy on the base paths, however, and makes a good effort to stay out of double plays.

FIELDING:

During Davey Johnson's tenure, Sasser got a rap that he would never be a good defensive catcher. Sasser worked extensively with Mets coach Doc Edwards last year -- to the extent that he referred to Edwards as "a second father" -- and turned himself into a decent backstop. He has visibly improved his ball-blocking abilities, and handles himself well on plays at the plate. Sasser still has a maddening tendency to pump the ball repeatedly before throwing it, even when he's just playing catch on the sidelines. He is improving at throwing out baserunners, however, and even became the first Mets' catcher ever to toss out Vince Coleman.

OVERALL:

Waiting in line behind future Hall of Famer Gary Carter made Sasser look weak by comparison, but he is quickly rising out of that shadow. Often banged up, Sasser continued to be effective last year while playing with a sprained ankle, a badly bruised hand, and a strained elbow. This young backstop is no powder puff.

MACKEY SASSER

Position: C
Bats: L **Throws:** R
Ht: 6' 1" **Wt:** 210

Opening Day Age: 28
Born: 8/3/62 in Fort Gaines, GA
ML Seasons: 4

Overall Statistics

	G	AB	R	H	D	T	HR	RBI	SB	BB	SO	AVG
1990	100	270	31	83	14	0	6	41	0	15	19	.307
Career	246	602	59	176	38	3	8	82	0	28	45	.292

Where He Hits the Ball

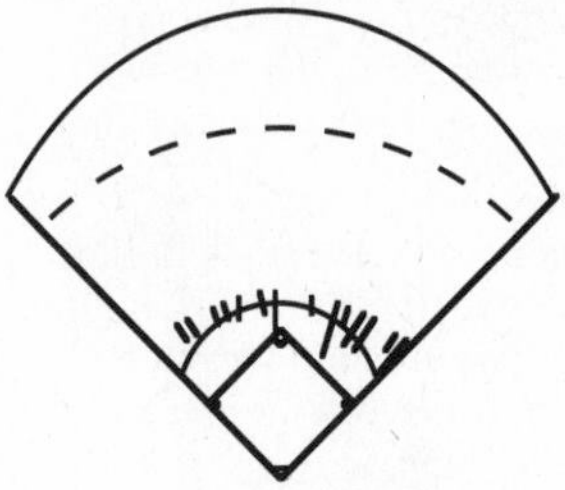

Vs. LHP

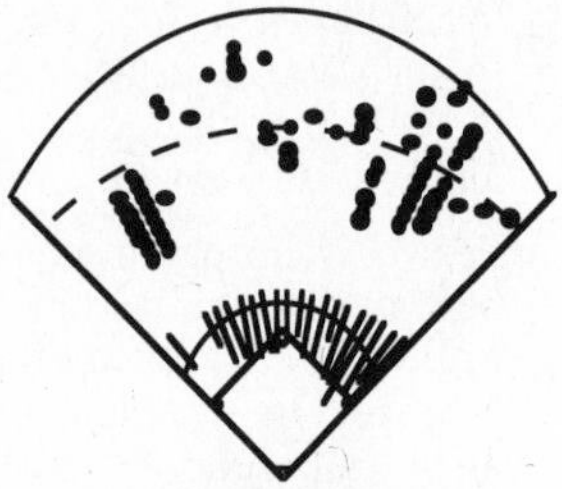

Vs. RHP

1990 Situational Stats

	AB	H	HR	RBI	AVG		AB	H	HR	RBI	AVG
Home	143	35	3	21	.245	LHP	53	11	1	7	.208
Road	127	48	3	20	.378	RHP	217	72	5	34	.332
Day	84	29	0	6	.345	Sc Pos	70	21	5	36	.300
Night	186	54	6	35	.290	Clutch	57	12	1	7	.211

1990 Rankings (National League)

➡ Led NL catchers in errors (14)

FUTURE MVP?

DARRYL STRAWBERRY

Position: RF
Bats: L **Throws:** L
Ht: 6' 6" **Wt:** 195

Opening Day Age: 29
Born: 3/12/62 in Los Angeles, CA
ML Seasons: 8

Overall Statistics

	G	AB	R	H	D	T	HR	RBI	SB	BB	SO	AVG
1990	152	542	92	150	18	1	37	108	15	70	110	.277
Career	1109	3903	662	1025	187	30	252	733	191	580	960	.263

Where He Hits the Ball

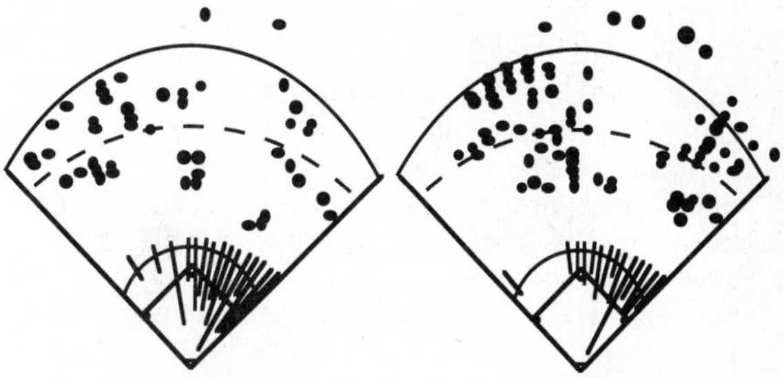

Vs. LHP Vs. RHP

1990 Situational Stats

	AB	H	HR	RBI	AVG		AB	H	HR	RBI	AVG
Home	268	68	24	67	.254	LHP	217	53	9	29	.244
Road	274	82	13	41	.299	RHP	325	97	28	79	.298
Day	179	54	8	37	.302	Sc Pos	148	45	12	74	.304
Night	363	96	29	71	.264	Clutch	88	21	5	11	.239

1990 Rankings (National League)

- 1st in HR frequency (14.7 ABs per HR)
- 2nd in home runs (37) and slugging percentage vs. right-handed pitchers (.594)
- 5th in RBIs (108) and on-base average vs. right-handed pitchers (.398)
- Led the Mets in home runs, total bases (281), RBIs, caught stealing (8), intentional walks (15), times on base (224), strikeouts (110), pitches seen (2,378), slugging percentage (.518), HR frequency and least GDPs per GDP situation (4.2%)
- Led NL right fielders in home runs, times on base, HR frequency and least GDPs per GDP situation

HITTING:

Always in the spotlight, Darryl Strawberry followed one of his biggest Met seasons by quickly signing a free agent contract with the Los Angeles Dodgers. Despite the fact that Strawberry had averaged 32 homers and 92 RBI in eight seasons in New York, the Mets did not seem especially concerned about losing him. The reaction among his old teammates was typically split: some criticized the Mets, others stuck knives in Strawberry.

Strawberry is the type of hitter who can carry a team when he's hot, but he has these . . . mood swings. Coming off a .225 season in 1989, he started slowly last year, but got red-hot right after Bud Harrelson replaced Davey Johnson as Mets manager. Strawberry was among the league leaders in most offensive categories at the All-Star break -- a .306 average with 21 homers - - and the Mets were looking like division winners. Strawberry cooled off after that, hitting .247 after the break, though he continued to hit with power and drive in runs. The Mets faded to second place, and fairly or unfairly, Strawberry got much of the blame.

Whether he's on a streak or mired in a slump, most pitchers hate to give in to Strawberry. If he knows a fastball is coming, he can drive it hard every time. Even on 3-2 and 3-1 counts, most pitchers will throw him breaking balls. A good slider down and away is a tough pitch for him to hit. A few teams will let their hardest throwers challenge Strawberry repeatedly. It is always a good idea to keep the pitches away, however.

BASERUNNING:

Strawberry was a consistent stealer of 25 to 30 bases per year until 1989. Now he runs less often. His success rate was a marginal 65% in 1990. He still has very good speed, but he doesn't have the natural instincts to read pitchers, take big-but-safe leads, and get a good jump. He makes occasional baserunning blunders.

FIELDING:

Strawberry's great athletic ability is least visible when he's in the field. Although he showed improvement in 1990, he still doesn't get a good jump or cover enough ground in right field, which makes one wonder how the Dodgers could consider using him in center. Often he looks confused and makes inappropriate plays.

OVERALL:

Strawberry now returns to his Los Angeles home, and will undoubtedly be primed to have a big year. At 29, he is more than halfway to 500 homers, and laid-back LA may be just the place for him.

TIM TEUFEL

Position: 2B/1B
Bats: R **Throws:** R
Ht: 6' 0" **Wt:** 175

Opening Day Age: 32
Born: 7/7/58 in Greenwich, CT
ML Seasons: 8

HITTING:

Tim Teufel is a natural platoon hitter. His batting average against lefties is normally 40 points higher than against righties, and his slugging percentage is often nearly 100 points higher. These differentials did not hold up last year, probably because the Mets tended to use Teufel mainly against the NL's best lefty pitchers. Facing mediocre lefties, they were usually happy to let Dave Magadan (for example) stay in the lineup.

Teufel is a good fastball hitter. The basic approach for most pitchers is to throw him a variety of pitches and move the ball around. Teufel is a good contact hitter. He is patient and has a good knowledge of the strike zone. He can foul off pitches repeatedly while waiting for the one he wants, and is happy to draw a walk as well. The main caution for pitchers: keep the ball away from Teufel. Don't give him anything up and in that he can turn on.

Teufel can handle all kinds of batting chores. He can get on base when leading off an inning. He can bunt a runner over. He can hit long flies to bring home a runner from third. And he can just plain get a base hit to keep a rally going. In his last 13 pinch-hit appearances of 1990, he had a double, two homers, a sacrifice fly, and a walk, with both homers coming in the ninth inning.

BASERUNNING:

Teufel has never been much of a base stealer. He has never swiped more than four in a season, and didn't even make an attempt last year. As a role player who often gets into tight games in crucial situations, however, Teufel must be alert and wily on the bases, and he fills that bill admirably.

FIELDING:

Originally a second baseman, Teufel is a versatile player who can be used at first, second, or third. His range is good at first and third, but a little below average at second. His throwing arm is adequate for all three positions. One aspect of fielding where Teufel continues to need development is the soft glove quality required of a first baseman.

OVERALL:

Teufel's value to the Mets has increased with the departures of hitters like Mike Marshall and Darryl Strawberry, the unspectacular offense of Keith Miller, and the problems of switch-hitters Howard Johnson and Gregg Jefferies against lefty pitching. Teufel figures to be a prominent role player, pinch hitter, and part-time infielder in 1991.

Overall Statistics

	G	AB	R	H	D	T	HR	RBI	SB	BB	SO	AVG
1990	80	175	28	43	11	0	10	24	0	15	33	.246
Career	759	2325	325	610	148	10	61	279	10	278	370	.262

Where He Hits the Ball

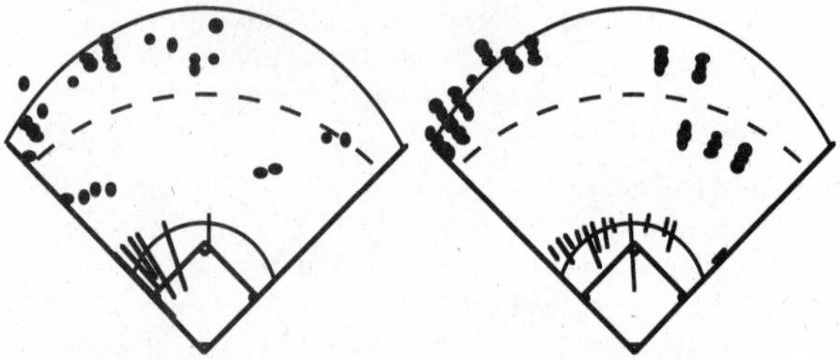

Vs. LHP Vs. RHP

1990 Situational Stats

	AB	H	HR	RBI	AVG		AB	H	HR	RBI	AVG
Home	64	16	4	12	.250	LHP	108	26	5	10	.241
Road	111	27	6	12	.243	RHP	67	17	5	14	.254
Day	69	20	5	15	.290	Sc Pos	45	9	2	13	.200
Night	106	23	5	9	.217	Clutch	39	9	1	5	.231

1990 Rankings (National League)

- Led the Mets in batting average on a 3-1 count (.429)

STAFF ACE

PITCHING:

Ever since Frank Viola uncorked a newly supercharged fastball at spring training in 1987, he has been one of the dominant pitchers in baseball, arguably the best lefty in the game today. In 1990 Viola won 20 games for the second time in three years. His 2.67 ERA further validated his emergence as the ace of the Mets staff.

Viola has excellent control and is easily capable of inside-outside, up and down movement within the strike zone. In addition to the fastball, he has a good slow curve, and a change-up that can be his out pitch. His fourth pitch is a slider that he uses only occasionally. Viola uses the fastball to set up the change; he doesn't want to show the change-up too frequently, or it loses its shock value. For a simple, different look and for keeping the hitters off balance, the Mets like Viola to use the slow curve more extensively. The two-pitch fastball/change repertoire is the most comfortable for Viola, but he gets in trouble when he forgets to mix in the slow curve. His curve gives the straight change a different, more surprising look. Viola did use the curve more in 1990 than he did in 1989, and the results were clearly visible.

Viola is a durable pitcher, but the Mets use him wisely. They only let him exceed 130 pitches three times last year, and he never went over 135. He threw seven complete games last year, even with the carefully-monitored pitch counts.

HOLDING RUNNERS, FIELDING, HITTING:

Baserunners struggle when they try to steal on Viola. In 1990, they got away with 25 stolen bases in 40 attempts, a below-average 63% success rate. In 1989, Viola had held the opposition to 59%, and in the American League his career average was around 50%. In the field, Viola is still improving at age 30. He had the second highest total chances among Mets' pitchers last year. At bat and on the bases, it is often obvious that his game was long ago impaired by the DH rule.

OVERALL:

The Mets gave up a lot of talent to get Frank Viola; so far they haven't been disappointed. He is learning the National League hitters faster than they are learning him, and with the help of the Mets coaching staff, he is becoming more of a senior-circuit style pitcher.

FRANK VIOLA

Position: SP
Bats: L **Throws:** L
Ht: 6' 4" **Wt:** 209

Opening Day Age: 30
Born: 4/19/60 in Hempstead, NY
ML Seasons: 9

Overall Statistics

	W	L	ERA	G	GS	Sv	IP	H	R	BB	SO	HR
1990	20	12	2.67	35	35	0	249.2	227	83	60	182	15
Career	137	110	3.70	307	306	0	2107.2	2077	960	608	1469	233

How Often He Throws Strikes

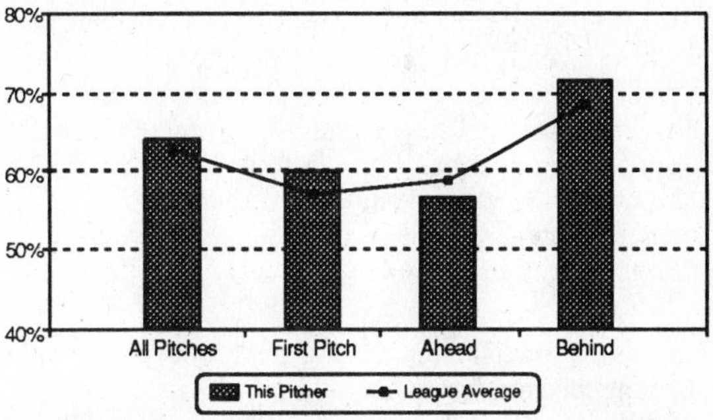

1990 Situational Stats

	W	L	ERA	Sv	IP		AB	H	HR	RBI	AVG
Home	12	5	2.44	0	125.2	LHB	183	47	1	12	.257
Road	8	7	2.90	0	124.0	RHB	755	180	14	60	.238
Day	9	5	2.44	0	103.1	Sc Pos	204	43	4	59	.211
Night	11	7	2.83	0	146.1	Clutch	63	14	1	2	.222

1990 Rankings (National League)

- 1st in games started (35), innings (249.2) and batters faced (1,016)
- 2nd in wins (20)
- 3rd in shutouts (3), wild pitches (11) and pitches thrown (3,684)
- 4th in ERA (2.67), strikeouts (182), runners caught stealing (15) and lowest slugging percentage allowed (.333)
- Led the Mets in ERA, wins, games started, complete games (7), shutouts, innings, batters faced, wild pitches, GDPs induced (17), lowest slugging percentage allowed (.333) and lowest stolen base percentage allowed (62.5%)

TODD HUNDLEY

Position: C
Bats: B **Throws:** R
Ht: 5'11" **Wt:** 170

Opening Day Age: 21
Born: 5/27/69 in Martinsville, VA
ML Seasons: 1

Overall Statistics

	G	AB	R	H	D	T	HR	RBI	SB	BB	SO	AVG
1990	36	67	8	14	6	0	0	2	0	6	18	.209
Career	36	67	8	14	6	0	0	2	0	6	18	.209

HITTING, FIELDING, BASERUNNING:

When the Mets needed a sub last spring for the injured Mackey Sasser, they brought up Todd Hundley from AA Jackson. The Mets' main interest was for some defense. Hundley's .209 average and two RBI were tiny numbers, but they could have been zeroes without causing heartbreak in the front office. Everyone knew that Hundley would be overmatched by major league pitching, and everyone was right. Even in the Southern League, Hundley was only a .265 hitter with 35 RBI.

Hundley, though not yet 22, has good poise for a young player; that would figure, as his father was former major league catcher Randy Hundley. He has decent speed and handles himself well on the bases, especially for a catcher with little experience. He stole five bases for Jackson, and gave his teammates some practical lessons in how to slide after he arrived in New York.

Unfortunately, Hundley's catching skills left something to be desired. He was out of his element trying to handle one of the best and most seasoned pitching staffs in baseball, and he often made rookie mistakes fielding the area around home plate. He is, of course, still very young, and the Mets weren't really discouraged by his performance.

OVERALL:

The Mets were desperate when they risked throwing Hundley into a major league pennant race. He gave a creditable account of himself taking all factors into consideration, and hopefully emerged with his confidence intact. He may need another year in the minors, but will be a good defensive catcher by 1992 at the latest.

DARREN REED

Position: CF
Bats: R **Throws:** R
Ht: 6' 1" **Wt:** 190

Opening Day Age: 25
Born: 10/16/65 in Ventura, CA
ML Seasons: 1

Overall Statistics

	G	AB	R	H	D	T	HR	RBI	SB	BB	SO	AVG
1990	26	39	5	8	4	1	1	2	1	3	11	.205
Career	26	39	5	8	4	1	1	2	1	3	11	.205

HITTING, FIELDING, BASERUNNING:

Darren Reed's development has been marked by experimentation. Over the years, he's tried all different kinds of hitting styles. Finally, in 1990, Reed and his coaches settled on one basic swing, intended to generate power rather than high average. The result: Reed hit 17 homers for Tidewater and joined the Mets on August 15. When asked to name one aspect of his game that improved enough to get him to the major leagues, Reed said simply, "The fly balls were going farther."

Hitting coach Mike Cubbage agrees that developing consistent power was the key to Reed's emergence: "The power potential was always there, but it was untapped." Reed is a good fastball hitter, with no gaps in his swing. He can cover the whole strike zone, but he has trouble with pitchers who change speeds effectively. The pitch that you don't want to throw him, obviously, is something he can pull.

On the bases, Reed has fair but unspectacular speed. He uses it well, however, and is an excellent percentage base stealer, swiping 26 bases in 32 attempts at Tidewater over the last two seasons. In the outfield, he has good range and an outstanding arm. He led the International League with 19 assists in 1989.

OVERALL:

Before 1990, Reed had a reputation for looking good in spring training, but then fizzling in Triple-A. At age 25, he has answered all questions about his motivation and durability, and is ready to help the Mets score more runs against left-handed pitching in 1991.

DAN SCHATZEDER

Position: RP
Bats: L **Throws:** L
Ht: 6' 0" **Wt:** 195

Opening Day Age: 36
Born: 12/1/54 in Elmhurst, IL
ML Seasons: 14

Overall Statistics

	W	L	ERA	G	GS	Sv	IP	H	R	BB	SO	HR
1990	1	3	2.20	51	2	0	69.2	66	23	23	39	2
Career	69	68	3.71	496	121	10	1311.0	1246	608	468	744	128

PITCHING, FIELDING, HITTING & HOLDING RUNNERS:

Still trying to fight for a pennant, the Mets acquired the well-travelled Dan Schatzeder last September to give them an extra left-handed situational reliever. The Astros were pleased with Schatzeder's work out of the pen (1-3, 2.39 ERA), but they faced losing him to free agency, and the Mets were willing to trade two prospects for him.

Schatzeder gave the Mets what they wanted. He yielded no runs in six appearances. Schatzeder's job was to come in and face one or two lefties; he averaged less than an inning per appearance. Schatzeder has the standard repertoire of a fastball, curve, slider, and change-up. He needs to spot the fastball carefully, because it's former velocity is now gone. Moving the ball around and dropping in a good hook are his keys to success.

Schatzeder typically does a good job holding runners, but they managed six stolen bases in seven tries last year. His fielding is only average, but his hitting is very good for a pitcher. At this stage of his career, he rarely gets to bat, however, and running the bases is not part of his game any more, either.

OVERALL:

Lefties who can throw strikes seem to have perpetual employment opportunities in the major leagues. Schatzeder staged a minor comeback in 1990, and could be a valuable contributor somewhere in 1991.

PAT TABLER

Position: RF/LF/DH
Bats: R **Throws:** R
Ht: 6' 2" **Wt:** 200

Opening Day Age: 33
Born: 2/2/58 in Hamilton, OH
ML Seasons: 10

Overall Statistics

	G	AB	R	H	D	T	HR	RBI	SB	BB	SO	AVG
1990	92	238	18	65	15	1	2	29	0	23	29	.273
Career	1071	3591	423	1027	180	24	46	475	16	335	524	.286

HITTING, FIELDING, BASERUNNING:

Pat Tabler's first two hits with the Mets were bases-loaded singles, giving him the phenomenal lifetime mark of .500 (40-for-80) with the sacks full. The Mets wanted Tabler to provide mature hitting talent in the heat of a pennant race, and he did just that.

Tabler is not much of a power hitter, instead trying to make contact and put the ball in play. He looks for a pitch he likes and attempts to hit it sharply. He is patient when it comes to choosing his pitch, but he would rather hit the ball than draw a walk. As indicated by his bases-loaded record, he understands that singles can generate plenty of RBI given the right opportunities.

On the base paths Tabler is just plain slow. He hasn't stolen a base since 1988, but was caught twice while with Kansas City last year. His biggest asset in the field is his ability to play first base and two outfield positions, but he is nothing special at any position.

OVERALL:

Tabler is probably better suited to the American League where the designated hitter rule can make use of his hitting ability without making demands on his limited fielding talents. A free agent at the end of the '90 season, his proven punch against lefties (.333 last year) figured to get him a few offers. The Mets were weak against southpaws last year, and are likely to make a bid.

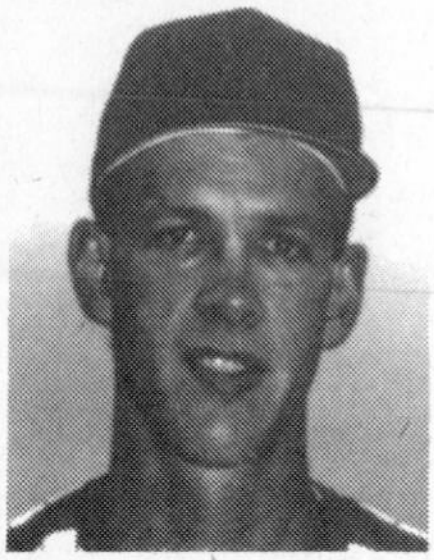

KELVIN TORVE

Position: 1B
Bats: L **Throws:** R
Ht: 6' 3" **Wt:** 185

Opening Day Age: 31
Born: 1/10/60 in Rapid City, SD
ML Seasons: 2

Overall Statistics

	G	AB	R	H	D	T	HR	RBI	SB	BB	SO	AVG
1990	20	38	0	11	4	0	0	2	0	4	9	.289
Career	32	54	1	14	4	0	1	4	0	5	11	.259

HITTING, FIELDING, BASERUNNING:

Kelvin Torve's first hit as a Met was a big one, a two-run pinch double that broke a tie against Philadelphia on August 9. He wasn't used a lot after that, but made an impression by hitting .289 in 38 at-bats, with four doubles.

Torve is a hard worker, professional in his approach. His hitting style uses the entire field. He doesn't try to do too much with any pitch. Hitting instructor Mike Cubbage describes him as a smart hitter who knows pitchers' strengths and weaknesses, and thinks through each at-bat, step by step. Torve is a streak hitter who can stay hot once he starts seeing the ball well. He finished third in the International League batting race with a .303 average last year.

Running is not a big part of Torve's game. His fielding is definitely above average, however. The Mets were originally attracted to Torve because of his soft glove and his ability to make good plays after coming in cold as a defensive replacement. In 1988 he made only two errors while playing an entire year at first base in the Twins' system.

OVERALL:

At 31, Torve is too old to be a prospect, but he's not too old to be a contributor on the 1991 Mets. He provides a tough left-handed bat off the bench, and a solid defensive replacement at first base. The departure of Darryl Strawberry improves Torve's chances to be a role player.

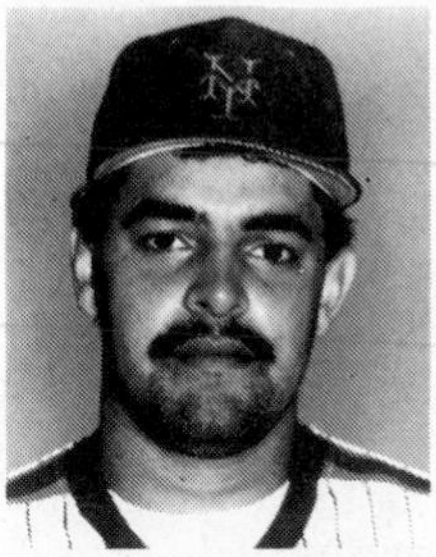

JULIO VALERA

Position: SP
Bats: R **Throws:** R
Ht: 6' 2" **Wt:** 185

Opening Day Age: 22
Born: 10/13/68 in San Sebastian, Puerto Rico
ML Seasons: 1

Overall Statistics

	W	L	ERA	G	GS	Sv	IP	H	R	BB	SO	HR
1990	1	1	6.92	3	3	0	13.0	20	11	7	4	1
Career	1	1	6.92	3	3	0	13.0	20	11	7	4	1

PITCHING, FIELDING, HITTING & HOLDING RUNNERS:

When the Mets needed to bolster their starting rotation for the pennant stretch last August, they displaced Ron Darling and brought up 21-year-old Julio Valera. It was a gutsy move that didn't pan out -- manager Bud Harrelson was widely criticized, in fact, for starting Valera against Pittsburgh in a crucial September contest. But the idea showed how much confidence New York has in this young righthander.

Valera has been playing winter ball in Puerto Rico for four years. He attracted scouts' attention by making major league hitters look bad while in winter ball, and he signed with the Mets at age 17. Valera has a live (87 to 88 MPH) sinking fastball, a slider, a good change-up, and a forkball. The forkball is a slow pitch which makes his straight change even more effective. He hides the ball well, is sneaky fast, and has above-average control of all his pitches.

Valera is good at holding runners. He is very aware of situations. His fielding is only fair, but he is improving in specific areas like covering first base quickly. He is not a great hitter.

OVERALL:

Valera is remarkable for his poise and mound savvy at a young age. He understands the subtle aspects of pitching better than many veterans. The short trial that he got in 1990 is not indicative of what to expect in 1991 and future years.

WALLY WHITEHURST

Position: RP
Bats: R **Throws:** R
Ht: 6' 3" **Wt:** 180

Opening Day Age: 27
Born: 4/11/64 in Shreveport, LA
ML Seasons: 2

Overall Statistics

	W	L	ERA	G	GS	Sv	IP	H	R	BB	SO	HR
1990	1	0	3.29	38	0	2	65.2	63	27	9	46	5
Career	1	1	3.50	47	1	2	79.2	80	34	14	55	7

PITCHING, FIELDING, HITTING & HOLDING RUNNERS:

Wally Whitehurst was frequently considered as a possible starter for the Mets in 1990, but he didn't start a single game. Whitehurst's big pitch is the curve, which he complements with an average fastball and an improving slider. One factor that kept him out of the starter's role is that he doesn't have a good change-of-pace pitch.

Whitehurst is a very aggressive pitcher who goes right after the hitters. His average of 13.9 pitches per inning last year was the lowest among Mets pitchers, and among the lowest in the National League. Whitehurst thrives on his ability to throw strikes and make the hitters put the ball in play in a location where it can be fielded. His strikeout-to-walk ratio last year -- 46 strikeouts, nine walks (two of them intentional) in 65.2 innings -- was outstanding, and even better than his minor league figures.

Whitehurst is very good at holding runners. His fielding ability is average, but he has a noticeable difficulty with balls hit right back at him. At bat and on the bases, he is nothing special.

OVERALL:

Whitehurst was a starter in the minors, and the Mets believe that he can be a starter in the big leagues, but there are a lot of pitchers in his way. In the meantime, he is a highly regarded asset in the bullpen, with an arm that bounces back well.

DARREL AKERFELDS

Position: RP
Bats: R **Throws:** R
Ht: 6' 2" **Wt:** 210

Opening Day Age: 28
Born: 6/12/62 in Denver, CO
ML Seasons: 4

PITCHING:

Darrel Akerfelds brought his knuckle-curve to the National League last year and became a four-month wonder before his arm wore out. Akerfelds pitched in 71 games, the fifth-highest total in the National League, and while that proved too much for his right arm, he did plenty of good pitching along the way.

Akerfelds was generous with walks and miserly with hits during the seaon. The key was getting ahead of the hitter. If Akerfelds got two strikes on a batter with two balls or less, they were doomed. Next would come the knuckle-curve, toppling as it approached the plate; the batter had to swing to protect himself, but could only miss the ball or top an easy infield out. The only problem with the pitch is that it normally dropped out of the strike zone. So until there were two strikes, hitters began to leave their bats on their shoulders whenever the pitch looked funny.

Akerfelds had excellent control of his other two pitches, a fastball and a slider. But pitching so often robbed these bread and butter pitches of speed and movement. He pitched well early because he pitched only twice a week, frequently getting three or four days rest between appearances. Through June 23, he gave up all of his earned runs but one when he had to pitch on consecutive days.

By mid-June, however, Akerfelds was the only Phillie getting anyone out. Leyva would use him as early as the seventh inning and leave him in to finish if he could. By the end of July, Akerfelds had made 46 appearances, and had nothing left. Late in the year, radar guns showed that his fastball had slowed by seven or eight MPH. When he lost his velocity, he had to spot his fastball on the edges, which meant that it was frequently a called ball.

HOLDING RUNNERS, FIELDING, HITTING:

Akerfelds' throws to bases can be adventures, and his delivery is easy to steal on. He is a genuine American League pitcher at the plate. He does hustle, though.

OVERALL:

Given 10 days rest in mid-September, Akerfelds pitched well once again. Joe Boever's live arm should fill Akerfelds' 1990 role and let Akerfelds produce as a good twice-a-week set-up/mop-up man. He must improve his control, however, as Leyva despises walks.

Overall Statistics

	W	L	ERA	G	GS	Sv	IP	H	R	BB	SO	HR
1990	5	2	3.77	71	0	3	93.0	65	45	54	42	10
Career	7	9	5.04	95	13	3	184.0	167	116	100	98	31

How Often He Throws Strikes

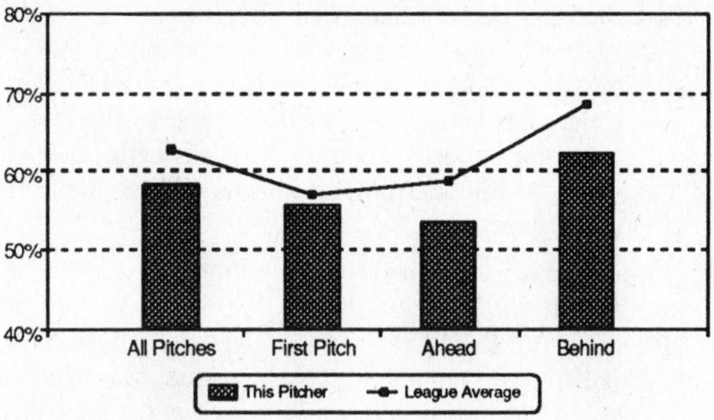

1990 Situational Stats

	W	L	ERA	Sv	IP		AB	H	HR	RBI	AVG
Home	5	0	2.88	1	50.0	LHB	159	31	7	30	.195
Road	0	2	4.81	2	43.0	RHB	165	34	3	18	.206
Day	1	0	3.68	0	14.2	Sc Pos	111	19	4	39	.171
Night	4	2	3.79	3	78.1	Clutch	136	21	2	10	.154

1990 Rankings (National League)

- 1st in first batter efficiency (.133)
- 5th in games pitched (71) and lowest batting average allowed vs. left-handed pitchers (.195)
- 8th in lowest percentage of inherited runners scored (26.3%)
- Led the Phillies in most stolen bases allowed (14), first batter efficiency and lowest percentage of inherited runners scored

JOE BOEVER

Position: RP
Bats: R **Throws:** R
Ht: 6' 1" **Wt:** 200

Opening Day Age: 30
Born: 10/4/60 in St. Louis, MO
ML Seasons: 6

PITCHING:

The Phils stole Joe Boever from the Braves because they knew that the reason Boever failed as a stopper would not prevent him from succeeding as a reliever. Boever held opponents to a 2.15 ERA, allowing no homers in 46 IP as a Phillie. As a Brave he recorded a 4.68 ERA, and surrendered a homer every seven innings pitched.

The difference was in his pattern of use. After acquiring Boever for Marvin Freeman, the Phillies used him on zero or one days rest in 23 of his 34 appearances. The Braves used him that often only 18 times in 33 appearances, because he was their stopper; they had to wait for save situations to use him. That kind of use doesn't suit Boever. He pitched 54 innings in 1990 on no or one days rest, with an ERA of 3.17; in the 34.1 innings he pitched with two or more days rest his ERA was 3.67 and he walked batters much more frequently.

Boever's mid-80s fastball is straight. He depends on its location and a uniform delivery which makes it difficult for hitters to pick up the pitch until it leaves his hand. His pitches are easier to read from the windup than the stretch. His best pitch is a palm ball which comes in slower than from Boever's arm speed would suggest, and then drops straight down like an old-fashioned overhand curve. It does not break 80 on the radar gun, but as Phils officials have said, "Any pitch that drops three feet doesn't have to be fast."

While Boever will throw the palm ball as often as twice per batter, its big break makes it unreliable when he runs a three ball count; that's why he walked 35 with the Braves. The trade also rejuvenated Boever's fastball. Working more frequently helped him standardize his rhythm and mechanics.

HOLDING RUNNERS, FIELDING, HITTING:

Boever is alert and fields his position well. His pickoff move is laborious and his best pitch is slow and sinks dramatically. When you hear that runners steal on pitchers, it's Boever they're talking about. At the plate, he made contact all three times he batted last year, the only Phils pitcher with a plate appearance who didn't strike out.

OVERALL:

The club's four projected 1991 starters averaged less than six innings per start in 1990. That will give Boever the heavy workload he needs to be effective. While they won't wait for save situations to use him, Boever could amass several if Roger McDowell slumps again.

Overall Statistics

	W	L	ERA	G	GS	Sv	IP	H	R	BB	SO	HR
1990	3	6	3.36	67	0	14	88.1	77	35	51	75	6
Career	8	20	3.64	187	0	36	247.1	232	104	113	196	22

How Often He Throws Strikes

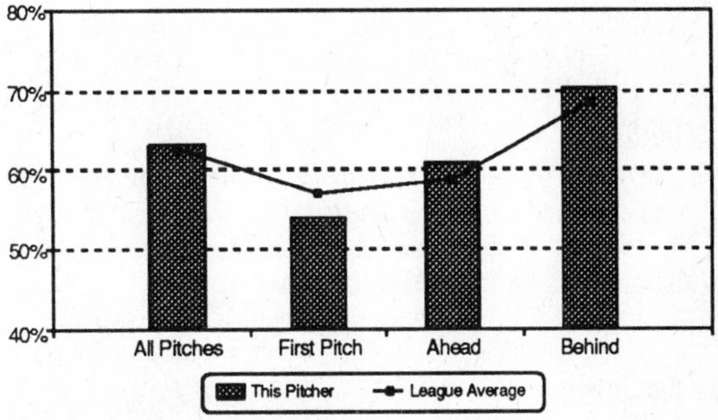

1990 Situational Stats

	W	L	ERA	Sv	IP		AB	H	HR	RBI	AVG
Home	2	3	4.10	5	52.2	LHB	176	32	1	24	.182
Road	1	3	2.27	9	35.2	RHB	155	45	5	21	.290
Day	1	0	4.97	4	25.1	Sc Pos	101	21	1	36	.208
Night	2	6	2.71	10	63.0	Clutch	190	39	3	22	.205

1990 Rankings (National League)

- 2nd in lowest batting average allowed vs. left-handed batters (.182)
- 8th in games pitched (67)

DON CARMAN

Position: RP
Bats: L **Throws:** L
Ht: 6' 3" **Wt:** 195

Opening Day Age: 31
Born: 8/14/59 in Oklahoma City, OK
ML Seasons: 8

PITCHING:

After six full seasons, 312 games and 53 wins, the Phils let Don Carman leave the team as a free agent, figuring that they would rather give a younger pitcher with an ERA over 4.00 (Carman's standard) an opportunity next year. Carman began last season as the Phils' left-handed middle reliever for two reasons: he has always had good success in his first inning of work, and he has always been very tough on lefties. It was a good idea, but it really didn't work.

Carman's best pitch is a hard fastball which tails near the plate and is especially tough on lefties. He throws it two-thirds of the time. His other pitch is an old-fashioned floppy curve. When the curve is working, Carman throws it up in the strike zone, so that it's still a strike when it finishes breaking. Unfortunately, the curve doesn't break once or twice a game, and when this happens it behaves like a batting practice fastball before (and after) it's hit. As a result, Carman has always been prone to the home run ball, and last year was no different, with 13 dingers allowed in only 86.2 innings.

Carman's problems with the curve are reflected in his truly bizarre stats versus lefty swingers last year. They batted only .175 off him (18-for-103), which indicates how tough he can be. But he made enough mistakes that the 18 hits included three doubles and seven homers. Carman will have to keep the ball in the park against lefties if he wants to stay in the majors.

HOLDING RUNNERS, FIELDING, HITTING:

Carman, a Steve Carlton-inspired martial arts devotee, has good balance, and ends his delivery in good shape to field the ball. His move to first is average, but he gets the ball to the plate rapidly, which helps discourage opposing runners. Long a joke as a hitter, Carman had his career year with the stick in 1990 going 3-for-11. After 204 lifetime at-bats, all he needs for a career cycle are the double, triple, and home run.

OVERALL:

Despite his problems last year, Carman held opposing hitters to a .218 average, which indicates that he's still very tough to hit. His problem is that he always seems to make one or two big mistakes. Carman may do well by going to the AL where the hitters don't know his stuff. Wherever he pitches, though, he'll have to throw more quality strikes.

Overall Statistics

	W	L	ERA	G	GS	Sv	IP	H	R	BB	SO	HR
1990	6	2	4.15	59	1	1	86.2	69	43	38	58	13
Career	53	52	4.06	312	102	10	883.1	805	436	359	581	107

How Often He Throws Strikes

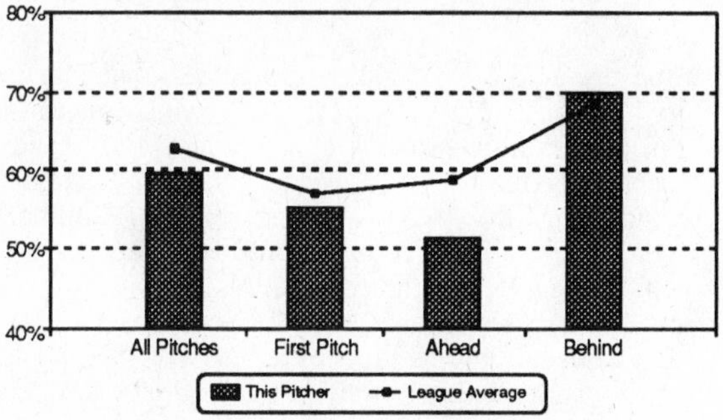

1990 Situational Stats

	W	L	ERA	Sv	IP		AB	H	HR	RBI	AVG
Home	5	0	3.50	0	43.2	LHB	103	18	7	22	.175
Road	1	2	4.81	1	43.0	RHB	213	51	6	24	.239
Day	3	1	4.11	0	30.2	Sc Pos	82	16	5	33	.195
Night	3	1	4.18	1	56.0	Clutch	63	11	1	6	.175

1990 Rankings (National League)

- 3rd in first batter efficiency (.149)
- Led the Phillies in hit batsmen (4) and holds (8)

PAT COMBS

Position: SP
Bats: L **Throws:** L
Ht: 6' 4" **Wt:** 205

Opening Day Age: 24
Born: 10/29/66 in Newport, RI
ML Seasons: 2

PITCHING:

In 16 of his 31 starts last year, Pat Combs averaged seven innings pitched, rang up an 8-2 record, and posted a 1.85 ERA. In his other 15 starts, he averaged under four innings per appearance, and went 2-8 with an ERA of 7.59. Watching him from one outing to the next, it was hard to believe this was the same fellow.

If you want to know which Pat Combs will show up, all you have to do is watch his curveball. If his left arm keeps trailing his body -- as if he were throwing Satchel Paige's old hesitation pitch -- then the ball will keep ending up high and outside, and he's going to have a tough outing. The problem is partly generated by Combs' change-up. He drags his arm slightly behind his body to deliver it, and in some games it seems that it triggers a flaw in his other pitches. When he avoids that problem, however, Combs can be a very effective pitcher.

At times last year, Combs lost confidence in his fastball and greatly reduced his use of it. Eventually he came up with a cut fastball, and the extra pitch helped make his regular fastball more effective. In September, he was throwing all five of his pitches (fastball, cut fastball, slider, curve, change) effectively, and as a result he rolled up four wins.

HOLDING RUNNERS, FIELDING, HITTING:

Combs gets the ball to the plate quickly, which helps keep baserunners close and gives his catcher a chance to throw out runners. While his follow-through does not leave him in good position to field the ball, he is a good athlete who can recover to make a play. His worst fault as a fielder is that he frequently will try to make a close play on a lead runner rather than take a sure out at first. As a hitter, Combs can put wood on the ball, and should improve as he gets more practice. He has no power, and is not a good bunter yet.

OVERALL:

Despite his .500 record and poor outings, Combs is on the way up. In his 1989 rise from Class A to Philadelphia, he simply overpowered those who faced him. Last season he had to make adjustments at the major league level; he did, and will continue to do so. Combs should move into the 12-15 win level in '91.

Overall Statistics

	W	L	ERA	G	GS	Sv	IP	H	R	BB	SO	HR
1990	10	10	4.07	32	31	0	183.1	179	90	86	108	12
Career	14	10	3.73	38	37	0	222.0	215	100	92	138	14

How Often He Throws Strikes

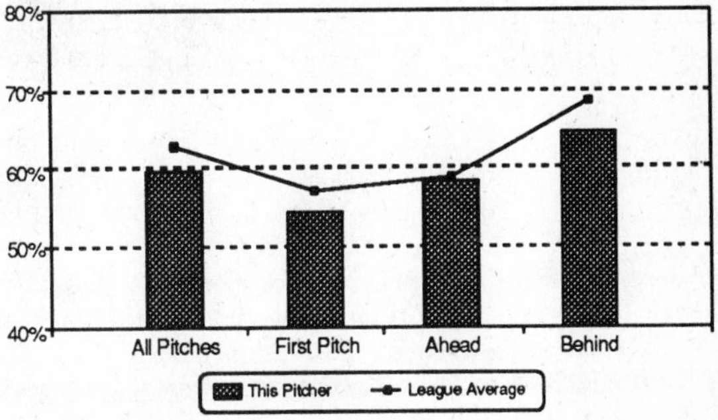

1990 Situational Stats

	W	L	ERA	Sv	IP		AB	H	HR	RBI	AVG
Home	4	2	3.05	0	82.2	LHB	135	35	5	20	.259
Road	6	8	4.92	0	100.2	RHB	561	144	7	61	.257
Day	3	4	3.66	0	46.2	Sc Pos	172	47	3	63	.273
Night	7	6	4.21	0	136.2	Clutch	45	9	1	2	.200

1990 Rankings (National League)

- 2nd in most walks allowed (86) and lowest stolen base percentage allowed (52.4%)
- 3rd lowest strikeout/walk ratio (1.3)
- 5th highest on-base average (.339)
- Led the Phillies in wins (10), games started (31), shutouts (2), innings (183.1), hits allowed (179), batters faced (800), walks allowed, hit batsmen (4), strikeouts (108), wild pitches (9), pitches thrown (2,962), runners caught stealing (10), lowest slugging percentage allowed (.375), groundball/flyball ratio (1.36), most run suppport per 9 innings (5.0), least HRs per 9 innings (.59), most strikeouts per 9 innings (5.3) and ERA at home (3.05)

HITTING:

Darren Daulton went into 1990 as an injury-diminished catcher with a .206 lifetime average. At the All-Star break last year, he was looking like the same old Daulton, with a .226 average and two homers. But then he rediscovered his bat, just in time to cash in on his impending free agency. Getting hot at exactly the right time, Daulton wound up with 12 homers, a .268 average -- and a three year, $6.7 million contract.

Daulton's emergence as a capable hitter was largely due to a sharp move by Manager Nick Leyva. Daulton is both patient and a good fastball hitter -- but, batting low in the order with weak hitters behind him, he often felt compelled to swing at bad breaking pitches in an effort to drive in runs. Right before the break, Leyva moved Daulton to the number-two spot in the batting order, and the difference was almost immediately noticeable. Coming up behind the base-stealing Lenny Dykstra, Daulton saw more fastballs. And batting high in the order, he wasn't afraid to take a walk.

Daulton went on to hit a nifty .317 (57-for-180) in the number-two spot. But that wasn't the only change that helped him. Daulton opened his stance a little more, which helped him pull the fastball better; the result was ten homers after the break. He also learned to slap outside breaking pitches to the opposite field, particularly against lefties. Daulton hit only one homer off a lefthander, but his .257 average against them helped him stay in the lineup.

BASERUNNING:

Daulton's recovery from knee problems show up clearly in the stolen base column. By studying pitchers and getting a good jump, he stole seven bases in eight attempts, easily the best performance of his career. He has slightly below-average speed, but a good first step. He's aggressive on the bases against weak outfield arms.

FIELDING:

In his second season as a regular, Daulton displayed reborn quickness at digging balls out of the dirt, and demonstrated an in-depth knowledge of both opposing hitters and his own pitchers. A hustling, aggressive backstop, Daulton will likely lead NL catchers in innings played again in '91.

OVERALL:

Daulton's mental game is clearly excellent. The question is whether his left knee can handle full-time duty again without weakening. And after playing five previous seasons without hitting higher than .225, he has to prove that his .268 average was no fluke.

DARREN DAULTON

Position: C
Bats: L **Throws:** R
Ht: 6' 2" **Wt:** 190

Opening Day Age: 29
Born: 1/3/62 in Arkansas City, KS
ML Seasons: 7

Overall Statistics

	G	AB	R	H	D	T	HR	RBI	SB	BB	SO	AVG
1990	143	459	62	123	30	1	12	57	7	72	72	.268
Career	472	1344	147	305	61	4	36	158	16	212	272	.227

Where He Hits the Ball

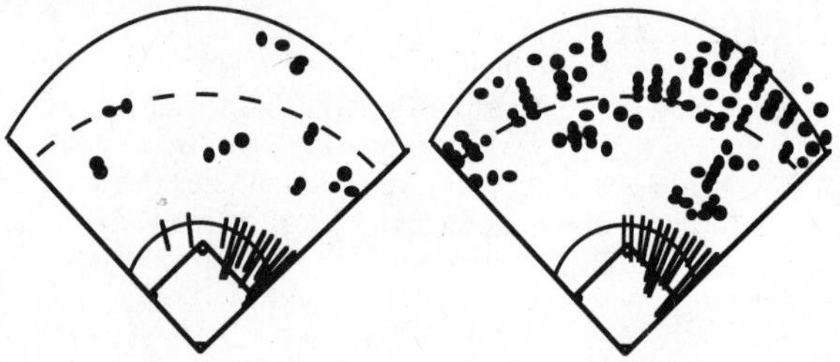

Vs. LHP Vs. RHP

1990 Situational Stats

	AB	H	HR	RBI	AVG		AB	H	HR	RBI	AVG
Home	224	56	5	24	.250	LHP	113	29	1	9	.257
Road	235	67	7	33	.285	RHP	346	94	11	48	.272
Day	108	32	3	18	.296	Sc Pos	117	33	3	42	.282
Night	351	91	9	39	.259	Clutch	85	22	3	13	.259

1990 Rankings (National League)

- 3rd highest percentage of runners caught stealing as a catcher (35.0%)
- 4th lowest batting average with the bases loaded (.091)
- 10th in walks (72)
- Led NL catchers in runs (62), doubles (30), walks, slugging percentage (.416), on-base average (.367), batting average (.272)/slugging percentage (.436)/on-base average (.363) vs. right-handed pitchers and batting average on the road (.285)

JOSE DeJESUS

Position: SP
Bats: R **Throws:** R
Ht: 6' 5" **Wt:** 175

Opening Day Age: 26
Born: 1/6/65 in Brooklyn, NY
ML Seasons: 3

PITCHING:

Jose DeJesus has the lowest cap brim and one of the liveliest fastballs in the National League. That's a frightening combination for opposing hitters, who are probably unsure if the wild young righthander even sees them. And with 73 walks allowed in 130 innings last year, maybe he doesn't.

After being obtained from Kansas City for Steve Jeltz before the '90 season, DeJesus began the year at AAA Scranton/Wilkes Barre. It was there that Phils' minor league instructor Jim Fregosi helped lighten the towering righthander's load. Fregosi told him to forget about the hitter, and DeJesus took the advice literally. He pulled his cap brim down so far that it hid his eyes, creating a tunnel between him and the catcher's wide glove. "Tunnel vision" is the right term: usually, DeJesus couldn't even remember what a given batter last did against him or even how he pitched him. With his new style, DeJesus was still wild, but he was also very tough to hit, holding opponents to a .211 batting average after his June recall to Philadelphia.

DeJesus has one great pitch: a high, hard fastball with a little sideways slide on the end. He can throw it to either corner. Unlike many dominant fastballs, it produces more fouls than swings and misses, and induces more ground balls than strikeouts. It was also more effective against lefties than it was against righties last year. DeJesus throws a slider, but as with the fastball, control is a problem. To help him cut down his walks and set up his fastball, DeJesus is scheduled to learn a change-up from Phils pitching coach Johnny Podres.

HOLDING RUNNERS, FIELDING, HITTING:

DeJesus is easy to steal on as he is slow delivering to the plate out of the stretch. His ungainly follow-through hampers him in fielding the ball. He has a good batting eye, and should become a passable hitter, although his bunting is awful.

OVERALL:

DeJesus' record last year was deceiving; he won nearly every game he had a chance to win. The Phils gave him four or more runs of support seven times, and he was 6-0 in those starts. In his other 15 starts, he received two or fewer runs to work with, and was 1-8. With his brim down, his fastball riding up and in, and better control, DeJesus should break double figures in wins in '91.

Overall Statistics

	W	L	ERA	G	GS	Sv	IP	H	R	BB	SO	HR
1990	7	8	3.74	22	22	0	130.0	97	63	73	87	10
Career	7	9	4.22	27	24	0	140.2	110	77	86	91	11

How Often He Throws Strikes

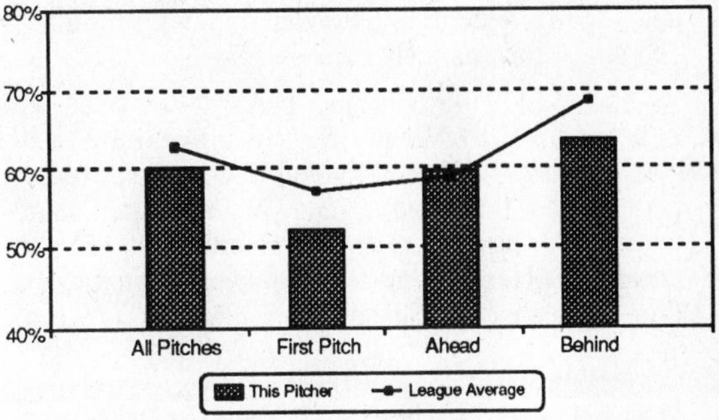

1990 Situational Stats

	W	L	ERA	Sv	IP		AB	H	HR	RBI	AVG
Home	2	5	3.68	0	71.0	LHB	300	57	4	20	.190
Road	5	3	3.81	0	59.0	RHB	159	40	6	28	.252
Day	2	3	6.04	0	28.1	Sc Pos	125	30	2	37	.240
Night	5	5	3.10	0	101.2	Clutch	38	7	0	1	.184

1990 Rankings (National League)

- → 4th lowest batting average allowed vs. left-handed batters (.190)
- → 8th most walks allowed (73)
- → Led the Phillies in lowest batting average allowed vs. left-handed batters

LENNY DYKSTRA

Position: CF
Bats: L **Throws:** L
Ht: 5'10" **Wt:** 170

Opening Day Age: 28
Born: 2/10/63 in Santa Ana, CA
ML Seasons: 6

HITTING:

Last year Lenny Dykstra fundamentally changed his approach to hitting, and became the best leadoff man in the National League. It began with a tiny adjustment. Hitting coach Denis Menke persuaded Dykstra to perch on the plate and point his back foot towards third. This opened his stance, corrected his balance, and improved his view of each pitch. In 1989, Dykstra lunged off an awkward back foot at breaking balls; in '90, he waited for the pitch and pounced, as able to single off an outside breaking pitch as he was to drive a inside fastball into the gap.

The other big change was Dykstra's built-up body. Having slumped late in the last three seasons, Dykstra premiered new muscles in '90 to conquer fatigue. The muscles turned out to be a springtime blessing because they enlarged Dykstra's ribs and chest, forcing him to cut down on his swing. Combined with his new, open stance, the abbreviated swing eliminated Dykstra's trademark fly balls.

Stronger and better balanced, Dykstra was over .400 as late as June 10. He hit over .400 all year long with men on base, and drew 14 intentional walks, which is very unusual for a leadoff man. While he tired somewhat as the season went on, Dykstra remained patient, hitting for placement more than power. As in the past, Dykstra declined in September.

BASERUNNING:

With his picture in the dictionary under the heading "full-throttle," Dykstra ran with the speed and brains to steal 33 bases in 38 attempts, and the hustle to cover his uniform with dirt by the middle of each game. The man is intense, to say the least.

FIELDING:

Dykstra has outstanding range, reads balls in front of him instantly and charges them confidently. His diving catches were electrifying. He is more tentative retreating, and plays deep to reduce the number of balls hit over his head. His quick release cannot make up for a weak arm, but he arrives at balls so quickly that few bases are lost due to this weakness.

OVERALL:

Dykstra once told a writer that he doesn't like baseball that much, but he loves to put on a show. He grimaces, grunts, pulls, tugs, fidgets, flexes -- and hits, runs, and fields too. Through accident, practice, and hard work, Dykstra became a fine leadoff man. He should remain a .280.-300 hitter, and one terrific exhibition.

Overall Statistics

	G	AB	R	H	D	T	HR	RBI	SB	BB	SO	AVG
1990	149	590	106	192	35	3	9	60	33	89	48	.325
Career	783	2628	432	739	159	23	43	232	166	307	290	.281

Where He Hits the Ball

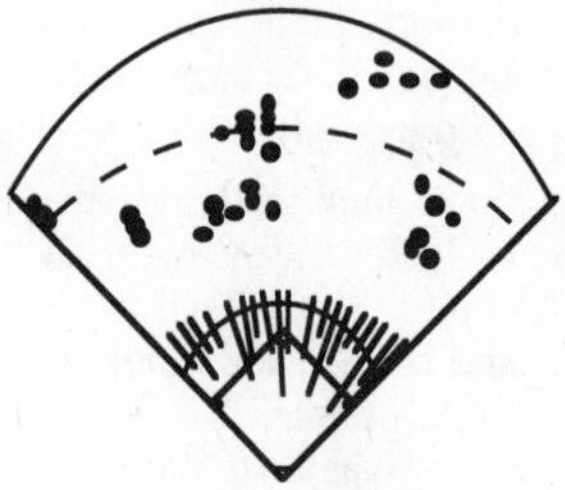

Vs. LHP

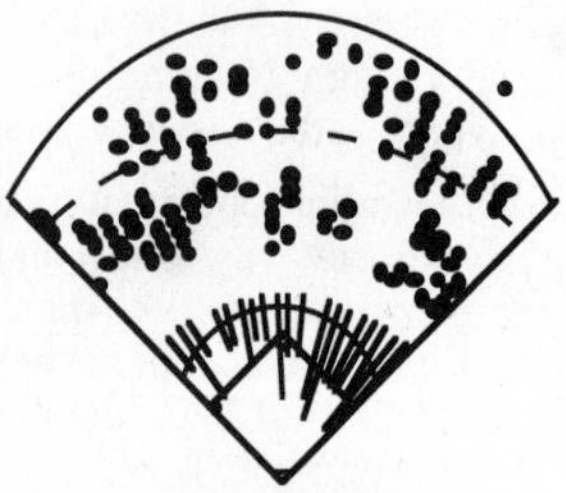

Vs. RHP

1990 Situational Stats

	AB	H	HR	RBI	AVG		AB	H	HR	RBI	AVG
Home	280	95	6	27	.339	LHP	200	58	1	17	.290
Road	310	97	3	33	.313	RHP	390	134	8	43	.344
Day	142	51	2	14	.359	Sc Pos	110	47	0	47	.427
Night	448	141	7	46	.315	Clutch	83	30	1	17	.361

1990 Rankings (National League)

- 1st in hits (192), times on base (288), on-base average (.418), batting average with runners in scoring position (.427), batting average vs. right-handed pitchers (.344), on-base average for a leadoff batter (.419), on-base average vs. right-handed pitchers (.435) and lowest percentage of swings that missed (5.9%)
- Led the Phillies in batting average (.325), at-bats (590), runs (106), hits, singles (145), doubles (35), total bases (260), stolen bases (33), walks (89), hit by pitch (7), pitches seen (2,551), plate appearances (691), slugging percentage (.441), on-base average, stolen base percentage (86.8%) and batting average with runners in scoring position

PITCHING:

Tommy Greene came to the Phils as part of last August's Dale Murphy deal with Atlanta. Pitcher Jeff Parrett went to the Braves in the trade, and at first, Greene took over Parrett's tenured position as an underachieving righthander with good stuff. But he pitched well late in the year, and the Phils think the 23-year-old Greene is more likely to develop than the 29-year old Parrett.

Greene's fortunes rise when his fastball does. Touted as a 90 MPH riser, the pitch was both slower (85-88) and straighter when Greene first arrived. In September he finally got it working, and the fastball had good movement against both left and right-handed batters. He won two of his last three starts, allowing 15 hits in 20 IP with a 2.70 ERA. Greene seemed more comfortable when he realized that his new park would hold high fastballs a lot better than the Launching Pad in Atlanta did.

Greene also throws a curve which either works beautifully or disastrously. He gets a lot of easy outs with it, but he also hangs far too many. To control the damage, Greene started throwing the curve on the outside corner, where his cripple pitches were more likely to stay in the park. He is also working on a change-up.

One problem the Phils face with Greene in 1991 is that he is out of options, and they will have to keep him on their roster or risk losing him. Unless he wins a rotation slot, he'll have to pitch in relief, an unfamiliar role for him. In the minors Greene made only one relief appearance in six seasons.

HOLDING RUNNERS, FIELDING, HITTING:

Greene's delivery is athletic, and he finishes it ready to pounce on the ball. A good fielder, he still needs to practice the quick-glove reaction plays that turf demands of a pitcher. Greene also has to work on holding runners. He is the Phils' best hitting pitcher, with some power and a good swing against most fastballs. He is good enough to be used as a pinch hitter.

OVERALL:

Greene may be handicapped by his lack of options. The pitching-poor Phils don't have 10 better pitchers, which could mean a forced course in relief pitching. But none of the four projected starters (Howell, Combs, DeJesus, and Mulholland) has ever had more than a few good months; if Greene gets hot, look for him to get his shot in the rotation.

TOMMY GREENE

Position: SP/RP
Bats: R **Throws:** R
Ht: 6' 5" **Wt:** 225

Opening Day Age: 24
Born: 4/6/67 in Lumberton, NC
ML Seasons: 2

Overall Statistics

	W	L	ERA	G	GS	Sv	IP	H	R	BB	SO	HR
1990	3	3	5.08	15	9	0	51.1	50	31	26	21	8
Career	4	5	4.75	19	13	0	77.2	72	43	32	38	13

How Often He Throws Strikes

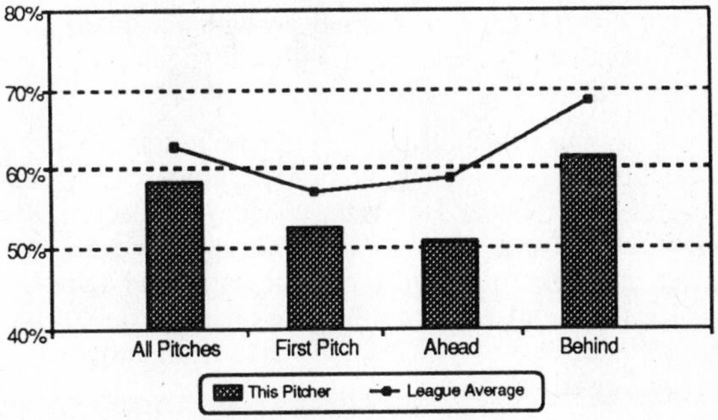

1990 Situational Stats

	W	L	ERA	Sv	IP		AB	H	HR	RBI	AVG
Home	2	2	4.86	0	33.1	LHB	105	33	4	14	.314
Road	1	1	5.50	0	18.0	RHB	90	17	4	13	.189
?											
Night	3	3	5.08	0	51.1	Clutch	3	0	0	0	.000

1990 Rankings (National League)

- Did not rank near the top or bottom in any category

CHARLIE HAYES

Position: 3B
Bats: R **Throws:** R
Ht: 6' 0" **Wt:** 190

Opening Day Age: 25
Born: 5/29/65 in Hattiesburg, MS
ML Seasons: 3

Overall Statistics

	G	AB	R	H	D	T	HR	RBI	SB	BB	SO	AVG
1990	152	561	56	145	20	0	10	57	4	28	91	.258
Career	246	876	82	224	35	1	18	100	7	39	144	.256

Where He Hits the Ball

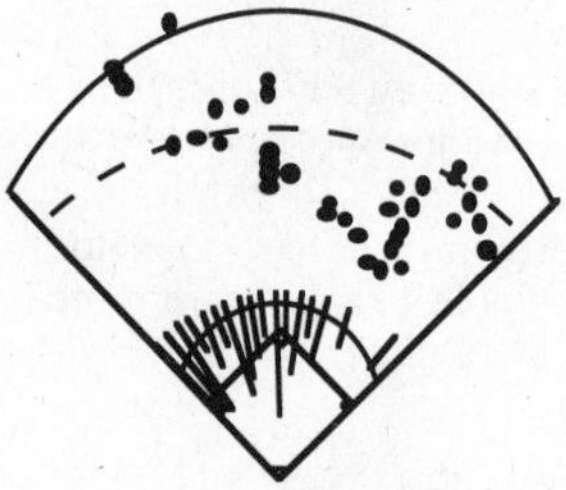

Vs. LHP

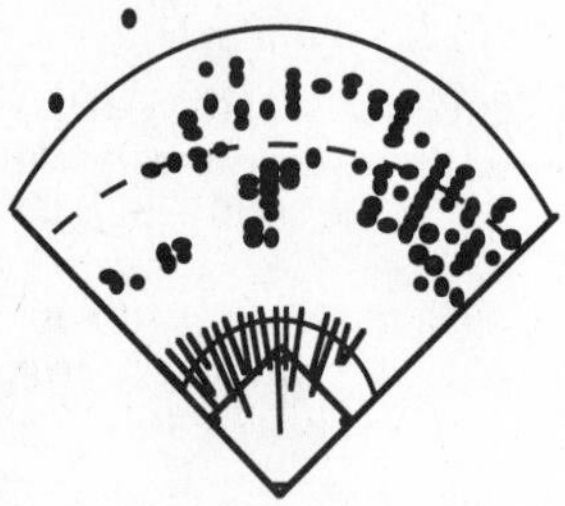

Vs. RHP

1990 Situational Stats

	AB	H	HR	RBI	AVG		AB	H	HR	RBI	AVG
Home	282	69	3	26	.245	LHP	193	57	5	22	.295
Road	279	76	7	31	.272	RHP	368	88	5	35	.239
Day	145	30	3	9	.207	Sc Pos	142	33	2	46	.232
Night	416	115	7	48	.276	Clutch	95	26	2	11	.274

1990 Rankings (National League)

- 1st in lowest slugging percentage vs. right-handed pitchers (.307)
- 4th lowest on-base average vs. right-handed pitchers (.277)
- 5th lowest batting average vs. right-handed pitchers (.239)
- 6th lowest on-base average (.293)
- 7th lowest batting average at home (.245)
- 9th lowest slugging percentage (.348)
- Led the Phillies in strikeouts (91), games (152), batting average vs. left-handed pitchers (.295) and slugging percentage vs. left-handed pitchers (.425)

HITTING:

After two seasons, the Phillies are beginning to wonder whether Charlie Hayes can develop into the 75-85 RBI man they projected him to become. The Phils gave Hayes a full shot last year, playing him in 152 games. But Hayes' batting average rose only one point, from .257 to .258. And though he logged nearly twice as many at-bats as he had in 1989, his home run output rose by only two (from eight to 10), and his RBI count increased by only 14 (from 43 to 57). Most discouraging of all, he got worse as the season went on. Hayes was hitting .280 at the All-Star break, but batted only .236 thereafter.

Last year Hayes began each at-bat with big strides and long uppercut swings, looking for a pitch to drive. It worked for half a season, but then opposing righthanders began to throw him cut fastballs, sliders, and change-ups early in the count. Hayes refused to cut down on his swing and go with the pitch, and became an easy out. He hit only .239 against righties last year.

Hayes has some hitting skills. In the minors he had a couple of .300 seasons, and he was always a dependable run producer. He has the talent to still become the number-five or six hitter the Phillies envisioned. But at this point he's still too much of a wild swinger. He'll have to learn to hit to the opposite field more often, instead of whaling away at the ball until he has two strikes on him.

BASERUNNING:

Hayes is adept at both take-out and evasive slides. He has only average speed, and takes a while to get up a head of steam. He's not much of a base stealing threat, with only four in eight attempts last year.

FIELDING:

Hayes showed potential in 1989, and long stretches of excellence in 1990. He has a howitzer arm, and good instincts as well. He may be the best in the majors on balls hit to his right. He is not as good on balls toward the shortstop hole, but if he can overcome a few of his careless mistakes, he'll challenge for a Gold Glove.

OVERALL:

Hayes' defensive improvement gives him a little time to work on his hitting. Right now, his glove is good enough to guarantee him a job. If he can improve his hitting as much as he has his fielding, he could become an All Star. If not, he may have Dave Hollins nipping at his heels.

HITTING:

Von Hayes suffered from two maladies last year: an artificial widening of the plate and a severely battered foot. Both ailments were self-inflicted, and both did a lot of damage. Last year Hayes saw his production drop in doubles (from 27 to 14), homers (from 26 to 17), RBI (from 78 to 73) and runs scored (from 93 to 70). He continued to be a productive performer, but not up to his past standards.

Hayes has always been a very selective hitter, taking numerous pitches and drawing a lot of walks. Last year, however, he took more called third strikes than ever before. Reverting to his old ways, Hayes blamed the umpires for bad calls, both on the field and in the newspapers. Finally, in mid-season, the Phillies had to tell him to stop arguing with umpires before it ruined his career.

A fine fastball hitter, Hayes has always been able to prolong an at-bat until he got the heater. Last year, with Ricky Jordan batting .241 behind him, the fastballs didn't come. Compounding his misery, Hayes kept fouling pitches off his foot and leg causing him to miss some 30 games. Pitchers hurt Hayes by challenging him high and inside. Over-anxious and not 100 percent physically, Hayes was unable to lay off these pitches as he had before.

Finally, the Phils traded for Dale Murphy, and Hayes was a benefactor; he started getting some fastballs over the plate again. From June 4 to August 4, Hayes hit one homer in 113 at-bats. After Murphy arrived in Philadelphia, Hayes hit four homers in a week, and added three more within a month.

BASERUNNING:

Hayes is still fast, though the days when he could steal 48 bases are long gone. He stole only 16 last year, but is still capable of 20 or more. He's an excellent baserunner, smarter and more effective than any Phillie except Lenny Dykstra. He always slides hard, and broke up more double plays than anyone on the team.

FIELDING:

Hayes hates playing left field where he played last year for the first time since 1987. He played well there, however, and will give the Phils good speed and range in left, and the arm of a right fielder wherever he plays.

OVERALL:

Over the winter, Hayes found himself in a familiar position -- as trade bait. Whether he remains in Philadelphia or not, he is smart enough -- and young enough at 32 -- to recapture most, if not all, of his past form.

VON HAYES

Position: RF/LF
Bats: L **Throws:** R
Ht: 6' 5" **Wt:** 180

Opening Day Age: 32
Born: 8/31/58 in Stockton, CA
ML Seasons: 10

Overall Statistics

	G	AB	R	H	D	T	HR	RBI	SB	BB	SO	AVG
1990	129	467	70	122	14	3	17	73	16	87	81	.261
Career	1324	4658	689	1269	250	34	139	646	233	644	708	.272

Where He Hits the Ball

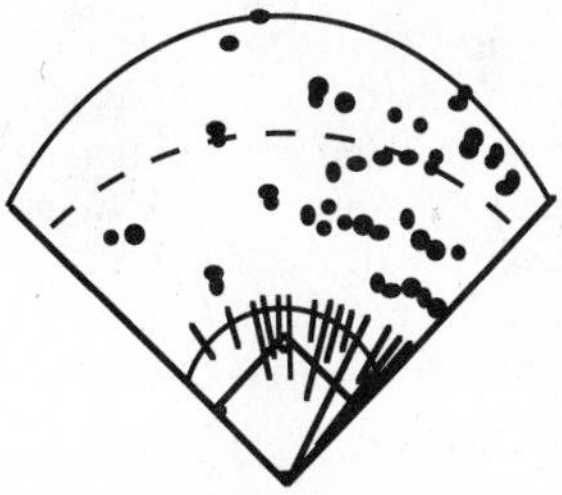

Vs. LHP

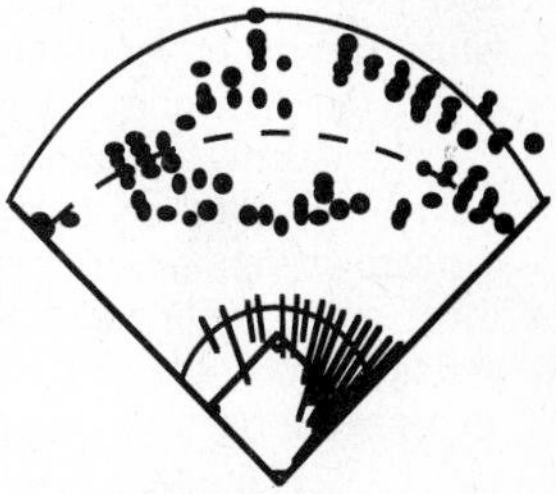

Vs. RHP

1990 Situational Stats

	AB	H	HR	RBI	AVG		AB	H	HR	RBI	AVG
Home	203	56	10	36	.276	LHP	179	49	6	28	.274
Road	264	66	7	37	.250	RHP	288	73	11	45	.253
Day	113	33	7	26	.292	Sc Pos	134	34	2	49	.254
Night	354	89	10	47	.251	Clutch	72	22	3	9	.306

1990 Rankings (National League)

- 5th in sacrifice flies (10) and walks (87)
- 7th in intentional walks (16) and pitches seen per plate appearance (3.92)
- Led the Phillies in home runs (17), RBIs (73), sacrifice flies, caught stealing (7), intentional walks, HR frequency (27.5 ABs per HR) and most pitches seen per plate appearance
- Led NL right fielders in walks, on-base average (.375), most pitches seen per plate appearance and highest percentage of pitches taken (59.9%)

DAVE HOLLINS

Position: 3B
Bats: B **Throws:** R
Ht: 6' 1" **Wt:** 195

Opening Day Age: 24
Born: 5/25/66 in Buffalo, NY
ML Seasons: 1

Overall Statistics

	G	AB	R	H	D	T	HR	RBI	SB	BB	SO	AVG
1990	72	114	14	21	0	0	5	15	0	10	28	.184
Career	72	114	14	21	0	0	5	15	0	10	28	.184

Where He Hits the Ball

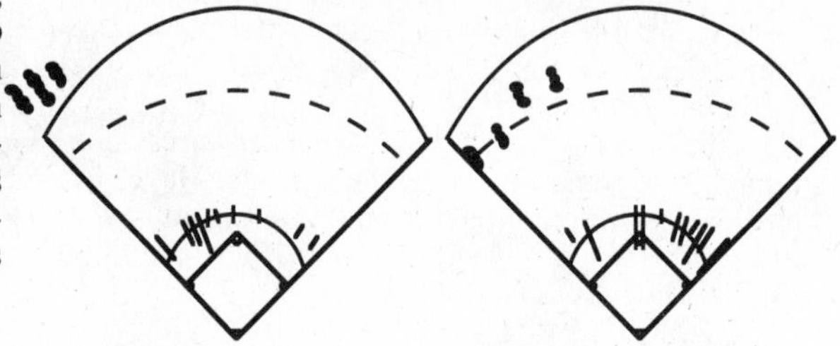

1990 Situational Stats

	AB	H	HR	RBI	AVG		AB	H	HR	RBI	AVG
Home	58	7	2	6	.121	LHP	46	8	3	7	.174
Road	56	14	3	9	.250	RHP	68	13	2	8	.191
Day	36	7	2	5	.194	Sc Pos	22	8	2	11	.364
Night	78	14	3	10	.179	Clutch	22	4	0	2	.182

1990 Rankings (National League)

➟ Did not rank near the top or bottom in any category

HITTING:

Plucked off the Padres roster during the winter draft, Dave Hollins showed the Phils enough bat and glove to etch his name into their future plans. Hollins batted only .184 in 114 scattered at-bats last year, but his five homers were a hopeful sign.

Throughout his career as a Padres' farmhand, Hollins hit for high averages with line drive power and a ton of walks. He displayed all three while leading the Mexican winter league in batting average and on-base percentage before the 1990 season. But last year Hollins surprised the Phils with his power. His five homers included three as a pinch hitter, and he had the best home run rate of any Phillie with 100+ plate appearances. He became the first Phillie to hit pinch hit home runs from both sides of the plate.

A switch-hitter, Hollins showed more power against lefties but reached base more often against righties, while hitting under .200 against both. He likes to crowd the plate and is a good fastball hitter who can extend his arms to smack a hard one to right or pull an inside pitch. Pitchers had their greatest success throwing him change-ups and breaking balls when he was ahead in the count and looking for a fastball. A selective hitter up until last year, Hollins should correct his over-eagerness with more experience.

BASERUNNING:

Hollins is smart, aggressive and runs well. Once he learns the NL's pitchers, catchers, and outfielders, he will be stealing 10-15 bases and taking near that many extra bases. Baserunning is a contact sport for Hollins, and he will probably have many more highlight-type collisions next year.

FIELDING:

On the quick plastic grass at the Vet, third baseman Hollins' footwork was slow at first, but he improved it to adequate. He has good hands, goes well to his left, and has a strong enough arm to make up for a release that needs to be smoothed out. He also impressed the Phils at first base, where his footwork and instincts seemed more natural than at his life-long position, third.

OVERALL:

Hollins may well start the season at AAA Scranton to get experience, but his good range of skills will get him back to the majors. He could be platooning at first with John Kruk by early June, would play third if Charlie Hayes were traded, and should be competing for Hayes' job by '92.

KEN HOWELL

Position: SP
Bats: R **Throws:** R
Ht: 6' 3" **Wt:** 228

Opening Day Age: 30
Born: 11/28/60 in Detroit, MI
ML Seasons: 7

Overall Statistics

	W	L	ERA	G	GS	Sv	IP	H	R	BB	SO	HR
1990	8	7	4.64	18	18	0	106.2	106	60	49	70	12
Career	38	48	3.95	245	54	31	613.1	534	296	275	549	46

How Often He Throws Strikes

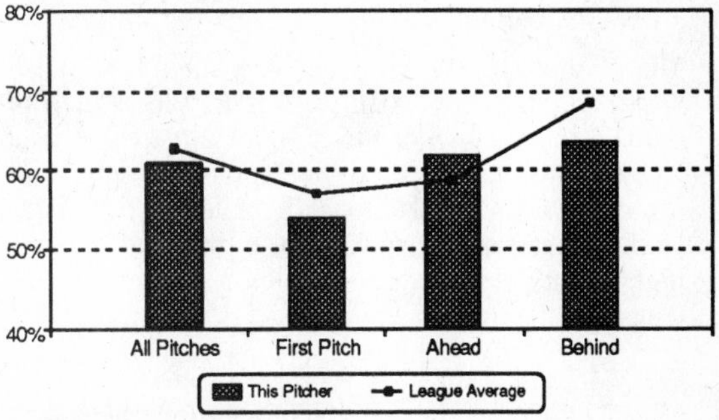

1990 Situational Stats

	W	L	ERA	Sv	IP		AB	H	HR	RBI	AVG
Home	4	4	5.43	0	61.1	LHB	257	77	7	43	.300
Road	4	3	3.57	0	45.1	RHB	150	29	5	10	.193
Day	2	0	3.57	0	17.2	Sc Pos	96	23	4	40	.240
Night	6	7	4.85	0	89.0	Clutch	34	7	2	3	.206

1990 Rankings (National League)

- 10th in wild pitches (8)
- Led the Phillies in sacrifice bunts as a hitter (8) and winning percentage (.533)

PITCHING:

In 1989, the oft-injured Ken Howell finally showed the talent that had made him the main man in trades involving Eddie Murray and Phil Bradley. In 1990, he showed that his physical problems were as real and recurring as his abilities.

The Phils made Howell their rotation anchor in 1990, and for the season's first two months, he pitched like one. Starting May 11, he averaged seven innings per start for eight games, winning six of them. At that point his record was a splendid 8-3, and he seemed capable of a 20-win season. Long a potential star, Howell had never won more than 12 games in a season.

But then Howell's right shoulder, which underwent surgery in 1988, wore down and began to plague him again. His soreness, located in the tendons which connect the arm to the shoulder in the bottom of his armpit, affected his mechanics. Howell began to use a bigger leg kick to take some of the burden from his arm. Unfortunately, that straightened and slowed his two money pitches, his fastball and slider, and Howell gave up more home runs than in '89 in half as many innings.

With the problems continuing, Howell's ERA rose to 4.64 -- more than a run higher than in 1989 -- and he finally had to go on the shelf after making only 18 starts. The doctors were unable to prescribe anything other than rest, so they gave him most of July off, and then shut him down for the year in August.

HOLDING RUNNERS, FIELDING, HITTING:

Howell's bulk makes him a slow-footed fielder. He frequently double-clutches the ball, and he often uses a wind-up to throw out bunters. His big leg kick gives runners a great lead and jump. From the stretch, however, he has a good move and swift delivery. Howell hit two doubles last year, one erased by rain, and shamed Nelson Santovenia by stealing a base. But he's no real threat at bat.

OVERALL:

Howell was off to a fine start last year before injuries derailed him, and that gives the Phillies hope. A full spring training should help him ease his shoulder into shape and shed the 15 extra pounds he carried in '90. He is a question mark as a number-one starter, but if he's healthy, he'll give the Phils a strong member of the rotation.

RICKY JORDAN

Position: 1B
Bats: R **Throws:** R
Ht: 6' 3" **Wt:** 210

Opening Day Age: 25
Born: 5/26/65 in Richmond, CA
ML Seasons: 3

Overall Statistics

	G	AB	R	H	D	T	HR	RBI	SB	BB	SO	AVG
1990	92	324	32	78	21	0	5	44	2	13	39	.241
Career	305	1120	136	311	58	4	28	162	7	43	140	.278

Where He Hits the Ball

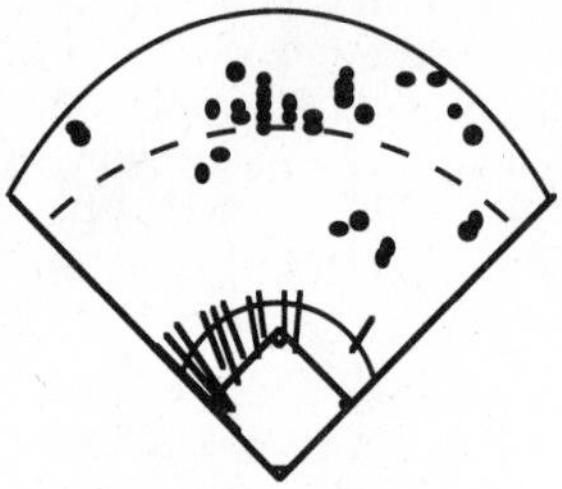

Vs. LHP

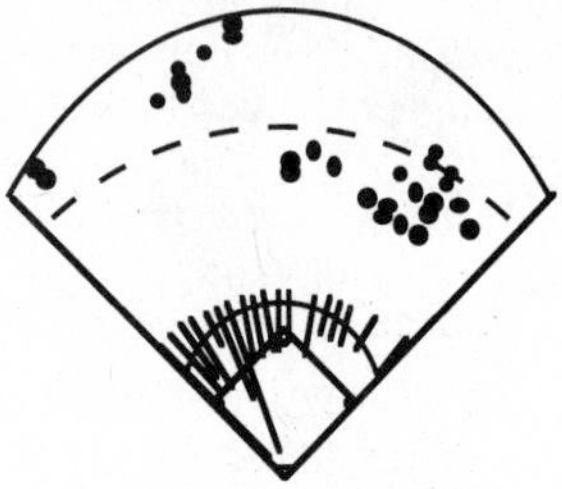

Vs. RHP

1990 Situational Stats

	AB	H	HR	RBI	AVG		AB	H	HR	RBI	AVG
Home	145	34	2	18	.234	LHP	118	29	2	12	.246
Road	179	44	3	26	.246	RHP	206	49	3	32	.238
Day	92	23	3	18	.250	Sc Pos	95	21	1	34	.221
Night	232	55	2	26	.237	Clutch	45	14	1	9	.311

1990 Rankings (National League)

- 1st in lowest slugging percentage while batting cleanup hitter (.375)
- Led the Phillies in batting average with the bases loaded (.333)

HITTING:

In 1990, Ricky Jordan lost his grip, sending more bats flying into the stands than baseballs. Plagued by finger and wrist injuries, Jordan couldn't keep his bottom hand anchored on the bat, and actually finished several swings by accidentally hurling his bat into the third base stands. A first baseman who puts Mr. Louisville into the seats more often than Mr. Spalding will get benched, as Jordan was, for John Kruk and Carmelo Martinez.

Jordan's problem is worse than embarrassing; it threatens his career. His weak grip took away his power and diminished his line drive stroke. A firm believer that major league hitters should drive every pitch and never walk, Jordan flexes, leans forward, and starts his bat early on most pitches, relying on his wrists to channel momentum. In 1990, his wrists weren't driving the ball anywhere. Instead, he became a weak fly ball hitter.

The Phillies blame Jordan's weakened bat on his wrists and note that he hit well in the second half of both 1988 and '89 when they were full strength. But Jordan's lack of plate discipline hurts him as much as his sore wrists do. National League pitchers have learned that Jordan swings even if the pitch is a foot high or outside or aimed at the knob of his bat. Even when healthy, Jordan gets himself out far too easily.

BASERUNNING:

Slowed by a nagging knee injury, Jordan became a station to station runner, which he will remain. He stole two bases in two attempts last year, but that was due to the element of surprise.

FIELDING:

Jordan's glove work demonstrated his ability to learn last season. He had always been handcuffed even by routine one-hop throws, but Jordan was drilled with low and bouncing throws all spring, and made several fine grabs during the season. He still has trouble judging when to take charge on balls to his right, making the pitcher's ability to cover first crucial, and he has a weak and inaccurate arm.

OVERALL:

Though injuries obviously hampered him last year, it's getting to be put-up-or-shut-up time for Jordan. The Phillies will give him a chance to show improvement this year, but he'll have to do it early. A hot-weather, late- season hitter, Jordan could establish his role on the team by the All-Star break. That might be too late, unless he gets his act together sooner.

HITTING:

A very consistent hitter, John Kruk batted exactly his lifetime average -- .291 -- in 1990. Kruk has now hit between .291 and .313 in four of his five seasons. His on-base percentages have been .403, .406, .369, .374 and .386. The last three years, he's belted nine, eight and seven homers, and scored 54, 53 and 52 runs. With Kruk, you pretty much know what you're going to get.

An opposite-field hitter who hit most of his '89 home runs to left center, Kruk looks for pitches up and away to drive, continually going the other way. Opposing pitchers have adjusted by routinely jamming him, but Kruk seldom turns and pulls an inside pitch for power. He had a 20-homer, 91-RBI year in 1987, but that appears to have been an accident of that lively-ball year. He seems to feel he's better going the other way, and it's hard to knock the results. Kruk adds to his value by getting on base frequently via the walk. But not the HBP: with his off-the-plate hitting style, Kruk has never been hit by a pitch in 634 major league games.

Kruk has had some good seasons against left-handed pitching in the past, but last year he batted nearly 100 points higher against righties. He hits for a little power against righties, but it's doubles and triples power, not the home run power you expect from a first baseman. Home runs are not his game; getting on base is.

BASERUNNING:

Kruk is an aggressive runner with decent straight-ahead speed. He loves to steal, but has to pick his spots. He was caught four out of his first six attempts last year. Then he stole three bases on Rich Gedman, and picked on other weak-armed catchers for eight steals in his last nine attempts.

FIELDING

Kruk is the Phils' best defensive left fielder and first baseman, and is usable in right. Despite his stocky body, he has good range in the outfield, and gets rid of the ball so quickly that he often prevents extra-base hits. At first base, he has everything except height.

OVERALL:

Kruk is a perfect symbol for the Phils as a whole: he reaches base, has some speed and is versatile, but lacks power. His on-base ability gives him offensive value, but he will probably be no more than a very valuable platoon player for the Phillies this year. With Ricky Jordan and now Wes Chamberlain around, he will likely be benched against most lefties.

JOHN KRUK

Position: LF/1B/RF
Bats: L **Throws:** L
Ht: 5'10" **Wt:** 195
Opening Day Age: 30
Born: 2/9/61 in Charleston, WV
ML Seasons: 5

Overall Statistics

	G	AB	R	H	D	T	HR	RBI	SB	BB	SO	AVG
1990	142	443	52	129	25	8	7	67	10	69	70	.291
Career	634	1903	264	553	85	19	48	284	38	311	342	.291

Where He Hits the Ball

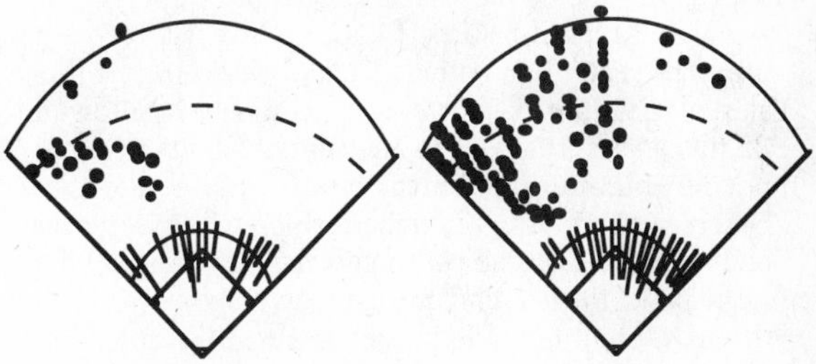

1990 Situational Stats

	AB	H	HR	RBI	AVG		AB	H	HR	RBI	AVG
Home	220	70	2	37	.318	LHP	117	26	2	15	.222
Road	223	59	5	30	.265	RHP	326	103	5	52	.316
Day	108	32	2	15	.296	Sc Pos	131	39	3	56	.298
Night	335	97	5	52	.290	Clutch	71	19	2	14	.268

1990 Rankings (National League)

- 3rd in on-base average vs. right-handed pitchers (.415)
- 5th lowest percentage of runs scored per time reached base (26.3%)
- 6th in triples (8)
- 7th in intentional walks (16) and on-base average (.386)
- Led the Phillies in triples, intentional walks and groundball/flyball ratio (1.92)
- Led NL left fielders in intentional walks, GDPs (11), on-base average vs. right-handed pitchers and batting average at home (.318)

ROGER McDOWELL

Position: RP
Bats: R **Throws:** R
Ht: 6' 1" **Wt:** 185

Opening Day Age: 30
Born: 12/21/60 in Cincinnati, OH
ML Seasons: 6

PITCHING:

In 1989, Roger McDowell was traded from the Mets, whose infield defense was poor, to the Phillies, a team whose infield was slightly above-average. The improved defense and a little luck made McDowell a tremendous stopper for the Phils. In 44 appearances after the trade, McDowell recorded 19 saves and a 1.11 ERA.

Unfortunately for him, McDowell's Philadelphia experience has exactly paralleled that of Lenny Dykstra, who came along with him from the Mets in the '89 Juan Samuel deal. The ground balls for each player found gloves consistently in 1989; in 1990 their grounders found holes. For much of last year, McDowell pitched about the same as he had in 1989. A sinker-baller, he depends on good infield defense, and didn't get nearly as much of it last year.

McDowell started the season reasonably well, recording eight saves in his first 14 appearances and having only one really bad outing. Then on May 16, the hits started to fall. In his next nine appearances he allowed 25 hits and eight walks in 12 innings; hitters ravaged not only his offerings, but his confidence. Pressing, he began overthrowing his sinker, which made it fly flat and straight. Then he overcompensated, bringing his right hand further and further down in his follow-through, but that made him miss the strike zone. He had to use his fastball too much, trying to run it in on hitters. Instead, it often was hit hard.

By the first week of June, McDowell had lost his position as stopper to a rotating group that included Darrel Akerfelds and eventually Joe Boever. Ironically enough, the demotion helped McDowell recover. Without the constant pressure of save situations, he regained his sinker, and his confidence as well. When restored to his stopper post in September, he saved five games with a 2.77 ERA.

HOLDING RUNNERS, FIELDING, HITTING:

McDowell is a heady fielder with a good sense of where to make plays on sacrifice bunts. However, he is erratic, with eight errors over the last two seasons. His move to first is only average. He's a fine hitter for a pitcher and can bunt when called upon, which is rare.

OVERALL:

McDowell's first half displays the perils of a sinker ball stopper on a team whose infield is average and declining. McDowell needs slick-fielding John Kruk at first and rapid improvement from Mickey Morandini at second to record a good season.

Overall Statistics

	W	L	ERA	G	GS	Sv	IP	H	R	BB	SO	HR
1990	6	8	3.86	72	0	22	86.1	92	41	35	39	2
Career	42	40	3.05	396	2	125	611.1	561	240	211	299	26

How Often He Throws Strikes

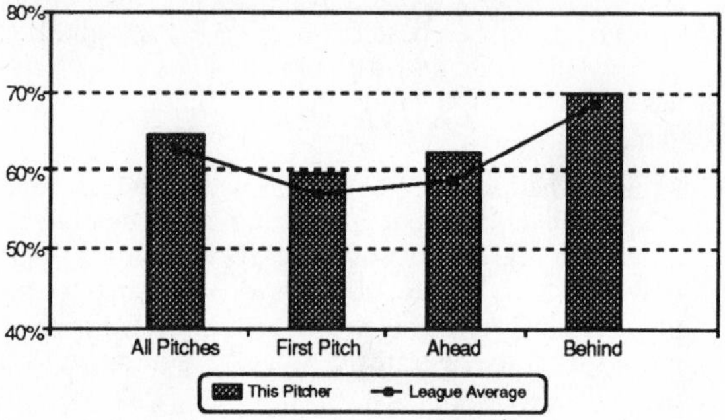

1990 Situational Stats

	W	L	ERA	Sv	IP		AB	H	HR	RBI	AVG
Home	3	4	5.40	10	36.2	LHB	183	60	2	35	.328
Road	3	4	2.72	12	49.2	RHB	139	32	0	15	.230
Day	2	2	1.38	7	26.0	Sc Pos	115	37	1	49	.322
Night	4	6	4.92	15	60.1	Clutch	186	61	1	36	.328

1990 Rankings (National League)

- 1st in games finished (60) and errors by a pitcher (5)
- 4th in games pitched (72)
- 5th in save opportunities (28), lowest save percentage (78.6%) and blown saves (6)
- Led the Phillies in games pitched, saves (22), games finished (60), GDPs induced (16), save opportunities, blown saves and most GDPs induced per GDP situation (17.0%)

MICKEY MORANDINI

Position: 2B
Bats: L **Throws:** R
Ht: 5'11" **Wt:** 170

Opening Day Age: 24
Born: 4/22/66 in Kittanning, PA
ML Seasons: 1

Overall Statistics

	G	AB	R	H	D	T	HR	RBI	SB	BB	SO	AVG
1990	25	79	9	19	4	0	1	3	3	6	19	.241
Career	25	79	9	19	4	0	1	3	3	6	19	.241

Where He Hits the Ball

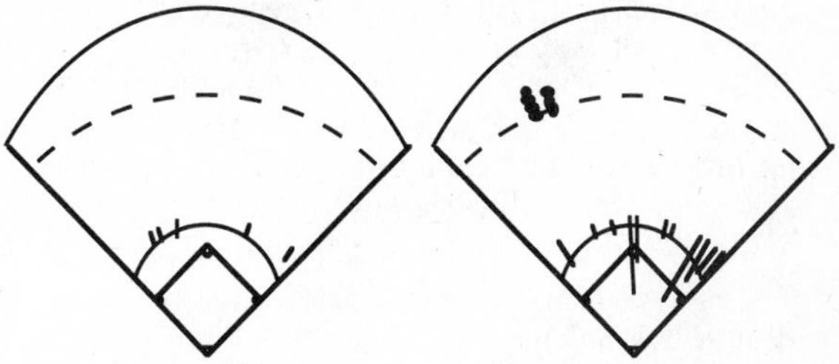

Vs. LHP **Vs. RHP**

1990 Situational Stats

	AB	H	HR	RBI	AVG		AB	H	HR	RBI	AVG
Home	47	14	1	3	.298	LHP	15	2	0	0	.133
Road	32	5	0	0	.156	RHP	64	17	1	3	.266
Day	21	6	0	0	.286	Sc Pos	13	3	0	2	.231
Night	58	13	1	3	.224	Clutch	12	5	0	0	.417

1990 Rankings (National League)

- Did not rank near the top or bottom in any category

HITTING:

When the Phillies traded Tom Herr to the Mets, they believed they were doing more than making a trade for two prospects. They were also exchanging an old Herr for a young one in Mickey Morandini, the second baseman they recalled from AAA Scranton/Wilkes-Barre. A lanky left-handed spray hitter who bunts well, Morandini excels at going with the pitch to move runners, and found enough gaps to hit .338 in A and AA ball in 1989. A member of the 1988 Olympic team, he walks frequently, and his power comes when he slices the ball down the lines or slaps it into the gaps for extra bases. Those are skills reminiscent of . . . Tommy Herr.

Unfortunately for the Phils, Morandini is not yet at Herr's level. He struck out in 16 percent of his plate appearances at AAA Scranton, and 22 percent of the time in 25 late-season major league games; that's twice as often as the young Herr, and about as often as the early Juan Samuel.

Morandini was overmatched initially both in AAA and the majors in '90. Halfway through the minor league season, he was hitting .223 with seven doubles and five stolen bases; in the second half he batted .296 with 17 doubles and 11 steals. The improvement came as Morandini learned to keep his weight back on curves and sliders, and to time fastballs and change-ups. In 87 major league plate appearances, Morandini was overmatched when faced with high inside fastballs. That's why he skipped winter ball to enroll in a strength-building program. He wants to introduce those pitches to the left field line this season.

BASERUNNING:

Morandini's first step is only fair, but he is swift, gets a good lead, and studies catchers and pitchers. He should pilfer 18-25 bases in '91. He was three-for-three for the Phils last September.

FIELDING:

Like most converted shortstops, Morandini has a strong arm, and ranges to his right better than to his left. Turning the double play from the second base side is still unfamiliar to him, and he needs to practice tracking down and taking charge of short fly balls. Morandini will soon be a fine second baseman, but in 1991, he'll still be learning.

OVERALL:

Morandini will bat eighth this year, and the Phils will be patient, not expecting him to be another Tom Herr just yet. They'll rest him against tough lefties for awhile, but Morandini should soon show the ability to play every day.

TERRY MULHOLLAND

Position: SP/RP
Bats: R **Throws:** L
Ht: 6' 3" **Wt:** 200

Opening Day Age: 28
Born: 3/9/63 in Uniontown, PA
ML Seasons: 4

PITCHING:

On August 15, Terry Mulholland turned around his season and perhaps his career when he threw a no-hitter against his old teammates, the San Francisco Giants. Mulholland didn't rest on his no-hit laurels. In his last ten starts, he allowed only 50 hits and 16 walks with a 1.99 ERA in 77 innings. Mulholland finished the year with a record of only 9-10, but his ERA was a fine 3.34. Going into 1990, he'd had a career record of 7-15 with a 4.67 ERA.

It was a big comeback from the first part of the 1990 season when Mulholland was first ineffective and then needed to go on the disabled list to rest his arm. When he returned from the DL, Mulholland possessed both greater strength and better mechanics; he also developed a better relationship with his catcher, Darren Daulton. While injured, Mulholland used Gus Hoefling's martial arts exercise program, and when he returned, he had not only had recovered his old velocity, but was throwing even harder. Even his slider had new bite. Mulholland's conditioning also enhanced his stamina, which had previously not gotten him past the sixth inning very often. He averaged nearly eight innings per start over his last ten outings.

A ground ball pitcher, Mulholland relies mostly on his sinking fastball and slider. He needs good location to be effective, and his control improved last year when he broke a longstanding habit of looking away from the plate during his delivery. Locking his eyes and concentration on his catcher, he was able to throw the fastball where he wanted it. Mulholland worked beautifully with Daulton, both on his mechanics and his game preparation. He gets ready for a game by planning in depth, more like a football coach than a pitcher.

HOLDING RUNNERS, FIELDING, HITTING:

Mulholland has a quick delivery to the plate, and a quick pickoff move. But his new policy of concentrating his attention on the hitter makes it easier to get a good jump on him. He leaves himself in good position to field, but has hard hands and an uncertain glove. He can't hit, run, or bunt, even at a pitcher's level of skill.

OVERALL:

In re-signing Darren Daulton, the Phils ensured that Mulholland would again work with his favorite battery-mate. A ground ball, non-strikeout pitcher on a team with average defense and hitting, Mulholland has the potential to win 12-to-15 games, but he'll need good support from his teammates both at the plate and in the field.

Overall Statistics

	W	L	ERA	G	GS	Sv	IP	H	R	BB	SO	HR
1990	9	10	3.34	33	26	0	180.2	172	78	42	75	15
Career	16	25	4.06	82	60	0	396.2	410	197	120	186	29

How Often He Throws Strikes

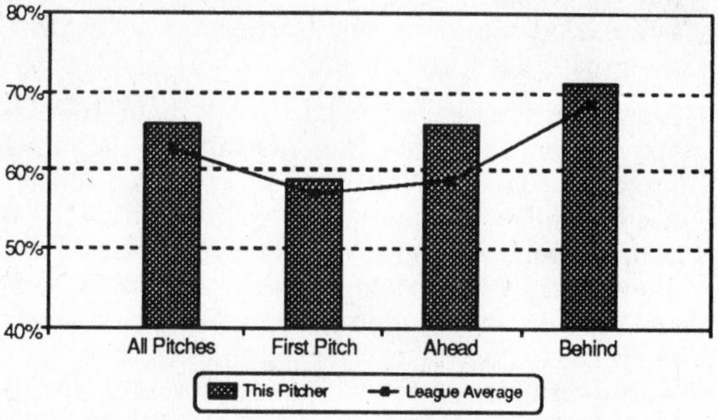

1990 Situational Stats

	W	L	ERA	Sv	IP		AB	H	HR	RBI	AVG
Home	3	4	2.66	0	71.0	LHB	101	28	2	12	.277
Road	6	6	3.78	0	109.2	RHB	582	144	13	61	.247
Day	2	5	4.22	0	42.2	Sc Pos	160	35	2	56	.219
Night	7	5	3.07	0	138.0	Clutch	56	16	2	5	.286

1990 Rankings (National League)

- 1st lowest stolen base percentage allowed (50.0%)
- 2nd least strikeouts per 9 innings (3.7)
- 4th least pitches thrown per batter (3.33)
- Led the Phillies in ERA (3.34), complete games (6), home runs allowed (15), GDPs induced (16), strikeout/walks ratio (1.8), lowest batting average allowed (.252), lowest on-base average allowed (.292), lowest stolen base percentage allowed, least pitches thrown per batter, most GDPs induced per 9 innings (.80) and lowest batting average allowed with runners in scoring position (.219)

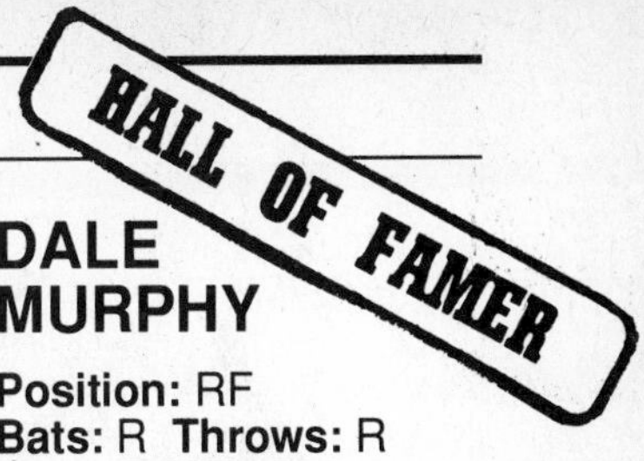

DALE MURPHY

Position: RF
Bats: R **Throws:** R
Ht: 6' 4" **Wt:** 215

Opening Day Age: 35
Born: 3/12/56 in Portland, OR
ML Seasons: 15

Overall Statistics

	G	AB	R	H	D	T	HR	RBI	SB	BB	SO	AVG
1990	154	563	60	138	23	1	24	83	9	61	130	.245
Career	1983	7312	1125	1958	315	38	378	1171	160	932	1627	.268

Where He Hits the Ball

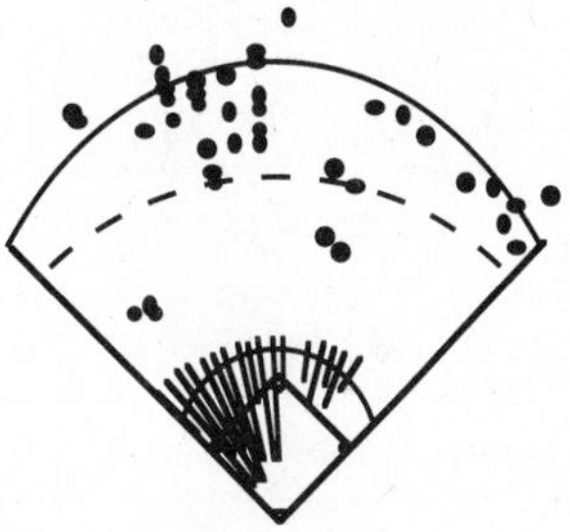

Vs. LHP

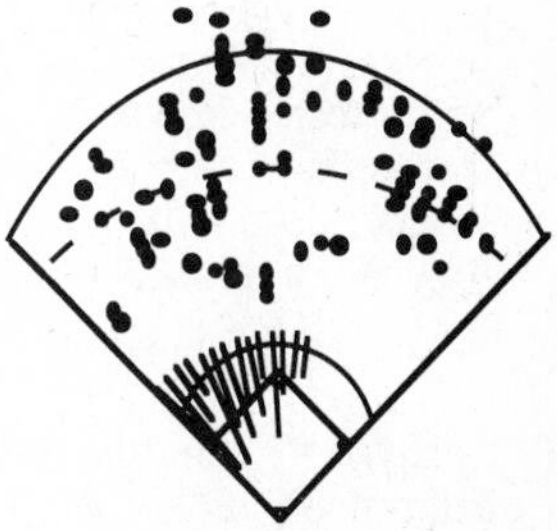

Vs. RHP

1990 Situational Stats

	AB	H	HR	RBI	AVG		AB	H	HR	RBI	AVG
Home	279	64	9	27	.229	LHP	180	56	14	38	.311
Road	284	74	15	56	.261	RHP	383	82	10	45	.214
Day	129	29	6	19	.225	Sc Pos	137	40	8	56	.292
Night	434	109	18	64	.251	Clutch	85	11	0	6	.129

1990 Rankings (National League)

- 1st in GDPs (22) and lowest batting average vs. right-handed pitchers (.214)
- 2nd in lowest slugging percentage vs. right-handed pitchers (.324), lowest on-base average vs. right-handed pitchers (.271) and lowest percentage of extra bases taken as a runner (25.8%)
- 3rd in strikeouts (130), most GDPs per GDP situation (21.4%), lowest batting average in the clutch (.129), highest slugging percentage vs. left-handed pitchers (.617), lowest batting average at home (.229) and highest percentage of swings that missed (29.5%)

HITTING:

After hitting 371 home runs for the Braves, Dale Murphy came to the Phils last August for Jeff Parrett. The Phillies' need for Murphy was obvious: he provided them with right-handed power to balance lefty swingers Lenny Dykstra, Von Hayes, John Kruk, and Darren Daulton. The big question was, could he still hit?

Murphy's bat provided the answer. After hitting only .232 in 97 games for the Braves, he batted .266 in 57 games for the Phils. Murphy had some trouble adjusting to his new park, and hit only one homer in Veterans Stadium after the deal. But he belted six on the road, and with 24 homers overall -- his ninth straight 20-plus season -- Murphy proved he's still a potent slugger. He also logged 83 RBI, the eighth time in nine years he's topped 80.

Physically, Murphy doesn't seem to have lost much, and his bat speed is still impressive. His production is lower than in his glory years; the culprits are his patience and his batting eye. Murphy often gets behind in counts by swinging at bad pitches. That forces him to hit defensively and swing for singles. Pitchers like to bust him up and in with fastballs and offer him low curveballs away and well out of the strike zone. Overanxious, Murphy is too often a sucker against righthanders' breaking balls. Against lefties, he's still the old Dale Murphy: 14 homers in only 180 at-bats last year, a .311 average, and a mighty .617 slugging percentage.

BASERUNNING:

A heady runner, Murphy showed the Phils a willingness to make seismic collisions at home plate. Though he's lost some speed, he remains very intelligent on the base paths. Murphy stole nine bases in 12 attempts last year -- all with Atlanta -- and the Phils would be very happy with a repeat performance.

FIELDING:

Once a fine center fielder, Murphy is a step slower but well suited to right field. He has a few problems charging balls and going to his right, but Lenny Dykstra's presence helps compensate for any loss of range. Murphy has the Phils' strongest outfield arm and a quick release which saves extra bases.

OVERALL:

Signed through 1992, Murphy will play right and bat fourth this year. He'll miss the Launching Pad, and will need to show more power at Veterans Stadium. But his recent level of performance -- 20 to 25 homers, 80 RBI -- would be more than satisfactory. If the Phils face a lot of lefties, he could do even better.

HITTING:

Randy Ready was the man Roberto Alomar supplanted at second base for the Padres in 1988. Now, the Phillies hope that he will provide a similar gateway to stardom for Mickey Morandini. In their '91 plans, the right-handed Ready will play second against some of the tougher lefties, and provide the Phils with an experienced, prepared pinch hitter. It's a role Ready is used to playing, and playing well.

Ready is a patient hitter who takes pitches, reaches base on walks and has shown both doubles and occasional home run power. The power was missing last year, however, as he dropped from eight homers to one, and from 23 extra-base hits to 11. Ready's struggles may have been due to some serious family problems: he spent a stressful summer caring for his disabled wife and participating in the final stages of a lawsuit against the doctor who had treated her. The suit was finally settled in early August, but the situation affected Ready all season. In fact, he slumped worse than ever after the settlement: his average dropped from .300 at the All-Star break to .277 by Aug. 2 to a final .244.

Whether his family situation was to blame or not, it was obvious that opposing pitchers were busting Ready inside, and he was unable to pull the ball. A determined student of hitting, Ready tried altering his stance, but that didn't help either.

BASERUNNING:

Ready is a conservative runner who will not normally challenge even average outfield arms. Like John Kruk, he'll try to steal a base on a poor catcher or lazy pitcher. He slides hard and has a high leg kick which assails middle infielders on double play relays.

FIELDING:

Ready is versatile, capable of playing second, third and the outfield. His fly ball judgement is not instinctive, and he sometimes has problems on sharply-hit balls. He's best at second base, with sure hands, a quick release and a strong arm. His range is a step less than most, and he's still learning to turn the double play well.

OVERALL:

Though he's not a full-time player, Ready is very valuable to the Phillies. He figures to get in his usual 100 games and at least 200 at bats while spelling the regulars at second, third and the outfield. He told club officials last year that they hadn't seen the real Randy Ready in '90; with his family situation more settled, he feels they will in 1991.

RANDY READY

Position: LF/2B
Bats: R **Throws:** R
Ht: 5'11" **Wt:** 180

Opening Day Age: 31
Born: 1/8/60 in San Mateo, CA
ML Seasons: 8

Overall Statistics

	G	AB	R	H	D	T	HR	RBI	SB	BB	SO	AVG
1990	101	217	26	53	9	1	1	26	3	29	35	.244
Career	560	1575	233	417	86	19	34	189	22	220	208	.265

Where He Hits the Ball

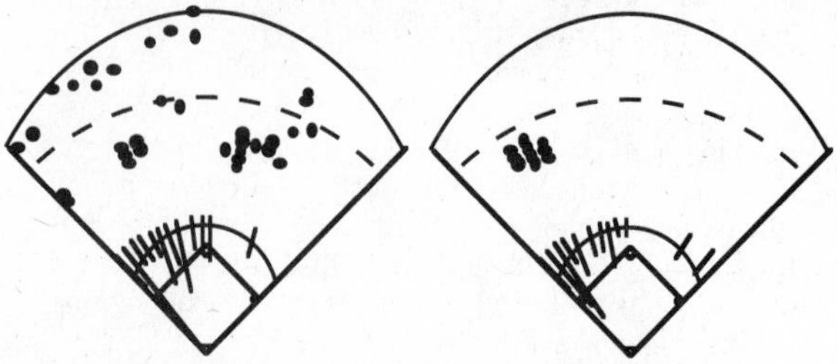

Vs. LHP   Vs. RHP

1990 Situational Stats

	AB	H	HR	RBI	AVG		AB	H	HR	RBI	AVG
Home	117	31	0	13	.265	LHP	128	32	1	15	.250
Road	100	22	1	13	.220	RHP	89	21	0	11	.236
Day	64	16	1	9	.250	Sc Pos	62	21	0	23	.339
Night	153	37	0	17	.242	Clutch	54	22	1	7	.407

1990 Rankings (National League)

- 1st lowest batting average with a 3-1 count (.000)
- 2nd highest batting average in the clutch (.407)
- 6th lowest batting average with the bases loaded (.100)
- Led the Phillies in least GDPs per GDP situation (5.2%) and highest batting average in the clutch

PITCHING:

When Bruce Ruffin came up to the Phillies in mid-season 1986, his pitching was so good that a few people were calling him a "young Steve Carlton." Since then, however, Ruffin has pitched like the old Steve Carlton, the one who spent his last few seasons ducking line drives. Ruffin has gone 18-33 over the last three seasons, winning only six games each year. His yearly ERAs have been a wrong-way progression: 2.46, 4.35, 4.43, 4.44, 5.38.

Over the last few years, Ruffin has spent about half of each season getting his mechanics straight. He's most effective throwing from a three-quarters motion, but he'd always let his arm droop down 'til he was throwing virtually sidearm. In the past, Ruffin would have his act together by the All-Star break, and then he'd pitch good ball. Entering 1990, his first half ERA was 4.59; his second half number was 3.49. Last season, June marked Ruffin's magic transformation, but this time it only lasted a month.

Ruffin won his last game July 2nd. After that, he allowed 46 earned runs in his final 50.2 innings. The opposition hit him hard even though his arm stayed up and even after he added a new change of pace. Righthanders who faced Ruffin had composite stats comparable to Will Clark's, and lefties -- whom he used to handle -- batted .292. No matter where Ruffin released the ball last year, he couldn't make his sinker drop sharply or his slider cut across the plate at the batter's knees. Hitters took the sinker for balls and pounded his fastball and slider. To keep from walking people, Ruffin made the opponents hit the ball. And hit it they did, hard and consistently.

HOLDING RUNNERS, FIELDING, HITTING:

There is not much wrong with the non-pitching parts of Ruffin's game. His delivery leaves him poised to field, and he pounces on bunts well. He works at holding runners because his breaking balls and sinkers give base stealers an advantage. Ruffin uses his quick move sparingly but effectively. He made progress as a hitter and bunter in '89, but fell back to awful at both in 1990.

OVERALL:

There's a good chance the Phils will deal Ruffin before the season starts. He's 27 and is still young enough to get his career on track again, but it's going to take a lot of work. A change of scenery might be the best thing for him.

BRUCE RUFFIN

Position: SP/RP
Bats: R **Throws:** L
Ht: 6' 2" **Wt:** 205

Opening Day Age: 27
Born: 10/4/63 in Lubbock, TX
ML Seasons: 5

Overall Statistics

	W	L	ERA	G	GS	Sv	IP	H	R	BB	SO	HR
1990	6	13	5.38	32	25	0	149.0	178	99	62	79	14
Career	38	51	4.22	167	119	3	770.0	855	425	321	394	54

How Often He Throws Strikes

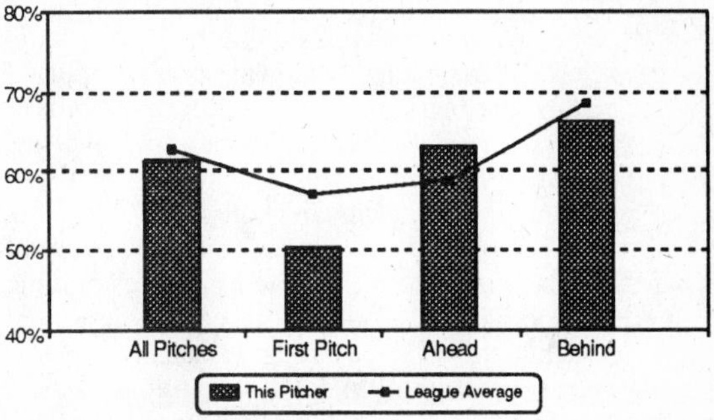

1990 Situational Stats

	W	L	ERA	Sv	IP		AB	H	HR	RBI	AVG
Home	5	7	5.40	0	78.1	LHB	120	35	0	29	.292
Road	1	6	5.35	0	70.2	RHB	479	143	14	61	.299
Day	2	2	5.13	0	47.1	Sc Pos	152	55	4	73	.362
Night	4	11	5.49	0	101.2	Clutch	17	5	0	1	.294

1990 Rankings (National League)

- 1st in highest batting average allowed with runners in scoring position (.362)
- 2nd lowest winning percentage (.316)
- 3rd highest batting average allowed vs. right-handed pitchers (.299)
- 8th in losses (13)
- Led the Phillies in losses

DICKIE THON

Position: SS
Bats: R **Throws:** R
Ht: 5'11" **Wt:** 175

Opening Day Age: 32
Born: 6/20/58 in South Bend, IN
ML Seasons: 12

Overall Statistics

	G	AB	R	H	D	T	HR	RBI	SB	BB	SO	AVG
1990	149	552	54	141	20	4	8	48	12	37	77	.255
Career	1061	3390	399	906	150	34	57	321	138	281	495	.267

Where He Hits the Ball

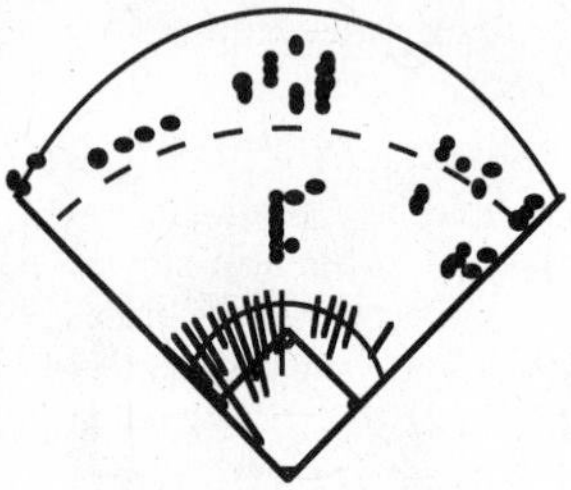

Vs. LHP

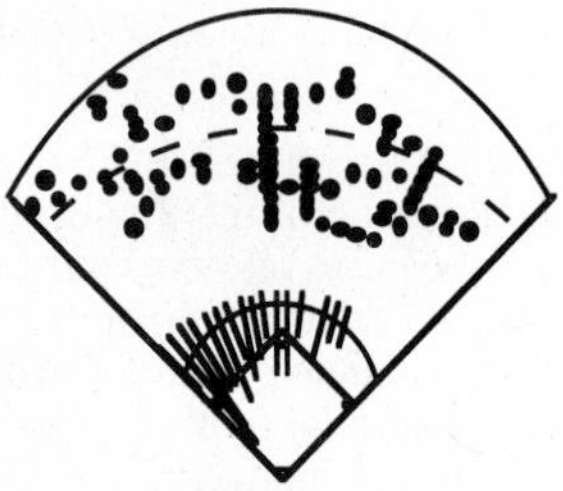

Vs. RHP

1990 Situational Stats

	AB	H	HR	RBI	AVG		AB	H	HR	RBI	AVG
Home	254	63	3	28	.248	LHP	202	53	5	21	.262
Road	298	78	5	20	.262	RHP	350	88	3	27	.251
Day	139	25	2	6	.180	Sc Pos	146	35	2	40	.240
Night	413	116	6	42	.281	Clutch	97	31	0	5	.320

1990 Rankings (National League)

- 1st in least pitches seen per plate appearance (3.10)
- 3rd lowest slugging percentage vs. right-handed pitchers (.326)
- 5th lowest on-base average vs. right-handed pitchers (.302)
- 7th in GDPs (14)
- 8th lowest batting average vs. right-handed pitchers (.251)
- Led the Phillies in GDPs and batting average on a 3-2 count (.308)
- Led NL shortstops in batting average in the clutch (.320)

HITTING:

In 1990, Dickie Thon tried to hit like a typical shortstop. For 1991, the Phils are hoping he'll hit like himself again. There was nothing wrong with Thon's batting figures (.255, eight homers, 48 RBI) last year, especially when compared with most other shortstops. But Thon showed in 1989 that he can do a lot better than that (.271, 15, 60).

Thon is the exception to the "use the whole field" rule. Unlike most hitters, Thon hits far better when he pulls the ball than when he tries to spray it around the diamond. Almost all of his power comes in rifle shots down the left field line or into the gap. But since Nick Leyva kept batting him behind men who reached base often, (Lenny Dykstra, John Kruk, Von Hayes), Thon decided last year to try to make more contact. He ended up pushing a lot of medium fly balls to right field, and his power output, one of his strengths, was curtailed.

Up to the All-Star break, Thon was spraying himself into mediocrity, batting .247 with only two homers. He then started pulling the ball again, and over the next month he batted .333, with four homers. But after an awful August week which Thon spent grounding into double plays and striking out -- the two banes of right-handed pull hitters -- he went back to spraying the ball, and hit only .234 for the season's last eight weeks. While this kind of change is usually due to a loss of bat speed, the Phils and Thon emphatically deny this, and state that Thon's pull-hitting power will return this season.

BASERUNNING:

A good percentage stealer, Thon doesn't get quite the jump he used to, but he's still a threat to swipe a base. He was 12-for-17 last year. He is a good student of pitcher's moves, and is aggressive running the bases.

FIELDING:

Sure-handed in the field, Thon's first step to his right is slower than that to his left, and he loses velocity on throws when he has to go towards third base. But he reads the ball off the bat well, and gloves balls behind second as smoothly as anyone.

OVERALL:

Thon makes nearly every play he reaches, and provides young second baseman Mickey Morandini with a strong veteran partner. If he can generate the bat speed to pull the ball for extra bases, Thon will be one of the best shortstops in the National League once again.

ROD BOOKER

Position: SS/2B
Bats: L **Throws:** R
Ht: 6' 0" **Wt:** 175

Opening Day Age: 32
Born: 9/4/58 in Los Angeles, CA
ML Seasons: 4

Overall Statistics

	G	AB	R	H	D	T	HR	RBI	SB	BB	SO	AVG
1990	73	131	19	29	5	2	0	10	3	15	26	.221
Career	145	221	35	56	9	3	0	21	7	26	37	.253

HITTING, FIELDING, BASERUNNING:

Rod Booker's value is in his versatility, not his bat. Booker backed up second, third, and shortstop for the Phillies last year; when he entered the game, the Phils defense did not suffer.

When Booker batted, however, the club's offense did. Facing mostly righty pitching, the 32-year-old left-handed slap hitter amassed almost as many strikeouts (26) as hits (29). That problem has a great deal to do with his age, according to long-time observers. Booker used to be able to handle hard pitches in on his hands or low and away; now he fouls them off. He used to be able to foul off two-strike hard sliders or sinkers, but now he misses them. Booker is, however a good curveball hitter; most of his hits come from slapping or poking offspeed breaking balls.

Booker's excellent first step from home makes him a threat to bunt for a base hit, and makes sacrifice bunts into bids for hits. His overall speed is good; he gets an excellent jump on pitchers and batted balls, and is alert for opportunities to take an extra base. Whether spot-starting or coming in as a late-inning defensive replacement, Booker has the arm to make the throws from third, a quick release, sure hands, and can turn the double play from either side of the bag.

OVERALL:

Booker is better defensively than Randy Ready and Mickey Morandini, and will remain the team's back-up middle infielder. His weak bat will ensure that Morandini plays at least against righties.

WES CHAMBERLAIN

Position: LF
Bats: R **Throws:** R
Ht: 6' 2" **Wt:** 210

Opening Day Age: 25
Born: 4/13/66 in Chicago, IL
ML Seasons: 1

Overall Statistics

	G	AB	R	H	D	T	HR	RBI	SB	BB	SO	AVG
1990	18	46	9	13	3	0	2	4	4	1	9	.283
Career	18	46	9	13	3	0	2	4	4	1	9	.283

HITTING, FIELDING, BASERUNNING:

The 1989 Eastern League MVP for his .306, 21 homer, 87 RBI season, Wes Chamberlain joined the Phillies last Aug. 30 and immediately became their best hitting prospect. Chamberlain and two other minor leaguers were acquired by the Phils for Carmelo Martinez when Pirates GM Larry Doughty accidentally left them on the wrong waiver list, and had to trade them or lose them for $50,000 each.

Chamberlain has two very different swings. He takes huge, long stride with a looping, arms-extended swing when he guesses he will see a high fastball; he has a short wristy swing when he expects to see a change or curve. It's almost as if, when the ball leaves the pitcher's hand, he has to quickly decide whether he's going to be Joe Carter or Felix Fermin. Not surprisingly, Chamberlain gets fooled a lot by offspeed stuff at this point in his career.

The Phillies were delighted by Chamberlain's speed and aggressiveness: his four stolen bases included a steal of third. He was not a good percentage stealer in the minors, however (14 for 33 this year), and needs to be more selective. Chamberlain's good wheels help him in the outfield where he can outrun occasional lapses in judgement.

OVERALL:

Talented but still very raw, Chamberlain has a lot to learn before he can become a successful major leaguer. His best hope to stick with the Phillies this year would be if Von Hayes is traded; it would be no great shock if he spent another year learning his lessons in Class AAA.

DARRIN FLETCHER

Position: C
Bats: L **Throws:** R
Ht: 6' 2" **Wt:** 195

Opening Day Age: 24
Born: 10/3/66 in Elmhurst, IL
ML Seasons: 2

Overall Statistics

	G	AB	R	H	D	T	HR	RBI	SB	BB	SO	AVG
1990	11	23	3	3	1	0	0	1	0	1	6	.130
Career	16	31	4	7	1	0	1	3	0	2	6	.226

HITTING, FIELDING, BASERUNNING:

Most 24-year-old catchers who had just hit .291 with 13 homers in AAA would be glad to be traded to a club whose starter was a lifetime .227 hitter. Unfortunately for Darrin Fletcher, the timing was a little slow. Darren Daulton's career year and three year, $6.7 million contract probably punched Fletcher's ticket to AAA Scranton for early '91.

Fletcher's play may change his venue by mid-season. A lefty hitter who crowds the plate and makes solid contact, Fletcher could be Mike Scioscia's slimmer, younger brother at bat. He bunts well and has good strike zone judgement. Compared to Daulton, he would hit for a higher average with less power, and he is slower than Daulton, but faster than Steve Lake.

Defensively, it will take Fletcher a while to learn NL hitters and his own pitchers. Daulton and Lake have a tremendous jump on him in this regard, because the Phils staff is made up of pitchers whose margin of error is slender. He did not throw well when challenged by base stealers in nine late-season games, and his confidence, game calling and comportment were questioned by veteran Phillies pitchers. He is young enough to improve on his shortcomings.

OVERALL:

Fletcher's defensive inexperience will cost him a spot this spring, but Lake's yearly injuries and Daulton's hitting history should put Fletcher into major league pinstripes to stay in 1991.

RON JONES

Position: LF
Bats: L **Throws:** R
Ht: 5'10" **Wt:** 200

Opening Day Age: 26
Born: 6/11/64 in Seguin, TX
ML Seasons: 3

Overall Statistics

	G	AB	R	H	D	T	HR	RBI	SB	BB	SO	AVG
1990	24	58	5	16	2	0	3	7	0	9	9	.276
Career	69	213	27	61	8	1	13	37	1	20	24	.286

HITTING, FIELDING, BASERUNNING:

Ron Jones' knees are the only thing between his bat and stardom, but so far they've been more than enough. After spending a year carefully rehabilitating the patella tendon he tore in April of 1989, Jones got hurt all over again last year, and played in only 24 games.

Jones started last season at AAA Scranton/Wilkes-Barre, then was brought up after playing 26 games. The Phils used him carefully. Manager Nick Leyva deployed Jones almost exclusively against righties, and Jones showed that his line drive stroke, power, and ability to draw walks had not been affected. When Von Hayes was briefly sidelined, Jones was looking forward to a solid week as the everyday right fielder. But on the second day of Hayes' injury, June 30, his left knee gave out as he spun his wheels trying to charge a line drive. It was back to surgeons and rehab for Jones.

Jones has recovered from previous injuries, and that gives the Phillies hope. Given the example of the last two years, he probably doesn't have a future as an outfielder, because lateral movement eventually incapacitates him. He still has good straight-ahead speed, and though he's not a big base stealing threat, his burly fullback's body is well suited to his aggressive approach to sliding into second base.

OVERALL:

Jones has to prove he can still hit, probably in the role of a left-handed pinch hitter this year. If his batting skills are undiminished, he is a good bet to be sent to the highest American League bidder as a designated hitter, where his knees will have fewer chances to undo his bat.

STEVE LAKE

Position: C
Bats: R **Throws:** R
Ht: 6' 1" **Wt:** 190

Opening Day Age: 34
Born: 3/14/57 in Inglewood, CA
ML Seasons: 8

Overall Statistics

	G	AB	R	H	D	T	HR	RBI	SB	BB	SO	AVG
1990	29	80	4	20	2	0	0	6	0	3	12	.250
Career	354	794	63	191	29	4	11	82	1	36	106	.241

HITTING, FIELDING, BASERUNNING:

At 34, Steve Lake is the quintessential backup catcher. His value is mainly defensive: calling games, handling pitchers, throwing out baserunners. He can hit a little: he's batted between .250 and .294 each of the last five years, no mean feat for a guy who rarely plays. But Lake has little power and doesn't walk much, so his offensive value is pretty limited.

Opposing pitchers have a straightforward approach to Lake. They throw him hard fastballs in the strike zone, and can often overpower him. He waits on curves and change-ups as well as anyone, looking to loft them over the infield for hits. Lake usually hits the ball on the ground, which makes him a good hit-and-run man. He's no threat to run, with one lifetime stolen base in one attempt. That was in 1985; since then, Lake has carefully protected his perfect stealing record.

Lake shines when he is behind, rather than beside, the plate. He offers a good target, and has an excellent knowledge of opposing hitters. Neither his 1989 knee injury or 1990 sprained hand appear to have affected his defense. Lake's outstanding arm and quick release make him death to opposing baserunners: he threw out 11 of 18 runners who tried to steal on him last year, and has nailed 104 of 187 base thieves in his career.

OVERALL:

Lake's right-handed bat, knowledge, and ability to stop an opponent's running game make him a good complement to Darren Daulton. But the arrival of Darrin Fletcher may push him to third-string status this year. Even in that role, he has value.

STEVE ONTIVEROS

Position: RP
Bats: R **Throws:** R
Ht: 6' 0" **Wt:** 180

Opening Day Age: 30
Born: 3/5/61 in Tularosa, NM
ML Seasons: 6

Overall Statistics

	W	L	ERA	G	GS	Sv	IP	H	R	BB	SO	HR
1990	0	0	2.70	5	0	0	10.0	9	3	3	6	1
Career	18	18	3.78	141	37	19	393.1	358	185	133	235	40

PITCHING, FIELDING, HITTING & HOLDING RUNNERS:

Steve Ontiveros' right elbow has kept him from pitching full-time since 1987. But Ontiveros claims that the Tommy John elbow procedure he underwent in July of '89 has completely rebuilt his elbow. The Phils think so, too, and have included Ontiveros in their 1991 plans. In fact, he could well be their number-five starter.

At 30, Ontiveros is the classic canny veteran who throws a little bit of everything. His primary pitch is a sinking cut fastball which he can throw to either side of the plate to both left and right-handed batters. He makes the fastball more effective by mixing in sliders and split-fingered fastballs. Because they are not thrown hard, all of these pitches are hittable; because they all move and are mixed intelligently by Ontiveros, who likes to call his own game, they are more likely to produce grounders and flies than liners and homers. Ontiveros gets into trouble when he leaves the ball up. But for the most part, he's pitched pretty well when he's been healthy.

Ontiveros is comfortable out of the stretch and is tough to steal on. Although he hustles, he is a poor hitter and fielder, and a negligible baserunner.

OVERALL:

If Ontiveros' shoulder holds up, he will make the team this spring. If the Phils don't acquire a fifth starter, he has the inside track on the job. If they do make a deal, he'll be a long relief man, and the first replacement when injury or ineffectiveness strikes a regular starter.

HITTING:

Wally Backman returned to the National League in 1990 after a one-year stint in Minnesota and found his career rejuvenated. Signed as a free agent by the Pittsburgh Pirates, Backman platooned at third base and hit leadoff against right-handed pitchers. Backman had a fine season in this role. He hit .346 over the season's first two months before tailing off to .292. That was a marked improvement over the .231 average he posted in his season with the Twins.

Backman was his usual slap-hitting self last year, but showed surprising power with 26 extra-base hits, the second-highest total of his career. He still has a good eye, drawing 42 walks in 361 plate appearances, and can bunt for a base hit. As he has throughout his career, the switch-hitter proved more valuable from the left side where he hit .303. He had a .194 average in just 31 at-bats as a righty. He likes low pitches batting from the left side, high pitches when batting righty. Backman is dangerous in the clutch and knocked in some big runs for the Pirates in 1990. He hit .350 with runners on base and .358 with men in scoring position.

BASERUNNING:

Hamstring injuries have robbed Backman of some speed and greatly reduced his base stealing ability. However, he did manage six steals in 1990 and pitchers must pay attention to him. Backman is a smart baserunner and is still able to take an extra base on singles and doubles.

FIELDING:

A second baseman for the majority of his career, Backman made a slow transition to third base and committed 12 errors. He let too many hard-hit balls get by him, was shaky on bunts, and often was lifted for a defensive replacement by the sixth inning. However, Backman can make the routine plays and has adjusted to making the long throw across the infield. Backman also saw time at his more familiar second base and exhibited good range and steady hands.

OVERALL:

Backman gave the Pirates decent play as a platoon third baseman and provided outstanding leadership in the clubhouse to a young team. However, he was a free agent at season's end and may not return to Pittsburgh. With Jose Lind entrenched at second and Jeff King ready to play every day at third, Backman's role in 1991 will be reduced if he rejoins the Pirates.

WALLY BACKMAN

Position: 3B/2B
Bats: B **Throws:** R
Ht: 5' 9" **Wt:** 168

Opening Day Age: 31
Born: 9/22/59 in Hillsboro, OR
ML Seasons: 11

Overall Statistics

	G	AB	R	H	D	T	HR	RBI	SB	BB	SO	AVG
1990	104	315	62	92	21	3	2	28	6	42	53	.292
Career	956	2983	454	831	125	19	10	219	113	334	433	.279

Where He Hits the Ball

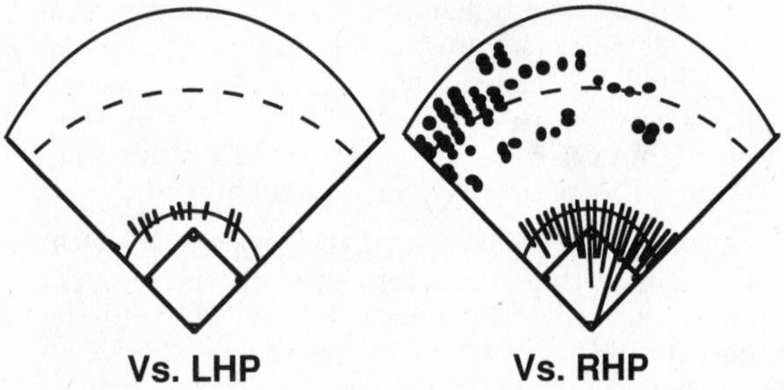

1990 Situational Stats

	AB	H	HR	RBI	AVG		AB	H	HR	RBI	AVG
Home	154	43	0	12	.279	LHP	31	6	0	3	.194
Road	161	49	2	16	.304	RHP	284	86	2	25	.303
Day	83	28	0	4	.337	Sc Pos	53	19	0	24	.358
Night	232	64	2	24	.276	Clutch	37	6	0	2	.162

1990 Rankings (National League)

- Did not rank near the top or bottom in any category

PITCHING:

The Pittsburgh Pirates expect Stan Belinda, a hard-throwing sidewinder, to be their closer of the future. Belinda had 66 saves in the equivalent of four minor league seasons, then set a Pirate rookie record with eight in 1990 after being called up on May 19.

Belinda seems to have what it takes to be a closer. His fastball reaches 94 MPH and it seems even faster because he delivers it from a difficult angle. Belinda also throws a below-average breaking ball and a forkball. Once he masters the forkball and develops a major league caliber offspeed pitch, he could be devastating.

Despite being a sidearm pitcher, Belinda does not induce as many ground balls as would be expected. He is a power pitcher, though he still has problems harnessing it. He struck out 55 batters in 58.1 innings but also walked 29. He should reduce the walks with experience. Belinda had an inconsistent season, which could be expected of a rookie. He pitched 13.2 scoreless innings over 12 appearances between June 24 and July 20, but had some rocky times in August when his ERA was 5.50. He bounced back in September and made contributions to the bullpen-by-committee that helped give the Pirates the National League East title.

Overall, Belinda allowed just nine of 41 inherited baserunners to score and had 9 holds. The baby-faced and crew-cut Belinda has great poise for a young pitcher. Though he blew five of his 13 save opportunities, he never sulked and held firm to his belief that he could get big-league hitters out.

HOLDING RUNNERS, FIELDING, HITTING:

As a short reliever, Belinda does not need to concentrate much on holding runners. However, he has a slow delivery and opponents were a perfect five-for-five in steal attempts last season. He needs to be a little more aware of runners. Because of his sidearm delivery, Belinda does not always land in good fielding position. He is quick off the mound and generally does not hurt himself with the glove, though. Belinda is no threat with the bat, going 0-for-5 with three strikeouts.

OVERALL:

Belinda had his ups and downs as a rookie but acquitted himself well. The Pirates have been grooming him for a closer's role since drafting him in 1986. He has never started a game as a professional. On a team that lacked a true closer in 1990, the opportunity is there for Belinda to take charge.

STAN BELINDA

Position: RP
Bats: R **Throws:** R
Ht: 6' 3" **Wt:** 185

Opening Day Age: 24
Born: 8/6/66 in Huntingdon, PA
ML Seasons: 2

Overall Statistics

	W	L	ERA	G	GS	Sv	IP	H	R	BB	SO	HR
1990	3	4	3.55	55	0	8	58.1	48	23	29	55	4
Career	3	5	3.93	63	0	8	68.2	61	31	31	65	4

How Often He Throws Strikes

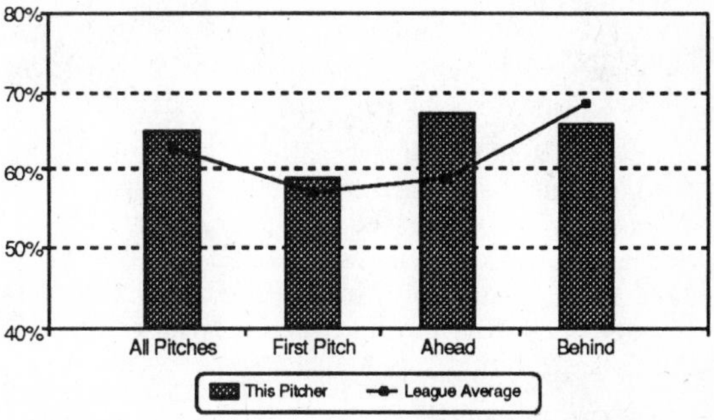

1990 Situational Stats

	W	L	ERA	Sv	IP		AB	H	HR	RBI	AVG
Home	1	2	4.97	2	25.1	LHB	91	16	1	10	.176
Road	2	2	2.45	6	33.0	RHB	120	32	3	14	.267
Day	0	1	5.28	3	15.1	Sc Pos	59	13	1	18	.220
Night	3	3	2.93	5	43.0	Clutch	124	28	1	15	.226

1990 Rankings (National League)

- 2nd in first batter efficiency (.146)
- 3rd in lowest percentage of inherited runners scored (22.0%)
- 9th in holds (9)
- Led the Pirates in games pitched (55), blown saves (5), first batter efficiency and lowest percentage of inherited runners scored

HITTING:

After two decades of searching for a long-term solution to their shortstop problem, it looks like the Pittsburgh Pirates have found the answer in Jay Bell. Bell was a solid player for the Pirates in 1990, his first full major league season.

Bell has brought the sacrifice bunt back to the game. Hitting out of the number-two slot in the batting order, Bell dropped down an incredible 39 sacrifice bunts in 1990. No one else in the major leagues had more than 17. Bell squares around early, before the pitcher releases the ball, yet is still able to sacrifice successfully.

Bell can do more than bunt, though. He is a decent hitter with gap power. He had 42 extra-base hits, including seven home runs, in 1990. Bell's power figures to improve as he matures and gets stronger. Bell likes high fastballs and prefers to pull the ball. However, he has improved at going the other way with power. He has trouble with low pitches, particularly outside breaking balls from righthanders.

A rather paradoxical part of Bell's hitting is his inordinate number of strikeouts; this is unexpected for a player who is an excellent bunter and hit-and-run man. He struck out 109 times in 583 at-bats in 1990. He becomes more of a free swinger with the bases empty, but will usually make contact with men on. He has played well in pressure situations.

BASERUNNING:

Bell has average speed but makes few mistakes on the base paths. He was able to steal 10 bases in 16 attempts last season. Though he usually plays it safe as a runner, he will take the extra base when the opportunity presents itself.

FIELDING:

Bell's range is only adequate but he knows how to play hitters and is helped by playing his home games on artificial turf. Though he made 22 errors in 1990, he had a string of 165 chances without a miscue. He also has a strong arm, which had led some scouts in the past to suggest that Bell would be better suited to third base. A switch is not necessary, though, as Bell is a competent major league shortstop.

OVERALL:

Bell gives the Pirates something they have lacked for years--solid play from a shortstop. Though not an Ozzie Smith or Barry Larkin, Bell does all the little things necessary to be a shortstop in the major leagues. He is only 25 years old and figures to be around for a long time.

JAY BELL

Position: SS
Bats: R **Throws:** R
Ht: 6' 1" **Wt:** 180

Opening Day Age: 25
Born: 12/11/65 in Eglin AFB, FL
ML Seasons: 5

Overall Statistics

	G	AB	R	H	D	T	HR	RBI	SB	BB	SO	AVG
1990	159	583	93	148	28	7	7	52	10	65	109	.254
Career	353	1204	166	296	57	12	14	117	21	115	243	.246

Where He Hits the Ball

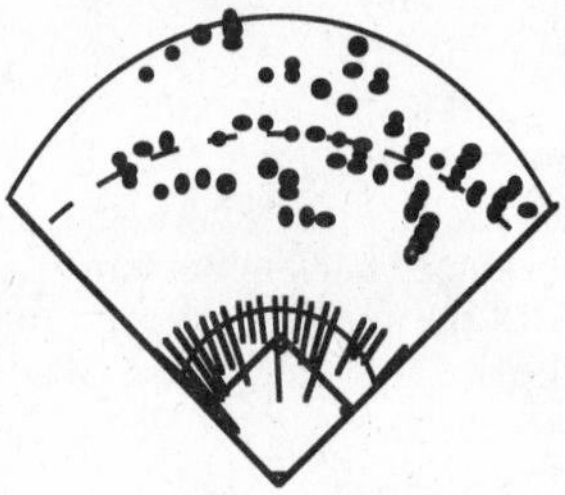

Vs. LHP

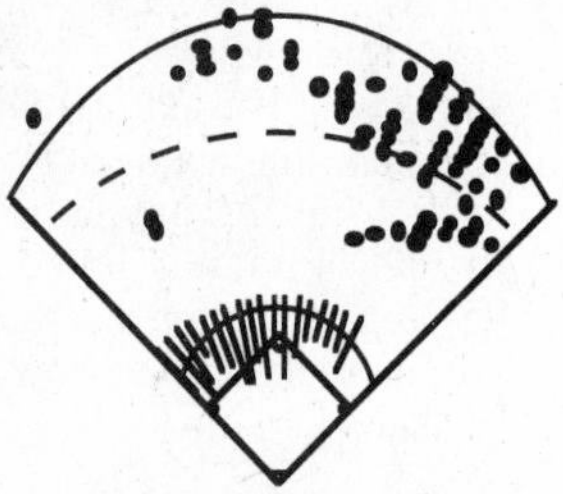

Vs. RHP

1990 Situational Stats

	AB	H	HR	RBI	AVG		AB	H	HR	RBI	AVG
Home	287	75	1	17	.261	LHP	251	69	2	17	.275
Road	296	73	6	35	.247	RHP	332	79	5	35	.238
Day	153	43	4	18	.281	Sc Pos	121	34	3	44	.281
Night	430	105	3	34	.244	Clutch	78	24	0	9	.308

1990 Rankings (National League)

- 1st in sacrifice bunts (39)
- 2nd in pitches seen (2,671) and bunts in play (51)
- 3rd in plate appearances (696)
- Led the Pirates in singles (106), triples (7), sacrifice bunts, hit by pitch (3), strikeouts (109), pitches seen (2,671), plate appearances, most pitches seen per plate appearance (3.84) and bunts in play
- Led NL shortstops in runs (93), doubles (28), sacrifice bunts, strikeouts, pitches seen, plate appearances, games (159) and bunts in play

BARRY BONDS

Position: LF
Bats: L **Throws:** L
Ht: 6' 1" **Wt:** 185

Opening Day Age: 26
Born: 7/24/64 in Riverside, CA
ML Seasons: 5

HITTING:

In his first four major league seasons, Barry Bonds showed the potential for becoming one of the game's top all-around players, but always fell short of expectations. No more. Bonds put it all together in 1990 and became the National League's Most Valuable Player.

Dropped from the leadoff spot to the number-five hole behind Bobby Bonilla, the multi-talented Bonds became the first player in baseball history to record this amazing combination: 30 homers, 50 stolen bases, 100 runs scored, 100 RBI and a .300 batting average. Inspired by the batting order switch and by losing a salary arbitration case prior to the season, Bonds proved wrong all the detractors who said he did not play hard and failed to produce in the clutch. In 1989, Bonds hit a measly .227 with runners in scoring position. However, in 1990 he hit a sizzling .377 in those situations in 1990 and .342 with runners on. He also showed consistency by never going more than two straight games without reaching base.

Bonds has outstanding power and can hit the ball out to any field. His weakness remains the inside fastball. Because of a looping swing, Bonds can be tied up with heat on the hands and often takes those pitches for strikes. Bonds is a rare left-handed power hitter in that he hits lefties as well as righties. He fared a bit better against lefthanders, hitting .304 against them in 1990 as opposed to .297 versus righthanders. Bonds also had an outstanding walk-strikeout ratio of 93-83.

BASERUNNING:

Bonds has greatly reduced the number of silly baserunning mistakes he used to make. Despite moving down in the order, he reached a career high with 52 steals in 1990 and became the first Pirate to steal 50 bases since Omar Moreno in 1979.

FIELDING:

Bonds is as smooth as any left fielder in the game; he is truly Gold Glove caliber. He effortlessly, almost nonchalantly, gets to balls and is adept at both coming in and going back on flies. In the past, Bonds' arm was considered suspect. However, he has registered 14 assists in each of the past two seasons.

OVERALL:

The Pirates tried to trade Bonds before the 1990 season. It's a good thing their plans went awry because the enigmatic Bonds finally put his power, speed and defense together to become one of the game's premier players. He can dominate for as long as he is so inclined.

Overall Statistics

	G	AB	R	H	D	T	HR	RBI	SB	BB	SO	AVG
1990	151	519	104	156	32	3	33	114	52	93	83	.301
Career	717	2601	468	688	156	26	117	337	169	377	448	.265

Where He Hits the Ball

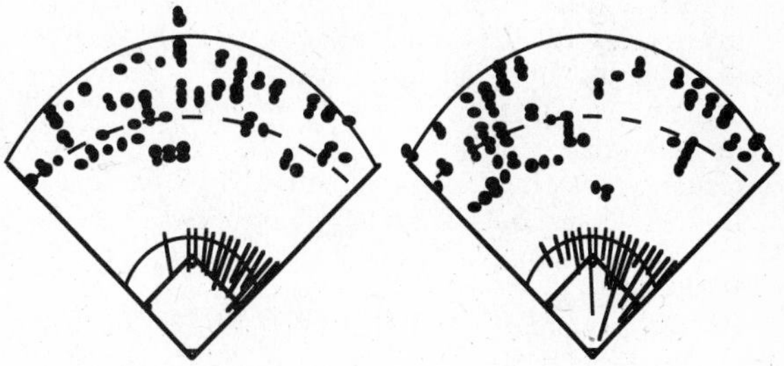

Vs. LHP Vs. RHP

1990 Situational Stats

	AB	H	HR	RBI	AVG		AB	H	HR	RBI	AVG
Home	239	66	14	46	.276	LHP	240	73	17	58	.304
Road	280	90	19	68	.321	RHP	279	83	16	56	.297
Day	138	39	12	30	.283	Sc Pos	138	52	7	79	.377
Night	381	117	21	84	.307	Clutch	82	24	3	9	.293

1990 Rankings (National League)

- 1st in slugging percentage (.564)
- 2nd in walks (93)
- 3rd in stolen bases (52), batting average with runners in scoring position (.377), highest percentage of pitches taken (62.9%) and steals of third (12)
- Led the Pirates in batting average (.301), home runs (33), stolen bases (52), caught stealing (13), walks, hit by pitch (3), times on base (252), slugging percentage, on-base average (.406), HR frequency (15.7 ABs per HR), stolen base percentage (80.0%), batting average with runners in scoring position and highest percentage of extra bases taken as a runner (53.7%)

BOBBY BONILLA

Position: RF/3B
Bats: B **Throws:** R
Ht: 6' 3" **Wt:** 230

Opening Day Age: 28
Born: 2/23/63 in New York, NY
ML Seasons: 5

Overall Statistics

	G	AB	R	H	D	T	HR	RBI	SB	BB	SO	AVG
1990	160	625	112	175	39	7	32	120	4	45	103	.280
Career	761	2717	408	757	157	31	98	426	26	307	430	.279

Where He Hits the Ball

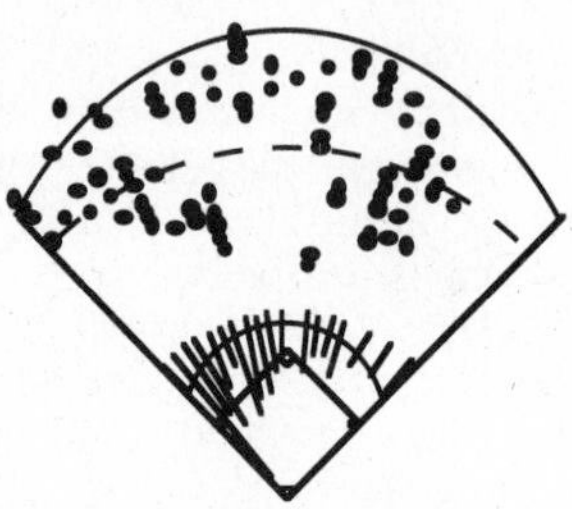

Vs. LHP

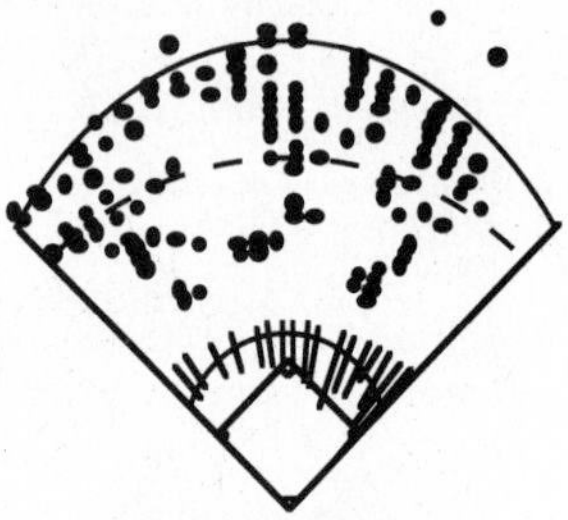

Vs. RHP

1990 Situational Stats

	AB	H	HR	RBI	AVG		AB	H	HR	RBI	AVG
Home	310	81	13	52	.261	LHP	280	73	14	48	.261
Road	315	94	19	68	.298	RHP	345	102	18	72	.296
Day	173	50	12	37	.289	Sc Pos	188	53	7	86	.282
Night	452	125	20	83	.277	Clutch	79	19	2	13	.241

1990 Rankings (National League)

- ➡ 1st in sacrifice flies (15) and most runs scored per time reached base (50.7%)
- ➡ 2nd in runs (112), doubles (39), total bases (324) and RBIs (12)
- ➡ 3rd in at-bats (625) and games (160)
- ➡ Led the Pirates in at-bats, runs, hits (175), doubles, triples (7), total bases, RBIs, sacrifice flies, games and runs scored per time reached base
- ➡ Led NL right fielders in at-bats, runs, doubles, total bases, RBIs, sacrifice flies, pitches seen (2,461), plate appearances (2,461), games, errors (12) and runs scored per time reached base

HITTING:

Already one of the top power hitters in the game, Bobby Bonilla improved even more in 1990 as he set career highs in home runs, RBI and runs scored. Two factors caused Bonilla's increased productivity. One was the Pirates moving Barry Bonds from the leadoff spot to the number-five hole directly behind him. This move forced pitchers to throw Bonilla more strikes. The second factor was moving from third base to right field. Bonilla is more comfortable in right field and no longer lets his defense affect his hitting.

Bonilla is a free swinger who looks for low fastballs. Seeing more pitches in the strike zone in 1990, he only drew 45 walks in 686 plate appearances. Bonilla is a better hitter from the left side of the plate, but showed marked improvement as a righty in the second half of 1990. Overall, Bonilla hit .296 with 18 homers and 72 RBIs in 345 at-bats as a left-handed hitter. He had a .261 average, 14 homers and 48 RBIs in 280 at-bats from the right side. Bonilla is basically a gap hitter, but has worked on generating more hip rotation in an effort to pull more pitches. He can be made to chase high pitches, particularly inside ones from lefties and outside ones from righties.

BASERUNNING:

Bonilla has pretty good speed for a big man, but usually plays it safe on the base paths. He goes into second base extremely hard to break up double plays. He stole only four bases last season and has just 26 in his 5-year career.

FIELDING:

After leading the National League in errors in his two full seasons as a regular third baseman, Bonilla was moved to right field last season. Though Bonilla still committed 12 errors, the highest total of any NL right fielder, he was not nearly the liability he was at the hot corner. Bonilla has a strong arm and decent range. However, he is sometimes shaky on fly balls and has problems with sinking liners. Bonilla also has experience at first base, which is likely his long-range position, as he has good reflexes and soft hands.

OVERALL:

Bonilla is one of the game's most durable players and has appeared in an average of 161 games a year over the past three seasons. He is also one of the game's most productive sluggers. Bonilla can become a free agent after the 1991 season and it is imperative for the Pirates to lock him up with a deal this year.

SID BREAM

Position: 1B
Bats: L **Throws:** L
Ht: 6' 4" **Wt:** 220

Opening Day Age: 30
Born: 8/3/60 in Carlisle, PA
ML Seasons: 8

Overall Statistics

	G	AB	R	H	D	T	HR	RBI	SB	BB	SO	AVG
1990	147	389	39	105	23	2	15	67	8	48	65	.270
Career	709	2133	249	562	135	10	60	307	40	242	316	.263

Where He Hits the Ball

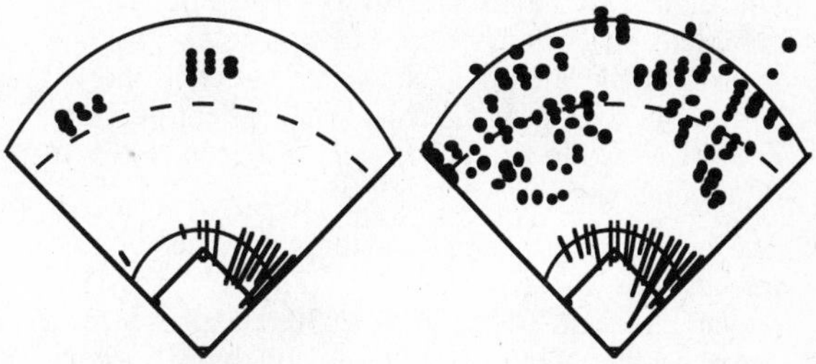

Vs. LHP   Vs. RHP

1990 Situational Stats

	AB	H	HR	RBI	AVG		AB	H	HR	RBI	AVG
Home	181	50	8	36	.276	LHP	96	25	2	12	.260
Road	208	55	7	31	.264	RHP	293	80	13	55	.273
Day	102	28	3	17	.275	Sc Pos	118	34	6	49	.288
Night	287	77	12	50	.268	Clutch	61	18	2	10	.295

1990 Rankings (National League)

- Led the Pirates in batting average with 2 strikes (.244)
- Led NL first basemen in sacrifice bunts (4)

HITTING:

Sid Bream came into the 1990 season as a huge question mark but wound up being one of the Pittsburgh Pirates' most consistent players. Bream underwent three knee operations in 1989, the last being a total reconstruction. Less than a week before the 1990 opener, Bream had doubts about his ability to come back. But he soon erased them; his hitting in many ways was even better than in his solid 1986-87-88 seasons.

After a slow start last year, Bream got rolling. Though limited to 389 at-bats as a platoon player, he had 15 homers, one short of his career high, and 67 RBIs. The Pirates were 15-0 in games when he homered. The Pirates rested Bream by sitting him out against most left-handed pitchers, though he hit a respectable .260 against southpaws.

A positive side effect of Bream's knee problems was the upper body strength he added during rehabilitation. As a result of the weight work, Bream now hits the ball farther than ever; his .455 slugging average last year was a career high. Bream has been a streak hitter throughout his career. However, he showed signs of being more consistent last season and did not strike out on as many bad pitches as he did in the past.

Primarily a pull hitter, Bream is a rare left-handed batter who likes pitches high in the strike zone. Pitchers will try to jam him inside in an attempt to get double play balls. However, Bream can turn on inside heaters and take them out of the park.

BASERUNNING:

Bream was never fast and the knee operations have made him even slower. However, pitchers will pay the price if they just forget about him. Bream managed eight stolen bases in 12 attempts last season because of his intelligence on the base paths.

FIELDING:

No one realized Bream's defensive value until he missed all but 19 games of the 1989 season. Though he has limited range, he rarely misplays a grounder and he snares any throw within his reach. Bream has an exceptionaliy strong arm for a first baseman and is outstanding on bunt coverage. He will sneak halfway down the line in sacrifice situations and willingly gamble on getting the lead runner.

OVERALL:

Bream was one of baseball's top comeback stories of the 1990 season. He enjoys Pittsburgh and the Pirates like his work ethic. He was a free agent this winter but figured to return to the Pirates.

STAFF ACE

DOUG DRABEK

Position: SP
Bats: R **Throws:** R
Ht: 6' 1" **Wt:** 185

Opening Day Age: 28
Born: 7/25/62 in Victoria, TX
ML Seasons: 5

PITCHING:

Doug Drabek went from a pretty good pitcher to a Cy Young Award winner in 1990. He was 22-6, led the National League in victories and became the Pittsburgh Pirates' first 20-game winner in 13 years. Beyond that, he led the Pirates in wins, starts, complete games, innings pitched and strikeouts while serving as the ace for the club which won the NL East.

Drabek throws four pitches and can usually get them all over for strikes. He has an average fastball, a nasty slider, a good curveball and a decent change-up. He mixes them up and is not afraid to throw any pitch in any situation. Drabek's best pitch is the slider, and former teammate Brian Fisher once described it as "the slider from hell." More often than not, Drabek will try to get the slider or curve in for a strike on the first pitch, then go to the fastball.

Drabek can go the distance, as evidenced by his nine complete games in 1990, and he rarely loses his effectiveness in the later innings. Drabek has control of all of his pitches; he walked just 2.2 batters per nine innings. When he's at his best, he'll induce batters to hit ground balls.

The bigger the game or situation, the better Drabek pitches. He was 12-3 following Pirates' losses last season and went 14-2 after June 30. He also threw a three-hit shutout over St. Louis to clinch the National League East, and recorded one of the two Pirate victories in the Championship Series against Cincinnati. Opponents hit only .220 with runners in scoring position and .153 in late-and-close situations.

HOLDING RUNNERS, FIELDING, HITTING:

For a righthander, Drabek is adept at holding runners. He pays close attention and has a quick, slide-step move. Drabek is an excellent athlete who was an all-state punter and high jumper in college. He springs off the mound to field bunts and saves many hits by spearing hard shots back through the box. Previously a poor hitter, Drabek became a force at the plate in 1990, hitting .214 with his first major league home run and six RBI. He also dropped down seven sacrifice bunts.

OVERALL:

Drabek put it all together in 1990 and emerged as one of the game's premier pitchers. He is just coming into his prime, too. He should be a big winner and a staff ace for years to come.

Overall Statistics

	W	L	ERA	G	GS	Sv	IP	H	R	BB	SO	HR
1990	22	6	2.76	33	33	0	231.1	190	78	56	131	15
Career	69	45	3.21	157	148	0	1003.0	890	394	271	577	92

How Often He Throws Strikes

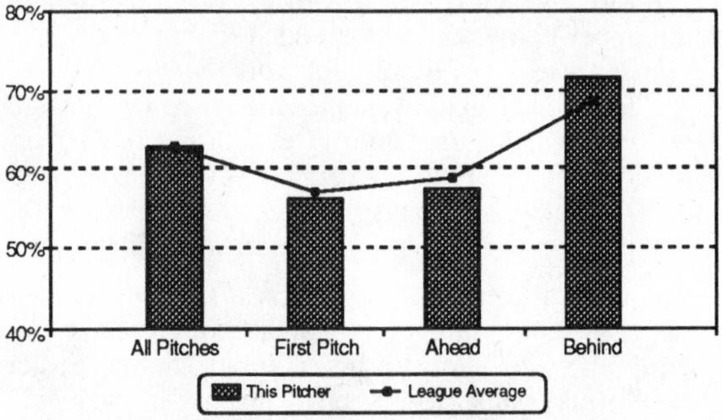

1990 Situational Stats

	W	L	ERA	Sv	IP		AB	H	HR	RBI	AVG
Home	11	3	3.00	0	120.0	LHB	538	131	10	47	.243
Road	11	3	2.51	0	111.1	RHB	308	59	5	18	.192
Day	9	1	2.30	0	70.1	Sc Pos	168	37	2	49	.220
Night	13	5	2.96	0	161.0	Clutch	72	11	1	2	.153

1990 Rankings (National League)

- 1st in wins (22) and winning percentage (.786)
- 2nd in complete games (9), lowest on-base average allowed (.274), least baserunners per 9 innings (9.7) and most run support per 9 innings (5.9)
- 3rd in shutouts (3), lowest slugging percentage allowed (.331) and ERA on the road (2.51)
- Led the Pirates in ERA (2.76), wins, games started (33), complete games, shutouts, innings (231.1), hits allowed (190), batters faced (918), walks allowed (56), strikeouts (131), stolen bases allowed (18), winning percentage and strikeout/walk ratio (2.3)

PITCHING:

For one-half of the 1990 season, Neal Heaton finally became the major league pitcher everyone thought he would be during an All-American career at the University of Miami. Heaton was one of the National League's top starting pitchers during the first half and was selected to his first All-Star game. Then came the second half. Heaton was eventually dropped from the rotation because of shoulder problems and ended the season as a seldom-used reliever.

The hard-throwing Heaton added an off-the-wall offspeed pitch in spring training: with the help of his new pitch, he opened the season by winning his first six starts and peaked with a 10-2 record. However, he immediately lost his next five starts on his way to a 2-7 finish. A strained rotator cuff reduced Heaton's effectiveness and he made only one start after August 20.

Heaton's bread and butter pitches are still the fastball and a hard slider. However, he developed a "screw-knuckle-change" that served as an offspeed pitch. Heaton releases the pitch like a screwball, grips it like a knuckleball and throws it at change-up speed. Previously, hitters could time Heaton because he threw each pitch at relatively the same velocity. But the offspeed pitch changed that.

The rotator cuff problem, though not serious enough for surgery, effectively ended Heaton's season. The Pirates feared risking his long-range health if they continued to start him. Even before the injury, Heaton was never a complete game pitcher. In the past three seasons, he finished only one of 53 starts. He pitched into the eighth inning just twice in 24 starts in 1990.

HOLDING RUNNERS, FIELDING, HITTING:

Heaton has a rather slow delivery, yet does a good job of shutting down the running game. He has a quick move to first and picks off his share of runners. He is also quick off the mound and is an above-average fielder. Heaton prides himself on hitting and often gets to the park early for extra batting practice. However, he struggled at the plate in 1990, going 2-for-43 (.047). He is occasionally used as a pinch runner and stole a base in that role last season.

OVERALL:

Heaton is a big question mark heading into this season. Is he the journeyman who was 61-81 in eight major league seasons prior to 1990? Is he the guy who made the National League All-Star team last season? Is he a sore-armed pitcher who can only be used as a reliever? The answers will come this season.

NEAL HEATON

Position: SP/RP
Bats: L **Throws:** L
Ht: 6' 1" **Wt:** 195

Opening Day Age: 31
Born: 3/3/60 in Jamaica, NY
ML Seasons: 9

Overall Statistics

	W	L	ERA	G	GS	Sv	IP	H	R	BB	SO	HR
1990	12	9	3.45	30	24	0	146.0	143	66	38	68	17
Career	73	92	4.35	290	201	10	1369.1	1440	727	469	619	146

How Often He Throws Strikes

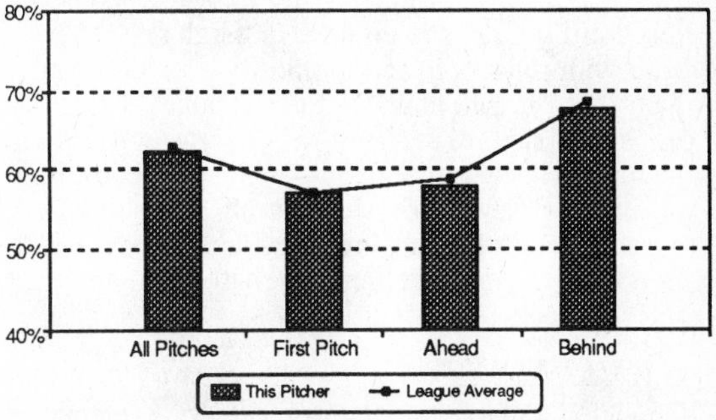

1990 Situational Stats

	W	L	ERA	Sv	IP		AB	H	HR	RBI	AVG
Home	6	5	3.02	0	80.1	LHB	90	28	4	9	.311
Road	6	4	3.97	0	65.2	RHB	453	115	13	48	.254
Day	5	2	2.84	0	44.1	Sc Pos	106	28	3	38	.264
Night	7	7	3.72	0	101.2	Clutch	21	9	1	5	.429

1990 Rankings (National League)

- 5th most runners caught stealing (13)
- Led the Pirates in home runs allowed (17), pickoff throws (117), runners caught stealing and lowest batting average allowed vs. right-handed batters (.254)

JEFF KING

Position: 3B
Bats: R **Throws:** R
Ht: 6' 1" **Wt:** 175

Opening Day Age: 26
Born: 12/26/64 in Marion, IN
ML Seasons: 2

Overall Statistics

	G	AB	R	H	D	T	HR	RBI	SB	BB	SO	AVG
1990	127	371	46	91	17	1	14	53	3	21	50	.245
Career	202	586	77	133	30	4	19	72	7	41	84	.227

Where He Hits the Ball

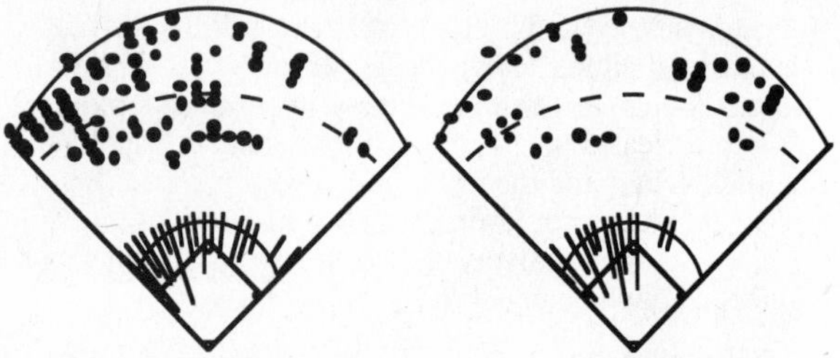

Vs. LHP Vs. RHP

1990 Situational Stats

	AB	H	HR	RBI	AVG		AB	H	HR	RBI	AVG
Home	179	49	9	30	.274	LHP	231	61	9	36	.264
Road	192	42	5	23	.219	RHP	140	30	5	17	.214
Day	116	30	5	17	.259	Sc Pos	112	26	3	38	.232
Night	255	61	9	36	.239	Clutch	60	7	0	4	.117

1990 Rankings (National League)

- 1st in lowest batting average in the clutch (.117) and lowest batting average on an 0-2 count (.000)
- 7th most GDPs per GDP situation (17.6%)

HITTING:

It has taken longer than the Pirates had originally hoped, but Jeff King has started showing signs of becoming a dependable major league player. The Pirates used the first pick in the 1986 amateur draft to select King, who was an All-American at the University of Arkansas. However, King did not spend his first full season in the major leagues until 1990.

After hitting .195 in 75 games as a rookie in 1989, King continued to struggle in the first half of '90. At the All-Star break, he was batting only .226 with three home runs and 16 RBI. But then he caught fire in the second half, batting .259 with 11 homers and 37 RBI. Spending the season as a platoon third baseman, King finally found confidence and patience in the second half of last season. He became more comfortable with offspeed pitches and was not overmatched by big-league fastballs, one of his weaknesses in the past.

King still struggles to produce in tough spots. He hit .232 with runners in scoring position in 1990 and a paltry .117 in late innings of close games. However, he showed signs of becoming a big-game player when he hit two home runs in a pivotal September meeting against the New York Mets. In all, King did well, especially considering that the Pirates have yet to figure out where to put him in the batting order. He hit in every spot but ninth in 1990.

BASERUNNING:

Though not blessed with blazing speed, King makes an impact on the bases. He has an innate talent for knowing exactly when he can take the extra base and almost never makes a poor judgement. He is not a base stealer, though, swiping only three in 1990.

FIELDING:

Because of a chronically bad shoulder, many had doubts about King making it as a third baseman. Though he was charged with 18 errors in 1990, King shows signs of being an above-average third baseman. He has quick reflexes, charges balls well and compensates for his shoulder with an accurate three-quarters delivery. King also adds versatility. He saw most of his action at first base as a rookie and has also played second base and shortstop in the major leagues.

OVERALL:

Labeled as uncaring and lazy in the minors, King is proving he can be a quality big-leaguer. He may never reach the stardom once expected, but he should be able to consistently hit 20 homers and drive in 80 runs a season.

PITCHING:

Rather quietly, Bob Kipper has become one of the National League's better left-handed middle relievers. Kipper has spent the past three seasons in the Pittsburgh Pirates' bullpen, and his win and save totals have been less than eye-popping. He is 10-12 with a modest total of seven saves. But another stat shows how tough Kipper has been: he's allowed only 6.5 hits per nine innings.

Kipper's fastball and slider are average but his change-up is exceptional. He throws it with the same motion as his other pitches and can make batters practically fall down in their futile attempts to hit it. Often, they wind up hitting little pop flies.

Though Kipper's specialty is getting left-handed hitters out, he was extremely effective against all batters in 1990, and actually fared a little better against righthanders. Lefties had a .225 batting average against him and righties hit only .178. Kipper, who bounced back strong after missing the first month with a sore elbow, was particularly tough in pressure situations last year. Opponents hit .162 with runners on, .180 with men in scoring position and .186 in close games.

Kipper is prone to wildness and home run balls. He has walked 3.6 per nine innings over the past three seasons and was touched for seven gopher balls in 62.2 innings in 1990. Those drawbacks prevented him from becoming an effective starting pitcher in the past. Kipper made an emergency start last season, his first in nearly three seasons, and was bombed for seven runs in 1.1 innings at Atlanta.

HOLDING RUNNERS, FIELDING, HITTING:

Kipper pays close attention to runners and has a quick move to first base. Sometimes, the move is a little too quick as evidenced by his league-high five balks in 1990. Kipper is a good fielder with quick reactions. He is good at fielding bunts and usually stops anything hit back through the middle. Though a fast runner, Kipper rarely gets on base to utilize his speed. As a reliever, he rarely gets to bat, which is OK since he was one-for-seven (.143) in 1990.

OVERALL:

Kipper was rushed to the major leagues and never cut it as a starting pitcher. In need of a lefthander in the bullpen, the Pirates made Kipper a reliever prior to the 1988 season. He has found a home in the bullpen and is one of the Pirates' unsung heroes.

BOB KIPPER

Position: RP
Bats: R **Throws:** L
Ht: 6' 2" **Wt:** 175

Opening Day Age: 26
Born: 7/8/64 in Aurora, IL
ML Seasons: 6

Overall Statistics

	W	L	ERA	G	GS	Sv	IP	H	R	BB	SO	HR
1990	5	2	3.02	41	1	3	62.2	44	24	26	35	7
Career	22	32	4.29	194	45	7	463.1	421	244	181	309	66

How Often He Throws Strikes

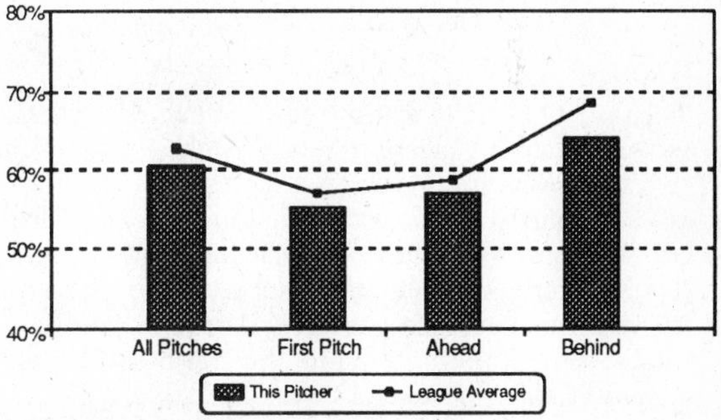

1990 Situational Stats

	W	L	ERA	Sv	IP		AB	H	HR	RBI	AVG
Home	4	1	2.70	0	30.0	LHB	80	18	0	7	.225
Road	1	1	3.31	3	32.2	RHB	146	26	7	19	.178
Day	3	0	0.56	2	16.0	Sc Pos	50	9	3	21	.180
Night	2	2	3.86	1	46.2	Clutch	59	11	1	6	.186

1990 Rankings (National League)

- 1st in balks (5)
- 4th in first batter efficiency (.162) and least GDPs induced per GDP situation (2.3%)
- Led the Pirates in balks

PITCHING:

Bill Landrum's fortunes took a turn for the worse in 1990 as quickly as they had turned for the better in 1989. In 1989, the journeyman came out of nowhere to become the Pittsburgh Pirates' closer. After posting only two saves in 59 previous major league relief appearances, Landrum had a club-high 26. That was a tough act for Landrum to follow, and he couldn't do it.

Landrum again led the Pirates in saves in 1990, but the total was 13, exactly half of what he had the previous season. Only one of those saves came after the All-Star break. Landrum's drop in productivity was in direct proportion to a drop in velocity. He lost about a foot off his fastball, falling from 92 to 87 MPH. Physical problems were the cause. Landrum pitched most of the season with a sore right knee on which he had arthroscopic surgery in 1988 to repair a torn ligament. The knee forced him to adjust his motion, thus putting extra strain on his shoulder.

The fastball, which Landrum cuts and gets downward movement on, is clearly his best pitch and induces strike outs and grounders. When its velocity diminishes, Landrum is in trouble. He throws a curveball and change-up but those are just for show. With a lessened fastball, Landrum seemed to lose some of the aggressiveness he gained in 1989. In previous stints with Cincinnati and the Chicago Cubs, Landrum was criticized for giving in to hitters, particularly when ahead in the count. He put himself in trouble early in 1990 by allowing leadoff hitters to compile a .355 batting average.

HOLDING RUNNERS, FIELDING, HITTING:

Landrum does not have a particularly good move to first base but compensates with a rather quick delivery home. Opponents were successful on eight of 10 steal attempts against him in 1990, though. Landrum is a good fielder who does the little things like cover first and back up bases. Landrum jokes about his inability to hit the ball out of the infield. However, he had a double in 1990 and scored his first major league run. That was Landrum's only hit, though, as he finished 1-for-9 (.111) with five strikeouts.

OVERALL:

Landrum disappeared as rapidly as he emerged. He probably pitched over his head a bit in 1989. However, if he can return to health in 1991, there's no reason to believe he can't be an effective reliever capable of closing games.

BILL LANDRUM

Position: RP
Bats: R **Throws:** R
Ht: 6' 2" **Wt:** 185

Opening Day Age: 33
Born: 8/17/57 in Columbia, SC
ML Seasons: 5

Overall Statistics

	W	L	ERA	G	GS	Sv	IP	H	R	BB	SO	HR
1990	7	3	2.13	54	0	13	71.2	69	22	21	39	4
Career	13	8	3.11	171	2	41	243.1	239	94	90	152	10

How Often He Throws Strikes

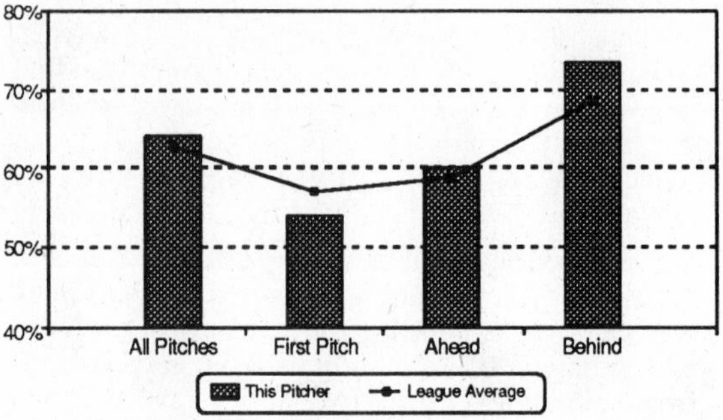

1990 Situational Stats

	W	L	ERA	Sv	IP		AB	H	HR	RBI	AVG
Home	4	2	1.93	7	37.1	LHB	138	38	2	16	.275
Road	3	1	2.36	6	34.1	RHB	125	31	2	13	.248
Day	1	0	2.70	1	13.1	Sc Pos	83	21	0	24	.253
Night	6	3	2.01	12	58.1	Clutch	126	34	1	16	.270

1990 Rankings (National League)

- ➟ 1st in worst first batter efficiency (.423)
- ➟ 8th in games finished (41)
- ➟ 9th in most GDPs induced per GDP situation (16.4%)
- ➟ Led the Pirates in saves (13), games finished and save opportunities (16)

MIKE LaVALLIERE

Position: C
Bats: L **Throws:** R
Ht: 5' 9" **Wt:** 190

Opening Day Age: 30
Born: 8/18/60 in Charlotte, NC
ML Seasons: 7

Overall Statistics

	G	AB	R	H	D	T	HR	RBI	SB	BB	SO	AVG
1990	96	279	27	72	15	0	3	31	0	44	20	.258
Career	533	1505	119	402	73	2	11	173	3	211	152	.267

Where He Hits the Ball

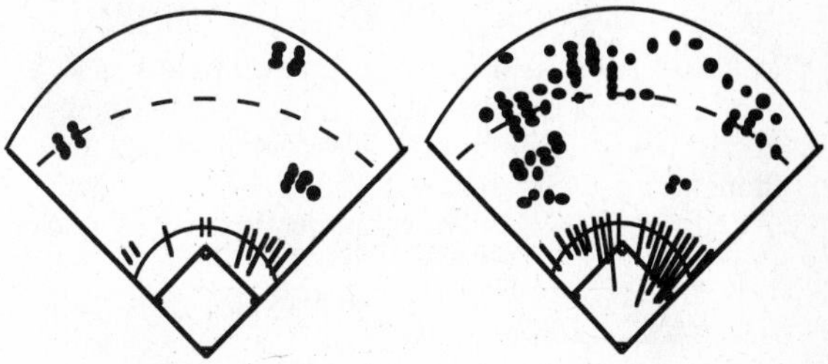

Vs. LHP   Vs. RHP

1990 Situational Stats

	AB	H	HR	RBI	AVG		AB	H	HR	RBI	AVG
Home	127	35	2	15	.276	LHP	56	21	2	11	.375
Road	152	37	1	16	.243	RHP	223	51	1	20	.229
Day	76	21	1	6	.276	Sc Pos	66	20	2	30	.303
Night	203	51	2	25	.251	Clutch	35	7	0	1	.200

1990 Rankings (National League)

➟ Did not rank near the top or bottom in any category

HITTING:

Mike LaValliere has long been considered a platoon player who sits against lefthanders. However, he is starting to show that maybe his rest should come against righties. After hitting .221 against southpaws in 1987 and .159 in the 1988, LaValliere has improved dramatically in the past two seasons. He had a .280 average against southpaws in 1989, then hit a smoking .375 in 1990.

Meanwhile, LaValliere's effectiveness against righthanders dropped in 1990 as he hit only .229 after seasons of .323, .284 and .321. LaValliere's success against lefthanders is the result of his learning how to go the other way with breaking balls. He was a pull hitter who liked fastballs earlier in his career, but is becoming adept at blooping singles into left field.

LaValliere is limited in the fact that he has little power and no speed. His three home runs in 1990 tied a career high. Thus, infielders play deep and outfielders play shallow. LaValliere compensates by showing outstanding patience. He drew 44 walks in 1990 while striking out only 20 times, the fourth straight season he has had more walks than strikeouts. He also comes up with big hits, batting .303 with runners in scoring position last season.

BASERUNNING:

The stocky LaValliere may be the slowest runner in the game. Three knee operations have done nothing to help his speed. He has only three lifetime steals (all in 1988) and has been thrown out eight times. LaValliere is fully aware of his limitations and does not take unnecessary chances.

FIELDING:

A former Gold Glove winner, LaValliere has a great rapport with pitchers. He has a sixth sense about which pitch to call in a certain situation and is a master psychologist, coddling and prodding his pitchers when necessary. LaValliere has a strong arm that is usually accurate. However, his throwing statistics suffered in 1990 as only 26 percent (36 of 140) of runners attempting to steal were caught. LaValliere's tendency to carry extra weight hampers his mobility.

OVERALL:

LaValliere is a solid singles' hitting catcher whose true value lies in his defense and handling of pitchers. He's a lot like Mike Scioscia, though he lacks Scioscia's occasional home run power; he's a good, solid catcher whose contributions are often overlooked. Valuing his efforts, the Pirates protected LaValliere's bad knees by starting him in 87 games last season. He must watch his weight, though, if he wants to have a long career.

JOSE LIND

Position: 2B
Bats: R **Throws:** R
Ht: 5'11" **Wt:** 170

Opening Day Age: 26
Born: 5/1/64 in Toabaja, Puerto Rico
ML Seasons: 4

HITTING:

The only thing preventing Jose Lind from becoming a star is his hitting. Though an extraordinary fielder, Lind is only an ordinary hitter as his .257 career batting average attests. Lind showed signs of becoming a good hitter in 1990. He started the season hitting the ball with authority and had a .339 average in early June. However, Lind skidded the rest of the season until his average finally came to rest at .261.

Lind has never been able to get totally comfortable at the plate. At times, he has tried to pull everything. On other occasions, he has concerned himself too much with taking each pitch to the opposite field. Therefore, pitchers will give Lind breaking balls away when he is in a pulling phase and inside fastballs when he is going through an opposite-field period. Lind started last season with a simple philosophy: see the ball and try to hit it hard up the middle. However, he fell back into the opposite-field groove in the second half.

Lind did have a career high 34 extra-base hits last season, but his power is minimal. He has five career home runs in 1846 at-bats. He does make contact, though, and is a good bunter. But he's a very undisciplined hitter, with only 16 unintentional walks last year.

BASERUNNING:

Batting eighth, Lind does not get very many steal attempts, but almost never gets caught when he tries. Lind was a perfect 8-for-8 last year and is 23-for-24 in the past two seasons. Lind is an alert baserunner. He can easily go from first to third on most singles and score from first on doubles.

FIELDING:

Lind does not possess blinding speed but his range and leaping ability are unmatched. He can get to any ball hit between the first and second base bags and will go into medium right field to steal pop flies. Though 5-foot-11, Lind can easily dunk a basketball and often climbs the ladder to turn line drives into outs. He also turns the double play well and has a good arm. He suffered from elbow problems and made 17 errors in 1989. However, he reduced that number to seven last season; when he started the year with 55 straight errorless games.

OVERALL:

Even if he doesn't hit, Jose Lind is a valuable player because of his great defensive ability. But if could get his average near .300, the sky would be the limit for the flashy second baseman.

Overall Statistics

	G	AB	R	H	D	T	HR	RBI	SB	BB	SO	AVG
1990	152	514	46	134	28	5	1	48	8	35	52	.261
Career	494	1846	201	474	81	16	5	156	40	124	203	.257

Where He Hits the Ball

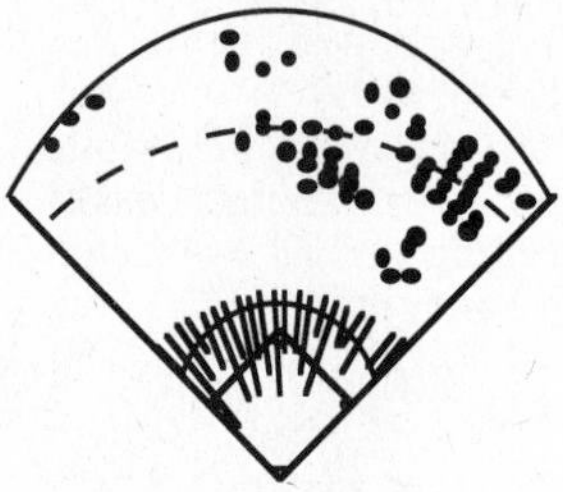

Vs. LHP

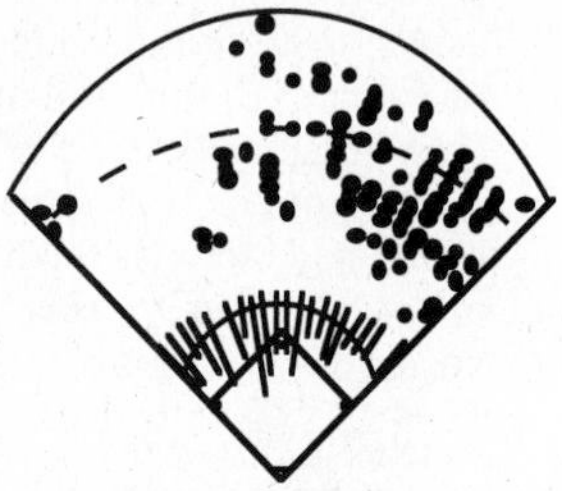

Vs. RHP

1990 Situational Stats

	AB	H	HR	RBI	AVG		AB	H	HR	RBI	AVG
Home	245	64	1	30	.261	LHP	216	50	1	19	.231
Road	269	70	0	18	.260	RHP	298	84	0	29	.282
Day	127	39	0	11	.307	Sc Pos	130	37	0	45	.285
Night	387	95	1	37	.245	Clutch	94	30	0	8	.319

1990 Rankings (National League)

- 1st in lowest HR frequency (514 ABs per HR)
- 2nd in GDPs (20)
- 4th in intentional walks (19) and lowest batting average on an 3-2 count (.083)
- Led the Pirates in intentional walks, GDPs, groundball/flyball ratio (1.64), batting average on an 0-2 count (.220), lowest percentage of swings that missed (11.1%) and highest percentage of swings put into play (50.5%)
- Led NL second basemen in intentional walks and GDPs

PITCHING:

Bob Patterson has gone from being a rookie, opening day starting pitcher to a Class AAA non-entity to contributing performer on a divisional champion -- all in the space of three years. Patterson finally stuck around for a full major league season in 1990 and gave Pittsburgh a solid effort out of the bullpen. Going 8-5 with five saves and 2.95 ERA in 55 appearances, he was an important part of the Pirates' bullpen-by-committee.

Patterson was the Pirates' starter in the 1987 season opener but was back in the minors six weeks later. He missed almost all of the 1988 season at AAA Buffalo because of a shoulder injury and wasn't even brought to spring training as a non-roster player in 1989. However, he pitched well in an '89 September call-up and re-established himself.

Patterson has a good curveball, a decent fastball and adequate offspeed stuff. The biggest reason for his sudden major league effectiveness is, quite simply, confidence. Previously, Patterson never had a firm belief he was capable of getting major-league hitters out. That has all changed. Patterson now challenges hitters and quickly gets a first strike. Patterson may have been the Pirates' most consistent reliever in a 1990 bullpen that was often shaky. His eight wins were one more than he had in his previous 41 games over four big-league seasons. He also had 8 holds, allowed only 12 of 39 inherited runners to score and gave up only 14 non-intentional walks in 94.2 innings.

A versatile pitcher, Patterson can start and pitch short, middle and long relief. He started five games for the Pirates last season, going 2-2, but was not as effective in that role as he was in the pen. The third time through the order, opponents had a .414 batting average against him. Patterson's ability to pitch long stints out of the bullpen paid off with four extra- inning victories.

HOLDING RUNNERS, FIELDING, HITTING:

Patterson pays attention to runners and keeps them close. Only five of nine were successful stealing against him last season. He is also a conscientious fielder who is unafraid to go after the lead runner on sacrifice attempts. Hitting is not a Patterson strong point, as a 1990 average of .053 (1-for-19) attests.

OVERALL:

Bob Patterson is a testament to perseverance. Even when everyone else gave up on him, Patterson kept pushing on. He was rewarded with a trip to the postseason and figures to be a key lefty in the Pirates' bullpen again this season.

BOB PATTERSON

Position: RP/SP
Bats: R **Throws:** L
Ht: 6' 2" **Wt:** 192

Opening Day Age: 31
Born: 5/16/59 in Jacksonville, FL
ML Seasons: 5

Overall Statistics

	W	L	ERA	G	GS	Sv	IP	H	R	BB	SO	HR
1990	8	5	2.95	55	5	5	94.2	88	33	21	70	9
Career	15	15	4.66	96	20	6	204.2	222	111	59	138	19

How Often He Throws Strikes

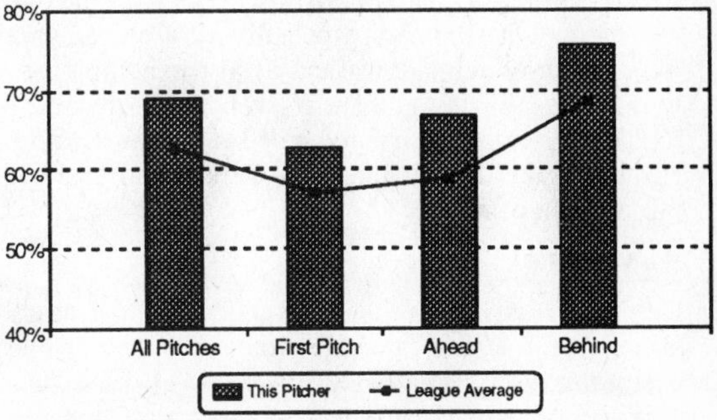

1990 Situational Stats

	W	L	ERA	Sv	IP		AB	H	HR	RBI	AVG
Home	4	1	2.70	3	53.1	LHB	103	21	1	8	.204
Road	4	4	3.27	2	41.1	RHB	251	67	8	28	.267
Day	1	1	3.05	2	20.2	Sc Pos	80	21	2	27	.262
Night	7	4	2.92	3	74.0	Clutch	96	22	1	10	.229

1990 Rankings (National League)

➟ Led the Pirates in games pitched (55)

GARY REDUS

Position: 1B
Bats: R **Throws:** R
Ht: 6' 1" **Wt:** 185

Opening Day Age: 34
Born: 11/1/56 in Tanner, AL
ML Seasons: 9

HITTING:

Always a useful player, Gary Redus can hit a home run or steal a base. At 34, his skills have declined somewhat, and he no longer does either well enough to warrant playing every day. But Redus has become very useful coming off the bench, and made a contribution to the Pirates' division title in 1990.

Though Redus has often been advised to take advantage of his speed by learning to hit the ball on the ground, he has preferred trying to drive the ball, and it's hard to criticize the results. Though he doesn't hit much for average, Redus can hit line drives to all fields and will often turn on the ball against left-handed pitchers. He has good power to the gaps and can hit the ball out of the park on occasion. Over 40 percent of his hits (24 of 56) went for extra bases last year, an excellent ratio.

Redus is primarily a high-ball hitter who likes the ball away from him. Pitchers, especially righties, can give him problems with down-and-away breaking stuff. Redus doesn't hit righthanders very well any more (.120 in '90) and is thus relegated to a platoon role. He will make the pitcher throw strikes and draws a fair amount of walks.

BASERUNNING:

Despite his advancing age, Redus hasn't lost much speed. He is still a first-rate stolen base threat and easily takes the extra base. His 11 stolen bases last year, however, were his lowest total since his 20-game debut with Cincinnati back in 1982, and his 69 percent success rate was the worst of his career.

FIELDING:

Redus has been asked by the Pirates to play out of position the past two seasons, platooning at first base. He has major problems there, particularly with handling off-target throws. He is an outfielder by trade and is adequate, but not great. He uses his speed well in the outfield, but his arm is below average.

OVERALL:

Redus was a free agent this winter. The Pirates, who now have Carmelo Martinez as a right-handed hitting first baseman, probably don't need Redus for that slot. But they've lost outfielder R.J. Reynolds to Japan, and Redus would be a logical replacement. Wherever he winds up, he figures to make a contribution. He has weaknesses, but his strengths are good enough that he is a valuable bench player.

Overall Statistics

	G	AB	R	H	D	T	HR	RBI	SB	BB	SO	AVG
1990	96	227	32	56	15	3	6	23	11	33	38	.247
Career	890	2830	490	706	151	42	74	283	290	409	583	.249

Where He Hits the Ball

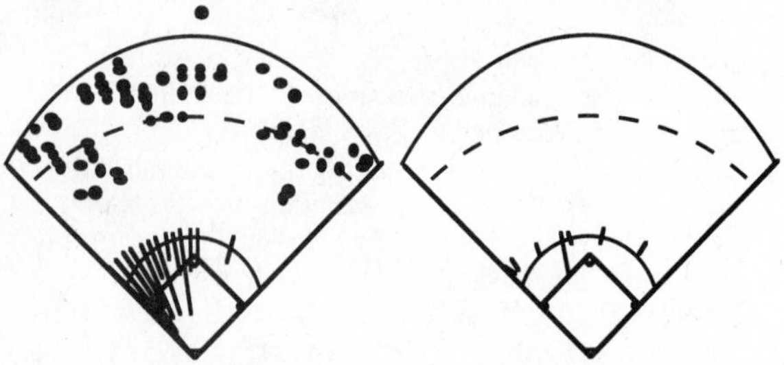

1990 Situational Stats

	AB	H	HR	RBI	AVG		AB	H	HR	RBI	AVG
Home	108	22	2	12	.204	LHP	202	53	6	23	.262
Road	119	34	4	11	.286	RHP	25	3	0	0	.120
Day	63	12	2	10	.190	Sc Pos	34	8	2	17	.235
Night	164	44	4	13	.268	Clutch	36	10	0	3	.278

1990 Rankings (National League)

- Led NL first basemen in steals of third (2)

DON SLAUGHT

Position: C
Bats: R **Throws:** R
Ht: 6' 1" **Wt:** 190

Opening Day Age: 32
Born: 9/11/58 in Long Beach, CA
ML Seasons: 9

Overall Statistics

	G	AB	R	H	D	T	HR	RBI	SB	BB	SO	AVG
1990	84	230	27	69	18	3	4	29	0	27	27	.300
Career	840	2596	275	706	159	22	54	285	13	181	383	.272

Where He Hits the Ball

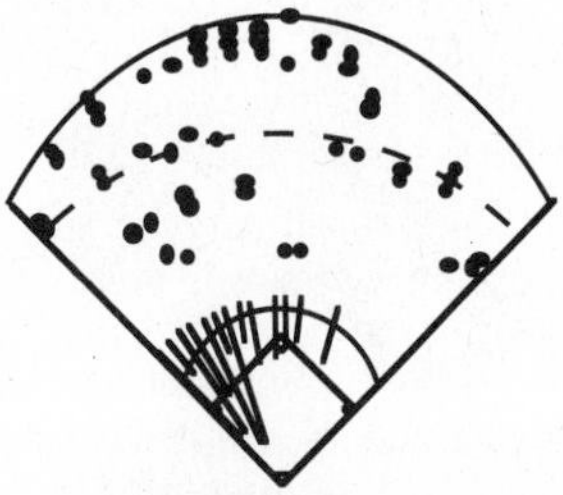

Vs. LHP

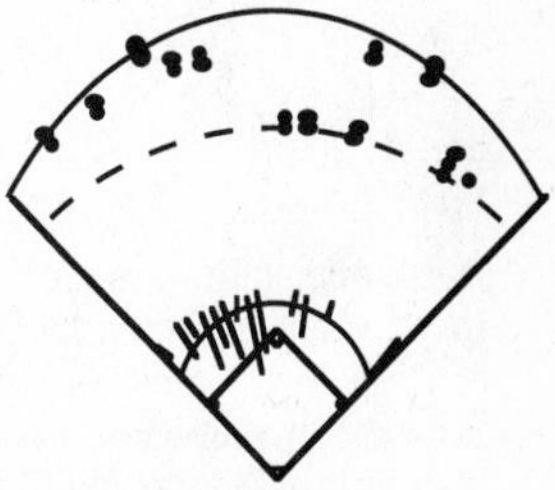

Vs. RHP

1990 Situational Stats

	AB	H	HR	RBI	AVG		AB	H	HR	RBI	AVG
Home	113	31	1	12	.274	LHP	164	52	2	17	.317
Road	117	38	3	17	.325	RHP	66	17	2	12	.258
Day	50	13	2	10	.260	Sc Pos	49	17	0	22	.347
Night	180	56	2	19	.311	Clutch	42	10	1	6	.238

1990 Rankings (National League)

- 1st in lowest batting average on a 3-1 count (.000)
- Led the Pirates in hit by pitch (3), batting average vs. left-handed pitchers (.317) and on-base average vs. left-handed pitchers (.393)
- Led NL catchers in hit by pitch and on-base average vs. left-handed pitchers

HITTING:

For the first half of the 1990 season, Don Slaught was a dangerous hitter for the Pittsburgh Pirates. In the second half, he did next to nothing. Acquired from the New York Yankees the previous winter, Slaught terrorized National League pitchers in his first trip through his new league. He had a .382 average at the All-Star break with four home runs and 20 RBI. However, he hit .206 with no homers and nine RBI thereafter.

As has often happened in his career, injuries slowed Slaught. He was hampered by hand problems in the second half as he sustained a sprained left thumb, a bruised right hand and a dislocated right ring finger. To compensate, Slaught dropped his hands at the plate, which caused reduced bat speed and too many pop-ups.

Slaught can be overpowered by a good fastball but handles breaking pitches well and feasts on mistakes. Though he hits to all fields, he has the ability to pull the ball when needed. Slaught is also developing a better eye and an improved ability to make contact. He had an identical number of walks and strikeouts, 27, in 1990. He was a good clutch hitter for the Pirates, posting a .347 average with runners in scoring position.

BASERUNNING:

To borrow an old cliche, Slaught runs pretty well for a catcher. In fact, he batted leadoff in one game last season. He did not steal a base in 1990, though, and has only two over the past four seasons. Slaught does not clog up the base paths and won't cost his team runs by trying to do too much.

FIELDING:

Though he improved his throwing while in the American League, Slaught struggled in the more speed-oriented National League. He threw out only 26 percent (22 of 84) of would-be base stealers and committed eight errors. Slaught also displayed a disturbing tendency of being unsure on pop fouls. Slaught lived down the label of not being a good pitch-caller or handler of pitchers. Pirate pitchers enjoyed working with him.

OVERALL:

Slaught platooned with Mike LaValliere behind the plate and was a good right-handed hitting catcher complement in the first half of 1990 for the Pirates. A free agent, Slaught's market value dropped with his poor second half. But he is a lifetime .272 hitter, and with seemingly every team in need of catching, Slaught should draw much interest.

PITCHING:

Though 1990 was a good year for the Pittsburgh Pirates, it was a frustrating one for John Smiley. The big lefthander had established himself as one of the game's most promising young starters in 1988 and '89. However, injuries led to an inconsistent 1990, and Smiley finished at 9-10 with a hefty 4.64 ERA. He had been a combined 25-19 with a 3.03 ERA over the previous two seasons.

Smiley came into the season recovering from arthroscopic surgery to remove bone chips from his left elbow the previous winter. Just when it seemed he was rounding into form, Smiley fractured his pitching hand in a car door accident on May 19 and missed six weeks.

A power pitcher with an awkward delivery, Smiley relies on a 90 MPH fastball and a hard slider. The fastball drops sharply, moving in on lefties and away from righties. He also throws a curveball and change-up. Smiley also has good control for a young lefty, and he's allowed just 2.1 walks per nine innings in his three seasons as a starter.

Poise and stamina were two of Smiley's strong points in previous seasons. Both left him at times in 1990. Smiley sometimes let his poor season get the best of him and became his own worst enemy. He particularly struggled early, allowing 25 first-inning runs in 25 starts. He completed just two games in 1990. After the second time around the order, opponents hit Smiley at a .326 clip.

HOLDING RUNNERS, FIELDING, HITTING:

Opposing baserunners take more liberties on Smiley than most other lefthanders. Because of an extremely high leg kick, Smiley is easy to run on and allowed 13 of 19 runners to steal successfully in 1990. The gangly Smiley's follow-through puts him in poor fielding position and he is not quick off the mound. He has made six errors in the last two seasons and can be negligent in backing up home plate and third base. Smiley's hitting also slipped last season after he drove in nine runs in '89. Smiley hit just .122 (6-for-49) with three RBI. He is a big man who takes big swings, though he had no extra-base hits last year.

OVERALL:

After tasting success, Smiley learned about failure last year. He is still only 26 and has some of the nastiest stuff of any young pitcher in the game. If he can get healthy, Smiley has the tools to bounce back and be a big winner.

JOHN SMILEY

Position: SP
Bats: L **Throws:** L
Ht: 6' 4" **Wt:** 195

Opening Day Age: 26
Born: 3/17/65 in Phoenixville, PA
ML Seasons: 5

Overall Statistics

	W	L	ERA	G	GS	Sv	IP	H	R	BB	SO	HR
1990	9	10	4.64	26	25	0	149.1	161	83	36	86	15
Career	40	34	3.73	163	85	4	646.1	593	297	185	405	61

How Often He Throws Strikes

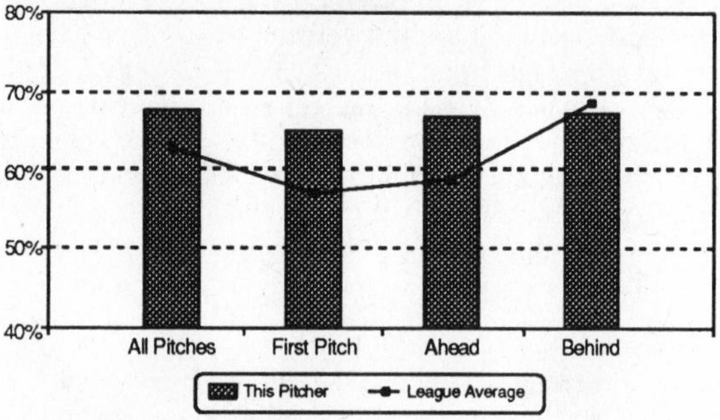

1990 Situational Stats

	W	L	ERA	Sv	IP		AB	H	HR	RBI	AVG
Home	3	4	3.80	0	64.0	LHB	93	28	3	14	.301
Road	6	6	5.27	0	85.1	RHB	492	133	12	55	.270
Day	4	2	4.54	0	39.2	Sc Pos	130	41	5	51	.315
Night	5	8	4.68	0	109.2	Clutch	40	8	2	4	.200

1990 Rankings (National League)

- 3rd worst ERA on the road (5.27)
- Led the Pirates in losses (10)

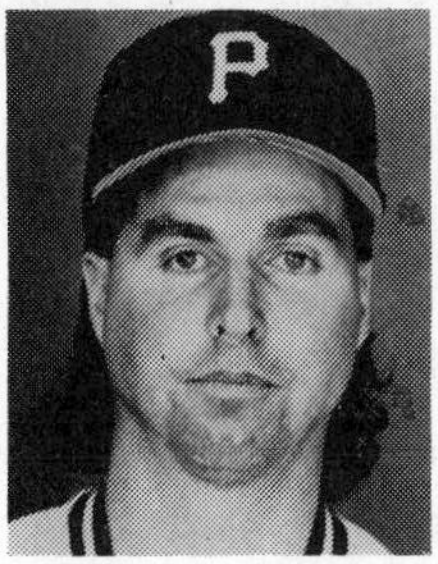

ZANE SMITH

Position: SP
Bats: L **Throws:** L
Ht: 6' 2" **Wt:** 195

Opening Day Age: 30
Born: 12/28/60 in Madison, WI
ML Seasons: 7

PITCHING:

Potential finally translated into results for Zane Smith in 1990. Long considered to have the promise of being a first-rate left-handed starter, Smith posted only his second winning record in six full major league seasons. He was 12-9 with the Montreal Expos and Pittsburgh Pirates and finished second in the National League with a 2.55 ERA.

Smith entered 1990 with a 39-59 career mark, mostly compiled while toiling for lowly Atlanta. He was clearly inspired by playing for a winner. Smith was 6-7 with a 3.23 ERA with Montreal but his August 8 trade to Pittsburgh spurred him to some of the best pitching of his career. He went 6-2 with a 1.30 ERA in 11 games as he helped the Pirates to the National League East title. Smith was a clutch performer for the Pirates, one-hitting the New York Mets in a key game on September 5 and pitching 18 consecutive scoreless innings between Aug. 31 and Sept. 10. As a Pirate, opponents hit just .162 against him with runners in scoring position.

A finesse pitcher, Smith does not overpower hitters but is a master of getting ground ball outs, particularly in double play situations. He had the highest ratio of double-play grounders per nine innings in baseball last year (1.42). Smith relies on a sharp-dropping sinker and also throws a good slider. He improved his change-up after coming to Pittsburgh and it has become an effective third pitch.

Smith is also 100 percent again after undergoing arthroscopic surgery to remove a bone chip from his left elbow late in the 1988 season. Montreal worked him back slowly, using him as a reliever in 1989 after acquiring him that July. However, Smith gained stamina as 1990 wore on and completed three of 10 starts for Pittsburgh.

HOLDING RUNNERS, FIELDING, HITTING:

Smith has only a decent move to first and he struggled to hold runners close last year. He is a slightly below-average fielder committing three errors in 1990. Smith is a good bunter and takes hitting seriously. He hit .162 (11-for-68) with three doubles and a triple and also had eight sacrifice hits.

OVERALL:

Smith's strong finish made him one of the hottest commodities in this winter's free agent market. As a 30-year-old lefty who seems on the verge of consistently winning big, Smith added millions to his value with the strong 1990 finish. Whether the Pirates would be willing to pay his asking price, however, was an open question.

Overall Statistics

	W	L	ERA	G	GS	Sv	IP	H	R	BB	SO	HR
1990	12	9	2.55	33	31	0	215.1	196	77	50	130	15
Career	51	68	3.66	223	159	3	1116.1	1101	541	435	652	62

How Often He Throws Strikes

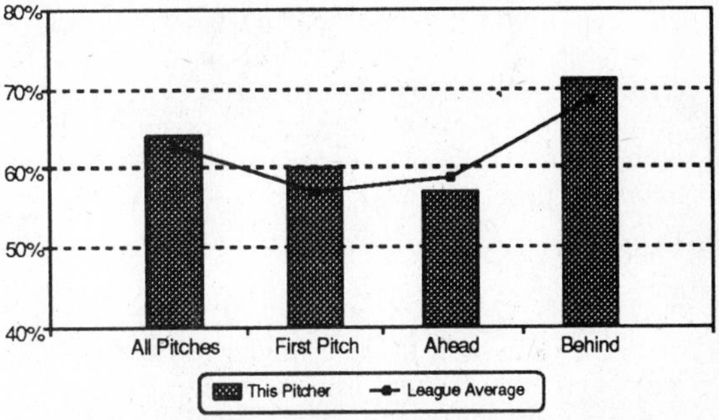

1990 Situational Stats

	W	L	ERA	Sv	IP		AB	H	HR	RBI	AVG
Home	9	3	2.05	0	118.1	LHB	116	19	1	8	.164
Road	3	6	3.15	0	97.0	RHB	685	177	14	60	.258
Day	1	1	2.52	0	25.0	Sc Pos	154	41	5	54	.266
Night	11	8	2.55	0	190.1	Clutch	88	19	2	9	.216

1990 Rankings (National League)

- 1st in GDPs induced (34), most GDPs induced per 9 innings (1.42), most GDPs induced per GDP situation (24.3%) and lowest batting average allowed vs. left-handed batters (.164)
- 2nd in ERA (2.55) and ERA at home (2.05)
- 3rd in groundball/flyball ratio (2.1) and highest stolen base percentage allowed (87.1%)
- 4th lowest run support per 9 innings (3.1)
- 5th in stolen bases allowed (27)

PITCHING:

Though the youthful-looking and soft-spoken Randy Tomlin appears more like a bat boy than a major league pitcher, he was a revelation for the Pittsburgh Pirates after a surprise promotion from Class AA. Tomlin was called up August 6 to start the first game of a doubleheader in Philadelphia. The plan was to send him right back to Harrisburg following the game. But a complete-game five-hitter threw a monkey wrench into that plan. Tomlin became a regular member of the rotation down the stretch and helped Pittsburgh to the National League East title. Tomlin's 4-4 record belied his 2.55 ERA. He allowed two earned runs or less in 10 of his 12 starts and issued only 12 walks in 77.2 innings.

Tomlin's success lies in deception. He has an awkward across-the-body delivery in which he slings the ball toward the plate. To opposing batters, it seems Tomlin is releasing his pitches from the vicinity of the first base dugout. His fastball, curve, slider and change-up are average but he changes speeds and throws strikes. The only thing out of the ordinary is how Tomlin grips his change, jamming the ball between his third and fourth fingers.

Despite his lack of a dominant pitch, Tomlin compensates with a great amount of moxie for a youngster. Tomlin completed two starts in 1990 but usually lost his effectiveness in the later innings. The first nine batters hit only .178 against him. However, the average rose to .216 the second time through the order and then to .278 thereafter.

HOLDING RUNNERS, FIELDING, HITTING:

Tomlin's delivery deceives baserunners as well as hitters. Base stealers had a terrible time trying to figure Tomlin out and stole only two bases in eight tries. Tomlin is an above-average fielder and, for a young player, does a fine job paying attention to details. Tomlin can fly but rarely gets on base to utilize his speed. He went just 1-for-25 (.040) with seven strikeouts. He also needs to work on his bunting.

OVERALL:

An 18th-round pick in the 1988 draft, Tomlin has made rapid progress to the major leagues. He made a good showing in the heat of a pennant race last season. He has only been around the league once, but the Pirates feel he will take a regular turn in their rotation for years to come.

RANDY TOMLIN

Position: SP
Bats: L **Throws:** L
Ht: 5'11" **Wt:** 179

Opening Day Age: 24
Born: 6/14/66 in Bainbridge, MD
ML Seasons: 1

Overall Statistics

	W	L	ERA	G	GS	Sv	IP	H	R	BB	SO	HR
1990	4	4	2.55	12	12	0	77.2	62	24	12	42	5
Career	4	4	2.55	12	12	0	77.2	62	24	12	42	5

How Often He Throws Strikes

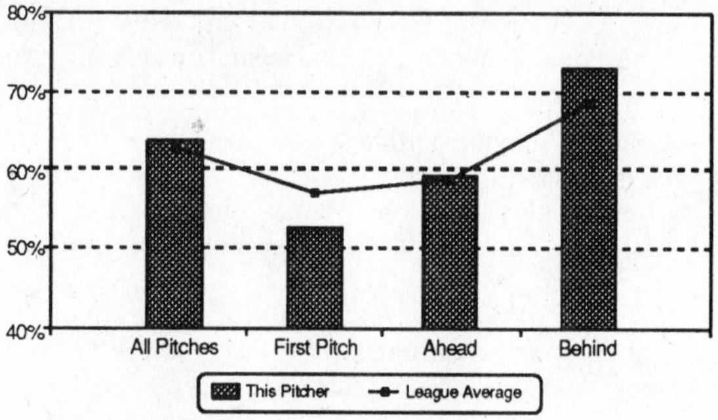

1990 Situational Stats

	W	L	ERA	Sv	IP		AB	H	HR	RBI	AVG
Home	2	3	3.02	0	50.2	LHB	45	12	2	5	.267
Road	2	1	1.67	0	27.0	RHB	235	50	3	15	.213
Day	0	3	4.07	0	24.1	Sc Pos	41	10	0	14	.244
Night	4	1	1.86	0	53.1	Clutch	16	5	1	1	.313

1990 Rankings (National League)

- Did not rank near the top or bottom in any category

ANDY VAN SLYKE

Position: CF
Bats: L **Throws:** R
Ht: 6' 2" **Wt:** 190
Opening Day Age: 30
Born: 12/21/60 in Utica, NY
ML Seasons: 8

HITTING:

Andy Van Slyke bounced back from an injury-plagued 1989 to re-establish himself as a premier player. Van Slyke rebounded from an '89 season in which he had a .237 batting average, nine home runs and 53 RBI to 1990 levels of .284, 17 and 77. He was at his best in the heat of the pennant race, coming up with 22 RBI in September.

Van Slyke quickly showed he was over the rib cage, shoulder and knee problems that bothered him in 1989 by belting two home runs on opening day. He remained a consistent force the rest of the season. Throughout his career, the knocks against Van Slyke were that he could not touch left-handed pitching and struck out too much. He improved on those weaknesses in 1990, hitting a respectable .261 against lefties with five homers, half of his previous career total. He also struck only 89 times following three consecutive triple-digit seasons.

Van Slyke can still be made to look bad by lefthanders on inside fastballs and breaking pitches away. However, after a lot of hard work, he is now able to hang in better against them. Van Slyke likes to pull the ball but can hit the ball deep to all parts of the park.

BASERUNNING:

Because of injuries, Van Slyke's stolen base totals have dipped in recent seasons. He had just 14 steals in 1990 but he was slowed by a sprained ankle late in the season. He was only caught four times. Van Slyke is a fast and daring baserunner who always looks to push things on the bases.

FIELDING:

When it comes to defensive center fielders, Van Slyke takes a back seat to no one. He has the speed, arm and instincts of a Gold Glove winner. Van Slyke makes remarkable catches in the gap look routine. He is not adverse to crashing into the wall or leaping above it. His arm is strong and deadly accurate and opponents do not even think of testing him. It is a rare occasion when he throws to the wrong base or misses a cutoff man.

OVERALL:

No one seems to enjoy playing baseball more than the ever-quotable Van Slyke. He goes all out at all times and is one of the game's most exciting players. In many respects, he has been the heart and soul of the Pirates' resurgence and they would be wise to keep him past 1991 when he is eligible for free agency.

Overall Statistics

	G	AB	R	H	D	T	HR	RBI	SB	BB	SO	AVG
1990	136	493	67	140	26	6	17	77	14	66	89	.284
Career	1098	3632	530	979	182	63	113	516	198	429	711	.270

Where He Hits the Ball

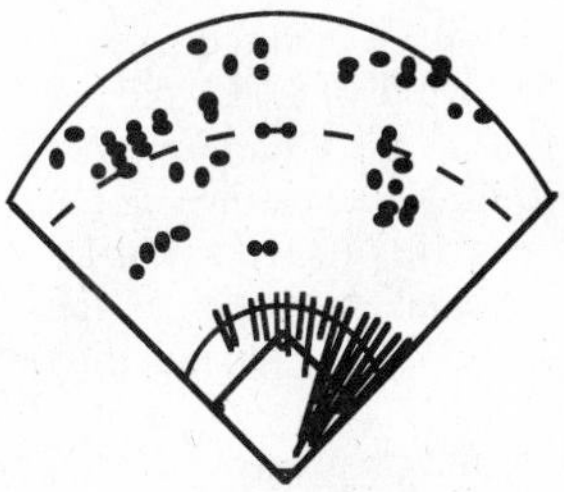
Vs. LHP

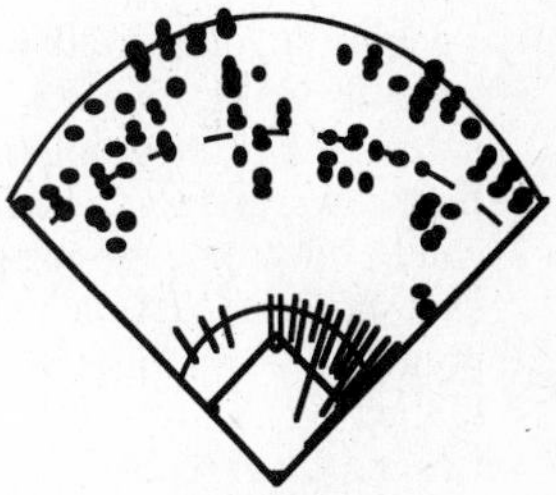
Vs. RHP

1990 Situational Stats

	AB	H	HR	RBI	AVG		AB	H	HR	RBI	AVG
Home	219	63	6	35	.288	LHP	188	49	5	28	.261
Road	274	77	11	42	.281	RHP	305	91	12	49	.298
Day	148	41	7	23	.277	Sc Pos	140	41	2	51	.293
Night	345	99	10	54	.287	Clutch	77	18	3	13	.234

1990 Rankings (National League)

- Led the Pirates in least GDPs per GDP situation (5.0%), batting average on a 3-1 count (.522) and batting average at home (.288)

PITCHING:

If Bob Walk could stay away from his old stomping grounds in Philadelphia, he would be fine. Walk has been placed on the disabled list three times in the past two seasons, each time a result of pulling a groin muscle while pitching at Veterans Stadium. Walk went on the DL twice in 1990, and it made for an inconsistent season in which he finished 7-5 with 12 no-decisions. He went two months and two days (May 18 to July 20) between his fourth and fifth wins and two more months (July 20 to Sept. 20) before his sixth victory.

Walk has a fastball that reaches 88 MPH, but relies on good control and mixing his pitches. He religiously tries to get either a curveball or slider over on the first pitch. If he gets a first strike, he becomes extremely effective. If not, he usually comes in with a hittable fastball or change-up.

Lacking stamina, Walk rarely will go past the sixth or seventh inning. He has completed only 12 of 188 career starts, including one of 24 in 1990. However, his one complete game of '90 showed why the veteran can be counted on in big games. He pitched a four-hit shutout in St. Louis on the final weekend of the regular season. Pirates manager Jim Leyland then tabbed Walk to start the opener of the National League Championship Series and he came up with a victory. Walk is also tough in the clutch, holding opposing hitters to a .220 average with runners in scoring position.

HOLDING RUNNERS, FIELDING, HITTING:

Walk has one of the best moves of any righthander in the game. It is deceptive -- so much so that it borders on a balk -- and effective. Only 12 of 21 opposing base stealers were successful with Walk on the mound last season. Though less than graceful-looking, Walk is a decent fielder, though he committed three errors in 1990. Walk loves to hit and run the bases, getting his uniform as dirty as that of a position player. He is a very good bunter and led the Pirate staff with 10 sacrifices in 1990. He hit .162 (6-for-37) with four RBI but struck out 13 times.

OVERALL:

After failing to live up to his early expectations with Philadelphia and Atlanta, Walk has served Pittsburgh's staff well the past five seasons. He will never be the ace but can be relied upon to take the ball every fifth day and give a decent effort.

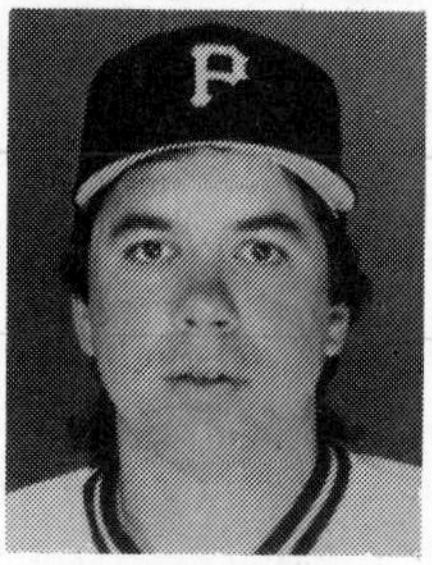

BOB WALK

Position: SP
Bats: R **Throws:** R
Ht: 6' 4" **Wt:** 217

Opening Day Age: 34
Born: 11/26/56 in Van Nuys, CA
ML Seasons: 11

Overall Statistics

	W	L	ERA	G	GS	Sv	IP	H	R	BB	SO	HR
1990	7	5	3.75	26	24	1	129.2	136	59	36	73	17
Career	73	59	3.91	257	188	3	1229.0	1221	601	458	641	100

How Often He Throws Strikes

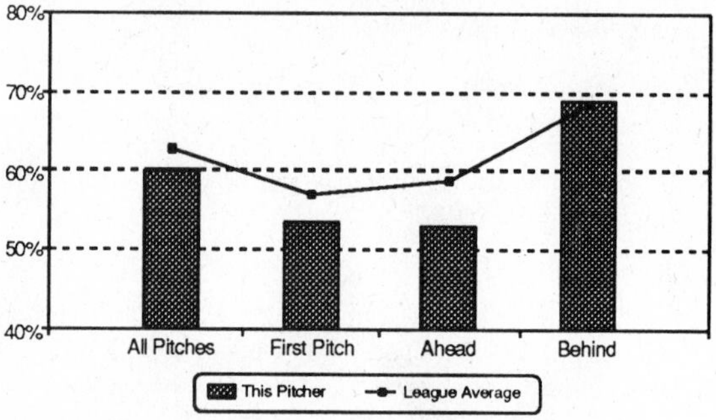

1990 Situational Stats

	W	L	ERA	Sv	IP		AB	H	HR	RBI	AVG
Home	3	3	3.90	0	60.0	LHB	300	78	9	32	.260
Road	4	2	3.62	1	69.2	RHB	203	58	8	19	.286
Day	2	1	4.72	1	40.0	Sc Pos	118	26	4	31	.220
Night	5	4	3.31	0	89.2	Clutch	24	4	0	0	.167

1990 Rankings (National League)

- Led the Pirates in home runs allowed (17) and hit batsmen (4)

DOUG BAIR

Position: RP
Bats: R **Throws:** R
Ht: 6' 0" **Wt:** 180

Opening Day Age: 41
Born: 8/22/49 in Defiance, OH
ML Seasons: 15

Overall Statistics

	W	L	ERA	G	GS	Sv	IP	H	R	BB	SO	HR
1990	0	0	4.81	22	0	0	24.1	30	15	11	19	3
Career	55	43	3.64	584	5	81	908.0	839	398	405	689	86

PITCHING, FIELDING, HITTING & HOLDING RUNNERS:

At 41, Doug Bair understands that while his marginal skills can no longer guarantee him a major league job, teams always need pitching at some point during the season. Bair has had to log some time in the minors during each of the last five seasons, but one major league club or another always gave him a call. Last year was no different, as Bair memorized all the airline arrival and departure times between Pittsburgh and AAA Buffalo. He began the season with the Pirates but was sent down and called up from Buffalo three additional times.

Bair was not overly effective however. He still throws hard, relying on a fastball and curveball. He also has a great work ethic and stays in excellent shape. However, age may finally be catching up to his velocity. His control also started to go in 1990 as he walked 11 in 24.1 innings. Like most veteran pitchers, Bair knows all the finer points of fielding. However, runners took liberties with him last season and were successful on six of seven steal attempts. Bair rarely bats but does not embarrass himself when he does.

OVERALL:

It has been quite a trip for Bair. He has pitched professionally for 20 seasons and played for eight major league and eight minor league clubs. He has also played on World Series winners in each league, getting a ring with St. Louis in 1982 and with Detroit in 1984. Age may be bringing Bair's fine journey to an end, though.

RAFAEL BELLIARD

Position: 2B
Bats: R **Throws:** R
Ht: 5' 6" **Wt:** 160

Opening Day Age: 29
Born: 10/24/61 in Pueblo Nuevo, Dominican Republic
ML Seasons: 9

Overall Statistics

	G	AB	R	H	D	T	HR	RBI	SB	BB	SO	AVG
1990	47	54	10	11	3	0	0	6	1	5	13	.204
Career	484	1051	115	229	16	9	1	72	35	85	168	.218

HITTING, FIELDING, BASERUNNING:

Rafael Belliard has had numerous chances to become the Pittsburgh Pirates' starting shortstop over the years. But his inability to hit has prevented him from being a regular. The Pirates finally gave up on him and gave the job to Jay Bell.

Belliard has compiled a weak .218 batting average in his career, with only 26 extra-base hits in 1051 at-bats. His only home run came back in 1987, the year everyone was hitting them out. Simply put, the diminutive Belliard is overpowered by major league pitching. He does not have the strength to handle fastballs, and good breaking pitches also elude his bat. Belliard did drive in five runs in a five-day span in 1990. However, he had only one RBI the rest of the season.

Belliard is speedy and a good baserunner, though his chances to show his running skills are rare. Defense has kept him in the major leagues. He is a superb shortstop with great range, outstanding hands and a good arm. He is also above average at second base and decent at third base.

OVERALL:

Belliard is great defensively but started only 13 games and had just 54 at-bats despite spending the entire 1990 season with the Pirates. He is a free agent and can only stick with a team that can afford to carry a good glove man.

JOHN CANGELOSI

Position: CF
Bats: B **Throws:** L
Ht: 5' 8" **Wt:** 150

Opening Day Age: 28
Born: 3/10/63 in Brooklyn, NY
ML Seasons: 6

Overall Statistics

	G	AB	R	H	D	T	HR	RBI	SB	BB	SO	AVG
1990	58	76	13	15	2	0	0	1	7	11	12	.197
Career	491	976	160	233	34	9	6	68	98	180	143	.239

HITTING, FIELDING, BASERUNNING:

Since showing great promise as a leadoff hitter in the first half of his rookie season with the Chicago White Sox in 1986, John Cangelosi has been hanging on with the Pirates as a fifth outfielder. Cangelosi won't be able to hold on to even that limited role if his average keeps sinking. Over the last four years he's batted .275, .254, .219, and then .197 in 1990.

Cangelosi batted 438 times with the White Sox in 1986. However, he has spent the past four years with the Pirates and has never received more than 182 at-bats in a season. He batted a career low 76 times last season. Cangelosi's greatest attribute is still his speed. However, he does not use it to his full advantage as a hitter. He is overaggressive at the plate and swings at too many bad pitches. He would serve the Bucs better by drawing a few more walks, something he used to do to perfection.

Cangelosi is a fast runner and a base stealing threat. But he has stolen only 48 bases over his four years with the Pirates, two less than he swiped for Chicago in '86. The old adage, "you can't steal first base," has been all too true with him recently. Cangelosi has good range in the field, but he is sometimes unsure on long drives and has a below-average arm.

OVERALL:

The scrappy Cangelosi is a favorite of Pirate manager Jim Leyland. However, Cangelosi's production continues to drop and it becomes more of a struggle for him to stay in the big leagues.

CARMELO MARTINEZ

Position: 1B/LF
Bats: R **Throws:** R
Ht: 6' 2" **Wt:** 220

Opening Day Age: 30
Born: 7/28/60 in Dorado, Puerto Rico
ML Seasons: 8

Overall Statistics

	G	AB	R	H	D	T	HR	RBI	SB	BB	SO	AVG
1990	83	217	26	52	9	0	10	35	2	30	42	.240
Career	895	2631	320	652	123	7	98	388	10	361	464	.248

HITTING, FIELDING, BASERUNNING:

Thus far, Carmelo Martinez' claim to fame as a Pittsburgh Pirate is that he almost indirectly cost General Manager Larry Doughty his job. In late August of last season, Doughty put outfield prospects Wes Chamberlain and Julio Peguero on waivers in order to clear spots on the 40-man roster. However, the waivers were not revocable and Philadelphia claimed both players. In a face-saving effort, Doughty traded the two along with another outfield prospect, Tony Longmire, to the Phillies for Martinez.

Martinez did provide some right-handed power in the season's final month and came through with a few big hits. A platoon player because of his struggles with righthanders, Martinez is a dead fastball hitter and has problems with almost all breaking stuff. He has a good eye, though, and can go deep. Ten of his 52 hits went for home runs last season.

Martinez is a plodding baserunner and goes station to station. He did steal two bases in three attempts last year, but that's about his limit. Defensively, Martinez is best suited to first base where he shows above-average skills. He can play left field and right field but has an awful time in the outfield. He does the best he can, but he lacks both range and a good throwing arm.

OVERALL:

The Pirates like Martinez' right-handed power. He could wind up platooning at first base in 1991, especially if the Bucs don't re-sign Gary Redus.

LLOYD McCLENDON

Position: LF
Bats: R **Throws:** R
Ht: 5'11" **Wt:** 195

Opening Day Age: 32
Born: 1/11/59 in Gary, IN
ML Seasons: 4

Overall Statistics

	G	AB	R	H	D	T	HR	RBI	SB	BB	SO	AVG
1990	53	110	6	18	3	0	2	12	1	14	22	.164
Career	262	578	70	137	24	1	19	79	12	70	90	.237

HITTING, FIELDING, BASERUNNING:

Lloyd McClendon went from 1989 hero to 1990 goat with the Chicago Cubs, but wound up spending the final three weeks of a National League East championship season with the Pittsburgh Pirates. It was the second straight year McClendon had played for the NL East champ, so he must figure he's a good-luck charm.

McClendon was an important role player for the Cubs as they won the division in 1989, hitting .286 with 12 homers in 259 at-bats. However, the Cubs felt McClendon became overweight in 1990 and lost bat speed. They gave him 107 at bats, then sent him to the minors for the month of August before dealing him to Pittsburgh in September. McClendon feasts on left-handed pitching and makes a good platoon player. Righties can give him fits, though, particularly with curveballs.

Though the stocky McClendon appears slow, that is deceptive and pitchers and outfielders must be alert when he is on base. McClendon is not great with the glove but provides versatility with his ability to catch and play first, third, left and right.

OVERALL:

McClendon was limited to three at-bats with the Pirates but homered in one of them. It's probably unrealistic to expect him to hit .286 again, as he did in 1989, but McClendon's lifetime totals -- 19 homers, 79 RBI, 70 runs scored and 70 walks in only 578 at-bats -- show what a useful player he can be. He could be an asset to the Pirates this season as a versatile right-handed hitting extra man.

VINCE PALACIOS

Position: RP
Bats: R **Throws:** R
Ht: 6' 3" **Wt:** 180

Opening Day Age: 27
Born: 7/19/63 in Mataloma, Mexico
ML Seasons: 3

Overall Statistics

	W	L	ERA	G	GS	Sv	IP	H	R	BB	SO	HR
1990	0	0	0.00	7	0	3	15.0	4	0	2	8	0
Career	3	3	4.19	20	7	3	68.2	59	32	26	36	4

PITCHING, FIELDING, HITTING & HOLDING RUNNERS:

Vicente Palacios resurrected his career with the Pittsburgh Pirates in the final month of the 1990 season. Palacios made the Pirates out of spring training in 1988 and was expected to be a key part of their future as a starting pitcher. After struggling early that season, he was sent to the minors and pitched in only seven major league games in 1988, and missed all of 1989 because of rotator cuff problems.

After two operations, Palacios bounced back strong at Class AAA Buffalo in 1990, going 13-7 with a 3.43 ERA in 28 starts. He was used in relief after his recall to Pittsburgh, however, pitching 15 scoreless innings and converting all three of his save opportunities. It was an important addition because the Pirate pen was struggling at the time, particularly from the right side.

Palacios has an above-average fastball, a good split-fingered pitch and adequate breaking stuff. He has regained the 90 MPH velocity he had before the injury. Palacios' biggest improvement has come in holding runners. He once was incredibly easy to run on with a slow delivery to home plate. But he greatly sped up the delivery and improved his move to first. He is no hitter, though.

OVERALL:

Palacios took control of a sometimes shaky Pirate bullpen down the stretch in 1990. The Bucs are looking for a closer, and a healthy Palacios might fit the bill. He could also make a contribution as a middle man or even as a starter.

TED POWER

Position: RP
Bats: R **Throws:** R
Ht: 6' 4" **Wt:** 220

Opening Day Age: 36
Born: 1/31/55 in Guthrie, OK
ML Seasons: 10

Overall Statistics

	W	L	ERA	G	GS	Sv	IP	H	R	BB	SO	HR
1990	1	3	3.66	40	0	7	51.2	50	23	17	42	5
Career	58	59	4.12	387	85	48	928.0	927	470	369	572	81

PITCHING, FIELDING, HITTING & HOLDING RUNNERS:

When he was healthy, the well-travelled Ted Power pitched well out of the Pittsburgh Pirates' bullpen in 1990. Though hampered by a strained triceps muscle in his pitching arm, Power was successful in all seven of his save opportunities and proved to be versatile by pitching long, middle and short relief. Power did not make a start during the regular season last year, the first time since 1985 that he'd been used exclusively out of the bullpen. He's made 85 starts in his ten-year career.

Even though he's now 36, Power lives up to his name. With a fastball in the 88 MPH range, he basically throws as hard as he can for as long as he can. When his fastball loses movement, Power struggles, because his slider, curveball and change-up are below average. Though he's had some success as a starter, Power is best suited to the bullpen since he relies so much on one pitch.

Power has a rather slow delivery to the plate but compensates by paying close attention to runners. A fine fielder, he has good quickness for a big man and gets off the mound rapidly. He is not much of a hitter, going 1-for-8 (.125) with five strikeouts in 1990.

OVERALL:

The Pirates had an option on Power's contract for 1991, but chose not to renew it, making him a free agent. Power will likely draw offers from other teams, as he is a veteran with starting and relieving experience. It's unlikely he'll be back with Pittsburgh.

VINCE COLEMAN

Position: LF
Bats: B **Throws:** R
Ht: 6' 0" **Wt:** 170

Opening Day Age: 29
Born: 9/22/61 in Jacksonville, FL
ML Seasons: 6

HITTING:

At 29, Vince Coleman is an enigma. He's the best base stealer in baseball, and because of that, he is a coveted leadoff man. But while Coleman had his best season at bat last year, his performance still disappointed many people -- including the Cardinals.

Coleman played in only 124 games last year, but still had some good numbers at the plate. A career .265 hitter, Coleman flirted with the .300 mark for much of the year before finishing with a .292 average. He used his great speed to good effect; his 31 infield hits led the club. He also showed more power than ever before, belting six homers and equalling his career-high with 33 extra-base hits. Coleman's nine triples tied for third in the NL, and he had a career high 15-game hitting streak.

The downside for Coleman is his mediocre ability to reach base, which has not improved enough. Coleman is the catalyst of the Cardinal attack, but he had a career low 35 walks, the second fewest of any Cardinal who played 120 games or more. His on-base percentage was only .340, the second best of his career but a very poor figure for a top leadoff man. Coleman has always struck out too often, and in 1990 his 88 strikeouts led the Cardinals. His strikeout-to-walk ratio of more than two-to-one was one of the worst for National League leadoff hitters.

BASERUNNING:

Still the top base thief in the game, Coleman led the majors with 77 steals; it was the sixth straight season he'd led the National League, tying Maury Wills' record. Baserunning is Coleman's signature mark in baseball. He was successful in 82 percent of his attempts last year, closely matching his 83 percent career average.

FIELDING:

Coleman has been underrated as an outfielder during his career. His speed compensates for some poor jumps, and he has always been an exceptional left fielder at catching foul flies against the wall. Though his arm isn't the greatest, his judgement is good in throwing to the proper base or cutoff man. Coleman's 12 assists were second among Cardinal outfielders.

OVERALL:

Coleman was a free agent at season's end, and the Cardinals were uncertain about re-signing him. The rival Mets were highly interested in obtaining his speedy services. He will certainly be missed by St. Louis if he doesn't come back. While Coleman's performance has often disappointed the Cards, the club does not have experienced hitters to fill his void at the top of the lineup.

Overall Statistics

	G	AB	R	H	D	T	HR	RBI	SB	BB	SO	AVG
1990	124	497	73	145	18	9	6	39	77	35	88	.292
Career	878	3535	566	937	106	56	15	217	549	314	628	.265

Where He Hits the Ball

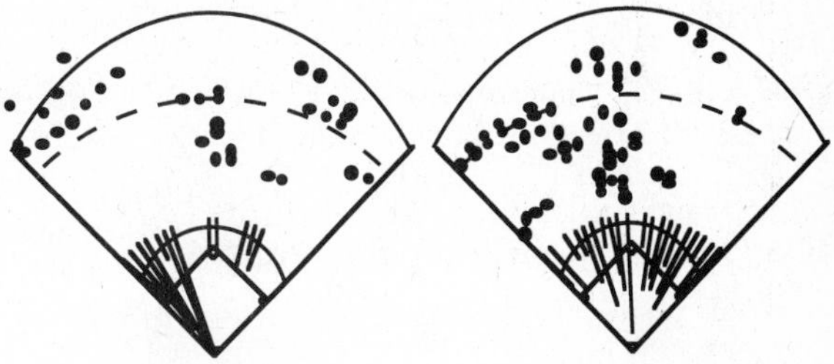

Vs. LHP   Vs. RHP

1990 Situational Stats

	AB	H	HR	RBI	AVG		AB	H	HR	RBI	AVG
Home	259	77	5	21	.297	LHP	191	50	5	18	.262
Road	238	68	1	18	.286	RHP	306	95	1	21	.310
Day	137	39	3	12	.285	Sc Pos	112	29	1	34	.259
Night	360	106	3	27	.294	Clutch	67	17	1	3	.254

1990 Rankings (National League)

- 1st in stolen bases (77) and steals of third (18)
- 3rd in triples (9)
- 5th in caught stealing (17) and bunts in play (28)
- 6th highest batting average on a 3-1 count (.600)
- Led the Cardinals in triples, stolen bases, caught stealing, strikeouts (88), runs scored per time reached base (40.1%), bunts in play and steals of third
- Led NL left fielders in triples, stolen bases, caught stealing, stolen base percentage (81.9%), batting average on a 3-1 count, bunts in play and steals of third

KEN DAYLEY

Position: RP
Bats: L **Throws:** L
Ht: 6' 0" **Wt:** 180

Opening Day Age: 32
Born: 2/25/59 in Jerome, ID
ML Seasons: 9

PITCHING:

Veteran reliever Ken Dayley started the 1990 season as one of the main candidates to replace the Cardinals' injured Todd Worrell as the team's main closer. Dayley was coming off a 1989 season in which he had a career high 12 saves, and the Cardinals hoped he could fill the role. However, Dayley was not very effective in save situations. He earned his first save April 18th and his second and final save September 25th. Meanwhile, the Cardinals were forced to acquire veteran Lee Smith to fill the void. For the season, Dayley was two-for-seven in save opportunities. But it was hardly a lost season for him. Dayley moved back into his familiar middle-relief/set-up role, and regained his old effectiveness.

Dayley has usually had great success facing left-handed batters, and is ordinarily brought in for that purpose. Part of his problem last year was that the situation reversed itself, as southpaws hit .283 against him while righties hit just .201. Three of the five home runs Dayley allowed were smacked by lefties. Because of this reversal, Dayley retired less than 70% of the first batters he faced. That went a long way in contributing to Dayley's allowance of 18 of 42 inherited runners to score, and partially explained why he failed as a closer.

A power pitcher, Dayley throws a curveball for his out pitch. It breaks very sharply and has a lot of velocity. Last year the curve became Dayley's strikeout pitch and ended a seasonal slide in Dayley's strikeout figures. Dayley also has a good fastball and an occasional change-up, but the curve remains his best pitch.

HOLDING RUNNERS, FIELDING, HITTING:

Though he's left-handed, Dayley has only a mediocre move to first. He is, however, an outstanding fielding pitcher. He has committed only one error during his career, which covers 375 games. He is not a hitting threat but does alright getting the sacrifice bunt down. On the base paths Dayley follows the coach's instructions and doesn't try to overextend himself.

OVERALL:

One of the Cardinals' many free agents after the 1990 season, Dayley has the kind of stuff that figured to interest other clubs. Needing a lefty in the bullpen to replace David Wells, Toronto signed him to a three year, six million dollar contract. Though never a high save-total closer, he was a very valuable contributor to the Cardinals' pennant-winning seasons of 1985 and 1987, and the Jays hope that a reliever like Dayley can help them to a pennant of their own in 1991. The departure of Dayley will force the Cards to continue to bring along their young pitchers.

Overall Statistics

	W	L	ERA	G	GS	Sv	IP	H	R	BB	SO	HR
1990	4	4	3.56	58	0	2	73.1	63	32	30	51	5
Career	33	45	3.62	375	33	39	568.2	556	268	216	401	42

How Often He Throws Strikes

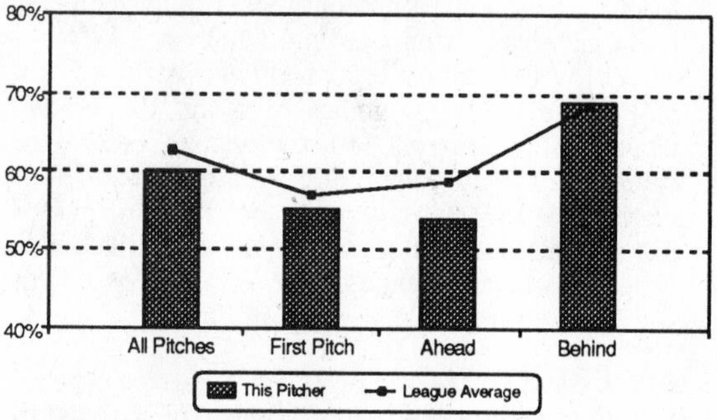

1990 Situational Stats

	W	L	ERA	Sv	IP		AB	H	HR	RBI	AVG
Home	3	1	3.23	0	39.0	LHB	106	30	3	15	.283
Road	1	3	3.93	2	34.1	RHB	164	33	2	23	.201
Day	2	1	2.93	0	27.2	Sc Pos	70	22	1	32	.314
Night	2	3	3.94	2	45.2	Clutch	124	34	4	23	.274

1990 Rankings (National League)

- → 4th in holds (14)
- → 5th in highest percentage of inherited runners scored (42.9%)
- → Led the Cardinals in holds, blown saves (5) and first batter efficiency (.225)

JOSE DeLEON

Position: SP
Bats: R **Throws:** R
Ht: 6' 3" **Wt:** 211

Opening Day Age: 30
Born: 12/20/60 in Rancho Viejo, La Vega, Dominican Republic
ML Seasons: 8

PITCHING:

After two winning seasons in St. Louis, Jose DeLeon reverted to his old nightmares in 1990. DeLeon's 19 losses equalled the highest total of his career, established during his horrible 1985 season, when he was 2-19 for Pittsburgh. As in 1985, his 19 losses led the league. They represented the most losses for a Cards' pitcher since 1970 when Steve Carlton went 10-19. In fact, Manager Joe Torre held DeLeon out of his last scheduled start just to avoid the possibility of him losing 20 games. DeLeon had just one win in his last 18 starts, and the Cardinals were 8-24 in his 32 starts.

Though he had a difficult season, DeLeon didn't really pitch as badly as his record indicates. His offense scored only 21 runs for him in his last 17 starts; starving for runs, he lost his confidence, and it showed. DeLeon was constantly pitching behind in the count, which will hurt the best of pitchers. He was trying to make the perfect pitch and as a result made the worst pitch.

DeLeon continues to rely mainly on two pitches, his fastball and his forkball. After working a career-high 244.2 innings in 1989, however, the velocity on his fastball wasn't as good as in the past. Neither was his location, as he had trouble controlling both pitches. DeLeon continued to be tough against right-handed batters, holding them to a .187 average. However, opposing teams stacked their line-ups with left-handed batters and they hit a resounding .286 against DeLeon. The Cardinals did not feel that DeLeon had arm trouble; they felt his arm was just tired.

HOLDING RUNNERS, FIELDING, HITTING:

DeLeon struggles with holding baserunners. His move to first is just average, but he has worked at quickening his move to the plate. He is an average fielding pitcher who doesn't make the outstanding play but also doesn't hurt himself in the field. He backs up the proper base and has his head in the game. As a batter, DeLeon swings hard, taking out some of his frustrations, but doesn't do much damage.

OVERALL:

DeLeon needs to forget 1990 entirely and rebound in 1991. He could easily be a candidate for the Comeback Player of the Year Award with his ability. DeLeon is the number-two pitcher in the Cardinal rotation that has to improve -- beginning with the first two staff members, Joe Magrane and DeLeon -- if the club is going to escape last place.

Overall Statistics

	W	L	ERA	G	GS	Sv	IP	H	R	BB	SO	HR
1990	7	19	4.43	32	32	0	182.2	168	96	86	164	15
Career	68	96	3.79	233	215	4	1417.0	1142	654	636	1225	107

How Often He Throws Strikes

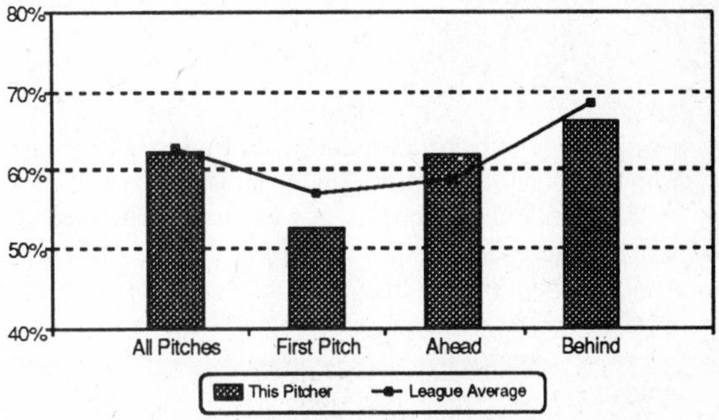

1990 Situational Stats

	W	L	ERA	Sv	IP		AB	H	HR	RBI	AVG
Home	3	9	5.55	0	84.1	LHB	405	116	8	56	.286
Road	4	10	3.48	0	98.1	RHB	278	52	7	30	.187
Day	2	3	4.21	0	47.0	Sc Pos	174	49	1	62	.282
Night	5	16	4.51	0	135.2	Clutch	45	12	1	5	.267

1990 Rankings (National League)

- 1st in losses (19), lowest winning percentage (.269), least run support per 9 innings (3.0) and worst ERA at home (5.55)
- 2nd in walks allowed (86) and lowest groundball/flyball ratio (.71)
- 5th worst ERA (4.43) and most strikeouts per 9 innings (8.1)
- Led the Cardinals in losses, games started (32), home runs allowed (15), walks allowed, strikeouts, strikeout/walk ratio (1.9), lowest batting average allowed (.246), lowest slugging percentage allowed (.370) and strikeouts per 9 innings

FRANK DiPINO

Position: RP
Bats: L **Throws:** L
Ht: 6' 0" **Wt:** 180

Opening Day Age: 34
Born: 10/22/56 in Syracuse, NY
ML Seasons: 10

PITCHING:

Middle relief pitcher Frank DiPino came back to earth in 1990 following his outstanding career year in 1989. DiPino had gone 9-0 in '89, and his 2.45 ERA that year was easily the best of his career. In '90, however, he was hit and hit hard, though he still recorded a winning record (5-2). It was a very tough season for the journeyman pitcher, who in 1989 had helped keep the Cardinals in contention all the way into September.

DiPino has several strengths as pitcher, but the main one is his durability. He's the rubber-armed type, capable of warming up almost every day and making frequent appearances. He's now worked in more than 60 games for five straight seasons, with varying degrees of effectiveness. Never the closer type, DiPino recorded three saves in five opportunities last year, all after the All-Star break when the Cards were out of contention. Whether finisher or mop-up man, he just goes out and does his job.

DiPino used to have a very good fastball, and he still throws a change, but he is now mainly dependent on his slider. Location is crucial to him, and though he didn't walk a lot of batters last year (12 of his 31 bases on balls were intentional), he was getting the ball up in the strike zone. He had to groove too many pitches, and the hitters teed off on him. As a result, he wasn't nearly as effective against left-handed hitters, always one of his strengths in the past. And after being invincible at Busch Stadium in 1989, holding opponents to a 1.58 ERA there in 1989, he was mediocre at home in 1990 with a 3.92 mark.

HOLDING RUNNERS, FIELDING, HITTING:

DiPino is not spectacular in the field and goes about his job rather routinely. He is not a good hitting pitcher. He has a good move to first which keeps runners close, giving his catcher a chance on the stolen base attempt.

OVERALL:

DiPino is now 34, with ten major league seasons of experience. His numbers were down in 1990. DiPino still has enough left in him to be useful and he has a veteran's savvy, but St. Louis, which is concentrating on younger players, might not be the best place for him. His best days are behind him now, and he could be on the bubble as far as the Cards are concerned.

Overall Statistics

	W	L	ERA	G	GS	Sv	IP	H	R	BB	SO	HR
1990	5	2	4.56	62	0	3	81.0	92	45	31	49	8
Career	34	37	3.80	494	6	56	673.0	643	318	260	502	51

How Often He Throws Strikes

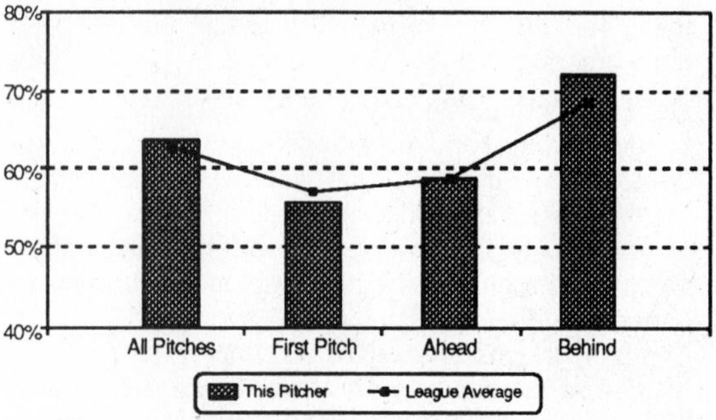

1990 Situational Stats

	W	L	ERA	Sv	IP		AB	H	HR	RBI	AVG
Home	3	2	3.92	3	41.1	LHB	133	39	2	18	.293
Road	2	0	5.22	0	39.2	RHB	180	53	6	40	.294
Day	2	0	4.66	1	19.1	Sc Pos	96	29	3	46	.302
Night	3	2	4.52	2	61.2	Clutch	65	22	2	21	.338

1990 Rankings (National League)

- 1st in worst percentage of inherited runners scored (56.8%)
- 4th worst first batter efficiency (.352)
- Led the Cardinals in games pitched (62)

BERNARD GILKEY

Position: LF
Bats: R **Throws:** R
Ht: 6' 0" **Wt:** 170

Opening Day Age: 24
Born: 9/24/66 in St. Louis, MO
ML Seasons: 1

HITTING:

A native of St. Louis, outfielder Bernard Gilkey is one of the players the Cardinals are depending on as they begin to rebuild for the future. An undrafted free agent, Gilkey started out at the bottom rung of the Cardinal ladder when he broke in by hitting only .204 at Class A Erie in 1985. But since then Gilkey has shown steady progress as he's moved through the Cards' minor league system. Last year he had his best season yet, hitting .295 at AAA Louisville. He continued to impress in his September trial with the big club, batting .297 in 64 at-bats.

Gilkey is an outfielder in the Vince Coleman mold, which is appropriate since he may well be asked to replace the free agent outfielder in 1991. Like Coleman, he relies on speed, but lacks power. Unlike Coleman, however, he's a patient hitter, willing to reach base with a walk. Gilkey had an outstanding .388 on-base percentage at Louisville, and posted a .375 OBP for the Cards in September. An excellent contact hitter, Gilkey has consistently had more walks than strikeouts -- 75 walks and 49 strikeouts at Louisville last year, eight walks and only five strikeouts for the Cards in his September trial.

More than anything, Gilkey has impressed the Cardinals with his steady improvement. Over the last three years, he's batted .244 at Class A Springfield, .278 at AA Arkansas, .295 at AAA Louisville and the .297 with the Cards last September.

BASERUNNING:

Blazing fast but still very raw, Gilkey has great potential for stealing bases, but his judgement is another matter. He stole 45 bases at Louisville, but was caught 32 times. A good student, Gilkey talked to Vince Coleman about baserunning and did much better with the Cards, swiping six in seven attempts. He planned to talk to Coleman more in the off season.

FIELDING:

With his great speed, Gilkey can cover a lot of ground in the outfield. He's still very inexperienced, however, and sometimes needs to use his speed to outrun his mistakes. Gilkey has a strong throwing arm and has led two minor leagues in assists.

OVERALL:

Gilkey's 1991 role with the Cards depends on several factors, most fundamentally their ability to re-sign Vince Coleman. If Coleman signs with another club, Gilkey looks like the logical replacement. If Coleman comes back to the Cards, Gilkey might get some more experience in AAA. In any case, he figures to see a lot of action in St. Louis before too long.

Overall Statistics

	G	AB	R	H	D	T	HR	RBI	SB	BB	SO	AVG
1990	18	64	11	19	5	2	1	3	6	8	5	.297
Career	18	64	11	19	5	2	1	3	6	8	5	.297

Where He Hits the Ball

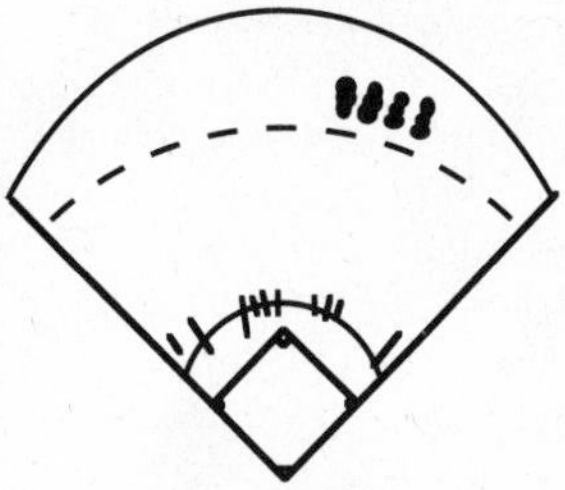

Vs. LHP

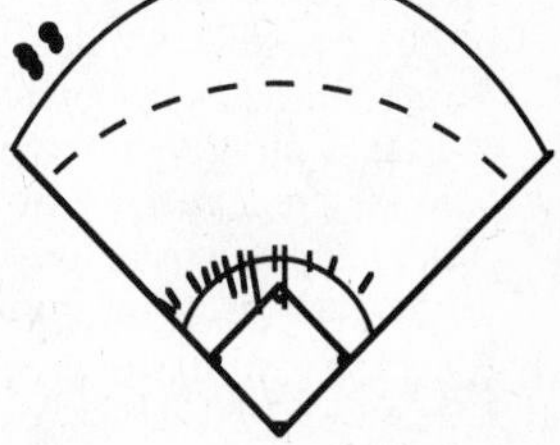

Vs. RHP

1990 Situational Stats

	AB	H	HR	RBI	AVG		AB	H	HR	RBI	AVG
Home	33	5	0	1	.152	LHP	29	8	0	0	.276
Road	31	14	1	2	.452	RHP	35	11	1	3	.314
Day	19	6	0	2	.316	Sc Pos	9	3	0	2	.333
Night	45	13	1	1	.289	Clutch	6	2	0	0	.333

1990 Rankings (National League)

- Did not rank near the top or bottom in any category

PEDRO GUERRERO

Position: 1B
Bats: R **Throws:** R
Ht: 6' 0" **Wt:** 195

Opening Day Age: 34
Born: 6/29/56 in San Pedro de Macoris, Dominican Republic
ML Seasons: 13

HITTING:

When healthy and playing for a contender, as was the case throughout most of 1989, Pedro Guerrero plays with an exuberance that can carry an entire ballclub. Such was not the case last season. The Cardinals were out of contention early, finishing last for the first time since 1918. Guerrero spent time on the 15-day disabled list with back problems, and struggled to reach 80 RBI. Even so, he led the club in that department.

In 1989 Guerrero's average with runners in scoring position was a robust .400, resulting in 117 RBI, but last year he collapsed to .252. Guerrero has a beautiful, short stroke, and is capable of adjusting to any pitch. But in 1990 he was over-anxious, chasing low and away breaking balls. His walks were down, and so was his production.

Playing in Busch Stadium, Guerrero has adjusted to hit line drives into the power alleys, rattling the ball off the outfield walls. Under Whitey Herzog, he began swinging for line drives instead of homers at Busch, and thus became a more potent hitter. But as the team struggled and the 1990 season wore on, Guerrero redeveloped his upper-cut swing. A lot of balls were caught at the wall, which was one reason for his decreased performance.

BASERUNNING:

Guerrero has no speed at all and his legs ache from previous knee injuries and playing on the artificial surface. He stole only two bases in 1989, and one in 1990. If Guerrero had average speed, a lot of his doubles would be triples. He will coast into second standing up rather than burst into full speed going for third. He is a smart baserunner on misplays but doesn't challenge outfielders.

FIELDING:

Guerrero is not as bad defensively as some critics claim. He doesn't have the range to get to balls some other first basemen get, but he is adequate. He plays near the line and cuts down on extra-base hits, but sacrifices some hits through the right side that Jose Oquendo can't reach.

OVERALL:

Guerrero is a great hitter playing for the wrong team. At this point in his career, a change in scenery could ignite the spark that he needs. He still has considerable trade value, and the American League would seem to be a place Guerrero could be productive for a few more years.

Overall Statistics

	G	AB	R	H	D	T	HR	RBI	SB	BB	SO	AVG
1990	136	498	42	140	31	1	13	80	1	44	70	.281
Career	1378	4819	679	1470	249	27	206	812	91	561	791	.305

Where He Hits the Ball

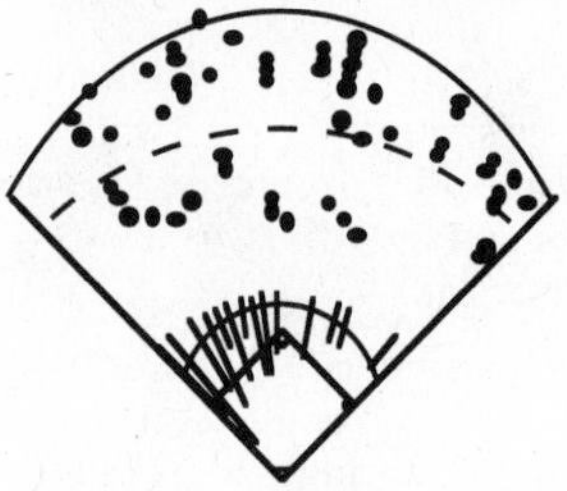

Vs. LHP

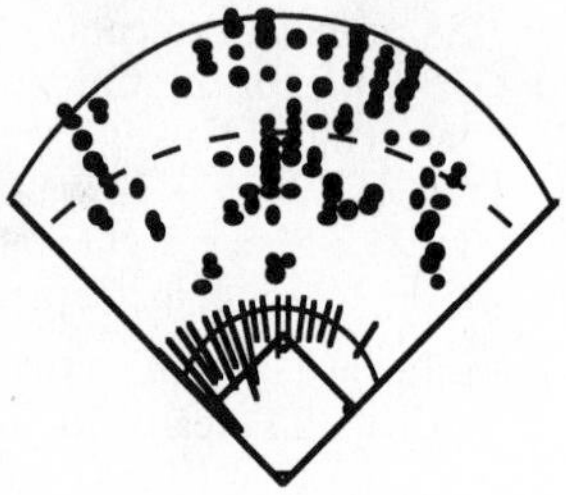

Vs. RHP

1990 Situational Stats

	AB	H	HR	RBI	AVG		AB	H	HR	RBI	AVG
Home	261	72	8	50	.276	LHP	168	46	4	30	.274
Road	237	68	5	30	.287	RHP	330	94	9	50	.285
Day	140	45	3	23	.321	Sc Pos	159	40	3	64	.252
Night	358	95	10	57	.265	Clutch	72	18	1	8	.250

1990 Rankings (National League)

- → 2nd least runs scored per time reached base (22.7%)
- → 3rd in sacrifice flies (11)
- → 7th in GDPs (14)
- → Led the Cardinals in RBIs (80), sacrifice flies, intentional walks (14), GDPs and batting average on the road (.287)
- → Led NL first basemen in errors (13)

PITCHING:

After going 7-15 in 1989, righthander Ken Hill started last year with the Cardinals and appeared in three games in relief before being optioned to AAA Louisville on April 28. Hill was not effective in his early work with the big club, giving up eight hits and seven runs in 3.2 innings for a 17.18 ERA. But the Cards still had high hopes for Hill and sent him down to get his bearings.

At Louisville, Hill began to put his game together. He spent three months at the AAA level and posted a 6-1 record with a 1.79 ERA in 12 starts. His control was better than ever. Hill allowed just 47 hits in 85.1 innings and struck out 104 batters while allowing only 27 walks. Hill struck out 10 or more in six of his 12 starts and set a Louisville record for strikeouts in a game with 15 against Indianapolis.

The Cardinals recalled Hill July 16 and immediately used him as a starter at New York. Hill struck out a career-high nine batters in 7.2 innings to gain his first win. He pitched masterfully, allowing only three hits and one run. But Hill still has a tendency to do very well in one start and then get blown out early in his next start. After that initial effort, his success did not continue. He did win five games in 1990, but his ERA was much higher than in 1989 at a hefty 5.49.

Hill's fastball and curveball both break hard, but he doesn't always know where. His control improved but is still below average; he got his walks down from 4.5 per nine innings in 1989 to 3.8 per nine last year. The Cardinals take that as a healthy sign for the future.

HOLDING RUNNERS, FIELDING, HITTING:

A good athlete who played basketball and soccer in high school, Hill is one of the best fielding pitchers in the National League. He will throw over to first base very often to keep the runner close, but that sometimes becomes harmful as Hill forgets to concentrate on the batter. At the plate, Hill has all the skills to become a good hitting pitcher. Hill will work the pitcher, fouling balls off until he gets a hittable pitch to put into play.

OVERALL:

Hill hasn't shown great results thus far, but he's just 25, and strong-armed. The Cardinals are rebuilding and figure to give him a chance to find his stuff this season. It would help immensely if he has better control over it this time around.

KEN HILL

Position: SP
Bats: R **Throws:** R
Ht: 6' 2" **Wt:** 175

Opening Day Age: 25
Born: 12/14/65 in Lynn, MA
ML Seasons: 3

Overall Statistics

	W	L	ERA	G	GS	Sv	IP	H	R	BB	SO	HR
1990	5	6	5.49	17	14	0	78.2	79	49	33	58	7
Career	12	22	4.32	54	48	0	289.1	281	150	138	176	16

How Often He Throws Strikes

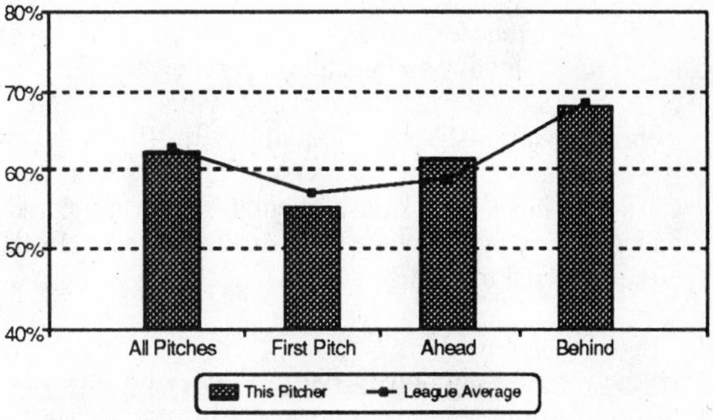

1990 Situational Stats

	W	L	ERA	Sv	IP		AB	H	HR	RBI	AVG
Home	2	2	6.75	0	28.0	LHB	185	49	4	21	.265
Road	3	4	4.80	0	50.2	RHB	114	30	3	18	.263
Day	3	3	4.17	0	41.0	Sc Pos	76	22	1	31	.289
Night	2	3	6.93	0	37.2	Clutch	26	11	0	3	.423

1990 Rankings (National League)

- Did not rank near the top or bottom in any category

REX HUDLER

Position: RF/LF
Bats: R **Throws:** R
Ht: 6' 2" **Wt:** 180

Opening Day Age: 30
Born: 9/2/60 in Tempe, AZ
ML Seasons: 6

Overall Statistics

	G	AB	R	H	D	T	HR	RBI	SB	BB	SO	AVG
1990	93	220	31	62	11	2	7	22	18	12	32	.282
Career	305	650	97	168	33	5	17	50	63	30	103	.258

Where He Hits the Ball

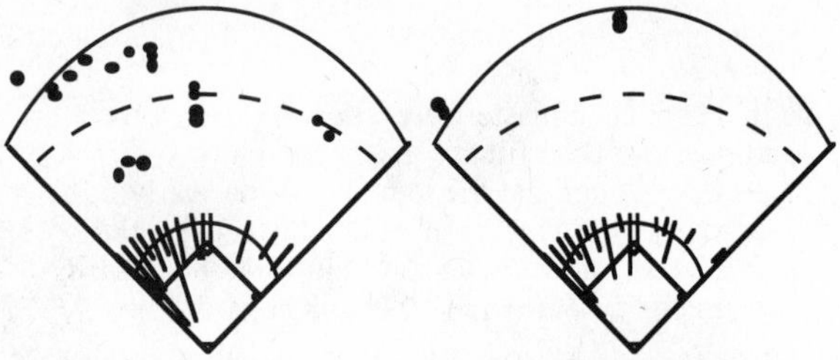

Vs. LHP **Vs. RHP**

1990 Situational Stats

	AB	H	HR	RBI	AVG		AB	H	HR	RBI	AVG
Home	89	22	2	7	.247	LHP	137	32	5	11	.234
Road	131	40	5	15	.305	RHP	83	30	2	11	.361
Day	73	28	2	9	.384	Sc Pos	55	14	1	14	.255
Night	147	34	5	13	.231	Clutch	42	12	3	5	.286

1990 Rankings (National League)

- ➡ 5th worst stolen base percentage (64.3%)
- ➡ 8th lowest on-base average vs. left-handed pitchers (.281)
- ➡ Led NL right fielders in bunts in play (17)

HITTING:

The most excitable player in baseball, Rex Hudler absolutely attacks the game. A former high school All-American football player, (he was offered a chance to play wide receiver at Notre Dame with Joe Montana), Hudler has a simple style of play: go as hard as you can as long as you can. He uses his fierce competitive nature and speed in the field, on the base paths, and at the plate.

Though used as a utility player with the Cardinals last year, Hudler was certainly an impact player. The Cards won 22 of 35 games (.629) he started after July 12. He hit a career high seven home runs, two of which came as a pinch hitter. He had eight bunt hits, and 15 infield hits.

Hudler will take lefthanders deep; 10 of his 13 home runs over the past two seasons have been belted off lefties. A high fastball hitter, he goes after the pitch with a vengeance, even when out of the strike zone. Rex-citable always swings hard. Hudler's overall average of .282 was greatly enhanced by his unexpected improvement hitting righthanders. In 1989 as an Expo, Rex hit only .220 versus righties; with the Cardinals in 1990 he smashed out a .361 average and had a slugging percentage of .530 against them. Both were Cardinal team highs.

BASERUNNING:

Hudler is a tremendously daring runner on the base paths. It's almost as if he doesn't stop running until he's tagged out. He stole 18 bases in 28 attempts (64%), often being thrown out at third after swiping second. Hudler runs with total abandon for his body, using head-first slides and body blocks to break up the double play.

FIELDING:

Hudler is the most versatile player on the St. Louis bench. He started games at six different positions -- first, second, third and all three outfield positions -- and also saw brief action as a substitute shortstop. Hudler is a capable defensive substitute, committing only five errors and recording three outfield assists. He uses his speed in the outfield to make highlight-film catches with diving plays.

OVERALL:

Hudler's enthusiasm for the game and his versatility make him a Cardinal fans' favorite. Besides his baseball skills, he brings a very talented singer to St. Louis. His wife, Jennifer, performed the National Anthem and the Canadian National Anthem at Busch Stadium to a resounding ovation of appreciation. The Cardinals hope both Hudlers will continue to perform well in 1991.

HITTING:

The Cardinals acquired switch-hitting outfielder Felix Jose last August 30, along with third baseman Stan Royer, in a trade with Oakland for the eventual National League batting champion, Willie McGee. Dal Maxvill, the Cardinal general manager, got lucky under the circumstances in acquiring Jose. There were few offers for McGee that held merit for St. Louis, and it didn't seem that the Cardinals would be able to sign him after the season. When Oakland center fielder Dave Henderson went down with an injury, the deal for McGee became a natural.

Thus far, it looks like both teams benefitted from the trade. McGee helped the A's wrap up the American League pennant; meanwhile, Jose proved he could hit with power from both sides of the plate. Jose showed his strength by belting a 463-foot home run into the upper deck of Busch Stadium September 19. It was the longest home run hit in St. Louis since systematic estimations of home run distances have been made at the park.

Jose is an undisciplined hitter, still prone to chasing breaking pitches out of the strike zone. He makes good contact from both sides of the plate and hits to all fields. Jose has the potential to be an excellent RBI man for the Cardinals. He can be placed anywhere from third through sixth in the lineup.

BASERUNNING:

Jose has good speed and can go from first to third on a hit. But thus far, his speed hasn't really translated into stolen bases, as Jose is still learning the art. Jose showed his potential by swiping 12 bases in 16 attempts last year.

FIELDING:

Jose has an excellent throwing arm and can play all three outfield positions. He is best in either left or right field and the Cardinals are projecting him to be their everyday right fielder. Jose's speed is a valuable asset in spacious Busch Stadium where he has the ability to cut off balls hit into the gaps and can catch up to soft flies down the outfield line.

OVERALL:

Jose may be a diamond in the rough. He has great natural ability and will only be 25 years old on opening day. Every aspect of his game is good now and will get much better with the discipline he should accrue through playing regularly. The Cardinals will have to live with some mistakes of inexperience, but are assured that Jose has a future.

FELIX JOSE

Position: RF/LF/CF
Bats: B **Throws:** R
Ht: 6' 1" **Wt:** 190

Opening Day Age: 25
Born: 5/8/65 in Santo Domingo, Dominican Republic
ML Seasons: 3

Overall Statistics

	G	AB	R	H	D	T	HR	RBI	SB	BB	SO	AVG
1990	126	426	54	113	16	1	11	52	12	24	81	.265
Career	154	489	59	126	19	1	11	58	13	28	95	.258

Where He Hits the Ball

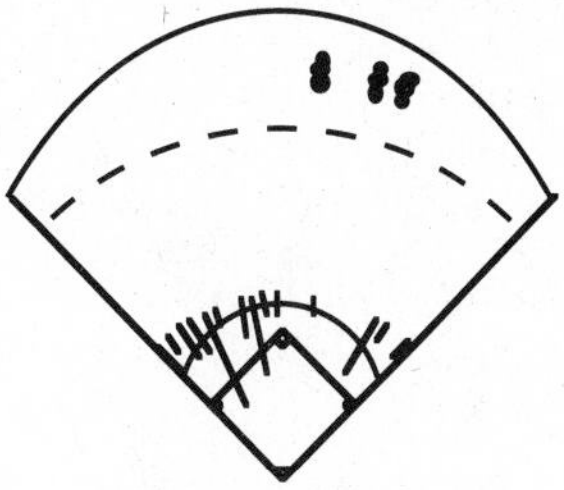

Vs. LHP

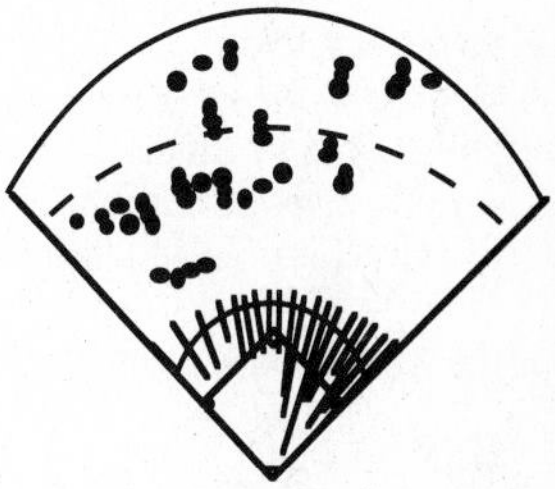

Vs. RHP

1990 Situational Stats

	AB	H	HR	RBI	AVG		AB	H	HR	RBI	AVG
Home	210	49	5	27	.233	LHP	103	31	2	16	.301
Road	216	64	6	25	.296	RHP	323	82	9	36	.254
Day	176	44	5	22	.250	Sc Pos	117	38	4	42	.325
Night	250	69	6	30	.276	Clutch	53	13	1	8	.245

1990 Rankings (National League)

- Did not rank near the top or bottom in any category

RAY LANKFORD

Position: CF
Bats: L **Throws:** L
Ht: 5'11" **Wt:** 180

Opening Day Age: 23
Born: 6/5/67 in Modesto, CA
ML Seasons: 1

HITTING:

Rookie center fielder Ray Lankford made his major league debut last August 21, moving nine-year veteran Willie McGee to right. Lankford lined a single off Atlanta righty John Smoltz in his first plate appearance, stole second base, then doubled in a run and scored in his last at-bat off lefty Kent Mercker. From that point forward, the trade of McGee became inevitable. Not letting up even after McGee was dealt to Oakland, Lankford wound up batting .286 in 39 games.

Lankford, a left-handed hitter, hit well against both lefties and righties last year. The new center fielder showed some surprising home run power against right-handed pitching with three home runs, all of which were hammered deep to right center, two coming at Busch. He had an impressive .452 slugging percentage, and 14 of his 36 hits went for extra-bases.

Lankford is an aggressive hitter, but one who rarely swings at bad pitches. At this point he can be fooled by a good major league change-up when behind in the count. Lankford sat out the last few games of the season last year, at his request and Torre's approval, to keep his rookie status for the 1991 season. Lankford should be a solid contender for the '91 Rookie of the Year Award.

BASERUNNING:

Lankford is an aggressive runner who can stretch a single into a double. At Modesto Junior College, he was the school's first running back to rush for 1,000 yards; obviously, he has the ability to break up double plays. Lankford's speed makes him a threat to steal when he chooses, and he was successful on eight of ten tries for the Cardinals.

FIELDING:

Lankford is a good defensive outfielder who has shown he can go after fly balls hit deep in the ballpark. If he has a weakness, it's his tendency to not take charge on pop flies, something Torre will get corrected. Lankford possesses a major league caliber arm that should improve with technique and experience. Faster baserunners will challenge him going from second to third on fly balls to medium-deep center.

OVERALL:

Lankford is the Cardinals' center fielder for the 1990s. The last six weeks of the season were a spring training session for the St. Louis ball club. Lankford played well and there's no reason to think that within a couple of seasons he won't be a steady .295 to .305 hitter with 30 doubles, 10 triples and 10 home runs or more.

Overall Statistics

	G	AB	R	H	D	T	HR	RBI	SB	BB	SO	AVG
1990	39	126	12	36	10	1	3	12	8	13	27	.286
Career	39	126	12	36	10	1	3	12	8	13	27	.286

Where He Hits the Ball

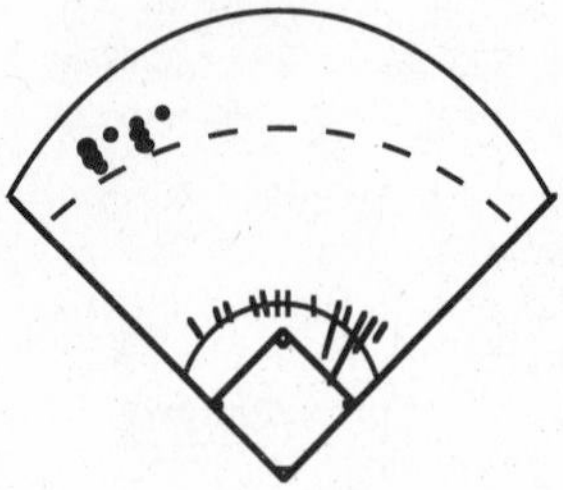

Vs. LHP

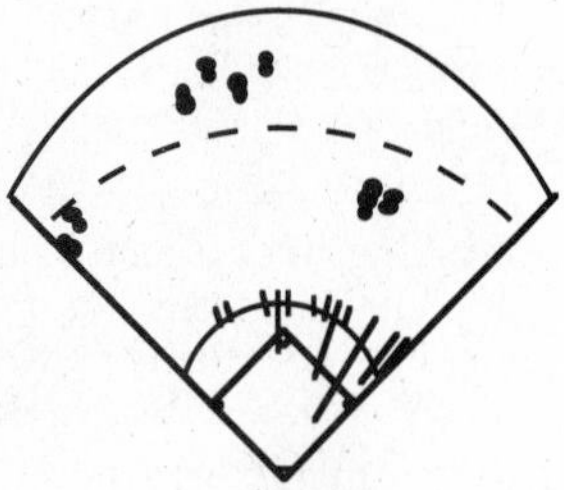

Vs. RHP

1990 Situational Stats

	AB	H	HR	RBI	AVG		AB	H	HR	RBI	AVG
Home	43	11	2	6	.256	LHP	45	14	0	1	.311
Road	83	25	1	6	.301	RHP	81	22	3	11	.272
Day	35	5	1	2	.143	Sc Pos	33	9	1	10	.273
Night	91	31	2	10	.341	Clutch	20	6	0	1	.300

1990 Rankings (National League)

- Did not rank near the top or bottom in any category

JOE MAGRANE

Position: SP
Bats: R **Throws:** L
Ht: 6' 6" **Wt:** 230

Opening Day Age: 26
Born: 7/2/64 in Des Moines, IA
ML Seasons: 4

PITCHING:

In his second season in 1988, Joe Magrane led the National League in earned run average. A year later Magrane was the top left-handed pitcher in the National League with 18 wins. The ace of the staff, the 6'-6" lefthander had matured into a dominant pitcher, and the Cards felt that their one-two punch of Magrane and Jose DeLeon would keep the club in contention. But last year the one-two punch got knocked out, as Magrane went 10-17 and DeLeon 7-19.

Magrane got off to a horrible start last year, losing his first six decisions. For the first time in his career he gave up more hits than innings pitched. Magrane's mental approach to the game became a factor as he made costly mistakes. With the Cardinals scoring just 33 runs in Magrane's 17 losses, he began to press. At the absolute wrong time, he would fail to cover first base or take command on the mound, giving in to a hitter or hurling a wild pitch. The results were usually catastrophic.

Magrane wasn't a total disaster last year. He won 10 games, second on the Card staff, and his ERA was respectable at 3.59. There wasn't a lot wrong with his stuff. Magrane throws a hard curve that breaks sharply down, often into the dirt, and hitters will chase it. He will throw the curve or his slider at any time in the count. Magrane's fastball can be intimidating, particularly coming from such a big hurler. But he wasn't always 100 percent physically last year. His left shoulder caused him some problems, and he was sidelined from September 4 to September 19 due to a strained shoulder.

HOLDING RUNNERS, FIELDING, HITTING:

Magrane has an excellent move to first and will throw over to catch the unaware baserunner. He can also take away hits up the middle with his size and quick reflexes. At the plate, Magrane is a definite home run threat and is a leader among the Cardinal pitchers in hits. He has been used as a pinch hitter and pinch runner.

OVERALL:

The anchor in the Cardinal rotation, Magrane has the talent to be a big winner. But it will tough for him to do it with this rebuilding ball club. There will be youthful mistakes behind him and the offensive support may not be there yet. He'll need to deal with adversity a little better than he did in 1990.

Overall Statistics

	W	L	ERA	G	GS	Sv	IP	H	R	BB	SO	HR
1990	10	17	3.59	31	31	0	203.1	204	86	59	100	10
Career	42	42	3.07	116	114	0	773.2	713	299	242	428	30

How Often He Throws Strikes

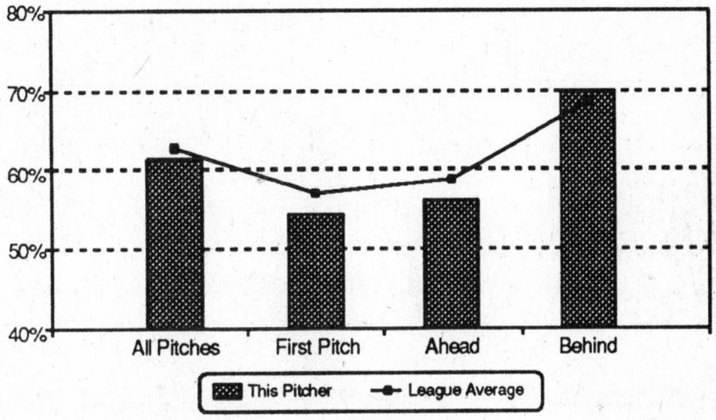

1990 Situational Stats

	W	L	ERA	Sv	IP		AB	H	HR	RBI	AVG
Home	4	10	4.27	0	116.0	LHB	150	43	1	14	.287
Road	6	7	2.68	0	87.1	RHB	624	161	9	56	.258
Day	4	3	3.64	0	47.0	Sc Pos	185	41	1	50	.222
Night	6	14	3.57	0	156.1	Clutch	66	24	2	14	.364

1990 Rankings (National League)

- 1st in runners caught stealing (16)
- 2nd in losses (17), hit batsmen (8) and least run support per 9 innings (3.01)
- 3rd in wild pitches (11) and least home runs allowed per 9 innings (.44)
- Led the Cardinals in ERA (3.59), complete games (3), shutouts (2), innings (203.1), hits allowed (204), batters faced (855), hit batsmen (8), wild pitches, pitches thrown (2,992), most stolen bases allowed (21), runners caught stealing, GDP induced (15), lowest on-base average allowed (.320), lowest stolen base percentage allowed (56.8%) and lowest batting average allowed with runners in scoring position (.222)

JOSE OQUENDO

Position: 2B
Bats: B **Throws:** R
Ht: 5'10" **Wt:** 156

Opening Day Age: 27
Born: 7/4/63 in Rio Piedras, Puerto Rico
ML Seasons: 7

HITTING:

Still only 27, Jose Oquendo continues to be an outstanding second baseman. Like a lot of Cardinals, Oquendo slumped at bat last year, dropping from .291 to .252. But the patient switch-hitter led the Cardinals with 74 walks, and there was nothing wrong with his .350 on-base percentage.

A slap hitter who patterned his swing after Rod Carew's, Oquendo has little power. Part of the reason his average dropped last year was that defenses played him very shallow. Outfielders were making routine plays on fly balls and line drives which otherwise would have dropped for hits. Pressing a little, Oquendo tried to hit the ball over their heads, especially when batting righty, which is his natural and more powerful side. After posting nearly identical figures from each side of the plate for the four seasons from 1986 through '89, Oquendo hit only .220 from the right side last year. He held his own batting lefty with a .269 mark.

A good breaking ball hitter, Oquendo hits from an exaggerated crouch when hitting lefty, and his strike zone is like a carnival target. Despite the fact that he usually bats eighth and that opposing pitchers hate to walk him, he still draws a considerable amount of bases on balls. Oquendo stands more straight up when hitting righty but still draws his share of walks from that side. All 11 of his career homers have come batting righty.

BASERUNNING:

Oquendo is no threat to steal. He has average speed but less-than-average running ability and nerve, whether stealing bases or running them.

FIELDING:

Along with Jose Lind, Oquendo is pressing Ryne Sandberg for Gold Glove status at second base. He doesn't quite have Lind's range, but his arm is the best at the position, and he made only three errors last year, a new record for second basemen playing in 150 or more games. Originally a shortstop, Oquendo will probably make the transition back to his old spot when Ozzie Smith leaves St. Louis.

OVERALL:

Oquendo is still the Cardinal's second baseman, but the Cards are high on rookie second-sacker Geronimo Pena. They will be looking for a place for Pena to play, and it would be no great surprise to see Oquendo move to shortstop before too long. Oquendo does whatever he can to help the team, offensively and defensively. He's one of the hardest workers in baseball, usually the first player at the park for a game.

Overall Statistics

	G	AB	R	H	D	T	HR	RBI	SB	BB	SO	AVG
1990	156	469	38	118	17	5	1	37	1	74	46	.252
Career	860	2379	248	629	80	14	11	195	32	308	280	.264

Where He Hits the Ball

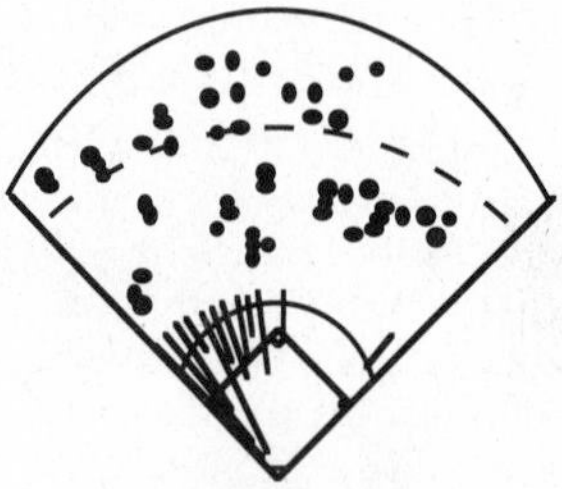

Vs. LHP

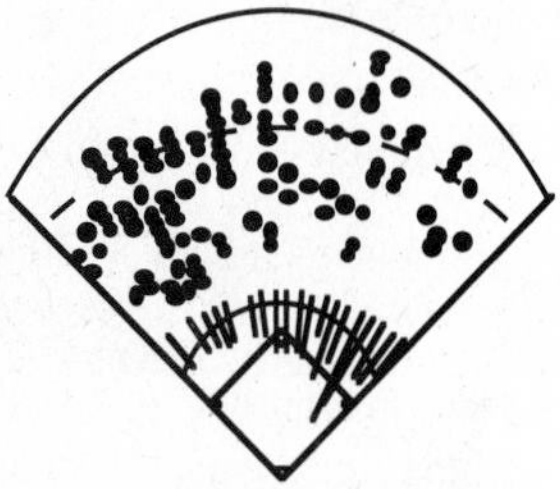

Vs. RHP

1990 Situational Stats

	AB	H	HR	RBI	AVG		AB	H	HR	RBI	AVG
Home	238	57	1	17	.239	LHP	164	36	1	7	.220
Road	231	61	0	20	.264	RHP	305	82	0	30	.269
Day	144	29	0	14	.201	Sc Pos	118	31	0	35	.263
Night	325	89	1	23	.274	Clutch	86	24	0	5	.279

1990 Rankings (National League)

- 1st in least runs scored per time reached base (19.8%)
- 3rd lowest slugging percentage vs. left-handed pitchers (.287)
- 4th lowest HR frequency (469 ABs per HR)
- 5th lowest slugging percentage (.316) and lowest batting average at home (.240)
- Led the Cardinals in walks (74) and games (156)
- Led NL second basemen in games and fielding percentage (.996)

TOM PAGNOZZI

Position: C
Bats: R **Throws:** R
Ht: 6' 1" **Wt:** 190

Opening Day Age: 28
Born: 7/30/62 in Tucson, AZ
ML Seasons: 4

Overall Statistics

	G	AB	R	H	D	T	HR	RBI	SB	BB	SO	AVG
1990	69	220	20	61	15	0	2	23	1	14	37	.277
Career	229	543	48	137	27	0	4	50	2	35	101	.252

Where He Hits the Ball

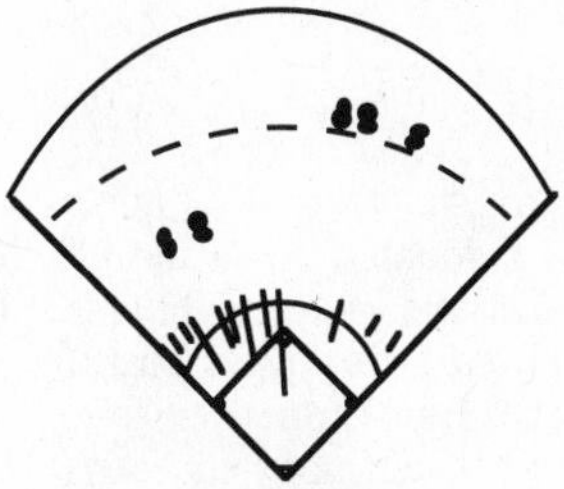

Vs. LHP

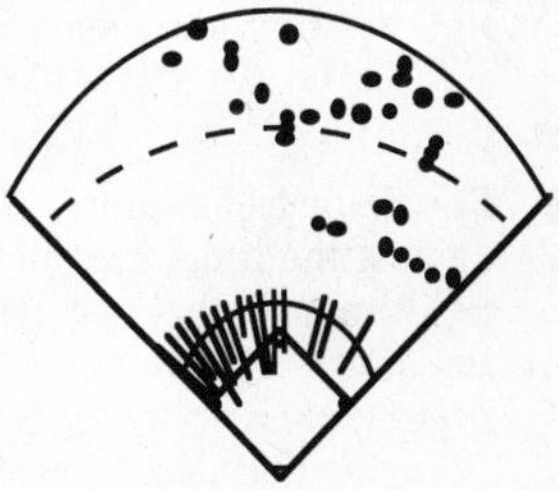

Vs. RHP

1990 Situational Stats

	AB	H	HR	RBI	AVG		AB	H	HR	RBI	AVG
Home	101	30	2	12	.297	LHP	82	24	1	9	.293
Road	119	31	0	11	.261	RHP	138	37	1	14	.268
Day	97	28	1	11	.289	Sc Pos	54	15	0	18	.278
Night	123	33	1	12	.268	Clutch	30	6	0	6	.200

1990 Rankings (National League)

➡ Did not rank near the top or bottom in any category

HITTING:

When manager Joe Torre moved catcher Todd Zeile to first base, then to third base, backup catcher Tom Pagnozzi probably did handstands for the opportunity to play every day. Last season, Pagnozzi finally showed he is no longer a "backup catcher," unless you don't need a catcher who throws well and can hit .270 to .280.

Given a chance to play regularly, Pagnozzi established career highs for hits, runs, doubles, walks, and RBI. Knowing he was going to be in the lineup was the key to Pagnozzi's success. He has never hit well as a pinch hitter, and starting sporadically never allowed him to get into a hitter's groove. Pagnozzi had always shown hitting potential in the past. He had batted .292 during his minor league career, and the Cardinals knew he had the potential to hit at the major league level. Pagnozzi has batted well in the two seasons in which he's been given some playing time, 1988 and 1990.

A right-handed hitter with occasional power, Pagnozzi improved last year when he stopped trying to pull everything. Pagnozzi can turn on a fastball, and he still hits line drives into left and center. His big change is that he will now go with the pitch and hit to the right side when he needs to. Pagnozzi hasn't been much of a home run threat thus far, with only four in 543 lifetime at-bats; however, he's hit as many as 14 homers in a minor league season, and he has the potential to hit more. Performing well in the clutch, Pagnozzi hit .278 with men in scoring position last year.

BASERUNNING:

Although he runs fairly well for a catcher, Pagnozzi is not much of a threat to steal bases. He was successful in one of two stolen base attempts last year. He's a fairly conservative baserunner, but avoided hitting into any double plays last year.

FIELDING:

After losing about 15 pounds before the 1990 season, Pagnozzi was noticeably quicker last year. He did not commit a passed ball all season. But the most important aspect of Pagnozzi's defense is his throwing ability. He has thrown out 55 of 145 (38%) would-be base stealers over his career and was 33 of 73 (45%) last season.

OVERALL

At age 28, Pagnozzi's stock skyrocketed with his 1990 performance. He goes into this season feeling that the catching job will be his, and that Todd Zeile will be the third baseman. Otherwise, Pagnozzi will demand to be traded.

TERRY PENDLETON

Position: 3B
Bats: B **Throws:** R
Ht: 5' 9" **Wt:** 178

Opening Day Age: 30
Born: 7/16/60 in Los Angeles, CA
ML Seasons: 7

Overall Statistics

	G	AB	R	H	D	T	HR	RBI	SB	BB	SO	AVG
1990	121	447	46	103	20	2	6	58	7	30	58	.230
Career	927	3433	404	888	155	24	44	442	99	252	430	.259

Where He Hits the Ball

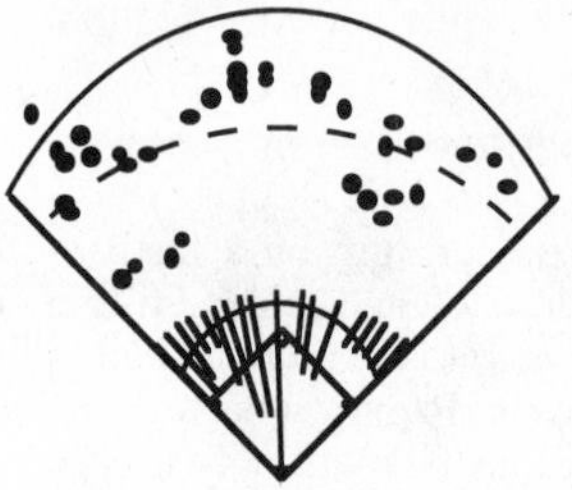

Vs. LHP

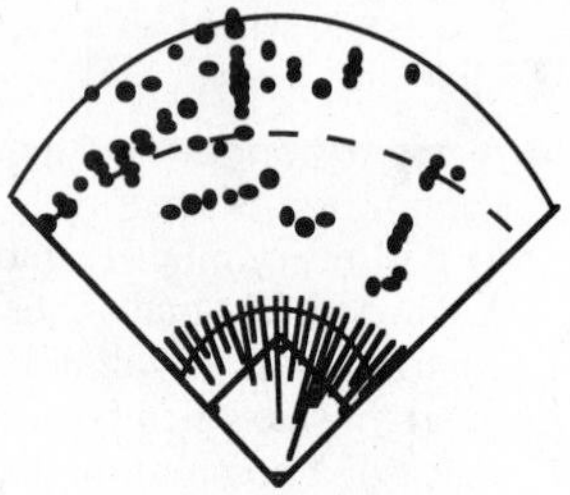

Vs. RHP

1990 Situational Stats

	AB	H	HR	RBI	AVG		AB	H	HR	RBI	AVG
Home	251	61	6	32	.243	LHP	158	33	4	23	.209
Road	196	42	0	26	.214	RHP	289	70	2	35	.242
Day	132	36	2	20	.273	Sc Pos	134	31	3	53	.231
Night	315	67	4	38	.213	Clutch	85	17	0	10	.200

1990 Rankings (National League)

- 2nd lowest on-base average vs. left-handed pitchers (.235)
- 5th highest batting average with the bases loaded (.500)
- 6th lowest batting average vs. left-handed pitchers (.209) and lowest batting average at home (.243)
- Led the Cardinals in batting average on a 3-2 count (.350)

HITTING:

Frustrating -- that's a one word description for what was probably Terry Pendleton's final season in St. Louis. The popular third baseman appeared in only 121 games last year and hit a career low .230. The sharp decline was strikingly similar to his 1988 season, a year in which Pendleton was plagued with injuries. As he struggled last year, the Cardinals pushed him aside and auditioned new third basemen. Pendleton started only two games after September 1.

Pendleton's offense is generated by slashing line drives through the infield and going with the pitch on the fast artificial surface. The switch-hitting third baseman generally hits better from the right side, although most of his home run power is left-handed. Last year, however, he hit for a better average from the left side, and had more power from the right. He likes the ball low when batting lefty, high when hitting righty. But he's always had a tendency to chase pitches out of the strike zone -- particularly high pitches when batting righty.

Pendleton had a career high five-hit game last June 26 against the Mets in which he doubled down the left field line, singled through the hole on the right side, lined one into center, and hit two shots past third. It was a typical hitting pattern for Pendleton when at his best. Unfortunately, he didn't have many moments like it last year.

BASERUNNING:

Pendleton is no longer the base stealing threat he was a few years ago. After stealing 80 bases in his first 534 major league games, he's swiped only 19 in his last 393. He's not a daring baserunner.

FIELDING:

A Gold Glove defender, Pendleton committed an unusually high 19 errors last year. Still, he is the best at racing into the bullpen after foul pop flies, making incredible over-the-shoulder catches. Pendleton also has a quick release and a great ability to charge slow rollers and bunts. He plays deep against pull hitters and takes away numerous doubles down the line.

OVERALL:

Pendleton was in the last year of his contract in 1990. The front office made no effort to negotiate with him during the season, and that obviously had an effect on his play. Pendleton always put the team ahead of his personal goals and never showed his emotions in a year in which he was all but forgotten. It's doubtful he'll be back with St. Louis, but he won't be easy to replace.

PITCHING:

Right-handed reliever Mike Perez has compiled a spectacular minor league record in his five seasons in the Cardinal system. In 1986, he broke in by recording a 2.97 ERA and striking out 72 batters in 72.2 innings in rookie ball. Shifted to the bullpen a year later, Perez set a minor league record with 41 saves at Class A Springfield; that year he compiled an 0.85 ERA and struck out 119 men in 84.1 innings. In 1988 he had 17 saves, a 2.08 ERA and 45 Ks in 43.1 innings at Class A St. Petersburg. The past two years, Perez has recorded 33 and 31 saves at AA Arkansas and AAA Louisville, respectively. He has continued to average a strikeout an inning. Perez finally made it to St. Louis last September, and pitched decently. Yet he's never been ranked as one of the Cards' top prospects. Why?

The answer is simple: he's not a hard thrower. Perez has a decent fastball, but nothing special. He does, however, have a very tricky motion. He hides the ball well, and batters have a very difficult time picking it up; in that way, he's similar to the Mets' Sid Fernandez, another pitcher who strikes out a lot of hitters without throwing exceptionally hard. Unlike Fernandez, who's never allowed many hits, Perez has permitted nearly one hit an inning over the last two years. And despite his hefty save totals, his minor league ERAs in 1989 and '90 were 3.64 and 4.28. With the Cards last September, Perez had a 3.95 ERA and fanned only five in 13.2 innings. It's an open question as to whether his stuff will baffle major league hitters as well as it did batters in the low minors.

HOLDING RUNNERS, FIELDING, HITTING:

Perez is a little on the stocky side and bounces around in front of the mound. Even so, he seems to be better than average fielding his position. His move to first is not great, and he looks like he's going to have problems holding runners. As a batter, Perez needs a lot of batting practice just to look like a hitter.

OVERALL:

Perez has an excellent chance to be on the Cardinals' opening day roster this year. The team's middle relief pitching was very shaky in 1990, and St. Louis will be looking at prospects closely. Despite his lack of a 90 MPH fastball, Perez' record is so intriguing that he figures to get a long look to show what he can do.

MIKE PEREZ

Position: RP
Bats: R **Throws:** R
Ht: 6' 0" **Wt:** 185

Opening Day Age: 26
Born: 10/19/64 in Yauco, Puerto Rico
ML Seasons: 1

Overall Statistics

	W	L	ERA	G	GS	Sv	IP	H	R	BB	SO	HR
1990	1	0	3.95	13	0	1	13.2	12	6	3	5	0
Career	1	0	3.95	13	0	1	13.2	12	6	3	5	0

How Often He Throws Strikes

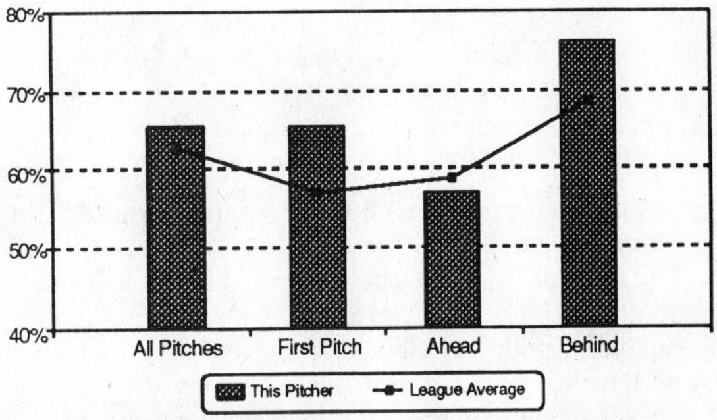

1990 Situational Stats

	W	L	ERA	Sv	IP		AB	H	HR	RBI	AVG
Home	1	0	4.26	1	6.1	LHB	27	7	0	2	.259
Road	0	0	3.68	0	7.1	RHB	23	5	0	5	.217
Day	0	0	13.50	0	2.0	Sc Pos	12	4	0	7	.333
Night	1	0	2.31	1	11.2	Clutch	18	3	0	2	.167

1990 Rankings (National League)

- Did not rank near the top or bottom in any category

BRYN SMITH

Position: SP
Bats: R **Throws:** R
Ht: 6' 2" **Wt:** 205

Opening Day Age: 35
Born: 8/11/55 in Marietta, GA
ML Seasons: 10

PITCHING:

The Cardinals signed free agent starter Bryn Smith before the 1990 season to a three-year contract worth about six million dollars. St. Louis' expectations were high for Smith, who was expected to be one of the missing pieces in a drive toward another division title. Manager Whitey Herzog said, "He should make me be eight games smarter because he beat St. Louis four times a year as an Expo." Herzog, who left the Cardinals in midseason, didn't look that smart when Smith won only nine games and recorded a mediocre 4.27 ERA in an injury-riddled season.

Though he did his best, Smith only won back-to-back starts one time for St. Louis on May 11 and May 16th. In truth, his work wasn't all that bad. The Cardinals didn't give much offensive support to Smith; in his eight losses, they scored just nine runs. Smith was on the disabled list from July 28 to September 5, and it's very likely he was pitching with a sore right shoulder before that. Smith is the type of player who will go out and do battle for the club under the worst of conditions. Even with all his problems, he was one of the few Cardinal hurlers to record a winning record.

Smith has always been a finesse hurler, working the corners and depending on changing speeds and excellent control. His best pitch is probably his palm ball, an offspeed pitch, and he also has an effective sinking fastball. Smith had elbow surgery in 1986, and since he'll be 36 late this season, the Cards have to be a little nervous about his shoulder problems last year.

HOLDING RUNNERS, FIELDING, HITTING:

Smith is a heads-up ballplayer who thinks about what he has to do on the mound. He has a decent move to first, but runners were very successful stealing against him last year (21 of 25). He fields his position very well. As a hitter he led the Cards' pitchers with ten hits and 11 sacrifice bunts.

OVERALL:

There are a lot of pitching staffs that would love to have a Bryn Smith. He is a thinking man's pitcher who knows what has to be done to gain a victory. Smith has a 13-6 career mark at Busch Stadium, and as a veteran pitcher on what will probably be a young staff, he should be a very steadying influence. If he's healthy.

Overall Statistics

	W	L	ERA	G	GS	Sv	IP	H	R	BB	SO	HR
1990	9	8	4.27	26	25	0	141.1	160	81	30	78	11
Career	90	79	3.37	310	218	6	1541.2	1470	673	371	916	119

How Often He Throws Strikes

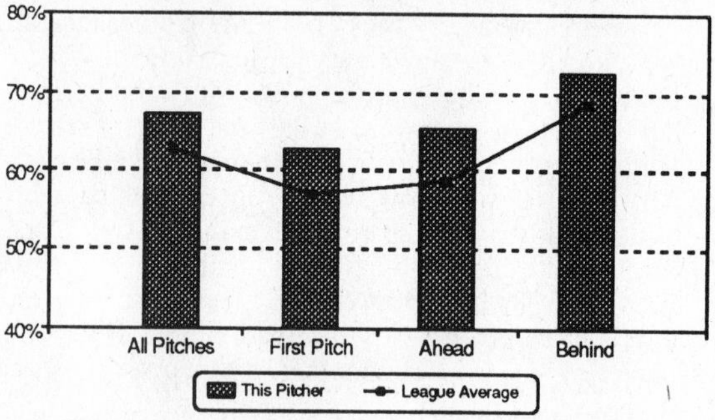

1990 Situational Stats

	W	L	ERA	Sv	IP		AB	H	HR	RBI	AVG
Home	6	4	3.84	0	84.1	LHB	339	102	3	41	.301
Road	3	4	4.89	0	57.0	RHB	220	58	8	32	.264
Day	2	3	4.29	0	42.0	Sc Pos	145	45	2	61	.310
Night	7	5	4.26	0	99.1	Clutch	22	7	0	0	.318

1990 Rankings (National League)

- 2nd highest batting average allowed with runners in scoring position (.310)
- 7th in sacrifice bunts as a hitter (11)
- Led the Cardinals in sacrifice bunts as a hitter, stolen bases allowed (21) and ERA at home (3.84)

STOPPER

LEE SMITH

Position: RP
Bats: R **Throws:** R
Ht: 6' 6" **Wt:** 245

Opening Day Age: 33
Born: 12/4/57 in Jamestown, LA
ML Seasons: 11

PITCHING:

The Cardinals acquired veteran right-handed relief ace Lee Smith last May 4 in a trade with the Boston Red Sox for outfielder Tom Brunansky. It may have been the best trade St. Louis has made since Dal Maxvill became general manager. Smith saved 27 games for the Cards, totaled 31 for the year, and his overall ERA of 2.06 was his best since 1983, when he was a kid of 25. Better yet, Maxvill signed Smith, who was in his free agent year, to a multi-year contract, proving it wasn't just a stopgap deal.

When Smith arrived in St. Louis, the Cardinal bullpen was in a shambles; no one had proven to be effective as the closer. Smith solved the problem, winning or saving 43 percent of the Cardinals' 70 victories. Returning to the National League after a two year absence, Smith resumed his role as the most intimidating closer in the circuit, though Randy Myers -- and now Rob Dibble -- might disagree. Smith is bigger than either, has that menacing look on his face, and still throws his fastball in the high 90s.

Just five of 29 inherited baserunners scored when Smith entered a game for the Cardinals last season (six of 34 for the entire year). He was practically unhittable during a streak from June 28 to August 3 when he pitched 20 consecutive scoreless innings. On July 14th, during the streak, Smith struck out five San Francisco Giants in two innings to preserve a 2-1 victory for Joe Magrane. He had at least one strikeout in 37 of 53 games (70%) and had a better than three-to-one strikeout-to-walk ratio (70/20).

Consistently brilliant, Smith has now recorded 25 or more saves in eight straight seasons. For his career, he has averaged over a strikeout an inning, and despite pitching the bulk of his seasons in hitters' parks at Wrigley and Fenway, his lifetime ERA is 2.88.

HOLDING RUNNERS, FIELDING, HITTING:

A power pitcher with a slow delivery, Smith has always been easy to steal on. He is not very agile and looks heavier than his listed 245 pounds, but with his style of pitching, he's not going to get many fielding chances. He doesn't bat enough for his weak hitting to be a factor.

OVERALL:

Even at 33, Smith remains an undiminished, blow-'em-away power reliever. He now has 265 career saves, placing him fifth all-time and second only to Jeff Reardon among active pitchers. Even pitching for a club which might not win many games, Smith figures to pad that total this year.

Overall Statistics

	W	L	ERA	G	GS	Sv	IP	H	R	BB	SO	HR
1990	5	5	2.06	64	0	31	83.0	71	24	29	87	3
Career	55	62	2.88	650	6	265	919.1	787	328	363	923	54

How Often He Throws Strikes

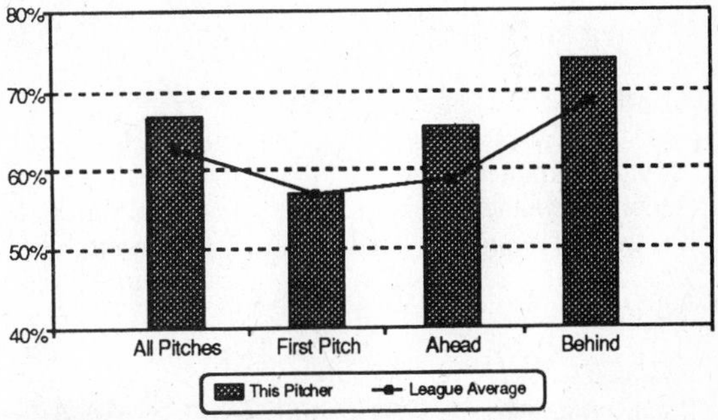

1990 Situational Stats

	W	L	ERA	Sv	IP		AB	H	HR	RBI	AVG
Home	3	3	2.49	12	47.0	LHB	180	42	3	19	.233
Road	2	2	1.50	19	36.0	RHB	130	29	0	7	.223
Day	2	0	0.76	12	35.2	Sc Pos	95	19	0	20	.200
Night	3	5	3.04	19	47.1	Clutch	256	61	3	24	.238

1990 Rankings (National League)

- 2nd in save percentage (84.4%)
- 3rd in saves (27) and save opportunities (32)
- 5th in games finished (45)
- Led the Cardinals in saves, games finished, save opportunities, save percentage and blown saves (5)

HALL OF FAMER

OZZIE SMITH

Position: SS
Bats: B **Throws:** R
Ht: 5'10" **Wt:** 155

Opening Day Age: 36
Born: 12/26/54 in Mobile, AL
ML Seasons: 13

Overall Statistics

	G	AB	R	H	D	T	HR	RBI	SB	BB	SO	AVG
1990	143	512	61	130	21	1	1	50	32	61	33	.254
Career	1926	7019	910	1798	297	52	19	600	464	807	454	.256

Where He Hits the Ball

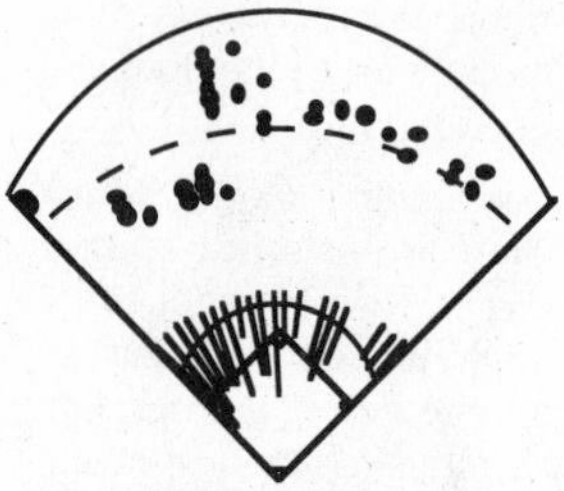

Vs. LHP

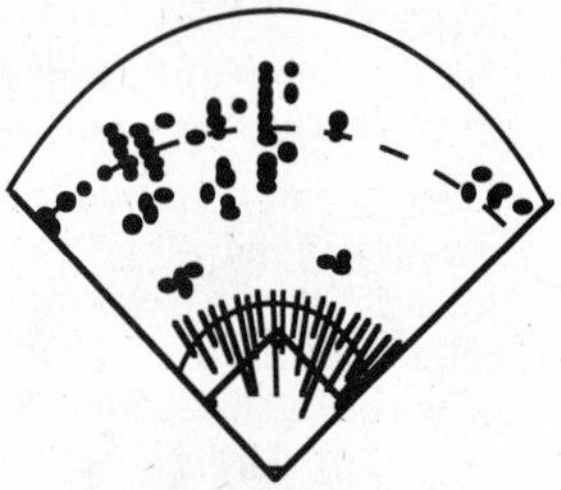

Vs. RHP

1990 Situational Stats

	AB	H	HR	RBI	AVG		AB	H	HR	RBI	AVG
Home	256	68	0	25	.266	LHP	201	58	1	23	.289
Road	256	62	1	25	.242	RHP	311	72	0	27	.232
Day	157	37	0	12	.236	Sc Pos	146	35	0	49	.240
Night	355	93	1	38	.262	Clutch	81	15	0	9	.185

1990 Rankings (National League)

- 2nd lowest HR frequency (512 ABs per HR), highest batting average with the bases loaded (.571) and highest percentage of swings put into play (59.3%)
- 3rd lowest slugging percentage (.305) and lowest percentage of swings that missed (7.1%)
- Led the Cardinals in at-bats (512), plate appearances (592) and stolen base percentage (84.2%)
- Led NL shortstops in sacrifice flies (10), stolen bases, groundball/flyball ratio, lowest percentage of swings that missed and highest percentage of swings put into play

HITTING:

As the Cardinals fell to the unaccustomed position of last place in 1990, a lot of the heat fell on Ozzie Smith. The most popular player in St. Louis since the days of Stan Musial, the effervescent Smith began catching flak as he and the team played poorly. Smith's average dropped to .254 last season, his worst year since 1983, and that seemed to perfectly mirror the Cardinals' struggles.

Smith got off to a slow start last year due to a pulled groin and a knee strain. He was hitting only .231 at the All-Star break, and was criticized for leading the All-Star balloting over Barry Larkin and Shawon Dunston. He was also blamed for the resignation of Whitey Herzog as Cardinal manager. Anonymous sources were spreading all kinds of rumors. Fortunately for Smith, he got himself together during the second half, batting a solid .278.

A spray hitter, Smith has always liked the ball upstairs, and he remains a dangerous high-ball hitter. He handles the bat extremely well, has excellent plate discipline, and doesn't strike out much. He is still rarely overmatched by hard throwers, and he makes excellent contact. Smith has been a national figure in the eyes of the sporting public, and that won't make it easy for the Cardinals if they feel the need to go with a younger player.

BASERUNNING:

In his fourteenth season, Smith is still an excellent base stealer. He has stolen 20 or more bases in each season of his career, and more than 30 in seven of the last eight. He has great baserunning instincts, is rarely thrown out on the paths, and will score from first on many hits.

FIELDING:

Even at his advanced age, Smith has not lost much range, and he remains a brilliant shortstop. He has been bothered by shoulder problems in recent years, but he rarely has to throw hard due to the quickness and agility he uses when fielding the ball and throwing in one motion. Smith knows both the Cardinal pitchers and the opposing hitters, and that knowledge generally makes up for whatever range he may have lost.

OVERALL:

Smith is a certain Hall of Famer who says he can play shortstop until he is 40 years old. He works very hard in drills and takes very good care of himself with a nutrition and strength program. Whether he'll remain the shortstop of the youth-oriented Cardinals, however, is another question.

SCOTT TERRY

Position: RP
Bats: R **Throws:** R
Ht: 5'11" **Wt:** 195

Opening Day Age: 31
Born: 11/21/59 in Hobbs, NM
ML Seasons: 5

Overall Statistics

	W	L	ERA	G	GS	Sv	IP	H	R	BB	SO	HR
1990	2	6	4.75	50	2	2	72.0	75	45	27	35	7
Career	20	24	3.91	171	40	7	419.0	415	203	144	210	34

How Often He Throws Strikes

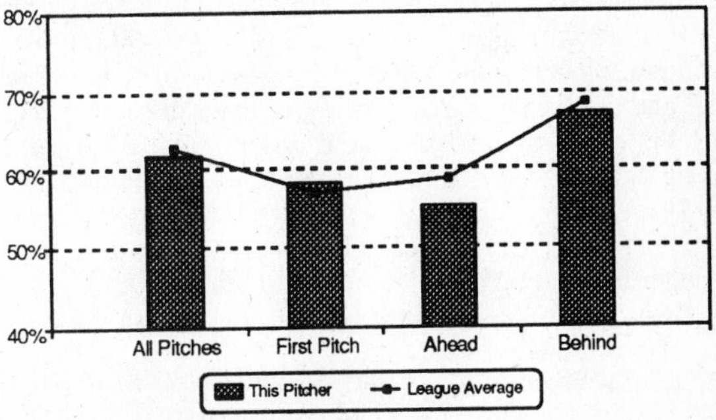

1990 Situational Stats

	W	L	ERA	Sv	IP		AB	H	HR	RBI	AVG
Home	1	3	4.04	1	35.2	LHB	130	35	4	26	.269
Road	1	3	5.45	1	36.1	RHB	154	40	3	23	.260
Day	0	1	6.23	0	13.0	Sc Pos	89	29	3	43	.326
Night	2	5	4.42	2	59.0	Clutch	43	13	1	10	.302

1990 Rankings (National League)

- 3rd least GDPs induced per GDP situation (1.7%)
- 5th worst first batter efficiency (.349)

PITCHING:

Scott Terry is a hard throwing righthander who can come out of the bullpen or give a team some starts when needed. Terry will take the ball when the manager gives him the opportunity. Last year, however, he often came up short, winning only two of eight decisions and recording a 4.75 ERA that was the second-highest of his career.

Injuries were mostly to blame for the bow-legged Terry's problems last year. Shoulder problems wreaked havoc on Terry during the season, and arthroscopic surgery was planned for the off season. Early in the year, Terry experienced pain in his shoulder, and at the All-Star break he had a hideous 7.52 ERA. There was more than a little talk that his career might be in jeopardy.

At that point, former Cardinal pitching coach Mike Roarke made some adjustments in Terry's delivery. Roarke changed Terry's motion so that he was pitching off a stiff back leg. Standing straight up and down, Terry was in a position where his arm was strong and he didn't have to worry about the lower half of his body. Roarke also got Terry to stop raising his hands over his head in the delivery, taking a lot of the pressure off his shoulder.

With his new delivery, Terry began to pitch a lot better. He allowed just 11 earned runs in his last 39.2 innings for a 2.50 ERA. Terry's basic stuff -- fastball, slider and change -- was always pretty good, and with his mechanical problems solved, he pitched a lot better.

HOLDING RUNNERS, FIELDING, HITTING:

Terry was originally signed as an outfielder, where he spent three-and-one-half seasons before switching to the mound. He has always done a good job of holding runners, and he's an excellent fielding pitcher whose motion is ideal for grabbing balls hit back through the box. As a former outfielder, Terry has better-than-average hitting skills and is not an automatic out at the plate.

OVERALL:

The Cardinals have some quality pitchers coming up from Louisville. Since Terry is 31 with a history of shoulder problems, St. Louis may give a lot of thought as to his future with the rebuilding club. Terry has a talented arm, however -- at least when it's healthy. His work during the last half of 1990 indicates that he can help somebody, even if it isn't the Cardinals.

BOB TEWKSBURY

Position: SP/RP
Bats: R **Throws:** R
Ht: 6' 4" **Wt:** 200

Opening Day Age: 30
Born: 11/30/60 in Concord, NH
ML Seasons: 5

Overall Statistics

	W	L	ERA	G	GS	Sv	IP	H	R	BB	SO	HR
1990	10	9	3.47	28	20	1	145.1	151	67	15	50	7
Career	21	22	3.90	74	54	1	360.1	405	183	78	139	24

How Often He Throws Strikes

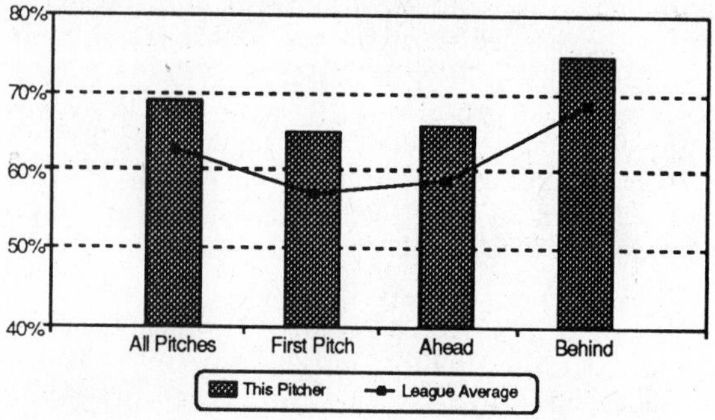

1990 Situational Stats

	W	L	ERA	Sv	IP		AB	H	HR	RBI	AVG
Home	4	5	3.66	0	66.1	LHB	339	94	4	37	.277
Road	6	4	3.30	1	79.0	RHB	226	57	3	22	.252
Day	4	3	4.04	0	49.0	Sc Pos	132	43	4	55	.326
Night	6	6	3.18	1	96.1	Clutch	24	4	0	0	.167

1990 Rankings (National League)

- 9th in shutouts (2)
- Led the Cardinals in complete games (3) and shutouts

PITCHING:

At 6'-4" and 200 pounds, Bob Tewksbury has the physical appearance of a hard thrower. However, Tewksbury is a pure control pitcher. His fastball has sometimes been clocked under 80 MPH. Regardless, Tewksbury knows how to win, and proved it by turning in a 10-9 record for the last-place Cardinals last year.

Tewksbury began the season in the Cardinal bullpen before being outrighted to AAA Louisville on May 9. At Louisville, Tewksbury did not walk a batter in his first 26 innings. He was 3-2 with a 2.43 ERA in six starts before the Cardinals brought him back on June 12 and put him in their rotation. Though he slumped a bit in September, Tewksbury was one of the Cardinals' most reliable hurlers from the time of his recall.

Tewksbury pitches like an artist painting the plate. He moves the ball up and down, inside and out, consistently keeping the batter off balance with change-ups and slow curves. His fastball is generally just out of the strike zone where the batter will swing but can't get a good cut. Tewksbury pitched two shutouts last year; they came in consecutive starts August 12 and August 17. In the second contest, he had a perfect game going against Houston until Franklin Stubbs got a double to lead off the eighth. Stubbs was the only batter to reach base.

The key to Tewksbury's success is his control. On August 29 at Cincinnati, Tewksbury was the first Cardinal to pitch a no walk, no strikeout complete game victory since Danny Cox did it in April 1987. For the year, he walked only 15 men in 145.1 innings -- an average of less than one per nine innings.

HOLDING RUNNERS, FIELDING, HITTING:

Tewksbury is an excellent fielding pitcher. He makes the play in front of him and is not afraid to throw out the baserunner on sacrifice attempts. He holds runners well, but his slow delivery to the plate is a hindrance for the catcher. At the plate and on the base paths, Tewksbury appears out of his element. He will swing the bat but only occasionally make contact. He is not a good bunter, either.

OVERALL:

Tewksbury has a fine arm that never suffers from over-burdening punishment. His philosophy of pitching is "let them hit it". He has thrown complete games in 80 pitches, and his games are often finished in two hours. He figures to be one of the mainstays of the Cardinal staff in 1991.

MILT THOMPSON

Position: RF/LF/CF
Bats: L **Throws:** R
Ht: 5'11" **Wt:** 170

Opening Day Age: 32
Born: 1/5/59 in Washington, DC
ML Seasons: 7

HITTING:

Long a steady offensive performer, Milt Thompson entered last season as an outfielder without a position. Thompson had made a strong impression on the Cardinals during 1989, his first year in St. Louis, by batting a solid .290 with 68 RBI. However, he'd seen most of his action in center field, and the Cards' regular center fielder, Willie McGee, was healthy once more. With faith in Thompson, the Cardinals opened up a position for him by trading right fielder Tom Brunansky to Boston on May 4 for reliever Lee Smith. However, Thompson turned out to be a total flop in right, hitting a career low .218.

After batting below .288 only once in six previous seasons, Thompson was in a funk last year, and for most of the season couldn't get to the .200 mark. He has always been a strong ground ball hitter, but last year he went overboard, trying to hit the ball on the ground even when pitchers were working the ball upstairs. He developed a swing that continually pushed the ball to second base, even against lefthanders' breaking balls. After making a strong showing against southpaws in 1989, batting .267, Thompson hit only .175 against lefthanders last year.

Though he had a miserable season last year, Thompson has the talent to rebound. He needs to restore the inside-out swing that was so effective for him in 1989, and use the whole field. Thompson seemed obsessed with hitting the ball on the ground last year. That's certainly a good strategy for a fast player on a turf field, but not when the only result is weak grounders to second.

BASERUNNING:

Thompson is very fast and has the ability to steal 30 or more bases a season. He has a career success rate over 79%, and was just above that with 25 steals in 30 attempts last year. Thompson is aggressive on the base paths and will take an extra base whenever he sees the opportunity.

FIELDING:

Thompson plays his best defense in left or center field. The angle in right field seemed to upset him at times last season. He has good range covering the gaps but does not possess a great arm.

OVERALL:

After the way he played last year, Thompson will have to be considered a backup platoon outfielder once again. In the past he has filled that role very capably, and if he can regain his batting stroke, he could wind up seeing a lot of playing time.

Overall Statistics

	G	AB	R	H	D	T	HR	RBI	SB	BB	SO	AVG
1990	135	418	42	91	14	7	6	30	25	39	60	.218
Career	756	2448	312	677	99	29	27	207	157	203	406	.277

Where He Hits the Ball

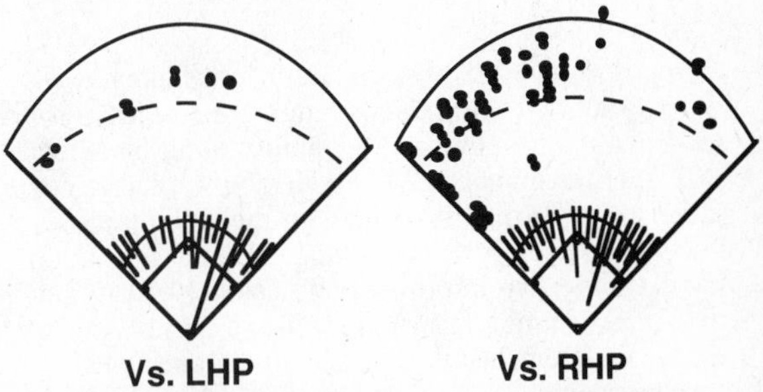

1990 Situational Stats

	AB	H	HR	RBI	AVG		AB	H	HR	RBI	AVG
Home	221	47	3	20	.213	LHP	120	21	0	4	.175
Road	197	44	3	10	.223	RHP	298	70	6	26	.235
Day	138	32	2	8	.232	Sc Pos	90	19	1	20	.211
Night	280	59	4	22	.211	Clutch	76	17	1	10	.224

1990 Rankings (National League)

- 1st on lowest batting average vs. left-handed pitchers (.175), lowest slugging percentage vs. left-handed pitchers (.233), lowest on-base average vs. left-handed pitchers (.227) and lowest batting average on a 3-2 count (.000)
- 5th lowest batting average with 2 strikes (.140)
- Led the Cardinals in hit by pitch (5) and least GDPs per GDP situation (4.3%)
- Led NL right fielders in stolen bases (25)

HITTING:

Prized rookie Todd Zeile was heralded as the super star catcher of the future in almost every baseball publication last spring. A lot of pressure was put on Zeile, and all things considered, he handled it very well. Zeile's 15 homers led the club and were the most by a Cardinal rookie since Ken Boyer belted 18 and Bill Virdon 17 back in 1955. Forty-three of his 121 hits (36%) went for extra bases. Further, Zeile showed unusual patience for a young player by drawing 67 walks.

What Zeile did not handle as well was new manager Joe Torre's conviction that Zeile should be moved to third base. Torre wanted more power at third base than Terry Pendleton could provide, and felt that Zeile could realize his offensive potential more easily at a less demanding position. But Zeile wasn't quite ready for a change after less than one major league season as a catcher.

If he can settle into a position, Zeile looks like he can develop into an outstanding hitter. He already possesses good discipline and the ability to hit breaking balls. Former manager Whitey Herzog wanted to get Zeile to try to hit line drives up the middle more, rather than try to pull everything. Herzog wanted to instill confidence into his young catcher and to get him to use more of the field. Zeile often pressed in clutch situations last year, especially with runners in scoring position.

BASERUNNING:

With little speed, Zeile is no threat to steal, and won't be asked to do so very often. He did swipe two bases last year, but was tossed out four times. He's fairly aggressive on the base paths, however, taking as many extra bases as his feet will allow.

FIELDING:

Zeile played his first pro game at third base last September 5, and it's still too early to judge him at that position. He could still wind up as a catcher, another position he's still trying to master. Zeile looked a little raw behind the plate last year, but promising. He threw out 35 of 136 base stealers (26%).

OVERALL:

Zeile was troubled over the move to third and feels that Torre doesn't have confidence in him as a catcher. Zeile has good hands, good feet, and decent reflexes. It will take some time, but who knows better than Joe Torre about moving from catcher to third? Ex-catcher Torre won an MVP Award as the Cardinals' third baseman in 1971.

TODD ZEILE

Position: C/1B/3B
Bats: R **Throws:** R
Ht: 6' 1" **Wt:** 190

Opening Day Age: 25
Born: 9/9/65 in Van Nuys, CA
ML Seasons: 2

Overall Statistics

	G	AB	R	H	D	T	HR	RBI	SB	BB	SO	AVG
1990	144	495	62	121	25	3	15	57	2	67	77	.244
Career	172	577	69	142	28	4	16	65	2	76	91	.246

Where He Hits the Ball

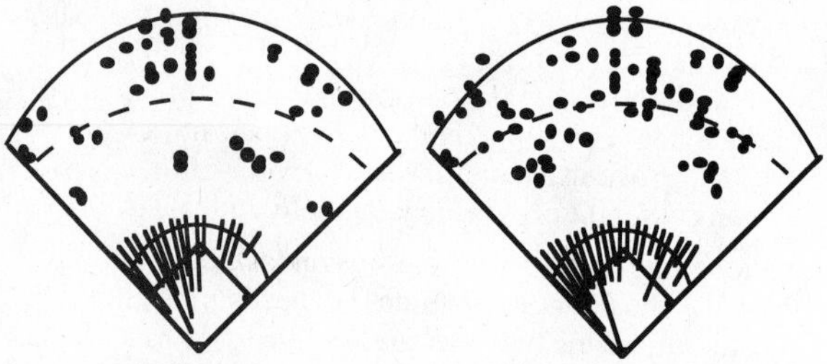

Vs. LHP Vs. RHP

1990 Situational Stats

	AB	H	HR	RBI	AVG		AB	H	HR	RBI	AVG
Home	233	61	8	26	.262	LHP	173	46	6	22	.266
Road	262	60	7	31	.229	RHP	322	75	9	35	.233
Day	106	27	4	16	.255	Sc Pos	129	21	2	35	.163
Night	389	94	11	41	.242	Clutch	88	18	1	6	.205

1990 Rankings (National League)

- 1st lowest batting avertage with runners in scoring position (.163)
- 2nd highest percentage of pitches taken (63.3%)
- Led the Cardinals in home runs (15), pitches seen (2,263), HR frequency (33 ABs per HR), pitches seen per plate appearance (3.97), slugging percentage vs. left-handed pitchers (.451) and highest percentage of pitches taken
- Led NL catchers in home runs, runs (62), total bases (197), HR frequency, pitches seen per plate appearance, most runs scored per time reached base (32.6%) and highest percentage of pitches taken

TIM JONES

Position: SS/2B
Bats: L **Throws:** R
Ht: 5'10" **Wt:** 172

Opening Day Age: 28
Born: 12/1/62 in Sumter, SC
ML Seasons: 3

Overall Statistics

	G	AB	R	H	D	T	HR	RBI	SB	BB	SO	AVG
1990	67	128	9	28	7	1	1	12	3	12	20	.219
Career	140	255	22	64	13	1	1	22	8	23	38	.251

HITTING, FIELDING, BASERUNNING:

Tim Jones is a better hitter than he showed last season, when he batted only .219. Jones got off to a very slow start at the plate last year and was virtually useless against southpaws, getting only one hit in 21 at-bats against lefties for the season. Jones had his useful moments during the season, however. He belted his first major league homer August 18 off Houston's Brian Fisher and recorded a career-high seven doubles. He also continued to show he's a good bunter, with the speed to beat out infield hits.

Jones is a versatile bench player, probably his best attribute. He made 21 starts at shortstop and six at second base last year, but also played third and even pitched (he gave up two runs in an inning and a third). Jones has also worked out in the off season at catching and is the Cardinals' emergency catcher. He caught one inning in 1988. Jones is used as a pinch runner and has the speed to steal. He was caught four times in seven attempts last year, however.

OVERALL:

Tim Jones is a classic Cardinal reserve player in the mold of a Mike Ramsey or Tom Lawless. He has the ability to come off the bench and fill in for injured or tiring middle infielders without disrupting the flow offensively or defensively.

TOM NIEDENFUER

Position: RP
Bats: R **Throws:** R
Ht: 6' 5" **Wt:** 224

Opening Day Age: 31
Born: 8/13/59 in St. Louis Park, MN
ML Seasons: 10

Overall Statistics

	W	L	ERA	G	GS	Sv	IP	H	R	BB	SO	HR
1990	0	6	3.46	52	0	2	65.0	66	26	25	32	3
Career	36	46	3.29	484	0	97	653.0	601	251	226	474	60

PITCHING, FIELDING, HITTING & HOLDING RUNNERS:

Unemployed after posting a 6.69 ERA with the Mariners in 1989, Tom Niedenfuer landed a job with the Cardinals last spring. The circumstances were unusual: Niedenfuer got his St. Louis shot after a phone call from his wife, actress Judy Landers, to then Cardinal manager Whitey Herzog. Herzog, of course, couldn't help remembering how Niedenfuer, then a Dodger, gave up the big home run to Jack Clark which had put the Cards in the 1985 World Series. Herzog was looking for a middle reliever, and agreed to give Niedenfuer a chance.

Herzog soon left St. Louis, but Niedenfuer stuck around, pitching better than his record (0-6) indicated, but not as well as his ERA (3.46) would have one believe. His fastball wasn't the same pitch National League hitters remembered from his Dodger days, but he was effective enough to appear in 52 games for the Cards. He pitched very well against righties, but had all kinds of problems against opposing lefthanders, who batted .330 against him. Niedenfuer was very good at preventing inherited runners from scoring, as only eight of 30 scored after he came into games.

Niedenfuer is decent at controlling the running game, and he is an adequate fielding pitcher. His range is a little below average. He never could hit, but he doesn't get much of a chance.

OVERALL:

Niedenfuer was unsigned for 1991, and with Herzog gone fishing, Niedenfuer's chances of coming back to St. Louis weren't great. He didn't pitch horribly last year, but his wife may have to get back on the phone this spring.

OMAR OLIVARES

Position: SP
Bats: R **Throws:** R
Ht: 6' 1" **Wt:** 185

Opening Day Age: 23
Born: 7/6/67 in Mayaguez, Puerto Rico
ML Seasons: 1

Overall Statistics

	W	L	ERA	G	GS	Sv	IP	H	R	BB	SO	HR
1990	1	1	2.92	9	6	0	49.1	45	17	17	20	2
Career	1	1	2.92	9	6	0	49.1	45	17	17	20	2

PITCHING, FIELDING, HITTING & HOLDING RUNNERS:

Young lefty Omar Olivares came to the Cards from San Diego last spring. Though not a hard thrower, Olivares is considered a definite prospect, and the Cards had to give up Alex Cole (who broke in with a bang for the Indians later in the year) and Steve Peters in order to get him.

Thus far, the Cards haven't been disappointed that they made the deal. Olivares went 10-11 with a 2.82 ERA at AAA Louisville last year, then came up to the big club and posted a 2.92 ERA in nine appearances, including six starts. Olivares showed off a good sinking fastball and a decent slider. With that equipment, he's capable of getting lots of ground ball outs. He's not afraid to pitch inside, and his stuff was very effective against left-handed hitters. He had problems with righties, who batted .301 against him.

A fine athlete, Olivares finishes his motion in good fielding position and helps himself with the glove. He also has a good pickoff move and is tough to steal on: runners stole only two bases in five attempts with him on the mound. He batted .370 at Wichita in 1989 and can help himself with the bat.

OVERALL:

Only 23, Olivares impressed the Cards with his work last year. He has an outside chance at earning a spot in the rotation this season, and definitely figures in the club's future plans. He'll need to improve his work against righties, however.

GERONIMO PENA

Position: 2B
Bats: B **Throws:** R
Ht: 6' 1" **Wt:** 170

Opening Day Age: 24
Born: 3/29/67 in Distrito Nacional, Dominican Republic
ML Seasons: 1

Overall Statistics

	G	AB	R	H	D	T	HR	RBI	SB	BB	SO	AVG
1990	18	45	5	11	2	0	0	2	1	4	14	.244
Career	18	45	5	11	2	0	0	2	1	4	14	.244

HITTING, FIELDING, BASERUNNING:

Rookie second baseman Geronimo Pena figures to be with the Cardinals on opening day 1991. The Cardinals are out of options on Pena and he has proven his ability to play second base in the majors. Pena batted only .249 at AAA Louisville last year and .244 in 18 games with the Cardinals, but the club feels he has the potential to do a lot better.

Though only 24, Pena has overcome a lot of adversity in his career. He was on the disabled list for three months in 1989 with a broken wrist suffered during spring training, but came back to hit .296 with 33 extra-base hits in 77 games for AA Arkansas. Last year, Pena had a bout with tuberculosis, which sapped his strength, then missed more time with a hand injury. He was still able to play 118 games. The illness and injury affected his hitting, as did a brief, unsuccessful shift to third base. In the past, he's demonstrated a quick bat with surprising power, and excellent patience for a young hitter. Pena had a .517 slugging average at Arkansas in '88.

Pena has great speed for his size and has stolen as many as 80 bases in a season. He is a good defensive second baseman, with the skills to play regularly there.

OVERALL:

Pena would have an excellent chance to be a regular this year, but Jose Oquendo stands in his way. Pena's best chance would come if the Cards were to trade Ozzie Smith and move Oquendo to short. Otherwise, he'll have to learn to be a bench player until his opportunity finally arrives.

DENNY WALLING

Position: 3B
Bats: L **Throws:** R
Ht: 6' 1" **Wt:** 185

Opening Day Age: 37
Born: 4/17/54 in Neptune, NJ
ML Seasons: 16

Overall Statistics

	G	AB	R	H	D	T	HR	RBI	SB	BB	SO	AVG
1990	78	127	7	28	5	0	1	19	0	8	15	.220
Career	1244	2898	370	794	141	30	49	378	44	305	308	.274

HITTING, FIELDING, BASERUNNING:

Denny Walling has lasted 16 seasons in the majors for one simple reason: he can hit. Now used mainly as a substitute, Walling last year became only the thirteenth player in major league history to record 100 career pinch hits. But that was one of the few highlights in a season in which Walling managed only a .220 average, his worst figure since 1982.

Walling has always been a good fastball hitter, often going after the first pitch in an attempt to get a hard one to hit. But the years have robbed him of bat speed, and he can now sometimes be overpowered by hard throwers. He's still dangerous, and his 28 hits last year produced 19 RBI. He's a disciplined hitter and a good contact man; he gets his share of walks, but seldom strikes out.

Walling has never had much speed, and he's slower now than ever, with no stolen bases since 1988. He's strictly station-to-station on the bases. He can still fill in at third, first and left field, but basically does so only in an emergency. Walling won't embarrass himself and played errorless ball last year, but he doesn't have much range.

OVERALL:

Walling was a free agent after the 1990 season, and it seemed unlikely that the Cards would try to re-sign him. His skills, narrow as they are, are more suited for a contending club looking for a lefty pinch swinger. But after his 1990 performance, Walling will have to prove he can still hit.

CRAIG WILSON

Position: 3B
Bats: R **Throws:** R
Ht: 5'11" **Wt:** 175

Opening Day Age: 26
Born: 11/28/64 in Anne Arundel County, MD
ML Seasons: 2

Overall Statistics

	G	AB	R	H	D	T	HR	RBI	SB	BB	SO	AVG
1990	55	121	13	30	2	0	0	7	0	8	14	.248
Career	61	125	14	31	2	0	0	8	0	9	16	.248

HITTING, FIELDING, BASERUNNING:

Craig Wilson did everything he could to make an impression on new manager Joe Torre last season. Wilson is a hard-nosed player in the field and at the plate, and Torre, the same type of guy, liked his attitude. Torre also liked the fact that Wilson hit .391 (nine-for-23) with four RBI as a pinch hitter.

Wilson has always impressed Cardinal management with his hitting. He batted .358 at Class A St. Petersburg in 1987, .317 in 55 games at AA Arkansas in 1989 and .291 in 75 games when moved up to AAA Louisville later that year. Wilson is not a home run hitter, and never belted more than eight in a minor league season. He's a gap hitter who can fight off the inside pitch and then take an outside pitch and line it into right. He's a good contact hitter with the discipline to lay off bad pitches.

Wilson played left, right, second, third and first for Torre last year, and committed only one error. He feels most comfortable at second and third base. He has good range as an infielder, having led all American Association third basemen in total chances in 1988. Wilson is not considered a base stealer, though he swiped 44 for St. Pete in 1986. He doesn't get a big lead or a good jump.

OVERALL:

Wilson will go to spring training to try to earn a spot with the team. He auditioned for the third base job before Torre moved Zeile to third, and he's still a possibility there if Zeile moves back to catcher. But he's more likely to stick around as a utility man.

HITTING:

At 24, Shawn Abner is still knocking on the major league door. The first player chosen in the 1984 draft by the usually-astute New York Mets, Abner was dealt to the Padres two years later as part of the package for Kevin McReynolds. The Mets gave up on Abner rather quickly, and now the Padres may be ready to do the same thing. Last season, his first full season in San Diego, Abner played in 91 games, starting 40. He produced his best numbers, but that's not saying much. He batted only .245 with one homer and 15 RBI.

The general rap on Abner has always been that he could not hit a breaking pitch. But Abner has even had problems wrestling with a good fastball. With only seven homers in 416 lifetime at-bats, he lacks the power expected from an outfielder. His strike zone judgement isn't great, either.

Abner's only excuse can be that last season's total of 184 at-bats nearly matched his previous career major-league total of 232. Abner wonders what he might accomplish if he was ever given 400 at-bats in a single season. Given what he's done with the chances he's had so far, that prospect is hardly appealing to San Diego.

BASERUNNING:

What Abner lacks in ability, he unfortunately doesn't make up for with heady play. Last year, he was one of at least three players who forgot how many outs there were or what the count was in either a baserunning or fielding situation. After a strike call, Abner wandered off second base and was picked off. He is a speedy runner, but his lack of fundamental skills are costly.

FIELDING:

Fielding is Abner's one area to shine. A decent outfielder with good speed, he is one the club's best defensive center fielders. In his brief major league tenure he has turned in several spectacular catches that have saved games. He has a decent, but erratic, throwing arm.

OVERALL:

Abner has long contended that it is impossible for him to develop as a hitter when he spends so much time on the bench. There is validity to that point. But up until now, he certainly hasn't made the most of the time he has been given. He is still only 24, but the Padres have patiently waited for four years hoping Abner would develop. After last season, they have probably given up the ghost.

SHAWN ABNER

Position: CF/LF
Bats: R **Throws:** R
Ht: 6' 1" **Wt:** 190

Opening Day Age: 24
Born: 6/17/66 in Hamilton, OH
ML Seasons: 4

Overall Statistics

	G	AB	R	H	D	T	HR	RBI	SB	BB	SO	AVG
1990	91	184	17	45	9	0	1	15	2	9	28	.245
Career	201	416	41	91	19	1	7	41	4	20	75	.219

Where He Hits the Ball

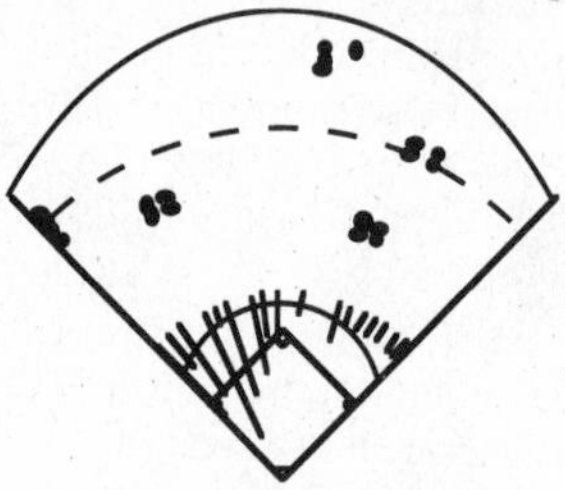

Vs. LHP

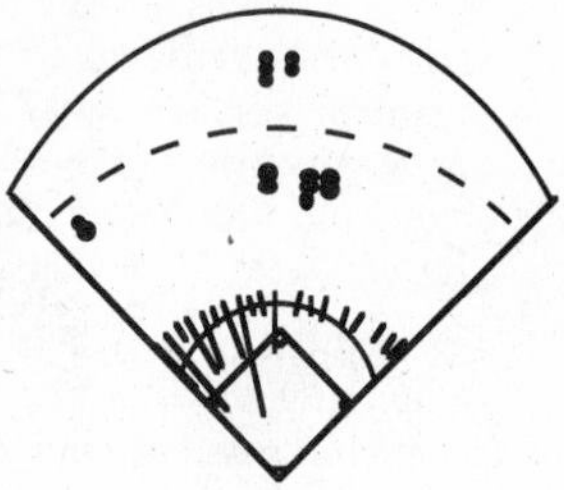

Vs. RHP

1990 Situational Stats

	AB	H	HR	RBI	AVG		AB	H	HR	RBI	AVG
Home	94	19	1	6	.202	LHP	101	23	0	10	.228
Road	90	26	0	9	.289	RHP	83	22	1	5	.265
Day	64	18	0	6	.281	Sc Pos	40	12	1	15	.300
Night	120	27	1	9	.225	Clutch	33	7	0	2	.212

1990 Rankings (National League)

- Did not rank near the top or bottom in any category

ROBERTO ALOMAR

Position: 2B
Bats: B **Throws:** R
Ht: 6' 0" **Wt:** 175

Opening Day Age: 23
Born: 2/5/68 in Ponce, Puerto Rico
ML Seasons: 3

Overall Statistics

	G	AB	R	H	D	T	HR	RBI	SB	BB	SO	AVG
1990	147	586	80	168	27	5	6	60	24	48	72	.287
Career	448	1754	246	497	78	12	22	157	90	148	231	.283

Where He Hits the Ball

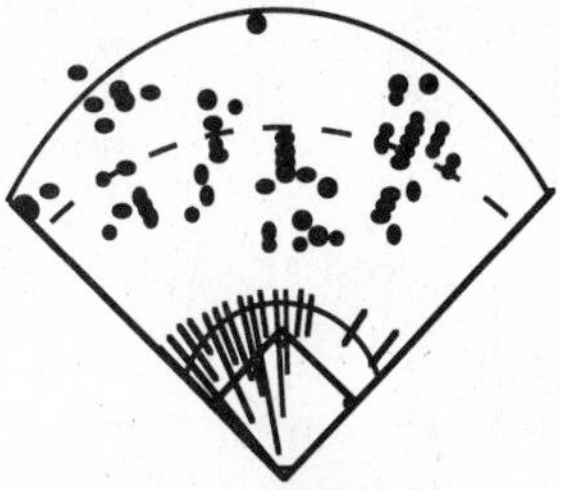
Vs. LHP

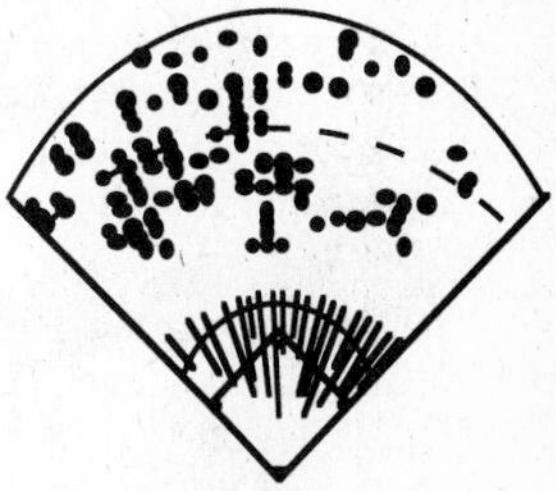
Vs. RHP

1990 Situational Stats

	AB	H	HR	RBI	AVG		AB	H	HR	RBI	AVG
Home	298	85	4	36	.285	LHP	204	53	3	17	.260
Road	288	83	2	24	.288	RHP	382	115	3	43	.301
Day	167	55	1	20	.329	Sc Pos	139	47	2	50	.338
Night	419	113	5	40	.270	Clutch	105	24	0	12	.229

1990 Rankings (National League)

- 4th highest batting average with a 3-2 count (.396)
- 5th in GDPs (16), batting average with runners in scoring position (.338) and lowest slugging percentage vs. right-handed pitchers (.382)
- Led the Padres in pitches seen per plate appearance (3.78), batting average with runners in scoring position and batting average with a 3-2 count
- Led NL second basemen in singles (130), pitches seen (2,444), batting average on a 3-2 count, batting average on the road (.288), errors (17) and highest percentage of extra bases taken as a runner

HITTING:

In three seasons, Roberto Alomar has become one of baseball's best-hitting second basemen. Very consistent, Alomar has hit 24, 27 and 27 doubles in his three seasons; hit nine, seven and six homers; scored 84, 82 and 80 runs; and drawn 47, 53 and 48 walks. Alomar's .287 average last year was down eight points from his 1989 figure, but the Padres aren't complaining.

The switch-hitting Alomar might be even more of an offensive force if he could improve his hitting from the right side. Repeating his previous pattern, Alomar batted much higher as a left-handed hitter last year (.301) than he did as a righty (.260). Alomar has spent a lot of time trying to improve his right-handed hitting, but thus far his work hasn't produced results. Fortunately, he hits well enough from the right side to avoid any thoughts of platooning.

Alomar's other Achilles heel as a hitter still remains his free-swinging nature. He still chases too many bad pitches, and his 48 walks last year were a low total for a guy who hits at the top of the order. Still, Alomar has become an excellent all around hitter. He can drive the ball and hit line drives to all fields.

BASERUNNING:

Very fast, Alomar has the potential to develop into a top base stealer. He led the Padres with a career high 42 swipes in 1989, but slipped to 24 steals last season; however, his success rate increased from 71 to 77 percent. Alomar runs the bases both aggressively and intelligently, and is often sent on the hit-and-run.

FIELDING:

Despite tremendous range, Alomar needs to polish his fielding. He's committed 63 errors in his three seasons, a tremendously high total for a second baseman. Fortunately, he's headed in the right direction, as he dropped from 28 errors in 1989 to 19 last year. Often the victim of his own great range, Alomar will frequently throw the ball away after making a great play. He needs to pause and think before making a needless throw.

OVERALL:

In three seasons, Alomar has still only given a hint of how good he might become. He possesses a good attitude -- the combination of will, talent and drive that makes a star athlete. He takes criticism well and is very manageable. So far, his only drawback is that he seems to lose some concentration when he becomes fatigued during the middle of the long season.

ANDY BENES

Position: SP
Bats: R **Throws:** R
Ht: 6' 6" **Wt:** 235

Opening Day Age: 23
Born: 8/20/67 in Evansville, IN
ML Seasons: 2

PITCHING:

The first player chosen in the 1988 amateur draft, Andy Benes was rushed to the major leagues late in his first professional season (1989) after working in only 21 minor league games. Benes was an almost immediate hit, going 6-3 during the last two months of '89. Last year, however, he looked like an inexperienced young pitcher as he turned in a 10-11 record.

Benes arrived in San Diego on Aug. 10, 1989 with a flat fastball and without a breaking pitch worth a darn. In addition, Benes' first two pro seasons were complicated by brief bouts with tendinitis in his right shoulder and elbow. When Benes joined the big club, former pitching coach Pat Dobson liked the righthander's arm, but not much else. Dobson went right to work, junking Benes' curveball and teaching him two new pitches, a slider and change up.

But the major leagues are rarely a good venue for that kind of training. In 1990, the result was a season of inconsistency. Benes, accustomed to striking out a batter per inning, found that he couldn't overpower major league hitters as easily.

One wonders, if at 6-6, 235 pounds, Benes is being miscast as a starter. Perhaps he is simply the prototypical stud reliever. Give him the ball to close the sure out for one inning and let him throw as hard as he can. Has anyone heard of Rob Dibble?

HOLDING RUNNERS, FIELDING, HITTING:

Equipped with a slide-step toward first base, Benes is still average at keeping the runner close. He is capable enough at fielding his position and has only committed one error as a Padre. He's also a pretty good hitter. Benes homered during his first month as a major leaguer, and has demonstrating decent bunting ability.

OVERALL:

At 23, Benes has shown two things: a great arm, and great inconsistency. His inexperience hasn't helped him, and he'll have to start over again this year with a new pitching coach. But Benes was also very inconsistent as a collegian at the University of Evansville. He struggled as a junior, turning in a 5.10 ERA, then pitched so well as a senior that he became the top pick in the draft. The Padres may have to ride out some rough moments before Benes settles down and becomes a top pitcher. Certainly, he has the potential.

Overall Statistics

	W	L	ERA	G	GS	Sv	IP	H	R	BB	SO	HR
1990	10	11	3.60	32	31	0	192.1	177	87	69	140	18
Career	16	14	3.58	42	41	0	259.0	228	115	100	206	25

How Often He Throws Strikes

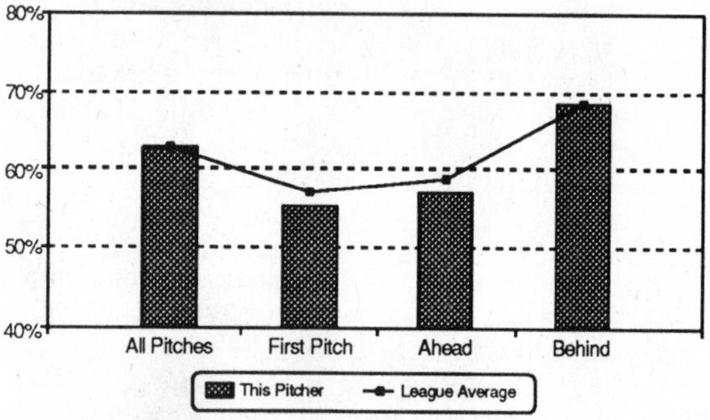

1990 Situational Stats

	W	L	ERA	Sv	IP		AB	H	HR	RBI	AVG
Home	6	4	3.93	0	89.1	LHB	431	108	9	41	.251
Road	4	7	3.32	0	103.0	RHB	299	69	9	30	.231
Day	0	3	2.89	0	46.2	Sc Pos	173	36	2	51	.208
Night	10	8	3.83	0	145.2	Clutch	50	16	3	8	.320

1990 Rankings (National League)

- → 1st in balks (5)
- → 4th lowest batting average allowed with runners in scoring position (.208)
- → 6th highest stolen percentage allowed (82.1%)
- → 8th highest ERA at home (3.93)
- → Led the Padres in walks allowed (69), balks, stolen bases allowed (23), most strikeouts per 9 innings (6.6) and lowest batting average allowed with runners in scoring position

JOE CARTER

Position: CF/1B/LF
Bats: R **Throws:** R
Ht: 6' 3" **Wt:** 215

Opening Day Age: 31
Born: 3/7/60 in Oklahoma City, OK
ML Seasons: 8

HITTING:

Joe Carter was the prize catch of the winter meetings when then San Diego general manager Jack McKeon wrestled him away from Cleveland for catcher Sandy Alomar, Jr., outfielder Chris James and third baseman Carlos Baerga. One wondered if the price was too high then. One still wonders if the price was too steep today.

On the surface, Carter had a good season. His 115 RBI led the club and was second-best in franchise history behind the 118 Dave Winfield racked up in 1979. His 24 homers were second best behind Jack Clark's 25, giving the Padres a pair of players with more than 20 homers for the first time since 1986. But looking below the surface, how much better a year could Carter have had?

For long stretches, Carter went into batting funks when he lunged at pitches outside of the strike zone. An aggressive, first-ball hitter, he often didn't have the patience to take a look at a few extra pitches. And he insists on pulling everything, whether on the inside or outside part of the plate. The result of all this was a career-low .232 batting average, making his RBI total of 115 even more remarkable as it came on the strength of just 147 hits.

BASERUNNING:

Carter is one of those athletes who literally takes your breath away when he romps from first to third on a single. A 30-30 player in 1987, last season Carter was a solid base stealer, adding 22 steals to his home run total of 24. Though he fell short of the 30 steals that he's capable of, you can't knock his 79% success percentage.

FIELDING:

A half season is enough of a look to recognize the fact that Carter doesn't cut it in center field. He doesn't break well on the ball, either moving back or forward. Perhaps an unconscious problem, Carter seems to slow down as he runs toward the warning track and extends his glove toward the fence chasing the ball down. Carter seems more suited to left; he has fewer problems there, and his weaknesses (lack of range, inability to hit the cutoff man) are better masked.

OVERALL:

Carter's success seems hindered only by self-imposed limitations. Some people, though, wonder if he has the heart. The jury is still out. In Carter's case, his own desire may mean the difference between having a Hall of Fame career or a nice career.

Overall Statistics

	G	AB	R	H	D	T	HR	RBI	SB	BB	SO	AVG
1990	162	634	79	147	27	1	24	115	22	48	93	.232
Career	1024	3941	541	1032	192	24	175	646	149	217	630	.262

Where He Hits the Ball

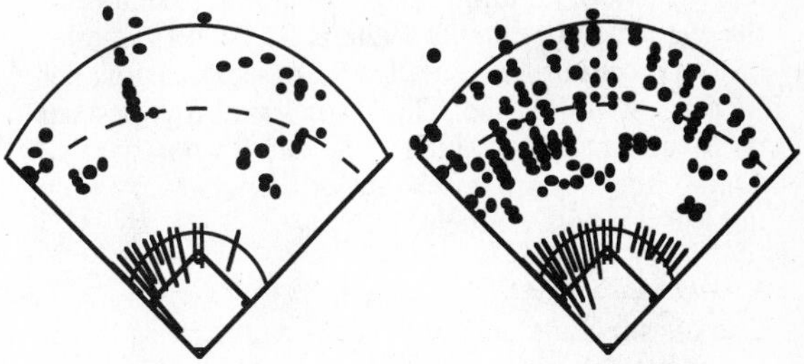

Vs. LHP Vs. RHP

1990 Situational Stats

	AB	H	HR	RBI	AVG		AB	H	HR	RBI	AVG
Home	322	71	12	53	.220	LHP	203	40	7	32	.197
Road	312	76	12	62	.244	RHP	431	107	17	83	.248
Day	188	39	7	32	.207	Sc Pos	192	51	7	87	.266
Night	446	108	17	83	.242	Clutch	123	27	4	22	.220

1990 Rankings (National League)

- 1st in at-bats (634), games (162) and lowest batting average at home (.221)
- 2nd in lowest batting average (.232), hit by pitch (7), plate appearances (697) and lowest batting average vs. left-handed pitchers (.197)
- 3rd in RBIs (115)
- Led the Padres in at-bats, total bases (248), RBIs, sacrifice files (8), hit by pitch, strikeouts (93), plate appearances, games and highest percentage of extra bases taken as a runner (58.1%)
- Led NL center fielders in at-bats, RBIs, intentional walks (18), hit by pitch, GDPs (12), games and fielding percentage (.990)

HITTING:

Still one of baseball's great power hitters, Jack Clark managed to belt 25 home runs last year despite playing in only 115 games. Along the way he feuded with teammates, missed considerable time with injuries, and went through long slumps and hot streaks. With Jack Clark, life is never dull.

Still a great fastball hitter, Clark looks for a hard one to pull during every at-bat. Pitchers throw him a lot of junk, but Clark has enormous discipline and will make the hurler throw strikes. He's led the National League in walks during each of the last three seasons that he's been in the league. Of course, Clark also takes a lot of called strikes and swings through a lot of fastballs. As a result, he strikes out as many or more times than he walks.

Because of a bevy of injuries, plus an end of the year suspension for arguing with an umpire, Clark came to the plate just 440 times in 1990. He walked 104 times, or 24 percent of the time. On 91 other occasions, or 21 percent of the time, Clark struck out. In 6 percent of his appearances, he hit a home run. It's not true that Clark either walks, strikes out or homers every time up. But it's close enough.

BASERUNNING:

Clark is slow, and not always alert on the bases. How many guys blow a sacrifice fly by leaving third base early, not once, but three times in the same year? Clark is a very aggressive baserunner, but not a threat to steal.

FIELDING:

An outfielder for most of his career, Clark still hasn't mastered first base. Despite a great right fielder's arm, he often makes throwing mistakes. He has decent range, but knocked himself out for a month in early May when he wrenched his back lunging to stab a grounder.

OVERALL:

Still a great slugger, Clark has always prided himself on his leadership ability. But that ability became a negative last season. His season-long hassle with Tony Gwynn, which became public after a May 24 players-only clubhouse meeting during which Clark chastised Gwynn for his approach to the game, caused a wide schism among the players. It did nothing at all to make the Padres a contending team. The real question is: are the home runs Clark still generates on occasion worth all the extraneous baggage?

JACK CLARK

Position: 1B
Bats: R **Throws:** R
Ht: 6' 3" **Wt:** 205

Opening Day Age: 35
Born: 11/10/55 in New Brighton, PA
ML Seasons: 16

Overall Statistics

	G	AB	R	H	D	T	HR	RBI	SB	BB	SO	AVG
1990	115	334	59	89	12	1	25	62	4	104	91	.266
Career	1773	6109	1011	1652	303	38	307	1060	76	1110	1221	.270

Where He Hits the Ball

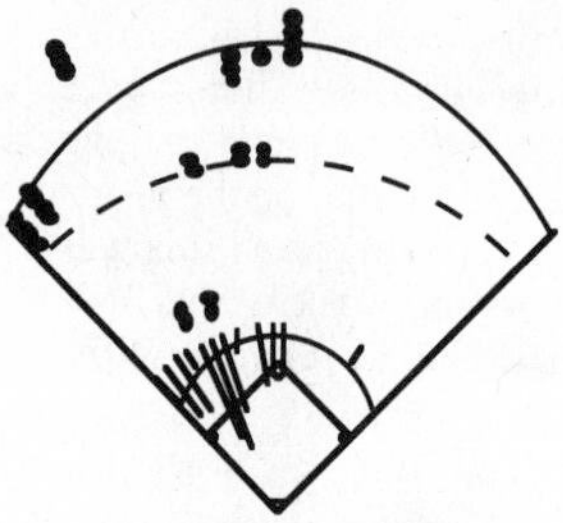

Vs. LHP

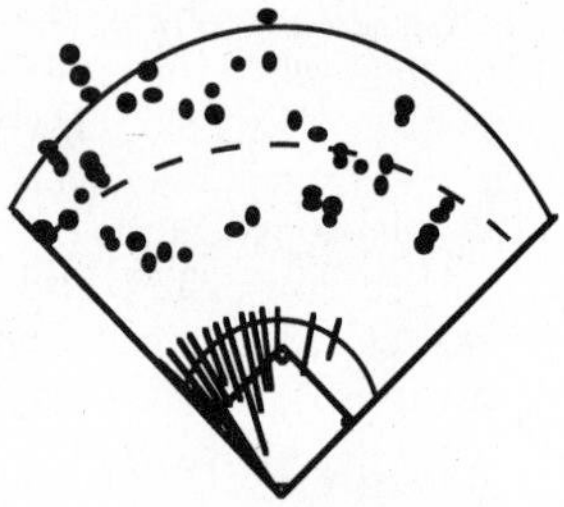

Vs. RHP

1990 Situational Stats

	AB	H	HR	RBI	AVG		AB	H	HR	RBI	AVG
Home	176	45	16	39	.256	LHP	114	43	9	21	.377
Road	158	44	9	23	.278	RHP	220	46	16	41	.209
Day	88	21	8	16	.239	Sc Pos	90	25	6	39	.278
Night	246	68	17	46	.276	Clutch	60	12	4	6	.200

1990 Rankings (National League)

- 1st in walks (104), slugging percentage vs. left-handed pitchers (.667) and on-base average vs. left-handed pitchers (.541)
- 2nd in batting average vs. left-handed pitchers (.377)
- 3rd lowest percentage of swings put into play (34.9%)
- Led the Padres in home runs (25), walks, batting average/slugging percentage/on-base average vs. left-handed pitchers, batting average on a 3-1 count (.429) and highest percentage of pitches taken (61.2%)
- Led NL first basemen in walks and batting average/slugging percentage/on-base average vs. left-handed pitchers

HITTING:

Tony Gwynn's streak of three consecutive National League batting titles came to an end last season as he "slumped" to .309. Gwynn still had a fine season, but not by his past standards. Last year, he spent too much time not hitting like Tony Gwynn.

A left-handed hitter, Gwynn has made a living driving outside pitches to the opposite field. He's a meticulous worker, one who videotapes opposing pitchers, and he's always preached hitting the ball where it's pitched. But last season, he was so far out in front of the ball that he hit many harmless grounders to the right side. That may have been the reason Gwynn hit 20 points below his career average.

Batting third last year, Gwynn felt under pressure to produce more runs. He did accumulate 72 RBI, a career high. But he had a tendency to be overanxious at the plate; he walked only 44 times, his lowest total since becoming a regular in 1984. Gwynn much prefers batting second, and it's easy to see why: freed of the responsibility to be an RBI man, he can revert to his natural, all-fields, style.

BASERUNNING:

At age 30 and playing 10 pounds overweight, Gwynn slumped from 40 steals to just 17 in 25 attempts last year; he was, however, more conservative with Jack Clark and Joe Carter coming up behind him. Once an over-eager baserunner who ran himself into a lot of outs, Gwynn has markedly improved his judgement in recent years.

FIELDING:

A three-time Gold Glove winner, Gwynn was happy last year that he didn't have to play center field. Instead he spent the season in his preferred spot, right. The extra weight appeared to affect his range at times, and he did not always seem able to reach balls he once gobbled up. But Gwynn still deserves to be rated among the league's best in right field. He has the ability to check base runners with a good arm.

OVERALL:

Gwynn's work habits, once second to none, deteriorated a bit last season after he became involved in contract hassles with management and became the focal point of season-long clubhouse rancor. For the first time, his approach to the game was questioned by teammates, notably Jack Clark and Mike Pagliarulo. Gwynn was called a "selfish" player who was more interested in winning batting titles than games. Though he tried, Gwynn was not able to rise above the fray. He'll try to answer his critics in 1991.

TONY GWYNN

Position: RF
Bats: L **Throws:** L
Ht: 5'11" **Wt:** 199

Opening Day Age: 30
Born: 5/9/60 in Los Angeles, CA
ML Seasons: 9

Overall Statistics

	G	AB	R	H	D	T	HR	RBI	SB	BB	SO	AVG
1990	141	573	79	177	29	10	4	72	17	44	23	.309
Career	1201	4651	696	1531	221	61	49	488	238	426	256	.329

Where He Hits the Ball

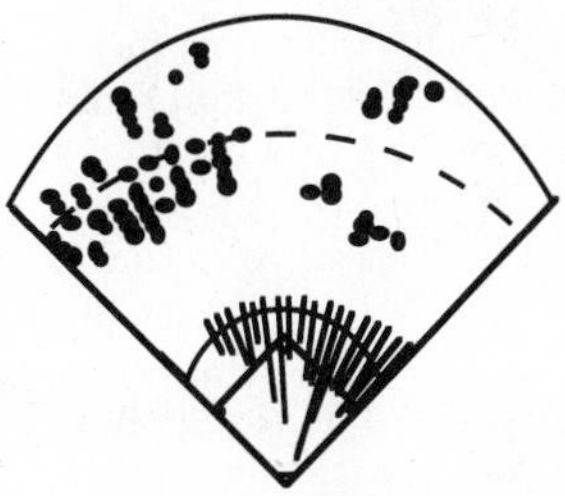

Vs. LHP

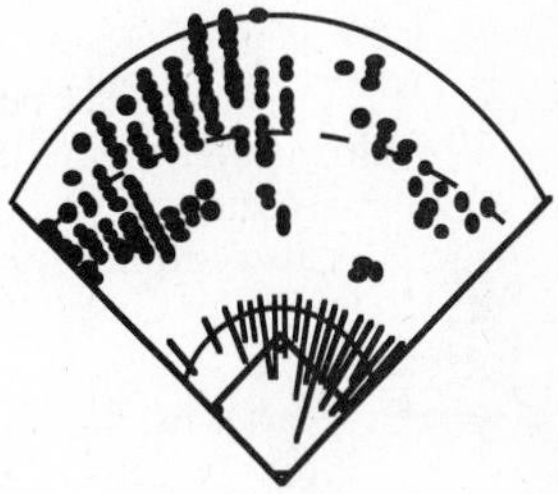

Vs. RHP

1990 Situational Stats

	AB	H	HR	RBI	AVG		AB	H	HR	RBI	AVG
Home	306	95	2	42	.310	LHP	228	64	3	28	.281
Road	267	82	2	30	.307	RHP	345	113	1	44	.328
Day	169	44	1	16	.260	Sc Pos	151	46	0	59	.305
Night	404	133	3	56	.329	Clutch	106	30	1	7	.283

1990 Rankings (National League)

- 1st in batting average on an 0-2 count (.435) and highest percentage of swings put into play (61.5%)
- 2nd in triples (10), batting average with 2 strikes (.282) and lowest percentage of swings that missed (6.5%)
- 3rd in intentional walks (20) and batting average with the bases loaded (.556)
- Led the Padres in hits (177), singles (134), triples, intentional walks, groundball/flyball ratio (2.1) and batting average with 2 strikes
- Led NL right fielders in hits, singles, triples, sacrifice bunts (7), groundball/flyball ratio and batting average with runners in scoring position (.305)

PITCHING:

Last August, Atlee Hammaker's nearly nine-year association with the San Francisco Giants came to an end. Despite a costly long-term contract, manager Roger Craig and general manager Al Rosen decided they and Hammaker had reached the end of the line. It wasn't so much Hammaker's 4-5 record or 4.28 ERA. It was a difference in philosophy.

Hammaker, once a quality left-handed starter before arm, shoulder and knee injuries took their toll, resisted Craig's insistence that he move to the bullpen. Thus the Giants and the player with the club's longest term of service parted ways. Two weeks later, on Aug. 24, purveying the offers that came in from the Cincinnati Reds and New York Mets (both pennant contenders) and the Padres (mired in fourth place), Hammaker decided to move his act of split-finger fastballs and breaking pitches on to San Diego.

For the long term, Hammaker views the career move as a chance to possibly become a starter again. From the Padres' point a view, the move was not much of a gamble. Because of Hammaker's San Francisco contract, the acquisition hardly cost the Padres anything at all. Despite one San Diego start in which he ran out of gas in the sixth inning and three losses in eight relief appearances, the Padres moved immediately at the end of the season to pick up the option on Hammaker's contract. If he makes the club this spring in any capacity, Hammaker will cost the Padres just $100,000 of his incentive-laden $1 million pact. But at 33, the question is how much Hammaker actually has left.

HOLDING RUNNERS, FIELDING, HITTING:

After a career-high .368 season in 1989, Hammaker went back to basics in 1990 when he batted .105, a mere 14 points below his career batting average. He has a mediocre move to first base that does not scare opposing base runners. He's also a mediocre fielder, but he did not commit an error in the 34 games he appeared in last season.

OVERALL:

Oft-injured, Hammaker is very fragile. Even his chaotic 1990 season ended a week early when he had to leave a game, ironically back at Candlestick Park, with a sore muscle in the rear of his left shoulder. For the coming season, the Padres are looking to fill one, perhaps two spots in their starting rotation. It may make the spring of 1991 Atlee Hammaker's very last stand.

ATLEE HAMMAKER

Position: RP/SP
Bats: B **Throws:** L
Ht: 6' 2" **Wt:** 200

Opening Day Age: 33
Born: 1/24/58 in Carmel, CA
ML Seasons: 9

Overall Statistics

	W	L	ERA	G	GS	Sv	IP	H	R	BB	SO	HR
1990	4	9	4.36	34	7	0	86.2	85	44	27	44	8
Career	59	66	3.60	233	151	5	1066.1	1031	477	276	610	92

How Often He Throws Strikes

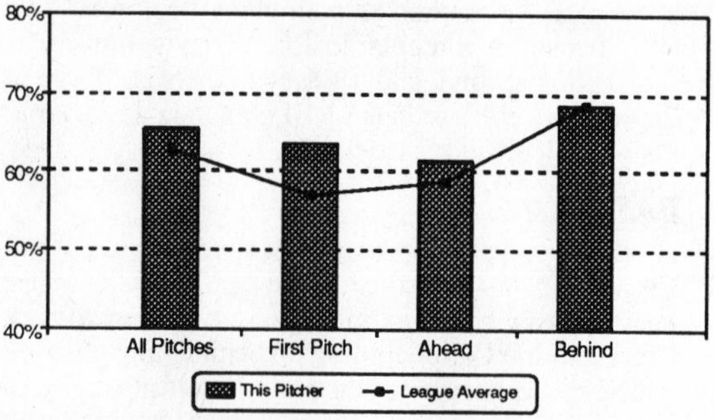

1990 Situational Stats

	W	L	ERA	Sv	IP		AB	H	HR	RBI	AVG
Home	3	5	4.81	0	48.2	LHB	67	13	2	5	.194
Road	1	4	3.79	0	38.0	RHB	261	72	6	31	.276
Day	1	3	3.62	0	32.1	Sc Pos	55	22	2	28	.400
Night	3	6	4.80	0	54.1	Clutch	74	20	3	10	.270

1990 Rankings (National League)

- Did not rank near the top or bottom in any category

PITCHING:

In his second full major league season, Greg Harris became the Padres' top right-handed closer -- a role he had filled on a part-time basis in 1989. But Harris shouldn't become too comfortable with relief work. For the coming season, new general manager Joe McIlvaine has already stated that he and manager Greg Riddoch are interested in placing Harris in the starting rotation for good.

Coming through the Padres' system, Harris had been an effective starter. But since reaching the big leagues in September of 1988, he has made only nine starts, eight of them coming in 1989 when a back injury to Eric Show compelled then-manager Jack McKeon to place Harris in the rotation. In 1990, the departure of relief ace Mark Davis kept Harris in the pen. He teamed with left hander Craig Lefferts as the club's one-two closing combination. Harris responded with eight wins and nine saves in a club-high 73 appearances. In two seasons as a reliever, both as a closer and set-up man, Harris has won 13 games and saved another 15.

Like most young power pitchers, Harris was able to blow away hitters with just his fastball for a long time in the minors. That's not as easy at the major league level, and former Padres' pitching coach Pat Dobson spent a lot of time on Harris' other pitches. Harris has always had an excellent curveball, and he now uses it just as much -- and often more effectively -- as his fastball.

By the middle of last season, Harris must have been doing something right. From June 9 through June 28, Harris made 10 appearances without giving up a run. Overall, his 2.30 ERA was the best of any pitcher on the club.

HOLDING RUNNERS, FIELDING, HITTING:

Though primarily a power pitcher, Harris does a fair job of holding runners. He has a good move to first base. He also fields his position pretty well. Harris batted just 12 times last season and picked up only one hit, a triple.

OVERALL:

After two full seasons, Harris has shown himself to be an excellent major league pitcher. The Padres consider him one of their few untouchables, feeling that he and Andy Benes are their most promising young pitchers. Now Harris is looking forward to starting, which has always been his preference. He has the stuff to be a big winner.

GREG W. HARRIS

Position: RP
Bats: R **Throws:** R
Ht: 6' 2" **Wt:** 190

Opening Day Age: 27
Born: 12/1/63 in Greensboro, NC
ML Seasons: 3

Overall Statistics

	W	L	ERA	G	GS	Sv	IP	H	R	BB	SO	HR
1990	8	8	2.30	73	0	9	117.1	92	35	49	97	6
Career	18	17	2.40	132	9	15	270.1	211	81	104	218	14

How Often He Throws Strikes

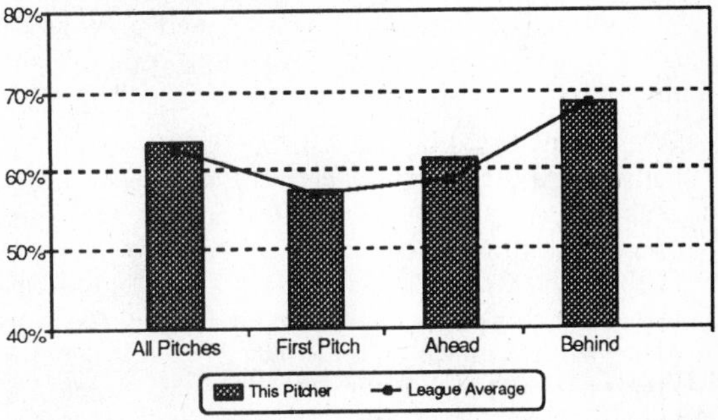

1990 Situational Stats

	W	L	ERA	Sv	IP		AB	H	HR	RBI	AVG
Home	4	4	2.10	3	55.2	LHB	223	62	2	26	.278
Road	4	4	2.48	6	61.2	RHB	196	30	4	21	.153
Day	4	4	5.20	3	36.1	Sc Pos	114	22	0	37	.193
Night	4	4	1.00	6	81.0	Clutch	259	56	2	30	.216

1990 Rankings (National League)

- 2nd highest percentage of inherited runners scored (50.0%)
- 3rd in games pitches (73) and blown saves (7)
- 6th in holds (10)
- Led the Paders in games pitched, hit batsmen (4), holds and blown saves

PITCHING:

For the Padres, the free agent derby that netted Bruce Hurst in December, 1988 for three years at $5.25 million, may have been a bit extravagant. Hurst, 15-11 with a 2.65 ERA and 179 strikeouts in 1989, slumped to 11-9 with a 3.14 ERA and 162 whiffs last season. Those are good figures, especially considering the way his teammates have performed, but the Padres have been somewhat disappointed in Hurst. They thought they were acquiring a big game pitcher.

Perhaps their expectations were unrealistic, and maybe the disappointment with Hurst stems from his poor showing in the first half of 1990. However, in the second half, Hurst pitched masterfully. He's primarily a breaking ball pitcher with only a modest fastball. Hurst mixes his pitches very intelligently, utilizing his forkball, slider and slow curve while spotting the fastball, and he has outstanding control. At his best, he can zero in on hitters' weaknesses, and he gets a lot of strikeouts for a pitcher who's not an especially hard thrower.

When Hurst has struggled with the Padres -- and he's had some stretches of ineffectiveness -- it's been because he could not consistently put his breaking pitches over for strikes. Hitters were able to sit on his fastball, and the result was that he allowed 21 homers last year, many of them game losers. Perhaps the tone of the '90 season was set for Hurst on opening day. He took a no-hitter into the 7th, then gave up a three-run homer to Hubie Brooks in the 8th to lose the game.

In 1989, Hurst also suffered from tendinitis in the left shoulder. But he had no arm problems last season. Pitching coach Pat Dobson, who is now with Kansas City, made several mechanical adjustments in Hurst's delivery, relieving the pressure that evidently had caused the shoulder problems.

HOLDING RUNNERS, FIELDING, HITTING:

Hurst is no terror at the plate. Coming up in the American League, he never had to hit during the regular season until 1989. He proved to be abominable. Last season, he went 6-for-67 (all singles) and drove in the first run of his career. Hurst is competent at fielding his position; his move to first base is outstanding. Hurst picked off 10 runners in 1989, tops on the club. Runners stuck closer to first last year, but he still nailed three.

OVERALL:

Hurst may not be a Roger Clemens, but he's still a very good pitcher. As the Padres struggle to get back into contention, his experience will be very important. Unlike most of his teammates, he's been to the mount before, pitching in two playoffs and winning a pair of World Series games for Boston in 1986.

BRUCE HURST

Position: SP
Bats: L **Throws:** L
Ht: 6' 3" **Wt:** 215

Opening Day Age: 33
Born: 3/24/58 in St. George, UT
ML Seasons: 11

Overall Statistics

	W	L	ERA	G	GS	Sv	IP	H	R	BB	SO	HR
1990	11	9	3.14	33	33	0	223.2	188	85	63	162	21
Career	114	93	3.91	303	283	0	1927.2	1971	916	608	1384	210

How Often He Throws Strikes

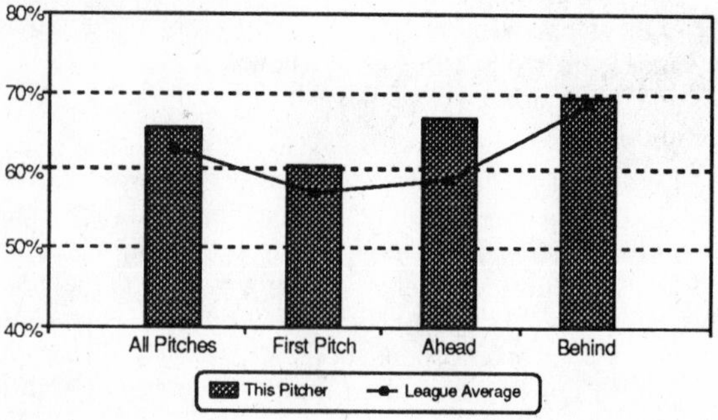

1990 Situational Stats

	W	L	ERA	Sv	IP		AB	H	HR	RBI	AVG
Home	7	3	2.66	0	122.0	LHB	165	38	7	23	.230
Road	4	6	3.72	0	101.2	RHB	658	150	14	49	.228
Day	1	4	4.27	0	65.1	Sc Pos	174	39	5	51	.224
Night	10	5	2.67	0	158.1	Clutch	95	29	4	17	.305

1990 Rankings (National League)

- ➡ 1st in shutouts (4)
- ➡ 2nd in complete games (9)
- ➡ 5th in home runs allowed (21), GDPs induced (21), most GDPs induced per 9 innings (.85), lowest batting average allowed vs. right- handed batters (.228)
- ➡ Led the Paders in games started (33), complete games, shutouts, strikeouts (162), pitches thrown (3,109), pickoff throws (177), GDPs induced, lowest batting average allowed (.228), lowest on-base percentage allowed (.284), groundball/flyball ratio (1.53) and most GDPs induced per 9 innings

CRAIG LEFFERTS

Position: RP
Bats: L **Throws:** L
Ht: 6' 1" **Wt:** 210

Opening Day Age: 33
Born: 9/29/57 in Munich, West Germany
ML Seasons: 8

Overall Statistics

	W	L	ERA	G	GS	Sv	IP	H	R	BB	SO	HR
1990	7	5	2.52	56	0	23	78.2	68	26	22	60	10
Career	39	44	2.95	528	5	77	762.1	668	283	227	482	72

How Often He Throws Strikes

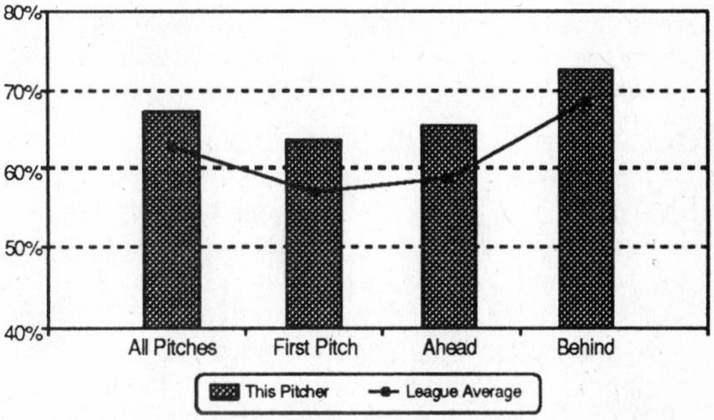

1990 Situational Stats

	W	L	ERA	Sv	IP		AB	H	HR	RBI	AVG
Home	4	2	2.39	11	37.2	LHB	87	18	1	5	.207
Road	3	3	2.63	12	41.0	RHB	211	50	9	28	.237
Day	4	3	3.64	6	29.2	Sc Pos	88	21	3	25	.239
Night	3	2	1.84	17	49.0	Clutch	235	53	8	31	.226

1990 Rankings (National League)

- 3rd in worst save percentage (76.7%) and blown saves (7)
- 4th in saves (23), save opportunities (30) and lowest percentage of inherited runners scored (22.2%)
- 6th in games finished (44)
- 8th in first batter efficiency (.196)
- Led the Padres in saves, games finished, save opportunities, blown saves, first batter efficiency and lowest percentage of inherited runners scored

PITCHING:

For the Padres, the big question going into the 1990 season was whether Craig Lefferts could make everyone forget the sad fact that they no longer had Mark Davis in the bullpen. Davis was all-everything in 1989: National League Cy Young Award winner and saver of 44 games in 48 opportunities, Davis had a hand in 54 percent of the Padres victories.

When Davis' free-agent negotiations broke down in San Diego, the Padres turned to Lefferts who had already played for the club from 1984 until he was traded to San Francisco on July 4, 1987. Armed with a promise that he would be given the job as the Padres' closer, Lefferts signed a three-year, $5.2 million contract.

For most of the year, Lefferts responded. He was not 1989-vintage Mark Davis, but Lefferts was certainly capable. He saved a career high 23 games. His 2.52 ERA was his lowest since 1984. He inherited 45 base runners and allowed just 10 to score, the fourth best such ratio in the league. Using his famous screwball as an out pitch, Lefferts usually did what he needed to do: throw strikes and keep the ball down in the strike zone.

Only once did Lefferts hit a dead-arm period. That came after former manager Jack McKeon used him five times in six games, and it seemed to confirm the notion that Lefferts has an arm that needs rest. He did have elbow problems in 1987 and shoulder problems in 1989. But he's worked as many as 83 games in a season, and he's averaged 66 appearances a year in his eight-season career.

HOLDING RUNNERS, FIELDING, HITTING:

As a late-inning reliever, Lefferts receives a rare at-bat. Last season he had four, with one hit. He had one hit. But he'll never forget the pinch hit appearance he took at San Diego on April 25, 1986 against former Giants' reliever Greg Minton: Lefferts' 12th-inning homer won the game. As a lefthander, he has a good move to first base. A capable fielder, he was flawless last season.

OVERALL:

Lefferts may find himself sharing the closer's role this season. New general manager Joe McIlvaine has already stated his feeling that Lefferts is going to need some help. It's an old story for Lefferts. He's one of those guys who is neither here nor there. Though he is capable enough of doing a competent job, management always seems to be looking for someone else.

PITCHING:

In 1989, Derek Lilliquist was a key member of Atlanta's young pitching corps. Along with John Smoltz, Tom Glavine and Marty Clary, Lilliquist was supposed to give the Braves the nucleus of great starting pitching for years to come. But Atlanta's first-round pick (sixth overall) in the June 1987 draft turned out to be a bust. He went from an 8-10 record and 3.97 ERA in 1989 to the minors early in 1990. By the All-Star break, he was out of the organization. On July 12, Lilliquist, a 25 year old lefthander who once harbored so much promise, was dealt for Mark Grant, a righthander of little note.

For the Padres it was just a matter of trading bodies -- the proverbial swap of their own problems for the problems of someone else. Would a new environment help Lilliquist keep the ball in the strike zone better? Would a new pitching coach (Pat Dobson) teach Lilliquist not to telegraph his pitches? With one-half a Padres season behind him (16 appearances and seven starts), the jury is still out.

Because of the failures of Eric Show and Calvin Schiraldi as starters, Lilliquist was eventually given the fifth spot in the rotation. Though his overall numbers were 5-11 with a 5.31 ERA, he made significant improvement with the Padres, where he was 3-3 (3-2 as a starter). He depends on good control to be effective, and he was finally able to get good location on both his fastball and his curve. Perhaps 1991 will be the year he finally arrives.

HOLDING RUNNERS, FIELDING, HITTING:

Managers love having Lilliquist's bat in the lineup. An accomplished hitter at the University of Georgia where he batted .301 with 19 homers and 60 RBIs during his junior year, Lilliquist batted .256 (11-for-43) last season with a pair of homers (both in the same game) and three RBIs. Though he has little mobility on the mound, he fields his position well and makes few mistakes. He is adept at holding a baserunner close to first.

OVERALL:

With so much of San Diego's pitching staff under siege, Lilliquist has a real opportunity to pitch himself into the rotation this spring. With the loss of Show and possibly Dennis Rasmussen to free agency, the Padres may be left with just three starters -- Bruce Hurst, Andy Benes and Ed Whitson. Now, Lilliquist has the opportunity to win a starting spot again. He has the second chance he didn't receive from the Braves.

DEREK LILLIQUIST

Position: SP/RP
Bats: L **Throws:** L
Ht: 6' 0" **Wt:** 200

Opening Day Age: 25
Born: 2/20/66 in Winter Park, FL
ML Seasons: 2

Overall Statistics

	W	L	ERA	G	GS	Sv	IP	H	R	BB	SO	HR
1990	5	11	5.31	28	18	0	122.0	136	74	42	63	16
Career	13	21	4.54	60	48	0	287.2	338	161	76	142	32

How Often He Throws Strikes

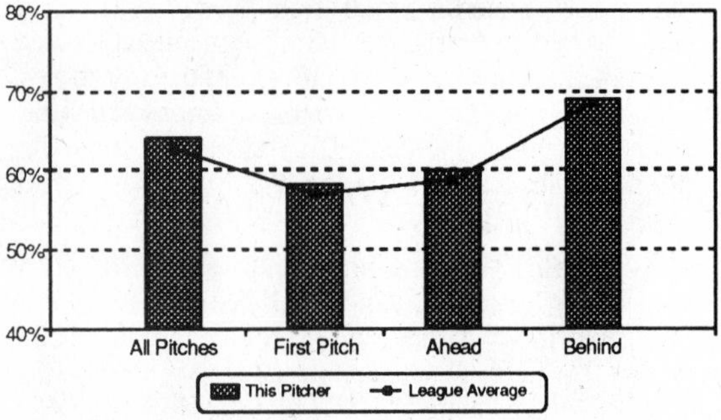

1990 Situational Stats

	W	L	ERA	Sv	IP		AB	H	HR	RBI	AVG
Home	2	6	4.71	0	57.1	LHB	92	30	3	8	.326
Road	3	5	5.85	0	64.2	RHB	386	106	13	51	.275
Day	1	3	4.59	0	33.1	Sc Pos	113	30	5	42	.265
Night	4	8	5.58	0	88.2	Clutch	34	8	0	1	.235

1990 Rankings (National League)

→ 3rd lowest winning percentage (.313)

HITTING:

The 1989 season he played in Detroit marked the beginning of the end for Fred Lynn, who is now 39 and clearly at the end of his career. The former American League All-Star batted just .241 for the Tigers, but more significantly, his power numbers disappeared. He belted only 11 homers, a career low for a non-injury season.

Lynn hoped the downturn in the Tigers' fortunes might be related to the slip in his own fortunes. So he signed with the Padres, a team that figured to be a contender. Lynn, who keeps himself in marvelous shape, came into the abbreviated spring training hoping to win a starting spot. He hit like gangbusters, batting .480 with a pair of homers in the cactus league. Come opening day, Lynn was in the starting lineup at Dodger Stadium and homered. But that was the high point.

After falling into a slump, Lynn was relegated to a role as a left-handed pinch hitter. His bat speed wasn't really there any more, as the numbers attest -- another .240 season with six homers and 23 RBI to show for 196 at-bats. Lynn, who can't wrestle a good fastball or even a modest breaking ball any longer, was not the answer. In the end, one wondered why he was even part of the question.

BASERUNNING:

Lynn is a slow-footed runner who tries to make up for his lack of speed with good intentions and a cunning grasp of fundamentals. But all the smarts in the world are not going to keep a guy like Lynn from clogging up the base paths.

FIELDING:

Once a premier center fielder, Lynn is now no longer even an adequate left fielder. He still has a good arm, but even had problems with that last season, stemming from tendinitis in his left shoulder. His range is very limited at this point in his career.

OVERALL:

Last year, Lynn did have the maturity and ability to step off the bench and act as a decent pinch hitter. But his club-leading .344 average (11-for-32) with a homer and six RBI in that department wasn't enough to keep him around. At season's end, the Padres declined to offer Lynn salary arbitration off a base contract worth $500,000. For the second straight winter, Lynn became a free agent. His pinch hitting ability may land him one more contract.

FRED LYNN

Position: LF
Bats: L **Throws:** L
Ht: 6' 1" **Wt:** 190

Opening Day Age: 39
Born: 2/3/52 in Chicago, IL
ML Seasons: 17

Overall Statistics

	G	AB	R	H	D	T	HR	RBI	SB	BB	SO	AVG
1990	90	196	18	47	3	1	6	23	2	22	44	.240
Career	1969	6925	1063	1960	388	43	306	1111	72	857	1116	.283

Where He Hits the Ball

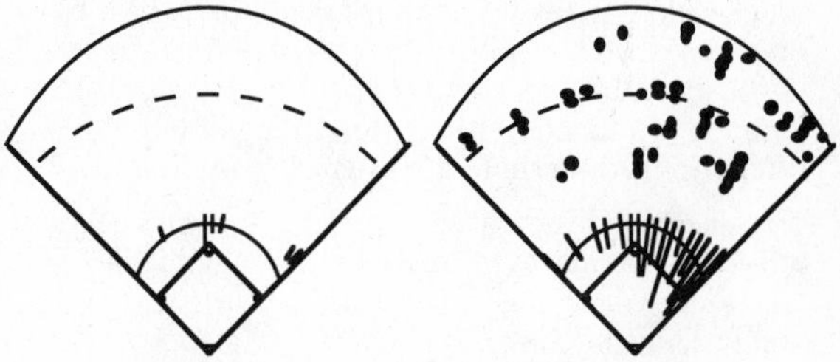

Vs. LHP Vs. RHP

1990 Situational Stats

	AB	H	HR	RBI	AVG		AB	H	HR	RBI	AVG
Home	112	27	2	15	.241	LHP	20	5	0	1	.250
Road	84	20	4	8	.238	RHP	176	42	6	22	.239
Day	56	15	3	5	.268	Sc Pos	44	10	0	16	.227
Night	140	32	3	18	.229	Clutch	44	13	1	5	.295

1990 Rankings (National League)

- Did not rank near the top or bottom in any category

HITTING:

Whatever happened to Mike Pagliarulo? Looking at him now, one would never guess that this is the same left-handed hitting slugger who belted 28 homers for the Yankees in 1986, and 32 a year later. Pagliarulo did hit a career high .254 last year, but with only seven homers. In three seasons since his 32-homer year, he's managed only 29 more. The Padres hoped that Pagliarulo's problems were mainly psychological, and that getting him out of New York might revive his power stroke. They were wrong.

Going into last season, then-manager Jack McKeon promised Pagliarulo the starting job at third base. The idea didn't last long. After Pagliarulo had a disastrous spring training at the plate, McKeon installed Bip Roberts as the everyday third baseman in the early going. In May, with Jack Clark injured, Joe Carter filling in at first base and Roberts shifted to left field, Pagliarulo was finally given his opportunity. But by-midseason, after nearly a month in which Pags did not drive in a run, new manager Greg Riddoch had seen enough. Riddoch resorted to giving journeyman Eddie Williams a short, but ill-fated trial.

For the second straight season, Pagliarulo claimed to be uncomfortable at the plate. For a long time, pitchers stopped throwing him fastballs, and he got nothing but breaking pitches. But last year they stopped being afraid of challenging him with hard stuff. Pagliarulo didn't respond to the challenge.

BASERUNNING:

Pagliarulo was never a base stealer with the Yankees, and he hasn't been one with the Padres, either, swiping only one in four attempts in 1990. However, he does run the bases aggressively. He's not averse to getting his uniform dirty on a rolling block at second base to break up a double play.

FIELDING:

Once considered a fine glove man, Pagliarulo now has two-step range. One to his left, the other to his right. He is, however, strong at coming in on the ball and making the bare-handed play, particularly on the bunt. His arm, once strong, has been weakened by elbow problems.

OVERALL:

At 31, Pagliarulo may be beyond redemption. That's too bad, because he's one of those selfless, gutty players who are an important cog on any championship team. Unfortunately for Pagliarulo, he became embroiled in the middle of Jack Clark's feud with Tony Gwynn. But his numbers did not warrant the influence he wielded in the clubhouse.

MIKE PAGLIARULO

Position: 3B
Bats: L **Throws:** R
Ht: 6' 2" **Wt:** 195

Opening Day Age: 31
Born: 3/15/60 in Medford, MA
ML Seasons: 7

Overall Statistics

	G	AB	R	H	D	T	HR	RBI	SB	BB	SO	AVG
1990	128	398	29	101	23	2	7	38	1	39	66	.254
Career	881	2820	332	651	141	14	115	389	10	280	615	.231

Where He Hits the Ball

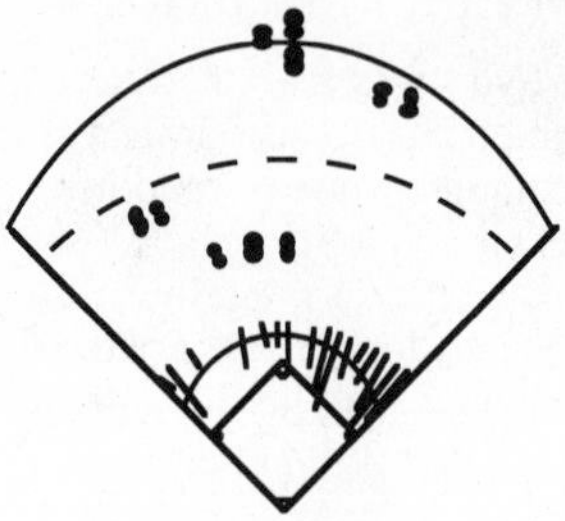

Vs. LHP

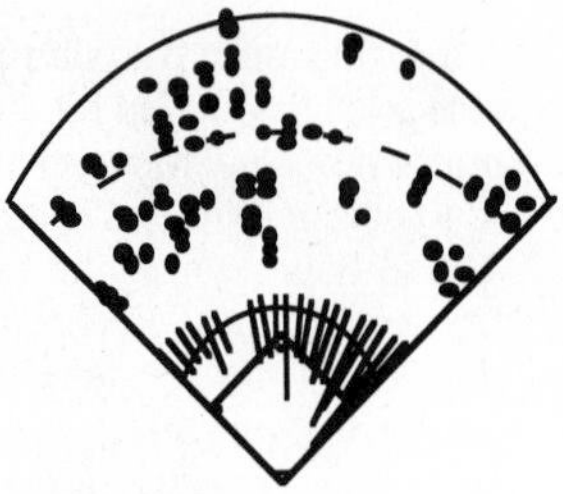

Vs. RHP

1990 Situational Stats

	AB	H	HR	RBI	AVG		AB	H	HR	RBI	AVG
Home	169	46	1	14	.272	LHP	101	25	4	13	.248
Road	229	55	6	24	.240	RHP	297	76	3	25	.256
Day	119	30	2	6	.252	Sc Pos	94	21	0	29	.223
Night	279	71	5	32	.254	Clutch	64	15	2	5	.234

1990 Rankings (National League)

- 4th in most GDPs per GDP situation (19.4%)
- 9th lowest batting average on the road (.240)

HITTING:

The question of whether Mark Parent could hit in the big leagues was probably irrevocably answered last season. The answer is no. Given a chance to play due to Benito Santiago's injury last year, Parent hit only .222.

In two previous seasons with the Padres, the big right-handed hitter had batted only .195 and .191. But he'd shown some flashes, especially in the power department. In 259 total at-bats -- less than half a season's work -- he'd belted an impressive 13 homers. Last year, however, with Santiago missing 53 mid-summer games due to a broken left forearm, Parent didn't hit for average, and he didn't hit for power, either. He managed only three homers in 189 at-bats.

At 6'-5" and 224 pounds, Parent has the physical equipment to hit the ball a long way. Before last year, he'd been a very undisciplined hitter, swinging at a lot of bad balls in an effort to jerk one out of the park. Last year, he shortened his stroke and laid off the bad pitches. As a result, he drew more walks and struck out less often. But making better contact didn't help Parent hit for a decent average. The main consequence of his new style was that he lost his power.

BASERUNNING:

The massive Parent is a traditional lumbering catcher. He is a base clogger. He compensates for his lack of speed by usually exhibiting a fundamental appreciation for the game. Parent will rarely hurt you by making a bad judgement or a foolish mistake.

FIELDING:

It was Parent's defense, not his hitting, which got him to the major leagues. But any comparison to Santiago all but evaporated when he was given increased exposure last season. Parent does have a decent arm, but he's no Santiago. His size helps make him effective at blocking the plate, and he's fairly agile for a big man, allowing only one passed ball last year. His strongest point is his ability to call a game.

OVERALL:

Parent's failure to hit last season probably doomed him to a backup role. At times he has asked to be traded, but when the club has made attempts, it has found no takers. With Tom Lampkin now in a Padres uniform, Parent may be hard pressed to maintain even his backup job for the 1991 season.

MARK PARENT

Position: C
Bats: R **Throws:** R
Ht: 6' 5" **Wt:** 224

Opening Day Age: 29
Born: 9/16/61 in Ashland, OR
ML Seasons: 5

Overall Statistics

	G	AB	R	H	D	T	HR	RBI	SB	BB	SO	AVG
1990	65	189	13	42	11	0	3	16	1	16	29	.222
Career	178	487	35	96	18	0	16	54	2	31	98	.197

Where He Hits the Ball

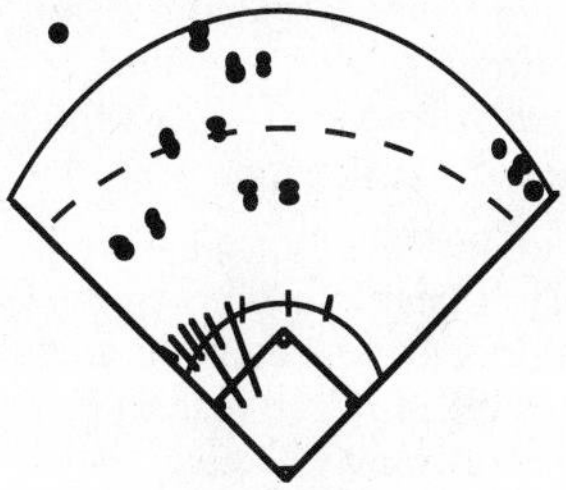

Vs. LHP

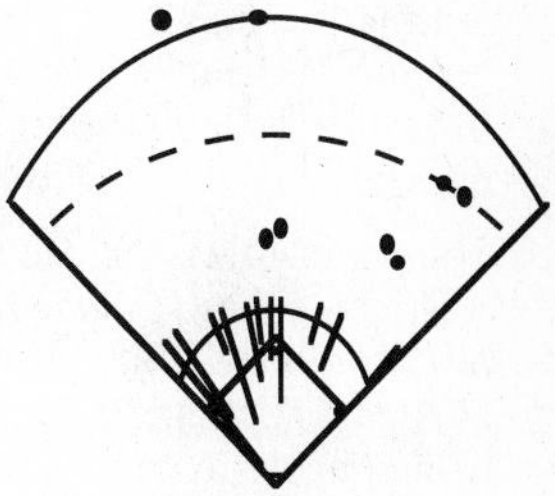

Vs. RHP

1990 Situational Stats

	AB	H	HR	RBI	AVG		AB	H	HR	RBI	AVG
Home	68	16	1	3	.235	LHP	85	26	2	7	.306
Road	121	26	2	13	.215	RHP	104	16	1	9	.154
Day	85	19	0	8	.224	Sc Pos	48	10	0	13	.208
Night	104	23	3	8	.221	Clutch	27	7	0	0	.259

1990 Rankings (National League)

➟ Did not rank near the top or bottom in any category

PITCHING:

Nearly 32, Dennis Rasmussen has been a regular major league starter for five seasons. He's been a decent workman, averaging over 13 wins per year while working at least 180 innings in every season. But in San Diego, Rasmussen really hasn't pitched well since 1988, when he came over from the Reds and went 14-4 in 20 starts over the remainder of the year. Rasmussen posted a 2.55 ERA for the Padres in '88, but since then he's faded, with marks of 4.26 and 4.51 the last two years. After 1990's 11-15 performance, his ability to remain a major league starter is in jeopardy.

Never a hard thrower, Rasmussen has been criticized in the past for a supposed unwillingness to challenge hitters. Pete Rose, his manager at Cincinnati, was his main critic, and that's how Rasmussen ended up in San Diego. The Padres' pitching coach, Pat Dobson, felt that Rasmussen's problems were mechanical. He got the lefthander to stop dropping his shoulder, a habit which made Rasmussen's arm swing across his body, causing the ball to miss the strike zone.

The new delivery helped a lot in 1988, but since then Rasmussen has struggled. He's been challenging the hitters more -- but the hitters have taken up the challenge, belting 28 homers off him last year. Even using his big-breaking curve, often an effective pitch in the past, didn't help. Last year lefties, whom he used to eat up, batted .333 against him. For two months, from July 1st to August 31st, Rasmussen won only once in 12 starts, losing nine times in the process. By the end of the season, manager Greg Riddoch had seen just about enough.

HOLDING RUNNERS, FIELDING, HITTING:

Though left-handed, Rasmussen does not have a great move to first. However, he did an adequate job holding runners in 1990. Big and hulking, he lacks mobility in the field. Formerly a weak hitter, Rasmussen had an unexpectedly great year at the plate. He led all Padres pitchers with a .290 batting average (18-for-62), driving in eight runs in the process.

OVERALL:

Rasmussen is one those pitchers who will drive you crazy by teasing you. On June 26 at Houston, he threw his first shutout in two years and only the third of his career. Then, he went into one of his trademark tail-spins. During those spins, he slows down his motion and drives infielders nuts with his creeping tempo. A free agent, he might attract some interest, but his value has sharply declined.

DENNIS RASMUSSEN

Position: SP
Bats: L **Throws:** L
Ht: 6' 7" **Wt:** 225

Opening Day Age: 31
Born: 4/18/59 in Los Angeles, CA
ML Seasons: 8

Overall Statistics

	W	L	ERA	G	GS	Sv	IP	H	R	BB	SO	HR
1990	11	15	4.51	32	32	0	187.2	217	110	62	86	28
Career	80	60	4.13	210	200	0	1232.1	1184	625	443	730	154

How Often He Throws Strikes

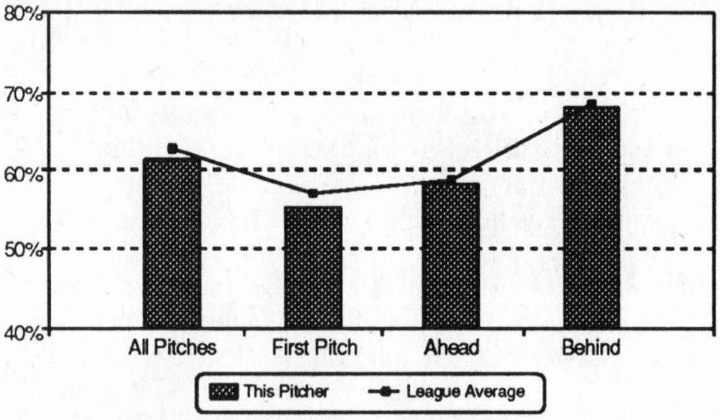

1990 Situational Stats

	W	L	ERA	Sv	IP		AB	H	HR	RBI	AVG
Home	5	9	4.37	0	101.0	LHB	108	36	5	17	.333
Road	6	6	4.67	0	86.2	RHB	634	181	23	77	.285
Day	3	5	4.83	0	59.2	Sc Pos	167	47	5	66	.281
Night	8	10	4.36	0	128.0	Clutch	32	12	1	5	.375

1990 Rankings (National League)

- ➟ 1st in home runs allowed (28), most runners caught stealing (16), highest batting average allowed (.292), highest slugging percentage allowed (.451), most HRs allowed per 9 innings (1.34)
- ➟ 2nd highest on-base average allowed (.348) and most baserunners allowed per 9 innings (13.5)
- ➟ 3rd in losses (15) and highest run support per 9 innings (5.7)
- ➟ Led the Padres in losses, hits allowed (217), home runs allowed, wild pitches (9), runners caught stealing, lowest stolen base percentage allowed (56.8%) and run support per 9 innings

HITTING:

It took him awhile, but Bip Roberts has evolved into a viable offensive force and leadoff hitter. Roberts had a painful debut for the Padres in 1986, hitting a weak .253 and looking very overmatched. Sent back to the minors for two years, he returned for good and surprised everyone by hitting .301 in 117 games in 1989. Roberts proved he was no fluke by batting .309 in 149 games last season, tying Tony Gwynn for the club lead.

But the numbers do not tell the entire story. With his combination of speed and ability to get on base, Roberts became the Padres' best leadoff man since Alan Wiggins was banished from the club in 1985 because of continued drug abuse.

Only 5-7, Roberts has become a much more disciplined hitter since spending two years at AAA Las Vegas. He makes the pitcher throw strikes and isn't afraid to take a walk. Always a good fastball hitter, he's become more adept at hitting the breaking ball. He has also demonstrated an ability to hit from both sides of the plate. He was a better righty swinger in 1989, more effective from the left side in 1990.

Utilizing an off season weight-lifting program, Roberts even put some pop on the ball in 1990. His nine homers and 44 RBI were both career highs. Previously, Roberts had hit four homers and driven in just 37 runs in his entire major league career.

BASERUNNING:

A good student of the game, Roberts has improved enormously as a base stealer. He was 14 for 26 stealing in 1986, 21 for 32 in 1989, and then led the club by swiping 46 in 58 attempts last year. His performance was all the more impressive because he does not possess blinding speed. Often sent on the hit-and-run, Roberts scored a club-leading 104 runs in 1990.

FIELDING:

Though capable of playing several positions, Roberts really doesn't play any of them very well. He's best at second base, but Roberto Alomar stands in his way there. So he's been forced to spend most of his time in left field or at third base. He's adequate at best, with a weak throwing arm.

OVERALL:

Roberts showed great perseverance by reviving his career after failing on his first try. When he was cut during spring training of 1987, he easily could have faded into oblivion. Instead, Roberts began to learn the game better and become a team player. He's now one of the Padres' mainstays.

BIP ROBERTS

Position: LF/3B/SS
Bats: B **Throws:** R
Ht: 5' 7" **Wt:** 160

Opening Day Age: 27
Born: 10/27/63 in Berkeley, CA
ML Seasons: 4

Overall Statistics

	G	AB	R	H	D	T	HR	RBI	SB	BB	SO	AVG
1990	149	556	104	172	36	3	9	44	46	55	65	.309
Career	372	1135	220	335	56	13	13	81	81	119	141	.295

Where He Hits the Ball

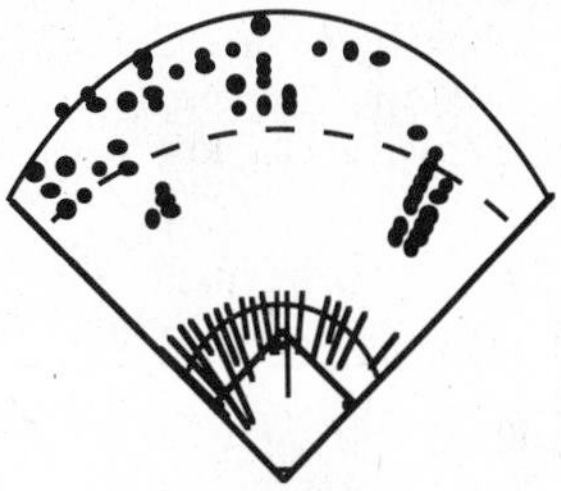

Vs. LHP

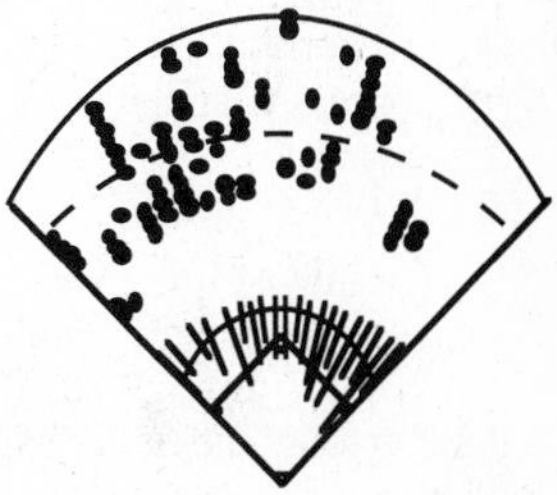

Vs. RHP

1990 Situational Stats

	AB	H	HR	RBI	AVG		AB	H	HR	RBI	AVG
Home	287	81	4	17	.282	LHP	221	65	4	16	.294
Road	269	91	5	27	.338	RHP	335	107	5	28	.319
Day	157	43	4	17	.274	Sc Pos	100	28	3	34	.280
Night	399	129	5	27	.323	Clutch	94	25	1	10	.266

1990 Rankings (National League)

- 2nd highest batting average on the road (.338)
- 5th highest batting average vs. right-handed pitchers (.319)
- Led the Padres in batting average (.309), runs (104), doubles (36), stolen bases (46), caught stealing (12), times on base (233), slugging percentage (.433), on-base average (.375), stolen base percentage (79.3%), runs scored per time reached base (44.6%), bunts in play (16) and steals of third (7)
- Led NL left fielders in batting average, at-bats (556), runs, hits (172), singles (124), doubles, sacrifice bunts (8), hit by pitch (6) and plate appearances (629)

PITCHING:

To say that Rich Rodriguez was a surprise call-up by the Padres on June 29 is an understatement. Rodriguez was not on the club's 40-man major league winter roster, nor was he a non-roster invitee to spring training. The first time the lefthander put on a Padres uniform was the evening his contract was purchased from Class AAA Las Vegas.

Rodriguez was brought up as a byproduct of the Padres' fruitless middle-inning relief pitching. Neither Mark Grant, Calvin Schiraldi nor Eric Show were getting the job done during the opening months of the season. Furthermore, Craig Lefferts, the designated closer, was the club's only lefthander coming out of the pen.

Rodriguez impressed early with his calm, cool effort under fire. Throwing an array of breaking pitches with his over-the-top delivery, he stranded 12 of the first 14 baserunners he inherited, earning immediate praise from former manager Jack McKeon and former pitching coach Pat Dobson. He keeps the ball low and doesn't allow many home run balls.

A product of the New York Mets organization, Rodriguez was buried behind other pitchers when he was coming through the Mets system. Almost always used in relief, he never had either the high save totals or low ERAs that attract a lot of attention. But the Padres liked his toughness, and picked him up before the 1989 season. They're glad they did, as Rodriguez became a mainstay during the second half of the '90 season. He finished with a 1-1 record and 2.83 ERA to show for 32 relief appearances.

HOLDING RUNNERS, FIELDING, HITTING:

Because of his role, he came to the plate just three times last season. At 28, he is a fundamentally sound player capable of fielding his position and holding runners close. He played errorless ball last year.

OVERALL:

On a rare high after a particularly good appearance by Rodriguez, manager Greg Riddoch likened Rodriguez' toughness and appearance on the mound to New York Mets reliever John Franco. Told of the comparison, Rodriguez was impressed. "He says I'm like Franco?" Rodriguez said. "I'm honored to be compared to Julio Franco." The point is, if Rodriguez can have another season in middle relief like last season, Riddoch will be grateful to compare Rodriguez to Rich Rodriguez.

RICH RODRIGUEZ

Position: RP
Bats: L **Throws:** L
Ht: 5'10" **Wt:** 194

Opening Day Age: 28
Born: 3/1/63 in Downey, CA
ML Seasons: 1

Overall Statistics

	W	L	ERA	G	GS	Sv	IP	H	R	BB	SO	HR
1990	1	1	2.83	32	0	1	47.2	52	17	16	22	2
Career	1	1	2.83	32	0	1	47.2	52	17	16	22	2

How Often He Throws Strikes

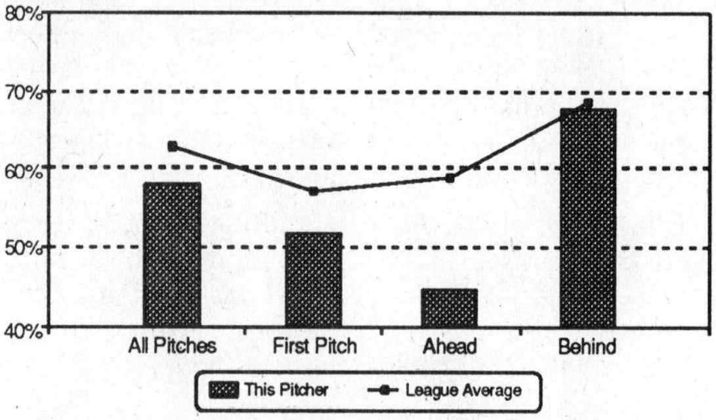

1990 Situational Stats

	W	L	ERA	Sv	IP		AB	H	HR	RBI	AVG
Home	1	0	2.57	0	28.0	LHB	65	15	0	7	.231
Road	0	1	3.20	1	19.2	RHB	116	37	2	15	.319
Day	1	0	2.70	0	10.0	Sc Pos	47	15	0	18	.319
Night	0	1	2.87	1	37.2	Clutch	63	14	0	2	.222

1990 Rankings (National League)

- Did not rank near the top or bottom in any category

BENITO SANTIAGO

Position: C
Bats: R **Throws:** R
Ht: 6' 1" **Wt:** 185

Opening Day Age: 26
Born: 3/9/65 in Ponce, Puerto Rico
ML Seasons: 5

Overall Statistics

	G	AB	R	H	D	T	HR	RBI	SB	BB	SO	AVG
1990	100	344	42	93	8	5	11	53	5	27	55	.270
Career	531	1906	215	506	81	12	58	246	52	95	350	.265

Where He Hits the Ball

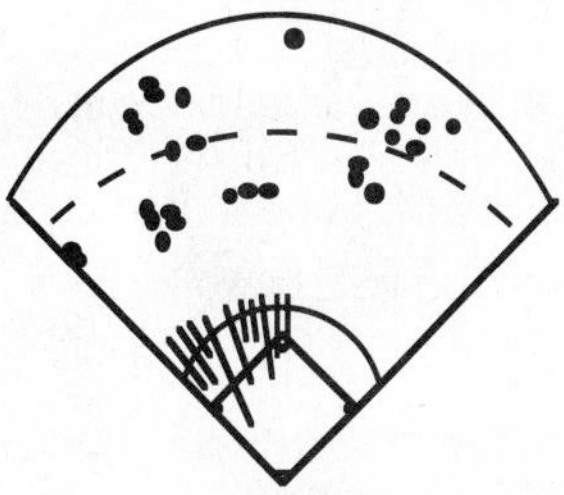

Vs. LHP

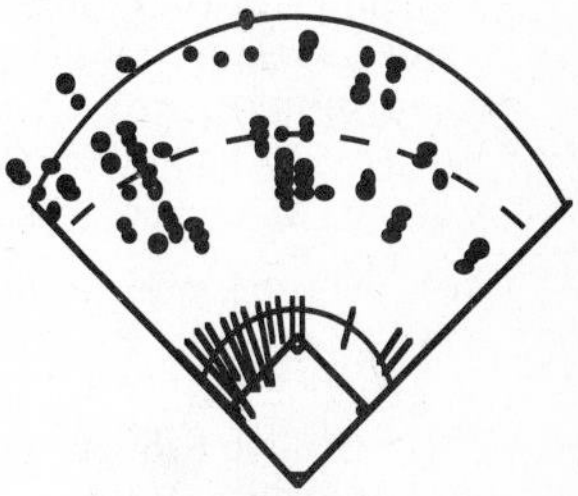

Vs. RHP

1990 Situational Stats

	AB	H	HR	RBI	AVG		AB	H	HR	RBI	AVG
Home	189	54	5	26	.286	LHP	116	32	1	12	.276
Road	155	39	6	27	.252	RHP	228	61	10	41	.268
Day	68	25	4	13	.368	Sc Pos	90	22	6	46	.244
Night	276	68	7	40	.246	Clutch	67	29	3	8	.433

1990 Rankings (National League)

- 1st in batting average in the clutch (.433)
- Led the Padres in least GDPs per GDP situation (6.3%) and batting average in the clutch
- Led NL catchers in triples (5), sacrifice flies (7), hit by pitch (3), batting average in the clutch and highest percentage of extra bases taken as a runner (50.0%)

HITTING:

The first nine weeks of last season marked Benito Santiago's emergence as a patient big-league hitter. Flushed from winning a $1.2 million contract through arbitration, Santiago came out of the gate wailing. He hit for power, average and drove in runs. He walked a little more and struck out a lot less.

Then, making a pinch hit appearance against San Francisco's Jeff Brantley on June 14, Santiago's season came to a screeching halt. Ducking a high, inside pitch, Santiago threw up his left arm to protect his face. The ball broke his forearm in three places. Santiago did not return until August 10, missing his second consecutive All-Star appearance in the process. By then, his season and the club's season were virtually over.

But though he played in only 100 games, Santiago showed improvement in several areas. His .270 average was his best in three seasons, and his .323 on base percentage was only one point short of his previous career high. His walk total of 27, modest as it was, was a career high, and his 55 strikeouts were by far his fewest. Santiago finally had some success laying off high fastballs, and as a result, became a better hitter.

BASERUNNING:

Santiago is certainly not the traditional cumbersome catcher on the base paths. When given the opportunity, he can steal a few bases. He was just five-for-ten last year, but the injury probably cut down on his running. He's also a fine and aggressive baserunner.

FIELDING:

Santiago is still the best throwing catcher in baseball. His arm is so potent that it often intimidates the opposition. With Santiago behind the plate for 129 games in 1989, opponents attempted just 129 steals. With Santiago missing 62 games last season, opponents attempted 192. The other parts of his game still need work, however. He makes a lot of errors trying to pick runners off, and his ability to call a game is still questioned. As he continues to master the game mentally, his defensive stock will soar.

OVERALL:

With the departure of Sandy Alomar, Jr. to Cleveland, the club made the obvious decision that the future rests with Santiago behind the plate. Before the injury, Santiago responded with renewed zeal and complete confidence. His value to the club was underscored during the 53 games he missed. Going into the game in which he was injured, the Padres were 30-27, just six games out of first. Upon his return, the club was 51-59, 12-1/2 games out.

PITCHING:

Calvin Schiraldi does not want to be a relief pitcher. There are those ugly memories of the 1986 World Series. Game Six. Schiraldi on the mound against the New York Mets. Boston one strike away from its first championship since 1918. Schiraldi is still looking for that strike. Schiraldi was equally as ineffective in Game Seven.

Now, spin the clock ahead three seasons. Schiraldi, a member of the Padres, is given the choice of pitching to Cincinnati's Eric Davis with Herm Winningham on second, first base open and the 1989 season on the line. Schiraldi pitches to Davis, who doubles in Winningham. The Padres are eliminated from the National Western division race.

Is it any wonder that Schiraldi does not have the mental makeup to be a closer? Despite a decent fastball and six-foot five-inches of supposed right-handed fury, he just doesn't have what it takes. Yet, when spring training of 1990 came around, former manager Jack McKeon had already set his starting rotation. And where was Schiraldi? In the bullpen.

That decision proved to be a disaster. He worked 34 games as a reliever, finishing the season with eight losses, one save and a 4.41 ERA. By the time new manager Greg Riddoch gave him a late-season shot at starting, it was too late. Schiraldi was awful. From August 5 to September 8, Schiraldi made seven consecutive starts. He was 0-5 with a 5.79 ERA. What to they do now with Calvin Schiraldi?

HOLDING RUNNERS, FIELDING, HITTING:

Schiraldi has a slow and lackluster move to first base. He's also slow getting off the mound to field his position. He made three errors last season, tied with Dennis Rasmussen for tops on the club among pitchers. A decent hitting pitcher, Schiraldi batted .190 (4-for-21) with a homer, only one of the two homers hit by Padre pitchers last season.

OVERALL:

Schiraldi left Chicago escaping Don Zimmer's doghouse, mostly because Zimmer had the distinct impression that Schiraldi just did not care. Schiraldi seemed to belie that notion by winning three key starts in the '89 stretch run right after the Padres obtained him from the Cubs. But last year, he was a different person. Schiraldi does not particularly appear to be in good physical shape, nor does he appear rabid about doing his job. It is a combination that may lead to Schiraldi, now 28, seeking another profession before he is 30 years old.

CALVIN SCHIRALDI

Position: RP/SP
Bats: R **Throws:** R
Ht: 6' 5" **Wt:** 215

Opening Day Age: 28
Born: 6/16/62 in Houston, TX
ML Seasons: 7

Overall Statistics

	W	L	ERA	G	GS	Sv	IP	H	R	BB	SO	HR
1990	3	8	4.41	42	8	1	104.0	105	59	60	74	11
Career	32	38	4.22	232	47	21	548.2	517	279	262	470	59

How Often He Throws Strikes

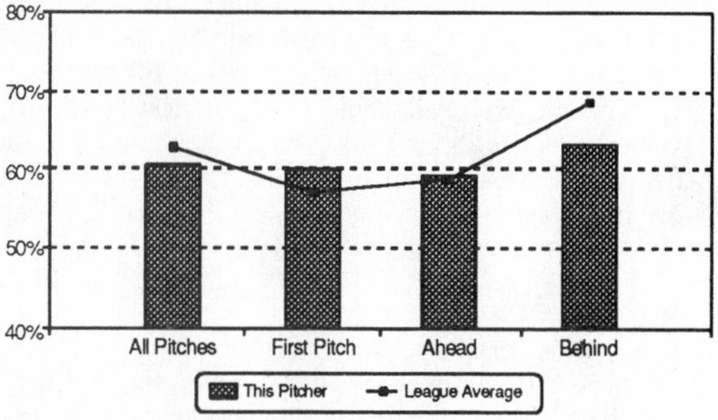

1990 Situational Stats

	W	L	ERA	Sv	IP		AB	H	HR	RBI	AVG
Home	2	5	4.24	1	63.2	LHB	207	55	7	33	.266
Road	1	3	4.69	0	40.1	RHB	190	50	4	30	.263
Day	1	2	5.28	0	29.0	Sc Pos	120	35	2	50	.292
Night	2	6	4.08	1	75.0	Clutch	65	17	1	9	.262

1990 Rankings (National League)

- Did not rank near the top or bottom in any category

PITCHING:

The winningest pitcher is San Diego Padres history, Eric Show has probably posted his last victory for the club. Show won only six games last year, his lowest total since breaking in back in 1981. His ERA of 5.76 was his worst ever, by a large margin. Show will be 35 shortly after the 1991 season starts, and he had major back surgery only two years ago. But Show thinks he can still be a winner.

Show's 1990 season was full of emotional rancor as he attempted to come back only six months after the surgery. With the club struggling out of the gate, former manager Jack McKeon gave Show a month to unwind. But Show was so erratic that after an 0-5 start he was dumped from the starting rotation of which he had been a member since 1983. The demotion didn't sit well with Show. After blasting both McKeon and pitching coach Pat Dobson, he was left to rot in the pen until McKeon was fired on July 11.

With Greg Riddoch in charge, Show ended the season as a middle reliever. And by season's end, he seemed to have put his physical problems behind him. After a 1-8 start, Show went 5-0 with a save in his final 22 appearances. On the final day of the season, Riddoch gave Show what was undoubtedly his last start as a Padre. On October 3 in Los Angeles, he became the only Padre pitcher to ever win 100 games.

Once almost exclusively a fastballer, Show evolved into more of a junkballer under the tutelage of Dobson. He now throws both a sinker and change-up, and if healthy has enough stuff to still be successful.

HOLDING RUNNERS, FIELDING, HITTING:

Show used to have a lot of problems holding runners, but he's had more success since starting to use a slide step. He has killed himself in the field, though, by not thinking. His failure to cover first base on an early-season ground ball was one of the reasons McKeon lost faith in him. Show has always been a fine hitter and can help himself with the stick.

OVERALL:

Show was a free agent after the 1990 season, and the Padres expressed no interest in trying to re-sign him. His penchant for speaking his mind was a big factor in that decision. He still seems able to pitch, and with something to prove and a chip on his shoulder, Show wants to show the Padres they made a mistake.

ERIC SHOW

Position: RP/SP
Bats: R **Throws:** R
Ht: 6' 1" **Wt:** 190

Opening Day Age: 34
Born: 5/19/56 in Riverside, CA
ML Seasons: 10

Overall Statistics

	W	L	ERA	G	GS	Sv	IP	H	R	BB	SO	HR
1990	6	8	5.76	39	12	1	106.1	131	74	41	55	16
Career	100	87	3.59	309	230	7	1603.1	1464	703	593	951	166

How Often He Throws Strikes

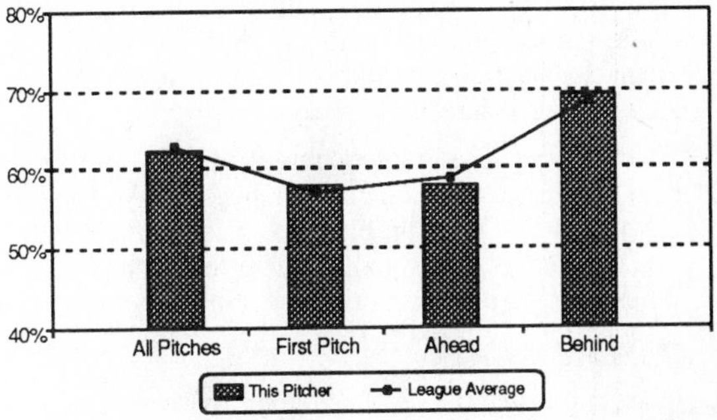

1990 Situational Stats

	W	L	ERA	Sv	IP		AB	H	HR	RBI	AVG
Home	3	5	6.22	0	50.2	LHB	234	74	8	34	.316
Road	3	3	5.34	1	55.2	RHB	194	57	8	38	.294
Day	1	1	5.59	0	19.1	Sc Pos	117	38	4	55	.325
Night	5	7	5.79	1	87.0	Clutch	44	10	1	4	.227

1990 Rankings (National League)

- Led the Padres in hit batsmen (4)

GARRY TEMPLETON

Position: SS
Bats: B **Throws:** R
Ht: 5'11" **Wt:** 190

Opening Day Age: 35
Born: 3/24/56 in Lockey, TX
ML Seasons: 15

Overall Statistics

	G	AB	R	H	D	T	HR	RBI	SB	BB	SO	AVG
1990	144	505	45	125	25	3	9	59	1	24	59	.248
Career	1967	7445	868	2035	319	104	67	702	239	365	1054	.273

Where He Hits the Ball

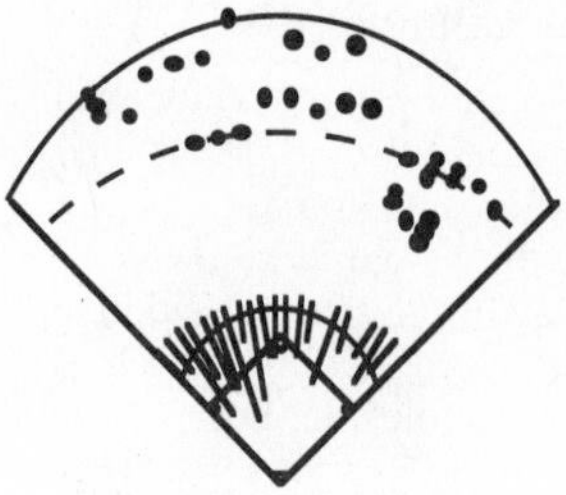

Vs. LHP

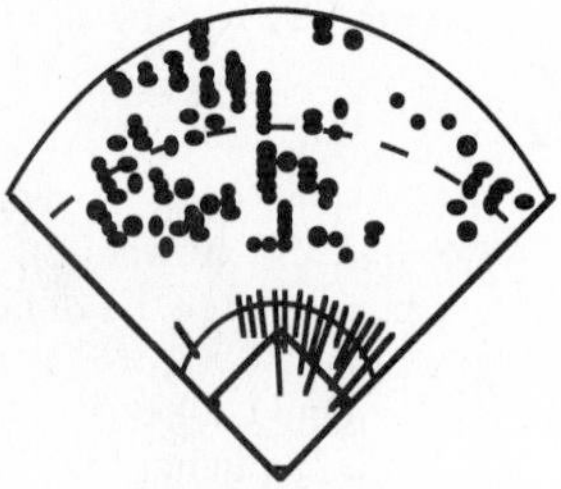

Vs. RHP

1990 Situational Stats

	AB	H	HR	RBI	AVG		AB	H	HR	RBI	AVG
Home	255	63	6	36	.247	LHP	189	48	4	29	.254
Road	250	62	3	23	.248	RHP	316	77	5	30	.244
Day	123	34	4	20	.276	Sc Pos	122	35	5	50	.287
Night	382	91	5	39	.238	Clutch	104	25	2	16	.240

1990 Rankings (National League)

- 2nd in lowest on-base average (.280) and lowest percentage of pitches taken (40.9%)
- 4th in GDPs (17) and least pitches seen per plate appearance (3.19)
- 8th in most GDPs per GDP situation (17.4%)
- 9th lowest batting average at home (.247)
- Led the Padres in GDPs
- Led NL shortstops in GDPs, batting average on a 3-2 count (.348) and errors (26)

HITTING:

Once a good enough player to be traded even-up for Ozzie Smith, Garry Templeton is now nearing the end of his career. Though both his hitting and fielding can't match his glory days, Templeton remained the Padres' regular shortstop last year, at age 34. He may be the shortstop again this year because no replacement is on the horizon.

A .273 lifetime hitter, Templeton batted only .248 last year, his lowest average since 1987. But he drove in 59 runs, his highest total since 1982, and he matched his career high with nine homers. He showed good pop for a shortstop by belting 37 extra-base hits.

That's the plus side. The minuses are that Templeton has always had terrible plate discipline, and his chronic knee problems have robbed him of the speed that was once a major part of his game. Templeton loves to hit the fastball, and he'll swing at one whether it's in the strike zone or not. He has enough hitting talent that he doesn't strike out much, but his impatience has made him far less valuable.

With an arthritic left knee, Templeton can no longer beat out leg hits like he could in his heyday with the Cardinals. The knee problem has also hampered him as a left-handed hitter, to the extent that he has sometimes considered batting righty exclusively.

BASERUNNING:

Once a consistent 25 to 35 stolen base man, Templeton has lost so much speed that he was able to swipe only one sack in each of the last two seasons, while getting tossed out a total of seven times. He's also had to become a much more cautious baserunner.

FIELDING:

Having lost considerable range to age and knee problems, Templeton compensates with his intelligence and ability to play the hitters. The left knee gives him a lot of problems on balls hit up the middle. He still has a very strong arm, but it's erratic, and Templeton made 26 errors last year.

OVERALL:

Considered a moody troublemaker during his Cardinal days, Templeton has been a club leader with the Padres and the team captain since 1987. He's helped a lot of the younger Padres, especially Bip Roberts and Roberto Alomar, and he could still be a major contributor even in a minor role. Whether he'll be the regular shortstop this year depends on whether the Padres, who have no heir-apparent, make a deal.

ED WHITSON

Position: SP
Bats: R **Throws:** R
Ht: 6' 3" **Wt:** 195

Opening Day Age: 35
Born: 5/19/55 in Johnson City, TN
ML Seasons: 14

PITCHING:

At 35, Ed Whitson is improving with age. The last five years, his ERAs have gone down: 6.23, 4.73, 3.77, 2.66, 2.60. Meanwhile, his winning percentages have gone up: .400, .435, .542, .593, .609. Look out, Nolan Ryan.

Last year was the finest of Whitson's 14-year career. Pitching for a bad ball club, he won 14 games; no other Padre won more than 11. He challenged for the ERA crown before finishing third with a career low 2.60. He threw a career high three shutouts, and he was the anchor of a shaky pitching staff. With Bruce Hurst, Dennis Rasmussen and Andy Benes all having problems at various stages in the season, Whitson was the club's only reliable starter who was consistently good for the entire year.

Could this be the same Ed Whitson who was basically laughed out of New York in 1986 after a horrendous tenure with the Yankees? It is, and it isn't. Whitson was never an overpowering pitcher, but as he's gotten older, he's learned to use his stuff a lot more intelligently. Developing a change-up was the key factor, for it helped set up his slider and curve. Whitson also throws his fastball at several speeds making hitters constantly adjust.

Whitson needs good control to be effective, and last year it was almost impeccable. He allowed only 1.8 walks per nine innings. With great location he was able keep the ball in the park, which was one of his major problems in the past. After permitting 22 home runs in 1989, he allowed only 13 in 1990. He's also proving to be a very durable hurler. Whitson has made at least 32 starts and pitched at least 200 innings for each of the last four years.

HOLDING RUNNERS, FIELDING, HITTING:

Whitson is average in all areas. He will help himself on occasion at the plate, and last season he finally hit his first homer in his 12th major league season. He's an okay fielder, but sometimes reacts slowly to balls hit up the middle and gets nailed with liners. Using the slide step, as do most Padre pitchers, he's become better at holding runners.

OVERALL:

Whitson has come a long way since his years with the Yankees, which seemed to throw his whole career off track. He lost his confidence in the Big Apple, and it took awhile for him to regain it. Now the confidence seems to be back to stay -- and so does Whitson, as a winning pitcher.

Overall Statistics

	W	L	ERA	G	GS	Sv	IP	H	R	BB	SO	HR
1990	14	9	2.60	32	32	0	228.2	215	73	47	127	13
Career	122	117	3.75	439	321	8	2162.0	2147	998	681	1226	198

How Often He Throws Strikes

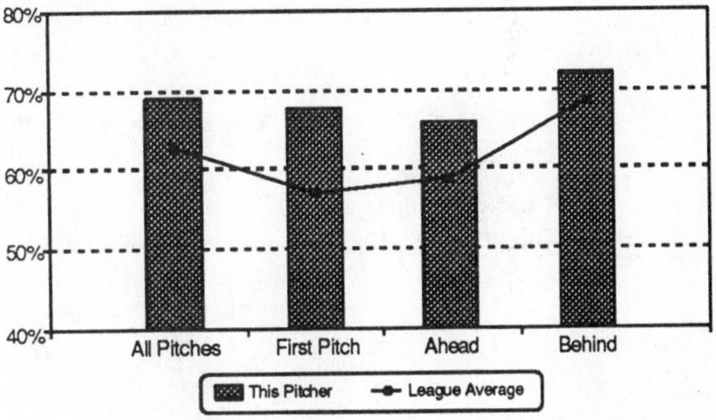

1990 Situational Stats

	W	L	ERA	Sv	IP		AB	H	HR	RBI	AVG
Home	5	6	2.65	0	125.2	LHB	527	143	6	37	.271
Road	9	3	2.53	0	103.0	RHB	328	72	7	29	.220
Day	5	3	3.39	0	74.1	Sc Pos	175	45	3	53	.257
Night	9	6	2.22	0	154.1	Clutch	69	23	2	7	.333

1990 Rankings (National League)

- 1st in least pitches thrown per batter (3.21)
- 3rd in ERA (2.60) and shutouts (3)
- 4th in ERA on the road (2.53)
- 7th in wins (14), innings (228.2), strikeout/walk ratio (2.7)
- Led the Padres in ERA, wins, innings, batter faced (918), winning percentage (.609), strikeout/walk ratio, lowest slugging percentage allowed (.347), least pitches thrown per batter and least HRs allowed per 9 innings (.51)

JERALD CLARK

Position: 1B
Bats: R **Throws:** R
Ht: 6' 4" **Wt:** 189

Opening Day Age: 27
Born: 8/10/63 in Crockett, TX
ML Seasons: 3

Overall Statistics

	G	AB	R	H	D	T	HR	RBI	SB	BB	SO	AVG
1990	52	101	12	27	4	1	5	11	0	5	24	.267
Career	75	157	17	38	7	1	6	21	0	8	37	.242

HITTING, FIELDING, BASERUNNING:

For the last three years the Padres have been wondering what do with Jerald Clark. A good minor league hitter who batted .301 in 107 games for Class AAA Las Vegas in 1988 and .313 in 107 games for Vegas in 1989, Clark just cannot seem to make the grade in the major leagues.

Because of the expanded post-lockout rosters, Clark made the club out of spring training last season for the first time and even had a four-hit game in a rare start. But by July 3, Clark was shipped back to the minors again, where he remained until the final eight weeks of the Padres season.

Part of his problem is his fielding. Clark is an average baserunner, but is a below average outfielder who can cost his team a game with a key bad play. Consequently, his value as a defensive replacement is nil. The Padres even tried him as a first baseman last season where he made eight uneventful starts. But the real mystery is his inability to hit in the major leagues. With San Diego, he hit .200 in 1988, .195 in 1989 and then .267 in 101 at-bats last season. A wild swinger, he belted five homers but also drew only five walks last year.

OVERALL:

Clark finished the year with a rush, going 5-for-12 with three homers and seven RBIs in his final three games of the season. He can be fooled with a breaking pitch, can be beat by a good fastball, and is a defensive liability. But he has some hitting skills, and his future may rest in the American League as a designated hitter.

JOEY CORA

Position: SS/2B
Bats: B **Throws:** R
Ht: 5' 8" **Wt:** 150

Opening Day Age: 25
Born: 5/14/65 in Caguas, Puerto Rico
ML Seasons: 3

Overall Statistics

	G	AB	R	H	D	T	HR	RBI	SB	BB	SO	AVG
1990	51	100	12	27	3	0	0	2	8	6	9	.270
Career	140	360	40	90	11	2	0	16	24	35	35	.250

HITTING, FIELDING, BASERUNNING:

A first round draft choice out of Vanderbilt in 1985, Joey Cora has not lived up to expectations. In 1987, the Padres tried to make Cora their starting second baseman. But he wasn't ready to make the jump from double-A to the majors, and well before mid-season he was back in the minors. He has been a bit player ever since. He did hit .270 in 100 at-bats last year, but with no power and no walks.

Cora has had some good years at Class AAA Las Vegas. Part of the problem with his transition to the majors is that, after blowing his initial opportunity, Roberto Alomar was installed at Cora's natural position of second base.

The Padres have experimented with Cora at shortstop and third base. But at 5'-8", 150 pounds, Cora is too small and his arm is too weak for him to be really effective on the left side of the diamond. The Padres like Cora's speed and ability to steal bases -- a Pacific Coast League-leading 40 in 1989, eight in 11 attempts for the Padres last year. But in San Diego, he may be the odd man out.

OVERALL:

Every time Cora tries to perform under the big-league microscope he seems to cave in under the pressure, making silly physical errors and even more costly mental mistakes. He needs a fresh start somewhere, and a shot at a starting job at second base. Given that kind of platform elsewhere, it would be interesting to see if he could make the grade.

DARRIN JACKSON

Position: CF
Bats: R **Throws:** R
Ht: 6' 0" **Wt:** 185

Opening Day Age: 27
Born: 8/22/63 in Los Angeles, CA
ML Seasons: 5

Overall Statistics

	G	AB	R	H	D	T	HR	RBI	SB	BB	SO	AVG
1990	58	113	10	29	3	0	3	9	3	5	24	.257
Career	240	487	58	121	22	3	13	49	8	23	89	.248

HITTING, FIELDING, BASERUNNING:

Along with Shawn Abner, Darrin Jackson gives the Padres a pair of players capable of running down fly balls in center field. Jackson's arrival two seasons ago allowed former manager Jack McKeon to move Tony Gwynn back to right field for the remainder of that season. With both Jackson and Abner on the bench and the arrival of Joe Carter for the '90 season Gwynn was finally able to play an entire season in right, his preferred position.

Jackson, 27, has not developed as a hitter, and last year the Padres had to ship him out to Class AAA Las Vegas in late June to work on his stroke. Jackson did hit better when he returned a month later, but he still needs a lot of work. His strike zone judgement is terrible, and he chases a lot of bad breaking pitches, especially against righthanders. Jackson does have some home run power, and he possesses excellent speed. He was three-for-three as a base stealer last year, and could develop that part of his game even more.

OVERALL:

Since trading center fielder Kevin McReynolds to the Mets in 1986, the Padres have not had a permanent fixture in a position that most experts consider to be one of the most important on the field. Joe Carter, the incumbent, has the bat, but his glove is much better suited to left. Jackson doesn't seem to have enough hitting skills to win the job, but the Padres can certainly utilize his defensive ability.

TOM LAMPKIN

Position: C
Bats: L **Throws:** R
Ht: 5'11" **Wt:** 185

Opening Day Age: 27
Born: 3/4/64 in Cincinnati, OH
ML Seasons: 2

Overall Statistics

	G	AB	R	H	D	T	HR	RBI	SB	BB	SO	AVG
1990	26	63	4	14	0	1	1	4	0	4	9	.222
Career	30	67	4	14	0	1	1	4	0	5	9	.209

HITTING, FIELDING, BASERUNNING:

With All-Star catcher Benito Santiago on the disabled list because of a broken left forearm, Tom Lampkin was acquired from Cleveland last July 11 as a backup catcher to Mark Parent. The trade, for outfielder Alex Cole, proved to be for very short term and very short-sighted.

Lampkin provided the Padres with another limited backup catcher. He bats left-handed and provides much more speed on the bases than the lumbering Parent. He has a little power, but not much, and good strike zone judgement. Lampkin doesn't figure to hit much for average. Nonetheless the Padres parted with center fielder Cole to get him. Thoroughly embarrassing San Diego, Cole stole 40 bases for the Indians in less than three months and was given the key to the city in the process.

Lampkin wasn't given anything except a ticket to Class AAA Las Vegas, where the Padres sent him just weeks after Santiago's return. His season ended there days later when he tore ligaments in his thumb and had to undergo surgery.

OVERALL:

Former general manager Jack McKeon liked Lampkin enough that he sought to have him included in the Joe Carter deal. At the time, Indians general manager Hank Peters didn't want to let Lampkin go. The Padres finally had to part with Cole in order to get him. Lampkin obviously has some value, but unless Santiago gets hurt again, he'll either be a little-used number-three catcher, or end up back in Triple A again. Meanwhile, Alex Cole will probably be the opening day center fielder for the Tribe.

PHIL STEPHENSON

Position: 1B
Bats: L **Throws:** L
Ht: 6' 1" **Wt:** 195

Opening Day Age: 30
Born: 9/19/60 in Guthrie, OK
ML Seasons: 2

Overall Statistics

	G	AB	R	H	D	T	HR	RBI	SB	BB	SO	AVG
1990	103	182	26	38	9	1	4	19	2	30	43	.209
Career	130	220	30	47	9	1	6	21	3	35	48	.214

HITTING, FIELDING, BASERUNNING:

A career minor leaguer in the Chicago Cubs and Oakland organizations, Phil Stephenson finally got a full year in the majors during 1990, his ninth professional season. Stephenson made the Padres out of spring training as a left-handed pinch hitter and backup first baseman to the brittle Jack Clark. On account of Clark's various injuries, Stephenson was given 35 starts at first base. But his key rolse for the club was as a pinch hitter. He only went 7- for-35, but he had 10 walks, in that capacity. Overall, though, Stephenson revealed why he had spent so many years toiling down on the farm. He batted just .209 with only four homers and 19 RBI. He drew a few walks, but also struck out a lot. He is so easy to pitch to that at times, there seem like there are holes in his swing as wide as the Grand Canyon.

A journeyman player, Stephenson actually is more adept with his glove than he is with his bat. He committed just one error at first base. He is a slow baserunner.

OVERALL:

Stephenson is a nice guy to have around as a late-inning defensive player at first base or as a pinch hitter. He's the type who harbors no illusions about his ability and seems content enough to fill a limited role. Easy going with a decent sense of humor, he won't walk around boring holes in the clubhouse if he doesn't play for weeks on end. He will probably be able to maintain a reserve position this season on what has been a weak Padre bench.

KEVIN BASS

Position: RF
Bats: B **Throws:** R
Ht: 6' 0" **Wt:** 180

Opening Day Age: 31
Born: 5/12/59 in Redwood City, CA
ML Seasons: 9

Overall Statistics

	G	AB	R	H	D	T	HR	RBI	SB	BB	SO	AVG
1990	61	214	25	54	9	1	7	32	2	14	26	.252
Career	1008	3349	426	916	170	30	85	428	113	220	440	.274

Where He Hits the Ball

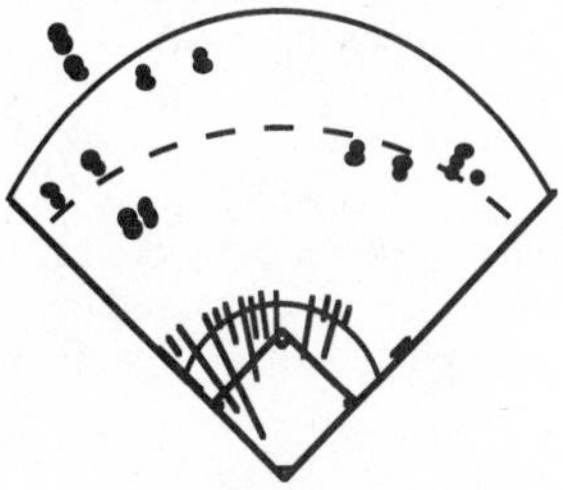

Vs. LHP

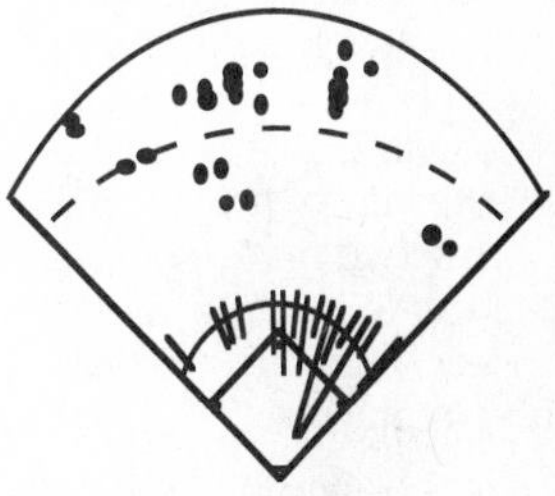

Vs. RHP

1990 Situational Stats

	AB	H	HR	RBI	AVG		AB	H	HR	RBI	AVG
Home	115	26	3	16	.226	LHP	90	23	5	16	.256
Road	99	28	4	16	.283	RHP	124	31	2	16	.250
Day	72	17	2	11	.236	Sc Pos	50	20	2	25	.400
Night	142	37	5	21	.261	Clutch	38	10	1	5	.263

1990 Rankings (National League)

- Did not rank near the top or bottom in any category

HITTING:

Kevin Bass went into 1990 thinking he was about to enjoy the most fulfilling season of his career. He signed a three-year contract with the Giants, partly because he was reared in nearby Menlo Park, and partly because he saw himself taking advantage of the hitter-friendly gales at Candlestick Park -- a far cry from the lifeless air of the Houston Astrodome.

Alas, Bass had little opportunity to enjoy his homecoming season. An injury to his left knee put him on the disabled list on May 26, and he didn't return to the Giants until September. Even when he did play, he seemed unable to trust the knee, and his work from both sides of the plate did not reflect the confidence that had made him a .276 career hitter.

Perhaps because he was trying to prove too much -- he also missed much of spring training because of a hamstring problem -- Bass found himself lunging at pitches he ordinarily could be expected to take. He saw a steady diet of back-door breaking balls from both sides of the plate, and because his timing was off, he had trouble laying off such pitches. Bass did show some signs of regaining his rhythm late in the season.

BASERUNNING:

Even when Bass' knee wasn't bothering him, the Giants took few chances with him in 1990, and he wasn't looking to steal or take the extra base on many occasions. Under normal circumstances, however, he is a better-than-average baserunner in all respects, and capable of 20 or more steals in a season.

FIELDING:

One of the Giants' main considerations in acquiring Bass was solving a long-standing defensive problem in right field, the toughest of the three outfield positions at Candlestick. Bass' work in that respect met expectations. He always has had a strong arm, and did a better job of hitting his cutoff man than he had with the Astros. He has very good range.

OVERALL:

The Giants found adequate replacements for Bass during his absence, so it can't be said that his return to pre-1989 form is a must for the Giants to be successful in 1991. Such a comeback, however, would be a major plus, and manager Roger Craig has flatly stated that a healthy Kevin Bass will be his regular right fielder in 1991. But at age 31, Bass is approaching the point where another injury-plagued season could jeopardize his future in baseball.

PITCHING:

Steve Bedrosian began the 1990 season as the relief closer for the defending National League champions. By midseason, his future as a major league closer was in question. By the end of the season, he was doing some of the best pitching of his career.

For a while last year, Bedrosian was doing his worst pitching since he became a full-time reliever for the Phillies in 1986. Seven straight bad outings, including four blown save opportunities in a row, prompted manager Roger Craig to make Jeff Brantley the closer at the end of May. But Bedrosian recovered his stuff later in the season, and was returned to the closer's role in August when Brantley was injured. He pitched superbly in September to finish with 17 saves.

Bedrosian is one of the most mechanics-conscious pitchers in baseball, and felt that mechanical flaws were causing his problems. One was his habit of extending his arm before shifting his body weight, another that he was too compact with his leg kick. As a result, Bedrosian simply couldn't hit the corners with any of his pitches. His hard slider, which he uses to set up his fastball, frequently came in flat and belt high. When he missed early in the count, he tended to lose aggressiveness and let up on his fastball to get it over the plate.

Bedrosian does not consider himself exclusively a power pitcher anymore, but there were times last season when Craig thought he would have been better off worrying less about his mechanics and his control and instead try to take a here's-my-best, hit-it-if-you-can approach.

HOLDING RUNNERS, FIELDING, HITTING:

Bedrosian has a decent pickoff move, but doesn't pay as much attention to baserunners as he should -- probably because he's been so intent on correcting his pitching problems. He is a good athlete who is aggressive in fielding bunts and trying for force outs. Bedrosian doesn't hit with any particular distinction.

OVERALL:

To Bedrosian's credit, he made no excuses for his 1990 performance. He was much admired for the manner in which he maintained his level of effort despite the fact his three-year-old son, Cody, was diagnosed in May as having leukemia. There were indications late in the season that he was recovering his form. Still, the Giants must take a wait-and-see approach this spring with Bedrosian before making him the primary San Francisco closer again.

STEVE BEDROSIAN

Position: RP
Bats: R **Throws:** R
Ht: 6' 3" **Wt:** 205

Opening Day Age: 33
Born: 12/6/57 in Methuen, MA
ML Seasons: 10

Overall Statistics

	W	L	ERA	G	GS	Sv	IP	H	R	BB	SO	HR
1990	9	9	4.20	68	0	17	79.1	72	40	44	43	6
Career	65	70	3.31	552	46	178	989.2	841	402	439	779	89

How Often He Throws Strikes

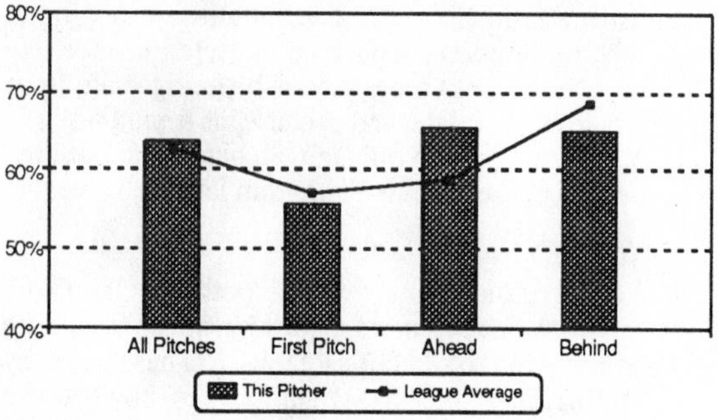

1990 Situational Stats

	W	L	ERA	Sv	IP		AB	H	HR	RBI	AVG
Home	8	4	3.54	11	48.1	LHB	170	45	4	24	.265
Road	1	5	5.23	6	31.0	RHB	129	27	2	12	.209
Day	6	3	3.92	6	39.0	Sc Pos	102	24	2	28	.235
Night	3	6	4.46	11	40.1	Clutch	179	41	3	21	.229

1990 Rankings (National League)

- 3rd in games finished (53)
- 4th lowest save percentage (77.3%)
- 5th lowest inherited runners scored (22.6%)
- 6th in games pitched (68)
- Led the Giants in games pitched, games finished, blown saves (5), first batter efficiency (.229) and lowest percentage of runners scored

JEFF BRANTLEY

Position: RP
Bats: R **Throws:** R
Ht: 5'11" **Wt:** 180
Opening Day Age: 27
Born: 9/5/63 in Florence, AL
ML Seasons: 3

PITCHING:

With Steve Bedrosian ineffective for much of last season, Giants manager Roger Craig used Jeff Brantley as if his arm could absorb any workload. Unfortunately for Brantley and the Giants, it couldn't. Brantley led National League relievers in innings pitched much of the season, and received a deserved berth on the NL All-Star team. But his shoulder began to flare up in late July, and he hardly pitched at all during the final two months of the season. Still, Brantley finished eighth in the NL with 19 saves.

Brantley and Craig both denied that Brantley simply wore out. But his problems began after he stopped throwing over the top and started coming at a three-quarter angle -- usually the surest sign that a pitcher is suffering from arm fatigue.

Because his best pitch is a sinking split-finger fastball, Brantley throws a lot of ground balls, and that's ideal at Candlestick Park with its bog-like infield. He'll usually try to set up that pitch by coming inside with hard stuff, then away with breaking balls. He has no qualms about moving men off the plate if he thinks they're crowding it; one of his inside fastballs broke Benito Santiago's arm early in the season.

Brantley will throw his breaking ball for strikes, but he'll usually try to do so only when it's early in the count. He doesn't change speeds too often; location and aggression rather than timing to throw off batters' timing are the keys to his success. He's extremely tough-minded and won't back down and throw a pitch over the middle of the plate, even when he's behind in the count.

HOLDING RUNNERS, FIELDING, HITTING:

Brantley probably is as tough against baserunners as any pitcher on the Giants' staff. He will go over to first incessantly, has a very quick move to first, and his motion is free 'of frills. Brantley also helps himself afield, where he handles bunts and comebackers with excellent instincts. Brantley doesn't often get a chance to hit, but can handle the bat adequately in bunting situations.

OVERALL:

After last season, the Giants will probably have to rethink their extensive use of Brantley. But there's no reason his shoulder shouldn't hold up as long as he's not overworked. He's an ideal set-up man and a better-than-competent closer, and Craig loves Brantley because he's such a battler.

Overall Statistics

	W	L	ERA	G	GS	Sv	IP	H	R	BB	SO	HR
1990	5	3	1.56	55	0	19	86.2	77	18	33	61	3
Career	12	5	3.17	123	2	20	204.2	200	81	76	141	15

How Often He Throws Strikes

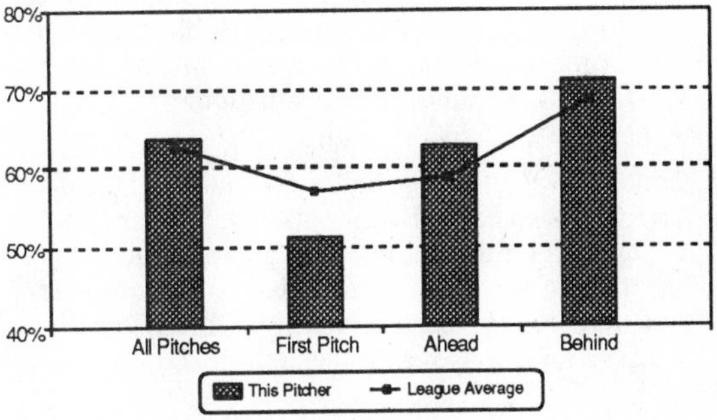

1990 Situational Stats

	W	L	ERA	Sv	IP		AB	H	HR	RBI	AVG
Home	4	1	1.77	9	40.2	LHB	190	51	1	13	.268
Road	1	2	1.37	10	46.0	RHB	131	26	2	9	.198
Day	4	3	2.10	5	34.1	Sc Pos	97	15	0	19	.155
Night	1	0	1.20	14	52.1	Clutch	221	53	2	14	.240

1990 Rankings (National League)

- 6th lowest save percentage (79.2%)
- 7th lowest percentage of inherited runners scored (24.4%)
- 8th in saves (19) and save opportunities (24)
- Led the Giants in saves, save opportunities, holds (8), save percentage and blown saves (5)

JOHN BURKETT

Position: SP
Bats: R **Throws:** R
Ht: 6' 2" **Wt:** 180

Opening Day Age: 26
Born: 11/28/64 in New Brighton, PA
ML Seasons: 2

PITCHING:

No pitcher in the National League surprised more people in 1990 than John Burkett -- and his employers were as surprised as anybody. Burkett made his major league debut with the Giants in 1987, then spent the next two seasons in the minors. He was called up last April only because the Giants, crippled by injuries, had no other choice; the front office at the time had no long-range plans for him. Burkett changed that in a hurry by winning seven of his first eight decisions. He finished with a 14-7 record to lead the Giants staff in wins, and demonstrated that his 200-plus bowling average isn't his only claim to athletic notoriety.

Earlier in his career, Burkett was a one-dimensional pitcher who tried to overpower hitters without really having the power to do it. His fastball is in the 88 to 90 MPH range, at best, but he has improved his other pitches and his location to the point where he'll tell you he doesn't have an out pitch. Burkett has confidence in his fastball, curve, change-up and split-finger fastball, regardless of the situation.

Burkett is a nibbler who moves the ball in and out. He almost never leaves the ball in the middle of the plate, and works so carefully that manager Roger Craig at times must remind him to be aggressive and not give the hitters too much credit. Burkett also has done much to reduce his excitability, which sometimes causes him to rush his mechanics.

HOLDING RUNNERS, FIELDING, HITTING:

Burkett still needs a lot of work on the non-pitching aspects of his game. He does not hold runners well, although he throws to first frequently. He has a sort of jump move that some managers have said is a borderline balk, and he tips it off by dropping his hands and his left knee before he wheels. Burkett is not quick on his feet and sometimes is a trifle sluggish moving off the mound. He is a terrible hitter.

OVERALL:

Burkett's rookie success should not obscure the fact that he appeared to be a career Class AAA pitcher before 1990. He doesn't have overwhelming stuff, and he must continue his maturing process. Burkett isn't a guy who can be expected to win 20 games, but he has become a solid, intelligent pitcher who should function well as a third or fourth starter.

Overall Statistics

	W	L	ERA	G	GS	Sv	IP	H	R	BB	SO	HR
1990	14	7	3.79	33	32	1	204.0	201	92	61	118	18
Career	14	7	3.81	36	32	1	210.0	208	96	64	123	20

How Often He Throws Strikes

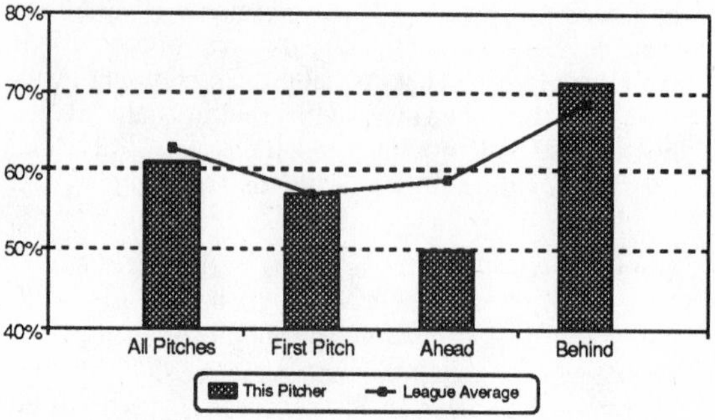

1990 Situational Stats

	W	L	ERA	Sv	IP		AB	H	HR	RBI	AVG
Home	6	2	3.98	0	104.0	LHB	464	118	10	50	.254
Road	8	5	3.60	1	100.0	RHB	317	83	8	28	.262
Day	8	2	3.25	0	105.1	Sc Pos	170	41	5	57	.241
Night	6	5	4.38	1	98.2	Clutch	59	18	0	5	.305

1990 Rankings (National League)

- 2nd in pickoff throws (280)
- 5th most run support per 9 innings (5.6)
- 6th in winning percentage (.667) and worst ERA at home (3.98)
- 7th in wins (14)
- Led the Giants in ERA (3.79), wins, games started (32), innings (204.0), hits allowed (201), batters faced (857), home runs allowed (18), hit batsmen (4), strikeouts (118), pitches thrown (3,137), pickoff throws and winning percentage

BRETT BUTLER

Position: CF
Bats: L **Throws:** L
Ht: 5'10" **Wt:** 170

Opening Day Age: 33
Born: 6/15/57 in Los Angeles, CA
ML Seasons: 10

Overall Statistics

	G	AB	R	H	D	T	HR	RBI	SB	BB	SO	AVG
1990	160	622	108	192	20	9	3	44	51	90	62	.309
Career	1360	5001	850	1424	189	83	39	362	358	654	527	.285

Where He Hits the Ball

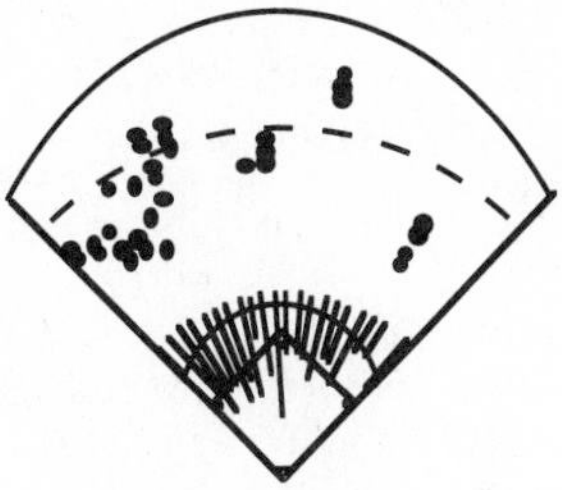

Vs. LHP

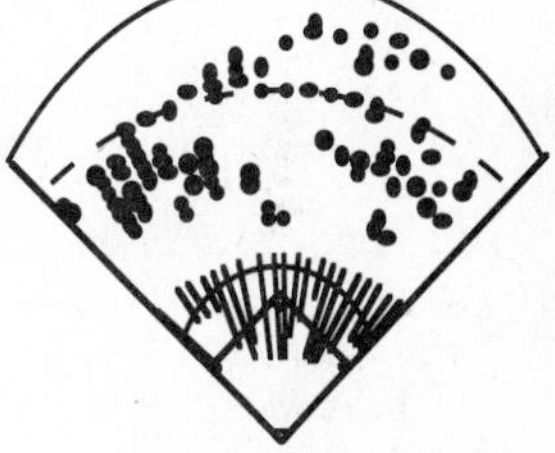

Vs. RHP

1990 Situational Stats

	AB	H	HR	RBI	AVG		AB	H	HR	RBI	AVG
Home	312	105	3	25	.337	LHP	245	74	1	20	.302
Road	310	87	0	19	.281	RHP	377	118	2	24	.313
Day	248	73	3	17	.294	Sc Pos	104	29	0	37	.279
Night	374	119	0	27	.318	Clutch	98	26	1	9	.265

1990 Rankings (National League)

- 1st in hits (192), singles (160), times on base (288), pitches seen (2,902), plate appearances (732) and bunts in play (55)
- 2nd in groundball/flyball ratio (2.2)
- 3rd in runs (108), triples (9), walks (90) and games (160)
- Led the Giants in batting average (.309), at-bats (622), runs, hits, singles, triples, stolen bases (51), caught stealing (19), walks, times on base, pitches seen, games, on-base average (.397), groundball/flyball ratio, stolen base percentage (72.9%) and bunts in play

HITTING:

Brett Butler's eighth full major league season ended with most of his numbers similar to that of his previous seven -- and some numbers even better. His 192 hits represented a career high and tied for the NL lead. However, Butler's season hardly was a continuum of consistency. He batted .366 in April before plummeting to .182 in May, when the Giants dropped to last place. He stabilized after that, but dropped back to the .280s in August before finishing with a flurry that landed him at .309 for the season.

Butler adeptly uses all fields, hitting the ball consistently on the ground to maximize his speed -- especially when he takes outside pitches to the opposite field. He hits the ball more frequently to the left field corner than to the right field corner, and shows line drive capability when he gets a pitch down and in. Late last season, though, he started looking to pull more pitches on the inside segment of the plate, and that enabled him to take advantage of the way teams played him.

Generally, pitchers have the most success against Butler when they pitch him up and in; he's an excellent low-ball hitter. He's also a patient hitter who draws a lot of walks, and an outstanding bunter, with 21 bunt hits last year to lead the NL.

BASERUNNING:

Butler had a typical Butler base stealing season in 1990, swiping 51 in 70 attempts. He studies pitchers' moves diligently, and although he doesn't have Vince Coleman speed, he gets a quick jump and knows how to slide and avoid infielders' tags. He's also an aggressive runner in non-stealing situations.

FIELDING:

Butler is a strong defensive outfielder with excellent quickness and range. He's not afraid to risk his body on dives and collisions. Even though he's short, he has surprising leaping ability. Butler's only liability is his arm, which is accurate but weak.

OVERALL:

Butler reportedly was being shopped around in May, partly because of his slump that month and partly because of some ill-advised comments he made about the devil singling the Giants out for misfortune. But don't look for him to go anywhere, even though he's scheduled to be one of the "new look" free agents. He's the only legitimate base stealing threat the Giants have, he's one of the best leadoff men in the league, and his defensive expertise is vital in the tricky conditions of Candlestick Park.

HALL OF FAMER

HITTING:

The New York Mets -- along with most baseball people -- believed the zing was gone from Gary Carter's bat after he batted .183 in 1989. The San Francisco Giants gave Carter a chance to prove his detractors wrong, and he took advantage in resounding style. Fresh-legged and enthusiastic after arthroscopic knee surgery, Carter surprised everyone by keeping his average in the .280 range for most of the year before slumping to his final .254 figure. He also showed he still has line drive power to left field, and became a valuable platoon man with left-handed hitting Terry Kennedy.

Carter remains a predominantly down-the-line pull hitter who likes the ball on the inside part of the plate. He has developed excellent plate judgment over the years, and usually will lay off the inside fastball that he can't handle. He's also good at holding back on the breaking ball outside the strike zone. Pitchers have the most success pitching him low and away with sliders, although it's still dangerous to hang a breaking ball on the outside portion of the plate against him.

BASERUNNING:

Carter is slow, but he doesn't hobble about as he did in his final seasons with the Mets. He even stole a base last year when the batter missed a sign on a hit-and-run. He's a smart baserunner who will take a fielder head-on when he has to, but won't go out of his way looking for contact.

FIELDING:

Carter's ability to work with young, inexperienced pitchers was one reason the Giants were able to hang in the pennant race most of the season despite setting a franchise record for most pitchers used. He's an expert at turning the mitt up so that it looks like the Holland Tunnel to his pitcher, and the fact he doesn't move around unnecessarily serves two purposes: it offers less distraction for the pitcher, and it gives the umpire a good look at the strike zone. Carter has a quick release, but doesn't throw as well as he once did.

OVERALL:

Rookie Steve Decker's strong September showing meant that the Giants would probably not re-sign free agent Carter. But he did everything the Giants expected off the field, and much more than they expected on it. He did nothing to damage his Hall of Fame credentials, and it appears he has at least a couple of productive seasons left at age 36.

GARY CARTER

Position: C
Bats: R **Throws:** R
Ht: 6' 2" **Wt:** 210
Opening Day Age: 37
Born: 4/8/54 in Culver City, CA
ML Seasons: 17

Overall Statistics

	G	AB	R	H	D	T	HR	RBI	SB	BB	SO	AVG
1990	92	244	24	62	10	0	9	27	1	25	31	.254
Career	2100	7438	979	1969	339	30	313	1170	37	793	934	.265

Where He Hits the Ball

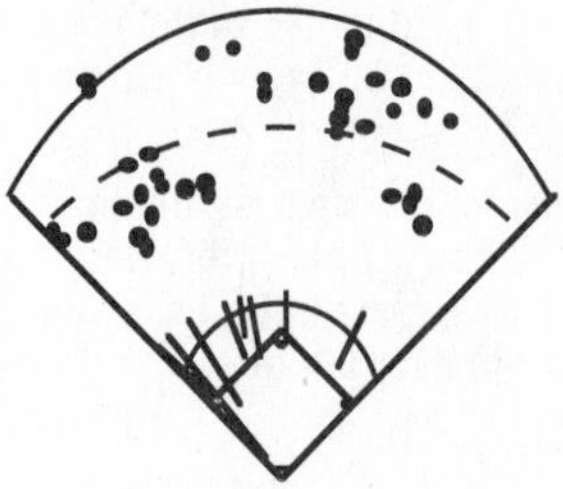

Vs. LHP

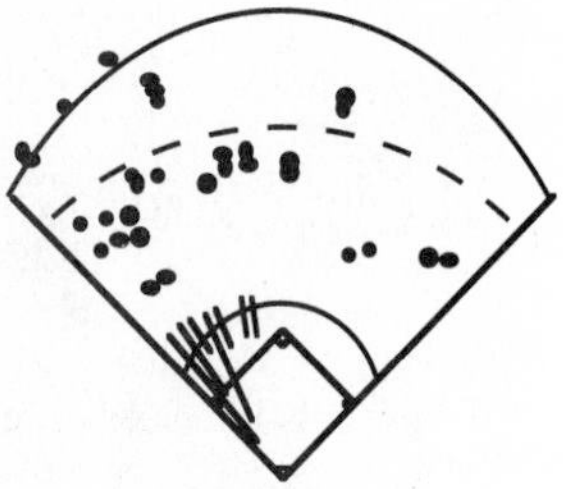

Vs. RHP

1990 Situational Stats

	AB	H	HR	RBI	AVG		AB	H	HR	RBI	AVG
Home	127	39	6	19	.307	LHP	127	30	3	11	.236
Road	117	23	3	8	.197	RHP	117	32	6	16	.274
Day	94	27	5	17	.287	Sc Pos	65	15	1	18	.231
Night	150	35	4	10	.233	Clutch	51	13	1	4	.255

1990 Rankings (National League)

- 4th in least GDPs per GDP situation (3.9%)
- Led the Giants in least GDPs per GDP situation
- Led NL catchers in least GDPs per GDP situation

WILL CLARK

Position: 1B
Bats: L **Throws:** L
Ht: 6' 1" **Wt:** 190

Opening Day Age: 27
Born: 3/13/64 in New Orleans, LA
ML Seasons: 5

Overall Statistics

	G	AB	R	H	D	T	HR	RBI	SB	BB	SO	AVG
1990	154	600	91	177	25	5	19	95	8	62	97	.295
Career	736	2700	452	815	150	27	117	447	34	319	503	.302

Where He Hits the Ball

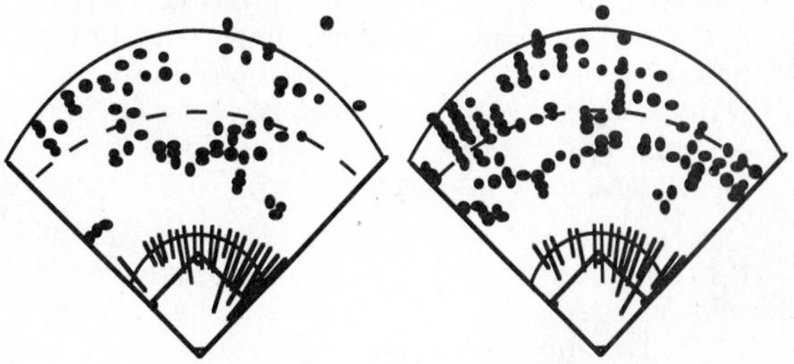

Vs. LHP **Vs. RHP**

1990 Situational Stats

	AB	H	HR	RBI	AVG		AB	H	HR	RBI	AVG
Home	296	94	8	44	.318	LHP	249	79	9	47	.317
Road	304	83	11	51	.273	RHP	351	98	10	48	.279
Day	239	64	9	39	.268	Sc Pos	172	50	4	73	.291
Night	361	113	10	56	.313	Clutch	94	25	4	16	.266

1990 Rankings (National League)

- 2nd in sacrifice flies (13)
- 5th in pitches seen (2,480)
- 6th in times on base (242)
- 7th in plate appearances (678)
- 8th in hits (177) and singles (128)
- Led the Giants in sacrifice flies and batting average vs. left-handed pitchers (.317)
- Led NL first basemen in at-bats (600), RBIs (95), sacrifice flies, pitches seen and plate appearances

HITTING:

Will Clark's 1990 season wasn't up to his or the Giants' expectations, even though it certainly wasn't a collapse. The explanation for his diminished numbers was fairly simple: he was hitting fly balls and grounders instead of line drives. The reason for that wasn't known until early September, when Clark revealed he had played most of the season with a nerve problem in his foot. He couldn't plant without pain, and had to undergo surgery after the season.

Partly because of his injury, and partly because he was dropping his hands instead of pulling them through the ball, Clark at mid-season developed a loop in his swing. One result was that he hit a lot of fly balls to left field when he tried to go with the outside pitch. Another result was that he hit on top of the ball and grounded out frequently when he tried to pull.

Clark still kept his average respectable, but his power output dropped. He did not hit a single home run in 123 at-bats from June 29 until August 11, and at one point manager Roger Craig sat Clark down and told him to relax and not try to carry the team by making every at-bat perfect. Clark usually was pitched up and away, often with back-door curves and sliders. He had some trouble with change-ups last year.

BASERUNNING:

Because he has often played with knee problems, Clark has lost a step since he first began his major league career in 1986. He still can steal an occasional base (eight in '90), however, and the Giants will hit-and-run with him on base. He is extremely combative on the base paths.

FIELDING:

Clark's aggressive style carries over to his play at first base, where he has become an accomplished performer. He is very fluid around the bag, and likes to throw the ball, although an elbow injury during his rookie season took away some of his arm strength. His range around the bag, though, is only average, mainly because of his knee problems.

OVERALL:

Last year, Clark found himself in an adjustment mode because few pitchers would give him a pitch in the zone he wanted. But he's still this generation's answer to Stan Musial, and with his personality and a surgically repaired foot, it can be expected that the statistical drop he experienced in 1990 will serve as a challenge that will return him to MVP-level status in 1991.

KELLY DOWNS

Position: SP
Bats: R **Throws:** R
Ht: 6' 4" **Wt:** 200

Opening Day Age: 30
Born: 10/25/60 in Ogden, UT
ML Seasons: 5

Overall Statistics

	W	L	ERA	G	GS	Sv	IP	H	R	BB	SO	HR
1990	3	2	3.43	13	9	0	63.0	56	26	20	31	2
Career	36	32	3.55	113	92	1	588.0	541	252	190	399	39

How Often He Throws Strikes

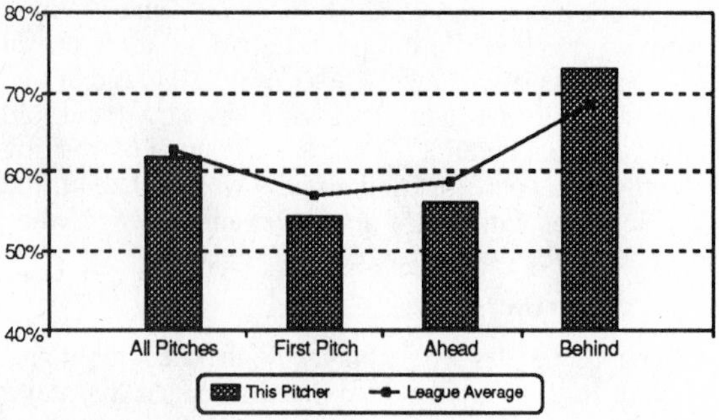

1990 Situational Stats

	W	L	ERA	Sv	IP		AB	H	HR	RBI	AVG
Home	2	0	2.10	0	34.1	LHB	152	37	1	16	.243
Road	1	2	5.02	0	28.2	RHB	88	19	1	8	.216
Day	1	0	1.85	0	24.1	Sc Pos	66	16	0	20	.242
Night	2	2	4.42	0	38.2	Clutch	23	4	0	1	.174

1990 Rankings (National League)

- Did not rank near the top or bottom in any category

PITCHING:

The season during which Kelly Downs' career could have ended instead turned out to be a new beginning. During his previous four seasons with the Giants, Downs was one of the team's few non-finesse pitchers. He had such velocity and movement on his fastball that manager Roger Craig once said of Downs that he was a threat to pitch a no-hitter anytime he started a game.

However, Downs' mechanics were terrible, and that was why he was so maddeningly inconsistent. He threw across his body, depending on arm speed while not using his lower body well, and he finished his motion in such a way that his shoulder was jarred violently. This latter problem was directly responsible for his torn rotator cuff. Downs streamlined his mechanics during his rehabilitation period, and the results were encouraging to the Giants after he returned to the team in August. He comes straight over the top now, he doesn't overthrow and he is able to spot the ball inside and outside with more accuracy. Craig is of the opinion that Downs has also become a smarter pitcher because of his surgery.

Downs still can throw in the 90 to 92 MPH range, and his two power pitches -- his riding fastball and his split-finger fastball -- remain his signature pitches. But he now mixes in a change-up that makes it difficult for hitters to sit on the fastball. He'll also change speeds on the splitter, which he throws with more velocity than most pitchers.

HOLDING RUNNERS, FIELDING, HITTING:

Downs held runners well before he was hurt, but last year 11 of 12 baserunners were successful stealing on him. The injuriy actually had a positive effect on Downs' fielding. Instead of lurching off the mound as he once did, Downs now squares himself to the plate, enabling him to pounce on bunts and field his position as well as anybody on the Giants' staff. Downs isn't a very good hitter, but he can be depended upon to get a bunt down when asked.

OVERALL:

The shoulder problems that have cut short Downs' past two seasons apparently were corrected by his rotator-cuff surgery. Add Downs' athleticism and intelligence, and the sum could be the consistency that Downs had lacked throughout his career. The Giants are counting on him to be one of their starters in 1991.

SCOTT GARRELTS

Position: SP
Bats: R **Throws:** R
Ht: 6' 4" **Wt:** 205

Opening Day Age: 29
Born: 10/30/61 in Urbana, IL
ML Seasons: 9

Overall Statistics

	W	L	ERA	G	GS	Sv	IP	H	R	BB	SO	HR
1990	12	11	4.15	31	31	0	182.0	190	91	70	80	16
Career	68	52	3.23	344	86	48	939.2	790	381	404	695	69

How Often He Throws Strikes

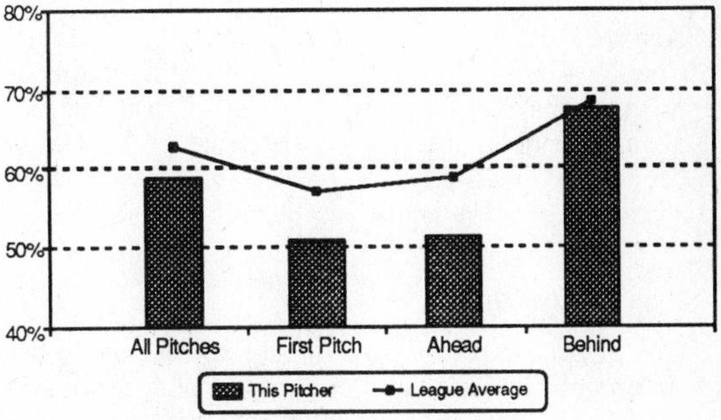

1990 Situational Stats

	W	L	ERA	Sv	IP		AB	H	HR	RBI	AVG
Home	6	7	3.83	0	103.1	LHB	397	119	8	44	.300
Road	6	4	4.58	0	78.2	RHB	301	71	8	34	.236
Day	3	3	3.59	0	62.2	Sc Pos	158	42	5	59	.266
Night	9	8	4.45	0	119.1	Clutch	66	17	2	7	.258

1990 Rankings (National League)

- 1st in lowest strikeout/walk ratio (1.1)
- 2nd most GDPs induced per 9 innings (1.1)
- 4th in GDPs induced (22) and least strikeouts per 9 innings (4.0)
- 6th highest batting average allowed (.272) and highest on-base average allowed (.339)
- 7th worst ERA (4.15) and highest slugging percentage allowed (.404)
- Led the Giants in losses (11), complete games (4), shutouts (2), walks allowed (70), wild pitches (7), GDPs induced, least pitches thrown per batter (3.50), least HRs allowed per 9 innings (.79) and GDPs induced per 9 innings

PITCHING:

Of all the mysteries surrounding the Giants' pitching staff in 1990 -- and the entire season was one continuous intrigue for them -- perhaps the most confounding was the way Scott Garrelts began the season as a cruel parody of his 1989 self. After all, Garrelts was coming off a 14-5 season during which he won the National League ERA title. In 1990, he lost six of his first seven decisions and his ERA on June 1 was 6.88. Just as abruptly, he recovered his 1989 form, and his denouement came in July when he came within one out of no-hitting Cincinnati. He finished 12-11, but with a 4.15 ERA.

Manager Roger Craig and pitching coach Norm Sherry tried numerous mechanical antidotes, most notably an effort to make Garrelts' motion more compact. Craig and Sherry also admonished Garrelts to be more aggressive in terms of pitching the inside corner -- a complaint that has been lodged against Garrelts by some of his own teammates. They feel Garrelts doesn't protect them enough with retaliatory "message" pitches. Another theory concerning Garrelts' temporary demise had to do with the retirement of Dave Dravecky. The two were close friends and shared strong religious convictions, and it was believed that Garrelts missed Dravecky's presence in the clubhouse more than the other Giants.

In any case, Garrelts was more aggressive on the inside part of the plate in the latter part of the season. He stopped pushing the ball and his motion seemed less strained after his 1-6 start. Garrelts, who already had a decent slider, also incorporated an off speed breaking ball into his repertoire.

HOLDING RUNNERS, FIELDING, HITTING:

Garrelts has an average move to first, but his attention sometimes drifts when runners are on base. The same can be said of his fielding. He has been known to mess up some easy chances, most often by trying to get an unlikely force out in a sacrifice situation. Garrelts isn't a high average hitter, even for a pitcher, but he'll get in his hacks.

OVERALL:

Garrelts enters 1991 as the senior Giant in terms of continuous service. That's somewhat surprising when considering his yearly performances which have been continuous swerves from great to terrible and back again. To Garrelts' credit, though, he fought through one of the most difficult periods of his career in 1990. The Giants are hoping he'll be able to attain a modicum of consistency in 1991; if he does, he could improve upon his 1989 stats.

TERRY KENNEDY

Position: C
Bats: L **Throws:** R
Ht: 6' 4" **Wt:** 224

Opening Day Age: 34
Born: 6/4/56 in Euclid, OH
ML Seasons: 13

HITTING:

Terry Kennedy spent much of the first two months of last season among the National League batting average leaders. He slumped in June and July, but came on again with a .314 August and finished at .277 -- his best average since 1983. His once-feared power has diminished drastically (only two home runs), and he was overmatched against the few lefthanders he faced. Even so, he proved he can make the adjustment from long-ball slugger to improvisational hitter.

Kennedy has a catcher's strike-zone knowledge, and he hardly ever swings at a fastball outside the strike zone. Consequently, he hits the ball to center field and the adjoining gaps most of the time. Against breaking pitches on the outside part of the plate, he'll often try to flick the ball down the left field line, and much of his early success was related to his ability to adjust to the fact most pitchers were working him away.

Kennedy still has some power, but he has a lot of trouble with fastballs in on his hands. Most lefthanders pitch him this way, and he has almost no success against them. Kennedy is a patient hitter who will go deep into counts, and will foul off pitch after pitch in search of the low-and-over delivery on which he thrives.

BASERUNNING:

One of the slowest players in baseball, Kennedy has stolen only six bases in 11 major league seasons. He obviously doesn't take many chances, but he's heady and won't take his team out of any innings. He's a hard-nosed sort who won't sidestep a take-out or home plate collision.

FIELDING:

Kennedy never has reminded anybody of Bob Boone behind the plate. He isn't flexible and sometimes has to reach for pitches that most catchers can shift their legs to block. His arm strength and release quickness are only fair, and he's easy to steal on if he doesn't get any help from his pitchers. On the plus side, he's intelligent, works well with pitchers and umpires and mentally catalogues the hitters.

OVERALL:

Kennedy probably never will be an everyday catcher again at age 34, but he's lithe enough to catch 100 games for at least another year or two. He and Gary Carter formed a solid, intelligent catching platoon, and unless Giant catcher of the future, Steve Decker, takes the job away this spring, look for Kennedy to remain the Giants' regular catcher against righthanded pitchers.

Overall Statistics

	G	AB	R	H	D	T	HR	RBI	SB	BB	SO	AVG
1990	107	303	25	84	22	0	2	26	1	31	38	.277
Career	1422	4808	462	1273	237	11	110	615	6	354	824	.265

Where He Hits the Ball

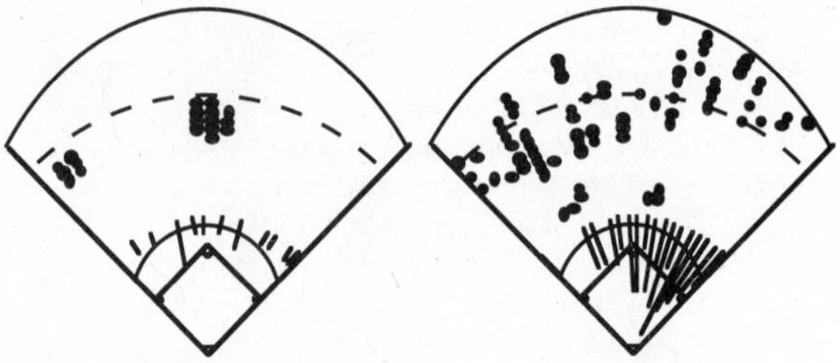

Vs. LHP Vs. RHP

1990 Situational Stats

	AB	H	HR	RBI	AVG		AB	H	HR	RBI	AVG
Home	148	43	2	18	.291	LHP	32	6	0	1	.188
Road	155	41	0	8	.265	RHP	271	78	2	25	.288
Day	129	37	1	9	.287	Sc Pos	63	15	1	23	.238
Night	174	47	1	17	.270	Clutch	45	17	0	3	.378

1990 Rankings (National League)

- 3rd lowest percentage of extra bases taken as a runner (26.5%)
- 5th highest batting average in the clutch (.378)
- Led the Giants in batting average in the clutch
- Led NL catchers in batting average on a 3-2 count (.286)

MIKE KINGERY

Position: RF/LF
Bats: L **Throws:** L
Ht: 6' 0" **Wt:** 180

Opening Day Age: 30
Born: 3/29/61 in St. James, MN
ML Seasons: 5

Overall Statistics

	G	AB	R	H	D	T	HR	RBI	SB	BB	SO	AVG
1990	105	207	24	61	7	1	0	24	6	12	19	.295
Career	375	969	122	256	49	10	15	105	24	77	129	.264

Where He Hits the Ball

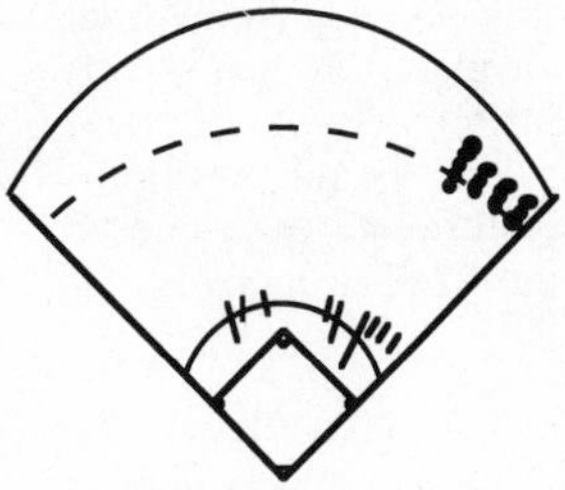

Vs. LHP

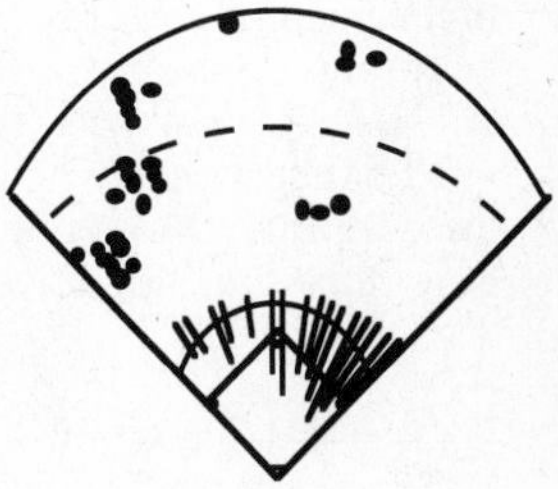

Vs. RHP

1990 Situational Stats

	AB	H	HR	RBI	AVG		AB	H	HR	RBI	AVG
Home	107	29	0	13	.271	LHP	25	10	0	4	.400
Road	100	32	0	11	.320	RHP	182	51	0	20	.280
Day	89	32	0	14	.360	Sc Pos	51	18	0	23	.353
Night	118	29	0	10	.246	Clutch	33	11	0	8	.333

1990 Rankings (National League)

- 5th highest percentage of extra bases taken as a runner (58.8%)
- Led the Giants in steals of third (2) and highest percentage of extra bases taken as a runner
- Led NL right fielders in highest percentage of extra bases taken as a runner

HITTING:

Giants manager Roger Craig, when asked why the team signed Mike Kingery as a free agent early last season, jokingly replied that it was because Kingery is balding and soon will look like his manager. The joke might have been on the Giants had they not signed Kingery, who had been released by the Seattle Mariners. While with the Mariners, he regressed after a promising (.280-9-52) rookie season in 1987.

Kingery, a left-handed hitter, played sparingly until Rick Leach was given a drug suspension early in August. At that point, Kingery took over the right field job against right-handed pitchers and his average soared. He was particularly effective in September, hitting .371 in 27 games. He also batted .353 with runners in scoring position.

Kingery has a tight, frill-free stroke that makes him a good breaking ball hitter, and his wrists are quick enough that he can react to the inside fastball. He showed no obvious weakness as a hitter, although the Giants would have liked him to take a few more pitches because he has such a good eye. He likes the ball down and in, which was one reason he batted .400 against the few left-handed pitchers he faced.

BASERUNNING:

Kingery doesn't have outstanding speed, but it's above average and he knows what to do with it. He stole six bases in seven tries last year, making up for his lack of speed by reading pitchers well and gauging their moves. He's only moderately aggressive in terms of taking the extra base, but he goes in hard on double play take-outs.

FIELDING:

The Giants knew they were getting an excellent defensive outfielder in Kingery, and he didn't disappoint them. He played right field as if he had grown up playing in Candlestick Park's maddening winds, and did a good job getting to balls in the corner. Kingery has such good range that he is considered the Giants' number-two center fielder, after Brett Butler. He throws with both velocity and accuracy.

OVERALL:

Kingery had a breakthrough season in 1990, and he proved to be one of the Giants' most complete, intelligent players. With Kevin Bass healthy and Leach apparently back in the picture, the Giants' outfield is crowded. But look for Kingery to stick around as an extra outfielder. He showed the Giants that he is capable of returning to his 1987 form.

PITCHING:

On a staff comprised largely of overachievers, Mike LaCoss perhaps is the best example of a pitcher who makes up in guile and toughness what he lacks in pure talent. LaCoss, 34, has been a .500 pitcher throughout his 11-season major league career, but he almost never has an outing that takes his team out of a game. His relatively poor strikeout-to-walk ratio (39 of each in '90) belies the fact that he's almost always around the plate, and at his best, he is right around the lower limit of the strike zone. That makes him ideal for Candlestick Park, where the high infield grass slows balls that are hit on the ground.

LaCoss is a fastball-sinker-slider pitcher who has cut down on the use of the split-finger fastball because of arm problems that he had in 1989. He doesn't change speeds much, and he concentrates on inducing ground balls. He prefers to work hitters low and inside early in the count, then zero in on the outside corner once he has moved the hitter off the plate. One can usually tell from LaCoss' back leg if he is about to have a good outing; because he is so tall, he must get good back-leg drive to keep the ball down. If he doesn't have good back-leg drive, he finishes high, and so does the ball.

HOLDING RUNNERS, FIELDING, HITTING:

LaCoss is among the Giants' poorer pitchers in most non-pitching phases of the game. Because of his build, he is somewhat awkward, and he uncoils slowly. That makes him an easy mark for most baserunners, although he has an adequate move to first and usually will help the catcher by paying a lot of attention to runners. LaCoss also fields his position awkwardly; he finishes spread out, and that makes it difficult for him to react to balls hit back up the middle. LaCoss is almost useless as a hitter; he had only one hit all last season. He is, however, a fine bunter.

OVERALL:

LaCoss never has been a big winner and has shown a tendency to be injury-prone. But Giants manager Roger Craig and general manager Al Rosen have always liked LaCoss because he never backs down to hitters. He's likely to be the Giants' fourth or fifth starter in 1990, and has added value because he has shown he can pitch in middle or short relief if necessary.

MIKE LaCOSS

Position: SP
Bats: R **Throws:** R
Ht: 6' 4" **Wt:** 200

Opening Day Age: 34
Born: 5/30/56 in Glendale, CA
ML Seasons: 13

Overall Statistics

	W	L	ERA	G	GS	Sv	IP	H	R	BB	SO	HR
1990	6	4	3.94	13	12	0	77.2	75	37	39	39	5
Career	97	98	3.93	397	238	12	1692.1	1725	846	701	753	95

How Often He Throws Strikes

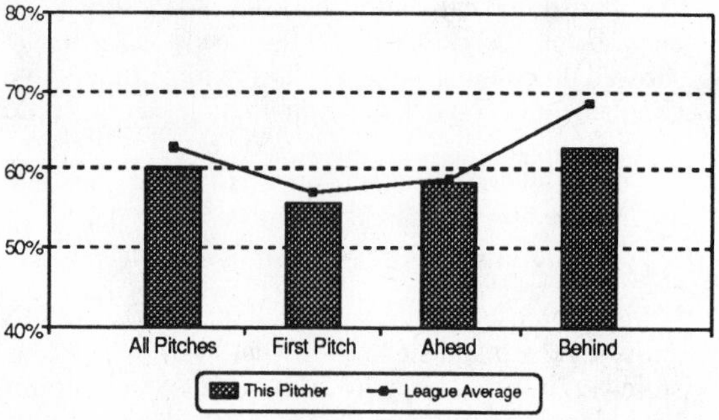

1990 Situational Stats

	W	L	ERA	Sv	IP		AB	H	HR	RBI	AVG
Home	2	2	3.67	0	27.0	LHB	179	44	3	16	.246
Road	4	2	4.09	0	50.2	RHB	111	31	2	16	.279
Day	1	1	1.72	0	15.2	Sc Pos	72	19	2	26	.264
Night	5	3	4.50	0	62.0	Clutch	21	2	0	0	.095

1990 Rankings (National League)

- Led the Giants in sacrifice bunts as a hitter (8)

GREG LITTON

Position: RF/2B
Bats: R **Throws:** R
Ht: 6' 0" **Wt:** 175

Opening Day Age: 26
Born: 7/13/64 in New Orleans, LA
ML Seasons: 2

HITTING:

A right-handed hitting utility man, Greg Litton was used largely as a platoon player with Rick Leach and later Mike Kingery in right field last year while Kevin Bass was injured. Litton's .245 hitting was about what the Giants expected from him. He went to the opposite field well when he was pitched on the outer half, and showed some power to both gaps. He usually was played slightly around to right, and in the gaps.

Fastballs on his fists bother Litton. He handles breaking pitches adequately overall, but his weakness with fastballs set him up for change-ups and breaking balls low and away because he tries to open up too quickly in an effort to adjust to the inside pitches. He is a first-ball hitter who needs to draw more walks and cut down on his strikeouts. The Giants also would like him to hit the ball more on the ground.

BASERUNNING:

Litton has slightly better-than-average speed, but he is not a good baserunner. He tends to be tentative on the bases, although he goes in hard on double play breakups. He is not a base stealing threat. In fact, he was picked off in more than one non-stealing situation last season. This is the area of his game in which he probably needs the most improvement.

FIELDING:

Litton, a career utility man, has played every position except pitcher, center field and first base during two seasons with the Giants. He came up as a second baseman, but turned out to be surprisingly adept in right field. He showed a very strong, accurate arm and didn't seemed cowed by the winds that make right field the most treacherous of the three outfield positions at Candlestick. His range is acceptable, and he doesn't hesitate to leave his feet or crash into walls in pursuit of flies.

OVERALL:

In 1990, Greg Litton turned out to be the right-handed hitting clone of Ernest Riles, another useful utility man. Litton has one dimension that Riles lacks: he took up catching a couple of seasons ago, and that makes him particularly valuable to a manager who maneuvers personnel as much as Craig does. Litton will probably never play regularly in the major leagues, at least not until he hits for a higher average and begins to draw more walks and use his speed.

Overall Statistics

	G	AB	R	H	D	T	HR	RBI	SB	BB	SO	AVG
1990	93	204	17	50	9	1	1	24	1	11	45	.245
Career	164	347	29	86	14	4	5	41	1	18	74	.248

Where He Hits the Ball

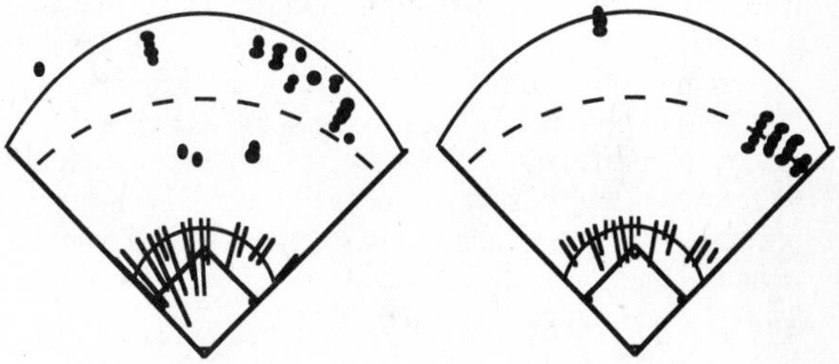

Vs. LHP **Vs. RHP**

1990 Situational Stats

	AB	H	HR	RBI	AVG		AB	H	HR	RBI	AVG
Home	102	29	0	15	.284	LHP	139	39	1	15	.281
Road	102	21	1	9	.206	RHP	65	11	0	9	.169
Day	75	21	1	10	.280	Sc Pos	62	15	0	23	.242
Night	129	29	0	14	.225	Clutch	50	12	0	9	.240

1990 Rankings (National League)

- Did not rank near the top or bottom in any category

KEVIN MITCHELL

Position: LF
Bats: R **Throws:** R
Ht: 5'11" **Wt:** 210

Opening Day Age: 29
Born: 1/13/62 in San Diego, CA
ML Seasons: 6

Overall Statistics

	G	AB	R	H	D	T	HR	RBI	SB	BB	SO	AVG
1990	140	524	90	152	24	2	35	93	4	58	87	.290
Career	688	2378	369	661	125	19	135	412	24	274	439	.278

Where He Hits the Ball

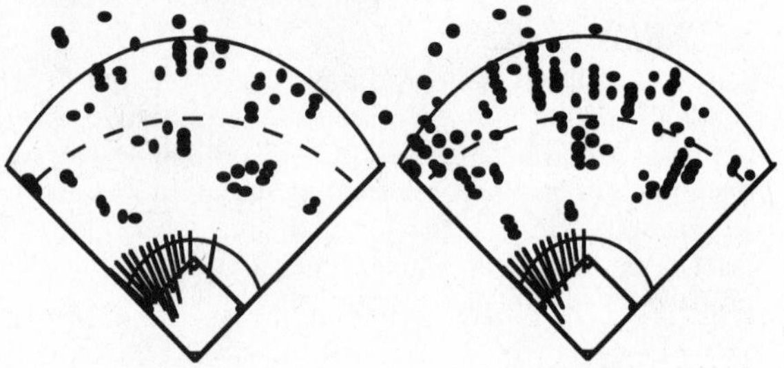

Vs. LHP   Vs. RHP

1990 Situational Stats

	AB	H	HR	RBI	AVG		AB	H	HR	RBI	AVG
Home	241	67	15	39	.278	LHP	170	52	10	29	.306
Road	283	85	20	54	.300	RHP	354	100	25	64	.282
Day	206	61	10	32	.296	Sc Pos	154	34	2	49	.221
Night	318	91	25	61	.286	Clutch	88	31	8	17	.352

1990 Rankings (National League)

- 2nd in HR frequency (15.0 ABs per HR)
- 3rd in home runs (35), slugging percentage (.544) and lowest groundball/flyball ratio (.74)
- Led the Giants in home runs, slugging percentage, HR frequency and batting average on the road (.300)
- Led NL left fielders in home runs, HR frequency, batting average in the clutch (.352), batting average vs. left-handed pitchers (.306), slugging percentage vs. right-handed pitchers (.542) and on-base average vs. left-handed pitchers (.395)

HITTING:

Kevin Mitchell was only slightly less of a threat in 1990 than he was during his MVP season in 1989. He challenged for the National League home run title, finishing with 35, and was among the league leaders in RBIs until a chronic wrist problem and some leg injuries curtailed his effectiveness late in the season. He submitted to three cortisone shots during the season and had wrist surgery two days before the end of the season.

Mitchell has become a hitter who can manipulate the bat as well as use it as a bludgeon. He likes to extend his arms and will take the outside pitch to right field, although he has a tendency to reach for outside pitches and get under them for fly balls and pop-ups. He usually is played slightly around to left and, of course, very deep.

Mitchell stands almost on top of the plate and opens up to the ball; by doing that, the inside pitch becomes almost an up-the-middle offering for him. Opponents tend to jam him, partly because he stands so close to the plate and partly because his wrist problems are well known. He has improved as a curveball hitter because he keeps his hands and weight centered even as he is opening his hips. It's best to pitch him low and away and to change speeds constantly.

BASERUNNING:

Mitchell has surprising speed and runs the bases very aggressively -- sometimes too aggressively. He is thrown out on the bases more often than manager Roger Craig would like, although Craig certainly would never complain about the way Mitchell approaches home plate collisions and double play take-outs. He doesn't get a great jump on pitchers and was only four for 11 in steal tries last year.

FIELDING:

Mitchell's defense in left field is only slightly above average. He gives full effort in the field, is sure-handed and will go into the wall without hesitation. His problem is that his range is somewhat limited, especially to his right. His arm is also weak, although he doesn't miss many cutoff men.

OVERALL:

Mitchell, who assured his future with the Giants by signing a four-year, $15 million contract on August 31, is a tough, hard-nosed individual who will play injured without complaint. Expect him to be in a Giants uniform for a long time to come.

PITCHING:

No pitcher on the Giants -- and perhaps no pitcher in the major leagues -- was hurt more by last year's spring training lockout than Rick Reuschel. Now 41, Reuschel has habitually been a slow starter, partly because he's a heavy-set man whose legs and muscle tone need to be strengthened during the spring. He didn't get much of a chance to work out due to the lockout, and at no time during the early part of the season did he resemble the pitcher who was the National League's starting pitcher in the 1989 All-Star Game.

After losing six of eight decisions, Reuschel suffered a knee injury on May 27 and underwent arthroscopic surgery that prompted talk of retirement. He returned to the roster September 17 and pitched a few games thereafter. He was impressive, and manager Roger Craig indicated that Big Daddy's spot in the rotation is his to lose this spring.

Reuschel at his best carves the plate like a chef slicing a rump roast. He changes speeds constantly, mixing in an occasional curve or slider, and can sink the ball or ride it depending on the need. However, Reuschel must set up his changes in speed with a no-nonsense fastball, which he still can throw in the 90 MPH range. The lack of spring training hurt him most in velocity: he couldn't throw the fastball with his usual authority, and hitters began waiting for the reduced-speed pitches. He's almost always around the plate, inviting first-pitch swinging, and once the hitters stopped respecting his fastball, Reuschel couldn't fool anybody.

HOLDING RUNNERS, FIELDING, HITTING:

Because Reuschel's motion is so compact, it's very difficult for baserunners to get a good jump on him. He has a very quick slide-step move and lets runners know that he has their attention by throwing to first frequently. The portly Reuschel is surprisingly agile around the mound, plays the bunt well and has no trouble covering first base. He's more dangerous at the plate than most pitchers, although he's more inclined to take pitches and try to draw walks than to hack.

OVERALL:

Despite his advanced age, there's no reason to think Reuschel can't regain his 1989 effectiveness if his knee is OK and if he has the benefit of a full spring training. He'll need to work more on conditioning than he has in the past, however. Don't count him out just yet.

RICK REUSCHEL

Position: SP
Bats: R **Throws:** R
Ht: 6' 3" **Wt:** 240

Opening Day Age: 41
Born: 5/16/49 in Quincy, IL
ML Seasons: 18

Overall Statistics

	W	L	ERA	G	GS	Sv	IP	H	R	BB	SO	HR
1990	3	6	3.93	15	13	1	87.0	102	40	31	49	8
Career	214	189	3.37	553	528	5	3539.0	3571	1489	928	2011	221

How Often He Throws Strikes

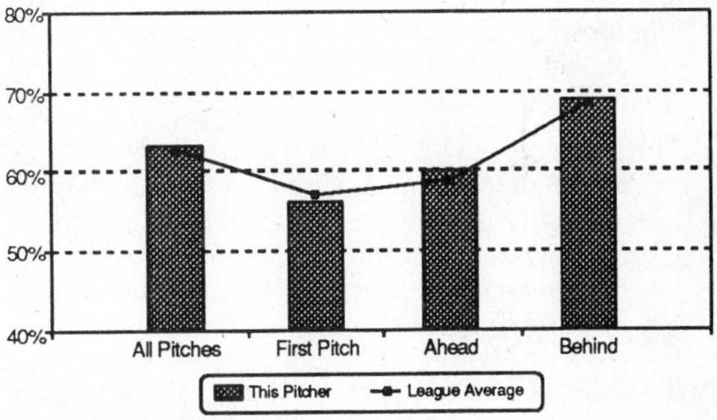

1990 Situational Stats

	W	L	ERA	Sv	IP		AB	H	HR	RBI	AVG
Home	2	1	3.14	0	43.0	LHB	206	67	6	23	.325
Road	1	5	4.70	1	44.0	RHB	137	35	2	15	.255
Day	2	3	4.12	0	39.1	Sc Pos	81	20	1	28	.247
Night	1	3	3.78	1	47.2	Clutch	27	6	1	4	.222

1990 Rankings (National League)

- 8th highest batting average allowed vs. left-handed batters (.325)

HITTING:

In 1990, Ernest Riles found himself in a situation that he admitted was frustrating at times. Riles can do so many things that Giants' manager Roger Craig didn't want to risk starting him because he was so indispensable off the bench. Riles, 30, was perhaps the National League's most dangerous pinch hitter in 1990. He had eight pinch hits in 12 tries during one stretch, and he led the major leagues with four pinch hit home runs, tying a club record. He became only the second player in the franchise's 109-year history to have back-to-back pinch hit home runs.

Riles' success as a pinch hitter can be traced to the one-chance syndrome. Coming in cold, knowing that he'll probably get only one at-bat, and knowing that the pitcher probably will be around the plate with him, Riles usually swings at the first pitch that faintly resembles a strike. He has a big swing that can make him look bad against breaking balls, but he's a good adjustment hitter who will put the ball in play somewhere when he's hacking in earnest.

The problem is that Riles lost that combative attitude when he started last year. He took too many pitches and too often found himself behind in the count, whereupon pitchers threw him more curveballs that caught him off balance.

BASERUNNING:

Riles has good speed and is an intelligent baserunner. He'll take the extra base and, like most of the Giants, goes in hard in take-out and collision situations. The Giants don't ask him to try to steal, which is just as well since he's been thrown out 23 times in 38 lifetime attempts.

FIELDING:

Riles started at second base, shortstop and third base during the 1990 season and is capable of playing the outfield. Riles, by instinct, is a second baseman, and his range is his greatest asset. He doesn't have a particularly strong arm, but it is accurate and he gets rid of the ball in a hurry. He has sure hands and an excellent first step toward the ball.

OVERALL:

The Giants, to the surprise of many, have gotten good value in the trade that brought Riles to San Francisco in exchange for Jeffrey Leonard. Though he's an extremely valuable bench player, he's made no secret of the fact he would like to play more. The Giants have other utility men, and it's possible they will trade Riles to a team that would make him a starter.

ERNEST RILES

Position: 2B/SS
Bats: L **Throws:** R
Ht: 6' 1" **Wt:** 180

Opening Day Age: 30
Born: 10/2/60 in Bainbridge, GA
ML Seasons: 6

Overall Statistics

	G	AB	R	H	D	T	HR	RBI	SB	BB	SO	AVG
1990	92	155	22	31	2	1	8	21	0	26	26	.200
Career	678	2019	259	534	75	16	37	228	15	191	316	.264

Where He Hits the Ball

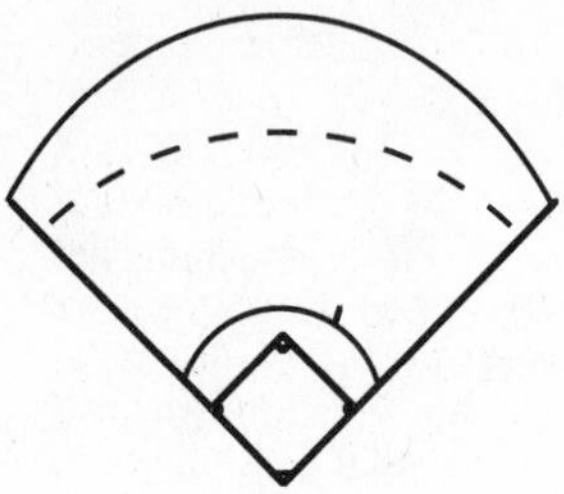

Vs. LHP

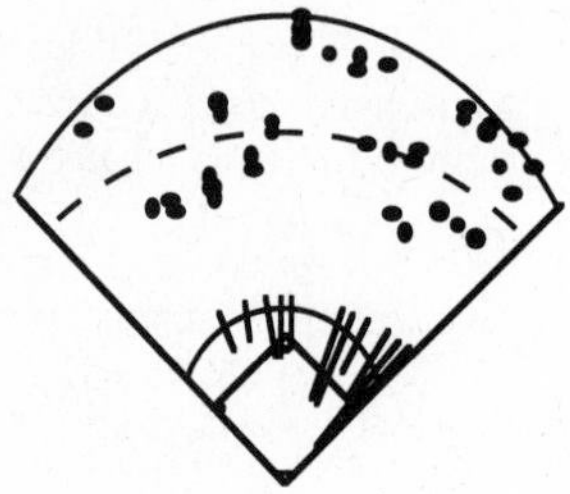

Vs. RHP

1990 Situational Stats

	AB	H	HR	RBI	AVG		AB	H	HR	RBI	AVG
Home	72	17	7	14	.236	LHP	8	2	1	3	.250
Road	83	14	1	7	.169	RHP	147	29	7	18	.197
Day	50	7	0	3	.140	Sc Pos	37	7	2	14	.189
Night	105	24	8	18	.229	Clutch	28	4	1	2	.143

1990 Rankings (National League)

- 1st in worst batting average on a 3-1 count (.000)

PITCHING:

The fact that Don Robinson -- alias "Don Cortisone" -- is even pitching at age 33 is something of a phenomenon. He has undergone seven operations, pitches with a massive knee brace and has an arthritic hip. One writer described his body as looking like "the French countryside after the Third Battle of the Marne." Nevertheless, Robinson endures, and his 1990 season was a pretty good one, although it was shortened by knee surgery and ended with a 4.57 ERA inflated by a handful of horrid outings.

Robinson has good overall stuff -- sinking fastball, curve, slider, change -- that he varies by altering his arm angles and speeds. He throws fairly hard and is almost always around the plate. It's best to come to the plate ready to hit because Robinson walks few, strikes out few and usually doesn't throw a lot of pitches in a game.

Robinson is something of a rarity in that he seems to do his best work when he's behind in the count. That's because he's primarily a fly ball pitcher. If a hitter gets ahead in the count and sees a fastball in the upper part of the strike zone, he'll usually go after it. This plays into Robinson's hands, because he changes speeds so well that he induces a lot of harmless flies. With that style, however, Robinson also gives up a lot of homers.

HOLDING RUNNERS, FIELDING, HITTING:

Robinson is one of the most difficult Giants to take baserunning liberties against. He doesn't have a quick release, but he has a deceptive move that he doesn't telegraph, and he'll vary his techniques to keep the runner guessing. Robinson doesn't look athletic, but he fields his position decently. He's also one of the best hitting pitchers in the major leagues. He has 12 career homers, including a pinch homer last year that was the first pinch hit HR by a pitcher since 1971.

OVERALL:

Of all the Giants pitchers who were injured during 1990, Don Robinson was probably missed the most. The team missed his penchant for doing his best pitching in the most important games, and they missed his needling and good humor in the clubhouse. When he returned, he probably was the closest thing the Giants had to a cornerstone starting pitcher. Robinson's hip problem, in particular, always makes him vulnerable to injury, but as long as he's healthy, manager Roger Craig won't hesitate to send him to the mound.

DON ROBINSON

Position: SP
Bats: R **Throws:** R
Ht: 6' 4" **Wt:** 231

Opening Day Age: 33
Born: 6/8/57 in Ashland, KY
ML Seasons: 13

Overall Statistics

	W	L	ERA	G	GS	Sv	IP	H	R	BB	SO	HR
1990	10	7	4.57	26	25	0	157.2	173	84	41	78	18
Career	102	93	3.70	479	202	56	1776.1	1703	807	586	1147	156

How Often He Throws Strikes

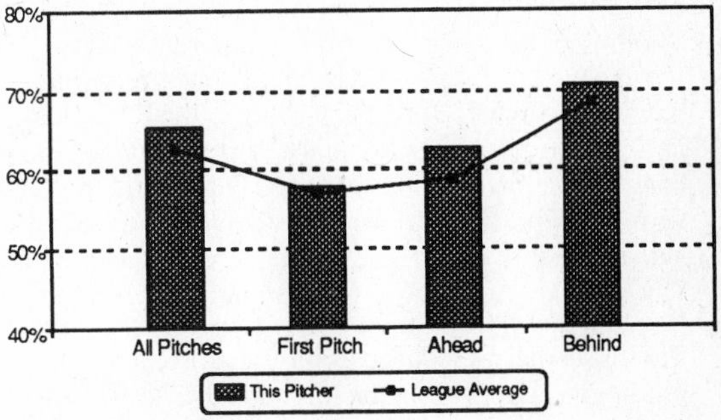

1990 Situational Stats

	W	L	ERA	Sv	IP		AB	H	HR	RBI	AVG
Home	4	1	5.04	0	60.2	LHB	369	105	12	43	.285
Road	6	6	4.27	0	97.0	RHB	249	68	6	35	.273
Day	2	2	5.07	0	60.1	Sc Pos	143	44	6	57	.308
Night	8	5	4.25	0	97.1	Clutch	77	20	0	6	.260

1990 Rankings (National League)

- 4th highest batting average allowed with runners in scoring position (.308)
- 5th in pickoff throws (209)
- Led the Giants in complete games (4), home runs allowed (18), stolen bases allowed (19) and runners caught stealing (8)

HITTING:

Robby Thompson as a hitter gives the Giants some things most teams don't expect from their second baseman. That's both good and bad. On the plus side, Thompson has fine power for a middle infielder. He's given the Giants three double-figure home run seasons in the past four, and his total of 15 in 1990 was a career high, as was his RBI total of 56.

The downside to Thompson's batting portfolio is the fact he continues to strike out at an alarming rate, though his 96 Ks in 1990 were an improvement over his total of 133 in '89. He doesn't have a lot of plate discipline, and he has a constricted, too-much-arm swing that makes it difficult for him to extend the bat against an outside fastball. When he hits the ball to right, he's generally merely jabbing under it; most of the fly balls he hits to the right side are pop-ups or easy fly balls.

Thompson has excellent power down the left-field line and up the left-center field alley. He's quick-handed enough to turn on the high, inside fastball, he's assertive enough to make a pitcher pay for a hanging curveball, and he gets the bat around quickly enough to hit the low, inside fastball through the left side of the infield.

BASERUNNING:

Thompson hasn't let his chronic back problems affect his aggressiveness on the base paths. He'll take a chance, sometimes unnecessarily, when trying to take the extra base, and he goes into take-out situations without qualms. He's had an excellent success rate in his steal attempts in recent years, going 14-for-18 last year.

FIELDING:

Thompson's strength is that he probably turns the double play as well as any second baseman in the National League. He is utterly fearless and can get something on his throw from virtually any arm angle. Thompson's range is perhaps slightly below average, especially to his right. He uses his instincts rather than his quickness to get to the hole between first and second. His arm strength is very good.

OVERALL:

Craig finds himself sitting Thompson down a lot more than Thompson would like -- either because of Thompson's ailing back or his frequent strikeout binges. Thompson nevertheless remains one of the best overall second basemen in the NL. Craig likes his toughness and his ability to respond to pressure. Thompson's back problems, however, make his long-range status somewhat iffy.

ROBBY THOMPSON

Position: 2B
Bats: R **Throws:** R
Ht: 5'11" **Wt:** 170

Opening Day Age: 28
Born: 5/10/62 in West Palm Beach, FL
ML Seasons: 5

Overall Statistics

	G	AB	R	H	D	T	HR	RBI	SB	BB	SO	AVG
1990	144	498	67	122	22	3	15	56	14	34	96	.245
Career	711	2491	359	639	125	28	52	245	68	207	543	.257

Where He Hits the Ball

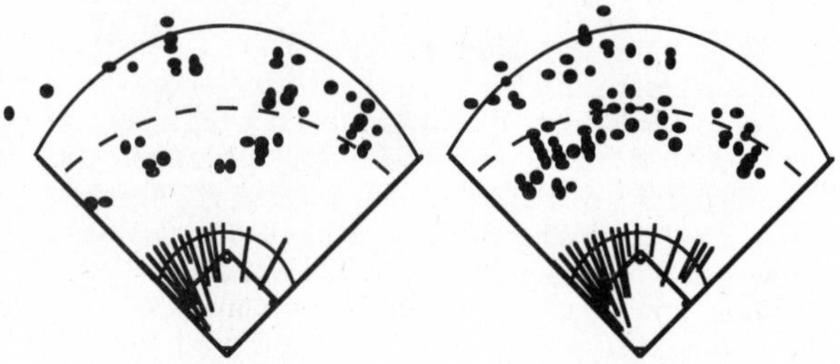

Vs. LHP　　Vs. RHP

1990 Situational Stats

	AB	H	HR	RBI	AVG		AB	H	HR	RBI	AVG
Home	248	66	8	37	.266	LHP	183	50	8	27	.273
Road	250	56	7	19	.224	RHP	315	72	7	29	.229
Day	207	53	7	26	.256	Sc Pos	121	30	3	41	.248
Night	291	69	8	30	.237	Clutch	88	21	3	13	.239

1990 Rankings (National League)

- 4th lowest batting average on the road (.224)
- 6th in hit by pitch (6)
- 7th lowest on-base percentage (.299)
- 9th lowest batting average (.245)
- Led the Giants in sacrifice bunts (8) and batting average with the bases loaded (.308)
- Led NL second basemen in sacrifice bunts and hit by pitch (6)

PITCHING:

One of many well-worn pitchers acquired in desperation by the Giants in 1990, Mark Thurmond turned out to be one of their most valuable fire-sale pickups. Thurmond, 34, was acquired from the Houston organization in April and was called up by the Giants on May 4. He was used mostly in middle relief, but later in the season emerged as a lefty-vs.-lefty specialist, and even served as the closer for a while when Steve Bedrosian was being shelled and Jeff Brantley was suffering from shoulder problems. He functioned adequately, and at times splendidly, before he was sidelined late in August by a neck problem.

Thurmond has an ordinary fastball, curve, slider, and change-up; the key for him is changing speeds. He is neither fast nor precise enough to overpower hitters or paint the corners, but he's most effective when he keeps hitters off balance with changes of speed. He's good at not putting the same pitch in the same place during a given at-bat.

Thurmond faces many lefties, and he usually tries to get them leaning with a slider or a curve outside, and then he busts the fastball inside. He also throws the change to set up the fastball, and his pattern generally is effective because the hitters don't know quite what to expect from him. He has less success against right-handed batters, who are less apt to open up early against him when he throws offspeed pitches.

HOLDING RUNNERS, FIELDING, HITTING:

Thurmond is well below average for a lefthander with regard to holding runners. He has a very slow delivery that makes him easy to run against, and he doesn't pay as much attention to runners as he should. He fields his position acceptably, but is slow to cover first because he's off balance when he delivers the ball. Thurmond is a terrible hitter, even for a pitcher.

OVERALL:

Thurmond has pitched for five organizations in the past five years, and never has approached the level of excellence he attained in 1984, when he helped the Padres to the World Series. But he is a good bet to win a place on the 1991 Giants' staff, mainly because manager Roger Craig has said he wants at least two and preferably three lefthanders in the bullpen. He had a decent season in 1990 before hurting his neck, and Craig tends to lean toward veterans like Thurmond over younger pitchers.

MARK THURMOND

Position: RP
Bats: L **Throws:** L
Ht: 6' 0" **Wt:** 190

Opening Day Age: 34
Born: 9/12/56 in Houston, TX
ML Seasons: 8

Overall Statistics

	W	L	ERA	G	GS	Sv	IP	H	R	BB	SO	HR
1990	2	3	3.34	43	0	4	56.2	53	26	18	24	6
Career	40	46	3.69	314	97	21	837.2	890	395	262	320	69

How Often He Throws Strikes

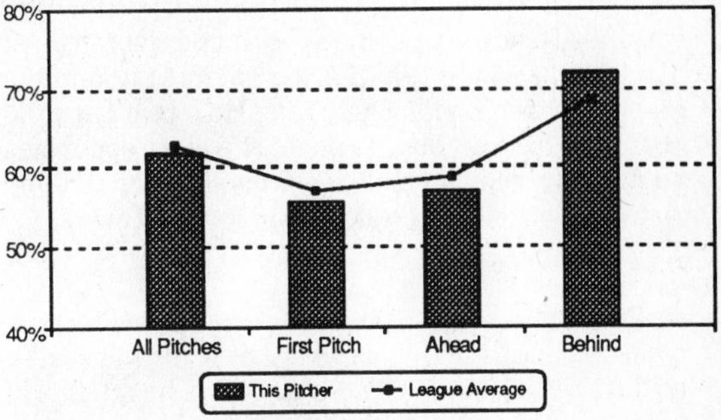

1990 Situational Stats

	W	L	ERA	Sv	IP		AB	H	HR	RBI	AVG
Home	2	1	3.00	1	27.0	LHB	60	14	3	10	.233
Road	0	2	3.64	3	29.2	RHB	146	39	3	22	.267
Day	0	2	3.60	2	25.0	Sc Pos	62	13	0	23	.210
Night	2	1	3.13	2	31.2	Clutch	77	15	2	13	.195

1990 Rankings (National League)

- 11th in holds (8)
- Led the Giants in holds

JOSE URIBE

Position: SS
Bats: B **Throws:** R
Ht: 5'10" **Wt:** 165

Opening Day Age: 31
Born: 1/21/60 in San Cristobal, Dominican Republic
ML Seasons: 7

HITTING:

For six seasons, Jose Uribe has quietly provided the Giants with a dependable-if-unobtrusive number-eight hitter. A career .241 hitter entering last season, Uribe surprised many by batting .308 in April and .293 in May. A .184 July dropped him back to a more accustomed level, and manager Roger Craig returned to his habit of pinch hitting for Uribe late in games.

Uribe, a switch-hitter, has always had problems from the left side, and even became a righty-only swinger for a time in 1989. As a lefthander, Uribe is a punch hitter who tries to go to the left side and hit the ball on the ground. He does both those things fairly well, and gets a lot of leg and seeing-eye hits. However, he has trouble with breaking balls and hasn't shown he can consistently fight off pitches up and in. What little power he has -- and it's very little -- is from the left side.

Uribe also tends to go to the left side as a right-handed hitter, but he winds up hitting the ball into the air more often than the Giants would like. He's best when he goes with the low, outside pitch, and most opponents go with the standard pattern for number-eight hitters -- fastball up and in, breaking ball low and away.

BASERUNNING:

Uribe still has better-than-average speed, but is more quick than fast. He isn't a base stealing threat because he doesn't use that quickness as well as he might. He tends to be tentative on the base paths.

FIELDING:

Uribe has been the glue holding the Giants' infield together since becoming their regular shortstop in 1985. He compensates for his relative lack of quickness to his right by squaring slightly around in that direction as the ball is pitched. That helps Uribe get to balls in the hole that his range -- which is only average -- might otherwise preclude him from reaching. Uribe is extremely sure-handed, and has both a quick release and an accurate arm.

OVERALL:

Uribe will probably be able to stave off challenges to his job for another year. At 31, though, he isn't getting any quicker, and the Giants' organization has three outstanding prospects -- Andres Santana, Mike Benjamin and Royce Clayton -- nearing readiness at his position. The Giants probably will look seriously at moving Uribe into a utility role or out of the organization by 1992 or 1993.

Overall Statistics

	G	AB	R	H	D	T	HR	RBI	SB	BB	SO	AVG
1990	138	415	35	103	8	6	1	24	5	29	49	.248
Career	837	2618	256	635	81	29	16	191	68	214	362	.243

Where He Hits the Ball

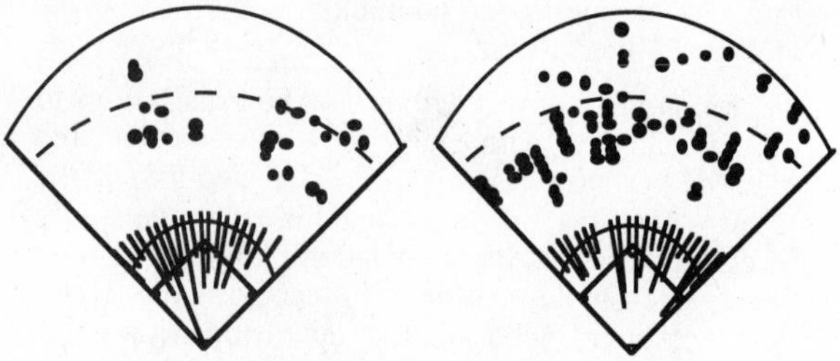

Vs. LHP   Vs. RHP

1990 Situational Stats

	AB	H	HR	RBI	AVG		AB	H	HR	RBI	AVG
Home	197	44	0	8	.223	LHP	142	40	0	7	.282
Road	218	59	1	16	.271	RHP	273	63	1	17	.231
Day	167	36	0	7	.216	Sc Pos	102	22	1	21	.216
Night	248	67	1	17	.270	Clutch	57	12	0	2	.211

1990 Rankings (National League)

- 3rd lowest batting average with the bases loaded (.077)
- 8th lowest slugging percentage vs. left-handed pitchers (.324)
- 9th lowest batting average with runners in scoring position (.216)
- Led the Giants in intentional walks (13), batting average on an 0-2 count (.235)
- Led NL shortstops in caught stealing (9) and intentional walks (13)

FUTURE MVP?

MATT D. WILLIAMS

Position: 3B
Bats: R **Throws:** R
Ht: 6' 2" **Wt:** 205

Opening Day Age: 25
Born: 11/28/65 in Bishop, CA
ML Seasons: 4

HITTING:

It was easy to forget that 1990 was Matt Williams' first full season in the major leagues. Even though he's only 25, he physically looks at least 10 years older. He also hit like a time-tested veteran throughout most of the season, leading the National League in RBIs with 122 and maintaining a decent average despite a few epochal slumps that already have given him a reputation as a streaky hitter.

Though he had an outstanding season in 1990, Williams still hasn't had much success adjusting to breaking balls. His strikeout total of 138 was the second-highest in the league, and most of them came when he guessed fastball and found himself flailing at a breaking ball. Manager Roger Craig surprisingly had him initiate hit-and-run plays on several occasions, reasoning that it might help Williams concentrate better on making contact instead of trying to hit the ball through the ozone layer.

Despite Williams' trouble with the curveball, though, don't hang one to him. He has quick wrists and can hit the ball out in any direction if he keeps his weight back. His best power -- and he has loads of it -- is to left-center, but he will hit the fastball up the middle and to the opposite field.

BASERUNNING:

Williams is not an accomplished baserunner, and took the Giants out of a number of innings by overestimating his speed, which is average. Like most of the Giants, he is willing to try a take-out and doesn't shy from home plate confrontations. The Giants do not ask him to steal often, although they occasionally hit-and-run with him on base.

FIELDING:

Craig calls Williams the best defensive third baseman in the National League; it probably is true that Williams can match his arm strength and sure-handedness with anybody. Craig doesn't mention however, that Williams' range isn't that much above average, although he does a good job on pop flies in Candlestick Park's vast foul ground. Despite this, he is among the best defensive third basemen in baseball.

OVERALL:

Even when Williams got off to a .130 start in 1989 and was sent to the minors in May, Craig and general manager Al Rosen kept assuring people that he would be an All-Star before long. Williams proved them correct in 1990. He's one of the best young power hitters in baseball, and probably the best third baseman the Giants have had since moving to San Francisco in 1958.

Overall Statistics

	G	AB	R	H	D	T	HR	RBI	SB	BB	SO	AVG
1990	159	617	87	171	27	2	33	122	7	33	138	.277
Career	379	1310	163	308	60	6	67	212	12	71	319	.235

Where He Hits the Ball

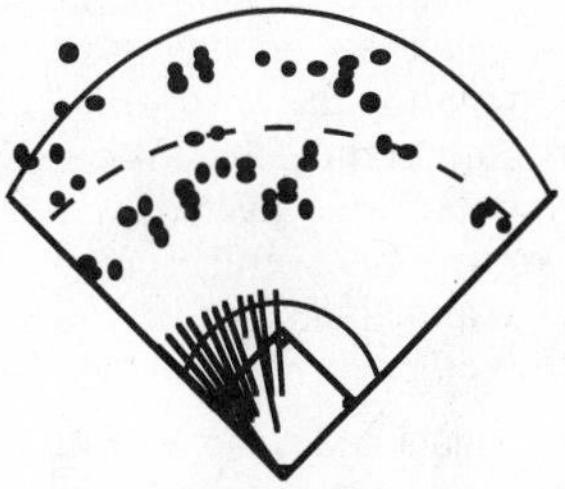

Vs. LHP

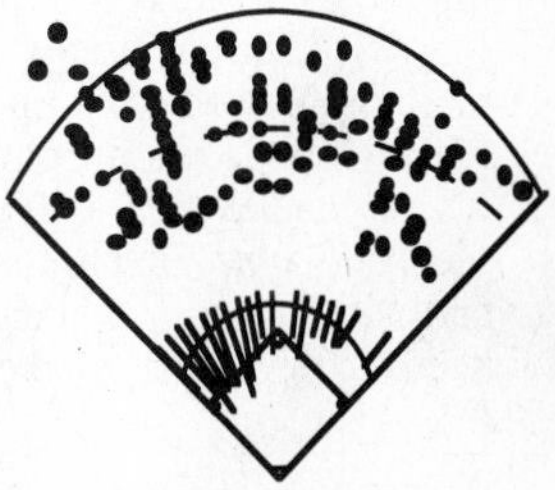

Vs. RHP

1990 Situational Stats

	AB	H	HR	RBI	AVG		AB	H	HR	RBI	AVG
Home	303	82	20	63	.271	LHP	208	59	12	48	.284
Road	314	89	13	59	.283	RHP	409	112	21	74	.274
Day	257	75	17	56	.292	Sc Pos	157	52	11	90	.331
Night	360	96	16	66	.267	Clutch	100	23	3	13	.230

1990 Rankings (National League)

- 1st in RBIs (122) and lowest percentage of pitches taken (40.3%)
- 2nd in hit by pitch (7), strikeouts (138)
- 4th in home runs (33), total bases (301) and highest percentage of swings that missed (29.4%)
- Led the Giants in doubles (27), total bases, RBIs, hit by pitch, strikeouts, GDPs (13) and batting average with runners in scoring position (.331)
- Led NL third basemen in home runs, total bases, RBIs, hit by pitch, strikeouts, slugging percentage (.488), HR frequency (18.7 ABs per HR) and batting average with runners in scoring position

PITCHING:

At the start of the 1990 season, the Giants didn't seem to have any use for Trevor Wilson. However, by the end of the season, they had used him in a multitude of capacities. Wilson spent parts of the 1988 and 1989 season with the Giants, and did not distinguish himself during those call-ups or during spring training last year. The Giants sent him down at the start of the season, and came close to trading him (and not Russ Swan) to Seattle for Gary Eave.

That turned out to be one of the Giants' best non-decisions of the year. Wilson went to Phoenix with instructions to develop pitches to complement his fastball. After successfully doing so, he was brought back early in the season and proceeded to win his first six decisions as a starter.

Then Wilson bogged down. He tended to come up high in the strike zone with his fastball because of his low leg kick and drops his hands lower than most pitchers. Wilson often missed high in the strike zone, forcing him to pitch from behind in the count. When his mechanics were right, however, the fastball was plenty tough. Wilson also throws an average curve and will dabble with a change and slider, but he still needs to develop a good offspeed pitch.

Late in the season, when the Giants had a shortage of lefthanders in the bullpen, manager Roger Craig moved Wilson to the set-up relief role. The confrontational nature of relief pitching seemed to fit Wilson well, because his best pitch still is his fastball. Craig has indicated that Wilson could well begin 1991 in the bullpen.

HOLDING RUNNERS, FIELDING, HITTING:

Because Wilson's motion enables him to square his shoulders to the plate after his release, he is a good fielder. His move to first good, and opponents have trouble running on him. Wilson at the plate makes decent contact for somebody who has done little batting. He takes his hacks, although he is somewhat less than graceful.

OVERALL:

The Giants have more starters than they need, and the use of Wilson in the rotation last year was a stopgap measure -- his 6-0 start notwithstanding. Look for the Giants to use him as one of their left-handed set-up men this season, and as a spot starter only if they again have injury problems. He should be prominent in the Giants' plans for 1991.

TREVOR WILSON

Position: SP/RP
Bats: L **Throws:** L
Ht: 6' 0" **Wt:** 175
Opening Day Age: 24
Born: 6/7/66 in Torrance, CA
ML Seasons: 3

Overall Statistics

	W	L	ERA	G	GS	Sv	IP	H	R	BB	SO	HR
1990	8	7	4.00	27	17	0	110.1	87	52	49	66	11
Career	10	12	4.09	45	25	0	171.2	140	86	81	103	14

How Often He Throws Strikes

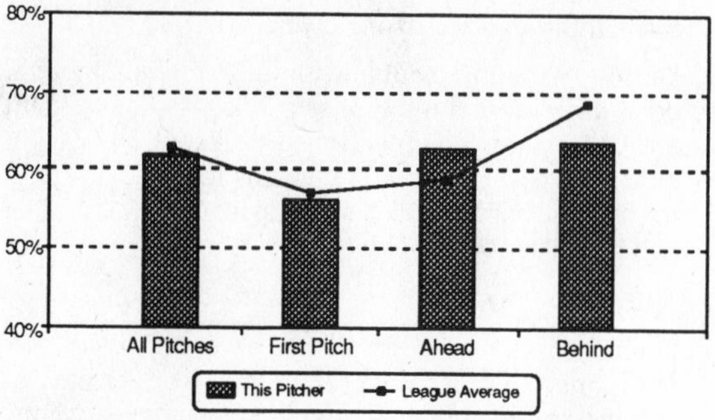

1990 Situational Stats

	W	L	ERA	Sv	IP		AB	H	HR	RBI	AVG
Home	5	3	2.88	0	68.2	LHB	64	14	1	8	.219
Road	3	4	5.83	0	41.2	RHB	335	73	10	36	.218
Day	4	1	4.06	0	31.0	Sc Pos	71	24	5	37	.338
Night	4	6	3.97	0	79.1	Clutch	54	8	0	1	.148

1990 Rankings (National League)

- 3rd lowest batting average allowed vs. right-handed batters (.218)
- Led the Giants in shutouts (2), runners caught stealing (8) and lowest batting average allowed vs. right-handed batters

DAVE ANDERSON

Position: SS/2B
Bats: R **Throws:** R
Ht: 6' 2" **Wt:** 191

Opening Day Age: 30
Born: 8/1/60 in Louisville, KY
ML Seasons: 8

Overall Statistics

	G	AB	R	H	D	T	HR	RBI	SB	BB	SO	AVG
1990	60	100	14	35	5	1	1	6	1	3	20	.350
Career	722	1716	210	410	64	10	14	122	47	190	285	.239

HITTING, FIELDING, BASERUNNING:

In 1990, Dave Anderson had by far the best offensive season of his major league career, hitting a remarkable .350 in 100 at-bats. Anderson, signed as a free agent after seven seasons with Los Angeles, showed himself to be an all-fields hitter who could milk a count until he got the pitch he wanted. He became a particularly good breaking ball hitter in 1990 because his mechanics virtually are waste-free. That helped him stay on-balance when pitchers changed speeds on him.

Anderson was a fine baserunner early in his career before back problems began to manifest themselves. He still runs adequately and doesn't make mental mistakes on the bases, but isn't much of a threat to steal. He can play all four infield positions, and received starts at first base, second base and shortstop in 1990. He originally was a shortstop, but seems most comfortable at second base now because that position accentuates his strength -- his range -- while minimizing his weakness -- a relatively weak arm. Anderson does get rid of the ball quickly, though, and has sure hands.

OVERALL:

When Anderson signed a two-year free agent contract with the Giants before last season, he probably expected to improve on his total of 87 games played for the Dodgers in 1989. Instead, he played in fewer games than in any year since his rookie season. Nevertheless, his versatility -- not to mention is .350 average -- proved valuable to the Giants, and he seemed to mature as a hitter during the limited playing time he did receive. He was a positive influence in the clubhouse, and should contribute in 1991 much as he did in 1990.

BILL BATHE

Position: C
Bats: R **Throws:** R
Ht: 6' 2" **Wt:** 200

Opening Day Age: 30
Born: 10/14/60 in Downey, CA
ML Seasons: 3

Overall Statistics

	G	AB	R	H	D	T	HR	RBI	SB	BB	SO	AVG
1990	52	48	3	11	0	1	3	12	0	7	12	.229
Career	121	183	15	39	4	1	8	29	0	9	39	.213

HITTING, FIELDING, BASERUNNING:

Bill Bathe was the Giants' most frequently-used right-handed pinch hitter in 1990, and if he remains with the team next year, it will be because manager Roger Craig has decided he can keep a player exclusively for that purpose. Bathe had two home runs and 11 RBI as a pinch hitter in 1990. He isn't much of a contact hitter, and he lunges after outside breaking balls. On the plus side, he knows the strike zone fairly well for a power hitter and he'll sit on the fastball, hitting it a long way if it's over the plate and above the knees.

Bathe came up as a catcher in the Oakland organization and has played first base and the outfield as well. But his days as a candidate for a regular job are probably over. He never has overcome an arm injury suffered two years ago, and, in any case, the Giants have a surplus of catchers in their organization. Bathe is ponderous on the bases and is no threat to steal or to take an extra base.

OVERALL:

Craig likes Bathe's ability to come off the bench cold and provide a quality at-bat, but the question is whether the Giants can afford the luxury of carrying a player who can do little except pinch hit. At age 30, Bathe probably can't be expected to learn any new skills, although he conceivably could be kept as a third catcher. His major league future, if any, could be as a designated hitter in the American League.

STEVE DECKER

Position: C
Bats: R **Throws:** R
Ht: 6' 3" **Wt:** 205

Opening Day Age: 25
Born: 10/25/65 in Rock Island, IL
ML Seasons: 1

Overall Statistics

	G	AB	R	H	D	T	HR	RBI	SB	BB	SO	AVG
1990	15	54	5	16	2	0	3	8	0	1	10	.296
Career	15	54	5	16	2	0	3	8	0	1	10	.296

HITTING, FIELDING, BASERUNNING:

A strapping young catcher, 25-year-old Steve Decker began the 1990 season toiling for the Giants' Class AA farm club at Shreveport. By the end of the year he was playing in San Francisco, and his work was so good that it was a big factor in the Giants' decision not to renew Gary Carter's contract.

A 21st-round draft choice in 1988, Decker has moved up the ladder quickly. He's never hit less than .289 at any of his three minor league stops, and this year he displayed some power for the first time with 22 doubles, 15 homers and 80 RBIs. No wild swinger, he only struck out 64 times at Shreveport and showed good patience by drawing 40 walks in 116 games. He was hardly overawed in his major league trial, either. Decker belted two doubles and three homers in 54 Giant at-bats while batting .296.

What really impressed the Giants, however, was Decker's defensive work. He handled veteran pitchers like Rick Reuschel and Mike LaCoss without missing a beat. Displaying a strong arm, he threw out six of 19 base stealers, and at 6'-3" and 205, he obviously has plate-blocking ability.

OVERALL:

The Giants don't want to rush Decker, but he impressed them so much that they're giving him a full shot at making the club this year. He'll probably platoon with Terry Kennedy, at least for awhile. Former major league catcher Clint Hurdle, who saw Decker all year in the Texas League, calls him "a catcher from the old school -- a big solid kid who throws well and can swing the bat." Keep an eye on this kid.

RICK LEACH

Position: RF
Bats: L **Throws:** L
Ht: 6' 0" **Wt:** 195

Opening Day Age: 33
Born: 5/4/57 in Ann Arbor, MI
ML Seasons: 10

Overall Statistics

	G	AB	R	H	D	T	HR	RBI	SB	BB	SO	AVG
1990	78	174	24	51	13	0	2	16	0	21	20	.293
Career	799	1719	205	460	100	10	18	183	8	176	217	.268

HITTING, FIELDING, BASERUNNING:

Rick Leach's season-ending suspension on August 2 forces the Giants to answer a difficult question: do they want to take a chance on a 33-year-old who twice has been disciplined for drug abuse? Before his suspension, Leach had hit well, and his cheerfulness and raucous sense of humor had helped the Giants compensate for the retirement of Bob Brenly and Mike Krukow, who had been the resident clubhouse wits.

Leach is a line drive hitter with little home run power, and Candlestick Park couldn't be better suited for him. The capricious winds, which usually blow out to right field, helped him parachute numerous bloop hits beyond the infield and provided the extra push that helped singles become gap doubles. Leach batted .341 at Candlestick Park.

When on the bases, Leach reminds people of his Michigan football days, when he ran the option offense with daring and disdain for contact. He was perhaps the Giants' most aggressive baserunner, though he isn't especially fast. Leach also performed well in right field, easily the toughest of the three fields to play at Candlestick because of the sun and wind. He reacts quickly to the ball, although his range is somewhat limited. His arm strength is only slightly above average.

OVERALL:

Despite Leach's drug history, the Giants, who appreciated his efforts last year, have invited him to spring training as a non-roster player. Look for Leach to return to the Giants in 1991, though probably in the fourth outfielder role for which the Giants originally acquired him.

RANDY O'NEAL

Position: RP
Bats: R **Throws:** R
Ht: 6' 2" **Wt:** 195

Opening Day Age: 30
Born: 8/30/60 in Ashland, KY
ML Seasons: 7

Overall Statistics

	W	L	ERA	G	GS	Sv	IP	H	R	BB	SO	HR
1990	1	0	3.83	26	0	0	47.0	58	23	18	30	3
Career	17	19	4.35	142	46	3	440.2	461	240	149	248	48

PITCHING, FIELDING, HITTING & HOLDING RUNNERS:

Among the many marginal pitchers who will be seeking to make the Giants' staff in 1991, Randy O'Neal has one of the best chances to stick. The reason has little to do with O'Neal's 1990 showing, which wasn't much different from his mediocre work over parts of six previous seasons with four other clubs. O'Neal sticks out now because he has developed a knuckleball, and the pitch looks good enough that manager Roger Craig considers O'Neal a candidate for a starting role.

O'Neal, 31, has been tinkering with the knuckleball for several years, but never attempted to polish it. The Giants didn't even know he had the pitch until he almost injured some of his teammates with it while playing catch. At Craig's urging, O'Neal began to throw it in the bullpen. San Francisco catcher Bill Bathe, who has caught Joe Niekro, said O'Neal's knuckler already compares favorably to Niekro's.

O'Neal also throws a fastball, slider, and split-finger pitch, so he does not need to be totally dependent on the knuckler. He is well-coordinated for his size, and fields his position fairly well. He didn't pay as much attention to baserunners as Craig would have liked, but his move is considered good. He has had little opportunity to swing the bat.

OVERALL:

The Giants sent O'Neal to winter ball to work on his knuckler, and expect him to make a strong bid for a job on the 1991 staff. Craig would rather use him as a starter than as a reliever because of the eccentric nature of the knuckleball.

FRANCISCO OLIVERAS

Position: RP
Bats: R **Throws:** R
Ht: 5'10" **Wt:** 170

Opening Day Age: 28
Born: 1/31/63 in Santurce, Puerto Rico
ML Seasons: 2

Overall Statistics

	W	L	ERA	G	GS	Sv	IP	H	R	BB	SO	HR
1990	2	2	2.77	33	2	2	55.1	47	22	21	41	5
Career	5	6	3.65	45	10	2	111.0	111	50	36	65	13

PITCHING, FIELDING, HITTING & HOLDING RUNNERS:

Francisco Oliveras had two stints with the Giants last year after being acquired early in June from the Minnesota organization. His first stint showed why nine previous professional seasons had yielded him only 12 major league appearances. The second showed that he has a chance to contribute to the Giants in 1991.

Oliveras went on the disabled list in July with shoulder trouble; at the time, there was no reason to suggest that he would pitch again for the Giants. However, he had a 2.03 ERA after coming off the DL, and finished at 2.77 -- second-best on the staff. Used mostly in middle relief with occasional set-up assignments, Oliveras depended on his fastball, which is above average in velocity and darts downward when he is coming straight over the top. His injury forced him to change his delivery to throw more over-the-top. Oliveras also throws a slider, mostly to right-handed hitters, and began working with a split-finger fastball in August and September. He doesn't have much in the way of an off speed pitch.

Oliveras has a deliberate motion that makes him relatively easy to steal on. He fields his position well and handled most bunts acceptably. He showed little sign of being able to wield a bat in his few opportunities.

OVERALL:

Oliveras showed enough during the final two months of the season to merit consideration for a berth on the 1991 staff. He is versatile enough to function in almost any role, and he has a live, moving fastball. He has a chance to make the '91 Giants and perhaps be an important contributor.

About STATS, Inc.

It all starts with the **system**. The STATS scoring method, which includes pitch-by-pitch information and the direction, distance, and velocity of each ball hit into play, yields an immense amount of information. Sure, we have all the statistics you're used to seeing, but where other statistic sources quit, STATS is just getting started.

Then, there's the **network**. Our information is timely because our game reporters send their information by computer as soon as the game is over. Statistics are checked, rechecked, updated, and are available daily.

Analysis comes next. STATS constantly searches for new ways to use this wealth of information to open windows into the workings of Baseball. Accurate numbers, intelligent computer programming, and a large dose of imagination all help coax the most valuable information from its elusive cover.

Finally, distribution!

STATS has served Major League teams for 11 years now including the Athletics, White Sox and Yankees. The boxscores that STATS provides exclusively to *USA Today* have revolutionized what Baseball fans expect from a boxscore. *The National*, *Sports Illustrated*, and *The Sporting News* regularly feature STATS, Inc. *ESPN's* nightly baseball coverage is supported by a full-time STATS statistician and supplemented by on-site assistance for their Sunday night broadcasts. We provide statistics for *Earl Weaver Baseball*, *Rotisserie Baseball*, the nationally syndicated newspaper game *Dugout Derby*, and other baseball games and fantasy leagues all over the country.

For the baseball fan, STATS publishes monthly and year-end reports on each Major League team. We offer a host of year-end statistical breakdowns on paper or disk that cover hitting, pitching, catching, baserunning, throwing, and more. STATS produces custom reports on request.

Computer users with modems can access the STATS computer for information with **STATS On-line**. If you own a computer with a modem, there is no other source with the scope of baseball information that STATS can offer.

STATS and Bill James enjoy an on-going affiliation that has produced several baseball products including ***STATS 1991 Major League Handbook*** and ***Bill James Fantasy Baseball***, the ultimate baseball game written by Bill James himself which allows you to manage your own team and compete with other team owners around the country.

Keep an eye out for other exciting future projects.

It is the purpose of STATS, Inc. to make the best possible Baseball information available to all Baseball interests: fans, players, teams, or media. Write to:

STATS, Inc.
7366 North Lincoln Ave.
Lincolnwood, IL 60646-1708

. . . or call us at 1-708-676-3322. We can send you a STATS brochure, a free Bill James Fantasy Baseball information kit, and/or information on STATS On-line.

To maintain its information, STATS hires people around the country to cover games using STATS scoring method. If you are interested in applying for a game reporter's position, please write or call STATS.

Also available from STATS, Inc. is ***The STATS 1991 Baseball Scoreboard***. The first edition of this book in 1990 took the nation's Baseball fans by storm. This all new edition, available by order directly from STATS, is back with the same great writing, eye-popping new graphics and amazing stats you won't find anywhere else.

A

B

C

D

E

F

G

L

M

N

O

P

T

U

V

W

Y

Z

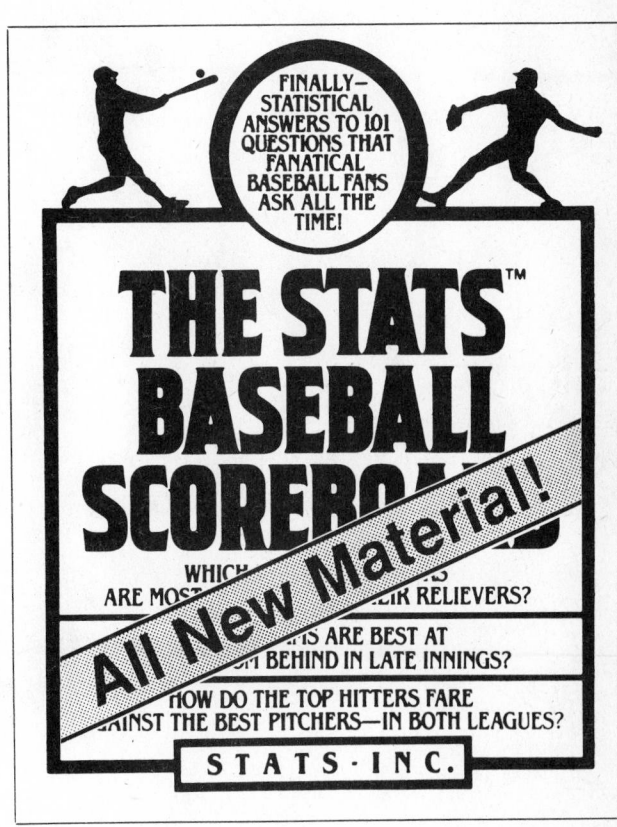

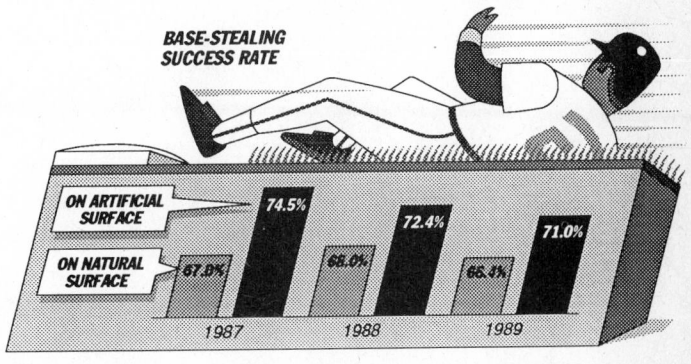